STARTING OUT WITH

Visual Basic®

Seventh Edition

STARTING OUT WITH

Visual Basic®

Seventh Edition

Tony Gaddis
Haywood Community College

Kip Irvine
Florida International University

PEARSON

Boston   Columbus   Indianapolis   New York   San Francisco   Hoboken
Amsterdam   Cape Town   Dubai   London   Madrid   Milan   Munich   Paris   Montréal   Toronto
Delhi   Mexico City   São Paulo   Sydney   Hong Kong   Seoul   Singapore   Taipei   Tokyo

Vice President, Editorial Director, ECS: Marcia Horton
Acquisitions Editor: Matt Goldstein
Editorial Assistant: Kristy Alaura
Vice President of Marketing: Christy Lesko
Director of Field Marketing: Tim Galligan
Product Marketing Manager: Bram Van Kempen
Field Marketing Manager: Demetrius Hall
Marketing Assistant: Jon Bryant
Director of Product Management: Erin Gregg
Team Lead, Program and Project Management:
 Scott Disanno
Program Manager: Carole Snyder
Project Manager: Greg Dulles

Senior Specialist, Program Planning and Support:
 Maura Zaldivar-Garcia
Cover Designer: Joyce Cosentino Wells
Manager, Rights and Permissions: Rachel Youdelman
Project Manager, Rights and Permissions: William Opaluch
Cover Image: *Stargatechris/123RF*
Inventory Manager: Meredith Maresca
Media Project Manager: Renata Butera
Full-Service Project Manager: Jogender Taneja/iEnergizer
 Aptara®, Inc.
Composition: iEnergizer Aptara®, Inc.
Printer/Binder: Edwards Brothers, Inc.
Cover Printer: Phoenix Color

Credits and acknowledgments borrowed from other sources and reproduced, with permission, in this textbook appear on the Credits page at the end of the text.

Many of the designations by manufacturers and sellers to distinguish their products are claimed as trademarks. Where those designations appear in this book, and the publisher was aware of a trademark claim, the designations have been printed in initial caps or all caps.

The programs and applications presented in this book have been included for their instructional value. They have been tested with care, but are not guaranteed for any particular purpose. The publisher does not offer any warranties or representations, nor does it accept any liabilities with respect to the programs or applications.

MICROSOFT AND/OR ITS RESPECTIVE SUPPLIERS MAKE NO REPRESENTATIONS ABOUT THE SUITABILITY OF THE INFORMATION CONTAINED IN THE DOCUMENTS AND RELATED GRAPHICS PUBLISHED AS PART OF THE SERVICES FOR ANY PURPOSE. ALL SUCH DOCUMENTS AND RELATED GRAPHICS ARE PROVIDED "AS IS" WITHOUT WARRANTY OF ANY KIND. MICROSOFT AND/OR ITS RESPECTIVE SUPPLIERS HEREBY DISCLAIM ALL WARRANTIES AND CONDITIONS WITH REGARD TO THIS INFORMATION, INCLUDING ALL WARRANTIES AND CONDITIONS OF MERCHANTABILITY. WHETHER EXPRESS, IMPLIED OR STATUTORY, FITNESS FOR A PARTICULAR. PURPOSE, TITLE AND NON-INFRINGEMENT. IN NO EVENT SHALL MICROSOFT AND/OR ITS RESPECTIVE SUPPLIERS BE LIABLE FOR ANY SPECIAL, INDIRECT OR CONSEQUENTIAL DAMAGES OR ANY DAMAGES WHATSOEVER RESULTING FROM LOSS OF USE, DATA OR PROFITS, WHETHER IN AN ACTION OF CONTRACT. NEGLIGENCE OR OTHER TORTIOUS ACTION, ARISING OUT OF OR IN CONNECTION WITH THE USE OR PERFORMANCE OF INFORMATION AVAILABLE FROM THE SERVICES.

THE DOCUMENTS AND RELATED GRAPHICS CONTAINED HEREIN COULD INCLUDE TECHNICAL INACCURACIES OR TYPOGRAPHICAL ERRORS CHANGES ARE PERIODICALLY ADDED TO THE INFORMATION HEREIN. MICROSOFT AND/OR ITS RESPECTIVE SUPPLIERS MAY MAKE IMPROVEMENTS AND/OR CHANGES IN THE PRODUCT(S) AND/OR THE PROGRAM(S) DESCRIBED HEREIN AT ANY TIME PARTIAL SCREEN SHOTS MAY BE VIEWED IN FULL WITHIN THE SOFTWARE VERSION SPECIFIED.

MICROSOFT® WINDOWS®, AND MICROSOFT OFFICE® ARE REGISTERED TRADEMARKS OF THE MICROSOFT CORPORATION IN THE U.S.A AND OTHER COUNTRIES. THIS BOOK IS NOT SPONSORED OR ENDORSED BY OR AFFILIATED WITH THE MICROSOFT CORPORATION.

Library of Congress Cataloging-in-Publication Data
Names: Gaddis, Tony, author. | Irvine, Kip R., author.
Title: Starting out with Visual Basic / Tony Gaddis, Haywood Community
    College, Kip Irvine, Florida International University.
Description: Seventh edition. | Boston : Pearson, 2016. | Includes
    bibliographical references and index.
Identifiers: LCCN 2016000100 | ISBN 9780134400150 | ISBN 0134400151
Subjects: LCSH: Visual Basic (Computer program language)
Classification: LCC QA76.73.M53 G33 2016 | DDC 005.26/8—dc23 LC record available at
    http://lccn.loc.gov/2016000100

10 9 8 7 6 5 4 3 2

PEARSON

ISBN 10:   0-13-440015-1
ISBN 13: 978-0-13-440015-0

Contents in Brief

Contents

Chapter 3   Variables and Calculations 125

Chapter 4   Making Decisions 233

Chapter 5   **Lists and Loops   309**

Preface

Welcome to *Starting Out with Visual Basic*, Seventh Edition. This book is intended for use in an introductory programming course. It is designed for students who have no prior programming background, but even experienced students will benefit from its depth of detail and the chapters covering databases, Web applications, and other advanced topics. The book is written in clear, easy-to-understand language and covers all the necessary topics of an introductory programming course. The text is rich in concise, practical, and real-world example programs, so the student not only learns how to use the various controls, constructs, and features of Visual Basic, but also learns why and when to use them.

Changes in the Seventh Edition

- **The book is completely updated for Visual Basic 2015**—This book was revised and tested using Visual Studio 2015 Community Edition.
- **Chapter 2 has been completely rewritten**—Chapter 2 still covers the same topics, but the chapter has been rewritten with fresh new tutorials and a more streamlined organization.
- **Chapter 3 has been reorganized**—We have reorganized Chapter 3 so the material on variables, data types, and calculations appears first, followed by the material on GUI creation. As a result, there is a stronger emphasis on coding fundamentals. Several new tutorials have also been added to the chapter.
- **A New Section on the PrintDialog Control**—Chapter 9 has a new section on the PrintDialog control, which allows the user to select a printer, or a PDF driver, if one is installed on the system.
- **Coverage of the CType Method**—Chapter 12 now has a section on the CType method, which provides convenient type conversion for objects.
- **New programming Problems**—Many new programming problems have been added throughout the book.
- **Code improvements**—Throughout the book, many of the code examples have been improved.

A Look at Visual Basic: Past and Present

The first version of Visual Basic was introduced in 1991. Prior to its introduction, writing a GUI interface for an application was no small task. Typically, it required hundreds of lines of C code for even the simplest *Hello World* program. Additionally, an understanding of graphics, memory, and complex system calls was often necessary. Visual Basic was revolutionary because it significantly simplified this process. With Visual Basic, a programmer could visually design an application's user interface. Visual Basic would then generate the code necessary to display and operate the interface. This allowed the programmer to spend less time writing GUI code and more time writing code to perform meaningful tasks.

The evolution of Visual Basic from version 1 to version 6 followed a natural progression. Each new release was an improved version of the previous release, providing additional features and enhancements. Visual Basic versions offered backward compatibility, where code written in an older version was compatible with a newer version of the Visual Basic development environment.

In 2002, Microsoft released a new object-oriented software platform known as .NET. The .NET platform consists of several layers of software that sit above the operating system and provide a secure, managed environment in which programs can execute. In addition to providing a managed environment for applications to run, .NET also provided new technologies for creating Internet-based programs and programs that provide services over the Web. Along with the introduction of the .NET platform, Microsoft introduced a new version of Visual Basic known as VB .NET 2002, which allowed programmers to write desktop applications or Web applications for the .NET platform.

VB .NET was not merely a new and improved version of VB 6, however. VB .NET was a totally new programming environment, and the Visual Basic language was dramatically revised. The changes were substantial enough that programs written in earlier versions of Visual Basic were not compatible with VB .NET. Microsoft provided a utility that could be used to convert older Visual Basic applications to the new VB .NET syntax, but the results were not always perfect. Although this was frustrating for some Visual Basic developers, Microsoft reasoned the changes were necessary to ensure that Visual Basic continued to evolve as a modern, professional programming environment.

Microsoft has continued to enhance and improve Visual Basic by regularly releasing new versions. The versions, which are named after the year in which they were released, are Visual Basic 2003, Visual Basic 2005, Visual Basic 2008 and so forth. At the time this book was written, the current release was Visual Basic 2015. You can see a complete list of the enhancements that have been made to this version of Visual Basic, as well as past versions, on this web page: msdn.microsoft.com/en-us/library/we86c8x2.aspx.

Organization of the Text

The text teaches Visual Basic step-by-step. Each chapter covers a major set of programming topics, introduces controls and GUI elements, and builds knowledge as the student progresses through the book. Although the chapters can be easily taught in their existing sequence, there is some flexibility. The following diagram suggests possible sequences of instruction.

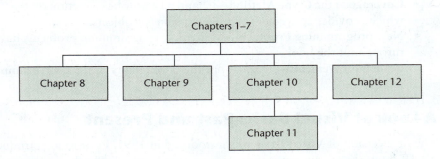

Chapters 1 through 7 cover the fundamentals of program design, flow control, modular programming, and the most important Visual Basic controls. The instructor may then continue in any order with Chapters 8, 9, 10, or 12. Part of Chapter 11 relies on database concepts, so it should be covered after Chapter 10.

Brief Overview of Each Chapter

Chapter 1: Introduction to Programming and Visual Basic. This chapter provides an introduction to programming, the programming process, and Visual Basic. GUI programming and the event-driven model are explained. The components of programs, such as keywords, variables, operators, and punctuation are covered, and tools such as flowcharts and pseudocode are presented. The student gets started using the Visual Basic environment in a hands-on tutorial.

Chapter 2: Creating Applications with Visual Basic. In this chapter the student learns to create forms with labels, buttons, and picture boxes and learns to modify control properties. The student is introduced to Visual Basic code, and learns to write simple event-driven applications that respond to button clicks, or provide interaction through clickable images. This chapter introduces the *Visual Studio Help* system, and provides a tutorial on simple debugging. The importance of commenting code is also discussed.

Chapter 3: Variables and Calculations. Variables, constants, and the Visual Basic data types are introduced. The student learns to gather input and create simple arithmetic statements. The intricacies of GUI design are introduced as the student learns about grouping controls with group boxes, assigning keyboard access keys, and setting the tab order. The student is introduced to exceptions and learns to write simple exception handlers. Debugging techniques for locating logic errors are covered.

Chapter 4: Making Decisions. The student learns about relational operators and how to control the flow of a program with the `If... Then`, `If...Then... Else`, and `If... Then... ElseIf` statements. Logical operators are introduced, and the `Select Case` statement is covered. Important applications of these constructs are discussed, such as testing numeric values, strings, and determining if a value lies within a range, and validating user input. Several string-handling functions and string methods are discussed. Radio buttons and check boxes are also introduced.

Chapter 5: Lists and Loops. This chapter begins by showing the student how to use input boxes as a quick and simple way to gather input. Next, list boxes and combo boxes are introduced. The chapter covers repetition control structures: the `Do While`, `Do Until`, and `For... Next` loops. Counters, accumulators, running totals, and other loop-related topics are discussed. The student also learns how to generate random numbers.

Chapter 6: Procedures and Functions. The student learns how and why to modularize programs with general-purpose procedures and functions. Arguments, parameters, and return values are discussed. Debugging techniques for stepping into and over procedures are introduced.

Chapter 7: Multiple Forms, Modules, and Menus. This chapter shows how to add multiple forms to a project and how to create a module to hold procedures and functions that are not associated with a specific form. It covers creating a menu system, with commands and submenus that the user may select from.

Chapter 8: Arrays and More. This chapter discusses both single dimension and multidimensional variable arrays. Many array programming techniques are presented, such as summing all the elements in an array, summing all the rows or columns in a two-dimensional array, searching an array for a specific value, sorting arrays, and using parallel arrays. The Enabled property, timer controls, and control anchoring and docking are also covered.

Chapter 9: Files, Printing, and Structures. This chapter begins by discussing how to save data to sequential text files and then read the data back into an application. The OpenFileDialog, SaveFileDialog, FontDialog, and ColorDialog controls are introduced. The PrintDocument control is discussed, with a special focus on printing reports. The chapter shows the student how to create user-defined data types with structures.

Chapter 10: Working with Databases. This chapter introduces basic database concepts. The student learns how to display a database table in a DataGridView control and write applications that display, sort, and update database data. The Structured Query Language (SQL) is introduced. An application that shows how to display database data in list boxes, text boxes, labels, and combo box is presented. The chapter concludes with an overview of Language Integrated Query (LINQ).

Chapter 11: Developing Web Applications. This chapter shows the student how to create ASP.NET applications that run on Web Browsers such as Internet Explorer, Chrome, Firefox, and Safari. Using Microsoft Visual Studio, or Microsoft Visual Web Developer, the student learns how to use Web server controls and Web forms to build interactive, database-driven Web applications.

Chapter 12: Classes, Collections, and Inheritance. This chapter introduces classes as a tool for creating abstract data types. The process of analyzing a problem and determining its classes is discussed, and techniques for creating objects, properties, and methods are introduced. Collections are presented as structures for holding groups of objects. The *Object Browser*, which allows the student to see information about the classes, properties, methods, and events available to a project, is also covered. The chapter concludes by introducing inheritance, and shows how to create a class that is based on an existing class.

Appendix A: Advanced User Interface Controls and Techniques. Discusses many of the more advanced controls available in Visual Basic, as well as several helpful programming techniques. This appendix also provides a summary of common user interface design guidelines.

Appendix B: Windows Presentation Foundation (WPF). Introduces the student to the Windows Presentation Framework (WPF), and includes a tutorial in which the student creates a simple WPF application.

Appendix C: Converting Mathematical Expressions to Programming Statements. Shows the student how to convert a mathematical expression into a Visual Basic programming statement.

Appendix D: Answers to Checkpoints. Students may test their progress by comparing their answers to Checkpoints with the answers provided. The answers to all Checkpoints are included.

Appendix E: Glossary. Provides a glossary of the key terms presented in the text.

The following appendixes can be downloaded from the book's companion Web site at www.pearsonhighered.com/cs-resources.

Appendix F: Visual Basic Function and Method Reference. Provides a reference for the functions and methods that are covered in the text. The exceptions that may be caused by these functions and methods are also listed.

Appendix G: Binary and Random-Access Files. Describes programming techniques for creating and working with binary and random-access data files.

Features of the Text

Concept Statements. Each major section of the text starts with a concept statement. This statement concisely summarizes the meaning of the section.

Tutorials. Each chapter has several hands-on tutorials that reinforce the chapter's topics. Many of these tutorials involve the student in writing applications that can be applied to real-world problems.

VideoNote

VideoNotes. A series of online videos, developed specifically for this book, are available for viewing at http://www.pearsonhighered.com/gaddisvb/. Icons appear throughout the text alerting the student to videos about specific topics.

Checkpoints. Checkpoints are questions placed at intervals throughout each chapter. They are designed to query the student's knowledge immediately after learning a new topic. Answers to all the Checkpoints are provided in Appendix D.

Notes. Notes are short explanations of interesting or often misunderstood points relevant to the topic being discussed.

Tips. Tips advise the student on the best techniques for approaching different programming problems and appear regularly throughout the text.

Warnings. Warnings caution the student about certain Visual Basic features, programming techniques, or practices that can lead to malfunctioning programs or lost data.

Review Questions and Exercises. In the tradition of all Gaddis texts, each chapter presents a thorough and diverse set of review questions and exercises. These include traditional fill-in-the-blank, true or false, multiple choice, and short answer questions. There are also unique tools for assessing a student's knowledge. For example, *Find the Error* questions ask the student to identify syntax or logic errors in brief code segments. *Algorithm Workbench* questions ask the student to design code segments to satisfy a given problem. There are also *What Do You Think?* questions that require the student to think critically and contemplate the topics presented in the chapter.

Programming Challenges. Each chapter offers a pool of programming exercises designed to solidify the student's knowledge of the topics at hand. In most cases, the assignments present real-world problems to be solved. When applicable, these exercises also include input validation rules.

Supplements

Student

The following supplementary material is bundled with the book:

- Source code and files required for the chapter tutorials are available at the book's companion website: `www.pearsonhighered.com/cs-resources`.
- The website also contains Appendix F, *Visual Basic Function and Method Reference*, and Appendix G, *Binary and Random-Access Files*.

Instructor

The following supplements are available to qualified instructors:

- Answers to all Review Questions in the text
- Solutions for all Programming Challenges in the text
- PowerPoint presentation slides for every chapter
- Test bank
- Test generation software that allows instructors to create customized tests

For information on how to access these supplements, visit the Pearson Education Instructor Resource Center at `http://www.pearsonhighered.com/irc/`.

Online Practice and Assessment with MyProgrammingLab

MyProgrammingLab is a web-based service that helps students fully grasp the logic, semantics, and syntax of programming. Through practice exercises and immediate, personalized feedback, MyProgrammingLab improves the programming competence of beginning students who often struggle with the basic concepts and paradigms of popular high-level programming languages. A self-study and homework tool, the MyProgrammingLab course for Visual Basic consists of roughly two hundred small practice exercises covering introductory topics such as variables, calculations, decision statements, loops, procedures, arrays, and more. For students, the system automatically detects errors in the logic and syntax of their code submissions and offers targeted hints that enable students to figure out what went wrong. For instructors, a comprehensive gradebook tracks correct and incorrect answers and stores the code inputted by students for review.

For a full demonstration, to see feedback from instructors and students, or to get started using MyProgrammingLab in your course, visit `www.myprogramminglab.com`.

Web Resources

Self-assessment quizzes, PowerPoint slides, source code files, and glossary flashcards are available on the Companion Website for *Starting Out with Visual Basic* at `www.pearsonhighered.com/cs-resources`.

Acknowledgments

There were many helping hands in the development and publication of this text. The authors would like to thank the following faculty reviewers for their helpful suggestions and expertise during the production of this edition:

Paul T. Bladek, *Edmonds Community College*

Mohammad Dadashzadeh, *Oakland University*

Travis Dalton, *Columbia College (SC)*

Martha Gibson, *Central Texas College*

Linda Lau, *Longwood University*

Gregory Ramsay, *Morgan State University*

JoAnne Strickland, *Solano Community College*

Joaquin Velez, *San Diego Community College District*

Erik Wynters, *Bloomsburg University of Pennsylvania*

Youlong Zhuang, *Columbia College of Missouri*

Reviewers of the Previous Editions

Achla Agarwal, *Bossier Parrish Community College*

Ronald Bass, *Austin Community College*

Ronald Beauchemin, *Springfield Technical Community College*

Zachory T. Beers, *Microsoft Corporation*

Robert M. Benavides, *Collin County Community College District*

Paul Bladek, *Edmonds Community College*

Douglas Bock, *Southern Illinois University at Edwardsville*

Skip Bottom, *J. Sargeant Reynolds Community College*

Harold Broberg, *Indiana Purdue University*

Nancy Burns, *Professor of Computer Science, Chipola College*

Arthur E. Carter, *Radford University*

Mara Casado, *State College of Florida, Manatee-Sarasota*

Joni Catanzaro, *Louisiana State University*

Jesse Cecil, *College of the Siskiyous*

Dr. Robert Coil, *Cincinnati State Community and Technical College*

Carol A. DesJardins, *St. Clair County Community College*

Sallie Dodson, *Radford University*

William J. Dorin, *Indiana University*

Robert Ekblaw, *SUNY Albany*

Rose M. Endres, *City College of San Francisco*

Jean Evans, *Brevard Community College*

Mark Fienup, *University of Northern Iowa*

Pierre M. Fiorini, PhD, *University of Southern Maine*

Arlene Flerchinger, *Chattanooga State Technical Community College*

Lawrence Fudella, *Erie Community College*

Gail M. Gehrig, *Florida Community College at Jacksonville*

Jayanta Ghosh, *Florida Community College*

Iskandar Hack, *Indiana University—Purdue University at Fort Wayne*

Tom Higginbotham, *Southeastern Louisiana University*

Dennis Higgins, *SUNY Oneonta*

David M. Himes, *Oklahoma State University, Okmulgee*

Greg Hodge, *Northwestern Michigan College*

Corinne Hoisington, *Central Virginia Community College*

Jackie Horton, *University of Vermont*

May-Chuen Hsieh, *Southwest Tennessee Community College*

Lee A. Hunt, *Collin County Community College*

Darrel Karbginsky, *Chemeketa Community College*

Frank J. Kreimendahl, *University of New Hampshire*

Herb Kronholm, *Mid-State Technical College*

Phil Larschan, *Tulsa Community College*

Art Lee, *Lord Fairfax Community College*

Joo Eng Lee-Partridge, *Central Connecticut State University*

Jing Liu, *Southeastern Louisiana University*

Juan Marquez, *Mesa Community College*

Gary Marrer, *Glendale Community College*

Norman McNeal, *Dakota County Technical College*

George McOuat, *Hawaii Pacific University*

Joseph Merrell

Sylvia Miner, *Florida International University*

Billy Morgan, *Holmes Community College*

Joan P. Mosey, *Point Park College*

Solomon Negash, *Kennesaw State University*

Robert Nields, *Cincinnati State Community and Technical College*

Gregory M. Ogle

Christopher J. Olson, *Dakota State University*

Merrill B. Parker, *Chattanooga State Technical Community College*

Rembert N. Parker, *Anderson University*

Alison Pechenick, *University of Vermont*

Richard Pelletier, *San Diego City College*

Carol M. Peterson, *South Plains Community College*

Anita Philipp, *Oklahoma City Community College*

T. N. Rajashekhara, *Camden County College*

Mark Reis, *University of Virginia*

Malu Roldan, *San Jose State*

Pete Sanderson, *Otterbein University*

Judy Scholl, *Austin Community College*

Gurmukh Singh, *SUNY at Fredonia*

Anne Spalding, *Mesa State College*

Judith A. Stafford, *Tufts University*

Angeline Surber, *Mesa Community College*

Robert L. Terrell, *Walters State Community College*

Margaret Warrick, *Allan Hancock College*

Doug Waterman, *Fox Valley Technical College*

Elaine Yale Weltz, *Seattle Pacific University*

Floyd Jay Winters, *Program Director, Computer Science, College of Florida, Manatee-Sarasota*

Catherine Wyman, *DeVry Institute, Phoenix*

Erik Wynters, *Bloomsburg University of Pennsylvania*

Sheri L. York, *Ball State University*

The authors would like to thank their families for their tremendous support throughout this project. We would also like to thank everyone at Pearson who is part of the editorial, production, and marketing team. We are extremely fortunate to have Matt Goldstein as our editor. He has guided us through the delicate process of updating this book many times. We are also fortunate to have Demetrius Hall and Bram Van Kempen as Marketing Managers. Their hard work is truly inspiring, and they do a great job of getting this book out to the academic community. The production team, led by Greg Dulles, worked tirelessly to make this book a reality. Thanks to you all!

About the Authors

Tony Gaddis is the principal author of the *Starting Out with* series of textbooks. Tony has nearly two decades of experience teaching computer science courses, primarily at Haywood Community College in North Carolina. He is a highly acclaimed instructor who was previously selected as North Carolina's Community College *Teacher of the Year*, and has received the *Teaching Excellence* award from the National Institute for Staff and Organizational Development. Besides Visual Basic books, the *Starting Out with* series includes introductory books on programming logic and design, Alice, the C++ programming language, Java™, Python, Microsoft® Visual C#®, and MIT App Inventor, all published by Pearson.

Kip Irvine holds M.S. (computer science) and D.M.A. (music composition) degrees from the University of Miami. He was formerly on the faculty at Miami-Dade Community College, and is presently a member of the School of Computing and Information Sciences at Florida International University. His published textbooks include *COBOL for the IBM Personal Computer*, *Assembly Language for Intel-Based Computers*, *C++ and Object-Oriented Programming*, and *Advanced Visual Basic .NET*.

Attention Students

Installing Visual Studio

To complete the tutorials and programming problems in this book, you need to install Visual Studio 2015 on your computer.

We recommend that you download Visual Studio Community 2015 from the following Web site, and install it on your system:

www.visualstudio.com

Visual Studio Community 2015 is a free, full-featured development environment, and is a perfect companion for this textbook.

 NOTE: If you are working in your school's computer lab, there is a good chance that Microsoft Visual Studio has already been installed. If this is the case, your instructor will show you how to start Visual Studio.

Installing the Student Sample Program Files

The Student Sample Program files that accompany this book are available for download from the book's companion Web site at:

http://www.pearsonhighered.com/cs-resources

These files are required for many of the book's tutorials. Simply download the Student Sample Program files to a location on your hard drive where you can easily access them.

MyProgrammingLab™

Through the power of practice and immediate personalized feedback, MyProgrammingLab helps improve your students' performance.

PROGRAMMING PRACTICE

With MyProgrammingLab, your students will gain first-hand programming experience in an interactive online environment.

IMMEDIATE, PERSONALIZED FEEDBACK

MyProgrammingLab automatically detects errors in the logic and syntax of their code submission and offers targeted hints that enables students to figure out what went wrong and why.

GRADUATED COMPLEXITY

MyProgrammingLab breaks down programming concepts into short, understandable sequences of exercises. Within each sequence the level and sophistication of the exercises increase gradually but steadily.

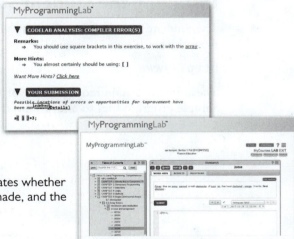

DYNAMIC ROSTER

Students' submissions are stored in a roster that indicates whether the submission is correct, how many attempts were made, and the actual code submissions from each attempt.

PEARSON eTEXT

The Pearson eText gives students access to their textbook anytime, anywhere.

STEP-BY-STEP VIDEONOTE TUTORIALS

These step-by-step video tutorials enhance the programming concepts presented in select Pearson textbooks.

For more information and titles available with **MyProgrammingLab**, please visit **www.myprogramminglab.com**.

1

Introduction to Programming and Visual Basic

TOPICS

Microsoft Visual Basic is a powerful software development system for creating applications that run on the Windows operating system. With Visual Basic, you can do the following:

- Create applications with graphical windows, dialog boxes, and menus
- Create applications that work with databases
- Create Web applications and applications that use Internet technologies
- Create applications that display graphics

Visual Basic, which is commonly referred to as VB, is a favorite tool among professional programmers. It provides tools to visually design an application's appearance, a modern programming language, and access to the latest Microsoft technologies. Powerful applications can be created with Visual Basic in a relatively short period of time.

Before plunging into learning Visual Basic, we will review the fundamentals of computer hardware and software, and then become familiar with the Visual Studio programming environment.

1.1   Computer Systems: Hardware and Software

CONCEPT: Computer systems consist of similar hardware devices and hardware components. This section provides an overview of computer hardware and software organization.

Hardware

The term **hardware** refers to a computer's physical components. A computer, as we generally think of it, is not an individual device, but rather a system of devices. Like the instruments in a symphony orchestra, each device plays its own part. A typical computer system consists of the following major components:

1. The central processing unit (CPU)
2. Main memory
3. Secondary storage devices
4. Input devices
5. Output devices

The organization of a computer system is shown in Figure 1-1.

Figure 1-1 The organization of a computer system

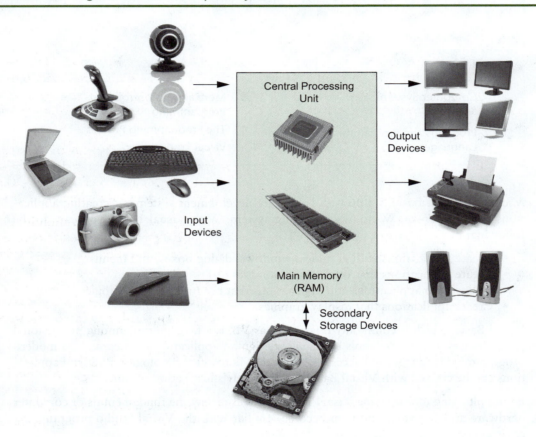

1. The CPU

When a computer is performing the tasks that a program tells it to do, we say that the computer is running or executing the program. The **central processing unit**, or **CPU**, is the part of a computer that actually runs programs. The CPU is the most important component in a computer because without it, the computer could not run software.

A **program** is a set of instructions that a computer's CPU follows to perform a task. The program's instructions are stored in the computer's memory, and the CPU's job is to fetch those instructions, one by one, and carry out the operations that they command. In memory, the instructions are stored as a series of **binary numbers**. A binary number is a sequence of 1s and 0s, such as

11011011

This number has no apparent meaning to people, but to the computer it might be an instruction to multiply two numbers or read another value from memory.

2. Main Memory

You can think of **main memory** as the computer's work area. This is where the computer stores a program while the program is running, as well as the data that the program is working with. For example, suppose you are using a word processing program to write an essay for one of your classes. While you do this, both the word processing program and the essay are stored in main memory.

Main memory is commonly known as **random-access memory**, or **RAM**. It is called this because the CPU is able to quickly access data stored at any random location in RAM. RAM is usually a volatile type of memory that is used only for temporary storage while a program is running. When the computer is turned off, the contents of RAM are erased. Inside your computer, RAM is stored in microchips.

3. Secondary Storage

Secondary storage is a type of memory that can hold data for long periods of time—even when there is no power to the computer. Frequently used programs are stored in secondary memory and loaded into main memory as needed. Important data, such as word processing documents, payroll data, and inventory figures, is saved to secondary storage as well.

The most common type of secondary storage device is the **disk drive**. A traditional disk drive stores data by magnetically encoding it onto a spinning circular disk. **Solid-state drives**, which store data in solid-state memory, are increasingly becoming popular. A solid-state drive has no moving parts, and operates faster than a traditional disk drive.

Most computers have some sort of secondary storage device, either a traditional disk drive or a solid-state drive, mounted inside their case. External storage devices are also available, which connect to one of the computer's communication ports, or plug into a memory slot. External storage devices can be used to create backup copies of important data or to move data to another computer. For example, **USB (Universal Serial Bus) drives** and **SD (Secure Digital) memory cards** are small devices that appear to the system as disk drives. They are inexpensive, reliable, and small enough to be carried in your pocket.

Optical devices such as the CD (compact disc) and the DVD (digital versatile disc) are also popular for data storage. Data is not recorded magnetically on an optical disc, but is encoded as a series of pits on the disc surface. CD and DVD drives use a laser to detect the pits and thus read the encoded data. Optical discs hold large amounts of data, and because recordable CD and DVD drives are now commonplace, they are good mediums for creating backup copies of data.

4. Input Devices

Input is any data the computer collects from the world outside of the computer. The device that collects the data and sends it to the computer is called an **input device**. Common input devices are the keyboard, mouse, touchscreen, scanner, and digital camera. Disk drives and optical drives can also be considered input devices because programs and data are retrieved from them and loaded into the computer's memory.

5. Output Devices

Output is any data the computer sends to the world outside of the computer. It might be a sales report, a list of names, a graphic image, or a sound. The data is sent to an **output device**, which formats and presents it. Common output devices are screens and printers. Storage devices can also be considered output devices because the CPU sends data to them in order to be saved.

Software

Software refers to the programs that run on a computer. There are two general categories of software: operating systems and application software. An **operating system** or **OS** is a set of programs that manages the computer's hardware devices and controls their processes. Windows, Mac OS, Android, iOS, and Linux are popular operating systems.

Application software refers to programs that make the computer useful to the user. These programs, which are generally called applications, solve specific problems or perform general operations that satisfy the needs of the user. Word processing, spreadsheet, and database packages are all examples of application software. As you work through this book, you will develop application software using Visual Basic.

 ## Checkpoint

1.1 List the five major hardware components of a computer system.

1.2 What is main memory? What is its purpose?

1.3 Explain why computers have both main memory and secondary storage.

1.4 What are the two general categories of software?

 # 1.2 Programs and Programming Languages

CONCEPT: A program is a set of instructions a computer follows in order to perform a task. A programming language is a special language used to write computer programs.

What Is a Program?

Computers are designed to follow instructions. A computer program is a set of instructions that enables the computer to solve a problem or perform a task. For example, suppose we want the computer to calculate someone's gross pay—a *Wage Calculator* application. Figure 1-2 shows a list of things the computer should do.

Collectively, the instructions in Figure 1-2 are called an **algorithm**. An algorithm is a set of well-defined steps for performing a task or solving a problem. Notice these steps are

Figure 1-2 Program steps—*Wage Calculator* application

1. Display a message on the screen: *How many hours did you work?*
2. Allow the user to enter the number of hours worked.
3. Once the user enters a number, store it in memory.
4. Display a message on the screen: *How much do you get paid per hour?*
5. Allow the user to enter an hourly pay rate.
6. Once the user enters a number, store it in memory.
7. Once both the number of hours worked and the hourly pay rate are entered, multiply the two numbers and store the result in memory as the gross pay.
8. Display a message on the screen that shows the gross pay. The message must include the result of the calculation performed in Step 7.

sequentially ordered. Step 1 should be performed before Step 2, and so on. It is important that these instructions are performed in their proper sequence.

States and Transitions

It is helpful to think of a running computer program as a combination of states and transitions. Each state is represented by a snapshot (like a picture) of the computer's memory. Using the *Wage Calculator* application example from Figure 1-2, the following is a memory snapshot taken when the program starts:

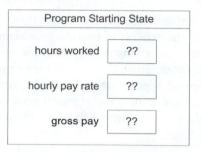

In Step 3, the number of hours worked by the user is stored in memory. Suppose the user enters the value 20. A new program state is created:

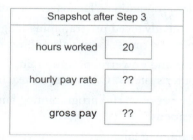

In Step 6, the hourly pay rate entered by the user is stored in memory. Suppose the user enters the value 25. The following memory snapshot shows the new program state:

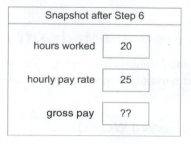

In Step 7, the application calculates the amount of money earned, saving it in memory. The following memory snapshot shows the new program state:

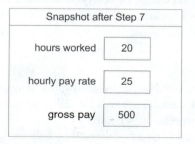

The memory snapshot produced by Step 7 represents the final program state.

Programming Languages

In order for a computer to perform instructions such as the wage calculator algorithm, the steps must be converted to a format the computer can process. As mentioned earlier, a program is stored in memory as a series of binary numbers. These numbers are known as **machine language instructions**. The CPU processes only instructions written in machine language. Our *Wage Calculator* application might look like the following at the moment when it is executed by the computer:

1010110111010100011110000110111010001110001110011010101110 *etc.*

The CPU interprets these binary or machine language numbers as commands. As you might imagine, the process of encoding an algorithm in machine language is tedious and difficult. **Programming languages,** which use words instead of numbers, were invented to ease this task. Programmers can write their applications in programming language statements, and then use special software called a **compiler** to convert the program into machine language. Names of some popular recent programming languages are shown in Table 1-1. This list is only a small sample—there are thousands of programming languages.

Table 1-1 Popular programming languages

Language	Description
Visual Basic, C#	Popular programming languages for building Windows and Web applications.
C, C++	Powerful advanced programming languages that emphasize flexibility and fast running times. C++ is also object-oriented.
Java	Flexible and powerful programming language that runs on many different computer systems. Often used to teach object-oriented programming.
Python	Simple, yet powerful programming language used for graphics and small applications.
PHP	Programming language used for creating interactive Web sites.
JavaScript	Scripting language used in Web applications that provides rich user interfaces for Web browsers.

What Is a Program Made Of?

All programming languages, including Visual Basic, have certain elements in common. Let's look at the major programming language elements that you will work with when writing a program.

Keywords (Reserved Words)

Each high-level language has its own set of words that the programmer must learn in order to use the language. The words that make up a high-level programming language are known as **keywords** or **reserved words**. Each keyword has a predefined meaning and cannot be used for any other purpose. As you work through this book you will learn many of the Visual Basic keywords and how to use them in a program.

Operators

In addition to keywords, programming languages have **operators** that perform various operations on data. For example, all programming languages have math operators that perform arithmetic. In Visual Basic, as well as most other languages, the + sign is an operator that adds two numbers. The following would add 12 and 75:

12 + 75

Variables

Programs use variables to store data in memory. A **variable** is a storage location in memory that is represented by a name. When a value is stored in a variable, it is stored in the computer's memory.

Programmers make up the names for all the variables that they use in a program. You will learn specific rules and guidelines for naming variables in Chapter 3, but for now just remember that a variable's name is a single word that indicates what the variable is used for. For example, a program that calculates the sales tax on a purchase might use a variable named tax to hold that value in memory. And a program that calculates the distance from Earth to a star might use a variable named distance to hold that value in memory. When a program stores a value in a variable, the value is actually stored in memory at the location represented by the variable.

Syntax

In addition to keywords and operators, each language also has its own **syntax**, which is a set of rules that must be strictly followed when writing a program. The syntax rules dictate how keywords, operators, and various punctuation characters must be used in a program. When you are learning a programming language, you must learn the syntax rules for that particular language.

NOTE: Human languages also have syntax rules. Do you remember when you took your first English class, and you learned all those rules about infinitives, indirect objects, clauses, and so forth? You were learning the syntax of the English language.

Although people commonly violate the syntax rules of their native language when speaking and writing, other people usually understand what they mean. Unfortunately, program compilers do not have this ability. If even a single syntax error appears in a program, the program cannot be compiled or executed.

Statements

The individual instructions that you write in a program are called **statements**. A programming statement can consist of keywords, operators, punctuation, and other allowable programming elements, arranged in the proper sequence to perform an operation. The statements that are written in a program are commonly called **source code**, or simply **code**.

Procedures

A **procedure** is a set of programming statements that exist within a program for the purpose of performing a specific task. The program executes the procedure when the task needs to be performed.

Comments (Remarks)

Not everything a programmer writes in a program is meant to be executed by the computer. Some parts of a program are **comments**, or **remarks**, that help the human reader of a program understand the purposes of program statements. In Visual Basic, any statement that begins with an apostrophe (') is considered a comment. When the Visual Basic compiler sees a statement that begins with an apostrophe, it recognizes it as a comment and it skips over it.

You should always add descriptive comments to your code. The extra time it takes is well spent. Sometimes you (the programmer) will have to reread and understand your own code. Comments are a great way to remind you of what you were thinking when you created the program. In addition, you may have to modify or maintain code written by another programmer and you will appreciate the time spent to write comments!

Graphical User Interfaces

When a computer program is needed to perform a task, a programmer is the person who develops the algorithm, and writes the programming statements that perform the algorithm's steps. Once the program is complete, it is made available to those who need to use it. The people who use the program are known as **users**.

Although a programmer works directly with a program's statements, users are typically not concerned with the program's inner workings. Users want to make sure they know how to operate the program when it is running, and that the program works as it should. The part of a program that users interact with is known as the **user interface**. On modern operating systems such as Windows, most of the programs that people use have a **graphical user interface**, or **GUI** (pronounced *gooey*). A graphical user interface typically consists of one or more windows that appear on the computer screen. A **window** is a rectangular area that contains other visual elements such as text, buttons that can be clicked with the mouse, boxes that accept keyboard input, and so forth. Let's look at an example. Follow the steps in Tutorial 1-1 to run a program that you can download from the book's companion Website, at www.pearsonhighered.com/gaddisvb.

Tutorial 1-1:
Running the *Wage Calculator* application

Step 1: Make sure you have downloaded the student sample programs from the textbook's companion Website, at www.pearsonhighered.com/gaddisvb. If you are working in your school's computer lab, your instructor will tell you where the files are located.

Step 2: Go to the folder containing the student sample programs for Chapter 1. Double-click the file *Wage Calculator.exe* (the *.exe* filename extension may not be visible). The program's window should display as shown in Figure 1-3. (Figure 1-3 shows the application running on a Windows 10 system. If you are using another version of Windows, the screen might appear differently.) Leave the program running as you continue to read. We will perform operations with the program in Tutorial 1-2.

Figure 1-3 A graphical user interface

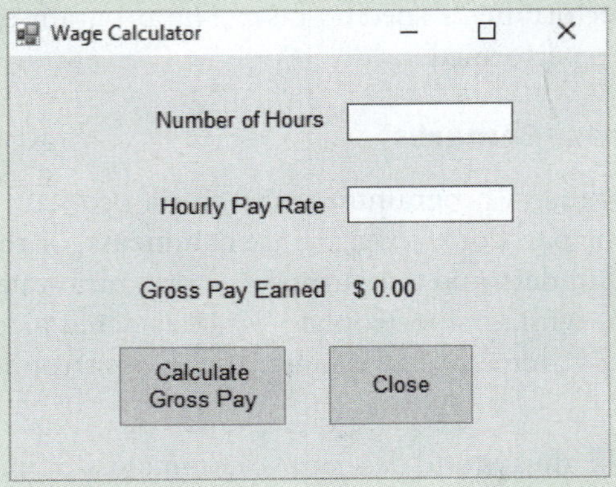

The program you executed in Tutorial 1-1 calculates an employee's gross pay. Notice that inside the program's window (shown in Figure 1-3) there are boxes for entering the number of hours worked and the hourly pay rate. There is also a button that calculates the gross pay when it is clicked with the mouse, and a button that closes the program (stops its execution). All of these elements are part of the program's GUI, and anyone operating the program will interact with these elements.

Objects and Controls

As a student studying Visual Basic, you will frequently encounter two terms: object and control. An **object** is an item in a program that contains data and has the ability to perform operations. The data an object contains is referred to as **properties**, or **attributes**. The operations an object can perform are called **methods**. (Recall that earlier we mentioned that a procedure is a set of programming statements that exist within a program for the purpose of performing a specific task. A method is a special type of procedure that belongs to an object.)

In the beginning of your studies you will learn how to use many different objects that are provided by Visual Basic to perform various operations in your programs. In Chapter 12, you will learn to define your own objects.

VideoNote

Forms, Controls, and Properties

A **control** is a specific type of object that usually appears in a program's graphical user interface. For example, each element appearing in the user interface in Figure 1-3 is a control. The window that contains the other elements is known as a **Form** control. The small boxes that accept keyboard input are known as **TextBox** controls. The areas that simply display text are known as **Label** controls. The buttons that perform operations when clicked with the mouse are known as **Button** controls. Figure 1-4 points out each of these controls in the user interface.

Figure 1-4 Types of controls

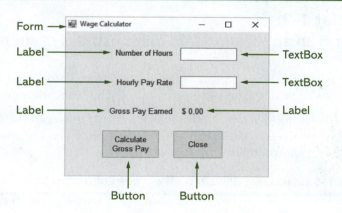

NOTE: Visual Basic is an **object-oriented programming (OOP)** language. A typical VB application uses numerous objects (such as GUI controls) that work together.

Properties

A GUI control's visual appearance is determined by the control's properties. A **property** is a piece of data that determines some characteristic of the control. For example, many controls have a **Text property** that determines the text that is displayed by the control. If you look at Figure 1-4, near the top of the form you see a Label control that displays the text *Number of Hours*. That Label control's Text property is set to the value *Number of*

Hours. Just below that Label is another Label control, and its Text property is set to the value *Hourly Pay Rate*.

Button controls also have a Text property. In Figure 1-4, the leftmost button's Text property is set to the value *Calculate Gross Pay*, and the rightmost button's Text property is set to the value *Close*. Forms have a Text property too, which determines the text that is displayed in the title bar at the top of the form. In Figure 1-4, the form's Text property is set to *Wage Calculator*. Part of the process of creating a Visual Basic application is deciding what values to store in each object's properties.

Event-Driven Programming

Programs that operate in a GUI environment must be **event-driven**. An event is an action that takes place within a program, such as the clicking of a control. All Visual Basic controls are capable of detecting various events. For example, a Button control can detect when it has been clicked and a TextBox control can detect when its contents have changed.

Names are assigned to all of the events that can be detected. For instance, when the user clicks a Button control, a Click event occurs. When the contents of a TextBox control changes, a TextChanged event occurs. If you wish for a control to respond to a specific event, you must write a set of programming statements known as an **event handler**. An event handler is a special type of procedure that executes when a specific event occurs. (Event handlers are also known as **event procedures**.) If an event occurs, and there is no event handler to respond to that event, the event is ignored.

Part of the Visual Basic programming process is designing and writing event handlers. Tutorial 1-2 demonstrates an event handler using the *Wage Calculator* application you executed in Tutorial 1-1.

Tutorial 1-2:
Running an application that demonstrates event handlers

Step 1:   With the *Wage Calculator* application from Tutorial 1-1 still running, enter the value **10** in the first TextBox control. This is the number of hours worked.

Step 2:   Press the ⎡Tab⎤ key. Notice that the cursor moves to the next TextBox control. Enter the value **25**. This is the hourly pay rate. The window should look like that shown in Figure 1-5.

Figure 1-5 Text boxes filled in on the *Wage Calculator* form

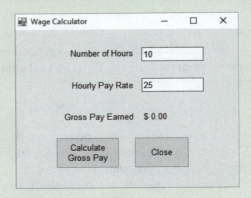

Step 3:   Click the *Calculate Gross Pay* button. Notice that in response to the mouse click, the application multiplies the values you entered in the TextBox controls and displays the result in a Label control. This action is performed by an event handler that responds to the button being clicked. The window should look like that shown in Figure 1-6.

Figure 1-6 Gross pay calculated

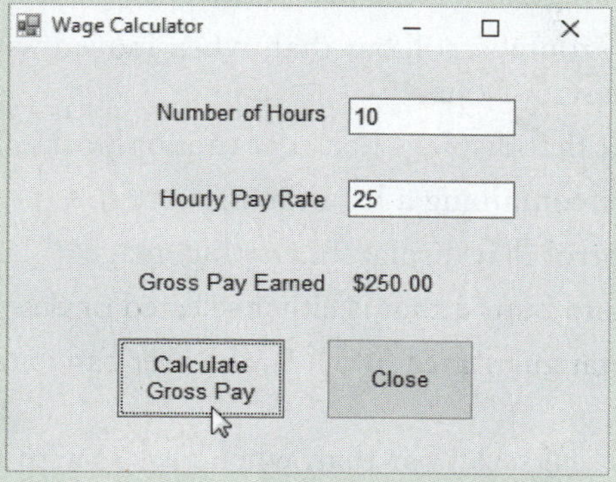

Step 4:   Next, click the *Close* button. The application responds to this event by terminating. This is because an event handler closes the application when the button is clicked.

This simple application demonstrates the essence of event-driven programming. In the next section, we examine the controls and event handlers more closely.

1.3 More about Controls and Programming

CONCEPT: As a Visual Basic programmer, you must design and create an application's GUI elements (forms and other controls) and the programming statements that respond to and/or perform actions (event handlers).

While creating a Visual Basic application, you will spend much of your time doing three things: creating the controls that appear in the application's user interface, setting the properties of the controls, and writing programming language statements that respond to events and perform other operations. In this section, we take a closer look at these aspects of Visual Basic programming.

Visual Basic Controls

In the previous section, you saw examples of several GUI elements, or controls. Visual Basic provides a wide assortment of controls for gathering input, displaying information, selecting values, showing graphics, and more. Table 1-2 lists some of the commonly used controls.

Table 1-2 Visual Basic controls

Control Type	Description
Button	A rectangular button-shaped object that performs an action when clicked with the mouse
CheckBox	A box that is checked or unchecked when clicked with the mouse
ComboBox	A control that is the combination of a ListBox and a TextBox
Form	A window, onto which other controls may be placed
GroupBox	A rectangular border that functions as a container for other controls
HScrollBar	A horizontal scroll bar that, when moved with the mouse, increases or decreases a value
Label	A box that displays text that cannot be changed or entered by the user
ListBox	A box containing a list of items
PictureBox	A control that displays a graphic image
RadioButton	A round button that is either selected or deselected when clicked with the mouse
TextBox	A rectangular area in which the user can enter text, or the program can display text
VScrollBar	A vertical scroll bar that, when moved with the mouse, increases or decreases a value

If you have any experience using Microsoft Windows, you are already familiar with most of the controls listed in Table 1-2. The student sample programs (available at www.pearsonhighered.com/gaddisvb) contains a simple demonstration program in Tutorial 1-3 that shows you how a few of them work.

Tutorial 1-3:
Running an application that demonstrates various controls

Step 1:   Make sure you have downloaded the student sample programs from the textbook's companion Website, at www.pearsonhighered.com/gaddisvb.

Step 2:   Navigate to the the *Chap1* folder.

Step 3:   Double-click the file *Controls Demo.exe*. (The *.exe* extension may not be visible on your system.)

Step 4:   Once the program loads and executes, the window shown in Figure 1-7 should appear on the screen.

Step 5:   The program presents several Visual Basic controls. Experiment with each one, noticing the following actions, which are performed by event handlers:

- When you click the small down arrow (⌄) in the ComboBox control, you see a list of pets. When you select one, the name of the pet appears below the combo box.
- When you click the CheckBox control, its text changes to indicate that the check box is checked or unchecked.
- When you click an item in the ListBox control, the name of that item appears below the list box.
- When you select one of the RadioButton controls, the text below them changes to indicate which one you selected. You may only select one at a time.

Figure 1-7 Control demonstration screen

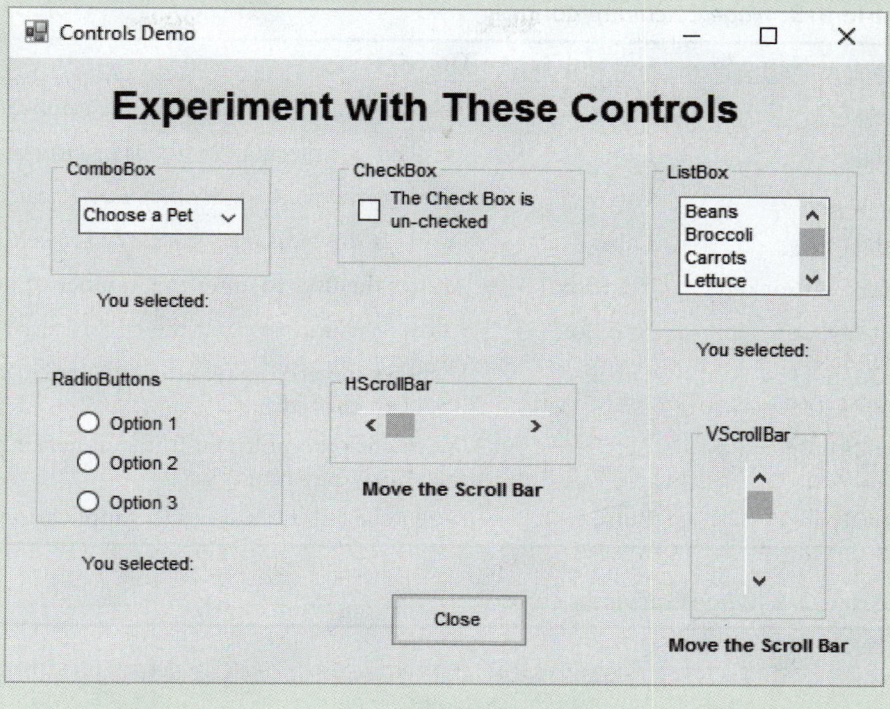

- You move the horizontal scroll bar (HScrollBar) and the vertical scroll bar (VScrollBar) by doing the following:
  - Clicking either of the small arrows at each end of the bar
  - Clicking inside the bar on either side of the slider
  - Clicking on the slider and while holding down the mouse button, moving the mouse to the right or left for the horizontal scroll bar, or up or down for the vertical scroll bar.

  When you move either of the scroll bars, the text below it changes to a number. Moving the scroll bar in one direction increases the number, and moving it in the other direction decreases the number.

Step 6: Click the *Close* button to end the application.

The Name Property

The appearance of a control is determined by its properties. Some properties, however, establish nonvisual characteristics. An example is the control's **Name property**. When the programmer wishes to manipulate or access a control in a programming statement, he or she must refer to the control by its name.

When you create a control in Visual Basic, it automatically receives a default name. The first Label control created in an application receives the default name `Label1`. The second Label control created receives the default name `Label2`, and the default names continue in this fashion. The first TextBox control created in an application is automatically named `TextBox1`. As you can imagine, the names for each subsequent TextBox control are `TextBox2`, `TextBox3`, and so on. You can change the control's default name to something more descriptive.

Table 1-3 lists all the controls, by name, in the *Wage Calculator* application (Section 1.2), and Figure 1-8 shows where each is located.

Table 1-3 *Wage Calculator* controls

Control Name	Control Type	Description
Form1	Form	The window that holds all of the application's other controls
Label1	Label	Displays the message *Number of Hours*
Label2	Label	Displays the message *Hourly Pay Rate*
Label3	Label	Displays the message *Gross Pay Earned*
txtHoursWorked	TextBox	Allows the user to enter the number of hours worked
txtPayRate	TextBox	Allows the user to enter the hourly pay rate
lblGrossPay	Label	Displays the gross pay, after the btnCalcGrossPay button has been clicked
btnCalcGrossPay	Button	When clicked, multiplies the number of hours worked by the hourly pay rate
btnClose	Button	When clicked, terminates the application

Figure 1-8 *Wage Calculator* controls

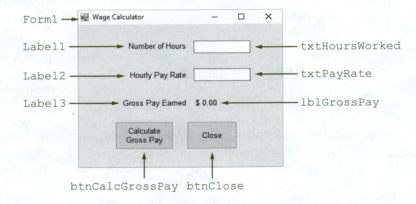

Control Naming Rules and Conventions

Four controls shown in Figure 1-8 (Form1, Label1, Label2, and Label3) still have their default names. The other five controls have programmer-defined names because those controls play an active role in the application's event handlers, and their names appear in the application's programming statements. Any control whose name appears in a programming statement should have a descriptive, programmer-defined name.

 NOTE: Some programmers prefer to give all the controls in their application meaningful names, including ones whose names do not appear in programming statements.

Although you have a great deal of flexibility in naming controls, you must follow these mandatory rules:

- The first character of a control name must be a letter or an underscore character (_).
- After the first character, the remaining characters may be letters, digits, or underscore characters (_).

It's important to remember that control names must be one word. They cannot contain spaces. Punctuation marks and other special symbols are also prohibited in control names.

In addition to these mandatory rules, there are three conventions that you should follow when naming controls:

1. The first three letters of the name should be a lowercase prefix indicating the control's type. In the *Wage Calculator* application, programmer-defined names use the following standard three-letter prefixes:
   - `lbl` indicates a Label control.
   - `txt` indicates a TextBox control.
   - `btn` indicates a Button control.

   There are standard prefixes for other controls as well. They are discussed in Chapter 2.

2. The first letter after the prefix should be uppercase. In addition, if the name consists of multiple words, the first letter of each word should be capitalized. This makes the name more readable. For example, `txtHoursWorked` is easier to read than `txthoursworked`.

3. The part of the control name that appears after the three-letter prefix should describe the control's purpose in the application. This makes the control name very helpful to anyone reading the application's programming statements. For example, it is evident that the `btnCalcGrossPay` control is a button that calculates the gross pay.

These are not mandatory rules, but they are standard conventions that many Visual Basic programmers follow. You should use these guidelines when naming the controls in your applications as well. Table 1-4 describes several fictitious controls and suggests appropriate programmer-defined names for them.

Table 1-4 Programmer-defined control name examples

Control Description	Suggested Name
A text box in which the user enters his or her age	`txtAge`
A button that, when clicked, calculates the total of an order	`btnCalcTotal`
A label that is used to display the distance from one city to another	`lblDistance`
A text box in which the user enters his or her last name	`txtLastName`
A button that, when clicked, adds a series of numbers	`btnAddNumbers`

S January 2015
Sept. 2014

 **Checkpoint**

1.5 What is an algorithm?

1.6 Why were computer programming languages invented?

1.7 What is an object? What is a control?

1.8 What does event-driven mean?

1.9 What is a property?

1.10 Why should the programmer change the name of a control from its default name?

1.11 If a control has the programmer-defined name `txtRadius`, what type of control is it?

1.12 What is the default name given to the first TextBox control created in an application?

1.13 Is `txtFirst+LastName` an acceptable control name? Why or why not?

1.4 The Programming Process

CONCEPT: The programming process consists of several steps, which include designing, creating, testing, and debugging activities.

Imagine building a bridge without a plan. How could it be any easier to create a complex computer program without designing its appearance and behavior? In this section, we introduce some of the most important knowledge you will gain from this book—how to begin creating a computer application. Regardless of which programming language you use in the future, good program design principles always apply.

Steps for Developing a Visual Basic Application

1. Clearly define what the application is to do.
2. Visualize the application running on the computer and design its user interface.
3. Determine the controls needed.
4. Define the values of each control's relevant properties.
5. Determine the event handlers and other code needed for each control.
6. Create a flowchart or pseudocode version of the code.
7. Check the flowchart or pseudocode for errors.
8. Start Visual Studio and create the forms and other controls identified in Step 3.
9. Use the flowcharts or pseudocode from Step 6 to write the actual code.
10. Attempt to run the application. Correct any syntax errors found and repeat this step as many times as necessary.
11. Once all syntax errors are corrected, run the program with test data for input. Correct any logic errors. Repeat this step as many times as necessary.

These steps emphasize the importance of planning. Just as there are good ways and bad ways to paint a house, there are good ways and bad ways to write a program. A good program always begins with planning.

With the *Wage Calculator* application as our example, let's look at each of these steps in greater detail.

1. Clearly define what the application is to do.

This step requires that you identify the purpose of the application, the information to be input, the processing to take place, and the desired output. For example, the requirements for the *Wage Calculator* application are as follows:

Purpose:	To calculate the user's gross pay
Input:	Number of hours worked, hourly pay rate
Process:	Multiply number of hours worked by hourly pay rate. The result is the user's gross pay
Output:	Display a message indicating the user's gross pay

2. Visualize the application running on the computer and design its user interface.

Before you create an application on the computer, first you should create it in your mind. Step 2 is the visualization of the program. Try to imagine what the computer screen will look like while the application is running. Then, sketch the form or forms in the application. For instance, Figure 1-9 shows a sketch of the form presented by the *Wage Calculator* application.

Figure 1-9 Sketch of the *Wage Calculator* form

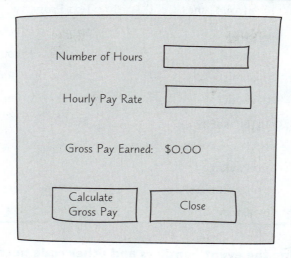

3. Determine the controls needed.

The next step is to determine the controls needed on each of the application's forms. You should assign names to all controls that will be accessed or manipulated in the application. Table 1-5 lists the controls in the *Wage Calculator* application.

Table 1-5 *Wage Calculator* controls

Control Type	Control Name	Description
Form	(Default)	A small form that will serve as the window onto which the other controls will be placed
Label	(Default)	Displays the message *Number of Hours*
Label	(Default)	Displays the message *Hourly Pay Rate*
Label	(Default)	Displays the message *Gross Pay Earned*
TextBox	txtHoursWorked	Allows the user to enter the number of hours worked
TextBox	txtPayRate	Allows the user to enter the hourly pay rate
Label	lblGrossPay	Displays the gross pay, after the btnCalcGrossPay button has been clicked
Button	btnCalcGrossPay	When clicked, multiplies the number of hours worked by the hourly pay rate; stores the result in a variable and displays it in the lblGrossPay label
Button	btnClose	When clicked, terminates the application

4. Define the values of each control's relevant properties.

Other than Name, Text is the only control property modified in the *Wage Calculator* application. Table 1-6 lists the value of each control's Text property.

Table 1-6 *Wage Calculator* control values

Control Type	Control Name	Text Property
Form	(Default)	`"Wage Calculator"`
Label	(Default)	`"Number of Hours"`
Label	(Default)	`"Hourly Pay Rate"`
Label	(Default)	`"Gross Pay Earned"`
Label	`lblGrossPay`	`"$0.00"`
TextBox	`txtHoursWorked`	`""`
TextBox	`txtPayRate`	`""`
Button	`btnCalcGrossPay`	`"Calculate Gross Pay"`
Button	`btnClose`	`"Close"`

5. Determine the event handlers and other code needed for each control.

Next, you should list the event handlers and other code that you will write. There are only two event handlers in the *Wage Calculator* application. Table 1-7 lists and describes them. Notice the Visual Basic names for the event handlers. `btnCalcGrossPay_Click` is the name of the event handler invoked when the `btnCalcGrossPay` button is clicked and `btnClose_Click` is the event handler that executes when the `btnClose` button is clicked.

Table 1-7 *Wage Calculator* event handlers

Event Handler Name	Description
`btnCalcGrossPay_Click`	Multiplies the number of hours worked by the hourly pay rate; these values are retrieved from the `txtHoursWorked` and `txtPayRate` TextBox controls and the result of the multiplication is stored in the `lblGrossPay` label's Text property
`btnClose_Click`	Terminates the application

6. Create a flowchart or pseudocode version of the code.

A **flowchart** is a diagram that graphically depicts the flow of a method. It uses boxes and other symbols to represent each step. Figure 1-10 shows a flowchart for the `btnCalcGrossPay_Click` event handler.

Figure 1-10 Flowchart for `btnCalcGrossPay_Click` event handler

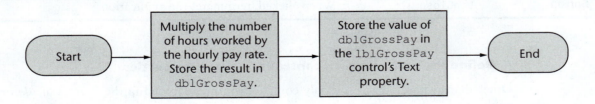

There are two types of boxes in the flowchart shown in Figure 1-10: ovals and rectangles. The flowchart begins with an oval labeled *Start* and ends with an oval labeled *End*. The rectangles represent a computational process or other operation. Notice that the symbols are connected with arrows that indicate the direction of the program flow.

Many programmers prefer to use pseudocode instead of flowcharts. **Pseudocode** is human-readable code that looks similar to programming language code. Although the computer cannot understand pseudocode, programmers often find it helpful to plan an algorithm in a language that's almost a programming language but still very readable by humans. The following is a pseudocode version of the btnCalcGrossPay_Click event handler:

Store Number of Hours Worked × Hourly Pay Rate in the grossPay variable.
Store the value of the grossPay variable in the lblGrossPay control's Text property.

7. Check the flowchart or pseudocode for errors.

In this phase the programmer reads the flowcharts and/or pseudocode from the beginning and steps through each operation, pretending that he or she is the computer. The programmer jots down the current contents of variables and properties that change and sketches what the screen looks like after each output operation. By checking each step, a programmer can locate and correct many errors.

8. Start Visual Studio and create the forms and other controls identified in Step 3.

This step is the first actual work done on the computer. Here, the programmer uses Visual Studio to create the application's user interface and arrange the controls on each form.

9. Use the flowcharts or pseudocode from Step 6 to write the actual code.

This is the second step performed on the computer. The flowcharts or pseudocode that was developed in Step 6 may be converted into code and entered into the computer using Visual Studio.

10. Attempt to run the application. Correct any syntax errors found and repeat this step as many times as necessary.

If you have entered code with syntax errors or typing mistakes, this step will uncover them. A **syntax error** is the incorrect use of a programming language element, such as a keyword, operator, or programmer-defined name. Correct your mistakes and repeat this step until the program runs.

11. Once all syntax errors are corrected, run the program with test data for input. Correct any logic errors. Repeat this step as many times as necessary.

Logic errors are mistakes that do not prevent an application from executing but cause it to produce incorrect results. For example, a mistake in a mathematical formula is a common type of **logic error**. When logic errors are found in a program, they must be corrected and the program retested. This step must be repeated until the program reliably produces satisfactory results.

Checkpoint

1.14 What four items should be identified when defining what a program is to do?

1.15 Describe the importance of good planning in the process of creating a Visual Basic application.

1.16 What does it mean to visualize a program running? What is the value of such an activity?

1.17 What is a flowchart?

1.18 What is pseudocode?

1.19 What is a logic error?

1.20 What is the purpose of testing a program with sample data or input?

1.21 How much testing should you perform on a new program?

1.5 Visual Studio

CONCEPT: Visual Studio consists of tools that you use to build Visual Basic applications. The first step in using Visual Basic is learning about these tools.

To follow the tutorials in this book and create Visual Basic applications, you will need to install **Visual Studio** on your computer. In this book, we are using Visual Studio 2015 Community edition. You can download Visual Studio Community edition for free from www.visualstudio.com.

Visual Studio is an **integrated development environment** (IDE), which means that it provides all the necessary tools for creating, testing, and debugging software. It can be used to create applications not only with Visual Basic, but also with other languages such as Visual C# and C++.

Visual Studio is a customizable environment. If you are working in your school's computer lab, there's a chance that someone else has customized the programming environment to suit his or her own preferences. If this is the case, the screens that you see may not match the ones shown in this book. For that reason it's a good idea to reset the programming environment before you create a Visual Basic application. Tutorial 1-4 guides you through the process.

Tutorial 1-4:
Starting Visual Studio and setting up the environment

VideoNote

Starting Visual Studio and Setting Up the Environment

Step 1: Depending on your operating system, use one of the following procedures to start Visual Studio:

- Windows 10: Open the Start menu, and then select *All Apps*. Scroll down in the list. When you see *Visual Studio 2015* appear, click it.
- Windows 8: On the Start screen, simply start typing Visual Studio. As you type, the search results will appear on the right edge of the screen. When you see *Visual Studio 2015* appear, click it.
- Windows 7: Click the Start button, and then select All Programs. Open the *Visual Studio 2015* program group, and click *Visual Studio 2015*.

Step 2: Figure 1-11 shows the Visual Studio environment. The screen shown in the figure is known as the *Start Page*. By default, the *Start Page* is displayed when you start Visual Studio, but you may or may not see it because it can be disabled. Notice the checkbox in the bottom left corner of the *Start Page* that reads *Show page on startup*. If this box is not checked, the *Start Page* will not be displayed when you start Visual Studio. If you do not see the *Start Page*, you can always display it by clicking *View* on the menu bar at the top of the screen, then clicking *Start Page*.

Figure 1-11 Visual Studio *Start Page*

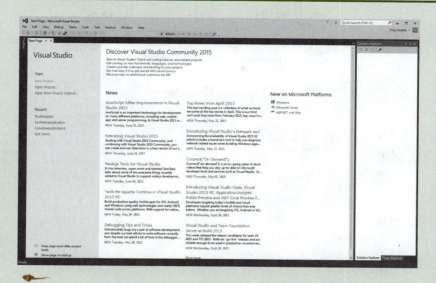

Step 3: In a school computer lab, it is possible that the Visual Studio environment has been set up for a programming language other than Visual Basic. To make sure that Visual Studio looks and behaves as described in this book, you should make sure that Visual Basic is selected as the programming environment. Perform the following:

- As shown in Figure 1-12, click *Tools* on the menu bar and then click *Import and Export Settings*. . . .
- On the screen that appears next, select *Reset all settings* and click the *Next* > button.
- On the screen that appears next, select *No, just reset settings, overwriting my current settings*, and then click the *Next* > button.
- The window shown in Figure 1-13 should appear next. Select *Visual Basic* and then click the *Finish* button.
- After a moment you should see a *Reset Complete* window. Click the *Close* button and continue with the next step in the tutorial.

Figure 1-12 Select *Tools*, then *Import and Export Settings* . . .

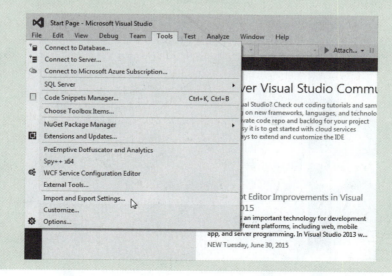

Figure 1-13 Select Visual Basic Development Settings

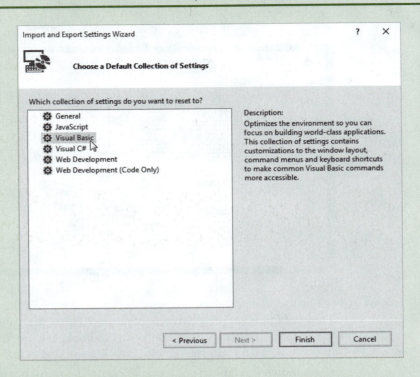

Step 4: Now you will reset Visual Studio's window layout to the default configuration. As shown in Figure 1-14, click *Window* on the menu bar and then click *Reset Window Layout*. Next you will see a dialog box asking *Are you sure you want to restore the default window layout for the environment?* Click *Yes*.

Figure 1-14 Resetting the window layout

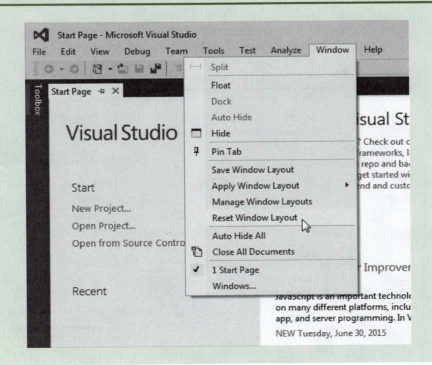

Step 5: Visual Basic has two settings known as *Option Explicit* and *Option Strict*, which many programmers prefer to turn on because they prevent certain types of programming errors. You will learn more about these settings in Chapter 3, but for now verify that they are currently turned on. Click *Tools* on the menu bar at the top of the screen, and then click *Options. . .*, as shown in Figure 1-15. This will display the *Options* window shown in Figure 1-16.

As shown in Figure 1-16, under *Projects and Solutions* (on the left side of the window), select *VB Defaults*. Then, verify that *Option Explicit* and *Option Strict* are set to *On*. Click the OK button to close the window.

The Visual Studio environment is now set up so you can follow the remaining tutorials in this book. If you are working in your school's computer lab, it is probably a good idea to go through these steps each time you start Visual Studio.

If you are continuing with the next tutorial, leave Visual Studio running. You can exit Visual Studio at any time by clicking *File* on the menu bar, and then clicking *Exit*.

Figure 1-15 Click *Tools,* and then *Options*

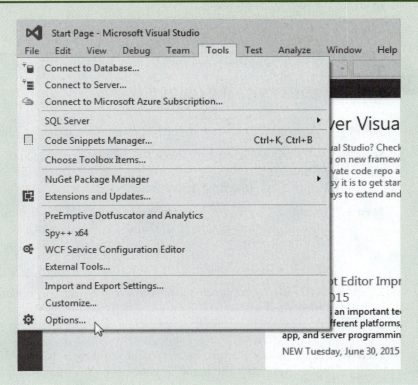

Figure 1-16 The *Options* window

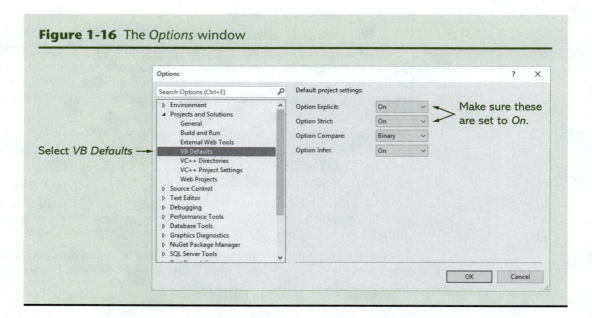

Select *VB Defaults* →

Make sure these are set to *On*.

Starting a New Project

Each Visual Basic application that you create is called a **project**. When you are ready to create a new application, you start a new project. Tutorial 1-5 leads you through the steps of starting a new Visual Basic project.

Tutorial 1-5:

Starting a new Visual Basic project

VideoNote

**Starting a
New Visual
Basic Project**

Step 1: If Visual Studio is not already running, start it as you did in Tutorial 1-4.

Step 2: As shown in Figure 1-17, click *File* on the menu bar at the top of the screen, and then select *New Project. . . .* After doing this, the *New Project* window shown in Figure 1-18 should be displayed.

Step 3: As shown in Figure 1-18, make sure *Installed > Templates > Visual Basic* is selected at the left side of the window. Then, select *Windows Forms Application*, in the center section of the window, as shown in the figure.

> **TIP:** If you don't see *Visual Basic* listed under *Templates*, look for it under *Other Languages*.

Step 4: At the bottom of the *New Project* window you see a *Name* text box. This is where you enter the name of your project. Visual Studio automatically fills this box with a default name. In Figure 1-18 the default name is *WindowsApplication1*. Change the project name to *My First Project*, as shown in Figure 1-19, and click the *OK* button.

Figure 1-17 Starting a new project

Figure 1-18 The *New Project* window

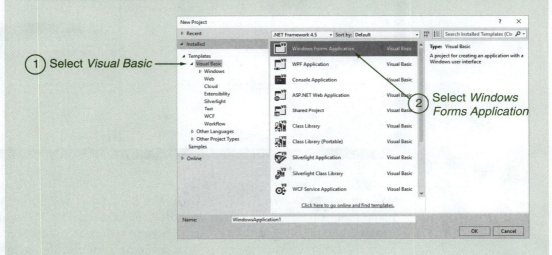

① Select *Visual Basic*

② Select *Windows Forms Application*

Figure 1-19 Changing the project name to *My First Project*

Change the project name to *My First Project*.

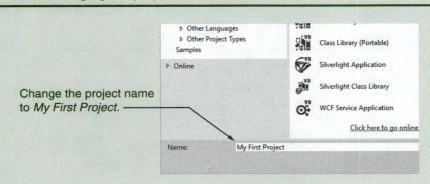

NOTE: As you work through this book you will create a lot of Visual Studio projects. As you do, you will find that default names such as *WindowsApplication1* do not help you remember what each project does. Therefore, you should always change the name of a new project to something that describes the project's purpose.

It might take a moment for the project to be created. Once it is, the Visual Studio environment should appear similar to Figure 1-20. Notice that the name of the project, *My First Project*, is displayed in the title bar at the top of the Visual Studio window.

Figure 1-20 The Visual Studio environment with a new project open

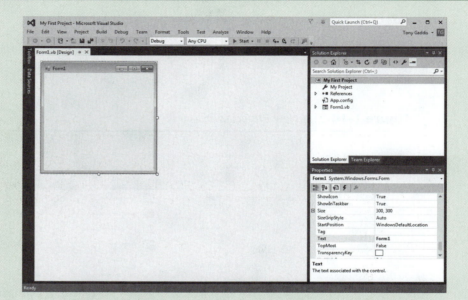

Step 5: Click *File* on the menu bar and then select *Save All*. The *Save Project* window will appear, as shown in Figure 1-21. The *Name* text box shows the project name that you entered when you created the project. The *Location* text box shows where a folder will be created on your system to hold the project. (The location shown on your system will be different from that shown in the figure.) If you wish to change the location, click the *Browse* button and select the desired drive and folder.

Click the *Save* button to save the project.

(Leave Visual Studio running so you can complete the next tutorial.)

Figure 1-21 The *Save Project* window

Save Project		? ✕
Name:	My First Project	
Location:	C:\Users\Tony\documents\visual studio 2015\Projects ⌄	Browse...
Solution Name:	My First Project	☑ Create directory for solution
		☐ Add to source control
		Save Cancel

The Visual Studio Environment

The Visual Studio environment consists of a number of windows that you will use on a regular basis. Figure 1-22 shows the locations of the following windows that appear within the Visual Studio environment: the *Designer* **window,** the *Solution Explorer* **window,** and the *Properties* **window.** Here is a brief summary of each window's purpose:

- The *Designer* Window
  You use the *Designer* window to create an application's graphical user interface. The *Designer* window shows the application's form, and it allows you to visually design its appearance by placing the desired controls that will appear on the form when the application executes.
- The *Solution Explorer* Window
  A **solution** is a container for holding Visual Basic projects. When you create a new VB project, a new solution is automatically created to contain it. The *Solution Explorer* window allows you to navigate among the files in a Visual Basic project.
- The *Properties* Window
  When you are creating a Visual Basic application, you use the *Properties* window to examine and change a control's properties.

Figure 1-22 The *Designer* window, *Solution Explorer* window, and *Properties* window

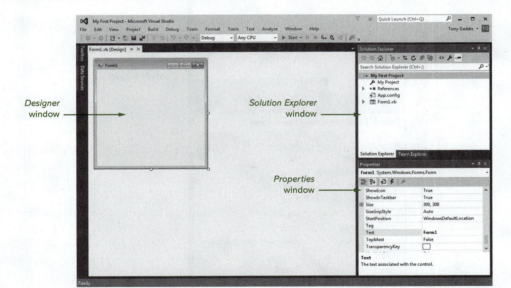

Visual Studio is a customizable environment. You can move these windows around, so they may not appear in the exact locations shown in Figure 1-22. You can also close the windows so they do not appear at all. If you do not see one or more of them, you can follow these steps to make them visible:

- If you do not see the *Designer* window, click *View* on the menu bar. On the *View* menu, click *Designer*. You can also press Shift+F7 on the keyboard. (You can also double-click the Form's filename inside the *Solution Explorer* window.)

- If you do not see the *Solution Explorer* window, click *View* on the menu bar. On the *View* menu, click *Solution Explorer*. You can also press Ctrl+Alt+L on the keyboard.
- If you do not see the *Properties* window, click *View* on the menu bar. On the *View* menu, click *Properties Window*. You can also press F4 on the keyboard.

Auto Hide

Many windows in Visual Studio have a feature known as **Auto Hide**. When you see the pushpin icon in a window's title bar, as shown in Figure 1-23, you know that the window has Auto Hide capability. You click the pushpin icon to turn Auto Hide on or off for a window.

Figure 1-23 *Auto Hide* pushpin icon

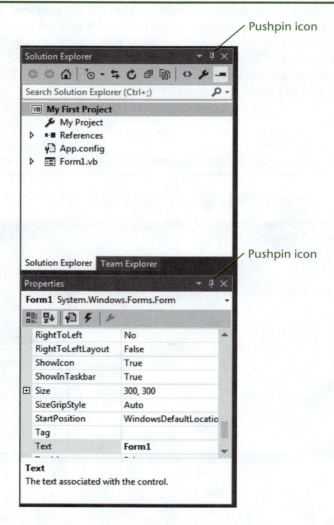

When Auto Hide is turned on, the window is displayed only as a tab along one of the edges of the Visual Studio window. This feature gives you more room to view your application's forms and code. Figure 1-24 shows how the *Solution Explorer* and *Properties* windows appear when their Auto Hide feature is turned on. Notice the tabs that read *Solution Explorer* and *Properties* along the right edge of the screen.

The Menu Bar and the Standard Toolbar

You've already used the Visual Studio menu bar several times. This is the bar at the top of the Visual Studio window that provides menus such as *File, Edit, View, Project,* and so

Figure 1-24 The *Solution Explorer* and *Properties* windows hidden

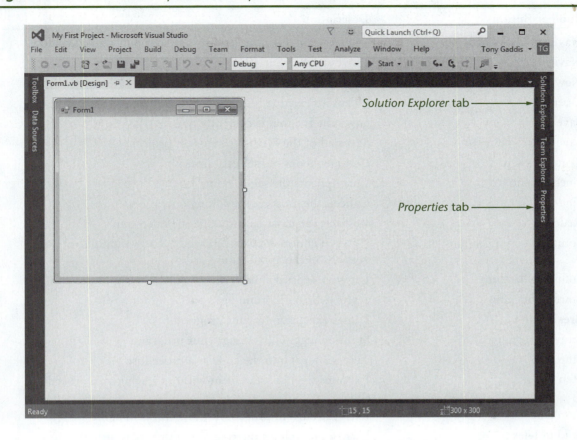

forth. As you progress through this book, you will become familiar with many of the menus. Below the menu bar is the standard toolbar. The **standard toolbar** contains buttons that execute frequently used commands. All commands that are displayed on the toolbar may also be executed from a menu, but the standard toolbar gives you quicker access to them. Figure 1-25 identifies the standard toolbar buttons and Table 1-8 gives a brief description of each.

Figure 1-25 Visual Studio standard toolbar buttons

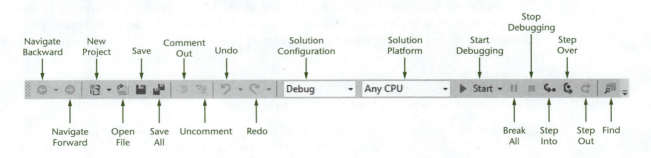

Table 1-8 Visual Studio toolbar buttons

Toolbar Button	Description
Navigate Backward	Moves to the previously active tab in the *Designer* window
Navigate Forward	Moves to the next active tab in the *Designer* window
New Project	Creates a new project
Open File	Opens an existing file
Save	Saves the file that is currently open
Save All	Saves all of the files in the current project
Comment Out	Comments out the selected lines
Uncomment	Uncomments the selected lines
Undo	Cancels the most recent editing operation
Redo	Restores the most recently undone operation
Solution Configurations	Lets you choose between creating Debug and Release versions of the application
Solution Platform	Lets you select the platform on which the application will run
Start Debugging	Starts debugging (running) your program
Break All	Pauses execution of your program
Stop Debugging	Stops debugging (running) your program
Step Into	Traces (steps) into the code in a procedure
Step Over	Executes the next statement without tracing into procedure calls
Step Out	Exits the current procedure while still debugging
Find in Files	Lets you search for a string in multiple files, usually those belonging to your project

 NOTE: Menu items and buttons cannot be used when they are grayed out.

The *Toolbox*

The *Toolbox* is a window that allows you to select the controls that you want to use in an application's user interface. When you want to place a Button, Label, TextBox, or other control on an application's form, you select it in the *Toolbox*. You will use the *Toolbox* extensively as you develop Visual Basic applications.

The *Toolbox* typically appears on the left side of the Visual Studio environment. If the *Toolbox* is in Auto Hide mode, its tab will appear as shown in Figure 1-26. Figure 1-27 shows the *Toolbox* opened, with Auto Hide turned off.

Figure 1-26 The *Toolbox* tab (Auto Hide turned on)

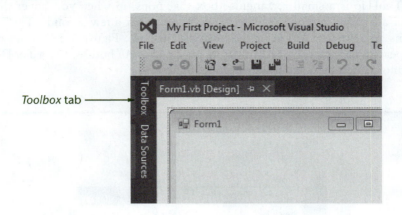

Toolbox tab ⟶

Figure 1-27 The *Toolbox* opened (Auto Hide turned off)

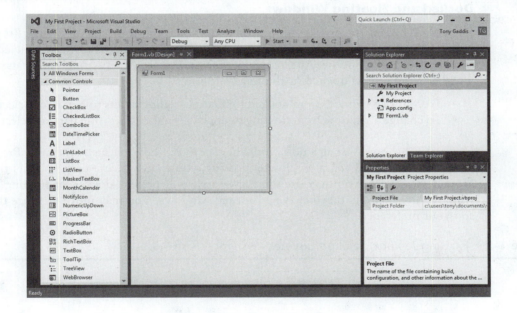

The *Toolbox* is divided into sections, and each section has a name. In Figure 1-27 you can see the *All Windows Forms* and *Common Controls* sections. If you scroll the *Toolbox*, you will see many other sections. Each of the sections can be opened or closed. If you want to open a section of the *Toolbox*, you simply click on its name tab. To close the section, click on its name tab again. In Figure 1-27, the *Common Controls* section is open. You use the *Common Controls* section to access controls that you frequently need, such as Buttons, Labels, and TextBoxes. You can move any section to the top of the list by dragging its name with the mouse.

Using ToolTips

A **ToolTip** is a small rectangular box that pops up when you hover the mouse pointer over a button on the toolbar or in the *Toolbox* for a few seconds. The ToolTip box contains a short description of the button's purpose. Figure 1-28 shows the ToolTip that appears when the cursor is left sitting on the *Save All* button. Use a ToolTip whenever you cannot remember a particular button's function.

Figure 1-28 *Save All* ToolTip

Docked and Floating Windows

Figure 1-27, seen previously, shows the *Toolbox, Solution Explorer,* and *Properties* windows when they are **docked**, which means they are attached to one of the edges of the Visual Studio window. Alternatively, the windows can be **floating**. You can control whether a window is **docked** or floating as follows:

- To change a window from docked to floating, right-click its title bar and select *Float*.
- To change a window from floating to docked, right-click its title bar and select *Dock*.

Figure 1-29 shows Visual Studio with the *Toolbox, Solution Explorer,* and *Properties* windows floating. When a window is floating, you can click and drag it by its title bar around the screen. You may use whichever style you prefer—docked or floating. When windows are floating, they behave as normal windows. You may move or resize them to suit your preference.

Figure 1-29 Floating *Toolbox, Solution Explorer,* and *Properties* windows

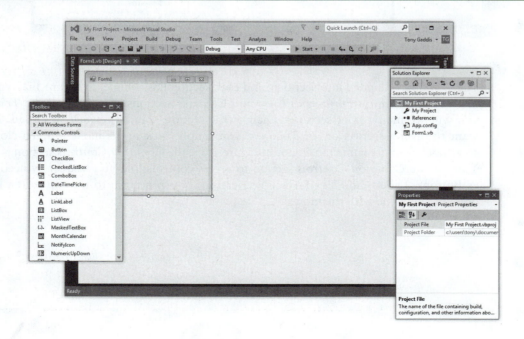

NOTE: A window cannot float if its Auto Hide feature is turned on.

 TIP: Remember, you can always reset the window layout by clicking *Window* on the menu bar, and then selecting *Reset Window Layout*. If you accidentally close the *Designer* window, the *Solution Explorer* window, or the *Properties* window, you can use the *View* menu to redisplay them.

Accessing the Visual Studio Documentation

You can access the full online documentation for Visual Studio by clicking *Help* on the menu bar, and then selecting *View Help*. (Or, you can press Ctrl+F1.) This launches your Web browser and opens the online **Microsoft Developer Network (MSDN) Library**. The MSDN Library provides complete documentation for Visual Basic, as well as the other programming languages included in Visual Studio. You will also find code samples, tutorials, articles, and access to Microsoft instructional videos.

 ## Tutorial 1-6:
Becoming familiar with Visual Studio

VideoNote

Becoming Familiar with Visual Studio

This exercise will give you practice interacting with the *Solution Explorer* window, the *Properties* window, and the *Toolbox*.

Step 1: Visual Studio should still be running on your computer from the previous tutorial. If it is, continue to Step 2.

If Visual Studio is not running on your computer, repeat the steps in Tutorial 1-5 to start a new project. This time, however, name the project *My Second Project*. (This is necessary because you've already created a project named *My First Project*.)

Step 2: Practice turning the Auto Hide feature on and off for the *Solution Explorer* window, the *Properties* window, and the *Toolbox*. Recall from our previous discussion that clicking the pushpin icon in each window's title bar turns Auto Hide on and off. When you are finished practicing, make sure Auto Hide is turned off for each of these windows. Your screen should look like Figure 1-27.

Step 3: Practice floating and docking the *Solution Explorer* window, the *Properties* window, and the *Toolbox*. Recall from our previous discussion that you can make any of these windows float by right-clicking its title bar and selecting *Float*. You dock a floating window by right-clicking its title bar and selecting *Dock*.

Step 4: The *Toolbox, Solution Explorer*, and *Properties* windows each have a *Close* button ([x]) in their upper right corner. Close each of these windows by clicking its *Close* button.

Step 5: Use commands from the *View* menu to restore the *Solution Explorer*, the *Properties* window, and the *Toolbox*.

Step 6: Exit Visual Studio by clicking *File* on the menu bar and then clicking *Exit*. You may see a dialog box asking whether you wish to save changes to a number of items. Click *Yes*.

Checkpoint

1.22   Briefly describe the purpose of the *Solution Explorer* window.

1.23   Briefly describe the purpose of the *Properties* window.

1.24   Briefly describe the purpose of the standard toolbar.

1.25   What is the difference between the toolbar and the *Toolbox*?

1.26   What is a ToolTip?

Summary

1.1 Computer Systems: Hardware and Software

- The major hardware components of a computer are the central processing unit (CPU), main memory, secondary storage devices, input devices, and output devices. Computer programs are stored in machine language, as a series of binary numbers.
- Main memory holds the instructions for programs that are running and data programs are working with. RAM is usually volatile, used only for temporary storage.
- The two general categories of software are operating systems and application software.

1.2 Programs and Programming Languages

- Although a computer can process only programs written in machine language, programmers use languages such as Visual Basic to write programs. They then use a compiler to translate their programs to machine language.
- Keywords (reserved words), operators, variables, syntax, statements, and comments are some of the programming language elements that you will work with when writing a program.
- The part of the program that the user interacts with is called the user interface. Modern systems use graphical user interfaces (GUIs).
- An object is an item in a program that contains data and has the ability to perform operations.
- A control is a type of object that usually appears in a program's graphical user interface.
- There are several types of controls available in Visual Basic. Applications in this chapter contained forms, Labels, TextBoxes, Buttons, CheckBoxes, RadioButtons, ListBoxes, ComboBoxes, and scroll bars.
- The appearance of a screen object, such as a form or other control, is determined by the object's properties.
- An event-driven program is one that responds to events or actions that take place while the program is running.

1.3 More about Controls and Programming

- All controls have a name. Programmers manipulate or access a control in a programming statement by referring to the control by its name. When a programmer creates a control in Visual Basic, it automatically receives a default name.
- Any control whose name appears in a programming statement should have a descriptive, programmer-defined name. Although programmers have a great deal of flexibility in naming controls, they should follow some standard guidelines.

1.4 The Programming Process

- This section outlines the steps for designing and creating a Visual Basic application.

1.5 Visual Studio

- Visual Studio consists of tools used to build Visual Basic applications.
- Visual Basic can be used to create many different types of applications.

Key Terms

algorithm
application software
attributes
Auto Hide
binary numbers
Button control
central processing unit (CPU)
CheckBox control
code
ComboBox control
comments
compiler
control
Designer window
disk drive
docked window
event-driven
event handler
event procedure
floating window
flowchart
Form
graphical user interface (GUI)
GroupBox control
hardware
HScrollBar control
input
input device
integrated development
  environment (IDE)
keywords
Label control
ListBox control
logic error
machine language instructions
main memory
methods
Microsoft Developer Network
  (MSDN) Library
Name property

object
object-oriented programming (OOP)
operating system (OS)
operators
output
output device
PictureBox control
procedure
program
programming languages
project
properties
Properties window
property
pseudocode
RadioButton control
random-access memory (RAM)
remarks
reserved words
SD (Secure Digital) memory cards
secondary storage
software
Solution Explorer window
solid-state drives solution
source code
standard toolbar
statement
syntax
syntax error
Text property
TextBox control
Toolbox window
ToolTip
USB (Universal Serial Bus) drives
user
user interface
variable
Visual Studio
VscrollBar control
window

Review Questions and Exercises

Fill-in-the-Blank

1. The job of the _____ is to fetch instructions, carry out the operations commanded by the instructions, and produce some outcome or resultant information.

2. A(n) _____ is an example of a secondary storage device.

3. The two general categories of software are _____ and _____.

4. A program is a set of _____.

5. Since computers cannot be programmed in natural human language, algorithms must be written in a(n) _____ language.

6. _____ is the only language computers can process directly, without any conversion required.

7. Words that have predefined meaning in a programming language are called _____.

8. A(n) _____ is a name that represents a storage location in memory.

9. _____ are characters or symbols that perform operations on one or more operands.

10. A(n) _____ is part of an application's code but is ignored by the compiler. It is intended for documentation purposes only.

11. Rules that must be followed when writing a program are called _____.

12. _____ is data the computer collects from the world outside of the computer.

13. _____ is data the computer sends to the world outside of the computer.

14. A(n) _____ is a set of well-defined steps for performing a task or solving a problem.

15. A(n) _____ is a diagram that graphically illustrates the flow of a program.

16. _____ is human-readable code that looks similar to programming language code.

17. A(n) _____ is a piece of data that determines some characteristic, such as color or size, of a control.

18. If you do not see the *Solution Explorer* or *Properties* windows in Visual Studio, you may use the _____ menu to make them visible.

19. You click the pushpin icon in a window's title bar to turn the _____ feature on or off.

20. You use the _____ to place Buttons, Labels, TextBoxes, and other controls on an application's forms.

21. The _____ window allows you to navigate among the files in your project.

22. The _____ window allows you to examine and change a control's color, size, and other characteristics.

23. When windows are _____, it means they are attached to one of the edges of the Visual Studio main window.

24. To dock a floating window, right-click its title bar and then select _____.

25. To reset the Visual Studio window layout, you select *Reset Window Layout* from the _____ menu.

26. An alternative way to select Visual Studio menu commands is to use the _____.

27. The _____ window shows your application's form. This is where you design your application's user interface by placing controls on the form that appears when your application executes.

28. When you want to place a Button, Label, TextBox, or other control on an application's form, use the mouse to select it in the _____ and drag it onto the form in the *Designer* window.

29. You can access the full documentation for Visual Studio by clicking _____ on the menu bar, and then selecting *View Help*.

30. A(n) _____ is a small box that is displayed when you hold the mouse cursor over a button on the toolbar or in the *Toolbox* for a few seconds.

Short Answer

1. What is the difference between main memory and secondary storage?
2. What is the difference between operating system software and application software?
3. What is an object?
4. What is a control?
5. Briefly describe what an event-driven program is.
6. From what you have read in this chapter, describe the difference between a Label control and a TextBox control. When is it appropriate to use one or the other?
7. When creating a Visual Basic application, you will spend much of your time doing what three things?
8. What is a form?
9. Summarize the mandatory rules that you must follow when naming a control.
10. What is a keyword?
11. What is the purpose of inserting comments in a program?
12. What is language syntax?
13. What is a syntax error?
14. What is a logic error?
15. What is an operator?
16. What is a flowchart?
17. What is pseudocode?
18. What default name will Visual Basic give to the first Label control that you place on a form? What default name will Visual Basic assign to the first TextBox control that you place on a form?
19. What property determines the text that is displayed by a Label control?
20. What is Auto Hide? How do you turn Auto Hide on or off?
21. What is the *Toolbox* window in Visual Studio?
22. What is the standard toolbar in Visual Studio?
23. What is a ToolTip?
24. If you do not see the *Solution Explorer* window in Visual Studio, how do you display it?
25. If you do not see the *Properties* window in Visual Studio, how do you display it?
26. Figure 1-30 shows the Visual Studio IDE. What are the names of the four areas indicated in the figure?

Figure 1-30 The Visual Studio IDE

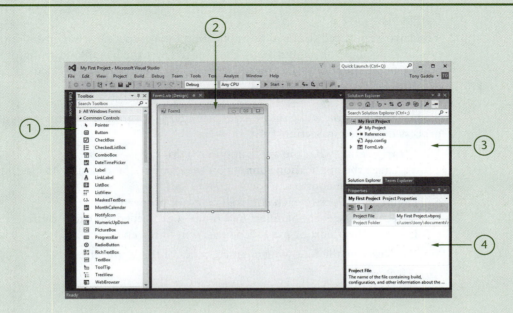

What Do You Think?

1. Are each of the following control names legal or illegal? If a name is illegal, indicate why.
   a. `txtUserName`
   b. `2001sales`
   c. `lblUser Age`
   d. `txtName/Address`
   e. `btnCalcSubtotal`

2. What type of control does each of the following prefixes usually indicate?
   a. `btn`
   b. `lbl`
   c. `txt`

3. For each of the following controls, make up a legal name that conforms to the standard control name convention described in this chapter.
   a. A TextBox control in which the user enters his or her last name
   b. A Button control that, when clicked, calculates an annual interest rate
   c. A Label control used to display the total of an order
   d. A Button control that clears all the input fields on a form

4. The following control names appear in a Visual Basic application used in a retail store. Indicate what type of control each is and guess its purpose.
   a. `txtPriceEach`
   b. `txtQuantity`
   c. `txtTaxRate`
   d. `btnCalcSale`
   e. `lblSubTotal`
   f. `lblTotal`

Programming Challenges

1. Carpet Size

You have been asked to create an application for a carpet sales and installation business. The application should allow the user to enter the length and width of a room and calculate the room's area in square feet. The formula for this calculation is

$$Area = Length \times Width$$

In this exercise, you will gain practice using Steps 1 through 6 of the programming process described in Section 1.4:

1. Clearly define what the application is to do.
2. Visualize the application running on the computer and design its user interface.
3. Determine the controls needed.
4. Define the values of each control's relevant properties.
5. Determine the event handlers and other code needed for each control.
6. Create a flowchart or pseudocode version of the code.

Step 1: Describe the following characteristics of this application:

>Purpose
>Input
>Process
>Output

Step 2: Draw a sketch of the application's form and place all the controls that are needed.

Step 3: Make a list of the controls you included in your sketch. List the control type and the name of each control.

Step 4: List the value of the Text property for each control, as needed. (Remember, some controls do not have a Text property.)

Step 5: List each method needed. Give the name of each method and describe what each method does.

Step 6: For each method you listed in Step 5, draw a flowchart or write pseudocode.

2. Available Credit

A retail store gives each of its customers a maximum amount of credit (commonly known as a credit limit). A customer's available credit is determined by subtracting the amount of credit used by the customer from the customer's maximum amount of credit. As you did in Programming Challenge 1, perform Steps 1 through 6 of the programming process to design an application that determines a customer's available credit.

3. Sales Tax

Perform Steps 1 through 6 of the programming process to design an application that gets from the user the amount of a retail sale and the sales tax rate. The application should calculate the amount of the sales tax and the total of the sale.

4. Account Balance

Perform Steps 1 through 6 of the programming process to design an application that gets from the user the starting balance of a savings account, the total dollar amount of the deposits made to the account, and the total dollar amount of withdrawals made from the account. The application should calculate the account balance.

2 Creating Applications with Visual Basic

TOPICS

2.1 Getting Started with Forms and Controls

CONCEPT: The first step in creating a Visual Basic application is creating the application's graphical user interface. You use the Visual Studio Designer, *Toolbox*, and *Properties* window to build the application's form with the desired controls, and set each control's properties.

In this chapter, you will create your first Visual Basic application. Your first application will consist of three components: a Form, a Button control, and a Label control. Before you start creating the application, however, you need to learn some fundamental concepts about creating user interfaces in Visual Studio. In this section, you will learn the basics of editing forms and creating controls.

The Application's Form

When you start a new Visual Basic project, Visual Studio automatically creates an empty form and displays it in the *Designer*. Figure 2-1 shows an example. Think of the empty form as a blank canvas that can be used to create the application's user interface. You can add controls to the form, change the form's size, and modify many of its characteristics. When the application runs, the form will be displayed on the screen.

Figure 2-1 A new project with a blank form displayed in the *Designer*

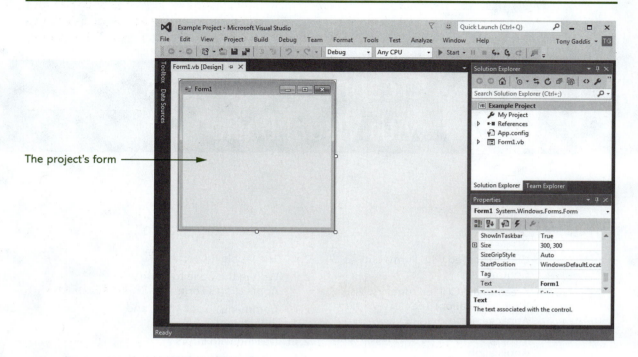

If you take a closer look at the form, you will notice that it is enclosed by a thin dotted line, known as a **bounding box**. As shown in Figure 2-2, the bounding box has small **sizing handles** that appear on the form's right edge, bottom edge, and lower-right corner. When a bounding box appears around an object in the *Designer*, it indicates that the object is selected and is ready for editing.

Figure 2-2 The form's bounding box and sizing handles

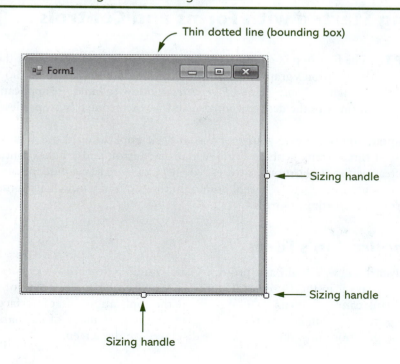

Initially the form's size is 300 pixels wide by 300 pixels high. You can easily resize the form with the mouse. When you position the mouse cursor over any edge or corner that has a sizing handle, the cursor changes to a two-headed arrow (⟺). Figure 2-3 shows examples. When the mouse cursor becomes a two-headed arrow, you can click and drag the mouse to resize form.

Figure 2-3 Using the mouse to resize the form

You learned in Chapter 1 that each form and control must have a name that identifies it. The blank form that Visual Studio initially creates in a new project is named Form1. Later in this book, you will learn how to change a form's name, but for now, you will keep the default name, Form1.

The *Properties* Window

The appearance and other characteristics of a GUI object are determined by the object's properties. When you select an object in the *Designer*, that object's properties are displayed in the *Properties* window. For example, when the Form1 form is selected, its properties are displayed in the *Properties* window as shown in Figure 2-4.

TIP: Recall from Chapter 1 that if the *Properties* window is in Auto Hide mode, you can click its tab to open it. If you do not see the *Properties* window, click *View* on the menu bar. On the *View* menu, click *Properties*.

The area at the top of the *Properties* window shows the name of the object that is currently selected. You can see in Figure 2-4 that the name of the selected object is Form1. Below that is a scrollable list of properties. The list of properties has two columns: the left column shows each property's name, and the right column shows each property's value. For example, look at the form's Size property in Figure 2-4. Its value is *300, 300*. This means that the form's size is 300 pixels wide by 300 pixels high. Next, look at the form's Text property. The Text property determines the text that is displayed in the form's title bar (the bar that appears at the top of the form). Its current value is *Form1*, so the text *Form1* is displayed in the form's title bar.

When a form is created, its Text property is initially set to the same value as the form's name. When you start a new project, the blank form that appears in the *Designer* will always be named Form1, so the text *Form1* will always appear in the form's title bar. In most cases, you want to change the value of the form's Text property to something more

Figure 2-4 The *Properties* window shows the selected object's properties

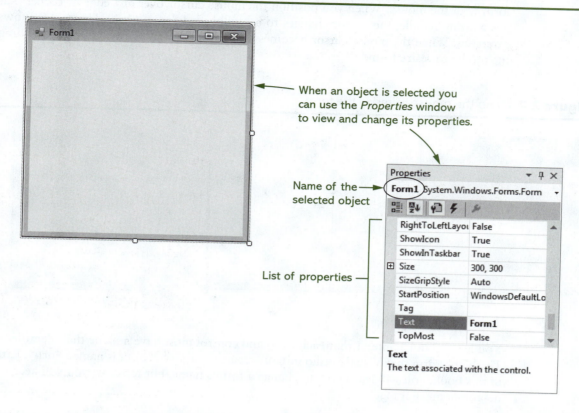

When an object is selected you can use the *Properties* window to view and change its properties.

Name of the selected object

List of properties

meaningful. For example, assume the Form1 form is currently selected. You can perform the following steps to change its Text property to *My First Program*.

- In the *Properties* window, locate the Text property.
- Double-click the word *Form1* that currently appears as the Text property's value, and then use the ⎡Delete⎤ key to delete it.
- Then, type *My First Program* in its place and press the ⎡Enter⎤ key. The text *My First Program* will now appear in the form's title bar, as shown in Figure 2-5.

> **NOTE:** Changing an object's Text property does not change the object's name. For example, if you change the Form1 form's Text property to *My First Program*, the form's name is still Form1. You have only changed the text that is displayed in the form's title bar.

Earlier we discussed how to use the mouse to resize a form in the *Designer*. An alternative method is to change the form's Size property in the *Properties* window. For example, assume the Form1 form is currently selected. You can perform the following steps to change its size to 400 pixels wide by 100 pixels high.

- In the *Properties* window, locate the Size property.
- Click inside the area that holds the Size property's value and delete the current value.
- Then, type *400, 100* in its place and press the ⎡Enter⎤ key. The form will be resized as shown in Figure 2-6.

Figure 2-5 The form's Text property value is displayed in the form's title bar

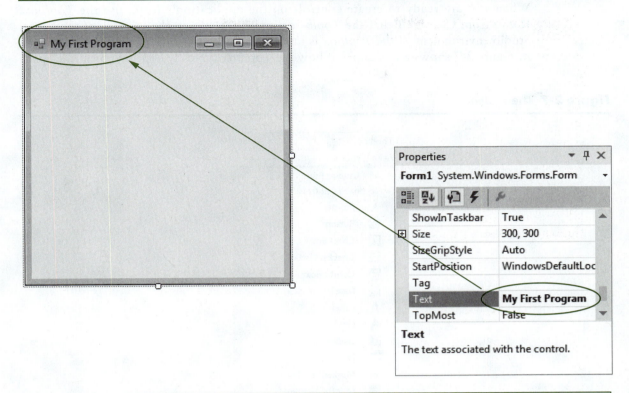

 NOTE: Notice in Figure 2-6 that the **Alphabetical button** ( ) is selected near the top of the *Properties* window. This causes the properties to be displayed in alphabetical order. Alternatively, the **Categorized button** ( ) can be selected, which causes the properties to be displayed in groups. The alphabetical listing is the default selection, and most of the time, it makes it is easier to locate specific properties.

Figure 2-6 The form's size changed to 400 by 100

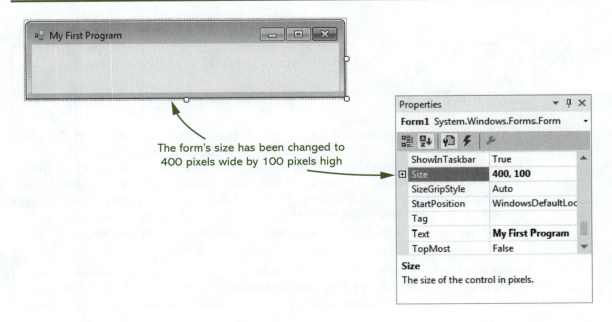

Adding Controls to a Form

When you are ready to create controls on the application's form, use the *Toolbox*. Recall from Chapter 1 that the *Toolbox* usually appears on the left side of the Visual Studio environment. If the *Toolbox* is in Auto Hide mode, you can click its tab to open it. Figure 2-7 shows an example of how the *Toolbox* typically appears when it is open.

Figure 2-7 The *Toolbox*

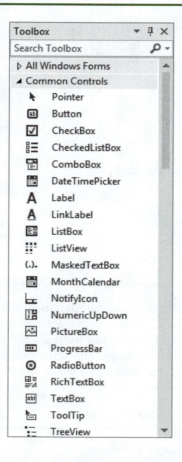

 TIP: If you do not see the *Toolbox* or its tab, click *View* on the menu bar, then click *Toolbox*.

The *Toolbox* shows a scrollable list of controls that you can add to a form. To add a control to a form, you simply find it in the *Toolbox*, and then double-click it. The control will be created on the form. For example, suppose you want to create a Button control on the form. You find the Button tool in the *Toolbox*, as shown in Figure 2-8, double-click it, and a Button control will appear on the form. Likewise, if you want to create a Label control on the form, you locate the Label tool in the *ToolBox* as shown in Figure 2-9. Double-click the Label tool, and a Label control will be created on the form.

 TIP: You can also click and drag controls from the *Toolbox* onto the form.

Figure 2-8 Creating a Button control

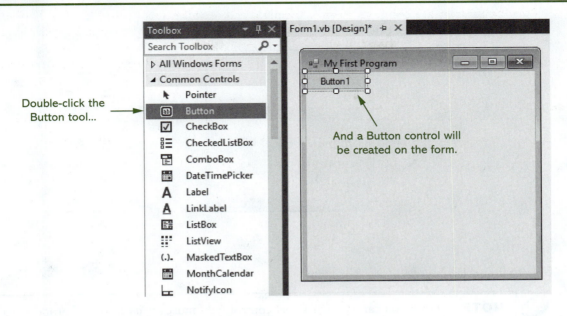

Double-click the
Button tool...

And a Button control will
be created on the form.

Figure 2-9 Creating a Label control

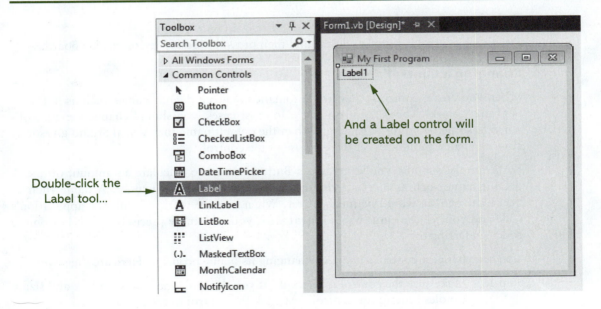

Double-click the
Label tool...

And a Label control will
be created on the form.

Resizing and Moving Controls

Take a closer look at the Button control that is shown on the form in Figure 2-8. Notice that it is enclosed in a bounding box with sizing handles. When you select a control and sizing handles appear around it, you can use the mouse to resize the control. You can also use the mouse to move a control to a new location on the form. Position the mouse cursor inside the control, and when the mouse cursor becomes a four-headed arrow (⊕), click and drag the control to a new location. Figure 2-10 shows a form with a Button control that has been enlarged and moved.

Figure 2-10 A Button control resized and moved

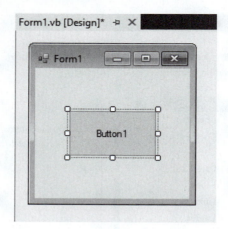

 NOTE: Before you can resize a Label control, you must set its AutoSize property to False. We will discuss the Label control's AutoSize property in greater detail later in this chapter.

Deleting a Control

Deleting a control is simple: select it and then press the ⌨Delete key on the keyboard.

Changing a Control's Name

When you create controls, they are automatically given default names such as Button1, Button2, Label1, Label2, and so forth. In most cases, you should change the control's name to something more meaningful than the default name that Visual Studio gives it. A control's name should reflect the purpose of the control.

For example, suppose you've created a Button control to calculate an amount of tax. A default name such as Button1 doesn't convey the button's purpose. A name such as btnCalculateTax would be much better. When you are working with the application's code and you see the name btnCalculateTax, you will know precisely which button the code is referring to.

You can change a control's name by changing its Name property. Here are the steps:

Step 1:   Make sure the control is selected. (If you don't see the bounding box and sizing handles around the control, just click the control to select it.)

Step 2:   In the *Properties* window, scroll up to the top of the list of properties. You should see the Name property as shown in Figure 2-11. (The Name property is enclosed in parentheses to make it appear near the top of the alphabetical list of properties. This makes it easier to find.)

Step 3:   Click inside the area that holds the Name property's value and delete the current name. Then, type the new name in its place and press the ⌨Enter key. You have successfully changed the name of the control.

Figure 2-12 shows the *Properties* window after a Button control's name has been changed to btnCalculateTax.

Figure 2-11 The Name property

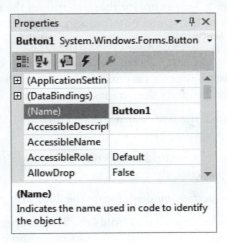

Figure 2-12 The Name property changed to `btnCalculateTax`

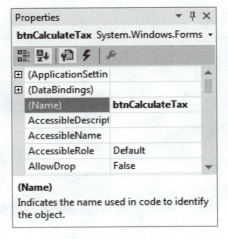

When It Is Acceptable to Keep the Default Name

As you work through this book, you will notice that occasionally we keep a control's default name. The only time we keep a control's default name is when the control's name will not appear in the application's code. This will be the case when a control exists for visual purposes only, and it doesn't *do* anything while the application is running. For example, you might create a Label control to display instructions that tell the user what to do. As the application runs, the label's text never changes, and the control's name never appears in any of the code that you write for the application. In this case, it is acceptable to keep the control's default name.

 NOTE: Keep in mind that some programmers prefer that all the controls in their applications have meaningful names, including controls whose names do not appear in code. If your instructor requires it, be sure to give every control a meaningful name.

More about the Text Property

Some controls have a Text property that determines the text that the control displays on the screen. For example, Forms, Buttons, and Labels have a Text property that works in the following manner:

- A Form's Text property determines the text that is displayed in the Form's title bar.
- A Button's Text property determines the text that is displayed on the Button.
- A Label's Text property determines the text that is displayed by the Label.

If you want to change the text that is displayed by one of these controls, you can change the control's Text property. Here are the steps:

Step 1:   Make sure the control is selected. (If you don't see a bounding box around the control, just click the control to select it.)

Step 2:   In the *Properties* window, locate the Text property.

Step 3:   Click inside the area that holds the Text property's value and delete the current value. Then, type the new text in its place and press the Enter key. The new text will be displayed.

Figure 2-13 shows an example of how changing a Button control's Text property changes the text displayed on the face of the button.

Figure 2-13   A Button control's Text property changed

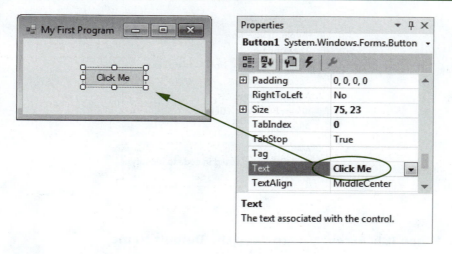

The Text Property and the Name Property

If a control has a Text property, its Text property is initially set to the same value as the control's name. For example, if you create a Button control, and its default name is `Button1`, then the control's Text property will also be set to Button1. Likewise, if you create a Label control, and its default name is `Label1`, then the control's Text property will be set to Label1. This sometimes causes confusion. It is important to remember that the Name property and the Text property are two different things. A control's Name property identifies the control in code, and a control's Text property determines the text the control displays on the screen. When you change a control's Name property, it does not affect the control's Text property, or vice-versa.

Using the *Properties* Window to Select Controls

The box appearing at the top of the *Properties* window, shown in Figure 2-14, shows the name of the currently selected control. This is referred to as the **object box**. In the figure, the Label1 control is currently selected in the object box. If you click inside the object box, a drop-down list will appear showing the names of all of the objects in the form. Figure 2-15 shows an example. You can click the name of an object in the drop-down list to select it. This has the same effect as selecting a control in the *Designer* window. The selected object's properties will be displayed in the *Properties* window.

Figure 2-14 Name of the currently selected control

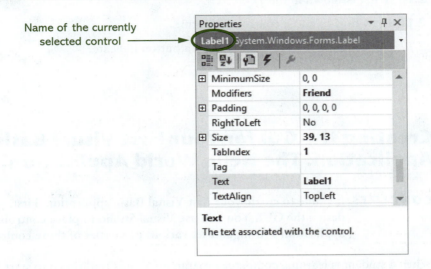

Figure 2-15 Drop-down list of the form's controls

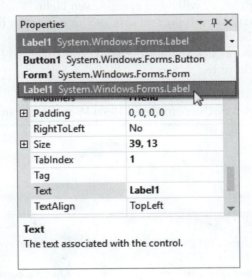

Checkpoint

2.1 When you start a new Visual Basic project, what object is automatically created and displayed in the *Designer*?

2.2 How can you tell that an object is selected and ready for editing in the *Designer*?

2.3 What is the purpose of an object's sizing handles?

2.4 What must each form and control in an application's GUI have to identify it?

2.5 What is the purpose of the *Properties* window?

2.6 What does the Alphabetical button do when selected in the *Properties* window?

2.7 What does the Categorized button do when selected in the *Properties* window?

2.8 What does a form's Text property determine?

2.9 What does a form's Size property determine?

2.10 What is shown in the *Toolbox*?

2.11 How do you add a control to a form?

2.12 What should the text displayed on a button indicate?

2.2 Creating the GUI for Your First Visual Basic Application: The Hello World Application

CONCEPT: It's time to create your first Visual Basic application. First, you will design the GUI. You will use Visual Studio to place controls on the application's form, and set various properties of those controls.

When a student is learning computer programming, it is traditional to start by learning to write a Hello World program. A **Hello World program** is a simple program that displays the words "Hello World" on the screen. In this chapter, you will create your first Visual Basic application, which will be an event-driven Hello World program. When the finished application runs, it will display the form shown on the left in Figure 2-16. Notice that the form displays the text *Click the button*, and it contains a button that reads *Display Message*. When you click the button, the text changes to *Hello World*, as shown in the image on the right in the figure.

Figure 2-16 Screens displayed by the completed Hello World program

Before the button is clicked   After the button is clicked

As shown in Figure 2-17, the GUI for the Hello World application consists of three components:

- A Form named Form1.
- A Button control named btnDisplayMessage. The purpose of the Button control is to cause the message *Hello World* to be displayed.
- A Label control named lblMessage. Initially, it displays the text *Click the button*. When the user clicks the Button control, the Label control's text changes to *Hello World*.

Figure 2-17 The controls in the Hello World program

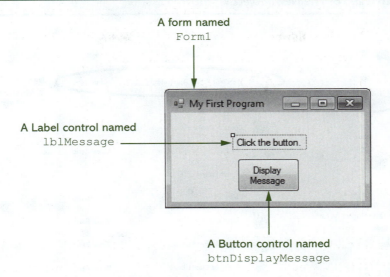

A form named
`Form1`

A Label control named
`lblMessage`

A Button control named
`btnDisplayMessage`

The process of creating this application is divided into two parts. First, you will create the application's GUI, and second, you will write the code that causes the *Hello World* message to appear when the user clicks the button. Tutorial 2-1 leads you through the process of creating the GUI.

VideoNote

Creating the GUI for the Hello World application

Tutorial 2-1:
Creating the GUI for the *Hello World* application

Step 1: Start Visual Studio.

Step 2: Start a new project by clicking *File* on the menu bar, then selecting *New Project....*

Step 3: The *New Project* window should appear. As shown in Figure 2-18, make sure *Visual Basic* is selected under *Installed > Templates* (on the left side of the window). Then, select *Windows Forms Application* as the type of application (in the center part of the window). In the *Name* text box (at the bottom of the window), change the name of the project to *Hello World*. Click the *OK* button to create the project.

Step 4: Make sure the *Toolbox*, the *Solution Explorer*, and the *Properties* window are visible, and that Auto Hide is turned off for each of these windows. The Visual Studio environment should appear as shown in Figure 2-19.

Step 5: Change the `Form1` form's Text property to *My First Program* as shown in Figure 2-20.

Step 6: The form's default size is too large for this application, so you need to make it smaller. Use the technique discussed in section 2.1 of this chapter to adjust the form's size with the mouse. The form should appear similar to that shown in Figure 2-21. (Don't worry about the form's exact size. Just make it appear similar to Figure 2-21.)

Step 7: Now you are ready to add a Button control to the form. Locate the Button tool in the *Toolbox* and double-click it. A Button control should appear on the form as shown in Figure 2-22. Move the Button control so that it appears in the approximate location shown in Figure 2-23.

Figure 2-18 The *New Project* window

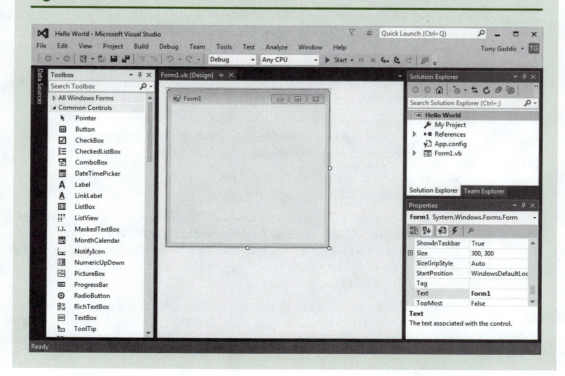

Figure 2-19 The Visual Studio environment

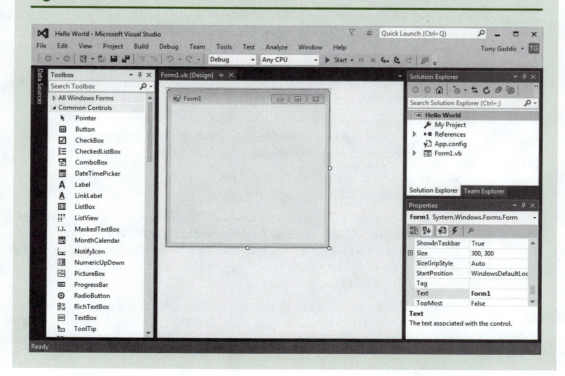

Figure 2-20 The form's Text property changed to *My First Program*

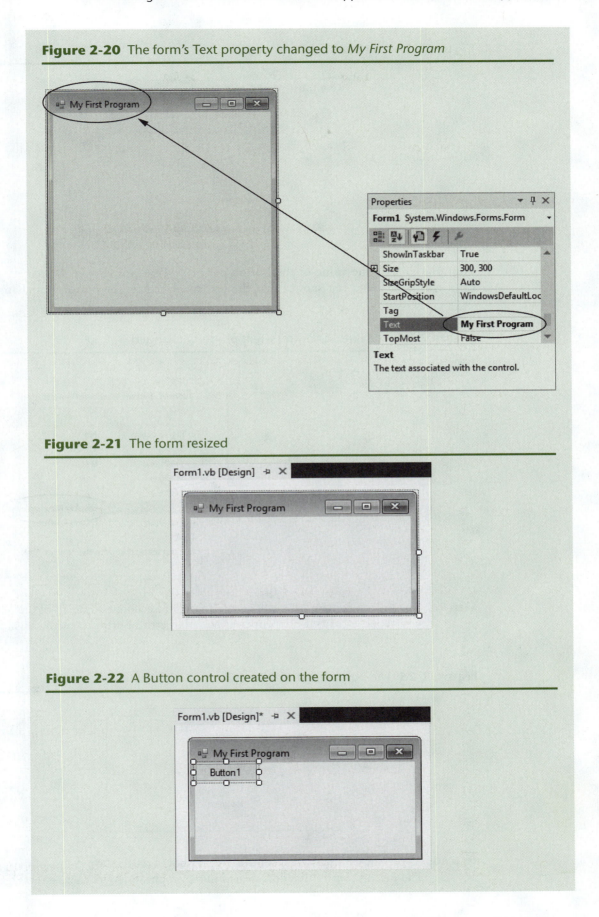

Figure 2-21 The form resized

Figure 2-22 A Button control created on the form

Figure 2-23 The Button control moved

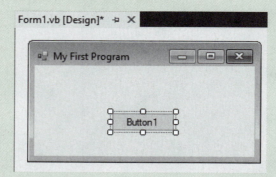

Step 8: Change the value of the Button control's Text property to *Display Message*. After doing this, notice that the text displayed on the button has changed, as shown in Figure 2-24.

Figure 2-24 The Button control's Text property changed

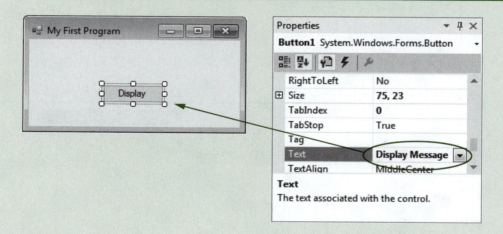

Step 9: The Button control isn't quite large enough to accommodate all of the text that you typed into its Text property, so enlarge the Button control, as shown in Figure 2-25.

Figure 2-25 The Button control enlarged

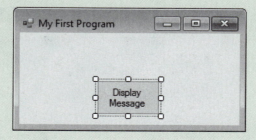

Step 10: As previously discussed, a control's name should reflect the purpose of the control. The Button control that you created in this application will cause a message to be

displayed when it is clicked. The name `Button1` doesn't convey that purpose, however. Change the Button control's Name property to `btnDisplayMessage`. The Properties window should appear as shown in Figure 2-26.

Step 11: Now you are ready to add the Label control. Locate the Label tool in the *Toolbox* and double-click it. A Label control should appear on the form as shown in Figure 2-27.

Figure 2-26 The Button control's Name property changed to `btnDisplayMessage`

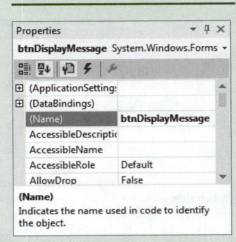

Figure 2-27 A Label control created on the form

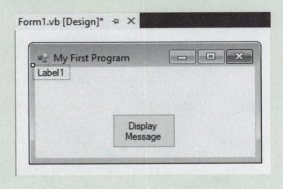

Step 12: Change the value of the Label control's Text property to *Click the button*. After doing this, notice that the text displayed by the label has changed, as shown in Figure 2-28.

Figure 2-28 The Label control's Text property changed

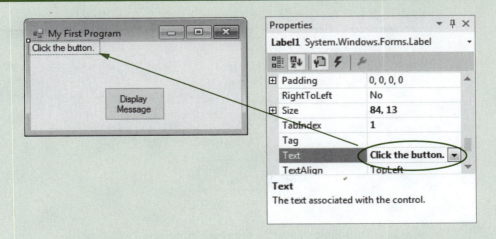

Step 13: Move the Label control so that it appears in the approximate location shown in Figure 2-29.

Step 14: Change the Label control's Name property to `lblMessage`. The *Properties* window should appear as shown in Figure 2-30.

Figure 2-30 The Label control's Name property changed to `lblMessage`

Figure 2-29 The Label control moved

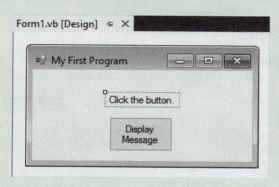

Step 15: Click *File* on the Visual Studio menu bar, then click *Save All* to save the project. You will see the *Save Project* dialog box the first time you save the project. Make sure the correct location is selected, and click the *Save* button.

Step 16: You're only partially finished with the application, but you can run it now to see how the GUI looks on the screen. To run the application, press the F5 key on the keyboard, or click the *Start Debugging* button (▶) on the toolbar. This causes the application to be compiled and executed. You will notice the Visual Studio environment will change its appearance somewhat, and you will see the application's form appear on the screen as shown in Figure 2-31. (Figure 2-31 shows the application running on Windows 10. If you are using a previous version of Windows, the form will look different.)

Figure 2-31 The application running

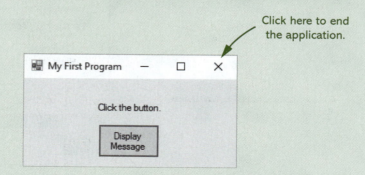

Although the application is running, it isn't capable of doing anything other than displaying the form. If you click the *Display Message* button, nothing will happen. That's because you haven't yet written the code that executes when the button is clicked. You will do that in the next tutorial. To end the application, click the standard Windows close button in the form's upper-right corner. (If you are running Windows 10, the close button will appear as ✕. If you are running a previous version of Windows, the close button will appear as [x].)

Step 17: Leave Visual Studio running for Tutorial 2-2, which takes you through the process of writing an event handler for the `btnDisplayMessage` button.

2.3 Writing the Code for the Hello World Application

CONCEPT: A lot of the code you write in Visual Basic applications will be event handlers. Event handlers respond to specific events that take place while an application is running. In the Hello World application, you will write an event handler that displays a message when the user clicks a button.

VideoNote

Responding to Events

In Tutorial 2-1 you created the GUI for your Hello World application. An application is more than a user interface, however. If you want your application to perform any meaningful actions, you have to write code. For example, if you run the Hello World application right now and click the `btnDisplayMessage` button, nothing will happen. That's because you haven't written the code for the button's event handler.

Recall from Chapter 1 that an event handler is a special type of procedure that executes when a specific event occurs. In the Hello World application, you need to write an event handler that executes when the user clicks the `btnDisplayMessage` button. To create the event handler, you simply double-click the `btnDisplayMessage` button in the *Designer*, as shown in Figure 2-32. This causes the *Code* window to open as shown in Figure 2-33.

The *Code* window is a text-editing window in which you write code. Notice that some code already appears in the window. Let's briefly discuss this code. First, notice that the first and last lines of code read:

```
Public Class Form1
End Class
```
Successinsiden.Hvlapply

Figure 2-32 Double-click the `btnDisplayMessage` control in the *Designer*

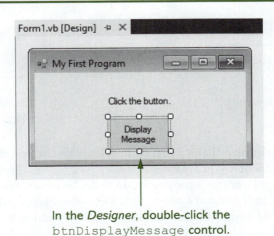

In the *Designer*, double-click the
`btnDisplayMessage` control.

Figure 2-33 The *Code* window

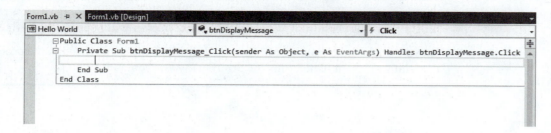

These statements are the beginning and the end of a **class declaration** for the Form1 form. You'll learn more about class declarations in Chapter 12. For now, you just need to know that all of the code for the Form1 form (and all controls on the Form1 form) must appear inside this class declaration.

Next, notice that inside the class declaration, the following two lines of code appear:

```
Private Sub btnDisplayMessage_Click(sender As Object, e As EventArgs) Handles btnDisplayMessage.Click
End Sub
```

This is a **code template** for the btnDisplayMessage button's Click event handler. The template, which has been conveniently written for you, consists of the first and last lines of the event handler's code. Your job is to fill in the code that goes between these two lines. When the application is running, any code that you write between these two lines will be executed when the btnDisplayMessage button is clicked.

For now you do not need to understand all parts of the event handler template code. At this point, you need to understand only the following concepts:

- The event handler begins with the line that starts with Private Sub, and it ends with the line that reads End Sub.
- As shown in Figure 2-34, the event handler's name is btnDisplayMessage_Click. At the end of the first line are the words Handles btnDisplayMessage.Click. This tells us that the code handles the Click event when it happens to the btnDisplayMessage control.

Now you know how to create an empty Click event handler for a Button control. But what code do you write inside the event handler? In the Hello World application, you will write code that displays the message *Hello World* in the lblMessage control.

Figure 2-34 A closer look at the event handler code

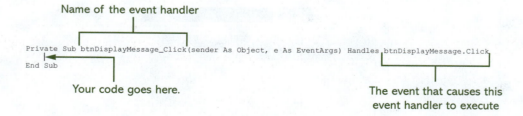

You've already learned that a Label control displays the text that is stored in the control's Text property. When you create a control, you use the *Properties* window to initially store values in the control's properties. In code, however, you use **assignment statements** to store values in a control's properties. The following assignment statement stores the text *Hello World* in the lblMessage control's Text property:

```
lblMessage.Text = "Hello World"
```

The equal sign (=) is known as the **assignment operator** . It assigns the value that appears on its right side to the item that appears on its left side. In this example, the item on the left side of the assignment operator is the expression `lblMessage.Text`. This is the `lblMessage` control's Text property. The value on the right side of the assignment operator is `"Hello World"`. The value `"Hello World"` is a **string**, which is a piece of data that is a sequence of one or more characters. When this statement executes, the string `"Hello World"` is assigned to the `lblMessage` control's Text property. This causes the text *Hello World* to be displayed in the Label control.

Notice in the previously shown assignment statement that the string `"Hello World"` is enclosed in double quotation marks. It is important to remember that the quotation marks are not part of the string. They are required in the code to indicate the beginning and the end of the string. When the statement executes, the text that appears between the quotation marks will be assigned to the Label control's Text property. Likewise, when the text is displayed the double quotation marks will not appear.

Figure 2-35 shows the completed Click event handler for the `btnDisplayMessage` button in the Hello World application. Figure 2-36 shows the application's form after the user has clicked the button. Notice that the text Hello World is displayed by the Label control.

Figure 2-35 The completed Click event handler

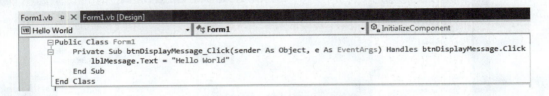

Figure 2-36 The Hello World application's form after the user has clicked the button

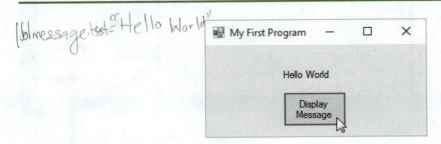

> **NOTE:** The first line of the event handler template is a long line of code. Because this line of code is so long, we will sometimes leave out the part that appears inside the parentheses, as shown here:
>
> To simplify the way code appears in this book,
we sometimes leave out the code that appears here.
>
> ```
> Private Sub btnDisplayMessage_Click(...) Handles btnDisplayMessage.Click
>
> End Sub
> ```
>
> We do this to simplify the appearance of the code in the book.

Now you know everything necessary to complete the Hello World application. In Tutorial 2-2 you will open the project and add a Click event handler for the `btnDisplayMessage` control. Inside the event handler you will write an assignment statement that stores the text *Hello World* in the `lblMessage` control's Text property. When you run the application, the text *Hello World* will be displayed by the label when the user clicks the button.

VideoNote

Writing the code for the Hello World application

Tutorial 2-2:
Writing code for the *Hello World* application

Step 1: If Visual Studio is not already running, start it. Open the *Hello World* project that you started in Tutorial 2-1. The application's form should appear in the *Designer*, as shown in Figure 2-37.

Figure 2-37 The *Hello World* project loaded with Form1 shown in the *Designer*

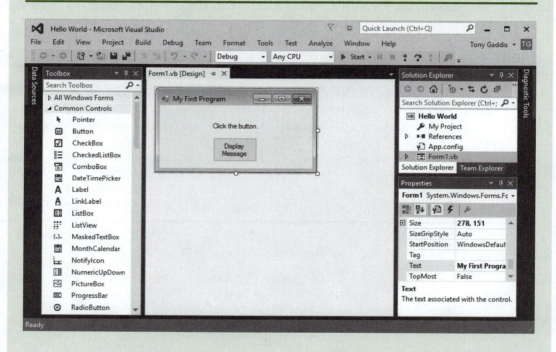

Step 2: In the *Designer*, double-click the `btnDisplayMessage` control. This should cause the *Code* window to appear as shown in Figure 2-38. Notice that an empty event handler named `btnDisplayMessage_Click` has been created.

Figure 2-38 *Code* window with an empty event handler

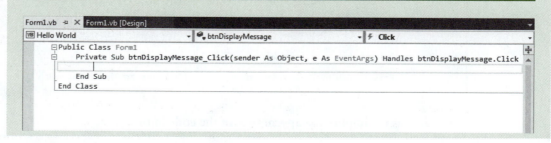

Step 3:   Inside the `btnDisplayMessage_Click` event handler, type the following statement exactly as it is shown:

```
lblMessage.Text = "Hello World"
```

When you have finished, the *Code* window should look like Figure 2-39.

Figure 2-39 Statement written inside the event handler

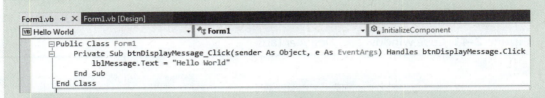

 NOTE: Did you notice that as soon as you started typing the statement, a box containing code popped up on the screen, at the point where you were typing? This is known as the **IntelliSense** list box. IntelliSense is a feature of Visual Studio that helps you write code faster. Later in this chapter we have included a section that explains more about IntelliSense. Until you've had time to read that section, just ignore the IntelliSense boxes.

Step 4:   Save the project.

Step 5:   Press the ⟨F5⟩ key on the keyboard, or click the *Start Debugging* button (▶) on the toolbar to compile and run the application.

 NOTE: If you typed the statement correctly inside the `btnDisplayMessage_Click` event handler (in Step 3), the application should run. If you did not type the statement correctly, however, a window will appear reporting build errors. If that happens, click the *No* button in the window, then correct the statement so it appears exactly as shown in Figure 2-39.

When the application runs, it will display the form shown on the left in Figure 2-40. When you click the button, the text changes to *Hello World*, as shown in the image on the right in the figure.

Figure 2-40 The *Hello World* application running

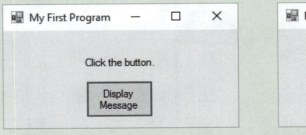   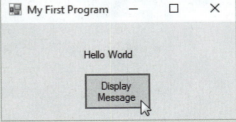

Before the button is clicked   After the button is clicked

Step 6:   To end the application, click the standard Windows close button (✕) in the form's upper-right corner.

Switching between the *Code* Window and the *Designer*

When you open the *Code* window, it appears in the same part of the screen as the *Designer*. While developing a Visual Basic application, you will often find yourself needing to switch back and forth between the *Designer* and the *Code* window. One way to quickly switch between the two windows is to use the tabs shown in Figure 2-41. In the figure, notice that the leftmost tab reads *Form1.vb*. That is the tab for the *Code* window. The rightmost tab reads *Form1.vb [Design]*. That is the tab for the *Designer*. (The tabs may not always appear in this order.) To switch between the *Designer* and the *Code* window, you simply click the tab for the desired window.

Figure 2-41 *Code* window and *Designer* tabs

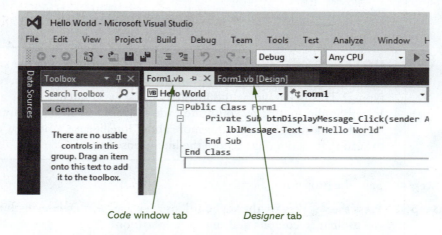

Code window tab   Designer tab

You can also use the *Solution Explorer* to open the *Code* window. Simply right-click Form1.vb in the *Solution Explorer*. A pop-up menu will appear, as shown in Figure 2-42. On the pop-up menu, click *View Code*. The code for Form1 will be displayed in the *Code* window.

Figure 2-42 *Code* window and *Designer* tabs

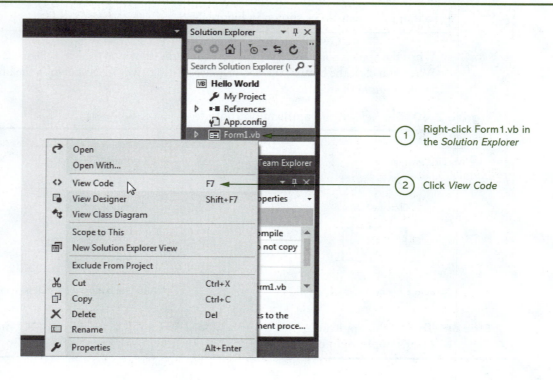

If you detach the *Code* window and move it to another part of the screen, you can see the *Code* window and the *Designer* at the same time. As shown in Figure 2-43, click the *Code* window tab and drag it to the desired location on the screen. (If you have multiple monitors connected to your computer, you can even drag the *Code* window to a different monitor.) To return the *Code* window to its position within the IDE, right-click the tab for the source code file in the *Code* window and select *Move to Main Document Group*. This is shown in Figure 2-44.

Figure 2-43 Detaching the *Code* window by clicking and dragging

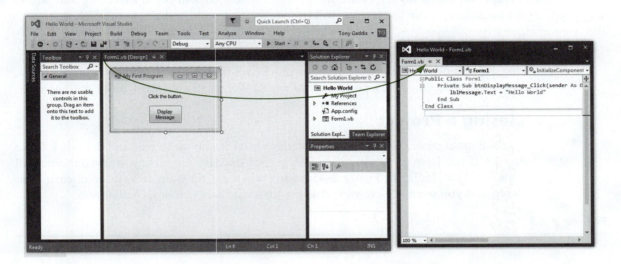

Figure 2-44 Returning the *Code* window to its docked position

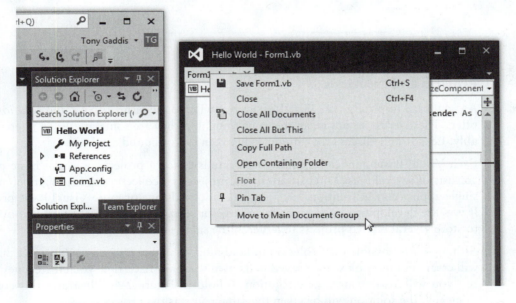

Design Mode, Run Mode, and Break Mode

Visual Studio has three modes in which it operates as you develop and test an application. The three modes are design mode, run mode, and break mode. You have already experienced **design mode**. This is the mode in which you create an application. When you are placing controls on an application's form or writing Visual Basic code, Visual Studio is operating in design mode. (Design mode is also known as **design time**.)

When you are ready to run an application that you are developing, you can execute it without leaving the Visual Studio environment. This puts Visual Studio in **run mode** (also known as **runtime**). The application will be running on the computer, and you can interact with it as the user. There are three ways to run an application from the Visual Studio environment:

- Click the *Start Debugging* button (▶) on the toolbar
- Click *DEBUG* on the menu bar, then select *Start Debugging*
- Press the F5 key

When you perform one of these actions, the Visual Basic compiler will begin compiling the application. If no errors are found, the application will begin executing and Visual Studio will enter run mode. You will experience run mode in the next tutorial.

Break mode is a special mode that allows you to momentarily suspend a running application for testing and debugging purposes. It is also the mode that Visual Studio enters when a running application encounters a runtime error. (Recall from Chapter 1 that a runtime error is an error that occurs while a program is running.) We will discuss break mode in Chapter 3.

Closing a Project

To close the current project, click *File* on the Visual Studio menu bar, and then click *Close Project*. If you have made changes to the project since the last time you saved it, you will see a window similar to Figure 2-45 asking whether you want to save or discard your changes. If you want to save your changes (in most cases you do), click *Save*.

Figure 2-45 *Save Changes* window

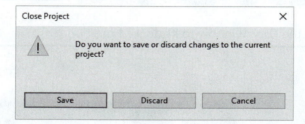

Projects and Solutions

As you learn to program in Visual Basic, you will see the terms *project* and *solution* used often. These terms do not mean the same thing, but they are sometimes used interchangeably. Let's briefly discuss the difference between a project and a solution.

Each Visual Basic application that you create is called a **project**. A Visual Basic project consists of several files. You can think of a project as a collection of files that belong to a single application. A **solution** is a container that holds one or more Visual Basic projects. If you are developing applications for a large organization, you might find it convenient to store several related projects together in the same solution.

Although it is possible for a solution to hold more than one project, each project that you will create in this book will be saved in its own solution. Each time you create a new project, you will also create a new solution to hold it. Figure 2-46 illustrates this concept. Typically, the solution will be given the same name as the project.

How Solutions and Projects Are Typically Organized on the Disk

When you save a project the first time in Visual Studio, you see the *Save Project* window shown in Figure 2-47. The window shows the project name, the location on the disk where the project will be saved, and the solution name. By default the solution's name will be the same as the project's name. Notice the *Browse. . .* button that appears next to the location. You can click this button to select a different location, if you wish.

Figure 2-46 Solution and project organization

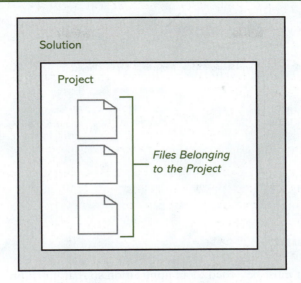

Figure 2-47 Specifying the project name, solution name, and location

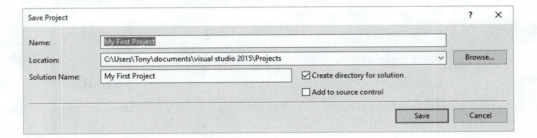

Also notice the *Create directory for solution* check box. It is a good idea to leave this box checked. It causes a directory (folder) for the solution to be created at the specified location. Inside that directory, another directory (folder) will be created for the project.

Let's use Figure 2-47 to see an example of how the files for the *My First Project* solution and project will be organized on the disk. Notice that in Figure 2-47 the following location is shown for the solution:

```
C:\Users\Tony\documents\visual studio 2015\Projects\
```

On your system, the location will not be exactly the same as this, but it will be something similar. At this location, a **solution folder** named *My First Project* will be created. If we use Windows to look inside that folder, we will see the two items shown in Figure 2-48. Notice that one of the items is another folder named *My First Project*. That is the **project folder**, which contains various files related to the project. The other item is the **solution file**. In Windows, you can double-click the solution file to open the project in Visual Studio.

Opening an Existing Project

If Visual Studio is already running, you can perform the following steps to open an existing project:

- Click *File* on the Visual Studio menu bar, then select *Open Project. . . .*
- The *Open Project* window will appear. Navigate to the desired solution folder, select the solution file, and click *Open*.

Figure 2-48 Contents of the *My First Project* solution folder

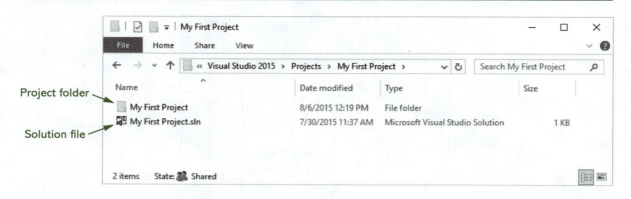

Checkpoint

2.13   What must be added to an application so that it can provide responses to actions by users?

2.14   How do you create an event handler for a button?

2.15   What is the *Code* window?

2.16   What is a string?

2.17   What is the assignment operator? What does it do?

2.18   How do you switch between the *Designer* and the code editor?

2.19   What are the three modes that Visual Studio operates in as you develop and test an application?

2.20   What is a project?

2.21   What is a solution?

2.4 More About Label Controls

CONCEPT: A Label control displays text on a form. Label controls have various properties that affect the control's appearance. Label controls can be used to display unchanging text, or program output.

When you create Label controls, they are automatically given default names such as `Label1`, `Label2`, and so forth. A Label control's Text property is initially set to the same value as the Label control's name. So, a Label control will display its own name when it is created, as shown by the example in Figure 2-49. When a Label control is selected in the *Designer*, you can use the *Properties* window to change its Text property. Figure 2-50 shows a Label control after its Text property has been changed to *Programming in Visual Basic is fun!*

You can also use the *Properties* window to change a Label control's name. If you are going to refer to the control in the application's code, you should change the control's name to something more meaningful than the default name that Visual Studio gives it.

Figure 2-49 Creating a Label control

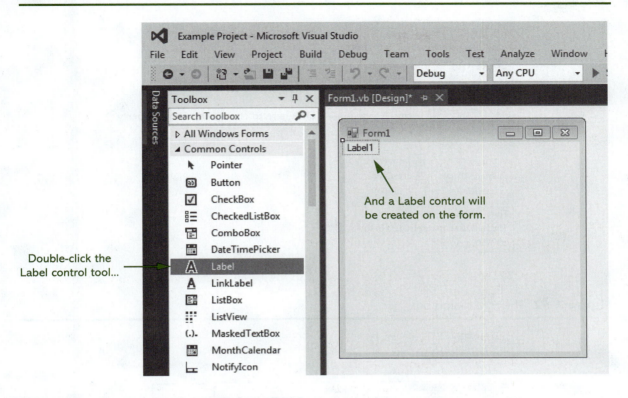

Figure 2-50 A Label control displaying a message

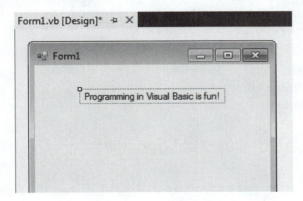

The Font Property

If you want to change the appearance of a Label control's text, you can change the control's Font property. The **Font property** allows you to set the font, font style, and size of the control's text. When you select the Font property in the *Properties* window, you will notice that an ellipses button (...) appears next to the property's value, as shown in Figure 2-51. When you click the ellipses button, the *Font* dialog box appears, as shown in Figure 2-52. Select a font, font style, and size, and click *OK*. The text displayed by the control will be updated with the selected attributes. For example, Figure 2-53 shows a Label control with the following Font property attributes:

Font: Lucida Handwriting
Font Style: Italic
Size: 10 point

Figure 2-51 The Font property

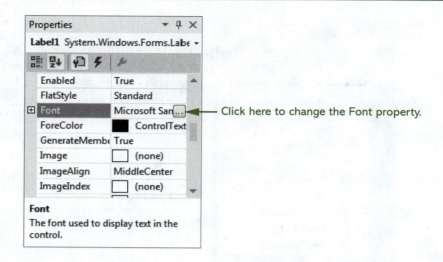

Click here to change the Font property.

Figure 2-52 The *Font* dialog box

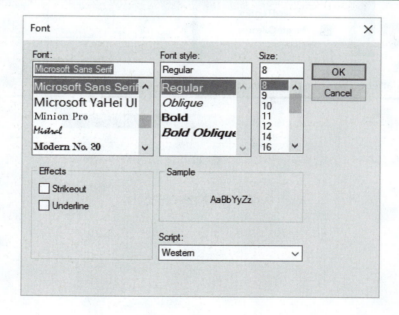

Figure 2-53 A label's appearance with altered font attributes

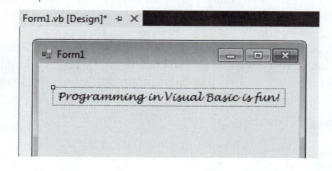

The BorderStyle Property

Label controls have a **BorderStyle property** that allows you to display a border around the control's text. The BorderStyle property may have one of three values: None, FixedSingle, or Fixed3D. The property is set to None by default, which means that no border will appear around the control's text. If the BorderStyle property is set to FixedSingle, the control's text will be outlined with a thin border. If the BorderStyle property is set to Fixed3D, the control's text will have a recessed 3D appearance. Figure 2-54 shows an example of Label controls with each BorderStyle setting.

Figure 2-54 BorderStyle examples

To change the BorderStyle property, select it in the *Properties* window and then click the down-arrow button (⌄) that appears next to the property's value. As shown in Figure 2-55, a drop-down list will appear containing the three possible values for this property. Select the desired value and the control's text will be updated.

Figure 2-55 BorderStyle selections

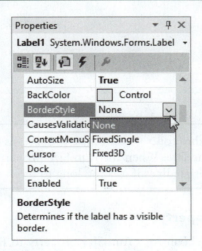

The AutoSize Property

Label controls have an **AutoSize property** that controls the way they can be resized. The AutoSize property is a **Boolean property**, which means that it can be set to one of two possible values: True or False. By default, a Label control's AutoSize property is set to True, which means that the control automatically resizes itself to accommodate the size of the text it displays. For example, look at the three Label controls in Figure 2-56. Each of the controls displays different amounts of text at different font sizes. Because each control's BorderStyle property is set to FixedSingle, you can see that each control is just large enough to accommodate its text.

Figure 2-56 Label controls with AutoSize set to True

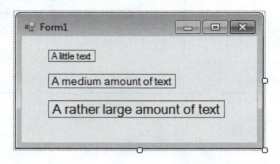

When a Label control's AutoSize property is set to True, you cannot manually change the size of the control by clicking and dragging its bounding box. If you want to manually change the size of a Label control, you have to set its AutoSize property to False. When AutoSize is set to False, sizing handles will appear around the control, allowing you to click and drag the bounding box to resize the control. Figure 2-57 shows an example. In the figure, the Label control has been resized, so it is much larger than the text it displays.

Figure 2-57 Label control with AutoSize set to False

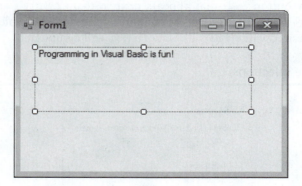

 NOTE: When a Label control's AutoSize property is set to True, the label's text will always appear on one line. When the AutoSize property is set to False, the label's text will wrap across multiple lines if it is too long to fit on one line.

The TextAlign Property

When you set a Label control's AutoSize property to False and then manually resize the control, it sometimes becomes necessary to change the way the label's text is aligned. By default, a label's text is aligned with the top and left edges of the label's bounding box. For example, look at the label shown in Figure 2-57. Notice how the text is positioned in the label's upper-left corner.

What if we want the text to be aligned differently within the label? For example, what if we want the text to be centered in the label or positioned in the lower-right corner? We can change the text's alignment in the label with the **TextAlign property.** The TextAlign property may be set to any of the following values: TopLeft, TopCenter, TopRight, MiddleLeft,

MiddleCenter, MiddleRight, BottomLeft, BottomCenter, or BottomRight. Figure 2-58 shows nine Label controls, each with a different TextAlign value.

Figure 2-58 Text alignments

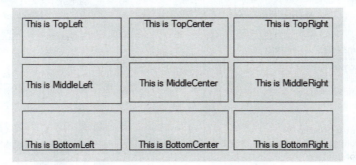

To change the TextAlign property, select it in the *Properties* window and then click the down-arrow button (∨) that appears next to its value. This causes a dialog box with nine buttons, as shown in the left image in Figure 2-59, to appear. As shown in the right image in the figure, the nine buttons represent the valid settings of the TextAlign property.

Figure 2-59 Setting the TextAlign property

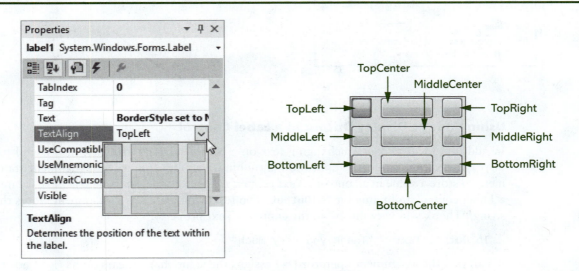

Changing the Background and Foreground Colors

You can use a Label control's **ForeColor property** to change the color of the label's text. You can also use the control's **BackColor property** to change the control's background color. When you select either the ForeColor or BackColor property in the *Properties* window, a down-arrow button (∨) appears next to the property's value. Click the down-arrow button and a drop-down list of colors appears, as shown in Figure 2-60.

Notice that the drop-down list has three tabs: *Custom*, *Web*, and *System*. The *System* tab lists colors defined in the current Windows configuration. The *Web* tab lists colors displayed with consistency in Web browsers. The *Custom* tab displays a color palette, as shown in Figure 2-61.

Figure 2-60 Drop-down list of colors

Figure 2-61 Custom color palette

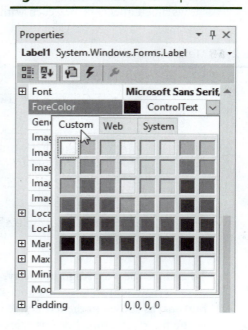

Using Code to Display Output in a Label Control

In addition to displaying unchanging text on a form, Label controls are also useful for displaying output while an application is running. In code, you use an assignment statement to store a value in a control's Text property. For example, suppose you have created a Label control and named it lblOutput. The following assignment statement stores the string "Thank you very much" in the control's Text property.

```
lblOutput.Text = "Thank you very much"
```

Recall that the assignment operator (=) assigns the value that appears on its right side to the item that appears on its left side. In this example, the item on the left side of the assignment operator is the expression lblOutput.Text. This is simply the lblOutput control's Text property. The value on the right side of the assignment operator is the string "Thank you very much". When this statement executes, the string "Thank you very much" is assigned to the lblOutput control's Text property. When this statement executes, the text *Thank you very much* is displayed in the Label control.

 WARNING! When writing assignment statements, remember that the item receiving the value must be on the left side of the = operator. The following statement, for example, is wrong and will cause an error when you compile the program:

```
"Thank you very much" = lblOutput.Text   ← ERROR!
```

NOTE: The standard notation for referring to a control's property in code is:

ControlName.PropertyName

The Text Property Accepts Strings Only

Strings are a type of data that you will use commonly in programming. You learned earlier in this chapter that a string is a sequence of one or more characters. Strings are meant to hold text items such as names, addresses, messages, and so on. When a string is written into a program's code, it is always enclosed in quotation marks. The quotation marks are not part of the string, but simply mark the beginning and end of the sequence of characters.

In programming, when a piece of data is written into a program's code, it is called a **literal**, because the data is literally written into the program. A string that is written into a program's code (and enclosed in quotation marks) is called a **string literal**.

It is important to point out that a control's Text property can accept strings only. You cannot assign a number to the Text property. For example, let's assume that an application has a Label control named `lblResult`. The following statement will cause an error because it is attempting to store the number 5 in the `lblResult` control's Text property:

```
lblResult.Text = 5    ← ERROR!
```

This does not mean that you cannot display a number in a label, however. If you put quotation marks around the number, it becomes a string literal. The following statement will work:

```
lblResult.Text = "5"
```

NOTE: The only time it is necessary to enclose a string in quotation marks is when you type the string into a program's code. For example, when you are using the *Properties* window in Visual Studio to store a value in a control's Text property, you do not enclose the value in quotation marks. If you did, the quotation marks would be displayed by the control.

Clearing a Label

In code, if you want to clear the text that is displayed in a Label control, assign an empty string (`""`) to the control's Text property, as shown here:

```
lblAnswer.Text = ""
```

As an alternative, you can clear a Label control by assigning the special value `String.Empty` to the control's Text property. Here is an example:

```
lblAnswer.Text = String.Empty
```

 **Checkpoint**

2.22 When you create a Label control, what is the control's Text property initially set to?

2.23 What is the default value of a label's BorderStyle property?

2.24 How do you change the BorderStyle property of a control in the *Properties* window?

2.25   What property determines whether a label can be resized?

2.26   What property determines the way text is aligned in a Label control?

2.27   What happens when you modify a Label control's BackColor property?

2.28   What happens when you modify a Label control's ForeColor property?

2.29   What three color categories are available when you edit a control's BackColor property?

2.30   What is a literal?

2.31   A string literal must be enclosed in what characters?

2.32   A control's Text property can accept data only of what type?

2.33   In code, how do you clear the text that is displayed in a Label control?

2.5   Creating Multiple Event Handlers

CONCEPT: Most applications that you will develop will have multiple event handlers, responding to different events.

The *Hello World* application that you developed in Tutorials 2-1 and 2-2 has only one button with a Click event handler. Many applications that you will develop will have multiple buttons, each with its own Click event handler. For example, the form shown in Figure 2-62 has three Button controls. As shown in the figure, the controls are named `btnFirst`, `btnSecond`, and `btnThird`.

Figure 2-62 A form with multiple Button controls

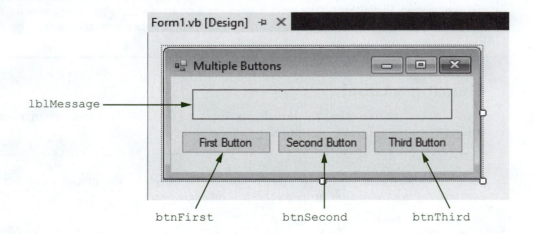

To create Click event handlers for the buttons, you simply double-click each Button control in the *Designer* and an empty event handler will be created in the form's source code file. The names of the Click event handlers will be `btnFirst_Click`, `btnSecond_Click`, and `btnThird_Click`. Figure 2-63 shows an example of the form's source code after the three event handlers have been created. Notice that each of the event handlers assigns a different string to the `lblMessage` Label control, causing a different message to be displayed on the screen. Figure 2-64 shows the application's form at runtime, after each button has been clicked.

Figure 2-63 Source code with three Click event handlers

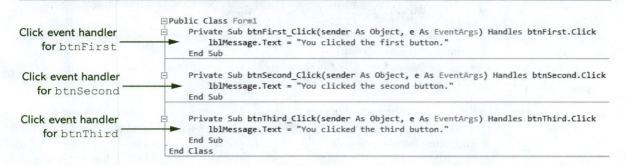

Click event handler for `btnFirst`

Click event handler for `btnSecond`

Click event handler for `btnThird`

```
Public Class Form1
    Private Sub btnFirst_Click(sender As Object, e As EventArgs) Handles btnFirst.Click
        lblMessage.Text = "You clicked the first button."
    End Sub

    Private Sub btnSecond_Click(sender As Object, e As EventArgs) Handles btnSecond.Click
        lblMessage.Text = "You clicked the second button."
    End Sub

    Private Sub btnThird_Click(sender As Object, e As EventArgs) Handles btnThird.Click
        lblMessage.Text = "You clicked the third button."
    End Sub
End Class
```

Figure 2-64 The application running

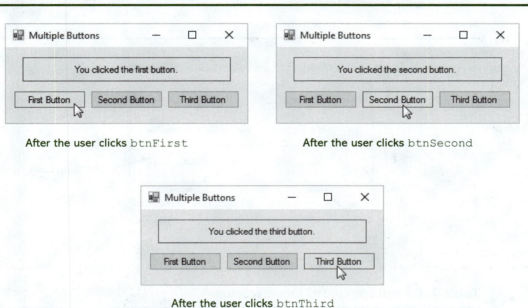

After the user clicks `btnFirst`

After the user clicks `btnSecond`

After the user clicks `btnThird`

In Tutorial 2-3 you will create an application that has multiple buttons, each with its own Click event handler.

Tutorial 2-3:
Creating the *Language Translator* application

VideoNote
Creating the Language Translator application

In this tutorial you will create an application that displays the phrase "Good Morning" in different languages. The form will have three buttons: one for Italian, one for Spanish, and one for German. When the user clicks any of these buttons, the translated phrase will appear in a Label control.

Step 1: Start Visual Studio and begin a new Visual Basic Windows Forms Application project named *Language Translator*. As a reminder, here are the steps for creating the project:

• Click *File* on the menu bar, then select *New Project*. . . .

- The *New Project* window should appear. Make sure *Visual Basic* is selected under *Installed* > *Templates* (on the left side of the window).
- Select *Windows Forms Application* as the type of application (in the center part of the window).
- In the *Name* text box (at the bottom of the window), change the name of the project to *Language Translator*. Click the *OK* button to create the project.

Step 2: Set up the application's form as shown in Figure 2-65. Notice that the form's Text property is set to *Language Translator*. The form has two Label controls and three Button controls. The names of the controls are shown in the figure. As you place each of the controls on the form, refer to Table 2-1 for the relevant property settings.

Figure 2-65 The *Language Translator* form

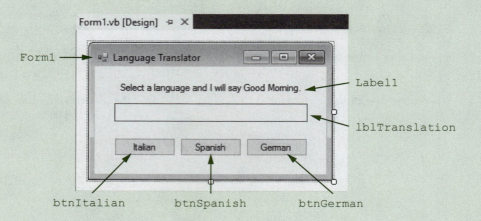

Table 2-1 Form and control property settings

Control Name	Control Type	Property Settings
Form1 (Default name)	Form	**Text:** *Language Translator* **Size:** 300, 175 (or approximately these values)
Label1 (Default name)	Label	**Text:** *Select a language and I will say Good Morning.*
lblTranslation	Label	**AutoSize:** False **BorderStyle:** FixedSingle **Font:** Microsoft Sans Serif (Style: Bold, Size:10 point) **Text:** (The contents of the Text property have been erased.) **TextAlign:** MiddleCenter
btnItalian	Button	**Text:** *Italian*
btnSpanish	Button	**Text:** *Spanish*
btnGerman	Button	**Text:** *German*

Step 3: Once you have the form and its controls set up, you can create the Click event handlers for the Button controls. In the *Designer*, double-click the `btnItalian` control. This will open the *Code* window, and you will see an empty event handler named `btnItalian_Click`. Write the following statement inside the event handler:

```
lblTranslation.Text = "Buongiorno"
```

Step 4: Switch your view back to the *Designer* and double-click the `btnSpanish` control. In the *Code* window, you will see an empty event handler named `btnSpanish_Click`. Write the following statement inside the event handler:

```
lblTranslation.Text = "Buenos Dias"
```

Step 5: Switch your view back to the *Designer* and double-click the `btnGerman` control. In the *Code* window, you will see an empty event handler named `btnGerman_Click`. Write the following statement inside the event handler:

```
lblTranslation.Text = "Guten Morgen"
```

Step 6: The form's code should now appear as shown in the following code listing. Please note that the boldface lines are the ones that you typed. Make sure the code you typed appears exactly as shown in those lines.

```
Public Class Form1
    Private Sub btnItalian_Click(...) Handles btnItalian.Click
        lblTranslation.Text = "Buongiorno"
    End Sub

    Private Sub btnSpanish_Click(...) Handles btnSpanish.Click
        lblTranslation.Text = "Buenos Dias"
    End Sub

    Private Sub btnGerman_Click(...) Handles btnGerman.Click
        lblTranslation.Text = "Guten Morgen"
    End Sub

End Class
```

Step 7: Save the project by clicking *File*, and then clicking *Save All*. (Alternatively, you can click the button.)

Step 8: Press the F5 key on the keyboard, or click the *Start Debugging* button (▶) on the toolbar to compile and run the application.

> **NOTE:** If you typed the statements correctly inside the event handlers, the application should run. If you did not type the statements inside the event handlers correctly, a window will appear reporting build errors. If that happens, click the *No* button in the window, then correct the code so that it appears exactly as previously shown.

Figure 2-66 shows the application's form when it starts running, and after you have clicked each of the Button controls. After you have tested each button, close the application's form.

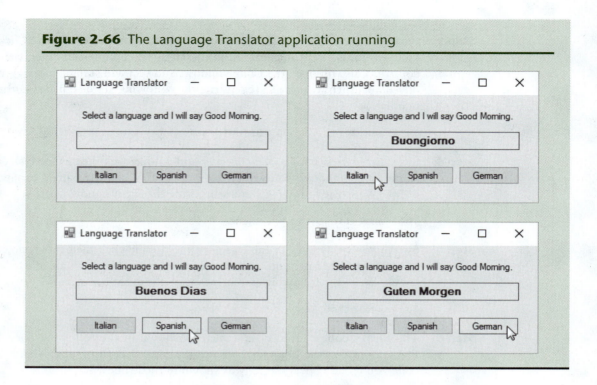

Figure 2-66 The Language Translator application running

2.6 Making Sense of IntelliSense

VideoNote
Using Intel-liSense

CONCEPT: As you type code in the Visual Studio code editor, IntelliSense boxes pop up to assist you. You can use the IntelliSense boxes to automatically complete some programming statements after typing only the first few characters.

IntelliSense is a feature of Visual Studio that provides automatic code completion as you write programming statements. Once you learn how to use IntelliSense, it helps you write code faster. If you've worked through the previous tutorials in this chapter, you've already encountered IntelliSense. For example, in Step 3 of Tutorial 2-3, you were instructed to write the following statement in the btnItalian_Click event handler:

```
lblTranslation.Text = "Buongiorno"
```

Did you notice that as soon as you started typing the statement, a box popped up on the screen? This is known as an IntelliSense list box. The content of the list box changes as you type. Figure 2-67 shows the IntelliSense list box after you have typed the characters lb.

Figure 2-67 IntelliSense list box displayed

```
Form1.vb* ↔ × Form1.vb [Design]*
[VB] Language Translator                              ⌄ ⚇ btnItalian
    ⊟Public Class Form1
    ⊟    Private Sub btnItalian_Click(sender As Object, e As EventArgs)
💡         lb
      End  ⚇ lblTranslation
    End Clas ⚙ LBound
```

The IntelliSense system is anticipating what you are about to type, and as you type characters, the content of the list box is reduced. The list box shown in Figure 2-67 shows all the names starting with `lb` that might be a candidate for the statement you are typing. Notice that `lblTranslation` is selected in the list box. With that item selected, you can press the Tab key on the keyboard, and the `lb` that you previously typed becomes `lblTranslation`.

Next, when you type a period, an IntelliSense list pops up showing every property and method belonging to the `lblTranslation` control. Type `te` and the Text property becomes selected, as shown in Figure 2-68. When you press the Tab key to select the Text property, your statement automatically becomes `lblTranslation.Text`. At this point, you can continue typing until you have completed the statement.

Figure 2-68 IntelliSense list box after typing ".te"

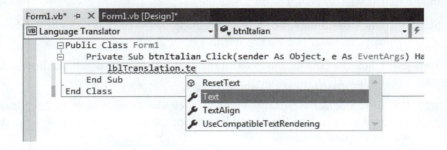

Now that you have an idea of how IntelliSense works, you are encouraged to experiment with it as you write code in future projects. With a little practice, it will become intuitive.

2.7 PictureBox Controls

CONCEPT: A PictureBox control displays a graphic image on a form. PictureBox controls have properties to control the way the image is displayed. A PictureBox control can have a Click event handler that responds when the user clicks the control at run time.

You can use a **PictureBox control** to display a graphic image on a form. A PictureBox control can display images that have been saved in the bitmap, GIF, JPEG, metafile, or icon graphics formats.

In the *Toolbox*, the PictureBox tool is located in the *Common Controls* group. When you double-click the tool, an empty PictureBox control is created on the form, as shown in Figure 2-69. Although the control does not yet display an image, it has a bounding box that shows its size and location, as well as sizing handles. When you create PictureBox controls, they are automatically given default names such as `PictureBox1`, `PictureBox2`, and so forth. If you will refer to the PictureBox control in the application's code, you should change the default name to something more meaningful.

Figure 2-69 An empty PictureBox control

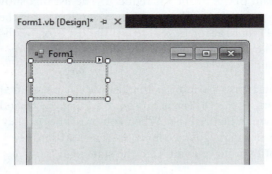

Once you have created a PictureBox control, you use its **Image property** to specify the image that it will display. Follow these steps:

Step 1: Click the Image property in the *Properties* window. An ellipses button (⌑) will appear, as shown on the left in Figure 2-70.

Step 2: Click the ellipses button and the *Select Resource* window, shown on the right in Figure 2-70, will appear.

Step 3: In the *Select Resource* window, click the *Import* button. An *Open* dialog box will appear. Use the dialog box to locate and select the image file that you want to display.

Step 4: After you select an image file, you will see its contents displayed in the *Select Resource* window. This indicates that the image has been imported into the project. Figure 2-71 shows an example of the *Select Resource* window after we have selected and imported an image.

Step 5: Click the *OK* button in the *Select Resource* window, and the selected image will appear in the PictureBox control. Figure 2-72 shows an example. Depending on the size of the image, you might see only part of it displayed. This is the case in Figure 2-72 because the image is larger than the PictureBox control. Your next step is to set the SizeMode property and adjust the size of the control.

Figure 2-70 The Image property's *Select Resource* window

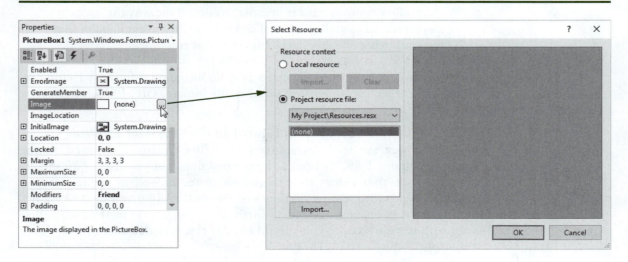

Figure 2-71 An image selected and imported

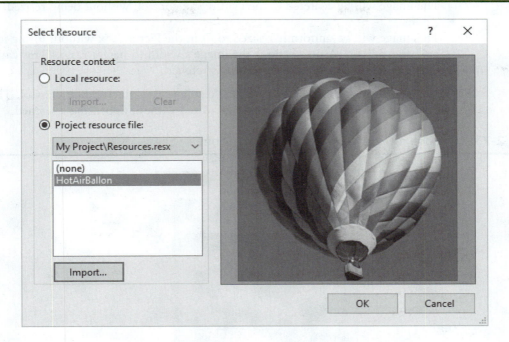

Figure 2-72 The image displayed in the PictureBox control

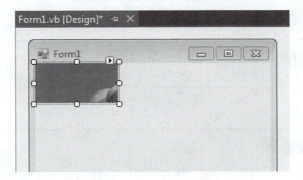

The SizeMode Property

The PictureBox control's **SizeMode property** specifies how the control's image is to be displayed. It can be set to one of the following values:

- **Normal**
  This is the default value. The image will be positioned in the upper-left corner of the PictureBox control. If the image is too big to fit in the PictureBox control, it will be clipped.
- **StretchImage**
  The image will be resized both horizontally and vertically to fit in the PictureBox control. If the image is resized more in one direction than the other, it will appear stretched.
- **AutoSize**
  The PictureBox control will be automatically resized to fit the size of the image.

- **CenterImage**
  The image will be centered in the PictureBox control, without being resized.
- **Zoom**
  The image will be uniformly resized to fit in the PictureBox without losing its original aspect ratio. (**Aspect ratio** is the image's width to height ratio.) This causes the image to be resized without appearing stretched.

Figure 2-73 shows an example of an image displayed in a PictureBox control. The control's SizeMode is set to Zoom, so it can be resized without appearing stretched.

Figure 2-73 An image resized with SizeMode set to Zoom

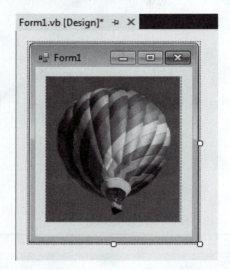

 NOTE: PictureBox controls also have a BorderStyle property that works just like a Label control's BorderStyle property.

 Tutorial 2-4:
Creating the *Guess the President* application

In this tutorial you will create an application that displays a photo of former US president Theodore Roosevelt, and asks the user to think of the president's name. When the user clicks a button, the president's name is displayed on the form. Figure 2-74 shows the application's form in the Designer, with the names of each control.

(The image file that you will use is included in this book's student sample programs. Make sure you have downloaded the student sample programs from the book's companion Web site at www.pearsonhighered.com/gaddis. The file is named President.jpg, and you will find it in the *Images* folder.)

Step 1: Start Visual Studio and begin a new Visual Basic Windows Forms Application project named *Guess the President*. As a reminder, here are the steps for creating the project:

- Click *File* on the menu bar, then select *New Project. . .*
- The *New Project* window should appear. Make sure *Visual Basic* is selected under *Installed > Templates* (on the left side of the window).

Figure 2-74 The *Guess the President* form in the *Designer*

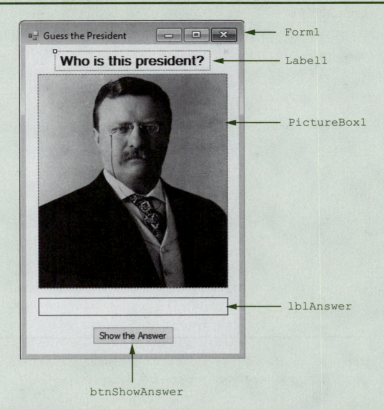

Select *Windows Forms Application* as the type of application (in the center part of the window).

- In the *Name* text box (at the bottom of the window), change the name of the project to *Guess the President*. Click the *OK* button to create the project.

Step 2: Set up the application's form as shown in Figure 2-74. Notice that the form's Text property is set to *Guess the President*. The form has a PictureBox control, two Label controls and a Button control. The names of the controls are shown in the figure. As you place each of the controls on the form, refer to Table 2-2 for the relevant property settings.

Step 3: Once you have the form and its controls set up, you can create the Click event handler for the Button control. In the *Designer*, double-click the btnShowAnswer control. This will open the *Code* window, and you will see an empty event handler named btnShowAnswer_Click. Write the following statement inside the event handler:

```
lblAnswer.Text = "Theodore Roosevelt"
```

Step 4: The form's code should now appear as shown in the following code listing. The line that appears in boldface is the one that you typed. Make sure the code you typed appears exactly like the one shown here.

```
Public Class Form1
    Private Sub btnShowAnswer_Click(...) Handles btnShowAnswer.Click
        lblAnswer.Text = "Theodore Roosevelt"
    End Sub
End Class
```

Step 5: Save the project by clicking *File*, and then clicking *Save All*. (Alternatively, you can click the button.)

Table 2-2 Form and control property settings

Control Name	Control Type	Property Settings
Form1 (Default name)	Form	**Text:** *Guess the President* **Size:** 280, 435
Label1 (Default name)	Label	**Text:** *Who is this president?* **Font:** Microsoft Sans Serif (Style: Bold, Size: 12 point)
PictureBox1 (Default name)	PictureBox	**Image:** Select and import the President.jpg file from the *Images* folder of the student sample programs. **SizeMode:** Zoom **Size:** 235, 275
lblAnswer	Label	**AutoSize:** False **BorderStyle:** FixedSingle **Font:** Microsoft Sans Serif (Style: Bold, Size: 12 point) **Text:** (The contents of the Text property have been erased.) **TextAlign:** MiddleCenter
btnShowAnswer	Button	**Text:** *Show the Answer*

Step 6: Press the [F5] key on the keyboard, or click the *Start Debugging* button (▶) on the toolbar to compile and run the application.

Figure 2-75 shows the application's form when it starts running, and after you have clicked the Button controls. After you have tested the button, close the application's form.

Figure 2-75 The *Guess the President* application running

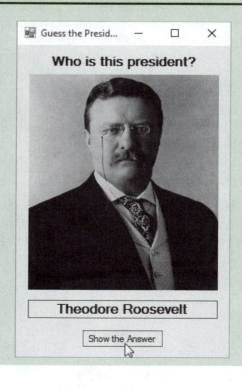

NOTE: If you typed the statements correctly inside the event handlers, the application should run. If you did not type the statements inside the event handlers correctly, a window will appear reporting build errors. If that happens, click the *No* button in the window, then correct the code so that it appears exactly as previously shown.

Creating Clickable Images with PictureBox Controls

You have learned that buttons can have Click event handlers. A Click event handler is executed when the user clicks the button. Other controls, such as PictureBoxes and labels, may also have Click event handlers. In Tutorial 2-5 you write Click event handlers for a group of PictureBox controls.

Tutorial 2-5:
Writing Click event handlers for PictureBox controls

In this tutorial you will create an application that displays the flags of Finland, France, and Germany in PictureBox controls. When the user clicks any of these PictureBoxes, the name of that flag's country will appear in a Label control.

(The image files that you will use are included in this book's student sample programs. Make sure you have downloaded the student sample programs from the book's companion Web site at www.pearsonhighered.com/gaddis. The files are named Finland.jpg, France.jpg, and Germany.jpg, and you will find them in the *Images/Flags* folder.)

Step 1: Start Visual Studio and begin a new Windows Forms Application project named *Flags*.

Step 2: Set up the application's form as shown in Figure 2-76. Notice that the form's Text property is set to *Flags*. The names of the controls are shown in the figure. Refer to Table 2-3 for each control's relevant property settings.

Figure 2-76 The *Flags* form in the *Designer*

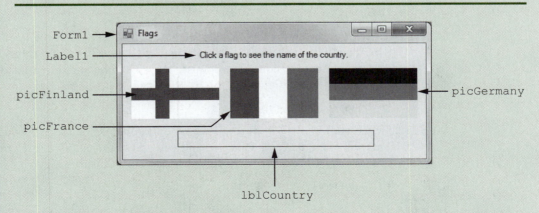

Step 3: Once you have the form and its controls set up, you can create the Click event handlers for the PictureBox controls. In the *Designer*, double-click the picFinland

Table 2-3 Control property settings

Control Name	Control Type	Property Settings
Form1 (Default name)	Form	**Text:** *Flags* **Size:** 430, 200 (or approximately these values)
Label1 (Default name)	Label	**Text:** *Click a flag to see the name of the country.*
picFinland	PictureBox	**Image:** Select and import the Finland.jpg file from the *Images* folder of the student sample programs. **BorderStyle:** FixedSingle **SizeMode:** AutoSize
picFrance	PictureBox	**Image:** Select and import the France.jpg file from the *Images* folder of the student sample programs. **BorderStyle:** FixedSingle **SizeMode:** AutoSize
picGermany	PictureBox	**Image:** Select and import the Germany.jpg file from the *Images* folder of the student sample programs. **BorderStyle:** FixedSingle **SizeMode:** AutoSize
lblCountry	Label	**AutoSize:** False **BorderStyle:** FixedSingle **Font:** Microsoft Sans Serif (Style: Bold, Size:10 point) **Text:** (The contents of the Text property have been erased.) **TextAlign:** MiddleCenter

control. This will open the *Code* window, and you will see an empty event handler named picFinland_Click. Write the following statement inside the event handler:

```
lblCountry.Text = "Finland"
```

Step 4: Switch your view back to the *Designer* and double-click the picFrance control. This will open the *Code* window, and you will see an empty event handler named picFrance_Click. Write the following statement inside the event handler:

```
lblCountry.Text = "France"
```

Step 5: Switch your view back to the *Designer* and double-click the picGermany control. This will open the *Code* window, and you will see an empty event handler named picGermany_Click. Write the following statement inside the event handler:

```
lblCountry.Text = "Germany"
```

Step 6: The form's code should now appear as shown in the following code listing. The code that you typed appears in boldface. Make sure the code that you typed appears exactly as shown in those lines.

```
Public Class Form1
    Private Sub picFinland_Click(...) Handles picFinland.Click
        lblCountry.Text = "Finland"
    End Sub

    Private Sub picFrance_Click(...) Handles picFrance.Click
        lblCountry.Text = "France"
    End Sub

    Private Sub picGermany_Click(...) Handles picGermany.Click
        lblCountry.Text = "Germany"
    End Sub

End Class
```

Step 7: Save the project by clicking *File*, and then clicking *Save All*. (Alternatively, you can click the ![] button.)

Step 8: Press the [F5] key on the keyboard, or click the *Start Debugging* button (▶) on the toolbar to compile and run the application.

Figure 2-77 shows the application's form when it starts running, and after you have clicked the PictureBox controls. After you have clicked each flag to make sure the application works correctly, close the application's form.

Figure 2-77 The *Flags* application running

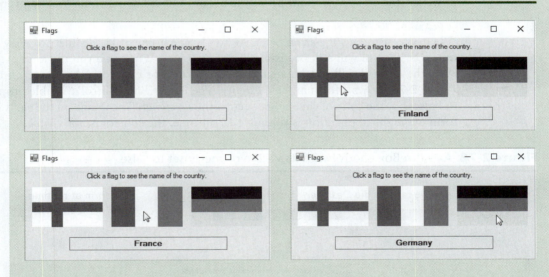

 NOTE: If you typed the statements correctly inside the event handlers, the application should run. If you did not type the statements inside the event handlers correctly, a window will appear reporting build errors. If that happens, click the *No* button in the window, then correct the code so that it appears exactly as previously shown.

Checkpoint

2.34 What is a PictureBox control used for?

2.35 Where is the PictureBox tool located in the *Toolbox*?

2.36 How do you display an image in the PictureBox?

2.37 What is the default value of the PictureBox control's SizeMode property?

2.38 How does setting the SizeMode property to Zoom affect the image that is to be displayed in the PictureBox control?

2.39 How do you create a clickable image?

2.8 The Visible Property

CONCEPT: A control's Visible property can be set to either True or False. If a control's Visible property is set to True, the control is visible on the form at runtime. If a control's Visible property is set to False, the control is invisible on the form at runtime.

Most controls have a **Visible property** that determines whether the control is visible on the form at runtime. The Visible property is a Boolean property, which means it can be set only to the values True or False. If a control's Visible property is set to True, the control will be visible on the form at runtime. If a control's Visible property is set to False, however, the control will not be visible at runtime. By default, the Visible property is set to True.

When you use the *Properties* window to change a control's Visible property at design time, the control will still be visible in the *Designer*. When you run the application, however, the control will not be visible on the form. For example, the image on the left in Figure 2-78 shows a form in the *Designer*. The PictureBox control's Visible property is set to False, but the control can still be seen in the *Designer*. The image on the right shows the form while the application is running. At runtime, the control is not visible.

Figure 2-78 A PictureBox control with its Visible property set to False

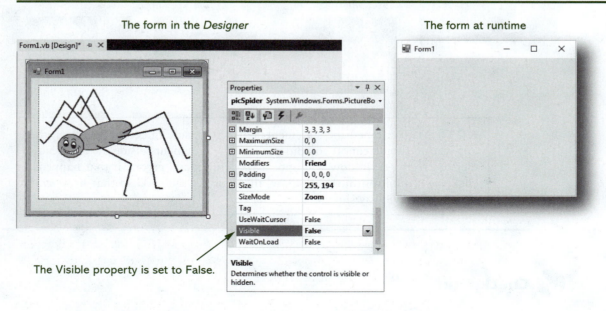

A control's Visible property can also be modified in code by an assignment statement, which makes it possible to hide or display a control while the application is running. For

example, the PictureBox control shown in Figure 2-78 is named `picSpider`. The following statement sets the control's Visible property to `True`:

```
picSpider.Visible = True
```

When this statement executes, the `picSpider` control will become visible. Likewise, the following statement sets the control's Visible property to `False`:

```
picSpider.Visible = False
```

When this statement executes, the `picSpider` control will become invisible.

Tutorial 2-6:
Creating the *Card Flip* application

In this tutorial, you will create an application that simulates a card being flipped over. When the application runs, it will display the form shown on the left in Figure 2-79. The form initially displays the back of a poker card. When the user clicks the *Show the Card Face* button, the card will be flipped over to show its face, as shown in the form on the right. When the user clicks the *Show the Card Back* button, the card is flipped back over to show its back.

The simulation of the card being flipped will be accomplished using the following logic:

- When the user clicks the *Show the Card Face* button, the PictureBox showing the card's back will be made invisible and the PictureBox showing the card's face will be made visible.
- When the user clicks the *Show the Card Back* button, the PictureBox showing the card's face will be made invisible and the PictureBox showing the card's back will be made visible.

Figure 2-79 The Card Flip application

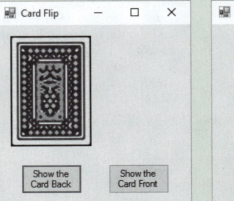

(The image files that you will use are included in this book's student sample programs. Make sure you have downloaded the student sample programs from the book's companion Web site at `www.pearsonhighered.com/gaddis`. The files are named Backface_Blue. jpg and Ace_Spades.jpg, and you will find them in the *Images/Poker Cards* folder.)

Step 1:   Start Visual Studio and begin a new Windows Forms Application project named *Card Flip*.

Step 2: Set up the application's form as shown in Figure 2-80. The names of the controls are shown in the figure. Use the *Properties* window to make the property settings shown in Table 2-4. (In particular, note that the picCardBack control's Visible property is set to True, and the picCardFace control's Visible property is set to False.)

Figure 2-80 The application's form

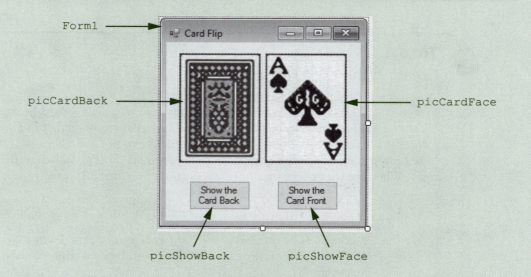

Table 2-4 Control property settings

Control Name	Control Type	Property Settings
Form1	Form	**Text:** Card Flip **Size:** 255, 266 (Or, manually resize the form to approximately match the form shown in Figure 2-80.)
picCardBack	PictureBox	**Image:** Select and import the Backface_Blue.jpg file from the *Images/Poker Cards* folder of the student sample programs. **Size:** 100, 140 **SizeMode:** Zoom **Visible:** True
picCardFace	PictureBox	**Image:** Select and import the Ace_Spades.jpg file from the *Images/Poker Cards* folder of the student sample programs. **Size:** 100, 140 **SizeMode:** Zoom **Visible:** False
btnShowBack	Button	**Text:** *Show the Card Back* (Manually resize the button to accommodate the text, as shown in Figure 2-80.)
btnShowFace	Button	**Text:** *Show the Card Face* (Manually resize the button to accommodate the text, as shown in Figure 2-80.)

Step 3: Once you have the form and its controls set up, you can create the Click event handlers for the Button controls. In the *Designer*, double-click the btnShowBack control. This will open the code editor, and you will see an empty event handler named btnShowBack_Click. Write the following statements inside the event handler:

```
picCardBack.Visible = True
picCardFace.Visible = False
```

Step 4: Switch your view back to the *Designer* and double-click the btnShowFace control. This will open the code editor, and you will see an empty event handler named btnShowFace_Click. Write the following statements inside the event handler:

```
picCardBack.Visible = False
picCardFace.Visible = True
```

Step 5: The form's code should now appear as follows. The lines that appear in bold-face are the ones that you typed. Make sure the code you typed matches those exactly.

```
Public Class Form1
    Private Sub btnShowBack_Click(...) Handles btnShowBack.Click
        picCardBack.Visible = True
        picCardFace.Visible = False
    End Sub

    Private Sub btnShowFace_Click(...) Handles btnShowFace.Click
        picCardBack.Visible = False
        picCardFace.Visible = True
    End Sub

End Class
```

Step 6: Save the project. Then, press the F5 key on the keyboard, or click the *Start Debugging* button ( ) on the toolbar to compile and run the application.

Test the application by clicking the buttons. When you click the *Show the Card Face* button, you should see the card's face (and the back of the card should be invisible). When you click the *Show the Card Back* button, you should see the card's back (and the card's face should be invisible). When you are finished, close the application.

> **NOTE:** If you typed the statements correctly inside the event handlers, the application should run. If you did not type the statements inside the event handlers correctly, a window will appear reporting build errors. If that happens, click the *No* button in the window, then correct the code so that it appears exactly as previously shown.

Sequential Execution of Statements

In Tutorial 2-6, the event handlers that you created each contained more than one statement. For example, here is the btnShowBack_Click method:

```
Private Sub btnShowBack_Click(...) Handles btnShowBack.Click
    picCardBack.Visible = True
    picCardFace.Visible = False
End Sub
```

This event handler has two assignment statements. When the event handler executes, the statements inside the event handler execute in the order that they appear, from the beginning to the end of the event handler. This statement executes first:

```
picCardBack.Visible = True
```

And then this statement executes:

```
picCardFace.Visible = False
```

When the application is running, however, you can't really tell that the statements are executing in this order simply by watching the action take place on the screen. When you click the showBackButton control, the Click event handler executes so quickly that it appears as though both statements execute simultaneously. It's important for you to understand, however, that the statements execute one at a time, in the order that they appear in the method.

In this particular method, it doesn't really matter which assignment statement is written first. If we reverse the order of the statements, we will not be able to see the difference on the screen because the application executes so quickly. In most applications, however, the order in which you write the statements in the event handlers is critically important. In Chapter 3 you will start writing event handlers that perform several steps, and in most cases, the steps must be performed in a specific order. Otherwise, the program will not produce the correct results.

Checkpoint

2.40 What does a control's Visible property do?

2.41 Does the value of a control's Visible property change how the image appears in the *Designer*?

2.42 Suppose an application has a PictureBox control named picPrize. Write an assignment statement that will make the PictureBox invisible.

2.43 If an event handler contains more than one statement, in what order are the statements executed?

2.9 Writing the Code to Close an Application's Form

CONCEPT: To close an application's form in code, you use the statement Me.Close().

All of the applications that you created in this chapter's tutorials required the user to click the standard Windows close button (✕) to close the application. The standard Windows close button appears in the upper-right corner of almost every window. In many applications, however, you will want to give the user an alternative way to close the application. For example, you might want to create an *Exit* button that closes the application when it is clicked.

To close an application's form, you execute the following statement:

```
Me.Close()
```

This statement is an example of a **method call**. Recall from Chapter 1 that objects have methods, which are operations that an object can perform. If you want to execute one of an object's methods, you have to call that method.

An application's form (which is an object) has a method named `Close`. When a form's `Close` method is called, it causes the form to close. If an application has only one form, closing the form also ends the application's execution.

In the statement `Me.Close()`, the keyword `Me`, which appears to the left of the period, is shorthand for referring to the current form. On the right side of the period, the word `Close` is the name of the method we are calling. Next is a set of parentheses, which always appear after the name of the method in a method call.

Let's look at an example of how this statement can be used. Figure 2-81 shows the form and code from a project named *Exit Button Demo*. The Button control that you see on the form is named `btnExit`. In the form's code you can see that we've created a Click event handler for the button. When the user clicks the button, it closes the form, thus closing the application.

Figure 2-81 A form with an *Exit* button

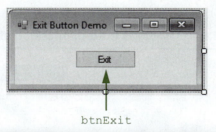

btnExit

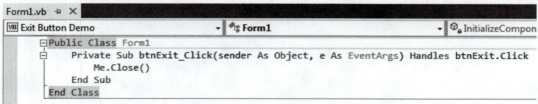

In Tutorial 2-7 you will add an *Exit* button to the *Guess the President* application that you created in Tutorial 2-4.

Tutorial 2-7:

Adding an *Exit* button to the *Guess the President* application

Step 1: Start Visual Studio and open the *Guess the President* project. As a reminder, here are the steps for opening the project:

- Click *File* on the menu bar, then select *Open Project. . . .*
- In the *Open Project* dialog box, navigate to the location where the *Guess the President.sln* file is located.
- Select the *Guess the President.sln* file and click the *Open* button to open the project.

TIP: Sometimes, when you open an existing project, the `Form1` form might not appear in the *Designer*. When this happens, simply double-click *Form1.vb* in the *Solution Explorer*, as shown in Figure 2-82.

Figure 2-82 Double-clicking *Form1.vb* in the Solution Explorer

Double-click *Form1.vb* in
the Solution Explorer to open
`Form1` in the Designer.

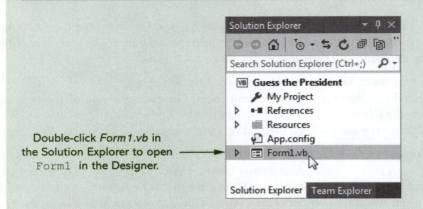

Step 2:   Move the `btnShowAnswer` button to the left, as shown in Figure 2-83.

Figure 2-83 The `btnShowAnswer` button repositioned

Step 3:   Add another Button control to the form. Change the new Button control's name
to `btnExit`, and set its Text property to *Exit*. Position the button as shown in
Figure 2-84.

Figure 2-84 The `btnExit` button created

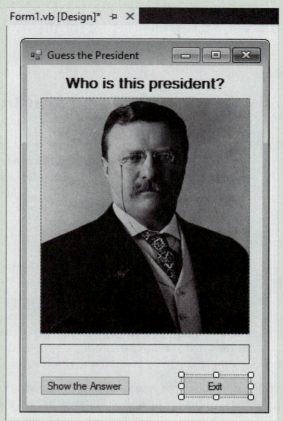

Step 4: Double-click the `btnExit` button to create a Click event handler. The *Code* window should open, showing a Click event handler template named `btnExit_Click`. Type the following statement inside the event handler:

```
Me.Close()
```

The application's code should now appear as follows. The line that you typed is shown in boldface.

```
Public Class Form1
    Private Sub btnShowAnswer_Click(...) Handles btnShowAnswer.Click
        lblAnswer.Text = "Theodore Roosevelt"
    End Sub

    Private Sub btnExit_Click(...) Handles btnExit.Click
        Me.Close()
    End Sub
End Class
```

Step 5: Save the project. Then, press the F5 key on the keyboard, or click the *Start Debugging* button (▶) on the toolbar to compile and run the application.

Test the application by clicking the *Exit* button. The application should stop running.

 NOTE: If you did not type the statement inside the event handler correctly, a window will appear reporting build errors. If that happens, click the *No* button in the window, then correct the code so that it appears exactly as previously shown.

Checkpoint

2.44 What is the purpose of the `Me.Close()` statement?

2.45 The keyword `Me` is shorthand for referring to what?

2.10 Comments, Blank Lines, and Indentation

CONCEPT: Comments are brief notes that are placed in a program's source code, explaining how parts of the program work. Programmers commonly use blank lines and indentation in program code to give the code visual organization, and make it easier to read.

Comments

Comments are short notes that are placed in different parts of a program, explaining how those parts of the program work. Comments are not intended for the compiler, and they do not affect the way the program executes. Comments are intended for any person who is reading the code and trying to understand what it does. You should get into the habit of writing comments in your application code. The comments will almost certainly save you time in the future when you have to modify or debug the program. Even large and complex applications can be made easy to read and understand if they are properly commented.

In Visual Basic, you begin a comment with an apostrophe ('). Anything appearing after the apostrophe, to the end of the line, is ignored by the Visual Basic compiler. The following code sample shows how we might use comments in the `btnShowBack_Click` event handler from Tutorial 2-6. Each comment explains what the very next line of code does.

```
Private Sub btnShowBack_Click(...) Handles btnShowBack.Click
    ' Make the image of the back of the card visible.
    picCardBack.Visible = True
    ' Make the image of the face of the card invisible.
    picCardFace.Visible = False
End Sub
```

A comment does not have to occupy an entire line. Anything appearing after the apostrophe ('), to the end of the line, is ignored. So, a comment can appear after an executable statement. The following code sample shows an example.

```
Private Sub btnShowBack_Click(...) Handles btnShowBack.Click
    picCardBack.Visible = True  ' Show the back of the card
    picCardFace.Visible = False ' Show the face of the card
End Sub
```

As a beginning programmer, you might resist the idea of writing a lot of comments in your programs. After all, it's a lot more interesting to write code that actually does something! However, you would be wise to take the extra time to write comments. They will almost certainly save you time in the future when you have to modify or debug the program. Even large and complex programs can be made easy to read and understand if they are properly commented.

NOTE: From this point forward, we will write comments as we write code. It's best to comment code as you write it because the code's purpose is fresh in your mind.

Using Blank Lines and Indentation to Make Your Code Easier to Read

Programmers commonly use blank lines and indentations in their code to create a sense of visual organization. This is similar to the way that authors visually arrange the text on the pages of a book. Instead of writing each chapter as one long series of sentences, they break it into paragraphs that are visually separated on the page. This does not change the information in the book, but it makes it easier to read.

For example, look at the following code sample. Notice that inside the event handler we have inserted a blank line to visually separate the code into two sets of statements. The blank line is not required, but it makes the code easier for humans to read. Programmers commonly insert blank lines at various places to make the code easier to read.

```
Private Sub btnShowBack_Click(...) Handles btnShowBack.Click
    ' Make the image of the back of the card visible.
    picCardBack.Visible = True

    ' Make the image of the face of the card invisible.
    picCardFace.Visible = False
End Sub
```

Programmers also use indentation to visually organize code. You may have noticed that in the *Code* window, all of the statements that appear inside an event handler are indented. In fact, Visual Studio is normally set up to automatically indent the code that you write in this fashion.

As you have worked through the tutorials in this chapter, you have probably noticed that Visual Studio automatically indents the code that you write inside event handlers. Indenting the statements inside a procedure is a common programming practice that makes code much easier for human eyes to read.

Although indenting the statements inside a procedure is not required (the code will still execute, even if it is not indented), it visually sets the statements apart. As a result, you can tell at a glance which statements are inside the procedure. This is helpful, especially when a program has a lot of procedures.

 Checkpoint

2.46 What purpose do comments serve?

2.47 What character does a comment begin with in Visual Basic?

2.48 Do comments affect the way that a program executes?

2.49 Why do programmers insert blank lines and indentations in their code?

 2.11 Dealing with Errors

CONCEPT: Programmers spend a lot of time finding and correcting errors in their code. In general, there are three types of software errors: syntax errors, runtime errors, and logic errors. The compiler reports syntax errors, but runtime and logic errors can be found only through the process of testing and debugging the program.

In general, there are three types of errors that a computer program can have: syntax errors, runtime errors, and logic errors. An important part of learning to program is learning how to deal with each type of error.

Syntax Errors

Writing code requires a lot of precision. Even small errors, like typing a comma in the wrong place, will prevent an application's code from compiling and executing. These types of mistakes are known as **syntax errors**.

The Visual Studio *Code* window does a good job of reporting syntax errors soon after you type them. When you enter a statement into the editor, Visual Studio analyzes it, and if a syntax error is found, it is underlined with a jagged line. Figure 2-85 shows an example. If you hold the mouse cursor over the jagged a line, a description of the error will pop up in a small window. The description usually gives you enough information to determine the cause of the error, and how to fix it.

Figure 2-85 Error underlined

```
Private Sub btnExit_Click(sender As Object, e As EventArgs) Handles btnExit.Click
    Me.Clos()
End Sub
```

This jagged line indicates an error.

If a syntax error exists in a project's code and you attempt to compile and execute it (by pressing the [F5] key on the keyboard, or clicking the *Start Debugging* button (▶) on the toolbar), you will see the window shown in Figure 2-86, reporting build errors. Click the *No* button to close the window, and you will the *Error List* shown in Figure 2-87.

Notice that the *Error List* window shows a description of each error, the source code file that contains the error, the line number and column number of the error, and the name of the project. If you double-click an error message displayed in the *Error List* window, the *Code* window will highlight the code that caused the error.

Figure 2-86 Window reporting build errors

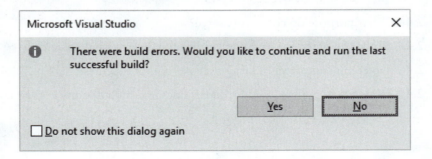

Figure 2-87 *Error List* window

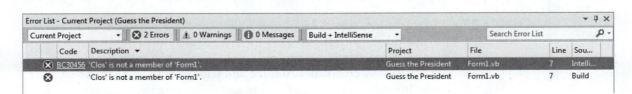

Runtime Errors

A **runtime error** is an unexpected error that occurs while a program is running. It usually happens when the program attempts to perform an operation that the computer cannot carry out. For example, a runtime error will occur if a program tries to read data from a file that does not exist. A runtime error will also occur if a program divides a number by zero, because it is mathematically impossible to do so.

These types of runtime errors usually cause the program to abruptly halt. When that happens, an error message is typically displayed. The error message may, or may not, give you an idea of what went wrong. Either way, you will have to use testing and debugging techniques to locate the source of the error. We will discuss testing and debugging momentarily.

Logic Errors

Like a runtime error, a **logic error** happens while a program is running. It is an error that causes the program to produce the wrong results, or behave in an unexpected manner. A program can be free of syntax errors, but, if the logical steps that it performs are not correct, the program will not do what it is supposed to do.

For example, suppose a program performs a calculation, and the code has a mathematical mistake. Mathematical mistakes (other than division by zero) do not cause a program to halt, but cause it to produce incorrect results.

Logic errors can be difficult to find. Because logic errors do not cause error messages to be displayed, their cause is not always apparent. Finding and fixing a logic error usually requires a bit of detective work on the part of the programmer. That's where the testing and debugging process comes in.

Testing and Debugging

The only way to find logic errors and runtime errors in your code is to **test** the application. To test an application, you run it many times, providing sample input and verifying that the output is correct. If the output is not correct, you know there is a logic error somewhere in your code. To find the logic error, you must debug the application.

Debugging is the process of analyzing your code to determine where the error is taking place. The best way to debug your code is with the help of a debugger. A **debugger** is a tool that lets you step through a program, or part of a program, executing its code one line at a time. As you execute each line of code, you can observe the data that the program stores in memory, as well as the values of control properties. This process helps you to locate the code that is causing the error. Once you know where the error is, you can take steps to fix it.

Visual Studio provides a powerful debugger that you can use to debug Visual Basic applications. You will begin to learn about the Visual Studio debugger in Chapter 3.

 **Checkpoint**

2.50 What are the three general types of errors that a computer program can have?

2.51 How can you tell that Visual Studio has found a syntax error?

2.52 What happens if you hold the mouse cursor over a jagged line in the code editor?

2.53 What happens if you attempt to compile and execute a program that contains syntax errors?

2.54 What type of error usually causes the program to abruptly halt?

2.55 What is an example of a runtime error?

2.56 What is a logic error?

2.57 How do you find runtime and logic errors in a program?

2.12 Displaying User Messages at Runtime

CONCEPT: There are numerous techniques for displaying messages to the user of an application. Label controls, Message Boxes, and StatusStrip controls are convenient ways to display messages to the user at runtime.

Most applications display messages to the user while the application is running. In this chapter, you have already learned how to display messages with Label controls. You simply assign a string to the Label control's Text property. In addition to Label controls, you can also use Message Boxes and StatusStrip controls.

Displaying Message Boxes

A **message box** is a small window, sometimes referred to as a **dialog box**, that displays a message. Figure 2-88 shows an example of a message box displaying the message *Thanks for clicking the button!* Notice that the message box also has an *OK* button. When the user clicks the *OK* button, the message box closes.

Figure 2-88 A message box

Visual Basic provides a method named `MessageBox.Show` that you can use to display a message box. If you want to execute the `MessageBox.Show` method, you write a statement that calls (or executes) the method. The following statement shows an example of how you would call the `MessageBox.Show` method to display the message box shown in Figure 2-88:

```
MessageBox.Show("Thanks for clicking the button!")
```

When you call the `MessageBox.Show` method, you write the string that you want to display inside the parentheses. In this example the string literal `"Thanks for clicking the button!"` is written inside the parentheses.

TIP: Remember that string literals are enclosed in double-quotation marks in code, but the quotation marks are not part of the string. When the message is displayed (as shown in Figure 2-88), the double-quotation marks do not appear.

Tutorial 2-8:
Displaying Message Boxes

In the student sample programs folder named *Chap2\French Numbers* you have a project named *French Numbers*. The project has been started for you, and in this tutorial you will complete it by writing the necessary event handlers.

When the project is complete, it will display the French words for the numbers 1 through 5, which are shown here:

1	un
2	deux
3	trois
4	quatre
5	cinq

The application's form has five button controls, displaying the numbers 1 through 5. The completed application will allow the user to click any of the buttons to select a number, and a message box will appear displaying the French word for the selected number. For example, if the user clicks the 2 button, a message box will appear displaying the word *deux*.

Step 1: Open the *French Numbers* project from the student sample programs folder named *Chap2\French Numbers*. Figure 2-89 shows the application's form, with the names of each Button control.

Figure 2-89 The *French Numbers* form

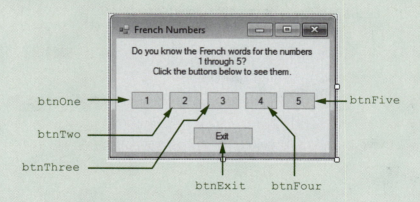

Step 2: Create Click event handlers for all of the button controls. When each button is clicked, it should display a message box showing the French word for the button's number, as described here:

- When the btnOne button is clicked, a message box should appear displaying *un*.
- When the btnTwo button is clicked, a message box should appear displaying *deux*.
- When the btnThree button is clicked, a message box should appear displaying *trois*.
- When the btnFour button is clicked, a message box should appear displaying *quatre*.
- When the btnFive button is clicked, a message box should appear displaying *cinq*.

In addition, write a Click event handler for the btnExit button that closes the form. When you have finished writing all of the event handlers, your code should be similar to the following. The code that you typed appears in bold. (Your event handlers might appear in a different order than those shown here, depending on the order in which you double-click each button in the *Designer* window.)

```
Public Class Form1
    Private Sub btnOne_Click(...) Handles btnOne.Click
        ' Display the French word for one.
        MessageBox.Show("un")
    End Sub

    Private Sub btnTwo_Click(...) Handles btnTwo.Click
        ' Display the French word for two.
        MessageBox.Show("deux")
    End Sub

    Private Sub btnThree_Click(...) Handles btnThree.Click
        ' Display the French word for three.
        MessageBox.Show("trois")
    End Sub

    Private Sub btnFour_Click(...) Handles btnFour.Click
        ' Display the French word for four.
        MessageBox.Show("quatre")
    End Sub

    Private Sub btnFive_Click(...) Handles btnFive.Click
        ' Display the French word for five.
        MessageBox.Show("cinq")
    End Sub

    Private Sub btnExit_Click(...) Handles btnExit.Click
        ' Close the form.
        Me.Close()
    End Sub

End Class
```

Step 3: Save the project, and then execute it. Test each button on the form to make sure it displays the correct word in a message box, as shown in Figure 2-90.

Figure 2-90 Message boxes that should be displayed by the *French Numbers* application

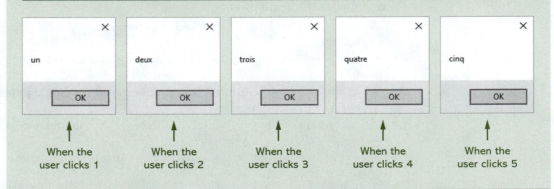

un	deux	trois	quatre	cinq
When the user clicks 1	When the user clicks 2	When the user clicks 3	When the user clicks 4	When the user clicks 5

The StatusStrip Control

The **StatusStrip control**, which is similar to a Label, is used to display program status messages to the user. As you have seen, the `MessageBox.Show` function grabs the user's attention and forces him or her to close the message box before continuing the program. However, a message displayed in a StatusStrip control appears in such a way that the user is not interrupted.

Figure 2-91 shows an example of the French Numbers program that allows the user to click the numbered buttons and see the French equivalents displayed in a StatusStrip control at the bottom of the form. The user has just clicked the number 2, so the word *deux* appears in the status line.

Figure 2-91 Using a StatusStrip control to display the number selected by the user

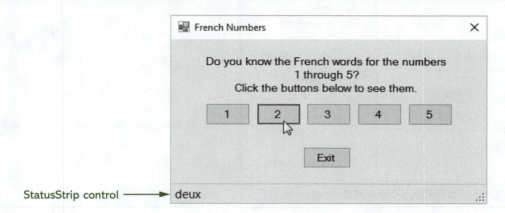

In the previous version of this program (with pop-up message boxes), the user had to click once on a number to display the message box with the French word, and then click a second time to remove the message box from the screen. In this new version, the user clicks only once to select a number. This approach helps the user to move quickly between the numbered buttons.

A StatusStrip control offers an ideal way to display messages under the following conditions:

1. The message being displayed is not a critical system error that forces the user to interrupt what he or she was doing.
2. The user will be clicking buttons multiple times within a short period of time. By not using a message box, you avoid forcing the user to click a second time just to clear the box from the screen.

Adding a StatusStrip and a Label to a Form

Two steps are involved in setting up a StatusStrip control with a label to hold messages:

Step 1.   Drag the StatusStrip control from the *Menus & Toolbars* section of the *Toolbox* window onto an existing form, as shown in Figure 2-92. The StatusStrip will attach itself to the bottom of the form. This is called *docking the control*.

Step 2.   Click the area on the left side of the StatusStrip, and a drop-down list will appear with the names of several types of controls, as shown in Figure 2-93. Select the *StatusLabel* member of this list.

This will cause a **ToolStripStatusLabel control** to be added to the StatusStrip, with a name such as *ToolStripStatusLabel1*. In the *Properties* window, give it a meaningful name such as lblStatus. Then, erase the contents of its Text property. The label will seem to disappear when in design mode. It will only appear at runtime when you assign a value to its Text property.

Figure 2-92 Drag the StatusStrip control from the *Toolbox*

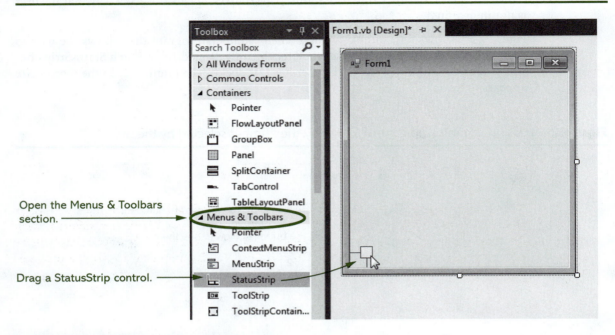

Open the Menus & Toolbars section.

Drag a StatusStrip control.

Figure 2-93 StatusStrip control drop-down list

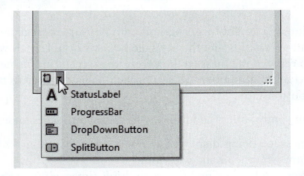

French Numbers Example

The following code is taken from an alternate version of Tutorial 2-8, found in the student sample programs folder named *Chap2\French StatusStrip Numbers*. Each of the MessageBox.Show statements in the original version of the program has been replaced by an assignment to a StatusLabel named lblStatus.Text:

```
Public Class Form1
    Private Sub btnOne_Click(...) Handles btnOne.Click
        ' Display the French word for one.
        lblStatus.Text = "un"
    End Sub

    Private Sub btnTwo_Click(...) Handles btnTwo.Click
        ' Display the French word for two.
        lblStatus.Text = "deux"
    End Sub
```

```
Private Sub btnThree_Click(...) Handles btnThree.Click
    ' Display the French word for three.
   lblStatus.Text = "trois"
End Sub

Private Sub btnFour_Click(...) Handles btnFour.Click
    ' Display the French word for four.
   lblStatus.Text = "quatre"
End Sub

Private Sub btnFive_Click(...) Handles btnFive.Click
    ' Display the French word for five.
   lblStatus.Text = "cinq"
End Sub

Private Sub btnExit_Click(...) Handles btnExit.Click
    ' Close the form.
   Me.Close()
End Sub

End Class
```

The sample programs in remaining chapters in this book will use both pop-up message boxes and labels to display error messages. In general, messages boxes are favored when the user's work flow must be interrupted by some critical event. The StatusStrip will be used to gently remind the user either to correct his or her input, or to display program status information.

 **Checkpoint**

2.58 What is a message box?

2.59 Write a statement that displays a message box showing the message *Welcome to our hotel!*

2.60 The following statement is not written correctly. What is wrong with it?
`MessageBoxShow("Invalid password")`

2.61 What is a StatusStrip control?

2.13 Customizing an Application's Form

CONCEPT: You can customize various aspects of a Form by setting its FormBorderStyle, MinimizeBox, MaximizeBox, and ControlBox properties. You can also lock the controls on a form, which prevents them from being moved or deleted.

The FormBorderStyle Property

Forms have a property named **FormBorderStyle** that controls the appearance of the form's border, and determines whether the user can resize the form. Sometimes you may want to prevent users from resizing your application's form at runtime, because doing so would distort the appearance of your user interface. Table 2-5 describes the values that you can assign to a form's FormBorderStyle property. (Note that *Sizable* is the default setting.)

Table 2-5 The FormBorderStyle property settings

Setting	Description
None	The form has no border.
FixedSingle	The form is not resizable, and uses a border that is a single line. The form is displayed with Minimize, Maximize, and Close buttons on its title bar. Although the form may be maximized and minimized, it may not be resized by its edges or corners.
Fixed3D	The form is not resizable and uses a border that has a 3D appearance. The form is displayed with Minimize, Maximize, and Close buttons on its title bar. Although the form may be maximized and minimized, it may not be resized by its edges or corners.
FixedDialog	The form is not resizable. It is displayed with Minimize, Maximize, and Close buttons on its title bar. Although the form may be maximized and minimized, it may not be resized by its edges or corners.
Sizable	This is the default setting for FormBorderStyle. The form is displayed with Minimize, Maximize, and Close buttons on its title bar. The form may be resized, but the controls will not move unless you set certain property values.
FixedToolWindow	The form is not resizable. It is displayed with only a Close button. The text that is displayed in the title bar appears in a reduced font size.
SizeableToolWindow	The form is not resizable. It is displayed with only a Close button. The text that is displayed in the title bar appears in a reduced font size.

MinimizeBox, MaximizeBox, and ControlBox

Forms have three possible buttons in the upper-right corner: a *Minimize* button (–) that hides the window and displays an icon on the Windows task bar, a *Maximize* (□) button that fills the entire display with the current window, and a *Close* (✕) button that closes the window completely. A sample is shown in Figure 2-94. You can use a Form's MinimizeBox, MaximizeBox, and ControlBox properties to control whether these buttons appear when your application is running:

- The form's **MinimizeBox property** can be set to True or False. When set to True, the Minimize button appears on the form. When set to False, the Minimize button does not appear on the form.
- The form's **MaximizeBox property** can be set to True or False. When set to True, the Maximize button appears on the form. When set to False, the Maximize button does not appear on the form.
- The form's **ControlBox property** can be set to True or False. When False, all buttons disappear from the upper-right corner of the form. This property overrides the values of MinimizeBox and MaximizeBox.

Locking Controls

Once you have placed all the controls in their proper positions on a form, it is usually a good idea to lock them. When you lock the controls on a form, they cannot be accidentally moved at design time. They must be unlocked before they can be moved.

To lock all the controls on a form, place the cursor over an empty spot on the form and right-click. A small menu pops up. One of the selections on the menu is *Lock Controls*.

In Tutorial 2-9 we modify the value of the form's FormBorderStyle property so that the user cannot minimize, maximize, or resize the window. We will also lock the controls on the form.

Figure 2-94 Minimize, Maximize, and Close buttons on a form

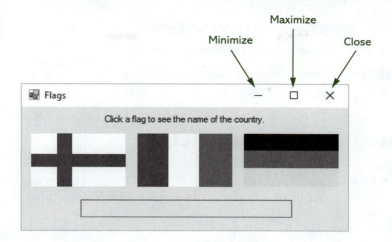

Minimize   Maximize   Close

Tutorial 2-9:
Setting the FormBorderStyle property and locking the controls on a form

Step 1: Start Visual Studio and open the *Guess the President* project that you created in Tutorial 2-4. Select the Form1 form and find the FormBorderStyle property in the *Properties* window.

Step 2: Click the FormBorderStyle property. A down-arrow button (⌄) appears. Click the down-arrow button to see a list of values.

Step 3: Click *FixedSingle*.

Step 4: Start the application and test the new border style. Notice that you can move the window, but you cannot resize it by its edges or its corners.

Step 5: Click the *Exit* button to end the application.

Step 6: Now you will lock the controls. Place the cursor over an empty spot on the form and right-click. A small menu pops up.

Step 7: Click the *Lock Controls* command.

Step 8: Select any control on the form and try to move it. Because the controls are locked, you cannot move them.

Step 9: Save the project.

When you are ready to move the controls, just right-click over an empty spot on the form and select the *Lock Controls* command again. This toggles (reverses) the locked state of the controls.

NOTE: You can still delete a locked control.

TIP: A single control may be locked by setting its Locked property to True. It may be unlocked by setting its Locked property to False.

Checkpoint

2.62 What happens when you lock the controls on a form?

2.63 How do you lock the controls on a form?

2.64 How do you unlock the controls on a form?

2.14 Using Visual Studio Help

CONCEPT: An extensive collection of online documentation and context-sensitive help is available from within Visual Studio.

You can access the documentation for Visual Studio by clicking *Help* on the menu bar, and then selecting *View Help*. (Or, you can press Ctrl+F1 on the keyboard.) This launches your Web browser and opens the online **Microsoft Developer Network (MSDN) Library**. The MSDN Library provides complete documentation for Visual Basic, as well as the other programming languages included in Visual Studio. You will also find code samples, tutorials, articles, and access to Microsoft Channel 9 Videos.

Context-Sensitive Help

The MSDN Library contains a vast amount of documentation on Visual Studio and Visual Basic. Because it contains so much information, it is often easier to find what you are looking for by using context-sensitive help. **Context-sensitive help** is help on a single topic that you are currently working on. You get context-sensitive help by selecting an item in the *Designer* window, *Code* window, *Properties* window, *Toolbox*, etc., and then pressing the F1 key. Your Web browser will launch, displaying help on the item that is selected.

For example, Figure 2-95 shows some code displayed in the *Code* window. Notice that the = operator has been selected (highlighted) in one of the lines of code. If we press the F1 key while the = operator is selected, we will see a help screen similar to Figure 2-96, displayed in a Web browser.

Notice that the left pane in the browser shows a list of topics that you can click on to get additional help. You can also use the search box that appears at the top of the left pane to search for help on specific items.

Figure 2-95 The = operator selected in the *Code* window

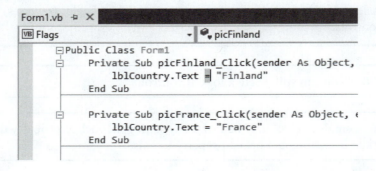

Figure 2-96 Help with the = operator

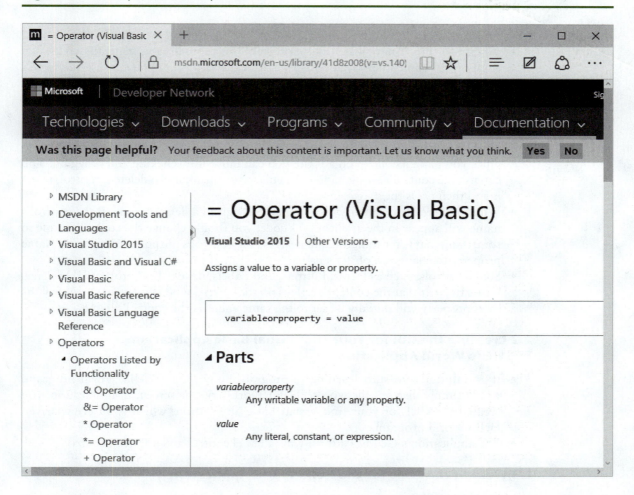

Summary

2.1 Getting Started with Forms and Controls

- When you start a new Visual Basic project, Visual Studio automatically creates an empty form named Form1, and displays it in the *Designer*. You can use the form's sizing handles to resize the form, and you can use the *Toolbox* to create controls on the form.
- When you select an object in the *Designer* window, that object's properties are displayed in the *Properties* window. You use the *Properties* window to change the object's properties.
- Once you place a control on a form, you can move it by clicking and dragging. You can use the control's sizing handles to enlarge or shrink it. To delete a control, select it and then press the ⟨Delete⟩ key.
- When you create a control, it is automatically given a default name. If the control's name will appear in the application's code, you should change the control's name to something that is meaningful, and describe the control's purpose. You use the Name property to change an object's name.
- Some controls, such as forms, Buttons, and Labels, have a Text property that determines the text that the control displays on the screen. When you create a control, its Text property will initially be set to the same value as the control's name.

2.2 Creating the GUI for Your First Visual Basic Application: The Hello World Application

- It is traditional to start learning to program by writing a Hello World program, which simply displays the words "Hello World" on the screen. In this section, you created the GUI for your first Visual Basic application, which is an event-driven Hello World program.
- The application's GUI has a form with a Label control and a Button control.

2.3 Writing the Code for the Hello World Application

- In this section, you wrote the code for your Hello World program. The code consisted of a Click event handler for the Button control.
- In the Click event handler, you wrote a statement that assigns the string "Hello World" to the Label control's Text property. As a result, the event handler displays the text *Hello World* in the Label control when the user clicks the button.
- You switch between the *Designer* and the *Code* window by using the tabs that appear at the top of the *Designer*. You can also detach the *Code* window and move it to a different part of the screen. That allows you to see both the *Designer* and the *Code* window at the same time.
- Visual Studio has three modes in which it operates as you develop an application: design mode, run mode, and break mode. In design mode, you create an application. In run mode, you are executing an application. In break mode, a running application's execution is momentarily suspended for testing and debugging purposes.
- Each Visual Basic application that you create is a project. A Visual Basic project is a collection of files that belong to a single application. Each project will belong to a solution.

2.4 More About Label Controls

- If you want to change the appearance of a Label control's text, you can change the control's Font property.
- The BorderStyle property determines the type of border that is displayed around a Label control. The possible values are None, FixedSingle, or Fixed3D.

- The AutoSize property determines whether a label will change size automatically to accommodate the amount of text in its Text property, or remain a fixed size.
- The TextAlign property determines how the text in a label is aligned, and may be set to any of the following values: TopLeft, TopCenter, TopRight, MiddleLeft, MiddleCenter, MiddleRight, BottomLeft, BottomCenter, or BottomRight.
- A Label control's ForeColor property determines the color of the label's text. A Label control's BackColor property determines the control's background color.
- In code, if you want to change the text that a Label control displays, you assign a string to a Label control's Text property. The Text property accepts strings only.
- If you want to clear the text that is displayed by a Label control, assign an empty string ("") or the special value `String.Empty` to the control's Text property.

2.5 Creating Multiple Event Handlers

- Many of the applications that you will develop will have multiple buttons, each with its own Click event handler.
- To create Click event handlers for multiple buttons, double-click each Button control in the *Designer* so an empty event handler will be created in the form's source code file.

2.6 Making Sense of IntelliSense

- As you type code in the Visual Studio code editor, IntelliSense boxes pop up to assist you. You can use the IntelliSense boxes to automatically complete some programming statements after typing only the first few characters.

2.7 PictureBox Controls

- A PictureBox control displays a graphic image on a form.
- PictureBox controls have properties to control the way the image is displayed.
- A PictureBox control can have a Click event handler that responds when the user clicks the control at run time.

2.8 The Visible Property

- A control's Visible property can be set to either True or False.
- If a control's Visible property is set to True, the control is visible on the form at runtime.
- If a control's Visible property is set to False, the control is invisible on the form at runtime.
- In this section, you also saw examples of event handlers that contain more than one programming statement. When an event handler containing multiple statements executes, the statements are executed in the order they appear, from the beginning to the end of the event handler.

2.9 Writing the Code to Close an Application's Form

- To close an application's form in code, you use the statement `Me.Close()`.

2.10 Comments, Blank Lines, and Indentation

- Comments are brief notes that are placed in a program's source code, explaining how parts of the program work.
- In Visual Basic, you begin a comment with an apostrophe ('). Anything appearing after the apostrophe, to the end of the line, is ignored by the Visual Basic compiler.
- Programmers commonly use blank lines and indentation in program code to give the code visual organization, and make it easier to read.

2.11 Dealing with Errors

- In general, there are three types of software errors: syntax errors, runtime errors, and logic errors.
- The Visual Studio *Code* window checks each line of code for syntax errors as soon as you enter it. When a syntax error is found, it is underlined with a jagged blue line.
- A runtime error is an unexpected error that occurs while a program is running. It usually happens when the program attempts to perform an operation that the computer cannot carry out. These types of runtime errors usually cause the program to abruptly halt.
- A logic error is an error in the logical steps that a program performs to complete a task. A logic error causes the program to produce the wrong results, or behave in an unexpected manner.
- The most effective way to find logic errors and runtime errors in your code is to test the application. If a logic error or runtime error occurs, you debug the application. Debugging is the process of analyzing your code to determine where the error is taking place. The best way to debug your code is with the help of a debugger.

2.12 Displaying User Messages at Runtime

- A message box is a small window that displays a message.
- In Visual Basic you call the `MessageBox.Show` method to display a message box.
- The StatusStrip control allows you to display messages on a form, without displaying a dialog box that must be closed by the user.

2.13 Customizing an Application's Form

- A form's BorderStyle property controls the appearance of the form's border, and determines whether the user can resize the form.
- You can use a Form's MinimizeBox, MaximizeBox, and ControlBox properties to determine whether the form has a minimize button, a maximize button, and a close button.

2.14 Using Visual Studio Help

- You access the Visual Studio Documentation and the MSDN Library by clicking *Help* on the menu bar, and then selecting *View Help*. (Or, you can press Ctrl+F1 on the keyboard.)
- You can get context-sensitive help on a single item that is currently selected in the *Designer* window, *Code* window, *Properties* window, *Toolbox*, etc., and then pressing the F1 key.

Key Terms

Alphabetical button
aspect ratio
assignment operator
assignment statement
AutoSize property
BackColor property
Boolean property
BorderStyle property
bounding box
break mode
Categorized button

class declaration
code template
Code window
comments
context-sensitive help
ControlBox property
debugger
debugging
design mode
design time
dialog box

Font property
ForeColor property
FormBorderStyle property
Hello World program
Image property
IntelliSense
literal
logic error
message box
method call
MaximizeBox property
Microsoft Developer Network
   (MSDN) Library
MinimizeBox property
object box
PictureBox control
project

project folder
run mode
runtime
runtime error
SizeMode property
sizing handles
solution
solution file
solution folder
StatusStrip control
string
string literal
syntax errors
test
TextAlign property
ToolStripStatusLabel control
Visible property

Review Questions

Multiple Choice

1. A(n) _____ is the thin dotted line that encloses an object in the *Designer*.
   a. selection marker
   b. control binder
   c. bounding box
   d. object container

2. The small squares that appear on the right edge, bottom edge, and lower-right corner of a form's bounding box are called _____.
   a. sizing hooks
   b. form edges
   c. bounding tags
   d. sizing handles

3. _____ is the name of the blank form that Visual Studio initially creates in a new project.
   a. `Form1`
   b. `Main`
   c. `New1`
   d. `Blank`

4. The _____ property holds the text that is displayed on the face of the button.
   a. Name
   b. Text
   c. Tag
   d. Face

5. A(n) _____ is a procedure that executes when a specific event takes place while an application is running.
   a. action process
   b. event handler
   c. runtime procedure
   d. event method

6. The statement `MessageBox.Show` is an example of a(n) _____.
   a. method call
   b. namespace
   c. Click event
   d. event handler

7. In programming we use the term "string" to mean _____.
   a. many lines of code
   b. parallel memory locations
   c. string of characters
   d. virtually anything

8. A piece of data that is written into a program's code is a(n) _____.
   a. identifier
   b. specifier
   c. keyword
   d. literal

9. The time during which you build the GUI and write the application's code is referred to as _____.
   a. runtime
   b. design time
   c. code time
   d. planning

10. The time during which an application is executing is referred to as _____.
    a. go time
    b. design time
    c. execution
    d. runtime

11. When you want to display text on a form, you use a _____ control.
    a. Button
    b. PictureBox
    c. Label
    d. TextBox

12. The _____ property allows you to set the font, font style, and size of the control's text.
    a. Style
    b. AutoSize
    c. Text
    d. Font

13. A(n) _____ property can be set to one of two possible values: True or False.
    a. Boolean
    b. Logical
    c. Binary
    d. Dual

14. Label controls have a(n) _____ property that determines whether or not they can be resized.
    a. Stretch
    b. AutoSize
    c. Dimension
    d. Fixed

15. The _____ property can be used to change the text's alignment in the label.
    a. TextPosition
    b. AutoAlign
    c. TextCenter
    d. TextAlign

16. In code, you use a(n) _____ to store a value in a control's property.
    a. Click event
    b. method call
    c. assignment statement
    d. Boolean value

17. The equal sign (=) is known as the _____.
    a. duplication symbol
    b. assignment operator
    c. value operator
    d. property position

18. The standard notation for referring to a control's property in code is _____.
    a. *ControlName.PropertyName*
    b. *ControlName=PropertyName*
    c. *PropertyName.ControlName*
    d. *PropertyName=ControlName*

19. _____ is a feature of Visual Studio that provides automatic code completion as you write programming statements.
    a. AutoCode
    b. AutoComplete
    c. IntelliSense
    d. IntelliCode

20. You can use a _____ control to display a graphic image on a form.
    a. Graphics
    b. PictureBox
    c. Drawing
    d. ImageBox

21. Once you have created a PictureBox control, you use its _____ property to specify the image it will display.
    a. Image
    b. Source
    c. DrawSource
    d. ImageList

22. The PictureBox control's _____ property specifies how the control's image is to be displayed.
    a. RenderMode
    b. DrawMode
    c. SizeMode
    d. ImageMode

23. _____ is the image's width to height ratio.
    a. Aspect ratio
    b. Size ratio
    c. Projection ratio
    d. Area ratio

24. Most controls have a _____ property that determines whether the control can be seen on the form at run time.
    a. Render
    b. Viewable
    c. Visible
    d. Draw

25. _____ are short notes placed in program code, explaining how the code works.
    a. Hidden statements
    b. Comments
    c. Bookmarks
    d. Descriptors

26. Programmers commonly use blank lines and indentations in their code to create a sense of _____.
    a. logic
    b. visual organization
    c. documentation
    d. program flow

27. To close an application's form in code, you use the statement _____.
    a. `Close();`
    b. `Close.This();`
    c. `Close()`
    d. `this.Close();`

True or False
1. T F: Changing an object's Text property also changes the object's name.
2. T F: When a form is created, its Text property is initially set to the same value as the form's name.
3. T F: The form's title is displayed in the bar along the top of a form.
4. T F: A Label control's Text property is initially set to the same value as the Label control's name.
5. T F: When a Label control's AutoSize property is set to True, you can manually change the size of the control by clicking and dragging its bounding box.
6. T F: By default, a label's text is aligned with the bottom and right edges of the label's bounding box.
7. T F: Label controls are useful for displaying output while an application is running.
8. T F: The assignment operator assigns the value that appears on its left side to the item that appears on its right side.
9. T F: You cannot modify a control's Text property with code.
10. T F: PictureBox controls also have a BorderStyle property that works just like a Label control's BorderStyle property.
11. T F: Buttons are the only controls that can respond to Click events.
12. T F: The Visible property is a Binary property, which means it can be set only to the value 1 or 0.
13. T F: A control is hidden in the *Designer* window if its Visible property is set to *False*.
14. T F: You can delete a locked control.
15. T F: When you lock the controls on a form, the user must enter a password before the application will run.

16. T F: Comments are ignored by the Visual Basic compiler.

17. T F: To close an application's form in code, you use the statement `Close.Me()`

18. T F: In the *Code* window, Visual Studio examines each statement as you type it, and reports any syntax errors that are found.

Short Answer

1. What does a bounding box indicate about an object in the *Designer*?

2. What happens when you position the mouse cursor over an edge or corner of a bounding box that has sizing handles?

3. What determines an object's appearance and other characteristics?

4. What is shown by each column in the *Properties* window?

5. What steps must you perform to change a form's Text property?

6. What steps must you perform to change a form's Size property in the *Properties* window?

7. How do you move a control to a new location on the form using the mouse?

8. What steps do you perform to change a Button control's Text property?

9. In code, what characters surround a string literal?

10. Briefly describe the difference between design time and runtime.

11. Describe the appearance of a Label control if its BorderStyle property is set to Fixed3D.

12. What does it mean when a Label control's AutoSize property is set to True?

13. What values can be assigned to the TextAlign property?

14. How do you clear the text that is displayed in a Label control in code?

15. What are the different image formats that a PictureBox control can display?

16. List the values that the SizeMode property of a PictureBox control can be set to.

17. How does Visual Studio help you to quickly correct syntax errors?

Algorithm Workbench

1. What statement would you write to display *Good Afternoon* in a message box?

2. What statement would you write to display your name in a message box?

3. Suppose an application's GUI has a Label control named `lblDog`. Write a statement that causes *Fido* to be displayed in the `lblDog` control.

4. Suppose an application's GUI has a Label control named `lblOutput`. Write a statement that clears any text that happens to be displayed by the control.

5. Suppose an application's GUI has a PictureBox control named `picMyPicture`. Write a statement that makes the control invisible at runtime.

What Do You Think?

1. Why, in the *Properties* window, do you change some properties with a drop-down list or a dialog box, while you change others by typing a value?

2. Why is it a good idea to equip a form with a button that terminates the application, if the form already has a standard Windows *Close* button in the upper right corner?

3. What is the benefit of creating PictureBox controls that respond to mouse clicks?

Find the Error

1. Open the *Error1* project from the student sample programs folder named *Chap2\\Error1*. Run the application. When Visual Studio reports an error, find and fix the error.

2. Open the *Error2* project from the student sample programs folder named *Chap2\\Error2*. Run the application. When Visual Studio reports an error, find and fix the error.

Programming Challenges

VideoNote

The Latin Translator Problem

1. **Latin Translator**

   Look at the following list of Latin words and their meanings.

Latin	English
sinister	left
dexter	right
medium	middle

   Create an application that translates the Latin words to English. The form should have three buttons, one for each Latin word. When the user clicks a button, the application should display the English translation in a Label control. The screens shown in Figure 2-97 show an example of the application running. The top-left screen shows the application when it starts. The other screens show the application after the user has clicked one of the buttons.

Figure 2-97 The Latin Translator application

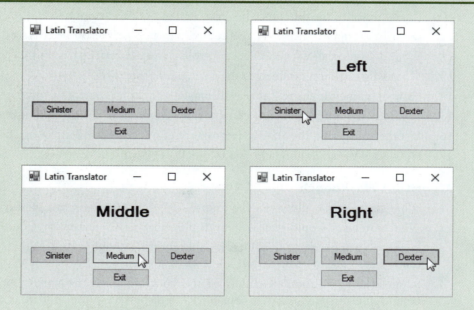

2. **Math Tutor Application**

   Create an application that displays a simple math problem in a Label control. The form should have a button that displays the answer to the math problem. It should also have a button that closes the application. The leftmost screen in Figure 2-98 shows the application's form before the button is clicked to display the answer. The rightmost screen shows the application's form after the button has been clicked.

Figure 2-98 The Math Tutor application

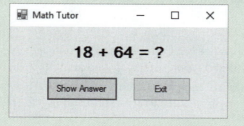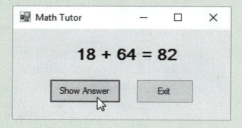

3. **Card Identifier**

Make sure you have downloaded the student sample programs from this book's companion Web site at www.pearsonhighered.com/gaddis. In the student sample programs, you will find a folder named *Images\Poker Cards*. In that folder, you will find image files for a complete deck of poker cards. Create an application with five PictureBox controls. Each PictureBox should display a different card from the set of images. When the user clicks any of the PictureBox controls, the name of the card should be displayed in a Label control. Figure 2-99 shows an example of the application running. The image on the left shows the application's form when it starts running. The image on the right shows the form after the user has clicked the two of clubs card.

Figure 2-99 Card Identifier application

4. **Orion Constellation**

Make sure you have downloaded the student sample programs from this book's companion Web site at www.pearsonhighered.com/gaddis. In the *Images* folder, you will find an image file named Orion.bmp, which contains a diagram of the Orion constellation. Orion is one of the most famous constellations in the night sky.

Create an application that displays the Orion image in a PictureBox control as shown on the left in Figure 2-100. The application should have a button that, when clicked, displays the names of each of the stars, as shown on the right in Figure 2-100. The application should have another button that, when clicked, hides the star names. The names of the stars are: *Betelgeuse, Meissa, Alnitak, Alnilam, Mintaka, Saiph*, and *Rigel*.

Hint: Place the PictureBox control with the Orion image on the form. Then, place Label controls containing the star names on top of the PictureBox. Use the Properties window to set each of the Label control's Visible property to False. That will cause the labels to be invisible when the application runs. The *Show Star Names* button will set each of the Label control's Visible property to True, and the *Hide Star Names* button will set each of the Label control's Visible property to False.

Figure 2-100 The Orion Constellation application

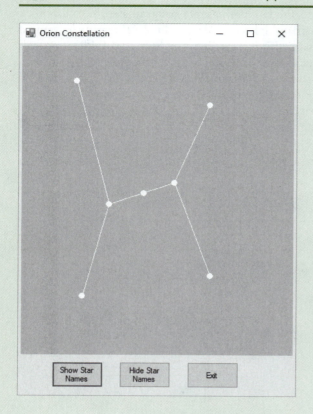

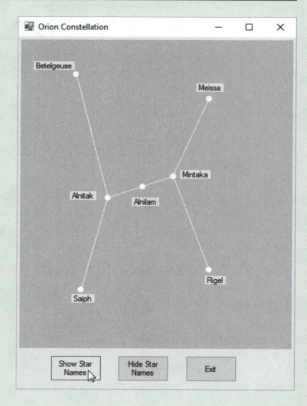

Design Your Own Forms

5. **State Abbreviations**

The following table shows lists of six states and their official abbreviations.

State	Abbreviation
Virginia	VA
North Carolina	NC
South Carolina	SC
Georgia	GA
Alabama	AL
Florida	FL

Create an application that allows the user to select a state and then displays that state's official abbreviation. The form should have six buttons, one for each state. When the user clicks a button, the application displays the state's abbreviation in a Label control.

6. **Heads or Tails**

In the student sample programs that accompany this book, you will find a folder named *Images\Coins* that contains images showing the heads and tails sides of a coin. Create an application with a *Show Heads* button and a *Show Tails* button. When the user clicks the *Show Heads* button, an image of the heads side of a coin should appear. When the user clicks the *Show Tails* button, an image of the tails side of a coin should appear.

7. **Clickable Number Images**

In the *Chap02* folder, in the student sample program files, you will find the image files shown in Figure 2-101. Create an application that displays these images in PictureBox controls. The application should perform the following actions:

- When the user clicks the 1 image, the application should display the word *One* in a message box.
- When the user clicks the 2 image, the application should display the word *Two* in a message box.
- When the user clicks the 3 image, the application should display the word *Three* in a message box.
- When the user clicks the 4 image, the application should display the word *Four* in a message box.
- When the user clicks the 5 image, the application should display the word *Five* in a message box.

Figure 2-101 Image files

One.bmp   Two.bmp   Three.bmp   Four.bmp   Five.bmp

8. **Joke and Punch line**

A joke typically has two parts: a setup and a punch line. For example, this might be the setup for a joke:

How many programmers does it take to change a light bulb?

And this is the punch line:

None. That's a hardware problem.

Think of your favorite joke and identify its setup and punch line. Then, create an application that has a Label and two buttons on a form. One of the buttons should read "Setup" and the other button should read "Punch line." When the *Setup* button is clicked, display the joke's setup in the Label control. When the *Punch line* button is clicked, display the joke's punch line in the Label control.

3 Variables and Calculations

This chapter covers the use of **text boxes** to gather input from users. It also discusses the use of variables, named constants, type conversion functions, and mathematical calculations. You will be introduced to the GroupBox control as a way to organize controls on an application's form. The *Format* menu commands, which allow you to align, size, and center controls, are also discussed. You will learn about the form's Load event, which happens when a form is loaded into memory, and debugging techniques for locating logic errors.

3.1 Gathering Text Input

CONCEPT: The TextBox control is a rectangular area that can accept keyboard input from the user.

Many of the programs that you will write from this point forward will require the user to enter data. The data entered by the user will then be used in some sort of operation. One of the primary controls that you will use to get data from the user is the TextBox control.

A **TextBox control** appears as a rectangular area on a form. When the application is running, the user can type text into a TextBox control. The program can then retrieve the text that the user entered and use that text in any necessary operations. Tutorial 3-1 examines an application that uses a TextBox control.

Tutorial 3-1:
Using a TextBox control

Step 1: Open the *Greetings* project from the student sample programs folder named *Chap3\Greetings*.

Step 2: Click the *Start* button (▶) to run the application. The application's form appears, as shown in Figure 3-1. The TextBox control is the white rectangular area beneath the label that reads *Enter Your Name*.

Notice that the TextBox control shows a blinking text cursor, indicating it is ready to receive keyboard input.

Figure 3-1 *Greetings* project initial form

Figure 3-2 *Greetings* project completed form

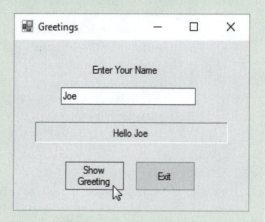

Step 3: Type your name. As you enter characters on the keyboard, they appear in the TextBox control.

Step 4: Click the *Show Greeting* button. The message *Hello* followed by the name you entered appears in a label below the TextBox control. The form now appears similar to the one shown in Figure 3-2.

Step 5: Click inside the TextBox control and use the Delete and/or Backspace key to erase the name you entered. Enter another name, and then click the *Show Greeting* button. Notice that the greeting message changes accordingly.

Step 6: Click the *Exit* button to close the application. You have returned to design mode.

Step 7: Look at the application's form in the *Designer* window. Figure 3-3 shows the form with its controls.

Notice that the name of the TextBox control starts with txt, which we use as the prefix for TextBox controls. Like the Label control, the TextBox control has a Text property. However, the Label control's Text property is only for displaying information—the user cannot directly alter its contents. The TextBox control's Text property is for input purposes. The user can alter it by typing characters into the TextBox control. Whatever the user types into the TextBox control is stored, as a string, in its Text property.

Figure 3-3 *Greetings* project form with controls labeled

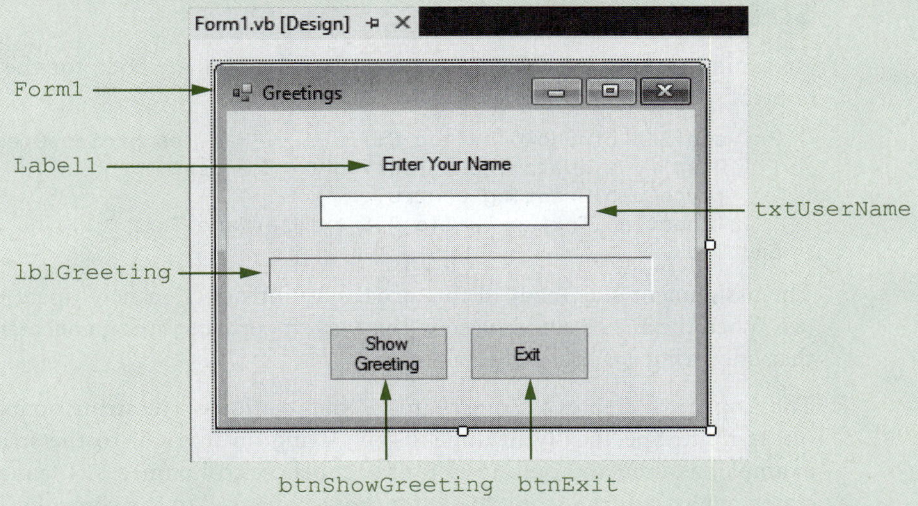

Using the Text Property in Code

You access a TextBox control's Text property in code the same way you access other properties. For example, assume an application has a Label control named `lblInfo` and a TextBox control named `txtInput`. The following statement assigns the contents of the TextBox control's Text property into the Label control's Text property.

```
lblInfo.Text = txtInput.Text
```

The following statement shows another example. It displays the contents of the `txtInput` control's Text property in a message box:

```
MessageBox.Show(txtInput.Text)
```

Clearing a Text Box

Recall from Chapter 1 that an object contains methods, which are actions the object performs. If you want to execute an object's method, you write a statement that calls the method. The general format of such a statement is

```
Object.Method
```

Object is the name of the object and *Method* is the name of the method that is being called.

A TextBox control is an object and has a variety of methods that perform operations on the text box or its contents. One of these methods is `Clear`, which clears the contents of the text box's Text property. The general format of the `Clear` method is

```
TextBoxName.Clear()
```

TextBoxName is the name of the TextBox control. Here is an example:

```
txtInput.Clear()
```

When this statement executes, the Text property of `txtInput` is cleared and the text box appears empty on the screen.

You can also clear a text box by assigning the predefined constant `String.Empty` to its Text property. Here is an example:

```
txtInput.Text = String.Empty
```

Once this statement executes, the Text property of txtInput is cleared and the text box appears empty on the screen.

String Concatenation

Returning to the *Greetings* application, let's look at the code for the btnShowGreeting control's Click event handler:

```
Private Sub btnShowGreeting_Click(...) Handles btnShowGreeting.Click
    ' Display a customized greeting to the user
    ' in the lblGreeting control.
    lblGreeting.Text = "Hello " & txtUserName.Text
End Sub
```

The assignment statement in this procedure introduces a new operator: the ampersand (&). When the ampersand is used in this way, it performs **string concatenation**. This means that one string is appended to another.

The & operator creates a string that is a combination of the string on its left and the string on its right. Specifically, it appends the string on its right to the string on its left. For example, assume an application uses a Label control named lblMessage. The following statement assigns the string "Good morning Charlie" to the control's Text property:

```
lblMessage.Text = "Good morning " & "Charlie"
```

In our *Greetings* application, if the user types *Mary* into the txtUserName control, the control's Text property is set to *Mary*. So the statement

```
lblGreeting.Text = "Hello " & txtUserName.Text
```

assigns the string "Hello Mary" to lblGreeting's Text property.

Look again at the assignment statement. Notice there is a space in the string literal after the word *Hello*. This prevents the two strings being concatenated from running together.

In a few moments, it will be your turn to create an application using TextBox controls and string concatenation. Tutorial 3-2 leads you through the process.

Using ControlChars.CrLf to Display Multiple Lines

If you want to display multiple lines of information in a message box, use the constant **ControlChars.CrLf** (CrLf stands for *carriage return line feed*). Concatenate it with the string you wish to display, where you wish to begin a new line (as shown in this example):

```
MessageBox.Show("This is line 1" & ControlChars.CrLf &
                "This is line 2")
```

This statement causes two lines of output to appear in a message box. When Visual Basic displays the string "This is line 1" & ControlChars.CrLf & "This is line 2", it interprets **ControlChars.CrLf** as a command to begin a new line of output.

Tutorial 3-2:
Building the *Date String* application

VideoNote

Building the
Date String
application

In this tutorial you will create an application that lets the user enter the following information about today's date:

- The day of the week
- The name of the month
- The numeric day of the month
- The year

When the user enters the information and clicks a button, the application displays a date string such as Saturday, December 17, 2016.

Step 1:   Start Visual Studio and create a new Windows Forms Application named *Date String*.

Step 2:   Create the form shown in Figure 3-4, using the following instructions:

- You insert TextBox controls by double-clicking the TextBox icon in the *Toolbox*. When a TextBox control is created, it will be given a default name. As with other controls, you can change a TextBox control's name by modifying its Name property.
- Give each control the name indicated in the figure. The labels that display *Enter the day of the week*, *Enter the month*, *Enter the day of the month*, and *Enter the year* will not be referred to in code, so they may keep their default names.
- Set the lblDateString label's AutoSize property to *False*, its BorderStyle property to *Fixed3D*, and its TextAlign property to *MiddleCenter*. Resize the label as shown in Figure 3-4, and delete the contents of the label's Text property.
- Set the form's Text property to *Date String*.

Figure 3-4 *Date String* form

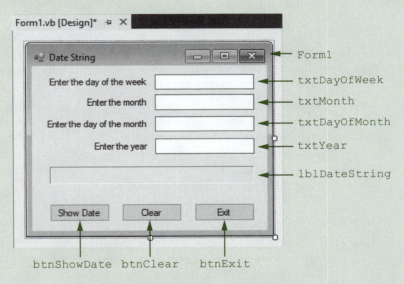

Step 3:   Next, you will write code for the btnShowDate button's Click event handler. Double-click the button to create the code template, and then enter the lines shown in bold:

```
Private Sub btnShowDate_Click(...) Handles btnShowDate.Click
    ' Concatenate the input and build the date string.
    lblDateString.Text = txtDayOfWeek.Text & ", " &
        txtMonth.Text & " " &
        txtDayOfMonth.Text & ", " &
        txtYear.Text
End Sub
```

This example introduces a new programming technique: breaking up a long statement into multiple lines. Quite often, you will find yourself writing statements that are too long to fit entirely inside the *Code* window. Your code will be hard to read if you have to scroll the *Code* window to the right to view long statements. In addition, if you or your instructor chooses to print your code, the statements that are too long to fit on one line of the page will wrap around to the next line and make your code look unorganized. For these reasons, it is usually best to break a long statement into multiple lines.

When typing most statements, you can simply press the [Enter] key when you reach an appropriate point to continue the statement on the next line. Remember, however, that you cannot break up a keyword, quoted string, or a name (such as a variable name or a control name).

Step 4: Switch back to the *Designer* window and double-click the btnClear button to create a code template for its Click event handler. Then enter the following bold code to complete the event handler:

```
Private Sub btnClear_Click(...) Handles btnClear.Click
    ' Clear the Text Boxes and lblDateString.
    txtDayOfWeek.Clear()
    txtMonth.Clear()
    txtDayOfMonth.Clear()
    txtYear.Clear()
    lblDateString.Text = String.Empty
End Sub
```

Let's review this code. The btnClear button allows the user to start over with a form that is empty of previous values. The btnClear_Click event handler clears the contents of all the TextBox controls and the lblDateString label. To accomplish this, the procedure calls each TextBox control's Clear method, and then assigns the special value String.Empty to lblDateString's Text property. (The value String.Empty represents an empty string. Assigning String.Empty to a label's Text property clears the value displayed by the label.)

Step 5: Switch back to the *Designer* window and double-click the btnExit button to create a code template for its Click event handler. Then enter the following bold code to complete the event handler:

```
Private Sub btnExit_Click(...) Handles btnExit.Click
    ' Close the form.
    Me.Close()
End Sub
```

Step 6: Save the project.

Step 7: Click the *Start* button (▶) to run the application. With the application running, enter the requested information into the TextBox controls and click the *Show Date* button. Your form should appear similar to the one shown in Figure 3-5.

Figure 3-5 Running the *Date String* application

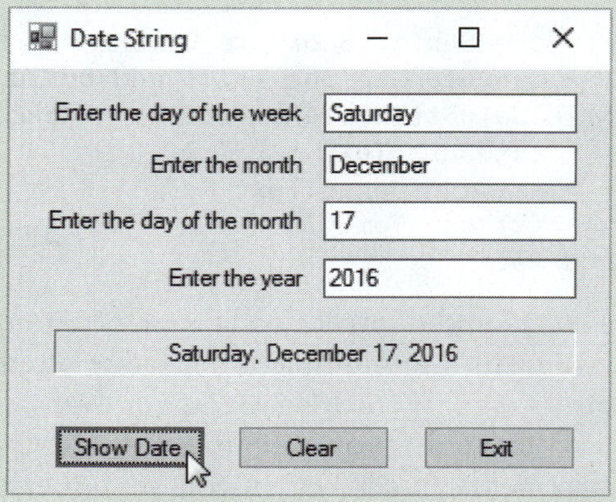

Step 8: Click the *Clear* button to test it, and then enter new values into the TextBox controls. Click the *Show Date* button.

Step 9: Click the *Exit* button to close the application.

Checkpoint

3.1 What TextBox control property holds text entered by the user?

3.2 Assume an application has a label named `lblMessage` and a TextBox control named `txtInput`. Write the statement that takes text the user entered into the TextBox control and assigns it to the label's Text property.

3.3 If the following statement is executed, what will the `lblGreeting` control display?
`lblGreeting.Text = "Hello " & "Jonathan, " & "how are you?"`

3.4 What is string concatenation?

3.2 Variables and Data Types

CONCEPT: Variables hold data that may be manipulated, used to manipulate other data, or remembered for later use.

VideoNote
Introduction to Variables

A **variable** is a storage location in computer memory that holds data while a program is running. It is called a variable because the data it holds can be changed by statements in the program.

You have already seen programs that store data in properties belonging to Visual Basic controls. While properties hold values that are associated with a specific control, variables are used for general purpose data storage in memory. Generally speaking, you can do a number of things with variables:

- Copy and store values entered by the user so the values can be manipulated
- Perform arithmetic on numeric values
- Test values to determine that they meet some criterion
- Temporarily hold and manipulate the value of a control property
- Remember data for later use in a program

Think of a variable as a name that represents a location in the computer's random-access memory (RAM). When a value is stored in a variable, it is actually stored in RAM. You use the assignment operator (=) to store a value in a variable, just as you do with a control property. For example, suppose a program uses a variable named `intLength`. The following statement stores the value 112 in that variable:

```
intLength = 112
```

When this statement executes, the value 112 is stored in the memory location the name `intLength` represents. As another example, assume the following statement appears in a program that uses a variable named `strGreeting` and a TextBox control named `txtName`:

```
strGreeting = "Good morning " & txtName.Text
```

Suppose the user has already entered *Holly* into the `txtName` TextBox control. When the statement executes, the variable `strGreeting` is assigned the string `"Good morning Holly"`.

Declaring Variables

A **variable declaration** is a statement that creates a variable in memory when a program executes. The declaration indicates the name you wish to give the variable and the type of data the variable will hold. Here is the general form of a variable declaration:

```
Dim VariableName As DataType
```

Here is an example of a variable declaration:

```
Dim intLength As Integer
```

Let's look at each part of this statement, and its purpose:

- The `Dim` keyword tells Visual Basic that a variable is being declared.
- `intLength` is the name of the variable.
- `As Integer` indicates the variable's data type, we know it will be used to hold integer numbers.

You can declare multiple variables with one `Dim` statement, as shown in the following statement. It declares three variables, all holding integers:

```
Dim intLength, intWidth, intHeight As Integer
```

 NOTE: The keyword `Dim` stands for "dimension." This is a term for declaring a variable that goes back to some of the earliest programming languages.

Variable Names

It is your responsibility as the programmer to make up the names of the variables that you use in a program. You must follow these rules when naming a variable in Visual Basic:

- The first character must be a letter or an underscore character. (We do not recommend that you start a variable name with an underscore, but if you do, the name must also contain at least one letter or numeric digit.)
- After the first character, you may use letters, numeric digits, and underscore characters. (You cannot use spaces, periods, or other punctuation characters in a variable name.)
- Variable names cannot be longer than 1,023 characters.
- Variable names cannot be Visual Basic keywords. Keywords have reserved meanings in Visual Basic, and their use as variable names would confuse the compiler.

Type Prefixes

In this book we normally begin variable names with a three- or four-letter prefix that indicates the variable's data type. For example, the variable name `intLength` begins with the three-letter prefix `int`, which indicates that it is an Integer variable. Earlier we used the name `strGreeting` as an example variable name. That name begins with the prefix `str`, indicating that it is a String variable.

The practice of beginning a variable name with a prefix is not required, but it is intended to make code more understandable. For example, when you are reading your own, or someone else's, code, and you see a variable name such as `intUnitsSold`, you immediately know that it is an Integer variable because of the `int` prefix.

The convention of using type prefixes in variable names has historically been popular among Visual Basic programmers, but not all programmers follow this practice. Your instructor may or may not require you to use them. Regardless of whether you use them or not, be consistent in the approach that you adopt.

Table 3-1 shows the prefixes that we use in this book, the Visual Basic data types that they are used with, and examples of each used in variable names. (We will discuss the commonly used data types in greater detail momentarily.)

Table 3-1 Recommended prefixes for variable names

Variable Type	Prefix	Examples
Boolean	bln	blnContinue, blnHasRows
Byte	byt	bytInput, bytCharVal
Char	chr	chrSelection, chrMiddleInitial
Date, DateTime	dtm or dat	dtmBirthDate, datPublicationDate
Decimal	dec	decWeeklySalary, decGrossPay
Double	dbl	dblAirVelocity, dblPlanetMass
Integer	int	intCount, intDaysInPayPeriod
Long	lng	lngElapsedSeconds
Object	obj	objStudent, objPayroll
Short	shrt	shrtCount
Single	sng	sngTaxRate, sngGradeAverage
String	str	strLastName, strAddress

Use Descriptive Variable Names

In addition to following the Visual Basic rules, you should always choose names for your variables that give an indication of what they are used for. For example, a String variable that holds a customer's name might be named strCustomerName, and an Integer variable that holds a car's speed might be named intSpeed. You may be tempted to give variables names like x and b2, but names like these give no clue as to what the variable's purpose is.

Because a variable's name should reflect the variable's purpose, programmers often find themselves creating names that are made of multiple words. For example, consider the following variable names:

```
inthoursworked
strcustomername
inthotdogssoldtoday
```

Unfortunately, these names are not easily read by the human eye because the words aren't separated. Because we can't have spaces in variable names, we need to find another way to separate the words in a multiword variable name and make it more readable to the human eye.

One way to do this is to use the camel case naming convention. **Camel case** names are written in the following manner:

- The variable name starts with lowercase letters.
- The first character of the second and subsequent words is written in uppercase.

For example, the following variable names are written in camel case:

```
intHoursWorked
strCustomerName
intHotDogsSoldToday
```

This style of naming is called camel case because the uppercase characters that appear in a name may suggest a camel's humps. The camel case convention is widely used, not only in Visual Basic, but in other languages as well. We will use the camel case convention for variable names in this book.

Assigning Values to Variables

A value is put into a variable with an assignment statement. For example, the following statement assigns the value 20 to the variable `intUnitsSold`:

```
intUnitsSold = 20
```

The = operator is called the assignment operator. A variable name must always appear on the left side of the assignment operator. For example, the following would be incorrect:

```
20 = intUnitsSold
```

On the right side of the operator, you can put a literal, another variable, or a mathematical expression that matches the variable's type. In the following, the contents of the variable on the right side of the = sign is assigned to the variable on the left side:

```
intUnitsSold = intUnitsOnHand
```

Suppose `intUnitsOnHand` already equals 20. Then Figure 3-6 shows how the value 20 is copied into the memory location represented by `intUnitsSold`.

Figure 3-6 Assigning `intUnitsOnHand` to `intUnitsSold`

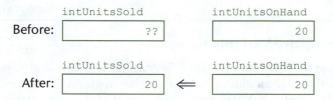

The assignment operator changes only the left operand. The right operand (or expression) does not change value. Sometimes your program will contain a series of statements that pass a value from one variable to the next. When the following statements execute, all three variables will contain the same value, 50:

```
Dim intA, intB, intC As Integer
intA = 50
intB = intA
intC = intB
```

A variable can hold only one value at a time. If you assign a new value to the variable, the new value replaces the variable's previous contents. There is no way to "undo" this operation. For example:

```
Dim intA, intB As Integer
intA = 50
intA = 99
```

After the second assignment statement, `intA` equals 99. The value 50 no longer exists in memory.

Integer Data Types

Integers are whole numbers such as −5, 26, 12345, and 0. Visual Basic has four data types, listed in Table 3-2, for holding integers. (For your convenience the table also shows the type prefix that we will use for variables of each of these data types.) Unsigned integers can hold only positive values (zero is considered positive). Signed integers can hold both positive and negative values.

Table 3-2 Integer data types

Type	Naming Prefix	Description
Byte	byt	Holds an unsigned integer value in the range 0 to 255
Short	shrt	Holds a signed integer in the range –32,768 to +32,767
Integer	int	Holds a signed integer in the range –2,147,483,648 to +2,147,483,647
Long	lng	Holds a signed integer in the range –9,223,372,036,854,775,808 to +9,223,372,036,854,775,807

The following code example shows variables of the different integer types being declared and assigned values:

```
Dim bytInches As Byte
Dim shrtFeet as Short
Dim intMiles As Integer
Dim lngNationalDebt As Long

bytInches = 26
shrtFeet = 32767
intMiles = 2100432877
lngNationalDebt = 4000000000001
```

Each type has a different storage size and range of possible values it can hold. Most of the time, you will use the Integer data type for integer-type values. Its name is easy to remember, and Integer values are efficiently processed by the computer.

Integer Literals

When you write an integer literal in your program code, Visual Basic assumes the literal is type Integer if the value fits within the allowed range for the Integer data type. A value larger than that will be assumed to be type Long. On rare occasions you may want to override the literal's default type. You do this by appending one of the following special characters to the end of the number:

I Integer literal
L Long integer literal
S Short integer literal

In the following code example, an integer literal uses the L character to identify it as type Long:

```
Dim lngCounter As Long
lngCounter = 10000L
```

In the following, an integer literal uses the S character to identify it as type Short:

```
Dim shrtFeet as Short
shrtFeet = 1234S
```

TIP: You cannot embed commas in numeric literals. The following, for example, causes an error: `intMiles = 32,767`

Floating-Point Data Types

Values that have fractional parts and use a decimal point must be stored in one of Visual Basic's floating-point data types. Table 3-3 lists the floating-point data types, showing their naming prefixes and descriptions.

Table 3-3 Floating-point data types

Type	Naming Prefix	Description
Single	sng	Holds a signed single precision real number with 7 significant digits, in the range of approximately plus or minus 1.0×10^{38}
Double	dbl	Holds a signed double precision real number with 15 significant digits, in the range of approximately plus or minus 1.0×10^{308}
Decimal	dec	Holds a real number with 29 significant digits after the decimal point, in the range of approximately plus or minus 79,228,162,514,264,337, 593,543,950,335

Floating-Point Literals

If a numeric literal is written with a decimal point, and it fits within the range of a Double, then the numeric literal is treated as a Double. (See Table 3-3 for the minimum and maximum values of a Double.) For example, the numeric literals 3.14 and 127.896 are treated as Doubles.

Floating-point literals can also be written in scientific notation. The number 47281.97, for example, would be written in scientific notation as 4.728197×10^4. Visual Basic requires the letter E just before the exponent in scientific notation. So, our sample number would be written in Visual Basic like this:

```
4.728197E+4
```

The + sign after the E is optional. Here is an example of a value having a negative exponent:

```
4.623476E−2
```

Scientific notation is particularly useful for very large numbers. Instead of writing a value such as 1234000000000000000000000000000.0, for example, it is easier to write 1.234E+31.

Assigning Numeric Literals to Decimal Variables

When Option Strict is set to *On*, you cannot assign a Double value to a Decimal variable. Consequently, the following code will cause an error at compile-time because the literal 28.75 is treated as a Double:

```
Dim decPayRate As Decimal
decPayRate = 28.75          'This will cause an error.
```

To fix this error, you must append the letter D to the numeric literal. Here is an example:

```
Dim decPayRate As Decimal
decPayRate = 28.75D
```

When the letter D appears at the end of a numeric literal, the compiler will treat the numeric literal as a Decimal.

Significant Digits

The significant digits measurement for each floating-point data type is important for certain kinds of calculations. Suppose you were simulating a chemical reaction and needed to calculate the number of calories produced. You might produce a number such as 1.234567824724. If you used a variable of type Single, only the first seven digits would be kept in computer memory, and the remaining digits would be lost. The last digit would be rounded upward, producing 1.234568. This loss of precision happens because the computer uses a limited amount of storage for floating-point numbers. If you did the same chemical reaction calculation using a variable of type Double, the entire result would be safely held in the number, with no loss of precision.

The Decimal data type is used in financial calculations when you need a great deal of precision. This data type helps prevent rounding errors from creeping into repeated calculations.

The following code demonstrates each floating-point data type:

```
Dim sngTemperature As Single
Dim dblWindSpeed As Double
Dim decBankBalance As Decimal

sngTemperature = 98.6
dblWindSpeed = 35.373659262
decBankBalance = 1234567890.1234567890123456789D
```

Boolean Data Type

A Boolean type variable can hold only one of two possible values: *True* or *False*. The values True and False are built-in Visual Basic keywords. The word *Boolean* is named after George Boole, a famous mathematician of the nineteenth century. (His Boolean algebra is the basis for all modern computer arithmetic.)

We use Boolean variables to hold information that is either true or false. The standard naming prefix for Boolean variables is `bln`. Here is an example:

```
Dim blnIsRegistered As Boolean
blnIsRegistered = True
```

We will begin using Boolean variables in Chapter 4.

Char Data Type

Variables of the Char data type can hold a single Unicode character. Unicode characters are the set of values that can represent a large number of international characters in different languages. To assign a character literal to a Char variable, enclose the character in double quotations marks, followed by a lowercase "c". The standard naming prefix for Char variables is `chr`. The following is an example:

```
Dim chrLetter As Char
chrLetter = "A"c
```

String Data Type

A variable of type String can hold between zero and about 2 billion characters. The characters are stored in sequence. A string literal, as you have seen earlier, is always enclosed in quotation marks. In the following code, a string variable is assigned various string literals:

```
Dim strName As String
strName = "Jose Gonzalez"
```

The standard naming prefix for String variables is `str`.

An empty string literal can be coded as "" or by the special identifier named `String.Empty`:

```
strName = ""
strName = String.Empty
```

Date Data Type

A variable of the Date data type can hold date and time information. Date variables are assigned a prefix of `dtm` or `dat`. You can assign a date literal to a Date variable, as shown here:

```
Dim dtmBirth As Date
dtmBirth = #5/1/2016#
```

Notice that the Date literal is enclosed in # symbols. A variety of date and time formats is permitted. All of the following Date literals are valid:

```
#12/10/2016#
#8:45:00 PM#
#10/20/2016 6:30:00 AM#
```

A Date literal can contain a date, a time, or both. When specifying a time, if you omit AM or PM, the hours value is assumed to be based on a 24-hour clock. If you supply a date without the time, the time portion of the variable defaults to 12:00 AM.

In Tutorial 3-3, you will assign text to a variable.

Tutorial 3-3:
Assigning text to a variable

In this tutorial, you will modify a program that assigns the contents of text boxes to a String variable.

Step 1: Open the *Variable Demo* project from the student sample programs folder named *Chap3\Variable Demo*.

Step 2: View the Form1 form in the *Designer* window, as shown in Figure 3-7.

Step 3: Double-click the *Show Name* button, which opens the *Code* window and creates a template for the button's Click event handler. Type the following lines, shown in bold:

```
Private Sub btnShowName_Click(...) Handles btnShowName.Click
    ' Declare a string variable to hold the full name.
    Dim strFullName As String

    ' Combine the first and last names and assign the
    ' result to strFullName.
    strFullName = txtFirstName.Text & " " & txtLastName.Text

    ' Display the full name in the lblFullName label.
    lblFullName.Text = strFullName
End Sub
```

Figure 3-7 *Variable Demo* application, Form1

Step 4: In the *Designer* window, double-click the *Clear* button and insert the following lines in the *Code* window (shown in bold):

```
Private Sub btnClear_Click(...) Handles btnClear.Click
    '  Clear TextBox controls and the Label.
    txtFirstName.Clear()
    txtLastName.Clear()
    lblFullName.Text = String.Empty
End Sub
```

Step 5: In the *Designer* window, double-click the *Exit* button and insert the following lines in the *Code* window (shown in bold):

```
Private Sub btnExit_Click(...) Handles btnExit.Click
    '  Close the form.
    Me.Close()
End Sub
```

Step 6: Save the project.

Step 7: Run the program, type in a name, and click the *Show Name* button. The output should look similar to that shown in Figure 3-8.

Figure 3-8 *Variable Demo* application, running

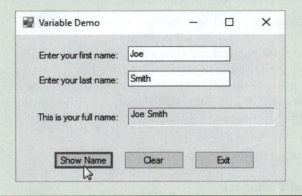

 TIP: **Code outlining** is a Visual Studio tool that lets you expand and collapse sections of code. As your programs get longer, it is sometimes helpful to collapse procedures you have already written. Then you can concentrate on new sections of code. For example, notice that a minus sign (–) appears next to the heading of the btnShowName_Click procedure in the *Variable Demo* application. If you click the minus sign, it collapses the event handler into a single line of code showing its name. You can modify outlining options by right-clicking in the *Code* window and selecting *Outlining*.

Variable Declarations and the IntelliSense Feature

When you are entering a variable declaration, Visual Studio's IntelliSense feature helps you fill in the data type. Suppose you begin to type a variable declaration such as the following:

```
Dim decPayRate As
```

If you press the [Spacebar] at this point, a list box appears with all the possible data types in alphabetical order. When the list box appears, type the first few letters of the data type name, and the box will highlight the data type that matches what you have typed. For example, after you type *dec* the Decimal data type will be highlighted. Press the [Tab] key to select the highlighted data type.

> **TIP:** You can use the arrow keys or the mouse with the list box's scroll bar to scroll through the list. Once you see the desired data type, double-click it with the mouse.

Default Values and Initialization

When a variable is first created it is assigned a default value. Variables with a numeric data type (such as Byte, Decimal, Double, Integer, Long, and Single) are assigned the value 0. Boolean variables are initially assigned the value False, and Date variables are assigned the value 12:00:00 AM, January 1 of year 1. String variables are automatically assigned a special value called `Nothing`.

You may also specify a starting value in the `Dim` statement. This is called **initialization**. Here is an example:

```
Dim intUnitsSold As Integer = 12
```

This statement declares `intUnitsSold` as an Integer and assigns it the starting value 12. Here are other examples:

```
Dim strLastName As String = "Johnson"
Dim blnIsFinished As Boolean = True
Dim decGrossPay As Decimal = 2500
Dim chrMiddleInitial As Char = "E"c
```

Forgetting to initialize variables can lead to program errors. Unless you are certain a variable will be assigned a value before being used in an operation, always initialize it. This principle is particularly true with string variables. Performing an operation on an uninitialized string variable often results in a runtime error, causing the program to halt execution because the value `Nothing` is invalid for many operations. To prevent such errors, always initialize string variables or make sure they are assigned a value before being used in other operations. A good practice is to initialize String variables with an empty string, as shown in the following statement:

```
Dim strName As String = String.Empty
```

Local Variables

In the examples we have looked at so far, the variables are declared inside event handlers. When a variable is declared inside of a procedure, such as an event handler, it is referred to as a **local variable**. A local variable belongs to the procedure in which it is declared, and only statements inside that procedure can access the variable. (The term *local* is meant to indicate that the variable can be used only locally, within the procedure in which it is declared.)

An error will occur if a statement in one procedure attempts to access a local variable that belongs to another procedure. For example, assume that an application has the following two event handlers:

```
Private Sub Button1_Click(...) Handles Button1.Click
    ' Declare an Integer variable named intValue.
    Dim intValue As Integer

    ' Assign a value to the variable.
    intValue = 25
End Sub

Private Sub Button2_Click(...) Handles Button2.Click
    ' Attempt to assign a value to the intValue variable.
    ' This will cause an error!
    intValue = 0
End Sub
```

The `intValue` variable that is declared inside the `Button1_Click` event handler is a local variable that belongs to that procedure. However, the assignment statement inside the `Button2_Click` event handler attempts to store a value in `intValue` variable. This will cause an error because the `intValue` variable is local to the `Button1_Click` procedure, and statements outside that procedure cannot access it. If we try to compile this code, we still get the following error message: *'intValue' is not declared.*

What if we declared `intValue` again in the `Button2_Click` event handler? Then the program would compile with no errors, but we would have created two different variables having the same name. Each variable is separate from the other:

```
Private Sub Button1_Click(...) Handles Button1.Click
    ' Declare an Integer variable named intValue.
    Dim intValue As Integer

    ' Assign a value to the variable.
    intValue = 25
End Sub

Private Sub Button2_Click(...) Handles Button2.Click
    ' Declare an Integer variable named intValue.
    Dim intValue As Integer

    ' Attempt to assign a value to the intValue variable.
    intValue = 0
End Sub
```

In this case, the `Button1_Click` event handler has a local variable named `intValue`, and the `Button2_Click` event handler has its own local variable named `intValue`. Variables in different procedures can have the same name because they are isolated from each other.

Scope

The term **scope** means the part of a program in which a variable may be accessed. Every variable has a scope, and a variable is visible only to statements in its scope. A local variable's scope begins at the `Dim` statement that declares the variable, and ends at the end of the procedure in which the variable is declared. The variable cannot be accessed by statements outside this region. That means that a local variable cannot be accessed by statements outside the procedure, or by statements that are inside the procedure but before the `Dim` statement that declares the variable.

For example, look at the following event handler code. This procedure attempts to assign a value to a variable before the variable is declared:

```
Private Sub Button1_Click(...) Handles Button1.Click
    strName = "Jane" 'ERROR!
    Dim strName As String
End Sub
```

If we try to compile this code, we will get the error message *Local variable 'strName' cannot be referred to before it is declared.*

Duplicate Variable Names

Earlier you saw that two variables with the same name can be declared in different procedures. That is because the scope of the two variables is separate. You cannot, however, declare two variables with the same name in the same scope. For example, look at the following event handler:

```
Private Sub Button1_Click(...) Handles Button1.Click
    ' Declare an Integer variable named intValue.
    Dim intValue As Integer = 0
```

```
   ' Declare another Integer variable named intValue.
   ' ERROR!
   Dim intValue As Integer = 25
End Sub
```

This procedure declares two local variables named `intValue`. The second `Dim` statement will cause an error because a variable named `intValue` has already been declared. If we try to compile this code we will get the error message *Local variable 'intValue' is already declared in the current block*.

 **Checkpoint**

3.5   What is a variable?

3.6   Write a variable declaration for an Integer variable named **intUnitsSold**.

3.7   Which of the following variable names are written with the convention used in this book?
   a. decintrestrate
   b. InterestRateDecimal
   c. decInterestRate

3.8   Indicate whether each of the following is a legal variable name. If it is not, explain why.
   a. count
   b. rate*Pay
   c. deposit.amount
   d. down_payment

3.9   What default value is assigned to each of the following variables?
   a. Integer
   b. Double
   c. Boolean
   d. Byte
   e. Date

3.10   Write a Date literal for the following date and time: 5:35:00 PM on February 20, 2017.

3.11   *Bonus question*: Find out which famous Microsoft programmer was launched into space in 2007. Was this programmer connected in any way to Visual Basic?

 3.3   **Performing Calculations**

    CONCEPT: **Visual Basic has powerful arithmetic operators that perform calculations with numeric variables and literals.**

VideoNote

Problem Solving with Variables

There are two basic types of operators in Visual Basic: unary and binary. These reflect the number of operands an operator requires. A **unary operator** requires only a single operand. The negation operator, for example, produces the negative of its operand:

```
-5
```

It can be applied to a variable. The following line negates the value in `intCount`:

```
-intCount
```

A **binary operator** works with two operands. The addition operator (+) is binary because it uses two operands. The following mathematical expression adds the values of two numbers:

```
5 + 10
```

The following adds the values of two variables:

```
intA + intB
```

Table 3-4 lists the binary arithmetic operators in Visual Basic. Addition, subtraction, multiplication, division, and exponentiation can be performed on both integer and floating-point data types. Only two operations (integer division and modulus) must be performed on integer types.

Table 3-4 Arithmetic operators in Visual Basic

Operator	Operation
+	Addition
–	Subtraction
*	Multiplication
/	Floating-point division
\	Integer division
MOD	Modulus (remainder from integer division)
^	Exponentiation (x^y = x^y)

Addition

The addition operator (+) adds two values, producing a sum. The values can be literals or variables. The following are examples of valid addition expressions:

```
intA + 10
20 + intB
```

The question is, what happens to the result? Ordinarily, it is assigned to a variable, using the assignment operator. In the following statement, intC is assigned the sum of the values from intA and intB:

```
intC = intA + intB
```

This operation happens in two steps. First, the addition takes place. Second, the sum is assigned to the variable on the left side of the = sign.

The following example adds the contents of two Double variables that hold rainfall measurements for the months of March and April:

```
dblCombined = dblMarchRain + dblAprilRain
```

Subtraction

The subtraction operator (–) subtracts the right-hand operand from the left-hand operand. In the following, the variable intC will contain the difference between intA and intB:

```
intC = intA - intB
```

Alternatively, the difference might be assigned back to the variable intA:

```
intA = intA - intB
```

The following statement uses Decimal variables. It subtracts an employee's tax amount from his or her gross pay, producing the employee's net pay:

```
decNetPay = decGrossPay - decTax
```

Addition and Subtraction in Applications

How can addition and subtraction statements be useful in an application? Suppose a college registration program needs to add the credits completed by a student during two semesters (Fall and Spring). First, the variables would be declared:

```
Dim intFallCredits, intSpringCredits, intTotalCredits As Integer
```

Then the application would assign values to `intSpringCredits` and `intFallCredits`, perhaps by asking for their input from the user. Finally, the program would calculate the total credits for the year:

```
intTotalCredits = intFallCredits + intSpringCredits
```

Multiplication

The multiplication operator (*) multiplies the right-hand operand by the left-hand operand. In the following statement, the variable `intC` is assigned the product of multiplying `intA` and `intB`:

```
intC = intA * intB
```

The following statement uses Decimal variables to multiply an item's price by the sales tax rate, producing a sales tax amount:

```
decTaxAmount = decItemPrice * decTaxRate
```

Floating-Point Division

The floating-point division operator (/) divides one floating-point value by another. The result, called the quotient, is also a floating-point number. For example, the following statement divides the total points earned by a basketball team by the number of players, producing the average points per player:

```
dblAverage = dblTotalPoints / dblNumPlayers
```

NOTE: You should be careful that you do not divide a number by zero. Doing so produces the special value `Infinity`, which cannot be used in subsequent calculations.

Integer Division

The integer division operator (\) divides one integer by another, producing an integer result. For example, suppose we know the number of minutes it will take to finish a job, and we want to calculate the number of hours that are contained in that many minutes. The following statement uses integer division to divide the `intMinutes` variable by 60, giving the number of hours as a result:

```
intHours = intMinutes \ 60
```

Integer division does not save any fractional part of the quotient. The following statement, for example, produces the integer 3:

```
intQuotient = 10 \ 3
```

Modulus

The modulus operator (`MOD`) performs integer division and returns only the remainder. The following statement assigns 2 to the variable named `intRemainder`:

```
intRemainder = 17 MOD 3
```

Note that 17 divided by 3 equals 5, with a remainder of 2. Suppose a job is completed in 174 minutes, and we want to express this value in both hours and minutes. First, we can use integer division to calculate the hours (2):

```
intTotalMinutes = 174
intHours = intTotalMinutes \ 60
```

Next, we use the MOD operator to calculate the remaining minutes (54):

```
intMinutes = intTotalMinutes Mod 60
```

Now we know that the job was completed in 2 hours, 54 minutes.

Exponentiation

Exponentiation calculates a variable x taken to the power of y when written in the form $x \wedge y$. The value it returns is of type Double. For example, the following statement assigns 25.0 to dblResult:

```
dblResult = 5.0 ^ 2.0
```

You can use integers as operands, but the result will still be a Double:

```
dblResult = intX ^ intY
```

Negative and fractional exponents are permitted.

Combined Assignment Operators

Quite often, programs have assignment statements in the following form:

```
intNumber = intNumber + 1
```

On the right-hand side of the assignment operator, 1 is added to intNumber. The result is then assigned to intNumber, replacing the value that was previously stored there. Similarly, the following statement subtracts 5 from intNumber.

```
intNumber = intNumber - 5
```

Table 3-5 shows examples of similar statements. Assume that the variable x is set to 6 prior to each statement's execution.

Table 3-5 Assignment statements (Assume x = 6 prior to each statement's execution)

Statement	Operation Performed	Value of x after the Statement Executes
x = x + 4	Adds 4 to x	10
x = x - 3	Subtracts 3 from x	3
x = x * 10	Multiplies x by 10	60
x = x / 2	Divides x by 2	3

Assignment operations are common in programming. For convenience, Visual Basic offers a special set of operators designed specifically for these jobs. Table 3-6 shows the **combined assignment operators**, or **compound operators**.

Table 3-6 Combined assignment operators

Operator	Example Usage	Equivalent To
+=	x += 2	x = x + 2
-=	x -= 5	x = x - 5
*=	x *= 10	x = x * 10
/=	x /= y	x = x / y
\=	x \= y	x = x \ y
&=	strName &= lastName	strName = strName & lastName

Operator Precedence

It is possible to build **mathematical expressions** with several operators. The following statement assigns the sum of 17, x, 21, and y to the variable `intAnswer`.

```
intAnswer = 17 + x + 21 + y
```

Some expressions are not that straightforward, however. Consider the following statement:

```
dblOutcome = 12 + 6 / 3
```

What value will be stored in `dblOutcome`? If the addition takes place before the division, then `dblOutcome` will be assigned 6. If the division takes place first, `dblOutcome` will be assigned 14. The correct answer is 14 because the division operator has higher **precedence** than the addition operator.

Mathematical expressions are evaluated from left to right. When two operators share an operand, the operator with the highest precedence executes first. Multiplication and division have higher precedence than addition and subtraction, so 12 + 6 / 3 works like this:

- 6 is divided by 3, yielding a result of 2.
- 12 is added to 2, yielding a result of 14.

It can be diagrammed as shown in Figure 3-9.

Figure 3-9 `dblOutcome = 12 + 6 / 3`

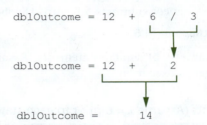

The precedence of the arithmetic operators, from highest to lowest, is as follows:

1. Exponentiation (the ^ operator)
2. Multiplication and division (the * and / operators)
3. Integer division (the \ operator)
4. Modulus (the MOD operator)
5. Addition and subtraction (the + and – operators)

The multiplication and division operators have the same precedence. This is also true of the addition and subtraction operators. When two operators with the same precedence share an operand, the operator on the left executes before the operator on the right.

Table 3-7 shows some example mathematical expressions with their values.

Table 3-7 Mathematical expressions and their values

Expression	Value
5 + 2 * 4	13
2^3 * 4 + 3	35
10 / 2 – 3	2
8 + 12 * 2 – 4	28
6 – 3 * 2 + 7 – 1	6

Grouping with Parentheses

Parts of a mathematical expression may be grouped with parentheses to force some operations to be performed before others. In the following statement, the sum of *x*, *y*, and *z* is divided by 3. The result is assigned to `dblAverage`.

```
dblAverage = (x + y + z) / 3
```

Without the parentheses, however, *z* would be divided by 3, and the result added to the sum of *x* and *y*. Table 3-8 shows more expressions and their values.

Table 3-8 Additional mathematical expressions and their values

Expression	Value
(5 + 2) * 4	28
10 / (5 − 3)	5
8 + 12 * (6 − 2)	56
(6 − 3) * (2 + 7) / 3	9

More about Mathematical Operations: Converting Mathematical Expressions to Programming Statements

In algebra, the mathematical expression $2xy$ describes the value 2 times *x* times *y*. Visual Basic, however, requires an operator for any mathematical operation. Table 3-9 shows some mathematical expressions that perform multiplication and the equivalent Visual Basic expressions.

Table 3-9 Visual Basic equivalents of mathematical expressions

Mathematical Expression	Operation	Visual Basic Equivalent
$6B$	6 times *B*	6 * B
(3)(12)	3 times 12	3 * 12
$4xy$	4 times *x* times *y*	4 * x * y

 **Checkpoint**

3.12 What value will be stored in `dblResult` after each of the following statements executes?
   a. `dblResult = 6 + 3 * 5`
   b. `dblResult = 12 / 2 − 4`
   c. `dblResult = 2 + 7 * 3 − 6`
   d. `dblResult = (2 + 4) * 3`
   e. `dblResult = 10 \ 3`
   f. `dblResult = 6 ^ 2`

3.13 What value will be stored in `intResult` after each statement executes?
   a. `intResult = 10 MOD 3`
   b. `intResult = 47 MOD 15`

3.14 How is integer division different from floating-point division?

3.15 What will be the final value of dblResult in the following sequence?

```
Dim dblResult As Double = 3.5
dblResult += 1.2
```

3.16 What will be the final value of dblResult in the following sequence?

```
Dim dblResult As Double = 3.5
dblResult *= 2.0
```

 ## 3.4   Mixing Different Data Types

Implicit Type Conversion

When you assign a value of one data type to a variable of another data type, Visual Basic attempts to convert the value being assigned to the data type of the receiving variable. This is known as an **implicit type conversion**. Suppose we want to assign the integer 5 to a variable of type Single named sngNumber:

```
Dim sngNumber As Single = 5
```

When the statement executes, the integer 5 is automatically converted into a single-precision real number, which is then stored in sngNumber. This conversion is a **widening conversion** because no data is lost.

Narrowing Conversions

If you assign a real number to an integer variable, Visual Basic attempts to perform a **narrowing conversion**. Often, some data is lost. For example, the following statement assigns 12.2 to an integer variable:

```
Dim intCount As Integer = 12.2   'intCount = 12
```

Assuming for the moment that Visual Basic is configured to accept this type of conversion, the 12.2 is rounded downward to 12. Similarly, the next statement rounds upward to the nearest integer when the fractional part of the number is .5 or greater:

```
Dim intCount As Integer = 12.5   'intCount = 13
```

Another narrowing conversion occurs when assigning a Double value to a variable of type Single. Both hold floating-point values, but Double permits more significant digits:

```
Dim dblOne As Double = 1.2342376
Dim sngTwo As Single = dblOne     'sngTwo = 1.234238
```

The value stored in sngTwo is rounded up to 1.234238 because variables of type Single can only hold seven significant digits.

Option Strict

Visual Basic has a configuration option named *Option Strict* that determines whether certain implicit data type conversions are legal. If you set *Option Strict* to *On*, only widening conversions are permitted (such as Integer to Single). Figure 3-10 shows how implicit conversion between numeric types must be in a left-to-right direction in the diagram. A Decimal value can be assigned to a variable of type Single, an Integer can be assigned to a variable of type Double, and so on. If, on the other hand, *Option Strict* is set to *Off*, all types of numeric conversions are permitted, with possible loss of data.

Figure 3-10 *Conversions permitted with Option Strict On*

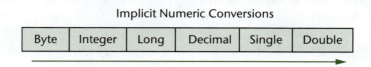

Implicit Numeric Conversions

Byte	Integer	Long	Decimal	Single	Double

To set *Option Strict* for a single project, right-click the project name in the *Solution Explorer* window, select *Properties*, and then select the *Compile* tab, as shown in Figure 3-11. From the *Option Strict* drop-down list, you can select *On* or *Off*.

We recommend setting *Option Strict* to *On*, so Visual Basic can catch errors that result when you accidentally assign a value of the wrong type to a variable. When set to *On*, *Option Strict* forces you to use a conversion function, making your intentions clear. This approach helps to avoid runtime errors. A function is a special type of procedure, explained on page 152.

Figure 3-11 *Project Properties* page

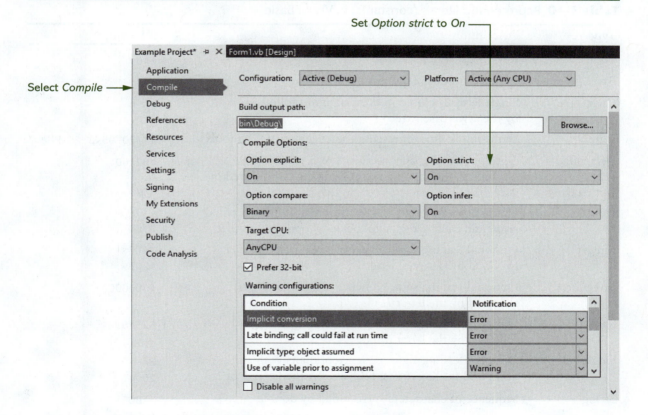

Type Conversion Runtime Errors

The following statement does not compile with *Option Strict* set to *On*:

```
Dim intCount As Integer = "abc123"
```

But if *Option Strict* has been set to *Off*, a program containing this statement will compile without errors. Then, when the program executes, it will stop when it reaches this statement because the string "abc123" contains characters that prevent the string from being converted to a number. The program will generate a runtime error message. Recall from Chapter 2 that runtime errors are errors that occur while the application is running. The type of error in this case is also known as a **type conversion error** or **type mismatch error**.

Runtime errors are harder to catch than syntax errors because they occur while a program is running. Particularly in programs where the user has a number of choices (mouse clicks, keyboard input, menus, and so on), it is very difficult for a programmer to predict when runtime errors might occur. Nevertheless, there are certain conversion functions shown in the next section that reduce the chance of this type of mishap.

> **TIP:** Can the best-trained programmers avoid runtime errors? To discover the answer to that question, spend some time using commercial Web sites and notice all the little things that go wrong. Software reliability is particularly hard to guarantee when users have lots of choices.

Literals

Literals (also known as constants) have specific types in Visual Basic. Table 3-10 lists the more common types. Many literals use a suffix character (*C*, *D*, *@*, *R*, *I*, *L*, *F*, *S*, !) to identify their type.

Table 3-10 Representing literals (constants) in Visual Basic

Type	Description	Example
Boolean	Keywords *True* and *False*	`True`
Byte	Sequence of decimal digits between 0 and 255	`200`
Char	Single letter enclosed in double quotes followed by the lowercase letter *C*	`"A"c`
Date	Date and/or time representation enclosed in # symbols	`#1/20/05 3:15 PM#`
Decimal	Optional leading sign, sequence of decimal digits, optional decimal point and trailing digits, followed by the letter *D* or *@*	`+32.0D` `64@`
Double	Optional leading sign, sequence of digits with a decimal point and trailing digits, followed by optional letter *R*	`3.5` `3.5R`
Integer	Optional leading sign, sequence of decimal digits, followed by optional letter *I*	`-3054I` `+26I`
Long	Optional leading sign, sequence of decimal digits, followed by the letter *L*	`40000000L`
Short	Optional leading sign, sequence of decimal digits, followed by the letter *S*	`12345S`
Single	Optional leading sign, sequence of digits with a decimal point and trailing digits, followed by the letter *F* or !	`26.4F` `26.4!`
String	Sequence of characters surrounded by double quotes	`"ABC"` `"234"`

It's important to know literal types because you often assign literal values to variables. If the receiving variable in an assignment statement has a different type from the literal, an implied conversion takes place. If *Option Strict* is *On*, some conversions are automatic and others generate errors. You need to understand why.

Most of the time, you will be inclined to use no suffix with numeric literals. As long as the receiving variable's data type is compatible with the literal's data type, you have no problem:

```
Dim lngCount As Long = 25              'Integer assigned to Long
Dim dblSalary As Double = 2500.0       'Double assigned to Double
```

In the following example, however, we're trying to assign a Double to a Decimal, which is not permitted when *Option Strict* is *On*:

```
Dim decPayRate As Decimal = 35.5          'Double to Decimal (?)
```

If you know how to create numeric literals, all you have to do is append a *D* to the number. The following is valid:

```
Dim decPayRate As Decimal = 35.5D
```

Named Constants

You have seen several programs and examples where numbers and strings are expressed as literal values. For example, the following statement contains the literal numeric value 0.129:

```
dblPayment = dblPrincipal * 0.129
```

Suppose this statement appears in a banking program that calculates loan information.

In such a program, two potential problems arise. First, it is not clearly evident to anyone other than the original programmer what the number 0.129 is. It appears to be an interest rate, but in some situations there are other fees associated with loan payments. How can you determine the purpose of this statement without painstakingly checking the rest of the program?

The second problem occurs if this number is used in other calculations throughout the program and must be changed periodically. Assuming the number is an interest rate, if the rate changes from 12.9% to 13.2% the programmer will have to search through the source code for every occurrence of the number.

Both of these problems can be addressed by using named constants. A **named constant** is like a variable whose content is read-only, and cannot be changed by a programming statement while the program is running. The following is the general form of a named constant declaration:

```
Const ConstantName As DataType = Value
```

Here is an example of a named constant declaration:

```
Const dblINTEREST_RATE As Double = 0.129
```

It looks like a regular variable declaration except for the following differences:

- The word `Const` is used instead of `Dim`.
- An initialization value is required.
- By convention, all letters after the prefix are capitals.
- Words in the name are separated by the underscore character.

The keyword `Const` indicates that you are declaring a named constant instead of a variable. The value given after the = sign is the value of the constant throughout the program's execution.

A value must be assigned when a named constant is declared or an error will result. An error will also result if any statements in the program attempt to change the contents of a named constant.

One advantage of using named constants is that they help make programs self-documenting. The statement

```
dblPayment = dblPrincipal * 0.129
```

can be changed to read

```
dblPayment = dblPrincipal * dblINTEREST_RATE
```

A new programmer can read the second statement and know what is happening. It is evident that dblPrincipal is being multiplied by the interest rate.

Another advantage to using named constants is that consistent changes can easily be made to the program. Let's say the interest rate appears in a dozen different statements throughout the program. When the rate changes, the value assigned to the named constant in its declaration is the only value that needs to be modified. If the rate increases to 13.2% the declaration is changed to the following:

```
Const dblINTEREST_RATE as Double = 0.132
```

Every statement that uses dblINTEREST_RATE will use the new value.

It is also useful to declare named constants for common values that are difficult to remember. For example, any program that calculates the area of a circle must use the value *pi*, which is 3.14159. This value could easily be declared as a named constant, as shown in the following statement:

```
Const dblPI as Double = 3.14159
```

Explicit Type Conversions

Let's assume for the current discussion that *Option Strict* is set to *On*. If you try to perform anything other than a widening conversion, your code will not compile. Visual Basic has a set of conversion functions to solve this problem.

What Is a Function?

A **function** is a special type of procedure. When you call a function, you typically send data to the function as input. The function performs an operation using that data, and then it sends a value back as output. Figure 3-12 illustrates this idea.

Figure 3-12 A function receives input and produces a single output

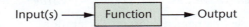

When we send a piece of data as input to a function, we typically say that we are passing the data as an **argument**. When a function sends a value back as output, we typically say that the function is **returning a value**.

For example, one of the Visual Basic conversion functions is named CInt. (You can think of this as standing for "Convert to Integer.") If you have a non-integer value that you need to convert to an integer, you can call the CInt function, passing the value as an argument. The CInt function will return that value, converted to an integer. Here is a code sample that shows how the CInt function works:

```
' Declare two variables.
Dim dblRealNumber as Double = 3.2
Dim intWholeNumber As Integer = 0

' Assign the Double value to the Integer variable.
intWholeNumber = CInt(dblRealNumber)
```

The last statement assigns the value of the Double variable, dblRealNumber, to the Integer variable, intWholeNumber. Let's take a closer look. On the right side of the = operator is the expression CInt(dblRealNumber). This expression calls the CInt function, passing the value of dblRealNumber, which is 3.2, as an argument.

The CInt function converts the value 3.2 to an integer by dropping the .2. (Dropping the fractional part of a number is called **truncation**.) The value 3 is then returned from the function. The assignment operator then assigns the value 3 to the `intWholeNumber` variable, as shown in Figure 3-13.

Figure 3-13 Using the `CInt` function

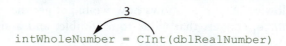

intWholeNumber = CInt(dblRealNumber)

The value 3 is returned from the `CInt` function and
assigned to the `intWholeNumber` variable.

Visual Basic Conversion Functions

Table 3-11 lists the Visual Basic conversion functions that we will use most often. The input to each conversion function is an expression, which is another name for a constant, a variable, or a mathematical expression (such as 2.0 + 4.2). The following situations require a conversion function:

- When assigning a wider numeric type to a narrower numeric type. In Figure 3-10 (page 149), the arrow pointing from left to right indicates automatic conversions. Any conversion in the opposite direction requires a call to a conversion function. Examples are Long to Integer, Decimal to Long, Double to Single, and Double to Decimal.
- When converting between Boolean, Date, Object, String, and numeric types. These all represent different categories, so they require conversion functions.

Table 3-11 Commonly used type conversion functions

Function	Description
CDate(*expr*)	Converts a String expression containing a valid date, such as "10/14/2016 1:30:00 PM", to a Date. Input can also be a Date literal, such as #10/14/2016 1:30:00 PM#.
CDbl(*expr*)	Converts an expression to a Double. If the input expression is a String, a leading currency symbol ($) is permitted, as are commas. The decimal point is optional.
CDec(*expr*)	Converts an expression to a Decimal. If the input expression is a String, a leading currency symbol ($) is permitted, as are commas. The decimal point is optional.
CInt(*expr*)	Converts an expression to an Integer. If the input expression is a String, a leading currency symbol ($) is permitted, as are commas. The decimal point is optional, as are digits after the decimal point.
CStr(*expr*)	Converts an expression to a String. Input can be a mathematical expression, a Boolean value, a date, or any numeric data type.

VideoNote

Converting TextBox Input

Converting TextBox Input

The conversion functions listed in Table 3-11 are commonly used to convert values that the user has entered into TextBox controls. Anything entered by the user into a TextBox is stored as a string in the control's Text property. If the user has entered a numeric value into a TextBox, and you want to use that value in a calculation, you will have to convert it from a string to an appropriate numeric data type.

For example, suppose a payroll application uses a TextBox named `txtHoursWorked` to get the number of hours worked, and a TextBox named `txtPayRate` to get the hourly pay rate. If the application needs to use the values held in these controls in a calculation, the values must be converted to a numeric type. The following statement shows how we might get the value that has been entered into txtHoursWorked, convert that value to an Integer, and assign it to a variable named intHoursWorked:

```
intHoursWorked = CInt(txtHoursWorked.Text)
```

And, the following statement shows how we might get the value that has been entered into txtPayRate, convert that value to a Double, and assign it to a variable named dblPayRate:

```
dblPayRate = CDbl(txtPayRate.Text)
```

After these conversions have taken place, the intHoursWorked and dblPayRate variables can be used in calculations.

The value of a TextBox control's Text property can be converted to other values as well. For example, a TextBox can be used to get a date from the user, and then the control's Text property can be converted to the Date data type. For example, assume that an application has a TextBox named txtBirthday, and the user has entered a date such as *11/15/2016*. The following statement declares a Date variable named dtmBirthday and initialized it with the value in the TextBox:

```
Dim dtmBirthday As Date = CDate(txtBirthDay.Text)
```

Here's an example that declares a Decimal variable named decAccountBalance and initializes it with the value entered into the txtAccountBalance TextBox:

```
Dim decAccountBalance As Decimal = CDec(txtAccountBalance.Text)
```

Converting Floating-Point Numbers to Integers

The CInt function is required when assigning any floating-point type to an integer. Here is an example showing a Double being converted to an integer:

```
Dim dblAmount As Double = 3.4
Dim intAmount As Integer = CInt(dblAmount)
```

Here is an example showing a Single being converted to an integer:

```
Dim sngAmount As Single = 1.2
Dim intAmount As Integer = CInt(sngAmount)
```

And, here is an example showing a Decimal being converted to an integer:

```
Dim decAmount As Decimal = 9.1
Dim intAmount As Integer = CInt(decAmount)
```

Converting Doubles and Singles to Decimals

As previously mentioned, when *Option Strict* is set to *On*, a Double value cannot be assigned directly to a Decimal variable. A Single value cannot be assigned directly to a Decimal either. You can, however, use the CDec function to explicitly convert a Double or a Single to a Decimal. The following shows an example with a Double being converted to a Decimal:

```
Dim dblAmount As Double = 123.45
Dim decAmount As Decimal = CDec(dblAmount)
```

And the following shows an example with a Single being converted to a Decimal:

```
Dim sngAmount As Single = 4.5
Dim decAmount As Decimal = CDec(sngAmount)
```

If You Want to Know More: `CInt` and Rounding

The `CInt` function converts an expression to an Integer. If the input value contains digits after the decimal point, a special type of rounding occurs, called *banker's rounding*. Here's how it works:

- If the digit after the decimal point is less than 5, the digits after the decimal point are removed from the number. We say the number is *truncated*.
- If the digit after the decimal point is a 5, the number is rounded toward the nearest even integer.
- If the digit after the decimal point is greater than 5 and the number is positive, it is rounded to the next highest integer.
- If the digit after the decimal point is greater than 5 and the number is negative, it is rounded to the next smallest integer.

Invalid Conversions

What happens if you call a conversion function, passing a value that cannot be converted? Here's an example:

```
Dim dblSalary As Double
dblSalary = CDbl("xyz")
```

The program stops with a runtime error, displaying the dialog box shown in Figure 3-14. The specific type of error, also known as an exception, is called an *InvalidCastException*. The text inside the list box consists of hyperlinks, which take you to specific *Visual Studio Help* pages. Later in this chapter, you will learn how to catch errors like this so the program won't stop.

Figure 3-14 Error displayed when trying to perform an invalid conversion from String to Double

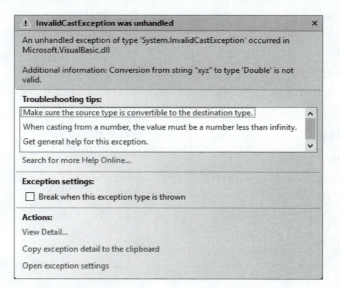

Tutorial 3-4:

Creating the *Tip Calculator* application

In this tutorial you will create an application that calculates a 15%, 20%, or 25% tip for a meal purchased at a restaurant. Figure 3-15 shows the application's form in the *Designer*. When the application runs, the user enters the total amount of the bill into the `txtBillAmount` control and then clicks one of the buttons to calculate the tip. There are three buttons: `btnFifteen` calculates a 15% tip, `btnTwenty` calculates a 20% tip, and `btnTwentyFive` calculates a 25% tip. The amount of the tip is displayed in the `lblTip` control.

Figure 3-15 The *Tip Calculator* form

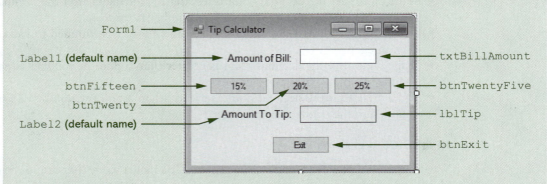

Step 1: Start Visual Studio and begin a new Visual Basic Windows Forms Application project named *Tip Calculator*.

Step 2: Set up the application's form as shown in Figure 3-15. The names of the controls are shown in the figure. As you place each of the controls on the form, refer to Table 3-12 for the relevant property settings.

Table 3-12 Form and control property settings

Control Name	Control Type	Property Settings
Form1 (Default name)	Form	**Text:** *Tip Calculator* **Size:** 300, 210 (or approximately these values)
Label1 (or Default name)	Label	**Font:** Microsoft Sans Serif (Size: 10 point) **Text:** *Amount of Bill:*
txtBillAmount	TextBox	None
btnFifteen	Button	**Text:** *15%*
btnTwenty	Button	**Text:** *20%*
btnTwentyFive	Button	**Text:** *25%*
Label2 (or Default name)	Label	**Font:** Microsoft Sans Serif (Size: 10 point) **Text:** *Amount To Tip:*
lblTip	Label	**AutoSize:** False **BorderStyle:** FixedSingle **Font:** Microsoft Sans Serif (Size: 10 point) **Text:** (The contents of the Text property have been erased.) **TextAlign:** MiddleCenter
btnExit	Button	**Text:** *Exit*

Step 3: Once you have the form and its controls set up, you can create the Click event handlers for the Button controls. In the *Designer*, double-click the `btnFifteen` control. This will open the *Code* window, and you will see an empty event handler named `btnFifteen_Click`. Complete the event handler by writing the code shown in bold here. (Do not write the line numbers! They are shown for reference only, to help us discuss specific lines of code.)

```
 1 Private Sub btnFifteen_Click(...) Handles btnFifteen.Click
 2    ' Variable declarations
 3    Dim dblBill As Double = 0.0
 4    Dim dblTip As Double = 0.0
 5
 6    ' Get the amount of the bill.
 7    dblBill = CDbl(txtBillAmount.Text)
 8
 9    ' Calculate a 15 percent tip.
10    dblTip = dblBill * 0.15
11
12    ' Display the tip.
13    lblTip.Text = CStr(dblTip)
14 End Sub
```

Let's take a closer look at the code you wrote for this event handler. Lines 3 and 4 declare the following variables:

- The dblBill variable, declared in line 3, will hold the amount of the bill. We will get this value from the user.
- The dblTip variable, declared in line 4, will hold the amount of the tip. We will calculate this amount.

In line 7 we get the amount of the bill from the txtBillAmount control's Text property, and assign that value to the dblBill variable. Notice that we use the CDbl function to convert the control's Text property to a Double. This is necessary because the Text property is a string. If we need to perform math with the Text property's value, we have to convert it to a numeric type.

In line 10 we calculate the 15 percent tip. We multiply the dblBill variable by 0.15 and assign the result to the dblTip variable.

In line 13 we display the tip by assigning the dblTip variable's value to the lblTip control's Text property. Notice that we use the CStr function to convert the dblTip variable to a string. This is necessary because the Text property is a string, and dblTip is a Double. Before we can assign dblTip to the Text property, we need to convert its value to a string.

Step 4: Switch back to the *Designer*, and double-click the btnTwenty control. This will switch your view back to the *Code* window, and you will see an empty event handler named btnTwenty_Click. Complete the event handler by writing the code shown in bold here. (Again, do not write the line numbers! They are shown for reference only, to help us discuss specific lines of code.)

```
 1 Private Sub btnTwenty_Click(...) Handles btnTwenty.Click
 2    ' Variable declarations
 3    Dim dblBill As Double = 0.0
 4    Dim dblTip As Double = 0.0
 5
 6    ' Get the amount of the bill.
 7    dblBill = CDbl(txtBillAmount.Text)
 8
 9    ' Calculate a 20 percent tip.
10    dblTip = dblBill * 0.2
11
12    ' Display the tip.
13    lblTip.Text = CStr(dblTip)
14 End Sub
```

Notice that this event handler is very similar to the Click event handler that you wrote for the btnFifteen control, in Step 3. The only differences are the comment shown in line 9, and the calculation that is performed in line 10. In line 10, you multiply dblBill by 0.2, to calculate a 20 percent tip.

Step 5: Switch back to the *Designer*, and double-click the btnTwentyFive control. This will switch your view back to the *Code* window, and you will see an empty event handler named btnTwentyFive_Click. Complete the event handler by writing the code shown in bold here. (Again, do not write the line numbers! They are shown for reference only, to help us discuss specific lines of code.)

```
 1 Private Sub btnTwentyFive_Click(...) Handles btnTwentyFive.Click
 2   ' Variable declarations
 3   Dim dblBill As Double = 0.0
 4   Dim dblTip As Double = 0.0
 5
 6   ' Get the amount of the bill.
 7   dblBill = CDbl(txtBillAmount.Text)
 8
 9   ' Calculate a 25 percent tip.
10   dblTip = dblBill * 0.25
11
12   ' Display the tip.
13   lblTip.Text = CStr(dblTip)
14 End Sub
```

Notice that this event handler is very similar to the Click event handlers that you wrote for the btnFifteen control in Step 3, and the btnTwenty control in Step 4. The only differences are the comment shown in line 9, and the calculation that is performed in line 10. In line 10, you multiply dblBill by 0.25, to calculate a 25% tip.

Step 6: Switch back to the *Designer*, and double-click the btnExit control. This will switch your view back to the *Code* window, and you will see an empty event handler named btnExit_Click. Complete the event handler by writing the code shown in bold here.

```
Private Sub btnExit_Click(...) Handles btnExit.Click
  ' Close the form.
  Me.Close()
End Sub
```

Step 7: Save the project. Then, press the [F5] key on the keyboard, or click the *Start Debugging* button (▶) on the toolbar to compile and run the application.

Test the application by entering *100* for the amount of the bill, and clicking each tip percentage button to see the amount of the tip. As shown in Figure 3-16, the application should display 15.00 as 15%, 20.00 as 20%, and 25.00 as 25%. Experiment with other values to confirm that the application is correct. When you are finished, click the *Exit* button to close the application.

Figure 3-16 The *Tip Calculator* application running

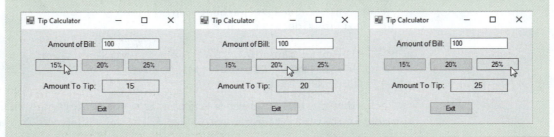

If You Want to Know More: Full Set of VB Conversion Functions

Table 3-11, shown earlier (p. 153), lists the Visual Basic conversion functions that you will use most frequently. For your reference, Table 3-13 contains a more complete list of Visual Basic conversion functions, including some that you will use only occasionally.

Table 3-13 Visual Basic type conversion functions

Function	Description
CBool(*expr*)	Converts an expression to a Boolean value. The expression must be a number, a string that represents a number, or the strings "True" or "False". Otherwise a runtime error is generated. If the expression is nonzero, the function returns *True*. Otherwise it returns *False*. For example, CBool(10) and CBool("7") return *True*, while CBool(0) and CBool("0") return *False*. If the argument is the string "True", the function returns *True*, and if the expression is the string "False", the function returns *False*.
CByte(*expr*)	Converts an expression to a Byte, which can hold the values 0 through 255. If the argument is a fractional number, it is rounded. If the expression cannot be converted to a value in the range of 0–255, a runtime error is generated.
CChar(*expr*)	Converts a string expression to a Char. If the string contains more than one character, only the first character is returned. For example, CChar("xyz") returns the character *x*.
CDate(*expr*)	Converts an expression to a Date. String expressions must be valid Date literals. For example, CDate("#10/14/2016 1:30:00 PM#") returns a Date with the value *1:30 PM, October 14th, 2016*. If the expression cannot be converted to a Date value, a runtime error is generated.
CDbl(*expr*)	Converts a numeric or string expression to a Double. If the expression converts to a value outside the range of a Double, or is not a numeric value, a runtime error is generated.
CDec(*expr*)	Converts a numeric or string expression to a Decimal. The CDec function can convert strings starting with a $ character, such as $1,200.00. Commas are also permitted. If the expression converts to a value outside the range of a Decimal, or is not a numeric value, a runtime error is generated.
CInt(*expr*)	Converts a numeric or string expression to an Integer. If the expression converts to a value outside the range of an Integer, or is not a numeric value, a runtime error is generated. Rounds to nearest integer.
CLng(*expr*)	Converts a numeric or string expression to a Long (long integer). If the expression converts to a value outside the range of a Long, or is not a numeric value, a runtime error is generated.
CObj(*expr*)	Converts an expression to an Object.
CShort(*expr*)	Converts a numeric or string expression to a Short (short integer). If the expression converts to a value outside the range of a Short, or is not a numeric value, a runtime error is generated.
CSng(*expr*)	Converts a numeric or string expression to a Single. If the expression converts to a value outside the range of a Single, or is not a numeric value, a runtime error is generated. The input expression may contain commas, as in "1,234."
CStr(*expr*)	Converts a numeric, Boolean, Date, or string expression to a String. Input can be an arithmetic expression, a Boolean value, a date, or any numeric data type.

Checkpoint

3.17 After the statement `dblResult = 10 \ 3` executes, what value will be stored in `dblResult`?

3.18 After each of the following statements executes, what value will be stored in `dblResult`?
   a. `dblResult = 6 + 3 * 5`
   b. `dblResult = 12 / 2 - 4`
   c. `dblResult = 2 + 7 * 3 - 6`
   d. `dblResult = (2 + 4) * 3`

3.19 What value will be stored in `dblResult` after the following statement executes?
`dblResult = CInt("28.5")`

3.20 Will the following statement execute or cause a runtime error?
`dblResult = CDbl("186,478.39")`

3.21 What is a named constant?

3.22 Assuming that `intNumber` is an integer variable, what value will each of the following statements assign to it?
   a. `intNumber = 27`
   b. `intNumber = CInt(12.8)`
   c. `intNumber = CInt(12.0)`
   d. `intNumber = (2 + 4) * 3`

3.23 Which function converts the string `"860.2"` to value of type Double?

3.24 How would the following strings be converted by the `CDec` function?
   a. `48.5000`
   b. `$34.95`
   c. `2,300`
   d. `Twelve`

3.5 Formatting Numbers and Dates

Users of computer programs generally like to see numbers and dates displayed in an attractive, easy to read format. Numbers greater than 999, for instance, should usually be displayed with commas and decimal points. The value 123456.78 would normally be displayed as "123,456.78".

> **TIP:** Number formatting is dependent on the locale that is used by the computer's Microsoft Windows operating system. *Localization* refers to the technique of adapting your formats for various regions and countries of the world. For example, in North America a currency value is formatted as 123,456.78. In many European countries, the same value is formatted as 123.456,78. In this book, we will display only North American formats, but you can find help on using other types of formats by looking for the topic named *localization* in Visual Studio help.

`ToString` Method

All numeric and date data types in Visual Basic contain the `ToString` **method**. This method converts the contents of a variable to a string. The following code segment shows an example of the method's use.

```
Dim intNumber As Integer = 123
lblNumber.Text = intNumber.ToString()
```

In the second statement the number variable's `ToString` method is called. The method returns the string `"123"`, which is assigned to the Text property of `lblNumber`.

By passing a formatting string to the `ToString` method, you can indicate what type of format you want to use when the number or date is formatted. The following statements create a string containing the number `1234.5` in Currency format:

```
Dim dblSample As Double
Dim strResult As String
dblSample = 1234.5
strResult = dblSample.ToString("c")
```

When the last statement executes, the value assigned to `strResult` is `"$1,234.50"`. Notice that an extra zero was added at the end because currency values usually have two digits to the right of the decimal point. The value `"c"` is called a format string. Table 3-14 shows the format strings used for all types of floating-point numbers (Double, Single, and Decimal), assuming the user is running Windows in a North American locale. The format strings are not case sensitive, so you can code them as uppercase or lowercase letters. If you call `ToString` using an integer type (Byte, Integer, or Long), the value is formatted as if it were type Double.

Table 3-14 Standard numeric format strings

Format String	Description
N or n	Number format
F or f	Fixed-point scientific format
E or e	Exponential scientific format
C or c	Currency format
P or p	Percent format

Number Format

Number format (n or N) displays numeric values with thousands separators and a decimal point. By default, two digits display to the right of the decimal point. Negative values are displayed with a leading minus (–) sign. Example:

```
–2,345.67
```

Fixed-Point Format

Fixed-point format (f or F) displays numeric values with no thousands separator and a decimal point. By default, two digits display to the right of the decimal point. Negative values are displayed with a leading minus (–) sign. Example:

```
–2345.67
```

Exponential Format

Exponential format (e or E) displays numeric values in scientific notation. The number is normalized with a single digit to the left of the decimal point. The exponent is marked by the letter e, and the exponent has a leading + or – sign. By default, six digits display to the right of the decimal point, and a leading minus sign is used if the number is negative. Example:

```
–2.345670e+003
```

Currency Format

Currency format (c or C) displays a leading currency symbol (such as $), digits, thousands separators, and a decimal point. By default, two digits display to the right of the decimal point. Negative values are surrounded by parentheses. Example:

```
($2,345.67)
```

Percent Format

Percent format (p or P) causes the number to be multiplied by 100 and displayed with a trailing space and % sign. By default, two digits display to the right of the decimal point. Negative values are displayed with a leading minus (–) sign. The following example uses –.2345:

```
-23.45 %
```

Specifying the Precision

Each numeric format string can optionally be followed by an integer that indicates how many digits to display after the decimal point. For example, the format n3 displays three digits after the decimal point. Table 3-15 shows a variety of numeric formatting examples, based on the North American locale.

Table 3-15 Numeric formatting examples (North American locale)

Number Value	Format String	ToString( ) Value
12.3	n3	12.300
12.348	n2	12.35
1234567.1	n	1,234,567.10
123456.0	f2	123456.00
123456.0	e3	1.235e+005
.234	p	23.40%
–1234567.8	c	($1,234,567.80)

Rounding

Rounding can occur when the number of digits you have specified after the decimal point in the format string is smaller than the precision of the numeric value. Suppose, for example, that the value 1.235 were displayed with a format string of n2. Then the displayed value would be 1.24. If the next digit after the last displayed digit is 5 or higher, the last displayed digit is rounded *away from zero*. Table 3-16 shows examples of rounding using a format string of n2.

Table 3-16 Rounding examples, using the n2 display format string

Number Value	Formatted As
1.234	1.23
1.235	1.24
1.238	1.24
–1.234	–1.23
–1.235	–1.24
–1.238	–1.24

Integer Values with Leading Zeros

Integer type variables (Byte, Integer, or Long) have a special format string, D (or d), that lets you specify the minimum width for displaying the number. Leading zeros are inserted if necessary. Table 3-17 shows examples.

Table 3-17 Formatting integers, using the D (d) format string

Integer Value	Format String	Formatted As
23	D	23
23	D4	0023
1	D2	01

Formatting Dates and Times

When you call the ToString method using a Date or DateTime variable, you can format it as a short date, short time, long date, and so on. Table 3-18 lists the most commonly used format strings for dates and times. The following example creates a string containing "8/23/2016", called the short date format.

```
Dim dtmSample As Date = "#8/23/2016#"
Dim strResult As String = dtmSample.ToString("d")
```

Date/time format strings are case sensitive.

Table 3-18 Common date/time formats

Format String	Description
d	Short date format, which shows the month, day, and year. An example is "8/23/2016".
D	Long date format, which contains the day of the week, month, day, and year. An example is "Tuesday, August 23, 2016".
t	Short time format, which shows the hours and minutes. An example is "3:22 PM".
T	Long time format, which contains the hours, minutes, seconds, and an AM/PM indicator. An example is "3:22:00 PM".
F	Full (long) date and time. An example is "Tuesday August 23, 2016 3:22:00 PM".

Tutorial 3-5:
Creating the *Sale Price Calculator* Application with Currency Formatting

If you are writing a program that works with a percentage, you have to make sure that the percentage's decimal point is in the correct location before doing any math with the percentage. This is especially true when the user enters a percentage as input. Most users will enter the number 50 to mean 50%, 20 to mean 20%, and so forth. Before you perform any calculations with such a percentage, you have to divide it by 100 to move its decimal point to the left two places.

Suppose a retail business is planning to have a storewide sale where the prices of all items will be reduced by a specified percentage. In this tutorial, you will create an application to calculate the sale price of an item after the discount is subtracted. Here is the algorithm, expressed as pseudocode:

1. *Get the original price of the item.*
2. *Get the discount percentage. (For example, 20 would be entered for 20%.)*
3. *Divide the percentage amount by 100 to move the decimal point to the correct location.*
4. *Multiply the percentage by the original price. This is the amount of the discount.*

5. *Subtract the discount from the original price. This is the sale price.*
6. *Display the sale price.*

Figure 3-17 shows the application's form, in the *Designer*, with the names of all the controls. When the application runs, the user will enter an item's original price into the `txtOriginalPrice` control and the discount percentage into the `txtDiscountPercentage` control. When the user clicks the `btnCalculate` control, the application will calculate the item's sale price and display the result in the `lblSalePrice` control. The `btnExit` control closes the application's form.

Figure 3-17 The *Sale Price Calculator* form

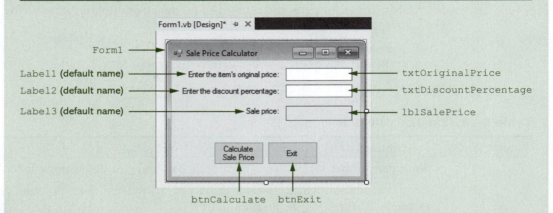

Step 1: Start Visual Studio and begin a new Visual Basic Windows Forms Application project named *Sale Price Calculator.*

Step 2: Set up the application's form as shown in Figure 3-17. The names of the controls are shown in the figure. As you place each of the controls on the form, refer to Table 3-19 for the relevant property settings.

Table 3-19 Control property settings

Control Name	Control Type	Property Settings
Form1	Form	**Size:** 300, 220 (approximately) **Text:** *Sale Price Calculator*
Label1 (or other default name)	Label	**Text:** *Enter the item's original price:*
Label2 (or other default name)	Label	**Text:** *Enter the discount percentage:*
Label3 (or other default name)	Label	**Text:** *Sale price:*
txtOriginalPrice	TextBox	No properties changed
txtDiscountPercentage	TextBox	No properties changed
lblSalePrice	Label	**AutoSize:** False **BorderStyle:** FixedSingle **Text:** (The contents of the Text property have been erased.) **TextAlign:** MiddleCenter
btnCalculate	Button	**Text:** *Calculate Sale Price*
btnExit	Button	**Text:** *Exit*

Step 3: Once you have set up the form with its controls, you can create the Click event handlers for the Button controls. In the *Designer*, double-click the btnCalculate control. This will open the *Code* window, and you will see an empty event handler named btnCalculate_Click. Complete the btnCalculate_Click event handler by typing the bold code shown in here. (Remember, do not write the line numbers! They are shown for reference only, to help us discuss specific lines of code.)

```
 1 Private Sub btnCalculate_Click(...) Handles btnCalculate.Click
 2    Dim decOriginalPrice As Decimal = 0        ' Original price
 3    Dim decDiscountPercentage As Decimal = 0   ' Discount percentage
 4    Dim decDiscountAmount As Decimal = 0       ' Amount of discount
 5    Dim decSalePrice As Decimal = 0            ' Sale price
 6
 7    ' Get the item's original price.
 8    decOriginalPrice = CDec(txtOriginalPrice.Text)
 9
10    ' Get the discount percentage.
11    decDiscountPercentage = CDec(txtDiscountPercentage.Text)
12
13    ' Move the percentage's decimal point left 2 spaces.
14    decDiscountPercentage = decDiscountPercentage / 100
15
16    ' Calculate the amount of the discount.
17    decDiscountAmount = decOriginalPrice * decDiscountPercentage
18
19    ' Calculate the sale price.
20    decSalePrice = decOriginalPrice - decDiscountAmount
21
22    ' Display the sale price.
23    lblSalePrice.Text = decSalePrice.ToString("c")
24 End Sub
```

Let's take a closer look at the code:

Line 2: This statement declares a Decimal variable named decOriginalPrice. This variable will hold the item's original price.

Line 3: This statement declares a Decimal variable named decDiscountPercentage. This variable will hold the discount percentage.

Line 4: This statement declares a Decimal variable named decDiscountAmount. This variable will hold the amount of discount that will be taken from the item's original price. This amount will be calculated.

Line 5: This statement declares a Decimal variable named decSalePrice. This variable will hold the item's sale price. This amount will be calculated.

Line 8: This statement converts the txtOriginalPrice control's Text property to a Decimal and assigns the result to the decOriginalPrice variable.

Line 11: This statement converts the txtDiscountPercentage control's Text property to a Decimal and assigns the result to the decDiscountPercentage variable.

Line 14: This statement divides decDiscountPercentage by 100 and stores the result back in decDiscountPercentage. This moves the decimal point in the decDiscountPercentage variable to the left two places.

Line 17: This statement calculates the amount of the discount. It multiplies decOriginalPrice by decDiscountPercentage and assigns the result to decDiscountAmount.

Line 20: This statement calculates the item's sale price. It subtracts the `decDiscountAmount` variable from the `decOriginalPrice` variable and assigns the result to the `decSalePrice` variable.

Line 23: This statement displays the item's sale price as a currency amount. It converts the `decSalePrice` variable to a string and assigns the result to the `lblSalePrice` control's Text property. Notice that the format string `"c"` is passed to the `decSalePrice` variable's `ToString` method.

Step 4: Switch your view back to the *Designer* and double-click the `btnExit` button. In the *Code* window, you will see an empty event handler named `btnExit_Click`. Complete the `btnExit_Click` event handler by typing the bold code shown here.

```
Private Sub btnExit_Click(...) Handles btnExit.Click
  ' Close the form.
  Me.Close()
End Sub
```

Step 5: Save the project. Then, press the F5 key on the keyboard, or click the *Start Debugging* button (▶) on the toolbar to compile and run the application. Test the application by entering values into the TextBoxes and clicking the *Calculate Sale Price* button. The sale price should be displayed, similar to Figure 3-18. Click the *Exit* button and the form should close.

Figure 3-18 The *Sale Price Calculator* application

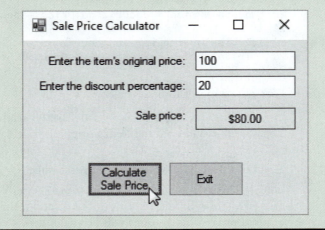

Checkpoint

3.25 Write a statement that uses the `ToString` method to convert the contents of a variable named `dblSalary` to a Currency format.

3.26 For each of the following numeric formats, identify the format string used as the input parameter when calling the `ToString` method.
   a. Currency
   b. Exponential scientific
   c. Number
   d. Percent
   e. Fixed-point

3.27 How can you make the ToString method display parentheses around a number in Currency format when the number is negative?

3.28 In the following table, fill in the expected values returned by the ToString function when specific numeric values are used with specific format strings.

Number Value	Format String	ToString( ) Value
12.3	n4	
12.348	n1	
1234567.1	n3	
123456.0	f1	
123456.0	e3	
.234	p2	
−1234567.8	c3	

3.29 Show an example of formatting a Date variable in Long Time format when calling the ToString method.

3.30 Show an example of formatting a Date variable in Long Date format when calling the ToString method.

3.6 Class-Level Variables

CONCEPT: Class-level variables are accessible to all procedures in a class.

Recall that a variable's scope is the part of the program in which the variable is visible. All of the variables you have created so far have had local scope, meaning that each was declared and used inside a procedure. Local variables are not visible to statements outside the procedure in which they are declared.

It's also possible to declare a class-level variable, which is accessible to all of the procedures in a class. Recall from Chapter 2 that a form's code appears inside a class. For example, suppose a project has a form named Form1. When you open the form in the *Code* window, you see that its code is contained inside a class declaration such as this:

```
Public Class Form1

    Event handlers appear here. . .

End Class
```

A class-level variable is declared inside a class declaration, but not inside any procedure. Class-level variables have class scope because they are visible to all statements inside the class. For example, look at the following code. The application's form has two Button controls: btnSetValue and btnShowValue.

```
1   Public Class Form1
2     ' Declare a class-level variable.
3     Dim intValue As Integer
4
5     Private Sub btnSetValue_Click(...) Handles btnSetValue.Click
6       intValue = 99
7     End Sub
8
```

```
 9  Private Sub btnShowValue_Click(...) Handles btnShowValue.Click
10      MessageBox.Show(intValue.ToString())
11  End Sub
12 End Class
```

Notice that the declaration of the `intValue` variable in line 3 is inside the class, but is not inside of either event handler. The variable has class scope, so it is visible to both of the event handlers. When the `btnSetValue_Click` procedure executes, the statement in line 6 assigns 99 to the variable. When the `btnShowValue_Click` procedure executes, the statement in line 10 displays the variable's value in a message box. (In the *Chap3* folder of student sample programs you will find the previously shown code in a project named *Class-Level Variable Demo*.)

Most programmers agree that you should not overuse class-level variables. Although they make it easy to share values between procedures, their use can also lead to problems. Here are some of the reasons:

- While debugging, if you find that the wrong value is being stored in a class-level variable, you will have to track down each statement in the class that uses the variable to determine where the bad value is coming from. In a class with lots of code, this can be tedious and time-consuming.
- When two or more procedures modify the same class-level variable, you must ensure that one procedure cannot upset the accuracy or correctness of another procedure by modifying the variable.
- Class-level variables can make a program hard to understand. A class-level variable can be modified by any statement in the class. If you are to understand any part of the class that uses a class-level variable, you have to be aware of all the other parts of the class that access that variable.

Class-Level Constants

Although you should be careful not to overuse class-level variables, it is generally acceptable to use class-level constants. A class-level constant is a named constant declared with the `Const` keyword, at the class level. Because a constant's value cannot be changed during the program's execution, you do not have to worry about many of the potential hazards that are associated with the use of class-level variables.

Tutorial 3-6:
Creating the *Change Counter* application

In this tutorial, you will create the *Change Counter* application. The application will display images of four coins, having the values 5 cents, 10 cents, 25 cents, and 50 cents. Each time the user clicks on a coin image, the value of that coin is added to a total, and the total is displayed. Figure 3-19 shows the application's form in the *Designer*, with the names of all the controls.

Step 1:   Start Visual Studio and begin a new Visual Basic Windows Forms Application project named *Sale Price Calculator*.

Step 2:   Set up the application's form as shown in Figure 3-19. The names of the controls are shown in the figure. As you place each of the controls on the form, refer to Table 3-20 for the relevant property settings.

Figure 3-19 The *Change Counter* form

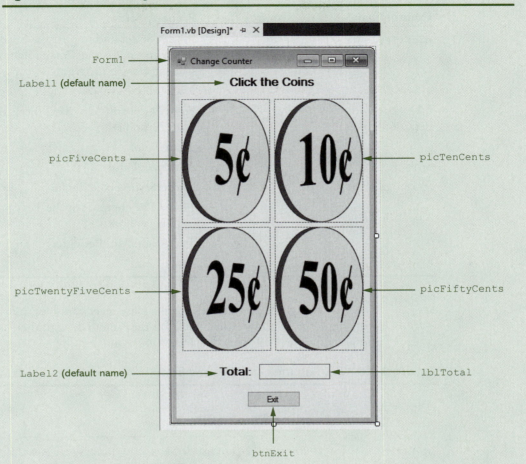

Form1.vb [Design]* ⊕ ✕

Form1 → Change Counter

Label1 (default name) → **Click the Coins**

picFiveCents → 5¢   10¢ ← picTenCents

picTwentyFiveCents → 25¢   50¢ ← picFiftyCents

Label2 (default name) → **Total:** [   ] ← lblTotal

Exit

btnExit

Table 3-20 Control property settings

Control Name	Control Type	Property Settings
Form1	Form	**Size:** 290, 550 (approximately) **Text:** *Change Counter*
Label1 (or other default name)	Label	**Font:** Microsoft Sans Serif (Style: Bold, Size: 12 point) **Text:** *Click the Coins*
picFiveCents	PictureBox	**Image:** Select and import the 5cents.png file from the *Images\Coins* folder of the student sample programs. **SizeMode:** AutoSize
picTenCents	PictureBox	**Image:** Select and import the 10cents.png file from the *Images\Coins* folder of the student sample programs. **SizeMode:** AutoSize
picTwentyFiveCents	PictureBox	**Image:** Select and import the 25cents.png file from the *Images\Coins* folder of the student sample programs. **SizeMode:** AutoSize

(continued)

Table 3-20 Control property settings (*continued*)

Control Name	Control Type	Property Settings
picFiftyCents	PictureBox	**Image:** Select and import the 50cents.png file from the *Images\Coins* folder of the student sample programs.
		SizeMode: AutoSize
Label2 (or other default name)	Label	**Font:** Microsoft Sans Serif (Style: Bold, Size: 12 point)
		Text: *Total:*
lblTotal	Label	**AutoSize:** False
		BorderStyle: FixedSingle
		Text: (The contents of the Text property have been erased.)
		TextAlign: MiddleCenter
btnExit	Button	**Text:** *Exit*

Step 3: Now you will write declarations for the class-level variables, but first you must open the *Code* window. Click *View* on the menu bar, and then select *Code*, as shown in Figure 3-20. This opens the *Code* window.

Figure 3-20 Opening the *Code* Window from the *View* menu

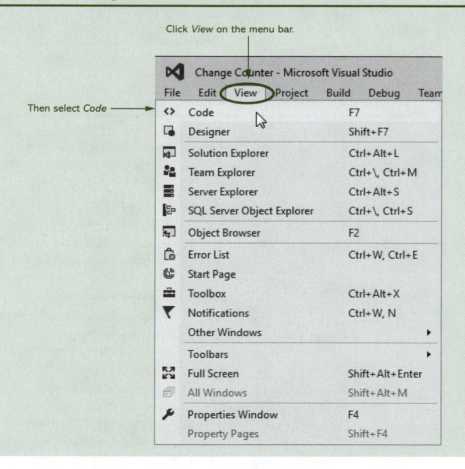

Step 4: Write the declarations for the class-level constants, shown here in bold. (Remember, do not write the line numbers! They are shown for reference only, to help us discuss specific lines of code.)

```
1 Public Class Form1
2   ' Class-level constants for the coin values
3   Dim decFIVE_CENTS_VALUE As Decimal = 0.05D
4   Dim decTEN_CENTS_VALUE As Decimal = 0.1D
5   Dim decTWENTY_FIVE_CENTS_VALUE As Decimal = 0.25D
6   Dim decFIFTY_CENTS_VALUE As Decimal = 0.5D
7
8 End Class
```

Let's take a closer look at each of the declarations:

- Line 3 declares a Decimal constant named decFIVE_CENTS_VALUE, initialized with the value 0.05D. This constant represents the value of the 5¢ coin.
- Line 4 declares a Decimal constant named decTEN_CENTS_VALUE, initialized with the value 0.1D. This constant represents the value of the 10¢ coin.
- Line 5 declares a Decimal constant named decTWENTY_FIVE_CENTS_VALUE, initialized with the value 0.25D. This constant represents the value of the 25¢ coin.
- Line 6 declares a Decimal constant named decFIFTY_CENTS_VALUE, initialized with the value 0.5D. This constant represents the value of the 50¢ coin.

Step 5: Now you will declare a class-level variable named decTotal, initialized with 0. You will use this variable to keep the total value of the coins that the user clicks. Type the lines that are shown here in bold.

```
Public Class Form1
  ' Class-level constants for the coin values
  Dim decFIVE_CENTS_VALUE As Decimal = 0.05D
  Dim decTEN_CENTS_VALUE As Decimal = 0.1D
  Dim decTWENTY_FIVE_CENTS_VALUE As Decimal = 0.25D
  Dim decFIFTY_CENTS_VALUE As Decimal = 0.5D

  ' Class-level variable to hold the total,
  ' initialized with 0.
  Dim decTotal As Decimal = 0.0D
End Class
```

Step 6: Now you will create the Click event handlers for the PictureBox controls. Switch your view back to the *Designer* and double-click the picFiveCents control. This will open the code editor, and you will see an empty event handler named picFiveCents_Click. Complete the picFiveCents_Click event handler by typing the code shown in bold here. (Remember, do not write the line numbers! They are shown for reference only, to help us discuss specific lines of code.)

```
1 Private Sub picFiveCents_Click(...) Handles picFiveCents.Click
2   ' Add the value of 5 cents to the total.
3   decTotal = decTotal + decFIVE_CENTS_VALUE
4
5   ' Display the total, formatted as currency.
6   lblTotal.Text = decTotal.ToString("c")
7 End Sub
```

This is what the code does:

- The statement in line 3 adds the value of the decFIVE_CENTS_VALUE constant to the decTotal variable.
- This statement in line 6 converts the decTotal variable to a string, and assigns the result to the lblTotal control's Text property. The "c" format string causes the number to be formatted as currency.

Step 7: Switch your view back to the *Designer* and double-click the picTenCents control. This will open the code editor, and you will see an empty event handler named picTenCents_Click. Complete the picTenCents_Click event handler by typing the code shown in bold here. (Remember, do not write the line numbers! They are shown for reference only, to help us discuss specific lines of code.)

```
1 Private Sub picTenCents_Click(...) Handles picTenCents.Click
2    ' Add the value of 10 cents to the total.
3    decTotal = decTotal + decTEN_CENTS_VALUE
4
5    ' Display the total, formatted as currency.
6    lblTotal.Text = decTotal.ToString("c")
7 End Sub
```

This is what the code does:

- The statement in line 3 adds the value of the decTEN_CENTS_VALUE constant to the decTotal variable.
- This statement in line 6 converts the decTotal variable to a string, and assigns the result to the lblTotal control's Text property. The "c" format string causes the number to be formatted as currency.

Step 8: Switch your view back to the *Designer* and double-click the picTwentyFive-Cents control. This will open the code editor, and you will see an empty event handler named picTwentyFiveCents_Click. Complete the picTwentyFive-Cents_Click event handler by typing the code shown in bold here. (Again, do not write the line numbers! They are shown for reference only, to help us discuss specific lines of code.)

```
1 Private Sub picTwentyFiveCents_Click(...) Handles picTenCents.Click
2    ' Add the value of 25 cents to the total.
3    decTotal = decTotal + decTWENTY_FIVE_CENTS_VALUE
4
5    ' Display the total, formatted as currency.
6    lblTotal.Text = decTotal.ToString("c")
7 End Sub
```

This is what the code does:

- The statement in line 3 adds the value of the decTWENTY_FIVE_CENTS_VALUE constant to the decTotal variable.
- This statement in line 6 converts the decTotal variable to a string, and assigns the result to the lblTotal control's Text property. The "c" format string causes the number to be formatted as currency.

Step 9: Switch your view back to the *Designer* and double-click the picFiftyCents control. This will open the code editor, and you will see an empty event handler named picFiftyCents_Click. Complete the picFiftyCents_Click event handler by typing the code shown in bold here. (Again, do not write the line numbers! They are shown for reference only, to help us discuss specific lines of code.)

```
1 Private Sub picFiftyCents_Click(...) Handles picTenCents.Click
2    ' Add the value of 50 cents to the total.
3    decTotal = decTotal + decFIFTY_CENTS_VALUE
4
5    ' Display the total, formatted as currency.
6    lblTotal.Text = decTotal.ToString("c")
7 End Sub
```

This is what the code does:

- The statement in line 3 adds the value of the decFIFTY_CENTS_VALUE constant to the decTotal variable.
- This statement in line 6 converts the decTotal variable to a string, and assigns the result to the lblTotal control's Text property. The "c" format string causes the number to be formatted as currency.

Step 10: Switch your view back to the *Designer* and double-click the btnExit button. In the *Code* window, you will see an empty event handler named btnExit_Click. Complete the btnExit_Click event handler by typing the bold code shown here.

```
Private Sub btnExit_Click(...) Handles btnExit.Click
    ' Close the form.
    Me.Close()
End Sub
```

Step 11: Save the project. Then, press the F5 key on the keyboard, or click the *Start Debugging* button (▶) on the toolbar to compile and run the application. Test the application by clicking the coin images, in any order you wish. The total shown on the form should update by the correct amount each time you click a coin. When you are finished, click the *Exit* button and the form should close.

 Checkpoint

3.31 What is the difference between a class-level variable and a local variable?

3.32 Where do you declare class-level variables?

 **3.7** **Exception Handling**

CONCEPT: A well-engineered program should report errors and try to continue. Or, it should explain why it cannot continue, and then shut down. In this section, you learn how to recover gracefully from errors, using a technique known as exception handling.

An **exception** is an unexpected error that occurs while a program is running, causing the program to abruptly halt. Exceptions are typically caused by circumstances outside of the programmer's control. In Tutorial 3-7 you will run an application and deliberately cause an exception.

 Tutorial 3-7:
Exception Demonstration

VideoNote
Exception
Demonstration

Step 1: Open the *Exception Demo* project from the Chapter 3 sample programs folder named *Exception Demo*. Figure 3-21 shows the application's form in the *Designer*. The TextBox control's name is txtSalary, and the Button control's name is btnOk.

Figure 3-21 The *Exception Demo* application's form

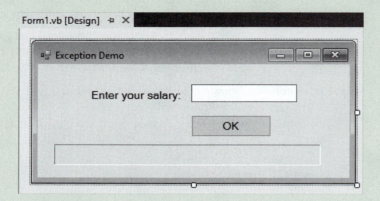

Step 2: Open the *Code* window and look at the btnOk button's Click event handler. The code is shown here, with line numbers inserted for reference purposes:

```
1 Private Sub btnOk_Click(...) Handles btnOk.Click
2   ' Declare a variable to hold the user's salary.
3   Dim decSalary As Decimal
4
5   ' Get the user's input and convert it to a Decimal.
6   decSalary = CDec(txtSalary.Text)
7
8   ' Display the user's salary.
9   lblResult.Text = "Your salary is " & decSalary.ToString("c")
10 End Sub
```

Line 3 declares a Decimal variable named decSalary. Line 6 uses the CDec function to convert the txtSalary control's Text property to a Decimal, and assigns the result to the decSalary variable. Line 9 displays a message showing the value of decSalary formatted as currency.

Step 3: Run the application. Enter *4000* in the TextBox and click the *OK* button. You should see the message *Your salary is $4000.00.*

Step 4: Change the contents of the TextBox to *Four Thousand*, as shown in Figure 3-22.

Figure 3-22 *Four Thousand* entered into the TextBox

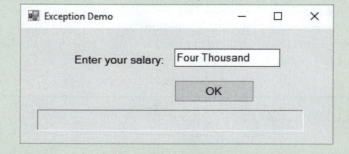

Because the string *Four Thousand* cannot be converted by the CDec function, an exception will occur when you click the *OK* button. Test it by clicking the *OK* button. The application will halt and you will see the error window shown in Figure 3-23.

Figure 3-23 The resulting error window

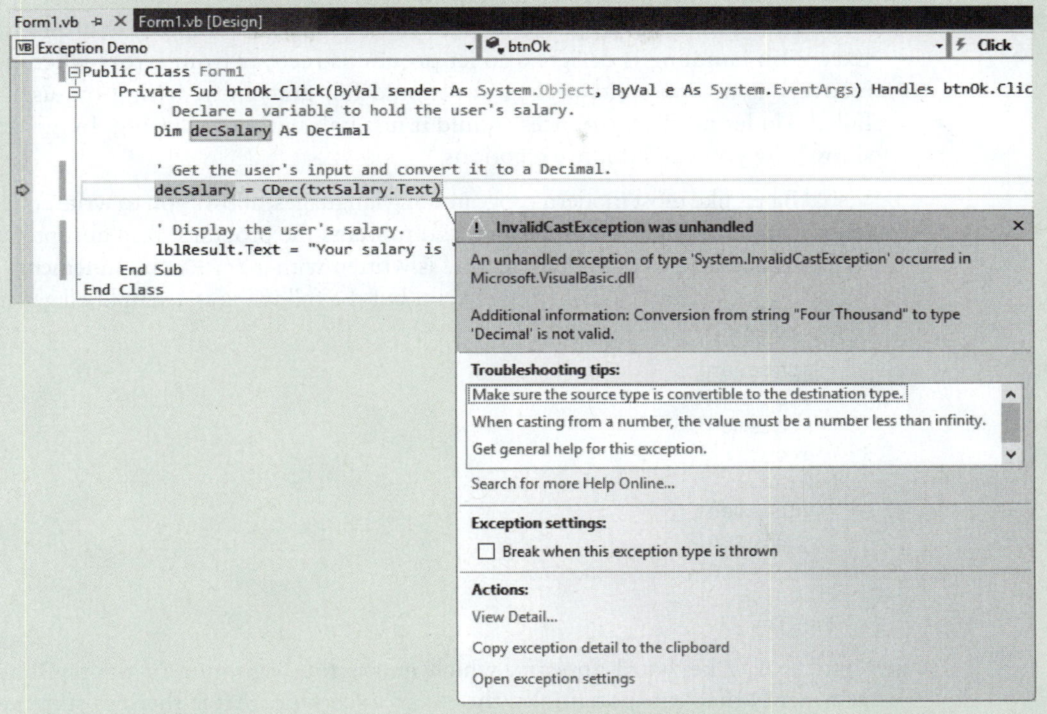

A lot of information is displayed in the error window. Before continuing, take note of the following:

- The window's title bar shows the message *InvalidCastException was unhandled*. All exceptions have a name, and the name of the exception that just occurred is InvalidCastException. Anytime a conversion function such as CDec fails to convert a value, it causes an InvalidCastException to occur. This message also tells us that the exception was *unhandled*. That means that the program doesn't have any code to take care of the exception. It simply allowed it to happen, and as a result the application halted.
- Just below the window's title bar you see the error message *Conversion from string "Four Thousand" to type 'Decimal' is not valid*. This tells us exactly what happened to cause the exception.
- In the *Code* window, the statement that caused the exception is highlighted.

Step 5: Close the error window. The application is now in break mode, which is used for debugging. We will discuss break mode in greater detail later in this chapter. For now, just exit break mode by performing *one* of the following actions:

- Click the *Stop Debugging* button (■) on the toolbar.
- Click *Debug* on the menu bar, and then select *Stop Debugging*.
- Press Ctrl+Alt+Break on the keyboard.

When an exception occurs, programmers commonly say an *exception was thrown*. As you were following the steps in Tutorial 3-7, an exception known as an InvalidCastException was thrown when the CDec function attempted to convert the string "Four Thousand" to a Decimal value. When an exception is thrown, it should be handled by your program code. If the exception is unhandled (as was the case in Tutorial 3-7), the program halts.

Failure Can Be Graceful

Exceptions are typically thrown because of events outside the programmer's control. A disk file may be unreadable, for example, because of a hardware failure. The user may enter invalid data, as happened in Tutorial 3-7. Or, the computer may be low on memory. Exception handling is designed to let programs recover from errors when possible. Or, if recovery is not possible, a program should fail gracefully, letting the user know why it failed. Under no circumstances should it just halt without warning. In this section we will show how you can handle exceptions.

Visual Basic, like most modern programming languages, allows you to write code that responds to exceptions when they are thrown, and prevents the program from abruptly crashing. Such code is called an **exception handler** and is written with a **Try–Catch statement**. There are several ways to write a Try-Catch statement, but the following is a simplified general format:

```
Try
   statement
   statement
   statement
   etc...
Catch
   statement
   statement
   statement
   etc...
End Try
```

First the Try keyword appears, which marks the beginning of the **try block**. These are statements that can potentially throw an exception. After the last statement in the try block, a **catch block** appears, containing one or more statements. When a Try-Catch statement executes, the statements in the try block are executed in sequential order. If a statement in the try block throws an exception, the program immediately begins executing statements in the catch block. After the last statement in the catch block has executed, the program resumes execution with any statements appearing after the End Try keywords. Finally, it is important to remember that as soon as an exception is thrown, all remaining statements in the try block are skipped.

Let's see how a Try-Catch statement can be used in the *Exception Demo* application. A modified version of the btnOk_Click procedure is shown here, with line numbers inserted for reference:

```
1 Private Sub btnOk_Click(...) Handles btnOk.Click
2    ' Declare a variable to hold the user's salary.
3    Dim decSalary As Decimal
4
5    Try
6       ' Get the user's input and convert it to a Decimal.
7       decSalary = CDec(txtSalary.Text)
8
9       ' Display the user's salary.
10      lblResult.Text = "Your salary is " & decSalary.ToString("c")
11   Catch
12      ' Display an error message.
13      lblResult.Text = "Please try again, and enter a number."
14   End Try
15 End Sub
```

In this code, when the statement in line 7 throws an exception, the program immediately jumps to the Catch clause in line 11 and begins executing the statements in the catch block. The catch block displays a message in line 13, and that's the end of the Try-Catch statement. Figure 3-24 illustrates this sequence of events.

Figure 3-24 Sequence of events in the `Try-Catch` statement

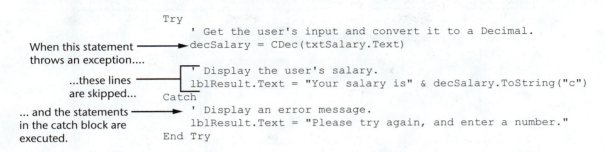

```
                         Try
                             ' Get the user's input and convert it to a Decimal.
When this statement ───────→ decSalary = CDec(txtSalary.Text)
throws an exception....
                             ' Display the user's salary.
   ...these lines ─────────→   lblResult.Text = "Your salary is" & decSalary.ToString("c")
   are skipped...        Catch
... and the statements ───→    ' Display an error message.
in the catch block are         lblResult.Text = "Please try again, and enter a number."
executed.                End Try
```

We encourage you to modify the `btnOk_Click` procedure in the *Exception Demo* project by adding the `Try-Catch` statement as previously shown. Then, run the application again. If you enter 4000 in the TextBox and click the *OK* button, you will see the message *Your salary is $4000.00*, just as you did before. If you enter something that cannot be converted to a Decimal, such as the string *Four Thousand*, you will see the message shown in Figure 3-25. This message is displayed by the statement shown previously in line 13 (in the catch block).

Figure 3-25 Message displayed by the exception handler

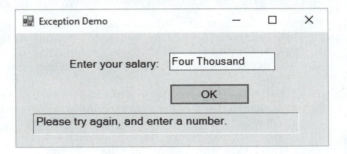

VideoNote

Salary Calculator **project** with exception handling

Tutorial 3-8:
Salary Calculator project with exception handling

The student sample programs folder contains a partially completed project named *Salary Calculator*. When the project is complete, it will allow the user to input a person's annual salary and number of pay periods per year. With the click of a button, the program will calculate the amount of salary the user should receive per pay period.

In this tutorial you will complete the project. First, you will implement the program without exception handling, test it, and note how runtime errors occur. Then, you will add exception handling to the program and test it again.

Step 1: Open the *Salary Calculator* project from the Chapter 3 sample programs folder named *Salary Calculator*. Figure 3-26 shows the application's form with the names of the several controls.

Figure 3-26 *Salary Calculator* form

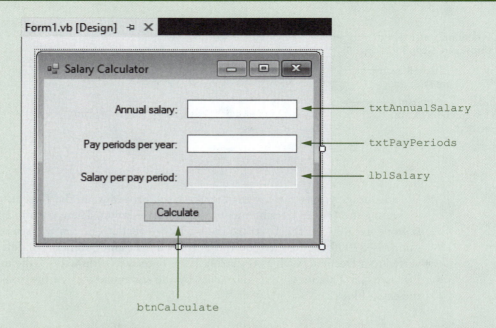

Step 2: Double-click the `btnCalculate` button to open the *Code* window. Insert the following bold code shown in the lines 2 through 14 into its Click event handler. (Don't enter the line numbers! They are shown only for reference.)

```
1 Private Sub btnCalculate_Click(...) Handles btnCalculate.Click
2    Dim decAnnualSalary As Decimal ' Annual salary
3    Dim intPayPeriods As Integer   ' Number of pay periods
4    Dim decSalary As Decimal       ' Salary per pay period
5
6    ' Get the annual salary and number of pay periods.
7    decAnnualSalary = CDec(txtAnnualSalary.Text)
8    intPayPeriods = CInt(txtPayPeriods.Text)
9
10   ' Calculate the salary per pay period.
11   decSalary = decAnnualSalary / intPayPeriods
12
13   ' Display the salary per pay period.
14   lblSalary.Text = decSalary.ToString("c")
15 End Sub
```

Let's go over the code that you just wrote:

- Lines 2 through 4 declare the local variables used in the procedure.
- Line 7 uses the `CDec` function to convert the value of the `txtAnnualSalary` control's Text property to a Decimal, and assigns the result to the `decAnnualSalary` variable.
- Line 8 uses the `CInt` function to convert the value of the `txtPayPeriods` control's Text property to an Integer, and assigns the result to the `intPayPeriods` variable.
- Line 11 divides `decAnnualSalary` by `intPayPeriods` to calculate the salary per pay period. The result is assigned to the `decSalary` variable.
- Line 14 uses the `ToString("c")` method to convert `decSalary` to a string, formatted as currency. The resulting string is assigned to the `lblSalary` control's Text property.

Step 3: Save and run the program. Enter **75000** for the annual salary and **26** for the pay periods per year. When you click *Calculate*, the output should be $2,884.62.

Step 4: Now you will purposely cause an exception. Erase the contents of the *Pay periods per year:* text box and click the *Calculate* button. You should see an error window appear, like the one shown in Figure 3-27, saying *InvalidCastException was unhandled*. Notice the error message in the window reads *Conversion from string "" to type Integer is not valid*. Also notice the statement that caused the error (line 8 in the previously shown code).

Figure 3-27 Exception reported

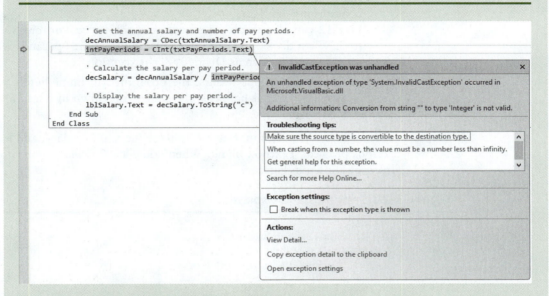

Close the error window and click the *Stop Debugging* button (■) on the Visual Studio toolbar. The program should return to design mode.

Step 5: Your next task is to add exception handling to the program to prevent the type of runtime error you just saw. You never want a program to halt like this when the user enters bad data. Revise the code in the btnCalculate_Click procedure so it looks like the following. (The new code is shown in bold. As before, don't enter the line numbers. They are shown only for reference.)

```
1   Private Sub btnCalculate_Click() Handles btnCalculate.Click
2      Dim decAnnualSalary As Decimal     ' Annual salary
3      Dim intPayPeriods As Integer       ' Number of pay periods
4      Dim decSalary As Decimal           ' Salary per pay period
5
6      Try
7         ' Get the annual salary and number of pay periods.
8         decAnnualSalary = CDec(txtAnnualSalary.Text)
9         intPayPeriods = CInt(txtPayPeriods.Text)
10
11        ' Calculate the salary per pay period.
12        decSalary = decAnnualSalary / intPayPeriods
13
14        ' Display the salary per pay period.
15        lblSalary.Text = decSalary.ToString("c")
```

```
16       Catch
17          ' Display an error message.
18          MessageBox.Show("Error: Be sure to enter nonzero " &
19                          "numeric values.")
20       End Try
21    End Sub
```

Now, the statements that can potentially throw an exception are placed inside the try block:

- Line 8 can throw an InvalidCastException if the txtAnnualSalary control contains invalid data.
- Line 9 can throw an InvalidCastException if the txtPayPeriods control contains invalid data.
- Line 12 can also throw an exception if the intPayPeriods variable is set to 0. When division by zero happens, if one of the operands is a Decimal, an exception known as DivideByZeroException occurs.

If any of these exceptions occurs, the program will immediately jump to the Catch clause. When that happens, the statement shown in lines 18 and 19 will display an error message.

Step 6: Save and run the program. Enter *75000* for the annual salary, and leave the pay periods per year TextBox blank. When you click *Calculate*, you should see the message shown in Figure 3-28.

Figure 3-28 Error message displayed

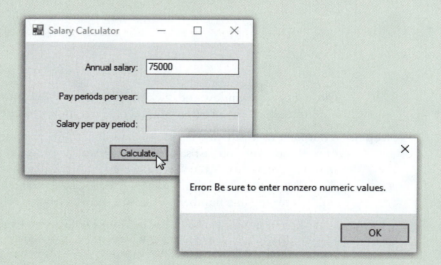

Step 7: Now let's see what happens when the program divides by zero. Leave 75000 as the annual salary and enter *0* for the pay periods per year. When you click *Calculate*, you should again see the message shown in Figure 3-28.

Using Nested Try-Catch Statements

As you saw in Tutorial 3-8, a procedure might contain several statements that potentially can throw an exception. If you look back at Step 5 of that tutorial, you see that lines 9, 10, and 13 each can potentially throw an exception. Regardless of which line throws an exception, the catch block displays the same error message (in lines 19 and 20). If you want to handle the exceptions separately with a unique error message displayed for each one, you can create a set of nested Try-Catch statements. (When we use the term *nested*, we mean that one Try-Catch statement appears inside another.)

The following code shows how this can be done. This is a modified version of the btnCalculate_Click procedure in Tutorial 3-8.

```
1  Private Sub btnCalculate_Click(...) Handles btnCalculate.Click
2     Dim decAnnualSalary As Decimal  ' Annual salary
3     Dim intPayPeriods As Integer    ' Number of pay periods per year
4     Dim decSalary As Decimal        ' Salary per pay period
5
6     Try
7        ' Get the annual salary.
8        decAnnualSalary = CDec(txtAnnualSalary.Text)
9
10          Try
11             ' Get the number of pay periods.
12             intPayPeriods = CInt(txtPayPeriods.Text)
13
14             Try
15                ' Calculate the salary per pay period.
16                decSalary = decAnnualSalary / intPayPeriods
17
18                ' Display the salary per pay period.
19                lblSalary.Text = decSalary.ToString("c")
20             Catch
21                ' Error message for division-by-zero.
22                MessageBox.Show("Pay periods cannot be zero.")
23             End Try
24
25          Catch
26             ' Error message for invalid pay periods.
27             MessageBox.Show("Pay periods must be an integer.")
28          End Try
29
30       Catch
31          ' Error message for invalid salary.
32          MessageBox.Show("Enter a numeric value for salary.")
33       End Try
34  End Sub
```

Let's take a closer look at this code:

- The first Try statement appears in line 6. Inside the try block, line 8 attempts to convert txtAnnualSalary.Text to a Decimal. If an exception is thrown, the program will jump to the Catch clause in line 30. When that happens, line 32 displays an error message prompting the user to enter a numeric value for the salary, and the procedure ends.
- If txtAnnualSalary.Text is successfully converted to a Decimal in line 8, the program continues to the nested Try statement in line 10. Line 12 attempts to convert txtPayPeriods.Text to an Integer. If an exception is thrown, the program will jump to the Catch clause in line 25. When that happens, line 27 displays an error message indicating that pay periods must be an integer, and the procedure ends.
- If txtPayPeriods.Text is successfully converted to a Decimal in line 12, the program continues to the nested Try statement in line 14. Then, line 16 divides decAnnualSalary by intPayPeriods. If intPayPeriods happens to be zero, an exception is thrown and the program jumps to the Catch clause in line 20. When that happens, line 22 displays an error message indicating that pay periods cannot be zero, and the procedure ends.
- If the division operation in line 16 is successful, then line 19 displays the salary in the lblSalary control.

(In the *Chap3* folder of student sample programs you will find the previously shown code in a project named *Nested Try*.)

If You Want to Know More: Using Multiple Catch Clauses to Handle Multiple Types of Errors

Another way to handle different types of exceptions separately, with a unique error message displayed for each one, is to have a Catch clause for each type of exception.

The following code shows how this can be done. This is a modified version of the btnCalculate_Click procedure in Tutorial 3-8. Notice that the Try-Catch statement has two Catch clauses: one for InvalidCastExceptions (line 18) and one for DivideByZeroExceptions (line 22). If the code inside the try block throws an InvalidCastException, the program will jump to the catch block in line 18, perform the statements there, and then exit. If the code inside the try block throws a DivideByZeroException, the program will execute the Catch block starting in line 22, and then exit.

```
 1 Private Sub btnCalculate_Click() Handles btnCalculate.Click
 2    Dim decAnnualSalary As Decimal    ' Annual salary
 3    Dim intPayPeriods As Integer       ' Number of pay periods per year
 4    Dim decSalary As Decimal           ' Salary per pay period
 5
 6    Try
 7       ' Get the annual salary and number of pay periods.
 8       decAnnualSalary = CDec(txtAnnualSalary.Text)
 9       intPayPeriods = CInt(txtPayPeriods.Text)
10
11       ' Calculate the salary per pay period.
12       decSalary = decAnnualSalary / intPayPeriods
13
14       ' Display the salary per pay period.
15       lblSalary.Text = decSalary.ToString("c")
16
17    Catch ex As InvalidCastException
18       ' An invalid value as entered.
19       MessageBox.Show("Error: Input must be numeric.")
20
21    Catch ex As DivideByZeroException
22       ' Zero was entered for pay periods.
23       MessageBox.Show("Error: Enter nonzero values.")
24    End Try
25 End Sub
```

This is a more complex way of handling exceptions, and it requires you to know the names of the exception types that you want to handle ahead of time. A simple way to do this is to run the program without the Try-Catch statement and deliberately cause the exceptions to occur. You can then see the name of the exception in the error window that appears. (In the *Chap3* folder of student sample programs you will find the previously shown code in a project named *Multiple Exceptions*.)

If You Want to Know More: Displaying an Exception's Default Error Message

It's possible for your program to retrieve the default error message for an exception. This is the error message that you see in the error window that appears when an exception is unhandled.

When an exception occurs, an object known as an **exception object** is created in memory. The exception object has various properties that contain data about the exception. When you write a Catch clause, you can optionally assign a name to the exception object, as shown here:

```
Catch ex As Exception
```

This Catch clause specifies that the name ex refers to the exception object. Inside the catch block, we can use the name ex to access the exception object's properties. One of these is the Message property, which contains the exception's default error message. The following code shows how this can be done. This is another modified version of the btnCalculate_Click procedure in Tutorial 3-8.

```
1 Private Sub btnCalculate_Click(...) Handles btnCalculate.Click
2   Dim decAnnualSalary As Decimal ' Annual salary
3   Dim intPayPeriods As Integer   ' Number of pay periods
4   Dim decSalary As Decimal       ' Salary per pay period
5
6   Try
7     ' Get the annual salary and number of pay periods.
8     decAnnualSalary = CDec(txtAnnualSalary.Text)
9     intPayPeriods = CInt(txtPayPeriods.Text)
10
11    ' Calculate the salary per pay period.
12    decSalary = decAnnualSalary / intPayPeriods
13
14    ' Display the salary per pay period.
15    lblSalary.Text = decSalary.ToString("c")
16
17  Catch ex As Exception
18    ' Display the default error message.
19    MessageBox.Show(ex.Message)
20  End Try
21 End Sub
```

The statement in line 19 displays the exception object's Message property in a message box. Figure 3-29 shows some examples.

Figure 3-29 Examples of default exception messages

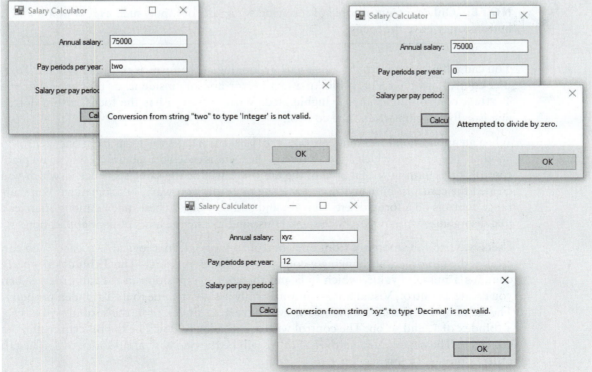

Checkpoint

3.33 What is an exception?

3.34 What is an exception handler?

3.35 What kind of code does the try block of a `Try-Catch` statement contain?

3.36 What causes the program to jump to the `Catch` clause of a `Try-Catch` statement?

3.37 How can you display the default error message when an exception is thrown?

3.38 Write a `Try-Catch` statement for an application that calculates the sum of two whole numbers and displays the result. The application uses two TextBox controls named `txtValue1` and `txtValue2` to gather the input, a Label control named `lblSum` to display the result, and a Button control to activate the calculation.

3.8 More GUI Details

In Chapter 2 you learned the basics of creating a GUI by placing controls on a form and setting various properties. In this section, you will learn to fine-tune many aspects of an application's GUI.

Controlling a Form's Tab Order

When an application is running and a form is displayed, one of the form's controls always has the **focus**. The control having the focus is the one that receives the user's keyboard input. For example, when a TextBox control has the focus, it receives the characters that the user enters on the keyboard. When a button has the focus, pressing the (Enter) key executes the button's Click event handler.

NOTE: Only controls capable of receiving some sort of input, such as text boxes and buttons, may have the focus.

You can tell which control has the focus by looking at the form at runtime. When a TextBox control has the focus, a blinking text cursor appears inside it, or the text inside the TextBox control might appear highlighted. When a button has the focus, a thin dotted line usually appears around the control.

When an application is running, pressing the (Tab) key changes the focus from one control to another. The order in which controls receive the focus is called the **tab order**. When you place controls on a form in Visual Studio, the tab order will be the same sequence in which you created the controls. In many cases this is the tab order you want, but sometimes you rearrange controls on a form, delete controls, and add new ones. These modifications often lead to a disorganized tab order, which can confuse and irritate the users of your application.

Users want to tab smoothly from one control to the next, in a logical sequence. You can modify the tab order by changing a control's TabIndex property. The **TabIndex property** contains a numeric value, which indicates the control's position in the tab order. When you create a control, Visual Studio automatically assigns a value to its TabIndex property. The first control you create on a form will have a TabIndex of 0, the second will have a TabIndex of 1, and so on. The control with a TabIndex of 0 will be the first control in the tab order. The next control in the tab order will be the one with a TabIndex of 1. The tab order continues in this sequence.

You may change the tab order of a form's controls by selecting them, one-by-one, and changing their TabIndex property in the *Properties* window. An easier method, however, is to click *View* on the Visual Studio menu bar, and then click *Tab Order*. This causes the form to be displayed in **tab order selection mode**. The image on the left in Figure 3-30 shows a form in the normal view, and the image on the right shows the form in tab order selection mode. We have also inserted the names of the TextBox and Button controls in the image on the right, for reference purposes. The form in the figure is from a project named *Tab Order Demo*, in the *Chap3* folder of the student sample programs.

Figure 3-30 A form displayed in tab order selection mode

Normal view   Tab order selection mode

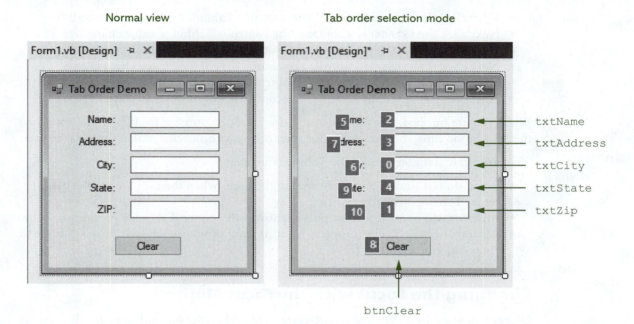

btnClear

In tab order selection mode, each control's existing TabIndex value is displayed in a small box, in the control's upper-left corner. Notice the following in the image on the right in Figure 3-30:

- The txtName control's TabIndex is 2.
- The txtAddress control's TabIndex is 3.
- The txtCity control's TabIndex is 0.
- The txtState control's TabIndex is 4.
- The txtZip control's TabIndex is 1.
- The btnClear control's TabIndex is 8.

NOTE: Although the Label controls have TabIndex values, those values are irrelevant in this example because Label controls cannot receive the focus.

As you look at Figure 3-30, think about the order in which the controls will receive the focus when the application runs.

- The txtCity control has the lowest TabIndex value (0), so it will receive the focus first.
- If you press the [Tab] key, the focus will jump to the txtZip control because it has the next lowest TabIndex value (1).
- Press the [Tab] key again, and the focus will jump to the txtName control (TabIndex is set to 2).

- Press the Tab key again, and the focus will jump to the `txtAddress` control (TabIndex is set to 3).
- Press the Tab key again, and the focus will jump to the `txtState` control (TabIndex is set to 4).
- Press the Tab key again, and the focus will jump to the `btnClear` control (TabIndex is set to 8).

This is a very confusing tab order, and should be arranged. When a form is displayed in tab order selection mode, you establish a new tab order by simply clicking the controls with the mouse, in the order you want. To fix the disorganized tab order shown in Figure 3-30, we would perform the following:

- First, click the `txtName` control. The control's TabIndex value changes to 0.
- Next click the `txtAddress` control. The control's TabIndex value changes to 1.
- Next click the `txtCity` control. The control's TabIndex value changes to 2.
- Next click the `txtState` control. The control's TabIndex value changes to 3.
- Next click the `txtZip` control. The control's TabIndex value changes to 4.
- Next click the `btnClear` control. The control's TabIndex value changes to 5.

When you are finished, exit tab order selection mode by pressing the Esc key. Now when the application runs, the focus will shift smoothly in an order that makes sense to the user.

Here are a few last notes about the TabIndex property:

- If you do not want a control to receive the focus when the user presses the Tab key, set its **TabStop property** to *False*.
- An error will occur if you assign a negative value to the TabIndex property in code.
- A control whose Visible property is set to *False* or whose Enabled property is set to *False* cannot receive the focus.

Changing the Focus with the Focus Method

Often, you want to make sure a particular control has the focus. For example, look at the *Tab Order Demo* form shown previously in Figure 3-30. The purpose of the *Clear* button is to clear any input that the user has entered, and reset the form so that it is ready to accept a new set of input. When the *Clear* button is clicked, the TextBox controls should be cleared and the focus should return to the `txtName` control. This would make it unnecessary for the user to click the TextBox control in order to start entering another set of information.

In code, you move the focus to a control by calling the **Focus method**. The method's general syntax is:

```
ControlName.Focus()
```

where *ControlName* is the name of the control. For instance, you move the focus to the `txtName` control with this statement:

```
txtName.Focus()
```

After the statement executes, the `txtName` control will have the focus. Here is an example of how the `btnClear` control's Click event handler could be written:

```
1 Private Sub btnClear_Click(...) Handles btnClear.Click
2    ' Clear the TextBox controls.
3    txtName.Text = String.Empty
4    txtAddress.Text = String.Empty
5    txtCity.Text = String.Empty
6    txtState.Text = String.Empty
7    txtZip.Text = String.Empty
```

```
 8
 9     ' Set the focus to txtName.
10     txtName.Focus()
11 End Sub
```

The statements in lines 3 through 7 clear the contents of the TextBox controls. Then, the statement in line 10 sets the focus to the txtName control.

Assigning Keyboard Access Keys to Buttons

An **access key**, also known as a **mnemonic**, is a key that is pressed in combination with the Alt key to access a control such as a button quickly. When you assign an access key to a button, the user can trigger a Click event either by clicking the button with the mouse or by using the access key. Users who are quick with the keyboard prefer to use access keys instead of the mouse.

You assign an access key to a button through its Text property. For example, assume an application has a button whose Text property is set to *Exit*. You wish to assign the access key Alt + X to the button, so the user may trigger the button's Click event by pressing Alt + X on the keyboard. To make the assignment, place an ampersand (&) before the letter *x* in the button's Text property: E&xit. Figure 3-31 shows how the Text property appears in the *Properties* window.

Figure 3-31 Text property E&xit

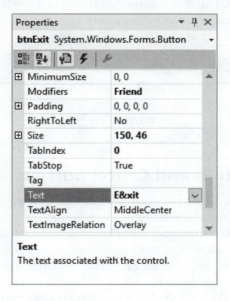

Although the ampersand is part of the Button control's Text property, it is not displayed on the button. With the ampersand in front of the letter *x*, the letter will appear underlined as shown in Figure 3-32. This indicates that the button may be clicked by pressing Alt + X on the keyboard. (You will see the underlining at design time. At run time, however, the underlining may not appear until the user presses the Alt key.)

Figure 3-32 Button control with E&xit Text property

NOTE: Access keys do not distinguish between uppercase and lowercase characters. There is no difference between [Alt]+[X] and [Alt]+[X].

Suppose we had stored the value &Exit in the button's Text property. The ampersand is in front of the letter *E*, so [Alt]+[E] becomes the access key. The button will appear as shown in Figure 3-33.

Figure 3-33 Button control with &Exit Text property

Exit

Assigning the Same Access Key to Multiple Buttons

Be careful not to assign the same access key to two or more buttons on the same form. If two or more buttons share the same access key, a Click event is triggered for the first button created when the user presses the access key.

Displaying the & Character on a Button

If you want to display an ampersand character on a button use two ampersands (&&) in the Text property. Using two ampersands causes a single ampersand to display and does not define an access key. For example, if a button's Text property is set to Save && Exit the button will appear as shown in Figure 3-34.

Figure 3-34 Button control with Save && Exit Text property

Save & Exit

Accept Buttons and Cancel Buttons

An **accept button** is a button on a form that is automatically clicked when the user presses the [Enter] key. A **cancel button** is a button on a form that is automatically clicked when the user presses the [Esc] key. Forms have two properties, AcceptButton and CancelButton, which allow you to designate an accept button and a cancel button. When you select these properties in the *Properties* window, a down-arrow button () appears, which displays a drop-down list when clicked. The list contains the names of all the buttons on the form. You select the button that you want to designate as the accept button or cancel button.

Any button that is frequently clicked should probably be selected as the accept button. This will allow keyboard users to access the button quickly and easily. *Exit* or *Cancel* buttons are likely candidates to become cancel buttons.

Selecting and Moving Multiple Controls

It is possible to select multiple controls in the *Designer* and work with them all at once. For example, you can select a group of controls and move them all to a different location on the form. You can also select a group of controls and change some of their properties.

Select multiple controls by using one of the following techniques:

- Position the cursor over an empty part of the form near the controls you wish to select. Click and drag a selection box around the controls. This is shown in Figure 3-35. When you release the mouse button, all the controls that are partially or completely enclosed in the selection box will be selected.
- Hold down the Ctrl key while clicking each control you wish to select.

After using either of these techniques, all the controls you have selected will appear with sizing handles. You may now move them, delete them, or use the *Properties* window to set many of their properties to the same value.

Figure 3-35 Selecting multiple controls by clicking and dragging the mouse

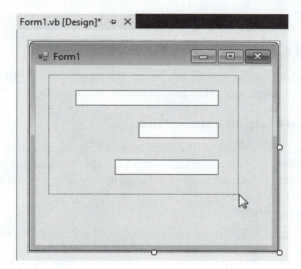

 TIP: In a group of selected controls, it is easy to deselect a control that you have accidentally selected. Simply hold down the Ctrl key and click the control you wish to deselect.

Organizing Controls with Group Boxes and Panels

A **group box** is a rectangular area with a thin border and an optional title in its upper-left corner. It is a container that can hold other controls. You can use group boxes to create a sense of visual organization on a form. In Visual Studio, you use the **GroupBox control** to create a group box with an optional title.

The GroupBox control is found in the *Toolbox*, in the *Containers* section. When you create a GroupBox control, you can set its Title property to the text that you want displayed in the GroupBox's upper-left corner. If you don't want a title displayed on the GroupBox, you can clear the contents of its Text property.

The form in Figure 3-36 shows an example of a GroupBox control. The control's Text property is set to *Personal Data*, and a group of other controls are inside the GroupBox.

Creating a Group Box and Adding Controls to It

Suppose you've just created a GroupBox control. To add another control to the GroupBox, select the GroupBox control and then double-click the desired tool in the Toolbox to place another control inside the group box.

Figure 3-36 A GroupBox containing other controls

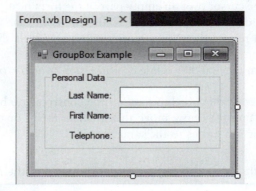

Moving an Existing Control to a Group Box

If an existing control is not inside a GroupBox, but you want to move it to the GroupBox, just use the mouse to drag the control inside the GroupBox.

Moving and Resizing a GroupBox

If a GroupBox is selected in the *Designer*, a four-headed arrow (⊕) will appear in the GroupBox's upper-left corner. Click and drag the four-headed arrow to move the Group-Box. Any controls that are inside the GroupBox will be moved with it.

Deleting a GroupBox

To delete a GroupBox, simply select it in the *Designer* and then press the ⌜Delete⌟ key. Any controls that are inside the GroupBox will be deleted as well.

Group Box Tab Order

The value of a control's TabIndex property is handled differently when the control is placed inside a GroupBox control. GroupBox controls have their own TabIndex property, and the TabIndex values of the controls inside the group box are relative to the GroupBox control's TabIndex property. For example, Figure 3-37 shows a GroupBox control displayed in tab order selection mode. As you can see, the GroupBox control's TabIndex is set to 0. The TabIndex of the controls inside the group box are displayed as 0.0, 0.1, 0.2, and so on.

Figure 3-37 GroupBox TabIndex values

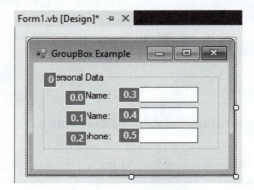

NOTE: The TabIndex properties of the controls inside the group box will not appear this way in the *Properties* window. They will appear as 0, 1, 2, and so on.

Panels

A **Panel control** is a rectangular container for other controls, like a GroupBox. Here are the primary differences between a Panel and a GroupBox:

- A Panel cannot display a title, and does not have a Text property.
- A Panel's border can be specified by its BorderStyle property. The available settings are None, FixedSingle, and Fixed3D. The property is set to None by default, which means that no border will appear. If the BorderStyle property is set to FixedSingle, the control will be outlined with a thin border. If the BorderStyle property is set to Fixed3D, the control will have a recessed 3D appearance.

Figure 3-38 shows an example of a form with a Panel. The Panel's BorderStyle property is set to Fixed3D.

Figure 3-38 A Panel containing other controls

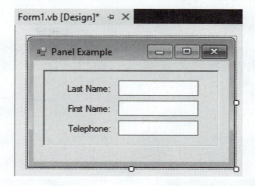

 **Checkpoint**

3.39 What is meant when it is said that a control has the focus?

3.40 What happens if you press the ⟨Enter⟩ key while a Button control has the focus?

3.41 How do you display a form in tab order selection mode? How do you exit tab order selection mode?

3.42 What happens when a control's TabStop property is set to *False*?

3.43 Write a programming statement that gives the focus to a TextBox control named `txtNumber`.

3.44 How do you assign an access key to a Button control?

3.45 How do you display an ampersand (&) character on a Button control?

3.46 What is an accept button? What is a cancel button? How do you establish these buttons on a form?

3.47 When a GroupBox control is deleted, what happens to the controls that are inside?

3.48 How are the TabIndex properties of the controls inside the group box organized?

3.49 How is a Panel control different from a GroupBox control?

3.9 The Load Event

CONCEPT: When an application's form loads into memory, an event known as the Load event (also known as the *Form Load*) takes place. You can write an event handler for the Load event, and that handler will execute just before the form is displayed.

When you run an application, the application's startup form is loaded into memory and an event known as the **Load event** takes place. The Load event takes place before the form is displayed on the screen. If you want to execute some code at this point, you can write the code in the form's Load event handler.

To create a Load event handler for a form, double-click any area of the form in the *Designer* window, where there is no other control. The *Code* window will open with a template for the form's Load event handler. This is demonstrated in Figure 3-39. Any code that you write in the Load event handler will be executed just before the form is displayed on the screen.

Figure 3-39 Creating a form's Load event handler

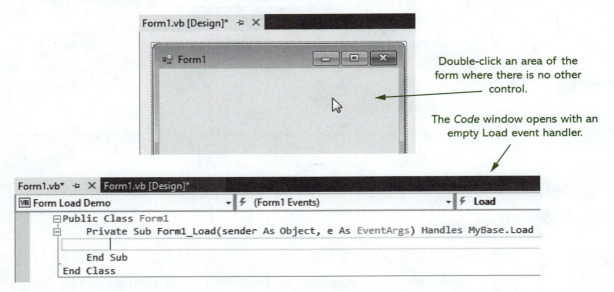

For example, in Tutorial 3-9 you will write code in a form's Load event handler to get the current date from the system, and display it on the form. Visual Basic provides the functions listed in Table 3-21, which allow you to retrieve the current date, time, or both from your computer. (We discussed functions on page 152.)

Table 3-21 Date and time functions

Function	Description
Now	Returns the current date and time from the system
TimeOfDay	Returns the current time from the system, without the date
Today	Returns the current date from the system, without the time

The following code demonstrates how to use the Now function:

```
Dim dtmSystemDate As Date
dtmSystemDate = Now
```

After the code executes, `dtmSystemDate` will contain the current date and time, as reported by the system. The `TimeOfDay` function retrieves only the current time from the system, demonstrated by the following code.

```
Dim dtmSystemTime As Date
dtmSystemTime = TimeOfDay
```

After the statement executes, `dtmSystemTime` will contain the current time, but not the current date. Instead, it will contain the date January 1 of year 1. The `Today` function retrieves only the current date from the system, demonstrated by the following statement:

```
dtmSystemDate = Today
```

After the statement executes, `dtmSystemDate` will contain the current date, but will not contain the current time. Instead, it will contain the time 00:00:00.

You can use the `ToString` method to directly format the results of a Date/Time function. For example, assume that an application has a Label control named `lblOutput`. Look at the following code:

```
lblOutput.Text = Today.ToString("D")
```

This statement calls the `Today` function to get the date, and uses the `ToString` method to format it as a long date. The result is assigned to the `lblOutput` control's Text property. Here's another example:

```
lblOutput.Text = Now.ToString("F")
```

This statement calls the `Now` function to get the current date and time, and uses the `ToString` method to format it as a full date and time. The result is assigned to the `lblOutput` control's Text property.

Tutorial 3-9:
Getting the system date in the Load event handler

In this tutorial, you will create an application that uses the form's Load event handler to get the system date, and display it in a Label control.

Step 1: Start Visual Studio and begin a new Visual Basic Windows Forms Application project named *Form Load Demo*.

Step 2: Set up the application's form as shown in Figure 3-40. The names of the controls are shown in the figure. As you place each of the controls on the form, refer to Table 3-22 for the relevant property settings.

Figure 3-40 The *Form Load Demo* application's form

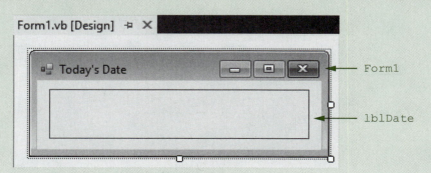

Table 3-22 Control property settings

Control Name	Control Type	Property Settings
Form1	Form	**Size:** 300, 110 (approximately) **Text:** *Today's Date*
lblDate	Label	**AutoSize:** False **BorderStyle:** FixedSingle **Font:** Microsoft Sans Serif (Style: Bold, Size: 14 point) **Size:** 260, 50 (approximately) **Text:** (The contents of the Text property have been erased.) **TextAlign:** MiddleCenter

Step 3: Double-click any area of the form that is not occupied by the Label control. The *Code* window will open, with an empty code template for the Form1_Load event handler. Complete the Form1_Load event handler by typing the code shown in bold here. (Remember, do not write the line numbers! They are shown for reference only, to help us discuss specific lines of code.)

```
1 Private Sub Form1_Load(...) Handles MyBase.Load
2    ' Get the current date from the system.
3    Dim dtmSystemDate = Today
4
5    ' Display the date.
6    lblDate.Text = dtmSystemDate.ToString("d")
7 End Sub
```

The statement in line 3 declars a Date variable named dtmSystemDate. The variable is initialized with the value that is given by the Today function, which is the system date. The statement in line 6 converts the variable's value to a string (formatted as a short date, with the "d" formatting string). The result is assigned to the lblDate control's Text property.

Step 4: Save the project. Then, press the F5 key on the keyboard, or click the *Start Debugging* button (▶) on the toolbar to compile and run the application. Figure 3-41 shows an example of how the application's form should appear.

Figure 3-41 The *Form Load Demo* application

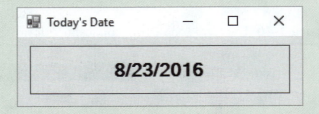

 **Checkpoint**

3.50 What event happens just before a form is displayed on the screen?

3.51 How do you create a Load event handler for a form?

3.52 What Visual Basic function would you use to get the current date and time from the system?

3.53 What Visual Basic function would you use to get the current time from the system, without the date?

3.54 What Visual Basic function would you use to get the current date from the system, without the time?

3.10 Focus on Program Design and Problem Solving: Building the *Room Charge Calculator* Application

A guest staying at the Highlander Hotel may incur the following types of charges:

- Room charges, based on a per-night rate
- Room service charges
- Telephone charges
- Miscellaneous charges

The manager of the Highlander Hotel has asked you to create an application that calculates the guest's total charges. Figure 3-42 shows how the application's form should appear when the application is running.

Figure 3-42 Sample output from the *Room Charge Calculator* application

Pseudocode for the `btnCalculate_Click` **Procedure**

Many programmers like to use pseudocode to express the steps in an application in an informal manner. There are no rigid rules for writing pseudocode, so you can write it in a conversational way, or you can keep it very brief. Fortunately, you do not have to follow any Visual Basic syntax rules! Here is our first attempt at pseudocode for the Calculate_Click procedure.

```
try:
    declare variables
    clear the error message label
    calculate the basic room charge
    calculate the additional charges
    calculate the subtotal
    calculate the tax
    calculate the grand total
    display all calculated values
catch input errors:
    display a reminder that input must be numeric
```

This code helps us to organize the sequence of actions clearly in our mind before beginning to write code. More details need to be added to this pseudocode. First, let's show how the basic room charge is calculated:

```
Basic room charge is equal to:
    number of nights * nightly room charge
```

Next, we show how to calculate the additional charges:

```
Additional charges are equal to:
    room service + telephone + miscellaneous
```

Next, we calculate the subtotal:

```
Subtotal is equal to:
    basic room charge + additional charges
```

The grand total is calculated next:

```
Grand total is equal to:
    subtotal * tax rate
```

Finally, the procedure displays all calculated values:

```
Display room charges, additional charges, subtotal,
    tax, and grand total
```

 TIP: Once you start typing your program into the computer, your mind will be distracted by all the Visual Basic language rules, controls, and other Visual Studio commands. That is why it is important to have written pseudocode first, to organize your program's logic, before you start typing. Some people prefer to use flowcharts to design their program logic, which we will do next.

Creating the Visual Interface

When creating a visual interface for any application, you should take into account the following ideas:

All user interfaces should be designed to help the user, not the programmer. The purpose of the application should be immediately clear by looking at the interface. The user has a certain goal in mind when using your application, and he or she needs to know whether this application suits this goal.

The spacing, alignment, and use of color should be visually appealing to the majority of people who are using your application. Of course, people vary in their tastes quite a bit, so what might be appealing to a 15-year-old playing a video game might not go over as well for an adult in a business office. People who look at screens all day usually like to see colors that do not tire their eyes.

Assuming that users need to enter some data, their attention should be immediately drawn to the form's input fields. They should not have to spend time trying to figure out what to do. The input fields should have a contrasting background color (in our case, white) that makes them look different from all other controls on the form.

After users have entered the data, consider how they will know what to do next. Fortunately, users are accustomed to looking for buttons. In our current application, we want users to click the *Calculate Charges* button, so we place it on the left side of the bottom row. (In Western European countries, users generally read from left to right.)

Output fields (in our case the Total Charges) should be grouped together and given a background color suggesting that the user cannot type into these fields. In our current design, the output Label controls have a gray background.

The rightmost button on the bottom row is labeled *Exit*, which is fairly common in many user interfaces.

Figure 3-43 shows how the controls are arranged on the form with names. You can use this diagram when designing the form and assigning values to the Name property of each control. Table 3-24, located at the end of this section, can also be used as a reference.

Figure 3-43 Named controls

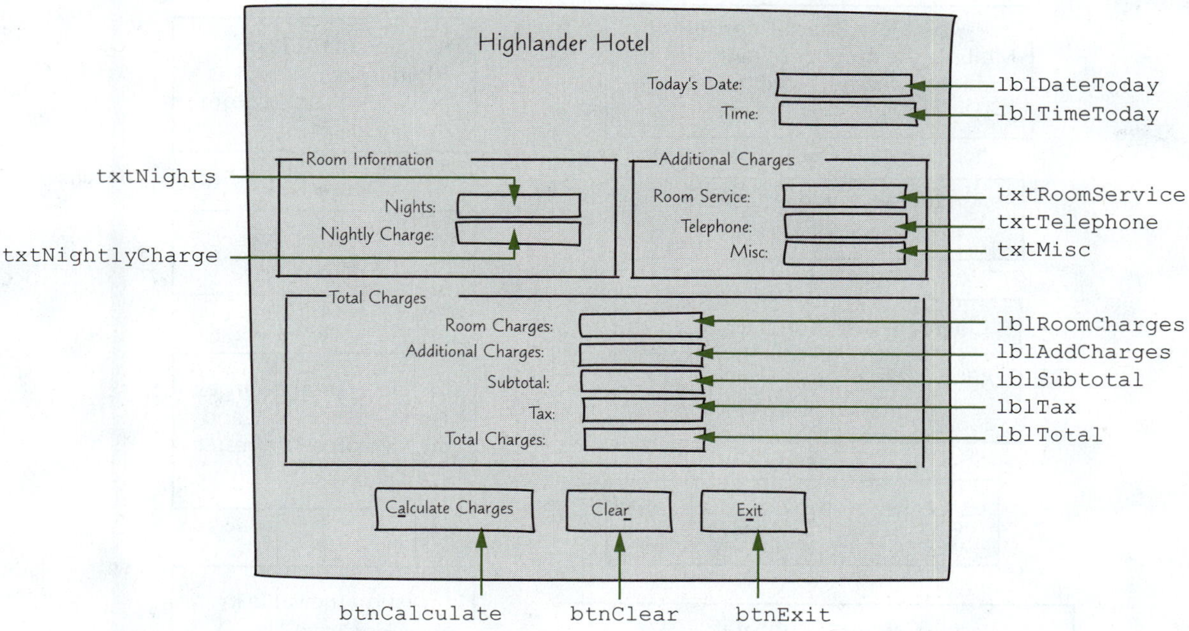

Table 3-23 lists and describes the event handlers needed for this application. Notice that a Load event handler is needed for the form.

Table 3-23 Event handlers in the *Room Charge Calculator* application

Method	Description
btnCalculate_Click	Calculates the room charges, additional charges, subtotal (room charges plus additional charges), 8% tax, and the total charges. These values are assigned to the Text properties of the appropriate labels.
btnClear_Click	Clears the TextBox controls, and the labels used to display summary charge information. This procedure also resets the values displayed in the lblDateToday and lblTimeToday labels.
btnExit_Click	Ends the application
Form1_Load	Initializes the lblDateToday and lblTimeToday labels with the current system date and time

Figure 3-44 shows the flowchart for the btnCalculate_Click procedure. The procedure uses the following Decimal variables:

    decRoomCharges
    decAddCharges
    decSubtotal
    decTax
    decTotal

Figure 3-44 Flowchart for btnCalculate_Click

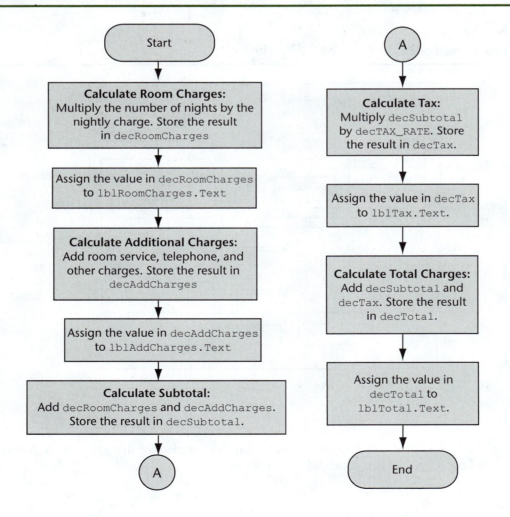

The procedure also uses a named constant, decTAX_RATE, to hold the tax rate.

The flowchart in Figure 3-44 uses a new symbol: Ⓐ

This is called the **connector symbol** and is used when a flowchart is broken into two or more smaller flowcharts. This is necessary when a flowchart does not fit on a single page or must be divided into sections. A connector symbol, which is a small circle with a letter or number inside it, allows you to connect two flowcharts. In the flowchart shown in Figure 3-44, the Ⓐ connector indicates that the second flowchart segment begins where the first flowchart segment ends.

The flowcharts for the btnClear_Click, btnExit_Click, and Form1_Load procedures are shown in Figures 3-45, 3-46, and 3-47, respectively.

Recall that the form's Load procedure executes each time the form loads into memory. Tutorial 3-10 shows you how to create the *Room Charge Calculator* application.

Figure 3-45 Flowchart for btnClear_Click

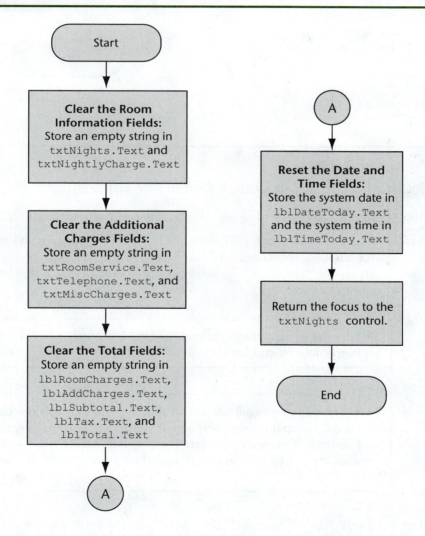

Figure 3-46 Flowchart for `btnExit_Click`

Figure 3-47 Flowchart for Form1_Load procedure

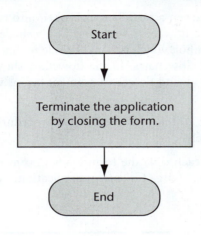

Tutorial 3-10:
Beginning the *Room Charge Calculator* application

Step 1:   Create a new Windows Forms Application project named *Room Charge Calculator*.

Step 2:   Figure 3-43 (on page 197) showed a sketch of the application's form, including the names of the named controls. Refer to this figure as you set up the form and create the controls. Once you have completed the form, it should appear as shown in Figure 3-48.

> **TIP:** Most of the controls are contained inside group boxes. Refer to Section 3.8 for instructions on creating controls inside a group box.

> **TIP:** The TextBox controls are all the same size, and all the Label controls that display output are the same size. If you are creating many similar instances of a control, it is easier to create the first one, set its size and properties as needed, copy it to the clipboard, and then paste it onto the form to create another one.

Step 3:   Table 3-24 (on page 205) lists the relevant property settings of all the controls on the form. Refer to this table and make the necessary property settings.

Figure 3-48 The *Room Charge Calculator* form

Step 4: Now you will write the application's event handlers, beginning with the form's `Load event handler`. Double-click any area of the form not occupied by another control. The *Code* window should open with a code template for the `Form1_Load` procedure. Complete the procedure by typing the following code shown in bold:

```
Private Sub Form1_Load(...) Handles MyBase.Load
  ' Get today's date from the system and display it.
  lblDateToday.Text = Now.ToString("D")

  ' Get the current time from the system and display it.
  lblTimeToday.Text = Now.ToString("T")
End Sub
```

Step 5: Double-click the *Calculate Charges* button. The *Code* window should open with a code template for the `btnCalculate_Click` procedure. Complete the procedure by typing the bold code shown in the following. (Do not type the line numbers. They are shown for reference only.)

```
1  Private Sub btnCalculate_Click(...) Handles btnCalculate.Click
2    ' Declare variables for the calculations.
3    Dim decRoomCharges As Decimal      ' Room charges total
4    Dim decAddCharges As Decimal       ' Additional charges
5    Dim decSubtotal As Decimal         ' Subtotal
```

```
6      Dim decTax As Decimal                    ' Tax
7      Dim decTotal As Decimal                  ' Total of all charges
8      Const decTAX_RATE As Decimal = 0.08D  ' Tax rate
9
10     Try
11       ' Calculate and display the room charges.
12       decRoomCharges = CDec(txtNights.Text) *
13           CDec(txtNightlyCharge.Text)
14       lblRoomCharges.Text = decRoomCharges.ToString("c")
15
16       ' Calculate and display the additional charges.
17       decAddCharges = CDec(txtRoomService.Text) +
18           CDec(txtTelephone.Text) +
19           CDec(txtMisc.Text)
20       lblAddCharges.Text = decAddCharges.ToString("c")
21
22       ' Calculate and display the subtotal.
23       decSubtotal = decRoomCharges + decAddCharges
24       lblSubtotal.Text = decSubtotal.ToString("c")
25
26       ' Calculate and display the tax.
27       decTax = decSubtotal * decTAX_RATE
28       lblTax.Text = decTax.ToString("c")
29
30       ' Calculate and display the total charges.
31       decTotal = decSubtotal + decTax
32       lblTotal.Text = decTotal.ToString("c")
33     Catch
34       ' Error message
35       MessageBox.Show("All input must be valid numeric values.")
36     End Try
37   End Sub
```

Lines 3 through 8 declare the variables used by this method. Lines 12–14 calculate and display the basic room charges. Lines 17–20 calculate the additional charges, such as telephone and room service. Lines 23–24 add together the room charges and additional charges, displaying a subtotal. Lines 27–28 calculate and display the taxes, and lines 31–32 calculate and display the final totals. If the user forgets to input a value or enters a nonnumeric value, line 35 will display an error message on the status strip at the bottom of the form, as shown in Figure 3-49. In order to keep our program code as short as possible we display a single error message relating to all the input fields. A useful improvement would be to create a separate Try-Catch statement for each input field and display a specific error message for each input field. This would provide more effective feedback to the user. This improvement will be suggested as a Programming Challenge at the end of the chapter.

Exception handling was used in this procedure to check for invalid input. If the user enters an invalid value in any of the text boxes, the message shown in Figure 3-49 will appear, and then the user will be able to reenter the input. Imagine how much better this is than letting the program halt unexpectedly.

Figure 3-49 Message displayed by the exception handler

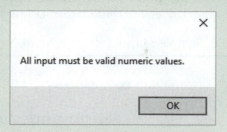

Step 6: Open the *Design* window and double-click the *Clear* button. The *Code* window should open with a code template for the btnClear_Click procedure. Complete the procedure by typing the following code shown in bold.

```
Private Sub btnClear_Click(...) Handles btnClear.Click
    ' Clear the room info fields.
    txtNights.Clear()
    txtNightlyCharge.Clear()

    ' Clear the additional charges fields.
    txtRoomService.Clear()
    txtTelephone.Clear()
    txtMisc.Clear()

    ' Clear the decTotal fields.
    lblRoomCharges.Text = String.Empty
    lblAddCharges.Text = String.Empty
    lblSubtotal.Text = String.Empty
    lblTax.Text = String.Empty
    lblTotal.Text = String.Empty

    ' Get today's date from the operating system and display it.
    lblDateToday.Text = Now.ToString("D")

    ' Get the current time from the operating system and display it.
    lblTimeToday.Text = Now.ToString("T")

    ' Reset the focus to the first field.
    txtNights.Focus()
End Sub
```

Step 7: Open the *Design* window and double-click the *Exit* button. The *Code* window should open with a code template for the btnExit_Click procedure. Complete the procedure by typing the following code shown in bold.

```
Private Sub btnExit_Click(...) Handles btnExit.Click
    ' Close the form.
    Me.Close()
End Sub
```

Step 8: Save the project.

Step 9:   Run the application. If there are errors, compare your code with that shown, and correct them. Once the application runs, enter test values, as shown in Figure 3-50, for the charges and confirm that it displays the correct output.

Figure 3-50 Sample output from the *Room Charge Calculator* application

Table 3-24 lists each control, along with any relevant property values.

Table 3-24 Named controls in *Room Charge Calculator* form

Control Type	Control Name	Property	Property Value
Label	(Default)	Text: Font:	*Highlander Hotel* *MS sans serif, bold, 18 point*
Label	(Default)	Text:	*Today's Date:*
Label	lblDateToday	Text: AutoSize: Font.Bold:	(Initially cleared) *False* *True*
Label	(Default)	Text:	*Time:*
Label	lblTimeToday	Text: AutoSize: Font.Bold:	(Initially cleared) *False* *True*

(continued)

Control Type	Control Name	Property	Property Value
Group box	(Default)	Text:	*Room Information*
Label	(Default)	Text:	*Nights:*
TextBox	txtNights	Text:	(Initially cleared)
Label	(Default)	Text:	*Nightly Charge:*
TextBox	txtNightlyCharge	Text:	(Initially cleared)
Group box	(Default)	Text:	*Additional Charges*
Label	(Default)	Text:	*Room Service:*
TextBox	txtRoomService	Text:	(Initially cleared)
Label	(Default)	Text:	*Telephone:*
TextBox	txtTelephone	Text:	(Initially cleared)
Label	(Default)	Text:	*Misc:*
TextBox	txtMisc	Text:	(Initially cleared)
Group box	(Default)	Text:	*Total Charges*
Label	(Default)	Text:	*Room Charges:*
Label	lblRoomCharges	Text:	(Initially cleared)
		AutoSize:	*False*
		BorderStyle:	*Fixed3D*
Label	(Default)	Text:	*Additional Charges:*
Label	lblAddCharges	Text:	(Initially cleared)
		AutoSize:	*False*
		BorderStyle:	*Fixed3D*
Label	(Default)	Text:	*Subtotal:*
Label	lblSubtotal	Text:	(Initially cleared)
		AutoSize:	*False*
		BorderStyle:	*Fixed3D*
Label	(Default)	Text:	*Tax:*
Label	lblTax	Text:	(Initially cleared)
		AutoSize:	*False*
		BorderStyle:	*Fixed3D*
Label	(Default)	Text:	*Total Charges:*
Label	lblTotal	Text:	(Initially cleared)
		AutoSize:	*False*
		BorderStyle:	*Fixed3D*
Button	btnCalculate	Text:	*C&alculate Charges*
Button	btnClear	Text:	*Clea&r*
Button	btnExit	Text:	*E&xit*

Changing Colors with Code (Optional Topic)

Chapter 2 showed how to change the foreground and background colors of a control's text by setting the ForeColor and BackColor properties in the *Properties* window. In addition to using the *Properties* window, you can also store values in these properties with code. Visual Basic provides numerous values that represent colors and can be assigned to the ForeColor and BackColor properties in code. The following are a few of the values:

```
Color.Black
Color.Blue
Color.Cyan
Color.Green
Color.Magenta
Color.Red
Color.White
Color.Yellow
```

For example, assume an application has a Label control named lblMessage. The following code sets the label's background color to black and foreground color to yellow:

```
lblMessage.BackColor = Color.Black
lblMessage.ForeColor = Color.Yellow
```

Visual Basic also provides values that represent default colors on your system. For example, the value SystemColors.Control represents the default control background color and SystemColors.ControlText represents the default control text color. The following statements set the lblMessage control's background and foreground to the default colors.

```
lblMessage.BackColor = SystemColors.Control
lblMessage.ForeColor = SystemColors.ControlText
```

In Tutorial 3-11, you will modify the *Room Charge Calculator* application so that the total charges are displayed in white characters on a blue background. This will make the total charges stand out visually from the rest of the information on the form.

Tutorial 3-11:
Changing a label's colors

In this tutorial, you will modify two of the *Room Charge Calculator* application's event handlers: btnCalculate_Click and btnClear_Click. In the btnCalculate_Click procedure, you will add code that changes the lblTotal control's color settings just after the total charges are displayed. In the btnClear_Click procedure, you will add code that reverts lblTotal's colors back to their normal state.

Step 1: With the *Room Charge Calculator* project open, open the *Code* window and scroll to the btnCalculate_Click event handler.

Step 2: The btnCalculate_Click procedure is shown as follows. Add the three lines shown in bold:

```
Private Sub btnCalculate_Click(...) Handles btnCalculate.Click
    ' Declare variables for the calculations.
    Dim decRoomCharges As Decimal          ' Room charges total
    Dim decAddCharges As Decimal           ' Additional charges
    Dim decSubtotal As Decimal             ' Subtotal
    Dim decTax As Decimal                  ' Tax
    Dim decTotal As Decimal                ' Total of all charges
    Const decTAX_RATE As Decimal = 0.08D   ' Tax rate

    Try
        ' Calculate and display the room charges.
        decRoomCharges = CDec(txtNights.Text) *
                    CDec(txtNightlyCharge.Text)
        lblRoomCharges.Text = decRoomCharges.ToString("c")

        ' Calculate and display the additional charges.
        decAddCharges = CDec(txtRoomService.Text) +
                    CDec(txtTelephone.Text) +
                    CDec(txtMisc.Text)
        lblAddCharges.Text = decAddCharges.ToString("c")

        ' Calculate and display the subtotal.
        decSubtotal = decRoomCharges + decAddCharges
        lblSubtotal.Text = decSubtotal.ToString("c")

        ' Calculate and display the tax.
        decTax = decSubtotal * decTAX_RATE
        lblTax.Text = decTax.ToString("c")

        ' Calculate and display the total charges.
        decTotal = decSubtotal + decTax
        lblTotal.Text = decTotal.ToString("c")

        ' Change the colors for the total charges.
        lblTotal.BackColor = Color.Blue
        lblTotal.ForeColor = Color.White
    Catch
        ' Error message
        MessageBox.Show("All input must be valid numeric values.")
    End Try
End Sub
```

Step 3: The `btnClear_Click` event handler is shown as follows. Add the three lines shown in bold:

```
Private Sub btnClear_Click(...) Handles btnClear.Click
    ' Clear the room info fields.
    txtNights.Clear()
    txtNightlyCharge.Clear()

    ' Clear the additional charges fields.
    txtRoomService.Clear()
    txtTelephone.Clear()
    txtMisc.Clear()
```

```
                    ' Clear the decTotal fields.
                    lblRoomCharges.Text = String.Empty
                    lblAddCharges.Text = String.Empty
                    lblSubtotal.Text = String.Empty
                    lblTax.Text = String.Empty
                    lblTotal.Text = String.Empty

                    ' Get today's date from the system and display it.
                    lblDateToday.Text = Now.ToString("D")

                    ' Get the current time from the system and display it.
                    lblTimeToday.Text = Now.ToString("T")

                    ' Reset the lblTotal control's colors.
                    lblTotal.BackColor = SystemColors.Control
                    lblTotal.ForeColor = SystemColors.ControlText

                    ' Reset the focus to the first field.
                    txtNights.Focus()
                End Sub
```

Step 4: Save the project.

Step 5: Run and test the application. When you click the *Calculate Charges* button, the value displayed in the lblTotal label should appear in white text on a blue background. When you click the *Clear* button, the color of the lblTotal label should return to normal.

3.11 More About Debugging: Locating Logic Errors

CONCEPT: Visual Studio allows you to pause a program and then execute statements one at a time. After each statement executes, you may examine variable contents and property values.

A **logic error** is a mistake that does not prevent an application from running, but causes the application to produce incorrect results. Mathematical mistakes, assigning a value to the wrong variable, or assigning the wrong value to a variable are examples of logic errors. Logic errors can be difficult to find. Finding and fixing a logic error usually requires a bit of detective work on the part of the programmer. Fortunately, Visual Studio provides you with debugging tools that make locating logic errors easier.

Visual Studio allows you to set breakpoints in your program code. A **breakpoint** is a line you select in your source code. When the application is running and it reaches a breakpoint, the application pauses and enters break mode. While the application is paused, you may examine variable contents and the values stored in certain control properties.

Visual Studio allows you to **single-step** through an application's code once its execution has been paused by a breakpoint. This means that the application's statements execute one at a time, under your control. After each statement executes, you can examine variable and property values. This process allows you to identify the line or lines of code causing the error. In Tutorial 3-12, you single-step through an application's code.

Tutorial 3-12:
Single-stepping through an application's code at runtime

In this tutorial, you will open the *Average Race Times* application, and test it for logic errors. The application is simple: it lets the user enter the finishing times for three runners, and then click a button to calculate their average time. To determine whether the application correctly calculates an average, you will perform a simple test. You will enter the value 25 for each runner, and then click the button to calculate the average. The result should also be 25. If the application produces any other value, then you know that a logic error exists somewhere in the application's code.

Step 1: Open the *Average Race Times* project from the student sample programs folder named *Chap3\Average Race Times*.

Step 2: Run the application. The application's form appears, as shown in Figure 3-51.

Figure 3-51 *Average Race Times* form

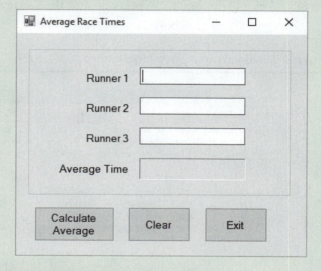

Step 3: This application allows you to enter the finishing times of three runners in a race and then see their average time. Enter **25** as the time for all three runners.

Step 4: Click the *Calculate Average* button. The application displays the incorrect value 58.3 as the average time. (The correct value should be 25.)

Step 5: Click the *Exit* button to stop the application.

Step 6: Open the *Code* window (click *View* on the menu bar, and then select *Code*) and locate the following line of code, which appears in the btnCalculate_Click event handler:

    dblRunner1 = CDbl(txtRunner1.Text)

This line of code is where we want to pause the execution of the application. We must make this line a breakpoint.

Step 7: Click the mouse in the left margin of the *Code* window, next to the line of code, as shown in Figure 3-52.

Figure 3-52 Click the mouse in the left margin of the *Code* window

Click the mouse pointer here. ⟶

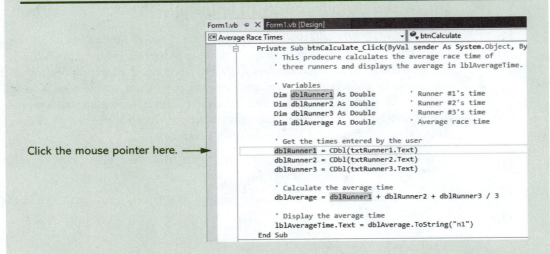

Step 8: Notice that a red dot appears next to the line in the left margin, and the line of code becomes highlighted. This is shown in Figure 3-53.

Figure 3-53 Breakpoint code highlighted

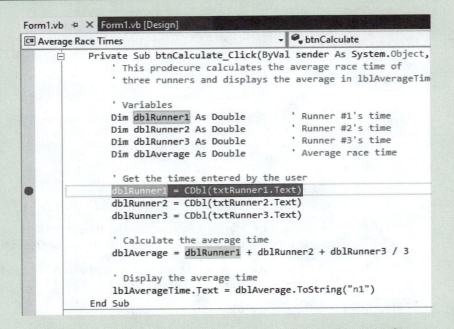

The dot indicates that a breakpoint has been set on this line. Another way to set a breakpoint is to move the text cursor to the line you wish to set as a breakpoint, and then press F9.

Step 9: Now that you have set the breakpoint, run the application. When the form appears, enter **25** as the time for each runner.

Step 10: Click the *Calculate Average* button. When program execution reaches the breakpoint, it goes into break mode and the *Code* window reappears. The breakpoint line is shown with yellow highlighting and a small yellow arrow appears in the left margin, as shown in Figure 3-54.

Figure 3-54 Breakpoint during break mode

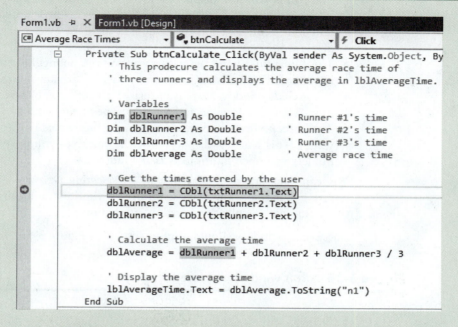

The yellow highlighting and small arrow indicate the application's current execution point. The **execution point** is the next line of code that will execute. (The line has not yet executed.)

 NOTE: If the highlighting and arrow appear in a color other than yellow, the color options on your system may have been changed.

Step 11: To examine the contents of a variable or control property, hover the cursor over the variable or the property's name in the *Code* window. A small box will appear showing the variable or property's contents. For example, Figure 3-55 shows the result of hovering the mouse pointer over the expression txtRunner1.Text in the highlighted line. The box indicates that the property is currently set to "25".

Figure 3-55 txtRunner1.Text property contents revealed

```
        ' Get the times entered by the user
        dblRunner1 = CDbl(txtRunner1.Text)
        dblRunner2 = CDbl(txtRunner2.Text     txtRunner1.Text  Q  ▾ "25"  ◻
        dblRunner3 = CDbl(txtRunner3.Text)

        ' Calculate the average time
        dblAverage = dblRunner1 + dblRunner2 + dblRunner3 / 3
```

Step 12: Now hover the mouse pointer over the variable name dblRunner1. A box appears indicating that the variable is set to 0. Because the highlighted statement has not yet executed, no value has been assigned to this variable.

Step 13: You may also examine the contents of variables with the *Autos*, *Locals*, and *Watch* windows.

A description of each window follows:

- The *Autos* **window** displays a list of the variables appearing in the current statement, the three statements before, and the three statements after the current statement. The current value and the data type of each variable are also displayed.
- The *Immediate* **window** allows you to type debugging commands using the keyboard. This window is generally used by advanced programmers.
- The *Locals* **window** displays a list of all the variables in the current procedure. The current value and the data type of each variable are also displayed.
- The *Watch* **window** allows you to add the names of variables you want to watch. This window displays only the variables you have added. Visual Studio lets you open multiple *Watch* windows.

You can open any of these windows by selecting *Debug* on the menu bar, then selecting *Windows*, and then selecting the window that you want to open. Use this technique to open the *Locals* window now.

The *Locals* window should appear, similar to Figure 3-56.

Figure 3-56 *Locals* window displayed

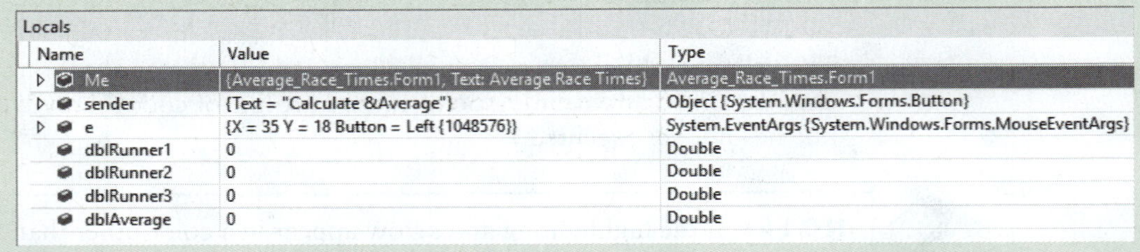

Locals		
Name	Value	Type
▷ ⚙ Me	{Average_Race_Times.Form1, Text: Average Race Times}	Average_Race_Times.Form1
▷ ⚙ sender	{Text = "Calculate &Average"}	Object {System.Windows.Forms.Button}
▷ ⚙ e	{X = 35 Y = 18 Button = Left {1048576}}	System.EventArgs {System.Windows.Forms.MouseEventArgs}
⚙ dblRunner1	0	Double
⚙ dblRunner2	0	Double
⚙ dblRunner3	0	Double
⚙ dblAverage	0	Double

Step 14: Now you are ready to single-step through each statement in the event handler. To do this, use the **Step Into command**. (The *Step Over* command, which is similar to *Step Into*, is covered in Chapter 6.) You activate the *Step Into* command by one of the following methods:
- Press the F8 key.
- Select *Debug* from the menu bar, and then select *Step Into* from the *Debug* menu.

When you activate the *Step Into* command, the highlighted statement is executed. Press the F8 key now. Look at the *Watch* window and notice that the dblRunner1 variable is now set to 25. Also notice that the next line of code is now highlighted.

Step 15: Press the F8 key two more times. The variables dblRunner1, dblRunner2, and dblRunner3 should display values of 25 in the *Locals* window.

Step 16: The following statement, which is supposed to calculate the average of the three scores, is now highlighted:

```
dblAverage = dblRunner1 + dblRunner2 + dblRunner3 / 3
```

After this statement executes, the average of the three numbers should display next to dblAverage. Press F8 to execute the statement.

Step 17: Notice that the *Locals* window now reports that db1Average holds the value 58.333333333333336. This is not the correct value, so there must be a problem with the math statement that just executed. Can you find it? The math statement does not calculate the correct value because the division operation takes place before any of the addition operations. You must correct the statement by inserting a set of parentheses.

From the menu, select *Debug*, and then click *Stop Debugging* to halt the application. In the *Code* window, insert a set of parentheses into the math statement so it appears as follows:

```
db1Average = (db1Runner1 + db1Runner2 + db1Runner3) / 3
```

Step 18: Next, you will clear the breakpoint so the application will not pause again when it reaches that line of code. To clear the breakpoint, use one of the following methods:
- Click the mouse on the breakpoint dot in the left margin of the *Code* window.
- Press Ctrl+Shift+F9.
- Select *Debug* from the menu bar, and then select *Delete All Breakpoints* from the *Debug* menu.

Step 19: Run the application again. Enter **25** as each runner's time, and then click the *Calculate Average* button. This time the correct average, 25, is displayed.

Step 20: Click the *Exit* button to stop the application.

If You Want to Know More: Debugging Commands in the Toolbar

Visual Studio provides a toolbar for debugging commands, shown in Figure 3-57.

Figure 3-57 *Debug* toolbar commands

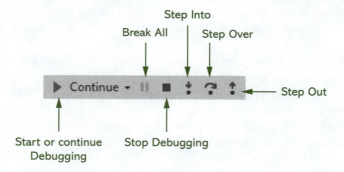

Checkpoint

3.55 What is the difference between a syntax error and a logic error?

3.56 What is a breakpoint?

3.57 What is the purpose of single-stepping through an application?

Summary

3.1 Gathering Text Input

- Words and characters typed into a TextBox control are stored in the control's Text property. The standard prefix for TextBox control names is txt.
- The & operator is used to perform string concatenation.

3.2 Variables and Data Types

- The assignment operator (=) is used to store a value in a variable, just as with a control property. A variable's data type determines the type of information that the variable can hold.
- Rules for naming variables are enforced by the Visual Basic compiler. Naming conventions, on the other hand, are not rigid—they are based on a standard style of programming.
- When a variable is first created in memory, Visual Basic assigns it an initial value, which depends on its data type. You may also initialize a variable, which means that you specify the variable's starting value.
- Variables of the Date (DateTime) data type can hold a date and time. You may store values in a Date variable with date literals, strings, or user input.
- Each Visual Basic data type has a method named ToString that returns a string representation of the variable calling the method.

3.3 Performing Calculations

- A unary operator has only one operand. An example is the negation operator (minus sign).
- A binary operator has two operands. An example is the addition operator (plus sign).
- The \ symbol identifies the integer division operator.
- The * symbol identifies the multiplication operator.
- The ^ symbol identifies the exponentiation operator.
- The MOD operator returns the remainder after performing integer division.
- When two operators share an operand, the operator with the highest precedence executes first. Parts of a mathematical expression may be grouped with parentheses to force some operations to be performed before others.
- A combined assignment operator combines the assignment operator with another operator.
- A variable's scope determines where a variable is visible and where it can be accessed by programming statements.
- A variable declared inside a procedure is called a local variable. This type of variable is only visible from its declaring statement to the end of the same procedure. If a variable is declared inside a class, but outside of any procedure, it is called a class-level variable. If a variable is declared outside of any class or procedure, it is called a global variable.

3.4 Mixing Different Data Types

- Implicit type conversion occurs when you assign a value of one data type to a variable of another data type. Visual Basic attempts to convert the value being assigned to the data type of the destination variable.
- A narrowing conversion occurs when a larger type is assigned to a smaller type. An example is when a real number is assigned to an integer type variable.
- A widening conversion occurs when data of a smaller type is assigned to a variable of a larger type. An example is when assigning any type of integer to a Double.

- The *Option Strict* statement determines whether certain implicit conversions are legal. When *Option Strict* is *On*, only widening conversions are permitted. When *Option Strict* is *Off*, both narrowing and widening conversions are permitted.
- A type conversion or type mismatch error is generated when an automatic conversion is not possible.
- An explicit type conversion is performed by one of Visual Basic's conversion functions. The conversion functions discussed in this chapter are `CDate` (convert to date), `CDbl` (convert to Double), `CDec` (convert to Decimal), `CInt` (convert to Integer), and `CStr` (convert to String).
- The `CInt` function performs a special type of rounding called banker's rounding.
- Visual Basic provides several type conversion functions, such as `CInt` and `CDbl`, which convert expressions to other data types.

3.5 Formatting Numbers and Dates

- Ordinarily, numeric values should be formatted when they are displayed. Formatting gives your programs a more professional appearance.
- The `ToString` method converts the contents of a variable into a string.
- You can pass a format string as an input argument to the `ToString` method. The format string can be used to configure the way a number or date is displayed.
- Number format (`n` or `N`) displays numeric values with thousands separators and a decimal point.
- Fixed-point format (`f` or `F`) displays numeric values with no thousands separator and a decimal point.
- Exponential format (`e` or `E`) displays numeric values in scientific notation. The number is normalized with a single digit to the left of the decimal point.
- Currency format (`c` or `C`) displays a leading currency symbol (such as $), digits, thousands separators, and a decimal point.
- Percent format (`p` or `P`) causes the number to be multiplied by 100 and displayed with a trailing space and % sign.
- You can use the `ToString` method to format dates and times. Several standard formats were shown in this chapter: short date, long date, short time, long time, and full date and time.

3.6 Class-Level Variables

- Class-level variables are declared inside a class declaration (such as a form's class), but not inside of any procedure.
- Class-level variables are accessible to all of the procedures in a class.

3.7 Exception Handling

- Exception handling is a structured mechanism for handling errors in Visual Basic programs.
- Exception handling begins with the `Try` keyword, followed by one or more catch blocks, followed by `End Try`.
- Some types of errors are preventable by the programmer, such as dividing by zero. Other errors may be caused by user input, which is beyond the control of the programmer.
- When a program throws an exception, it generates a runtime error. An unhandled exception causes a program to terminate and display an error message.
- You can write exception handlers that catch exceptions and find ways for the program to recover. Your exception handler can also display a message to the user.
- Exception handlers can handle multiple types of exceptions by specifically identifying different types of exceptions with different catch blocks.

3.8 More GUI Details

- The control that has the focus receives the user's keyboard input or mouse clicks.
- The focus is moved by calling the Focus method.
- The order in which controls receive the focus when the [Tab] key is pressed at runtime is called the tab order. When you place controls on a form, the tab order will be the same sequence in which you created the controls. You can modify the tab order by changing a control's TabIndex property.
- Tab order selection mode allows you to easily view the TabIndex property values of all the controls on a form.
- If you do not want a control to receive the focus when the user presses the [Tab] key, set its TabStop property to *False*.
- You assign an access key to a button by placing an ampersand (&) in its Text property. The letter that immediately follows the ampersand becomes the access key. That letter appears underlined on the button.
- Forms have two properties named AcceptButton and CancelButton. AcceptButton refers to the control that will receive a Click event when the user presses the [Enter] key. CancelButton refers to the control that will receive a Click event when the user presses the [Esc] key.
- A GroupBox control, which is used as a container for other controls, appears as a rectangular border with an optional title. You can create the GroupBox first and then create other controls inside it. Alternatively, you can use the mouse to drag existing controls inside the GroupBox.
- A Panel control is a container, like a GroupBox. A Panel, however, does not display a title, and it has a BorderStyle property that allows you to customize the appearance of the control's border.

3.9 The Load Event

- When an application's form loads into memory, an event known as the Load event takes place.
- You can write an event handler for the Load event, and that handler will execute just before the form is displayed.
- The Now function retrieves the current date and time from the computer system. The TimeOfDay function retrieves the current time. The Today function retrieves the current date.

3.10 Focus on Program Design and Problem Solving: Building the *Room Charge Calculator* Application

- The *Room Charge Calculator* application calculates charges for guests at an imaginary hotel. It combines many of the techniques introduced in this chapter, such as type conversion functions, formatting numbers, and formatting dates.
- Visual Basic provides numerous values that represent colors. These values may be used in code to change a control's foreground and background colors.

3.11 More About Debugging: Locating Logic Errors

- A logic error is a programming mistake that does not prevent an application from compiling, but causes the application to produce incorrect results.
- A runtime error occurs during a program's execution—it halts the program unexpectedly.
- A breakpoint is a line of code that causes a running application to pause execution and enter break mode. While the application is paused, you may perform debugging operations such as examining variable contents and the values stored in control properties.
- Single-stepping is the debugging technique of executing an application's programming statements one at a time. After each statement executes, you can examine variable and property contents.

Key Terms

accept button
access key
argument
Autos window
binary operator
breakpoint
camel case
cancel button
catch block
catch clause
code outlining
combined assignment operators
compound operators
connector symbol
exception
exception handler
exception object
execution point
focus
Focus method
function
GroupBox control
Immediate window
implicit type conversion
initialization
Load event
local variable
Locals window
logic error

mathematical expression
mnemonic
named constant
narrowing conversion
Option Strict
Panel control
precedence
returning a value
scope (of a variable)
single-step
Step Into command
string concatenation
tab order
tab order selection mode
TabIndex property
TabStop property
text box
TextBox control
ToString method
truncation
try block
Try-Catch statement
type conversion error
type mismatch error
unary operator
variable
variable declaration
Watch window
widening conversion

VideoNote

Building a *Kayak Rental* Application

Video Tutorial: Building a *Kayak Rental* Application

In each chapter, from Chapter 3 onward, we will present a sequence of video tutorials that promote an accelerated learning experience. Each group of tutorials combines topics from the current and previous chapters to build an application that integrates visual design and interaction principles. Students who wish to accelerate their learning may use these videos to summarize and apply essential topics in these chapters. The videos are available on the book's companion Web site, which you can access from www.pearsonhighered.com/gaddis.

In this sequence of video tutorials, we show how to build a simple *Kayak Rental* application. The user's interface is oriented toward a store employee, whose goal is to interact with a customer and select an appropriate kayak with related equipment. The store clerk also wants to calculate the rental price. Because the customer is also looking at the screen, we want the program to present an attractive and easy to use interface.

- Part 1: Designing the user interface
- Part 2: Gathering information from the user
- Part 3: Finishing the calculations

Review Questions and Exercises

Fill-in-the-Blank

1. The _____ control allows you to capture input the user has typed on the keyboard.

2. _____ is a commonly used prefix for TextBox control names.

3. _____ means that one string is appended to another.

4. A(n) _____ is a storage location in the computer's memory, used for holding information while the program is running.

5. A(n) _____ is a statement that causes Visual Basic to create a variable in memory.

6. A variable's _____ determines whether a variable can hold a string, an integer, a date, or some other kind of data.

7. A(n) _____ variable is declared inside a procedure.

8. When Option Strict is set to _____, only widening conversions are permitted.

9. A(n) _____ is a specialized routine that performs a specific operation and then returns a value.

10. The _____ function converts an expression to an integer.

11. The _____ format string, when passed to the ToString method, produces a number in Currency format.

12. A(n) _____ is information that is passed to a function when the function is called.

13. When two operators share an operand, the operator with the highest _____ executes first.

14. A named _____ is like a variable whose content is read-only; it cannot be changed while the program is running.

15. The control that has the _____ is the one that receives the user's keyboard input or mouse clicks.

16. The order in which controls receive the focus is called the _____.

17. You can modify the tab order by changing a control's _____ property.

18. If you do not want a control to receive the focus when the user presses the Tab key, set its _____ property to *False*.

19. An access key is a key that you press in combination with the _____ key to access a control such as a button quickly.

20. You define a button's access key through its _____ property.

21. A(n) _____ is a container for other controls that appears as a rectangular border with an optional title.

22. A(n) _____ is a container for other controls that displays no title and has a customizable border.

23. A form's _____ procedure executes each time a form loads into memory.

24. A(n) _____ is a line of code that causes a running application to pause execution and enter break mode.

True or False

Indicate whether the following statements are true or false.

1. T F: The TextBox control's Text property holds the text entered by the user into the TextBox control at runtime.
2. T F: You can access a TextBox control's Text property in code.
3. T F: The string concatenation operator automatically inserts a space between the joined strings.
4. T F: A local variable may be accessed by any other procedure in the same Form file.
5. T F: When a string variable is created in memory, Visual Basic assigns it the initial value 0.
6. T F: A variable's scope is the time during which the variable exists in memory.
7. T F: A variable declared inside a procedure is only visible to statements inside the same procedure.
8. T F: The CDbl function converts a number to a string.
9. T F: If the CInt function cannot convert its argument, it causes a runtime error.
10. T F: The multiplication operator has higher precedence than the addition operator.
11. T F: A named constant's value can be changed by a programming statement while the program is running.
12. T F: Only controls capable of receiving input, such as TextBox and Button controls, may have the focus.
13. T F: You can cause a control to be skipped in the tab order by setting its TabPosition property to *False*.
14. T F: A runtime error will occur if you assign a negative value to the TabIndex property in code.
15. T F: A control whose Visible property is set to *False* still receives the focus.
16. T F: GroupBox and Label controls have a TabIndex property, but they are skipped in the tab order.
17. T F: When you assign an access key to a button, the user can trigger a Click event by typing [Alt]+ the access key character.
18. T F: The statement lblMessage.BackColor = Color.Green will set lblMessage control's background color to green.
19. T F: You can select multiple controls simultaneously with the mouse.
20. T F: You can change the same property for multiple controls simultaneously.
21. T F: To group controls in a group box, add the controls to a form first, then draw the group box around them.
22. T F: While single-stepping through an application's code in debugging mode, the highlighted execution point is the line of code that has already executed.

Multiple Choice

1. When the user types input into a TextBox control, in which property is it stored?
    a. Input
    b. Text
    c. Value
    d. Keyboard

2. Which character is the string concatenation operator?

   a. &
   b. *
   c. %
   d. @

3. You declare a named constant with which keyword?

   a. `Constant`
   b. `Const`
   c. `NamedConstant`
   d. `Dim`

4. Which of the following is the part of a program in which a variable is visible and may be accessed by a programming statement?

   a. segment
   b. lifetime
   c. scope
   d. module

5. If a variable named `dblTest` contains the value 1.23456, then which of the following values will be returned by the expression `dblTest.ToString("N3")`?

   a. 1.23456
   b. 1.235
   c. 1.234
   d. +1.234

6. If the following code executes, which value is assigned to `strA`?

   ```
   Dim dblTest As Double = 0.25
   Dim strA As String = dblTest.ToString("p")
   ```

   a. "0.25"
   b. "2.50"
   c. "25.00%"
   d. "0.25"

7. In code, you move the focus to a control with which method?

   a. `MoveFocus`
   b. `SetFocus`
   c. `ResetFocus`
   d. `Focus`

8. Which form property allows you to specify a button to be clicked when the user presses the Enter key?

   a. DefaultButton
   b. AcceptButton
   c. CancelButton
   d. EnterButton

9. Which form property allows you to specify a button that is to be clicked when the user presses the Esc key?

   a. DefaultButton
   b. AcceptButton
   c. CancelButton
   d. EnterButton

10. You can modify a control's position in the tab order by changing which property?
    a. TabIndex
    b. TabOrder
    c. TabPosition
    d. TabStop

11. You assign an access key to a button through which property?
    a. AccessKey
    b. AccessButton
    c. Mnemonic
    d. Text

12. A group box's title is stored in which property?
    a. Title
    b. Caption
    c. Text
    d. Heading

Short Answer

1. Describe the difference between the Label control's Text property and the TextBox control's Text property.

2. How do you clear the contents of a TextBox control?

3. What is the difference between the Single and Integer data types?

4. Create variable names that would be appropriate for holding each of the following information items:
    a. The number of backpacks sold this week
    b. The number of pounds of dog food in storage
    c. Today's date
    d. An item's wholesale price
    e. A customer's name
    f. The distance between two galaxies, in kilometers
    g. The number of the month (1 = January, 2 = February, and so on)

5. Why should you always make sure that a String variable is initialized or assigned a value before it is used in an operation?

6. When is a local variable destroyed?

7. How would the following strings be converted by the CDec function?
    a. "22.9000"
    b. "1xfc47uvy"
    c. "$19.99"
    d. "0.05%"
    e. String.Empty

8. Briefly describe how the CDec function converts a string argument to a number.

9. Complete the following table by providing the value of each mathematical expression:

Expression	Value
5 + 2 * 8	_____
20 / 5 − 2	_____
4 + 10 * 3 − 2	_____
(4 + 10) * 3 − 2	_____

10. Assuming that the variable `dblTest` contains the value 67521.584, complete the following table, showing the value returned by each function call:

Function Call	Return Value
`dblTest.ToString("d2")`	_____
`dblTest.ToString("c2")`	_____
`dblTest.ToString("e1")`	_____
`dblTest.ToString("f2")`	_____

11. What is the focus when referring to a running application?

12. Write a statement that sets the focus to the `txtPassword` control.

13. How does Visual Basic automatically assign the tab order to controls?

14. How does a control's TabIndex property affect the tab order?

15. How do you assign an access key to a button?

16. How does assigning an access key to a button change the button's appearance?

17. Describe one way to select multiple controls in design mode.

18. Describe three ways to set a breakpoint in an application's code.

What Do You Think?

1. Should a programming language automatically insert a space between strings concatenated with the & operator?

2. Why can't you perform arithmetic operations on a string, such as `"28.9"`?

3. Suppose a number is used in calculations throughout a program and must be changed every few months. What benefit is there to using a named constant to represent the number?

4. Should Label controls be capable of receiving the focus?

5. Why should the tab order of controls in your application be logical?

6. Why assign access keys to buttons?

7. What is the significance of showing an underlined character on a button?

8. Generally speaking, which button should be set as a form's default button?

9. How can you get your application to execute a group of statements each time a form is loaded into memory?

10. How can you place an existing control in a group box?

11. Visual Basic automatically reports syntax errors. Why doesn't it automatically report logic errors?

Find the Error

1. Open the *Chap3\ Error1\ Error1* project from the student sample programs folder. The `btnSum_Click` event handler has an error. Fix the error so the application correctly displays the sum of the numbers.

2. Open the *Chap3\ Error2\ Error2* project from the student sample programs folder. The application has an error. Find the error and fix it.

3. Open the *Chap3\ Error3\ Error3* project from the student sample programs folder. The `btnCalculate_Click` procedure contains an unusual error. Find the error and fix it.

Algorithm Workbench

1. Create a flowchart that shows the necessary steps for making the cookies in the following recipe:

    Ingredients:

1/2 cup butter	1/2 teaspoon vanilla
1 egg	1/2 teaspoon salt
1 cup sifted all-purpose flour	1/2 teaspoon baking soda
1/2 cup brown sugar	1/2 cup chopped nuts
1/2 cup sugar	1/2 cup semisweet chocolate chips

    Steps:
    Preheat oven to 375°.
    Cream the butter.
    Add the sugar and the brown sugar to the butter and beat until creamy.
    Beat the egg and vanilla into the mixture.
    Sift and stir the flour, salt, and baking soda into the mixture.
    Stir the nuts and chocolate chips into the mixture.
    Shape the mixture into 1/2-inch balls.
    Place the balls about one inch apart on a greased cookie sheet.
    Bake for 10 minutes.

2. A hot dog, still in its package, should be heated for 40 seconds in a microwave. Draw a flowchart showing the necessary steps to cook the hot dog.

3. The following pseudocode algorithm for the event handler `btnCalcArea_Click` has an error. The event handler is supposed to calculate the area of a room's floor. The area is calculated as the room's width (entered by the user into `txtWidth`), multiplied by the room's length (entered by the user into in `txtLength`). The result is displayed with the label `lblArea`. Find the error and correct the algorithm.

    1. Multiply the `intWidth` variable by the `intLength` variable and store the result in the `intArea` variable.
    2. Assign the value in `txtWidth.Text` to the `intWidth` variable.
    3. Assign the value in `txtLength.Text` to the `intLength` variable.
    4. Assign the value in the `intArea` variable to `lblArea.Text`.

4. The following steps should be followed in the event handler `btnCalcAvailCredit_Click`, which calculates a customer's available credit. Construct a flowchart that shows these steps.

    1. Assign the value in the TextBox control `txtMaxCredit` to the variable `decMaxCredit`.
    2. Assign the value in the TextBox control `txtUsedCredit` to the variable `decUsedCredit`.
    3. Subtract the value in `decUsedCredit` from `decMaxCredit`. Assign the result to `decAvailableCredit`
    4. Assign the value in `decAvailableCredit` to the label `lblAvailableCredit`.

5. Convert the flowchart you constructed in Exercise 4 into Visual Basic code.

6. Design a flowchart or pseudocode for the event handler `btnCalcSale_Click`, which calculates the total of a retail sale. Assume the program uses `txtRetailPrice`, a TextBox control that holds the retail price of the item being purchased, and `decTAX_RATE`, a constant that holds the sales tax rate. The event handler uses the items above to calculate the sales tax for the purchase and the total of the sale. Display the total of the sale in a label named `lblTotal`.

7. Convert the flowchart or pseudocode you constructed in Exercise 6 into Visual Basic code.

Programming Challenges

The *Miles per Gallon Calculator* Problem

1. **Miles per Gallon Calculator**

   Create an application that calculates a car's gas mileage. The formula for calculating the miles that a car can travel per gallon of gas is:

   $$MPG = \frac{miles}{gallons}$$

   In the formula *MPG* is miles-per-gallon, *miles* is the number of miles that can be driven on a full tank of gas, and *gallons* is the number of gallons that the tank holds.

   The application's form should have TextBox controls that let the user enter the number of gallons of gas the tank holds and the number of miles the car can be driven on a full tank. When the *Calculate MPG* button is clicked, the application should display the number of miles that the car can be driven per gallon of gas. The form should also have a *Clear* button that clears the input and results, and an *Exit* button that ends the application. If the user fails to enter numeric values, display an appropriate error message and do not attempt to perform calculations. The application's form should appear as shown in Figure 3-58.

Figure 3-58 *Miles per Gallon Calculator* in the *Designer*

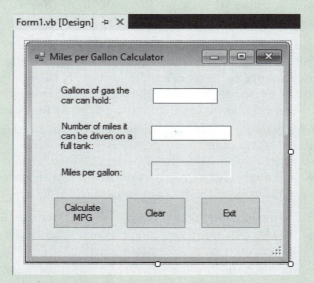

Use the following set of test data to determine if the application is calculating properly:

Gallons	Miles	Miles per Gallon
10	375	37.50
12	289	24.08
15	190	12.67

2. **Stadium Seating**

There are three seating categories at a high school athletic stadium. For a baseball game, Class A seats cost $15 each, Class B seats cost $12 each, and Class C seats cost $9 each. Create an application that allows the user to enter the number of tickets sold for each class. The application should be able to display the amount of income generated from each class of ticket sales and the total revenue generated. If the user fails to enter numeric values, display an appropriate error message and do not attempt to perform calculations. The application's form should resemble the one shown in Figure 3-59.

Figure 3-59 *Stadium Seating* form in the *Designer*

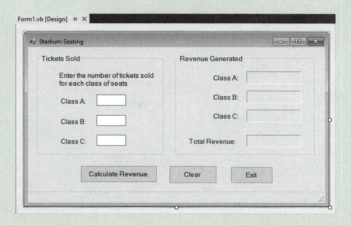

Use the following test data to determine if the application is calculating properly:

Ticket Sales	Revenue
Class A: 320	Class A: $4,800.00
Class B: 570	Class B: $6,840.00
Class C: 890	Class C: $8,010.00
	Total Revenue: $19,650.00
Class A: 500	Class A: $7,500.00
Class B: 750	Class B: $9,000.00
Class C: 1,200	Class C: $10,800.00
	Total Revenue: $27,300.00
Class A: 100	Class A: $1,500.00
Class B: 300	Class B: $3,600.00
Class C: 500	Class C: $4,500.00
	Total Revenue: $9,600.00

3. **Weekly Temperature Average**

   Create an application that lets the user enter weekly temperature readings over a five-week period. Once the values are entered, the user clicks the *Calculate Average* button, and the application should display the average in a Label control. The application's form should resemble the one shown in Figure 3-60. If the user fails to enter numeric values, display an appropriate error message and do not perform the calculation.

Figure 3-60 *Weekly Temperature Average form in the* Designer

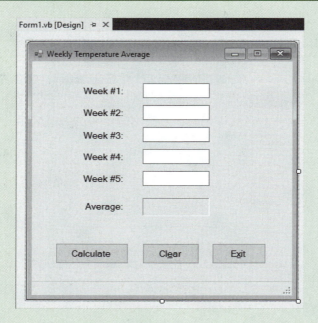

4. **Theater Revenue**

   A movie theater only keeps a percentage of the revenue earned from ticket sales. The remainder goes to the movie company. Create an application that calculates and displays the following figures for one night's box office business at a theater:

   a. *Gross revenue for adult tickets sold.* This is the amount of money taken in for all adult tickets sold.

   b. *Net revenue for adult tickets sold.* This is the amount of money from adult ticket sales left over after the payment to the movie company has been deducted.

   c. *Gross revenue for child tickets sold.* This is the amount of money taken in for all child tickets sold.

   d. *Net revenue for child tickets sold.* This is the amount of money from child ticket sales left over after the payment to the movie company has been deducted.

   e. *Total gross revenue.* This is the sum of gross revenue for adult and child tickets sold.

   f. *Total net revenue.* This is the sum of net revenue for adult and child tickets sold.

   The application's form should resemble the one shown in Figure 3-61.

Figure 3-61 *Theater Revenue* form in the *Designer*

Assume the theater keeps 20% of its box office receipts. Use a named constant in your code to represent this percentage. If the user fails to enter numeric values, display an appropriate error message and do not attempt to perform calculations. Use the following test data to determine if the application is calculating properly:

Ticket Sales		Revenue	
Price per Adult Ticket:	$6.00	Gross Adult Ticket Sales:	$720.00
Adult Tickets Sold:	120	Gross Child Ticket Sales:	$288.00
Price per Child Ticket:	$4.00	Total Gross Revenue:	$1,008.00
Child Tickets Sold:	72	Net Adult Ticket Sales:	$144.00
		Net Child Ticket Sales:	$57.60
		Total Net Revenue:	$201.60

5. **Room Charge Calculator Error Display**

   In the *Room Charge Calculator* application presented earlier in this chapter, the same error message was displayed whenever a user neglected to enter numeric data into any of the input fields. Redesign the code in the program so that a unique error message is displayed for each input field.

6. **Simple Calculator Exceptions**

   Improve the *Simple Calculator* application from Tutorial 3-8 so it displays an error message in a Label control if the user enters nonnumeric values into the text boxes.

7. **Sailboat Races**

   The Upper West View Yacht club sponsors sailboat races every weekend for its fleet of SuperGee sailboats, and wants to determine which boat is the winner out of every four races. The scoring system is simple: a boat finishing in first position (first place) receives 1 point; a boat in second place receives 2 points, and so on. At the end of four races, the boats are ranked in ascending order by number of points, so the boats with the lowest points win.

   Your task is to write an application that lets the user input the finishing position for each of three boats for four races. The program will then display the total points for each boat. Here are some specific requirements:

   - Validate all text boxes to make sure the user enters integer values.
   - Use a StatusStrip with a label to display an error message. When the user corrects an error and clicks the *Calculate* button again, clear any existing error message.
   - Set TabIndex properties so that the focus will move between input fields in a logical manner.
   - Do not allow the user to maximize or resize the form.

Figure 3-62 shows a sample of the program as the user is entering all valid values. In any single race, no place value should appear twice, although you currently do not have the programming tools to enforce this rule. For Race 1 in the sample, for example, the values 1, 2, and 3 each only appear once. *Hint: to avoid an excessive amount of typing when coding this solution, rely on the copy and paste commands with the Windows clipboard. The key combinations are Ctrl-C (copy) and Ctrl-V (paste).*

Figure 3-62 User input at runtime to the *Sailboat Races* program

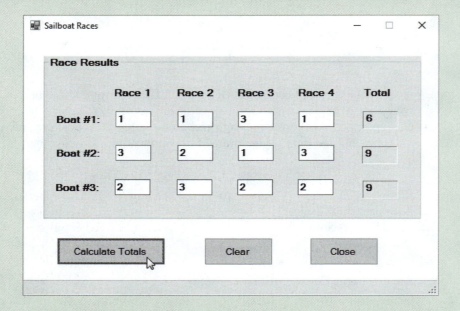

8. **Converting Celsius to Fahrenheit**

   Create an application that converts Celsius to Fahrenheit. The formula is $F = 1.8 * C + 32$ where F is the Fahrenheit temperature and C is the Celsius temperature. If the user fails to enter numeric values, display an appropriate error message and do not attempt to perform calculations. Use the following test data to determine if the application is calculating properly:

Celsius	Fahrenheit
100	212
0	32
56	132.8

9. **Currency Converter**

   Create an application that converts U.S. dollar amounts to pounds, euros, and yen. The following conversion factors are not accurate, but you can use them in your application:

   1 dollar = 0.68 pound
   1 dollar = 0.83 euro
   1 dollar = 108.36 yen

   In your code, declare named constants to represent the conversion factors for the different types of currency. For example, you might declare the conversion factor for yen as follows:

   ```
   Const dblYEN_FACTOR As Double = 108.36
   ```

Use the named constants in the mathematical conversion statements. If the user fails to enter numeric values, display an appropriate error message and do not attempt to perform calculations. Use the following test data to determine whether the application is calculating properly:

Dollars	Conversion	Values
$100.00	Pounds:	68
	Euros:	83
	Yen:	10,836
$ 25.00	Pounds:	17
	Euros:	20.75
	Yen:	2,709
$ 1.00	Pounds:	0.68
	Euros:	0.83
	Yen:	108.36

10. **Monthly Sales Taxes**

A retail company must file a monthly sales tax report listing the total sales for the month, and the amount of state and county sales tax collected. The state sales tax rate is 4% and the county sales tax rate is 2%. Create an application that allows the user to enter the total sales for the month. From this figure, the application should calculate and display the following:

a. The amount of county sales tax
b. The amount of state sales tax
c. The total sales tax (county plus state)

In the application's code, represent the county tax rate (0.02) and the state tax rate (0.04) as named constants. Use the named constants in the mathematical statements. If the user fails to enter numeric values, display an appropriate error message and do not attempt to perform calculations. Use the following test data to determine whether the application is calculating properly:

Total Sales	Tax Amounts	
9,500	County sales tax:	$190.00
	State sales tax:	$380.00
	Total sales tax:	$570.00
5,000	County sales tax:	$100.00
	State sales tax:	$200.00
	Total sales tax:	$300.00
15,000	County sales tax:	$300.00
	State sales tax:	$600.00
	Total sales tax:	$900.00

11. **Calculating Property Taxes**

A county collects property taxes on the assessment value of property, which is 60% of the property's actual value. If, for example, an acre of land is valued at $10,000, its assessment value is $6,000. The property tax rate is $0.64 for each $100 of the assessment value. Therefore, the tax for an acre assessed at $6,000 will be $38.40. Create an application that displays the assessment value and property tax when a user enters the actual value of a property. If the user fails to enter numeric values, display an appropriate error message and do not attempt to perform calculations. Use the following test data to determine if the application is calculating properly:

Actual Property Value	Assessment and Tax	
100,000	Assessment value:	60,000.00
	Property tax:	384.00
75,000	Assessment value:	45,000.00
	Property tax:	288.00
250,000	Assessment value:	150,000.00
	Property tax:	960.00

12. **Pizza Pi**

Joe's Pizza Palace needs an application to calculate the number of slices a pizza of any size can be divided into. The application should do the following:

a. Allow the user to enter the diameter of the pizza, in inches.
b. Calculate the number of slices that can be cut from a pizza that size.
c. Display a message that indicates the number of slices.

To calculate the number of slices that can be cut from the pizza, you must know the following facts:

a. Each slice should have an area of 14.125 inches.
b. To calculate the number of slices, divide the area of the pizza by 14.125.

The area of the pizza is calculated with the following formula:

$$Area = \pi r^2$$

NOTE: π is the Greek letter pi. 3.14159 can be used as its value. The variable r is the radius of the pizza. Divide the diameter by 2 to get the radius.

If the user fails to enter numeric values, display an appropriate error message and do not attempt to perform calculations. Use the following test data to determine if the application is calculating properly:

Diameter of Pizza	Number of Slices
22 inches	27
15 inches	13
12 inches	8

13. **Distance Traveled**

Assuming there are no accidents or delays, the distance that a car travels down the interstate can be calculated with the following formula:

$$Distance = Speed \times Time$$

Create a VB application that allows the user to enter a car's speed in miles-per-hour. If the user fails to enter numeric values, display an appropriate error message and do not attempt to perform calculations. When a button is clicked, the application should display the following:

• The distance the car will travel in 5 hours
• The distance the car will travel in 8 hours
• The distance the car will travel in 12 hours

14. **Body Mass Index**

    Create a VB application that lets the user enter his or her weight (in pounds) and height (in inches). If the user fails to enter numeric values, display an appropriate error message and do not attempt to perform calculations. The application should calculate the user's body mass index (BMI). The BMI is often used to determine whether a person is overweight or underweight for his or her height. A person's BMI is calculated with the following formula:

$$BMI = weight \times 703/height^2$$

15. **How Much Insurance?**

    Many financial experts advise that property owners should insure their homes or buildings for at least 80% of the amount it would cost to replace the structure. Create a VB application that lets the user enter the replacement cost of a building and then displays the minimum amount of insurance he or she should buy for the property. If the user fails to enter numeric values, display an appropriate error message and do not attempt to perform calculations.

16. **How Many Calories?**

    Assume that a bag of cookies holds 40 cookies. The calorie information on the bag claims that there are 10 servings in the bag and that a serving equals 300 calories. Create a VB application that lets the user enter the number of cookies he or she actually ate and then reports the number of total calories consumed. If the user fails to enter a numeric value, display an appropriate error message and do not attempt to perform calculations.

4 Making Decisions

TOPICS

In this chapter, you will learn how programs use If...Then, If...Then...Else, and If...Then...ElseIf statements to make decisions. You will learn how to compare values using relational operators and build complex comparisons using logical operators. You will be introduced to the Select Case statement, radio buttons (which allow the user to select one choice from many possible choices), and check boxes (which allow the user to make on/off or yes/no types of selections). You will learn more about message boxes, which display messages to the user, and the process of input validation.

4.1 The Decision Structure

CONCEPT: The decision structure allows a program's logic to have more than one path of execution.

In the programs you have written so far, statements execute sequentially. This means that statements are executed one after the other, in the order in which they appear.

You might think of sequentially executed statements as the steps you take as you walk down a road. To complete the journey, you must start at the beginning and take each step, one after the other, until you reach your destination. This is illustrated in Figure 4-1.

Figure 4-1 Sequence instruction

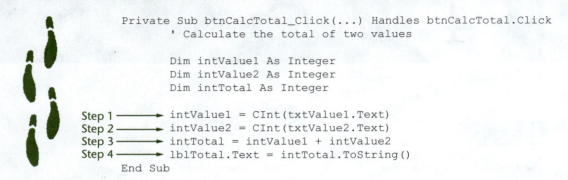

```
Private Sub btnCalcTotal_Click(...) Handles btnCalcTotal.Click
    ' Calculate the total of two values

    Dim intValue1 As Integer
    Dim intValue2 As Integer
    Dim intTotal As Integer

Step 1 ——→  intValue1 = CInt(txtValue1.Text)
Step 2 ——→  intValue2 = CInt(txtValue2.Text)
Step 3 ——→  intTotal = intValue1 + intValue2
Step 4 ——→  lblTotal.Text = intTotal.ToString()
End Sub
```

This type of code is called a **sequence structure** because the statements are executed in sequence, without branching in another direction. Programs often need more than one path of execution because many algorithms require a program to execute some statements only under certain circumstances. This can be accomplished with a **decision structure**.

Decision Structures in Flowcharts and Pseudocode

In a decision structure's simplest form, an expression is tested for a true or false value. If the expression is true, an action is performed. If the expression is false, the action is not performed. Figure 4-2 shows a flowchart segment for a decision structure. The diamond symbol represents a yes/no question, or a true/false expression. If the answer to the question is *yes* (or if the expression is true), the program follows one path. If the answer to the question is *no* (or the expression is false), the program follows another path.

In the flowchart, the action *Wear a coat* is performed only when it is cold outside. If it is not cold outside, the action is skipped. The action is **conditionally executed** because it is performed only when a certain condition (*cold outside*) exists. Figure 4-3 shows a more elaborate flowchart, where three actions are taken, only when it is cold outside.

Decision structures can also be expressed as pseudocode. For example, the decision structure shown in Figure 4-2 can be expressed as

> *If it is cold outside Then*
> *   Wear a coat.*
> *End If*

The *End If* statement marks the end of the decision structure in pseudocode. The statements appearing between *If . . . Then* and *End If* are executed only when it is cold outside. The decision structure shown in Figure 4-3, which conditionally executes three actions, can be expressed as

> *If it is cold outside Then*
> *   Wear a coat.*
> *   Wear a hat.*
> *   Wear gloves.*
> *End If*

Figure 4-2 Simple decision structure flowchart

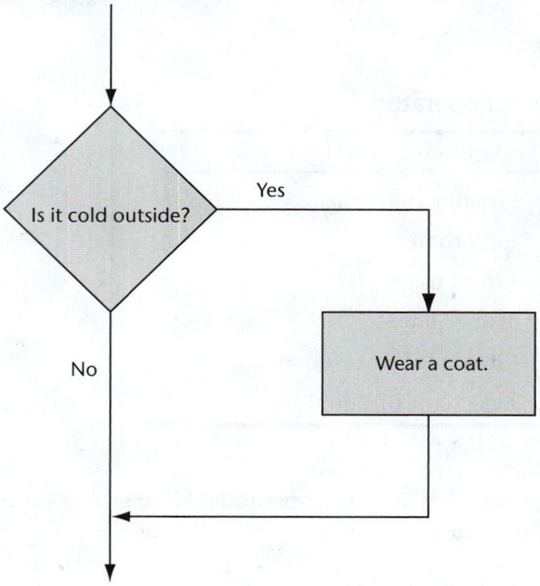

Figure 4-3 Three-action decision structure flowchart

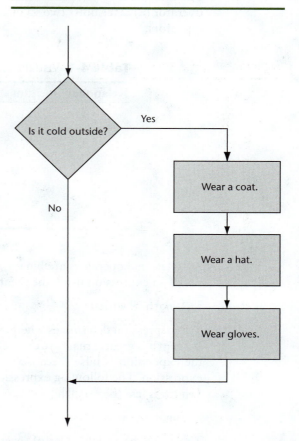

The If . . . Then **Statement**

4.2

CONCEPT: The If . . . Then statement causes other statements to execute only when an expression is true.

VideoNote

The If . . . Then Statement

One way to code a decision structure in Visual Basic is with the If . . . Then statement. Here is the general form of the If . . . Then statement.

```
If expression Then
    statement
    (more statements may follow)
End If
```

The If . . . Then statement is really very simple: if the *expression* is true, the statement or statements that appear between the If . . . Then and the End If are executed. Otherwise, the statements are skipped.

Boolean Expressions and Relational Operators

The expression that is tested in an If . . . Then statement can be either True or False. Such an expression is known as a **Boolean expression**. Special operators known as relational operators are commonly used in Boolean expressions. A **relational operator** determines whether a specific relationship exists between two values. For example, the greater-than operator (>) determines whether one value is greater than another value. The equal to operator (=) determines two values are the same. Table 4-1 lists the Visual Basic relational operators.

Table 4-1 Visual Basic relational operators

Relational Operator	Meaning
>	Greater than
<	Less than
=	Equal to
<>	Not equal to
>=	Greater than or equal to
<=	Less than or equal to

All relational operators are binary, which means they use two operands. Here is an example of an expression using the greater than operator:

```
length > width
```

This expression determines whether the value of `length` is greater than the value of `width`. If `length` is greater than `width`, the value of the expression is true. Otherwise, the value of the expression is false. Because the expression can be only true or false, it is a Boolean expression. The following expression uses the less than operator (<) to determine whether `length` is less than `width`:

```
length < width
```

Table 4-2 shows examples of several relational expressions that compare the variables x and y.

Table 4-2 Boolean expressions using relational operators

Relational Expression	Meaning
$x > y$	Is x greater than y?
$x < y$	Is x less than y?
$x >= y$	Is x greater than or equal to y?
$x <= y$	Is x less than or equal to y?
$x = y$	Is x equal to y?
$x <> y$	Is x not equal to y?

The = operator, when used in a relational expression, determines whether the operand on its left is equal to the operand on its right. If both operands have the same value, the expression is true. Assuming that a is 4, the expression $a = 4$ is true and the expression $a = 2$ is false.

There are two operators that can test more than one relationship at the same time. The >= operator determines whether the operand on its left is greater than or equal to the operand on the right. Assuming that a is 4, b is 6, and c is 4, the expressions $b >= a$ and $a >= c$ are true, and $a >= 5$ is false. When using this operator, the > symbol must precede the = symbol, with no space between them.

The <= operator determines whether the left operand is less than or equal to the right operand. Once again, assuming that *a* is 4, *b* is 6, and *c* is 4, both *a* <= *c* and *b* <= 10 are true, but *b* <= *a* is false. When using this operator, the < symbol must precede the = symbol, with no space between them.

The <> operator is the *not equal* operator. It determines whether the operand on its left is not equal to the operand on its right, which is the opposite of the = operator. As before, assuming *a* is 4, *b* is 6, and *c* is 4, both *a* <> *b* and *b* <> *c* are true because a is not equal to b and b is not equal to *c*. However, *a* <> *c* is false because a is equal to *c*. Values compared by a relational expression need not be exactly the same type. Suppose we compare a variable of type Single to an integer constant, as in the following:

```
sngTemperature > 40
```

In this example, the integer 40 is temporarily converted to a Single so the comparison can take place. You do not have to worry about doing this conversion. It is carried out automatically by the Visual Basic compiler. Similarly, we might want to compare a Double to a Single, as in the following:

```
dblTemperature < sngBoilingPoint
```

The value of `sngBoilingPoint` is automatically converted to type Double so the values can be compared.

Putting It All Together

Let's look at an example of an If...Then statement:

```
If decSales > 50000 Then
    lblResult.Text = "You've earned a bonus!"
End If
```

This statement uses the > operator to determine whether `decSales` is greater than 50000. If expression `decSales` > 50000 is true, the message *You've earned a bonus!* is displayed to the user.

The following example conditionally executes multiple statements.

```
If decSales > 50000 Then
    lblResult.Text = "You've earned a bonus!"
    decCommissionRate = 0.12
    intDaysOff = intDaysOff + 1
End If
```

Here are some specific rules to remember about the multiline If...Then statement:

- A Boolean expression must appear between If and Then.
- The words If and Then must appear on the same line.
- Nothing other than a comment can appear after the Then keyword, on the same line.
- The End If statement must be on a line by itself. Only a comment may follow it on the same line.

Tutorial 4-1 examines an application that uses the If...Then statement.

Tutorial 4-1:
Examining an application that uses the `If...Then` statement

Step 1: Open the *Test Score Average 1* project from the student sample programs folder named *Chap4\Test Score Average 1*.

Step 2: Run the application. The form appears, as shown in Figure 4-4.

Step 3: Enter the following test scores in the three text boxes: **80, 90, 75**.

Step 4: Click the *Calculate Average* button. The average test score is displayed.

Step 5: Click the *Clear* button, and then enter the following test scores in the three text boxes: **100, 97, 99**.

Step 6: Click the *Calculate Average* button. This time, in addition to the average test score being displayed, the message *Congratulations! Great Job!* also appears. The form appears, as shown in Figure 4-5.

Figure 4-4 *Test Score Average* form

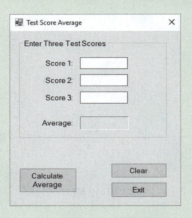

Figure 4-5 Average and message displayed

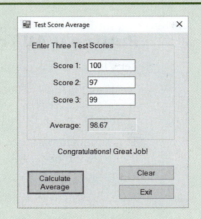

Step 7: Click the *Exit* button to terminate the application.

Step 8: Open the *Code* window and find the `btnCalculate_Click` event handler. The code is as follows:

```
Private Sub btnCalculate_Click(...) Handles btnCalculate.Click
    ' Variables to hold scores and the average score
    Dim dblScore1 As Double
    Dim dblScore2 As Double
    Dim dblScore3 As Double
    Dim dblAverage As Double

    ' Constants
    Const NUM_SCORES As Integer = 3
    Const dblHIGH_SCORE As Double = 95.0

    Try
        ' Assign the TextBox scores to the variables.
        dblScore1 = CDbl(txtScore1.Text)
        dblScore2 = CDbl(txtScore2.Text)
        dblScore3 = CDbl(txtScore3.Text)
```

```
                ' Calculate the average score.
                dblAverage = (dblScore1 + dblScore2 + dblScore3) / NUM_SCORES

                ' Display the average, rounded to 2 decimal places.
                lblAverage.Text = dblAverage.ToString("n2")

                ' If the score is high, compliment the student.
                If dblAverage > dblHIGH_SCORE Then
                    lblMessage.Text = "Congratulations! Great Job!"
                End If
            Catch
                ' Display an error message.
                lblMessage.Text = Scores must be numeric."
            End Try
        End Sub
```

Notice that at the end of the try block, the following `If...Then` statement appears:

```
    If dblAverage > dblHIGH_SCORE Then
        lblMessage.Text = "Congratulations! Great Job!"
    End If
```

This statement determines whether the average is greater than 95, and if so, displays *Congratulations! Great Job!* in the `lblMessage` label.

Programming Style and the `If...Then` Statement

When you type an `If...Then` statement, Visual Studio automatically indents the conditionally executed statements. This is not a syntax requirement, but a programming style convention. For example, compare the following statements:

```
If decSales > 50000 Then
    lblMessage.Text = "You've earned a bonus!"
    decCommissionRate = 0.12
    intDaysOff = intDaysOff + 1
End If

If decSales > 50000 Then
lblMessage.Text = "You've earned a bonus!"
decCommissionRate = 0.12
intDaysOff = intDaysOff + 1
End If
```

Both `If...Then` statements produce the same result. The first example, however, is more readable to the human eye than the second because the conditionally executed statements are indented.

NOTE: If the automatic indenting feature has been turned off, you can turn it on by clicking *Tools* on the menu bar, then clicking *Options*. In the *Options* window, perform the following:

- Click *Text Editor* in the left pane, then click *Basic*, then click *Tabs*. Make sure *Smart* is selected in the dialog box under *Indenting*.
- In the left pane, click *Advanced*. Make sure *Automatic Insertion of end constructs* and *Pretty listing (reformatting) of code* are both checked.

Using Relational Operators with Math Operators

It is possible to use a relational operator and math operators in the same expression. Here is an example:

```
If intX + intY > 20 Then
    lblMessage.Text = "It is true!"
End If
```

When a relational operator appears in the same expression as one or more math operators, the math operators always execute first. In this statement, the + operator adds intX and intY. The result is compared to 20 using the > operator. Here is another example:

```
If intX + intY > intA - intB Then
    lblMessage.Text = "It is true!"
End If
```

In this statement, the result of intX + intY is compared, using the > operator, to the result of intA - intB.

Most programmers prefer to use parentheses to clarify the order of operations. Relying on operator precedence rules is risky because the rules are hard to remember. Here is a preferred way to write the foregoing If...Then statement:

```
If (intX + intY) > (intA - intB) Then
    lblMessage.Text = "It is true!"
End If
```

Using Function Calls with Relational Operators

It is possible to compare the return value of a function call with another value, using a relational operator. Here is an example:

```
If CInt(txtInput.Text) < 100 Then
    lblMessage.Text = "It is true!"
End If
```

This If...Then statement calls the CInt function to get the integer value of txtInput.Text. The function's return value is compared to 100 by the < operator. If the result of CInt(txtInput.Text) is less than 100, the assignment statement is executed.

Using Boolean Variables as Flags

A **flag** is a Boolean variable that signals when some condition exists in the program. When the flag is set to *False*, it indicates the condition does not yet exist. When the flag is set to *True*, it means the condition does exist. Look at the following code, which uses a Boolean variable named blnQuotaMet.

```
If blnQuotaMet Then
    lblMessage.Text = "You have met your sales quota"
End If
```

The preceding statement assigns the string "You have met your sales quota" to lblMessage.Text if the Boolean variable equals *True*. If blnQuotaMet is *False*, the assignment statement is not executed. It is not necessary to use the = operator to compare the variable to *True*. The statement is equivalent to the following:

```
If blnQuotaMet = True Then
    lblMessage.Text = "You have met your sales quota"
End If
```

Checkpoint

4.1 Assuming *x* is 5, *y* is 6, and *z* is 8, indicate whether each of the following relational expressions equals *True* or *False*:

a.	$x = 5$	T	F	e.	$z <> 4$	T	F
b.	$7 <= (x + 2)$	T	F	f.	$x >= 6$	T	F
c.	$z < 4$	T	F	g.	$x <= (y * 2)$	T	F
d.	$(2 + x) <> y$	T	F				

4.2 In the following `If...Then` statement, assume that `blnIsInvalid` is a Boolean variable. Exactly what condition is being tested?

```
If blnIsInvalid Then
    ' Do something
End If
```

4.3 Do both of the following `If...Then` statements perform the same operation, even though their indentations are different?

```
If decSales > 10000 Then
    decCommissionRate = 0.15
End If

If decSales > 10000 Then
decCommissionRate = 0.15
End If
```

4.4 Of the two `If...Then` statements shown in Checkpoint 4.3, which is preferred, and why?

4.3 The `If...Then...Else` Statement

CONCEPT: The `If...Then...Else` statement executes one group of statements if the Boolean expression is true and another group of statements if the Boolean expression is false.

VideoNote

The If...
Then...Else
Statement

The `If...Then...Else` statement is an expansion of the `If...Then` statement. Here is its format:

```
If condition Then
    statement
    (more statements may follow)
Else
    statement
    (more statements may follow)
End If
```

As in an `If...Then` statement, a Boolean expression is evaluated. If the expression is true, a statement or group of statements is executed. If the expression is false, a separate group of statements is executed, as in the following.

```
If dblTemperature < 40 Then
    lblMessage.Text = "A little cold, isn't it?"
Else
    lblMessage.Text = "Nice weather we're having!"
End If
```

The `Else` clause specifies a statement or group of statements to be executed when the Boolean expression is false. In the preceding example, if the expression `dblTemperature < 40` is false, the statement appearing after the `Else` clause is executed.

The If...Then...Else statement follows only one of the two paths. If you think of the statements in a computer program as steps taken down a road, consider the If...Then...Else statement as a fork in the road. Instead of being a momentary detour, like an If...Then statement, the If...Then...Else statement causes the program execution to follow one of two exclusive paths. Figure 4-6 shows a flowchart for this type of decision structure.

Figure 4-6 Flowchart for If...Then...Else statement

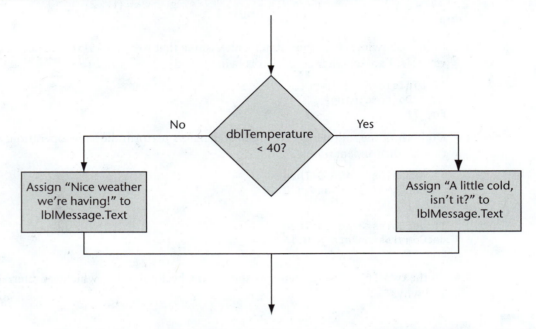

The logic shown in the flowchart in Figure 4-6 can also be expressed in pseudocode:

If temperature < 40 Then
  Display the message "A little cold, isn't it?"
Else
  Display the message "Nice weather we're having!"
End If

In Tutorial 4-2 you complete an application that uses the If...Then...Else statement.

VideoNote

Completing an application that uses the If... Then... Else statement

Tutorial 4-2:
Completing an application that uses the
If...Then...Else statement

Step 1: Open the *Test Score Average 2* project from the student sample programs folder named *Chap4\Test Score Average 2*. (This is a modification of the *Test Score Average 1* application from Tutorial 4-1.)

Step 2: Double-click the *Calculate Average* button. The *Code* window will open and show the btnCalculate_Click event handler, which is shown as follows. Complete the event handler by writing the code shown in bold:

```
Private Sub btnCalculate_Click(...) Handles btnCalculate.Click
    ' Variables to hold scores and the average score
    Dim dblScore1 As Double
    Dim dblScore2 As Double
    Dim dblScore3 As Double
    Dim dblAverage As Double
```

```
' Constants
Const NUM_SCORES As Integer = 3
Const dblHIGH_SCORE As Double = 95.0

Try
    ' Copy the TextBox scores into the variables.
    dblScore1 = CDbl(txtScore1.Text)
    dblScore2 = CDbl(txtScore2.Text)
    dblScore3 = CDbl(txtScore3.Text)

    ' Calculate the average score.
    dblAverage = (dblScore1 + dblScore2 + dblScore3) / NUM_SCORES

    ' Display the average, rounded to 2 decimal places.
    lblAverage.Text = dblAverage.ToString("n2")

    ' If the score is high, give the student praise.
    ' Otherwise, give some encouragement.
    If dblAverage > dblHIGH_SCORE Then
        lblMessage.Text = "Congratulations! Great Job!"
    Else
        lblMessage.Text = "Keep trying!"
    End If
Catch
    ' Display an error message.
    lblMessage.Text = "Scores must be numeric."
End Try
End Sub
```

Now the application will display one of two possible messages. If the user's average score is greater than 95, the message *Congratulations! Great Job!* will appear. Otherwise, the message *Keep trying!* will appear.

Step 3: Save the project.

Step 4: Run the application and input the following test scores in the three text boxes: **80, 90, 75.**

Step 5: Click the *Calculate Average* button. As shown in Figure 4-7, the average test score is displayed, and the message *Keep trying!* appears.

Figure 4-7 *Test Score Average* form with message displayed

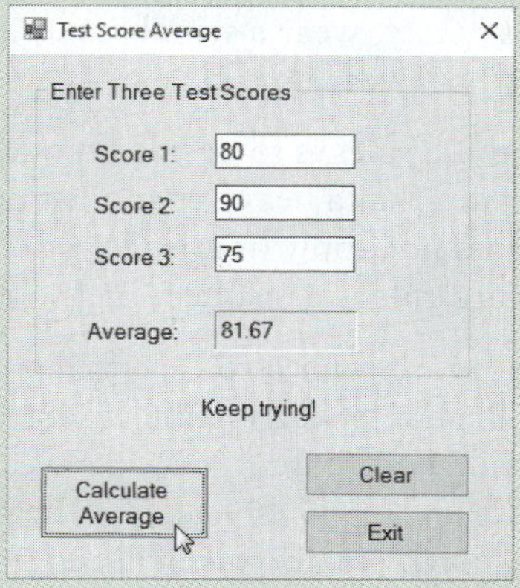

Step 6: Click the *Clear* button, and then enter the following test scores in the three text boxes: **100, 97, 99.**

Step 7: Click the *Calculate Average* button. This time, the message *Congratulations! Great job!* appears.

Step 8: Click the *Exit* button to terminate the application.

Checkpoint

4.5 Look at each of the following code segments. What value will the `If...Then...Else` statements store in the variable `intY`?

a.
```
intX = 0
If intX < 1 Then
  intY = 99
Else
  intY = 0
End If
```

b.
```
intX = 100
If intX <= 1 Then
  intY = 99
Else
  intY = 0
End If
```

c.
```
intX = 0
If intX <> 1 Then
  intY = 99
Else
  intY = 0
End If
```

4.4 The `If...Then...ElseIf` Statement

CONCEPT: The `If...Then...ElseIf` statement is like a chain of `If...Then...Else` statements. They perform their tests, one after the other, until one of them is found to be true.

We make certain mental decisions by using sets of different but related rules. For example, we might decide which type of coat or jacket to wear by consulting the following rules:

- If it is very cold, wear a heavy coat.
- Else, if it is chilly, wear a light jacket.
- Else, if it is windy, wear a windbreaker.
- Else, if it is hot, wear no jacket.

The purpose of these rules is to decide on one type of outer garment to wear. If it is cold, the first rule dictates that a heavy coat must be worn. All the other rules are then ignored. If the first rule does not apply (if it isn't cold) the second rule is consulted. If that rule does not apply, the third rule is consulted, and so on.

The way these rules are connected is very important. If they were consulted individually, we might go out of the house wearing the wrong jacket or, possibly, more than one jacket. For instance, if it is windy, the third rule says to wear a windbreaker. What if it is both windy and very cold? Will we wear a windbreaker? A heavy coat? Both? Because of the order in which the rules are consulted, the first rule will determine that a heavy coat is needed. The remaining rules will not be consulted, and we will go outside wearing the most appropriate garment.

This type of decision making is also common in programming. In Visual Basic, it is accomplished with the `If...Then...ElseIf` statement. Here is its general format:

```
If condition Then
   statement
   (more statements may follow)
ElseIf condition Then
   statement
   (more statements may follow)
(put as many ElseIf statements as necessary)
Else
   statement
   (more statements may follow)
End If
```

This construction is like a chain of If...Then...Else statements. The Else part of one statement is linked to the If part of another. The chain of If...Then...Else statements becomes one long statement. In Tutorial 4-3, you complete an application that uses the If...Then...ElseIf statement.

Tutorial 4-3:

Completing an application that uses the
If...Then...ElseIf statement

VideoNote

Completing an application that uses the If...Then... ElseIf statement

In this tutorial, you will begin with the program from Tutorial 4-2 and add controls and program code that display the student's letter grade (*A, B, C, D, F*).

Step 1: Open the *Test Score Average 2* project you modified in Tutorial 4-2.

Step 2: Drag the form's border downward about one-half inch, and drag the lblMessage control and the three Button controls downward on the form to make space for a new row of controls.

Step 3: Drag the lower border of the group box downward about one-half inch to make room for a label that will display the student's letter grade.

Step 4: Inside the group box add the new Label controls shown in Figure 4-8. When you add the label on the left, set its Text property to *Grade:*. When you add the label on the right, set its Name property to lblGrade, its AutoSize property to *False*, and set its BorderStyle property to *Fixed3D*.

Figure 4-8 Adding the *Grade* label inside the group box

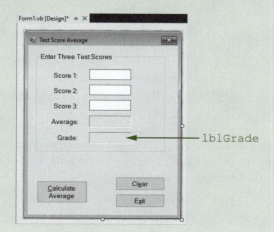

Step 5: Double-click the *Calculate Average* button. The *Code* window will open and show the btnCalculate_Click event handler, which is shown as follows. Complete the event handler by writing the code shown in bold:

```
Private Sub btnCalculate_Click(...) Handles btnCalculate.Click
    ' Variables to hold scores and the average score
    Dim dblScore1 As Double
    Dim dblScore2 As Double
    Dim dblScore3 As Double
    Dim dblAverage As Double

    ' Constants
    Const NUM_SCORES As Integer = 3
    Const dblHIGH_SCORE As Double = 95.0

    Try
        ' Assign the TextBox scores to the variables.
        dblScore1 = CDbl(txtScore1.Text)
        dblScore2 = CDbl(txtScore2.Text)
        dblScore3 = CDbl(txtScore3.Text)

        ' Calculate the average score.
        dblAverage = (dblScore1 + dblScore2 + dblScore3) / NUM_SCORES

        ' Display the average, rounded to 2 decimal places.
        lblAverage.Text = dblAverage.ToString("n2")

        ' Display the letter grade.
        If dblAverage < 60 Then
            lblGrade.Text = "F"
        ElseIf dblAverage < 70 Then
            lblGrade.Text = "D"
        ElseIf dblAverage < 80 Then
            lblGrade.Text = "C"
        ElseIf dblAverage < 90 Then
            lblGrade.Text = "B"
        ElseIf dblAverage <= 100 Then
            lblGrade.Text = "A"
        End If

        ' If the score is high, give the student praise.
        ' Otherwise, give some encouragement.
        If dblAverage > dblHIGH_SCORE Then
            lblMessage.Text = "Congratulations! Great Job!"
        Else
            lblMessage.Text = "Keep trying!"
        End If
    Catch
        ' Display an error message.
        lblStatus.Text = "Scores must be numeric."
    End Try
End Sub
```

The If...Then...ElseIf statement that you wrote has a number of notable characteristics. Let's analyze how it works. First, the Boolean expression dblAverage < 60 is tested:

```
If dblAverage < 60 Then
    lblGrade.Text = "F"
```

If dblAverage is less than 60, *F* is assigned to lblGrade.Text, and the rest of the ElseIf statements are ignored. If dblAverage is not less than 60, the next ElseIf statement executes:

```
If dblAverage < 60 Then
   lblGrade.Text = "F"
ElseIf dblAverage < 70 Then
   lblGrade.Text = "D"
```

The first If...Then statement filtered out all grades less than 60, so when this ElseIf statement executes, dblAverage must be 60 or greater. If dblAverage is less than 70, *D* is assigned to lblGrade.Text and the remaining ElseIf statements are ignored. The chain of events continues until one of the expressions is true, or the End If statement is encountered. Figure 4-9 uses a flowchart to describe the logic.

Figure 4-9 Flowchart for determining the student's letter grade

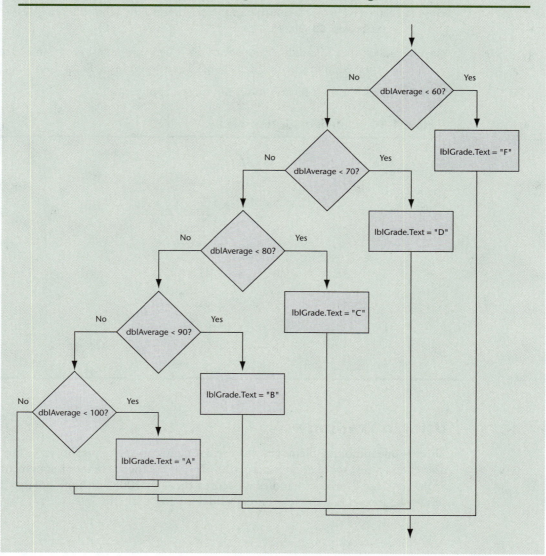

Step 6: Scroll down to the `btnClear_Click` event handler and add the statement shown here in bold:

```
Private Sub btnClear_Click(...) Handles btnClear.Click
  ' Clear the Text Boxes and Labels.
  txtScore1.Clear()
  txtScore2.Clear()
  txtScore3.Clear()
  lblAverage.Text = String.Empty
  lblMessage.Text = String.Empty
  lblGrade.Text = String.Empty

  ' Reset the focus.
  txtScore1.Focus()
End Sub
```

This statement will clear the contents of the `lblGrade` label when the user clicks the *Clear* button.

Step 7: Save the project, run the application, and input the following test scores in the text boxes: **80, 90, 75.**

Step 8: Click the *Calculate Average* button. The average test score and letter grade are displayed, along with the message *Keep trying!* (see Figure 4-10).

Step 9: Click the *Exit* button to terminate the application.

Figure 4-10 Student grade displayed

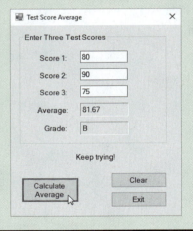

Using a Trailing Else

There is one minor problem with the test averaging applications shown so far: What if the user enters a test score greater than 100? The `If...Then...ElseIf` statement in the *Test Score Average 2* project handles all scores through 100, but none greater. Figure 4-11 shows the form when the user enters values greater than 100.

Figure 4-11 *Test Score Average 2* application showing values greater than 100

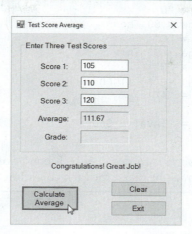

The program does not give a letter grade because there is no code to handle a score greater than 100. Assuming that any grade over 100 is invalid, we can fix the program by placing an `Else` at the end of the `If...Then...ElseIf` statement, as follows:

```
' Display the letter grade.
If dblAverage < 60 Then
   lblGrade.Text = "F"
ElseIf dblAverage < 70 Then
   lblGrade.Text = "D"
ElseIf dblAverage < 80 Then
   lblGrade.Text = "C"
ElseIf dblAverage < 90 Then
   lblGrade.Text = "B"
ElseIf dblAverage <= 100 Then
   lblGrade.Text = "A"
Else
   lblGrade.Text = "Invalid Score"
End If
```

The trailing `Else` catches any value that falls through the cracks. It provides a default response when the `If...Then` or none of the `ElseIf` statements finds a true condition.

TIP: When writing an `If...Then...ElseIf` statement, code the structure of the statement first, identifying all the conditions to be tested. For example, the code in our example might initially be written as follows:

```
If dblAverage < 60 Then
ElseIf dblAverage < 70 Then
ElseIf dblAverage < 80 Then
ElseIf dblAverage < 90 Then
ElseIf dblAverage <= 100 Then
Else
End If
```

This creates the framework of the statement. Next, insert the conditionally executed statements, as shown in bold in the following code:

```
If dblAverage < 60 Then
   lblGrade.Text = "F"
```

```
ElseIf dblAverage < 70 Then
    lblGrade.Text = "D"
ElseIf dblAverage < 80 Then
    lblGrade.Text = "C"
ElseIf dblAverage < 90 Then
    lblGrade.Text = "B"
ElseIf dblAverage <= 100 Then
    lblGrade.Text = "A"
Else
    lblGrade.Text = "Invalid Score"
End If
```

A good design approach is to decide which conditions must be tested first, and then decide what actions must be taken for each condition.

✔ Checkpoint

4.6 The following If...Then...ElseIf statement has several Boolean expressions that test the variable intX. Assuming intX equals 20, how many times will the following statement compare intX before it finds a Boolean expression that is true?

```
If intX < 10 Then
    intY = 0
ElseIf intX < 20 Then
    intY = 1
ElseIf intX < 30 Then
    intY = 2
ElseIf intX < 40 Then
    intY = 3
Else
    intY = -1
End If
```

4.7 In the following If...Then...ElseIf statement, if the variable intX equals 5, how many times will the code assign a value to intY?

```
If intX < 10 Then
    intY = 0
ElseIf intX < 20 Then
    intY = 1
ElseIf intX < 30 Then
    intY = 2
ElseIf intX < 40 Then
    intY = 3
End If
```

Look carefully at the following set of If...Then statements. If the variable intX equals 5, how many times will the code assign a value to intY?

```
If intX < 10 Then
    intY = 0
End If
If intX < 20 Then
    intY = 1
End If
If intX < 30 Then
    intY = 2
End If
If intX < 40 Then
    intY = 3
End If
```

4.5 Nested If Statements

CONCEPT: A nested If statement is an If statement inside the conditional block of another If statement. (In this section, we use the term If statement to refer to an If...Then, If...Then...Else, or If...Then...ElseIf statement.)

A **nested If statement** is an If statement that appears inside another If statement. In Tutorial 4-4, you will examine an application that uses nested If statements. The application determines whether a bank customer qualifies for a special loan. The customer must meet one of the following qualifications:

- Earn $30,000 per year or more and have worked in his or her current job for more than two years.
- Have worked at his or her current job for more than five years.

VideoNote

Completing an application with a nested If statement

Tutorial 4-4:
Completing an application with a nested If statement

Step 1: Open the *Loan Qualifier* project from the student sample programs folder named *Chap4\Loan Qualifier*.

Step 2: Open Form1 in the *Design* window. It should appear as shown in Figure 4-12.

Figure 4-12 *Loan Qualifier* application

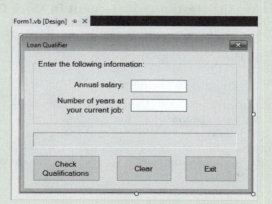

Step 3: Double-click the *Check Qualifications* button. The *Code* window will open and show the code template for the btnCheckQual_Click event handler. Complete the event handler by writing the code shown here in bold:

```
Private Sub btnCheckQual_Click(...) Handles btnCheckQual.Click
    ' Variables to hold input data.
    Dim dblSalary As Double
    Dim intYearsOnJob As Integer

    Try
        ' Get the user's input.
        dblSalary = CDbl(txtSalary.Text)
        intYearsOnJob = CInt(txtYearsOnJob.Text)

        ' Determine whether the applicant qualifies
        ' for the special loan.
        If dblSalary > 30000 Then
            If intYearsOnJob > 2 Then
                lblMessage.Text = "The applicant qualifies."
```

```
          Else
            lblMessage.Text = "The applicant does not qualify."
          End If
        Else
          If intYearsOnJob > 5 Then
            lblMessage.Text = "The applicant qualifies."
          Else
            lblMessage.Text = "The applicant does not qualify."
          End If
        End If

      Catch ex As Exception
        ' Display an error message.
        lblMessage.Text = "Please enter numeric values."
      End Try
    End Sub
```

Step 4: Save and run the application. Enter **45000** for salary and **3** for years at current job. Click the *Check Qualifications* button. The message *The applicant qualifies.* should appear on the form.

Step 5: Enter **15000** for salary and **3** for years at current job. Click the *Check Qualifications* button. The message *The applicant does not qualify.* appears on the form.

Step 6: Experiment with other values. When you are finished, click the *Exit* button to terminate the application.

Examining the Nested `If` Statement in More Depth

In the *Loan Qualifier* project, the outermost `If` statement tests the following expression:

```
If dblSalary > 30000 Then
```

If this expression is true, the nested `If` statement shown in bold is executed:

```
If dblSalary > 30000 Then
  If intYearsOnJob > 2 Then
    lblMessage.Text = "The applicant qualifies."
  Else
    lblMessage.Text = "The applicant does not qualify."
  End If
Else
  If intYearsOnJob > 5 Then
    lblMessage.Text = "The applicant qualifies."
  Else
    lblMessage.Text = "The applicant does not qualify."
  End If
End If
```

However, if the expression `dblSalary > 30000` is not true, the `Else` part of the outermost `If` statement causes its nested `If` statement, shown in bold, to execute:

```
If dblSalary > 30000 Then
  If intYearsOnJob > 2 Then
    lblMessage.Text = "The applicant qualifies."
  Else
    lblMessage.Text = "The applicant does not qualify."
  End If
```

```
  Else
    If intYearsOnJob > 5 Then
      lblMessage.Text = "The applicant qualifies."
    Else
      lblMessage.Text = "The applicant does not qualify."
    End If
End If
```

Figure 4-13 shows a flowchart for these nested If statements.

Figure 4-13 Flowchart of nested If statements

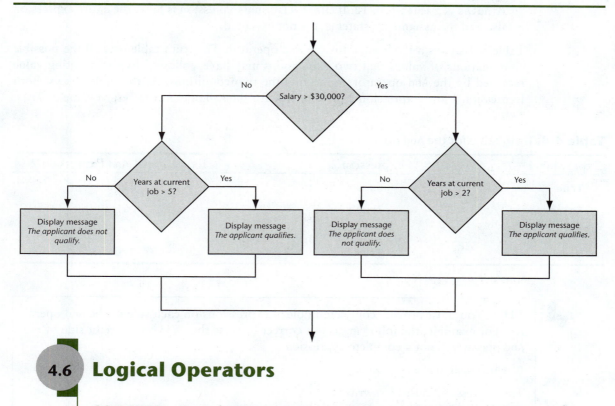

4.6 Logical Operators

CONCEPT: Logical operators combine two or more Boolean expressions into a single expression.

Logical operators can combine multiple Boolean expressions into a compound Boolean expression. Each individual Boolean expression might be very simple. But then, you can combine them using logical operators (also called Boolean operators) to make complex decisions. Table 4-3 lists Visual Basic's logical operators.

Table 4-3 Visual Basic logical operators

Operator	Effect
And	Combines two expressions into one. Both expressions must be true for the overall expression to be true.
Or	Combines two expressions into one. One or both expressions must be true for the overall expression to be true. It is only necessary for one to be true, and it does not matter which.
Xor	Combines two expressions into one. One expression (not both) must be true for the overall expression to be true. If both expressions are true, or both expressions are false, the overall expression is false.
Not	Reverses the logical value of an expression: makes a true expression false and a false expression true.

The And Operator

The **And operator** combines two expressions into one. Both expressions must be true for the overall expression to be true. The following If statement uses the And operator:

```
If intTemperature < 20  And  intMinutes > 12 Then
   lblMessage.Text = "The temperature is in the danger zone."
End If
```

In this statement, the two relational expressions are combined into a single expression. The assignment statement is executed only if intTemperature is less than 20 and intMinutes is greater than 12. If either relational expression is false, the entire expression is false and the assignment statement is not executed.

Table 4-4 shows a truth table for the And operator. The truth table lists all the possible combinations of values that two expressions may have, followed by the resulting value returned by the And operator connecting the two conditions. As the table shows, both Expression 1 and Expression 2 must be true for the And operator to return value of *True*.

Table 4-4 Truth table for the And operator

Expression 1	Expression 2	Expression 1 And Expression 2
True	False	False
False	True	False
False	False	False
True	True	True

TIP: You must provide complete Boolean expressions on each side of the And operator. For example, the following is not correct because the code on the right side of the And operator is not a complete expression:

```
intTemperature > 0 And < 100
```

The expression must be rewritten as follows:

```
intTemperature > 0 And intTemperature < 100
```

Short-Circuit Evaluation with AndAlso

When the And operator appears in a compound Boolean expression, Visual Basic evaluates both expressions on the left and right side of the And operator. Consider the following example in which the first expression compares dblX to zero and the second expression calls a Boolean function named CheckValue:

```
If dblX > 0  And  CheckValue(dblX) Then
   lblResult.Text = "Expression is True"
Else
   lblResult.Text = "Expression is False"
End If
```

When this code executes, the expression dblX > 0 will be tested, and then the CheckValue function is called. In some situations, however, it shouldn't be necessary to call the CheckValue function to determine the value of the compound Boolean expression. If the expression dblX > 0 is false, then the compound expression is also false, so the function call can be skipped. Such behavior is called *short-circuit evaluation*. In Visual Basic you use the **AndAlso operator** to achieve short-circuit evaluation. In the following example, assuming that dblX is less than or equal to zero, CheckValue is not called and *Expression is False* is displayed:

```
If dblX > 0 AndAlso  CheckValue(dblX) Then
   lblResult.Text = "Expression is True"
Else
   lblResult.Text = "Expression is False"
End If
```

The Or **Operator**

The **Or operator** combines two expressions into one. One or both expressions must be true for the overall expression to be true. It is only necessary for one to be true, and it does not matter which. The following If statement uses the Or operator:

```
If intTemperature < 20 Or  intTemperature > 100 Then
   lblMessage.Text = "The temperature is in the danger zone."
End If
```

The assignment statement will be executed if intTemperature is less than 20 or intTemperature is greater than 100. If either relational test is true, the entire expression is true and the assignment statement is executed.

Table 4-5 is a truth table for the Or operator.

Table 4-5 Truth table for the Or operator

Expression 1	Expression 2	Expression 1 or Expression 2
True	False	True
False	True	True
False	False	False
True	True	True

All it takes for an Or expression to be true is for one of the subexpressions to be true. It doesn't matter if the other subexpression is true or false.

> **TIP:** You must provide complete Boolean expressions on both sides of the Or operator. For example, the following is not correct because the code on the right side of the Or operator is not a complete Boolean expression:
>
> ```
> intTemperature < 0 Or > 100
> ```
>
> The expression must be rewritten as follows:
>
> ```
> intTemperature < 0 Or intTemperature > 100
> ```

Short Circuit-Evaluation with OrElse

When the Or operator appears in a compound Boolean expression, Visual Basic evaluates both expressions on the left and right side of the Or operator. Consider the following example, in which the first expression compares dblX to zero; the second calls a Boolean function named CheckValue:

```
If dblX = 0  Or  CheckValue(dblX) Then
   lblResult.Text = "Expression is True"
End If
```

When this code executes, the expression dblX = 0 will be tested, and then the CheckValue function is called. In some situations, however, it shouldn't be necessary to call the CheckValue function to determine the value of the compound expression. If the expression dblX = 0 is true, then we know that the compound expression is true, so the function call can be skipped. As previously mentioned, this type of evaluation is known as short-circuit evaluation, and it can be performed with the OrElse operator.

In the following example, if dblX equals zero, the CheckValue function is not called:

```
If dblX = 0  OrElse  CheckValue(dblX) Then
   lblResult.Text = "Expression is True"
End If
```

See the *ShortCircuit* application in the student sample programs folder named *Chap4\ShortCircuit* for an example of the OrElse operator.

The Xor **Operator**

Xor stands for *exclusive or*. The **Xor operator** takes two expressions as operands and creates an expression that is true when one, but not both, of the subexpressions is true. The following If statement uses the Xor operator:

```
If decTotal > 1000  Xor  decAverage > 120 Then
   lblMessage.Text = "You may try again."
End If
```

The assignment statement will be executed if decTotal is greater than 1000 or decAverage is greater than 120, but not both. If both relational tests are true, or neither is true, the entire expression is false. Table 4-6 shows a truth table for the Xor operator.

Table 4-6 Truth table for the Xor operator

Expression 1	Expression 2	Expression 1 Xor Expression 2
True	False	True
False	True	True
False	False	False
True	True	False

TIP: You must provide complete Boolean expressions on both sides of the Xor operator. For example, the following is not correct because the code on the right side of the Xor operator is not a complete Boolean expression:

```
value < 0 Xor > 100
```

The expression must be rewritten as follows:

```
value < 0 Xor value > 100
```

The Not Operator

The **Not operator** takes a Boolean expression and reverses its logical value. In other words, if the expression is true, the Not operator returns *False*, and if the expression is false, it returns *True*. The following If statement uses the Not operator:

```
If Not intTemperature > 100 Then
    lblMessage.Text = "You are below the maximum temperature."
End If
```

First, the expression intTemperature > 100 is tested to be true or false. Then the Not operator is applied to that value. If the expression intTemperature > 100 is true, the Not operator returns *False*. If it is false, the Not operator returns *True*. This example is equivalent to asking *Is intTemperature not greater than 100?* Table 4-7 shows a truth table for the Not operator.

Table 4-7 Truth table for the Not operator

Expression	Not Expression
True	False
False	True

Checking Numeric Ranges with Logical Operators

When your program is determining whether a number is inside a numeric range, it's best to use the And operator. For example, the following If statement checks the value in intX to determine whether it is in the range of 20 through 40:

```
If intX >= 20 And intX <= 40 Then
    lblMessage.Text = "The value is in the acceptable range."
End If
```

The expression in the If statement is true only when intX is greater than or equal to 20 *and* less than or equal to 40. The value in intX must be within the range of 20 through 40 for this expression to be true.

When your program is determining whether a number is outside a range, it's best to use the Or operator. The following statement determines whether intX is outside the range of 20 through 40:

```
If intX < 20 Or intX > 40 Then
    lblMessage.Text = "The value is outside the acceptable range."
End If
```

It is important not to get these logical operators confused. For example, the following expression cannot be true because no value exists that is both less than 20 and greater than 40.

```
If intX < 20 And intX > 40 Then
    lblMessage.Text = "The value is outside the acceptable range."
End If
```

If You Want to Know More about Using Not, And, Or, and Xor Together

It is possible to write an expression containing more than one logical operator. For example, examine the following If statement:

```
If intX < 0 And intY > 100 Or intZ = 50 Then
    ' Perform some statement.
End If
```

Logical operators have an order of precedence. The Not operator has the highest precedence, followed by the And operator, followed by the Or operator, followed by the Xor operator. So, in the example statement, the following expression is evaluated first:

```
intX < 0 And intY > 100
```

The result of this expression is then applied to the Or operator to carry out the rest of the condition. For example, if the first expression (using And) is true, the remainder of the condition will be tested as follows:

```
True Or intZ = 50
```

If the first expression (using And) is false, however, the remainder of the condition will be tested as follows:

```
False Or intZ = 50
```

Always use parentheses in logical expressions to clarify the order of evaluation. The following If statement confirms that the And operator executes before the Or operator:

```
If (intX < 0 And intY > 100) Or intZ = 50 Then
    ' Perform some statement.
End If
```

You can use parentheses to force one expression to be tested before others. For example, look at the following If statement:

```
If intX < 0 And (intY > 100 Or intZ = 50) Then
    ' Perform some statement.
End If
```

In the statement, the expression (intY > 100 Or intZ = 50) is tested first.

If You Want to Know More about Using Math Operators with Relational and Logical Operators

It is possible to write expressions containing math, relational, and logical operators. For example, look at the following code segment:

```
intA = 5
intB = 7
intX = 100
intY = 30
If (intX > (intA * 10)) And (intY < (intB + 20)) Then
    ' Perform some statement.
End If
```

In statements containing complex conditions, math operators execute first. After the math operators, relational operators execute. Logical operators execute last. Let's use this order to step through the evaluation of the condition shown in our sample If statement. First, the math operators execute, causing the statement to become

```
If (intX > 50) And (intY < 27) Then
```

Next, the relational operators execute, causing the statement to become

```
If True And False Then
```

Since True And False equals *False*, the condition is false.

 **Checkpoint**

4.8 The following truth table shows various combinations of the values *True* and *False* connected by a logical operator. Complete the table by indicating whether the result of each combination is *True* or *False*.

Logical Expression	Result
True And False	_____
True And True	_____
False And True	_____
False And False	_____
True Or False	_____
True Or True	_____
False Or True	_____
False Or False	_____
True Xor False	_____
True Xor True	_____
Not True	_____
Not False	_____

 4.7 **Comparing, Testing, and Working with Strings**

CONCEPT: Visual Basic provides various methods in the String class that make it easy to work with strings. This section shows you how to use relational operators to compare strings, and discusses several functions and string methods that perform tests and manipulations on strings.

In the preceding examples, you saw how numbers can be compared using the relational operators. You can also use relational operators to compare strings. For example, look at the following code segment, in which strName1 and strName2 are string variables.

```
strName1 = "Mary"
strName2 = "Mark"
If strName1 = strName2 Then
   lblMessage.Text = "The names are the same"
Else
   lblMessage.Text = "The names are NOT the same"
End If
```

The = operator tests strName1 and strName2 to determine whether they are equal. Since the strings "Mary" and "Mark" are not equal, the Else part of the If statement will cause the message *The names are NOT the same* to be assigned to lblMessage.Text.

You can compare string variables with string literals as well. The following code sample uses the <> operator to determine if strMonth is not equal to *October*:

```
If strMonth <> "October" Then
   ' statement
End If
```

You can also use the >, <, =, and <= operators to compare strings. Before we look at these operators, though, we must understand how characters are stored in memory.

Computers do not actually store characters, such as *A*, *B*, *C*, and so on, in memory. Instead, they store numeric codes that represent the characters. Visual Basic uses **Unicode**, which is a numbering system that represents all letters of the alphabet (lowercase and uppercase), the printable digits 0 through 9, punctuation symbols, and special characters. Each character is stored in memory as its corresponding Unicode number. When the computer is instructed to print the value on the screen, it displays the character that corresponds to the numeric code.

NOTE: Unicode is an international encoding system that is extensive enough to represent all the characters of most of the world's alphabets.

In Unicode, letters are arranged alphabetically. Because *A* comes before *B*, the numeric code for the letter *A* is less than the code for the letter *B*. In the following If statement, the relational expression "A" < "B" is true.

```
If "A" < "B" Then
  ' Do something
End If
```

TIP: When comparing strings, make sure they are consistent in their use of uppercase and lowercase letters. Avoid comparing "jones" to "Adams" or "BAKER", for example. The ordering of strings is affected by the choice of uppercase and lowercase letters.

When you use relational operators to compare strings, the strings are compared character-by-character. For example, look at the following code segment:

```
strName1 = "Mary"
strName2 = "Mark"
If strName1 > strName2 Then
  lblMessage.Text = "Mary is greater than Mark"
Else
  lblMessage.Text = "Mary is not greater than Mark"
End If
```

The > operator compares each character in the strings "Mary" and "Mark", beginning with the first, or leftmost, characters, as shown in Figure 4-14.

Figure 4-14 String comparison

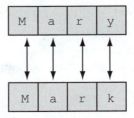

Here is how the comparison takes place:

1. The *M* in *Mary* is compared with the *M* in *Mark*. Since these are the same, the next characters are compared.
2. The *a* in *Mary* is compared with the *a* in *Mark*. Since these are the same, the next characters are compared.

3. The *r* in *Mary* is compared with the *r* in *Mark*. Since these are the same, the next characters are compared.
4. The *y* in *Mary* is compared with the *k* in *Mark*. Since these are not the same, the two strings are not equal. The character *y* is greater than *k*, so it is determined that *Mary* is greater than *Mark*.

NOTE: If one of the strings in a relational comparison is shorter in length than the other, Visual Basic treats the shorter character as if it were padded with blank spaces. For example, suppose the strings `"High"` and `"Hi"` were compared. The string `"Hi"` would be treated as if it were four characters in length, with the last two characters being spaces. Because the space character has a lower value than the alphabetic characters in Unicode, `"Hi"` would be less than `"High"`.

Testing for No Input

You can determine whether the user has entered a value into a text box by comparing the TextBox control's Text property to the predefined constant `String.Empty` as shown here:

```
If txtInput.Text = String.Empty Then
   lblMessage.Text = "Please enter a value"
Else
   ' The txtInput control contains input, so
   ' perform an operation with it here.
End If
```

The predefined constant `String.Empty` represents an **empty string**, which is a string that contains no characters.

The `If` statement copies the string *Please enter a value* to `lblMessage` if the `txtInput` control contains no input. The statements following the `Else` clause are executed only if `txtInput` contains a value. You can use this technique to determine whether the user has provided input for a required field before performing operations on that field.

NOTE: The technique we used in the preceding `If` statement does not detect a string that contains only spaces. A space is a character, just as the letter *A* is a character. If the user types only spaces into a text box, you will have to trim away the spaces to determine if any other characters were typed. Later in this section, we will discuss functions for trimming spaces from strings.

The ToUpper and ToLower Methods

The `ToUpper` and `ToLower` methods are both members of the `String` class, so they may be called with any string variable or expression. The **ToUpper method** returns the uppercase equivalent of a string. Here is the method's general format:

```
StringExpression.ToUpper()
```

StringExpression can be any string variable or string expression. In the following example, `strLittleWord` and `strBigWord` are string variables:

```
strLittleWord = "Hello"
strBigWord = strLittleWord.ToUpper()
```

After the statement executes, strBigWord will contain "HELLO" in uppercase letters. Notice that the original string, "Hello" had one uppercase letter—the initial *H*. The ToUpper method converts only lowercase characters. Characters that are already uppercase and characters that are not alphabet letters are not converted.

> **TIP:** The ToUpper method does not modify the value of the string, but returns the string's uppercase equivalent. For example, after the statements in the previous example execute, strLittleWord still contains the original string "Hello".

The **ToLower method** works just like the ToUpper method, except it returns a lowercase version of a string. Here is the method's general format:

```
StringExpression.ToLower()
```

In the following example, strBigTown and strLittleTown are string variables:

```
strBigTown = "NEW YORK"
strLittleTown = strBigTown.ToLower()
```

After the statements execute, the variable strLittleTown contains the string "new york". The ToLower method converts only uppercase characters. Characters that are already lowercase, and characters that are not alphabet letters, are not converted.

> **TIP:** Like ToUpper, the ToLower method does not modify the original string.

You may also use the ToUpper and ToLower methods with a control's Text property. In the following example strLastName is a string variable:

```
strLastName = txtLastName.Text.ToUpper()
```

The ToUpper and ToLower methods are helpful in performing string comparisons. String comparisons in Visual Basic are *case sensitive*, meaning that uppercase letters are not considered the same as their lowercase counterparts. In other words, *A* is not the same as *a*. This can lead to problems when you construct If statements that compare strings. Tutorial 4-5 leads you through such an example.

Tutorial 4-5:
Examining an application that performs string comparisons

Step 1: Open the *Secret Word* project from the student sample programs folder named *Chap4\ Secret Word*.

Step 2: Run the application. The form shown in Figure 4-15 appears.

This application asks you to enter the secret word, which might be similar to a password in some programs. The secret word is *PROSPERO*.

Step 3: Enter **prospero** in all lowercase letters, and click the *Ok* button. You will see the message *Wrong! That is NOT the secret word!*

4.7 Comparing, Testing, and Working with Strings   **263**

Figure 4-15 *Secret Word* form

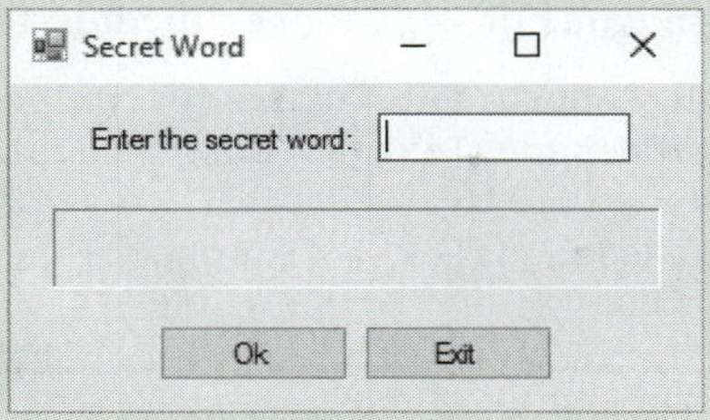

Step 4: Enter **Prospero** with an uppercase *P*, followed by all lowercase letters. Click the *Ok* button. Once again, you see the message *Wrong! That is NOT the secret word!*

Step 5: Enter **PROSPERO** in all uppercase letters and click the *Ok* button. This time you see the message *Congratulations! That is the secret word!*

Step 6: Click the *Exit* button to close the application.

Step 7: Open the *Code* window and look at the btnOk_Click event handler. The code is as follows:

```
Private Sub btnOk_Click(...) Handles btnOk.Click
  ' Compare the input entered with the secret word.
  If txtInput.Text = "PROSPERO" Then
    lblMessage.Text = "Congratulations! That is the secret word!"
  Else
    lblMessage.Text = "Wrong! That is NOT the secret word!"
  End If
End Sub
```

The If...Then...Else statement compares the string entered by the user to *PROSPERO* in all uppercase letters. But what if the programmer intended to accept the word without regard to case? What if *prospero* in all lowercase letters is valid as well? One solution would be to modify the If statement to test for all the other possible values. However, to test for all the possible combination of lowercase and uppercase letters would require a large amount of code.

A better approach is to convert the text entered by the user to all uppercase letters, and then compare the converted text to *PROSPERO*. When the user enters the word *prospero* in any combination of uppercase or lowercase characters, this test will return *True*. Modify the code by adding a call to the ToUpper method, as shown in bold in the following code.

```
If txtInput.Text.ToUpper() = "PROSPERO" Then
  lblMessage.Text = "Congratulations! That is the secret word!"
Else
  lblMessage.Text = "Wrong! That is NOT the secret word!"
End If
```

Step 8: Run the application. When the form appears, enter **prospero** in all lowercase letters and click the *Ok* button. This time you see the message *Congratulations! That is the secret word!* You can experiment with various combinations of uppercase and lowercase letters. As long as you type the word *prospero* the application will recognize it as the secret word.

Step 9: Close the project.

The ToLower method can also be used in Tutorial 4-5 to accomplish the same result, as shown in bold in the following code. Just make sure you compare the return value of the ToLower method to an all lowercase string.

```
If txtInput.Text.ToLower() = "prospero"  Then
   lblMessage.Text = "Congratulations! That is the secret word!"
Else
   lblMessage.Text = "Wrong! That is NOT the secret word!"
End If
```

The IsNumeric Function

The **IsNumeric function** accepts a string as its argument and returns *True* if the string contains a number. The function returns *False* if the string's contents cannot be recognized as a number. Here is the function's general use:

```
IsNumeric(StringExpression)
```

Here is an example:

```
Dim strNumber As String
strNumber = "576"
If IsNumeric(strNumber) Then
   lblMessage.Text = "It is a number"
Else
   lblMessage.Text = "It is NOT a number"
End If
```

In this statement, the expression IsNumeric(strNumber) returns *True* because the contents of strNumber can be recognized as a number. In the following code segment, however, the expression returns *False*:

```
strNumber = "123abc"
If IsNumeric(strNumber) Then
   lblMessage.Text = "It is a number"
Else
   lblMessage.Text = "It is NOT a number"
End If
```

When you want the user to enter numeric data, the IsNumeric function is useful for checking user input and confirming that it is valid.

Determining the Length of a String

The **Length property**, a member of the String class, returns the number of characters in a string. Here is an example:

```
Dim strName As String = "Herman"
Dim intNumChars As Integer
intNumChars = strName.Length
```

The code stores 6 in intNumChars because the length of the string "Herman" is 6.

You can also determine the length of a control's Text property, as shown in the following code:

```
If txtInput.Text.Length > 20 Then
   lblMessage.Text = "Please enter no more than 20 characters."
End If
```

There are many situations in which Length is useful. One example is when you must display or print a string and have only a limited amount of space.

> **WARNING:** If you attempt to get the length of an uninitialized string variable, an exception (runtime error) occurs. You can prevent this error by initializing string variables with an empty string, as shown in the following statement:
>
> ```
> Dim str As String = String.Empty
> ```

Optional Topic: Trimming Spaces from Strings

Sometimes it is necessary to trim leading and/or trailing spaces from a string before performing other operations on the string, such as a comparison. A **leading space** is a space that appears at the beginning, or left side, of a string. For instance, the following string has three leading spaces:

```
"   Hello"
```

A **trailing space** is a space that appears at the end, or right side, of a string, after the non-space characters. The following string has three trailing spaces:

```
"Hello   "
```

The String class has three methods for removing spaces: TrimStart, TrimEnd, and Trim. Here is the general format of each method:

```
StringExpression.TrimStart()
StringExpression.TrimEnd()
StringExpression.Trim()
```

The **TrimStart method** returns a copy of the string expression with all leading spaces removed. The **TrimEnd method** returns a copy of the string expression with all trailing spaces removed. The **Trim method** returns a copy of the string expression with all leading and trailing spaces removed. The following is an example:

```
strGreeting = "   Hello   "
lblMessage1.Text = strGreeting.TrimStart()
lblMessage2.Text = strGreeting.TrimEnd()
lblMessage3.Text = strGreeting.Trim()
```

In this code, the first statement assigns the string "   Hello   " (with three leading spaces and three trailing spaces) to the named variable, strGreeting. In the second statement, the TrimStart method is called. Its return value, "Hello   ", is assigned to lblMessage1.Text. In the third statement, the TrimEnd method is called. Its return value, "   Hello", is assigned to lblMessage2.Text. In the fourth statement, the Trim method is called. Its return value, "Hello", is assigned to lblMessage3.Text.

These methods do not modify the string variable, but return a modified copy of the variable. To actually modify the string variable you must use a statement such as the following:

```
strGreeting = strGreeting.Trim()
```

After this statement executes, the strGreeting variable no longer contains leading or trailing spaces.

Like the Length property, these methods may also be used with a control's Text property. The following is an example:

```
Dim strName As String
strName = txtName.Text.Trim()
```

The Substring Method

The **Substring method** returns a substring, or a string within a string. There are two formats:

```
StringExpression.Substring(Start)
StringExpression.Substring(Start, Length)
```

The positions of the characters in *StringExpression* are numbered, with the first character at position 0. In the first format shown for the method, an integer argument, *Start*, indicates the starting position of the string to be extracted from *StringExpression*. The method returns a string containing all characters from the *Start* position to the end of *StringExpression*. For example, look at the following code:

```
Dim strLastName As String
Dim strFullName As String = "George Washington"
strLastName = strFullName.Substring(7)
```

After this code executes, the variable strLastName will contain the string "Washington" because "Washington" begins at position 7 in strFullName, and continues to the end of the string.

In the second format shown for Substring, a second integer argument, *Length*, indicates the number of characters to extract, including the starting character. For example, look at the following code:

```
Dim strFirstName As String
Dim strFullName As String = "George Washington"
strFirstName = strFullName.Substring(0, 6)
```

In this code, the Substring method returns the six characters that begin at position 0 in strFullName. After the code executes, the variable strFirstName contains the string "George".

Optional Topic: The IndexOf Method

The **IndexOf method** searches for a character or a string within a string. The method has three general formats:

```
StringExpression.IndexOf(SearchString)
StringExpression.IndexOf(SearchString, Start)
StringExpression.IndexOf(SearchString, Start, Count)
```

In the first format, *SearchString* is the string or character to search for within *StringExpression*. The method returns the character position, or index, of the first occurrence of *SearchString* if it is found within *StringExpression*. If *SearchString* is not found, the method returns –1. For example, look at the following code:

```
Dim strName As String = "Angelina Adams"
Dim intPosition As Integer
intPosition = strName.IndexOf("e")
```

After this code executes, the variable position equals 3 because the character *e* is found at character position 3.

 NOTE: With the IndexOf method, the first character position is 0.

In the second format shown for `IndexOf`, a second argument, *Start*, is an integer that specifies a starting position within *StringExpression* for the search to begin. The following is an example:

```
Dim strName As String = "Angelina Adams"
Dim intPosition As Integer
intPosition = strName.IndexOf("A", 1)
```

After the code executes, the variable `intPosition` equals 9. The `IndexOf` method begins its search at character position 1 (the second character), so the first *A* is skipped.

NOTE: The version of the `IndexOf` method used here performs a case sensitive search. When searching for *A* it does not return the position of *a*.

In the third format shown for `IndexOf`, a third argument, *Count*, is an integer specifying the number of characters within *StringExpression* to search. Here is an example:

```
Dim strName As String = "Angelina Adams"
Dim intPosition As Integer
intPosition = strName.IndexOf("A", 1, 7)
```

After the code executes, the variable position equals –1. The `IndexOf` method searches only 7 characters, beginning at character 1. Because *A* is not found in the characters searched, the method returns –1.

WARNING: An exception (runtime error) will occur if the starting position argument passed to `IndexOf` is negative or specifies a nonexistent position. Get the length of the string before calling `IndexOf` to ensure the index is in a valid range.

The following code shows how to use the `IndexOf` method to determine if a search string exists within a string:

```
Dim strName As String = "Angelina Adams"
If strName.IndexOf("Adams") = -1 Then
  lblMessage.Text = "Adams is not found"
End If
```

Tutorial 4-6 completes a string searching application.

Tutorial 4-6:
Completing a string searching application

In this tutorial, you will write code that implements a string searching program. You will have an opportunity to try the `IsNumeric`, `Trim`, and `IndexOf` methods. The user interface is already created, so you can concentrate on the program code that makes it work. Here are its basic features:

- A string is shown at the top of the form, as shown in Figure 4-16, containing various character patterns (*abc*, *ABC*, *00123*, and so on). It uses a blue font, which appears gray on the printed page.
- The user inputs a string into the text box, indicating which substring the user wants to find.
- The user clicks the *Go* button, as shown in Figure 4-17.

- The program displays the position in which the substring was found. You can verify the accuracy of the result by inspecting the numbers in the scale line below the string shown in blue.
- The user can change the starting index position of the search from 0 to another value. In Figure 4-18, the user has selected index position 4 to begin searching. The next matching occurrence of *ABC* is found at index 20.
- If the user enters a nonnumeric index, an error message box pops up, as shown in Figure 4-19.

Figure 4-16 *String Finder* application, when started

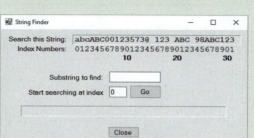

Figure 4-17 User enters substring the user wants to find, clicks *Go* button

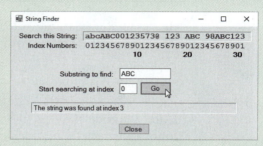

Figure 4-18 Searching for *ABC* starting at index position 4

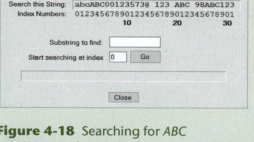

Figure 4-19 User has entered a nonnumeric index

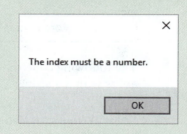

Step 1:   Open the *String Finder* project from the student sample programs folder named *Chap4\String Finder*.

Step 2:   Open Form1 in the *Designer* window. Click each control and view its name in the *Properties* window. When you begin writing code, you will want to know the control names.

Step 3:   Double-click the *Go* button. The *Code* window will open and show the code template for the btnGo_Click event handler. Complete the event handler by writing the code shown here in bold:

```
Private Sub btnGo_Click(...) Handles btnGo.Click
    ' Variable declarations
    Dim intStartIndex As Integer ' Starting index of the search
    Dim intFoundIndex As Integer ' Index of the found substring

    ' Determine whether the starting index is numeric.
    If IsNumeric(txtStartIndex.Text) Then

        ' Determine whether a string to search for was entered.
        If txtToFind.Text.Length > 0 Then
```

```
            ' Get the starting index for the search.
            intStartIndex = CInt(txtStartIndex.Text)

            ' Search for the substring.
            intFoundIndex = lblString.Text.IndexOf(txtToFind.Text,
                                               intStartIndex)

            ' Indicate whether the search string was found.
            If intFoundIndex = -1 Then
              lblResults.Text = "The string was not found."
            Else
              lblResults.Text = "The string was found at index " &
                               intFoundIndex
            End If

          Else
            ' Display an error message for an empty search string.
            MessageBox.Show("Enter a string to search for.")
          End If
        Else
          ' Display an error message for a non-numeric index.
          MessageBox.Show("The index must be a number.")
        End If
    End Sub
```

Step 4: Save and run the program. Search for the substring *ABC* starting at index 0. The program should find the string at position 3.

Step 5: Search for *ABC* starting at index 4. The program should find the string at position 20.

Checkpoint

4.9 Are each of the following relational expressions *True* or *False*?
   a. "ABC" > "XYZ"   _____
   b. "AAA" = "AA"   _____
   c. "ABC123" < "abc123"   _____

4.10 Match the description in the right column with the method or function in the left column.

_____ IsNumeric	a.	Returns the uppercase equivalent of a string.
_____ ToLower	b.	Returns the number of characters in a string.
_____ ToUpper	c.	Returns a copy of a string without trailing spaces.
_____ Length	d.	Returns a copy of a string without leading or trailing spaces.
_____ TrimStart	e.	Searches for the first occurrence of a character or string within a string.
_____ Substring	f.	Accepts a string as its argument and returns *True* if the string contains a number.
_____ IndexOf	g.	Returns the lowercase equivalent of a string.
_____ TrimEnd	h.	Extracts a string from within a string.
_____ Trim	i.	Returns a copy of a string without leading spaces.

4.8 The Select Case **Statement**

CONCEPT: In a Select Case statement, one of several possible actions is taken, depending on the value of an expression.

The If...Then...ElseIf statement allows your program to branch into one of several possible paths. It performs a series of tests and branches when one of these tests is true. The **Select Case statement**, which is a similar mechanism, tests the value of an expression only once, and then uses that value to determine which set of statements to branch to. Following is the general format of the Select Case statement. The items inside the brackets are optional.

```
Select Case TestExpression
  [Case ExpressionList
    [one or more statements]]
  [Case ExpressionList
    [one or more statements]]
  [Case Else
    [one or more statements]]
End Select
```

Case statements may be repeated as many times as necessary.

The first line starts with Select Case and is followed by a test expression. The test expression may be any numeric or string expression that you wish to test.

Starting on the next line is a sequence of one or more Case statements. Each Case statement follows this general form:

```
Case  ExpressionList
    one or more statements
```

After the word Case is an expression list, so-called because it may hold one or more expressions. Beginning on the next line, one or more statements appear. These statements are executed if the value of the test expression matches any of the expressions in the Case statement's expression list.

A Case Else comes after all the Case statements. This branch is selected if none of the Case expression lists match the test expression. The entire Select Case construct is terminated with an End Select statement.

 WARNING: The Case Else section is optional. If you leave it out, however, your program will have nowhere to branch to if the test expression doesn't match any of the expressions in the Case expression lists.

Here is an example of the Select Case statement:

```
Select Case CInt(txtInput.Text)
  Case 1
    MessageBox.Show("Day 1 is Monday.")
  Case 2
    MessageBox.Show("Day 2 is Tuesday.")
  Case 3
    MessageBox.Show("Day 3 is Wednesday.")
```

```
        Case 4
          MessageBox.Show("Day 4 is Thursday.")
        Case 5
          MessageBox.Show("Day 5 is Friday.")
        Case 6
          MessageBox.Show("Day 6 is Saturday.")
        Case 7
          MessageBox.Show("Day 7 is Sunday.")
        Case Else
          MessageBox.Show("That value is invalid.")
      End Select
```

Let's look at this example more closely. The test expression is `CInt(txtInput.Text)`. The `Case` statements `Case 1`, `Case 2`, `Case 3`, `Case 4`, `Case 5`, `Case 6`, and `Case 7` mark where the program is to branch to if the test expression is equal to the values 1, 2, 3, 4, 5, 6, or 7. The `Case Else` section is branched to if the test expression is not equal to any of these values.

Suppose the user has entered 3 into the `txtInput` text box, so the expression `CInt(txtInput.Text)` is equal to 3. Visual Basic compares this value with the first `Case` statement's expression list:

```
      Select Case CInt(txtInput.Text)
➡️      Case 1
          MessageBox.Show("Day 1 is Monday.")
```

The only value in the expression list is 1, and this is not equal to 3, so Visual Basic goes to the next `Case`:

```
      Select Case CInt(txtInput.Text)
        Case 1
          MessageBox.Show("Day 1 is Monday.")
➡️      Case 2
          MessageBox.Show("Day 2 is Tuesday.")
```

Once again, the value in the expression list does not equal 3, so Visual Basic goes to the next `Case`:

```
      Select Case CInt(txtInput.Text)
        Case 1
          MessageBox.Show("Day 1 is Monday.")
        Case 2
          MessageBox.Show("Day 2 is Tuesday.")
➡️      Case 3
          MessageBox.Show("Day 3 is Wednesday.")
```

This time, the value in the `Case`'s expression list matches the value of the test expression, so the `MessageBox.Show` statement on the next line executes. (If there had been multiple statements appearing between the `Case 3` and `Case 4` statements, all would have executed.) After the `MessageBox.Show` statement executes, the program jumps to the statement immediately following the `End Select` statement.

Flowcharting the `Select Case` Statement

The flowchart segment in Figure 4-20 shows the general form of a `Select Case` statement. The diamond represents the test expression, which is compared to a series of values. The path of execution follows the value matching the test expression. If none of the values matches a test expression, the default path is followed (`Case Else`).

Figure 4-20 General form of a `Select Case` statement

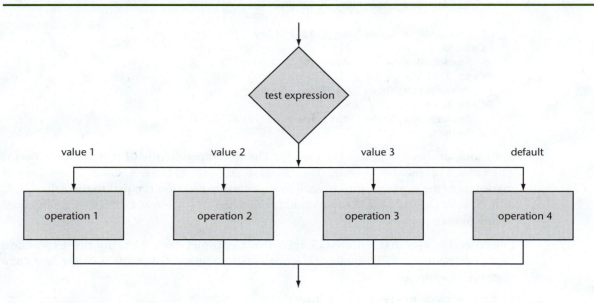

More About the Expression List

The `Case` statement's expression list can contain multiple expressions, separated by commas. For example, the first `Case` statement in the following code compares `intNumber` to 1, 3, 5, 7, and 9, and the second `Case` statement compares it to 2, 4, 6, 8, and 10. In the following code, assume that `strStatus` is a string variable:

```
Select Case intNumber
  Case 1, 3, 5, 7, 9
    strStatus = "Odd"
  Case 2, 4, 6, 8, 10
    strStatus = "Even"
  Case Else
    strStatus = "Out of Range"
End Select
```

The `Case` statement can also test string values. In the following code, assume that `strAnimal` is a string variable:

```
Select Case strAnimal
  Case "Dogs", "Cats"
    MessageBox.Show("House Pets")
  Case "Cows", "Pigs", "Goats"
    MessageBox.Show("Farm Animals")
  Case "Lions", "Tigers", "Bears"
    MessageBox.Show("Oh My!")
End Select
```

You can use relational operators in the `Case` statement, as shown by the following example. The `Is` keyword represents the test expression in the relational comparison.

```
Select Case dblTemperature
  Case Is <= 75
    blnTooCold = True
  Case Is >= 100
    blnTooHot = True
  Case Else
    blnJustRight = True
End Select
```

Finally, you can determine whether the test expression falls within a range of values. This requires the To keyword, as shown in the following code.

```
Select Case intScore
  Case Is >= 90
    strGrade = "A"
  Case 80 To 89
    strGrade = "B"
  Case 70 To 79
    strGrade = "C"
  Case 60 To 69
    strGrade = "D"
  Case 0 To 59
    strGrade = "F"
  Case Else
    MessageBox.Show("Invalid Score")
End Select
```

The numbers used on each side of the To keyword are included in the range. So, the statement Case 80 To 89 matches the values 80, 89, or any number in between.

TIP: The To keyword works properly only when the smaller number appears on its left and the larger number appears on its right. You can write an expression such as 10 To 0, but it will not function properly at runtime.

Tutorial 4-7 examines a sales commission calculator application.

Tutorial 4-7:
Examining *Crazy Al's Sales Commission Calculator* application

Crazy Al's Computer Emporium is a retail seller of computers and tech gadgets. The sales staff at Crazy Al's works strictly on commission. At the end of the month, each salesperson's commission is calculated according to Table 4-8.

For example, a salesperson with $16,000 in monthly sales earns a 12% commission ($1,920.00). A salesperson with $20,000 in monthly sales earns a 14% commission ($2,800.00).

Table 4-8 Sales commission rates

Sales This Month	Commission Rate
Less than $10,000	5%
$10,000 – $14,999	10%
$15,000 – $17,999	12%
$18,000 – $21,999	14%
$22,000 or more	16%

Because the staff is paid once per month, Crazy Al's allows each employee to take up to $1,500 per month in advance pay. When sales commissions are calculated, the amount of each employee's advance pay is subtracted from the commission. If any salesperson's commission is less than the amount of the advance, he or she must reimburse Crazy Al's for the difference.

Here are two examples:

- Beverly's monthly sales were $21,400, so her commission is $2,996. She took $1,500 in advance pay. At the end of the month she gets a check for $1,496.
- John's monthly sales were $12,600, so his commission is $1,260. He took $1,500 in advance pay. At the end of the month he must pay back $240 to Crazy Al's.

In this tutorial, you will complete an application that will determine a salesperson's commission. The application's form has already been created for you, and is shown in Figure 4-21.

Figure 4-21 *Crazy Al's Commission Calculator* form

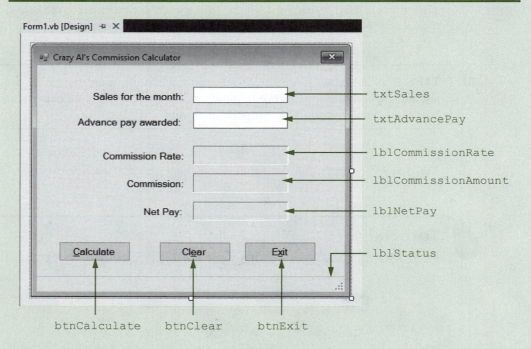

Step 1: Open the *Crazy Al* project from the student sample programs folder named *Chap4\Crazy Al*.

Step 2: Double-click the btnCalculate button, and complete its Click event handler by writing the bold code shown here. As you are writing the code, notice that the Select Case construct has a Case statement for each level of sales in the commission table.

```
Private Sub btnCalculate_Click(...) Handles btnCalculate.Click
    ' Variable declarations
    Dim decSalesAmount As Decimal            ' Monthly sales amount
    Dim decAdvancePayAmount As Decimal       ' Advance pay taken
    Dim decCommissionRate As Decimal         ' Commission rate
    Dim decCommissionAmount As Decimal       ' Commission
    Dim decNetPay As Decimal                 ' Net pay

    Try
        ' Clear any previous error messages.
        lblStatus.Text = String.Empty
```

```
        ' Get the amount of sales.
        decSalesAmount = CDec(txtSales.Text)

        ' Get the amount of advance pay.
        decAdvancePayAmount = CDec(txtAdvancePay.Text)

        ' Determine the commission rate.
        Select Case decSalesAmount
            Case Is < 10000
                decCommissionRate = 0.05D

            Case 10000 To 14999
                decCommissionRate = 0.1D

            Case 15000 To 17999
                decCommissionRate = 0.12D

            Case 18000 To 21999
                decCommissionRate = 0.14D

            Case Is >= 22000
                decCommissionRate = 0.15D
        End Select

        ' Calculate the commission and net pay amounts.
        decCommissionAmount = decSalesAmount * decCommissionRate
        decNetPay = decCommissionAmount - decAdvancePayAmount

        ' Display the rate, commission, and net pay.
        lblCommissionRate.Text = decCommissionRate.ToString("p")
        lblCommissionAmount.Text = decCommissionAmount.ToString("c")
        lblNetPay.Text = decNetPay.ToString("c")

    Catch
        ' Display an error message alerting user to invalid input.
        lblStatus.Text = "Please enter numeric values."
    End Try
End Sub
```

Step 3: Save the project, and then run the application.

Step 4: Enter 32000 as the amount of sales for this month (first text box), and Enter 2000 as the amount of advance pay taken (second text box). Click the *Calculate* button. You should see the commission rate, commission, and net pay information, as shown in Figure 4-22.

Step 5: Click the *Clear* button to reset the contents of the input and display fields. Experiment with other values for sales and advance pay. When you are finished, click the *Exit* button to end the application.

Figure 4-22 Calculations filled in

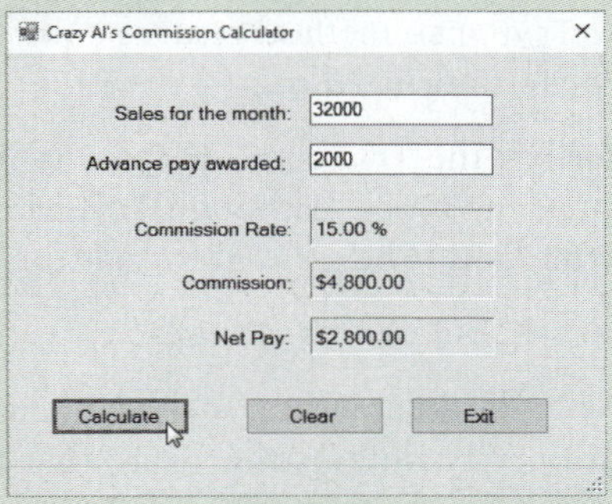

 **Checkpoint**

4.11 Convert the following `If...Then...ElseIf` statement into a `Select Case` statement.

```
If intQuantity >= 0 And intQuantity <= 9 Then
    decDiscount = 0.1
ElseIf intQuantity >= 10 And intQuantity <= 19 Then
    decDiscount = 0.2
ElseIf intQuantity >= 20 And intQuantity <= 29 Then
    decDiscount = 0.3
ElseIf intQuantity >= 30 Then
    decDiscount = 0.4
Else
    MessageBox.Show("Invalid Data")
End If
```

 4.9   Introduction to Input Validation

CONCEPT: Input validation is the process of inspecting input values and determining whether they are valid.

The accuracy of a program's output is only as good as the accuracy of its input. Therefore, it is important that your applications perform input validation on the values entered by the user. **Input validation** is the process of inspecting input values and determining whether they are valid. In this section we will discuss ways of using decision structures to prevent data conversion exceptions, and determine whether numeric values entered by the user fall within an acceptable range.

Preventing Data Conversion Exceptions

In Chapter 3 you learned that an exception will occur if you try to convert the contents of a TextBox to a number, but the TextBox contains nonnumeric data. We introduced the `Try-Catch` statement, and you saw how to use it to handle those exceptions when they occur. Now that you know how to use the `If...Then` statement, you have more validation techniques at your disposal.

The **TryParse method** lets you determine whether a string (such as a TextBox's Text property) contains a value that can be successfully converted to a specific data type. You can use this method *before* attempting to perform the actual conversion, to avoid unwanted runtime errors. *Parsing a string* means to analyze it, and determine whether the string can be converted to a specific data type. If the conversion is possible, it is completed, and the `TryParse` method returns *True* (a Boolean value). If the conversion is not possible, `TryParse` returns *False*.

Table 4-9 describes the `TryParse` method as it occurs in the Integer, Double, Decimal, Single, and DateTime types. Although `TryParse` appears in all of these types, it is essentially the same method. The general format for `TryParse` is

```
Type.TryParse(source, destination)
```

Type can be a standard data type, such as Integer, Double, Decimal, Single, or DateTime. The *source* parameter contains the string that is about to be converted. The *destination* parameter is the variable that will receive the converted value. The method returns a Boolean result.

Table 4-9 TryParse methods

Method	Description
Integer.TryParse	Accepts two arguments: a string (argument 1) and an Integer variable (argument 2). The method attempts to convert the string (argument 1) to an Integer. If successful, the converted value is assigned to the Integer variable (argument 2) and the method returns *True*. If the conversion is not successful, the method returns *False*.
Double.TryParse	Accepts two arguments: a string (argument 1) and Double variable (argument 2). The method attempts to convert the string (argument 1) to a Double. If successful, the converted value is assigned to the Double variable (argument 2) and the method returns *True*. If the conversion is not successful, the method returns *False*.
Decimal.TryParse	Accepts two arguments: a string (argument 1) and a Decimal variable (argument 2). The method attempts to convert the string (argument 1) to a Decimal. If successful, the converted value is assigned to the Decimal variable (argument 2) and the method returns *True*. If the conversion is not successful, the method returns *False*.
Single.TryParse	Accepts two arguments: a string (argument 1) and a Single variable (argument 2). The method attempts to convert the string (argument 1) to a Single. If successful, the converted value is assigned to the Single variable (argument 2) and the method returns *True*. If the conversion is not successful, the method returns *False*.
DateTime.TryParse	Accepts two arguments: a string (argument 1) and a DateTime variable (argument 2). The method attempts to convert the string (argument 1) to a DateTime value. If successful, the converted value is assigned to the DateTime variable (argument 2) and the method returns *True*. If the conversion is not successful, the method returns *False*.

Because the TryParse method returns either *True* or *False*, it is commonly called as the Boolean expression in an If...Then statement. The following code snippet shows an example using the Integer.TryParse method. The lines are numbered for reference purposes. As you read the code, assume txtInput is the name of a TextBox control.

```
1  Dim intNumber As Integer
2
3  If Integer.TryParse(txtInput.Text, intNumber) Then
4    lblResult.Text = "The value is " + intNumber
5  Else
6    lblResult.Text = "Cannot convert to an integer"
7  End If
```

The purpose of this code snippet is to convert the value of txtInput's Text property to an Integer and assign that value to the intNumber variable, which is declared in line 1. In line 3, the If...Then statement calls the Integer.TryParse method, passing txtInput.Text as argument 1 and intNumber as argument 2. Here's what happens:

- If txtInput.Text is successfully converted to an Integer, the resulting value is assigned to the intNumber variable, and the method returns True. That causes the statement in line 4 to execute.
- If txtInput.Text cannot be converted to an Integer, the method returns False. That causes the statement in line 6 (after the Else clause) to execute.

In the following example, we attempt to convert the contents of `txtSalary.Text` into a Decimal value and store it in `decSalary`:

```
If Not Decimal.TryParse(txtSalary.Text, decSalary) Then
    lblStatus.Text = "Not a valid number"
End If
```

If the conversion fails, the sample code displays an error message.

In Tutorial 4-8 you will look at a simple application that uses the `Integer.TryParse` and `Decimal.TryParse` methods to validate data entered by the user.

VideoNote

Validating Input with TryParse

Tutorial 4-8:
Examining an application that uses `TryParse` for input validation

Step 1: Open the *Gross Pay* project from the student sample programs folder named *Chap4\Gross Pay*. Figure 4-23 shows the application's form in the *Designer*. This is a simple program that allows you to enter the number of hours worked and your hourly pay rate. When you click the *Calculate Gross Pay* button, your gross pay is calculated and displayed.

Step 2: Run the application. Enter an invalid value such as *xyz9* for the hours worked, and then click the *Calculate Gross Pay* button. Notice that the message *Enter a valid integer for hours* worked appears in a label on the form.

Figure 4-23 The *Gross Pay* application's form

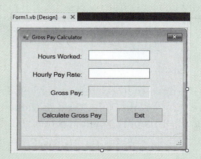

Step 3: Enter *40* for the hours worked (a valid number), and then enter an invalid value such as *abc44* for the hourly pay rate. Click the *Calculate Gross Pay* button. Notice that a message appears, this time showing the message *Enter a valid value for hourly pay rate*.

Step 4: With *40* still entered for the hours worked, change the hourly pay rate to *50*. Click the *Calculate Gross Pay* button. This time $2,000.00 is displayed as the gross pay.

Step 5: Click the *Exit* button to exit the application.

Step 6: Switch to the *Code* window and locate the `btnCalculate_Click` event handler. The code is shown here, with line numbers inserted for reference:

```
1 Private Sub btnCalculate_Click(...) Handles btnCalculate.Click
2    ' Declare variables
3    Dim intHours As Integer      ' Hours worked
4    Dim decPayRate As Decimal    ' Hourly pay rate
5    Dim decGrossPay As Decimal   ' Gross pay
6
7    ' Clear any previously displayed message.
8    lblStatus.Text = String.Empty
9
10   ' Get the hours worked.
11   If Integer.TryParse(txtHours.Text, intHours) Then
12     ' Get the hourly pay rate.
13     If Decimal.TryParse(txtPayRate.Text, decPayRate) Then
14       ' Calculate the gross pay.
15       decGrossPay = intHours * decPayRate
16
17       ' Display the gross pay.
18       lblGrossPay.Text = decGrossPay.ToString("c")
19     Else
20       ' Display pay rate error message.
21       lblStatus.Text = "Enter a valid value for hourly pay rate."
22     End If
23   Else
24     ' Display hours worked error message.
25     lblStatus.Text = "Enter a valid integer for hours worked."
26   End If
27 End Sub
```

Let's take a closer look at the code:

- Lines 3 through 5 declare the variables `intHours` (to hold hours worked), `decPayRate` (to hold the hourly pay rate), and `decGrossPay` (to hold the gross pay).
- Line 8 clears any message that might have been previously displayed in the `lblStatus` Label control.
- The `If...Then` statement that begins in line 11 calls `Integer.TryParse` to convert `txtHours.Text` to an Integer and assign the result to `intHours`. If the conversion fails, the program jumps to the `Else` clause in line 23, and the message *Enter a valid integer for hours worked,* is displayed in line 25. If the conversion is successful, however, the program continues with the `If...Then` statement in line 13.
- The `If...Then` statement that begins in line 13 calls `Decimal.TryParse` to convert `txtPayRate.Text` to a Decimal and assign the result to `decPayRate`. If the conversion fails, the program jumps to the `Else` clause in line 19, and the message *Enter a valid value for hourly pay rate.* is displayed in line 21. If the conversion is successful, however, the program continues with the calculation in line 15.
- Line 15 multiplies `intHours` by `decPayRate` and assigns the result to `decGrossPay`.
- Line 18 displays the value of `decGrossPay`, in Currency format.

Checking Numeric Ranges

In addition to checking for valid conversions, you sometimes need to check numeric input values to make sure they fall within a range. For example, suppose you are running the *Gross Pay* application from Tutorial 4-8, and instead of entering 40 as the number of hours, you accidentally enter 400. The program doesn't know that you made a mistake, so it uses the incorrect data you entered to calculate the gross pay.

This error could be avoided by using an If...Then statement to test the number of hours to make sure it is a reasonable value. For example, there are 168 hours in a week, so the maximum number of hours a person can work in a week is 168. The following If...Then statement determines whether the variable intHours is in the range of 0 through 168:

```
If intHours >= 0 And intHours <= 168 Then
   decGrosspay = intHours * decPayRate
Else
   lblStatus.Text = "Invalid number of hours."
End If
```

In this code, we used the And logical operator to create the following Boolean expression:

```
intHours >= 0 And intHours <= 168
```

This expression's value is true only if the value of intHours is within the range of 0 through 168.

It's also possible to enter an invalid value for the hourly pay rate. Suppose the company's maximum hourly pay rate is 45. Only values in the range of 0 through 45 are valid, so we could add another If...Then statement (shown here in bold) that validates the value of the decPayRate variable:

```
If intHours >= 0 And intHours <= 168 Then
   If decPayRate >= 0 And decPayRate <= 45.0 Then
      decGrosspay = intHours * decPayRate
   Else
      lblStatus.Text = "Invalid pay rate."
   End If
Else
   lblStatus.Text = "Invalid number of hours."
End If
```

In the previous examples we determined whether a value was within a range. Sometimes you want to know if a value is outside of a range. In that case it is better to use the Or operator to create a logical expression. For example, suppose you've written an application that is a car driving simulator, and the intSpeed variable holds the car's current speed. In the simulation, the minimum speed limit is 35 and the maximum speed limit is 60. To determine whether intSpeed is outside this range, we could use the following logic:

```
If intSpeed < 35 Or intSpeed > 60 Then
   lblStatus.Text = "Speed violation!"
End If
```

It's important to use the correct logical expression when testing for a range of values. Can you tell, for example, why the following expression would never be true?

```
' This is an error!
If intSpeed < 35 And intSpeed > 60 Then
   lblStatus.Text = "Speed violation!"
End If
```

The expression can never be true because intSpeed cannot be less than 35 and at the same time be greater than 60.

4.10 Focus on GUI Design: Radio Buttons and Check Boxes

CONCEPT: Radio buttons appear in groups of two or more, allowing the user to select just one of several options. A check box allows the user to individually select an item regardless of whether other check boxes are selected.

Radio Buttons

Radio buttons are useful when you want the user to select one choice from several possible choices. Figure 4-24 shows a group of radio buttons. The user can select either Coffee, Tea, or Soft Drink by clicking the appropriate button.

A radio button is selected when the user clicks on it, and it is deselected when the user clicks on some other radio button within the same group. Each radio button has a small circle that appears filled in when the radio button is selected and appears empty when the radio button is deselected.

The **RadioButton control** displays a single radio button. RadioButton controls are normally grouped in one of the following ways:

- All radio buttons inside a GroupBox control are members of the same group.
- All radio buttons located on a form but not inside a GroupBox control are members of the same group.

Figure 4-25 shows two forms. The form on the left has three radio buttons that belong to the same group. The form on the right has two groups of radio buttons.

At runtime, only one radio button in a group may be selected at a time, which makes them mutually exclusive. Clicking on a radio button selects it and automatically deselects any other radio button in the same group.

Figure 4-24 Radio buttons

Figure 4-25 Forms with radio buttons

NOTE: The name *radio button* refers to the old car radios that had push buttons for selecting stations. Only one button could be pushed in at a time. When you pushed a button, it automatically popped out any other button that had been selected before.

Radio Button Properties

Radio buttons have a Text property, which holds the text that is displayed next to the radio button's circle. For example, the radio buttons in the leftmost form in Figure 4-25 have their Text properties set to *Coffee*, *Tea*, and *Soft Drink*.

Radio buttons have a Boolean property named Checked. The **Checked property** is set to *True* when the radio button is selected and *False* when the radio button is deselected. Their default value is *False*.

Working with Radio Buttons in Code

The commonly used prefix for a radio button control's name is *rad*. You determine whether a radio button is selected by testing its Checked property. In the following example code, assume that radCoffee, radTea, and radSoftDrink are radio buttons within the same group:

```
If radCoffee.Checked = True Then
  lblResult.Text = "You selected coffee"
ElseIf radTea.Checked = True Then
  lblResult.Text = "You selected tea"
ElseIf radSoftDrink.Checked = True Then
  lblResult.Text = "You selected a soft drink"
End If
```

Because the Checked property is Boolean, the code we just wrote can be simplified:

```
If radCoffee.Checked Then
  lblResult.Text = "You selected coffee"
ElseIf radTea.Checked Then
  lblResult.Text = "You selected tea"
ElseIf radSoftDrink.Checked Then
  lblResult.Text = "You selected a soft drink"
End If
```

Radio Buttons have a **CheckedChanged event** that is generated when the user selects or deselects a radio button. If you double-click a radio button in the *Designer* window, a code template for the CheckedChange event handler is created in the *Code* window.

Tab Indexes and Access Keys

Radio button controls have a position in the form's tab order, which may be changed with the TabIndex property. As with other controls, you can assign an access key to a radio button by placing an ampersand (&) in the Text property, just before the character you wish to serve as the access key. The character will appear underlined on the form. At runtime, when the user presses the [Alt]+*access key* combination, the focus shifts to the radio button, and the radio button is selected.

Selecting a Radio Button in Code

You can use code to select a radio button, using an assignment statement to set the desired radio button's Checked property to *True*. For example:

```
radChoice1.Checked = True
```

 TIP: If you set a radio button's Checked property to *True* in design mode (with the *Properties* window), it becomes the default radio button for that group. It is selected when the application starts up and it remains selected until the user or application code selects another radio button.

Check Boxes

A *check box* appears as a small box, labeled with a caption. An example is shown in Figure 4-26.

Figure 4-26 Check box

The **CheckBox control** displays a check box. When a check box is selected, a small check mark appears inside the box. Unlike radio buttons, check boxes are not mutually exclusive. When there are multiple check boxes on a form or in a group box, any number of them can be selected at a given time. We say they are *mutually independent*.

The prefix that we use for a CheckBox control's name is chk. Like radio buttons, check boxes have a Checked property. When a check box is selected, or checked, its Checked property is set to *True*. When a check box is deselected, or unchecked, its Checked property is set to *False*. Here is a summary of other characteristics of the check box:

- A check box's caption is stored in the Text property.
- A check box's place in the tab order may be modified with the TabIndex property. When a check box has the focus, a thin dotted line appears around its text. You can check or uncheck it by pressing the Spacebar.
- You may assign an access key to a check box by placing an ampersand (&) in the Text property, just before the character that you wish to serve as the access key.
- You can use code to select or deselect a check box. Simply use an assignment statement to set the desired check box's Checked property. For example:

      chkChoice4.Checked = True

- You may set a check box's Checked property at design time.
- Like radio buttons, check boxes have a CheckedChanged event that is generated whenever the Checked property changes. If you have written a CheckedChanged event handler for the check box, it will execute whenever the user checks or unchecks the check box.

In Tutorial 4-9, you complete the code for an application that demonstrates radio buttons and check boxes.

Tutorial 4-9:
Completing an application with radio buttons and check boxes

Step 1:   Open the *Radio Button Check Box Demo* project from the student sample programs folder named *Chap4\Radio Button Check Box Demo*.

Step 2:   Run the program to see the form shown in Figure 4-27. Stop the program.

Figure 4-27 *Radio Button Check Box Demo* form

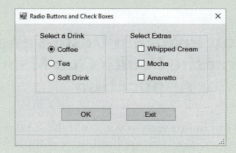

Step 3: Double-click the *OK* button and insert the following bold code into the btnOk_Click event handler:

```
Private Sub btnOk_Click(...) Handles btnOk.Click
  ' Determine which radio button is selected.
  If radCoffee.Checked = True Then
    lblResult.Text = "You selected coffee"
  ElseIf radTea.Checked = True Then
    lblResult.Text = "You selected tea"
  ElseIf radSoftDrink.Checked = True Then
    lblResult.Text = "You selected a soft drink"
  End If

  ' Determine which check boxes are selected.
  If chkWhipped.Checked = True Then
    lblResult.Text &= ", and Whipped Cream"
  End If

  If chkMocha.Checked = True Then
    lblResult.Text &= ", and Moca"
  End If

  If chkAmaretto.Checked = True Then
    lblResult.Text &= ", and Amaretto"
  End If
End Sub
```

Step 4: Save the project and run the application.

Step 5: Click one of the drinks, and then click one or two of the extras from the check boxes. When you click the *OK* button, you should see a list of your selections. Experiment by clicking different radio buttons and check boxes. Note the results you see after clicking the *OK* button.

 Checkpoint

4.12 Write a Boolean expression that equals true when the radio button named radBlue has been selected.

4.13 If several radio buttons are placed on a form, not inside group boxes, how many of them may be selected at any given time?

4.14 Write a Boolean expression that equals true when a check box named chkCream has been selected.

4.15 If several check boxes appear on a form, how many of them may be selected at any given time?

4.16 How can the user check or uncheck a check box that has the focus by using the keyboard?

4.11 Focus on Program Design and Problem Solving: Building the *Health Club Membership Fee Calculator* Application

CONCEPT: In this section you build the *Health Club Membership Fee Calculator* application. It will use features discussed in this chapter, including decision structures, radio buttons, and check boxes.

The Bay City Health and Fitness Club charges the following monthly membership rates:

Standard adult membership:	$40/month
Child (age 12 and under):	$20/month
Student:	$25/month
Senior citizen (age 65 and over):	$30/month

The club also offers the following optional services, which increase the base monthly fee:

Yoga lessons:	add $10 to the monthly fee
Karate lessons:	add $30 to the monthly fee
Personal trainer:	add $50 to the monthly fee

The manager of the club has asked you to create a *Health Club Membership Fee Calculator* application. It should allow the user to select a membership rate, select optional services, and enter the number of months of the membership. It should calculate the member's monthly and total charges for the specified number of months. The application should also validate the number of months entered by the user. An error message should be displayed if the user enters a number less than 1 or greater than 24. (Membership fees tend to increase every two years, so there is a club policy that no membership package can be purchased for more than 24 months at a time.)

Table 4-10 describes the input values for this application, with appropriate restrictions. For example, the number of months entered by the user must be validated before performing any calculations. Similarly, Table 4-11 describes the two types of output for this application, showing how the values are calculated.

Table 4-10 Describing inputs for the *Health Club Membership* application

Input	Type of Input	Restrictions
Type of membership	Radio button group	Only one type of membership may be selected.
Yoga option	Check box	
Karate option	Check box	
Personal trainer option	Check box	
Number of months	Text box	Must be an integer between 1 and 24.

Table 4-11 Describing outputs for the *Health Club Membership* application

Output	Generated By
Monthly fee	User's selection of the type of membership plus user's selected options (yoga, karate, personal trainer).
Total fee	Calculated as the monthly fee multiplied by the number of months.

Figure 4-28 shows a sketch of the application's form. The figure also shows the name of each control with a programmer-defined name.

Table 4-12 lists each control, along with any relevant property settings.

Figure 4-28 Sketch of the *Health Club Membership Fee Calculator* form

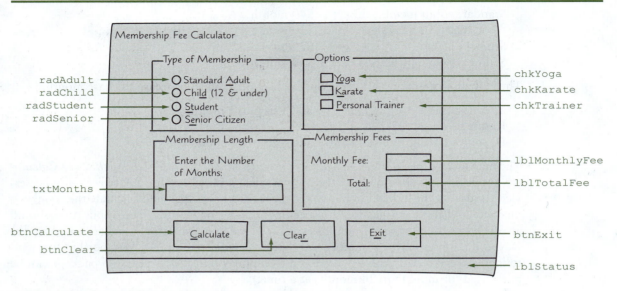

Table 4-12 *Health Club Membership Fee Calculator* controls

Control Type	Control Name	Property	Property Value
Form	(Default)	Text:	*Membership Fee Calculator*
Group box	(Default)	Text:	*Type of Membership*
Radio button	radAdult	Text:	*Standard &Adult*
		Checked:	*True*
Radio button	radChild	Text:	*Chil&d (12 && under)*
Radio button	radStudent	Text:	*&Student*
Radio button	radSenior	Text:	*S&enior Citizen*
Group box	(Default)	Text:	*Options*
Check box	chkYoga	Text:	*&Yoga*
Check box	chkKarate	Text:	*&Karate*
Check box	chkTrainer	Text:	*&Personal Trainer*
Group box	(Default)	Text:	*Membership Length*
Label	(Default)	Text:	*Enter the Number of Months:*
Text box	txtMonths	Text:	
Group box	(Default)	Text:	*Membership Fees*
Label	(Default)	Text:	*Monthly Fee:*
Label	(Default)	Text:	*Total:*
Label	lblMonthlyFee	BorderStyle:	*Fixed3D*
		Text:	Initially cleared
		AutoSize:	*False*
Label	lblTotalFee	BorderStyle:	*Fixed3D*
		Text:	Initially cleared
		AutoSize:	*False*
Button	btnCalculate	Text:	*&Calculate*
Button	btnClear	Text:	*Clea&r*
Button	btnExit	Text:	*E&xit*
StatusStrip	(Default)	Text:	
ToolStripStatusLabel	lbStatus	Text:	

Table 4-13 lists and describes the event handlers needed for this application.

Table 4-13 *Health Club Membership Fee Calculator* event handlers

Event Handler	Description
btnCalculate_Click	First, this handler validates the number of months entered by the user. Then, if the input is valid, it calculates the monthly fees and the total fee for the time period. Charges for optional services are included. If the input is not valid, an error message is displayed and no calculations are performed.
btnClear_Click	Clears the text box, output labels, and check boxes, and resets the radio buttons so that radAdult is selected.
btnExit_Click	Closes the application window.

Figure 4-29 shows a simplified flowchart for the btnCalculate_Click event handler, without reflecting details such as input validation.

The number of months entered by the user is tested to determine whether it is valid. If the number of months is valid, the fees are calculated.

The first two processes in the calculation are (1) calculate the base monthly fee, and (2) calculate and add the cost of optional services. Each of these processes can be expanded into more detailed flowcharts. Figure 4-30 shows a more detailed view of the *calculate the base monthly fee* process.

Figure 4-29 Flowchart for btnCalculate_Click

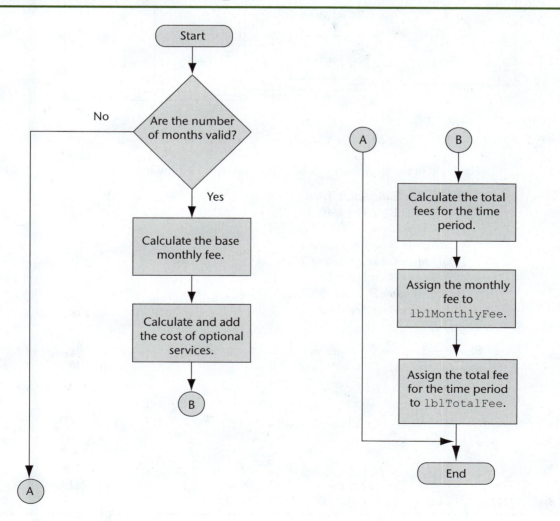

Figure 4-30 Flowchart of *calculate the base monthly fee* process

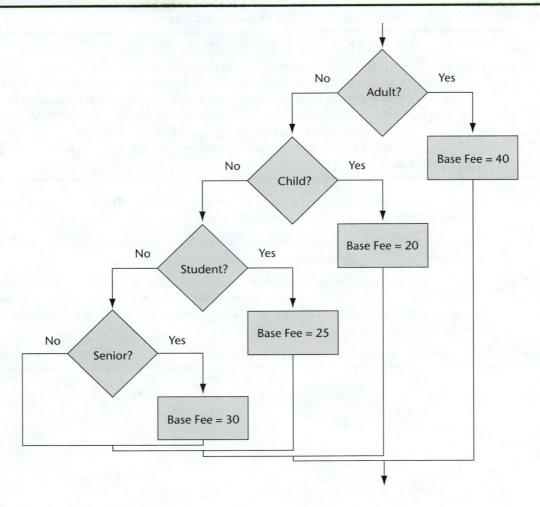

The logic in the flowchart can be expressed by the following pseudocode:

> *If Member is an Adult Then*
>   *Monthly Base Fee = 40*
> *ElseIf Member is a Child Then*
>   *Monthly Base Fee = 20*
> *ElseIf Member is a Student Then*
>   *Monthly Base Fee = 25*
> *ElseIf Member is a Senior Citizen Then*
>   *Monthly Base Fee = 30*
> *End If*

Figure 4-31 shows a more detailed view of the *calculate and add the cost of optional services* process.

Figure 4-31 Flowchart of *calculate and add the cost of optional services* process

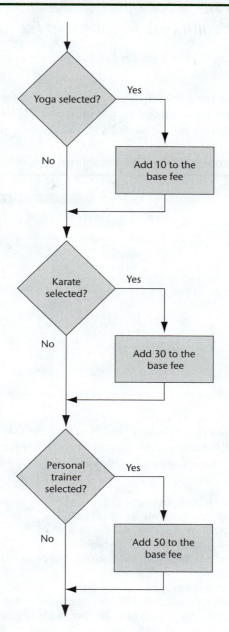

The logic in the flowchart can be expressed with the following pseudocode:

> *If Yoga is selected Then*
>   *Add 10 to the monthly base fee*
> *End If*
> *If Karate is selected Then*
>   *Add 30 to the monthly base fee*
> *End If*
> *If Personal Trainer is selected Then*
>   *Add 50 to the monthly base fee*
> *End If*

Tutorial 4-10 builds the *Health Club Membership Fee Calculator* application.

Tutorial 4-10:
Building the *Health Club Membership Fee Calculator* application

Step 1: Create a new Windows application project named *Health Club Membership Fee Calculator*.

Step 2: Set up the form as shown in Figure 4-32. Create the group boxes, radio buttons, and check boxes. Refer to the previously shown sketch in Figure 4-28 for the control names and Table 4-12 for the relevant property settings of each control.

Figure 4-32 *Membership Fee Calculator* form

Step 3: In the *Designer* window, double-click the *Calculate* button to create the code template for the btnCalculate_Click event handler. Type the code shown here in bold. (Don't type the line numbers. We have inserted them for reference only.)

```
1 Private Sub btnCalculate_Click(...) Handles btnCalculate.Click
2    Dim decBaseFee As Decimal          ' Base Monthly Fee
3    Dim decTotalFee As Decimal         ' Total Membership Fee
4    Dim intMonths As Integer           ' Number of months
5    Dim blnInputOk As Boolean = True
6
7    ' Constants for base fees.
8    Const decADULT_FEE As Decimal = 40D
9    Const decCHILD_FEE As Decimal = 20D
10   Const decSTUDENT_FEE As Decimal = 25D
11   Const decSENIOR_FEE As Decimal = 30D
12
13   ' Constants for additional fees.
14   Const decYOGA_FEE As Decimal = 10D
15   Const decKARATE_FEE As Decimal = 30D
16   Const decTRAINER_FEE As Decimal = 50D
17
18   ' Validate and convert the number of months.
19   lblStatus.Text = String.Empty
20   If Integer.TryParse(txtMonths.Text, intMonths) = False Then
21       lblStatus.Text = "Months must be an integer."
22       blnInputOk = False
23   End If
24
```

```
25     ' Validate the number of months.
26     If intMonths < 1 Or intMonths > 24 Then
27         lblStatus.Text = "Months must be in the range 1 - 24."
28         blnInputOk = False
29     End If
30
31     If blnInputOk = True Then
32         ' Determine the base monthly fee.
33         If radAdult.Checked = True Then
34             decBaseFee = decADULT_FEE
35         ElseIf radChild.Checked = True Then
36             decBaseFee = decCHILD_FEE
37         ElseIf radStudent.Checked = True Then
38             decBaseFee = decSTUDENT_FEE
39         ElseIf radSenior.Checked = True Then
40             decBaseFee = decSENIOR_FEE
41         End If
42
43         ' Check for additional services.
44         If chkYoga.Checked = True Then
45             decBaseFee += decYOGA_FEE
46         End If
47
48         If chkKarate.Checked = True Then
49             decBaseFee += decKARATE_FEE
50         End If
51
52         If chkTrainer.Checked = True Then
53             decBaseFee += decTRAINER_FEE
54         End If
55
56         ' Calculate the total fee.
57         decTotalFee = decBaseFee * intMonths
58
59         ' Display the fees.
60         lblMonthlyFee.Text = decBaseFee.ToString("c")
61         lblTotalFee.Text = decTotalFee.ToString("c")
62     End If
63 End Sub
```

Let's take a moment to go over this code. Lines 2 through 5 declare the following variables:

- The decBaseFee variable will hold the member's base monthly fee ($40 for an adult, $20 for a child, $25 for a student, or $30 for a senior citizen).
- The decTotalFee variable will hold the member's total monthly fee.
- The intMonths variable will hold the number of months of membership.
- The blnInputOk variable will act as a flag to indicate whether the number of months entered by the user is a valid integer in the range of 1 through 24. If the number of months is valid, the variable will be set to True. Otherwise, the variable will be set to False.

Lines 8 through 11 declare the following constants:

- decADULT_FEE specifies the monthly base fee for an adult membership.
- decCHILD_FEE specifies the monthly base fee for a child membership.
- decSTUDENT_FEE specifies the monthly base fee for a student membership.
- decSENIOR_FEE specifies the monthly base fee for a senior citizen membership.

Lines 14 through 16 declare the following constants:

- `decYOGA_FEE` specifies the additional monthly fee for yoga lessons.
- `decKARATE_FEE` specifies the additional monthly base fee for karate lessons.
- `decTRAINER_FEE` specifies the additional monthly base fee for a personal trainer.

The `If` statement in line 20 calls `Integer.TryParse` to convert the value `txtMonths.Text` to an Integer and assign the result to the `intMonths` variable. If the conversion fails, the program will assign an error message to a label (`lblStatus`) and line 22 assigns the value False to `blnInputOk`. If the conversion succeeds, the program continues to the next `If` statement in line 26.

Earlier, we specified that the number of months must be in the range of 1 through 24. The `If...Then` statement in line 26 determines whether the value of `intMonths` falls within this range. If it does not, the program will display an error message and line 28 assigns the value False to `blnInputOk`. If the conversion succeeds, we reach line 31, which determines whether `blnInputOk` is set to True. If so, the number of months is valid.

The user has selected a radio button on the application's form to specify the type of membership. The `If` statement in line 33 determines which radio button was selected and assigns an appropriate value to the `decBaseFee` variable.

Next, a series of three `If...Then` statements appears in lines 44 through 54. These statements determine whether any of the check boxes for additional services (yoga lessons, karate lessons, or a personal trainer) have been selected. If any have been selected, the `decBaseFee` variable is increased by the necessary amount.

Next, line 57 calculates the total fee by multiplying the monthly fee by the number of months. The result is assigned to the `decTotalFee` variable. Line 50 displays the monthly fee, and line 61 displays the total fee.

Step 4: Go back to the *Designer* window, and double-click the *Clear* button to create the code template for the `btnClear_Click` event handler. Type the code shown here in bold.

```
Private Sub btnClear_Click(...) Handles btnClear.Click
    ' Reset the Adult radio button.
    radAdult.Checked = True

    ' Clear the check boxes.
    chkYoga.Checked = False
    chkKarate.Checked = False
    chkTrainer.Checked = False

    ' Clear the number of months.
    txtMonths.Clear()

    ' Clear the fee labels.
    lblMonthlyFee.Text = String.Empty
    lblTotalFee.Text = String.Empty
    lblStatus.Text = String.Empty

    ' Give txtMonths the focus.
    txtMonths.Focus()
End Sub
```

Step 5: Go back to the *Designer* window, and double-click the *Exit* button to create the code template for the btnExit_Click event handler. Type the code shown here in bold.

```
Private Sub btnExit_Click(...) Handles btnExit.Click
    ' Close the form.
    Me.Close()
End Sub
```

Step 6: Save the project, and then run it. (If you mistyped something, and as a result have any syntax errors, correct them.)

Step 7: With the application running, enter the test data shown in Table 4-14 and confirm that it displays the correct output.

Table 4-14 Test values for the *Health Club Membership Fee Calculator* application

Type of Membership	Monthly Fee	Total
Standard adult with yoga, karate, and personal trainer for 6 months	$130.00	$780.00
Child with karate for 3 months	$50.00	$150.00
Student with yoga for 12 months	$35.00	$420.00
Senior citizen with karate and personal trainer for 8 months	$110.00	$880.00

Step 8: End the application.

Summary

4.1 The Decision Structure

- Programs often need more than one path of execution. Many algorithms require a program to execute some statements only under certain circumstances. The decision structure accomplishes this.

4.2 The `If...Then` Statement

- The `If...Then` statement can cause other statements to execute under certain conditions.
- Boolean expressions, such as those created using relational operators, can be evaluated only as *True* or *False*.
- Math operators and function calls can be used with relational operators.

4.3 The `If...Then...Else` Statement

- The `If...Then...Else` statement executes one group of statements if a condition is true and another group of statements if the condition is false.

4.4 The `If...Then...ElseIf` Statement

- The `If...Then...ElseIf` statement is like a chain of `If...Then...Else` statements that perform their tests, one after the other, until one of them is found to be true.

4.5 Nested `If` Statements

- A nested `If` statement is an `If` statement in the conditionally executed code of another `If` statement.

4.6 Logical Operators

- Logical operators connect two or more relational expressions into one (using `And`, `Or`, `AndAlso`, `OrElse`, or `Xor`), or reverse the logic of an expression (using `Not`).
- When determining whether a number is inside a numeric range, it's best to use the `And` operator.
- When determining whether a number is outside a range, it's best to use the `Or` operator.

4.7 Comparing, Testing, and Working with Strings

- Relational operators can be used to compare strings.
- An empty string is represented by the constant `String.Empty`, or by two quotation marks, with no space between them.
- The `IsNumeric` function accepts a string as its argument and returns *True* if the string contains a number. The function returns *False* if the string's contents cannot be recognized as a number.
- The `Substring` method extracts a specified number of characters from within a specified position in a string.
- The `IndexOf` method is used to search for a character or a string within a string.

4.8 The `Select Case` Statement

- The `Select Case` statement tests the value of an expression only once, and then uses that value to determine which set of statements to branch to.

4.9 Introduction to Input Validation

- The accuracy of a program's output depends on the accuracy of its input. It is important that applications perform input validation on the values entered by the user.

4.10 Focus on GUI Design: Radio Buttons and Check Boxes

- Radio buttons appear in groups and allow the user to select one of several possible options. Radio buttons placed inside a group box are treated as one group, separate and distinct from any other groups of radio buttons. Only one radio button in a group can be selected at any time.
- Clicking on a radio button selects it and automatically deselects any other radio button selected in the same group.
- Check boxes allow the user to select or deselect items. Check boxes are not mutually exclusive. There may be one or more check boxes on a form, and any number of them can be selected at any given time.

4.11 Focus on Program Design and Problem Solving: Building the *Health Club Membership Fee Calculator* Application

- This section outlines the process of building the *Health Club Membership Fee Calculator* application using the features discussed in the chapter.

Key Terms

And operator
AndAlso operator
Boolean expression
CheckBox control
CheckedChanged event
Checked property
conditionally executed (statement)
decision structure
empty string
flag
If...Then
If...Then...Else
If...Then...ElseIf
IndexOf method
input validation
IsNumeric function
leading space
Length property
logic error

logical operators
nested If statement
Not operator
Or operator
OrElse operator
RadioButton control
relational operator
Select Case statement
sequence structure
Substring method
ToLower method
ToUpper method
trailing space
Trim method
TrimEnd method
TrimStart method
TryParse method
Unicode
Xor operator

Video Tutorial: Improving the *Kayak Rental* Application

In this sequence of video tutorials, we improve on the *Kayak Rental* application by helping the clerk to make decisions. CheckBox and RadioButton controls are added to the interface to give the user more flexibility when choosing equipment. Finally, we validate the user's input to check for invalid data. When designing the user interface, we constantly keep in mind the user's goals, as well as the user's mental model of how the application works.

- Part 1: Enhancing the user interface with new controls
- Part 2: Checking for incorrect input
- Part 3: Testing the application

Review Questions and Exercises

Fill-in-the-Blank

1. A(n) _____ structure allows a program to execute some statements only under certain circumstances.

2. A(n) _____ operator determines if a specific relationship exists between two values.

3. Boolean expressions can only be evaluated as _____ or _____.

4. A(n) _____ is a Boolean variable that signals when some condition exists in the program.

5. The _____ statement will execute one group of statements if the condition is true, and another group of statements if the condition is false.

6. The _____ statement is like a chain of `If...Then...Else` statements. They perform their tests, one after the other, until one of them is found to be true.

7. A(n) _____ `If` statement is an `If` statement that appears inside another `If` statement.

8. _____ operators connect two or more relational expressions into one or reverse the logic of an expression.

9. The _____ method returns the uppercase equivalent of a string.

10. The _____ returns a lowercase version of a string.

11. The _____ function accepts a string as its argument and returns *True* if the string contains a number, or *False* if the string's contents cannot be recognized as a number.

12. The _____ method returns the number of characters in a string.

13. The _____ method returns a copy of a string without leading spaces.

14. The _____ method returns a copy of a string without trailing spaces.

15. The _____ method returns a copy of the string without leading or trailing spaces.

16. The _____ method extracts a specified number of characters from within a specified position in a string.

17. The value _____ can be concatenated with a string to produce multiple line displays.

18. A(n) _____ statement tests the value of an expression only once, and then uses that value to determine which set of statements to branch to.

19. _____ is the process of inspecting input values and determining whether they are valid.

20. _____ controls usually appear in groups and allow the user to select one of several possible options.

21. _____ controls may appear alone or in groups and allow the user to make yes/no or on/off selections.

True or False

Indicate whether the following statements are true or false.

1. T F: It is not possible to write a Boolean expression that contains more than one logical operator.

2. T F: It is not possible to write Boolean expressions that contain math, relational, and logical operators.

3. T F: You may use the relational operators to compare strings.

4. T F: Clicking on a radio button selects it and leaves any other selected radio button in the same group selected as well.

5. T F: Radio buttons that are placed inside a group box are treated as one group, separate and distinct from any other groups of radio buttons.

6. T F: When a group of radio buttons appears on a form (outside of a group box), any number of them can be selected at any time.

7. T F: You may have one or more check boxes on a form, and any number of them can be selected at any given time.

8. T F: The `If...Then` statement is an example of a sequence structure.

9. T F: An `If...Then` statement will not execute unless the conditionally executed statements are indented.

10. T F: The `Substring` method returns a lowercase copy of a string.

Multiple Choice

1. Relational operators allow you to _____ numbers.
   a. add
   b. multiply
   c. compare
   d. average

2. This statement can cause other program statements to execute only under certain conditions.
   a. `Conditional`
   b. `Decide`
   c. `If`
   d. `Execute`

3. This is a Boolean variable that signals when a condition exists.
   a. Relational operator
   b. Flag
   c. Arithmetic operator
   d. Float

4. This statement is like a chain of `If` statements. They perform their tests, one after the other, until one of them is found to be true.

    a. `If...Then`
    b. `If...Then...ElseIf`
    c. `Chain...If`
    d. `Relational`

5. When placed at the end of an `If...Then...ElseIf` statement, this provides default action when none of the `ElseIf` statements have true expressions.

    a. Trailing `If`
    b. Trailing `Select`
    c. Trailing `Otherwise`
    d. Trailing `Else`

6. When an `If` statement is placed inside another `If statement`, it is known as this type of statement.

    a. Nested `If`
    b. Complex `If`
    c. Compound `If`
    d. Invalid `If`

7. This operator connects two Boolean expressions into one. One or both expressions must be true for the overall expression to be true. It is only necessary for one to be true, and it does not matter which.

    a. `And`
    b. `Or`
    c. `Xor`
    d. `Not`

8. This operator connects two Boolean expressions into one. Both expressions must be true for the overall expression to be true.

    a. `And`
    b. `Or`
    c. `Xor`
    d. `Not`

9. This operator reverses the logical value of an Boolean expression. It makes a true expression false and a false expression true.

    a. `And`
    b. `Or`
    c. `Xor`
    d. `Not`

10. This operator connects two Boolean expressions into one. One, and only one, of the expressions must be true for the overall expression to be true. If both expressions are true, or if both expressions are false, the overall expression is false.

    a. `And`
    b. `Or`
    c. `Xor`
    d. `Not`

11. When determining whether a number is inside a numeric range, it's best to use this logical operator.

    a. `And`
    b. `Or`
    c. `Xor`
    d. `Not`

12. When determining whether a number is outside a range, it's best to use this logical operator.
    a. `And`
    b. `Or`
    c. `Xor`
    d. `Not`

13. In code you should test this property of a radio button or a check box to determine whether it is selected.
    a. Selected
    b. Checked
    c. On
    d. Toggle

14. This method attempts to convert a value to an Integer.
    a. `NumericConvert`
    b. `IntegerConvert`
    c. `Integer.TryParse`
    d. `Integer.TryConvert`

15. `strName` is a string variable. This expression returns the length of the string stored in `strName`.
    a. `Length(strName)`
    b. `strName.Length`
    c. `strName.StringSize`
    d. `CharCount(strName)`

Short Answer

1. Describe the difference between the `If...Then...ElseIf` statement and a series of `If...Then` statements.

2. In an `If...Then...ElseIf` statement, what is the purpose of a trailing `Else`?

3. What is a flag and how does it work?

4. Briefly describe how the `And` operator works.

5. Briefly describe how the `Or` operator works.

6. How is the `Xor` operator different from the `Or` operator?

7. How is the `AndAlso` operator different from the `And` operator?

8. How is the `OrElse` operator different from the `Or` operator?

What Do You Think?

1. Why are the relational operators called *relational*?

2. When writing an `If...Then` statement to determine whether a number is inside a range, would you use the `And` operator or the `Or` operator in the Boolean expression?

3. Why does Visual Studio automatically indent the conditionally executed statements in a decision structure?

4. Explain why you cannot convert the following If...Then...ElseIf statement into a Select Case statement.

```
If dblTemperature = 100 Then
    intX = 0
ElseIf intPopulation > 1000 Then
    intX = 1
ElseIf dblRate < .1 Then
    intX = -1
End If
```

Find the Error

1. For each of the following Visual Basic code snippets, identify the syntax error.

   a.
   ```
   If intX > 100
       lblResult.Text = "Invalid Data"
   End If
   ```
   b.
   ```
   Dim str As String = "Hello"
   Dim intLength As Integer
   intLength = Length(str)
   ```
   c.
   ```
   If intZ < 10 Then
       lblResult.Text = "Invalid Data"
   ```
   d.
   ```
   Dim str As String = "123"
   If str.IsNumeric Then
       lblResult.Text = "It is a number."
   End If
   ```
   e.
   ```
   Select Case intX
       Case < 0
           lblResult.Text = "Value too low."
       Case > 100
           lblResult.Text = "Value too high."
       Case Else
           lblResult.Text = "Value just right."
   End Select
   ```

Algorithm Workbench

1. Read the following instructions for cooking a pizza, and then design a flowchart with a decision structure that shows the necessary steps to cook the pizza with either thin and crispy or thick and chewy crust.
   a. For thin and crispy crust, do not preheat the oven. Bake pizza at 450 degrees for 15 minutes.
   b. For thick and chewy crust, preheat the oven to 400 degrees. Bake pizza for 20 minutes.

2. Write an If...Then statement that assigns 0 to intX when intY is equal to 20.

3. Write an If...Then statement that multiplies decPayRate by 1.5 when intHours is greater than 40.

4. Write an If...Then statement that assigns 0.2 to decCommissionRate when decSales is greater than or equal to $10,000.00.

5. Write an If...Then statement that sets the variable intFees to 50 when the Boolean variable blnIsMax equals *True*.

6. Write an `If...Then...Else` statement that assigns 1 to `intX` when `intY` is equal to 100. Otherwise it should assign 0 to `intX`.

7. The string variable `strPeople` contains a list of names, such as *Bill Jim Susan Randy Wilma* and so on. Write code that searches people for *Gene*. If *Gene* is found in `strPeople`, display a message in a Label control indicating that *Gene* was found.

8. Write an `If...Then` statement that prints the message *The number is valid* if the variable `sngSpeed` is within the range 0 through 200.

9. Write an `If...Then` statement that prints the message *The number is not valid* if the variable `sngSpeed` is outside the range 0 through 200.

10. Convert the following `If...Then...ElseIf` statement into a `Select Case` statement.

```
If intSelection = 1 Then
    lblStatus.Text = "Pi times radius squared"
ElseIf intSelection = 2 Then
    lblStatus.Text = "Length times width"
ElseIf intSelection = 3 Then
    lblStatus.Text = "Pi times radius squared times height"
ElseIf intSelection = 4 Then
    lblStatus.Text = "Well, okay then, good bye!"
Else
    lblStatus.Text = "Your selection was not recognized"
End If
```

Programming Challenges

1. **Larger and Smaller**

   Create an application that allows the user to enter two integers on a form similar to the one shown in Figure 4-33. The application should determine which value is larger than the other, or it should determine that the values are equal. Before comparing the numbers, use the `TryParse` method to verify that both inputs are valid integers. If an error is found, display an appropriate message to the user. Use a Label control to display all messages. The *Exit* button should close the window.

Figure 4-33 *Larger and Smaller* form

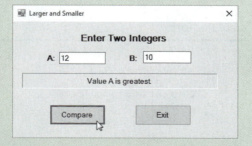

2. **Roman Numeral Converter**

   Create an application that allows the user to enter an integer between 1 and 10 into a text box on a form similar to the one shown in Figure 4-34. Use a `Select Case` statement to identify which Roman numeral is the correct translation of the integer. Display the Roman numeral in a Label control. If the user enters an invalid value, display an appropriate error message and do not attempt the conversion. Include an *Exit* button that closes the window.

Figure 4-34 *Roman Numeral Converter* form

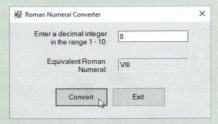

The following table lists the Roman numerals for the numbers 1 through 10.

Number	Roman Numeral
1	I
2	II
3	III
4	IV
5	V
6	VI
7	VII
8	VIII
9	IX
10	X

Input validation: Do not accept a number less than 1 or greater than 10. If the user enters a number outside this range, display an error message.

3. **Fat Percentage Calculator**

Create an application that allows the user to enter the number of calories and fat grams in a food. The application should display the percentage of the calories that come from fat. If the calories from fat are less than 30% of the total calories of the food, it should also display a message indicating the food is low in fat. (Display the message in a label or a message box.) The application's form should appear similar to the one shown in Figure 4-35.

One gram of fat has 9 calories, so:
  *Calories from fat = fat grams * 9*

The percentage of calories from fat can be calculated as:
  Percentage of calories from fat = Calories from fat / total calories

Figure 4-35 *Fat Gram Calculator* form

Input validation: Make sure the number of calories and fat grams are numeric, and are not less than 0. Also, the number of calories from fat cannot be greater than the total number of calories. If that happens, display an error message indicating that either the calories or fat grams were incorrectly entered.

Use the following test data to determine if the application is calculating properly:

Calories and Fat	Percentage Fat
200 calories, 8 fat grams	Percentage of calories from fat: 36%
150 calories, 2 fat grams	Percentage of calories from fat: 12% (a low-fat food)
500 calories, 30 fat grams	Percentage of calories from fat: 54%

4. **Weekly Temperatures with Validation**

   Programming Challenge 3 in Chapter 3 asked you to create an application that asks the user to enter weekly temperature readings over a five-week period. In this version of the application, you will perform more detailed input validation. Once the values are entered and the user clicks the *Calculate Average* button, check each input field for two criteria:

   1. The temperature must be numeric
   2. The temperature must be between −50 and +130

   If any single input field is incorrect, you must identify the field and the error by printing a message in the StatusStrip control and moving the focus to the incorrect field.

5. **Software Sales**

   Software companies often offer their customers the option to lease the software yearly or purchase it for a one-time fee. Also, they offer numerous add-on options such as technical support, training, and cloud backup services. Your task is to write a program that offers the user these types of options, using radio buttons and check boxes. A sample is shown in Figure 4-36. The prices you will use are listed in the following table:

Yearly lease	$5,000
One-Time Purchase	$20,000
Level-3 Technical Support	$3,500
On-Site Training	$2,000
Cloud Backup	$300

   Include buttons that clear all selections and close the form.

Figure 4-36 *Software Sales* application

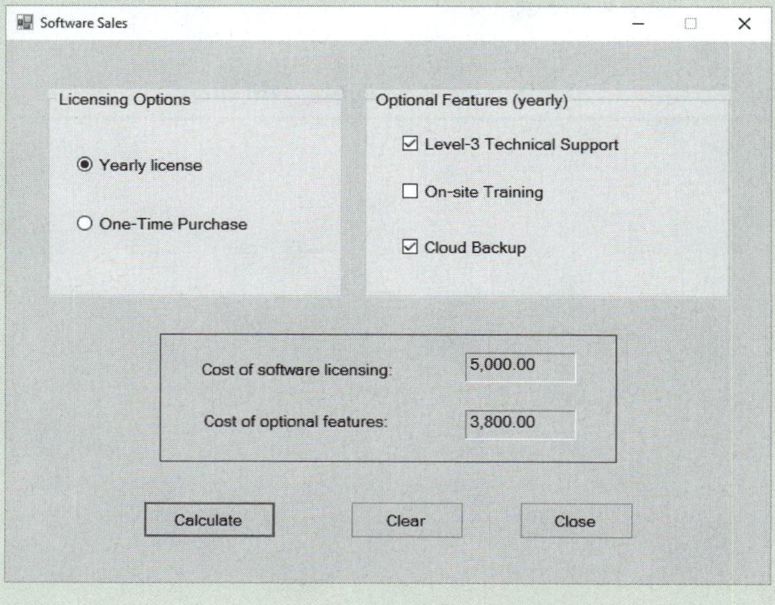

6. **Sailboat Race Ranking**

Programming Challenge 7 in Chapter 3 asked you to create an application that tracks the performance of sailboats in five races. That version of the application only calculated the total points for each boat. In this new version, you are asked to rank the boats, assigning them first, second, and third place. Also, you will need to perform the following input validations:

1. All input values must be valid integers.
2. In any column (a single race), the three integers must add up to 6 (1 + 2 + 3, in any order). We assume there are no tie scores.

When one of these input validations fails, display an appropriate message in the status bar. You do not need to customize the message for each input field, but you must explain the nature of the error (nonnumeric, or duplicate values for a single race). Figure 4-37 shows a sample of the program as the user is entering values, and has incorrectly entered the rankings for Race #1. If all inputs are correct, display the rankings, as shown in the sample in Figure 4-38. It is possible for two or more boats to have the same total race score. In that case, display the word "TIE" on the status bar, and turn the font color for all three scores to the color Red. An example of tie scores is shown in Figure 4-39. *Note: There are six ways of arranging the rankings of three sailboats, so your nested IF statement must be able to create these arrangements. The arrangements are: (1,2,3),(1,3,2),(2,1,3),(2,3,1),(3,1,2), and (3,2,1).*

Figure 4-37 Validating user input, *Sailboat Race Ranking* program

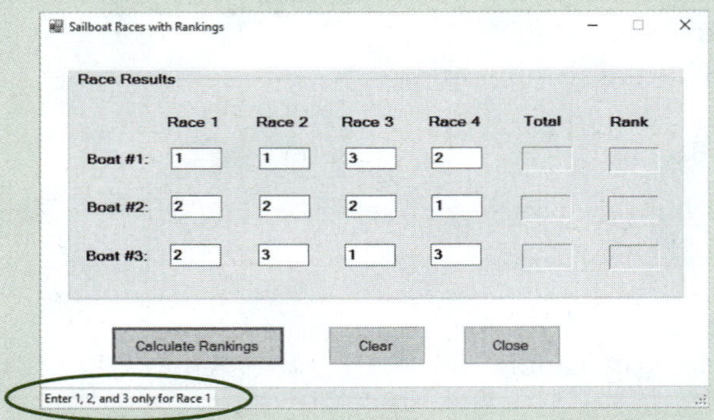

Error Message

Figure 4-38 Sample output for the *Sailboat Race Ranking* program

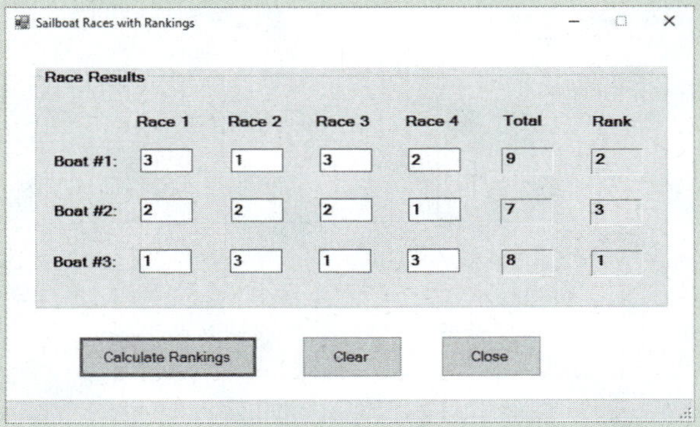

Figure 4-39 *Sailboat Race Ranking* with tied scores

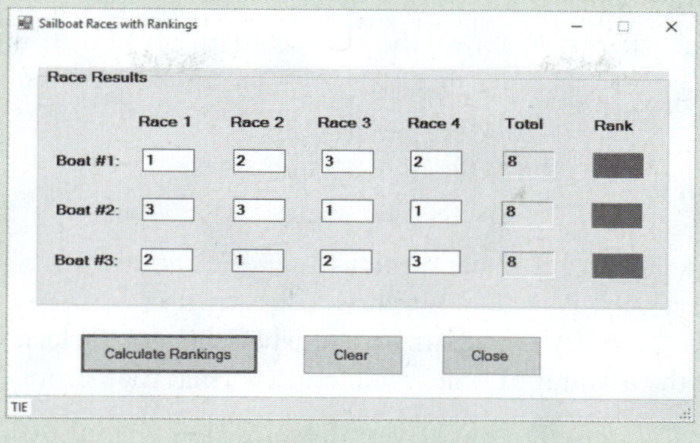

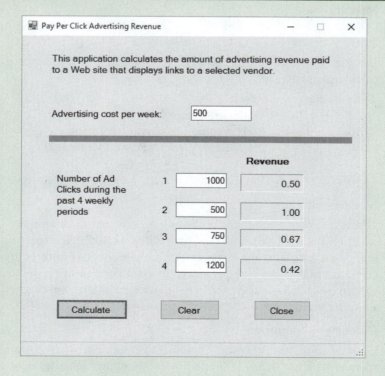

7. **Pay Per Click Advertising Revenue**

   Many Web sites have advertisements that help to generate revenue by keeping track of how many times users click on the ads. The process is called Pay Per Click (PPC), which directs traffic to Web sites run by vendors (sellers of services and merchandise). According to one well-known source, PPC revenue is calculated by dividing the cost of advertising by the number of times users click on an advertisement. Your task is to create an application that calculates weekly PPC revenue. Align all text boxes and labels holding calculated results on the right side. Implement input validation on all numeric inputs, and display an error message if a field is nonnumeric. A sample user interface design is shown in Figure 4-40.

Figure 4-40 *Pay Per Click Advertising Revenue* Application

Design Your Own Forms

8. Speed of Sound

The following table shows the approximate speed of sound in air, water, and steel.

Medium	Speed
Air	1,100 feet per second
Water	4,900 feet per second
Steel	16,400 feet per second

Create an application that displays a set of radio buttons allowing the user to select air, water, or steel. Provide a text box to let the user enter the distance a sound wave will travel in the selected medium. Then, when the user clicks a button, the program should display the amount of time it will take. Format the output to two decimal places.

Input validation: Do not accept distances less than 0. Always check for nonnumeric data.

Use the following test data to determine if the application is calculating properly:

Medium and Distance	Speed of Sound
Air, 10,000 feet	9.09 seconds
Water, 10,000 feet	2.04 seconds
Steel, 10,000 feet	0.61 seconds

9. Freezing and Boiling Points

The following table lists, in degrees Fahrenheit, the freezing and boiling points of several substances. Create an application that allows the user to enter a temperature. The program should then display a list of the substances that freeze at that temperature, followed by a list of substances that will boil at the same temperature.

Substance	Freezing Point	Boiling Point
Ethyl alcohol	−173°	172°
Mercury	−38°	676°
Oxygen	−362°	−306°
Water	32°	212°

Use the following test data and sample outputs to determine if the application is calculating properly:

Temperature	Results
−20°	Water will freeze and oxygen will boil.
−50°	Mercury and water will freeze and oxygen will boil.
−200°	Ethyl alcohol, mercury, and water will freeze and oxygen will boil.
−400°	Ethyl alcohol, mercury, oxygen, and water will freeze.

10. Name Formatting

Create an application that lets the user enter a person's name as a last name, comma, and first name. An example is "Fernandez, Frank". Redisplay the name as the first name, a space, and the last name. An example is "Frank Fernandez". Display an error message if the user forgets to insert a comma in the input name. The output should be correct whether or not the user includes a space after the comma in the input string. Be sure to test the program both ways.

11. Commas in Numbers

Users of computer programs often like to enter numbers with commas inserted in the middle, such as "1,234,000,688". Most computer languages consider this format to be nonnumeric. Write a program that inputs a number containing no more than three commas, and produces a string containing the same number without the commas.

12. **Museum Tours**

    Write a program that lets the user select items from different guided tours at a large museum. Use RadioButton controls to ask the user to select a spoken language for the tour, such as English, German, or Chinese. Then use CheckBox controls to select various sections of the museum, such as Ancient Mesopotamia, Ancient Europe, Medieval Europe, East Asia, and so on. After the users have made their selections, they click a *Continue* button, which causes the application to display the cost of the tour, the language, and the list of museum sections they plan to visit.

13. **Searching for Vacation Rentals**

    When searching for a vacation rental, it is most useful to narrow down the search from the thousands of available properties. Create an application that helps the user by using CheckBox controls as a list of neighborhood names in Paris, such as: Marais, Latin Quarter, Champs-Élysées, Sacre-Coeur, Bastille, and Les Halles. Also, include a list of CheckBox controls containing options, such as: Boutique Hotel, Large Hotel, Studio, 2-Bed Apartment, 1-Bed Apartment. In this way, the user would be able to search multiple neighborhoods for many different types of rental units. After the user makes his or her selections and clicks a *Continue* button, display a comma-separated string that lists all of their searching criteria.

14. **Mass and Weight**

    Scientists measure an object's mass in kilograms and its weight in newtons. If you know the amount of mass of an object, you can calculate its weight, in newtons, with the following formula:

    $$Weight = mass \times 9.8$$

    Create a VB application that lets the user enter an object's mass and calculates its weight. If the object weighs more than 1000 newtons, display a message indicating that it is too heavy. If the object weighs less than 10 newtons, display a message indicating that it is too light.

15. **Book Club Points**

    Serendipity Booksellers has a book club that awards points to its customers based on the number of books purchased each month. The points are awarded as follows:
    - If a customer purchases 0 books, he or she earns 0 points.
    - If a customer purchases 1 book, he or she earns 5 points.
    - If a customer purchases 2 books, he or she earns 15 points.
    - If a customer purchases 3 books, he or she earns 30 points.
    - If a customer purchases 4 or more books, he or she earns 60 points.
      Create a VB application that lets the user enter the number of books that he or she has purchased this month and displays the number of points awarded.

16. **Body Mass Index Program Enhancement**

    In Programming Challenge 15 in Chapter 3 you were asked to create a VB application that calculates a person's body mass index (BMI). Recall from that exercise that the BMI is often used to determine whether a person with a sedentary lifestyle is overweight or underweight for their height. A person's BMI is calculated with the following formula:

    $$BMI = weight \times 703 / height^2$$

    In the formula, weight is measured in pounds and height is measured in inches. Enhance the program so it displays a message indicating whether the person has optimal weight, is underweight, or is overweight. A sedentary person's weight is considered to be optimal if his or her BMI is between 18.5 and 25. If the BMI is less than 18.5, the person is considered to be underweight. If the BMI value is greater than 25, the person is considered to be overweight.

17. **Magic Dates**

The date June 10, 1960, is special because when we write it in the following format, the month times the day equals the year.

6/10/60

Create a VB application that lets the user enter a month (in numeric form), a day, and a two-digit year. The program should then determine whether the month times the day is equal to the year. If so, it should display a message saying the date is magic. Otherwise it should display a message saying the date is not magic.

5 Lists and Loops

TOPICS

This chapter begins by showing you how to use input boxes, which provide a quick and simple way to ask the user to enter data. List boxes and combo boxes are also introduced. Next, you learn to write loops, which cause blocks, or sequences of programming statements to repeat. You will also learn how to generate random numbers and use them for various purposes in a program. Finally, we cover the ToolTip control, which allows you to display pop-up messages when the user moves the mouse over controls.

5.1 Input Boxes

CONCEPT: Input boxes provide a simple way to gather input without placing a text box on a form.

An **input box** is a quick and simple way to ask the user to enter data. Figure 5-1 shows an example. In the figure, an input box displays a message to the user and provides a text box for the user to enter input. The input box also has *OK* and *Cancel* buttons.

You can display input boxes with the `InputBox` function. When the function is called, an input box such as the one shown in Figure 5-1 appears on the screen. Here is a simplified general format:

```
InputBox(Prompt [, Title] [, Default])
```

Figure 5-1 Input box that requests the user's name

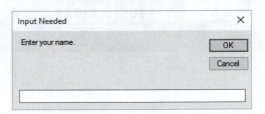

The brackets in the general format are shown around the `Title and Default` arguments to indicate that they are optional. The first argument, `Prompt`, is a string that is displayed to the user in the input box. Normally, the string asks the user to enter a value. The optional arguments, `Title` and `Default`, are described as follows.

- `Title` is a string that appears in the input box's title bar. If you do not provide a value for `Title`, the name of the project appears.
- `Default` is a string to be initially displayed in the input box's text box. If you do not provide a value for `Default`, the input box's text box is left empty.

If the user clicks the input box's *OK* button or presses the (Enter) key, the function returns the string value from the input box's text box. If the user clicks the *Cancel* button, the function returns an empty string. To retrieve the value returned by the `InputBox` function, use the assignment operator to assign it to a variable. For example, the following code displays the input box shown previously in Figure 5-1.

```
Dim strUsername As String
strUsername = InputBox("Enter your name.", "Input Needed")
```

After this code executes, the value the user entered in the input box is stored as a string in `strUserName`. As another example, the following statement displays the input box shown in Figure 5-2, and converts the string entered by the user into a numeric value.

```
strUserInput = InputBox("Enter the distance.", "Provide a Value")
dblDistance = CDbl(strUserInput)
```

Figure 5-2 Input box prompting for a distance

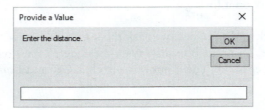

You can also provide an optional third argument to the `InputBox` function, to specify a default input value. The value that you provide as the third argument will be displayed in the input box. The following code shows an example.

```
strUserInput = InputBox("Enter the distance.", "Provide a Value", "100")
```

When this code executes, the input box shown in Figure 5-3 will be displayed. Notice that the value 100 is already filled in as the default input.

Figure 5-3 Input box with default input

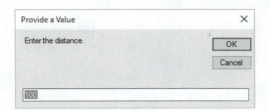

 NOTE: In most applications, the InputBox function should not be used as the primary method of input because it draws the user's attention away from the application's form. It also complicates data validation, because the box closes before validation can take place. Despite these drawbacks, it is a convenient tool for developing and testing applications.

 **Checkpoint**

Carefully examine the input box in Figure 5-4 and complete Checkpoint items 5.1 and 5.2.

Figure 5-4 Input box that requests a number from the user

5.1 Write a statement that displays the input box.

5.2 Write a statement that displays the input box and assigns its return value to an integer variable only if the user clicks the *OK* button.

5.2 List Boxes

CONCEPT: List boxes display a list of items and allow the user to select an item from the list.

The ListBox Control

A **ListBox control** displays a list of items and also allows the user to select one or more items from the list. (Informally, we refer to this control as a *list box*.) Figure 5-5 shows a form with two list boxes. At runtime, the user may select one of the items, causing the item to appear selected.

Figure 5-5 List box examples

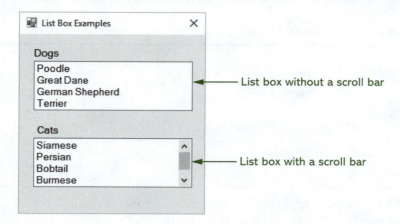

> List box without a scroll bar

> List box with a scroll bar

One of the list boxes in Figure 5-5 does not have a scroll bar, but the other one does. A scroll bar appears when the list box contains more items than can be displayed in the space provided. In the figure, the top list box has four items (Poodle, Great Dane, German Shepherd, and Terrier), and all items are displayed. The bottom list box shows four items (Siamese, Persian, Bobtail, and Burmese), but because it has a scroll bar, we know there are more items in the list box than those four.

Creating a ListBox Control

You create a ListBox control using either of the following methods:

- Double-click the ListBox icon in the *Toolbox* window to cause a ListBox control to appear on the form. Move the control to the desired location and resize it, if necessary.
- Click the ListBox icon in the *Toolbox* window and use the mouse to draw the List-Box control on the form with the desired location and size.

In design mode, a ListBox control appears as a rectangle. The size of the rectangle determines the size of the list box. The prefix that we will use in a ListBox control's name is lst, where the first character is a lowercase letter *L*. Let's discuss some of the list box's important properties and methods.

The Items Property

The entries in a list box are stored in a property named Items. You can store values in the **Items property** (also known as the Items collection) at design time or at runtime. To store values in the Items property at design time, follow these steps:

1. Make sure the ListBox control is selected in the *Designer* window.
2. In the *Properties* window, the setting for the Items property is displayed as *(Collection)*. When you select the Items property, an ellipsis button (. . .) appears.
3. Click the ellipsis button. The *String Collection Editor* dialog box appears, as shown in Figure 5-6.
4. Type the values that are to appear in the list box into the *String Collection Editor* dialog box. Type each value on a separate line by pressing the [Enter] key after each entry.
5. When you have entered all the values, click the *OK* button.

Figure 5-6 The *String Collection Editor* dialog box

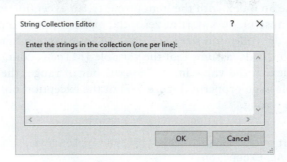

The Items.Count Property

You can use the **Items.Count property** to determine the number of items stored in the list box. When there are no items in the Items property, the Items.Count property equals 0. For example, assume an application has a list box named lstEmployees. The following If...Then statement displays a message when there are no items in the list box:

```
If lstEmployees.Items.Count = 0 Then
   lblStatus.Text = "There are no items in the list!"
End If
```

The following statement assigns the number of items in the list box to the variable intNumEmployees:

```
intNumEmployees = lstEmployees.Items.Count
```

Item Indexing

The Items property is a collection of objects, in which each has an *index*, or number. The first object in the collection has index 0, the next has index 1, and so on. The last index value is *n* – 1, where *n* is the number of items in the collection. When you access the Items property in code, you must supply an integer index. In the following example, the expression refers to the first item in the list box:

```
lstEmployees.Items(0)
```

If you want to retrieve an item from the Items property and assign it to a variable, you must explicitly convert the item to the same data type as the variable. For example, suppose we want to get the first item in the lstEmployees list box and assign it to strName, a string variable. We would call the item's ToString method as shown here:

```
strName = lstEmployees.Items(0).ToString()
```

This statement gets the item stored at lstEmployees.Items(0), calls the item's ToString method, and assigns the resulting string to the strName variable.

Let's look at another example. Suppose an application has a list box named lstRoomNumbers that contains a list of room numbers. The following statement shows how to assign the second item in the list box to an Integer variable named intRoomNumber:

```
intRoomNumber = CInt(lstRoomNumbers.Items(1))
```

This statement gets the item stored at lstRoomNumbers.Items(1), converts it to an Integer with the CInt function, and assigns the resulting value to the intRoomNumber variable.

Handling Exceptions Caused by Indexes

When you use an index with the Item property, an exception is thrown if the index is out of range. Because indexes start at zero, the highest index number you can use is always one less than the collection size. You can use an exception handler to trap such an error. In the following code, assume that the variable intIndex contains a value that we want to use as an index. If the value in intIndex is out of range, the exception is handled. We display the Message property (Figure 5-7) of the exception object to give the user an idea of what went wrong.

```
Try
   strInput = lstMonths.Items(intIndex).ToString()
Catch ex As Exception
   MessageBox.Show(ex.Message)
End Try
```

Figure 5-7 Exception thrown by out of range index

Many programmers prefer to handle indexing errors using an If statement. The following code is an example in which we compare the index (in a variable named intIndex) to the Count property of the Items collection:

```
If intIndex >= 0 And intIndex < lstMonths.Items.Count Then
   strInput = lstMonths.Items(intIndex).ToString()
Else
   MessageBox.Show("Index is out of range: " & intIndex)
End If
```

The SelectedIndex Property

When the user selects an item in a list box, the item's index is stored in the **SelectedIndex** property. If no item is selected, SelectedIndex equals −1. You can use the SelectedIndex property's value as an index to retrieve the selected item from the Items property. For example, assume an application has a list box named lstLocations. The following code segment uses an If . . . Then statement to determine whether the user has selected an item in the list box. If an item was selected, the code copies the item from the Items property to the string variable strLocation.

```
If lstLocations.SelectedIndex <> −1 Then
   strLocation = lstLocations.Items(lstLocations.SelectedIndex).
      ToString()
End If
```

 TIP: To prevent a runtime error, always test the SelectedIndex property to make sure it does not equal −1 before using it with the Items property to retrieve an item.

You can also use the SelectedIndex property to deselect an item by setting it to −1. For example, the following statement deselects any selected item in lstLocations:

```
lstLocations.SelectedIndex = −1
```

The SelectedItem Property

Whereas the SelectedIndex property contains the index of the currently selected item, the **SelectedItem property** contains the item itself. For example, suppose the list box lstFruit contains *Apples*, *Pears*, and *Bananas*. If the user has selected *Pears*, the following statement copies the string *Pears* to the variable strSelectedFruit:

```
strSelectedFruit = lstFruit.SelectedItem.ToString()
```

Because the SelectedItem is type Object, you must call its ToString method if you want to assign it to a String variable.

The Sorted Property

You can use the list box's **Sorted property** to cause the items in the Items property to be displayed alphabetically. This Boolean property is set to *False* by default, causing the items to be displayed in the order they were inserted into the list. When set to *True*, the items are sorted alphabetically.

The Items.Add Method

To store values in the Items property with code at runtime, use the **Items.Add** method. Here is the general format:

```
ListBox.Items.Add(Item)
```

ListBox is the name of the list box control. *Item* is the value to be added to the Items property. For example, suppose an application has a list box named lstStudents. The following statement adds the string "Sharon" to the end of the list box.

```
lstStudents.Items.Add("Sharon")
```

You can add virtually any type of values to a list box, including objects. For example, the following statements add Integer, Decimal, and Date objects to list boxes.

```
Dim intNum As Integer = 5
Dim decGrossPay As Decimal = 1200D
Dim datStartDate As Date = #12/18/2016#
lstNumbers.Items.Add(intNum)
lstWages.Items.Add(decGrossPay)
lstDates.Items.Add(datStartDate)
```

When you add an object other than a string to a list box, the text displayed in the list box is the string returned by the object's ToString method.

The Items.Insert Method

To insert an item at a specific position, you must use the Items.Insert method. Here is the general format of the **Items.Insert method**:

```
ListBox.Items.Insert(Index, Item)
```

ListBox is the name of the list box control. *Index* is an integer argument that specifies the position where *Item* is to be placed in the Items property. *Item* is the item to add to the list.

For example, suppose the list box lstStudents contains the following items, in the order they appear: *Bill*, *Joe*, *Geri*, and *Sharon*. Since *Bill* is the first item, its index is 0. The index for *Joe* is 1, for *Geri* is 2, and for *Sharon* is 3. Now, suppose the following statement executes.

```
lstStudents.Items.Insert(2, "Jean")
```

This statement inserts *Jean* at index 2. The string that was previously at index 2 (*Geri*) is moved to index 3, and the string previously at index 3 (*Sharon*) is moved to index 4. The items in the Items property are now *Bill*, *Joe*, *Jean*, *Geri*, and *Sharon*.

The `Items.Remove` and `Items.RemoveAt` Methods

The `Items.Remove` and `Items.RemoveAt` methods both remove one item from a list box's Items property. Here is the general format of both methods:

```
ListBox.Items.Remove(Item)
ListBox.Items.RemoveAt(Index)
```

ListBox is the name of the list box control. With the `Items.Remove` method, *Item* is the item you wish to remove. For example, the following statement removes the string *Industrial Widget* from the `lstInventory` list box.

```
lstInventory.Items.Remove("Industrial Widget")
```

If you specify an item that is not in the list box, nothing is removed.

The `Items.RemoveAt` method removes the item at a specific index. For example, the following statement removes the item at index 4 from the `lstInventory` list box:

```
lstInventory.Items.RemoveAt(4)
```

 WARNING: If you specify an invalid index with the `Items.RemoveAt` method, an exception will be thrown.

The `Items.Clear` Method

The `Items.Clear` method erases all the items in the Items property. Here is the method's general format:

```
ListBox.Items.Clear()
```

For example, assume an application has a list box named `lstCars`. The following statement erases all items in the list.

```
lstCars.Items.Clear()
```

In Tutorial 5-1, you create an application with two list boxes.

Tutorial 5-1:
Creating list boxes

Step 1:   Create a new Windows Forms Application project named *List Boxes*. Change the form's Text property to *List Box Demo*.

Step 2:   On the form, create a list box as shown in Figure 5-8. Notice that the default name of the list box is `ListBox1`. Also notice that the name of the list box is displayed in the list box at design time. It will not appear there at runtime.

Step 3: Change the name of the list box to `lstMonths`.

Step 4: With the list box selected, click the Items property in the *Properties* window. Then click the ellipsis button (⊡) that appears.

Step 5: The *String Collection Editor* dialog box will appear. Type the following names of the months, with one name per line: `January, February, March, April, May, June, July, August, September, October, November,` and `December`. When you are finished, the dialog box should appear as shown in Figure 5-9. Click the *OK* button to close the dialog box.

Figure 5-8 A list box

Figure 5-9 *String Collection Editor* with months filled in

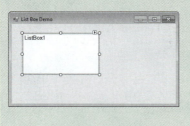

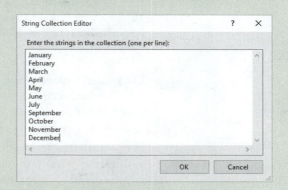

Step 6: Create another list box and make it the same size as the first one. Change its name to `lstYears`. Enter the following items in its Items property: **2016, 2017, 2018, 2019,** and **2020**.

Step 7: Create two buttons on the form. Name the first `btnOk`, and change its Text property to *OK*. Name the second `btnReset` and change its Text property to *Reset*. The form should look similar to Figure 5-10.

Figure 5-10 The form with two list boxes and two buttons

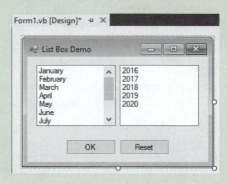

Step 8: Double-click the btnOk button to generate a Click event handler code template. Complete the event handler by writing the following bold code shown in lines 2 through 15.

```
 1 Private Sub btnOk_Click(...) Handles btnOk.Click
 2   Dim strInput As String ' Holds selected month and year
 3
 4   If lstMonths.SelectedIndex = -1 Then
 5     ' No month is selected
 6     MessageBox.Show("Select a month.")
 7   ElseIf lstYears.SelectedIndex = -1 Then
 8     ' No year is selected
 9     MessageBox.Show("Select a year.")
10   Else
11     ' Get the selected month and year
12     strInput = lstMonths.SelectedItem.ToString() &
13       " " & lstYears.SelectedItem.ToString()
14     MessageBox.Show("You selected " & strInput)
15   End If
16 End Sub
```

Let's take a closer look at the code. The If statement in line 4 determines whether lstMonths.SelectedIndex is equal to –1, which would mean that the user has not selected anything from the lstMonths list box. If that is true, line 6 displays a message box telling the user to select a month.

If the user has selected an item from lstMonths, the ElseIf clause in line 7 determines whether lstYears.SelectedIndex is equal to –1, which would mean that the user has not selected anything from the lstYears list box. If that is true, line 9 displays a message box telling the user to select a year.

If the user has selected items in both lstMonths and lstYears, the program jumps to the Else clause in line 10. The statement that appears in lines 12 and 13 creates a string containing the selected month, followed by a space, followed by the selected year. For example, if the user selected *April* in lstMonths and *2017* in lstYears, the string "April 2017" would be created and assigned to the strInput variable. Then line 14 displays the string in a message box.

Step 9: Double-click the btnReset button to add a Click event handler code template. Write the following code shown in bold:

```
Private Sub btnReset_Click(...) Handles btnReset.Click
  ' Reset the list boxes.
  lstMonths.SelectedIndex = -1
  lstYears.SelectedIndex = -1
End Sub
```

When this button is clicked, the SelectedIndex property of both list boxes is set to –1. This deselects any selected items.

Step 10: Run the application. Without selecting any item in either list box, click the *OK* button. A message box appears instructing you to *Select a month*.

Step 11: Select *March* in lstMonths, but do not select an item from lstYears. Click the *OK* button. This time a message box appears instructing you to *Select a year*.

Step 12: With *March* still selected in `lstMonths`, select *2018* in `lstYears`. Click the *OK* button. Now a message box appears with the message *You selected March 2018*. Click the message box's *OK* button to dismiss it.

Step 13: Click the *Reset* button. The items you previously selected in `lstMonths` and `lstYears` are deselected.

Step 14: Close the application and save it.

More about the Items Collection

You've learned that a list box's Items property is a special type of container known as a *collection*. Collections are commonly used to store groups of objects, and as you learn more about Visual Basic, you will see that collections are used in many places. What you have learned about a list box's Items collection applies to other collections as well. Table 5-1 lists several important collection methods and properties.

Table 5-1 Several methods and properties of collections

Method or Property	Description
`Add(item As Object)`	Method: adds *item* to the collection, returning its index position.
`Clear( )`	Method: removes all items in the collection. No return value.
`Contains(value As Object)`	Method: returns *True* if *value* is found at least once in the collection.
`Count`	Property: returns the number of items in the collection. Read-only, so you can read it but not change it.
`IndexOf(value As Object)`	Method: returns the Integer index position of the first occurrence of *value* in the collection. If *value* is not found, the return value is −1.
`Insert(index As Integer, item As Object)`	Method: insert *item* in the collection at position *index*. No return value.
`Item(index As Integer)`	Property: returns the object located at position *index*.
`Remove(value As Object)`	Method: removes *value* from the collection. No return value.
`RemoveAt(index As Integer)`	Method: removes the item at the specified *index*. No return value.

You have already seen examples of the Add, Clear, Insert, Remove, and RemoveAt methods. Let's look at examples of the remaining methods and properties shown in the table. Assume that `lstMonths` is the same list box that you created in Tutorial 5-1. The following If...Then statement determines whether the `lstMonths` list box's Items property contains "March". If so, it displays the message "March is found in the list." Otherwise, it displays "March is NOT found in the list."

```
If lstMonths.Items.Contains("March") Then
    MessageBox.Show("March is found in the list.")
Else
    MessageBox.Show("March is NOT found in the list.")
End If
```

In the following statement, `intIndex` is assigned the value 2 because *March* is located at index 2 in the collection.

```
intIndex = lstMonths.Items.IndexOf("March")
```

In the following statement, `strMonth` is assigned the string `"April"` because it is at index position 3 in the collection.

```
Dim strMonth As String = lstMonths.Items.Item(3).ToString()
```

 **Checkpoint**

5.3 What is the index of the first item stored in a list box's Items property?

5.4 Which list box property holds the number of items stored in the Items property?

5.5 If a list box has 12 items stored in it, what is the index of the 12th item?

5.6 Which list box property holds the item that has been selected from the list?

5.7 Which list box property holds the index of the item that has been selected from the list?

5.8 Assume `lstNames` is a list box and `strSelectedName` is a String variable. Write a statement that assigns the second item in `lstNames` to `strSelectedName`.

5.3   Introduction to Loops: The `Do While` Loop

CONCEPT: A loop is a repeating structure that contains a block of program statements.

Chapter 4 introduced decision structures, which direct the flow of a program along two or more paths. A **repetition structure**, or **loop**, causes one or more statements to repeat. Visual Basic has three types of loops: the `Do While` loop, the `Do Until` loop, and the `For...Next` loop. The difference among them is how they control the repetition.

VideoNote
The Do While Loop

The `Do While` Loop

The `Do While` loop has two important parts: (1) a Boolean expression that is tested for a *True* or *False* value, and (2) a statement or group of statements that is repeated as long as the Boolean expression is true. Figure 5-11 shows a flowchart of a `Do While` loop.

Figure 5-11 Flowchart of a Do While loop

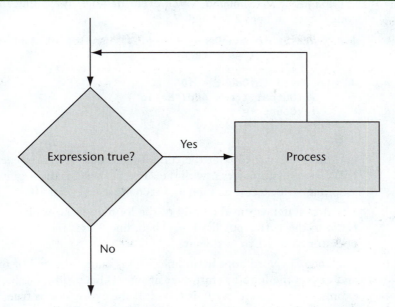

Notice the use of the diamond symbol for testing a Boolean expression. If the expression is true, the structure performs a process. Then it tests the Boolean expression again; if the expression is still true, the process is repeated. This continues as long as the Boolean expression is true when it is tested.

Here is the general format of the **Do While loop** in code:

```
Do While  BooleanExpression
   statement
   (more statements may follow)
Loop
```

The statement that reads Do While is the beginning of the loop, and the statement that reads Loop is the end of the loop. The statements that appear between these two lines are known as the *body of the loop*. When the loop runs, the *BooleanExpression* is tested. If it is true, then the statements in the body of the loop are executed. Then the loop starts over and the *BooleanExpression* is tested again. If it is still true, the statements in the body of the loop are executed. This cycle repeats until the *BooleanExpression* is false.

Because the statements in the body of the loop are executed only under the condition that the Boolean expression is true, they are called **conditionally executed statements**. The Do While loop works like an If statement that executes over and over. As long as the Boolean expression is true, the conditionally executed statements will repeat. Each repetition of the loop is called an **iteration**. In Tutorial 5-2, you complete an application that demonstrates the Do While loop.

Tutorial 5-2:
Completing an application that uses the Do While loop

VideoNote

Completing an application that uses the Do While loop

Step 1: Open the *Do While Demo* project from the student sample programs folder named *Chap5\Do While Demo*.

Step 2: In the *Designer* window for Form1, double-click the *Run Demo* button to display the *Code* window.

Step 3: Complete the `btnRunDemo_Click` event handler by writing the following bold code shown in lines 2 through 7.

```
1 Private Sub btnRunDemo_Click(...) Handles btnRunDemo.Click
2   Dim intCount As Integer = 0
3
4   Do While intCount < 10
5     lstOutput.Items.Add("Hello")
6     intCount += 1
7   Loop
8 End Sub
```

Let's take a closer look at the code. Line 2 declares an Integer variable named `intCount` and initializes it with the value 0. Line 4 is the beginning of a `Do While` loop that will execute as long as `intCount` is less than 10.

The first statement in the body of the loop appears in line 5. It adds the word *Hello* to the `lstOutput` list box. Then, line 6 uses the `+=` combined assignment operator to add 1 to `intCount`.

The `Loop` keyword appears in line 7. This marks the end of the `Do While` loop and causes the loop to start over at line 4. Each time the loop starts over, the expression `intCount < 10` is tested. If the expression is true, the statements in the body of the loop (lines 5 and 6) are executed. If the expression is false, the loop stops and the program resumes with the statement that immediately follows the `Loop` statement in line 7. (In this code, the event handler ends immediately after the loop.)

Step 4: Save and run the application. Click the *Run Demo* button. The output should appear as shown in Figure 5-12.

Figure 5-12 Output from the *Do While Demo* application

Infinite Loops

In all but rare cases, loops must contain within themselves a way to terminate. This means that something inside the `Do While` loop must eventually make the test expression false. The loop in the *Do While Demo* application stops when the variable `intCount` is no longer less than 10.

If a loop does not have a way of stopping, it is called an **infinite loop**. Infinite loops keep repeating until the program is interrupted. Here is an example:

```
intCount = 0
Do While intCount < 10
  lstOutput.Items.Add("Hello")
Loop
```

This loop will execute forever because it does not contain a statement that changes `intCount`. Each time the test expression is evaluated, `intCount` will still be equal to 0. In general, a loop that never stops causes a program to become unresponsive to user input.

Programming Style and Loops

When you code a loop, Visual Studio automatically indents the statements in the body of the loop. This is not a syntax requirement, but a programming style convention. For example, compare the following loops:

```
Do While intCount < 10
  lstOutput.Items.Add("Hello")
  intCount += 1
Loop
```

```
Do While intCount < 10
lstOutput.Items.Add("Hello")
intCount += 1
Loop
```

These two loops do the same thing, but the second one does not use proper indentation. In the first loop, you can quickly see which statements are repeated by the loop because they are indented.

NOTE: If the automatic indenting feature has been turned off, you can turn it on by clicking *Tools* on the menu bar, then clicking *Options*. In the *Options* window, perform the following:

- Expand *Text Editor* in the left pane, then expand *Basic*, then click *Tabs*. Make sure *Smart* is selected in the group box under *Indenting*.
- In the left pane, under *Basic*, click *Advanced*. Make sure *Automatic Insertion of end constructs* and *Pretty listing (reformatting) of code* are both checked.

Counters

A **counter** is a variable that is regularly incremented or decremented each time a loop iterates. To *increment* a variable means to add 1 to its value. To *decrement* a variable means to subtract 1 from its value.

The following statements increment the variable `intX`:

```
intX = intX + 1
intX += 1
```

The following statements decrement the variable `intX`.

```
intX = intX - 1
intX -= 1
```

Often, a program must control or keep track of the number of iterations a loop performs. For example, the loop in the *Do While Demo* application adds *Hello* to the list box 10 times. Let's look at part of the code again.

```
Do While intCount < 10
    lstOutput.Items.Add("Hello")
    intCount += 1
Loop
```

In the code, the variable `intCount`, which starts at 0, is incremented each time through the loop. When `intCount` reaches 10, the loop stops. As a counter variable, it is regularly incremented in each iteration of the loop. In essence, `intCount` keeps track of the number of iterations the loop has performed.

TIP: `intCount` must be properly initialized. If it is initialized to 1 instead of 0, the loop will iterate only nine times.

Pretest and Posttest `Do While` Loops

The `Do While` loop can be written as a pretest loop or a posttest loop. The difference between these two types of loop is as follows:

- In a **pretest loop**, the Boolean expression is tested first. If the expression is true, the loop then executes the statements in the body of the loop. This process repeats until the Boolean expression is false.
- In a **posttest loop**, the statements in the body of the loop are executed first, and then the Boolean expression is tested. If the Boolean expression is true, the loop repeats. If the Boolean expression is false, the loop stops.

The examples that you have seen so far have all been pretest loops. An important characteristic of a pretest loop is that it will never execute if its Boolean expression is false to start with. For example, look at the following code:

```
Dim intCount As Integer = 100
Do While intCount < 10
    MessageBox.Show("Hello World!")
    intCount += 1
Loop
```

In this code the variable `intCount` is initialized with the value 100. When the `Do While` loop begins to execute, it tests the expression `intCount < 10`. Because this expression is false to start with, the loop immediately ends. The statements in the body of the loop never execute.

The `Do While` loop can also be written as a posttest loop, using the following general format:

```
Do
    Statement
    (More statements may follow)
Loop While BooleanExpression
```

Notice that in this general format, the `While` *BooleanExpression* clause appears at the end, after the `Loop` keyword. A loop written this way is a posttest `Do While` loop, and it tests its Boolean expression after each loop iteration. The flowchart in Figure 5-13 shows the logic of a posttest `Do While` loop.

Figure 5-13 Logic of the posttest Do While loop

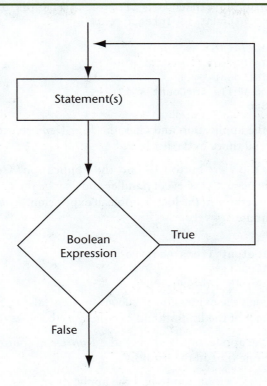

A posttest loop will always perform at least one iteration, even if its Boolean expression is false to start with. For example, look at the following code:

```
Dim intCount As Integer = 100
Do
   MessageBox.Show("Hello World!")
   intCount += 1
Loop While intCount < 10
```

In this code the variable intCount is initialized with the value 100. Then the loop begins to execute. Because this is a posttest loop, it first executes the statements in the body of the loop and then tests the expression intCount < 10. The expression is false, so the loop stops after the first iteration.

In Tutorial 5-3, you will modify the *Do While Demo* application to use a posttest loop.

Tutorial 5-3:
Modifying the *Do While Demo* application to use a posttest loop

Step 1: Open the *Do While Demo* project from the student sample programs folder named *Chap5\Do While Demo*.

Step 2: Open the *Code* window. When you wrote the btnRunDemo_Click event handler in Tutorial 5-2, you used a pretest Do While loop. In this step you will modify the loop so it is a posttest loop. Change the code to appear as follows. The modified lines of code are shown in bold.

VideoNote

Using a
posttest loop

```
            Private Sub btnRunDemo_Click(...) Handles btnRunDemo.Click
               Dim intCount As Integer = 0

               Do
                  lstOutput.Items.Add("Hello")
                  intCount += 1
               Loop While intCount < 10
            End Sub
```

Step 3: Run the application and click the *Run Demo* button. The loop should display *Hello* 10 times in the list box.

Step 4: Click the *Exit* button to end the application. Go back to the code for the btnRunDemo_Click event handler and change the less-than operator to a greater-than operator in the loop's Boolean expression. After doing this, the loop should appear as:

```
Do
   lstOutput.Items.Add("Hello")
   intCount += 1
Loop While intCount > 10
```

Although the expression intCount > 10 is false to begin with, the statements in the body of the loop should execute once because this is a posttest loop.

Step 5: Run the application and click the *Run Demo* button. The loop should display *Hello* one time in the list box.

Step 6: Click the *Exit* button to end the application.

Keeping a Running Total

Many programming tasks require you to calculate the total of a series of numbers. For example, suppose you are writing a program that calculates a business's total sales for a week. The program would read the sales for each day as input and calculate the total of those numbers.

Programs that calculate the total of a series of numbers typically use two elements:

- A loop that reads each number in the series.
- A variable that accumulates the total of the numbers as they are read.

The variable that is used to accumulate the total of the numbers is called an **accumulator**. It is often said that the loop keeps a **running total** because it accumulates the total as it reads each number in the series. Figure 5-14 shows the general logic of a loop that calculates a running total.

When the loop finishes, the accumulator will contain the total of the numbers that were read by the loop. Notice that the first step in the flowchart is to set the accumulator variable to 0. This is a critical step. Each time the loop reads a number, it adds it to the accumulator. If the accumulator starts with any value other than 0, it will not contain the correct total when the loop finishes.

Let's look at an example. The application in Tutorial 5-4 calculates a company's total sales for five days by taking daily sales figures as input and keeping a running total of them as they are gathered.

Figure 5-14 Logic for calculating a running total

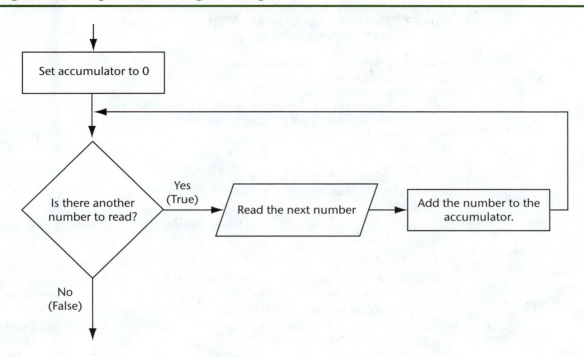

Tutorial 5-4:
Using a loop to keep a running total

In this tutorial, you will use an input box and a loop to enter five separate sales amount values. The values will be added to a total, which will be displayed.

Step 1: Open the *Running Total* project from the student sample programs folder named *Chap5\Running Total*.

Step 2: Open Form1 in design mode and double-click the *Enter Sales* button.

Step 3: Complete the btnEnterSales_Click event handler by writing the following bold code shown in lines 2 through 28.

```
 1 Private Sub btnEnterSales_Click(...) Handles btnEnterSales.Click
 2    Const intNUM_DAYS As Integer = 5  ' The number of days
 3    Dim intCount As Integer = 1       ' Loop counter
 4    Dim decSales As Decimal = 0       ' To hold daily sales
 5    Dim decTotal As Decimal = 0       ' To hold the total sales
 6    Dim strInput As String            ' To hold string input
 7
 8    ' Get the sales for each day.
 9    Do While intCount <= intNUM_DAYS
10      ' Get a daily sales amount from the user.
11      strInput = InputBox("Enter the sales for day " &
12                      intCount.ToString())
13
14      ' Convert the input to a Decimal.
```

```
15      If Decimal.TryParse(strInput, decSales) Then
16        ' Add the daily sales to the total sales.
17        decTotal += decSales
18
19        ' Add 1 to the loop counter.
20        intCount += 1
21      Else
22        ' Display an error message for invalid input.
23        MessageBox.Show("Enter a numeric value.")
24      End If
25    Loop
26
27    ' Display the total sales.
28    lblTotal.Text = decTotal.ToString("c")
29 End Sub
```

Let's take a closer look at the code. Here is a summary of the constant and variable declarations:

- Line 2 declares a constant named intNUM_DAYS, set to the value 5. This is the number of days of sales data we want to get from the user.
- Line 3 declares a variable named intCount that will be used as a loop counter. Notice that the variable is initialized with the value 1.
- Line 4 declares a variable named decSales that will be used to hold daily sales amounts.
- Line 5 declares a variable named decTotal that will hold the total sales. This is the accumulator variable. Notice that decTotal is initialized with the value 0. It is important that decTotal starts with the value 0 so the sum of all the sales amounts will be correct.
- Line 6 declares a variable named strInput that will hold the user's input, which is returned from the InputBox function.

The Do While loop that begins in line 9 executes as long as intCount is less than or equal to intNUM_DAYS. The statement in lines 11 and 12 displays an input box prompting the user to enter the sales for a specified day. (The first time the loop iterates, it will prompt the user to *Enter the sales for day 1*, the second time it will prompt *Enter the sales for day 2*, and so on.) The user's input is assigned, as a string, to the strInput variable.

Because the user's input is returned as a string, we need to convert it to a Decimal so we can perform math with it. That means that an exception will be thrown if the user has entered nonnumeric input. To prevent an exception, the If... Then statement in line 15 calls the Decimal.TryParse method to convert strInput to a Decimal and store the result in the decSales variable. Recall from Chapter 4 that this method returns True if the conversion is successful, or False if the value cannot be converted to a Decimal. If the method returns False, the program will jump to the Else clause in line 21, display the error message in line 23, and then the loop starts over. If the user's input is successfully converted to a Decimal, however, decSales is added to the decTotal variable in line 17, and 1 is added to intCount in line 20. The loop then starts over.

After the loop finishes, line 28 displays the total sales in the lblTotal label.

Step 4: Save and run the program. Click the *Enter Sales* button. The input box shown in Figure 5-15 asks the user to enter the sales for day 1. Enter 1000, and click the *OK* button. (If you prefer, you may press the [Enter] key.)

Figure 5-15 Input box

> Running Total   ×
>
> Enter the sales for day 1   OK
>
>   Cancel
>
> |

Step 5: The application will present input boxes asking for the sales for days 2, 3, 4, and 5. Enter the following amounts:

    Day 2:   2000
    Day 3:   3000
    Day 4:   4000
    Day 5:   5000

Step 6: After you enter the sales amount for all five days, the application should display the total sales as shown in Figure 5-16.

Step 7: End the program. You're finished.

Figure 5-16 Total sales displayed

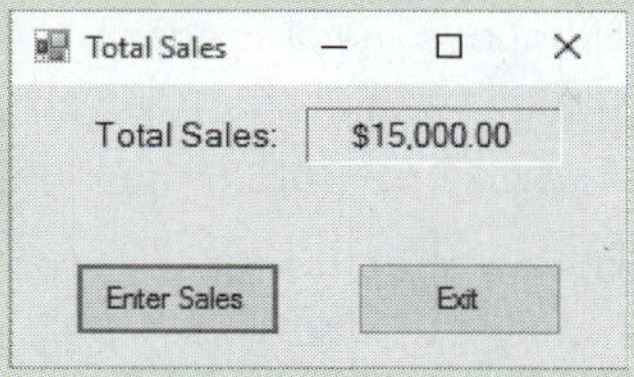

> ▦ Total Sales   —   □   ×
>
> Total Sales: $15,000.00
>
>   Enter Sales   Exit

Letting the User Control the Loop

Sometimes the user must decide how many times a loop should iterate. In Tutorial 5-5, you examine a modification of the *Running Total* application. This version of the program asks the user how many days he or she has sales figures for. The application then uses that value to control the number of times the Do While loop repeats.

Tutorial 5-5:
Examining an application that uses a user-controlled loop

Step 1: Open the *User Controlled* project from the student sample programs folder named *Chap5\User Controlled*.

Step 2: Run the application. When the form appears, click the *Enter Sales* button. The input box shown in Figure 5-17 appears.

Step 3: The input box asks you to enter the number of days you have sales figures for. Enter 3 and click the *OK* button (or press ⟨Enter⟩).

Figure 5-17 Input box

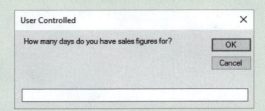

Step 4: Because you entered 3 for the number of days, the application presents three input boxes asking for the sales for days 1, 2, and 3. Enter the following values when asked:

Day 1: **1000**
Day 2: **2000**
Day 3: **3000**

Step 5: After you enter the sales figure for day 3, the application's form displays $6,000.00 as the total sales.

Step 6: Click the *Exit* button to terminate the application.

Step 7: Open the *Code* window and look at the btnEnterSales_Click event handler. Notice that this version of the code does not declare the constant intNUM_DAYS, as was used in Tutorial 5-4. This event handler has a new variable named intNumDays, declared as follows:

```
Dim intNumDays As Integer ' To hold the number of days
```

The following code that gets the number of days from the user, converts that input to an integer, and assigns the result to intNumDays:

```
' Get the number of days from the user.
strInput = InputBox("How many days do you have sales figures for?")

' Convert the user's input to an integer.
intNumDays = CInt(strInput)
```

After this code executes, intNumDays will hold the number of days specified by the user. Then, notice the first line of the Do While loop:

```
Do While intCount <= intNumDays
```

The loop repeats while intCount is less than or equal to intNumDays, the value specified by the user. As a result, the number of loop iterations will be equal to the number of days specified by the user.

Checkpoint

5.9 How many times will the following code segment display the message box?

```
Dim intCount As Integer = 0
Do While intCount < 10
  MessageBox.Show("I love Visual Basic!")
Loop
```

5.10 How many times will the following code segment display the message box?

```
Dim intCount As Integer = 0
Do While intCount < 10
  MessageBox.Show("I love Visual Basic!")
  intCount += 1
Loop
```

5.11 How many times will the following code segment display the message box?

```
Dim intCount As Integer = 100
Do
  MessageBox.Show("I love Visual Basic!")
  intCount += 1
Loop While intCount < 10
```

5.12 In the following code segment, which variable is the counter and which is the accumulator?

```
Dim intA As Integer
Dim intX As Integer
Dim intY As Integer
Dim intZ As Integer
Dim strInput As String
intX = 0
intY = 0
strInput = InputBox("How many numbers do you wish to enter?")
intZ = CInt(strInput)
Do While intX < intZ
  strInput = InputBox("Enter a number.")
  intA = CInt(strInput)
  intY += intA
  intX += 1
Loop
MessageBox.Show("The sum of those numbers is " & intY.ToString())
```

5.13 The following loop adds the numbers 1 through 5 to the lstOutput list box. Modify the loop so that instead of starting at 1 and counting to 5, it starts at 5 and counts backward to 1.

```
Dim intCount As Integer = 1
Do While intCount <= 5
  lstOutput.Items.Add(intCount)
  intCount += 1
Loop
```

5.14 Write a Do While loop that uses an input box to ask the user to enter a number. The loop should keep a running total of the numbers entered and stop when the total is greater than 300.

5.15 If you want a Do While loop always to iterate at least once, which form should you use, pretest or posttest?

5.4 The Do Until and For...Next Loops

CONCEPT: The Do Until loop iterates until its test expression is true. The For...Next loop uses a counter variable and iterates a specific number of times.

The Do Until Loop

The Do While loop iterates as long as a Boolean expression is true. Sometimes, however, it is more convenient to write a loop that iterates *until* an expression is true—that is, a loop that iterates as long as an expression is false, and then stops when the expression becomes true.

For example, consider a machine in an automobile factory that paints cars as they move down the assembly line. When there are no more cars to paint, the machine stops. If you were programming such a machine, you might want to design a loop that causes the machine to paint cars until there are no more cars on the assembly line.

A loop that iterates until a condition is true is known as a **Do Until loop**. The `Do Until` loop can be written as either a pretest or a posttest loop. Here is the general format of a pretest `Do Until` loop:

```
Do Until BooleanExpression
   Statement
   (More statements may follow)
Loop
```

Here is the general format of a posttest `Do Until` loop:

```
Do
   Statement
   (More statements may follow)
Loop Until BooleanExpression
```

In Tutorial 5-6, you examine an application that uses the `Do Until` loop. The application asks the user to enter test scores and then displays the average of the scores.

Tutorial 5-6:
Examining an application that uses the `Do Until` loop

Step 1: Open the *Test Scores* project from the student sample programs folder named *Chap5\Test Scores*.

Step 2: Run the application. The form appears, as shown in Figure 5-18.

Step 3: Click the *Get Scores* button. The input box shown in Figure 5-19 appears.

Figure 5-18 *Test Score Average* form   **Figure 5-19** Input box

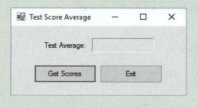
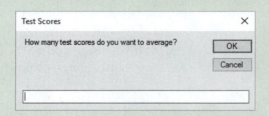

Step 4: Enter **5** for the number of test scores and click the *OK* button (or press [Enter]).

Step 5: Because you entered 5 for the number of test scores, the application presents five input boxes asking for scores 1, 2, 3, 4, and 5. Enter the following values when asked.

Test Score 1: **98**   Test Score 3: **100**   Test Score 5: **92**

Test Score 2: **87**   Test Score 4: **74**

Step 6: After you enter the fifth test score, the test score average 90.2 is displayed on the application form. Click the *Exit* button to end the application.

Step 7:   Open the *Code* window. The application's code is shown, with line numbers for reference, at the end of the tutorial. Let's look at the btnGetScores_Click event handler in greater detail:

- Local variables are declared in lines 6 through 11. Notice that the dblTotal variable (line 8) is initialized to 0. This variable is used as an accumulator. Also notice that the intCount variable (line 11) is initialized to 1. This variable is used as a loop counter.
- Line 14 displays the input box prompting the user for the number of test scores. The input is assigned to strInput.
- The If...Then statement in line 17 uses the Integer.TryParse method to convert strInput to an Integer, and store the result in intNumScores. If the conversion is successful, the Integer.TryParse method returns True and the program continues to line 20. If the conversion fails (because of invalid input), the Integer.TryParse method returns False, and the program jumps to the Else clause in line 45. If this happens, line 47 displays an error message, and the event handler ends.
- The Do Until loop that begins in line 20 iterates until intCount is greater than intNumScores. Inside the loop, lines 22 and 23 prompt the user for a test score, storing the user's input in strInput. The If...Then statement in line 26 uses the Double.TryParse method to convert strInput to a Double, and store the result in dblTestScore. If the conversion is successful, the Double.TryParse method returns True and the program continues to line 29. If the conversion fails (because of invalid input), the Double.TryParse method returns False, and the program jumps to the Else clause in line 33. If this happens, line 35 displays an error message, and the event handler ends.
- Line 29 uses the += operator to add dblTestScore to the accumulator variable dblTotal.
- Line 32 uses the += operator to add 1 to the counter variable intCount.
- After the loop has finished, the If...Then statement in line 40 determines whether intNumScores is greater than 0. If so, line 41 calculates the average test score, and line 42 displays the average in the lblAverage label.

```
1 Public Class Form1
2
3  Private Sub btnGetScores_Click(...) Handles btnGetScores.Click
4     ' This procedure gets the test scores, then calculates and
5     ' displays the average.
6     Dim intNumScores As Integer    ' The number of test scores
7     Dim dblTestScore As Double     ' To hold a test score
8     Dim dblTotal As Double = 0     ' Accumulator, initialized to 0
9     Dim dblAverage As Double       ' The average of the test scores
10    Dim strInput As String         ' To hold user input
11    Dim intCount As Integer = 1    ' Counter variable, initialized to 1
12
13    ' Prompt the user for the number of test scores.
14    strInput = InputBox("How many test scores do you want to average?")
15
16    ' Convert the input to an integer.
17    If Integer.TryParse(strInput, intNumScores) Then
18
19       ' Get the test scores.
20       Do Until intCount > intNumScores
```

```
21          ' Prompt the user for a score.
22          strInput = InputBox("Enter test score " &
23                              intCount.ToString())
24
25          ' Convert the input to a Double.
26          If Double.TryParse(strInput, dblTestScore) Then
27
28              ' Add the score to the accumulator.
29              dblTotal += dblTestScore
30
31              ' Add 1 to the counter.
32              intCount += 1
33          Else
34              ' Invalid test score.
35              MessageBox.Show("Enter a numeric test score.")
36          End If
37        Loop
38
39        ' Calculate and display the average.
40        If intNumScores > 0 Then
41            dblAverage = dblTotal / intNumScores
42            lblAverage.Text = dblAverage.ToString()
43        End If
44
45      Else
46        ' Invalid number of test scores.
47        MessageBox.Show("Enter an integer value for number of test scores.")
48      End If
49    End Sub
50
51    Private Sub btnExit_Click(...) Handles btnExit.Click
52      ' Close the form.
53      Me.Close()
54    End Sub
55 End Class
```

The For...Next **Loop**

VideoNote

The For...
Next Loop

The For...Next loop is ideal for situations that require a counter because it initializes, tests, and increments a counter variable. Here is the format of the **For...Next** loop:

```
For CounterVariable = StartValue To EndValue [Step Increment]
   statement
   (more statements may follow)
Next [CounterVariable]
```

As usual, the brackets are not part of the syntax, but indicate the optional parts. Let's look closer at the syntax.

- *CounterVariable* is the variable to be used as a counter. It must be a numeric variable.
- *StartValue* is the value the counter variable will be initially set to. This value must be numeric.
- *EndValue* is the value the counter variable is tested against just prior to each iteration of the loop. This value must be numeric.
- The Step *Increment* part of the statement is optional. If it is present, *Increment* (which must be a numeric expression) is the amount added to the counter variable at the end of each iteration. If the Step *Increment* part of the statement is omitted, the counter variable is incremented by 1 at the end of each iteration.

- The Next [*CounterVariable*] statement marks the end of the loop and causes the counter variable to be incremented. Notice that the name of the counter variable is optional.

Here is an example of the For...Next loop:

```
For intCount = 1 To 10
    MessageBox.Show("Hello")
Next
```

This loop executes the MessageBox.Show("Hello") statement 10 times. The following steps take place when the loop executes.

1. intCount is set to 1 (the start value).
2. intCount is compared to 10 (the end value). If intCount is less than or equal to 10, continue to Step 3. Otherwise the loop is exited.
3. The MessageBox.Show("Hello") statement in the body of the loop is executed.
4. intCount is incremented by 1.
5. Go back to Step 2 and repeat this sequence.

The flowchart shown in Figure 5-20 shows loop's actions.

 WARNING: It is incorrect to place a statement in the body of the For...Next loop that changes the counter variable's value. For example, the following loop increments intCount twice for each iteration.

```
' Warning!
For intCount = 1 To 10
    MessageBox.Show("Hello")
    intCount += 1
Next
```

Figure 5-20 Flowchart of For...Next loop

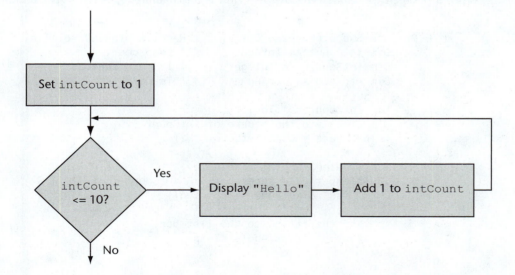

In Tutorial 5-7, you examine an application that demonstrates the For...Next loop.

 NOTE: Because the For...Next loop performs its test prior to each iteration, it is a pretest loop. Unlike the Do While and Do Until loops, this is the only form the For...Next loop may be written in.

Tutorial 5-7:
Examining an application that uses the `For...Next` loop

Step 1: Open the *For Next Demo 1* project from the student sample programs folder named *Chap5\For Next Demo 1*.

Step 2: Run the application. The form appears as shown in Figure 5-21.

Step 3: Click the *Run Demo* button. The form now appears as shown in Figure 5-22.

Figure 5-21 *For Next Demo 1* form

Figure 5-22 Results of `For...Next` loop

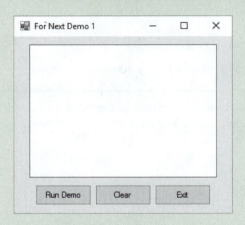

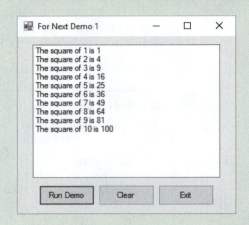

Step 4: Click the *Exit* button to terminate the application.

Step 5: Open the *Code* window and find the `btnRunDemo_Click` event handler. The code is as follows:

```
Private Sub btnRunDemo_Click(...) Handles btnRunDemo.Click
    Dim intCount As Integer      ' Loop counter
    Dim intSquare As Integer     ' To hold squares
    Dim strTemp As String        ' To hold output

    For intCount = 1 To 10
      ' Calculate the square of intCount.
      intSquare = CInt(intCount ^ 2)

      ' Create a string to display.
      strTemp = "The square of " & intCount.ToString() &
        " is " & intSquare.ToString()

      ' Add the string to the list box.
      lstOutput.Items.Add(strTemp)
    Next
End Sub
```

Figure 5-23 illustrates the order of the steps taken by the `For...Next` loop in this program.

Figure 5-23 Steps in For...Next loop

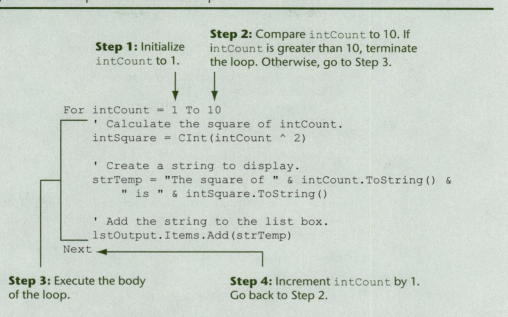

Step 1: Initialize intCount to 1.

Step 2: Compare intCount to 10. If intCount is greater than 10, terminate the loop. Otherwise, go to Step 3.

```
For intCount = 1 To 10
    ' Calculate the square of intCount.
    intSquare = CInt(intCount ^ 2)

    ' Create a string to display.
    strTemp = "The square of " & intCount.ToString() &
        " is " & intSquare.ToString()

    ' Add the string to the list box.
    lstOutput.Items.Add(strTemp)
Next
```

Step 3: Execute the body of the loop.

Step 4: Increment intCount by 1. Go back to Step 2.

In Tutorial 5-8, you complete a partially written application. The application will use a graphic image and a For...Next loop to perform a simple animation.

Tutorial 5-8:
Completing an application that uses the For...Next loop

Step 1: Open the *For Next Demo 2* project from the student sample programs folder named *Chap5\For Next Demo 2*.

Step 2: Open the application's form, as shown in Figure 5-24.

Figure 5-24 *For Next Demo 2* form

The spaceship graphic is displayed by a PictureBox control. The PictureBox control has a Left property that specifies the distance from the left edge of the form to the left edge of the PictureBox control. (The distance is measured in pixels.) In this tutorial, you will write a For...Next loop that makes the image move across the form by increasing the value of the PictureBox control's Left property.

NOTE: The PictureBox control's Left property does not appear in the *Properties* window. You access the Left property in code.

Step 3: Double-click the *Go!* button, and then complete the `btnGo_Click` event handler by writing the following bold code.

```
Private Sub btnGo_Click(...) Handles btnGo.Click
    Dim intCount As Integer ' Loop counter

    ' Move the image across the form.
    For intCount = 1 To 375
      picSpaceship.Left = intCount
    Next
End Sub
```

Look at the first line of the `For...Next` loop:

```
For intCount = 1 To 375
```

The start value for `intCount` is 1, and its end value is 375. Inside the loop, the following statement assigns the value of `intCount` to the PictureBox control's Left property:

```
picSpaceship.Left = intCount
```

As the loop iterates, the value in the Left property grows larger, which causes the PictureBox control to move across the form.

Step 4: Run the application. Each time you click the *Go!* button, the spaceship image should move from the form's left edge to its right edge.

Step 5: Click the *Exit* button to end the application. If you wish, open the *Code* window and experiment with different start and end values for the `For...Next` loop.

Specifying a Step Value

The **step value** is the value added to the counter variable at the end of each iteration of the `For...Next` loop. By default, the step value is 1. You can specify a different step value with the `Step` keyword. For example, look at the following code:

```
For intCount = 0 To 100 Step 10
    MessageBox.Show(intCount.ToString())
Next
```

In this loop, the starting value of `intCount` is 0 and the ending value of `intCount` is 100. The step value is 10, which means that 10 is added to `intCount` at the end of each iteration. During the first iteration `intCount` is 0, during the second iteration `intCount` is 10, during the third iteration `intCount` is 20, and so on.

You may also specify a negative step value if you want to decrement the counter variable. For example, look at the following loop:

```
For intCount = 10 To 1 Step -1
    MessageBox.Show(intCount.ToString())
Next
```

In this loop the starting value of `intCount` is 10 and the ending value of `intCount` is 1. The step value is –1, which means that 1 is subtracted from `intCount` at the end of each iteration. During the first iteration `intCount` is 10, during the second iteration `intCount` is 9, and so on.

Summing a Series of Numbers with the For...Next Loop

The For...Next loop can be used to calculate the sum of a series of numbers, as shown in the following code:

```
Dim intCount As Integer          ' Loop counter
Dim intTotal As Integer = 0      ' Accumulator

' Add the numbers 1 through 100.
For intCount = 1 To 100
   intTotal += intCount
Next

' Display the sum of the numbers.
MessageBox.Show("The sum of 1 through 100 is " & intTotal.ToString())
```

This code uses the variable intTotal as an accumulator and calculates the sum of the numbers from 1 through 100. The counter variable, intCount, has a starting value of 1 and an ending value of 100. During each iteration, the value of intCount is added to intTotal.

You may also let the user specify how many numbers to sum, as well as the value of each number. For example, look at the following code:

```
1    Dim intCount As Integer          ' Loop counter
2    Dim intMaxCount As Integer       ' To hold the maximum count
3    Dim dblTotal As Double = 0.0     ' Accumulator
4    Dim strInput As String           ' To hold user input
5    Dim dblNum As Double             ' To hold a number
6
7    ' Get the number of numbers to sum.
8    strInput = InputBox("How many numbers do you want to sum?")
9    intMaxCount = CInt(strInput)
10
11   ' Add the user-specified numbers.
12   For intCount = 1 To intMaxCount
13      ' Get a number.
14      strInput = InputBox("Enter a number.")
15      dblNum = CDbl(strInput)
16
17      ' Add the number to the accumulator.
18      dblTotal += dblNum
19   Next
20
21   ' Display the sum of the numbers.
22   MessageBox.Show("The sum of those numbers is " &
23                   dblTotal.ToString())
```

For simplicity, we have left out exception handlers or other code to validate the user input. Line 8 prompts the user for the number of numbers to sum, and line 9 stores the user's input in the intMaxCount variable. In line 12, which is the beginning of the For...Next loop, the intCount variable has a starting value of 1 and an ending value of intMaxCount. As a result, the number of iterations will be the value stored in intMaxCount.

In line 14, an input box is used to prompt the user for a number. In line 15, the value entered by the user is stored in the dblNum variable. Line 18 adds dblNum to the dblTotal variable, which is the accumulator.

Optional Topic: Breaking Out of a Loop

In rare circumstances, you might find it necessary to stop a loop before it goes through all of its iterations. Visual Basic provides the **Exit Do** statement, which allows you to prematurely break out of a Do While loop, and the **Exit For statement**, which allows you to prematurely break out of a For...Next loop. The way they work is simple:

- When a Do While loop is executing, if it encounters an Exit Do statement, the loop immediately ends.
- When a For...Next loop is executing, if it encounters an Exit For statement, the loop immediately ends.

You should do your best to avoid using these statements, however. They bypass the normal logic that terminates the loop and make the code more difficult to understand and debug.

Deciding Which Loop to Use

Although most repetitive algorithms can be written with any of the three types of loops, each works best in different situations.

The Do While Loop

Use the Do While loop when you wish the loop to repeat as long as the test expression is true. You can write the Do While loop as a pretest or posttest loop. Pretest Do While loops are ideal when you do not want the code in the loop to execute if the test expression is false from the beginning. Posttest loops are ideal when you always want the code in the loop to execute at least once.

The Do Until Loop

Use the Do Until loop when you wish the loop to repeat until the test expression is true. You can write the Do Until loop as a pretest or posttest loop. Pretest Do Until loops are ideal when you do not want the code in the loop to execute if the test expression is true from the beginning. Posttest loops are ideal when you always want the code in the loop to execute at least once.

The For...Next Loop

The For...Next loop is a pretest loop that first initializes a counter variable to a starting value. It automatically increments the counter variable at the end of each iteration. The loop repeats as long as the counter variable is not greater than an end value. The For...Next loop is primarily used when the number of required iterations is known.

 **Checkpoint**

5.16 How many times will the code inside the following loop execute? What will be displayed in the message box?

```
intX = 0
Do Until intX = 10
    intX += 2
Loop
MessageBox.Show(intX.ToString())
```

5.17 Write a For...Next loop that adds every fifth number, starting at zero, through 100, to the list box lstOutput.

5.18 Write a For...Next loop that repeats seven times, each time displaying an input box that asks the user to enter a number. The loop should also calculate and display the sum of the numbers entered.

5.19 Which type of loop is best to use when you know exactly how many times the loop should repeat?

5.20 Which type of loop is best to use when you want the loop to repeat as long as a condition exists?

5.21 Which type of loop is best to use when you want the loop to repeat until a condition exists?

5.5 Nested Loops

CONCEPT: A loop that is contained inside another loop is called a nested loop.

A **nested loop** is a loop inside another loop. A clock is a good example of something that works like a nested loop. The second hand, minute hand, and hour hand all spin around the face of the clock. The hour hand, however, makes only one revolution for every 60 of the minute hand's revolutions. And it takes 60 revolutions of the second hand for the minute hand to make one revolution. This means that for every complete revolution of the hour hand, the second hand revolves 3,600 times.

The following is a code segment with a For...Next loop that partially simulates a digital clock. It displays the seconds from 0 through 59 in a label named lblSeconds.

```
For intSeconds = 0 To 59
  lblSeconds.Text = intSeconds.ToString()
Next
```

We can add a minutes variable and another label, and nest the loop inside another loop that cycles through 60 minutes:

```
For intMinutes = 0 To 59
  lblMinutes.Text = intMinutes.ToString()
  For intSeconds = 0 To 59
    lblSeconds.Text = intSeconds.ToString()
  Next
Next
```

To make the simulated clock complete, another variable, label, and loop can be added to count the hours:

```
For intHours = 0 To 23
  lblHours.Text = intHours.ToString()
  For intMinutes = 0 To 59
    lblMinutes.Text = intMinutes.ToString()
    For intSeconds = 0 To 59
      lblSeconds.Text = intSeconds.ToString()
    Next
  Next
Next
```

The innermost loop will iterate 60 times for each iteration of the middle loop. The middle loop will iterate 60 times for each iteration of the outermost loop. When the outermost loop has iterated 24 times, the middle loop will have iterated 1,440 times and the innermost loop will have iterated 86,400 times.

The simulated clock example brings up a few points about nested loops:

- An inner loop goes through all of its iterations for each iteration of an outer loop.
- Inner loops complete their iterations before outer loops do.
- To get the total number of iterations of a nested loop, multiply the number of iterations of all the loops.

Checkpoint

5.22 What values will the following code segment add to the `lstNumbers` list box?

```
For intX = 1 To 3
    lstNumbers.Items.Add(intX)
    For intY = 1 To 2
        lstNumbers.Items.Add(intY)
    Next
Next
```

5.23 How many times will the value in `intY` be displayed in the following code segment?

```
For intX = 1 To 20
    For intY = 1 To 30
        MessageBox.Show(intY.ToString())
    Next
Next
```

5.6 Multicolumn List Boxes, Checked List Boxes, and Combo Boxes

CONCEPT: A multicolumn list box displays items in columns with a horizontal scroll bar, if necessary. A checked list box displays a check box next to each item in the list. A combo box performs many of the same functions as a list box, and it can also let the user enter text.

Multicolumn List Boxes

The ListBox control has a Multicolumn property that can be set to *True* or *False*. By default, it is set to *False*. If you set Multicolumn to *True*, it causes the list box to display its list in columns. You set the size of the columns, in pixels, with the ColumnWidth property. For example, suppose a form has a list box named `lstNumbers`, as shown in Figure 5-25.

The list box's Multicolumn property is set to *True*, and its ColumnWidth property is set to *30*. The following code adds the numbers 0 through 100 to a list box:

```
For intNumber = 0 To 100
    lstNumbers.Items.Add(intNumber)
Next
```

After the code executes, the list box appears as shown in Figure 5-26.

Notice that a horizontal scroll bar automatically appears in the list box. The user may scroll through the list and select a number.

Checked List Boxes

The CheckedListBox control is a variation of the ListBox control. It supports all ListBox properties and methods discussed in Section 5.2. Each item in a CheckedListBox control, however, is displayed with a check box next to it. Figure 5-27 shows an example.

An item in a checked list box may be selected and/or checked. Only one item in a checked list box may be selected at a given time, but multiple items may be checked.

Figure 5-25 List box

Figure 5-26 List box with multicolumn display

Figure 5-27 Checked list box

This is how the CheckOnClick property determines whether items become checked:

- When set to *False*, the user clicks an item once to select it, and then clicks it again to check it (or uncheck it, if it is already checked).
- When set to *True*, the user clicks an item only once to both select it and check it (or uncheck it, if it is already checked).

The CheckOnClick property is set to *False* by default. Because this setting makes working with the control a bit complicated, you may prefer setting it to *True* for most applications.

You can access the selected item in a checked list box exactly as you do with a regular list box: through the SelectedIndex and SelectedItem properties. These properties only indicate which item is selected, however, and do not report which items are checked. You access the checked items through the GetItemChecked method, which has the following general format:

```
CheckedListBox.GetItemChecked(Index)
```

CheckedListBox is the name of the CheckedListBox control. *Index* is the index of an item in the list. If the item is checked, the method returns *True*. Otherwise, it returns *False*. For example, assume an application has a checked list box name clbCities. (clb is the prefix for checked list boxes.) The following code counts the number of checked items:

```
Dim intIndex As Integer              ' List box index
Dim intCheckedCities As Integer = 0  ' To count the checked cities

' Step through the items in the list box, counting
' the number of checked items.
For intIndex = 0 To clbCities.Items.Count - 1
  If clbCities.GetItemChecked(intIndex) = True Then
    intCheckedCities += 1
  End If
Next

' Display the number of checked cities.
MessageBox.Show("You checked " & intCheckedCities.ToString() &
                " cities.")
```

As another example, assume an application uses the controls shown in Figure 5-28. The checked list box on the left is clbCities and the list box on the right is lstChecked. The *OK* button, btnOk, uses the following Click event handler:

```
Private Sub btnOk_Click(...) Handles btnOk.Click
  Dim intIndex As Integer ' List box index

  For intIndex = 0 To clbCities.Items.Count - 1
    If clbCities.GetItemChecked(intIndex) = True Then
      lstChecked.Items.Add(clbCities.Items(intIndex))
    End If
  Next
End Sub
```

The btnOk_Click event handler adds the items checked in the clbCities control to the lstChecked control. Figure 5-29 shows how the controls appear after the user has checked three cities and clicked the *OK* button.

Figure 5-28 Checked list box and a list box

Figure 5-29 Cities checked

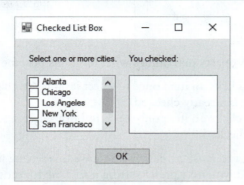

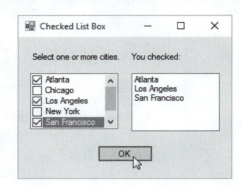

Combo Boxes

Combo boxes and list boxes are similar in the following ways:

- They both display a list of items.
- They both have Items, Items.Count, SelectedIndex, SelectedItem, and Sorted properties.
- They both have Items.Add, Items.Clear, Items.Remove, and Items.RemoveAt methods.
- All of these properties and methods work the same with combo boxes and list boxes.

Additionally, a combo box has a rectangular area that works like a text box. The user may either select an item from the combo box's list or type text into the combo box's text input area.

Like a text box, the combo box has a Text property. If the user types text into the combo box, the text is stored in the Text property. Also, when the user selects an item from the combo box's list, the item is copied to the Text property.

The prefix that we use for combo box names is cbo.

Combo Box Styles

There are three different styles of combo boxes: the drop-down combo box, the simple combo box, and the drop-down list combo box. You can select a combo box's style with its DropDownStyle property. Let's look at the differences of each style.

The Drop-Down Combo Box

DropDown is the default setting for the combo box DropDownStyle property. At run-time, a drop-down combo box appears like the one shown in Figure 5-30.

This style of combo box behaves like either a text box or a list box. The user may either type text into the box (like a text box) or click the down arrow (▾). If the user clicks the down arrow, a list of items drops down, as shown in Figure 5-31.

Now the user may select an item from the list. When the user selects an item, it appears in the text input area at the top of the box and is copied to the combo box's Text property.

NOTE: When typing text into the combo box, the user may enter a string that does not appear in the drop-down list.

Figure 5-30 A drop-down combo box

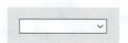

Figure 5-31 A list drops down when the user clicks the down arrow

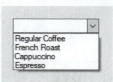

TIP: When the combo box has the focus, the user may also press [Alt] + [↓] to drop the list down. This is also true for the drop-down list combo box.

The Simple Combo Box

With the simple style of combo box, the list of items does not drop down but is always displayed. Figure 5-32 shows an example.

As with the drop-down combo box, this style allows the user to type text directly into the combo box or select from the list. When typing, the user is not restricted to the items that appear in the list. When an item is selected from the list, it is copied to the text input area and to the combo box's Text property.

The Drop-Down List Combo Box

When the DropDownList combo box style is selected, the user may not type text directly into the combo box. An item must be selected from the list. Figure 5-33 shows a drop-down list combo box. When the user clicks the down arrow, a list of items appears, as shown in Figure 5-34.

Figure 5-32 The simple combo box

Figure 5-33 The drop-down list combo box

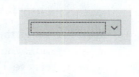

Figure 5-34 A list drops down when the user clicks the down arrow

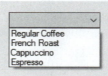

When the user selects an item from the list, it is copied to the text area at the top of the combo box and to the Text property. Because the user can only select items from the list, it is not possible to enter text that does not appear in the list.

Getting the User's Input from a Combo Box

As with the list box, you can determine which item has been selected from a combo box's list by retrieving the value in the SelectedIndex or SelectedItem properties. If the user has typed text into the combo box's text area, however, you cannot use the SelectedIndex or SelectedItem properties to get the text. The best way to get the user's input is with the Text property, which contains either the user's text input or the item selected from the list.

> **NOTE:** The drop-down list combo box's Text property is read-only. You cannot change its value with code.

List Boxes versus Combo Boxes

The following guidelines help you decide when to use a list box and when to use a combo box.

- Use a drop-down or simple combo box when you want to provide the user a list of items to select from but do not want to limit the user's input to the items on the list.
- Use a list box or a drop-down list combo box when you want to limit the user's selection to a list of items. The drop-down list combo box generally takes less space than a list box (because the list doesn't appear until the user clicks the down arrow), so use it when you want to conserve space on the form.

In Tutorial 5-9, you create three styles of combo boxes.

Tutorial 5-9:
Creating combo boxes

In this tutorial, you will create each of the three styles of combo boxes.

Step 1: Create a new Windows Forms Application project named *Combo Box Demo*.

Step 2: Set up the form like the one shown in Figure 5-35. Create three combo boxes: cboCountries (drop-down combo box), cboPlays (simple combo box), and cboArtists (drop-down list combo box).

Step 3: Enter the following items into the Items property of the cboCountries combo box: England, Ireland, Scotland, and Wales. Set the combo box's Sorted property to *True*.

Step 4: Enter the following items into the Items property of the cboPlays combo box: Hamlet, Much Ado about Nothing, Romeo and Juliet, A Comedy of Errors, and The Merchant of Venice. Set the combo box's Sorted property to *True*.

Step 5: Enter the following items into the Items property of the cboArtists combo box: Michelangelo, Raphael, and da Vinci.

Figure 5-35 *Combo Box Demo* form

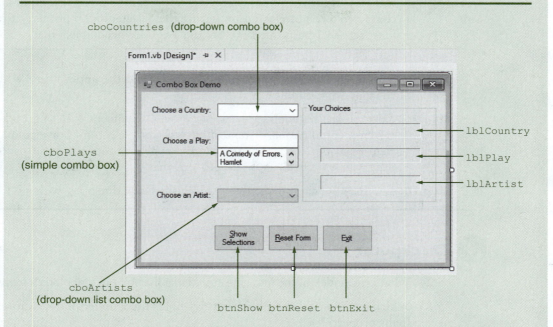

cboCountries (drop-down combo box)

cboPlays
(simple combo box)

lblCountry

lblPlay

lblArtist

cboArtists
(drop-down list combo box)

btnShow btnReset btnExit

Step 6: The btnShow_Click event handler should perform the following tasks:

- Copy the selected item or typed text from the cboCountries combo box to the lblCountry.Text property.
- Copy the selected item or typed text from the cboPlays combo box to the lblPlay.Text property.
- Copy the selected item from the cboArtists combo box to the lblArtist. Text property.

Enter the following code shown in bold for the btnShow_Click event handler:

```
Private Sub btnShow_Click(...) Handles btnShow.Click
    ' Display the combo box selections.
    lblCountry.Text = cboCountries.Text
    lblPlay.Text = cboPlays.Text
    lblArtist.Text = cboArtists.Text
End Sub
```

Step 7: The btnReset_Click event handler should deselect any items that are selected in the combo boxes. As with list boxes, this is accomplished by setting the SelectedIndex property to –1. The procedure should also set the Text property of lblCountry, lblPlay, and lblArtist to String.Empty. Enter the following code, shown in bold, for the btnReset_Click event handler.

```
Private Sub btnReset_Click(...) Handles btnReset.Click
    ' Reset the combo boxes.
    cboCountries.SelectedIndex = -1
    cboCountries.Text = String.Empty
    cboPlays.SelectedIndex = -1
    cboPlays.Text = String.Empty
    cboArtists.SelectedIndex = -1
    ' Note: cboArtists.Text is read-only.

    ' Reset the labels.
    lblCountry.Text = String.Empty
    lblPlay.Text = String.Empty
    lblArtist.Text = String.Empty
End Sub
```

> **NOTE:** If the user types characters into a combo box's text input area, those characters are not cleared by setting the SelectedIndex property to –1. You must set the Text property to `String.Empty` to accomplish that.

Step 8: The `btnExit_Click` event handler should end the application. Write the code for that event handler.

Step 9: Save the project and run the application. Experiment with the combo boxes by trying a combination of text input and item selection. For example, select an item from the `cboCountries` list and type text into the `cboPlays`' text input area. Click the `btnShow` button to see what you have entered.

Step 10: End the application when you are finished experimenting with it.

 Checkpoint

5.24   What is the index of the first item stored in a list box or combo box's Items property?

5.25   Which list box or combo box property holds the number of items stored in the Items property?

5.26   Which list box or combo box property holds the index of the item selected from the list?

5.27   What is the difference between a drop-down and drop-down list combo box?

5.28   What is the best method of getting the user's input from a combo box?

5.29   Suppose you want to place a list box on a form, but it would take up too much space. What other control might you use?

 5.7   Random Numbers

CONCEPT: Visual Basic provides tools to generate random numbers and initialize the sequence of random numbers with a random seed value.

Computer applications such as games and simulations often create what appear to be random events. A program simulating a traffic intersection, for example, might generate random numbers of simulated vehicles. Based on information provided during the simulation, planners can estimate the average amount of time drivers spend waiting at the stoplight. Similarly, random numbers can simulate the movements of stock prices, using various rules about how stock prices change.

Unfortunately, computers aren't capable of generating truly random numbers (unless you have an old, malfunctioning computer—then it might fail from time to time, generating truly random results). Instead, computers use carefully crafted formulas that are based on years of research to generate pseudo-random numbers. **Pseudo-random numbers** only seem to be random. For most applications that require random numbers, however, pseudo-random numbers work just as well.

To generate random numbers in Visual Basic, you have to create a special type of object known as a `Random` **object** in memory. `Random` objects have methods and properties that make generating random numbers fairly easy. Here is an example of a statement that creates a Random object:

```
Dim rand As New Random
```

This statement declares a variable named rand. The expression New Random creates a Random object in memory. After this statement executes, the rand variable will refer to the Random object. As a result, you will be able to use the rand variable to call the object's methods for generating random numbers. (There is nothing special about the variable name rand used in this example. You can use any legal variable name.)

The Next Method

Once you have created a Random object, you can call its **Next method** to get a random integer value. The following code shows an example:

```
' Declare an Integer variable.
Dim intNum As Integer

' Create a Random object.
Dim rand As New Random

' Get a random integer and assign it to intNum.
intNum = rand.Next()
```

After this code executes, the intNum variable will contain a random number. If you call the Next method with no arguments, as shown in this example, the returned integer is somewhere between 0 and 2,147,483,647. Alternatively, you can pass an argument that specifies an upper limit to the generated number's range. In the following statement, the value assigned to intNum is somewhere between 0 and 99:

```
intNum = rand.Next(100)
```

The random integer's range does not have to begin at zero. You can add or subtract a value to shift the numeric range upward or downward. In the following statement, we call the Next method to get a random number in the range of 0 through 9, and then we add 1 to it. So, the number assigned to intNum will be somewhere in the range of 1 through 10:

```
intNum = rand.Next(10) + 1
```

The following statement shows another example. It assigns a random integer to intNum between −50 and +49:

```
intNum = rand.Next(100) - 50
```

The NextDouble Method

You can call a Random object's **NextDouble method** to get a random floating-point value between 0.0 and 1.0 (not including 1.0). The following code shows an example:

```
' Declare a Double variable.
Dim dblNum As Double

' Create a Random object.
Dim rand As New Random

' Get a random number and assign it to dblNum.
dblNum = rand.NextDouble()
```

After this code executes, the dblNum variable will contain a random floating-point number in the range of 0.0 up to (but not including) 1.0. If you want the random number to fall within a larger range, multiply it by a scaling factor. The following statement assigns a random number between 0.0 and 500.0 to dblNum:

```
dblNum = rand.NextDouble() * 500.0
```

The following statement generates a random number between 100.0 and 600.0:

```
dblNum = (rand.NextDouble() * 500.0) + 100.0
```

In Tutorial 5-10 you will create a VB application that uses random numbers to simulate a coin toss.

Tutorial 5-10:
Creating the *Coin Toss* application

In this tutorial you will create an application that simulates the tossing of a coin. Each time the user tosses the coin, the application will use a Random object to get a random integer in the range of 0 through 1. If the random number is 0, it means the tails side of the coin is up, and if the random number is 1, it means the heads side is up. The application will display an image of a coin showing either the heads side or the tails side, depending on the value of the random number.

Step 1: Create a new Windows Forms application named *Coin Toss*.

Step 2: Set up the form with two PictureBox controls and two buttons, like the one shown in Figure 5-36. In the student sample programs, in the *Chap5* folder, you will find two image files named Heads.bmp and Tails.bmp. Set the picHeads control's Image property to the Heads.bmp file, and set the picTails control's Image property to the Tails.bmp file.

Step 3: Set the Visible property to *False* for both the picHeads control and the picTails control. (You will still see the images on the form in the *Designer* window, but they will be invisible when the application runs.)

Figure 5-36 The *Coin Toss* form

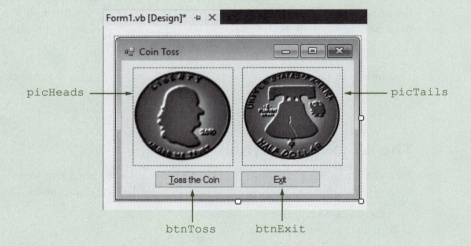

Step 4: Double-click the btnToss button to create a code template for its Click event handler. Complete the event handler by writing the following bold code shown in lines 2 through 20.

```
1   Private Sub btnToss_Click(...) Handles btnToss.Click
2       Dim intSideUp As Integer ' To indicate which side is up
3       Dim rand As New Random    ' Random number generator
4
```

```
 5     ' Get a random number in the range of 0 through 1.
 6     ' 0 means tails up, and 1 means heads up.
 7     intSideUp = rand.Next(2)
 8
 9     ' Display the side that is up.
10     If intSideUp = 0 Then
11         ' 0 means tails is up, so display the tails
12         ' image and hide the heads image.
13         picTails.Visible = True
14         picHeads.Visible = False
15     Else
16         ' 1 means heads is up, so display the heads
17         ' image and hide the tails image.
18         picHeads.Visible = True
19         picTails.Visible = False
20     End If
21 End Sub
```

Let's take a closer look at the code. Line 2 declares an Integer variable named intSideUp. This variable will hold a random number that indicates which side of the coin is up. Line 3 creates a Random object, using the name rand to refer to that object.

Line 7 calls the rand object's Next method, passing 2 as an argument. This means that the method will return a value in the range of 0 through 1. The random number is assigned to the intSideUp variable.

The If statement in line 10 determines whether intSideUp is equal to 0. If so, it means that the tails side of the coin is up, so line 13 makes the picTails control visible and line 14 makes the picHeads control invisible.

If the intSideUp variable is not equal to 0, then the heads side of the coin is up. In that case, the Else clause in line 15 takes over. Line 18 makes the picHeads control visible and line 19 makes the picTails control invisible.

Step 5: Write an event handler for the btnExit button. The button should close the form when it is clicked.

Step 6: Save the application, and then run it. Initially you will not see the coin on the form. When you click the *Toss the Coin* button, however, one of the two images (heads up or tails up) will be displayed, as shown in Figure 5-37. Click the button several times to simulate several coin tosses. When you are finished, exit the application.

Figure 5-37 The *Coin Toss* form with heads up and tails up

Random Number Seeds

The formula used to generate random numbers has to be initialized with a value known as a seed value. The **seed value** is used in the calculation that returns the next random number in the series. When a Random object is created in memory, it retrieves the system time from the computer's internal clock and uses that as the seed value. The system time is an integer that represents the current date and time, down to a hundredth of a second.

If a Random object uses the same seed each time it is created, it will always generate the same series of random numbers. Because the system time changes every hundredth of a second, it is the preferred value to use as the seed in most cases. However, you can specify a different integer value as the seed, if you desire, when you create a Random object. Here is an example:

```
Dim rand As New Random(1000)
```

In this example, the Random object that is created uses 1000 as the seed value. Each time a Random object is created with this statement, it will generate the same series of random numbers. That may be desirable when running specific tests and validations, but decidedly boring if the program is a computer game or simulation.

 Checkpoint

5.30 What does a Random object's Next method return?

5.31 What does a Random object's NextDouble method return?

5.32 Write code that creates a Random object and then assigns a random integer in the range of 1 through 100 to the variable intRandomNumber.

5.33 Write code that creates a Random object and then assigns a random integer in the range of 100 through 400 to the variable intRandomNumber.

5.34 What does a Random object use as its seed value if you do not specify one?

5.35 What happens if the same seed value is used each time a Random object is created?

5.8 Simplifying Code using the With...End With Statement

CONCEPT: The With...End With statement allows you to simplify a series of consecutive statements that perform operations using the same object.

Sometimes you must write several consecutive statements that perform operations on the same control or other object. The following code shows an example of several operations being performed with a text box named txtName:

```
txtName.Clear()
txtName.ForeColor = Color.Blue
txtName.BackColor = Color.Yellow
txtName.BorderStyle = BorderStyle.Fixed3D
```

In Visual Basic you can simplify this code using the **With...End With** statement, as shown here:

```
With txtName
    .Clear()
    .ForeColor = Color.Blue
```

```
      .BackColor = Color.Yellow
      .BorderStyle = BorderStyle.Fixed3D
   End With
```

Notice that in the `With...End With` statement we refer to the `txtName` control only once, in the first line. That eliminates the need to repeatedly type `txtName` at the beginning of each line that appears inside the statement.

5.9 ToolTips

> **CONCEPT:** ToolTips are a standard and convenient way of providing help to the users of an application. The ToolTip control allows you to assign pop-up hints to the other controls on a form.

A ToolTip is a small box displayed when the user holds the mouse cursor over a control. The box shows a short description of what the control does. Most Windows applications use ToolTips as a way of providing immediate and concise help to the user.

The **ToolTip control** allows you to create ToolTips for other controls on a form. Place a ToolTip control in your application just as you place other controls: double-click the ToolTip icon in the Toolbox. When you do so, a ToolTip control appears in an area at the bottom of the *Designer* window, as shown in Figure 5-38.

Figure 5-38 ToolTip control

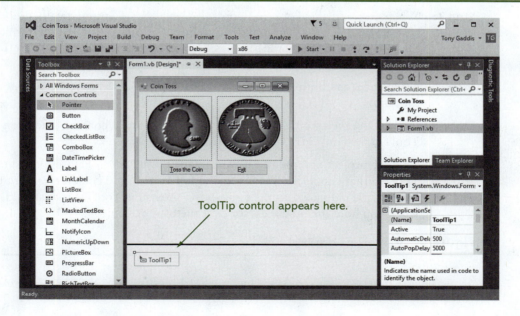

Because the ToolTip control is invisible at runtime, it does not appear on the form at design time. Instead, it appears in an area known as the component tray. The **component tray** is a resizable region at the bottom of the *Designer* window that holds invisible controls.

When you add a ToolTip control to a form, a new property is added to all the other controls. The new property is named *ToolTip on ToolTipControl*, where *ToolTipControl* is the name of the ToolTip control. For example, suppose you add a ToolTip control to a form and keep the default name *ToolTip1*. The new property that is added to the other controls will be named *ToolTip on ToolTip1*. This new property holds the string that is displayed as the control's ToolTip.

ToolTip Properties

You can select the ToolTip control in the component tray and then examine its properties in the *Properties* window. The InitialDelay property determines the amount of time, in milliseconds, that elapses between the user pointing the mouse at a control and the ToolTip's appearance. The default setting is 500. (One millisecond is 1/1000th of a second, so 500 milliseconds is half of a second.)

The AutoPopDelay property is also a measure of time in milliseconds. It determines how long a ToolTip remains on the screen once it is displayed. The default setting is 5000. The ReshowDelay property holds the number of milliseconds that will elapse between the displaying of different ToolTips as the user moves the mouse from control to control. The default setting is 100.

You can set these properties individually, or set them all at once with the AutomaticDelay property. When you store a value in the AutomaticDelay property, InitialDelay is set to the same value, AutoPopDelay is set to 10 times the value, and ReshowDelay is set to one-fifth the value. In Tutorial 5-11, you add ToolTips to an application.

Tutorial 5-11:
Adding ToolTips to an application

Step 1: Load the *Coin Toss* project that you completed in Tutorial 5-10 and open the form in the *Designer* window.

Step 2: Scroll down in the Toolbox until you find the ToolTip icon ( ). Double-click the icon to add a ToolTip control to the component tray. Notice that the default name of the ToolTip control is *ToolTip1*.

Step 3: When you add the ToolTip1 control, Visual Basic automatically adds a new property named *ToolTip on ToolTip1* to all other controls on the form. In the *Designer* window select the btnToss Button control, and then locate the ToolTip on ToolTip1 property in the *Properties* window.

Step 4: Set the btnToss Button control's ToolTip on ToolTip1 property to *Click to toss the coin*.

Step 5: In the *Designer* window select the btnExit Button control, and then set its ToolTip on ToolTip1 property to *Click to exit*.

Step 6: Save the project and the run it. The image on the left in Figure 5-39 shows the ToolTip that should appear when you hold the mouse cursor over the btnToss button, and the image on the right shows shows the ToolTip that should appear when you hold the mouse cursor over the btnExit button.

Figure 5-39 ToolTips displayed

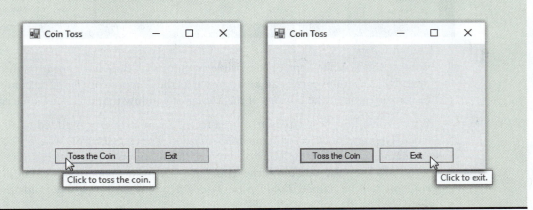

5.10 Focus on Program Design and Problem Solving: Building the *Vehicle Loan Calculator* Application

CONCEPT: In this section, you build the *Vehicle Loan Calculator* application. The application uses a loop, input validation, and ToolTips. This section also covers some of the Visual Basic intrinsic financial functions.

Visual Basic has several built-in functions for performing financial calculations. You will build a program named *Vehicle Loan Calculator*. It uses the following functions: Pmt, IPmt, and PPmt. Let's look at each function in detail before continuing with the case study.

The Pmt Function

The Pmt function returns the periodic payment amount for a loan. It assumes the loan has a fixed interest rate. Here is the general form of the **Pmt function** call:

```
Pmt(PeriodicInterestRate, NumberOfPeriods, -LoanAmount)
```

Descriptions of each argument follow:

1. *PeriodicInterestRate*: You usually know a loan's annual interest rate; this function, however, needs to know the loan's periodic interest rate. A loan is divided into periods, and you make a payment each period. The periodic interest rate is the rate of interest per period of the loan. For example, if you make monthly payments on a loan, the period is each month. If the annual interest rate is 9%, then the periodic interest rate is .09 divided by 12, which is .0075.
2. *NumberOfPeriods*: For a loan that requires monthly payments, this is the total number of months of the loan. For example, a three-year loan is given for 36 months.
3. *LoanAmount*: This is the amount being borrowed, which must be negative.

NOTE: The Pmt function can also be used to calculate payments on a savings plan. When using it for that purpose, specify the desired value of the savings as a positive number.

Here is an example of the function call:

```
dblPayment = Pmt(dblAnnInt / 12, 24, -5000)
```

In this statement, dblAnnInt contains the annual interest rate, 24 is the number of months of the loan, and the amount of the loan is $5,000. After the statement executes, dblPayment holds the fixed monthly payment amount.

The IPmt Function

The IPmt function returns the interest payment for a specific period on a loan. It assumes the loan has a fixed interest rate, with fixed monthly payments. Here is the general format of the **IPmt function** call:

```
IPmt(PeriodicInterestRate, Period, NumberOfPeriods, -LoanAmount)
```

Descriptions of each argument follow:

1. *PeriodicInterestRate*: As with the Pmt function, this function must know the periodic interest rate. (See the description of argument 1 for the Pmt function.)
2. *Period*: This argument specifies the period for which you wish to calculate the payment. The argument must be at least 1, and no more than the total number of periods of the loan.

3. *NumberofPeriods*: The total number of periods of the loan. (See the description of argument 2 for the Pmt function.)
4. *LoanAmount*: As with the Pmt function, the loan amount must be expressed as a negative number.

Here is an example of the function call:

```
dblInterest = IPmt(dblAnnInt / 12, 6, 24, -5000)
```

In this statement, dblAnnInt contains the annual interest rate, 6 is the number of the month for which you wish to calculate the payment, 24 is the number of months of the loan, and the amount of the loan is $5,000. After the statement executes, dblInterest holds the amount of interest paid in month 6 of the loan.

The PPmt Function

The PPmt function returns the principal payment for a specific period on a loan. It assumes the loan has a fixed interest rate, with fixed monthly payments. Here is the general format of the **PPmt function** call:

```
PPmt(PeriodicInterestRate, Period, NumberOfPeriods, -LoanAmount)
```

Descriptions of each argument follow:

1. *PeriodicInterestRate*: As with the Pmt function, this function must know the periodic interest rate. (See the description of argument 1 for the Pmt function.)
2. *Period*: This argument specifies the period for which you wish to calculate the payment. The argument must be at least 1, and no more than the total number of periods of the loan.
3. *NumberOfPeriods*: The total number of periods of the loan. (See the description of argument 2 for the Pmt function.)
4. *LoanAmount*: As with the Pmt function, the loan amount must be expressed as a negative number.

Here is an example of the function call:

```
dblPrincipal = PPmt(dblAnnInt / 12, 6, 24, -5000)
```

In this statement, dblAnnInt contains the annual interest rate, 6 is the number of the month for which you wish to calculate the payment, 24 is the number of months of the loan, and the amount of the loan is $5,000. After the statement executes, dblPrincipal holds the amount of principal paid in month 6 of the loan.

The Case Study

The Central Mountain Credit Union finances new and used vehicles for its members. A credit union branch manager asks you to write an application named *Vehicle Loan Calculator* that displays the following information for a loan:

- The monthly payment amount
- The amount of the monthly payment applied toward interest
- The amount of the monthly payment applied toward principal

We will assume that the credit union currently charges 8.9% annual interest for new vehicle loans and 9.5% annual interest on used vehicle loans.

Figure 5-40 shows the *Vehicle Loan Calculator* application at runtime. When the user selects the *Used* car radio button, the list box is cleared and the Annual interest rate changes. The user can then click the *Calculate* button to see the new interest and principal payments. A sample is shown in Figure 5-41. If the user neglects to enter a valid number into the three input fields, an error message reminds the user, as shown in Figure 5-42.

Figure 5-40 The *Vehicle Loan Calculator* application

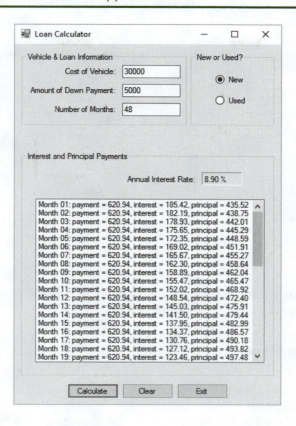

Figure 5-41 The Vehicle Loan Calculator, after selecting a used car loan

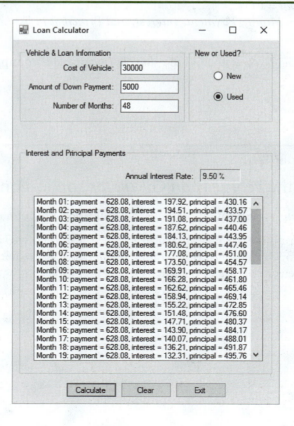

Figure 5-42 Error message in the *Vehicle Loan Calculator* application

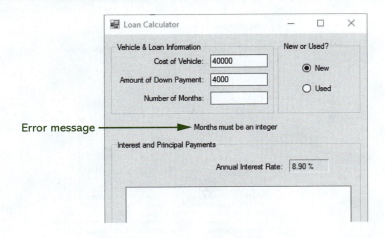

Error message ⟶ Months must be an integer

The following pseudocode shows the steps we will follow when calculating the monthly payments, interest amount, and principal payments.

> *Get VehicleCost from the form*
> *Get DownPayment from the form*
> *Get Months from the form*
>
> *Loan = VehicleCost – DownPayment*
> *MonthlyPayment = Pmt()*
> *For Count = 0 To Months*
>   *Interest = IPmt()*
>   *Principal = PPmt()*
>   *Display Month, Payment, Interest, and Principal in list box*
> *Next*

In Tutorial 5-12 you will build the *Vehicle Loan Calculator* application.

Tutorial 5-12:
Building the *Vehicle Loan Calculator* application

Step 1: Create a new Windows Forms Application project named *Loan Calculator*.

Step 2: Set up the form as shown in Figure 5-43. Refer to Table 5-2 for the important property settings. A few of the Label controls are not listed in the table because their values are evident from the figure.

Figure 5-43 The *Vehicle Loan Calculator* main form

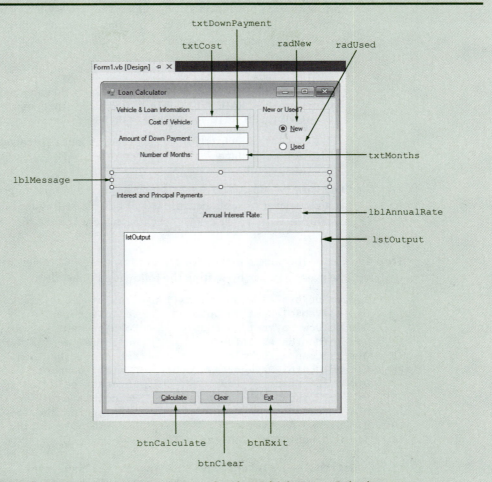

Table 5-2 Important property settings for the Vehicle Loan Calculator

Control Type	Control Name	Property	Property Value
Form	(Default)	Text	*Loan Calculator*
GroupBox	(Default)	Text	*Vehicle && Loan Information*
GroupBox	(Default)	Text	*New or Used?*
GroupBox	(Default)	Text	*Interest and Principal Payments*
TextBox	txtCost		
TextBox	txtDownPayment		
TextBox	txtMonths		
RadioButton	radNew	Text	*New*
RadioButton	radUsed	Text	*Used*
Label	lblAnnualRate	BorderStyle	*Fixed3D*
		AutoSize	*False*
Label	lblMessage	AutoSize	*False*
		TextAlign	*MiddleCenter*
ListBox	lstOutput		
Button	btnCalculate	Text	*Calculate*
Button	btnClear	Text	*Clear*
Button	btnExit	Text	*Exit*

Step 3: Once you have placed all the controls on the form and set their properties, you can write the application's code. Open the *Code* window and write the comments and class-level variable declarations shown as follows in bold. This code should not appear inside of any event handler.

```
Public Class Form1
  ' Class-level constants
  Const dblMONTHS_YEAR As Double = 12  ' Months per year
  Const dblNEW_RATE As Double = 0.05   ' Interest rate, new cars
  Const dblUSED_RATE As Double = 0.08  ' Interest rate, used cars

  ' Class-level variable to hold the annual interest rate
  Dim dblAnnualRate As Double = dblNEW_RATE
End Class
```

The variable, dblAnnualRate, which holds the annual interest rate, is declared as a class-level variable because it will be accessed by multiple procedures. It is initialized with dblNEW_RATE because a new vehicle loan will be selected by default.

Step 4: Create the code template for the btnCalculate_Click event handler. Complete the event handler by writing the following bold code.

```
1  Private Sub btnCalculate_Click() Handles btnCalculate.Click
2     Dim dblVehicleCost As Double      ' Vehicle cost
3     Dim dblDownPayment As Double      ' Down payment
4     Dim intMonths As Integer          ' Number of months for the loan
5     Dim dblLoan As Double             ' Amount of the loan
6     Dim dblMonthlyPayment As Double   ' Monthly payment
7     Dim dblInterest As Double         ' Interest paid for the period
8     Dim dblPrincipal As Double        ' Principal paid for the period
9     Dim intCount As Integer           ' Counter for the loop
10    Dim strOut As String              ' Used to hold a line of output
11    Dim blnInputOk As Boolean = True
12
13    ' Get the vehicle cost, validating at the same time.-
14    If Not Double.TryParse(txtCost.Text, dblVehicleCost) Then
15       lblMessage.Text = "Vehicle cost must be a number"
16       blnInputOk = False
17    End If
18
19    ' Get the down payment, validating at the same time.
20    If Not Double.TryParse(txtDownPayment.Text, dblDownPayment) Then
21       lblMessage.Text = "Down Payment must be a number"
22       blnInputOk = False
23    End If
24
25    ' Get the number of months, validating at the same time.
26    If Not Integer.TryParse(txtMonths.Text, intMonths) Then
27       lblMessage.Text = "Months must be an integer"
28       blnInputOk = False
29    End If
30
31    If blnInputOk = True Then
32       ' Calculate the loan amount and monthly payment.
33       dblLoan = dblVehicleCost - dblDownPayment
34       dblMonthlyPayment = Pmt(dblAnnualRate / dblMONTHS_YEAR,
35                              intMonths, -dblLoan)
36
37       ' Clear the list box and message label.
```

```
38        lstOutput.Items.Clear()
39        lblMessage.Text = String.Empty
40
41        For intCount = 1 To intMonths
42            ' Calculate the interest for this period.
43            dblInterest = IPmt(dblAnnualRate / dblMONTHS_YEAR,
44                            intCount, intMonths, -dblLoan)
45
46            ' Calculate the principal for this period.
47            dblPrincipal = PPmt(dblAnnualRate / dblMONTHS_YEAR,
48                            intCount, intMonths, -dblLoan)
49
50            ' Start building the output string with the month.
51            strOut = "Month " & intCount.ToString("d2")
52
53            ' Add the payment amount to the output string
54            strOut &= ": payment = " & dblMonthlyPayment.ToString("n2")
55
56            ' Add the interest amount to the output string.
57            strOut &= ", interest = " & dblInterest.ToString("n2")
58
59            ' Add the principal for the period.
60            strOut &= ", principal = " & dblPrincipal.ToString("n2")
61
62            ' Add the output string to the list box
63            lstOutput.Items.Add(strOut)
64        Next
65    End If
66 End Sub
```

The error checking in this procedure uses a Boolean variable named blnInputOk to verify the correctness of the user's input. The variable is initialized to True in line 11, so you start out assuming that all input is valid. But then in lines 16 and 22, the variable will be set to False if the user has incorrectly entered either the vehicle cost or the down payment. Finally, the code checks the value of the blnInputOk variable in line 31 before completing the calculations.

Step 5: Create the code template for the btnClear_Click event handler. Complete the event handler by writing the following bold code.

```
Private Sub btnClear_Click(...) Handles btnClear.Click
    ' Reset the interest rate.
    dblAnnualRate = dblNEW_RATE

    ' Clear the text boxes
    txtCost.Clear()
    txtDownPayment.Clear()
    txtMonths.Clear()

    ' Clear the list box.
    lstOutput.Items.Clear()

    ' Set default interest rate for new car loans.
    lblAnnualRate.Text = dblNEW_RATE.ToString("p")
    radNew.Checked = True

    ' Clear any error messages.
    lblMessage.Text = String.Empty

    ' Reset the focus to txtCost.
    txtCost.Focus()
End Sub
```

Step 6: Create the code template for the `btnExit_Click` event handler. Complete the event handler by writing the following bold code.

```
Private Sub btnExit_Click(...) Handles btnExit.Click
  ' Close the form.
  Me.Close()
End Sub
```

Step 7: Create the code template for the `radNew_CheckedChanged` event handler. (You can easily create the code template by opening the *Designer* window and double-clicking the `radNew` control.) Complete the event handler by writing the following bold code.

```
Private Sub radNew_CheckedChanged(...) Handles radNew.CheckedChanged
  ' If the New radio button is checked, then
  ' the user has selected a new car loan.
  If radNew.Checked = True Then
     dblAnnualRate    = dblNEW_RATE
     lblAnnualRate.Text = dblNEW_RATE.ToString("p")
     lstOutput.Items.Clear()
  End If
End Sub
```

Step 8: Create the code template for the `radUsed_CheckedChanged` event handler. (You can easily create the code template by opening the *Designer* window and double-clicking the `radUsed` control.) Complete the event handler by writing the following bold code.

```
Private Sub radUsed_CheckedChanged(...) Handles radUsed.CheckedChanged
  ' If the Used radio button is checked, then
  ' the user has selected a used car loan.
  If radUsed.Checked = True Then
     dblAnnualRate = dblUSED_RATE
     lblAnnualRate.Text = dblUSED_RATE.ToString("p")
     lstOutput.Items.Clear()
  End If
End Sub
```

Step 9: Save and run the application. Experiment with different values for the loan amount, down payment, and number of months.

Summary

5.1 Input Boxes

- Input boxes provide a simple way to gather input from the user.

5.2 List Boxes

- A list box control displays a list of items and allows the user to select one or more items from the list.

5.3 Introduction to Loops: The `Do While` Loop

- A repetition structure, or loop, causes one or more statements to repeat. Each repetition of a loop is called an iteration.
- The `Do While` loop has an expression that is tested for *True* or *False* value and a statement or group of statements that is repeated as long as an expression is true.

5.4 The `Do Until` and `For...Next` Loops

- The `Do Until` loop repeats until its test expression is true.
- The `For...Next` loop initializes, tests, and increments a counter variable.
- The `Do While` and `Do Until` loops may be written as either pretest or posttest loops. The `For...Next` loop is a pretest loop.
- The `Exit Do` and `Exit For` statements, when placed inside the body of a loop, stop the execution of the loop and cause the program to jump to the statement immediately following the loop.

5.5 Nested Loops

- A loop located inside another loop is called a nested loop. It is used when a task performs a repetitive operation and each iteration of that operation is itself a repetitive operation.

5.6 Multicolumn List Boxes, Checked List Boxes, and Combo Boxes

- A multicolumn list box displays items in columns with a horizontal scroll bar, if necessary.
- A checked list box displays a check box next to each item in the list.
- There are three different styles of combo box: the drop-down combo box, the simple combo box, and the drop-down list combo box. You select a combo box's style with its DropDownStyle property.

5.7 Random Numbers

- A Random object has methods that generate random sequences of numbers.
- A Random object's Next method returns the next random integer in a series.
- A Random object's NextDouble method returns a random value between 0.0 and 1.0.

5.8 Simplifying Code using the `With...End With` Statement

- The `With...End With` statement allows you to simplify a series of consecutive statements that perform operations using the same object.

5.9 ToolTips

- The ToolTip control allows you to create ToolTips (pop-up hints) for other controls on the same form.
- The ToolTip control is invisible at runtime; it appears in the component tray at design time.

5.10 Focus on Program Design and Problem Solving: Building the *Vehicle Loan Calculator* Application

- This section outlines the process of building the *Vehicle Loan Calculator* application using a loop.
- The Pmt function returns the periodic payment amount for a loan. The IPmt function returns the required interest payment for a specific period on a loan. The PPmt function returns the principal payment for a specific period on a loan.

Key Terms

accumulator	ListBox control
combo box	loop
component tray	nested loop
conditionally executed statements	Next method
counter	NextDouble method
Do Until loop	Pmt function
Do While loop	posttest loop
Exit Do statement	PPmt function
Exit For statement	pretest loop
For...Next loop	pseudo-random numbers
infinite loop	Random object
input box	repetition structure
IPmt function	running total
Items property	seed value
Items.Add method	SelectedIndex property
Items.Clear method	SelectedItem property
Items.Count property	Sorted property
Items.Insert method	step value
Items.Remove method	ToolTip control
Items.RemoveAt method	With...End With statement
iteration	

VideoNote

Improving the
Kayak Rental
Application

Video Tutorial: Improving the *Kayak Rental* Application

In this sequence of video tutorials, we improve on the *Kayak Rental* application by displaying lists of choices in CheckedListBox and ComboBox controls. These controls allow the user to pick from larger sets of kayaks and accessories. Our application uses loops to manipulate checked items. ToolTips are added to help the user understand the meanings of buttons and selection controls.

- Part 1: Adding CheckedListBox, ComboBox, and ToolTip controls

- Part 2: Calculating the rental costs

Review Questions and Exercises

Fill-in-the-Blank

1. A(n) _____ provides a simple way to gather input without placing a text box on a form.

2. A(n) _____ displays a list of items and allows the user to select an item from the list.

3. A(n) _____ causes one or more statements to repeat.

4. If a loop does not have a way of stopping, it is called a(n) _____ loop.

5. A(n) _____ is a variable that is regularly incremented or decremented each time a loop iterates.

6. A(n) _____ loop evaluates its test expression after each iteration.

7. Each repetition of the loop is called a(n) _____.

8. The _____ statement, when placed inside the body of a `Do While` loop, stops the execution of the loop and causes the program to jump to the statement immediately following the loop.

9. A loop that is inside another loop is called a(n) _____ loop.

10. A(n) _____ object has methods that can generate a sequence of random numbers.

11. The _____ method generates a random integer.

12. The _____ method generates a random floating-point value.

13. The _____ function returns the periodic payment amount for a loan.

14. The _____ function returns the principal payment for a specific period on a loan.

15. The _____ function returns the required interest payment for a specific period on a loan.

Multiple Choice

1. You display input boxes with this function.
    a. `InBox`
    b. `Input`
    c. `InputBox`
    d. `GetInput`

2. An input box returns the value entered by the user as this.
    a. String
    b. Integer
    c. Single
    d. Boolean

3. Visual Basic automatically adds this to a list box when it contains more items than can be displayed.
    a. Larger list box
    b. Scroll bar
    c. Second form
    d. Message box

4. A list box or combo box's index numbering starts at this value.
    a. 0
    b. 1
    c. −1
    d. any value you specify

5. This property holds the index of the selected item in a list box.

   a. Index
   b. SelectedItem
   c. SelectedIndex
   d. Items.SelectedIndex

6. This method erases one item from a list box.

   a. `Erase`
   b. `Items.Remove`
   c. `Items.RemoveItem`
   d. `Clear`

7. The `Do While` statement marks the beginning of a `Do While` loop, and the `Loop` statement marks the end. The statements between these are known as one of the following.

   a. Processes of the loop
   b. Functions of the loop
   c. Substance of the loop
   d. Body of the loop

8. This type of loop evaluates its test expression before each iteration.

   a. Out-test
   b. Pretest
   c. Posttest
   d. In-test

9. One of the following is a sum of numbers that accumulates with each iteration of a loop.

   a. Counter
   b. Running total
   c. Summation function
   d. Iteration count

10. This type of loop is ideal for situations that require a counter because it is specifically designed to initialize, test, and increment a counter variable.

    a. `Do While`
    b. `Do Until`
    c. `For...Next`
    d. `Posttest Do Until`

11. You do this to get the total number of iterations of a nested loop.

    a. Add the number of iterations of all the loops
    b. Multiply the number of iterations of all the loops
    c. Average the number of iterations of all the loops
    d. Get the number of iterations of the outermost loop

12. When this ListBox control's property is set to *True*, it causes the ListBox control to display its list in multiple columns.

    a. Columns
    b. Multicolumn
    c. ColumnList
    d. TableDisplay

13. This control has a rectangular area that functions like a text box.

    a. List box
    b. Drop-down list box
    c. Combo box
    d. Input label

14. This is the prefix that we use for combo box names.

    a. cbo
    b. com
    c. cbx
    d. cob

15. With this style of combo box, the list of items does not drop down, but is always displayed.

    a. Drop-down combo box
    b. Simple combo box
    c. Drop-down list combo box
    d. Simple drop-down combo list box

16. This combo box property will contain the user's text input or the item selected from the list.

    a. Input
    b. Caption
    c. List
    d. Text

17. Which of the following statements creates a Random object and initializes the sequence of random numbers with the seed value 25?

    a. InitRandom(25)
    b. Rnd(25)
    c. Dim rand As New Seed(25)
    d. Dim rand As New Random(25)

True or False

Indicate whether the following statements are true or false.

1. T F: If you do not provide a value for an input box's title, an error will occur.

2. T F: If the user clicks an input box's *Cancel* button, the function returns the number –1.

3. T F: The Items.RemoveAt method always removes the last item in a list box (the item with the highest index value).

4. T F: Infinite loops keep repeating until the program is interrupted.

5. T F: A loop's conditionally executed statements should be indented.

6. T F: A pretest loop always performs at least one iteration, even if the test expression is false from the start.

7. T F: The Do While loop may be written as either a pretest or posttest loop.

8. T F: In a For...Next loop, the *Counter Variable* must be numeric.

9. T F: The *Step Increment* part of the For...Next statement is optional.

10. T F: The For...Next loop is a posttest loop.

11. T F: In a nested loop, the inner loop goes through all of its iterations for each iteration of an outer loop.

12. T F: To create a checked list box, you draw a regular list box and set its Checked property to *True*.

13. T F: A drop-down list combo box allows the user to either select an item from a list or type text into a text input area.

14.   T F: If a Random object is initialized with the same seed value each time it is created, it will produce the same series of random numbers each time.

Short Answer

1.   What buttons automatically appear on an input box?

2.   What value is returned by the InputBox function if the user clicks the *Cancel* button?

3.   Write a statement that adds *Spinach* to the list box lstVeggies at index 2.

4.   Write a statement that removes the item at index 12 of the combo box named cboCourses.

5.   Describe the two important parts of a Do While loop.

6.   In general terms, describe how a Do While loop works.

7.   Why should you indent the statements in the body of a loop?

8.   Describe the difference between pretest loops and posttest loops.

9.   Why are the statements in the body of a loop called conditionally executed statements?

10.   What is the difference between the Do While loop and the Do Until loop?

11.   Which loop should you use in situations where you wish the loop to repeat as long as the test expression is true?

12.   Which type of loop should you use in situations where you wish the loop to repeat until the test expression is true?

13.   Which type of loop should you use when you know the number of required iterations?

14.   What feature do combo boxes have that list boxes do not have?

15.   With one style of combo box the user may not type text directly into the combo box, but must select an item from the list. Which style is it?

16.   With one style of combo box the Text property is read-only. Which style?

17.   What value does a Random object use as its seed if you do not specify a seed value?

What Do You Think?

1.   Why is it important to assign an initial value to a loop counter variable?

2.   Why should you be careful not to place a statement in the body of a For...Next loop that changes the value of the loop's counter variable?

3.   You need to write a loop that iterates until the user enters a specific value into an input box. Which type of loop should you choose? Why?

4.   You need to write a loop that will repeat 224 times. Which type of loop will you choose? Why?

5.   You need to write a loop that iterates as long as a variable has a specific value stored in it. Which type of loop will you choose? Why?

6.   Why is a computer's system time a good source of random seed values?

7.   You use the statement lstNames.Items.RemoveAt(6) to remove an item from a list box. Does the statement remove the sixth or seventh item in the list? Why?

8.   What kind of control(s) do you use when you want to provide the user a list of items to select from, but do not want to limit the user's input to the items on the list?

9.   What kind of control(s) do you use when you want to limit the user's selection to a list of items?

Find the Error

Identify the syntactically incorrect statements in the following:

1.
```
Loop
    intX = intX + 1
Do While intX < 100
```

2.
```
Do
    lstOutput.Items.Add("Hello")
    intX = intX + 1
While intCount < 10
```

3.
```
Loop Until intX = 99
    intX = intX + 1
Do
```

4.
```
For intX = 1
    lstOutput.Items.Add(intX)
Next
```

Algorithm Workbench

1. An event handler named `btnShow_Click` must add the numbers 1 through 20 to a list box named `lstNumbers`. Design a flowchart for this event handler.

2. Write the code that you would insert into the code template for the event handler described in Question 1.

3. Write a `Do While` loop that uses an input box to get a number from the user. The number should be multiplied by 10 and the result stored in the variable product. The loop should iterate as long as product contains a value less than 100.

4. Write a `Do While` loop that uses input boxes to get two numbers from the user. The numbers should be added and the sum displayed in a message box. An input box should ask the user whether he or she wishes to perform the operation again. If so, the loop should repeat; otherwise it should terminate.

5. Write a `For...Next` loop that adds the following set of numbers to the list box `lstNumbers`.
    0, 10, 20, 30, 40, 50 ... 1000

6. Write a loop that uses an input box to get a number from the user. The loop should iterate 10 times and keep a running total of the numbers entered.

7. Convert the following pretest `Do While` loop to a posttest `Do While` loop:
```
intX = 1
Do While intX > 0
  strInput = InputBox("Enter a number")
  intX = CInt(strInput)
Loop
```

8. Convert the following `Do While` loop to a `Do Until` loop:
```
strInput = String.Empty
Do While strInput.ToUpper <> "Y"
  strInput = InputBox("Are you sure you want to quit?")
Loop
```

9. Convert the following `Do While` loop to a `For...Next` loop:
```
intCount = 0
Do While intCount < 50
  lstOutput.Items.Add(intCount)
  intCount += 1
Loop
```

10. Convert the following `For...Next` loop to a `Do While` loop:

```
For intX = 50 To 0 Step -1
    lstOutput.Items.Add(intX)
Next
```

11. Rewrite the following statements so they appear inside a `With` block:

```
txtName.Text = "(unknown)"
txtName.Font.Size = 10
txtName.BackColor = Color.Red
```

Programming Challenges

VideoNote

The Sum of Numbers Problem

1. **Sum of Numbers**

   Create an application that displays a form similar to the one shown in Figure 5-44. When the *Enter Numbers* button is clicked, the application should display the input box shown in Figure 5-45.

   The input box asks the user to enter a positive integer value. Notice that the default input value is 10. When the *OK* button is clicked, the application should display a message box with the sum of all the integers from 1 through the value entered by the user, as shown in Figure 5-46.

Figure 5-44 *Sum of Numbers* form

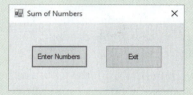

Figure 5-45 *Sum of Numbers* input box

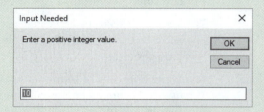

Figure 5-46 *Sum of Numbers* message box

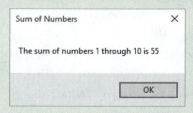

If the user enters a negative value, the application should display an error message. Use the following test data to determine if the application is calculating properly:

Value	Sum
5	15
10	55
20	210
100	5050

2. **Distance Calculator**

   If you know a vehicle's speed and the amount of time it has traveled, you can calculate the distance it has traveled as follows:

   $$Distance = Speed * Time$$

For example, if a train travels 40 miles per hour for 3 hours, the distance traveled is 120 miles. Create an application with a form similar to the one shown in Figure 5-47.

When the user clicks the *Calculate* button, the application should display an input box asking the user for the speed of the vehicle in miles-per-hour, followed by another input box asking for the amount of time, in hours, that the vehicle has traveled. Then it should use a loop to display in a list box the distance the vehicle has traveled for each hour of that time period. Figure 5-48 shows an example of what the application's form should look like.

Figure 5-47 *Distance Calculator*

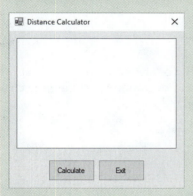

Figure 5-48 *Distance Calculator* completed

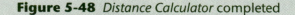
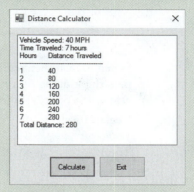

Use the following test data to determine if the application is calculating properly.

Vehicle Speed: 60
Hours Traveled: 7

Hours	Distance Traveled
1	60
2	120
3	180
4	240
5	300
6	360
7	420

3. **Workshop Selector**

Table 5-3 shows a training company's workshops, the number of days of each, and its registration fees.

Table 5-3 Workshops and registration fees

Workshop	Number of Days	Registration Fee
Handling Stress	3	$595
Time Management	3	$695
Supervision Skills	3	$995
Negotiation	5	$1,295
How to Interview	1	$395

The training company conducts its workshops in the six locations shown in Table 5-4. The table also shows the lodging fees per day at each location.

Table 5-4 Training locations and lodging fees

Location	Lodging Fees per Day
Austin	$95
Chicago	$125
Dallas	$110
Orlando	$100
Phoenix	$92
Raleigh	$90

When a customer registers for a workshop, he or she must pay the registration fee plus the lodging fees for the selected location. For example, here are the charges to attend the Supervision Skills workshop in Orlando:

Registration: $995
Lodging: $100 × 3 days = $300
Total: $1,295

Design an application with a form that resembles the one shown in Figure 5-49.

Figure 5-49 *Workshop Selector* form

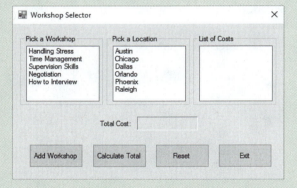

The application should allow the user to select a workshop from one list box and a location from another list box. When the user clicks the *Add Workshop* button, the application should add the total cost of the selected workshop at the selected location in the third list box. When the user clicks the *Calculate Total* button, the total cost of all the selected workshops should be calculated and displayed in the label. The *Reset* button should deselect the workshop and location from the first two list boxes, clear the third list box, and clear the total cost label.

4. **Hotel Occupancy**

The ElGrande Hotel has 8 floors and 30 rooms on each floor. Create an application that calculates the occupancy rate for each floor, and the overall occupancy rate for the hotel. The occupancy rate is the percentage of rooms occupied, and may be calculated by dividing the number of rooms occupied by the number of rooms. For example, if 18 rooms on the first floor are occupied, the occupancy rate is as follows:

$$18/30 = 0.6 \text{ or } 60\%$$

On startup, the application's form should appear similar to the one shown in Figure 5-50. Each time the user enters the occupancy for a single floor and clicks the *Save* button, the floor number in the ComboBox should increment automatically (just add 1 to its SelectedIndex property), and a new line should appear in the List-Box with the percentage occupancy. Also, the contents of the TextBox at the top of the form should clear automatically when the user clicks the *Save* button, so the user does not accidentally enter the same data twice in a row. The *Reset* button should clear all the appropriate controls on the form. The *Exit* button should end the application. Use the values shown in Figure 5-51 to confirm that your application is performing the correct calculations. Be sure to check for a non-integer value in the TextBox and notify the user if there is an error.

Figure 5-50 *Hotel Occupancy* form

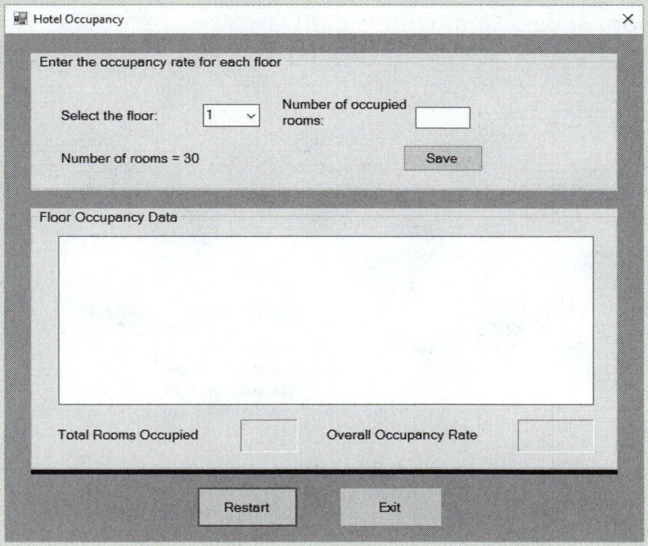

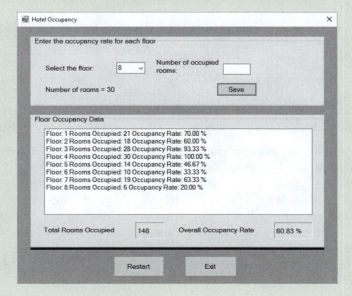

Figure 5-51 Completed *Hotel Occupancy* form

5. **Adding Students to a Club**

   Create an application that displays a list of student names in a ListBox. Use a second empty ListBox to represent the members of a student club. Use a button labeled *Add* to copy member names from the general list to the club list. Use a button labeled *Remove* to remove a student from the club list. Keep a running count of the number of names in the club list.

   The application should perform the following error-checking:

   - Do not permit the same person's name to be added twice.
   - Avoid throwing an exception if the user clicks the Add button before having selected a student name.
   - Avoid a runtime error if the user clicks the *Remove selected member* button, without having selected a member name.

   A sample of the program's interface is shown in Figure 5-52.

Figure 5-52 Application: *Adding Students to a Club*

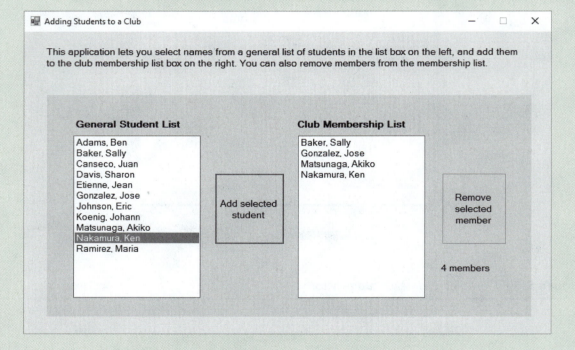

6. **Selecting Regions, States, and Cities**

   Many companies have branch offices through the country. In order for users of a Web site to locate company branches, they can select a region. Then the user is able to select from a list of states (or provinces) within the selected region. Finally, within a single state or province, city names can appear where the company has branch offices.

   Write an application that simulates this with three ComboBox controls. The regions will be named NorthEast, SouthEast, and NorthWest. When the user selects a region, add names of states from the selected region to the State selection ComboBox. When a state is selected, add cities from that state to the State selection ComboBox. You can select state and city names from the United States, or provinces and cities from your favorite country. Important: after having selected a region, state, and city, the user might decide to select a different region; in that case, you must clear the state and city lists. When the user selects a new state, you must clear the city list.

A sample of the interface is shown in Figure 5-53. (We used a Panel control to provide a contrasting background.)

Figure 5-53 Selecting Regions, States, and Cities

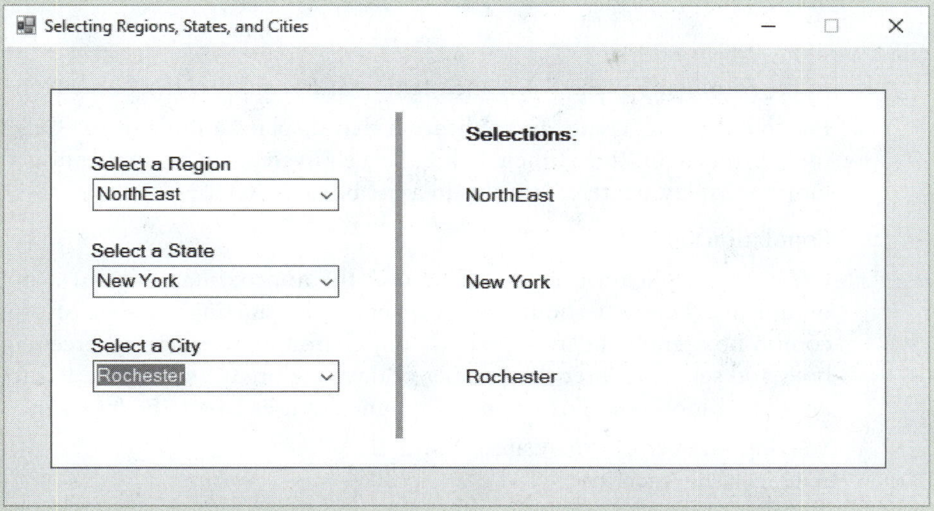

7. **Integer Math Tutor**

   Create an application that uses random integers to test the user's knowledge of arithmetic. Let the user choose from addition, subtraction, multiplication, and division. The integers used in the problems should range from 20 to 120. When giving feedback, use color to differentiate between a correct answer response, versus an incorrect answer response. Also check for non-integer input. Preparing division problems requires special consideration because the quotient must be an integer. Therefore, you can use a loop to generate new random values for the second operand until you find one that divides the first operand evenly. Use the Mod operator to verify that the integer division remainder is zero.

   Figure 5-54 shows a sample interface for this application.

Figure 5-54 Integer Math Tutor application

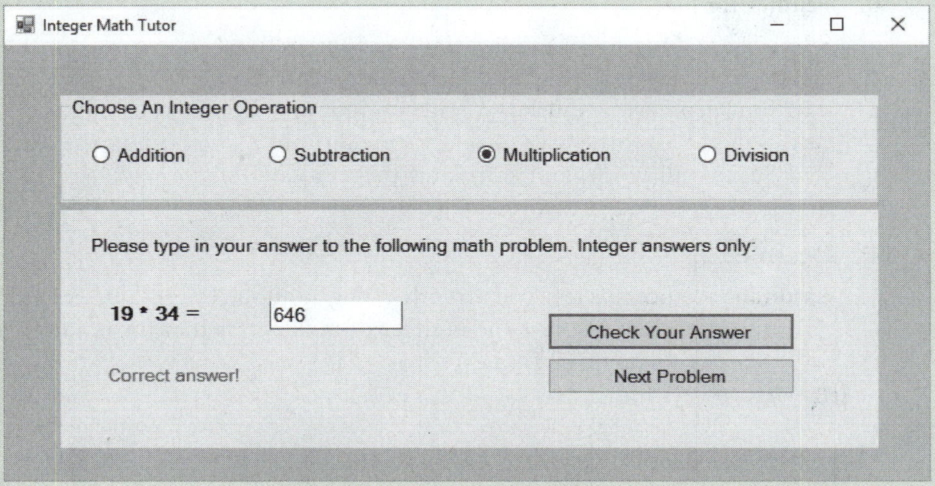

Design Your Own Forms

8. **Celsius to Fahrenheit Table**

   In Programming Challenge 8 of Chapter 3, you created an application that converts Celsius temperatures to Fahrenheit. Recall that the formula for performing this conversion is

   $$F = 1.8 * C + 32$$

   In the formula, F is the Fahrenheit temperature and C is the Celsius temperature.

   For this exercise, create an application that displays a table of the Celsius temperatures 0 through 20 and their Fahrenheit equivalents. The application should use a loop to display the temperatures in a list box.

9. **Population**

   Create an application that will predict the approximate size of a population of organisms. The user should select or enter the starting number of organisms in a combo box, enter the average daily population increase (as a percentage) in a text box, and select or enter the number of days the organisms will be left to multiply in another combo box. For example, assume the user enters the following values:

Starting number of organisms:	2
Average daily increase:	30%
Number of days to multiply:	10

   The application should display the following table of data.

Day	Approximate Population
1	2
2	2.6
3	3.38
4	4.394
5	5.7122
6	7.42586
7	9.653619
8	12.5497
9	16.31462
10	21.209

   Be sure to add appropriate ToolTips for each control on the form.

10. **Pennies for Pay**

    Susan is hired for a job, and her employer agrees to pay her every day. Her employer also agrees that Susan's salary is one penny the first day, two pennies the second day, four pennies the third day, and continuing to double each day. Create an application that allows the user to select or enter into a combo box the number of days that Susan will work, and calculates the total amount of pay she will receive over that period of time.

11. **Ocean Levels**

    Assuming the ocean's level is currently rising at about 1.5 millimeters per year, create an application that displays the number of millimeters that the ocean will have risen each year for the next 10 years.

12. **Burning Calories**

Suppose you have a treadmill with three different speeds (low, medium, high). Let us assume that low speed burns 3.5 calories, medium speed burns 4.5 calories, and high speed burns 6 calories per minute. Create an application that lets the user select the speed from a ComboBox control, and uses a loop to display the number of calories burned after 10, 15, 20, 25, and 30 minutes. Display the values in a ListBox control.

13. **Fibonacci Sequence**

The Fibonacci number sequence, said to have been invented by Leonardo di Pisa, is used in simulations and is found in nature. If you start with 0 and 1, the next integer (1) in the series is their sum; the next integer (2) is the sum of the previous two values (1 + 1). Write a program that uses a loop to display the first 100 Fibonacci numbers in a multicolumn list box with 12 rows and 4 columns. The last number should be 1,836,311,903.

14. **Budget Analysis**

Create an application that lets the user enter the amount that he or she has budgeted for a month. A loop should then use input boxes to prompt the user for his or her expenses for the month, and keep a running total. When the loop finishes, the program should display the amount that the user is over or under budget.

15. **Speed Conversion Chart**

Your friend Amanda, who lives in the United States, just bought an antique European sports car. The car's speedometer works in kilometers per hour. The formula for converting kilometers per hour to miles per hour is:

$$MPH = KPH * 0.6214$$

In the formula, *MPH* is the speed in miles per hour and *KPH* is the speed in kilometers per hour. Amanda is afraid she will get a speeding ticket, and has asked you to write a program that displays a list of speeds in kilometers per hour with their values converted to miles per hour. The list should display the speeds from 60 kilometers per hour through 130 kilometers per hour, in increments of 5 kilometers per hour. (In other words, it should display 60 kph, 65 kph, 70 kph, and so forth, up through 130 kph.)

16. **Dice Simulator**

Create an application that simulates rolling a pair of dice. When the user clicks a button, the application should generate two random numbers, each in the range of 1 through 6, to represent the value of the dice. Use PictureBox controls to display the dice. (In the student sample programs, in the *Chap5* folder, you will find six images named Die1.bmp, Die2.bmp, Die3.bmp, Die4.bmp, Die5.bmp, and Die6.bmp, that you can use in the PictureBoxes.)

17. **Random Number Guessing Game**

Create an application that generates a random number in the range of 1 through 100, and asks the user to guess what the number is. If the user's guess is higher than the random number, the program should display "Too high, try again." If the user's guess is lower than the random number, the program should display "Too low, try again." The program should use a loop that repeats until the user correctly guesses the random number.

18. **Random Number Guessing Game Enhancement**

Enhance the program that you wrote for Programming Challenge 18 so it keeps a count of the number of guesses that the user makes. When the user correctly guesses the random number, the program should display the number of guesses.

6 Procedures and Functions

TOPICS

A **procedure** is a collection of statements that performs a task. Event handlers, for example, are procedures. A **function** is a collection of statements that performs a task and then returns a value to the part of the program that executed it. You have already used many of Visual Basic's built-in functions such as `CInt` and `IsNumeric`.

This chapter discusses how to code general purpose procedures and functions. These procedures do not respond to events, but execute when they are called by other code statements. You will learn how to create, call, and pass arguments to these procedures as well as various techniques for debugging applications that use them.

In common object-oriented terminology, the term **method** is used to mean both procedures and functions.

6.1 Procedures

⌐**CONCEPT:** You can write your own general purpose procedures that perform specific tasks. General purpose procedures are not triggered by events, but are called from statements in other procedures.

A procedure is a collection of statements that performs a task. An event handler or event procedure is a type of procedure that is executed when an event, such as a mouse click, occurs while the program is running. This section discusses general purpose procedures that are not triggered by events, but executed by statements in other procedures.

By writing your own procedures, you can **modularize** an application's code, that is, break it into small, manageable procedures. Imagine a book with a thousand pages that was not divided into chapters or sections. Finding a single topic in the book would be very difficult. Real-world applications can easily have thousands of lines of code, and unless they are modularized, they can be very difficult to modify and maintain.

Procedures can reduce the amount of duplicated code in a program. If a specific task is performed in several places, a procedure for performing that task can be written once and executed anytime it is needed.

Tutorial 6-1 walks you through an example application that uses a procedure.

Tutorial 6-1:
Examining an application with a procedure

Step 1: Open the *Procedure Demo* project from the student sample programs folder named *Chap6\Procedure Demo*. The application's form is shown in Figure 6-1. The form has a list box named `lstOutput` and two buttons: `btnGo` and `btnExit`.

Figure 6-1 *Procedure Demo* form

Step 2: Open the *Code* window and find the procedure named `DisplayMessage`, which is shown here:

```
Sub DisplayMessage()
  ' This is a procedure that displays a message.
  lstOutput.Items.Add("")
  lstOutput.Items.Add("Hello from the DisplayMessage procedure.")
  lstOutput.Items.Add("")
End Sub
```

The declaration of a procedure begins with a `Sub` statement and ends with an `End Sub` statement. The code that appears between these two statements is the body of the procedure. When the `DisplayMessage` procedure executes, it displays a blank line in the list box, followed by the string `"Hello from the DisplayMessage procedure."`, followed by another blank line.

Figure 6-2 shows the parts of the `Sub` statement.

Figure 6-2 First line of `DisplayMessage` procedure

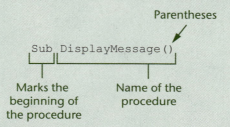

The first line of the procedure begins with the word Sub, followed by the name of the procedure, followed by a set of parentheses. In this procedure, the parentheses are empty. Later, you will see procedures having items inside the parentheses.

> **NOTE:** An event handler is associated with a control, so its name is commonly prefixed with the control's name. For example, the `btnGo` button's Click event handler is named `btnGo_Click`. Since a general purpose procedure is not associated with a control, we do not usually prefix its name with any control name.

Step 3: General purpose procedures are not executed by an event. Instead, they must be called. Look at the following code for the `btnGo_Click` event handler. The statement in line 7 calls the `DisplayMessage` procedure.

```
1 Private Sub btnGo_Click(...) Handles btnGo.Click
2   ' Display some text in the list box.
3   lstOutput.Items.Add("Hello from the btnGo_Click procedure.")
4   lstOutput.Items.Add("Now I am calling the DisplayMessage procedure.")
5
6   ' Call the DisplayMessage procedure.
7   DisplayMessage()
8
9   ' Display some more text in the list box.
10  lstOutput.Items.Add("Now I am back in the btnGo_Click procedure.")
11 End Sub
```

This type of statement, known as a **procedure call**, causes the procedure to execute. A procedure call is simply the name of the procedure that is to be executed. Parentheses follow the name of the procedure. You can also use the **Call keyword**, as shown here:

```
Call DisplayMessage()
```

The `Call` keyword is optional and is not used in this text.

When a procedure call executes, the application branches to the procedure and executes its body. When the procedure has finished, control returns to the procedure call and resumes executing at the next statement. Figure 6-3 illustrates how this application branches from the `btnGo_Click` procedure to the `DisplayMessage` procedure call, and returns to the `btnGo_Click` procedure.

Figure 6-3 Procedure call

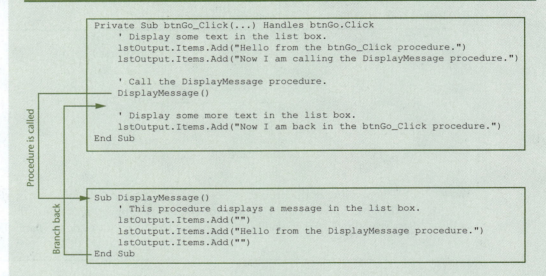

```
Private Sub btnGo_Click(...) Handles btnGo.Click
    ' Display some text in the list box.
    lstOutput.Items.Add("Hello from the btnGo_Click procedure.")
    lstOutput.Items.Add("Now I am calling the DisplayMessage procedure.")

    ' Call the DisplayMessage procedure.
    DisplayMessage()

    ' Display some more text in the list box.
    lstOutput.Items.Add("Now I am back in the btnGo_Click procedure.")
End Sub


Sub DisplayMessage()
    ' This procedure displays a message in the list box.
    lstOutput.Items.Add("")
    lstOutput.Items.Add("Hello from the DisplayMessage procedure.")
    lstOutput.Items.Add("")
End Sub
```

Procedure is called

Branch back

Step 4: Run the application. Click the *Go* button. The form should appear as shown in Figure 6-4.

Figure 6-4 Results of *Procedure Demo*

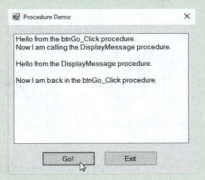

As you can see, the statements in the `btnGo_Click` event handler executed up to the `DisplayMessage` procedure call. At that point, the application branched to the `DisplayMessage` procedure and executed all of its statements. When the `DisplayMessage` procedure finished, the application returned to the `btnGo_Click` event handler and resumed executing at the line following the `DisplayMessage` call.

Step 5: Click the *Exit* button to end the application.

Declaring a Procedure

The general format of a **procedure declaration** is as follows:

```
[AccessSpecifier] Sub ProcedureName ([ParameterList])
   [Statements]
End Sub
```

The items shown in brackets are optional. *AccessSpecifier* specifies the accessibility of the procedure. This is an important issue because some applications have more than one form. When you use the `Private` access specifier, the procedure may be accessed only by other procedures declared in the same class or form. When a procedure begins with `Public`, it may also be accessed by procedures declared in other forms. If you leave out the access specifier, it defaults to `Public`. We will begin to use access specifiers in later chapters.

Following the keyword **Sub** is the name of the procedure. You should always give the procedure a name that reflects its purpose. You should also adopt a consistent style of using uppercase and lowercase letters. For procedure names, we use **Pascal casing**, which capitalizes the first character and the first character of each subsequent word in the procedure name. All other characters are lowercase. Using different styles of capitalization for variables and procedures lets the reader of your code know what type of entity a name belongs to.

Inside the parentheses is an optional *ParameterList*. A **parameter** is a special variable that receives a value being passed into a procedure. Later in this chapter, you will see procedures that use parameters to accept data passed into them.

The last line of a procedure declaration is the `End Sub` statement. Between the `Sub` statement and the `End Sub` statement, you write the statements that execute each time the procedure is called.

Tutorial 6-2 guides you through the process of writing procedures. In the tutorial, you will complete an application that uses two procedures, in addition to its event handlers.

Tutorial 6-2:

Creating and calling procedures

VideoNote

Creating and calling procedures

The *Chap6* folder in the student sample programs contains a partially created project named *Lights*. In this tutorial you will complete the project so it simulates a light being turned off or on. The project's form is shown in Figure 6-5.

Figure 6-5 The *Lights* project's form

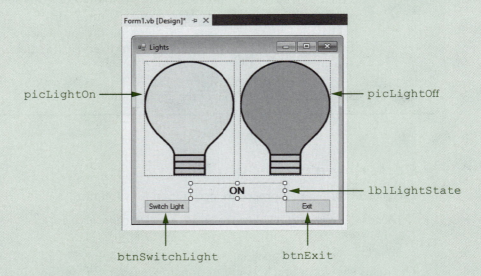

The form has the following controls:

- A PictureBox control named `picLightOn`, showing the image of a light bulb turned on. Initially, this PictureBox's Visible property is set to *True*.
- A PictureBox control name `picLightOff`, showing the image of a light bulb turned off. Initially, this PictureBox's Visible property is set to *False*.
- A Label control named `lblLightState` that will display either *"ON"* or *"OFF"*. Initially, this control's Text property is set to *"ON"*.
- A Button control named `btnSwitchLight` that turns the light off or on.
- A Button control named `btnExit` that closes the form.

When the user clicks the *Switch Light* button, the state of the light will be reversed. In other words, if the light is currently on, it will be turned off. If the light is currently off, it will be turned on.

When the light is turned on, the following actions will take place:

- The `picLightOn` control's Visible property is set to *True*.
- The `picLightOff` control's Visible property is set to *False*.
- The `lblLightState` label's Text property is assigned the string `"ON"`.

When the light is turned off, the following actions will take place:

- The `picLightOff` control's Visible property is set to *True*.
- The `picLightOn` control's Visible property is set to *False*.
- The `lblLightState` label's Text property is assigned the string `"OFF"`.

Step 1: Open the *Lights* project from the *Chap6* folder in the sample student programs.

Step 2: Open the *Code* window and type the following two procedures, shown in lines 3 through 23. (Don't type the line numbers. They are shown here for reference only.)

```
1 Public Class Form1
2
3   Sub TurnLightOn()
4     ' Display the "Light On" image.
5     picLightOn.Visible = True
6
```

```
 7        ' Hide the "Light Off" image.
 8        picLightOff.Visible = False
 9
10        ' Change the label text.
11        lblLightState.Text = "ON"
12     End Sub
13
14     Sub TurnLightOff()
15        ' Display the "Light Off" image.
16        picLightOff.Visible = True
17
18        ' Hide the "Light On" image.
19        picLightOn.Visible = False
20
21        ' Change the label text.
22        lblLightState.Text = "OFF"
23     End Sub
24 End Class
```

Before continuing, let's take a closer look at the code. Line 3 is the beginning of a procedure named TurnLightOn. The purpose of this procedure is to simulate the light turning on. When this procedure executes, line 5 makes the picLightOn control visible, line 8 hides the picLightOff control, and line 11 sets the lblLightState control's Text property to "ON".

Line 14 is the beginning of a procedure named TurnLightOff. The purpose of this procedure is to simulate the light turning off. When this procedure executes, line 16 makes the picLightOff control visible, line 19 hides the picLightOn control, and line 22 sets the lblLightState control's Text property to "OFF".

Step 3: Open the *Designer* window and double-click the btnSwitchLight button to create a code template for its Click event handler. Complete the event handler by writing the bold code, shown here in lines 2 through 7. (Don't type the line numbers. They are shown here for reference only.)

```
1 Private Sub btnSwitchLight_Click(...) Handles btnSwitchLight.Click
2    ' Reverse the state of the light.
3    If picLightOn.Visible = True Then
4       TurnLightOff()
5    Else
6       TurnLightOn()
7    End If
8 End Sub
```

Let's review this code. The If...Then statement in line 3 determines whether the picLightOn control is visible. If it is, it means the light is turned on, so the statement in line 4 calls the TurnLightOff procedure to turn the light off. Otherwise, the Else clause in line 5 takes over, and the TurnLightOn procedure is called on line 6 to turn the light on.

Step 4: Open the *Designer* window and double-click the btnExit button to create a code template for its Click event handler. Complete the event handler as shown here:

```
Private Sub btnExit_Click(...) Handles btnExit.Click
   ' Close the form.
   Me.Close()
End Sub
```

Step 5: Save the project, and then run the application. The form should initially appear as shown on the left in Figure 6-6. When you click the *Switch Light* button, the form should appear as shown on the right in the figure. Each time you click the *Switch Light* button, the state of the light should reverse.

Figure 6-6 Light on and off

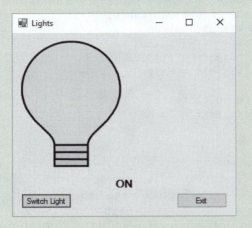
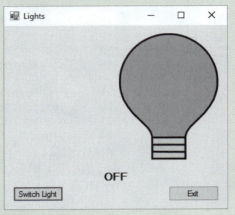

Step 6: When you are finished, exit the application.

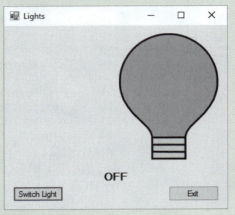 **Checkpoint**

6.1 Figure 6-7 shows an application's form.

The list box is named `lstOutput`. The buttons are named `btnGo` and `btnExit`. The application's procedures are as follows:

```
Private Sub btnGo_Click(...) Handles btnGo.Click
   Dim intNumber As Integer
   Dim strInput As String

   strInput = InputBox("Enter a number")
   intNumber = CInt(strInput)

   If intNumber < 10 Then
      Message1()
      Message2()
   Else
      Message2()
      Message1()
   End If
End Sub

Private Sub btnExit_Click(...) Handles btnExit.Click
   'Close the form.
   Me.Close()
End Sub
```

```
Sub Message1()
  lstOutput.Items.Add("Able was I")
End Sub

Sub Message2()
  lstOutput.Items.Add("I saw Elba")
End Sub
```

Suppose you run this application and click the btnGo button. What will the application display in the list box if you enter 10 in the input box? What if you enter 5?

Figure 6-7 *Checkpoint 6.1* application form

6.2 Would you say that the use of procedures (a) increases or (b) decreases the amount of duplicate code in programs?

6.2 Passing Arguments to Procedures

CONCEPT: When calling a procedure, you can pass it values known as arguments.

VideoNote
Passing
Arguments to
Procedures

Values passed to procedures are called **arguments**. You are already familiar with how to use arguments. In the following statement, the CInt function is called and an argument, txtInput.Text, is passed to it:

```
intValue = CInt(txtInput.Text)
```

There are two ways to pass an argument to a procedure: by value or by reference. Passing an argument **by value** means that only a copy of the argument is passed to the procedure. Because the procedure has only a copy, it cannot make changes to the original argument. When an argument is passed **by reference**, however, the procedure has access to the original argument and can make changes to it.

In order for a procedure to accept an argument, it must be equipped with a parameter. A parameter is a special variable that receives an argument being passed into a procedure. Here is an example procedure that uses a parameter:

```
Sub DisplayValue(ByVal intNumber As Integer)
  ' This procedure displays a value in a message box.
  MessageBox.Show(intNumber.ToString())
End Sub
```

Notice the statement inside the parentheses in the first line of the procedure (repeated below).

```
ByVal intNumber As Integer
```

This statement declares the variable `intNumber` as an integer parameter. The optional **ByVal** keyword indicates that arguments passed into the variable are passed by value. This parameter variable enables the `DisplayValue` procedure to accept an integer argument.

Here is an example of how you would call the procedure and pass an argument to it:

```
DisplayValue(5)
```

The argument, 5, is listed inside the parentheses. This value is passed into the procedure's parameter variable, `intNumber`. This is illustrated in Figure 6-8.

Figure 6-8 Passing 5 to `DisplayValue`

```
DisplayValue(5)                    The value 5
                              is copied into the
                              parameter variable
                                  intNumber.

Sub DisplayValue(ByVal intNumber As Integer)
    ' This procedure displays a value in a message box.
    MessageBox.Show(intNumber.ToString())
End Sub
```

You may also pass variables and the values of expressions as arguments. For example, the following statements call the `DisplayValue` procedure, passing various arguments:

```
DisplayValue(intX)
DisplayValue(intX * 4)
DisplayValue(CInt(txtInput.Text))
```

The first statement passes the value in the variable `intX` as the argument. The second statement passes the value of the expression `intX * 4` as the argument. The third statement passes the value returned from `CInt(txtInput.Text)` as the argument.

The `ByVal` keyword is optional. You can omit the `ByVal` keyword, and the parameter will be declared `ByVal` by default. For example, the `DisplayValue` procedure can be written like this:

```
Sub DisplayValue(intNumber As Integer)
    ' This procedure displays a value in a message box.
    MessageBox.Show(intNumber.ToString())
End Sub
```

When this procedure is called, any arguments passed to it will be passed by value.

 NOTE: Although you can omit the `ByVal` keyword in a parameter variable declaration, it is still a good idea to use it. Doing so clearly documents that arguments are passed to the parameter by value.

Tutorial 6-3 guides you through an application that demonstrates argument passing.

Tutorial 6-3:
Examining an application that demonstrates passing an argument to a procedure

Step 1: Open the *Argument Demo* project from the student sample programs folder named *Chap6\Argument Demo*. The application's form is shown in Figure 6-9. The application's form has four buttons: btnDemo1, btnDemo2, btnDemo3, and btnExit, as well as a ListBox control to display numeric values.

Figure 6-9 *Argument Demo* form

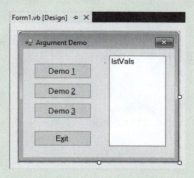

Step 2: In addition to the event handlers for each of the form's buttons, the application uses the DisplayValue procedure described earlier. Open the *Code* window and locate the btnDemo1_Click event handler. The code is as follows:

```
Private Sub btnDemo1_Click(...) Handles btnDemo1.Click
    'This event handler calls the DisplayValue procedure,
    'passing 5 as an argument.
    lstVals.Items.Clear()
    DisplayValue(5)
End Sub
```

This event handler calls DisplayValue with 5 as the argument.

Step 3: Locate the btnDemo2_Click event handler. The code is as follows:

```
Private Sub btnDemo2_Click(...) Handles btnDemo2.Click
    ' Call the DisplayValue procedure several times,
    ' passing different arguments each time.
    lstVals.Items.Clear()
    DisplayValue(5)
    DisplayValue(10)
    DisplayValue(2)
    DisplayValue(16)

    ' The value of an expression is passed to the
    ' DisplayValue procedure.
    DisplayValue(3 + 5)
End Sub
```

This event handler calls the DisplayValue procedure five times. Each procedure call is given a different argument. Notice the last procedure call:

```
DisplayValue(3 + 5)
```

This statement passes the value of an expression as the argument. When this statement executes, the value 8 is passed to DisplayValue.

Step 4: Locate the btnDemo3_Click event handler. The code is as follows:

```
Private Sub btnDemo3_Click(...) Handles btnDemo3.Click
    ' Use a loop to call the DisplayValue procedure
    ' passing a variable as the argument.
    lstVals.Items.Clear()
    Dim intCount As Integer

    For intCount = 1 To 10
        DisplayValue(intCount)
    Next
End Sub
```

This event handler has a local variable named intCount. It uses a For...Next loop to call the DisplayValue procedure ten times, each time passing the intCount variable as the argument.

Step 5: Locate the DisplayValue method, which adds the value it receives to the ListBox control:

```
Sub DisplayValue(ByVal intNumber As Integer)
    ' This procedure adds a value to the list box.
    lstVals.Items.Add(intNumber.ToString())
End Sub
```

Step 6: Run the application and click the *Demo 1* button. The value 5 appears in the list box.

Step 7: Click the *Demo 2* button. Five successive values are displayed, showing the values 5, 10, 2, 16, and 8.

Step 8: Click the *Demo 3* button. Ten successive values are displayed, showing the values 1 through 10.

Step 9: Click the *Exit* button to end the application.

Passing Multiple Arguments

Often, it is useful to pass more than one argument to a procedure. For example, the following is a procedure that accepts two arguments:

```
Sub ShowSum(ByVal intNum1 As Integer, ByVal intNum2 As Integer)
    Dim intSum As Integer ' Local variable to hold a sum

    ' Get the sum of the two arguments.
    intSum = intNum1 + intNum2

    ' Display the sum.
    MessageBox.Show("The sum is " & intSum.ToString())
End Sub
```

Assuming that intValue1 and intValue2 are Integer variables, the following is an example call to the ShowSum procedure:

```
ShowSum(intValue1, intValue2)
```

When a procedure with multiple parameters is called, the arguments are assigned to the parameters in left-to-right order, as shown in Figure 6-10.

Figure 6-10 Multiple arguments passed to multiple parameters

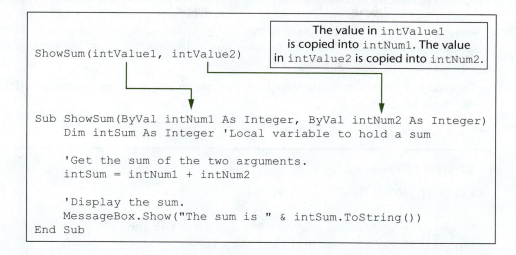

The following procedure call causes 5 to be assigned to the `intNum1` parameter and 10 to be assigned to `intNum2`:

```
ShowSum(5, 10)
```

However, the following procedure call causes 10 to be assigned to the `intNum1` parameter and 5 to be assigned to `intNum2`:

```
ShowSum(10, 5)
```

More about Passing Arguments by Reference

You have learned that when an argument is passed by value to a parameter only a copy of the argument is passed to the parameter variable. If the parameter's value is changed inside the procedure, it has no effect on the original argument.

When an argument is passed by reference, however, the procedure has access to the original argument. Any changes made to the parameter variable are actually performed on the original argument. You use the **ByRef** keyword in the declaration of a parameter variable to cause arguments to be passed by reference to the parameter. Here is an example:

```
Sub GetName(ByRef strName as String)
    ' Get the user's name
    strName = InputBox("Enter your name.")
End Sub
```

This procedure uses ByRef to declare the `strName` parameter. Any argument assigned to the parameter is passed by reference, and any changes made to `strName` are made to the argument passed into it. For example, assume the following code calls the procedure and displays the user name:

```
' Declare a string variable
Dim strUserName As String

' Get the user's name
GetName(strUserName)

' Display the user's name
MessageBox.Show("Your name is" & strUserName)
```

This code calls the `GetName` procedure and passes the string variable `strUserName`, by reference, into the `strName` parameter. The `GetName` procedure displays an input box instructing the user to enter his or her name. The user's input is stored in the `strName` variable. Because `strUserName` was passed by reference, the value stored in `strName` is stored in `strUserName`. When the message box is displayed, it shows the name entered by the user.

Tutorial 6-4 further demonstrates how passing an argument by reference differs from passing it by value.

Tutorial 6-4:
Working with `ByVal` and `ByRef`

In this tutorial, you examine a procedure that accepts an argument passed by value. Then you use the `ByRef` keyword to see how the procedure behaves differently.

Step 1: Open the *ByVal ByRef Demo* project from the student sample programs folder named *Chap6\ByVal ByRef Demo*. The application's form is shown in Figure 6-11. The form has a list box named `lstOutput` and two buttons named `btnGo` and `btnExit`.

Figure 6-11 *ByVal ByRef Demo* form

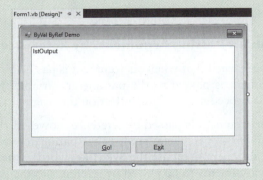

Step 2: Open the *Code* window and look at the `btnGo_Click` event handler.

```
Private Sub btnGo_Click(...) Handles btnGo.Click
    Dim intNumber As Integer = 100

    lstOutput.Items.Add("Inside btnGo_Click the value of " &
                        "intNumber is " &
                        intNumber.ToString())

    lstOutput.Items.Add("Now I am calling ChangeArg.")

    ChangeArg(intNumber)
    lstOutput.Items.Add("Now back in btnGo_Click, " &
                        "the value of intNumber is " &
                        intNumber.ToString())
End Sub
```

The variable `intNumber` is initialized to 100. This procedure calls the `ChangeArg` procedure and passes `intNumber` as the argument.

Step 3: Now look at the `ChangeArg` procedure. The code is as follows:

```
Sub ChangeArg(ByVal intArg As Integer)
  ' Display the value of intArg.
  lstOutput.Items.Add(" ")
  lstOutput.Items.Add("Inside the ChangeArg procedure, " &
                      "intArg is " & intArg.ToString())
  lstOutput.Items.Add("I will change the value of intArg.")

  ' Assign 0 to intArg.
  intArg = 0

  ' Display the value of intArg.
  lstOutput.Items.Add("intArg is now " & intArg.ToString())
  lstOutput.Items.Add(" ")
End Sub
```

Notice that the parameter variable, `intArg`, is declared `ByVal`.

Step 4: Run the application and click the *Go!* button. The form should appear as shown in Figure 6-12. Although the `ChangeArg` procedure sets `intArg` to 0, the value of `intNumber` did not change. This is because the `ByVal` keyword was used in the declaration of `intArg` (`intArg` was passed by value).

Figure 6-12 Results with argument passed by value

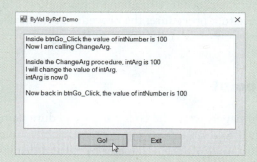

Step 5: Click the *Exit* button to end the application.

Step 6: Experiment by removing the `ByVal` keyword from the `ChangeArg` procedure and running the application again. The output should be exactly the same. Click the *Exit* button.

Step 7: Open the *Code* window. Insert `ByRef` before the parameter in the `ChangeArg` procedure. The first line of the procedure should now look like this:

```
Sub ChangeArg(ByRef intArg As Integer)
```

Step 8: Run the application again and click the *Go!* button. The form should appear as shown in Figure 6-13. This time, when `ChangeArg` sets `intArg` to 0, it changes the value of `intNumber` to 0. This is because the `ByRef` keyword was used in the declaration of `intArg`.

Figure 6-13 Results with argument passed by reference

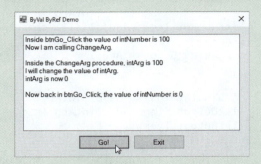

Step 9: Click the *Exit* button to end the application.

 NOTE: You have learned how to pass variables as arguments to procedures. You can also pass constants and expressions as arguments to procedures. Although you can pass both variable and nonvariable arguments by reference, only variable arguments can be changed by the procedure receiving the arguments. If you pass a nonvariable argument by reference to a procedure, the procedure cannot change the argument.

Checkpoint

6.3 On paper, write the code for a procedure named `TimesTen`. The procedure must have an Integer parameter variable named `intValue`. The procedure must multiply the parameter by 10 and display the result in a message box.

6.4 Write a statement that calls the `TimesTen` procedure you wrote in Checkpoint 6.3. Pass the number 25 as the argument.

6.5 On paper, write the code for a procedure named `PrintTotal`. The procedure must have the following parameters:

```
intNum1 As Integer
intNum2 As Integer
intNum3 As Integer
```

The procedure must calculate the total of the three numbers and display the result in a message box.

6.6 Write a statement that calls the `PrintTotal` procedure you wrote in Checkpoint 6.5. Pass the variables `intUnits`, `intWeight`, and `intCount` as the arguments. The three arguments will be assigned to the `intNum1`, `intNum2`, and `intNum3` parameters.

6.7 Suppose you want to write a procedure that accepts an argument and uses the argument in a mathematical operation. You want to make sure that the original argument is not altered. Should you declare the parameter `ByRef` or `ByVal`?

6.3 # Functions

CONCEPT: **A function returns a value to the part of the program that called the function.**

VideoNote

Functions

This section shows you how to write functions. Like a procedure, a function is a set of statements that perform a task when the function is called. In addition, a function returns a value that can be used in an expression.

In previous chapters, you called built-in Visual Basic functions many times. For instance, you used the CInt function to convert strings to integers. You also used the ToString function, which converts numbers to strings. Now you will learn to write your own functions that return values in the same way as built-in functions.

Declaring a Function

The general format of a function declaration is as follows:

```
[AccessSpecifier] Function FunctionName ([ParameterList]) As DataType
    [Statements]
End Function
```

A function declaration is similar to a procedure declaration. *AccessSpecifier* is optional and specifies the accessibility of the function. As with procedures, you may use the keywords Private, Public, Protected, Friend, and Protected Friend as access specifiers. If you do not include an access specifier, it defaults to Public. Next is the keyword Function, followed by the name of the function. Inside the parentheses is an optional list of parameters. Following the parentheses is As *DataType*, where *DataType* is any data type. The data type listed in this part of the declaration is the data type of the value returned by the function.

The last line of a function declaration is the End Function statement. Between the Function statement and the End Function statements, are statements that execute when the function is called. Here is an example of a completed function:

```
1 Function Sum(ByVal dblNum1 As Double, ByVal dblNum2 As Double) As Double
2     Dim dblResult As Double
3
4     ' Add the two arguments.
5     dblResult = dblNum1 + dblNum2
6
7     ' Return the result.
8     Return dblResult
9 End Function
```

This code shows a function named Sum that accepts two arguments, adds them, and returns their sum. (Everything you have learned about passing arguments to procedures applies to functions as well.) The Sum function has two parameter variables, dblNum1 and dblNum2, both of the Double data type. Notice that the words As Double appear after the parentheses. This indicates that the value returned by the function will be of the Double data type.

Inside the function, the statement shown in line 2 declares a local variable named dblResult. The statement shown in line 5 adds the parameter variables dblNum1 and dblNum2, and assigns the result to dblResult. The Return statement in line 8 causes the function to end execution and return a value to the part of the program that called the function. The general format of the Return statement, when used to return a value from a function, is as follows:

```
Return Expression
```

Expression is the value to be returned. It can be any expression having value, such as a variable, a constant, or a mathematical expression. In this case, the Sum function returns the value in the db1Result variable. However, we could have eliminated the db1Result variable, and returned the expression db1Num1 + db1Num2, as shown in the following code:

```
Function Sum(ByVal dblNum1 As Double, ByVal dblNum2 As Double) As Double
   Return dblNum1 + dblNum2
End Function
```

The data type of the Return statement's expression should be the same as the function's return type, or convertible to the function's return type. For example, if the Sum function returns a Double, the value of the Return statement's expression must be Double, or a type that automatically converts to Double. If the return value cannot be converted to the function's return data type, a runtime error occurs.

Calling a Function

Assuming that db1Total, db1Value1, and db1Value2 are variables of type Double, here is an example of how you might call the Sum function:

```
dblTotal = Sum(dblValue1, dblValue2)
```

This statement passes the variables db1Value1 and db1Value2 as arguments. It assigns the value returned by the Sum function to the variable db1Total. So, if db1Value1 is 20.0 and db1Value2 is 40.0, the statement assigns 60.0 to db1Total.

Figure 6-14 illustrates how the arguments are passed to the function and how a value is returned from the function.

Figure 6-14 Arguments passed and a value returned

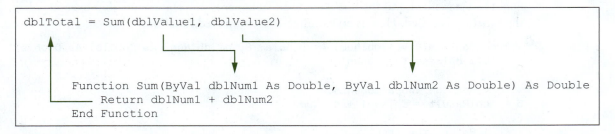

In Tutorial 6-5, you will create a simple application that uses a function to calculate the sale price of a retail item.

VideoNote

The *Sale Price Calculator* application

Tutorial 6-5:
The *Sale Price Calculator* application

In this tutorial you will create an application that calculates the sale price of a retail item. The application will allow the user to enter the item's regular retail price and the discount percentage. It will then calculate the sale price using the following formula:

$$Sale\ Price = Retail\ Price - (Retail\ Price \times Discount\ Percentage)$$

For example, if an item's retail price equals $100 and the discount percentage equals 25% (.25), the sale price will equal $75. Your application's code will contain a function named `CalculateSalePrice` that accepts the item's retail price and the discount percentage as arguments. The function will then return the calculated sale price.

Step 1: Start a new Windows Forms Application project named *Sale Price Calculator*. Set up the application's form as shown in Figure 6-15. The shaded area behind the input fields is a Panel control.

Figure 6-15 *Sale Price Calculator* form

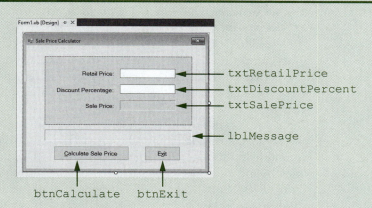

Step 2: Open the *Code* window and insert the following two class-level variable declarations, shown in bold (in lines 3 and 4)

```
1 Public Class Form1
2
3     Private decRetail As Decimal     ' To hold the retail price
4     Private decPercentage As Decimal ' To hold the discount percentage
5
6 End Class
```

Step 3: Now you will create the `ValidateInputFields` function, which uses the `TryParse` method to convert the two input fields into numbers. Type the code for the function inside the class, as shown in bold (in lines 6 through 21) in the following:

```
1 Public Class Form1
2
3     Private decRetail As Decimal     ' To hold the retail price
4     Private decPercentage As Decimal ' To hold the discount percentage
5
6     Private Function ValidateInputFields() As Boolean
7         'Try to convert each of the input fields. Return False if
8         'any field is invalid, and display a suitable error message.
9
10        If Not Decimal.TryParse(txtRetailPrice.Text, decRetail) Then
11            lblMessage.Text = "Retail price must be numeric"
12            Return False
13        End If
14
15        If Not Decimal.TryParse(txtDiscountPercent.Text, decPercentage) Then
16            lblMessage.Text = "Discount percentage must be numeric"
```

```
17              Return False
18          End If
19
20          Return True
21      End Function
22
23 End Class
```

This type of validation function follows a common pattern, which is to attempt to convert an input field; if the conversion fails, you can display an error message and return immediately with a value of *False*. The following pseudocode helps to express this logic:

Try to convert the input field to a number;
If the conversion fails,
  display an error message and return False immediately.

Line 10 calls the TryParse method to try to convert the retail price input field into a Decimal value. If the TryParse method returns *False*, line 11 displays an error message in a label before returning a value of *False* for the ValidateInputFields function in line 12. When you use the Return statement as in line 12, control passes out of the function immediately. On the other hand, if the call to the TryParse method in line 10 returns *True*, control passes to line 15 where the second field (discount percent) is converted to Decimal. If this conversion fails, lines 16 and 17 display a message and tell the ValidateInputFields function to return *False*. Finally, if line 20 is reached, all of the input fields must have been valid, so the ValidateInputFields function returns *True*.

Step 4: Now you will create the CalculateSalePrice function, whose job it is to calculate the sale price of an item after deducting the discount percentage. Type the code for the function inside the class, as shown in bold (in lines 23 through 30) in the following:

```
1 Public Class Form1
2
3      Private decRetail As Decimal     ' To hold the retail price
4      Private decPercentage As Decimal ' To hold the discount percentage
5
6      Private Function ValidateInputFields() As Boolean
7          'Try to convert each of the input fields. Return False if
8          'any field is invalid, and display a suitable error message.
9
10         If Not Decimal.TryParse(txtRetailPrice.Text, decRetail) Then
11             lblMessage.Text = "Retail price must be numeric"
12             Return False
13         End If
14
15         If Not Decimal.TryParse(txtDiscountPercent.Text, decPercentage) Then
16             lblMessage.Text = "Discount percentage must be numeric"
17             Return False
18         End If
19
20         Return True
21     End Function
22
23     Function CalculateSalePrice(ByVal decRetail As Decimal,
24                             ByVal decPercentage As Decimal) As Decimal
25         ' Calculate and return the sale price.
26         Dim decSalePrice As Decimal
```

```
27
28          decSalePrice = decRetail - (decRetail * decPercentage)
29          Return decSalePrice
30      End Function
31
32  End Class
```

This function has two parameters: decRetail and decPercentage. When the function is called, it receives a retail price and discount percentage. In line 26 we declare a local variable named decSalePrice to hold the calculated sale price. Line 28 calculates the sale price and assigns it to decSalePrice. Line 29 then returns the value of the decSalePrice variable.

Step 5: Switch to the *Designer* window and double-click the *Calculate* button to create a Click event handler. Complete the event handler with the bold code (shown in lines 33 through 42) in the following:

```
 1  Public Class Form1
 2
 3      Private decRetail As Decimal      ' To hold the retail price
 4      Private decPercentage As Decimal  ' To hold the discount percentage
 5
 6      Private Function ValidateInputFields() As Boolean
 7          'Try to convert each of the input fields. Return False if
 8          'any field is invalid, and display a suitable error message.
 9
10          If Not Decimal.TryParse(txtRetailPrice.Text, decRetail) Then
11              lblMessage.Text = "Retail price must be numeric"
12              Return False
13          End If
14
15          If Not Decimal.TryParse(txtDiscountPercent.Text, decPercentage) Then
16              lblMessage.Text = "Discount percentage must be numeric"
17              Return False
18          End If
19
20          Return True
21      End Function
22
23      Function CalculateSalePrice(ByVal decRetail As Decimal,
24                                  ByVal decPercentage As Decimal) As Decimal
25          ' Calculate and return the sale price.
26          Dim decSalePrice As Decimal
27
28          decSalePrice = decRetail - (decRetail * decPercentage)
29          Return decSalePrice
30      End Function
31
32      Private Sub btnCalculate_Click(...) Handles btnCalculate.Click
33          Dim decSalePrice As Decimal
34
35          ' Clear any previous message.
36          lblMessage.Text = String.Empty
37
38          ' If the input is valid, display the sale price.
39          If ValidateInputFields() Then
40              decSalePrice = CalculateSalePrice(decRetail, decPercentage)
41              lblSalePrice.Text = decSalePrice.ToString("c")
42          End If
43      End Sub
44  End Class
```

Line 33 declares decSalePrice, which will hold the calculated sale price. Line 36 clears any message that was previously displayed in the lblMessage control. Line 39 calls the ValidateInputFields function to check the input fields for valid values. If the function returns *True*, lines 40 and 41 are executed. Line 40 calculates the sale price, and line 41 displays the price in the lblSalePrice control, with currency formatting.

Step 6:   Switch to the *Designer* window and double-click the *Exit* button to create a Click event handler. Complete the event handler with the bold statement (shown in line 46) in the following:

```
 1 Public Class Form1
 2
 3     Private decRetail As Decimal      ' To hold the retail price
 4     Private decPercentage As Decimal ' To hold the discount percentage
 5
 6     Private Function ValidateInputFields() As Boolean
 7         'Try to convert each of the input fields. Return False if
 8         'any field is invalid, and display a suitable error message.
 9
10         If Not Decimal.TryParse(txtRetailPrice.Text, decRetail) Then
11             lblMessage.Text = "Retail price must be numeric"
12             Return False
13         End If
14
15         If Not Decimal.TryParse(txtDiscountPercent.Text, decPercentage) Then
16             lblMessage.Text = "Discount percentage must be numeric"
17             Return False
18         End If
19
20         Return True
21     End Function
22
23     Function CalculateSalePrice(ByVal decRetail As Decimal,
24                                 ByVal decPercentage As Decimal) As Decimal
25         ' Calculate and return the sale price.
26         Dim decSalePrice As Decimal
27
28         decSalePrice = decRetail - (decRetail * decPercentage)
29         Return decSalePrice
30     End Function
31
32     Private Sub btnCalculate_Click(...) Handles btnCalculate.Click
33         Dim decSalePrice As Decimal
34
35         ' Clear any previous message.
36         lblMessage.Text = String.Empty
37
38         ' If the input is valid, display the sale price.
39         If ValidateInputFields() Then
40             decSalePrice = CalculateSalePrice(decRetail, decPercentage)
41             lblSalePrice.Text = decSalePrice.ToString("c")
42         End If
43     End Sub
44
45     Private Sub btnExit_Click(...) Handles btnExit.Click
46         Me.Close()
47     End Sub
48 End Class
```

Step 7: Run and test the application. Enter 100 for the retail price and 0.25 for the discount percentage. When you click the *Calculate Sale Price* button, the application should display $75.00 as the sale price, as shown in Figure 6-16.

Figure 6-16 Calculated sale price

Functions That Return Nonnumeric Values

When writing functions, you are not limited to returning numeric values. You can return nonnumeric values, such as strings and Boolean values. For example, here is the code for a function that returns a String:

```
Function FullName(ByVal strFirst As String,
                  ByVal strLast As String) As String
    ' Local variable to hold the full name
    Dim strName As String

    ' Append the last name to the first name and
    ' assign the result to strName.
    strName = strFirst & " " & strLast

    ' Return the full name.
    Return strName
End Function
```

Here is an example of a call to this function:

```
strCustomer = FullName("John", "Martin")
```

After this call, the String variable `strCustomer` will hold `"John Martin"`.

Here is an example of a function that returns a Boolean value:

```
Function IsValid(intNum As Integer) As Boolean
    Dim blnStatus As Boolean

    If intNum >= 0 And intNum <= 100 Then
        blnStatus = True
    Else
        blnStatus = False
    End If

    Return blnStatus
End Function
```

This function returns *True* if its argument is within the range 0 to 100. Otherwise, it returns *False*. The following code segment has an `If...Then` statement with an example call to the function:

```
intValue = 20
If IsValid(intValue) Then
    lblStatus.Text = The value is within range."
Else
    lblStatus.Text = The value is out of range."
End If
```

When this code executes, it displays *The value is within range*. Here is another example:

```
intValue = 200
If IsValid(intValue) Then
    lblStatus.Text = The value is within range."
Else
    lblStatus.Text = The value is out of range."
End If
```

When this code executes, it displays *The value is out of range*.

Checkpoint

6.8 Look at the following function declaration and answer the questions below.

```
Function Distance(ByVal sngRate As Single,
                  ByVal sngTime As Single) As Single
```

   a.   What is the name of the function?
   b.   When you call this function, how many arguments do you pass to it?
   c.   What are the names of the parameter variables and what are their data types?
   d.   This function returns a value of what data type?

6.9 Write the first line of a function named `Days`. The function should return an integer value. It should have three integer parameters: `intYears`, `intMonths`, and `intWeeks`. All arguments should be passed by value.

6.10 Write an example function call statement for the function described in Checkpoint 6.9.

6.11 Write the first line of a function named `LightYears`. The function should return a value of the Single data type. It should have one parameter variable, `lngMiles`, of the Long data type. The parameter should be declared so that the argument is passed by value.

6.12 Write an example function call statement for the function described in Checkpoint 6.11.

6.13 Write the entire code for a function named `TimesTwo`. The function should accept an integer argument and return the value of that argument multiplied by two.

6.4   More about Debugging: Stepping Into, Over, and Out of Procedures and Functions

CONCEPT: Visual Studio debugging commands allow you to single-step through applications with procedure and function calls. The *Step Into* command allows you to single-step through a called procedure or function. The *Step Over* command allows you to execute a procedure or function call without single-stepping through its lines. The *Step Out* command allows you to execute all remaining lines of a procedure or function you are debugging without stepping through them.

In Chapter 3 you learned to set a breakpoint in your application's code and to single-step through the code's execution. Let's find out how to step into or step over a procedure or function and step out of a procedure or function.

When an application is in break mode, the **Step Into command** causes the currently highlighted line (the execution point) to execute. If that line contains a call to a procedure or a function, the next highlighted line is the first line in that procedure or function. In other words, the *Step Into* command allows you to single-step through a procedure or function when it is called. Activate the *Step Into* command using one of the following methods:

- Press the F8 key
- Select *Debug* from the menu bar, and then select *Step Into* from the *Debug* menu
- Click the *Step Into* button (⬇) on the *Debug Toolbar*, if the toolbar is visible

Like the *Step Into* command, the **Step Over command** causes the currently highlighted line to execute. If the line contains a procedure or function call, however, the procedure or function is executed without stepping through its statements. Activate the *Step Over* command using one of the following methods:

> **TIP:** Visual Studio can be configured in different ways. Under some configurations, the *Step Into* command from the *Debug* menu might be activated by the F11 function key, and the *Step Over* command may be activated by the F10 key. To find out which keys are used, look carefully at these commands when you click on the *Debug* menu.

- Press Shift+F8
- Select *Debug* from the menu bar, and then select *Step Over* from the *Debug* menu
- Click the *Step Over* button (⬇) on the *Debug Toolbar*, if the toolbar is visible

Use the **Step Out command** when single-stepping through a procedure or function, if you want the remainder of the procedure or function to complete execution without single-stepping. After the procedure or function has completed, the line following the procedure or function call is highlighted, and you may resume single-stepping. Activate the *Step Out* command using one of the following methods:

- Press Ctrl+Shift+F8
- Select *Debug* from the menu bar, and then select *Step Out* from the *Debug* menu
- Click the *Step Out* button (⬇) on the *Debug Toolbar*, if the toolbar is visible

In Tutorials 6-6, 6-7, and 6-8 you practice using each of these commands.

VideoNote

Practicing the *Step Into* command

Tutorial 6-6:
Practicing the *Step Into* command

In this tutorial, you use the *Sale Price Calculator* project to practice single-stepping through procedures and functions.

Step 1:   Open the *Sale Price Calculator* project from Tutorial 6-5.

Step 2:   Open the *Code* window and set a breakpoint at the line in the btn_Calculate_Click event handler shown in Figure 6-17.

Figure 6-17 Location of breakpoint

```
        Private Sub btnCalculate_Click() Handles btnCalculate.Click

            Dim decSalePrice As Decimal
            lblMessage.Text = String.Empty

            If ValidateInputFields() Then
                decSalePrice = CalculateSalePrice(decRetail, decPercentage)
                lblSalePrice.Text = decSalePrice.ToString("c")
            End If
        End Sub
```

 TIP: Set a breakpoint by clicking the mouse while the pointer is positioned in the left margin, next to the line of code. You can also move the text cursor to the line you wish to set as a breakpoint, and then press F9.

Step 3:   Run the application in debug mode, and enter 100 for the retail price and .25 for the discount percentage.

Step 4:   Click the *Calculate Sale Price* button. The application enters break mode with the breakpoint line highlighted.

Step 5:   Notice that the highlighted line contains a call to the CalculateSalePrice function. Press F8 to execute the *Step Into* command.

Step 6:   Because you pressed F8, the first line of the CalculateSalePrice function is highlighted next. You will now single-step through the statements inside the CalculateSalePrice function. Continue pressing the F8 key to single-step through the CalculateSalePrice function. When the End Function line is highlighted, press F8 once more to return to the line that called the function.

Step 7:   Press F5 or click *Debug* on the menu bar and then click *Continue* to exit break mode and resume normal execution. (Leave the project open in Visual Studio. You will use it in the next tutorial.)

Tutorial 6-7:
Practicing the *Step Over* command

Step 1: Make sure the *Sale Price Calculator* project is still open in Visual Studio from Tutorial 6-6. The breakpoint should still be set as shown in Figure 6-18.

Figure 6-18 Location of breakpoint

```
        Private Sub btnCalculate_Click() Handles btnCalculate.Click

            Dim decSalePrice As Decimal
            lblMessage.Text = String.Empty

            If ValidateInputFields() Then
                decSalePrice = CalculateSalePrice(decRetail, decPercentage)
                lblSalePrice.Text = decSalePrice.ToString("c")
            End If
        End Sub
```

Step 2: Run the application in debug mode and enter **100** for the retail price and **.25** for the discount percentage.

Step 3: Click the *Calculate Sale Price* button. The application enters break mode with the breakpoint line highlighted.

Step 4: Notice that the highlighted line contains a call to the `CalculateSalePrice` function. Press ⟨Shift⟩+⟨F8⟩ to execute the *Step Over* command. This executes the function call without stepping through it. The next line is now highlighted.

Step 5: Press ⟨F5⟩ or click *Debug* on the menu bar and then click *Continue* to exit break mode and resume normal execution. (Leave the project open in Visual Studio. You will use it in the next tutorial.)

Tutorial 6-8:
Practicing the *Step Out* command

Step 1: Make sure the *Sale Price Calculator* project is still open in Visual Studio from the previous tutorial. The breakpoint should still be set as shown in Figure 6-19.

Figure 6-19 Location of breakpoint

```
    Private Sub btnCalculate_Click() Handles btnCalculate.Click

        Dim decSalePrice As Decimal
        lblMessage.Text = String.Empty

        If ValidateInputFields() Then
            decSalePrice = CalculateSalePrice(decRetail, decPercentage)
            lblSalePrice.Text = decSalePrice.ToString("c")
        End If
    End Sub
```

Step 2: Run the application in debug mode and enter **100** for the retail price and **.25** for the discount percentage.

Step 3: Click the *Calculate Sale Price* button. The application enters break mode with the breakpoint line highlighted.

Step 4: Notice that the highlighted line contains a call to the `CalculateSalePrice` function. Press F8 to execute the *Step Into* command.

Step 5: Because you pressed F8, the first line of the `CalculateSalePrice` function is highlighted next. Press the F8 key once again to advance to the next line in the function.

Step 6: Instead of continuing to step through the function, you will now step out of the function. Press Ctrl+Shift+F8 to execute the *Step Out* command. Single-stepping is suspended while the remaining statements in the `CalculateSalePrice` function execute. You are returned to the `btnCalculate_Click` event handler, at the line containing the function call.

Step 7: Press F5 or click *Debug* on the menu bar and then click *Continue* to exit break mode and resume normal execution.

TIP: When the current execution point does not contain a procedure or function call, the *Step Into* and *Step Over* commands perform identically.

Checkpoint

6.14 Suppose you are debugging an application in break mode and are single-stepping through a function that has been called. If you want to execute the remaining lines of the function and return to the line that called the function, what command do you use? What key(s) do you press to execute this command?

6.15 Suppose you are debugging an application in break mode and the current
execution point contains a procedure call. If you want to single-step through the
procedure that is being called, what command do you use? What key(s) do you
press to execute this command?

6.16 Suppose you are debugging an application in break mode, and the current
execution point contains a function call. If you want to execute the line, but not
single-step through the function, what command do you use? What key(s) do you
press to execute this command?

6.5 Focus on Program Design and Problem Solving: Building the *Bagel and Coffee Price Calculator* Application

CONCEPT: In this section you build the *Bagel and Coffee Price Calculator*
application. It uses procedures and functions to calculate the total
of a customer order.

Brandi's Bagel House has a bagel and coffee delivery service for the businesses in her
neighborhood. Customers may call in and order white and whole wheat bagels with a
variety of toppings. Additionally, customers may order three different types of coffee.
Here is a complete price list:

Bagels:
White bagel	$1.25
Whole wheat bagel	$1.50

Toppings:
Cream cheese	$0.50
Butter	$0.25
Blueberry jam	$0.75
Raspberry jam	$0.75
Peach jelly	$0.75

Coffee:
Regular coffee	$1.25
Cappuccino	$2.00
Café au lait	$1.75

(*Note:* Delivery for coffee alone is not offered.)

Brandi, the owner, has asked you to write an application that her staff can use to record
an order as it is called in. The application should display the total of the order, including
6% sales tax. Figure 6-20 shows the application's form in the *Designer*, with the names of
various controls.

Figure 6-20 *Bagel and Coffee Price Calculator* form

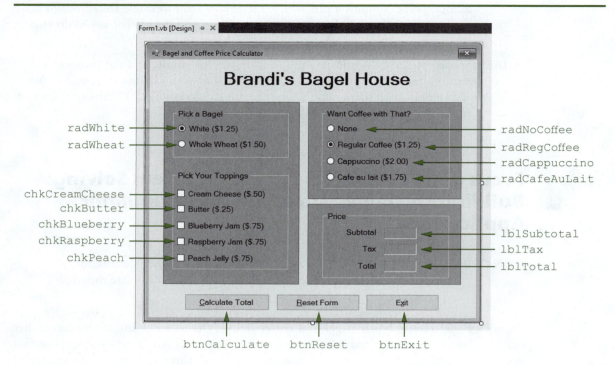

Table 6-1 lists each control, along with any relevant property settings.

Table 6-1 *Bagel and Coffee* Calculator controls

Control Type	Control Name	Property	Property Value
Form	(Default)	Text:	Bagel and Coffee Price Calculator
Label	(Default)	Text	*Brandi's Bagel House*
		Font	*Microsoft San Serif*, 24pt, style=Bold
		TextAlign	*MiddleCenter*
ToolTip	(Default)		(Retain all default property settings.)
Panel	(Default)	BackColor:	ActiveCaption (under *System*)
		BorderStyle:	FixedSingle
GroupBox	(Default)	Text:	*Pick a Bagel*
RadioButton	radWhite	Text:	*White ($1.25)*
		Checked:	*True*
		ToolTip on ToolTip1:	*Click here to choose a white bagel.*
RadioButton	radWheat	Text:	*Whole Wheat ($1.50)*
		ToolTip on ToolTip1:	*Click here to choose a whole wheat bagel.*
GroupBox	(Default)	Text:	*Pick Your Toppings*
CheckBox	chkCreamCheese	Text:	*Cream Cheese ($.50)*
		ToolTip on ToolTip1:	*Click here to choose cream cheese.*
CheckBox	chkButter	Text:	*Butter ($.25)*
		ToolTip on ToolTip1:	*Click here to choose butter.*

(continued)

Table 6-1 *Bagel and Coffee Calculator* controls (*continued*)

Control Type	Control Name	Property	Property Value
CheckBox	chkBlueberry	Text: ToolTip on ToolTip1:	*Blueberry Jam ($.75)* *Click here to choose blueberry jam.*
CheckBox	chkRaspberry	Text: ToolTip on ToolTip1:	*Raspberry Jam ($.75)* *Click here to choose raspberry jam.*
CheckBox	chkPeach	Text: ToolTip on ToolTip1:	*Peach Jelly ($.75)* *Click here to choose peach jelly.*
Panel	(Default)	BackColor: BorderStyle:	ActiveCaption (under *System*) FixedSingle
GroupBox	(Default)	Text:	*Want coffee with that?*
RadioButton	radNoCoffee	Text: ToolTip on ToolTip1:	None *Click here to choose no coffee.*
RadioButton	radRegCoffee	Text: Checked: ToolTip on ToolTip1:	*Regular Coffee ($1.25)* *True* *Click here to choose regular coffee.*
RadioButton	radCappuccino	Text: ToolTip on ToolTip1:	*Cappuccino ($2.00)* *Click here to choose cappuccino.*
RadioButton	radCafeAuLait	Text: ToolTip on ToolTip1:	*Cafe au lait ($1.75)* *Click here to choose cafe au lait.*
Panel	(Default)	BackColor: BorderStyle:	ActiveCaption (under *System*) FixedSingle
GroupBox	(Default)	Text:	*Price*
Label	(Default)	Text:	*Subtotal*
Label	lblSubtotal	Text: AutoSize: BorderStyle:	 *False* *Fixed3D*
Label	(Default)	Text:	*Tax*
Label	lblTax	Text: AutoSize: BorderStyle:	 *False* *Fixed3D*
Label	(Default)	Text:	*Total*
Label	lblTotal	Text: AutoSize: BorderStyle:	 *False* *Fixed3D*
Button	btnCalculate	Text: ToolTip on ToolTip1:	*&Calculate Total* *Click here to calculate the total of the order.*
Button	btnReset	Text: ToolTip on ToolTip1:	*&Reset Form* *Click here to clear the form and start over.*
Button	btnExit	Text: ToolTip on ToolTip1:	*E&xit* *Click here to exit.*

Table 6-2 lists and describes the methods (event handlers, procedures, and functions) used in this application.

Table 6-2 Methods for *Bagel and Coffee Calculator*

Method	Type of Method	Description
btnCalculate_Click	Event handler	Calculates and displays the total of an order. Calls the following functions: CalcBagelCost, CalcCoffeeCost, CalcToppingCost, and CalcTax.
btnExit_Click	Event handler	Ends the application.
btnReset_Click	Event handler	Resets the controls on the form to their initial values. Calls the following procedures: ResetBagels, ResetToppings, ResetCoffee, ResetPrice.
CalcBagelCost	Function	Returns the price of the selected bagel.
CalcToppingCost	Function	Returns the total price of the selected toppings.
CalcCoffeeCost	Function	Returns the price of the selected coffee.
CalcTax	Function	Accepts the amount of a sale as an argument. Returns the amount of sales tax on that amount. The tax rate is stored in a class-level constant, decTAX_RATE.
ResetBagels	Procedure	Resets the bagel type radio buttons to their initial value.
ResetToppings	Procedure	Resets the topping check boxes to unchecked.
ResetCoffee	Procedure	Resets the coffee radio buttons to their initial values.
ResetPrice	Procedure	Sets the Text property of the lblSubtotal, lblTax, and lblTotal labels to String.Empty.

The btnCalculate_Click event handler procedure calculates the total of an order and displays its price. Notice that very little math is actually performed in this procedure, however. It calls the CalcBagelCost, CalcToppingCost, CalcCoffeeCost, and CalcTax functions to get the values it needs. Here is the pseudocode:

subtotal = CalcBagelCost() + CalcToppingCost() + CalcCoffeeCost()
tax = CalcTax(subtotal)
total = subtotal + tax

lblSubtotal.Text = subtotal
lblTax.Text = tax
lblTotal.Text = total

The purpose of the btnReset event handler procedure is to reset all the radio buttons, check boxes, and labels on the form to their initial values. This operation has been broken into the following procedures: ResetBagels, ResetToppings, ResetCoffee, ResetPrice. When btnReset_Click executes, it calls these procedures. Here is the pseudocode:

ResetBagels()
ResetToppings()
ResetCoffee()
ResetPrice()

The CalcBagelCost function determines whether the user has selected white or whole wheat, and returns the price of that selection. Here is the pseudodode:

If White Is Selected Then
*   cost of bagel = 1.25*
Else
*   cost of bagel = 1.5*
End If
Return cost of bagel

The `CalcToppingCost` function examines the topping check boxes to determine which toppings the user has selected. The total topping price is returned. Here is the pseudocode:

> *cost of topping = 0.0*
> *If Cream Cheese Is Selected Then*
>   *cost of topping += 0.5*
> *End If*
> *If Butter Is Selected Then*
>   *cost of topping += 0.25*
> *End If*
> *If Blueberry Is Selected Then*
>   *cost of topping += 0.75*
> *End If*
> *If Raspberry Is Selected Then*
>   *cost of topping += 0.75*
> *End If*
> *If Peach Is Selected Then*
>   *cost of topping += 0.75*
> *End If*
> *Return cost of topping*

The `CalcCoffeeCost` function examines the coffee radio buttons to determine which coffee (if any) the user has selected. The price is returned. Here is the pseudocode:

> *If No Coffee Is Selected Then*
>   *cost of coffee = 0*
> *ElseIf Regular Coffee Is Selected Then*
>   *cost of coffee = 1.25*
> *ElseIf Cappuccino Is Selected Then*
>   *cost of coffee = 2*
> *ElseIf Café Au Lait Is Selected Then*
>   *cost of coffee = 1.75*
> *End If*
> *Return cost of coffee*

The `CalcTax` function accepts an argument, which is passed into the `amount` parameter variable. (The tax rate will be stored in a class-level constant.) The amount of sales tax is returned. Here is the pseudocode:

> *sales tax = amount * tax rate*
> *Return sales tax*

The `ResetBagels` procedure resets the bagel radio buttons to their initial values. Here is the pseudocode:

> *radWhite = Selected*
> *radWheat = Deselected*

The `ResetToppings` procedure unchecks all the topping check boxes. Here is the pseudocode:

> *chkCreamCheese = Unchecked*
> *chkButter = Unchecked*
> *chkBlueberry = Unchecked*
> *chkRaspberry = Unchecked*
> *chkPeach = Unchecked*

The `ResetCoffee` procedure resets the coffee radio buttons to their initial values. Here is the pseudocode:

> *radNoCoffee = Deselected*
> *radRegCoffee = Selected*
> *radCappuccino = Deselected*
> *radCafeAuLait = Deselected*

The `ResetPrice` procedure copies an empty string to `lblSubtotal`, `lblTax`, and `lblTotal`. Here is the pseudocode:

> *lblSubtotal.Text = String.Empty*
> *lblTax.Text = String.Empty*
> *lblTotal.Text = String.Empty*

In Tutorial 6-9, you build the *Bagel House* application.

Tutorial 6-9:
Building the *Bagel House* application

Step 1: Create a new Windows Forms Application project named *Bagel House*.

Step 2: Set up the form as shown in Figure 6-21. Refer to Figure 6-20 and Table 6-1 for specific details about the controls and their properties.

Step 3: Once you have placed all the controls on the form and set their properties, you can begin writing the code. Start by opening the *Code* window and writing the class-level declarations shown in bold:

```
Public Class Form1
  ' Class-level declarations
  Const decTAX_RATE As Decimal = 0.06D      ' Tax rate
  Const decWHITE_BAGEL As Decimal = 1.25D  ' Cost of a white bagel
  Const decWHEAT_BAGEL As Decimal = 1.5D   ' Cost of a whole wheat bagel
  Const decCREAM_CHEESE As Decimal = 0.5D   ' Cost of cream cheese topping
  Const decBUTTER As Decimal = 0.25D        ' Cost of butter topping
  Const decBLUEBERRY As Decimal = 0.75D     ' Cost of blueberry topping
  Const decRASPBERRY As Decimal = 0.75D     ' Cost of raspberry topping
  Const decPEACH As Decimal = 0.75D         ' Cost of peach topping
  Const decREG_COFFEE As Decimal = 1.25D    ' Cost of regular coffee
  Const decCAPPUCCINO As Decimal = 2D       ' Cost of cappuccino
  Const decCAFE_AU_LAIT As Decimal = 1.75D ' Cost of Cafe au lait
End Class
```

Step 4: Now write the `btnCalculate_Click`, `btnReset_Click`, and `btnExit_Click` event handlers, as follows:

```
Private Sub btnCalculate_Click(...) Handles btnCalculate.Click
  ' This procedure calculates the total of an order.
  Dim decSubtotal As Decimal      ' Holds the order subtotal
  Dim decTax As Decimal           ' Holds the sales tax
  Dim decTotal As Decimal         ' Holds the order total
```

Figure 6-21 *Brandi's Bagel House* form

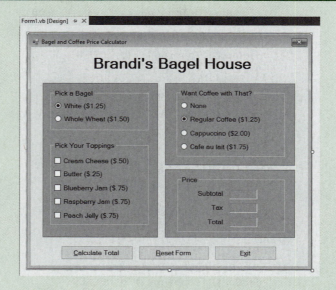

```
    decSubtotal = CalcBagelCost() + CalcToppingCost() + CalcCoffeeCost()
    decTax = CalcTax(decSubtotal)
    decTotal = decSubtotal + decTax

    lblSubtotal.Text = decSubtotal.ToString("c")
    lblTax.Text = decTax.ToString("c")
    lblTotal.Text = decTotal.ToString("c")
End Sub

Private Sub btnReset_Click(...) Handles btnReset.Click
    ' This procedure resets the controls to default values.
    ResetBagels()
    ResetToppings()
    ResetCoffee()
    ResetPrice()
End Sub

Private Sub btnExit_Click(...) Handles btnExit.Click
    ' Close the form.
    Me.Close()
End Sub
```

Step 5: Write the code for the following functions and procedures:

```
Function CalcBagelCost() As Decimal
    ' This function returns the cost of the selected bagel.
    Dim decBagel As Decimal

    If radWhite.Checked = True Then
        decBagel = decWHITE_BAGEL
    Else
        decBagel = decWHEAT_BAGEL
    End If

    Return decBagel
End Function
```

```
Function CalcToppingCost() As Decimal
   ' This function returns the cost of the toppings.
   Dim decCostOfTopping As Decimal = 0D

   If chkCreamCheese.Checked = True Then
      decCostOfTopping += decCREAM_CHEESE
   End If

   If chkButter.Checked = True Then
      decCostOfTopping += decBUTTER
   End If

   If chkBlueberry.Checked = True Then
      decCostOfTopping += decBLUEBERRY
   End If

   If chkRaspberry.Checked = True Then
      decCostOfTopping += decRASPBERRY
   End If

   If chkPeach.Checked = True Then
      decCostOfTopping += decPEACH
   End If

   Return decCostOfTopping
End Function

Function CalcCoffeeCost() As Decimal
   ' This function returns the cost of the selected coffee.
   Dim decCoffee As Decimal

   If radNoCoffee.Checked Then
      decCoffee = 0D
   ElseIf radRegCoffee.Checked = True Then
      decCoffee = decREG_COFFEE
   ElseIf radCappuccino.Checked = True Then
      decCoffee = decCAPPUCCINO
   ElseIf radCafeAuLait.Checked = True Then
      decCoffee = decDAFE_AU_LAIT
   End If

   Return decCoffee
End Function

Function CalcTax(ByVal decAmount As Decimal) As Decimal
   ' This function receives the sale amount and
   ' returns the amount of sales tax.
   Return decAmount * decTAX_RATE
End Function

Sub ResetBagels()
   ' This procedure resets the bagel selection.
   radWhite.Checked = True
End Sub

Sub ResetToppings()
   ' This procedure resets the topping selection.
   chkCreamCheese.Checked = False
   chkButter.Checked = False
```

```
            chkBlueberry.Checked = False
            chkRaspberry.Checked = False
            chkPeach.Checked = False
    End Sub

    Sub ResetCoffee()
        ' This procedure resets the coffee selection.
        radRegCoffee.Checked = True
    End Sub

    Sub ResetPrice()
        ' This procedure resets the price.
        lblSubtotal.Text = String.Empty
        lblTax.Text = String.Empty
        lblTotal.Text = String.Empty
    End Sub
```

Step 6: Save and run the program. If there are errors, use debugging techniques you have learned to find and correct them.

Step 7: When you're sure the application is running correctly, save it one last time.

Summary

6.1 Procedures

- The declaration for a procedure begins with a `Sub` statement and ends with an `End Sub` statement. The code that appears between these two statements is the body of the procedure.
- When a procedure is called, the application branches to that procedure and executes its statements. When the procedure has finished, the application branches back to the procedure call and resumes executing at the next statement.

6.2 Passing Arguments to Procedures

- A parameter is a special variable that receives an argument value passed into a procedure or function. If a procedure or function has a parameter, you must supply an argument when calling the procedure or function.
- When a procedure or function with multiple parameters is called, arguments are assigned to the parameters in left-to-right order.
- There are two ways to pass an argument to a procedure: by value or reference. Passing an argument by value means that only a copy of the argument is passed to the procedure. Because the procedure has only a copy, it cannot make changes to the original argument. When an argument is passed by reference, however, the procedure has access to the original argument and can make changes to it.

6.3 Functions

- A function returns a value to the part of the program that called it. Similar to a procedure, it is a set of statements that perform a task when the function is called.
- A value is returned from a function by the `Return` statement.

6.4 More about Debugging: Stepping Into, Over, and Out of Procedures and Functions

- Visual Studio debugging commands (*Step Into*, *Step Over*, and *Step Out*) allow you to step through application code and through called procedures and function.

6.5 Focus on Program Design and Problem Solving: Building the *Bagel and Coffee Price Calculator* Application

- This section outlines the process of building the *Bagel and Coffee Price Calculator* application, with a focus on program design and problem solving.

Key Terms

arguments	parameter
by reference (pass argument)	Pascal casing
by value (pass argument)	procedure
ByRef	procedure call
ByVal	procedure declaration
Call keyword	*Step Into* command
function	*Step Out* command
method	*Step Over* command
modularize	Sub (keyword)

Video Tutorial: Improving the *Kayak Rental* Application

In this sequence of video tutorials, we improve on the *Kayak Rental* application by creating more modular code. Because this chapter focuses on procedures (methods) and arguments, we use them to perform validation and calculations. This has the effect of making the code much more readable. As a bonus, we show that you can even pass controls as arguments to procedures. Finally, we spend some time with the Visual Studio debugger, showing how to set breakpoints, examine variables, and step into procedure calls.

- Part 1: Using procedure calls for calculations
- Part 2: Using procedure calls for validation
- Part 3: Learning more about the Visual Studio debugger

Review Questions and Exercises

Fill-in-the-Blank

1. A(n) _____ is a named block of code that performs a specific task and does not return a value.

2. A(n) _____ statement causes a procedure to be executed.

3. A(n) _____ is a named block of statements that executes and returns a value.

4. You return a value from a function with the _____ statement.

5. _____ local variables are not destroyed when a procedure returns.

6. Values passed to a procedure or function are called _____.

7. A(n) _____ is a special variable that receives an argument passed to a procedure or function.

8. When an argument is passed by _____ a copy of the argument is assigned to the parameter variable.

9. When an argument is passed by _____ the called procedure has access to the original argument and can modify its value.

10. The _____ debugging command allows you to single-step through a called procedure or function.

Multiple Choice

1. Which of the following terms means to divide an application's code into small, manageable procedures?
   a. Break
   b. Modularize
   c. Parameterize
   d. Bind

2. Which type of statement causes a procedure to execute?
   a. Procedure declaration
   b. Access specifier
   c. Procedure call
   d. Step Into

3. What happens when a procedure finishes executing?

    a. The application branches back to the procedure call and resumes executing at the next line
    b. The application terminates
    c. The application waits for the user to trigger the next event
    d. The application enters break mode

4. In what way is a function different from a procedure?

    a. A procedure returns a value, but a function does not return a value
    b. A function returns a value, but a procedure does not return a value
    c. A function must be executed in response to an event
    d. There is no difference

5. What is an argument?

    a. A variable that a parameter is passed into
    b. A value passed to a procedure or function when it is called
    c. A local variable that retains its value between procedure calls
    d. A reason not to create a procedure or function

6. What keyword is used in a parameter declaration to specify that the argument is passed by value?

    a. `ByVal`
    b. `Val`
    c. `Value`
    d. `AsValue`

7. When an argument is passed to a procedure this way, the procedure has access to the original argument and may make changes to it.

    a. By value
    b. By address
    c. By reference
    d. By default

8. Which of the following is a debugging command that causes a procedure or function to execute without single-stepping through the procedure's or function's code?

    a. *Step Into*
    b. *Step Through*
    c. *Jump Over*
    d. *Step Over*

9. Which of the following is a debugging command that is used when you are stepping through a procedure's code and you wish to execute the remaining statements in the procedure without single-stepping through them?

    a. *Jump Out*
    b. *Step Through*
    c. *Step Out*
    d. *Step Over*

True or False

Indicate whether the following statements are true or false.

1. T F: A general purpose procedure is associated with a specific control.
2. T F: You must use the `Call` keyword to execute a procedure.

3. T F: When a parameter is declared, its name may be preceded by the `ByVal` keyword, the `ByRef` keyword, or no keyword at all.

4. T F: You can pass more than one argument to a procedure or function.

5. T F: If you write a procedure or function with a parameter variable, you do not have to supply an argument when calling the procedure.

6. T F: If you are debugging an application in break mode and you want to single-step through a procedure that will be called in the highlighted statement, you use the *Step Over* command.

Short Answer

1. Why do local variables lose their values between calls to the procedure or function in which they are declared?

2. What is the difference between an argument and a parameter variable?

3. Where do you declare parameter variables?

4. If you are writing a procedure that accepts an argument and you want to make sure the procedure cannot change the value of the argument, how should you declare the matching procedure parameter?

5. When a procedure or function accepts multiple arguments, does it matter what order the arguments are passed in?

6. How do you return a value from a function?

What Do You Think?

1. What advantage is there to dividing an application's code into several small procedures?

2. When might you choose to define a local variable (inside a procedure) rather than defining it at the class level?

3. Give an example in which passing an argument by reference would be useful.

4. Suppose you want to write a procedure to perform an operation. How do you decide if the procedure should be a procedure or a function?

5. When debugging an application, why would you not want to single-step through every procedure or function?

Find the Error

Locate the errors in the following code examples:

1.
```
Sub DisplayValue(Dim intNumber As Integer)
    ' This displays a value.
    MessageBox.Show(intNumber.ToString())
End Sub
```

2. The following is a procedure:
```
Sub Greeting(ByVal strName As String)
    ' This procedure displays a greeting.
    MessageBox.Show("Hello " & strName)
End Sub
```

And the following is a call to the procedure:
```
Greeting()
```

3. The following is a function:

```
Function Product(ByVal intNum1 As Integer, ByVal intNum2
                    As Integer) As Integer
    Dim intResult As Integer
    intResult = intNum1 * intNum2
End Function
```

4. The following is a function:

```
Sub Sum(ByVal intNum1 As Single, ByVal intNum2 As Single)
        As Single
    Dim intResult As Single
    intResult = intNum1 + intNum2
    Return intResult
End Sub
```

Algorithm Workbench

1. The following statement calls a function named `Half` that returns a Decimal, which is half of the argument. Write the function.

```
decResult = Half(intNumber)
```

2. An application contains the following function:

```
Function Square(ByVal intValue As Integer) As Integer
    Return intValue ^ 2
End Function
```

Write a statement that passes the value 4 to this function and assigns its return value to a variable named `intResult`.

3. Write a procedure named `TimesTen` that accepts a single Integer argument. When the procedure is called, it should display the product of its argument multiplied by 10 in a message box.

4. An application contains the following procedure:

```
Sub Display(ByVal intArg1 As Integer, ByVal strArg2 As String,
        ByVal sngArg3 As Single)
    MessageBox.Show("Here are the values: " &
                intArg1.ToString() & " " &
                strArg2 & " " & sngArg3.ToString())
End Sub
```

Write a statement that calls the procedure and passes it the following variables:

```
Dim strName As String
Dim intAge As Integer
Dim sngIncome As Single
```

Programming Challenges

VideoNote
The *Retail Price Calculator* Problem

1. **Retail Price Calculator**

   Write an application that accepts from the user the wholesale cost of an item and its markup percentage. (For example, if an item's wholesale cost is $5 and its retail price is $10, then the markup is 100%.)

   The program should contain a function named `CalculateRetail` that receives the wholesale cost and markup percentage as arguments, and returns the retail price of the item. The application's form should look something like the one shown in Figure 6-22.

Figure 6-22 *Retail Price Calculator* form

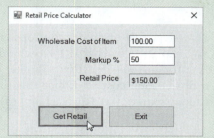

Figure 6-23 *Hospital Charges* form

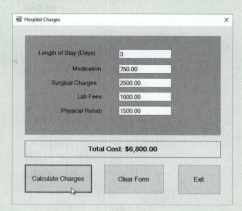

When the user clicks the *Get Retail* button, the program should do the following:

- Verify that the values entered by the user for the wholesale cost and the markup percent are numeric and not negative
- Call the `CalculateRetail` function
- Display the retail cost as returned from the function

2. **Hospital Charges**

Create an application that calculates the total cost of a hospital stay. The application should accept the following input:

- The number of days spent in the hospital, as an integer
- The amount of medication charges
- The amount of surgical charges
- The amount of lab fees
- The amount of physical rehabilitation charges

The hospital charges $350 per day. The application's form should resemble the one shown in Figure 6-23.

Create the following functions:

`CalcStayCharges`	Calculates and returns the base charges for the hospital stay. This is computed as $350 times the number of days in the hospital.
`CalcMiscCharges`	Calculates and returns the total of the medication, surgical, lab, and physical rehabilitation charges.
`CalcTotalCharges`	Calculates and returns the total charges.
`ValidateInputFields`	Checks the validity of the input fields by converting each to a numeric value and checking its range. If any input field is found to be invalid, this function displays an error message and returns a value of *False*.

Input Validation: Do not accept a negative value for length of stay, medication charges, surgical charges, lab fees, or physical rehabilitation charges. When displaying error messages, use a Label control and specifically name the missing field and the type of data to be entered (integer or numeric).

3. **Solar Panel Installation**

The Megawatt solar panel company installs solar panels on home rooftops. The base installation charge of $2,000 includes two panels. The charge for each additional panel is $300. The normal waiting time for installation is two weeks, but customers can pay an express charge of 5% of the total cost to reduce this time. Create an application that collects the required information from the user and calculates the charges for the installation.

The user should input the following information: first name, last name, phone, number of panels, deposit amount, and a check box for the express installation option. When the user clicks a button to view the charges, display a group box containing the following information: base installation charge, cost of installing additional panels, total installation cost, deposit amount, and balance due.

Error checking should include the following criteria:

- The name and phone fields cannot be blank
- The number of panels must be an integer between 1 and 1,000
- The deposit amount must be a numeric value greater than 0.

Use separate procedures and functions for validation and calculations whenever possible. For example, validation of user inputs should be performed in a separate Boolean function, called from the Click handler of the *Calculate Charges* button. Display error messages whenever appropriate.

When the application starts, as in Figure 6-24, the *Charges* group box should be invisible. After the user clicks the *Calculate Charges* button and all inputs are validated, the *Charges* group box should appear, as shown in Figure 6-25. If the deposit amount was greater than the total charges, change the caption of the final field from "Balance due" to "Refund". When the user clicks the *Clear* button, clear all inputs and hide the *Charges* group box.

Figure 6-24 Solar Panel Installation application, on startup

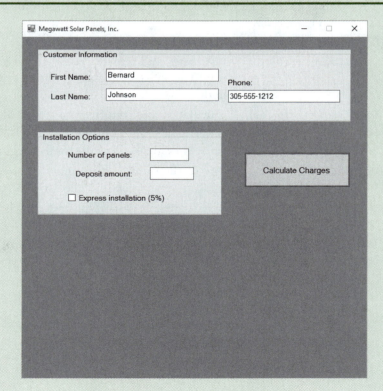

Figure 6-25 Solar Panel Installation, after calculating charges

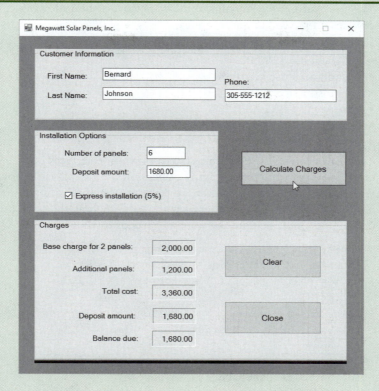

Test the application by varying the number of solar panels between 1 and 10, varying the deposit amount, and changing the express option. For example, in Figure 6-26, the user wants to install only one panel, but must pay the base installation price of $2,000.

Figure 6-26 Solar Panel Installation, installing one panel

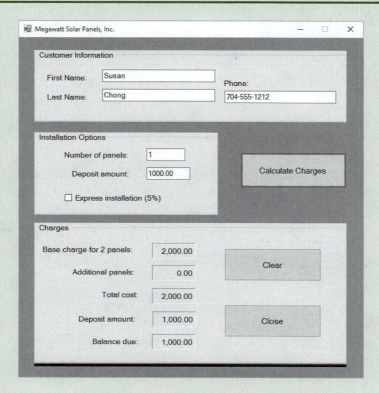

4. **TG Automotive**

The TG Automotive repair company performs the following routine maintenance services on passenger automobiles:

- Oil change—$36.00
- Lube job—$28.00
- Radiator flush—$50.00
- Transmission flush—$120.00
- Inspection—$15.00
- Muffler replacement—$200.00
- Tire rotation—$20.00

TG Automotive also performs other nonroutine services and charges for parts and labor ($60 per hour). Create an application that displays the total for a customer's visit to the shop. A sample user interface for the application appears in Figure 6-27. Your source code should contain functions, such as the ones listed here, that validate inputs and calculate the various parts of the bill:

```
' Verify that the two input values are valid
' numbers and neither is less than zero.
Function ValidateInputs() As Boolean


' Calculate all oil and lubrication charges.
Function CalcOilLubeCharges() As Decimal


'Calculate radiator and transmission flush charges.
Function CalcFlushCharges() As Decimal


' Calculate inspection, muffler, and tire
' rotation charges.
Function CalcMiscCharges() As Decimal


' Calculate and display the total of all charges,
' including labor, parts, and services.
Sub CalculateTotalCharges()
```

Figure 6-27 TG Automotive application form

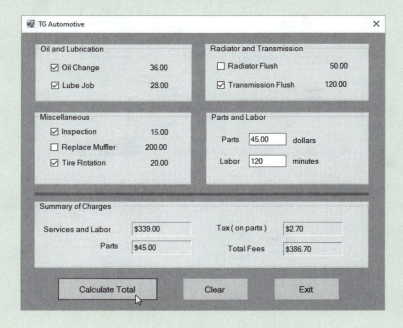

Also, create procedures, such as the ones listed here, that are called when the user clicks the *Clear* button:

```
' Reset the oil change and lube job check boxes.
Sub ClearOilLube()


' Clear the radiator and transmission flush check boxes.
Sub ClearFlushes()


' Clear the inspection, muffler replacement, and tire
' rotation check boxes.
Sub ClearMisc()


' Clear the parts and labor check boxes.
Sub ClearOther()
```

Design Your Own Forms

5. **Password Verifier**

   You will develop a software package that requires users to enter their passwords. Your software requires users' passwords to meet the following criteria:

   - The password should be at least six characters long
   - The password should contain at least one numeric digit and at least one alphabetic character

   Create an application that asks the user to enter a password. The application should use a function named `IsValid` to verify that the password meets the criteria. It should display a message indicating whether the password is valid or invalid.

   The `IsValid` function should accept a string as its argument and return a Boolean value. The string argument is the password to be checked. If the password is valid, the function should return *True*. Otherwise, it should return *False*.

> **TIP:** Refer to Chapter 4 for more information about working with strings.

6. **Travel Expenses**

   Create an application that calculates and displays the total travel expenses for a business trip. The user must provide the following information:

   - Number of days on the trip
   - Amount of airfare, if any
   - Amount paid for meals, if any
   - Amount of car rental fees, if any
   - Number of miles driven, if a private vehicle was used
   - Amount of parking fees, if any
   - Amount of taxi charges, if any
   - Conference or seminar registration fees, if any
   - Lodging charges, per night

The company reimburses travel expenses according to the following policy:

- $37 per day for meals
- Parking fees, up to $10.00 per day
- Taxi charges up to $20.00 per day
- Lodging charges up to $95.00 per day
- If a private vehicle is used, $0.27 per mile driven

The application should calculate and display the following:

- Total expenses incurred by the business person
- The total allowable expenses for the trip
- The excess that must be paid by the business person, if any
- The amount saved by the business person if the expenses were under the total allowed

The application should have the following functions:

CalcMeals	Calculates and returns the amount reimbursed for meals.
CalcMileage	Calculates and returns the amount reimbursed for mileage driven in a private vehicle.
CalcParkingFees	Calculates and returns the amount reimbursed for parking fees.
CalcTaxiFees	Calculates and returns the amount reimbursed for taxi charges.
CalcLodging	Calculates and returns the amount reimbursed for lodging.
CalcTotalReimbursement	Calculates and returns the total amount reimbursed.
CalcUnallowed	Calculates and returns the total amount of expenses that are not allowable, if any. These are parking fees that exceed $10.00 per day, taxi charges that exceed $20.00 per day, and lodging charges that exceed $95.00 per day.
CalcSaved	Calculates and returns the total amount of expenses under the allowable amount, if any. For example, the allowable amount for lodging is $95.00 per day. If a business person stayed in a hotel for $85.00 per day for five days, the savings would be $50.00.

Input validation: Do not accept negative numbers for any dollar amount or for miles driven in a private vehicle. Do not accept numbers less than 1 for the number of days.

7. **Falling Distance**

   When an object is falling because of gravity, the following formula can be used to determine the distance the object falls in a specific time period:

   $$d = \tfrac{1}{2}\, gt^2$$

   The variables in the formula are as follows: d is the distance in meters, g is 9.8, and t is the amount of time in seconds that the object has been falling.

   Create a VB application that allows the user to enter the amount of time that an object has fallen and then displays the distance that the object fell. The application should have a function named FallingDistance. The FallingDistance function should accept an object's falling time (in seconds) as an argument. The function should return the distance in meters that the object has fallen during that time interval.

8. **Kinetic Energy**

Martial arts experts know that the force needed to break several boards or bricks is based much more on speed than the weight of a hand or foot. This is why children (with training) can often break more boards than untrained adults. The physics formula for *kinetic energy* (shown below as *KE*) explains this phenomenon:

$$KE = \frac{1}{2}\, mv^2$$

In this formula, *m* equals the mass of an object (in kilograms), and *v* is the velocity in meters per second (measured as a change in distance over time). Because the velocity is squared, it is much more important in determining how much kinetic energy you produce! Your job is to create a VB application that allows the user to enter an object's mass and velocity and then displays the object's kinetic energy. The application should have a function named `KineticEnergy` that accepts a moving object's mass (in kilograms) and velocity (in meters per second) as arguments. The function should return the object's level of kinetic energy.

9. **Prime Numbers**

A prime number is a number that can be evenly divided by only itself and 1. For example, the number 5 is prime because it can be evenly divided by only 1 and 5. The number 6, however, is not prime because it can be evenly divided by 1, 2, 3, and 6.

Write a Boolean function named `IsPrime` which takes an integer as an argument and returns *true* if the argument is a prime number or *false* otherwise. Use the function in an application that lets the user enter a number and then displays a message indicating whether the number is prime.

TIP: Recall that the `MOD` operator divides one number by another and returns the remainder of the division. In an expression such as `intNum1 MOD intNum2`, the `MOD` operator will return 0 if `intNum1` is evenly divisible by `intNum2`.

10. **Prime Number List**

This exercise assumes you have already written the `IsPrime` function in Programming Challenge 9. Create another application that uses this function to display all of the prime numbers from 1 through 100 in a list box. The program should have a loop that calls the `IsPrime` function.

11. **Workshop Selector with Procedures**

Programming Challenge 3 in Chapter 5 asked you to create an application with list boxes so that users could select workshops and locations. Modify the application by creating separate procedures for the following tasks, and call them from the Click event handler for the *Add Workshop* button:

```
' Determine the registration fee and number of days based on
' the selected index of the workshops list box.
Sub SetDaysAndRegistrationFee()


' Set the logding fee per day based on the selected index of the
' location list box.
Sub SetLodgingFeePerDay()
```

12. **Weekly Temperature Average**

Programming Challenge 4 in Chapter 4 asked you to validate user input and calculate the average temperature from a list of temperatures entered into text boxes by the user. Improve the application by creating a single function that validates the user's input into a TextBox control. Call your function separately for every TextBox on the form. Here is a sample function declaration:

```
Function CheckTemperature(txtBox As TextBox, dblTemp As Double,
                                      id As String) As Boolean
```

If the input is found to be nonnumeric or out of range, display an error message and reposition the input focus on the appropriate text box. See the Chapter 4 description of the problem for the valid temperature ranges. Write a second procedure that only calculates and displays the temperature average. *Suggestion: You may find it easiest to declare some variables at the class level, outside of any procedure.*

13. **Rock, Paper, Scissors Game**

Create an application that lets the user play the game of "Rock, Paper, Scissors" against the computer. The program should work as follows:

(**1**) When the program begins, a random number in the range of 1 through 3 is generated. If the number is 1, then the computer has chosen rock. If the number is 2, then the computer has chosen paper. If the number is 3, then the computer has chosen scissors. (Don't display the computer's choice yet.)

(**2**) The user clicks a button to select his or her choice of rock, paper, or scissors.

(**3**) The computer's choice is displayed.

(**4**) A winner is selected according to the following rules:

- If one player chooses rock and the other player chooses scissors, then rock wins. (Rock smashes scissors.)
- If one player chooses scissors and the other player chooses paper, then scissors wins. (Scissors cuts paper.)
- If one player chooses paper and the other player chooses rock, then paper wins. (Paper covers rock.)
- If both players make the same choice, the game must be played again to determine the winner.

7 Multiple Forms, Modules, and Menus

TOPICS

This chapter shows how to add multiple forms to a project and how to create a module to hold procedures and functions. It also covers creating a menu system, as well as context menus, with commands and submenus that the user may select from.

7.1 Multiple Forms

CONCEPT: Visual Basic projects can have multiple forms. The startup form is the form that is displayed when the project executes. Other forms in a project are displayed by programming statements.

The applications you have created so far have only one form in their user interface. Visual Basic does not limit you to one form in a project, however. You may create multiple forms in a project to use as dialog boxes, display error messages, and so on. Then you can display these forms as they are needed.

A Windows Forms application typically has one form that is designated as the **startup form**. When the application executes, the startup form is automatically displayed. By default, the first form you create is the startup form. You will learn later in this chapter how to designate any form in a project as the startup form.

Form Files and Form Names

Each form in a Visual Basic project has a name that is stored in the form's Name property (viewable in the *Properties* window when the form is selected). As you already know, the first form in a project is automatically named Form1. When a form is created in a Visual Basic project, the code associated with the form is stored in a file that has the same name as the form, followed by the *.vb* extension. So, the code for a form named Form1 will be stored in a file named *Form1.vb*. The *Solution Explorer* window shows an entry for each form file in a project. Figure 7-1 shows the *Solution Explorer* window with an entry for the form named *Form1.vb*.

Figure 7-1 *Solution Explorer* window with entry for *Form1.vb*

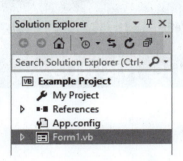

 NOTE: The code stored in a form file is the same code that you see when you open the form in the *Code* window.

Renaming an Existing Form File

If you use the *Solution Explorer* window to change a form's file name, the form's Name property changes automatically to match the file name. If, for example, you rename the file *Form1.vb* to *MainForm.vb*, the form's Name property changes from Form1 to MainForm.

On the other hand, if you change a form's Name property, the form's file name does not change automatically. To maintain consistency between the form's file name and its Name property, you should use the *Solution Explorer* to rename the form's file instead of changing the form's Name property. Here's how to rename a form file:

1. Right-click the form's file name in the *Solution Explorer* window.
2. A pop-up menu should appear, as shown in Figure 7-2. Select *Rename* from the pop-up menu.

Figure 7-2 Right-clicking the form file

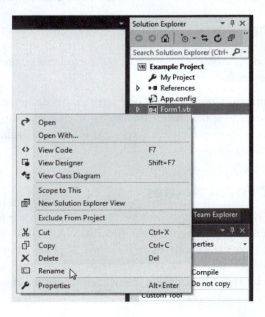

Figure 7-3 Form file renamed as *MainForm.vb*

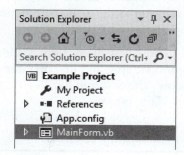

3. The name of the form file should be highlighted in the *Solution Explorer* window. Type the new name for the form file. Be sure to keep the *.vb* extension. Figure 7-3 shows an example where *Form1.vb* has been renamed *MainForm.vb*.

When you have multiple forms in an application, you should give each form a meaningful name. In a multi-form project, default form names such as Form1, Form2, etc., do not adequately describe the purpose of each form.

Adding a New Form to a Project

VideoNote
Creating and Displaying a Second Form

Follow these steps to add a new form to a project:

1. Click *Project* on the Visual Studio menu bar, and then select *Add Windows Form . . .* from the *Project* menu. The *Add New Item* window, shown in Figure 7-4, should appear.

Figure 7-4 *Add New Item* window

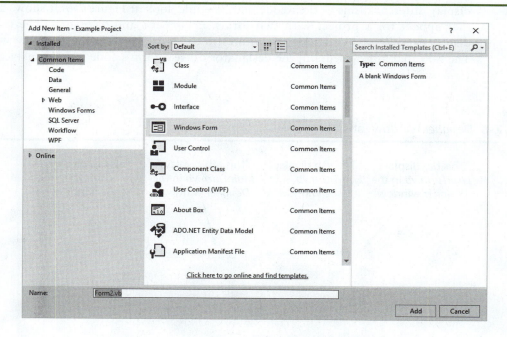

2. Near the bottom of the *Add New Item* window, a *Name* text box appears where you can specify the new form's file name. Initially, a default name will appear here. (Notice that in Figure 7-4 the default name *Form2.vb* appears. The actual name that appears on your screen may be different.) Change the default name that is displayed

in the *Name* text box to a more descriptive name. For example, if you wish to name the new form ErrorForm, enter *ErrorForm* in the *Name* text box. (Visual Studio will add the *.vb* file extension to the name automatically when it creates the form.)

3. Click the *Add* button.

After completing these steps, a new blank form is added to your project. The new form is displayed in the *Designer* window and an entry for the new form's file appears in the *Solution Explorer* window. The *Solution Explorer* window in Figure 7-5 shows two form files: *ErrorForm.vb* and *MainForm.vb*.

Figure 7-5 *Solution Explorer* window showing two forms

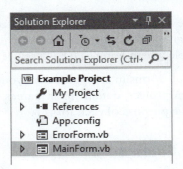

Switching between Forms and Form Code

At design time, you can easily switch to another form by double-clicking the form's entry in the *Solution Explorer* window. The form will be then displayed in the *Designer* window. You can also use the tabs that appear at the top of the *Designer* window to display different forms or their code. For example, look at Figure 7-6. It shows the tabs that appear for a project with two forms: ErrorForm and MainForm. The tabs that display the [*Design*] designator cause a form to be displayed in the *Designer* window. The tabs that appear without the designator cause a form's code to be displayed in the *Code* window.

Figure 7-6 *Designer* window tabs

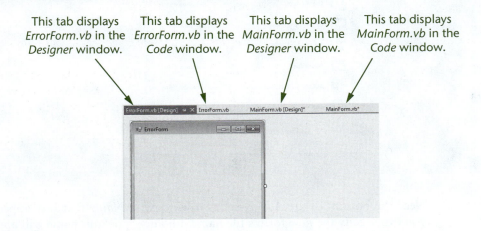

Removing a Form

If you wish to remove a form from a project and delete its file from the disk, follow these steps.

1. Right-click the form's entry in the *Solution Explorer* window.
2. On the pop-up menu, click *Delete*.

If you wish to remove a form from a project but you do not want to delete its file from the disk, follow one of these sets of steps.

1. Right-click the form's entry in the *Solution Explorer* window.
2. On the pop-up menu click *Exclude From Project*.

or

1. Select the form's entry in the *Solution Explorer* window.
2. Click *Project* on the menu, and click *Exclude From Project*.

Designating the Startup Form

The Form1 form is, by default, the startup form. It is automatically displayed when the application runs. To make another form the startup form, follow these steps:

1. In the *Solution Explorer* window, right-click the project name. Figure 7-7 shows the location of the project name in the window.

Figure 7-7 Project name in *Solution Explorer* window

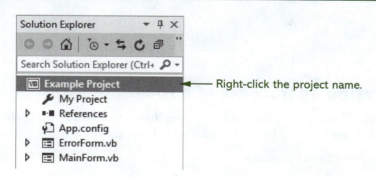

2. On the pop-up menu, click *Properties*. The project's properties page should appear, as shown in Figure 7-8.
3. Make sure the *Application* tab is selected at the left edge of the properties page, as shown in Figure 7-8. To change the startup form, click the down arrow (⊡) in the *Startup form* drop-down list. A list of all the forms in the project appears. Select the form that should display first when your program executes.
4. Save the project and click the *Close* button (✕) on the properties page tab.

Figure 7-8 Project's properties page

Application tab   Startup form

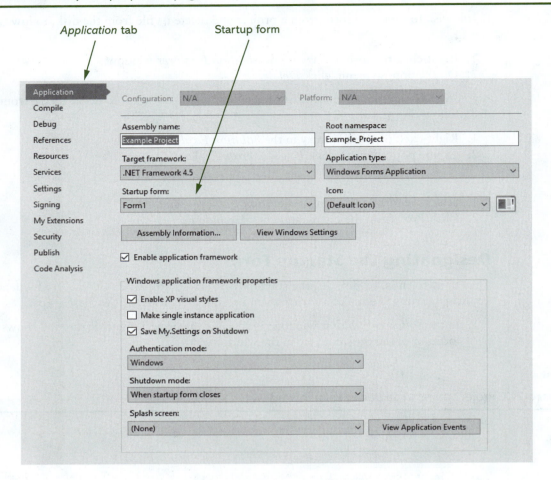

Creating an Instance of a Form

A form file contains all of a form's code. Recall that when you open a form in the *Code* window, the first and last lines of code look like the following:

```
Public Class FormName

End Class
```

In the first line, *FormName* is the form's name. Recall from Chapter 2 that these statements are the beginning and the end of a class declaration for the form. All of the code for the form (event handlers, procedures, functions, and class-level declarations) must appear inside this class declaration.

A form's class declaration by itself does not create a specific form, but is merely the description of a form. It is similar to the blueprint for a house. The blueprint itself is not a house, but is a detailed description of a house. When we use the blueprint to build an actual house, we can say we are building an instance of the house described by the blueprint. If we want, we can build several identical houses from the same blueprint. Each house is a separate instance of the house described by the blueprint. This idea is illustrated in Figure 7-9.

A form's class declaration serves a similar purpose. We can use it to create one or more instances of the form described by the class declaration, and then use the instance(s) to display the form on the screen.

Figure 7-9 Blueprints and instances of the blueprints

Blueprint that describes a house

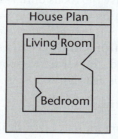

Instances of the house described by the blueprint

Displaying a Form

The first step in displaying a form is to create an instance of the form. You create an instance of a form with a `Dim` statement. The general format is as follows:

```
Dim ObjectVariable As New ClassName
```

ObjectVariable is the name of an object variable that references an instance of the form. An **object variable** is a variable that holds the memory address of an object and allows you to work with the object. *ClassName* is the form's class name. For example, assume that you have added a form to your project and named it `ErrorForm`. The following statement creates an instance of the form in memory:

```
Dim frmError As New ErrorForm
```

Let's examine what happens as a result of this statement. First, a variable named `frmError` is declared. Then, the part of the statement that reads `New ErrorForm` causes an instance of the `ErrorForm` form to be created in memory. The form's memory address is assigned to the `frmError` variable. (When an object variable holds the memory address of an object, we say that it references the object.) We may now use the `frmError` variable to perform operations with the form.

 NOTE: In this book we use the prefix `frm` in a variable name to indicate that the variable references a form.

This statement does not cause the form to be displayed on the screen. It only creates an instance of the form in memory and assigns its address to the object variable. To display the form on the screen, you must use the object variable to invoke one of the form's methods.

The ShowDialog and Show Methods

A form can be either modal or modeless. When a **modal form** is displayed, no other form in the application can receive the focus until the modal form is closed. The user must close the modal form before he or she can work with any other form in the application. A **modeless form**, on the other hand, allows the user to switch focus to another form while it is displayed. The **ShowDialog method** causes a form to be displayed as a modal form. When this method is called, the form is displayed and it receives the focus. The general format of the method call is as follows:

```
ObjectVariable.ShowDialog()
```

ObjectVariable is the name of an object variable that references an instance of a form. For example, the following code creates an instance of the ErrorForm form and displays it:

```
Dim frmError As New ErrorForm
frmError.ShowDialog()
```

To display a modeless form, use the **Show method**. The general format of the Show method is as follows:

```
ObjectVariable.Show()
```

ObjectVariable is the name of an object variable that references an instance of a form. For example, the following code creates an instance of the ErrorForm form and displays it as a modeless form:

```
Dim frmError As New ErrorForm
frmError.Show()
```

 TIP: Most of the time, forms shoud be modal. It is common for a procedure to display a form and then perform operations dependent on input gathered by the form. Therefore, you will normally use the ShowDialog method to display a form.

Closing a Form with the Close Method

Forms commonly have a button, such as *Close* or *Cancel*, which the user clicks to close the form. When the user clicks such a button, the form must call the Close method. The **Close method** closes a form and removes its visual part from memory.

When a form calls its own Close method, it typically does so with the **Me keyword**, as shown here:

```
Me.Close()
```

The word Me in Visual Basic is a special variable that references the currently executing object. For example, suppose a form has a Button control named btnExit, and the form's code contains the following event handler:

```
Private Sub btnExit_Click(...) Handles btnExit.Click
    Me.Close()
End Sub
```

Assume that an instance of the form has been created in memory and it is currently displayed on the screen. When this event handler executes, Me references the current instance of the form. So, the statement Me.Close() causes the current instance of the form to call its own Close method, thus closing the form.

The `Hide` Method

The **Hide method** makes a form or control invisible, but does not remove it from memory. It has the same effect as setting the Visible property to *False*. As with the `Close` method, a form uses the `Me` keyword to call its own `Hide` method, such as `Me.Hide()`. Use the `Hide` method when, instead of closing a form, you want to remove it temporarily from the screen. After hiding a form, you may redisplay it with the `ShowDialog` or `Show` methods.

Now that we've covered the basics of having multiple forms in a project, go through the steps in Tutorial 7-1. In the tutorial you will create a simple application that has two forms.

Tutorial 7-1:
Creating an application with two forms

Step 1:   Create a new Windows Forms Application project named *Multiform Practice*.

Step 2:   In the *Solution Explorer* window, rename the *Form1.vb* file to *MainForm.vb*. (Right-click *Form1.vb* and then select *Rename* from the pop-up menu.) Changing the form's file name in the *Solution Explorer* to *MainForm.vb* also changes the form's name to `MainForm`. The *Solution Explorer* window should appear as shown in Figure 7-10.

Step 3:   In the *Designer* window, set up the `MainForm` form as shown in Figure 7-11. Name the *Display Form* Button control `btnDisplayForm` and the *Exit* Button control `btnExit`.

Figure 7-10 *Solution Explorer* after changing *Form1.vb* to *MainForm.vb*

Figure 7-11 The `MainForm` form

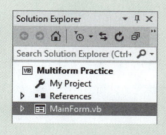

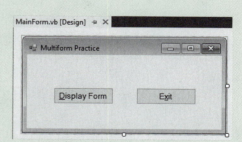

Step 4:   Perform the following steps to create another form named `MessageForm` in the project:

- Click *Project* on the menu bar, then select *Add Windows Form . . .*
- The *Add New Item* window will appear. Enter *MessageForm.vb* as the name.
- Click the *Add* button.

As shown in Figure 7-12, a new form named `MessageForm` will appear in the *Designer* window. Notice that an entry for *MessageForm.vb* appears in the *Solution Explorer*.

Figure 7-12 `MessageForm` added to the project

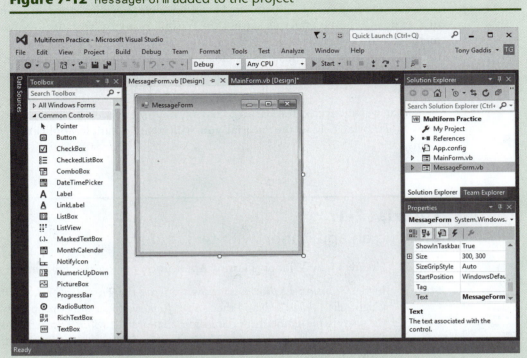

Step 5: In the *Designer* window, set up the `MessageForm` as shown in Figure 7-13. Name the Button control `btnClose`.

Figure 7-13 The `MessageForm` form

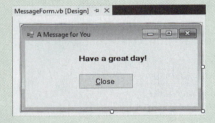

Step 6: Use the tabs at the top of the *Designer* window to switch to *MainForm.vb* [*Design*]. This brings up the `MainForm` in the *Designer* window.

Step 7: Double-click the `btnDisplayForm` button to create a code template for the button's Click event handler. Complete the event handler by writing the bold code shown here in lines 2 through 6. (Don't type the line numbers. They are shown for reference.)

```
1 Private Sub btnDisplayForm_Click(...) Handles btnDisplayForm .Click
2     ' Create an instance of MessageForm.
3     Dim frmMessage As New MessageForm
4
5     ' Display the form in modal style.
6     frmMessage.ShowDialog()
7 End Sub
```

Let's take a closer look at this code. Line 3 creates an instance of the `MessageForm` form in memory and assigns its address to the `frmMessage` variable. Line 6 uses the `frmMessage` variable to call the form's ShowDialog method. When this statement executes, it will display the form on the screen in modal style.

Step 8: Use the tabs at the top of the *Designer* window to switch back to *MainForm.vb* [*Design*]. This brings up the `MainForm` again in the *Designer* window.

Step 9: Double-click the `btnExit` button to create a code template for the button's Click event handler. Complete the event handler by writing the bold code shown here:

```
Private Sub btnExit_Click(...) Handles btnExit.Click
    ' Close the form.
    Me.Close()
End Sub
```

When this event handler executes, it will close the `MainForm` form, which will end the application.

Step 10: Use the tabs at the top of the *Designer* window to switch to *MessageForm.vb* [*Design*]. This brings up the `MessageForm` in the *Designer* window.

Step 11: Double-click the `btnClose` button to create a code template for the button's Click event handler. Complete the event handler by writing the bold code shown here:

```
Private Sub btnClose_Click(...) Handles btnClose.Click
    ' Close the form.
    Me.Close()
End Sub
```

When this event handler executes, it will close the `MessageForm` form.

Step 12: Save the project and then run it. The `MainForm` should appear, as shown on the left in Figure 7-14. Click the *Display Form* button. The `MessageForm` form should appear, as shown on the right in Figure 7-14.

> **NOTE:** Some early releases of Visual Studio 2015 have a bug that will cause the following error when you compile the project in Step 12: *'Form1' is not a member of 'MultiForm Practice'*. If you see this error message, download the document titled **Startup Form Issue in VS2015** from this book's companion Web site for a simple solution. The companion Web site is at www.pearsonhighered.com/gaddisvb.

Figure 7-14 The `MainForm` and the `MessageForm` forms displayed

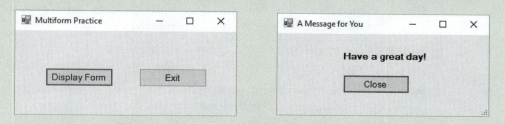

Step 13: On the `MessageForm`, click the *Close* button. This should close the `Message-Form`. Next, click the *Exit* button on the `MainForm` to end the application.

More about Modal and Modeless Forms

You have already learned that when a modal form is displayed, no other form in the application can receive the focus until the modal form is closed or hidden. There is another important aspect of modal forms. When a procedure calls the ShowDialog method to display a modal form, no subsequent statements in that procedure execute until the modal form is closed. This concept is illustrated in Figure 7-15.

Figure 7-15 Execution of statements after displaying a modal form

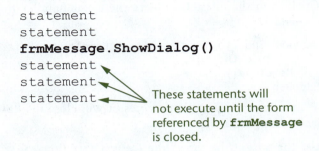

```
statement
statement
frmMessage.ShowDialog()
statement
statement
statement
```
These statements will not execute until the form referenced by **frmMessage** is closed.

When a procedure calls the Show method to display a modeless form, however, statements following the method call continue to execute after the modeless form is displayed. Visual Basic does not wait until the modeless form is closed before executing these statements. This concept is illustrated in Figure 7-16. Tutorial 7-2 demonstrates this difference between modal and modeless forms.

Figure 7-16 Execution of statements after displaying a modeless form

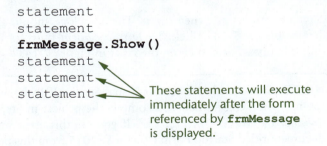

```
statement
statement
frmMessage.Show()
statement
statement
statement
```
These statements will execute immediately after the form referenced by **frmMessage** is displayed.

Tutorial 7-2:

Completing an application that displays modal and modeless forms

Step 1: Open the *Modal Modeless Demo* project from the student sample programs folder named *Chap7\Modal Modeless Demo*.

Step 2: Look at the *Solution Explorer* window, shown in Figure 7-17. The project has two forms, MainForm and MessageForm. MainForm is the startup form.

Step 3: Double-click the entry for *MainForm.vb* in the *Solution Explorer*. The form should appear in the *Designer* window, as shown in Figure 7-18.

Step 4: To look at the MessageForm form, double-click its entry in the *Solution Explorer* window, as shown in Figure 7-19. The *Close* button is named btnClose.

Figure 7-17 *Solution Explorer* window showing two forms

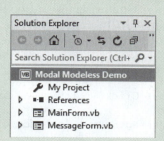

Figure 7-18 The `MainForm` form

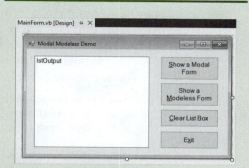

Figure 7-19 The `MessageForm` form

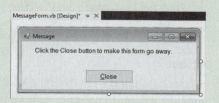

Step 5: Open the *Code* window to view the code for the `MessageForm` form. Look at the `btnClose_Click` event handler. Its code is as follows:

```
Private Sub btnClose_Click(...) Handles btnClose.Click
    ' Close the form.
    Me.Close()
End Sub
```

When this procedure executes, it closes the `MessageForm` form.

Step 6: Open `MainForm` in the *Designer* window and double-click the *Show a Modal Form* button. This will create a code template for the `btnShowModal_Click` event handler. Complete the event handler by typing the bold code shown in lines 2 through 12. (Don't type the line numbers. They are shown for reference.)

```
 1 Private Sub btnShowModal_Click(...) Handles btnShowModal.Click
 2     Dim intCount As Integer              ' Counter
 3     Dim frmMessage As New MessageForm    ' Instance of MessageForm
 4
 5     ' Show the message form in modal style.
 6     frmMessage.ShowDialog()
 7
 8     ' Display some numbers in the list box on the MainForm.
 9     ' This will happen AFTER the user closes the MessageForm.
10     For intCount = 1 To 10
11         lstOutput.Items.Add(intCount.ToString())
12     Next
13 End Sub
```

Let's take a closer look at the code. Line 2 declares `intCount`, an Integer variable that will be used as a counter. Line 3 creates an instance of the `MessageForm` form and assigns its address to a variable named `frmMessage`.

Line 6 uses the `frmMessage` variable to call the form's `ShowDialog` method. This displays the `MessageForm` in modal style, which means that no other statements in this event handler will execute until the `MessageForm` closes.

After the MessageForm closes, the For...Next loop in lines 10 through 12 executes. The loop displays the numbers 1 through 10 in the lstOutput list box.

Step 7: Open MainForm in the *Designer* window again and double-click the *Show a Modeless Form* button. This will create a code template for the btnShowModeless_Click event handler. Complete the event handler by typing the bold code shown in lines 2 through 12. (Don't type the line numbers. They are shown for reference.)

```
1 Private Sub btnShowModeless_Click(...) Handles btnShowModal.Click
2    Dim intCount As Integer          ' Counter
3    Dim frmMessage As New MessageForm ' Instance of MessageForm
4
5    ' Show the message form in modeless style.
6    frmMessage.Show()
7
8    ' Display some numbers in the list box on the MainForm.
9    ' This will happen while the MessageForm is still on the screen.
10   For intCount = 1 To 10
11       lstOutput.Items.Add(intCount.ToString())
12   Next
13 End Sub
```

The btnShowModeless_Click event procedure basically performs the same operation as the btnShowModal_Click procedure: It displays the Message-Form form and then displays the numbers 1 through 10 in the lstOutput list box. The only difference is that line 6 displays the MessageForm in modeless style, using the Show method. Therefore, the For...Next loop in lines 10 through 12 executes immediately after the MessageForm is displayed. The program does not wait for the user to close the MessageForm before executing the loop.

Step 8: Run the application. On the main form, click the *Show a Modal Form* button. The MessageForm form is displayed. Figure 7-20 shows the forms, positioned so you can see both of them. Notice that the For...Next loop has not executed because you do not see the numbers 1 through 10 printed on the main form.

Figure 7-20 The MainForm form and the modal MessageForm form

Step 9: Click the *Close* button on the MessageForm form to close the form. Now look at the MainForm form. As shown in Figure 7-21, the For...Next loop executes as soon as the MessageForm form is closed.

Figure 7-21 `MainForm` after the modal `MessageForm` form is closed

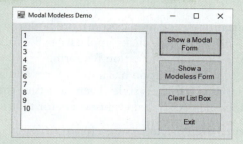

Step 10: Click the *Clear List Box* button to clear the numbers from the list box.

Step 11: Click the *Show a Modeless Form* button to display the `MessageForm` in modeless style. As shown in Figure 7-22, notice that the `For...Next` loop executes immediately after the form is displayed; it does not wait for you to click the `MessageForm` *Close* button.

Figure 7-22 `MainForm` form and the modeless `MessageForm` form

Step 12: Click the `MessageForm` *Close* button to close the form.

Step 13: Click the `MainForm`'s *Exit* button to end the application.

The Load, Activated, FormClosing, and FormClosed Events

There are several events associated with forms. In this section we will discuss the Load, Activated, FormClosing, and FormClosed events.

The Load Event

The Load event was introduced in Chapter 3, but a quick review is in order. Just before a form is displayed, a Load event occurs. If you need to execute code automatically just before a form is displayed, you can create a Load event handler, which will execute in response to the Load event. To write code in a form's Load event handler, double-click any area of the form where there is no other control. The *Code* window appears with a code template similar to the following:

```
Private Sub MainForm_Load(...) Handles MyBase.Load

End Sub
```

Complete the template with the statements you wish the procedure to execute.

The Activated Event

A form's Activated event occurs when the user switches the focus to the form from another form or application. Here are two examples of how the Activated event occurs:

- Application A and application B are both running, and a form in application A has the focus. The user clicks application B's form. When this happens, the Activated event occurs for application B's form.
- Suppose an application has a main form and a second form, and the second form is displayed in modeless style. Then each time the user clicks a form that does not have the focus, an Activated event occurs for that form.

The Activated event occurs when a form is initially displayed, following the Load event. If you need to execute code in any of these situations, you can create an Activated event handler, which executes in response to the Activated event. To create an **Activated event handler,** follow these steps:

1. Select a form in the *Designer* window.
2. Select the *Events* button in the *Properties* window toolbar (see Figure 7-23). This button looks like a lightning bolt.
3. Double-click the *Activated* event name in the *Properties* window. A code template for the Activated event handler will be created in the *Code* window, as shown in Figure 7-24.

Figure 7-23 Select the *Events* icon in the *Properties* window.

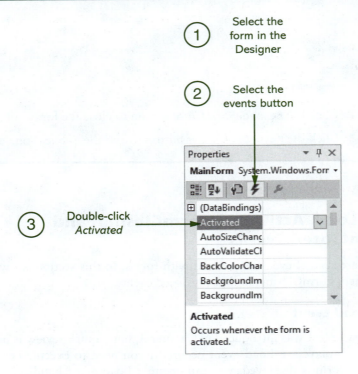

Figure 7-24 Activated event handler procedure

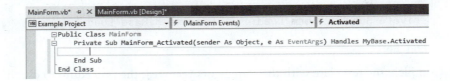

The FormClosing Event

The FormClosing event occurs when a form is in the process of closing, but before it has closed. It might be in response to the Close method being executed, the user pressing the Alt + F4 keys, or the user clicking the standard Windows *Close* button (✕) in the form's upper-right corner. To execute code in response to a form closing, such as asking the user if he or she really wants to close the form, create a **FormClosing event handler**. Here are the required steps:

1. Select a form in the *Designer* window.
2. Select the *Events* button in the *Properties* window toolbar.
3. Double-click the *FormClosing* event name in the *Properties* window.

After completing these steps, a code template for the FormClosing event handler is created in the *Code* window, as shown in the following example. Notice that we have shown the full parameter list that appears inside the event handler's parentheses:

```
Private Sub MainForm_FormClosing(sender As Object,
    e As System.Windows.Forms.FormClosingEventArgs)
    Handles Me.FormClosing

End Sub
```

One of the event handler's parameters is named e. It has a Boolean property named *Cancel*. If you set e.Cancel to *True*, the form will not close. Code showing an example of this technique follows:

```
Private Sub MainForm_FormClosing(sender As Object,
    e As System.Windows.Forms.FormClosingEventArgs)
    Handles Me.FormClosing

    If MessageBox.Show("Are you Sure?", "Confirm",
        MessageBoxButtons.YesNo) = DialogResult.Yes Then
        e.Cancel = False   ' Continue to close the form.
    Else
        e.Cancel = True    ' Do not close the form.
    End If
End Sub
```

The FormClosed Event

The FormClosed event occurs after a form has closed. If you need to execute code immediately after a form has closed, create a **FormClosed event handler** by following these steps:

1. Select a form in the *Designer* window.
2. Select the *Events* button in the *Properties* window toolbar.
3. Double-click the *FormClosed* event name in the *Properties* window.

After completing these steps, a code template for the FormClosed event handler will be created in the *Code* window.

 TIP: You cannot prevent a form from closing with the FormClosed event handler. You must use the FormClosing event handler to prevent a form from closing.

When you use the `Me.Close` method to close an application's startup form, the application fires the FormClosing and FormClosed events.

Accessing Controls on a Different Form

Once you have created an instance of a form, you can access controls on that form in code. For example, suppose an application has a form named GreetingsForm, and GreetingsForm has a Label control named `lblMessage`. The following code shows how you can create an instance of GreetingsForm, assign a value to the `lblMessage` control's Text property, and then display the form in modal style:

```
Dim frmGreetings As New GreetingsForm
frmGreetings.lblMessage.Text = "Good day!"
frmGreetings.ShowDialog()
```

The first statement creates an instance of GreetingsForm and assigns its address to the `frmGreetings` variable. At this point the form exists in memory, but it has not been displayed on the screen. The second statement assigns the string "Good day!" to the `lblMessage` control's Text property. Notice that the control's name is preceded by `frmGreetings`, followed by a dot. This tells Visual Basic that the control is not on the current form, but on the form that is referenced by `frmGreetings`. The third statement calls the form's ShowDialog method to display the form on the screen. When the form appears on the screen, the `lblMessage` control will display the text *Good Day!*

In Tutorial 7-3 you get a chance to create a multiform application in which code on one form creates an instance of another form and assigns values to controls on that form.

Tutorial 7-3:
Accessing a control on a different form

In this tutorial you will create an application that allows the user to select a food from the application's main form, and then display a second form that shows the selected food's nutritional information.

Step 1: Create a new Windows Forms Application project named *Food Facts*.

Step 2: In the *Solution Explorer* window, rename the *Form1.vb* file to *MainForm.vb*. (Right-click *Form1.vb* and then select *Rename* from the pop-up menu.) Changing the form's file name to *MainForm.vb* changes the form's name to `MainForm`. The *Solution Explorer* window should appear as shown in Figure 7-25.

Figure 7-25 *Solution Explorer* after changing *Form1.vb* to *MainForm.vb*

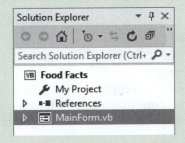

Step 3: In the *Designer* window, set up the `MainForm` form with the controls shown in Figure 7-26.

Figure 7-26 The `MainForm` form

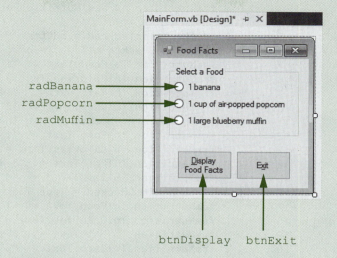

radBanana
radPopcorn
radMuffin

btnDisplay   btnExit

Step 4: Perform the following steps to create another form named `NutritionForm` in the project:

- Click *Project* on the menu bar, and then select *Add Windows Form . . .*
- The *Add New Item* window will appear. Enter *NutritionForm* as the name.
- Click the *Add* button.

Step 5: In the *Designer* window, set up the `NutritionForm` form with the controls shown in Figure 7-27. The Label controls named `lblFood`, `lblCalories`, `lblFat`, and `lblCarb` have the following property settings:

- *AutoSize* is set to *False*
- *BorderStyle* is set to *Fixed3D*

Figure 7-27 The `NutritionForm` form

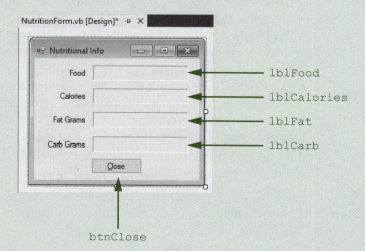

lblFood
lblCalories
lblFat
lblCarb

btnClose

Step 6: Open `MainForm` in the *Designer* window, and double-click the *Display Food Facts* button to create a code template for the button's Click event handler. Complete the event handler by writing the following bold code, shown in lines 2 through 24. (Don't type the line numbers; they are shown for reference.)

```
1 Private Sub btnDisplay_Click(...) Handles btnDisplay.Click
2     ' Create an instance of the NutritionForm.
3     Dim frmNutrition As New NutritionForm
4
5     ' Find the selected radio button.
6     If radBanana.Checked = True Then
7         frmNutrition.lblFood.Text =  "1 banana"
8         frmNutrition.lblCalories.Text =  "100"
9         frmNutrition.lblFat.Text =  "0.4"
10        frmNutrition.lblCarb.Text =  "27"
11    ElseIf radPopcorn.Checked = True Then
12        frmNutrition.lblFood.Text =  "1 cup air-popped popcorn"
13        frmNutrition.lblCalories.Text =  "31"
14        frmNutrition.lblFat.Text =  "0.4"
15        frmNutrition.lblCarb.Text =  "6"
16    ElseIf radMuffin.Checked = True Then
17        frmNutrition.lblFood.Text =  "1 large blueberry muffin"
18        frmNutrition.lblCalories.Text =  "385"
19        frmNutrition.lblFat.Text =  "9"
20        frmNutrition.lblCarb.Text =  "67"
21    End If
22
23    ' Display the NutritionForm.
24    frmNutrition.ShowDialog()
25 End Sub
```

Let's take a closer look at this code. Line 3 creates an instance of the Nutrition-Form form in memory and assigns its address to the frmNutrition variable. Keep in mind that although the form has been created in memory, it has not yet been displayed on the screen.

The If...Then statement in line 6 determines whether the radBanana radio button is selected. If so, the statements in lines 7 through 10 use the frmNutrition variable to assign values to the Label controls on the NutritionForm form. The values that are assigned are the nutritional values for a banana.

If the radBanana radio button is not selected, the ElseIf...Then clause in line 11 determines whether the radPopcorn radio button is selected. If so, the statements in lines 12 through 15 use the frmNutrition variable to assign values to the Label controls on the NutritionForm. The assigned values are the nutritional values for one cup of air-popped popcorn.

If neither the radBanana nor the radPopcorn radio button is selected, the ElseIf...Then clause in line 16 determines whether the radMuffin radio button is selected. If so, the statements in lines 17 through 20 use the frmNutrition variable to assign values to the Label controls on the NutritionForm. The values that are assigned are the nutritional values for one large blueberry muffin.

Line 24 uses the frmNutrition variable to call the form's ShowDialog method. When this statement executes, it will display the NutritionForm form on the screen in modal style.

Step 7: Create the following Click event handler for the MainForm form's btnExit button:

```
Private Sub btnExit_Click(...) Handles btnExit.Click
    ' Close the form.
    Me.Close()
End Sub
```

Step 8: Open NutritionForm in the *Designer* window, and double-click the *Close* button to create a code template for the button's Click event handler. Complete the event handler by writing the following bold code:

```
          Private Sub btnClose_Click(...) Handles btnClose.Click
              ' Close the form.
              Me.Close()
          End Sub
```

Step 9: Save the project and then run it. The `MainForm` should appear, as shown on the left in Figure 7-28. With the *1 banana* radio button selected, click the *Display Food Facts* button. The `NutritionForm` form should appear, as shown on the right in Figure 7-28.

 NOTE: Some early releases of Visual Studio 2015 have a bug that will cause the following error when you compile the project in Step 9: *'Form1' is not a member of 'Food Facts'*. If you see this error message, download the document titled **Startup Form Issue in VS2015** from this book's companion Web site for a simple solution. The companion Web site is at www.pearsonhighered.com/gaddisvb.

Figure 7-28 The `MainForm` and the `NutritionForm` forms displayed

Step 10: On the `NutritionForm` form, click the *Close* button. This should close the `NutritionForm` form. Try selecting the other radio buttons on the `MainForm` form and clicking the *Display Food Facts* button to see each item's nutritional information. When you are finished, click the *Exit* button on the `MainForm` form to end the application.

Class-Level Variables in a Form

Although a form's class-level variables are accessible to all statements in the form's class, they are not accessible by default to statements outside the form's class. For example, assume a project has a form named `AmountForm`, which has the following class-level variable declaration:

```
Dim dblTotal As Double          ' Class-level variable
```

The same project has another form that uses the following statements:

```
Dim frmAmount As New AmountForm
frmAmount.dblTotal = 100.0
```

Although the assignment statement has fully qualified the name of `dblTotal` by preceding it with the object variable name, the statement still cannot access it because class-level variables are private by default. The statement will cause an error when the project is compiled.

It is possible to make a class-level variable available to methods outside the class. This is done using the **Public** keyword. Here is an example:

```
Public dblTotal As Double          ' Class-level variable
```

Although class-level variables are automatically declared private by the `Dim` statement, you should explicitly declare them private with the **Private** keyword. Here is an example:

```
Private dblTotal As Double
```

NOTE: Class-level variables are usually declared `Private` unless a strong reason exists to do otherwise. Private variables help support an object-oriented design principle named *encapsulation*. This means to keep (or hide) information inside the class that does not need to be visible by the rest of the program.

Using `Private` and `Public` **Procedures in a Form**

Recall from Chapter 6 that a procedure or function may begin with an optional access specifier, such as `Public` or `Private`. When a procedure is labeled `Private`, it may be executed only by statements in the same form. When a procedure is labeled `Public`, it may also be executed by statements that are outside the form. If you do not provide an access specifier, the procedure defaults to `Public`. In projects that use multiple forms, you should always make the procedures in a form private unless you specifically want statements outside the form to execute the procedure.

Using a Form in More Than One Project

Once you create a form, you do not have to re-create it to use it in another project. After a form has been saved to a file, it may be used in other projects. Follow these steps to add an existing form to a project:

1. With the receiving project open in Visual Studio, click *Project* on the menu bar, and then click *Add Existing Item*.
2. The *Add Existing Item* dialog box appears. Use the dialog box to locate the form file that you want to add to the project. (Remember that form files end with the *.vb* extension.) When you locate the file, select it and click the *Open* button. A copy of the form is now added to the project and copied into your project's folder.

Checkpoint

7.1 How do you cause a form to be displayed automatically when your application executes?

7.2 What prefix do we use in this book when naming variables that will reference forms?

7.3 Describe the process of adding a new form to a project.

7.4 In Visual Studio only, describe the process of excluding a form from a project.

7.5 What is a form file? What file extension does a form file have?

7.6 What is the difference between a modal form and a modeless form?

7.7 Suppose a project has an object variable named `frmResults`, which references an instance of a form. Write the statement that uses the `frmResults` variable to display the form in modal style.

7.8 Write a statement that displays the form referenced by `frmResults` in modeless style.

7.9 In which event handler do you write code if you want it to execute when the user switches to a form from another form or from another application?

7.10 Suppose a project has a form named `InfoForm` with a label named `lblCustomer`. The following declaration statement appears in the `MainForm` form:

```
Dim frmInfo As New InfoForm
```

The frmInfo variable references an instance of InfoForm. Write a statement that uses the frmInfo variable to copy the string *Jim Jones* to the lblCustomer Label control on the InfoForm form.

7.11 What is the Me keyword used for?

7.12 Suppose you want to declare a class-level variable of the Double data type named dblAverage in a form. Assuming you want code in other forms to access it, write the variable declaration.

7.2 Modules

CONCEPT: A module contains code—declarations and procedures—that are used by other files in a project.

When you create a large application with multiple forms, quite often you will find that the code in several different forms needs to call the same function or procedure. For example, suppose you are creating an application for a retail business and in one of the application's forms you write a function that calculates the sales tax on a purchase. Later you discover that event handlers in several other forms need to call the same function. Do you duplicate the sales tax function in each of the forms that need to call it? That's one approach. A better approach, however, is to store the sales tax function in some location where all the forms can access it. Then you can reduce the amount of duplicated code and make it easier to maintain the application if you ever need to modify the sales tax function. In Visual Basic, such a location is known as a module.

A **module** is a Visual Basic file that contains only code. That is to say, it contains only procedures, functions, and declarations of variables and constants. Any Public procedures, functions, and declarations that appear in a module are global, which means they are accessible to all of the forms in the same project. Module files use the *.vb* extension. When a module is added to a project, its name appears in the *Solution Explorer* along with the entries for the project's form files.

NOTE: You do not write event handlers in a module. Modules only contain general-purpose procedures, functions, and declarations that are available to all forms in a project.

Module Names and Module Files

The content of a module begins with a Module statement and ends with an End Module statement. The general format follows:

```
Module ModuleName
   [Module Contents]
End Module
```

ModuleName is the name of the module. This can be any valid identifier. If you have only one module in your project you should give it a name that clearly relates it to the project. For example, if a project is named *Order Entry*, then its module might be named OrderEntryModule. It is possible to have multiple modules in a project. For example, you might have one module containing math procedures and another module containing procedures for retrieving information from a database. If your project has multiple modules, give each module a name that describes its purpose.

When you create a module, its code is stored in a file named with the *.vb* extension. Normally, the name of the file is the same as the name of the module. Therefore, a module named `OrderEntryModule` should be saved to the file *OrderEntryModule.vb*.

Let's look at a sample module. The following code shows the contents of a module named `RetailMath`. (The line numbers are not part of the module. They are shown only for reference.)

```
1 Module RetailMath
2     ' Global constant for the tax rate
3     Public Const decTAX_RATE As Decimal = 0.07D
4
5     ' The SalesTax function returns the sales tax on a purchase.
6     Public Function SalesTax(ByVal decPurchase As Decimal) As Decimal
7         Return decPurchase * decTAX_RATE
8     End Function
9 End Module
```

Line 3 declares a module-level constant named `decTAX_RATE`. (It's module-level because it is not declared inside any procedure or function.) Notice that the declaration begins with the word `Public`. This means that the constant is accessible to code outside the module. As a result, the code in any form in the same project has access to this constant.

In lines 6 through 8 a function named `SalesTax` appears. Notice that the function header in line 6 also begins with the word `Public`. This means that the function can be called by code outside the module. As a result, the code in any form in the same project may call this function.

Procedures, functions, and declarations can be declared as `Private`, which means that they can be accessed only by code in the same module.

Adding a Module

Follow these steps to add a module to a project.

1. Click *Project* on the menu bar and then click *Add Module....* The *Add New Item* window shown in Figure 7-29 should appear. Notice that in the figure, the name

Figure 7-29 *Add New Item* dialog box

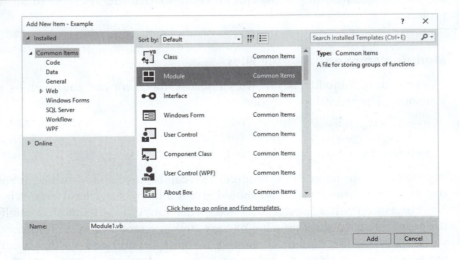

Module1.vb appears in the *Name* text box. In this example, *Module1.vb* is the default name for the file that the module will be stored in, and *Module1* is the default name for the module.

> **NOTE:** The default name may be different, depending on the number of modules already in the project.

2. Change the default name that is displayed in the *Name* text box to the name you wish to give the new module file. For example, if you wish to name the new module `MainModule`, enter *MainModule.vb* in the *Name* text box.
3. Click the *Add* button.

> **NOTE:** When you name the module file, be sure to keep the *.vb* extension.

A new, empty module will be added to your project. The module is displayed in the *Code* window, and an entry for the new module appears in the *Solution Explorer* window. The *Solution Explorer* window in Figure 7-30 shows two forms and one module: `ErrorForm`, `MainForm`, and `ExampleProjectModule`.

Figure 7-30 *Solution Explorer* window showing two forms and one module

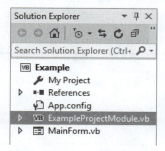

Once you have added a module to your project, you type code directly into it using the *Code* window.

Module-Level Variables

A variable declared inside a module, but not inside a procedure or function, is called a **module-level variable**. The same rules about the scope of class-level variables in a form apply to module-level variables in a module.

- A module-level variable in a module is accessible to any procedure or function in the module.
- If a module-level variable is declared with the `Dim` or `Private` keyword, the variable is not accessible to statements outside the module. Such a variable has **module scope**.
- If a module-level variable is declared with the `Public` keyword, it is accessible to statements outside the module.

A module-level variable declared `Public` is also known as a **global variable** because it can be accessed globally, by any statement in the application.

> **TIP:** Some programmers prefix the names of global variables with the characters `g_`. This documents the variable's scope. For example, a global Decimal variable that holds the amount of a purchase might be named `g_decPurchaseAmount`.

TIP: Although global variables provide an easy way to share data among procedures, forms, and modules, they should be used with caution. While debugging an application, if you find that the wrong value is being stored in a global variable, you will have to track down every statement that accesses it to determine where the bad value is coming from. Also, when two or more procedures modify the same variable, you must be careful that one procedure's actions do not upset the correctness of another procedure.

Tutorial 7-4 examines an application that uses a module.

Tutorial 7-4:
Examining an application that uses a module

In this tutorial you will examine the *Converter* application, which performs simple conversions between metric and English units. The application has three forms and a module that contains all of the conversion functions.

Step 1: Open the *Converter* project from the student sample programs folder named *Chap7\Converter*.

Step 2: Before we examine the application's code, let's see it in action. Run the application. The main form appears, as shown in Figure 7-31.

Figure 7-31 The application's main form

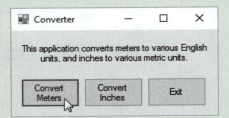

Step 3: Click the *Convert Meters* button. The *Meters To English* form appears, as shown on the right in Figure 7-32. This form has a TextBox for you to enter a number of meters. Enter a number in the TextBox, and then click the *Convert to Inches* button. A message box appears showing the equivalent number of inches. Close the message box, and then try the *Convert to Feet* and *Convert to Yards* buttons. When you are finished, click the *Close* button to close the *Meters To English* form.

Figure 7-32 The application's main form and the *Meters To English* form

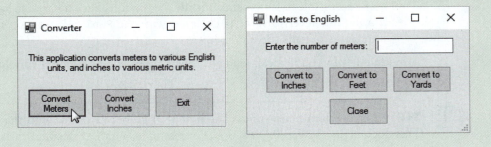

Step 4: Back on the main form, click the *Convert Inches* button. The *Inches To Metric* form appears, as shown on the right in Figure 7-33. This form has a TextBox for you to enter a number of inches. Enter a number in the TextBox, and then click the *Convert to Millimeters* button. A message box appears showing the equivalent number of millimeters. Close the message box, and then try the *Convert to Centimeters* and *Convert to Meters* buttons. When you are finished click the *Close* button to close the *Inches To Metric* form.

Figure 7-33 The application's main form and the *Inches To Metric* form

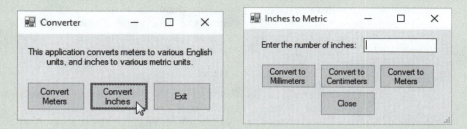

Step 5: Back on the application's main form, click the *Exit* button to end the application.

Step 6: Look in the *Solution Explorer*, as shown in Figure 7-34, and notice that the project has the following *.vb* files:

- *InchesToMetricForm.vb*–This is the form file for the form named `InchesToMetricForm`.
- *MainForm.vb*–This is the form file for the form named `MainForm`.
- *MathModule.vb*–This is a module file that contains functions and constants for the mathematical conversions.
- *MetersToEnglishForm.vb*–This is the form file for the form named `MetersToEnglishForm`.

Figure 7-34 *Solution Explorer*

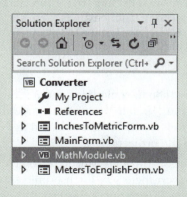

Step 7: Double-click the entry for *MathModule.vb* in the *Solution Explorer*. This opens the *MathModule.vb* file in the *Code* window. The file's contents are shown here, with line numbers added for reference:

```
1 Module MathModule
2     ' Constants for the meters to English conversion factors
3     Public Const dblMETERS_TO_INCHES As Double = 39.37
4     Public Const dblMETERS_TO_FEET As Double = 3.28
5     Public Const dblMETERS_TO_YARDS As Double = 1.09
6
```

```
 7    ' Constants for the inches to metric conversion factors
 8    Public Const dblINCHES_TO_MM As Double = 25.4
 9    Public Const dblINCHES_TO_CM As Double = 2.54
10    Public Const dblINCHES_TO_METERS As Double = 0.0254
11
12    ' The MetersToInches function accepts a number of meters as
13    ' an argument and returns the equivalent number of inches.
14    Public Function MetersToInches(ByVal dblMeters As Double) As Double
15        Return dblMeters * dblMETERS_TO_INCHES
16    End Function
17
18    ' The MetersToFeet function accepts a number of meters as
19    ' an argument and returns the equivalent number of feet.
20    Public Function MetersToFeet(ByVal dblMeters As Double) As Double
21        Return dblMeters * dblMETERS_TO_FEET
22    End Function
23
24    ' The MetersToYards function accepts a number of meters as
25    ' an argument and returns the equivalent number of yards.
26    Public Function MetersToYards(ByVal dblMeters As Double) As Double
27        Return dblMeters * dblMETERS_TO_YARDS
28    End Function
29
30    ' The InchesToMM function accepts a number of inches as
31    ' an argument and returns the equivalent number of millimeters.
32    Public Function InchesToMM(ByVal dblInches As Double) As Double
33        Return dblInches * dblINCHES_TO_MM
34    End Function
35
36    ' The InchesToCM function accepts a number of inches as
37    ' an argument and returns the equivalent number of centimeters.
38    Public Function InchesToCM(ByVal dblInches As Double) As Double
39        Return dblInches * dblINCHES_TO_CM
40    End Function
41
42    ' The InchesToMeters function accepts a number of inches as
43    ' an argument and returns the equivalent number of meters.
44    Public Function InchesToMeters(ByVal dblInches As Double) As Double
45        Return dblInches * dblINCHES_TO_METERS
46    End Function
47 End Module
```

The MathModule module contains all of the code for the application's conversion functions. A summary of the code follows. Note that all of the constants and functions in the file are declared as Public, which makes them globally accessible in the project.

- Lines 3 through 5 declare some constants that are used in the formulas to convert meters to English units.
- Lines 8 through 10 declare some constants that are used in the formulas to convert inches to metric units.
- The MetersToInches function appears in lines 14 through 16. This function accepts a number of meters as an argument and returns the equivalent number of inches.
- The MetersToFeet function appears in lines 20 through 22. This function accepts a number of meters as an argument and returns the equivalent number of feet.

- The `MetersToYards` function appears in lines 26 through 28. This function accepts a number of meters as an argument and returns the equivalent number of yards.
- The `InchestoMM` function appears in lines 32 through 34. This function accepts a number of inches as an argument and returns the equivalent number of millimeters.
- The `InchesToCM` function appears in lines 38 through 40. This function accepts a number of inches as an argument and returns the equivalent number of centimeters.
- The `InchesToMeters` function appears in lines 44 through 46. This function accepts a number of inches as an argument and returns the equivalent number of meters.

Step 8: Now let's see how the functions in *MathModule.vb* are called by statements in the application's forms. Open the form `MetersToEnglishForm` in the *Code* window. (A fast way to do this is to right-click *MetersToEnglish.vb* in the *Solution Explorer*, and then select *View Code* from the pop-up menu.)

Figure 7-35 shows the `btnMetersToInches_Click` event handler. Notice the statement that calls the `MetersToInches` function, which is stored in the *MathModule.vb* file.

Figure 7-35 A call to the `MetersToInches` function

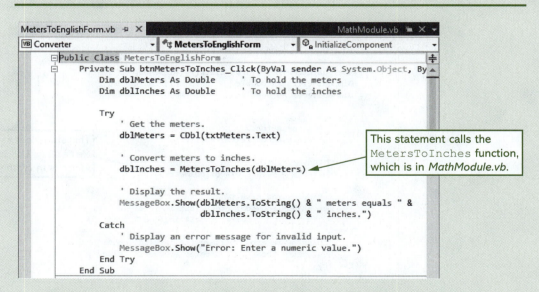

Scroll down to the the `btnMetersToFeet_Click` event handler, which is shown in Figure 7-36. Notice the statement that calls the `MetersToFeet` function, which is stored in the *MathModule.vb* file.

Now scroll down to the the `btnMetersToYards_Click` event handler, which is shown in Figure 7-37. Notice the statement that calls the `MetersToYards` function, which is stored in the *MathModule.vb* file.

Figure 7-36 A call to the `MetersToFeet` function

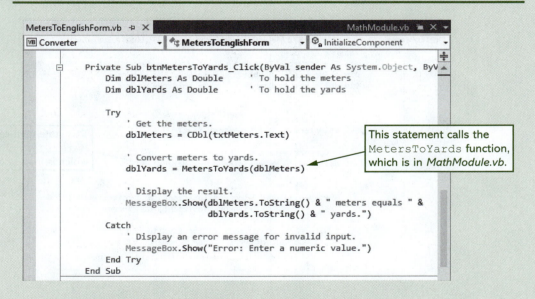

```vb
Private Sub btnMetersToFeet_Click(ByVal sender As System.Object, ByVa
    Dim dblMeters As Double    ' To hold the meters
    Dim dblFeet As Double      ' To hold the feet

    Try
        ' Get the meters.
        dblMeters = CDbl(txtMeters.Text)

        ' Convert meters to feet.
        dblFeet = MetersToFeet(dblMeters)

        ' Display the result.
        MessageBox.Show(dblMeters.ToString() & " meters equals " &
                        dblFeet.ToString() & " feet.")
    Catch
        ' Display an error message for invalid input.
        MessageBox.Show("Error: Enter a numeric value.")
    End Try
End Sub
```

> This statement calls the `MetersToFeet` function, which is in *MathModule.vb*.

Figure 7-37 A call to the `MetersToYards` function

```vb
Private Sub btnMetersToYards_Click(ByVal sender As System.Object, ByV
    Dim dblMeters As Double    ' To hold the meters
    Dim dblYards As Double     ' To hold the yards

    Try
        ' Get the meters.
        dblMeters = CDbl(txtMeters.Text)

        ' Convert meters to yards.
        dblYards = MetersToYards(dblMeters)

        ' Display the result.
        MessageBox.Show(dblMeters.ToString() & " meters equals " &
                        dblYards.ToString() & " yards.")
    Catch
        ' Display an error message for invalid input.
        MessageBox.Show("Error: Enter a numeric value.")
    End Try
End Sub
```

> This statement calls the `MetersToYards` function, which is in *MathModule.vb*.

Step 9: Now let's see how the functions in *MathModule.vb* are called by statements in the `InchesToMetricForm` form. Open the form `InchesToMetricForm` in the *Code* window. At the top of the file you should see the `btnInchesToMM_Click` event handler as shown in Figure 7-38. Notice the statement that calls the `InchesToMM` function, which is stored in the *MathModule.vb* file.

Figure 7-38 A call to the `InchesToMM` function

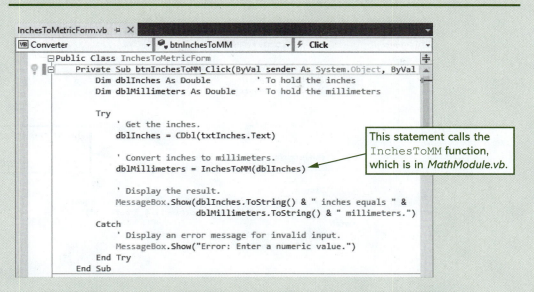

Scroll down to the the `btnInchesToCM_Click` event handler, which is shown in Figure 7-39. Notice the statement that calls the `InchesToCM` function, which is stored in the *MathModule.vb* file.

Figure 7-39 A call to the `InchesToCM` function

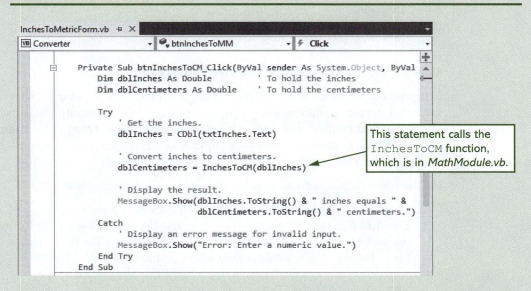

Now scroll down to the the `btnInchesToMeters_Click` event handler, which is shown in Figure 7-40. Notice the statement that calls the `InchesToMeters` function, which is stored in the *MathModule.vb* file.

Figure 7-40 A call to the `InchesToMeters` function

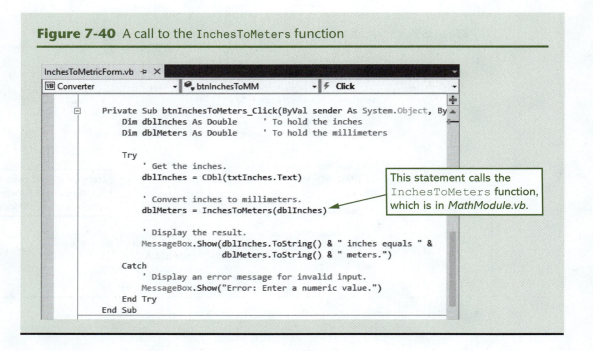

This statement calls the `InchesToMeters` function, which is in *MathModule.vb*.

NOTE: It's worth pointing out that the *Converter* application uses the *MathModule.vb* file not only for sharing common functions between two forms, but it is also for organizing all of the mathematical functions together, in the same module. It's possible to have multiple modules in the same application, with each module containing related procedures, functions, and declarations.

Using a Module in More Than One Project

It is possible to use a module in more than one project. For example, suppose you have created a project with a module that contains several commonly used math functions. Later, you find yourself working on a new project that needs many of the same functions. Instead of rewriting the functions (or copying and pasting them), you can simply add the module to the new project.

Follow these steps to add an existing standard module to a project.

1. Click *Project* on the menu bar, and then click *Add Existing Item*.
2. The *Add Existing Item* dialog box appears. Use the dialog box to locate the module file you want to add to the project. When you locate the file, select it and click the *Open* button. The module is now added to the project.

 **Checkpoint**

7.13 What do modules contain?

7.14 With what file extension are modules saved?

7.15 Describe the steps you take to add a new module to a project.

7.16 How can modules be used to organize code in a multiform project?

7.17 How do you add an existing module to a project?

7.3 Menus

CONCEPT: Visual Basic allows you to create a system of drop-down menus for any form in your application. You use the menu designer to create a menu system.

VideoNote

Creating
a Menu

In the applications you have studied so far, the user performs tasks primarily by clicking buttons. When an application has several operations for the user to choose from, a menu system is more commonly used than buttons. A **menu system** is a collection of commands organized in one or more drop-down menus. The **menu designer** allows you to visually create a custom menu system for any form in an application.

Before you learn how to use the menu designer, you must learn about the typical components of a menu system. Look at the Example Menu System shown in Figure 7-41.

Figure 7-41 Example Menu System

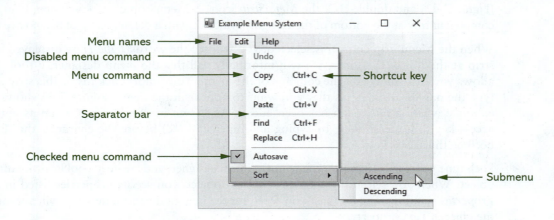

The menu system in the figure consists of the following items.

- **Menu names**—Each drop-down menu has a name. The menu names are listed on a menu strip that appears just below the form's title bar. The menu names in Figure 7-41 are *File*, *Edit*, and *Help*. The user may activate a menu by clicking the menu name. In the figure, the *Edit* menu has been activated. Menu items may also be assigned access keys (such as <u>F</u> for File, <u>E</u> for Edit, and <u>H</u> for Help). The user may also activate a menu by entering ⟮Alt⟯ + its access key.
- **Menu command**—Menus have commands. The user selects a command by clicking it, entering its access key, or entering its shortcut key.
- **Shortcut key**—A **shortcut key** is a key or combination of keys that causes a menu command to execute. Shortcut keys are shown on a menu to the right of their corresponding commands. For example, in Figure 7-41, ⟮Ctrl⟯+⟮C⟯ is the shortcut key for the *Copy* command. Here is the primary difference between a shortcut key and an access key: a menu command's access key works only while the menu is open, but a shortcut key may be executed at any time while the form is active.
- **Disabled menu command**—You can cause a menu command to be disabled when you do not want the user to select it. A disabled menu command appears in dim lettering (grayed out) and cannot be selected. In Figure 7-41, the *Undo* command is disabled.
- **Checked menu command**—A checked menu command is usually one that turns an option on or off. A check mark appears to the left of the command, indicating the

option is turned on. When no check mark appears to the left of the command, the option is turned off. The user toggles a checked menu command each time he or she selects it. In Figure 7-41, *Autosave* is a checked menu command.

- **Submenu**—Some of the commands on a menu are actually the names of submenus. You can tell when a command is the name of a submenu because a right arrow (▸) appears to its right. Activating the name of a submenu causes the submenu to appear. For example, in Figure 7-41, clicking the *Sort* command causes a submenu to appear.
- **Separator bar**—A **separator bar** is a horizontal bar used to separate groups of commands on a menu. In Figure 7-41, separator bars are used to separate the *Copy*, *Cut*, and *Paste* commands into one group, the *Find* and *Replace* commands into another group, and the *Sort* command in a box by itself. Separator bars are used only as visual aids and cannot be selected by the user.

The MenuStrip Control

An application's menu system is constructed with a **MenuStrip control**. When your form is displayed in the *Designer* window, find the *Menus & Toolbars* section of the *Toolbox* window (Figure 7-42) and double-click the *MenuStrip* icon. A MenuStrip control will appear in the component tray at the bottom of the *Designer* window, with a default name of MenuStrip1.

When the MenuStrip control is selected, you will see the words *Type Here* displayed in a strip at the top of the form. We will informally call this the **menu designer**, a tool that allows you to visually edit the contents of the menu. You simply click inside this strip and type the names of the items that you want to appear in the menu. Figure 7-43 shows an example where a *File* menu has been added. As shown in the figure, you can assign an access key to a menu name by typing an ampersand (&) before the character that is to become the access key.

Each time you add an item to a menu in the menu designer, you create a **ToolStripMenuItem object**. When you select a ToolStripMenuItem object, you see its properties listed in the *Properties* window. The text that you typed for the item in the menu designer will appear in the object's Text property.

ToolStripMenuItem objects are given default names (stored in their Name properties) when they are created, but it is recommended that you change these names to reflect each item's position in the menu system hierarchy. For example, look at the menu system sketch in Figure 7-44. Table 7-1 lists the recommended names of this menu system's ToolStripMenuItem objects, along with the contents of their Text properties.

Figure 7-42 *Menus & Toolbars* section of the *Toolbox*

Figure 7-43 Inserting text into a menu item

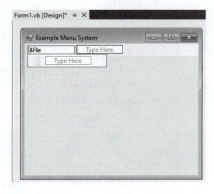

Figure 7-44 Example menu system sketch

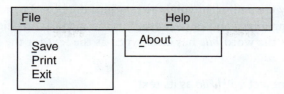

Table 7-1 ToolStripMenuItem objects and their Text properties

ToolStripMenuItem Name	Text Property
mnuFile	&File
mnuFileSave	&Save
mnuFilePrint	&Print
mnuFileExit	E&xit
mnuHelp	&Help
mnuHelpAbout	&About

The menu item names listed in Table 7-1 indicate where in the menu hierarchy each control belongs. The names of objects corresponding to commands on the *File* menu all begin with mnuFile. For example, the *Save* command on the *File* menu is named mnuFileSave. Likewise, the object for the *About* command on the *Help* menu is named mnuHelpAbout.

ToolStripMenuItem objects also respond to events. You can make a menu functional by writing Click event procedures for its objects.

How to Use the Menu Designer

Once you have placed a MenuStrip control in a form's component tray, you can use the menu designer to create menu items. Start the menu designer by selecting the MenuStrip control. Figure 7-45 shows a form with a MenuStrip control selected in the component tray, and the menu designer started. The designer appears on the form in the location that the menu system will appear.

Figure 7-45 MenuStrip control selected and menu designer started

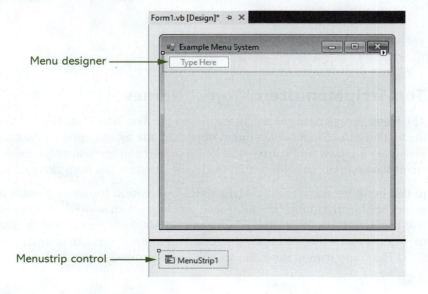

Notice in Figure 7-45 that the words *Type Here* appear in a small box in the menu designer. This marks the position of the first menu item. A ToolStripMenuItem object is automatically created when you type text into the box. The text you type is stored in the item's Text property and is displayed on the menu strip. Figure 7-46 shows the menu designer after the word *File* has been typed as the text for the first menu item.

Figure 7-46 MenuStrip object with *File* as its text

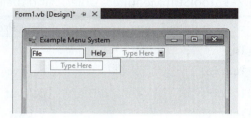

Notice that the menu designer now shows two new *Type Here* boxes, one below and one to the right of the first object. Simply click in one of the boxes to select it, and then type the text that you wish to appear at that position.

Figure 7-47 shows the menu designer with a more complete menu system. The menu system has *File*, *Edit*, and *Help* menus. The *Edit* menu is displayed.

Figure 7-47 Menu designer with many items

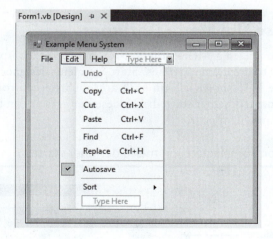

ToolStripMenuItem Object Names

The menu designer assigns default names to the ToolStripMenuItem objects as you create them. You can change a menu item object's name by changing its Name property in the *Properties* window. In Figure 7-48, the *Properties* window shows the properties of a ToolStripMenuItem object. Notice that the Name property has been changed to mnuEditCopy.

In this book we use a hierarchical naming convention for menu items. For example, the names of all entries under the *File* menu will begin with *mnuFile*. Entries in the *Edit* menu will begin with *mnuEdit*. Individual items within these menus will dictate the remaining part of the name. For example, the *Exit* item in the *File* menu is usually named *mnuFileExit*. The *Copy* item in the *Edit* menu is usually named *mnuEditCopy*.

Figure 7-48 *Properties* window showing a ToolStripMenuItem object's properties

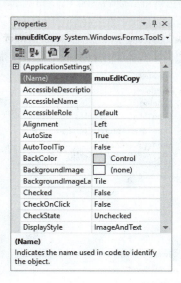

Shortcut Keys

As previously stated, a shortcut key is a key or combination of keys that causes a menu command to execute. Table 7-2 lists some commonly used shortcut keys in Windows applications.

Table 7-2 Some commonly used shortcut keys in Windows applications

Shortcut Key	Command
Ctrl + S	Save
Ctrl + P	Print
Ctrl + C	Copy
Ctrl + X	Cut
Ctrl + V or Shift + Insert	Paste

Shortcut keys are shown on a menu to the right of their corresponding commands. To create a shortcut key for a menu item, click the down arrow that appears next to the **Shortcut-Keys property** in the *Properties* window. A dialog appears as shown in Figure 7-49. The *Key* drop-down list shows all the available shortcut keys and allows you to select a key from the list. The dialog also allows you to select the Ctrl, Shift, or Alt key (or any combination of these). For example, if you want to assign Ctrl + S as a shortcut key, you would select the S key in the drop-down list and place a check next to Ctrl.

You must also make sure that the **ShowShortcut property** is set to *True*. When set to *False*, the item's shortcut key will not be displayed.

Checked Menu Items

Some programs have menu items that simply turn a feature on or off. For example, suppose you are creating an application that functions as an alarm clock, and you want the

Figure 7-49 Setting a shortcut key

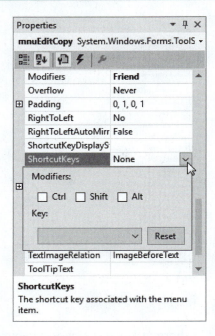

user to be able to turn the alarm on or off with a menu item. A common approach would be to have a checked menu item for the alarm. When a check mark appears next to the menu item, it indicates that the alarm is on. When the check mark is not displayed next to the menu item, it indicates that the alarm is off. When the user clicks the menu item, it toggles its state between on and off. This type of menu item is called a checked menu item.

To give a menu item the ability to become checked or unchecked when it is clicked by the user, you set the item's **CheckOnClick property** to *True*. You can then set the **Checked property** to either *True* or *False* to specify how the item should initially appear when the application runs. If you set the Checked property to *True*, the item will appear with a check mark next to it. If you set the Checked property to *False*, no check mark will be shown.

In code you can use the Checked property to determine whether a menu item is checked. If the Checked property is set to *True*, it means the item is checked. If the Checked property is set to *False*, it means the item is unchecked. The following code shows an example. This code tests the Checked property of a menu item named `mnuSettingsAlarm`. If the item is checked, a message box is displayed.

```
If mnuSettingsAlarm.Checked = True Then
    MessageBox.Show("WAKE UP!")
End If
```

Disabled Menu Items

A disabled menu item appears dimmed, or *grayed out*, and may not be selected by the user. You may disable a menu item by setting its Enabled property to *False*. For example, applications that provide *Cut*, *Copy*, and *Paste* commands usually disable the *Paste* command until something is cut or copied. So, the *Paste* menu item's Enabled property can be set to *False* at design time (in the *Properties* window) and then set to *True* in code after the *Cut* and *Copy* commands have been used. Assuming that the *Paste* menu item is named `mnuEditPaste`, the following code enables it:

```
mnuEditPaste.Enabled = True
```

Separator Bars

You can insert a separator bar into a menu in either of the following ways:

- Right-click an existing menu item. On the pop-up menu that appears, select *Insert*, and then select *Separator*. A separator bar will be inserted above the menu item.
- Type a hyphen (–) as a menu item's Text property.

Submenus

When an existing menu item is selected in the menu designer, a *Type Here* box is displayed to its right. Figure 7-50 shows an example. This box allows you to create a submenu item. When you create a submenu, a right arrow (▶) will automatically be displayed next to the menu item that is the parent of the submenu.

Figure 7-50 Creating a submenu

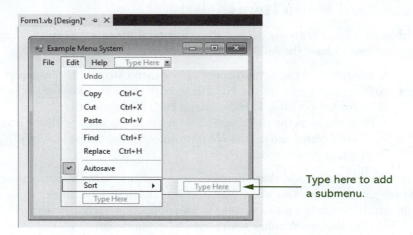

Type here to add a submenu.

Inserting Menu Items in an Existing Menu

If you need to insert a new menu item above an existing menu item, start the menu designer and then right-click the existing menu item. On the pop-up menu that appears, select *Insert*, and then select *MenuItem*. A new menu item will be inserted above the existing menu item.

If you need to insert a new menu item at the bottom of an existing menu, start the menu designer and simply select the desired menu or submenu. A *Type Here* box automatically appears at the bottom.

Deleting Menu Items

To delete a menu item, start the menu designer and perform one of the following procedures:

- Right-click the menu item you wish to delete. On the pop-up menu, select *Delete*.
- Select the menu item you wish to delete, and then press the Delete key.

Rearranging Menu Items

You can move a menu item by clicking and dragging. Simply select it in the menu designer and drag it to the desired location.

ToolStripMenuItem Click Event

You do not have to write code to display a menu or a submenu. When the user clicks a menu item that displays a menu or a submenu, Visual Basic automatically causes the menu or submenu to appear.

If a menu item does not have a menu or submenu to display, you make it functional by providing a Click event procedure for it. For example, assume a menu system has a *File* menu with an *Exit* command, which causes the application to end. The menu item for the *Exit* command is named mnuFileExit. Here is the code for the object's Click event procedure:

```
Private Sub mnuFileExit_Click(...) Handles mnuFileExit.Click
  ' Close the form.
  Me.Close()
End Sub
```

To write a Click event procedure for a menu item, start the menu designer, then double-click the desired menu item. A code template for the Click event procedure will be created.

Standard Menu Items

Although all applications do not have identical menu systems, it is standard for most applications to have the following menu items:

- A *File* menu as the leftmost item on the menu strip, with the access key Alt+F.
- An *Exit* command on the *File* menu, with the access key Alt+X and optionally the shortcut key Alt+Q. This command ends the application.
- A *Help* menu as the rightmost item on the menu strip, with the access key Alt+H.
- An *About* command on the *Help* menu, with the access key Alt+A. This command displays an *About* box.

You should always add these items to your menu systems because most Windows users expect to see them. You should also assign shortcut keys to the most commonly used commands. Study the menu system in an application such as Microsoft Word or Microsoft Excel to become familiar with a typical menu design.

In Tutorial 7-5, you learn to use the menu designer by building a simple menu system.

Tutorial 7-5:
Building a menu

In this tutorial, you create an application that demonstrates how a label appears in different colors. You build a menu system that allows the user to select a color, which is then applied to a Label control. Figure 7-51 shows a sketch of the menu system.

Figure 7-51 Sketch of menu system

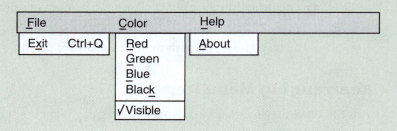

Step 1: Create a new Windows Forms Application project named *Menu Demo*.

Step 2: Change the form's Text property to *Menu Demo*. Place a label named **lblMessage** on the form and set its *Text* property to *Hello World!*, as shown in Figure 7-52.

Step 3: Double-click the *MenuStrip* tool in the *Toolbox* to add a MenuStrip control to the form.

   The control, which appears in the component tray, should be selected. If it is not, select it. The menu designer should now be running, as shown in Figure 7-53.

Figure 7-52 *Menu Demo* form

Figure 7-53 Form with menu designer running

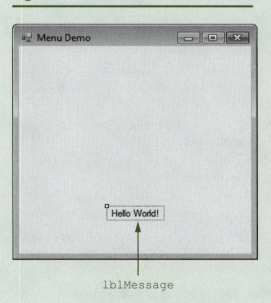

lblMessage

Step 4: First, you will create the *File* menu item. In the *Type Here* box, type **&File**. Press the Enter key to create the object. The text *File* should now appear on the menu strip.

Step 5: Set the Name property for the menu item you just created. Use the mouse to select the word *File* on the menu. The menu item's properties should be displayed in the *Properties* window. Change the Name property to **mnuFile**.

Step 6: Next, you will create the *Exit* menu item on the *File* menu. Use the mouse to select the *Type Here* box below the *File* menu item. Type **E&xit** and press Enter to create the object. The text *Exit* should now appear on the *File* menu, as shown in Figure 7-54.

Step 7: Next, you must set the properties for the menu item you just created. Use the mouse to select the word *Exit*. The menu item's properties should be displayed in the *Properties* window. Change the Name property to **mnuFileExit**. In the ShortcutKeys property select Ctrl+Q.

Step 8: Now you are ready to add the *Color* menu item. In the *Type Here* box shown in Figure 7-55 type **&Color** and press Enter.

Figure 7-54 *Exit* menu item created

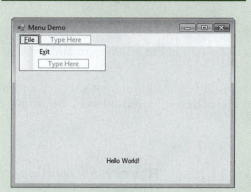

Figure 7-55 Where to type &Color

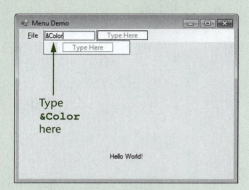

Step 9: Set the Name property for the menu item you just created. Use the mouse to select the word *Color* on the menu. The menu item's properties should be displayed in the *Properties* window. Change the Name property to **mnuColor**.

Step 10: Next, you will add the first four menu items to the *Color* menu. Below the **mnuColor** menu item, add an object whose Text reads **&Red** and whose Name property is **mnuColorRed**.

Below the **mnuColorRed** object, add an object whose Text reads **&Green** and whose Name property is **mnuColorGreen**.

Below the **mnuColorGreen** object, add an object whose Text reads **&Blue** and whose Name property is **mnuColorBlue**.

Below the **mnuColorBlue** object, add an object whose Text reads **Blac&k** and whose Name property is **mnuColorBlack**.

Step 11: The menu sketch shown in Figure 7-51 (displayed earlier) shows a separator bar just below the word *Black* on the *Color* menu. Create the separator bar by typing a hyphen (–) in the *Type Here* box below the **mnuColorBlack** object.

Step 12: Below the separator bar, add an object whose Text reads **Visible** and whose Name property is **mnuColorVisible**. This object's CheckOnClick and Checked properties should both be set to *True*. The *Color* menu should now appear as shown in Figure 7-56.

Step 13: To the right of the *Color* menu item, add the *Help* menu item with the text **&Help** and the name **mnuHelp**.

Step 14: Below the word *Help*, add a menu item with the text **&About** and the name **mnuHelpAbout**. When finished, the *Help* menu should appear as shown in Figure 7-57.

Figure 7-56 Completed *Color* menu

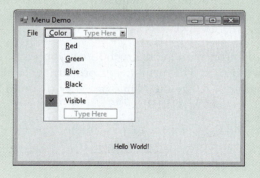

Figure 7-57 Completed *Help* menu

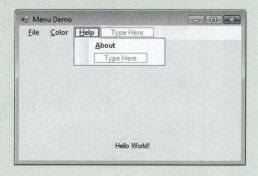

Step 15: Now you will write Click event procedures for the appropriate menu items, starting with `mnuFileExit`. In the menu designer, double-click the word *Exit*, which is on the *File* menu. The *Code* window opens with a code template for the `mnuFileExit_Click` event procedure. Complete the procedure by typing the code shown in bold, as follows:

```
Private Sub mnuFileExit_Click(...) Handles mnuFileExit.Click
    ' Close the form.
    Me.Close()
End Sub
```

Step 16: Follow this same procedure to write the event procedures for the items on the *Color* menu. The code for the event procedures is as follows:

```
Private Sub mnuColorRed_Click(...) Handles mnuColorRed.Click
    ' Set the label's foreground color to red.
    lblMessage.ForeColor = Color.Red
End Sub
Private Sub mnuColorGreen_Click(...) Handles mnuColorGreen.Click
    ' Set the label's foreground color to green.
    lblMessage.ForeColor = Color.Green
End Sub
Private Sub mnuColorBlue_Click(...) Handles mnuColorBlue.Click
    ' Set the label's foreground color to blue.
    lblMessage.ForeColor = Color.Blue
End Sub
Private Sub mnuColorBlack_Click(...) Handles mnuColorBlack.Click
    ' Set the label's foreground color to black.
    lblMessage.ForeColor = Color.Black
End Sub
Private Sub mnuColorVisible_Click(...) Handles mnuColorVisible.Click
    ' Make the label visible or invisible
    If mnuColorVisible.Checked = True Then
        lblMessage.Visible = True
    Else
        lblMessage.Visible = False
    End If
End Sub
```

Let's take a closer look at the `mnuColorVisible_Click` procedure. This procedure tests the `mnuColorVisible` object's Checked property to determine whether the menu item is checked. If it is checked, the user wants to make the label visible so the `lblMessage.Visible` property is set to *True*. Otherwise, the `lblMessage.Visible` property is set to *False*.

Step 17: The *Help* menu has one item: *About*. Most applications have this command, which displays a dialog box known as an *About* box. An **About** box usually shows some brief information about the application. Write the following code, shown in bold, for the `mnuHelpAbout` menu item's Click event procedure:

```
Private Sub mnuHelpAbout_Click(...) Handles mnuHelpAbout.Click
    ' Display a simple About box.
    MessageBox.Show("A Simple Menu System Demo")
End Sub
```

Step 18: Save the project and run it. Try selecting different colors to see how they make the label appear. Also test the *Visible* command and the *About* command. When finished, type Ctrl+Q to exit the application.

Context Menus

A **context menu**, or pop-up menu, is displayed when the user right-clicks a form or control. To create a context menu, you must add a ContextMenuStrip control to a form. You do this just as you add other controls: double-click the *ContextMenuStrip* icon in the *Toolbox* window. A ContextMenuStrip control is then created in the form's component tray. The first such control will have the default name `ContextMenuStrip1`, the second will have the default name `ContextMenuStrip2`, and so on.

Once you have added a ContextMenuStrip control to a form, you select it and then add items to it with the menu designer, just as you do with a regular menu. After you have built the context menu, you add Click event procedures for its menu items. Then, you associate the context menu with a control by setting the control's ContextMenuStrip property to the name of the ContextMenuStrip control. At runtime, the context menu will pop up when the user right-clicks the control. For example, Figure 7-58 shows a context menu displayed when the user right-clicks a Label control.

Figure 7-58 *Context* menu

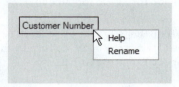

Checkpoint

7.18 Briefly describe each of the following menu system components:
   a. Menu name
   b. Menu command
   c. Disabled menu command
   d. Checked menu command
   e. Shortcut key
   f. Submenu
   g. Separator bar

7.19 What is the difference between a menu item's access key and its shortcut key?

7.20 What prefix do we use for ToolStripMenuItem objects?

7.21 Suppose an application has a *File* menu with the following commands: *Save*, *Save As*, *Print*, and *Exit*. What name would you give each of the controls?

7.22 How do you assign an access key to a menu item?

7.23 What happens if you set a ToolStripMenuItem object's CheckOnClick property to *True*?

7.24 How do you disable a menu control in code?

7.25 How do you determine whether a check mark appears next to a menu item in code?

7.26 What event occurs when the user clicks on a menu item?

7.27 How does the user display a context menu?

7.28 How do you associate a context menu with a control?

7.4 Focus on Problem Solving: Building the *High Adventure Travel Agency Price Quote* Application

CONCEPT: In this section you build an application for the High Adventure Travel Agency. The application uses multiple forms, a module, and a menu system.

The High Adventure Travel Agency offers the following vacation packages for thrill-seeking customers.

- **Scuba Adventure:** This package provides six days at a Caribbean resort with scuba lessons. The price for this package is $3,000 per person.
- **Sky Dive Adventure:** This package provides individual sky diving lessons during a six-day vacation at a luxury lodge. The price for this package is $2,500 per person.

The travel agency gives a 10% discount for groups of five or more. You've been asked to create an application to calculate the charges for each package.

In Tutorial 7-6 you will create an application that has the following forms and modules:

- The `MainForm` form is the application's startup form. It will provide a menu that allows the user to select one of the vacation packages.
- The `ScubaForm` form will calculate the price of a scuba adventure travel package.
- The `SkyDiveForm` form will calculate the price of a sky dive adventure travel package.
- The `PriceCalcModule` module will contain global constants and a function that both the `ScubaForm` and `SkyDiveForm` forms will use to calculate discounts.

The `MainForm`

The `MainForm` form, at run time, is shown in Figure 7-59. The beach photo shown on the form is located in the student sample files, in the *Chap7* folder in a file named *High-Adventure.bmp*. You will display this image in a PictureBox control. Notice that the form

Figure 7-59 The *High Adventure* application's `MainForm`

Figure 7-60 The menu system

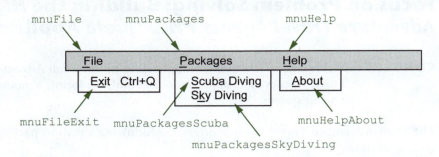

also has a MenuStrip control. Figure 7-60 shows a sketch of the menu system, along with the names that you will assign to each MenuItem control.

Here is a summary of the actions performed by the MenuItem controls:

- When the user clicks the `mnuFileExit` item, the application will end.
- When the user clicks the `mnuPackagesScuba` item, an instance of the `ScubaForm` form will be displayed. The `ScubaForm` form will calculate the price of a scuba adventure travel package.
- When the user clicks the `mnuPackagesSkyDiving` item, an instance of the `SkyDive-Form` form will be displayed. The `SkyDiveForm` form will calculate the price of a Sky dive adventure travel package.
- When the user clicks the `mnuHelpAbout` item, a simple *About* box will be displayed.

The `ScubaForm`

Figure 7-61 shows the `ScubaForm` form and lists the names that you will assign to various controls on the form. When you create the `lblDiscount` and `lblTotal` Label controls, you will set their AutoSize properties to False and their BorderStyle properties to FixedSingle. Here is a summary of the actions that the Button controls will perform:

- The `btnCalcTotal` button will use the value entered in the `txtNumberPeople` control to calculate and display the discount (if any) and the total cost for the scuba adventure vacation.
- The `btnReset` button will clear the text box and labels, and give the focus to `txtNumberPeople`.
- The `btnClose` button will close the form.

Figure 7-61 The `ScubaForm` form

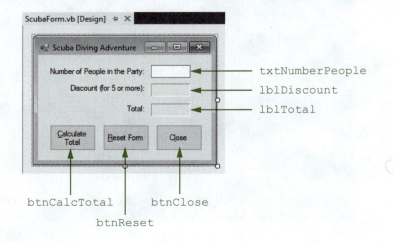

The SkyDiveForm

Figure 7-62 shows the SkyDiveForm form and lists the names that you will assign to various controls on the form. When you create the lblDiscount and lblTotal Label controls, you will set their AutoSize properties to False and their BorderStyle properties to FixedSingle. Here is a summary of the actions that the Button controls will perform:

- The btnCalcTotal button will use the value entered in the txtNumberPeople control to calculate and display the discount (if any) and the total cost for the sky dive adventure vacation.
- The btnReset button will clear Text properties of the txtNumberPeople, lblDiscount, and lblTotal controls, and give the focus to txtNumberPeople.
- The btnClose button will close the form.

Figure 7-62 The SkyDiveForm form

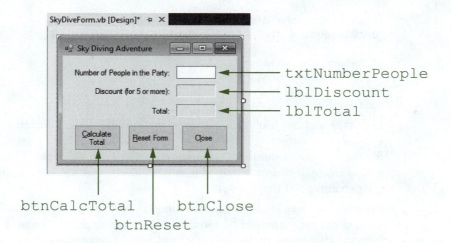

Tutorial 7-6:

Tutorial 7-6:
Building the *High Adventure Travel Agency Price Quote* application

Step 1: Create a new Windows Forms Application project named *High Adventure*.

Step 2: Change the name of the Form1 form to MainForm.

Step 3: Place a MenuStrip control on the form and create the MenuItem objects shown previously in Figure 7-60. Refer to this figure for the names of the MenuItem objects and the text that each object should display.

Step 4: Place a PictureBox control on the MainForm. Use the *HighAdventure.bmp* file, located in the *Chap7* folder of the student sample files, for the Image property.

Step 5: Create the ScubaForm form and place on it the controls shown previously in Figure 7-61. Refer to the figure for the names of the controls. When you create the lblDiscount and lblTotal Label controls, set their AutoSize properties to False and their BorderStyle properties to FixedSingle. (Don't worry about writing the event handlers for this form yet. You will do that at a later point.)

Step 6: Create the SkyDiveForm form and place on it the controls shown previously in Figure 7-62. Refer to the figure for the names of the controls. When you create the lblDiscount and lblTotal Label controls, set their AutoSize properties to False and their BorderStyle properties to FixedSingle. (Don't worry about writing the event handlers for this form yet. You will do that at a later point.)

Step 7: Create a module named *PriceCalcModule.vb*. Use the *Code* window to write the following code in the module. (Don't type the line numbers. They are shown only for reference.)

```
1 Module PriceCalcModule
2     ' Global constants
3     Public Const g_intMINIMUM_FOR_DISCOUNT As Integer = 5
4     Public Const g_decDISCOUNT_PERCENTAGE As Decimal = 0.1D
5
6     ' The CalcDiscount function accepts a package total
7     ' as an argument and returns the amount of discount
8     ' for that total.
9
10    Public Function CalcDiscount(decTotal As Decimal) As Decimal
11        Dim decDiscount As Decimal ' To hold the discount
12
13        ' Calculate the discount.
14        decDiscount = decTotal * g_decDISCOUNT_PERCENTAGE
15
16        ' Return the discount.
17        Return decDiscount
18    End Function
19 End Module
```

Let's take a closer look at the code in the module. Line 3 declares a global Integer constant named g_intMINIMUM_FOR_DISCOUNT. This constant will be used for the minimum number of people required for a discount. Line 4 declares a global Decimal constant named g_decDISCOUNT_PERCENTAGE. It will be used for the percentage of the discount.

Lines 10 through 18 show a public function named CalcDiscount. This function accepts the total amount of a vacation package as an argument. Line 14 calculates the discount for that amount, and line 17 returns the discount. This function will be called by statements in both the ScubaForm and SkyDiveForm forms.

Step 8: Now you will write the event handlers for the ScubaForm form. Open the ScubaForm form in the *Designer* window and create the code templates for the btnCalcTotal, btnReset, and btnClose buttons. The following shows how the form's code should appear after you have completed the event handlers. (The line numbers are shown only for reference.)

```
1 Public Class ScubaForm
2
3     Private Sub btnCalcTotal_Click(...) Handles btnCalcTotal.Click
4         ' Constant for the price per person for this package
5         Const decSCUBA_PRICE_PER_PERSON As Decimal = 3000D
6
7         ' Local variables
8         Dim intNumberPeople As Integer ' Number of people
9         Dim decDiscount As Decimal ' Amount of discount
10        Dim decTotal As Decimal ' Total cost
11
12        Try
13            ' Get the number of people.
14            intNumberPeople = CInt(txtNumberPeople.Text)
15
```

```
16            ' Get the total before any discount is applied.
17            decTotal = intNumberPeople * decSCUBA_PRICE_PER_PERSON
18
19            ' Determine whether a discount can be given.
20            If intNumberPeople > = g_intMINIMUM_FOR_DISCOUNT Then
21               ' Get the amount of the discount.
22               decDiscount = CalcDiscount(decTotal)
23
24               ' Subtract the discount from the total.
25               decTotal = decTotal - decDiscount
26            Else
27               ' The discount is $0.
28               decDiscount = 0D
29            End If
30
31            ' Display the results.
32            lblDiscount.Text = decDiscount.ToString("c")
33            lblTotal.Text = decTotal.ToString("c")
34         Catch ex As Exception
35            ' Error message for invalid input.
36            MessageBox.Show("Enter a valid integer for number of people.")
37         End Try
38      End Sub
39
40      Private Sub btnReset_Click(...) Handles btnReset.Click
41         ' Clear the text box and the display labels.
42         txtNumberPeople.Clear()
43         lblDiscount.Text = String.Empty
44         lblTotal.Text = String.Empty
45
46         ' Reset the focus.
47         txtNumberPeople.Focus()
48      End Sub
49
50      Private Sub btnClose_Click(...) Handles btnClose.Click
51         ' Close the form.
52         Me.Close()
53      End Sub
54 End Class
```

Let's take a closer look at the code. In the btnCalcTotal_Click event handler, line 5 declares the constant decSCUBA_PRICE_PER_PERSON to represent the price of the scuba package, per person. Line 8 declares the intNumberPeople variable to hold the number of people in the party. Line 9 declares the decDiscount variable to hold the discount, if one is given. Line 10 declares the decTotal variable to hold the total cost.

A Try-Catch statement begins in line 12. Inside the try block, line 14 reads the value entered by the user into the txtNumberPeople TextBox, converts it to an integer, and assigns the result to the intNumberPeople variable. If the user has entered an invalid value, an exception will be thrown and the program will jump to the Catch statement in line 34. If that happens, an error message is displayed by line 36 and the procedure ends.

If the value entered by the user is a valid integer, the total cost of the vacation (before any discount is given) is calculated in line 17 and assigned to the decTotal variable. Then the If . . . Then statement in line 20 determines whether five or more people are in the party. If so, the `CalcDiscount` function (which is stored in the module) is called in line 22 to get the amount of the discount. The value returned from the function is assigned to `decDiscount`. Then the discount is subtracted from the total in line 25. If there are less than five people in the party, the statement in line 28 sets `decDiscount` to 0. Line 32 displays the amount of the discount in the `lblDiscount` control, and line 33 displays the total cost in the `lblTotal` control.

The `btnReset_Click` event handler clears the Text properties of the `txtNumberPeople`, `lblDiscount`, and `lblTotal` controls in lines 42 through 44, and then gives the focus to the `txtNumberPeople` control in line 47.

The `btnClose_Click` event handler closes the form.

Step 9: Now you will write the event handlers for the SkyDiveForm form. Open the SkyDiveForm form in the *Designer* window, and create the code templates for the btnCalcTotal, btnReset, and btnClose buttons. The following shows how the form's code should appear after you have completed the event handlers. (The line numbers are shown only for reference.)

```
1  Public Class SkyDiveForm
2
3      Private Sub btnCalcTotal_Click(...) Handles btnCalcTotal.Click
4          ' Constant for the price per person for this package
5          Const decSKYDIVE_PRICE_PER_PERSON As Decimal = 2500D
6
7          ' Local variables
8          Dim intNumberPeople As Integer ' Number of people
9          Dim decDiscount As Decimal ' Amount of discount
10         Dim decTotal As Decimal ' Total cost
11
12         Try
13             ' Get the number of people.
14             intNumberPeople = CInt(txtNumberPeople.Text)
15
16             ' Get the total before any discount is applied.
17             decTotal = intNumberPeople * decSKYDIVE_PRICE_PER_PERSON
18
19             ' Determine whether a discount can be given.
20             If intNumberPeople >= g_intMINIMUM_FOR_DISCOUNT Then
21                 ' Get the amount of the discount.
22                 decDiscount = CalcDiscount(decTotal)
23
24                 ' Subtract the discount from the total.
25                 decTotal = decTotal - decDiscount
26             Else
27                 ' The discount is $0.
28                 decDiscount = 0D
29             End If
30
31             ' Display the results.
32             lblDiscount.Text = decDiscount.ToString("c")
33             lblTotal.Text = decTotal.ToString("c")
34         Catch ex As Exception
35             ' Error message for invalid input.
36             MessageBox.Show("Enter a valid integer for number of people.")
```

```
37                End Try
38        End Sub
39
40        Private Sub btnReset_Click(...) Handles btnReset.Click
41            ' Clear the text box and the display labels.
42            txtNumberPeople.Clear()
43            lblDiscount.Text = String.Empty
44            lblTotal.Text = String.Empty
45
46            ' Reset the focus.
47            txtNumberPeople.Focus()
48        End Sub
49
50        Private Sub btnClose_Click(...) Handles btnClose.Click
51            ' Close the form.
52            Me.Close()
53        End Sub
54 End Class
```

This code is very similar to the code that you wrote in Step 8, but let's take a moment to go over it. In the btnCalcTotal_Click event handler, line 5 declares the constant decSKYDIVE_PRICE_PER_PERSON to represent the price of the sky diving package, per person. Line 8 declares the intNumberPeople variable to hold the number of people in the party. Line 9 declares the decDiscount variable to hold the discount, if one is given. Line 10 declares the decTotal variable to hold the total cost.

A Try-Catch statement begins in line 12. Inside the try block, line 14 reads the value entered by the user into the txtNumberPeople TextBox, converts it to an integer, and assigns the result to the intNumberPeople variable. If the user has entered an invalid value, an exception will be thrown and the program will jump to the Catch statement in line 34. If that happens, an error message is displayed by line 36 and the procedure ends.

If the value entered by the user is a valid integer, the total cost of the vacation (before any discount is given) is calculated in line 17 and assigned to the decTotal variable. Then the If . . . Then statement in line 20 determines whether five or more people are in the party. If so, the CalcDiscount function (which is stored in the module) is called in line 22 to get the amount of the discount. The value returned from the function is assigned to decDiscount. Then the discount is subtracted from the total in line 25. If there are less than five people in the party, the statement in line 28 sets decDiscount to 0. Line 32 displays the amount of the discount in the lblDiscount control, and line 33 displays the total cost in the lblTotal control.

The btnReset_Click event handler clears the Text properties of the txtNumberPeople, lblDiscount, and lblTotal controls in lines 42 through 44, and then gives the focus to the txtNumberPeople control in line 47.

The btnClose_Click event handler closes the form.

Step 10: Now you will write the event handlers for the MainForm form. Open the Main-Form form in the *Designer* window and create code templates for each of the MenuItem objects. The following shows how the form's code should appear after you have completed the event handlers. (The line numbers are shown only for reference.)

```
1 Public Class MainForm
2
3   Private Sub mnuFileExit_Click(...) Handles mnuFileExit.Click
4     ' Close the form.
5     Me.Close()
6   End Sub
7
8   Private Sub mnuPackagesScuba_Click(...) Handles mnuPackagesScuba.Click
9     ' Create an instance of the ScubaForm.
10    Dim frmScuba As New ScubaForm
11
12    ' Display the ScubaForm in modal style.
13    frmScuba.ShowDialog()
14  End Sub
15
16  Private Sub mnuPackagesSkyDiving_Click(...) Handles mnuPackagesSkyDiving.Click
17    ' Create an instance of the SkyDiveForm.
18    Dim frmSkyDive As New SkyDiveForm
19
20    ' Display the SkyDiveForm in modal style.
21    frmSkyDive.ShowDialog()
22  End Sub
23
24  Private Sub mnuHelpAbout_Click(...) Handles mnuHelpAbout.Click
25    ' Display a simple About box.
26    MessageBox.Show("High Adventure Travel Price Quote System Version 1.0")
27  End Sub
28 End Class
```

Let's take a closer look at the code. In the mnuFileExit_Click event handler, line 5 closes the form, thus ending the application.

In the mnuPackagesScuba_Click event handler, line 10 creates an instance of the ScubaForm form in memory and assigns its address to the frmScuba variable. Then line 13 displays the form on the screen in modal style.

In the mnuPackagesSkyDiving_Click event handler, line 18 creates an instance of the SkyDiveForm form in memory and assigns its address to the frmSkyDive variable. Then line 21 displays the form on the screen in modal style.

In the mnuHelpAbout_Click event handler, line 26 displays a message box as a simple *About* box.

Step 11: Save the project and test the application. Make sure all the menu items work properly, and try different numbers of people for each of the packages to make sure the calculations are correct.

NOTE: Some early releases of Visual Studio 2015 have a bug that will cause the following error when you compile the project in Step 11: *'Form1' is not a member of 'High Adventure'*. If you see this error message, download the document titled **Startup Form Issue in VS2015** from this book's companion Web site for a simple solution. The companion Web site is at www.pearsonhighered. com/gaddisvb.

Summary

7.1 Multiple Forms

- Visual Basic projects can have multiple forms; one form is the startup form, displayed when the project executes. Other forms are displayed by programming statements.
- When you create a form, the code for that form is stored in a file ending with a *.vb* extension. Normally, the name of the file is the same as the name of the form. The form file contains the form class declaration, which is code that describes the form's properties and methods.
- The project's properties page allows you to designate a project's startup form.
- Before displaying a form, you must create an instance of the form. Then, you must call a method (Show or ShowDialog) to display the form. The Show method displays a form in modeless style. The ShowDialog method displays a form in modal style.
- When a modal form is displayed, no other form in the application can receive the focus until the modal form is closed. No other statements in the procedure that displayed the modal form will execute until the modal form is closed.
- A form's Close method removes it from the screen and from memory. A form typically uses the Me keyword to call its own Close method, as in Me.Close().
- The Load event occurs just before a form is displayed for the first time. A form's Activated event occurs when the user switches to the form from another form or another application. The FormClosing event occurs when a form is in the process of closing, but before it has closed. The FormClosed event is triggered after a form has closed. You may write event handlers that execute in response to any of these events.
- Code from one form can reference controls on a different form, as long as an instance of that form has been created in memory and its address has been assigned to a variable. You must fully qualify the name of the object by preceding it with the name of the variable that references the form, followed by a period.
- To make a form's class-level variable available to statements outside the form, declare it with the Public keyword. Although class-level variables are automatically declared private by the Dim statement, you should explicitly declare them private with the Private keyword.
- After a form has been saved to a form file, it may be used in other projects.

7.2 Modules

- A module contains code—declarations and procedures—that is used by other files in a project.
- A variable declared inside a module (between the Module and the End Module statements), but not inside a procedure or function, is a module-level variable. A module-level variable declared Public is also known as a global variable because it can be accessed globally by any statement in the application.
- You can use the same module in more than one project, as long as you include the file in each project.

7.3 Menus

- The MenuStrip control lets you create a system of drop-down menus on any form. You place a MenuStrip control on the form and then use the menu designer to create a menu system.
- An application's menu system is constructed from ToolStripMenuItem objects. When you create menu items, you name them with the mnu prefix.
- If you do not want the user to be able to select a menu item, set the item's Enabled property to *False* (either in design mode or in runtime code). When a menu control's CheckOnClick property is set to *True*, it will have the ability to become checked or

unchecked when clicked. When a menu control's Checked property equals *True*, a check mark appears on the menu next to the control's text.
- You make a ToolStripMenuItem object respond to clicks by providing it with a Click event handler.

7.4 Focus on Problem Solving: *Building the High Adventure Travel Agency Price Quote* Application

- This section outlines the process of building the *High Adventure Travel Agency Price Quote* application using multiple forms, a module, and a menu system.

Key Terms

About box	modeless form
Activated event handler	module
Checked property	module-level variable
CheckOnClick property	module scope
`Close` method	object variable
context menu	`Private` keyword
FormClosed event handler	`Public` keyword
FormClosing event handler	separator bar
global variable	shortcut key
`Hide` method	ShortcutKeys property
`Me` keyword	`Show` method
menu designer	`ShowDialog` method
menu system	ShowShortcut property
MenuStrip control	startup form
modal form	ToolStripMenuItem object

VideoNote

Adding menus and forms to the *Kayak Rental* Application

Video Tutorial: Adding Menus and Forms to the *Kayak Rental* Application

In this sequence of video tutorials, we improve on the *Kayak Rental* application by adding separate user interfaces for customers and managers. Each type of user will have his or her own window or form that matches his or her needs. In addition, we will provide security by requiring a password to access the non-customer forms.

- Part 1: Adding multiple forms to the *Kayak Rental* application
- Part 2: Adding the Manager Login window

Review Questions and Exercises

Fill-in-the-Blank

1. If a form is the _____, it is displayed first when the project executes.

2. When a(n) _____ form is displayed, no other form in the application can receive the focus until the form is closed.

3. A(n) _____ is a variable that holds the memory address of an object and allows you to work with the object.

4. The _____ method removes a form from the screen but does not remove it from memory.

5. The _____ method removes a form from the screen and releases the memory it is using.

6. The _____ method displays a form in modal style.

7. The _____ method displays a form in modeless style.

8. Modules contain no _____ procedures.

9. When a procedure declaration in a form file begins with _____, the procedure may only be accessed by statements in the same form.

10. To make a class-level variable available to statements outside the module, you declare it with the _____ keyword.

11. A module-level variable declared `Public` is also known as a(n) _____ variable.

12. You can disable a menu control in code by setting its _____ property to *False*.

13. When a menu item's _____ property equals *True*, a check mark appears on the menu next to the item's text.

14. A(n) _____ is a pop-up menu that is displayed when the user right-clicks a form or control.

Multiple Choice

1. Which of the following variable name prefixes do we use in this book for variables that reference forms?
   a. `fr`
   b. `frm`
   c. `for`
   d. `fm`

2. When this type of form is displayed, no other form in the application can receive the focus until the form is closed.
   a. modal
   b. modeless
   c. startup
   d. unloaded

3. When this type of form is displayed, statements following the method call continue to execute after the form is displayed.
   a. modal
   b. modeless
   c. startup
   d. unloaded

4. What does the `Hide` method do?
   a. Removes a form from the screen and removes it from memory
   b. Removes a form from the screen but does not remove it from memory
   c. Positions one form behind another one
   d. Removes a form from memory but does not remove it from the screen

5. This method makes a form invisible, but does not remove it from memory.
   a. `Remove`
   b. `Delete`
   c. `Close`
   d. `Hide`

6. If you want to declare `g_intTotal` in a module as a global variable, which of the following declarations would you use?

   a. `Dim g_intTotal As Integer`
   b. `Public g_intTotal As Integer`
   c. `Global g_intTotal As Integer`
   d. `Private g_intTotal As Integer`

7. Just before a form is initially displayed, this event occurs.

   a. InitialDisplay
   b. Load
   c. Display
   d. Create

8. This event occurs when the user switches to the form from another form or another application.

   a. Activated
   b. Load
   c. Switch
   d. Close

9. This event occurs as a form is in the process of closing, but before it has closed.

   a. FormClosed
   b. StartClose
   c. ShuttingDown
   d. FormClosing

10. This event occurs after a form has closed.

    a. FormClosed
    b. EndClose
    c. ShutDown
    d. FormClosing

11. A form uses this statement to call its own `Close` method.

    a. `Form.Close()`
    b. `Me.Close()`
    c. `Close(Me)`
    d. `ThisForm.Close()`

12. If a procedure or variable is used by more than one form, where should it be declared?

    a. Module
    b. Form file
    c. Multiprocess file
    d. Project file

13. If an application's menu system has a *Cut* command on the *Edit* menu, what should the MenuItem control for the command be named?

    a. `mnuCut`
    b. `mnuEdit`
    c. `mnuCutEdit`
    d. `mnuEditCut`

14. A menu command's _____ only works while the menu is open, while a(n) _____ may be executed at any time while the form is active.
    a. shortcut key, access key
    b. access key, shortcut key
    c. function key, control key
    d. alternate key, control key

15. Which of the following statements disables the mnuFilePrint object?
    a. mnuFilePrint.Disabled = True
    b. mnuFilePrint.Enabled = False
    c. mnuFilePrint.Available = False
    d. Disable mnuFilePrint

True or False

Indicate whether the following statements are true or false.

1. T F: By default, the first form you create is the startup form.

2. T F: The Show method displays a form in modeless style.

3. T F: Although the Hide method removes a form from the screen, it does not remove it from memory.

4. T F: If you have code that you want to execute every time a form displays, the form's Load event procedure is the best place to write it.

5. T F: The Activated event executes only once—when the form is initially displayed.

6. T F: The FormClosing event executes before a form has completely closed.

7. T F: It is not possible to access a control on another form in code.

8. T F: A menu command's shortcut key works only while the menu is open.

9. T F: If a menu control does not display a menu or submenu, you make it functional by providing a Click event handler for it.

10. T F: A context menu displays when the user double-clicks a control.

Short Answer

1. Describe the process of adding a new form to a project.

2. Describe the process of removing a form from a project, but not deleting the form file.

3. Describe the process of removing a form from a project and deleting the form file.

4. Describe the process of changing the startup form to another form.

5. What does the statement Me.Close() do?

6. What is the difference between the Load event and the Activated event?

7. Suppose you want to execute code when a form is about to close, but has not fully closed. Where should you place the code?

8. Suppose you want to execute code when a form has fully closed. Where should you place the code?

9. Suppose you wish to declare a variable in a module so all the forms in the project have access to it. How should you declare the variable?

10. Describe the steps for adding a module to a project.

11. What is the difference between a menu control's access key and its shortcut key?

12. How do you create a checked menu item?

13. In code, how do you determine whether a check mark appears next to a menu item?

14. What is a disabled menu item? How do you make a menu item disabled?

What Do You Think?

1. If you want to display multiple forms on the screen at one time and be able to interact with any of them at any time, do you display them as modal or modeless forms?

2. You want to write code that removes a form from the screen, but you still want to access controls on the form in code. How do you accomplish this?

3. Suppose a form is referenced by a variable named `frmStatus`, and the form has a Label control named `lblArrivalGate`. Write a statement that stores the string `"D West"` in the label's Text property from another form.

4. Suppose you have written a function, named `CircleArea`, which returns the area of a circle. You call the function from numerous procedures in different form modules. Should you store the function in a form or a module?

5. The following code creates instances of three forms in memory and then displays them. After the code executes, will all three forms be on the screen at the same time? Why or why not?

```
Dim frmFirst As New OneForm
Dim frmSecond As New TwoForm
Dim frmThird As New ThreeForm
frmFirst.Show()
frmSecond.Show()
frmThird.Show()
```

Find the Error

What is wrong with the following statements?

1. `Hide Me`

2. *Class-level declaration in ResultsForm:*
   ```
   Dim intNumber as Integer
   ```
   Statements in another form:
   ```
   Dim frmResults as New ResultsForm
   frmResults.intNumber = 100
   ```

3. ```
   Dim frmError As ErrorForm
   frmError.ShowDialog()
   ```

4. ```
   Module TestModule
       ' Declare a GLOBAL variable.
       Dim g_intCount As Integer
   End Module
   ```

Algorithm Workbench

1. An application has two forms named `MainForm` and `SecondForm`. The `SecondForm` form has a public class-level integer variable named `intReading`, and the `MainForm` form has a text box named `txtInput`. Assume the user has entered a value into the `txtInput` control on the `MainForm` form, and an event handler executes the following statement:
   ```
   Dim frmSecond As New SecondForm
   ```

   Write a statement that executes after this statement and stores the value entered in `txtInput` into the `intReading` variable (in the `SecondForm` form).

2. Here is the code template for a form's FormClosing event handler:

```
Private Sub MainForm_FormClosing(sender As Object,
   e As System.Windows.Forms.FormClosingEventArgs)
   Handles Me.FormClosing

End Sub
```

Suppose you want the form to close only if the user knows the secret word, which is *water*. Write statements in this procedure to ask the user to enter the secret word. If the user enters the correct secret word, the form should close. Otherwise, the form should not close. (Perform a case-insensitive test for the secret word.)

Programming Challenges

1. **Conference Registration System**

   Create an application that calculates the registration fees for a conference. The general conference registration fee is $895 per person. There is also an optional opening night dinner with a keynote address for $30 per person. Additionally, the optional preconference workshops listed in Table 7-3 are available.

Table 7-3 Optional preconference workshops

Workshop	Free
Introduction to E-commerce	$295
The Future of the Web	$295
Advanced Visual Basic	$395
Network Security	$395

The application should have two forms. The main form should appear similar to the one shown in Figure 7-63.

Figure 7-63 *Conference Registration System* main form

When the user clicks the *Select Conference Options* button, the form shown in Figure 7-64 should appear.

Figure 7-64 *Conference Options* form

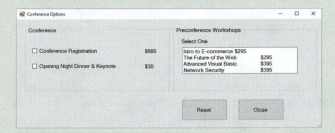

The *Conference Options* form allows the user to select the regular conference registration, the optional opening night dinner, and an optional preconference workshop. (The user cannot register for the optional events, however, without selecting the conference registration of $895.) When the *Close* button is clicked, this form should be removed from the screen and the total registration fee should appear on the main form.

> **TIP:** Use a module with a global variable to hold the total cost. That way, both forms will have access to the variable.

2. **Shopping Cart System**

   Design an application that works as a shopping cart system. The user should be able to add any of the following items to his or her shopping cart:

   Print Books (books on paper):
I Did It Your Way	$11.95
The History of Scotland	$14.50
Learn Calculus in One Day	$29.95
Feel the Stress	$18.50

   Audio Books (books on tape):
Learn Calculus in One Day	$29.95
The History of Scotland	$14.50
The Science of Body Language	$12.95
Relaxation Techniques	$11.50

   The application's main form should appear similar to the one shown in Figure 7-65.

Figure 7-65 *Shopping Cart* main form

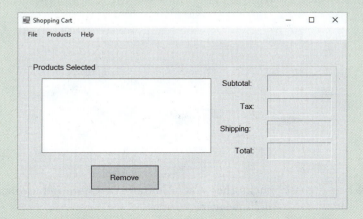

The list box shows all items in the shopping cart. There is a 6% sales tax on the total cost of the items in the shopping cart. Also, for each item in the shopping cart there is a $2.00 shipping charge. To remove an item from the shopping cart, the user selects it in the list box and clicks the *Remove* button. The subtotal, tax, shipping, and total fields should be adjusted accordingly. The main form's menu system is sketched in Figure 7-66.

Figure 7-66 *Shopping Cart* menu system

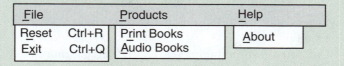

When the user selects *Reset* from the *File* menu, all items in the shopping cart should be removed, and the subtotal, tax, shipping, and total fields should be cleared. When the user selects *Exit* from the *File* menu, the application should end. When the user selects *About* from the *Help* menu, a simple *About* box should appear. When the user selects *Print Books* from the *Products* menu, the form in Figure 7-67 should appear.

Figure 7-67 *Print Books* form

To add one of the items in the list to the shopping cart, the user selects it and clicks the *Add Book to Cart* button. To cancel the operation, the user simply clicks the *Close* button without selecting a book. On the main form, when the user selects *Audio Books* from the *Products* menu, the form in Figure 7-68 should appear.

Figure 7-68 *Audio Books* form

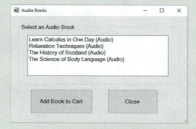

To add one of the items in the list to the shopping cart, the user selects it and clicks the *Add Book to Cart* button. To cancel the operation, the user simply clicks the *Close* button without selecting a book.

TIP: When the user selects either a print book or an audio book, use a module with global variables to hold the name and price of the selected book. That way, the main form will be able to retrieve the name and price after the other forms have closed.

3. **Cell Phone Packages**

Cell Solutions, a cell phone provider, sells the following packages:

800 minutes per month	$45.00 per month
1500 minutes per month	$65.00 per month
Unlimited minutes per month	$99.00 per month

Customers may also select the following options:

Email	$25.00 per month
Unlimited text messaging	$10.00 per month

The provider sells the following phones:

Model 100:	$29.95
Model 110:	$49.95
Model 200:	$99.95

(A 6% sales tax applies to the sale of a phone.)

Additionally, the provider offers individual plans and family plans. With the Individual plan, the customer gets one phone. With the Family plan, the customer gets as many phones of the same model as he or she desires, and all the phones share the same minutes. Email and text messaging fees are charged for each phone purchased under the Family plan.

Create an application that calculates a customer's plan cost. The application's main form should look similar to the one shown in Figure 7-69.

When the user clicks the *Individual* button, the form shown in Figure 7-70 should appear.

Figure 7-69 *Cell Phone Packages* form　　**Figure 7-70** *Individual Plan* form

 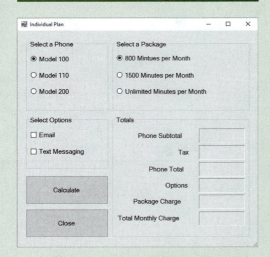

The user selects the phone model, options, and package. When the *Calculate* button is clicked, the charges are calculated and displayed.

When the user clicks the *Family* button on the main form, the form shown in Figure 7-71 should appear.

The user enters the number of phones, selects the phone model, options, and package. When the *Calculate* button is clicked, the charges are calculated and displayed.

Figure 7-71 *Family Plan* form

4. **Solar Panel Installation**

Programming Challenge 3 in Chapter 6 asked you to create an application related to a solar panel installation company. The application collected required information from the user and charged for installation. For this programming challenge, you are asked to improve the previous version of the application as follows:

1. Add a MenuStrip control with three top-level items: (1) File, (2) Customer, and (3) Installation.
2. Add two items to the File menu: (1) Clear and (2) Exit. These two items will duplicate the functions assigned to the buttons at the bottom of the form.
3. Add one item to the Customer menu: *Information*.
4. Add two items to the Installation menu: (1) Options and (2) Charges. Set the Enabled property of the *Charges* menu item to False.
5. Add a *Check for Errors* button to the *Installation Options* panel. When the user clicks this button, check the input fields in the panel, and if no errors are found in the input fields, display a message inside the panel saying the installation options have been verified. Also, enable the *Installation >> Charges* menu item.

Use the menus to control visibility of the GroupBox controls (panels), so the user will have fewer items to view at any one time. When the user selects the *Options* item from the Installation menu, display the appropriate panel. Only after both customer info and installation options have been entered, should you enable the *Charges* menu item and button.

When the program starts, as in Figure 7-72, the user is prompted for information about the customer. Other panels are hidden. If the user clicks on the *Installation >> Options* menu item without completing the customer fields, a message on the status bar explains that the customer fields must be filled in before continuing to the next step. In Figure 7-73, the user has entered some of the installation options, and then clicked the *Check for Errors* button. The message on the status bar reminds the user that the deposit amount is missing. In Figure 7-74, the user has fixed the problem and checked again, so the program displays a green confirmation message (*Installation options verified*) and quietly enables the *Installation >> Charges* menu item. In Figure 7-75, the user has selected the *Installation >> Charges* menu item. At this point, if the user were to click the *Clear* button, the lower two panels would disappear, leaving only the Customer Information panel with its text boxes cleared out.

Figure 7-72 The solar panel installation application, on startup

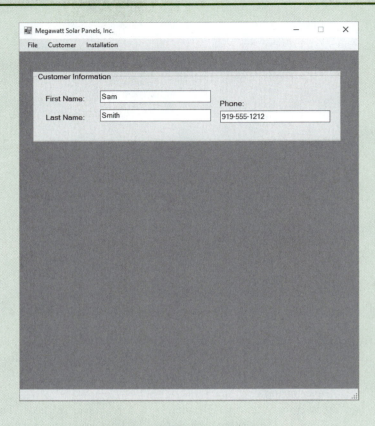

Figure 7-73 Solar panel installation options, checking for errors

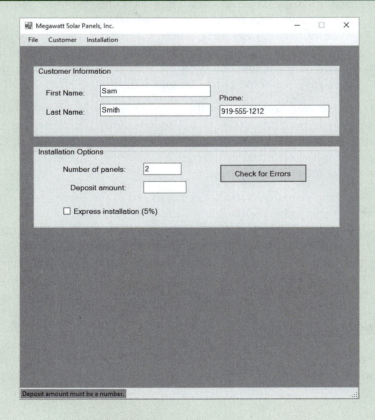

Figure 7-74 Verifying that the installation options are correct

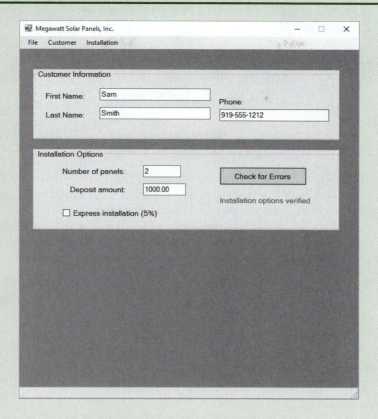

Figure 7-75 After selecting the *Installation >> Charges* menu item

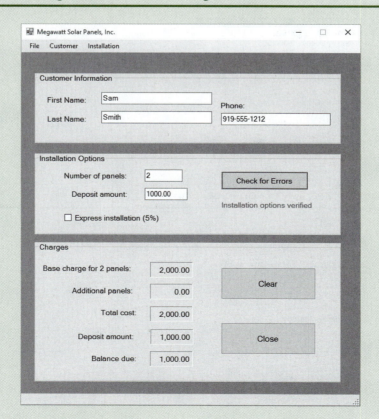

5. **Dorm and Meal Plan Calculator**

   Suppose a university has the following dormitories, offered at these prices:

   • Allen Hall $2,500 per semester
   • Pike Hall $2,200 per semester
   • Farthing Hall $2,100 per semester
   • University Suites $2,800 per semester

   Let us also assume the university also offers these meal plans:

   • 7 meals per week $1,560 per semester
   • 14 meals per week $2,095 per semester
   • Unlimited meals $2,500 per semester

   Create an application with a module and two forms. The module holds defined constants for the various dormitories and meal plans. The startup form holds the names of the dormitories, a set of buttons, a status bar, and labels that display semester charges, as shown in Figure 7-76. A second form holds the list of meal plans, and selection buttons, shown in Figure 7-77. When the user selects a dormitory and meal plan, the application should show the total charges for the semester on the startup form.

   Note: Use code statements in the Form Load event handler for each form to initialize the list boxes with the names of the dormitories or meal plans, along with their prices. This must be done at runtime, to allow future changes in the values of price constants to be displayed correctly in the list boxes.

Figure 7-76 Dorm and Meal Calculator—startup form

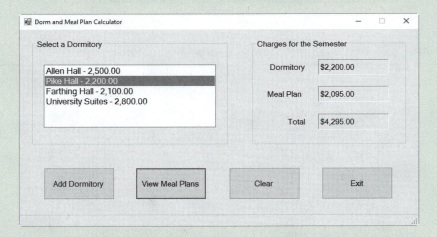

Figure 7-77 Dorm and Meal Calculator—meal plans

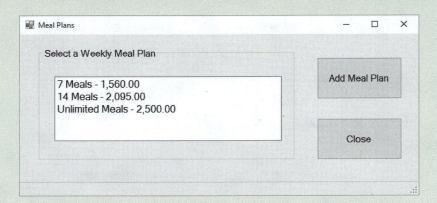

6. **TG Automotive with Dialog Window**

   In Chapter 6, Programming Challenge 4, you were asked to create an application that calculates charges for an automotive repair company. A significant drawback to the design of that program was that it was not expandable—you are limited to only the number of options that can easily fit on a single form. Real-world applications usually require a great deal of input selections, leading to the use of separate windows to get different types of input. In this Programming Challenge, you will create a separate form, such as the one shown in Figure 7-78, to get the user's oil and lubrication services selections. Notice that the price of each service is included in the Text property of each CheckBox control.

   Oil changes are now divided into two types: Crankcase oil and transmission oil. In the form shown in Figure 7-78, the user has selected two checkboxes and clicked the *Confirm Selections* button. Notice that a confirmation message containing the price appears on the status line. The message also instructs the user that he or she may now close the form. Upon returning to the application's main form, shown in Figure 7-79, the button caption has been updated to show the cost of the lubrication services previously selected by the user. If the user clicks the Clear button, you need to reset the caption of the oil and lubrication services button to its starting value (with no price). One of the concepts we demonstrate in this application is that button captions may be altered at runtime to give more information to users.

   It would be possible to use dialog windows to collect user input for each of the other service categories, but doing so would require lots of work. Instead, you will use a dialog window for only the oil and lubrication services category. *Suggestion: You will find it easiest to move some class-level variables and constants to a global code module so that they may be accessed from both the startup form and the Oil and Lubrication Services form.*

Figure 7-78 TG Automotive dialog window

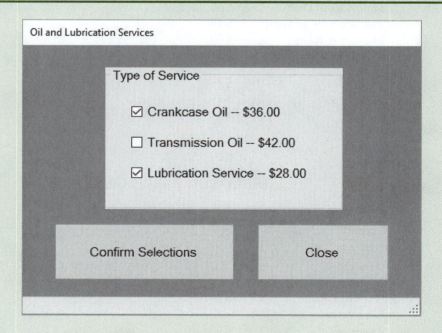

Figure 7-79 TG Automotive main window

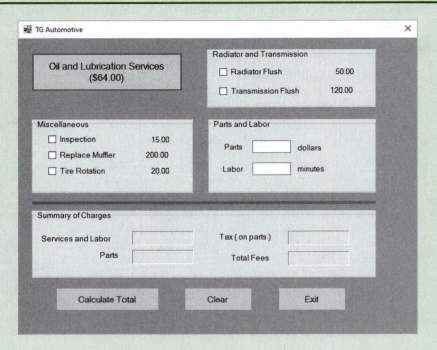

Design Your Own Forms

7. **Skateboard Designer**

The Skate Shop sells the following skateboard products.

Decks:

The Master Thrasher	$60
The Dictator of Grind	$45
The Street King	$50

Truck assemblies:

7.75 axle	$35
8 axle	$40
8.5 axle	$45

Wheel sets:

51 mm	$20
55 mm	$22
58 mm	$24
61 mm	$28

Additionally, the Skate Shop sells the following miscellaneous products and services:

Grip tape	$10
Bearings	$30
Riser pads	$ 2
Nuts & bolts kit	$ 3
Assembly	$10

Create an application that allows the user to select one deck from a form, one truck assembly from a form, and one wheel set from a form. The application should also have a form that allows the user to select any miscellaneous product, using check boxes. The application should display the subtotal, the amount of sales tax (at 6%), and the total of the order. Do not apply sales tax to assembly.

8. **Astronomy Helper**

Create an application that displays the following data about the planets of the solar system (including Pluto, which is no longer considered a planet). (For your information, the distances are shown in AUs, or astronomical units. 1 AU equals approximately 93 million miles. In your application simply display the distances as they are shown here, in AUs.)

Mercury

Type	Terrestrial
Average distance from the sun	0.387 AU
Mass	3.31×10^{23} kg
Surface temperature	−173°C to 430°C

Venus

Type	Terrestrial
Average distance from the sun	0.7233 AU
Mass	4.87×10^{24} kg
Surface temperature	472°C

Earth

Type	Terrestrial
Average distance from the sun	1 AU
Mass	5.967×10^{24} kg
Surface temperature	−50°C to 50°C

Mars

Type	Terrestrial
Average distance from the sun	1.5237 AU
Mass	0.6424×10^{24} kg
Surface temperature	−140°C to 20°C

Jupiter

Type	Jovian
Average distance from the sun	5.2028 AU
Mass	1.899×10^{27} kg
Temperature at cloud tops	−110°C

Saturn

Type	Jovian
Average distance from the sun	9.5388 AU
Mass	5.69×10^{26} kg
Temperature at cloud tops	−180°C

Uranus

Type	Jovian
Average distance from the sun	19.18 AU
Mass	8.69×10^{25} kg
Temperature above cloud tops	−220°C

VideoNote

The *Astronomy Helper* Problem

Neptune

Type	Jovian
Average distance from the sun	30.0611 AU
Mass	1.03×10^{26} kg
Temperature at cloud tops	−216°C

Pluto

Type	Low density
Average distance from the sun	39.44 AU
Mass	1.2×10^{22} kg
Surface temperature	−230°C

The application should have a separate form for each planet. On the main form, create a menu system that allows the user to select the planet he or she wishes to know more about.

8 Arrays and More

TOPICS

We introduce arrays in this chapter. An array is a single variable that can hold multiple values. A single-dimensional array is useful for storing and working with a single set of data, while a multidimensional array can be used to store and work with multiple sets of data. This chapter presents many array programming techniques, such as summing and averaging the elements in an array, summing all columns in a two-dimensional array, searching an array for a specific value, and using parallel arrays. The Enabled, Anchor, and Dock properties, and Timer controls, are also covered. The chapter concludes with an introduction to lists.

8.1 Arrays

CONCEPT: An array is a single variable that can hold multiple values. You store and work with values in an array by using a subscript.

Sometimes it is necessary for an application to store multiple values of the same type. Often it is better to create an array than several individual variables. All of the values stored within an array are called **elements,** and all elements in an array are of the same data type. You access the individual elements in an array using a subscript. A **subscript,** also known as an **index,** is an integer that identifies the position of a specific element within an array.

Subscript numbering begins at 0, so the subscript of the first element in an array is 0 and the subscript of the last element in an array is one less than the total number of elements. For example, consider an array of seven integers. The subscript of the first element in the array is 0 and the subscript of the last element in the array is 6.

Declaring an Array

You declare an array much like you declare a regular variable. Here is the general format of an array declaration:

```
Dim ArrayName (UpperSubscript) As DataType
```

Let's take a closer look at the syntax.

- *ArrayName* is the name of the array.
- *UpperSubscript* is the value of the array's highest subscript. This must be a positive integer, a positive named constant (of type Integer), or an Integer variable containing a positive integer.
- *DataType* is a Visual Basic data type.

Let's look at some examples.

```
Dim intHours(6) As Integer
```

This statement declares intHours as an array of integers. The number inside the parentheses, 6, indicates that the array's highest subscript is 6. Figure 8-1 shows that this array consists of seven elements with the subscripts 0 through 6. The figure shows that numeric array elements are initialized to the value 0. Notice that the array has a total of seven elements.

Figure 8-1 intHours array

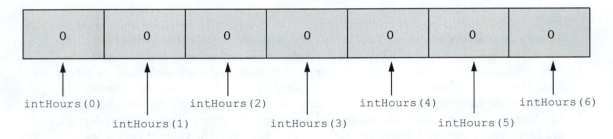

The following is another example of an array declaration:

```
Dim decPay(4) As Decimal
```

This statement declares decPay as an array of five Decimal values, as shown in Figure 8-2, with subscripts 0 through 4. The following example uses the contents of an Integer variable to specify the array size:

```
Dim intSize As Integer = 4
Dim decPay(intSize) As Decimal
```

Figure 8-2 decPay array

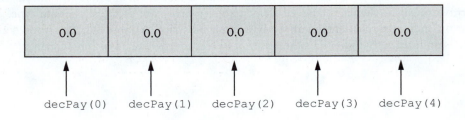

Implicit Array Sizing and Initialization

You can implicitly size an array by omitting the upper subscript in the declaration and providing an initialization list. An array initialization list is a set of numbers enclosed in a set of braces, with the numbers separated by commas. The following is an example of an array declaration that uses an initialization list:

```
Dim intNumbers() As Integer = { 2, 4, 6, 8, 10, 12 }
```

This statement declares `intNumbers` as an array of integers. The numbers 2, 4, 6, 8, 10, and 12 are stored in the array. The value 2 will be stored in element zero, 4 will be stored in element one, and so on. Notice that no upper subscript is provided inside the parentheses. The array is large enough to hold the values in the initialization list. In this example, the array has six elements, as shown in Figure 8-3.

Figure 8-3 `intNumbers` array

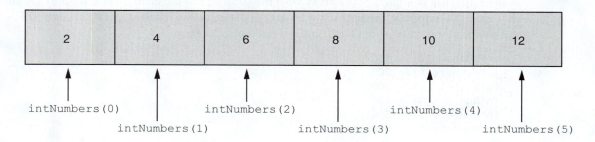

> **NOTE:** You cannot provide both an initialization list and an upper subscript in an array declaration.

Although we have shown only arrays of numbers up to this point, it is important to note that arrays often contain strings. The following code declares an implicitly sized array of strings.

```
Dim strFriends() As String = { "Joe", "Geri", "Bill", "Rose" }
```

You can initialize an array with empty strings, as shown here.

```
Dim strFriends() As String = { "", "", "", "" }
```

It is a good idea to initialize a string array, particularly if there is a chance that your program will access its elements before any data has been stored there. Performing an operation on a string array element results in a runtime error if no data has been stored in the element.

> **NOTE:** Like regular string variables, the uninitialized elements of a string array are set to the special value `Nothing`. Before doing any work with the elements of a string array, you must store values in them, even if the values are empty strings.

Using Named Constants as Subscripts in Array Declarations

To make programs easier to maintain and debug, programmers often use a named constant as the upper subscript in an array declaration, as shown in the following code:

```
Const intMAX_SUBSCRIPT As Integer = 100
Dim intArray(intMAX_SUBSCRIPT) As Integer
```

Quite often, when you write code that processes an array, you have to refer to the value of the array's upper subscript. You will see examples of this later in the chapter. When you declare a named constant to represent an array's upper subscript, you can use that constant any time that you need to refer to the array's last subscript in code. Then, if you ever need to modify the program so the array is a different size, you need only to change the value of the named constant.

Assigning Values to Array Elements

You can store a value in an array element with an assignment statement. On the left of the = operator, use the name of the array with the subscript of the element you wish to assign. For example, suppose intNumbers is an array of integers with subscripts 0 through 5. The following statements store values in each element of the array:

```
intNumbers(0) = 100
intNumbers(1) = 200
intNumbers(2) = 300
intNumbers(3) = 400
intNumbers(4) = 500
intNumbers(5) = 600
```

TIP: The expression intNumbers(0) is pronounced *intNumbers sub zero*.

Figure 8-4 shows the values assigned to the elements of the array after these statements execute.

Figure 8-4 intNumbers array with assigned values

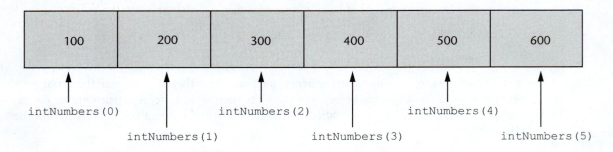

Accessing Array Elements with a Loop

VideoNote

Accessing Array Elements with a Loop

You can assign an integer to a variable and then use the variable as a subscript. This makes it possible to use a loop to cycle through an entire array, performing the same operation on each element. This can be helpful if you want to process the elements in a large array because writing individual statements would require a lot of typing.

For example, the following code declares `intSeries` as an array of 10 integers. The array's subscripts are 0 through 9. The `For...Next` loop stores the value 100 in each of its elements, beginning at subscript 0:

```
Const intMAX_SUBSCRIPT As Integer = 9
Dim intSeries(intMAX_SUBSCRIPT) As Integer
Dim intCount As Integer

For intCount = 0 To intMAX_SUBSCRIPT
   intSeries(intCount) = 100
Next
```

The variable `intCount`, used as the loop counter, takes on the values 0 through 9 as the loop repeats. The first time through the loop, `intCount` equals 0, so the statement `intSeries(intCount) = 100` assigns 100 to `intSeries(0)`. The second time the loop executes, the statement stores 100 in `intSeries(1)`, and so on. Figure 8-5 illustrates how the loop is set up so the counter variable begins with the first array subscript and ends with the last array subscript.

Figure 8-5 A `For...Next` loop using a counter variable to step through an array

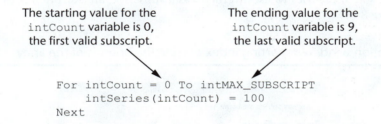

The following example uses a `Do While` loop to perform the same operation:

```
Const intMAX_SUBSCRIPT As Integer = 9
Dim intSeries(intMAX_SUBSCRIPT) As Integer
Dim intCount As Integer = 0

Do While intCount <= intMAX_SUBSCRIPT
   intSeries(intCount) = 100
   intCount += 1
Loop
```

We mentioned earlier that it is a good idea to initialize a string array if there is a chance that the program will access its elements before data has been stored there. It might be cumbersome, however, to provide a separate initializer for each array element. Instead, you can use a loop to initialize the array's elements. For example, the following code stores an empty string in each element of `strNames`, a 1000-element array of strings:

```
Const intMAX_SUBSCRIPT As Integer = 999
Dim strNames(intMAX_SUBSCRIPT) As String
Dim intCount As Integer

For intCount = 0 To intMAX_SUBSCRIPT
   strNames(intCount) = String.Empty
Next
```

Array Bounds Checking

The Visual Basic runtime system performs **array bounds checking**, meaning that it does not allow a statement to use a subscript outside the range of valid subscripts for an array.

For example, in the following declaration, the array named `intValues` has a subscript range of 0 through 10:

```
Const intMAX_SUBSCRIPT As Integer = 10
Dim intValues(intMAX_SUBSCRIPT) As Integer
```

If a statement uses a subscript that is less than 0 or greater than 10 with this array, the program will throw an exception.

The compiler does not display an error message at design time when you write a statement that uses an invalid subscript. For example, the loop in the following code uses out-of-range subscripts:

```
Const intMAX_SUBSCRIPT As Integer = 10
Dim intValues(intMAX_SUBSCRIPT) As Integer
Dim intIndex As Integer

For intIndex = 0 To 20
  intValues(intIndex) = 99
Next
```

At runtime, this loop executes until `intIndex` equals 11. At that point, when the assignment statement tries to use `intIndex` as a subscript, an exception is thrown, as shown in Figure 8-6.

Figure 8-6 Exception window reporting index outside the bounds of the array

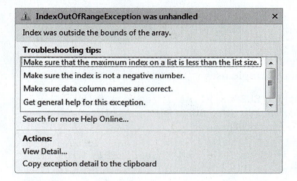

Tutorial 8-1:
Using an array to hold a list of random lottery numbers

In this tutorial you will create an application that randomly generates lottery numbers. When a button is clicked, the application will generate five 2-digit integer numbers and store them in an array. The contents of the array will then be displayed on the application's form in labels.

Step 1: Create a new Windows Forms Application project named *Lottery Numbers*.

Step 2: Set up the project's form with Label and Button controls as shown in Figure 8-7. Set the following properties for each of the Label controls:

- AutoSize = False
- BorderStyle = Fixed3D
- TextAlign = MiddleCenter
- Clear the Text property

Figure 8-7 The *Lottery Numbers* form

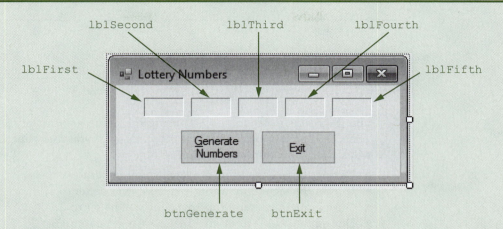

Step 3: Complete the code for the form's event handlers as shown in the following. (Don't type the line numbers. They are shown for reference.)

```
1 Public Class Form1
2    Private Sub btnGenerate_Click(...) Handles btnGenerate.Click
3       Const intMAX_SUBSCRIPT As Integer = 4       ' Maximum subscript
4       Dim intLottery(intMAX_SUBSCRIPT) As Integer ' Lottery array
5       Dim intCount As Integer                     ' Loop counter
6
7       ' Create a Random object.
8       Dim rand As New Random
9
10      ' Fill the array with random numbers.
11      ' Each number will be in the range 0-99.
12      For intCount = 0 To intMAX_SUBSCRIPT
13         intLottery(intCount) = rand.Next(100)
14      Next
15
16      ' Display the array elements in the labels.
17      lblFirst.Text = intLottery(0).ToString()
18      lblSecond.Text = intLottery(1).ToString()
19      lblThird.Text = intLottery(2).ToString()
20      lblFourth.Text = intLottery(3).ToString()
21      lblFifth.Text = intLottery(4).ToString()
22   End Sub
23
24   Private Sub btnExit_Click(...) Handles btnExit.Click
25      ' Close the form.
26      Me.Close()
27   End Sub
28 End Class
```

Let's take a closer look at the code for the btnGenerate_Click event handler. Line 3 declares the constant intMAX_SUBSCRIPT, set to the value 4, and line 4 declares an Integer array named intLottery. The constant intMAX_SUBSCRIPT is used as the upper subscript. As shown in Figure 8-8, the intLottery array will have five elements, and their subscripts will be 0 through 4. Line 5 declares a variable named intCount that will be used as a loop counter.

Figure 8-8 The `intLottery` array and its subscripts

intLottery(0) intLottery(1) intLottery(2) intLottery(3) intLottery(4)

Line 8 creates a `Random` object, using the name `rand` to refer to that object. Then, the `For...Next` loop in line 12 executes. If you study line 12 carefully you will see that the loop will iterate five times:

- During the first iteration, `intCount` will be set to 0.
- During the second iteration, `intCount` will be set to 1.
- During the third iteration, `intCount` will be set to 2.
- During the fourth iteration, `intCount` will be set to 3.
- During the fifth iteration, `intCount` will be set to 4.

The statement inside the loop in line 13 gets a random number in the range of 0 through 99 and assigns it to `intLottery(intCount)`. As a result,

- The first random number will be assigned to `intLottery(0)`.
- The second random number will be assigned to `intLottery(1)`.
- The third random number will be assigned to `intLottery(2)`.
- The fourth name random number will be assigned to `intLottery(3)`.
- The fifth random number will be assigned to `intLottery(4)`.

The statements in lines 17 through 21 display the values of the array elements by assigning their values to the Label controls. Notice that we call each array element's `ToString` method to convert its value to a string, as shown in line 17:

```
lblFirst.Text = intLottery(0).ToString()
```

The value stored in `intLottery(0)` is an integer, so the expression `intLottery(0).ToString()` converts that value to a string. The resulting string is then assigned to the `lblFirst` control's Text property. This technique is used to convert the remaining array elements to strings and assign their values to the other Label controls in lines 18 through 21.

Step 4: Save the project, and run the application. Click the *Generate Numbers* button. You should see random numbers displayed in each of the Label controls, similar to Figure 8-9.

Figure 8-9 Array elements displayed in the Label controls

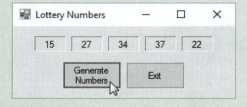

Using Array Elements to Store Input

Array elements can be used to hold data entered by the user. For example, the following code gets numbers from the user and stores them in the intSeries array:

```
Const intMAX_SUBSCRIPT As Integer = 9
Dim intSeries(intMAX_SUBSCRIPT) As Integer
Dim intCount As Integer

For intCount = 0 To intMAX_SUBSCRIPT
   intSeries(intCount) = CInt(InputBox("Enter a number."))
Next
```

In Tutorial 8-2 you will create an application that uses input boxes to read a sequence of strings as input, and stores those strings in an array.

VideoNote

Using an array to hold a list of names entered by the user

Tutorial 8-2:
Using an array to hold a list of names entered by the user

In this tutorial you will create an application that uses an array to hold five strings. The application will have a button that allows you to enter the names of five friends. It will store those names in the array and then display the contents of the array in a list box.

Step 1: Create a new Windows Forms Application project named *Friend List*.

Step 2: Set up the project's form with a ListBox and two Button controls as shown in Figure 8-10.

Figure 8-10 The *Friend List* project's form

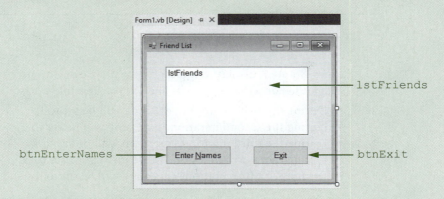

Step 3: Complete the code for the form's event handlers as shown in the following. (Don't type the line numbers. They are shown for reference.)

```
1  Public Class Form1
2     Private Sub btnEnterNames_Click(...) Handles btnEnterNames.Click
3        Const intMAX_SUBSCRIPT As Integer = 4    ' The max subscript
4        Dim strNames(intMAX_SUBSCRIPT) As String ' Array to hold names
5        Dim intCount As Integer                  ' Loop counter
6
7        ' Tell the user what we are about to do.
8        MessageBox.Show("I'm going to ask you to enter the " &
9                        "names of five friends.")
10
11       ' Get the names and store them in the array.
```

```
12          For intCount = 0 To intMAX_SUBSCRIPT
13              strNames(intCount) = InputBox("Enter a friend's name.")
14          Next
15
16          ' Clear the list box of its current contents.
17          lstFriends.Items.Clear()
18
19          ' Display the contents of the array in the list box.
20          For intCount = 0 To intMAX_SUBSCRIPT
21              lstFriends.Items.Add(strNames(intCount))
22          Next
23      End Sub
24
25      Private Sub btnExit_Click(...) Handles btnExit.Click
26          ' Close the form.
27          Me.Close()
28      End Sub
29 End Class
```

Let's take a closer look at the code for the btnEnterNames_Click event handler. Line 3 declares the constant intMAX_SUBSCRIPT, set to the value 4, and line 4 declares a string array named strNames. The constant intMAX_SUBSCRIPT is used as the upper subscript. As shown in Figure 8-11, the strNames array will have five elements, and their subscripts will be 0 through 4. Line 5 declares a variable named intCount that will be used as a loop counter.

Figure 8-11 The strNames array and its subscripts

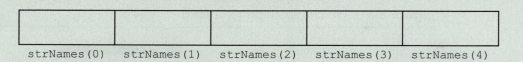

strNames(0)   strNames(1)   strNames(2)   strNames(3)   strNames(4)

Lines 8 and 9 display a message box preparing the user to enter five names. Then, the For...Next loop in line 12 executes five times:

- During the first iteration, intCount will be set to 0.
- During the second iteration, intCount will be set to 1.
- During the third iteration, intCount will be set to 2.
- During the fourth iteration, intCount will be set to 3.
- During the fifth iteration, intCount will be set to 4.

The statement inside the loop, in line 13, does the following: (1) It displays an input box prompting the user to enter a friend's name, and (2) it assigns the value entered by the user to strNames(intCount). As a result,

- The first name the user enters will be assigned to strNames(0).
- The second name the user enters will be assigned to strNames(1).
- The third name the user enters will be assigned to strNames(2).
- The fourth name the user enters will be assigned to strNames(3).
- The fifth name the user enters will be assigned to strNames(4).

Line 17 clears the contents of the 1stFriends list box. Then, another For...Next loop executes in line 20. Just like the previous For...Next loop, this loop uses the intCount variable to step through the elements of the strNames array. When this loop executes, the statement in line 21 adds an array element to the 1stFriends list box. After the loop has finished, each name that is stored in the strNames array will be displayed in the list box.

Step 4: Save the project, and run the application. Click the *Enter Names* button, and then enter five names in the resulting input boxes. After you enter the last one, you should see the names displayed in the list box, similar to Figure 8-12.

Figure 8-12 Names displayed in the list box

Getting the Length of an Array

Arrays have a read-only property named Length that holds the number of elements in the array. For example, assume the following declaration:

```
Dim strNames() As String = { "Joe", "Geri", "Rose" }
```

The strNames array has a total of 3 elements, with an upper subscript of 2. The array's Length property returns the value 3. The following is an example of code that uses the Length property:

```
For intCount = 0 to strNames.Length - 1
    MessageBox.Show(strNames(intCount))
Next
```

The code uses the expression strNames.Length - 1 as the loop's upper limit, because the value in the Length property is 1 greater than the array's upper subscript. As you will learn later, it is possible to change an array's size while an application is running. You can use the Length property to get the current value of an array's size.

Processing Array Contents

You can use array elements just like regular variables in operations. For example, assuming intHours is an array of Integers, the following statement multiplies intHours(3) by the variable decPayRate and stores the result in decGrossPay:

```
decGrossPay = intHours(3) * decPayRate
```

Assuming `intTallies` is an array of Integers, the following statement adds 1 to `intTallies(0)`:

```
intTallies(0) += 1
```

And, assuming `decPay` is an array of Decimals, the following statement displays `decPay(5)` in a message box:

```
MessageBox.Show(decPay(5).ToString())
```

In Tutorial 8-3 you will complete an application that performs calculations using array elements.

VideoNote

Using array elements in a calculation

Tutorial 8-3:
Completing an application that uses array elements in a calculation

JJ's House of Pizza has six employees, each paid $15 per hour. In this tutorial, you complete an application that stores the number of hours worked by each employee in an array. The application uses the values in the array to calculate each employee's gross pay.

Step 1: Open the *Simple Payroll* project located in the student sample programs folder named *Chap8\Simple Payroll*. Figure 8-13 shows the project's form as it appears in the *Designer*, which has already been created for you.

Figure 8-13 *Simple Payroll* form

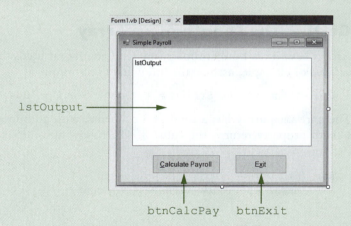

Step 2: Complete the code for the Button control event handlers as shown in the following. (Don't type the line numbers. They are shown for reference.)

```
1 Public Class Form1
2     Private Sub btnCalcPay_Click(...) Handles btnCalcPay.Click
3         ' Constants
4         Const decHOURLY_PAY_RATE As Decimal = 15D
5         Const intMAX_SUBSCRIPT As Integer = 5
6
7         ' Array and other variables
```

```
8              Dim dblHoursArray(intMAX_SUBSCRIPT) As Double
9              Dim intCount As Integer = 0    ' Loop counter
10             Dim decEmpPay As Decimal        ' To hold gross pay
11
12             ' Prepare the user to enter each employee's hours.
13             MessageBox.Show("I'm going to ask you for each " &
14                             "employee's hours worked.")
15
16             ' Get the hours worked by the employees.
17             Do While intCount < dblHoursArray.Length
18                Try
19                    dblHoursArray(intCount) =
20                        CDbl(InputBox("Employee number " &
21                                      (intCount + 1).ToString()))
22                    intCount += 1
23                Catch
24                    ' Display an error message for invalid hours.
25                    MessageBox.Show("Enter a valid number of " &
26                                    "hours for that employee.")
27                End Try
28             Loop
29
30             ' Clear the list box.
31             lstOutput.Items.Clear()
32
33             ' Calculate and display each employee's gross pay.
34             For intCount = 0 To dblHoursArray.Length - 1
35                decEmpPay = CDec(dblHoursArray(intCount) *
36                    decHOURLY_PAY_RATE)
37
38                lstOutput.Items.Add("Employee " &
39                                    (intCount + 1).ToString() &
40                                    " earned " &
41                                    decEmpPay.ToString("c"))
42             Next
43         End Sub
44
45     Private Sub btnExit_Click(...) Handles btnExit.Click
46         ' Close the form.
47         Me.Close()
48     End Sub
49 End Class
```

Let's take a closer look at the btnCalcPay_Click event handler. Here is a summary of the declarations that appear in lines 4 through 10:

- Line 4 declares the constant decHOURLY_PAY_RATE for the employee hourly pay rate.
- Line 5 declares the constant intMAX_SUBSCRIPT for the array's upper subscript.
- Line 8 declares dblHoursArray, an array of Doubles, to hold all of the employees' hours worked.
- Line 9 declares intCount, which will be used as a loop counter (initialized to 0) and to step through the dblHoursArray array.
- Line 10 declares decEmpPay, a Decimal to hold an employee's gross pay.

Lines 13 and 14 display a message box, letting the user know that we are about to ask for each employee's hours worked. The Do While loop that begins in line 17 uses the intCount variable to step through the dblHoursArray array. Recall that intCount was initialized with 0. The loop executes as long as intCount is less than dblHoursArray.length.

Inside the loop a Try-Catch statement is used to catch any exceptions that might occur if the user enters a non-numeric value. The statement that appears in lines 19 through 21 performs the following actions:

- It displays an input box prompting the user with an employee number.
- It uses the CDbl function to convert the user's input to a Double.
- It assigns the resulting value to the array element dblHoursArray(intCount).

If the user enters an invalid value, the program will branch to the Catch clause in line 23, display an error message in lines 25 and 26, and then the loop starts over. If the user enters a valid value, however, line 22 adds 1 to the intCount variable. The loop then starts over.

Once the user has entered values for all of the array elements, line 31 clears the list box, and then the For...Next loop in line 34 begins. This loop also uses the intCount variable to step through each array element. Lines 35 and 36 use an array element to calculate an employee's gross pay, and lines 38 through 41 add a string to the list box reporting the employee's gross pay.

Step 3: Save the project, and run the application. Click the *Calculate Payroll* button. A series of input boxes should appear, asking you to enter the number of hours worked for employees 1 through 6. Enter the following values in order:

Employee 1:	**10**
Employee 2:	**40**
Employee 3:	**20**
Employee 4:	**15**
Employee 5:	**10**
Employee 6:	**30**

After you enter the hours for employee 6, the form should appear, as shown in Figure 8-14.

Step 4: Click the *Exit* button to end the program.

Figure 8-14 *Simple Payroll* application, after entering hours for all employees

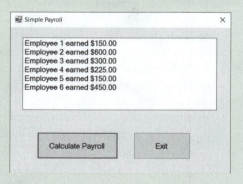

Accessing Array Elements with a For Each Loop

Visual Basic provides a special loop known as the **For Each loop**. The For Each loop can simplify array processing when your task is simply to step through an array, retrieving the value of each element. The loop can read the array elements, but it cannot modify their values. The For Each loop is written in the following general form:

```
For Each var As type In array
    statements
Next
```

In the general form, *var* is the name of a variable that will be created just for use with the loop, *type* is the data type of the array, and *array* is the name of an array. The loop will iterate once for every element in the array. Each time the loop iterates, it copies an array element to the *var* variable. For example, the first time the loop iterates, the *var* variable will contain the value of *array*(0); the second time the loop iterates, the *var* variable will contain the value of *array*(1); and so forth. This continues until the loop has stepped through all of the elements in the array.

For example, suppose we have the following array declaration:

```
Dim intArray() As Integer = {10, 20, 30, 40, 50, 60}
```

The following For Each loop displays all of the array values in a ListBox control named lstShow:

```
For Each intVal As Integer In intArray
    lstShow.Items.Add(intVal)
Next
```

Optional Topic: Using the For Each Loop with a ListBox

A For Each loop can also be used to process the items in a collection. Suppose we would like to search for a city name in the Items collection of a ListBox control named lstCities. We will assume that the user has entered a city name into a TextBox control named txtCity. Figure 8-15 shows an example of the program at runtime. Here are the statements that execute the search:

```
For Each strCity As String In lstCities.Items
  If strCity = txtCity.Text Then
    lblResult.Text = "The city was found!"
  End If
Next
```

Figure 8-15 Searching for a city name in a ListBox control

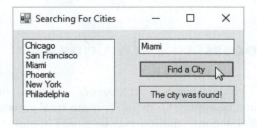

 **Checkpoint**

8.1 Write declaration statements for the following arrays:
   a. `intEmpNums`, an array of 100 integers
   b. `decPayRate`, an array of 24 Decimal values
   c. `intMiles`, an array of integers initialized to the values 10, 20, 30, 40, and 50
   d. `strNames`, an array of strings with an upper subscript of 12
   e. `strDivisions`, an array of strings initialized to the values "North", "South", "East", and "West"

8.2 Identify the error in the following declaration:

```
Dim intNumberSet(4) As Integer = { 25, 37, 45, 60 }
```

8.3 Look at the following array declarations and indicate the number of elements in each array:
   a. `Dim dblNums(100) As Double`
   b. `Dim intValues() As Integer = { 99, 99, 99 }`
   c. `Dim intArray(0) As Integer`

8.4 What is array bounds checking?

8.5 Assume that a procedure has the following array declaration:

```
Const intMAX_SUBSCRIPT As Integer = 25
Dim intPoints(intMAX_SUBSCRIPT) As Integer
```

Write a `For...Next` loop that displays each of the array's elements in message boxes.

8.6 Rewrite your answer to Checkpoint 8.5 using a `For...Each` loop.

8.7 What values are displayed in the message boxes by the following code? (Use a calculator if necessary.)

```
Const dblRATE As Double = 0.1
Const intMAX_SUBSCRIPT As Integer = 3
Dim intBalance(intMAX_SUBSCRIPT) As Integer
Dim intCount As Integer
Dim dblResult As Double

intBalance(0) = 100
intBalance(1) = 250
intBalance(2) = 325
intBalance(3) = 500

For intCount = 0 To intMAX_SUBSCRIPT
  dblResult = intBalance(intCount) * dblRATE
  MessageBox.Show(dblResult.ToString())
Next
```

8.2 Array Processing Techniques

CONCEPT: There are many uses for arrays, and many programming techniques can be applied to them. You can total values and search for data. Related information may be stored in multiple parallel arrays. In addition, arrays can be resized at runtime.

How to Total the Values in a Numeric Array

To total the values in a numeric array, use a loop with an accumulator variable. The loop adds the value in each array element to the accumulator. For example, assume the following array declaration exists in an application, and values have been stored in the array:

```
Const intMAX_SUBSCRIPT As Integer = 24
Dim intUnits(intMAX_SUBSCRIPT) As Integer
```

The following code adds each array element to the `intTotal` variable:

```
Dim intTotal As Integer = 0
Dim intCount As Integer

For intCount = 0 To (intUnits.Length – 1)
   intTotal += intUnits(intCount)
Next
```

NOTE: The first statement in the previous example sets `intTotal` to 0. Recall from Chapter 5 that an accumulator variable must be set to 0 before it is used to keep a running total or the sum will not be correct. Although Visual Basic automatically initializes numeric variables to 0, this statement emphasizes that `intTotal` must equal 0 before the loop starts.

The previous example demonstrated how to use a `For...Next` loop to total all of the values in a numeric array. You can also use a `For Each` loop, as shown in the following code. Assume `intUnits` is an Integer array.

```
Dim intTotal As Integer = 0

For Each intVal As Integer In intUnits
    intTotal += intVal
Next
```

After the loop finishes, `intTotal` will contain the total of all the elements in `intUnits`.

Calculating the Average Value in a Numeric Array

The first step in calculating the average value in an array is to sum the values. The second step is to divide the sum by the number of elements in the array. Assume the following declaration exists in an application, and values have been stored in the array:

```
Const intMAX_SUBSCRIPT As Integer = 24
Dim intUnits(intMAX_SUBSCRIPT) As Integer
```

The following loop calculates the average value in the `intUnits` array. The average is stored in the `dblAverage` variable.

```
Dim intTotal As Integer = 0
Dim dblAverage As Double
Dim intCount As Integer

For intCount = 0 To (intUnits.Length – 1)
   intTotal += intUnits(intCount)
Next

' Use floating-point division to compute the average.
dblAverage = intTotal / intUnits.Length
```

The statement that calculates the average (`dblAverage`) must be placed after the end of the loop. It should execute only once.

Finding the Highest and Lowest Values in an Integer Array

Earlier in this chapter, when explaining `For Each` loops, we showed you how to find the largest value in an array. Let's look at a similar example that uses a `For Next` loop and accesses each array element using a subscript. Assume that the following array declaration exists in an application, and that values have been stored in the array:

```
Dim intNumbers() As Integer = {1, 2, 3, 4, 5}
Dim intCount As Integer       ' Loop counter
Dim intHighest As Integer     ' To hold the highest value

' Get the first element.
intHighest = intNumbers(0)

' Search for the highest value.
For intCount = 1 To (intNumbers.Length - 1)
    If intNumbers(intCount) > intHighest Then
        intHighest = intNumbers(intCount)
    End If
Next
```

The code begins by assigning the value in the first array element to the variable `intHighest`. Next, the loop compares all remaining array elements, beginning at subscript 1, to `intHighest`. Each time it finds a value in the array greater than `intHighest`, the value is copied into `intHighest`. When the loop finishes, `intHighest` equals the largest value in the array.

Lowest Value

The following code, which finds the lowest value in the array, is very similar to the code for finding the highest value. When the loop finishes, `intLowest` equals the smallest value in the array.

```
Dim intNumbers() As Integer = {1, 2, 3, 4, 5}
Dim intCount As Integer       ' Loop counter
Dim intLowest As Integer      ' To hold the lowest value

' Get the first element.
intLowest = intNumbers(0)

' Search for the lowest value.
For intCount = 1 To (intNumbers.Length - 1)
    If intNumbers(intCount) < intLowest Then
        intLowest = intNumbers(intCount)
    End If
Next
```

Copying One Array's Contents to Another

Assume that an application has declared the following arrays and has already initialized the `intOldValues` array with values:

```
Const intMAX_SUBSCRIPT As Integer = 200
Dim intOldValues(intMAX_SUBSCRIPT) As Integer
Dim intNewValues(intMAX_SUBSCRIPT) As Integer
```

Suppose we want to copy the contents of the `intOldValues` array to the `intNewValues` array. We might be tempted to use a single assignment statement, such as the following:

```
intNewValues = intOldValues
```

Although this statement compiles, it does not copy the `intOldValues` array to the `intNewValues` array. Instead it causes the names `intNewValues` and `intOldValues` to reference the same array in memory.

Instead, we must use a loop to copy the individual elements from `intOldValues` to `intNewValues`, as shown in the following code:

```
For intCount = 0 To (intOldValues.Length-1)
   intNewValues(intCount) = intOldValues(intCount)
Next
```

Parallel Arrays

Sometimes it is useful to store related data in two or more related arrays, also known as **parallel arrays**. Let's start by declaring two arrays—one holding the names of training workshops, and the other the cost for each workshop:

```
Const intMAX As Integer = 4

Dim strWorkshops(intMAX) As String = {"Negotiating Skills",
   "Lowering Stress", "Teamwork", "Building Resumes"}

Dim decCosts(intMAX) As String = {500D, 450D, 720D, 250D}
```

The information for each workshop is stored in the same relative position in each array. For instance, the price of `strWorkshops(0)` is stored in `decCosts(0)`. In other words, the Negotiating Skills workshop costs $500.00. Or, to use another example, the price of `strWorkshops(2)` is stored in `decCosts(2)`. Figure 8-16 shows how these arrays match each other.

Figure 8-16 Matching workshops to costs using parallel arrays

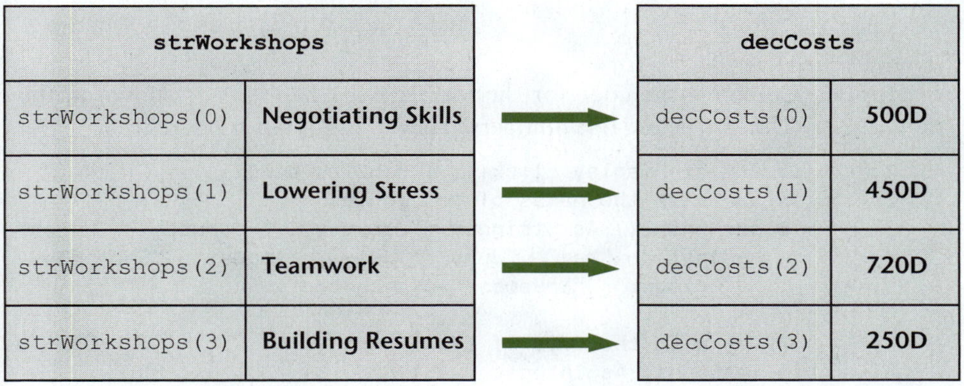

Having information in parallel arrays offers you a great convenience—you only need a single subscript to get related information. For example, the following loop displays each workshop name and its price in a list box:

```
For i As Integer = 0 to intMax - 1
   lstShow.Items.Add( strWorkshops(i) & " will cost " & decCosts(i) )
Next i
```

Tutorial 8-4 examines an application that uses parallel arrays: one to hold the names of the months, and one to hold the number of days in each month.

Tutorial 8-4:
Using parallel arrays

In this tutorial you will create an application that displays the number of days in each month. The application will use two parallel arrays: a string array that is initialized with the names of the months, and an Integer array that is initialized with the number of days in each month. When a button is clicked, the application will display its output in a list box.

Step 1: Create a new Windows Forms Application project named *Months and Days*.

Step 2: Set up the project's form with a ListBox and two Button controls as shown in Figure 8-17.

Figure 8-17 The *Months and Days* project's form

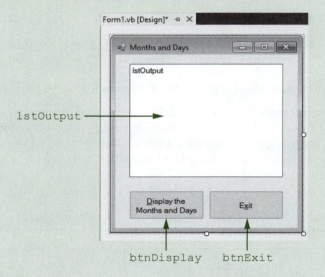

Step 3: Complete the code for the form's event handlers as shown in the following. (Don't type the line numbers. They are shown for reference.)

```
1 Private Sub btnDisplay_Click(...) Handles btnDisplay.Click
2     ' Array with the names of the months
3     Dim strMonths() As String = {"January", "February", "March",
4         "April", "May", "June", "July", "August", "September",
5         "October", "November", "December"}
6
7     ' Array with the days of each month
8     Dim intDays() As Integer = {31, 28, 31, 30, 31, 30,
9                                 31, 31, 30, 31, 30, 31}
10
11    ' Display a list of the months and days.
12    For intCount As Integer = 0 To strMonths.Length − 1
13        lstOutput.Items.Add(strMonths(intCount) & " has " &
14                            intDays(intCount).ToString() & " days.")
15    Next
16 End Sub
```

Let's take a closer look at the code for the `btnDisplay_Click` event handler. Lines 3 through 5 declare a String array named `strMonths`. The `strMonths` array is initialized with the names of the months, so it has twelve elements. Lines 8 and 9 declare an Integer array named `intDays`. The `intDays` array is initialized with the number of days in each month, so it also has twelve elements.

The `strMonths` and `intDays` arrays have the parallel relationship shown in Figure 8-18. In this relationship, `strMonths(i)` contains the name of a month, and `intDays(i)` contains the number of days in that same month.

Figure 8-18 Parallel arrays

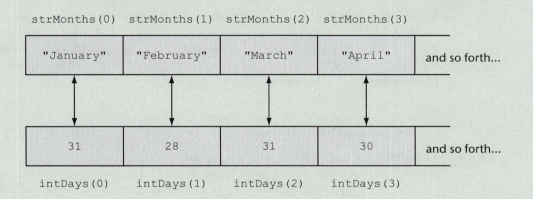

The `For...Next` loop that begins in line 12 uses the `intCount` variable to step through the parallel arrays, displaying a line of output in the `lstOutput` list box. In the first iteration the string `"January has 31 days."` will be added to the list box. In the second iteration the string `"February has 28 days."` will be added to the list box. This continues for each element in the arrays.

Step 4: Save the project, and run the application. Click the *Display the Months and Days* button. You should see the output shown in Figure 8-19.

Figure 8-19 Output displayed in the list box

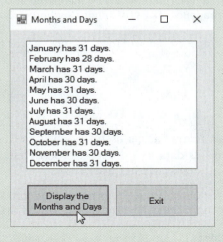

Step 5: Click the *Exit* button to end the application.

Parallel Relationships between Arrays, List Boxes, and Combo Boxes

Items stored in a list box or a combo box have a built-in index. The index of the first item is 0, the index of the second item is 1, and so on. Because this indexing scheme corresponds with the way array subscripts are used, it is easy to create parallel relationships between list boxes, combo boxes, and arrays.

For example, assume that an application has a list box named lstPeople. The following statements store three names in the list box:

```
lstPeople.Items.Add("Jean James")
lstPeople.Items.Add("Kevin Smith")
lstPeople.Items.Add("Joe Harrison")
```

When these statements execute, "Jean James" is stored at index 0, "Kevin Smith" is stored at index 1, and "Joe Harrison" is stored at index 2. Also assume the application has an array of strings named strPhoneNumbers. This array holds the phone numbers of the three people whose names are stored in the list box. The following statements store phone numbers in the array:

```
strPhoneNumbers(0) = "555-2987"
strPhoneNumbers(1) = "555-5656"
strPhoneNumbers(2) = "555-8897"
```

The phone number stored at element 0 ("555-2987") belongs to the person whose name is stored at index 0 in the list box ("Jean James"). Likewise, the phone number stored at element 1 belongs to the person whose name is stored at index 1 in the list box, and so on. When the user selects a name from the list box, the following statement displays the person's phone number:

```
MessageBox.Show(strPhoneNumbers(lstPeople.SelectedIndex))
```

The SelectedIndex property holds the index of the selected item in the list box. This statement uses the index as a subscript in the strPhoneNumbers array.

It is possible however, for the SelectedIndex property to hold a value outside the bounds of the parallel array. When no item is selected, the SelectedIndex property holds –1. The following code provides error checking:

```
With lstPeople
  If .SelectedIndex > -1 And
      .SelectedIndex < strPhoneNumbers.Length Then
    MessageBox.Show(strPhoneNumbers(.SelectedIndex))
  Else
    MessageBox.Show("That is not a valid selection.")
  End If
End With
```

Arrays That Point to Other Data

Another way arrays can be useful is when you need to look up information in another array that has its data in a different order. First, let's return to the arrays of workshops and costs used previously in this chapter:

```
Dim strWorkshops() As String = {"Negotiating Skills",
  "Lowering Stress", "Teamwork", "Building Resumes"}

Dim decCosts() As String = {500D, 450D, 720D, 250D}
```

Then, let us declare a list of cities in which training workshops are held:

```
Dim strCities() As String = {"Chicago", "Miami", "Atlanta",
    "Denver", "Topeka", "Indianapolis"}
```

We would like to match up workshops to cities. To do that, we create a location array that tells us where each workshop is located:

```
Dim intLocations() As Integer = {3, 0, 1, 4}
```

The number in each array position points to an entry in the strCites array. It tells us, for example, that the first workshop is in strCities(3), which is *Denver*. Or, the second workshop is in strCities(0), which is *Chicago*. The third workshop is in strCities(1), which is *Miami*, and the fourth workshop is in strCities(4), which is *Topeka*. Let's write all this information to a list box, as we did before, adding the workshop city name this time:

```
For i As Integer = 0 to strWorkshops.Length-1
    lstShow.Items.Add( strWorkshops(i) & " will cost " & decCosts(i) [#] &
    " and will be held in " & strCities(intLocations(i)))
Next i
```

To understand this code, we must take apart the expression strCities(intLocations(i)). Let's use the first time through the loop, when i = 0 as an example: intLocations(0) contains the value 3. Now, let's use this 3 to create the expression strCities(3). What is that equal to? We can look for the element in the strCities array that has subscript 3—it is Denver, as shown by Figure 8-20. Let's try another example: suppose i = 2. The expression intLocations(0) equals 1. If we use that number to create the expression strCities(1), we get the city named *Miami*.

Figure 8-20 Using the intLocation array to identify a city name

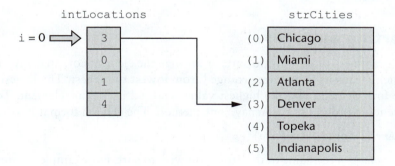

Searching Arrays

Applications not only store and process information stored in arrays, but also often search arrays for specific items. The most basic method of searching an array is the **sequential search**. It uses a loop to examine the elements in an array, one after the other, starting with the first. It compares each element with the value being searched for and stops when the value is found or the end of the array is reached. If the value being searched for is not in the array, the algorithm unsuccessfully searches to the end of the array.

The pseudocode for a sequential search is as follows:

found = False
subscript = 0
Do While found is False and subscript < array's length
    If array(subscript) = searchValue Then
        found = True
        position = subscript

```
      End If
      subscript += 1
   End While
```

In the pseudocode, *found* is a Boolean variable, *position* and *subscript* are integers, *array* is an array of any type, and *searchValue* is the value being searched for. When the search is complete, if the *found* variable equals *False,* the search value was not found. If *found* equals *True,* position contains the subscript of the array element containing the search value.

For example, suppose an application stores test scores in an array named *scores.* The following pseudocode searches the array for an element containing 100:

```
' Search for a 100 in the array.
found = False
count = 0
Do While Not found And count < scores.Length
   If scores(count) = 100 Then
      found = True
      position = count
   End If
   count += 1
Loop

' Was 100 found in the array?
If found Then
   Display "Congratulations! You made a 100 on test" & (position + 1)
Else
   Display "You didn't score a 100, but keep trying!"
End If
```

Sorting an Array

Programmers often want to sort, or arrange the elements of, an array in **ascending order,** which means its values are arranged from lowest to highest. The lowest value is stored in the first element, and the highest value is stored in the last element. To sort an array in ascending order, use the `Array.Sort` method. The general format is as follows:

```
Array.Sort(ArrayName)
```

ArrayName is the name of the array you wish to sort. For example, assume that the following declaration exists in an application:

```
Dim intNumbers() As Integer = {7, 12, 1, 6, 3}
```

The following statement will sort the array in ascending order:

```
Array.Sort(intNumbers)
```

After the statement executes, the array values are in the following order: `1, 3, 6, 7, 12`.

When you pass an array of strings to the `Array.Sort` method, the array is sorted in ascending order according to the Unicode encoding scheme, which we discussed in Chapter 3. Generally, the sort occurs in alphabetic order. But to be more specific about the order, numeric digits are first, uppercase letters are second, and lowercase letters are last. For example, assume the following declaration:

```
Dim strNames() As String = {"dan", "Kim", "Adam", "Bill"}
```

The following statement sorts the array in ascending order:

```
Array.Sort(strNames)
```

After the statement executes, the values in the array appear in this order: `"Adam"`, `"Bill"`, `"Kim"`, `"dan"`.

Dynamically Sizing Arrays

You can change the number of elements in an array at runtime, using the `ReDim` statement. The general format of the `ReDim` statement is as follows:

```
ReDim [Preserve] Arrayname (UpperSubscript)
```

The word `Preserve` is optional. If it is used, any existing values in the array are preserved. If `Preserve` is not used, existing values in the array are destroyed. *Arrayname* is the name of the array being resized. *UpperSubscript* is the new upper subscript and must be a positive whole number. If you resize an array and make it smaller than it was, elements at the end of the array are lost.

For example, the following statement resizes `strNames` so that 25 is the upper subscript:

```
ReDim Preserve strNames(25)
```

After this statement executes, `strNames` has 26 elements. Because the `Preserve` keyword is used, any values originally stored in `strNames` will still be there.

When you do not know at design time the number of elements you will need in an array, you can declare an array without a size and use the `ReDim` statement later to give it a size. For example, suppose you want to write a test-averaging application that averages any number of tests. You can initially declare the array with no size, as follows:

```
Dim dblScores() As Double
```

Currently, `dblScores` equals `Nothing`, but is capable of referencing an array of Double values. Later, when the application has determined the number of test scores, a `ReDim` statement will give the array a size. The following code shows an example of such an operation:

```
intNumScores = CInt(InputBox("Enter the number of test scores."))
If intNumScores > 0 Then
    ReDim dblScores (intNumScores - 1)
Else
    MessageBox.Show("You must enter 1 or greater.")
End If
```

This code asks the user to enter the number of test scores. If the user enters a value greater than 0, the `ReDim` statement sizes the array with `intNumScores - 1` as the upper subscript. (Because the subscripts begin at 0, the upper subscript is `intNumScores - 1`.)

 Checkpoint

8.8 Suppose `intValues` is an array of 100 integers. Write a `For...Next` loop that totals all the values stored in the array.

8.9 Suppose `intPoints` is an array of integers, but you do not know the size of the array. Write code that calculates the average of the values in the array.

8.10 Suppose `strSerialNumbers` is an array of strings. Write a single statement that sorts the array in ascending order.

8.11 What is displayed by the message boxes in the following code segment? (You may need to use a calculator.)

```
Const intMAX_SUBSCRIPT As Integer = 4
Dim intTimes(intMAX_SUBSCRIPT) As Integer
Dim intSpeeds(intMAX_SUBSCRIPT) As Integer
Dim intDists(intMAX_SUBSCRIPT) As Integer
Dim intCount As Integer

intSpeeds(0) = 18
intSpeeds(1) = 4
intSpeeds(2) = 27
intSpeeds(3) = 52
intSpeeds(4) = 100

For intCount = 0 To 4
    intTimes(intCount) = intCount
Next

For intCount = 0 To 4
    intDists(intCount) = intTimes(intCount) * intSpeeds(intCount)
Next

For intCount = 0 To 4
    MessageBox.Show(intTimes(intCount).ToString() & " " &
                    intSpeeds(intCount).ToString() & " " &
                    intDists(intCount).ToString())
Next
```

8.12 Assume that decSales is an array of 20 Decimal values. Write a statement that resizes the array to 50 elements. If the array has existing values, they should be preserved.

8.13 Assume that intValidNumbers is an array of integers. Write code that searches the array for the value 247. If the value is found, display a message indicating its position in the array. If the value is not found, display a message indicating so.

8.3 Procedures and Functions That Work with Arrays

CONCEPT: You can pass arrays as arguments to procedures and functions. You can return an array from a function. These capabilities allow you to write procedures and functions that perform general operations with arrays.

Passing Arrays as Arguments

Quite often you will want to write procedures or functions that process the data in arrays. For example, procedures can be written to store data in an array, display an array's contents, and sum or average the values in an array. Usually such procedures accept an array as an argument.

The following procedure accepts an integer array as an argument and displays the sum of the array's elements:

```
' The DisplaySum procedure displays the sum of the elements in the
' argument array.
```

```
Sub DisplaySum(ByVal intArray() As Integer)
   Dim intTotal As Integer = 0 ' Accumulator
   Dim intCount As Integer      ' Loop counter

   For intCount = 0 To (intArray.Length - 1)
      intTotal += intArray(intCount)
   Next

   MessageBox.Show("The total is " & intTotal.ToString())
End Sub
```

The parameter variable is declared as an array with no upper subscript specified inside the parentheses. The parameter is an object variable that references an array that is passed as an argument. To call the procedure, pass the name of an array, as shown in the following code:

```
Dim intNumbers() As Integer = { 2, 4, 7, 9, 8, 12, 10 }
DisplaySum(intNumbers)
```

When this code executes, the DisplaySum procedure is called and the intNumbers array is passed as an argument. The procedure calculates and displays the sum of the elements in intNumbers.

Passing Arrays by Value and by Reference

Array parameters can be declared ByVal or ByRef. Be aware, however, that the ByVal keyword does not restrict a procedure from accessing and modifying the argument array's elements. For example, look at the following SetToZero procedure:

```
' Set all the elements of the array argument to zero.
Sub SetToZero(ByVal intArray() As Integer)
   Dim intCount As Integer ' Loop counter

   For intCount = 0 To intArray.Length - 1
      intArray(intCount) = 0
   Next
End Sub
```

This procedure accepts an integer array as its argument and sets each element of the array to 0. Suppose we call the procedure, as shown in the following code:

```
Dim intNumbers() As Integer = { 1, 2, 3, 4, 5 }
SetToZero(intNumbers)
```

After the procedure executes, the intNumbers array will contain the values 0, 0, 0, 0, and 0.

Although the ByVal keyword does not restrict a procedure from accessing and modifying the elements of an array argument, it does prevent an array argument from being assigned to another array. For example, the following procedure accepts an array as its argument and then assigns the parameter to another array:

```
' Assign the array argument to a new array. Does this work?
Sub ResetValues(ByVal intArray() As Integer)
   Dim newArray() As Integer = { 0, 0, 0, 0, 0}
   intArray = newArray
End Sub
```

Suppose we call the procedure, as shown in the following code:

```
Dim intNumbers() As Integer = { 1, 2, 3, 4, 5 }
ResetValues(intNumbers)
```

After the procedure executes, the `intNumbers` array still contains the values 1, 2, 3, 4, and 5. If the parameter array had been declared with the `ByRef` keyword, however, the assignment would have affected the argument, and the `intNumbers` array would contain the values 0, 0, 0, 0, and 0 after the procedure executed.

Returning an Array from a Function

You can return an array from a function. For example, the following function prompts the user to enter four names. The names are then returned in an array.

```
' Get three names from the user and return them as an array
' of strings.
Function GetNames() As String()
    Const intMAX_SUBSCRIPT As Integer = 2
    Dim strNames(intMAX_SUBSCRIPT) As String
    Dim intCount As Integer

    For intCount = 0 To 3
        strNames(intCount) = InputBox("Enter name " &
            (intCount + 1).ToString())
    Next

    Return strNames
End Function
```

The function has a return type of `String()`, indicating that it returns an array of strings. The return value can be assigned to any array of strings. The following code shows the function's return value being assigned to `strCustomers`:

```
Dim strCustomers() As String
strCustomers = GetNames()
```

After the code executes, the `strCustomers` array contains the names entered by the user.

An array returned from a function must be assigned to an array of the same type. For example, if a function returns an array of integers, its return value can be assigned only to an array of integers. In Tutorial 8-5, you examine an application containing several functions that work with arrays.

Tutorial 8-5:
Examining an application that passes an array to procedures and functions

In this tutorial, you examine the *Sales Data* application, which asks the user for sales figures for five days. It calculates and displays the total sales, average sales, highest sales amount, and lowest sales amount.

Step 1: Open the *Sales Data* project located in the student sample programs folder named *Chap8\Sales Data*.

Step 2: Before we look at the code, let's see the application in action. Run the application. Figure 8-21 shows the project's form. Click the *Calculate Sales Data* button.

Figure 8-21 *Sales Data* form

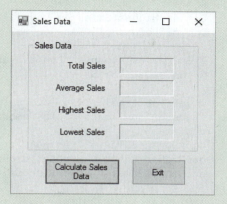

Step 3: A series of five input boxes will appear, asking you to enter the sales for days 1 through 5. Enter the following amounts for each input box:

Day 1:   **1000**

Day 2:   **2000**

Day 3:   **3000**

Day 4:   **4000**

Day 5:   **5000**

After you enter the sales amount for day 5, the application's form should appear as shown in Figure 8-22.

Figure 8-22 *Sales Data* form with sales data displayed

Step 4: Click the *Exit* button to end the application.

Step 5: Now we will examine the application's code. Open the *Code* window and look at the `btnCalculate_Click` event handler. The code is shown here, with line numbers for reference:

```
1 Public Class Form1
2
3     Private Sub btnCalculate_Click(...) Handles btnCalculate.Click
4         ' Create an array to hold sales amounts.
5         Const intMAX_SUBSCRIPT As Integer = 4
6         Dim decSales(intMAX_SUBSCRIPT) As Decimal
7
```

```
8            ' Other local variables
9            Dim decTotalSales As Decimal      ' To hold the total sales
10           Dim decAverageSales As Decimal    ' To hold the average sales
11           Dim decHighestSales As Decimal    ' To hold the highest sales
12           Dim decLowestSales As Decimal     ' To hold the lowest sales
13
14           ' Get sales amounts from the user.
15           GetSalesData(decSales)
16
17           ' Get the total sales, average sales, highest sales
18           ' amount and lowest sales amount.
19           decTotalSales = TotalArray(decSales)
20           decAverageSales = AverageArray(decSales)
21           decHighestSales = Highest(decSales)
22           decLowestSales = Lowest(decSales)
23
24           ' Display the results.
25           lblTotal.Text = decTotalSales.ToString("c")
26           lblAverage.Text = decAverageSales.ToString("c")
27           lblHighest.Text = decHighestSales.ToString("c")
28           lblLowest.Text = decLowestSales.ToString("c")
29       End Sub
30
```

Here is a summary of the declarations that appear in lines 5 through 12:

- Line 5 declares the constant intMAX_SUBSCRIPT, set to the value 4. This will be the upper subscript of the array that holds sales amount.
- Line 6 declares decSales as an array of Decimals, using intMAX_SUBSCRIPT as the upper subscript. The array has five elements, one for each day of sales.
- Line 9 declares decTotalSales as a Decimal, to hold the total sales amount.
- Line 10 declares decAverageSales as a Decimal, to hold the average sales amount.
- Line 11 declares decHighestSales as a Decimal, to hold the highest sales amount.
- Line 12 declares decLowestSales as a Decimal, to hold the lowest sales amount.

Line 15 calls the GetSalesData procedure, passing the decSales array as an argument. The GetSalesData procedure displays the input boxes prompting the user to enter sales amounts for each day. It stores the amounts entered by the user in the array that is passed as an argument.

Line 19 calls the TotalArray function, passing the decSales array as an argument. The function returns the total of the values in the array, and that value is assigned to the decTotalSales variable.

Line 20 calls the AverageArray function, passing the decSales array as an argument. The function returns the average of the values in the array, and that value is assigned to the decAverageSales variable.

Line 21 calls the Highest function, passing the decSales array as an argument. The function returns the highest value in the array, and that value is assigned to the decHighestSales variable.

Line 22 calls the Lowest function, passing the decSales array as an argument. The function returns the lowest value in the array, and that value is assigned to the decLowestSales variable.

The statements in lines 25 through 28 display the sales data in the Label controls on the application's form.

Just below the `btnCalculate_Click` event handler is the `GetSalesData` procedure, shown here with line numbers for reference:

```
31   ' The GetSalesData procedure accepts a Decimal array argument.
32   ' It fills the array with sales amounts entered by the user.
33
34   Sub GetSalesData(ByRef decSales() As Decimal)
35       Dim intCount As Integer = 0 ' Loop counter, set to 0
36
37       ' Fill the decSales array with values entered by the user.
38       Do While intCount < decSales.Length
39          Try
40              ' Get the sales for a day.
41              decSales(intCount) =
42                  CDec(InputBox("Enter the sales for day " &
43                               (intCount + 1).ToString()))
44              ' Increment intCount.
45              intCount += 1
46          Catch
47              ' Display an error message for invalid input.
48              MessageBox.Show("Enter a valid numeric value.")
49          End Try
50       Loop
51   End Sub
52
```

Line 35 declares `intCount`, which will be used as a loop counter and to step through the `decSales` array parameter. Notice that `intCount` is initialized to 0.

The `Do While` loop that begins in line 38 uses the `intCount` variable to step through the `decSales` array parameter. Recall that `intCount` was initialized with 0. The loop executes as long as `intCount` is less than `decSales.length`.

Inside the loop a `Try–Catch` statement is used to catch any exceptions that might occur if the user enters a non-numeric value. The statement that appears in lines 41 through 43 performs the following actions:

- It displays an input box prompting the user to enter the sales for a specific day.
- It uses the `CDec` function to convert the user's input to a Decimal.
- It assigns the resulting value to the array element `decSales(intCount)`.

If the user enters an invalid value, the program will branch to the `Catch` clause in line 46, display an error message in line 48, and then the loop starts over. If the user enters a valid value, however, line 45 adds 1 to the `intCount` variable. The loop then starts over. When the loop is finished, the `decSales` array parameter will contain the sales amounts entered by the user, and the procedure ends.

Next is the `TotalArray` function, shown here with line numbers for reference. The function accepts a Decimal array as an argument. It uses a loop to step through the array's elements, adding their values to an accumulator variable. The total of the array's elements is then returned.

```
53   ' The TotalArray function accepts a Decimal array as an
54   ' argument and returns the total of its values.
55
56   Function TotalArray(ByVal decValues() As Decimal) As Decimal
57       Dim decTotal As Decimal = 0  ' Accumulator
58       Dim intCount As Integer      ' Loop counter
```

```
59
60          ' Calculate the total of the array's elements.
61          For intCount = 0 To (decValues.Length - 1)
62              decTotal += decValues(intCount)
63          Next
64
65          ' Return the total.
66          Return decTotal
67      End Function
68
```

Next is the AverageArray function, shown here with line numbers for reference. The function accepts a Decimal array as an argument and returns the average of the array's values.

```
69      ' The AverageArray function accepts a Decimal array as an
70      ' argument and returns the total of its values.
71
72      Function AverageArray(ByVal decValues() As Decimal) As Decimal
73          Return TotalArray(decValues) / decValues.Length
74      End Function
75
```

Next is the Highest function, shown here with line numbers for reference. The function accepts a Decimal array as an argument and returns the highest value found in the array.

```
76      ' The Highest function accepts a Decimal array as an
77      ' argument and returns the highest value it contains.
78
79      Function Highest(ByVal decValues() As Decimal) As Decimal
80          Dim intCount As Integer    ' Loop counter
81          Dim decHighest As Decimal  ' To hold the highest value
82
83          ' Get the first value in the array.
84          decHighest = decValues(0)
85
86          ' Search for the highest value.
87          For intCount = 1 To (decValues.Length - 1)
88              If decValues(intCount) > decHighest Then
89                  decHighest = decValues(intCount)
90              End If
91          Next
92
93          ' Return the highest value.
94          Return decHighest
95      End Function
96
```

Next is the Lowest function, shown here with line numbers for reference. The function accepts a Decimal array as an argument and returns the lowest value found in the array.

```
97      ' The Lowest function accepts a Decimal array as an
98      ' argument and returns the lowest value it contains.
99
100     Function Lowest(ByVal decValues() As Decimal) As Decimal
101         Dim intCount As Integer    ' Loop counter
102         Dim decLowest As Decimal   ' To hold the lowest value
```

```
103
104            ' Get the first value in the array.
105            decLowest = decValues(0)
106
107            ' Search for the lowest value.
108            For intCount = 1 To (decValues.Length - 1)
109                If decValues(intCount) < decLowest Then
110                    decLowest = decValues(intCount)
111                End If
112            Next
113
114            ' Return the lowest value.
115            Return decLowest
116        End Function
117
```

Next is the `btnExit_Click` event handler, shown here with line numbers for reference:

```
118        Private Sub btnExit_Click(...) Handles btnExit.Click
119            ' Close the form.
120            Me.Close()
121        End Sub
122    End Class
```

8.4 Multidimensional Arrays

CONCEPT: You may create arrays with more than two dimensions to hold complex sets of data.

Two-Dimensional Arrays

The arrays presented so far have had only one subscript. An array with one subscript is called a **one-dimensional array** and is useful for storing and working with a single set of data. Sometimes, though, it is necessary to work with multiple sets of data. For example, in a grade-averaging program, a teacher might record all of one student's test scores in an array. If the teacher has 30 students, that means there must be 30 arrays to record the scores for the entire class. Instead of declaring 30 individual arrays, it would be better to declare a two-dimensional array.

A **two-dimensional array** is like an array of arrays. It can be used to hold multiple sets of values. Think of a two-dimensional array as having rows and columns of elements, as shown in Figure 8-23. This figure shows an array having three rows (numbered 0, 1, and 2) and four columns (numbered 0, 1, 2, and 3). There are a total of 12 elements in the array.

Figure 8-23 Rows and columns

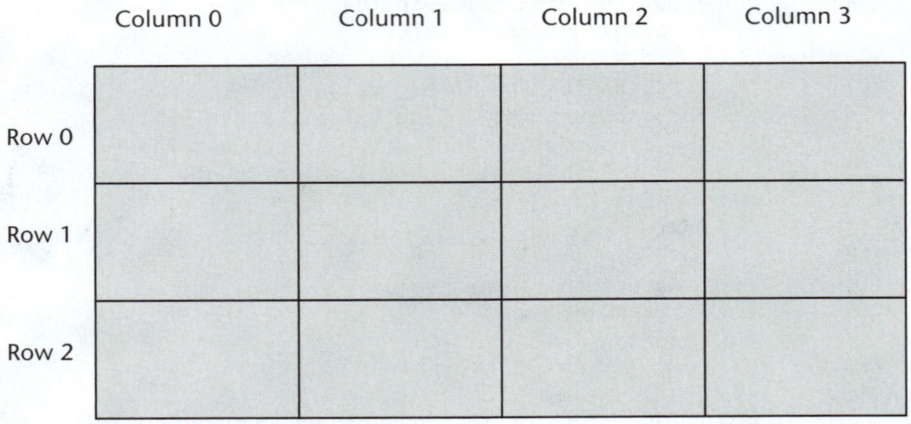

	Column 0	Column 1	Column 2	Column 3
Row 0				
Row 1				
Row 2				

To declare a two-dimensional array, two sets of upper subscripts are required, the first for the rows and the second for the columns. The general format of a two-dimensional array declaration is as follows:

```
Dim ArrayName (UpperRow,UpperColumn) As DataType
```

Let's take a closer look at the syntax.

- *ArrayName* is the name of the array.
- *UpperRow* is the value of the array's highest row subscript. This must be a positive integer.
- *UpperColumn* is the value of the array's highest column subscript. This must be a positive integer.
- *DataType* is a Visual Basic data type.

An example declaration of a two-dimensional array with three rows and four columns follows and is shown in Figure 8-24. The highest row subscript is 2 and the highest column subscript is 3.

```
Dim dblScores (2, 3) As Double
```

Figure 8-24 Declaration of a two-dimensional array

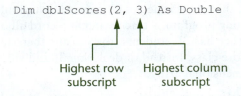

```
Dim dblScores(2, 3) As Double
```

Highest row subscript   Highest column subscript

As with one-dimensional arrays, it is a good practice to use named constants to specify the upper subscripts. Here is an example:

```
Const intMAX_ROW As Integer = 2
Const intMAX_COL As Integer = 3
Dim dblScores(intMAX_ROW, intMAX_COL) As Double
```

When data in a two-dimensional array is processed, each element has two subscripts, the first for its row and the second for its column. Using the dblScores array as an example, the elements in row 0 are referenced as follows:

```
dblScores(0, 0)
dblScores(0, 1)
dblScores(0, 2)
dblScores(0, 3)
```

The elements in row 1 are referenced as follows:

```
dblScores(1, 0)
dblScores(1, 1)
dblScores(1, 2)
dblScores(1, 3)
```

The elements in row 2 are referenced as follows:

```
dblScores(2, 0)
dblScores(2, 1)
dblScores(2, 2)
dblScores(2, 3)
```

Figure 8-25 illustrates the array with the subscripts shown for each element.

Figure 8-25 Subscripts for each element of the dblScores array

	Column 0	Column 1	Column 2	Column 3
Row 0	dblScores(0, 0)	dblScores(0, 1)	dblScores(0, 2)	dblScores(0, 3)
Row 1	dblScores(1, 0)	dblScores(1, 1)	dblScores(1, 2)	dblScores(1, 3)
Row 2	dblScores(2, 0)	dblScores(2, 1)	dblScores(2, 2)	dblScores(2, 3)

To access one of the elements in a two-dimensional array, you must use two subscripts. For example, the following statement stores the number 95 in dblScores(2, 1):

```
dblScores(2, 1) = 95
```

Programs often use nested loops to process two-dimensional arrays. For example, the following code prompts the user to enter a score, once for each element in the array:

```
For intRow = 0 To intMAX_ROW
  For intCol = 0 To intMAX_COL
    dblScores(intRow, intCol) = CDbl(InputBox("Enter a score."))
  Next
Next
```

And the following code displays all the elements in the dblScores array:

```
For intRow = 0 To intMAX_ROW
  For intCol = 0 To intMAX_COL
    lstOutput.Items.Add(dblScores(intRow, intCol).ToString())
  Next
Next
```

Implicit Sizing and Initialization of Two-Dimensional Arrays

As with a one-dimensional array, you may provide an initialization list for a two-dimensional array. Recall that when you provide an initialization list for an array, you cannot provide the upper subscript numbers. When initializing a two-dimensional array, you must provide the comma to indicate the number of dimensions. The following is an example of a two-dimensional array declaration with an initialization list:

```
Dim intNumbers(,) As Integer = { {1, 2, 3} ,
                                  {4, 5, 6} ,
                                  {7, 8, 9} }
```

Initialization values for each row are enclosed in their own set of braces. In this example, the initialization values for row 0 are {1, 2, 3}, the initialization values for row 1 are {4, 5, 6}, and the initialization values for row 2 are {7, 8, 9}. So, this statement declares an array with three rows and three columns.

The values are assigned to the intNumbers array in the following manner:

```
intNumbers(0, 0) is set to 1
intNumbers(0, 1) is set to 2
intNumbers(0, 2) is set to 3

intNumbers(1, 0) is set to 4
intNumbers(1, 1) is set to 5
intNumbers(1, 2) is set to 6

intNumbers(2, 0) is set to 7
intNumbers(2, 1) is set to 8
intNumbers(2, 2) is set to 9
```

Summing the Columns of a Two-Dimensional Array

You can use nested loops to sum the columns in a two-dimensional array. The following code sums each column of an array named intValues. The outer loop controls the column subscript and the inner loop controls the row subscript. The variable intTotal accumulates the sum of each column.

```
' Sum the columns.
For intCol = 0 To intMAX_COL
  ' Initialize the accumulator.
  intTotal = 0

  ' Sum all rows within this column.
  For intRow = 0 To intMAX_ROW
    intTotal += intValues(intRow, intCol)
  Next

  ' Display the sum of the column.
  MessageBox.Show(" Sum of column " & intCol.ToString() &
              " is " & intTotal.ToString())
Next
```

Tutorial 8-6:
Completing the *Seating Chart* application

In this tutorial, you will complete the *Seating Chart* application. When completed, the application will display an airplane seating chart and allow the user to select a seat number. The application will display the price of the selected seat.

Step 1: Open the *Seating Chart* project located in the student sample programs folder named *Chap8\Seating Chart*. Figure 8-26 shows the application's form, which

Figure 8-26 The *Seating Chart* application's form

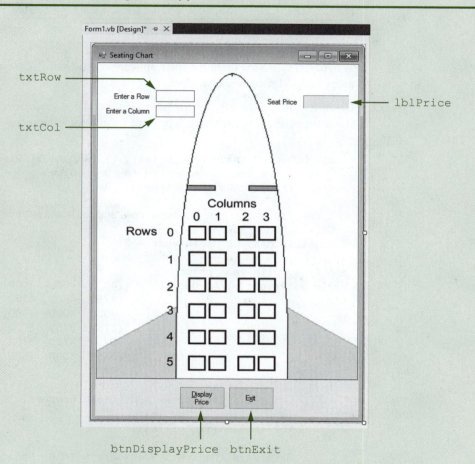

has already been created for you. The seating chart image (which is displayed in a `PictureBox` control) shows the seats on the plane, arranged in rows and columns. When the completed application runs, the user will enter valid row and column numbers in the `txtRow` and `txtCol` text boxes, and then click the *Display Price* button. The price of the selected seat will be displayed in the `lblPrice` label.

The following table shows the seat prices:

	Columns			
	0	1	2	3
Row 0	$450	$450	$450	$450
Row 1	$425	$425	$425	$425
Row 2	$400	$400	$400	$400
Row 3	$375	$375	$375	$375
Row 4	$375	$375	$375	$375
Row 5	$350	$350	$350	$350

When you write the code for the application, you will create a two-dimensional array to hold these values.

Step 2: Complete the code for the form's event handlers as shown in the following. (Don't type the line numbers. They are shown for reference.)

```
1 Public Class Form1
2     Private Sub btnDisplayPrice_Click(...) Handles btnDisplayPrice.Click
3         ' Variables for the selected row and column
4         Dim intRow, intCol As Integer
5
6         ' Constants for the maximum row and column subscripts
7         Const intMAX_ROW As Integer = 5
8         Const intMAX_COL As Integer = 3
9
10        ' Array with seat prices
11        Dim decPrices(,) As Decimal = {{450D, 450D, 450D, 450D},
12                                       {425D, 425D, 425D, 425D},
13                                       {400D, 400D, 400D, 400D},
14                                       {375D, 375D, 375D, 375D},
15                                       {375D, 375D, 375D, 375D},
16                                       {350D, 350D, 350D, 350D}}
17
18        Try
19            ' Get the selected row and column numbers.
20            intRow = CInt(txtRow.Text)
21            intCol = CInt(txtCol.Text)
22
23            ' Make sure the row and col are within range.
24            If intRow >= 0 And intRow <= intMAX_ROW Then
25                If intCol >= 0 And intCol <= intMAX_COL Then
26                    ' Display the selected seat's price.
27                    lblPrice.Text = decPrices(intRow,intCol).ToString("c")
28                Else
29                    ' Error message for invalid column.
```

```
30                    MessageBox.Show("Column must be 0 through " &
31                              intMAX_COL.ToString())
32             End If
33         Else
34             ' Error message for invalid row.
35             MessageBox.Show("Row must be 0 through " &
36                        intMAX_ROW.ToString())
37         End If
38     Catch
39         ' Error message for non-integer input.
40         MessageBox.Show("Row and column must be integers.")
41     End Try
42 End Sub
43
44 Private Sub btnExit_Click(...) Handles btnExit.Click
45     ' Close the form.
46     Me.Close()
47 End Sub
48 End Class
```

Let's take a closer look at the btnDisplayPrice_Click event handler. Line 4 declares the intRow and intCol variables. These will hold the row and column numbers that the user enters. Lines 7 and 8 declare the constants inMAX_ROW (set to 5) and intMAX_COL (set to 3). These values are the upper row and column numbers in the array that will hold the seat prices.

Lines 11 through 16 declare decPrices, a two-dimensional array of Decimals, initialized with the seat prices previously shown.

A Try–Catch statement begins in line 18 to deal with any non-numeric values entered by the user. In line 20 we get the row number entered by the user into the txtRow text box, convert it to an Integer, and store the result in the intRow variable. If an exception is thrown because of a non-numeric value, the program will jump to the Catch clause in line 38.

In line 21 we get the column number entered by the user into the txtCol text box, convert it to an Integer, and store the result in the intCol variable. If an exception is thrown because of a non-numeric value, the program will jump to the Catch clause in line 38.

Next we want to make sure the selected row and column numbers are within the correct range. The valid row numbers are 0 through 5, and the valid column numbers are 0 through 3. The If...Then statement in line 24 determines whether intRow is within the correct range. If it is not, the Else clause in line 33 displays an error message. If intRow is within the correct range, the If...Then statement in line 25 determines whether intCol is within the correct range. If it is not, the Else clause in line 28 displays an error message. Otherwise, the program continues with line 27. Line 27 uses intRow and intCol as subscripts to retrieve the selected seat's price from the decPrices array, and then displays that value in the lblPrice label.

Step 3: Save the project, and then run the application. Experiment by entering row and column numbers for different seats, and comparing the displayed price with the table previously shown. Figure 8-27 shows the application's form with row 2, column 3 selected. When you are finished, click the *Exit* button to end the application.

Figure 8-27 Row 2, column 3 selected

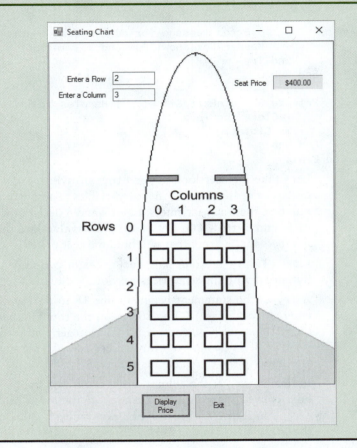

Three-Dimensional Arrays and Beyond

You can create arrays with up to 32 dimensions, but it is rare to have more than 3. The following is an example of a three-dimensional array declaration:

```
Dim decSeats(9, 11, 14) As Decimal
```

This array can be thought of as 10 sets of 12 rows, with each row containing 15 columns. This array might be used to store the prices of seats in an auditorium, in which there are 15 seats in a row, 12 rows in a section, and 10 sections in the room.

Figure 8-28 represents a three-dimensional array as pages of two-dimensional arrays.

Arrays with more than three dimensions are difficult to visualize but can be useful in some programming applications. For example, in a factory warehouse where cases of widgets are stacked on pallets, an array of four dimensions can store a part number for each widget. The four subscripts of each element can represent the pallet number, case number, row number, and column number of each widget. Similarly, an array with five dimensions could be used if there were multiple warehouses.

Figure 8-28 A three-dimensional array

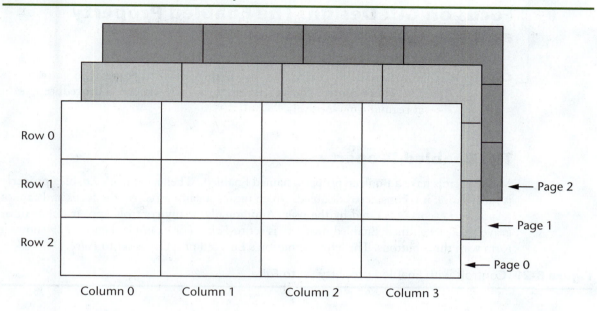

Checkpoint

8.14 Declare a two-dimensional array of integers named `intGrades`. It should have 30 rows and 10 columns.

8.15 How many elements are in the following array?

```
Dim decSales(5, 3) As Decimal
```

8.16 Write a statement that assigns 56893.12 to the first column of the first row of the `decSales` array declared in Checkpoint 8.15.

8.17 Write a statement that displays in a message box the contents of the last column of the last row of the array `decSales` declared in Checkpoint 8.15.

8.18 Declare a two-dimensional array of integers named `intSettings`, that is large enough to hold the following table of numbers:

```
12    24    32    21    42
14    67    87    65    90
19     1    24    12     8
```

8.19 How many rows and columns does the array declared in the following statement have?

```
Dim intMatrix(,) As Integer = { { 2, 4, 7, 0, 3} ,
{ 6, 5, 12, 8, 6} , { 9, 0, 14, 6, 0} ,
{ 16, 7, 9, 13, 10} }
```

8.20 A movie rental store keeps DVDs on 50 racks with 10 shelves each. Each shelf holds 25 DVDs. Declare a three-dimensional array of strings large enough to represent the store's storage system. Each element of the array holds a movie title.

8.5 Focus on GUI Design: The Enabled Property and the Timer Control

CONCEPT: You can disable controls by setting their Enabled property to *False*. The Timer control allows your application to execute a procedure at regular time intervals.

The Enabled Property

Most controls have a Boolean property named Enabled. When a control's **Enabled property** is set to *False*, it is considered disabled, which means it cannot receive the focus and cannot respond to events generated by the user. Additionally, many controls appear dimmed, or grayed out, when their Enabled property is set to *False*. For example, Figure 8-29 shows a form with three buttons. The leftmost button's Enabled property is set to *False*.

Figure 8-29 Controls with Enabled property set to *False*

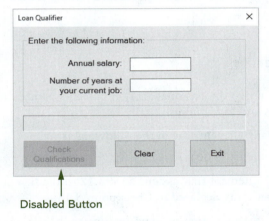

Disabled Button

By default, a control's Enabled property is set to *True*. If you change a control's Enabled property to *False* at design time, the control is initially disabled when the application runs.

You can also change the Enabled property's value with code at runtime. For example, assume an application has a radio button named radBlue. The following statement disables the control:

```
radBlue.Enabled = False
```

Sometimes you may not want the user to access controls. For example, consider an application that calculates the price of two different models of a new car. One model comes only in red, yellow, and black, while the other model comes only in white, green, and orange. As soon as the user selects a model, the application can disable colors not available for that model.

The Timer Control

The **Timer control** allows an application to automatically execute code at regular time intervals. It is useful when you want an application to perform an operation at certain times or after an amount of time has passed. For example, a Timer control can perform simple animation by moving a graphic image across the screen, or it can cause a form to be hidden after a certain amount of time.

Double-click the Timer icon in the *Toolbox* to place a Timer control on a form. (The Timer control is in the *Components* section of the *Toolbox*.) Because the Timer control is invisible at runtime, it appears in the component tray at design time. The prefix that we will use for a Timer control's name is tmr.

Timer Events

When you place a Timer control on a form, it responds to Tick events while the application is running. A Tick event is generated at regular time intervals. If the control has a Tick event handler, it is executed each time a Tick event occurs. Therefore, the code that you write in the Tick event handler executes at regular intervals.

To create a Tick event handler code template, double-click a Timer control that has been placed in the form's component tray.

Timer Control Properties

The Timer control has two important properties: Enabled and Interval. When the Enabled property is set to *True*, the Timer control responds to Tick events. When the Enabled property is set to *False*, the Timer control does not respond to Tick events (code in the control's Tick event handler does not execute).

The **Interval property** can be set to a value of 1 or greater. The value stored in the Interval property is the number of milliseconds that elapse between timer events. A millisecond is a thousandth of a second, so setting the Interval property to 1000 causes a timer event to occur every second.

In Tutorial 8-7, you examine an application that demonstrates a Timer control.

Tutorial 8-7:
The *Timer Demo*

Step 1: Open the *Timer Demo* project from the sample student programs folder named *Chap8\Timer Demo*. The application's form is shown in Figure 8-30. Notice that the Timer control appears as a stopwatch in the component tray.

Figure 8-30 *Timer Demo* form

Step 2: Run the application. The form shown in Figure 8-31 appears.

Figure 8-31 *Timer Demo* application running

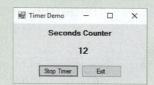

Step 3: The number appearing under the *Seconds Counter* label is initially set to 0, but it increments every second. After a few seconds, click the *Stop Timer* button to halt the timer.

Step 4: When you click the *Stop Timer* button, the button's text changes to *Start Timer*. Click the button again to start the timer.

Step 5: After a few seconds, click the *Exit* button to end the application.

Step 6: With the *Designer* window open, select the Timer control.

Step 7: With the Timer control selected, look at the *Properties* window. The name of the control is tmrSeconds. Its Enabled property is initially set to *True*, and its Interval property is set to *1000*.

Step 8: Open the *Code* window and notice that a class-level variable named intSeconds is declared.

Step 9: Look at the tmrSeconds_Tick event handler. The code is as follows:

```
Private Sub tmrSeconds_Tick(...) Handles tmrSeconds.Tick
    ' Update the seconds display by one second.
    intSeconds += 1
    lblCounter.Text = intSeconds.ToString()
End Sub
```

Each time the tmrSeconds_Tick event handler executes, it adds 1 to intSeconds and then copies its value to the lblCounter label. Because the Timer control's Interval property is set to *1000*, this event handler executes every second (unless the Timer control's Enabled property equals *False*).

Step 10: The button that stops and starts the timer is named btnToggleTimer. Look at the btnToggleTimer_Click event handler. The code is as follows:

```
Private Sub btnToggleTimer_Click(...) Handles btnToggleTimer.Click
    ' Toggle the timer.
    If tmrSeconds.Enabled = True Then
        tmrSeconds.Enabled = False
        btnToggleTimer.Text = "&Start Timer"
    Else
        tmrSeconds.Enabled = True
        btnToggleTimer.Text = "&Stop Timer"
    End If
End Sub
```

If tmrSeconds.Enabled equals *True*, the code sets it to *False* and changes the button's text to &*Start Timer*. Otherwise, it sets the property to *True* and changes the button's text to &*Stop Timer*.

In Tutorial 8-8 you will use a Timer control to create a game application.

Tutorial 8-8:
Creating the *Catch Me* game

In this tutorial you will create a game application that displays a button. Every second, the button will move to a new, random location on the application's form. The user wins the game when he or she clicks the button.

There are a few button and form properties that will prove useful:

- The current form is identified by the keyword `Me`.
- The width and height, in pixels, of a form or other control is controlled by its Width and Height properties.
- The position of a button within a form is controlled by its Top and Left properties. Vertical pixel coordinates start at 0 at the top of a form and grow in a downward direction, as shown in Figure 8-32.

Figure 8-32 Pixel coordinates in a Visual Basic form

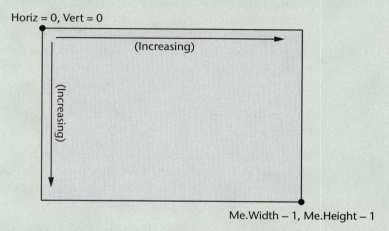

The *Catch Me* game application will have a Timer control with its Interval property set to *1000*. As a result, it will generate a Tick event once every second. The Timer control's Tick event handler will generate two random numbers and assign these random numbers to the Button control's Top and Left properties. As a result, the Button control will move to a random location on the form. The Button control's Click event handler will disable the Timer control (to stop the button from moving around on the form) and display a message indicating that the user won the game.

Step 1: Create a new Windows Forms Application project named *Catch Me*. Set up the application's form as shown in Figure 8-33. Name the Button control `btnCatchMe`, and center it vertically and horizontally in the form.

Figure 8-33 The *Catch Me* application's form

Step 2: Create a Timer control and name it `tmrGameTimer`. Set its Enabled property to *True* and its Interval property to *1000*.

Step 3:   The complete code for the application is shown at the end of this tutorial, with line numbers shown for reference. Double-click the `tmrGameTimer` control that you created in Step 2. This opens the *Code* window and creates a code template for the `tmrGameTimer_Tick` event handler. Complete the event handler by entering the code shown in lines 3 through 15.

Let's take a closer look at the code:

- Line 4 creates a Random object that we will use to generate random numbers.
- Line 7 declares two variables: `intNewLeft` and `intNewTop`. These variables will hold the random numbers for the button's new location.
- Line 10 generates a random integer and assigns it to `intNewLeft`. Notice that the argument passed to the `rand.Next` method is the expression `Me.Width – btnCatchMe.Width`. This will make sure that the random number is not a value that will place the Button control off the right edge of the form.
- Line 11 generates a random integer and assigns it to `intNewTop`. The expression `Me.Height – btnCatchMe.Height` will make sure that the random number is not a value that will place the Button control off the bottom edge of the form.
- Line 14 assigns `intNewLeft` to `btnCatchMe.Left`.
- Line 15 assigns `intNewTop` to `btnCatchMe.Top`.

Step 4:   In the *Designer* window, double-click the `btnCatchMe` Button control. This opens the *Code* window and creates a code template for the `btnCatchMe_Click` event handler. Complete the event handler by entering the code shown in lines 19 through 23.

Let's take a closer look at the code:

- Line 20 sets the Timer control's Enabled property to *False*. This stops the Timer from generating Tick events.
- Line 23 displays a message box letting the user know he or she won.

Step 5:   Save the project and run the application. After you've become more skilled at playing game, you can make it more challenging by changing the Timer control's Interval property to a lower value. This will decrease the amount of time between button moves.

```
 1 Public Class Form1
 2     Private Sub tmrGameTimer_Tick(...) Handles tmrGameTimer.Tick
 3         ' Create a Random object.
 4         Dim rand As New Random
 5
 6         ' Variables to hold XY coordinates
 7         Dim intNewLeft, intNewTop As Integer
 8
 9         ' Get random XY coordinates.
10         intNewLeft = rand.Next(Me.Width - btnCatchMe.Width)
11         intNewTop = rand.Next(Me.Height - btnCatchMe.Height)
12
13         ' Move the button to the new location.
14         btnCatchMe.Left = intNewLeft
15         btnCatchMe.Top = intNewTop
16     End Sub
17
18     Private Sub btnCatchMe_Click(...) Handles btnCatchMe.Click
19         ' Disable the timer.
20         tmrGameTimer.Enabled = False
21
22         ' Display a message.
23         MessageBox.Show("You win!")
24     End Sub
25 End Class
```

8.6 Focus on GUI Design: Anchoring and Docking Controls

CONCEPT: Controls have two properties, Anchor and Dock, which allow you to control the control's position on the form when the form is resized at runtime.

The Anchor Property

By default, when a user resizes a form at runtime, the positions of controls on the form do not change with respect to the top and left edges of the form. For example, in Figure 8-34, the image on the left shows the form before the user resizes it and the image on the right shows the form after the user resizes it.

Figure 8-34 A form before and after the user resizes it

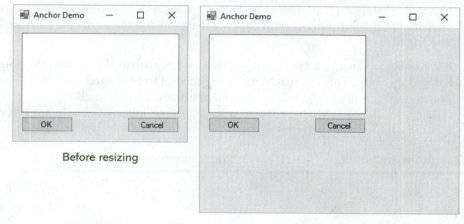

Before resizing

After resizing

When the user resizes the form, the positions of the list box and buttons do not change. Controls have an **Anchor property,** which allows you to anchor the control to one or more edges of a form. When a control is anchored to a form's edge, the distance between the control's edge and the form's edge remains constant when the form is resized at runtime.

When you click the Anchor property in the *Properties* window, the pop-up window shown in Figure 8-35 appears. Notice that the top and left bars are selected, indicating that the control

Figure 8-35 Anchor property selected

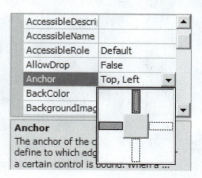

is anchored to the top and left edges of the form. This is the Anchor property's default setting. To change the Anchor property's setting, select the bars that correspond to the edges of the form you wish to anchor the control to. For example, Figure 8-36 shows how the Anchor property appears when the control is anchored to the bottom and right edges.

Figure 8-36 Anchor property set to the bottom and right edges

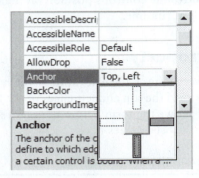

Figure 8-37 shows a form before and after it is resized. This time, the button controls are anchored to the bottom and right edges of the form and the list box is anchored to the top and left edges.

It is possible to anchor a control to opposing sides, such as the top and the bottom, or the left and the right. This approach causes the control to be resized when the form is resized. For example, look at Figure 8-38. The PictureBox control is anchored to all four edges of the form, and its SizeMode property is set to *StretchImage*. When the form is resized, the PictureBox control is resized.

Figure 8-37 Buttons anchored to the bottom and right edges of the form

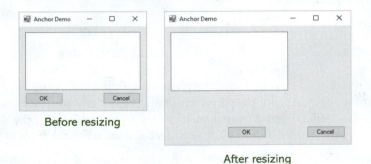

Figure 8-38 PictureBox control anchored to all four edges of the form

The Dock Property

When a control is docked, it is positioned directly against one of the edges of a form. Additionally, the length or width of a docked control is changed to match the length or width of the form's edge. For example, the form in Figure 8-39 has four docked buttons. A button is docked to each of the form's edges.

Figure 8-39 Form with docked buttons

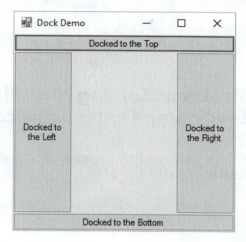

Buttons are automatically sized to fill up the edge to which they are docked. Use the **Dock property** to dock a control against a form's edge. In the *Properties* window, the pop-up window shown in Figure 8-40 appears. The figure illustrates how each button in the pop-up window affects the control. The square button in the center causes the control to fill the entire form.

Figure 8-40 Dock property selected

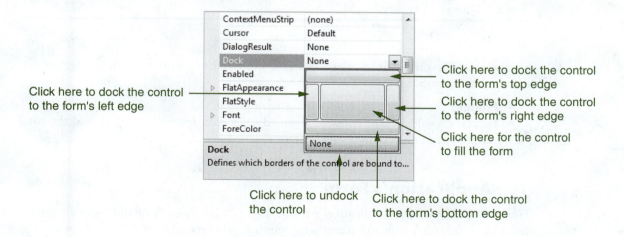

Checkpoint

8.21 Suppose a form has check box controls named chkFreePizza and chkFreeCola, and a radio button control named radLifeTimeMember. Write code that enables the check boxes if the radio button is selected.

8.22 If you want a Timer control to execute its Tick event handler every half second, what value must you store in its Interval property?

8.23 What is the purpose of the Anchor property?

8.24 What is the purpose of the Dock property?

8.7 Focus on Problem Solving: Building the *Demetris Leadership Center* Application

CONCEPT: In this section you build an application that uses data stored in parallel arrays.

The Demetris Leadership Center (DLC) publishes the books, videos, and MP3 audio books listed in Table 8-1.

Table 8-1 Demetris Leadership Center products

Product Title	Product Description	Product Number	Unit Price
Six Steps to Leadership	Book	914	$12.95
Six Steps to Leadership	MP3 Audio	915	$14.95
The Road to Excellence	Video	916	$18.95
Seven Lessons of Quality	Book	917	$16.95
Seven Lessons of Quality	MP3 Audio	918	$21.95

Suppose the vice president of sales has asked you to write a sales reporting program that does the following:

- Prompts the user for the units sold of each product
- Displays a sales report showing detailed sales data for each product and the total revenue from all products sold

The Application's Form

Figure 8-41 shows the application's form. Table 8-2 lists each of the form's controls (excluding the menu controls) along with relevant property settings.

Figure 8-41 Sketch of the application's form

Demetris Leadership Center
File Report Help
Sales Data
lstSalesData
Total Revenue
lblTotalRevenue

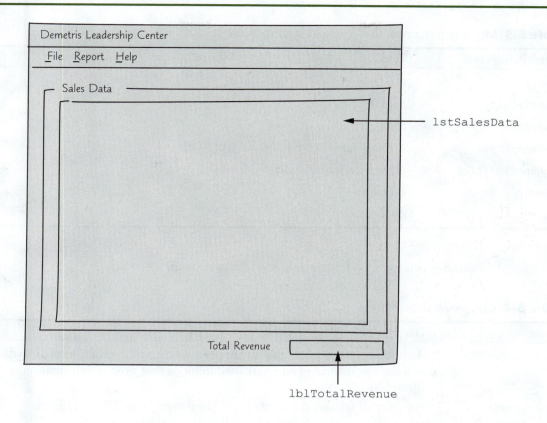

Table 8-2 Controls and property settings

Control Type	Control Name	Property	Property Value
Form	`Form1` (default)	Text:	*Demetris Leadership Center*
GroupBox	(Default)	Text:	*Sales Data*
Label	(Default)	Text:	*Total Revenue*
Label	`lblTotalRevenue`	Text:	
		AutoSize	*False*
		BorderStyle:	*Fixed3D*
ListBox	`lstSalesData`	AutoSize	*False*
MenuStrip	(Default)		See Table 8-3 for details

Figure 8-42 shows a sketch of the menu system on the application's form.

Figure 8-42 Menu system

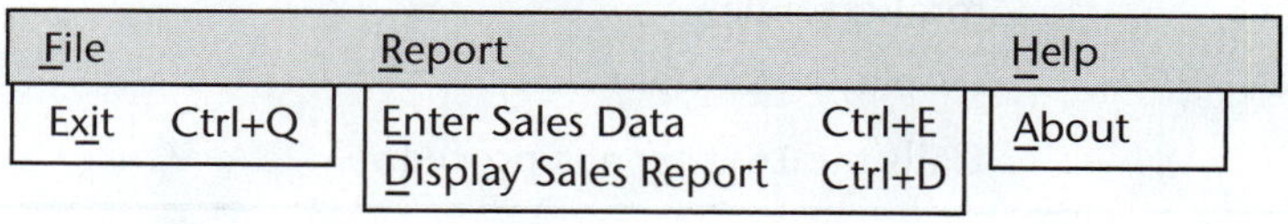

File
Report
Help
Exit Ctrl+Q
Enter Sales Data Ctrl+E
Display Sales Report Ctrl+D
About

Table 8-3 lists the menu item object names, text, and shortcut keys.

Table 8-3 Menu item names, text properties, and shortcut keys

Menu Item Name	Text	Shortcut Key
mnuFile	&File	
mnuFileExit	E&xit	Ctrl + Q
mnuReport	&Report	
mnuReportData	&Enter Sales Data	Ctrl + E
mnuReportDisplay	&Display Sales Report	Ctrl + D
mnuHelp	&Help	
mnuHelpAbout	&About	

Table 8-4 describes the form's class-level declarations.

Table 8-4 Class-level declarations

Name	Description
intMAX_SUBSCRIPT	A constant, set to 8, holding the upper subscript of the class-level arrays, and the upper limit of counters used in loops that process information in the arrays
strProdNames	An array of strings; this array holds the names of the DLC products
strDesc	An array of strings; this array holds the descriptions of the DLC products
intProdNums	An array of integers; this array holds the product numbers of the DLC products
decPrices	An array of Decimal variables; this array holds the prices of the DLC products
intUnitsSold	An array of integers; this array holds the number of units sold for each of the DLC products

The five arrays are parallel arrays, meaning that the same subscript can be used to access data relating to the same item. Table 8-5 lists and describes the methods in the form file.

Table 8-5 Methods

Method	Description
InitArrays	Procedure; assigns the names, descriptions, product numbers, and unit prices of the DLC products to the class-level arrays
mnuFileExit_Click	Ends the application
mnuReportData_Click	Prompts the user for sales data
mnuReportDisplay_Click	Calculates and displays the revenue for each product and the total revenue
mnuHelpAbout_Click	Displays an *About* box
Form1_Load	Calls the InitArrays procedure

In Tutorial 8-9, you build the *Demetris Leadership Center Sales Reporting* application.

Tutorial 8-9:
Building the *Demetris Leadership Center Sales Reporting* application

Step 1: Create a new Windows Forms Application project named *Demetris Sales*.

Step 2: Set up the form as shown in Figure 8-43.

Figure 8-43 The application's main form

Refer to Table 8-2 for the control names and their property settings, and to Figure 8-41 for the locations of the controls. Refer to Figure 8-42 for the menu layout and to Table 8-3 for the menu item properties. Be sure to select `frmMain` as the startup object.

Step 3: The following shows the code for the application. Use this as a reference as you complete the application. (Don't type the line numbers. They are shown for reference.)

```
1 Public Class Form1
2      ' This application displays a sales report for the Demetris
3      ' Leadership Center.
4
5      ' Class-level declarations
6      Const intMAX_SUBSCRIPT As Integer = 4          ' Upper subscript
7      Dim strProdNames(intMAX_SUBSCRIPT) As String   ' Product names
8      Dim strDesc(intMAX_SUBSCRIPT) As String        ' Descriptions
9      Dim intProdNums(intMAX_SUBSCRIPT) As Integer   ' Product numbers
10     Dim decPrices(intMAX_SUBSCRIPT) As Decimal     ' Unit prices
11     Dim intUnitsSold(intMAX_SUBSCRIPT) As Integer  ' Units sold
12
13     Private Sub Form1_Load(...) Handles MyBase.Load
14          ' Initialize the arrays with product data.
15          InitArrays()
16     End Sub
17
```

```
18    Private Sub InitArrays()
19        ' Initialize the arrays.
20        ' First product
21        strProdNames(0) = "Six Steps to Leadership"
22        strDesc(0) = "Book"
23        intProdNums(0) = 914
24        decPrices(0) = 12.95D
25
26        ' Second product
27        strProdNames(1) = "Six Steps to Leadership"
28        strDesc(1) = "MP3"
29        intProdNums(1) = 915
30        decPrices(1) = 14.95D
31
32        ' Third product
33        strProdNames(2) = "The Road to Excellence"
34        strDesc(2) = "Video"
35        intProdNums(2) = 916
36        decPrices(2) = 18.95D
37
38        ' Fourth product
39        strProdNames(3) = "Seven Lessons of Quality"
40        strDesc(3) = "Book"
41        intProdNums(3) = 917
42        decPrices(3) = 16.95D
43
44        ' Fifth product
45        strProdNames(4) = "Seven Lessons of Quality"
46        strDesc(4) = "MP3"
47        intProdNums(4) = 918
48        decPrices(4) = 21.95D
49    End Sub
50
51    Private Sub mnuFileExit_Click(...) Handles mnuFileExit.Click
52        ' Close the form.
53        Me.Close()
54    End Sub
55
56    Private Sub mnuReportData_Click(...) Handles mnuReportData.Click
57        Dim intCount As Integer = 0 ' Loop counter
58
59        Do While intCount <= intMAX_SUBSCRIPT
60            Try
61                ' Get the units sold for a product.
62                intUnitsSold(intCount) = CInt(
63                    InputBox("Enter units sold of product number " &
64                        intProdNums(intCount)))
65
66                ' Increment intCount.
67                intCount += 1
68            Catch
69                ' Error message for invalid input.
70                MessageBox.Show("Enter a valid integer.")
71            End Try
72        Loop
73    End Sub
74
```

```
75    Private Sub mnuReportDisplay_Click(...) Handles mnuReportDisplay.Click
76          ' Calculates and displays the revenue for each
77          ' product and the total revenue.
78          Dim intCount As Integer
79          Dim decRevenue As Decimal
80          Dim decTotalRevenue As Decimal
81
82          ' Display the sales report header.
83          lstSalesData.Items.Add("SALES REPORT")
84          lstSalesData.Items.Add("-------------------")
85
86          ' Display sales data for each product.
87          For intCount = 0 To intMAX_SUBSCRIPT
88
89              ' Calculate product revenue.
90              decRevenue = intUnitsSold(intCount) * decPrices(intCount)
91
92              ' Display the product data.
93              lstSalesData.Items.Add("Product Number: " &
94                                    intProdNums(intCount))
95              lstSalesData.Items.Add("Name: " &
96                                    strProdNames(intCount))
97              lstSalesData.Items.Add("Description: " &
98                                    strDesc(intCount))
99              lstSalesData.Items.Add("Unit Price: " &
100                                   decPrices(intCount).ToString("c"))
101             lstSalesData.Items.Add("Units Sold: " &
102                                   intUnitsSold(intCount).ToString())
103             lstSalesData.Items.Add("Product Revenue: " &
104                                   decRevenue.ToString("c"))
105             lstSalesData.Items.Add("")
106
107             ' Accumulate revenue.
108             decTotalRevenue = decTotalRevenue + decRevenue
109         Next
110
111         ' Display total revenue.
112         lblTotalRevenue.Text = decTotalRevenue.ToString("c")
113    End Sub
114
115    Private Sub mnuHelpAbout_Click(...) Handles mnuHelpAbout.Click
116          ' Display an About box.
117          MessageBox.Show("Displays a sales report for DLC.", "About")
118    End Sub
119 End Class
```

Step 4: Save the project.

Step 5: Run the application. On the application's form, click the *Report* menu, and then click *Enter Sales Data*. You will be prompted with input boxes to enter the units sold for each of the DLC products. Enter the following units' sold values:

Product number 914: **140**

Product number 915: **85**

Product number 916: **129**

Product number 917: **67**

Product number 918: **94**

Step 6: Click the *Report* menu, and then click *Display Sales Report*. Your form should now appear similar to the one shown in Figure 8-44. Scroll through the sales data displayed in the list box.

Figure 8-44 Sales report displayed

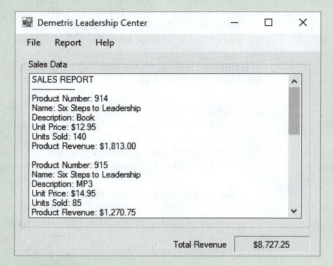

Step 7: Exit the application.

8.8 Using Lists to Hold Information (Optional Topic)

In Visual Basic you can use the **List** data type to hold a set of items. In many ways, a List is similar to an array, but a List has some advantages over an array. First, a list can grow dynamically as you add objects to it. You never have to dimension it to a certain size, as you do with an array. Second, it's easy to remove an item from a list, but very difficult to do the same with an array. Third, lists have a built-in searching function, which arrays do not.

The ListBox control, introduced in Section 5.2, has an Items property that contains a List. Therefore, you are already familiar with some of the operations on lists, such as Add, Remove, and Clear. Now you can create your own List objects and call the same methods you did with ListBox controls.

When you declare a List variable, you must specify the type of data that will be stored in the list. For example, this is how you would declare a list of strings:

```
Dim lstNames As List(Of String)
```

Whenever you create an object in Visual Basic, you must use the New keyword. Lists are objects, so you must use the New keyword as a way of telling Visual Basic that you want to create a new List object. Here is an example:

```
lstNames = New List(Of String)
```

Often, you will prefer to declare the List variable and create a List object at the same time. All you have to do is insert the New keyword into the variable declaration:

```
Dim lstNames As New List(Of String)
```

This is how you would declare and create a List of Integers:

```
Dim lstScores As New List(Of Integer)
```

And this is how you would create a List of Doubles:

```
Dim lstTemperatures As New List(Of Double)
```

Notice how a List always contains a single data type.

Choosing Identifier Names

When naming list variables, you may optionally begin the variable name with a prefix. Here are some examples:

```
Dim lstStrNames As List(Of String)
Dim lstIntScores As List(Of Integer)
```

The lst extension, however, is also used for ListBox controls. Alternately, you can use a prefix that indicates the data type of the items that will be stored in the list (such as int for Integer, dbl for Double, etc.), and use a plural noun to hint that it is a list. Here are some examples:

```
Dim strNames As List(Of String)
Dim intScores As List(Of Integer)
```

Identifier names are a matter of personal preference.

Common List Operations

Call the Add method to add an item to a list. For example:

```
Dim lstNames As New List(Of String)
lstNames.Add("Fred")
LSTNames.Add("Sam")
etc. ...
```

To remove an item, call the Remove method and pass the object you want to remove. Here's an example:

```
lstNames.Remove("Sam")
```

To remove all items, call the Clear method:

```
lstNames.Clear()
```

To get the size of a List, call its Count method:

```
Dim intCount As Integer
intCount = lstNames.Count()
```

You can use an index to access any existing list item. The lowest possible index value is 0. Let's assume our list contains "Fred" and "Sam". The following statements assign each name to a label control:

```
lblResult.Text = lstNames(0)    'returns: Fred
lblResult.Text = lstNames(1)    'returns: Sam
```

Similarly, you can replace a list item when using a subscript:

```
lstNames(0) = "Ben"
```

In the next tutorial, you will build a list based on names input by the user.

Tutorial 8-10:
Building a List from user input

In this tutorial, your will rewrite the application from Tutorial 8-2 that let the user input and save the names of friends. In this new version, the names will be saved in a List(Of String) object. After entering the names, the user can click a button and view all the names in a list box.

Step 1: Create a new Windows Forms application named *Friend List 2*. Place a Label, a ListBox, a TextBox, and two Button controls on the form. Use Figure 8-45 as a guide when naming the controls.

Figure 8-45 Controls in the *Friend List* application

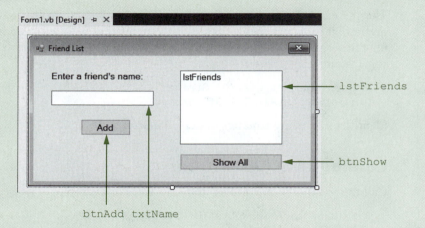

Step 2: Open the *Code* window and inside the form class write the class-level variable declaration shown here in bold (in line 2):

```
Public Class Form1
    Private lstNames As New List(Of String)

End Class
```

Step 3: Create the following Click handler for the *Add* button:

```
Private Sub btnAdd_Click(...) Handles btnAdd.Click
    ' Add the name to the List.
    lstNames.Add(txtName.Text)

    ' Clear the text box.
    txtName.Clear()
    txtName.Focus()
End Sub
```

The lstNames.Add statement adds the contents of the text box to the list of strings. The text box is cleared to prevent the user from accidentally clicking the button twice and adding the same name. The Focus method is called so the user can type a new name into the text box.

Step 4: Next, you will create a Click handler for the *Show All* button that copies the contents of the lstNames list to the list box named lstFriends:

```
Private Sub btnShow_Click(...) Handles btnShow.Click
    ' Display all names in the list box.
    Dim strName As String
```

```
          lstFriends.Items.Clear()

          For Each strName In lstNames
             lstFriends.Items.Add(strName)     'Add to list box
          Next
       End Sub
```

The list box is cleared, and then a `For Each` loop takes each name from `lstFriends` and adds it to the ListBox control.

Step 5: Run and test the application by entering several names into the text box and clicking the *Add* button after each name is entered.

Step 6: Click the *Show All* button. You should see all of the names you entered.

Accessing a List with a Subscript

Tutorial 8-10 used a `For-Each` loop to process all the elements in a list. This is a very easy technique, but sometimes you will want to use a loop counter to do the same thing. Let's take the code from the tutorial and show how it would be written using a counter:

```
Dim intIndex As Integer = 0
Dim strName As String

For intIndex = 0 To lstNames.Count - 1
  strName = lstNames(intIndex)
  lstFriends.Items.Add(strName)
Next
```

Searching for Items in a List

An easy way to search for item in a List is to use the `IndexOf` method. The `IndexOf` method accepts a value as an argument, and it searches for that value in the List. If the value is found, the method returns its index. If the value is not found, the method returns −1. The following code shows an example:

```
 1   ' Create a List of strings.
 2   Dim lstNames As New List(Of String)
 3   lstNames.Add("Chris")
 4   lstNames.Add("Kathryn")
 5   lstNames.Add("Bill")
 6
 7   ' Search for "Kathryn".
 8   Dim intPosition As Integer = lstNames.IndexOf("Kathryn")
 9
10   ' Was Kathryn found in the List?
11   If intPosition <> -1 Then
12       MessageBox.Show("Kathryn was found at index " &
13                       intPosition)
14   Else
15       MessageBox.Show("Kathryn was not found.")
16   End If
```

The statements in lines 2 through 5 create a List containing the strings `"Chris"`, `"Kathryn"`, and `"Bill"`. The statement in line 8 calls the `IndexOf` method to search for `"Kathryn"` in the List. The value that is returned from the method is assigned to the `intPosition` variable. After this statement executes, the `intPosition` variable will contain the index of `"Kathryn"`, or −1 if `"Kathryn"` was not found in the List. The `If...Then` statement in lines 11 through 16 displays one of two possible messages, depending on whether `"Kathryn"` was found. (If this code were executed, it would display the message *"Kathryn was found at index 1"*.)

There are two additional versions of the `IndexOf` method that allow you to specify the area of the List that should be searched. The following statement shows an example of one of these:

```
intPosition = lstNames.IndexOf("Diane", 2)
```

Notice that two arguments are passed to the `IndexOf` method. The first argument, "Diane", is the item to search for. The second argument, 2, is the starting index of the search. This specifies that the search should begin at index 2 and end at the last item in the List. (The beginning index is included in the search. If you pass an invalid index as an argument, an exception will occur.)

Here is an example of another version of the `IndexOf` method:

```
intPosition = lstNames.IndexOf("Diane", 2, 5)
```

In this example three arguments are passed to the `IndexOf` method. The first argument, "Diane", is the item to search for. The second argument, 2, is the starting index of the search. The third argument, 5, is the ending index of the search. This specifies that the search should begin at index 2 and end at index 5. (The beginning and ending indices are included in the search. If either index is invalid, an exception will occur.)

NOTE: The `IndexOf` method performs a sequential search to locate the specified item. If the List contains more than a thousand items, you may begin to notice a slight delay before the search finishes.

Summary

8.1 Arrays

- An array is a like a list of values given a single name. The values within an array are called elements and are of the same data type.
- Individual elements in an array are accessed through a subscript (or index), which is an integer that pinpoints a specific element within an array. Subscript numbering begins at zero. When you declare an array you can establish the array's size by specifying its upper subscript.
- You can implicitly size an array by omitting the upper subscript in the declaration statement, if you provide an initialization list. An array initialization list is a list of values enclosed in curly braces, with the values separated by commas.
- Array elements are processed in the same way as regular variables, but when working with array elements, you must provide subscripts.
- You can store an integer in a variable and then use the variable as a subscript. You can use a loop to cycle through an entire array, performing the same operation on each element.
- Visual Basic performs array bounds checking at runtime; it does not allow a statement to use a subscript outside the range of subscripts for an array.
- The For Each loop is a special loop designed specifically to access values from arrays and array-like structures.

8.2 Array Processing Techniques

- Arrays have a Length property that holds the number of elements in the array.
- To sum the numbers stored in an array, use a loop with an accumulator variable that adds all the elements. To average the numbers stored in an array, first sum all the values, and then divide the sum by the number of elements.
- To copy the values in one array to another, use a loop to copy the individual elements.
- You can create a parallel relationship between list boxes, combo boxes, and arrays.
- The sequential search algorithm uses a loop to examine the elements in an array. It compares each element with the value being searched for, and stops when the value is found or the end of the array is encountered. If the value being searched for is not in the array, the algorithm will unsuccessfully search to the end of the array.
- The Array.Sort method sorts the elements of an array in ascending order, which means the lowest value is stored in the first element and the highest value is stored in the last element.
- You can change the number of elements in an array at runtime with the ReDim statement.

8.3 Procedures and Functions That Work with Arrays

- Procedures and functions may be written to accept arrays as arguments. Functions may also be written to return arrays.

8.4 Multidimensional Arrays

- A single-dimensional array has one subscript and is useful for storing and working with a single set of data. Two-dimensional arrays can hold multiple sets of values. Think of a two-dimensional array as having rows and columns of elements.
- To declare a two-dimensional array, two sets of upper subscripts are required: the first one for the rows and the second one for the columns. A two-dimensional array may be implicitly sized by omitting the upper subscripts from the declaration and providing an initialization list.

- When data in a two-dimensional array is processed, each element has two subscripts: one for its row and one for its column. Nested loops can be used to sum the rows or columns of a two-dimensional numeric array.
- The For Each loop can be used to sum all the values in a numeric two-dimensional array.
- Visual Basic allows arrays of up to 32 dimensions.

8.5 Focus on GUI Design: The Enabled Property and the Timer Control

- When a control's Enabled property is set to *False*, it is considered disabled, which means it cannot receive the focus, cannot respond to events generated by the user, and appears dimmed or grayed out on the form.
- The Timer control is invisible at runtime. At design time it appears in the component tray. The standard prefix for a Timer control's name is tmr.
- The Timer control responds to Tick events. When a Tick event occurs, the Tick event handler is executed.
- When the Timer control's Enabled property is set to *True*, the Timer control responds to Tick events. When the Enabled property is set to *False*, the Timer control does not respond to Tick events and the code in the Tick event handler does not execute.
- The Timer control's Interval property can be set to a positive nonzero value that is the number of milliseconds to elapse between Tick events.

8.6 Focus on GUI Design: Anchoring and Docking Controls

- When a control is anchored to a form's edge, the distance between the control's edge and the form's edge remains constant, even when the user resizes the form.
- When a control is docked, it is positioned directly against one of the edges of a form. Additionally, the length or width of a docked control is changed to match the length or width of the form's edge.

8.7 Focus on Problem Solving: Building the *Demetris Leadership Center* Application

- This section outlines the process of building the *Demetris Leadership Center* application, which processes data used in parallel arrays.

8.8 Using Lists to Hold Information (Optional Topic)

- Lists are similar to arrays, but with certain advantages over arrays.
- A list can grow dynamically as you add objects to it.
- Items can be easily removed from a list.
- Lists have a built-in searching function.

Key Terms

Anchor property
array
array bounds checking
ascending order
Dock property
elements
Enabled property
For Each loop
index

Interval property
List
one-dimensional array
parallel arrays
sequential search
subscript
Timer control
two-dimensional array

Video Tutorial: Using Arrays to Look Up Information in the *Kayak Rental* Application

In this sequence of video tutorials, we improve on the *Kayak Rental* application by storing information about kayak rentals in parallel arrays. We will be able to use arrays to hold a history of rentals, look up rental rates, check on kayak types, and so on. Using arrays will reduce the amount of repetitive code and make the application code more professional. Finally, we will use a List object to hold the names of people who have signed up for a kayak tour.

- Part 1: Adding an array of kayak tour prices
- Part 2: Storing the rental history in an array
- Part 3: Letting customers choose from an array of kayaks
- Part 4: Building a list of people who have signed up for a tour

Review Questions and Exercises

Fill-in-the-Blank

1. You access the individual elements in an array through a(n) _____, which is a positive integer that identifies a specific position within an array.

2. The _____ loop is a special loop designed specifically to access values from arrays and array-like structures.

3. _____ arrays are two or more arrays that hold related data. The related elements in each array are accessed with a common subscript.

4. The _____ algorithm uses a loop to examine the elements in an array sequentially, starting with the first one.

5. The _____ statement resizes an array at runtime.

6. The _____ property holds the number of elements in an array.

7. Declaring a two-dimensional array requires two sets of _____.

8. When a control's _____ property is set to *False*, it is considered disabled.

9. The _____ property causes the distance between a control's edge and the form's edge to remain constant, even when the form is resized.

10. The _____ property causes a control to be positioned directly against one of the form's edges.

11. The _____ control allows an application to automatically execute code at regularly timed intervals.

12. The Timer control's _____ property specifies the number of milliseconds between timer events.

Multiple Choice

1. Which of the following describes the storage locations within an array?
   a. Boxes
   b. Elements
   c. Subvariables
   d. Intersections

2. Which of the following identifies a specific element within an array?

    a.   Element specifier
    b.   Determinator
    c.   Locator
    d.   Subscript

3. Which of the following is the lower subscript of an array?

    a.   1
    b.   { }
    c.   0
    d.   −1

4. When does array bounds checking occur?

    a.   Runtime
    b.   Design time
    c.   Break time
    d.   All of the above

5. Which of the following properties determines the number of elements in an array?

    a.   Size
    b.   Elements
    c.   Length
    d.   NumberElements

6. To access related data in a set of parallel arrays, how should you access the elements in the arrays?

    a.   Using the same array name
    b.   Using the same subscript
    c.   Using the index −1
    d.   Using the `GetParallelData` function

7. Which statement resizes the `intNumbers` array to 20 elements?

    a.   `ReDim intNumbers(19)`
    b.   `ReDim intNumbers(20)`
    c.   `Resize intNumbers() To 19`
    d.   `Resize intNumbers() To 20`

8. Which statement resizes the `intNumbers` array and does not erase the values already stored in the array?

    a.   `ReDim intNumbers(99)`
    b.   `ReDim Preserve intNumbers(99)`
    c.   `Preserve intNumbers(99)`
    d.   `ReSize Preserve intNumbers(99)`

9. Which of the following is an apt analogy for two-dimensional array elements?

    a.   Feet and inches
    b.   Books and pages
    c.   Lines and statements
    d.   Rows and columns

10. Which statement disables the control `lblResult`?

    a.   `lblResult.Disabled = True`
    b.   `Disable lblResult`
    c.   `lblResult.Enabled = False`
    d.   `lblResult.Dimmed = True`

11. The Timer control Interval property may be set to what type of value?
    a. 0 or greater
    b. A fractional number
    c. A negative number
    d. 1 or greater

12. Which of the following properties can you use to cause a control to fill an entire form?
    a. Fill
    b. Dock
    c. Anchor
    d. Stretch

13. Which of the following is similar to an array, but is not fixed in size?
    a. Unfixed array
    b. Adjustable array
    c. List
    d. Expandable variable

True or False

Indicate whether the following statements are true or false.

1. T F: The upper subscript of an array must be a positive whole number.
2. T F: Numeric array elements are automatically initialized to −1.
3. T F: You may not use a named constant as a subscript in an array declaration.
4. T F: Visual Basic allows you to use a variable as a subscript when processing an array with a loop.
5. T F: You get an error message at design time when you write code that attempts to access an element outside the bounds of an array.
6. T F: The value stored in an array's Length property is the same as the array's upper subscript.
7. T F: You should use a loop to copy the values of one array to another array.
8. T F: Parallel arrays are useful when working with related data of unlike types.
9. T F: The ReDim statement may be used with any array.
10. T F: The value stored in the Timer control's Interval property specifies an interval in seconds.
11. T F: It is possible to anchor a control to a form's opposing edges.
12. T F: When a control is docked to a form's edge, the width or height of the control is adjusted to match the size of the form's edge.
13. T F: A List's size automatically grows as you add items to it.

Short Answer

1. Write code that declares a string array with three elements and then stores your first, middle, and last names in the array's elements.

2. What values are displayed by the following code?
```
Const intMAX_SUBSCRIPT As Integer = 4
Dim intValues(intMAX_SUBSCRIPT) As Integer
Dim intCount As Integer
```

```
For intCount = 0 To intMAX_SUBSCRIPT
   intValues(intCount) = intCount + 1
Next
For intCount = 0 To intMAX_SUBSCRIPT
   MessageBox.Show(intValues(intCount).ToString())
Next
```

3. The following code segment declares a 20-element array of integers called `intFish`. When completed, the code should ask how many fish were caught by fisherman 1 through 20 and store this information in the array. Complete the program.

```
Sub FishCatchArray()
   Const intMAX_SUBSCRIPT As Integer = 19
   Dim intFish(intMAX_SUBSCRIPT) As Integer

   ' You must finish this procedure. It should ask how
   ' many fish were caught by fisherman 1 - 20 and
   ' store this information in the intFish array.
End Sub
```

4. What output is generated by the following code segment? (You may need to use a calculator.)

```
Const decRATE As Decimal = 0.1D
Const intMAX_SUBSCRIPT As Integer = 4
Dim decBalance(intMAX_SUBSCRIPT) As Decimal
Dim decDue As Decimal
Dim intCount As Integer

decBalance(0) = 100
decBalance(1) = 250
decBalance(2) = 325
decBalance(3) = 500
decBalance(4) = 1100

For intCount = 0 To intMAX_SUBSCRIPT
   decDue = decBalance(intCount) * decRATE
   MessageBox.Show(decDue.ToString())
Next
```

5. Write a statement that assigns 145 to the first column of the first row of the array declared in the following statement:

```
Dim intNumberArray(9, 11) As Integer
```

6. Write a statement that assigns 18 to the last column of the last row of the array declared in Question 5.

7. Assuming that an application uses a Timer control named `tmrClock`, write a statement that stops the timer from responding to timer events.

8. What advantages does a List have over an array?

What Do You Think?

1. The following code totals the values in two Integer arrays: `intNumberArray1` and `intNumberArray2`. Both arrays have 25 elements. Will the code print the correct sum of values for both arrays? Why or why not?

```
Dim intTotal As Integer = 0     ' Accumulator
For intCount = 0 To 24
   intTotal += intNumberArray1(intCount)
```

```
Next
MessageBox.Show("Total for intNumberArray1 is " &
                intTotal.ToString())
For intCount = 0 To 24
    intTotal += intNumberArray2(intCount)
Next
MessageBox.Show("Total for intNumberArray2 is " &
                intTotal.ToString())
```

2. How many elements are in the following array?

   `Dim dblSales (5, 3) As Double`

3. How many elements are in the following array?

   `Dim dblValues (3, 3) As Double`

4. Suppose an application uses a Timer control named `tmrControl`. Write a programming statement that sets the time between timer events at three seconds.

Find the Error

1. `Dim intReadings(-99) As Integer`

2.
   ```
   Dim intTable(10) As Integer ' Stores 11 values
   Dim intIndex As Integer
   Dim intMaxNum As Integer = 11
   For intIndex = 0 To intMaxNum
       intTable(intIndex) = CInt(InputBox("Enter the next value:"))
   Next
   ```

3. `Dim intValues(3) = { 2, 4, 6 }`

4.
   ```
   ' tmrTimer is a Timer control
   tmrTimer.Interval = 0
   ```

Algorithm Workbench

1. Assume `strNames` is a string array with 20 elements. Write a `For Each` loop that prints each element of the array.

2. Suppose you need to store information about 12 countries. Declare two arrays that may be used in parallel to store the names of the countries and their populations.

3. Write a loop that uses the arrays you declared in Question 2 to print each country's name and population.

4. The arrays `intNumberArray1` and `intNumberArray2` have 100 elements. Write code that copies the values in `intNumberArray1` to `intNumberArray2`.

5. Write the code for a sequential search that determines whether the value −1 is stored in the array named `intValues`. The code should print a message indicating whether the value was found.

6. Suppose an application stores the following data about employees:
   - Name, stored in a list box named `lstNames`
   - Employee number, stored in an array of strings named `strEmpNums`

   There is a parallel relationship between the list box and the array. Assume that the user has selected an employee's name from the list box. Write code that displays (in a message box) the employee number for the selected employee.

7. Write a function named `AverageDropOne()` that receives an array of integers and returns the average of the array after dropping the lowest value.

8. Assume that `dblValues` is a two-dimensional array of Doubles with 10 rows and 20 columns. Write a For Each statement that sums all the elements in the array and stores the sum in the variable `dblTotal`.

9. Write a function named `AverageDropK()` that receives an array of integers and a single integer K. The function returns the average of the array after dropping the K lowest values.

10. Suppose an application uses a two-dimensional array named `intDays`. Write code that sums each row in the array and displays the result.
```
Dim intDays(29, 5) As Integer
```

11. Write code that sums each column in the array in Question 10.

12. Create a function named `SumOdds` that returns the sum of the elements whose array indexes are odd. (We will consider zero to be even.)

13. Write code that creates a list of strings and stores the names of five of your friends.

Programming Challenges

1. **Largest/Smallest Array Values**

   Create an application that uses the InputBox method to let the user enter 10 integers into an array. The application should display the largest and smallest values stored in the array. Figure 8-46 shows an example of the application's form after all 10 values have been entered, with the largest and smallest values displayed.

Figure 8-46 *Largest/Smallest Array Values* form

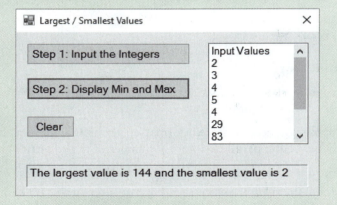

2. **Random Sentences**

   Create an application that produces random sentences as output. Create five arrays of strings, one each for nouns, adjectives, verbs, prepositions, and articles. Each array should hold several words of that part of speech. For example, the `strArticles` array could hold the strings `"the"` and `"a"`; the `strNouns` array could hold `"Martian"`, `"baby"`, `"skunk"`, `"computer"`, and `"mosquito"`; the `strPrepositions` array could hold `"around"`, `"through"`, `"under"`, `"over"`, and `"by"`; and so on.

   The application should generate sentences by randomly choosing eight words (randomly generating eight array indices) from these arrays, always constructing sentences by using the parts of speech in the following order: article, adjective, noun, verb, preposition, article, adjective, and noun.

   For example, a sentence might be "The shiny computer flew over a huge mosquito." In this example, "The" and "a" were randomly chosen from the articles array, "shiny" and "huge" from the adjectives array, "computer" and "mosquito" from the nouns array, "flew" from the verbs array, and "over" from the prepositions array. Be careful to produce sentences that have the proper spacing, uppercase and lowercase letters, and a period at the end.

Design your form with buttons to display the next sentence, to clear all sentences currently displayed, and to close the application. Display your sentences, one per line, in a list box. Allow enough room to display at least 10 sentences. Figure 8-47 shows an example of the form using a list box. The figure shows the form with three sentences generated.

Figure 8-47 *Random Sentences* form

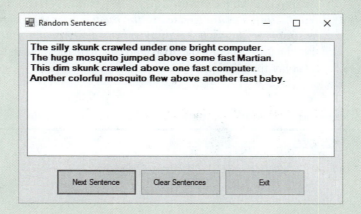

3. **PIN Verifier**

The National Commerce Bank has hired you to create an application that verifies a customer personal identification number (PIN). A valid PIN is a seven-digit number that meets the following specifications:

Digit 1: Must be in the range of 7 through 9
Digit 2: Must be in the range of 5 through 7
Digit 3: Must be in the range of 0 through 4
Digit 4: Must be in the range of 0 through 9
Digit 5: Must be in the range of 6 through 9
Digit 6: Must be in the range of 3 through 6
Digit 7: Must be in the range of 4 through 8

Notice that each digit must fall into a range of integers. Your application should have two arrays: intMinimum and intMaximum. The intMinimum array should hold the minimum value for each digit position, and the intMaximum array should hold the maximum value for each digit position.

The application should allow the user to enter seven digits on a form similar to the one shown in Figure 8-48. When the *Verify* button is clicked, the application should use the intMinimum and intMaximum arrays to verify that the numbers fall into acceptable ranges.

Figure 8-48 *PIN Verifier* form

4. **Calculate the Median**

Create an application that does the following:

1. Generates an array of randomly generated integers between 1 and 100. The length of the array should also be randomly generated as an integer between 5 and 10.
2. Sorts the array in ascending order.
3. Calculates and displays the median value, which is mathematically defined as the midpoint value. If the array has an odd number of values such as {2, 20, 35, 106, 117}, the median is the single integer in the middle (35). If the array has an even number of values, the median is the average of the two center values. For example, in the array {2, 20, 35, 37, 106, 117}, the median is (35 + 37) / 2.0 = 36.0. *Hint: be sure to declare the median variable as type Double. An example is shown in Figure 8-49, in which the array contains an even number of values.*
4. Let the user generate the array and calculate the median by clicking a single button.
5. Display the median in a Label control.

Figure 8-49 Calculating the Median value

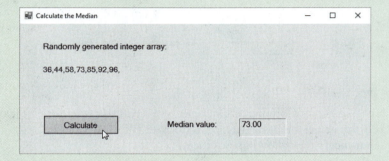

5. **Hotel Occupancy Using Lists or Arrays**

Programming Challenge 4 in Chapter 5 asked you to create an application that measured room occupancy percentages in a hotel. Briefly, it was described this way: *Create an application that calculates the occupancy rate for each floor, and the overall occupancy rate for the hotel. The occupancy rate is the percentage of rooms occupied, and may be calculated by dividing the number of rooms occupied by the number of rooms.* The implementation of this application in Chapter 5 was constrained by the inability to use arrays and lists, so we suggested that you automatically increment the combo box index to select floors in strict ascending sequence (1, 2, 3, etc.)

For this assignment, modify your previous application so that it uses an array (or a list) to hold the occupancy counts for all of the floors. This change to the program code will allow the user to select floor numbers in the combo box in any order. In Figure 8-50, for example, the user has selected the second and sixth floors, entering occupancy counts for each. In the figure, the user also clicked the *Totals* button. The ListBox was updated each time the user entered an occupancy count and clicked the *Save* button. The user may select floors in any order, even replacing a value for a floor that was entered before.

Figure 8-50 Hotel Occupancy rates

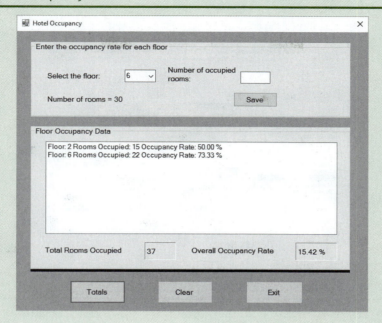

6. **Adding Students to Clubs**

VideoNote

Adding
students to
clubs.

Programming Challenge 5 in Chapter 5 asked you to create an application that added student names to a single club. As you recall, this was accomplished by copying each student's name from a list box containing all available students to a list box containing the names of the club members.

For this assignment, add a ComboBox control containing the names of four different clubs. When the user selects a club name from this combo box, the Club Membership list box must show only the members of the selected club. When the user adds new members to the club, the membership list for that club must be kept in an array or list so that it can be recalled if the user should select the club name at a later time. Any student may join multiple clubs, but a club cannot contain duplicate names. (We will assume that all student names in our sample data are unique.)

Figure 8-51 shows the user interface for this new application. The user has selected the Honors club from the combo box, so the list box on the right side of the form displays the members of the Honors club. The user can add new members or remove members. In Figure 8-52, the user has selected a different club (Computer), so the list of members is different. If the user were to select the Honors club again, the same list of members shown earlier in Figure 8-51 would appear.

You can implement this application using a two-dimensional array, where the club number (0, 1, 2) is the primary subscript, and the member index (from the list box) is the secondary subscript. Let's call this the *master array*. You can use a second (single-dimension) array to keep track of the number of students in each club, which will be useful when filling the Membership list box with the names of club members. This action happens whenever the user selects a different club name from the combo box. *Hint: whenever a person is added to or removed from a club, copy the contents of the Members list box into the master array of member names for all clubs.*

Figure 8-51 Adding students to the Honors club

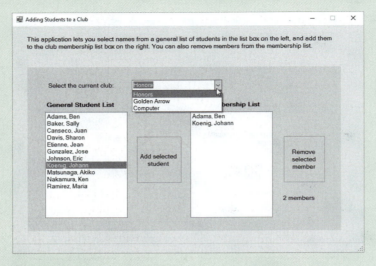

Figure 8-52 Selecting the Computer club

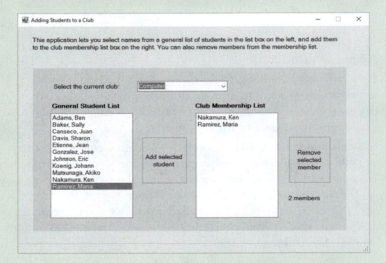

Design Your Own Forms

7. **Grade Book**

   Suppose a teacher has five students who have taken four tests. The teacher uses the following grading scale to assign a letter grade to a student, based on the average of his or her four test scores.

Test Score	Letter Grade
90–100	A
80–89	B
70–79	C
60–69	D
0–59	F

   Create an application that uses an array of strings to hold the five student names, an array of five strings to hold each student's letter grades, and five arrays of four single precision numbers to hold each student's set of test scores.

Equip the application with a menu or a set of buttons that allows the application to perform the following:

- Display a form that allows the user to enter or change the student names and their test scores.
- Calculate and display each student's average test score and a letter grade based on the average.

Input validation: Do not accept test scores less than zero or greater than 100.

8. **Grade Book Modification**

   Modify the *Grade Book* application in Programming Challenge 7 so it drops each student's lowest score when determining the test score averages and letter grades.

9. **Charge Account Validation**

   Create an application that allows the user to enter a charge account number. The application should determine whether the number is valid by comparing it to the numbers in the following list:

5658845	4520125	7895122	8777541	8451277	1302850
8080152	4562555	5552012	5050552	7825877	1250255
1005231	6545231	3852085	7576651	7881200	4581002

   The list of numbers should be stored in an array. A sequential search should be used to locate the number entered by the user. If the user enters a number that is in the array, the program should display a message indicating the number is valid. If the user enters a number that is not in the array, the program should display a message indicating the number is invalid.

VideoNote
The Lottery Simulation

10. **Lottery Simulation**

    Create an application that simulates a lottery. The application should have an array of five integers and should generate a random number in the range 0 through 9 for each element in the array. The array is permitted to contain duplicate values. The user should then enter five digits, which the application will compare to the numbers in the array. A form should be displayed showing how many of the digits matched. If all of the digits match, display a form proclaiming the user as a grand prize winner.

11. **Soccer Team Score Application**

    Suppose a soccer team needs an application to record the number of points scored by its players during a game. Create an application that asks how many players the team has and then asks for the names of each player. The program should declare an array of strings large enough to hold the player names and declare an array of integers large enough to hold the number of points scored by each player. The application should have a menu system or buttons that perform the following:

    - Display a form allowing the user to enter the players' names.
    - Display a form that can be used during a game to record the points scored by each player.
    - Display the total points scored by each player and by the team.

    Input validation: Do not accept negative numbers as points.

12. **Phone Number Lookup**

    Create an application that has two parallel arrays: a string array named `strPeople` that is initialized with the names of seven of your friends and a string array named `strPhoneNumbers` that is initialized with your friends' phone numbers. The program should allow the user to enter a person's name (or part of a person's name). It should then search for that person in the `strPeople` array. If the person is found, it should get that person's phone number from the strPhoneNumbers array and display it. If the person is not found in the strPeople array, the program should display a message indicating this.

13. **Finding a Numeric Pattern**

   Create an application that does the following:

   1. Generates and displays an array of 50 randomly generated integers between 1 and 20.
   2. Lets the user enter a sequence of 1 to 5 integers in a single text box.
   3. Searches the array for the first sequence of integers that matches the integer sequence entered by the user in Step 2.
   4. If a matching sequence is found, the program should display the index position of the match, or if no match is found, display a message such as "no match".

14. **Random String Shuffle**

   Create a procedure named RandomStringShuffle that receives an array of strings and rearranges its elements in random order. The usual way to do this is to loop through the array at least *N* times (if the array size is *N*). In each loop iteration, choose two subscripts (x, y) randomly between 0 and *N*-1. Use the subscripts to exchange the value of array(x) with array(y). Write a test program that creates and displays an array of 20 strings in alphabetic order. Next, your test program should call the RandomStringShuffle procedure, passing it the string array. Last of all, display the shuffled array.

15. **Tic-Tac-Toe Simulator**

   Create an application that simulates a game of tic-tac-toe. Figure 8-53 shows an example of the application's form. The form shown in the figure uses eight large Label controls to display the Xs and Os. The application should use a two-dimensional Integer array to simulate the game board in memory. When the user clicks the *New Game* button, the application should step through the array, storing a random number in the range of 0 through 1 in each element. The number 0 represents the letter O, and the number 1 represents the letter X. The form should then be updated to display the game board. The application should display a message indicating whether player X won, player Y won, or the game was a tie.

Figure 8-53 The *Tic-Tac-Toe* application

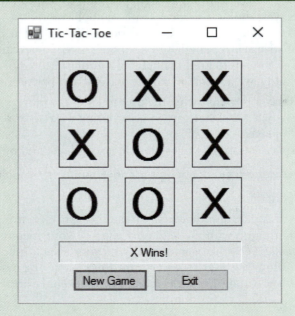

CHAPTER

9 Files, Printing, and Structures

TOPICS

This chapter shows you how to save data to sequential text files and then read the data back into an application. You will learn how to use the OpenFileDialog, SaveFileDialog, ColorDialog, and FontDialog controls. You can use these to equip your application with standard Windows dialog boxes for opening and saving files and for selecting colors and fonts. We discuss the PrintDocument control and how to print reports from your application. Finally, you learn how to package units of data together into structures.

9.1 Using Files

CONCEPT: A file is a collection of data stored on a computer disk. Data can be saved in a file and later reused.

Applications you have created so far require you to reenter data each time the program runs because the data kept in controls and variables is stored in RAM, and disappears once the program stops running. To retain data between the times it runs, an application must have a way of saving the data.

Data is saved in a **file**, on a computer disk. Once saved, the data remains after the program stops running and can be retrieved and used at a later time. In this chapter, you write applications that create files to save data. These applications do not rely on the user to reenter data each time the application runs.

The Process of Using a File

The following steps must be taken when a file is used by an application:

1. The file must be opened. If the file does not yet exist, opening it means creating it.
2. Data is written to the file or read from the file.
3. When the application is finished using the file, the file is closed.

When a Visual Basic application is actively working with data, the data is located in memory, usually in variables and/or control properties. When data is written to a file, it is copied from the variables or control properties, as shown in Figure 9-1.

Figure 9-1 Writing data to a file

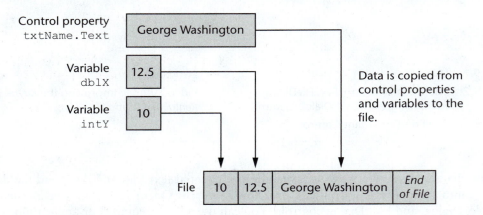

When data is read from a file, it is copied from the file into variables and/or control properties, as shown in Figure 9-2.

Figure 9-2 Reading data from a file

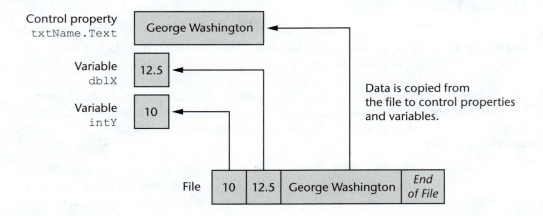

The terms input file and output file are often used. An **input file** is a file from which a program reads data. It is called an input file because the data stored in it serves as input to the program. An **output file** is a file into which a program writes data. It is called an output file because the program stores output in the file. In this book, we discuss the simplest type of data file, known as a **sequential-access file**. Sometimes this type of file is referred to as a **text file** because it can easily be created and modifed using a text editor such as Windows Notepad.

VideoNote

Writing Data to a File

Writing to Files with `StreamWriter` **Objects**

There are two ways to open a text file so you can write data to it: You can create a new file, or you can open an existing file so data can be appended to it. The actual writing to the file is performed by a **StreamWriter** object. There are two required steps:

1. Declare a `StreamWriter` variable.
2. If you want to create a new file, call `File.CreateText` and assign its return value to the `StreamWriter` variable. Or, if you want to append to an existing text file, call `File.AppendText` and assign its return value to the `StreamWriter` variable.

Before using `StreamWriter` objects, you should insert the following `Imports` statement at the top of your form's code file. This will make the **StreamWriter class** available to your program:

```
Imports System.IO
```

> **NOTE:** It is possible to omit the `Imports System.IO` statement, but then every reference to the `StreamWriter` class must use its fully qualified name, which is `System.IO.StreamWriter`.

Creating a Text File

First, we will show you how to create a new text file. Begin by declaring a `StreamWriter` variable, using the following general format:

```
Dim ObjectVar As StreamWriter
```

ObjectVar is the name of the object variable. You may use `Private` or `Public` in place of `Dim` if you are declaring the object variable at the class-level or module-level. Here's an example:

```
Dim phoneFile As StreamWriter
```

Next, call the **File.CreateText method**, passing it the name of a file. For example:

```
phoneFile = File.CreateText("phonelist.txt")
```

Notice how the return value from `File.CreateText` is assigned to the `StreamWriter` variable named `phoneFile`.

The filename you pass to the `File.CreateText` method can optionally contain a complete path, such as *C:\data\vbfiles\phonelist.txt*. If you use only a filename with no path, the file will be created in the same location as the application's executable file, which by default is your project's *\bin\Debug* folder.

If the file cannot be created, the `File.CreateText` method will throw an exception. This might happen if you specify a nonexistent path, or your application does not have the required permission to create a file in the specified location.

Opening an Existing File and Appending Data to It

If a text file already exists, you may want to add more data to the end of the file. This is called *appending* to the file. First, you declare a `StreamWriter` variable:

```
Dim phoneFile As StreamWriter
```

Then you call the **File.AppendText method**, passing it the name of an existing file. For example:

```
phoneFile = File.AppendText("phonelist.txt")
```

Any data written to the file will be written to the end of the file's existing contents.

If the file that you specify as an argument to the File.AppendText method does not exist, it will be created. If the file cannot be opened or created, the method will throw an exception. For example, an exception will occur if you specify a nonexistent path, or your application does not have the required permission to create a file in the specified location.

 WARNING: It is possible to move an application's executable file to a location other than the project's *bin* directory. Doing so changes the default location where the files are created.

Writing Data to a File

The **WriteLine method** of the StreamWriter class writes a line of data to a file. The following is the general format of the method:

```
ObjectVar.WriteLine(Data)
```

ObjectVar is the name of a StreamWriter object variable. *Data* represents constants or variables whose contents will be written to the file. The WriteLine method writes the data to the file and then writes a newline character immediately after the data. A **newline character** is an invisible character that separates text by breaking it into another line when displayed on the screen.

To further understand how the WriteLine method works, let's look at an example. Assume that an application opens a file and writes three students' first names and their scores to the file with the following code:

```
Dim studentFile As StreamWriter

Try
    ' Open the file.
    studentFile = File.CreateText("StudentData.txt")
    ' Write data to the file.
    studentFile.WriteLine("Jim")
    studentFile.WriteLine(95)
    studentFile.WriteLine("Karen")
    studentFile.WriteLine(98)
    studentFile.WriteLine("Bob")
    studentFile.WriteLine(82)
Catch
    MessageBox.Show("Error: The file cannot be created.")
End try
```

You can visualize the data being written to the file in the following manner:

Jim*<newline>*95*<newline>*Karen*<newline>*98*<newline>*Bob*<newline>*82*<newline>*

The newline characters are represented here as *<newline>*. You do not actually see the newline characters, but when the file is opened in a text editor such as Notepad, its contents appear as shown in Figure 9-3. As you can see from the figure, each newline character causes the data that follows it to be displayed on a new line.

 TIP: Each time the WriteLine method executes, it writes a separate line of text to the file.

In addition to separating the contents of a file into lines, the newline character also serves as a delimiter. A **delimiter** is an item that separates other items. When you write data to a file using WriteLine, newline characters are the delimiters. Later, you will see that data must be separated in order for it to be read from the file.

Figure 9-3 File contents displayed in Notepad

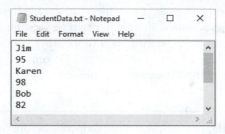

Writing a Blank Line to a File

The `WriteLine` method can write a blank line to a file by calling the method without an argument.

```
textFile.WriteLine()
```

The `Write` Method

The **Write method,** a member of the `StreamWriter` class, writes an item of data to a file without writing a newline character. The general format is as follows:

```
ObjectVar.Write(Data)
```

ObjectVar is the name of a `StreamWriter` object variable. *Data* represents the contents of a constant or variable that is to be written to the file. This method can be used to write data to a file without terminating the line with a newline character. For example, assume an application has a `StreamWriter` object variable named `outputFile`, as well as the following variables:

```
Dim strName As String = "Jeffrey Smith"
Dim intId As Integer = 47895
Dim strPhone As String = "555-7864"
```

The contents of all three variables are written to a single line in the file:

```
outputFile.Write(strName)
outputFile.Write(" ")
outputFile.Write(intId)
outputFile.Write(" ")
outputFile.WriteLine(strPhone)
```

The first statement writes the `strName` variable to the file. The second statement writes a space character (`" "`), the third statement writes the `intId` variable, and the fourth statement writes another space. The last statement uses the `WriteLine` method to write the phone number, followed by a newline character. Here is a sample of the output:

```
Jeffrey Smith 47895 555-7864
```

Closing a File

The opposite of opening a file is closing it. The `StreamWriter` class has a method named `Close` that closes a file. The following is the method's general format:

```
StreamWriter.Close()
```

After the method executes, the file that was referenced by `ObjectVar` is closed. For example, suppose `salesFile` is an object variable that references a `StreamWriter` object. The following statement closes the file associated with `salesFile`.

```
salesFile.Close()
```

To avoid losing data, your application should always close a file after it is finished using it. Computers typically create one or more buffers (memory areas) when a file is opened. When an application writes data to a file, that data is first written to the **buffer**. When the buffer is filled, all data stored there is written to the file. This technique improves the system's performance because writing data to memory is faster than writing it to a disk. The **Close method** writes any unsaved information remaining in the file buffer and releases memory allocated by the StreamWriter object.

 NOTE: Once a file is closed, you must reopen it before performing any operations on it.

In Tutorial 9-1, you examine an application that writes data about three fictional persons to a file.

 ## Tutorial 9-1:
Completing an application that writes data to a file

Step 1: Open the *File WriteLine Demo* project from the student sample programs folder named *Chap9\File WriteLine Demo*. The application form is shown in Figure 9-4.

Figure 9-4 *File WriteLine Demo* form

```
                            btnCreateFile btnExit
```

Step 2: Complete the code for the form's event handlers as shown in the following. (Don't type the line numbers. They are shown for reference.) Be sure to write the Imports statement shown in line 1.

```vb
1  Imports System.IO
2
3  Public Class Form1
4      Private Sub btnCreateFile_Click(...) Handles btnCreateFile.Click
5          ' Constant for the number of friends
6          Const intNUM_FRIENDS As Integer = 3
7
8          ' Local variables
9          Dim strFilename As String      ' File name
10         Dim strFriend As String        ' Name of a friend
11         Dim strPhone As String         ' To hold a phone number
12         Dim intCount As Integer        ' Loop counter
13         Dim friendFile As StreamWriter ' Object variable
14
```

```
15          ' Get the file name from the user.
16          strFilename = InputBox("Enter the filename.")
17
18          Try
19              ' Open the file.
20              friendFile = File.CreateText(strFilename)
21
22              ' Get the data and write it to the file.
23              For intCount = 1 To intNUM_FRIENDS
24                  ' Get a friend's name.
25                  strFriend = InputBox("Enter the name of friend " &
26                                      "number " & intCount.ToString())
27
28                  ' Get a friend's phone number.
29                  strPhone = InputBox("Enter the that friend's " &
30                                      "phone number.")
31
32                  ' Write the data to the file.
33                  friendFile.WriteLine(strFriend)
34                  friendFile.WriteLine(strPhone)
35              Next
36
37              ' Close the file.
38              friendFile.Close()
39          Catch
40              ' Error message
41              MessageBox.Show("That file cannot be created.")
42          End Try
43      End Sub
44
45      Private Sub btnExit_Click(...) Handles btnExit.Click
46          ' Close the form.
47          Me.Close()
48      End Sub
49 End Class
```

Let's examine the btnCreateFile_Click event handler closer. Here is a summary of the declarations that appear in lines 6 through 13:

- Line 6: The intNUM_FRIENDS constant is set to 3. This is the number of friends for whom we will store data.
- Line 9: The strFilename variable will hold the path and filename of the file that the application will create.
- Line 10: The strFriend variable will hold the name of a friend.
- Line 11: The strPhone variable will hold a friend's phone number.
- Line 12: The intCount variable will be used as a loop counter.
- Line 13: The friendFile variable is an object variable that will be used to open the file and write data to it.

Line 16 uses an input box to prompt the user to enter a filename. The filename is assigned to the strFilename variable.

The Try–Catch statement that begins in line 18 will catch any exceptions that are thrown. Line 20 tries to create the file specified by the path and filename entered by the user. If the file cannot be created, an exception is thrown and the program jumps to the Catch clause in line 39. If the file is successfully created, the For...Next loop in line 23 begins to execute. As the loop is written, it will iterate three times, with the intCount variable taking on the values 1 through 3.

Inside the loop, the statement in lines 25 through 26 uses an input box to prompt the user for a friend's name. The name entered by the user is assigned to the `strFriend` variable. Then the statement in lines 29 through 30 uses an input box to prompt the user for that friend's phone number. The phone number entered by the user is assigned to the `strPhone` variable. Line 33 writes the friend's name to the file, and line 34 writes the phone number to the file. Then, the loop starts over.

When the loop is finished, line 38 closes the file.

Step 3: Save the project. Run the application and click the *Create File* button. When prompted to enter the filename, provide the path of a disk location that can be written to. For example, if you enter *C:\MyFriends.txt*, the application will create the file *MyFriends.txt* in the root directory of drive C. If you enter *C:\Temp\MyFriends.txt* the application will create the file *MyFriends.txt* in the *C:\Temp* folder. Enter a path and filename and make a note of it because you will use the same file later in this tutorial and again in Tutorial 9-2.

NOTE: If you are working in a school computer lab, you may be restricted to saving files only at certain disk locations. Ask your instructor or lab manager for these locations.

Step 4: Enter the following names, ages, and addresses as you are prompted for this data. After you have entered the data for the third friend, the application returns to the main form. Click the *Exit* button.

	Name	Phone
Friend 1	Jim Weaver	555–1212
Friend 2	Mary Duncan	555–2323
Friend 3	Karen Warren	555–3434

Step 5: In Windows Explorer, locate the file that was created when you ran the application. Double-click the file's name to open it in the Notepad text editor. The contents of the file should appear as shown in Figure 9-5.

As you can see, each item is written to a separate line in the file because a newline character separates each item.

Step 6: Close the *Notepad* window that displays the text file.

Figure 9-5 Contents of the file displayed in Notepad

Appending Data to a File

When we **append** data to a file, we write new data immediately following existing data in the file. If an existing file is opened with the AppendText method, data written to the file is appended to the file. If the file does not exist, it is created. For example, assume the file *MyFriends.txt* exists and contains the following data, from Tutorial 9-1:

Jim Weaver
555-1212
Mary Duncan
555-2323
Karen Warren
555-3434

The following statments open the file in append mode and write additional data to the file:

```
' Declare an object variable
Dim friendFile As StreamWriter
' Open the file.
friendFile = File.AppendText("MyFriends.txt")
' Write the data.
friendFile.WriteLine("Bill Johnson")
friendFile.WriteLine("555-4545")
' Close the file.
friendFile.Close()
```

After this code executes, the *MyFriends.txt* file will contain the following data:

Jim Weaver
555-1212
Mary Duncan
555-2323
Karen Warren
555-3434
Bill Johnson
555-4545

Reading Files with StreamReader Objects

VideoNote

**Reading Data
from a File**

To read data from a sequential text file, use a **StreamReader object**. The **StreamReader class** provides methods for reading data from a file. The process of creating a Stream-Reader object is similar to that of creating a StreamWriter object, which we discussed in the previous section. First, you declare an object variable with a declaration statement in the following general format:

```
Dim ObjectVar As StreamReader
```

ObjectVar is the name of the object variable. As with other variables, you may use the Private or Public access specifier if you are declaring the object variable at the class level or module level.

Next, call the **File.OpenText method**, which creates an instance of the StreamReader object and stores its address in the object variable. The method's general format is as follows:

```
File.OpenText(Filename)
```

Filename is a string or a string variable specifying the path and/or name of the file to open. This method opens the file specified by *Filename* and returns a StreamReader object that may be used to read data from the file. If the file does not exist, or it cannot be opened for any reason, an exception will be thrown. The following code shows the two-step process of opening a file and assigning the StreamReader:

```
Dim customerFile As StreamReader
customerFile = File.OpenText("customers.txt")
```

The first statement declares an object variable named customerFile. The second statement opens the file *customers.txt* and returns the address of a StreamReader object that may be used to read data from the file. The address of the StreamReader object is assigned to the customerFile variable.

As in the case of the StreamWriter class, you need to write the following Imports statement at the top of your code file:

```
Imports System.IO
```

Reading Data from a File

The **ReadLine method** in the StreamReader class reads a line of data from a file. The general format of the method is as follows:

```
ObjectVar.ReadLine()
```

ObjectVar is the name of a StreamReader object variable. The method reads a line from the file associated with *ObjectVar* and returns the data as a string. For example, assume that customerFile is a StreamReader object variable and strCustomerName is a string variable. The following statement reads a line from the file and stores it in the variable:

```
strCustomerName = customerFile.ReadLine()
```

A StreamReader reads data in a forward-only direction. When the file is opened, its **read position,** the position of the next item to be read, is set to the first item in the file. As data is read, the read position advances through the file. For example, consider the file named *Quotation.txt*, as shown in Figure 9-6. As you can see from the figure, the file has three lines of text. Suppose a program opens the file with the following code:

```
Dim textFile As StreamReader
textFile = File.OpenText("Quotation.txt")
```

Figure 9-6 Text file with three lines

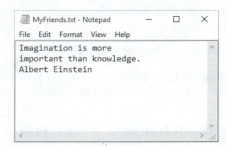

When this code opens the file, its read position is at the beginning of the first line, as illustrated in Figure 9-7.

Figure 9-7 Initial read position

Read position ⟶ Imagination is more
important than knowledge.
Albert Einstein

The following statement reads a line from the file, beginning at the current read position, and ending at the end-of-line marker:

```
strInput = textFile.ReadLine()
```

After the statement executes, the `strInput` variable contains the string `"Imagination is more"`. The invisible end-of-line marker is skipped, and the read position is placed at the beginning of the second line. Figure 9-8 illustrates the current read position.

Figure 9-8 Read position after first line is read

Imagination is more
Read position ⟶ important than knowledge.
Albert Einstein

If the `ReadLine` method is called again, the second line is read from the file and the file's read position is advanced to the third line. After all lines have been read, the read position will be at the end of the file.

Closing the File

Close an open `StreamReader` object by calling the `Close` method. The general format is as follows:

```
ObjectVar.Close()
```

In Tutorial 9-2, you complete an application that uses the `ReadLine` statement to read the file you created in Tutorial 9-1.

Tutorial 9-2:
Completing an application that reads a file

Step 1: Open the *File ReadLine Demo* project from the student sample programs folder named *Chap9\File ReadLine Demo*. The application's form, which has already been created for you, is shown in Figure 9-9.

Figure 9-9 *File ReadLine Demo* form

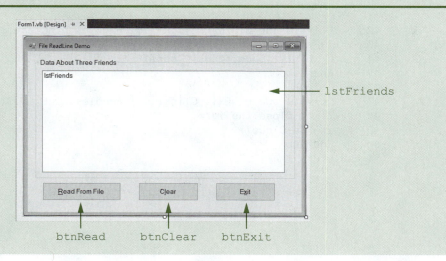

Step 2:   Complete the code for the form's event handlers as shown in the following. (Don't type the line numbers. They are shown for reference.) Be sure to write the Imports statement shown in line 1.

```
1 Imports System.IO
2
3 Public Class Form1
4     Private Sub btnRead_Click(...) Handles btnRead.Click
5         ' Constant for the number of friends
6         Const intNUM_FRIENDS As Integer = 3
7
8         ' Local variables
9         Dim friendFile As StreamReader   ' Object variable
10        Dim strFilename As String        ' File name
11        Dim strFriend As String          ' Name of a friend
12        Dim strPhone As String           ' To hold a phone number
13        Dim intCount As Integer          ' Loop counter
14
15        ' Get the file name from the user.
16        strFilename = InputBox("Enter the filename.")
17
18        Try
19            ' Open the file.
20            friendFile = File.OpenText(strFilename)
21
22            ' Read the data.
23            For intCount = 1 To intNUM_FRIENDS
24                ' Read a name and phone number from the file.
25                strFriend = friendFile.ReadLine()
26                strPhone = friendFile.ReadLine()
27
28                ' Display the data in the list box.
29                lstFriends.Items.Add("Friend Number " & intCount.ToString())
30                lstFriends.Items.Add("Name: " & strFriend)
31                lstFriends.Items.Add("Phone: " & strPhone)
32                lstFriends.Items.Add("") ' Add a blank line
33            Next intCount
34
35            ' Close the file.
36            friendFile.Close()
37        Catch
38            MessageBox.Show("That file cannot be opened.")
39        End Try
40    End Sub
41
42    Private Sub btnlear_Click(...) Handles btnClear.Click
43        ' Clear the list box.
44        lstFriends.Items.Clear()
45    End Sub
46
47    Private Sub btnExit_Click(...) Handles btnExit.Click
48        ' Close the form.
49        Me.Close()
50    End Sub
51 End Class
```

Let's examine the `btnRead_Click` event handler. Here is a summary of the declarations that appear in lines 6 through 13:

- Line 6: The `intNUM_FRIENDS` constant is set to 3. This is the number of friends for whom we will read data from the file.
- Line 9: The `friendFile` variable is an object variable that will be used to open the file and read data from it.
- Line 10: The `strFilename` variable will hold the path and filename of the file that the application will open.
- Line 11: The `strFriend` variable will hold the name of a friend that is read from the file.
- Line 12: The `strPhone` variable will hold a friend's phone number that is read from the file.
- Line 13: The `intCount` variable will be used as a loop counter.

Line 16 uses an input box to prompt the user to enter a filename. The filename is assigned to the `strFilename` variable.

The `Try–Catch` statement that begins in line 18 will catch any exceptions that are thrown. Line 20 tries to open the file specified by the path and filename entered by the user. If the file cannot be opened, an exception is thrown and the program jumps to the `Catch` clause in line 37. If the file is successfully created, the `For...Next` loop in line 23 begins to execute. As the loop is written, it will iterate three times, with the `intCount` variable taking on the values 1 through 3.

Inside the loop, the statement in line 25 reads a line of data from the file and assigns it to the `strFriend` variable, and line 26 reads the next line of data from the file and assigns it to the `strPhone` variable. Lines 29 through 32 add this friend's data to the list box, followed by a blank line. Then, the loop starts over. When the loop is finished, line 36 closes the file.

Step 3: Save the project. Run the application and click the *Read From File* button. An input box will appear asking for the filename. Enter the path and filename that you used to create the file in Step 3 of Tutorial 9-1. When you click the *OK* button on the input box, the data is read from the file and displayed in the list box, as shown in Figure 9-10. If you did not type the path and filename exactly as you did in Tutorial 9-1, you will see a message box indicating that the file was not found. In that case, click the *Read From File* button again, this time entering the correct path and filename.

Figure 9-10 Data displayed in the list box

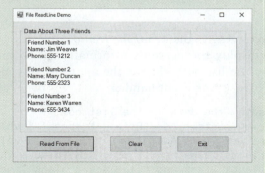

Step 4: Click the *Exit* button to end the application.

Determining Whether a File Exists

The `File.OpenText` method throws an exception if the file it is trying to open does not exist. To prevent an exception, you can call the **`File.Exists` method** to determine whether a file exists before you attempt to open it. The general format of the method is as follows:

```
File.Exists(Filename)
```

Filename is the name of a file, which may include the path. The method returns *True* if the file exists or *False* if the file does not exist. The following code shows an example of how to use the method to determine if a file exists prior to trying to open the file:

```
If File.Exists(strFilename) Then
    ' Open the file.
    inputFile = File.OpenText(strFilename)
Else
    MessageBox.Show(strFilename & " does not exist.")
End If
```

Using vbTab to Align Display Items

The predefined `vbTab` constant moves the print position forward to the next even multiple of 8. You can use it to align columns in displayed or printed output more effectively. The following is a simple example, displayed in a list box, of a reference line followed by three lines displaying tabs and characters:

```
ListBox1.Items.Add("012345678901234567890")
ListBox1.Items.Add("X" & vbTab & "X")
ListBox1.Items.Add("XXXXXXXXXXXX" & vbTab & "X")
ListBox1.Items.Add(vbTab & vbTab & "X")
```

In the output in Figure 9-11, the `vbTab` constant in the second line moves the print position forward to column 8 before displaying the letter *X*. (Print positions are numbered starting at 0.) In lines three and four, the print position moves to column 16 before displaying the final letter *X*.

Figure 9-11 Demonstrating tabs in a list box

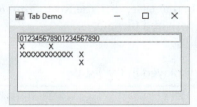

Briefly returning to the *ReadLine Demo* application from Tutorial 9-2, a slightly better way to display the person's information is to insert tabs between the labels and names in the list box. Here is the appropriately modified code from the loop inside the `btnRead_Click` event handler:

```
' Display the data in the list box.
lstFriends.Items.Add("Friend Number " & vbTab & intCount.ToString())
lstFriends.Items.Add("Name: " & vbTab & vbTab & strFriend)
lstFriends.Items.Add("Phone: " & vbTab & vbTab & strPhone)
lstFriends.Items.Add("") ' Add a blank line
```

The resulting output from this code appears in Figure 9-12.

Figure 9-12 *ReadLine Demo,* using tabs in the list box

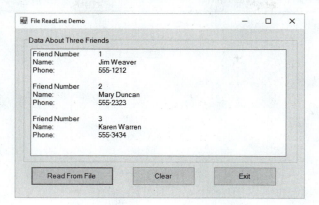

Detecting the End of a File

The *File ReadLine Demo* application in Tutorial 9-2 is designed to read exactly three records. This is because we know how many records are stored in the file. In many cases, however, the amount of data in a file is unknown. When this is the case, use the StreamReader object's **EndOfStream property** to determine when the end of the file has been reached. If the end of the file has been reached, the EndOfStream property will be set to *True*. Otherwise, it will be set to *False*.

The following example uses a Do Until loop that uses the EndOfStream property to determine when the end of the *Scores.txt* file has been reached. The loop reads all the lines from the file and adds them to the lstResults list box.

```
Dim scoresFile As StreamReader
Dim strInput As String
scoresFile = File.OpenText("Scores.txt")
Do Until scoresFile.EndOfStream
  strInput = scoresFile.ReadLine()
  lstResults.Items.Add(strInput)
Loop
scoresFile.Close()
```

Tutorial 9-3 examines an application that detects the end of a file.

Tutorial 9-3:
Examining an application that detects the end of a file

Step 1: Open the *File Demo* project from the student sample programs folder named *Chap9\File Demo*. Run the application. The form is shown in Figure 9-13.

VideoNote

Detecting the end of a file

Figure 9-13 *File Demo* form

Step 2: Click the *Create File* button. An input box appears and asks: *How many integers do you want to enter?* Enter **5** and press [Enter].

Step 3: Because you indicated you want to enter five numbers, the application will prompt you five times with an input box to enter a number. Enter the following numbers: **2**, **4**, **6**, **8**, and **10**. The application writes these numbers to a file.

Step 4: After you have entered the last number, click the *Read File* button. The application reads the numbers from the file and prints them in the list box, as shown in Figure 9-14. Click the *Exit* button to end the application.

Figure 9-14 *File Demo* form with numbers displayed

Step 5: Open the *Code* window. The first part of the form's class, including the btnCreate_Click event handler, is shown here with line numbers for reference.

```
1 Imports System.IO
2
3 Public Class Form1
4   ' Class-level constant for the filename
5   Private Const strFILENAME As String = "Numbers.txt"
6
7   Private Sub btnCreate_Click(...) Handles btnCreate.Click
8     ' Local variables
9     Dim outputFile As StreamWriter   ' Object variable
10    Dim intMaxNumbers As Integer     ' The number of values
11    Dim intCount As Integer = 0      ' Loop counter, set to 0
```

```
12        Dim intNumber As Integer          ' To hold user input
13
14      Try
15        ' Get the number of numbers from the user.
16        intMaxNumbers = CInt(InputBox("How many integers do " &
17                                        "you want to enter?"))
18
19        Try
20          ' Create the file.
21          outputFile = File.CreateText(strFILENAME)
22
23          ' Get the numbers and write then to the file.
24          Do While intCount < intMaxNumbers
25            Try
26              ' Get an integer.
27              intNumber = CInt(InputBox("Enter an integer."))
28
29              ' Write that integer to the file.
30              outputFile.WriteLine(intNumber)
31
32              ' Increment intCount.
33              intCount += 1
34            Catch
35              ' Error message for invalid integer.
36              MessageBox.Show("The last value you entered was not " &
37                              "a valid integer. Try again.").
38            End Try
39          Loop
40
41          ' Close the file.
42          outputFile.Close()
43
44        Catch
45          ' Error message for file creation error.
46          MessageBox.Show("Error creating the file " & strFILENAME)
47        End Try
48
49      Catch
50        ' Error message for invalid number of numbers.
51        MessageBox.Show("Enter a valid integer please.")
52      End Try
53   End Sub
54
```

Let's take a closer look at this code. Line 1 shows the Imports System.IO statement, and the form's class declaration begins in line 3. Line 5 declares a class-level constant named strFILENAME for the name of the file that we will be working with.

Here is a summary of the declarations that appear in lines 9 through 12:

- Line 9: The outputFile variable is an object variable that will be used to open the file and write data to it.
- Line 10: The intMaxNumbers variable will hold the number of integer values that will be written to the file.
- Line 11: The intCount variable will be used as a loop counter.
- Line 12: The intNumber variable will hold a number entered by the user, to be written to the file. Notice that we explicitly initialize intCount to 0.

Notice that a Try-Catch statement begins in line 14, and then lines 16 through 17 use an input box to prompt the user for the number of integer values that he or she wants to enter. If the user enters an invalid value, the CInt function in line 16 will throw an exception and the program will jump to the Catch clause in line 49.

If the user enters a valid integer value, the program can proceed to create the file. Notice that another Try-Catch statement begins in line 19, and then line 21 creates the file. If for any reason the file cannot be created, the File.CreateText method will throw an exception and the program will jump to the Catch clause in line 44.

If the file is successfully created, the program can proceed to get the numbers from the user and write them to the file. The Do While loop that begins in line 24 iterates as long as intCount is less than intMaxNumbers. Notice that inside the loop a Try-Catch statement begins in line 25, and then line 27 uses an input box to prompt the user for an integer. If the user enters an invalid value, the CInt function in line 27 will throw an exception and the program will jump to the Catch clause in line 34. If the user enters a valid integer, line 30 writes it to the file, and line 33 increments intCount. After the loop finishes, line 42 closes the file.

Step 6: Now scroll down and look at the btnRead_Click event handler, shown here with line numbers for reference:

```
55  Private Sub btnRead_Click(...) Handles btnRead.Click
56    ' Local variables
57    Dim inputFile As StreamReader ' Object variable
58    Dim strInput As String        ' To hold a line of input
59
60    Try
61      ' Open the file.
62      inputFile = File.OpenText(strFILENAME)
63
64      ' Clear the list box.
65      lstOutput.Items.Clear()
66
67      ' Read the file's contents.
68      Do Until inputFile.EndOfStream
69        ' Read a line from the file.
70        strInput = inputFile.ReadLine()
71
72        ' Add the line of input to the list box.
73        lstOutput.Items.Add(strInput)
74      Loop
75
76      ' Close the file.
77      inputFile.Close()
78    Catch
79      ' Error message for file open error.
80      MessageBox.Show(strFILENAME & " cannot be opened.")
81    End Try
82  End Sub
```

Let's take a closer look at this code. Here is a summary of the declarations that appear in lines 57 and 58:

- Line 57: The inputFile variable is an object variable that will be used to open the file and read data from it.
- Line 58: The strInput variable will hold a line of input that is read from the file.

Notice that a Try-Catch statement begins in line 60, and then line 62 opens the file. If the file cannot be opened, the File.OpenText method will throw an exception and the program will jump to the Catch clause in line 78. (This will happen, for example, if the user clicks the *Read File* button before the file has been created.)

If the file is successfully opened, line 65 clears the list box's contents. Then the `Do Until` loop in line 68 begins executing. The loop will iterate until the `inputFile.EndOfStream` property equals *True*, indicating that the end of the file has been reached. During each loop iteration, line 70 reads a line from the file and assigns it to the `strInput` variable, and line 73 adds `strInput` to the list box. After the loop finishes, line 77 closes the file.

Other StreamReader Methods

The `StreamReader` class also provides the `Read` and `ReadToEnd` methods, which we briefly discuss. The general format of the `Read` method is as follows:

```
ObjectVar.Read
```

ObjectVar is the name of a `StreamReader` object variable. The **Read method** reads only the next character from a file and returns the integer code for the character. To convert the integer code to a character, use the **Chr function**, as shown in the following code:

```
Dim textFile As StreamReader
Dim strInput As String = String.Empty
textFile = File.OpenText("names.txt")
Do While Not textFile.EndOfStream
  strInput &= Chr(textFile.Read)
Loop
textFile.Close()
```

This code opens the *names.txt* file. The `Do While` loop, which repeats until it reaches the end of the file, executes the following statement:

```
strInput &= Chr(textFile.Read)
```

This statement gets the integer code for the next character in the file, converts it to a character with the `Chr` function, and concatenates that character to the string variable `strInput`. When the loop has finished, the string variable `strInput` contains the entire contents of the file *names.txt*.

The general format of the `ReadToEnd` method is as follows:

```
ObjectVar.ReadToEnd
```

ObjectVar is the name of a `StreamReader` object variable. The **ReadToEnd method** reads and returns the entire contents of a file, beginning at the current read position. The following is an example:

```
Dim textFile As StreamReader
Dim strInput As String
textFile = File.OpenText("names.txt")
strInput = textFile.ReadToEnd()
textFile.Close()
```

The statement `strInput = textFile.ReadToEnd()` reads the file's contents and stores it in the variable `strInput`.

> **TIP:** **Modifying Data in a File.** People often want to know how they can change exist-
> ing data stored in a sequential file. Aside from appending to the end of a sequential file,
> you cannot easily modify its data while stored on a disk. Instead, you can read the file
> into memory, for example, into an array. You can then modify any of the array ele-
> ments, and write the array back to either the same file or a new file. The only limitation
> to this approach is that all the data must fit into memory while the program is running.
> If a set of data were really huge, this could be a problem, so most applications would
> instead use a database rather than a file. A database has built-in tools for modifying its
> contents without having to read all the data into memory.

Working with Arrays and Files

Saving the contents of an array to a file is easy. Use a loop to step through each element
of the array, writing its contents to the file. For example, assume an application has the
following array declaration:

```
Dim intValues() As Integer = {1, 2, 3, 4, 5, 6, 7, 8, 9, 10}
```

The following code opens a file named *Values.txt* and writes the contents of each element
of the values array to the file:

```
Dim outputFile As StreamWriter
outputFile = File.CreateText("Values.txt")
For Each intVal As Integer In intValues
    outputFile.WriteLine(intVal)
Next
outputFile.Close()
```

Reading the contents of a file into an array is equally straightforward. The following code
opens the *Values.txt* file and reads its contents into the elements of the intValues array:

```
Dim inputFile as StreamReader
inputFile = File.OpenText("Values.txt")
For intCount = 0 To (intValues.Length - 1)
    intValues(intCount) = CInt(inputFile.ReadLine())
Next
inputFile.Close()
```

There is problem with this code, however. It does not check for the end of file, so it assumes
the file contains enough values to fill the array. We can improve the code as follows:

```
Dim inputFile as StreamReader
Dim intIndex As Integer = 0
inputFile = File.OpenText("Values.txt")
Do Until inputFile.EndOfStream Or intIndex >= intValues.Length
    intValues(intIndex) = CInt(inputFile.ReadLine())
    intIndex = intIndex + 1
Loop
inputFile.Close()
```

This code uses a Do . . . Until loop that iterates until either the end of the file is reached,
or the array is filled up.

Checkpoint

9.1 What are the three steps in the process of using a file?

9.2 What type of object variable must you create to open a file for writing? For reading?

9.3 Write a statement that creates the file *Test.txt* so that you may write data to it. If the file already exists, its contents should be erased.

9.4 Write a statement that writes the contents of the variable `intX` to a line in the file you opened in Checkpoint 9.3.

9.5 Write a statement that opens the file *Test.txt* for reading.

9.6 Write a statement that reads a line from the file you opened in Checkpoint 9.5, into the variable `intX`.

9.7 How do you determine that a file already exists?

9.8 When reading a file, how does a program know it has reached end of the file?

9.2 The OpenFileDialog, SaveFileDialog, FontDialog, and ColorDialog Controls

CONCEPT: Visual Basic provides dialog controls that equip your applications with standard Windows dialog boxes for operations such as opening files, saving files, and selecting fonts and colors.

The OpenFileDialog and SaveFileDialog Controls

So far, the applications in this chapter that open a file either specify the filename as part of the code or require the user to enter the path and filename. Most Windows users, however, are accustomed to using a dialog box to browse their disk for a file to open or for a location to save a file. You can use the OpenFileDialog and SaveFileDialog controls to equip applications with standard dialog boxes used by most Windows applications.

The OpenFileDialog Control

The **OpenFileDialog control** displays a standard Windows *Open* dialog box, such as the one shown in Figure 9-15. The ***Open* dialog box** is useful in applications that work with files. It gives users the ability to browse for a file to open, instead of typing a long path and filename.

Figure 9-15 Windows *Open* dialog box

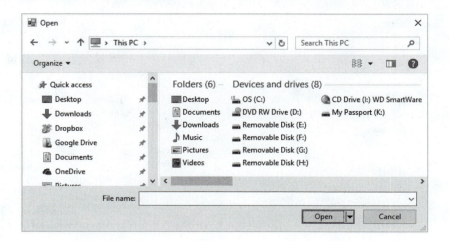

Adding the OpenFileDialog Control to Your Project

To place an OpenFileDialog control on a form, double-click the *OpenFileDialog* tool under the *Dialogs* tab in the *Toolbox* window. Because the control is invisible at runtime, it appears in the component tray at design time. We will use the prefix ofd when naming the control.

Displaying an *Open* Dialog Box

Display an *Open* dialog box by calling the OpenFileDialog control's ShowDialog method. The following is the method's general format:

```
ControlName.ShowDialog()
```

ControlName is the name of the OpenFileDialog control. For example, assuming ofdOpenFile is the name of an OpenFileDialog control, the following statement calls its ShowDialog method:

```
ofdOpenFile.ShowDialog()
```

ShowDialog returns one of the values Windows.Forms.DialogResult.OK or Windows.Forms.DialogResult.Cancel, indicating which button, *OK* or *Cancel*, the user clicked to close the dialog box. When the user selects a file with the *Open* dialog box, the file's path and name are stored in the control's **Filename property**.

The following code displays an *Open* dialog box and determines whether the user has selected a file. If so, the filename is displayed as follows:

```
If ofdOpenFile.ShowDialog() = Windows.Forms.DialogResult.OK Then
    MessageBox.Show(ofdOpenFile.FileName)
Else
    MessageBox.Show("You selected no file.")
End If
```

The Filter Property

The *Open* dialog box has a *Files of type* list box, which displays a filter that specifies the type of files visible in the dialog box. Filters typically use the wildcard character (*) followed by a file extension. For example, the *.txt filter specifies that only files ending in .txt (text files) are to be displayed. The *.doc filter specifies that only files ending in .doc (Microsoft Word files) are to be displayed. The *.* filter allows all files to be displayed.

The dialog box in Figure 9-16 shows a list box with *.txt and *.* filters.

Figure 9-16 *Open* dialog box with *.txt and *.* filters

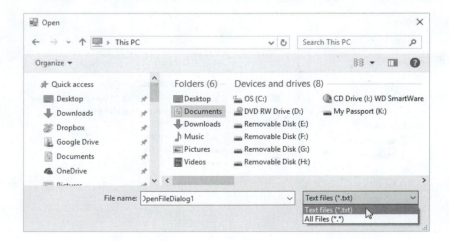

Use the **Filter property** to set the filters in the *Files of type* list box. This property can be set in the *Properties* window at design time, or by code at runtime. When storing a value in the Filter property, store a string containing a description of the filter and the filter itself. The description and the filter are separated with the pipe (|) symbol. For example, assuming an application has an OpenFileDialog control named ofdOpenFile, the following statement sets the Filter property for text files:

```
ofdOpenFile.Filter = "Text files (*.txt)|*.txt"
```

The part of the string appearing before the pipe symbol is a description of the filter, and is displayed in the *Files of type* list box. The part of the string appearing after the pipe symbol is the actual filter. In our example, the description of the filter is Text files (*.txt) and the filter is *.txt.

The pipe symbol is also used to separate multiple filters. For example, the following statement stores two filters in ofdOpenFile.Filter: *.txt and *.*:

```
ofdOpenFile.Filter = "Text files (*.txt)|*.txt|All Files (*.*)|*.*"
```

The description of the first filter is Text files (*.txt), and the filter is *.txt. The description of the second filter is All files (*.*), and the filter is *.*.

The InitialDirectory Property

By default, the *Open* dialog box displays the current directory (or folder). You can specify another directory to be initially displayed by storing its path in the **InitialDirectory property**. For example, the following code stores the path *C:\Data* in ofdOpenFile.InitialDirectory before displaying an *Open* dialog box:

```
ofdOpenFile.InitialDirectory = "C:\Data"
ofdOpenFile.ShowDialog()
```

When the *Open* dialog box is displayed, it shows the contents of the directory *C:\Data*.

If you want an *Open* dialog box to initially display the directory where the application's executable file is located, assign the value Application.StartupPath to the OpenFileDialog control's InitialDirectory property. Here's an example:

```
ofdOpenFile.InitialDirectory = Application.StartupPath
ofdOpenFile.ShowDialog()
```

The Title Property

You can change the default text displayed in the *Open* dialog box's title bar by storing a string in the control's **Title property**.

Using the *Open* Dialog Box to Open a File

The following code assumes ofdOpenFile is the name of an OpenFileDialog control. It demonstrates how to set the Filter, InitialDirectory, and Title properties, display the *Open* dialog box, retrieve the filename entered by the user, and open the file.

```
' Configure the Open dialog box and display it.
With ofdOpenFile
    .Filter = "Text files (*.txt)|*.txt|All files (*.*)|*.*"
    .InitialDirectory = "C:\Data"
    .Title = "Select a File to Open"
    If .ShowDialog() = Windows.Forms.DialogResult.OK Then
        inputFile = File.OpenText(.Filename)
    End If
End With
```

The SaveFileDialog Control

The **SaveFileDialog control** displays a standard Windows *Save As* dialog box. Figure 9-17 shows an example.

Figure 9-17 Windows *Save As* dialog box

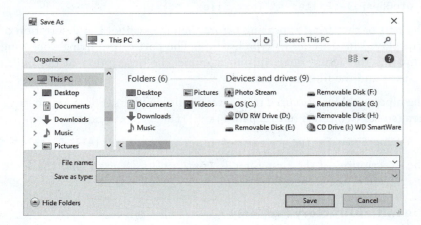

The *Save As* **dialog box** is useful in applications that work with files. It gives users the ability to browse their disks and to choose a location and name for the file.

The SaveFileDialog control has much in common with the OpenFileDialog control. Double-click the *SaveFileDialog* tool in the *Toolbox* to place the control on a form. Because the control is invisible at runtime, it appears in the component tray at design time. We will use the prefix sfd when naming the control.

Display a *Save As* dialog box by calling the SaveFileDialog control's ShowDialog method. The following is the method's general format:

```
ControlName.ShowDialog()
```

ControlName is the name of the SaveFileDialog control. For example, assuming sfdSaveFile is the name of a SaveFileDialog control, the following statement calls its ShowDialog method:

```
sfdSaveFile.ShowDialog()
```

This method returns one of the values `Windows.Forms.DialogResult.OK` or `Windows.-Forms.DialogResult.Cancel` indicating which button, *OK* or *Cancel*, the user clicked to dismiss the dialog box.

The Filename property holds the name of the file selected or entered by the user. The Filter, InitialDirectory, and Title properties work with the *Save As* dialog box the same way they do with the *Open* dialog box. The following code assumes that sfdSaveFile is the name of a common dialog control. It demonstrates how to set the Filter, InitialDirectory, and Title properties, display the *Save As* dialog box, retrieve the filename entered by the user, and open the file.

```
' Configure the Save As dialog box and display it.
With sfdSaveFile
    .Filter = "Text files (*.txt)|*.txt|All files (*.*)|*.*"
    .InitialDirectory = "C:\Data"
    .Title = "Save File As"
    ' If the user selected a file, open it for output.
    If.ShowDialog() = Windows.Forms.DialogResult.OK Then
```

```
        outputFile = System.IO.File.OpenText(.Filename)
    End If
End With
```

In Tutorial 9-4, you gain experience using the OpenFileDialog and SaveFileDialog controls by creating a simple text editor application. You will also learn about the TextBox control's MultiLine property, WordWrap property, and TextChanged event.

Tutorial 9-4:
Creating a *Simple Text Editor* application

In this tutorial, you will create a simple text editing application that allows you to create documents, save them, and open existing documents. The application will use a Multiline TextBox control to hold the document text. It will also use the menu system shown in Figure 9-18.

Figure 9-18 *Simple Text Editor* menu system

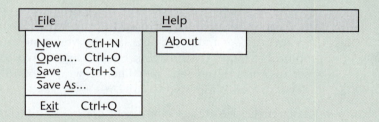

Table 9-1 lists the required menu items, showing the contents of their Text and ShortcutKeys properties.

Table 9-1 Menu items and their Text and ShortcutKeys properties

Menu Item Name	Text Property	ShortcutKeys Property
mnuFile	&File	(None)
mnuFileNew	&New	Ctrl + N
mnuFileOpen	&Open...	Ctrl + O
mnuFileSave	&Save	Ctrl + S
mnuFileSaveAs	Save &As...	(None)
mnuFileExit	E&xit	Ctrl + Q
mnuHelp	&Help	(None)
mnuHelpAbout	&About	(None)

Some of the menu item Text property values end with an ellipsis (. . .). It is a standard Windows convention for a menu item's text to end with an ellipsis if the menu item displays a dialog box.

Step 1: Create a new Windows Forms Application project named *Simple Text Editor*.

Step 2: Set the form's Text property to *Simple Text Editor*. Create a MenuStrip control on the form and add the menu items listed in Table 9-1. Set their Text and

ShortcutKeys properties to the values shown in the table. The form should appear similar to the one shown in Figure 9-19.

Figure 9-19 Initial *Simple Text Editor* form

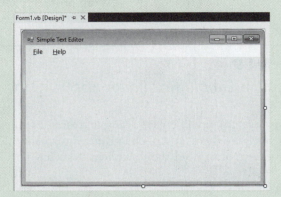

Step 3: Add a TextBox control to the form named `txtDocument`. TextBox controls have a Boolean property named **MultiLine**, which is set to *False* by default. When this property is set to *True*, the height of the TextBox control can be enlarged and its text can span multiple lines. Set the MultiLine property of the `txtDocument` control to *True*. TextBox controls also have a **WordWrap property** that, when set to *True*, causes long text lines to wrap around to the following line. By default, WordWrap is set to *True*.

Step 4: Enlarge the size of the `txtDocument` control so it fills most of the form, as shown in Figure 9-20.

Figure 9-20 *Simple Text Editor* form with text box enlarged

Step 5: Set the `txtDocument` control's Anchor property to *Top*, *Bottom*, *Left*, *Right*. This will cause the TextBox control to resize automatically if the user resizes the form.

Step 6: Add OpenFileDialog and SaveFileDialog controls to the form. (You will find these controls under the *Dialogs* group in the *Toolbox*.) Name the OpenFileDialog control `ofdOpenFile`. Name the SaveFileDialog control `sfdSaveFile`.

Step 7: Set the Title property of the `ofdOpenFile` control to *Open File*. Set the Title property of the `sfdSaveFile` control to *Save File As*. Set the Filter property to *Text Files (*.txt) | *.txt* for both controls.

Step 8: Now you are ready to write the code for the application. At the end of the tutorial you will find all of the code shown in one listing. (Don't type any of the line numbers. They are shown for reference only.) First, open the *Code* window and type the `Imports` statement shown in line 1.

Step 9: Inside the form's class declaration, type the comment and the class-level declarations shown in lines 4 through 6. The `strFilename` variable will hold the filename under which the text box's contents are saved. The `blnIsChanged` variable is a flag to indicate whether the text box's contents have been changed since the last time they were saved. We need this flag so we can warn the user any time he or she is about to clear the current document without saving it.

Step 10: Type the code for the `ClearDocument` procedure shown in lines 8 through 17. The `ClearDocument` procedure clears the `txtDocument` control's Text property, sets `strFilename` to an empty string, and sets `blnIsChanged` to *False*.

Step 11: Type the code for the `OpenDocument` procedure shown in lines 22 through 46. The `OpenDocument` procedure displays an *Open* dialog box, opens the file selected by the user, and reads its contents into the text box.

Step 12: Type the code for the `SaveDocument` procedure shown in lines 50 through 69. The `SaveDocument` procedure saves the contents of the text box to the file specified by the `strFilename` variable.

Step 13: Now you will write the code for the `txtDocument_TextChanged` event handler, shown in lines 71 through 74. This event handler will execute any time the `txtDocument` TextBox control's Text property changes. When that happens, we want to set the `blnIsChanged` variable to *True* to indicate that the current document has changed. Here's how to write the event handler:

In the *Code* window, select *txtDocument* in the class drop-down list box (which is in the upper-left area of the *Code* window), and then select *TextChanged* in the method name drop-down list box (which is in the upper-right area of the *Code* window). This will create a code template for the event handler. Simply type the contents of lines 72 and 73 to complete the event handler.

Step 14: Next, write the Click event handlers for the menu items. The code for all of the event handlers is shown in lines 76 through 141.

Step 15: Last, you will write the code for the `Form1_FormClosing` event handler, shown in lines 143 through 157. The purpose of this event handler is to warn the user if he or she attempts to exit the application without saving the contents of the text box. Here's how to create the correct event handler:

In the *Code* window, select *(Form1 Events)* in the class drop-down list box (in the upper-left area of the *Code* window), and then select *FormClosing* in the method name drop-down list box (in the upper-right area of the *Code* window). This will create a code template for the event handler. Simply type the contents of lines 144 through 156 to complete the event handler.

Step 16: Save and run the application. If you entered all the code correctly, you should see the form shown in Figure 9-21. Enter some text into the text box. Experiment with each of the menu commands to see if the application operates correctly. When you are finished, exit the application.

Figure 9-21 *Simple Text Editor* form

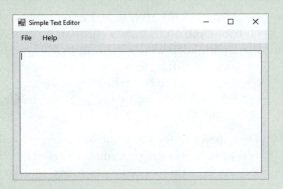

```
 1  Imports System.IO
 2
 3  Public Class Form1
 4      ' Class-level variables
 5      Private strFilename As String = String.Empty ' Document filename
 6      Dim blnIsChanged As Boolean = False           ' File change flag
 7
 8      Sub ClearDocument()
 9        ' Clear the contents of the text box.
10        txtDocument.Clear()
11
12        ' Clear the document name.
13        strFilename = String.Empty
14
15        ' Set isChanged to False.
16        blnIsChanged = False
17      End Sub
18
19      ' The OpenDocument procedure opens a file and loads it
20      ' into the TextBox for editing.
21
22      Sub OpenDocument()
23        Dim inputFile As StreamReader ' Object variable
24
25        If ofdOpenFile.ShowDialog = Windows.Forms.DialogResult.OK Then
26          ' Retrieve the selected filename.
27          strFilename = ofdOpenFile.FileName
28
29          Try
30            ' Open the file.
31            inputFile = File.OpenText(strFilename)
```

```
32
33              ' Read the file's contents into the TextBox.
34              txtDocument.Text = inputFile.ReadToEnd
35
36              ' Close the file.
37              inputFile.Close()
38
39              ' Update the isChanged variable.
40              blnIsChanged = False
41          Catch
42              ' Error message for file open error.
43              MessageBox.Show("Error opening the file.")
44          End Try
45        End If
46     End Sub
47
48     ' The SaveDocument procedure saves the current document.
49
50     Sub SaveDocument()
51        Dim outputFile As StreamWriter ' Object variable
52
53        Try
54           ' Create the file.
55           outputFile = File.CreateText(strFilename)
56
57           ' Write the TextBox to the file.
58           outputFile.Write(txtDocument.Text)
59
60           ' Close the file.
61           outputFile.Close()
62
63           ' Update the isChanged variable.
64           blnIsChanged = False
65        Catch
66           ' Error message for file creation error.
67           MessageBox.Show("Error creating the file.")
68        End Try
69     End Sub
70
71     Private Sub txtDocument_TextChanged(...) Handles txtDocument.TextChanged
72        ' Indicate the text has changed.
73        blnIsChanged = True
74     End Sub
75
76     Private Sub mnuFileNew_Click(...) Handles mnuFileNew.Click
77        ' Has the current document changed?
78        If blnIsChanged = True Then
79           ' Confirm before clearing the document.
80           If MessageBox.Show("The current document is not saved. " &
81                              "Are you sure?", "Confirm",
82                          MessageBoxButtons.YesNo) =
83                     Windows.Forms.DialogResult.Yes Then
84              ClearDocument()
85           End If
86        Else
```

```vb
 87               ' Document has not changed, so clear it.
 88               ClearDocument()
 89            End If
 90       End Sub
 91
 92       Private Sub mnuFileOpen_Click(...) Handles mnuFileOpen.Click
 93          ' Has the current document changed?
 94          If blnIsChanged = True Then
 95             ' Confirm before clearing and replacing.
 96             If MessageBox.Show("The current document is not saved. " &
 97                               "Are you sure?", "Confirm",
 98                               MessageBoxButtons.YesNo) =
 99                         Windows.Forms.DialogResult.Yes Then
100               ClearDocument()
101               OpenDocument()
102            End If
103          Else
104             ' Document has not changed, so replace it.
105            ClearDocument()
106            OpenDocument()
107          End If
108       End Sub
109
110       Private Sub mnuFileSave_Click(...) Handles mnuFileSave.Click
111          ' Does the current document have a filename?
112          If strFilename = String.Empty Then
113             ' The document has not been saved, so
114             ' use Save As dialog box.
115            If sfdSaveFile.ShowDialog = Windows.Forms.DialogResult.OK Then
116               strFilename = sfdSaveFile.FileName
117               SaveDocument()
118            End If
119          Else
120             ' Save the document with the current filename.
121            SaveDocument()
122          End If
123       End Sub
124
125       Private Sub mnuFileSaveAs_Click(...) Handles mnuFileSaveAs.Click
126          ' Save the current document under a new filename.
127          If sfdSaveFile.ShowDialog = Windows.Forms.DialogResult.OK Then
128            strFilename = sfdSaveFile.FileName
129            SaveDocument()
130          End If
131       End Sub
132
133       Private Sub mnuExit_Click(...) Handles mnuExit.Click
134          ' Close the form.
135          Me.Close()
136       End Sub
137
138       Private Sub mnuHelpAbout_Click(...) Handles mnuHelpAbout.Click
139          ' Display an about box.
140          MessageBox.Show("Simple Text Editor version 1.0")
141       End Sub
```

```
142
143    Private Sub Form1_FormClosing(...) Handles Me.FormClosing
144       ' If the document has been modified, confirm
145       ' before exiting.
146       If blnIsChanged = True Then
147          If MessageBox.Show("The current document is not saved. " &
148                            "Do you wish to discard your changes?",
149                            "Confirm",
150                            MessageBoxButtons.YesNo) =
151                        Windows.Forms.DialogResult.Yes Then
152             e.Cancel = False
153          Else
154             e.Cancel = True
155          End If
156       End If
157    End Sub
158 End Class
```

The ColorDialog and FontDialog Controls

The ColorDialog Control

The **ColorDialog control** displays a standard Windows *Color* dialog box. Figure 9-22 shows a default *Color* dialog box on the left. When the user clicks the *Define Custom Colors* button, the dialog box expands to become the fully open *Color* dialog box shown on the right.

Double-click the *ColorDialog* icon in the *Dialogs* section of the *Toolbox* to place the control on a form. Because the control is invisible at runtime, it appears in the component tray at design time. We will use the prefix cd when naming the control.

Figure 9-22 Windows *Color* dialog box

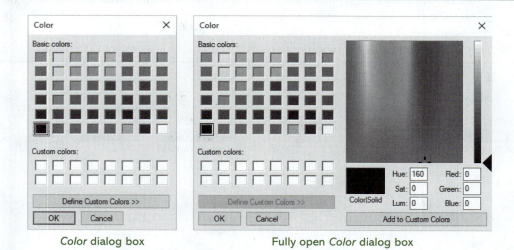

Color dialog box   Fully open Color dialog box

Display a *Color* dialog box by calling its `ShowDialog` method. For example, assuming `cdColor` is the name of a ColorDialog control, the following statement calls its `ShowDialog` method:

```
cdColor.ShowDialog()
```

This method returns one of the values, `Windows.Forms.DialogResult.OK` or `Windows.Forms.DialogResult.Cancel`, indicating which button, *OK* or *Cancel*, the user clicked to dismiss the dialog box. The Color property will hold a value representing the color selected by the user. This value can be used with control properties that designate color, such as ForeColor and BackColor. For example, the following code displays the *Color* dialog box and then sets the color of the text displayed by the `lblMessage` label to that selected by the user:

```
If cdColor.ShowDialog() = Windows.Forms.DialogResult.OK Then
    lblMessage.ForeColor = cdColor.Color
End If
```

By default, black is initially selected when the *Color* dialog box is displayed. If you wish to set the initially selected color, you must set the Color property to the desired color value. For example, the following code sets the initially selected color to blue:

```
cdColor.Color = Color.Blue
If cdColor.ShowDialog() = Windows.Forms.DialogResult.OK Then
    lblMessage.ForeColor = cdColor.Color
End If
```

The following code sets the initially selected color to the color of the `lblMessage` label before displaying the dialog box:

```
cdColor.Color = lblMessage.ForeColor
If cdColor.ShowDialog() = Windows.Forms.DialogResult.OK Then
    lblMessage.ForeColor = cdColor.Color
End If
```

The FontDialog Control

The **FontDialog control** displays a standard Windows *Font* dialog box. Figure 9-23 shows the default *Font* dialog box on the left, and a *Font* dialog box with a *Color* drop-down list on the right.

Figure 9-23 Windows *Font* dialog box

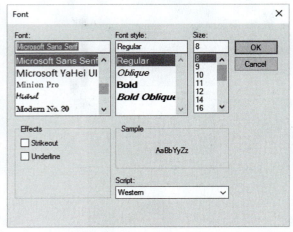
Default *Font* dialog box

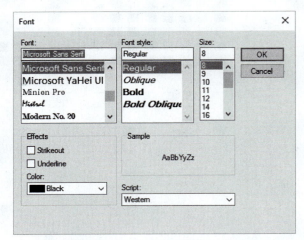
Font dialog box with color choices displayed

Double-click the *FontDialog* icon in the *Dialogs* section of the *Toolbox* to place the control on a form. Because the control is invisible at runtime, it appears in the component tray at design time. We will use the prefix `fd` when naming the control.

You display a *Font* dialog box by calling the FontDialog control's `ShowDialog` method. For example, assuming `fdFont` is the name of a FontDialog control, the following statement calls its `ShowDialog` method:

```
fdFont.ShowDialog()
```

By default, the *Font* dialog box does not allow the user to select a color. Color is controlled by the FontDialog control's ShowColor property, which can be set to *True* or *False*. When set to *True*, the *Font* dialog box appears with a *Color* drop-down list, shown on the right in Figure 9-23.

The `ShowDialog` method returns one of the values `Windows.Forms.DialogResult.OK` or `Windows.Forms.DialogResult.Cancel` indicating which button, *OK* or *Cancel*, the user clicked to dismiss the dialog box. The Font property will hold a value representing the font settings selected by the user. The Color property will hold a value representing the color selected by the user. For example, the following code displays the *Font* dialog box and then sets the `lblMessage` control's font to that selected by the user.

```
If fdFont.ShowDialog() = Windows.Forms.DialogResult.OK Then
   lblTest.Font = fdFont.Font
End If
```

The following code displays a *Font* dialog box with a drop-down list of colors. It then sets the `lblMessage` control's font and color to the values selected by the user.

```
fdFont.ShowColor = True
If fdFont.ShowDialog() = Windows.Forms.DialogResult.OK Then
   lblTest.Font = fdFont.Font
   lblTest.ForeColor = fdFont.Color
End If
```

Checkpoint

9.9 Why is it a good idea to use the *Open* and *Save As* dialog boxes in applications that work with files?

9.10 What is the purpose of the following OpenFileDialog and SaveFileDialog properties?
   Filter
   InitialDirectory
   Title
   Filename

9.11 Suppose you want an *Open* dialog box to have the following filters: text files (*.txt), Microsoft Word files (*.doc), and all files (*.*). What string would you store in the Filter property?

9.12 When the user selects a color with the *Color* dialog box, where is the color value stored?

9.13 When the user selects font settings with the *Font* dialog box, where are the font setting values stored?

9.14 How do you display a *Font* dialog box with a drop-down list of colors?

9.15 When the user selects a color with the *Font* dialog box, where is the color value stored?

9.3 The PrintDocument Control

CONCEPT: The PrintDocument control allows you to send output to the printer.

The **PrintDocument control** gives your application the ability to print output on the printer. Double-click the *PrintDocument* tool in the Printing section of the *Toolbox* window to place a PrintDocument control on a form. Because the control is invisible at runtime, it appears in the component tray at design time. We will use the prefix pd when naming the control.

The `Print` Method and the `PrintPage` Event

The PrintDocument control has a **Print method** that starts the printing process. The method's general format is as follows:

```
PrintDocumentControl.Print()
```

When the `Print` method is called, it triggers a PrintPage event. You must write code in the PrintPage event handler to initiate the actual printing. To create a PrintPage event handler code template, double-click the PrintDocument control in the component tray. The following is an example:

```
Private Sub pdPrint_PrintPage(...) Handles pdPrint.PrintPage

End Sub
```

Inside the **PrintPage event handler,** you can write code that sends text to the printer using a specified font and color, at a specified location. We will use the following general format to call the `e.Graphics.DrawString` method:

```
e.Graphics.DrawString(String, New Font(FontName, Size,
     Style), Brushes.Black, HPos, VPos)
```

String is the string to be printed. *FontName* is a string holding the name of the font to use. *Size* is the size of the font in points. *Style* is the font style. Valid values are `FontStyle.Bold`, `FontStyle.Italic`, `FontStyle.Regular`, `FontStyle.Strikeout`, and `FontStyle.Underline`. *HPos* is the horizontal position of the output. This is the distance of the output, in points, from the left margin of the paper. *VPos* is the vertical position of the output. This is the distance of the output, in points, from the top margin of the paper. The `Brushes.Black` argument specifies that output should be printed in black.

The following PrintPage event handler prints the contents of a TextBox control, txtInput, in a regular 12 point Times New Roman font. The horizontal and vertical coordinates of the output are 10 and 10.

```
Private Sub pdPrint_PrintPage(...) Handles pdPrint.PrintPage
     e.Graphics.DrawString(txtInput.Text, New Font("Times New Roman",
                  12, FontStyle.Regular), Brushes.Black, 10, 10)
End Sub
```

The following PrintPage event handler prints the string "Sales Report" in a bold 18 point Courier font. The horizontal and vertical coordinates of the output are 150 and 80.

```
Private Sub pdPrint_PrintPage(...) Handles pdPrint.PrintPage
     e.Graphics.DrawString("Sales Report", New Font("Courier",
                  18, FontStyle.Bold), Brushes.Black, 150, 80)
End Sub
```

The following PrintPage event handler prints the contents of a file. Assume that strFilename is a class-level string variable containing the name of the file whose contents are to be printed.

```
Private Sub pdPrint_PrintPage(...) Handles pdPrint.PrintPage
    Dim inputFile As StreamReader ' Object variable
    Dim intX As Integer = 10      ' X coordinate for printing
    Dim intY As Integer = 10      ' Y coordinate for printing
    Try
       ' Open the file.
       inputFile = File.OpenText(strFilename)
       ' Read all the lines in the file.
       Do While Not inputFile.EndOfStream
          ' Print a line from the file.
          e.Graphics.DrawString(inputFile.ReadLine(), New Font
             ("Courier", 10, FontStyle.Regular), Brushes.Black,
              intX, intY)
          ' Add 12 to intY.
          intY += 12
       Loop
       ' Close the file.
       inputFile.Close()
    Catch
       ' Error message for file open error.
       MessageBox.Show("Error: could not open file.")
    End Try
End Sub
```

The variables intX and intY specify the horizontal and vertical positions of each line of printed output. The statement intY += 12 inside the loop increases the vertical distance of each line by 12 points from the top of the page. The output is printed in a 10 point font, so there are 2 points of space between each line.

The PrintDialog Control

When you choose to print a document, most applications open a standard Windows *Print* dialog, such as the one shown in Figure 9-24. The *Print* dialog allows you to select a printer, the number of copies to print, and establish other settings. If you have the necessary software installed, you can choose to print to a PDF instead of a printer.

Figure 9-24 Standard Windows *Print* dialog

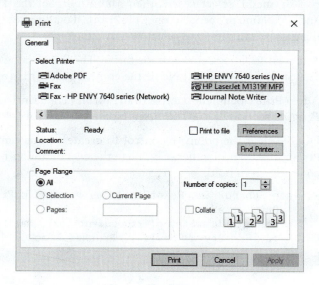

In your Visual Basic applications, you can use the **PrintDialog control** to display a standard Windows *Print* dialog. Double-click the *PrintDialog* tool in the Printing section of the *Toolbox* window to place a PrintDialog control on a form. Because the control is invisible at runtime, it appears in the component tray at design time. We will use the prefix pdd when naming the control.

In code, you display a *Print* dialog box by calling the PrintDialog control's ShowDialog method. Here is an example:

```
pddPrintDialog.ShowDialog()
```

The ShowDialog method returns one of these values:

- Windows.Forms.DialogResult.OK if the user clicked the *Print* button
- Windows.Forms.DialogResult.Cancel if the user clicked the *Cancel* button

The printer settings that the user selected in the dialog box (such as the name of the printer, the number of copies, the pages to print, etc.) will be stored in the PrintDialog control's **PrinterSettings property**. To use these settings, you assign the PrintDialog control's PrinterSettings property to the PrintDocument control's PrinterSettings property. In the following example, assume we have a PrintDialog control named pddPrintDialog, and PrintDocument control named pdPrint:

```
If pddPrintDialog.ShowDialog() = Windows.Forms.DialogResult.OK Then
    ' Get the printer settings.
    pdPrint.PrinterSettings = pddPrintDialog.PrinterSettings

    ' Print the document.
    pdPrint.Print()
End If
```

In Tutorial 9-5, you will modify the *Simple Text Editor* application you created in Tutorial 9-4 by adding a *Print* command to the *File* menu.

Tutorial 9-5:
Adding printing capabilities to the *Simple Text Editor* application

Step 1: Open the *Simple Text Editor* project you created in Tutorial 9-4.

Step 2: Add a *Print* menu item and separator bar to the *File* menu, as shown in Figure 9-25. To add the *Print* menu item, right-click on the *Exit* MenuItem. From the pop-up menu, select *Insert*, then *MenuItem*. Set the Text property to &Print and the Name property to mnuFilePrint. To add a separator bar, right-click on the *Exit* MenuItem, and select *Insert*, then *Separator*.

Step 3: Add a PrintDialog control to the form. (The PrintDialog control is in the *Printing* section of the *Toolbox*.) Name the control pddPrintDialog.

Step 4: Add a PrintDocument control to the form. (The PrintDocument control is in the *Printing* section of the *Toolbox*.) Name the control pdPrint.

Step 5: Double-click the pdPrint control to create a code template for the pdPrint_PrintPage event handler. Complete the event handler by entering the following code shown in bold:

```
Private Sub pdPrint_PrintPage(...) Handles pdPrint.PrintPage
    ' Print the contents of the text box.
    e.Graphics.DrawString(txtDocument.Text, New Font ("MS Sans Serif",
       12, FontStyle.Regular), Brushes.Black, 10, 10)
End Sub
```

Figure 9-25 Print menu item and separator bars added

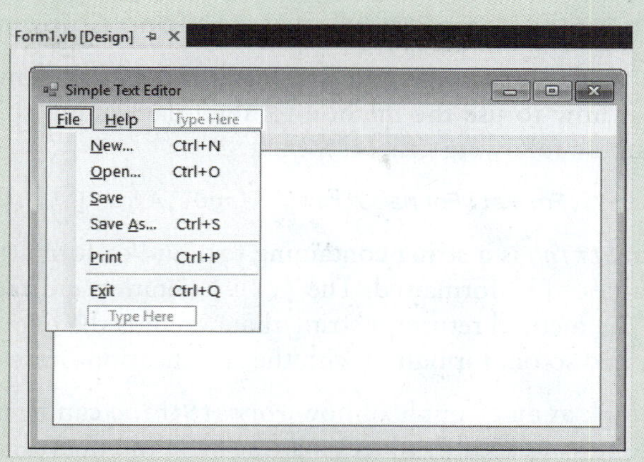

Step 6: Add the following mnuFilePrint_Click event procedure.

```
Private Sub mnuFilePrint_Click(...) Handles mnuFilePrint.Click
    ' Open the Print dialog.
    If pddPrintDialog.ShowDialog() = DialogResult.OK Then
        ' Get the printer settings.
        pdPrint.PrinterSettings = pddPrintDialog.PrinterSettings

        ' Print the document.
        pdPrint.Print()
    End If
```

Step 7: Save and run the application. Enter some text into the text box or load an existing file. Test the new *Print* command. The contents of the text box should be printed on the selected printer.

Step 8: Exit the application.

Formatted Reports with `String.Format`

Reports typically contain the following sections:

- A **report header**, printed first, contains the name of the report, the date and time the report was printed, and other general information about the data in the report.
- The **report body** contains the report's data and is often formatted in columns.
- An optional **report footer** contains the sum of one or more columns of data.

Printing Reports with Columnar Data

Report data is typically printed in column format, with each column having an appropriate heading. To properly align printed data in columns, you can use a monospaced font to ensure that all characters occupy the same amount of space, and use the `String.Format` method to format the data into columns. Let's take a closer look at each of these topics.

Monospaced Fonts

Most printers normally use proportionally spaced fonts such as MS sans serif. In a proportionally spaced font, the amount of space occupied by a character depends on the width of the character. For example, the letters *m* and *w* occupy more space than the letters *i* and *j*. Using proportionally spaced fonts, you may have trouble aligning data properly in columns. To remedy the problem, you can select a monospaced font such as Courier New. All characters in a monospaced font use the same amount of space on the printed page.

Using `String.Format` to Align Data along Column Boundaries

The `String.Format` method is a versatile tool for formatting strings. In this section, we discuss how to use the method to align data along column boundaries. The method is used in the following general format:

```
String.Format(FormatString, Arg0, Arg1 [,...])
```

FormatString is a string containing text and/or formatting specifications. *Arg0* and *Arg1* are values to be formatted. The [,...] notation indicates that more arguments may follow. The method returns a string that contains the data provided by the arguments *Arg0*, *Arg1*, and so on, formatted with the specifications found in *FormatString*.

Let's look at an example of how *FormatString* can be used to format data into columns. The following code produces a string with the numbers 10, 20, and 30 aligned into columns of ten characters wide each. The resulting string is stored in the variable `strTemp`.

```
Dim strTemp As String
Dim intX, intY, intZ As Integer
intX = 10
intY = 20
intZ = 30
strTemp = String.Format("{0, 10} {1, 10} {2, 10} ", intX, intY, intZ)
```

The string "{0, 10} {1, 10} {2, 10}" is the format string. The variable `intX` is argument 0, the variable `intY` is argument 1, and the variable `intZ` is argument 2. This is illustrated in Figure 9-26.

Figure 9-26 Arguments of the `String.Format` method

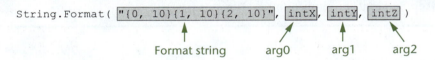

The contents of the format string specify how the data is to be formatted. In our example, the string has three sets of numbers inside curly braces. The first set is {0, 10}. This specifies that argument 0 (the variable `intX`) is to be placed in a column ten spaces wide. The second set is {1, 10}. This specifies that argument 1 (the variable `intY`) is to be placed in a column ten spaces wide. The third set, {2, 10}, specifies that argument 2 (the variable `intZ`) is to be placed in a column ten spaces wide. Figure 9-27 labels all these parts. There are no spaces between the sets.

Figure 9-27 Format specifications

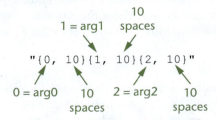

After the last statement in the previous code executes, the variable `strTemp` contains the string " 10 20 30". The numbers are placed in columns of ten spaces each, as illustrated in Figure 9-28. In our example, the numbers are right justified inside the columns. If you use a negative value for a column width in the format string, the column is left justified. For example, using the variables `intX`, `intY`, and `intZ` from the previous code example, the method call

```
String.Format("{0, -10} {1, -10} {2, -10} ", intX, intY, intZ)
```

produces the string "10 20 30 ".

Let's examine a code sample that prints a sales report with a header, two columns of data, and a footer. The data is printed from the following parallel arrays:

```
Dim strNames As String() = {"John Smith", "Jill McKenzie",
                            "Karen Suttles", "Jason Mabry",
                            "Susan Parsons"}
Dim decSales As Decimal() = {2500.0, 3400.0, 4200.0,
                             2200.0, 3100.0}
```

Figure 9-28 Column widths

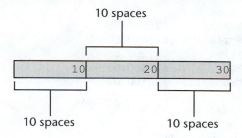

The `strNames` array contains five salespeople's names and the `decSales` array contains each salesperson's sales. The `For...Next` loop in the following event handler prints each line of data and uses an accumulator, `decTotal`, to sum the sales amounts. The contents of `decTotal` are printed in the footer to show the total sales.

```
Private Sub pdPrint_PrintPage(...) Handles pdPrint.PrintPage
    Dim intCount As Integer       ' Loop counter
    Dim decTotal As Decimal = 0   ' Accumulator
    Dim intVertPosition As Integer ' Vertical printing position

    ' Print the report header.
    e.Graphics.DrawString("Sales Report", New Font("Courier New", 12,
        FontStyle.Bold), Brushes.Black, 150, 10)

    e.Graphics.DrawString("Date and Time: " & Now.ToString(),
        New Font("Courier New", 12, FontStyle.Bold),
        Brushes.Black, 10, 38)

    ' Print the column headings.
    e.Graphics.DrawString(String.Format("{0, 20} {1, 20} ",
        "NAME", "SALES"), New Font("Courier New", 12,
        FontStyle.Bold), Brushes.Black, 10, 66)
```

```
                    ' Print the body of the report.
                    intVertPosition = 82
                    For intCount = 0 To 4
                        e.Graphics.DrawString(String.Format("{0, 20} {1, 20} ",
                            strNames(intCount), decSales(intCount).ToString("c")),
                            New Font("Courier New", 12, FontStyle.Regular),
                            Brushes.Black, 10, intVertPosition)

                        decTotal += decSales(intCount)
                        intVertPosition += 14
                    Next

                    ' Print the report footer.
                    e.Graphics.DrawString("Total Sales: " & decTotal.ToString("c"),
                        New Font("Courier New", 12, FontStyle.Bold),
                        Brushes.Black, 150, 165)
                End Sub
```

The report printed by this code appears similar to the following:

```
            Sales Report

    Date and Time: 10/14/2017 11:12:34 AM

                Name          Sales
            John Smith      $2,500.00
        Jill McKenzie       $3,400.00
        Karen Suttles       $4,200.00
          Jason Mabry       $2,200.00
        Susan Parsons       $3,100.00

        Total Sales:       $15,400.00
```

✔ Checkpoint

9.16 How do you trigger a PrintDocument control's PrintPage event?

9.17 Assume an application has a PrintDocument control named pdPrint. Write a statement in the control's PrintPage event handler that prints your first and last name in an 18 point bold MS sans serif font. Print your name at 100 points from the page's left margin and 20 points from the page's top margin.

9.18 Name the three sections most reports have.

9.19 What is the difference between a proportionally spaced font and a monospaced font?

9.20 Assume that an application has a PrintDocument control named pdPrint. Write a statement in the control's PrintPage event handler that prints the contents of the variables a and b in a 12 point regular Courier New font. The contents of a should be printed in a column 12 characters wide, and the contents of b should be printed in a column 8 characters wide. Print the data 10 points from the page's left margin and 50 points from the page's top margin.

9.21 Rewrite the answer you wrote to Checkpoint 9.20 so the contents of the variable a are left justified.

9.4 Structures

CONCEPT: Visual Basic allows you to create your own data types, into which you may group multiple data fields.

So far you have created applications that keep data in individual variables. If you need to group items, you can create arrays. Arrays, however, require elements to be of the same data type. Sometimes a relationship exists between items of different types. For example, a payroll system might use the variables shown in the following declaration statements:

```
Dim intEmpNumber As Integer     ' Employee number
Dim strFirstName As String      ' Employee's first name
Dim strLastName As String       ' Employee's last name
Dim dblHours As Double          ' Number of hours worked
Dim decPayRate As Decimal       ' Hourly pay rate
Dim decGrossPay As Decimal      ' Gross pay
```

All these variables are related because they can hold data about the same employee. The `Dim` statements, however, create separate variables and do not establish relationships.

Instead of creating separate variables that hold related data, you can group the related data. A **structure** is a data type you can create that contains one or more variables known as fields. The fields can be of different data types. Once a structure has been created, variables of the structure may be declared.

You create a structure at the class- or module-level with the **Structure** statement:

```
[AccessSpecifier] Structure StructureName
   FieldDeclarations
End Structure
```

AccessSpecifier is shown in brackets, indicating that it is optional. If you use the `Public` access specifier, the structure is accessible to statements outside the class or module. If you use the `Private` access specifier, the structure is accessible only to statements in the same class or module. *StructureName* is the name of the structure. *FieldDeclarations* is one or more declarations of fields, as regular `Dim` statements. The following is an example:

```
Structure EmpPayData
   Dim intEmpNumber As Integer
   Dim strFirstName As String
   Dim strLastName As String
   Dim dblHours As Double
   Dim decPayRate As Decimal
   Dim decGrossPay As Decimal
End Structure
```

This statement declares a structure named `EmpPayData`, having six fields.

TIP: Structure names and class names should begin with uppercase letters. This serves as a visual reminder that the structure or class name is not a variable name.

> **TIP:** If you want a structure to be available to multiple forms in a project, place the `Structure` statement, with the `Public` access specifier, in a module.

The `Structure` statement does not create a variable—it creates a new data type by telling Visual Basic what the data type contains. You declare variables of a structure using `Dim` statements, just as you would with any other data type. For example, the following statement declares a variable called `deptHead` as an `EmpPayData` variable:

```
Dim deptHead As EmpPayData
```

The `deptHead` variable can store six values because the `EmpPayData` data type is made of six fields, as illustrated in Figure 9-29.

Access the fields with the dot operator. For example, the following statements assign values to all six fields of the `deptHead` variable.

```
deptHead.intEmpNumber = 1101
deptHead.strFirstName = "Joanne"
deptHead.strLastName = "Smith"
deptHead.dblHours = 40.0
deptHead.decPayRate = 25
deptHead.decGrossPay = CDec(deptHead.dblHours) *
                       deptHead.decPayRate
```

Figure 9-29 `deptHead` variable

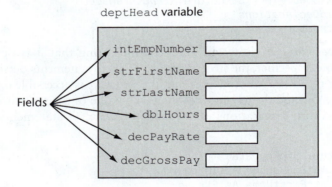

The following statement adds the `intEmpNumber` field to the `lstEmployeeList` list box:

```
lstEmployeeList.Items.Add(deptHead.intEmpNumber)
```

You can optionally use the `With` statement to simplify access to structure fields:

```
With deptHead
    .intEmpNumber = 1101
    .strFirstName = "Joanne"
    .strLastName = "Smith"
    .dblHours = 40.0
    .decPayRate = 25
    .decGrossPay = CDec(.dblHours) * .decPayRate
End With
```

Passing Structure Variables to Procedures and Functions

You can pass structure variables to procedures and functions. For example, the following procedure declares an `EmpPayData` parameter, passed by reference:

```
Sub CalcPay(ByRef employee As EmpPayData)
   ' This procedure accepts an EmpPayData variable
   ' as its argument. The employee's gross pay
   ' is calculated and stored in the grossPay
   ' field.
   With employee
      .decGrossPay =.dblHours * .decPayRate
   End With
End Sub
```

Arrays as Structure Members

Structures can contain array fields, but the arrays cannot be assigned initial sizes. An example is shown in the following statement:

```
Structure StudentRecord
   Dim strName As String
   Dim dblTestScores() As Double
End Structure
```

After declaring a structure variable, you can use the `ReDim` statement to establish a size for the array. Then you access the array elements with a subscript, as shown in the following example:

```
Dim student As StudentRecord
ReDim student.dblTestScores(4)
student.strName = "Mary McBride"
student.dblTestScores(0) = 89.0
student.dblTestScores(1) = 92.0
student.dblTestScores(2) = 84.0
student.dblTestScores(3) = 96.0
student.dblTestScores(4) = 91.0
```

Arrays of Structures

You may also declare an array of structures. For example, the following statement declares `employees` as an array of 10 `EmpPayData` variables:

```
Const intMAX_SUBSCRIPT As Integer = 9
Dim employees(intMAX_SUBSCRIPT) As EmpPayData
```

To access the individual elements in the array, use a subscript as shown in the following statement:

```
employees(0).intEmpNumber = 1101
```

When working with an array of structure variables in which the structure contains an array field, use the `ReDim` statement to establish a size for the array field of each element. For example, the `StudentRecord` discussed in the previous section has a field named `dblTestScores`, which is an array of five numbers. Suppose an application declares an array of `StudentRecord` variables as follows:

```
Const intMAX_SUBSCRIPT As Integer = 9
Dim students(intMAX_SUBSCRIPT) As StudentRecord
```

A loop, such as the following, can be used to set a size for each `testScores` array:

```
For intIndex = 0 To intMax_SUBSCRIPT
  ReDim students(intIndex).dblTestScores(4)
Next
```

You can use the array fields once they have been given a size. For example, the following statement stores 95 in `dblTestScores(0)` inside `students(5)`:

```
students(5).dblTestScores(0) = 95.0
```

Tutorial 9-6 examines an application that uses a structure.

Tutorial 9-6:
Examining an application with a structure

In this tutorial, you examine a modified version of the *File WriteLine Demo* project from Tutorial 9-1. This version of the project uses a structure to store the friend data.

Step 1: Open the *Structure File WriteLine Demo* project from the student sample programs folder named *Chap9\Structure File WriteLine Demo*.

Step 2: Open the *Code* window. The following statements declare the `FriendInfo` structure:

```
Structure FriendInfo
  Dim strName As String   ' To hold a name
  Dim strPhone As String  ' To hold a phone number
End Structure
```

Step 3: Look at the `btnCreateFile_Click` event handler. The procedure uses the structure variable `myFriend` to hold the names, ages, and addresses entered by the user. The `friendFile.WriteLine` statements write the contents of the structure variable's fields to the file.

```
Private Sub btnCreateFile_Click(...) Handles btnCreateFile.Click
  ' Constant for the number of friends
  Const intNUM_FRIENDS As Integer = 3

  ' Local variables
  Dim strFilename As String         ' File name
  Dim intCount As Integer           ' Loop counter
  Dim friendFile As StreamWriter    ' Object variable
  Dim myFriend As FriendInfo        ' Structure variable

  ' Get the file name from the user.
  strFilename = InputBox("Enter the filename.")

  Try
    ' Open the file.
    friendFile = File.CreateText(strFilename)

    ' Get the data and write it to the file.
    For intCount = 1 To intNUM_FRIENDS
      ' Get a friend's name.
      myFriend.strName = InputBox("Enter the name of friend " &
                                  "number " & intCount.ToString())
```

```
                ' Get a friend's phone number.
                myFriend.strPhone = InputBox("Enter the that friend's " &
                                             "phone number.")

                ' Write the data to the file.
                friendFile.WriteLine(myFriend.strName)
                friendFile.WriteLine(myFriend.strPhone)
            Next

                ' Close the file.
                friendFile.Close()
        Catch
            ' Error message
            MessageBox.Show("That file cannot be created.")
        End Try
    End Sub
```

Step 4: Run the application and, as you did in Tutorial 9-1, click the *Save Data to File* button. Enter a filename and data for three of your friends. The procedure saves the data.

Step 5: Exit the application.

Checkpoint

9.22 Write a statement that declares a structure named Movie. The structure should have fields to hold the following data about a movie.

The name of the movie
The director of the movie
The producer of the movie
The year the movie was released

9.23 Write a statement that declares a variable of the Movie structure that you created in Checkpoint 9.22.

9.24 Write statements that store the following data in the variable you declared in Checkpoint 9.23. (Do not use the With statement.)

The name of the movie: *Wheels of Fury*
The director of the movie: *Arlen McGoo*
The producer of the movie: *Vincent Van Dough*
The year the movie was released: *2017*

9.25 Rewrite the statements you wrote in Checkpoint 9.24 using the With statement.

Summary

9.1 Using Files

- Data is saved in a file, which is stored on a computer's disk.
- For an application to use a file, the file must be opened (which creates the file if it does not exist), data is either written to the file or read from the file, and the file is closed.
- When a sequential file is opened, its read position is set to the first item in the file. As data is read, the read position advances through the file.
- The contents of an array are saved to a file using a loop that steps through each element of the array, writing its contents to the file.
- By specifying a namespace with the `Imports` statement, you can refer to names in that namespace without fully qualifying them.
- The `File.CreateText` method creates a new file or replaces an existing one. The `File.AppendText` method opens a file so more data can be appended to the end of the file. The `File.OpenText` method opens a file for reading.

9.2 The OpenFileDialog, SaveFileDialog, FontDialog, and ColorDialog Controls

- The OpenFileDialog control displays a standard Windows *Open* dialog box. The SaveFileDialog control displays a standard Windows *Save As* dialog box. The ColorDialog control displays a standard Windows *Color* dialog box. The FontDialog control displays a standard Windows *Font* dialog box.

9.3 The PrintDocument Control

- The PrintDocument control allows your application to print output. You write the code that handles the printing in the `PrintPage` event handler. You trigger a Print-Page event by calling the `Print` method. You use the `e.Graphics.DrawString` method to send output to the printer.
- The PrintDialog control displays a standard Windows *Print* dialog box. It allows you to select a printer, as well as various printer settings, such as the number of copies to print, the pages to print, etc.
- Reports typically have a header, body, and footer.
- To align printed data properly in columns, you must use a monospaced font to ensure that all characters occupy the same amount of space; you use the `String.Format` method to format the data into columns.

9.4 Structures

- A structure is a defined data type that you create, which contains one or more variables known as fields. Fields can be of different data types. You can create a structure with the `Structure` statement. Once you have defined a structure, you may declare instances of it.

Key Terms

append	file
buffer	`File.AppendText` method
`Chr` function	`File.CreateText` method
`Close` method	`File.Exists` method
Color dialog box	`File.OpenText` method
ColorDialog control	Filename property
delimiter	Filter property
EndOfStream property	*Font* dialog box

FontDialog control
InitialDirectory property
input file
MultiLine property
newline character
Open dialog box
OpenFileDialog control
output file
`Print` method
PrintDialog control
PrintDocument control
`PrintPage` event handler
PrinterSettings property
Read method
read position
`ReadLine` method
`ReadToEnd` method

report body
report footer
report header
Save As dialog box
SaveFileDialog control
sequential-access file
`StreamReader` class
`StreamReader` object
`StreamWriter` class
`StreamWriter` object
structure
`Structure` statement
text file
Title property
WordWrap property
`Write` method
`WriteLine` method

VideoNote

Files and Colors in the *Kayak Rental* Application

Video Tutorial: Files and Colors in the *Kayak Rental* Application

In this sequence of video tutorials, we continue the *Kayak Rental* application. Because a kayak rental combines related information, we will use a Structure to hold this information in a convenient package. We will write the rental history to a data file and later read this file back into memory. The store manager will be given a way to customize the interface by choosing colors from dialog boxes. Finally, the store clerk will print a rental invoice on the printer.

- Part 1: Saving the rental history to a file and reading the rental history from a file.
- Part 2: Allowing the manager to customize colors, and printing a rental invoice.

Review Questions and Exercises

Fill-in-the-Blank

1. Before a file can be used, it must be _____.

2. When a file is opened, a(n) _____ is created, which is a small holding section of memory that data is first written to.

3. When it is finished using a file, an application should always _____ it.

4. To write data to a sequential file, use a(n) _____ object.

5. To read data from a sequential file, use a(n) _____ object.

6. The _____ method writes a line to a file.

7. The _____ method reads a line from a file.

8. The _____ character is a delimiter that marks the end of a line in a file.

9. The _____ control allows you to print data directly to the printer.

10. You write code that handles printing in the _____ event handler.

11. All of the characters printed with a(n) _____ font occupy the same amount of space.

12. The _____ control displays an *Open* dialog box for selecting or entering a filename.

13. The _____ control displays a *Save As* dialog box for selecting or entering a file.

14. The _____ control displays a *Color* dialog box for selecting a color.

15. The _____ control displays a *Font* dialog box for selecting a font.

16. A(n) _____ is a data type that you create, containing one or more variables, which are known as fields.

Multiple Choice

1. Which `Imports` statement is useful when you use the StreamWriter class?
   a. `Imports System.Input`
   b. `Imports VisualBasic.IO`
   c. `Imports System.IO`
   d. `Imports System.Files`

2. You use this type of object to write data to a file.
   a. `FileWriter`
   b. `OuputFile`
   c. `File`
   d. `StreamWriter`

3. You use this type of object to read data from a file.
   a. `FileReader`
   b. `StreamReader`
   c. `File`
   d. `Inputfile`

4. This method creates a file if it does not exist, and erases the contents of the file if it already exists.
   a. `File.OpenText`
   b. `File.AppendText`
   c. `File.CreateText`
   d. `File.OpenNew`

5. This method creates a file if it does not exist. If it already exists, data written to it will be added to the end of its existing contents.
   a. `File.OpenText`
   b. `File.AppendText`
   c. `File.CreateText`
   d. `File.OpenNew`

6. This statement writes a line of data to a file, terminating it with a newline character.
   a. `WriteLine`
   b. `SaveLine`
   c. `StoreLine`
   d. `Write`

7. This statement writes an item of data to a file, and does not terminate it with a new-line character.

   a. `WriteItem`
   b. `SaveItem`
   c. `StoreItem`
   d. `Write`

8. This statement reads a line from a file.

   a. `Read`
   b. `ReadLine`
   c. `GetLine`
   d. `Input`

9. You use this property to detect when the end of a file has been reached.

   a. `EndOfFile`
   b. `EndOfStream`
   c. `Eof`
   d. `FileEnd`

10. You use this method to determine if a file exists.

    a. `System.File.Exists`
    b. `IO.Exists`
    c. `File.Exists`
    d. `Exists.File`

11. Assuming that `ofdOpen` is an OpenFileDialog control, the following statement displays the dialog box.

    a. `ofdOpen.Display()`
    b. `Show(ofdOpen)`
    c. `ofdOpen.OpenDialog()`
    d. `ofdOpen.ShowDialog()`

12. This property determines the types of files displayed in an *Open* or a *Save As* dialog box.

    a. FileTypes
    b. Filter
    c. Types
    d. FileDisplay

13. This property determines the directory or folder first displayed in an *Open* or *Save As* dialog box.

    a. InitialDirectory
    b. InitialFolder
    c. Location
    d. Path

14. When the user selects a file with an *Open* or *Save As* dialog box, the file's path and name are stored in this property.

    a. Filename
    b. PathName
    c. File
    d. Item

15. When a PrintDocument control's `Print` method executes, it triggers this event.

    a. `StartPrint`
    b. `PrintPage`
    c. `PagePrint`
    d. `SendPage`

16. Inside the appropriate PrintDocument event handler you use this method to actually send output to the printer.

    a. `e.Graphics.DrawString`
    b. `e.PrintText`
    c. `e.Graphics.SendOutput`
    d. `Print`

17. You can use this method to align data into columns.

    a. `Align`
    b. `Format.Align`
    c. `Format.Column`
    d. `String.Format`

18. This statement allows you to create a data type that contains one or more variables, known as fields.

    a. `UserDefined`
    b. `DataType`
    c. `Structure`
    d. `Fields`

True or False

Indicate whether the following statements are true or false.

1. T F: A file must be opened before it can be used.

2. T F: An input file is a file that a program can write data to.

3. T F: To read a record stored in the middle or at the end of a sequential-access file, an application must read all records in the file before it.

4. T F: The `File.CreateText` method creates a `StreamReader` object and returns a reference to the object.

5. T F: If you specify only a filename when opening a file, Visual Basic will assume the file's location to be the folder containing the application's executable file (the file having an .exe extension).

6. T F: In addition to separating the contents of a file into lines, the newline character also serves as a delimiter.

7. T F: If you call the `WriteLine` method with no argument, it writes a blank line to the file.

8. T F: A file's read position is set to the end of the file when a file is first opened.

9. T F: The `ReadNext` method causes the read position to advance by one character.

10. T F: The Title property holds the name of the file the user selected with an *Open* or *Save As* dialog box.

11. T F: You can specify the font to use when sending output to the printer.

12. T F: You must use a proportionally spaced font when aligning data in columns.

13. T F: A structure may hold variables of different data types.

14. T F: `Structure` statements can appear inside a procedure or function.

15. T F: Structures may not contain arrays.

16. T F: You may declare an array of structure variables.

Short Answer

1. What are the three steps that must be taken when a file is used by an application?

2. What happens when you close a file with the `Close` method?

3. Where is the read position located when a file is first opened for reading?

4. What is the difference between the `StreamWriter` class's `WriteLine` method and the `StreamWriter` class's `Write` method?

5. What happens when you use the `File.OpenText` method to open a file that does not exist?

6. What has happened when a `StreamReader` object's `EndOfStream` property equals *True*?

7. What does the `StreamReader` class's `ReadLine` method return when it reads a blank line?

8. What does the `StreamReader` class's `Read` method return?

9. When working with a PrintDocument control, what is the difference between the `Print` method and the `PagePrint` event handler?

10. Within a class, where must `Structure` statements appear?

What Do You Think?

1. How do you think a file buffer increases system performance?

2. Why should you check the value of a `StreamReader` object's `EndOfStream` property before calling the `ReadLine` method?

3. You are using a `StreamReader` object's `ReadLine` method to read data from a file. After each line is read, it is added to a list box. What error can potentially occur, and how do you prevent it?

4. Suppose an application has forms named `MainForm` and `GetDataForm`, and a module named `MainModule`. Also, suppose you want a structure to be available only to procedures in the `MainModule` module. Where do you place the `Structure` statement, and which access specifier do you use: `Public` or `Private`?

5. Suppose an application properly aligns the contents of a report into columns using the `String.Format` method. But when the same report is printed on paper, the columns do not align as they should. What is the most likely cause of the problem?

Find the Error

Identify the errors in the following code snippets.

1.
```
Dim myFile As System.IO.StreamReader
myFile = File.CreateText("names.txt")
```

2.
```
If Not System.Exists(strFilename) Then
    MessageBox.Show(strFilename & " does not exist.")
End If
```

3. ```
   Do Until EndOfStream(myFile) = True
      strInput = myFile.ReadLine()
      lstResults.Items.Add(strInput)
   Loop
   ```

4. (Assume that ofdOpen is an OpenFileDialog control.)
   ```
   ofdOpen.Filter = "Text files (*.txt)&*.txt"
   ```

5. (Assume that pdPrint is a PrintDocument control.)
   ```
   Private Sub pdPrint_PrintPage(...) Handles pdPrint.PrintPage
      pdPrint.Print("Hello World!", New Font("Times New Roman",
         12, FontStyle.Regular), Brushes.Black, 10, 10)
   End Sub
   ```

6. The following Structure statement appears in a form:
   ```
   Structure PersonInfo
      Dim strName As String
      Dim intAge As Integer
      Dim strPhone As String
   End Structure
   ```

7. The following statement appears in the same form:
   ```
   PersonInfo.strName = "Jill Smith"
   ```

Algorithm Workbench

1. Suppose a file named *DiskInfo.txt* already exists, and you wish to add data to the data already in the file. Write the statements necessary to open the file.

2. Suppose you wish to create a new file named *NewFile.txt* and write data to it. Write the statements necessary to open the file.

3. Assuming an application uses a list box named lstInventory, write code that writes the contents of the list box to the file *Inventory.txt*.

4. Assuming an application has an array of integers named intNumbers, write code that writes the contents of the array to the file *numbers.txt*.

5. Write a Structure declaration that creates a structure to hold the following data about a savings account. The structure should be declared in a module and be available to all modules in the project.
   ```
   Account number (String)
   Account balance (Decimal)
   Interest rate (Double)
   Average monthly balance (Decimal)
   ```

6. Assume that CustomerData is a structure. The following statement declares customers as an array of ten CustomerData variables:
   ```
   Dim customers(9) As CustomerData
   ```
   Write a statement that stores "Jones" in the strLastName field of the customers(7).

7. Using the variables: strProductName, intProductNum, and decProductPrice, write a String.Format statement that returns a string with strProductName's value in a column of ten spaces, intProductNum's value in a column of eight spaces, and decProductPrice's value in a column of six spaces.

8. Assume an application uses an OpenFileDialog control named ofdOpen. Write statements that display an *Open* dialog box with the initial directory *C:\Gary\Images* and use the following filters: *JPEG images (*.jpg)* and *GIF images (*.gif)*.
   ```

Programming Challenges

1. **Creating Employee Data**

    Create an application that allows the user to enter the following employee data: First Name, Middle Name, Last Name, Employee Number, Department, Telephone Number, Telephone Extension, and E-mail Address. The valid values for department are Accounting, Administration, Marketing, MIS, and Sales. Once the data is entered, the user should be able to save it to a file. Figure 9-30 shows an example of the application's form. The form shown in Figure 9-30 has a combo box for selecting the department; a *Save Record* button, which writes the record to a file; a *Clear* button, which clears the text boxes; and an *Exit* button. Write code in the Form_ Load event handler that allows the user to enter the name of the file. If the file does not exist, a new one will be created. If the file already exists, the input data will be appended to the file.

Figure 9-30 *Employee Data* form for saving employee records

2. **Reading Employee Data**

    Create an application that reads the records stored in the file created by Programming Challenge 1.

    Write code in the form's Load event handler that allows the user to enter the name of the file, and opens the file. The form shown in Figure 9-31 has a *Next Record* button, which reads a record from the file and displays its fields; a *Clear* button,

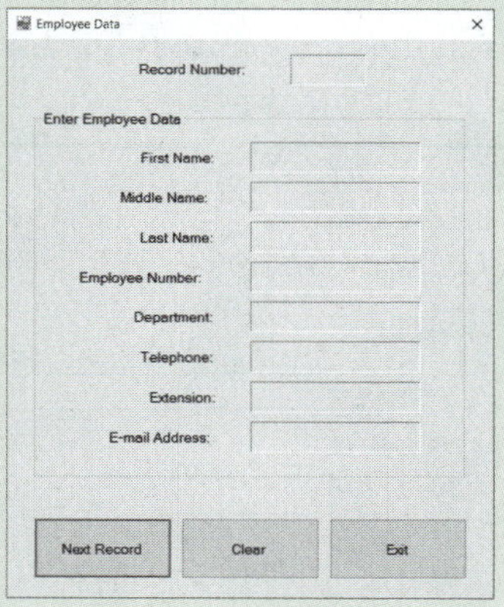

Figure 9-31 *Employee Data* form for reading employee records

which clears the labels; and an *Exit* button. When the user clicks the *Next Record* button, the application should read the next record from the file and display it. When the end of the file is encountered, a message should be displayed.

3. **Student Test Scores**

A teacher has six students and wants you to create an application that stores their grade data in a file and prints a grade report. The application should have a structure that stores the following student data: Name (a string), Test Scores (an array of five Doubles), and Average (a Double). Because the teacher has six students, the application should use an array of six structure variables.

The application should allow the user to enter data for each student, and calculate the average test score.

Figure 9-32 shows the application at runtime, containing sample values and calculated results.

Figure 9-32 *Student Test Scores* form

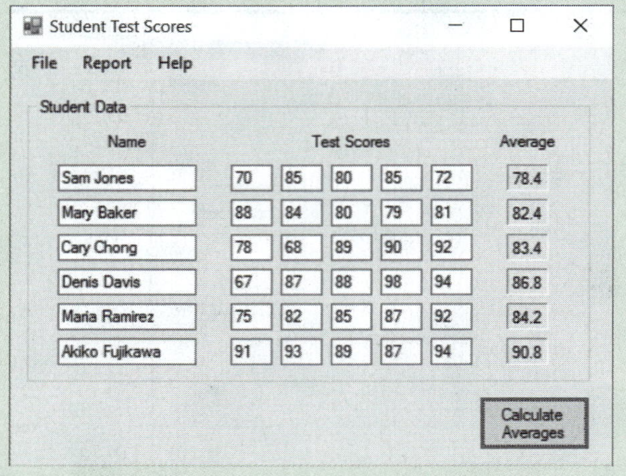

The user should be able to save the data to a file, read the data from the file, and print a report showing each student's test scores and average score. The form shown in Figure 9-32 uses a menu system. You may use buttons instead if you prefer.

Input validation: Do not accept test scores less than zero or greater than 100.

4. **Movie Collection**

Create an application that stores data about your movie collection in a file. The application should have a structure to hold the following fields: Movie Name, Year Produced, Running Time, and Rating. The application should allow the user to save the data to a file, search the file for a movie by name, and print a report listing all the movies records in the file. Figure 9-33 shows an example form.

Figure 9-33 *Movie Collection* form

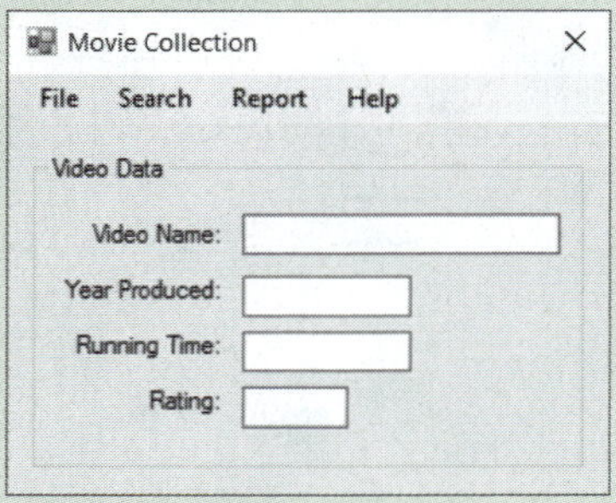

5. **TG Automotive**

Programming Challenge 6 in Chapter 7 asked you to create an application that calculates the cost of automobile servicing. In the current version of the program, you are asked to use the ColorDialog control to allow the user to customize the application's user interface. Figure 9-34 shows a sample of the *Customize Colors* dialog window.

Figure 9-34 Customizing the colors for the TG Automotive application

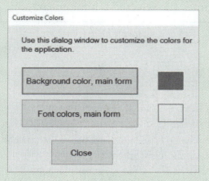

Design Your Own Forms

6. **Font and Color Tester**

Create an application that tests the way different fonts and color combinations appear. The application should display some text in a label, and have a menu with the items *Select Font* and *Select Color*.

The *Select Font* menu item should display a *Font* dialog box with a *Color* drop-down list. The application should change the text displayed in the label to the font and color selected in the dialog box.

The *Select Color* menu item should display a *Color* dialog box. The application should change the background color of the label to the color selected in the dialog box.

7. **Simple Text Editor Modification**

Modify the *Simple Text Editor* application that you created in this chapter by adding a *View* menu to the menu system. The *View* menu should have two items: *Font* and *Color*.

The *Font* menu item should display a *Font* dialog box with a *Color* drop-down list. The application should change the text displayed in the text box to the font and color selected in the dialog box.

The *Color* menu item should display a *Color* dialog box. The application should change the background color of the text box to the color selected in the dialog box.

8. **World Series Champions**

In the *Chap9* folder of the student sample programs, you will find the following files:

- Teams.txt—This file contains a list of several Major League baseball teams in alphabetical order. Each team listed in the file has won the World Series at least once.
- WorldSeriesWinners.txt—This file contains a chronological list of the World Series' winning teams from 1903 through 2012. (The first line in the file is the name of the team that won in 1903, and the last line is the name of the team that won in 2012. Note that the World Series was not played in 1904 or 1994.)

Create an application that displays the contents of the Teams.txt file in a ListBox control. When the user selects a team in the ListBox, the application should display the number of times that team has won the World Series in the time period from 1903 through 2012.

 TIP: Read the contents of the WorldSeriesWinners.txt file into a List or an array. When the user selects a team, an algorithm should step through the list or array counting the number of times the selected team appears.

9. **Name Search**

In the *Chap9* folder of the student sample programs, you will find the following files:

- GirlNames.txt—This file contains a list of the 200 most popular names given to girls born in the United States from 2000 through 2012.
- BoyNames.txt—This file contains a list of the 200 most popular names given to boys born in the United States from 2000 through 2012.

Create an application that reads the contents of the two files into two separate arrays or Lists. The user should be able to enter a boy's name, a girl's name, or both, and the application should display messages indicating whether the names were among the most popular.

10. **Population Data**

In the *Chap9* folder of the student sample programs, you will find a file named USPopulation.txt. The file contains the midyear population of the United States, in thousands, during the years 1950 through 1990. The first line in the file contains the population for 1950, the second line contains the population for 1951, and so forth. Create an application that reads the file's contents into an array or a List. The application should display the following data:

- The average annual change in population during the time period
- The year with the greatest increase in population during the time period
- The year with the least increase in population during the time period

11. **Image Viewer**

You can load an image into a PictureBox control at runtime by calling the `Image.FromFile` method. For example, assume that `picImage` is a PictureBox control and `filename` is a variable containing the name of a graphic file. The following statement loads the graphic file into the PictureBox control:

```
picImage.Image = Image.FromFile(filename)
```

Create an application that has a PictureBox control on a form. The PictureBox control should be configured so it fills the entire area of the form and resizes when the user resizes the form.

The application should have a *File* menu with an *Open* command. The *Open* command should display an *Open* dialog box, displaying files of the following graphic types:

- Bitmaps (*.bmp)
- JPEG images (*.jpg)
- GIF images (*.gif)

When the user selects a file with the *Open* dialog box, the application should display the image in the PictureBox control.

12. **Employee Data, Enhanced**

    Create an application that performs the following operations with the employee file created by the application in Programming Challenge 1:

    - Uses an *Open* dialog box to allow the user to select the file
    - Allows the user to enter a new employee record and then saves the record to the file
    - Allows the user to enter an employee number and searches for a record containing that employee number. If the record is found, the record is displayed.
    - Displays all records, one after the other
    - Prints an employee record

    Equip your application with either a menu system or a set of buttons to perform these operations.

13. **Hotel Occupancy Report**

    Programming Challenge 5 in Chapter 8 asked you to create a Hotel Occupancy application. For this assignment, you are asked to use the PrintDocument control to print a report with the title "Floor Occupancy Report" in 14-point bold type (any font). Then in non-bold 12-point type, print the contents of the ListBox control, each entry printed on a separate line. (To build a string containing lines of text, append the vbCrlf constant to each line.) Finally, at the bottom of the report, print two totals lines, one containing "Total rooms occupied: *nn*", and the other containing "Overall occupancy rate: *nn*%". (Substitute actual values for *nn*.)

14. **Adding Students to Clubs**

    Programming Challenge 6 in Chapter 8 asked you to create an application that lets users add students to clubs. For this assignment, when the main form closes, your program should automatically save the two-dimensional array of club membership lists into a data file. (Use the FormClosing event handler.) When the program starts, use the form's Load event handler to read the club names into the list box, and read the existing club membership data into the array variable.

    Here is a recommended format for the file, with sample data. The first line contains an integer *C* giving the number of clubs. The next *C* lines contain the names of the clubs. The next line contains an integer *n* giving the number of members in the first club. The next *n* lines contain the names of the members of this club. (In our sample below, the first club has three members.) The next line contains a new value for *n*, showing the number of members in the second club, and so on, until the end of the file. In our sample data, the second club contains two members:

```
3
Honors
Golden Arrow
Computer
3
Adams, Ben
Baker, Sally
Canseco, Juan
2
Koenig, Johann
Johnson, Eric
3
Matsunaga, Akiko
Nakamura, Ken
Ramirez, Maria
```

15. **Conference Registration System**

    Programming Challenge 1 in Chapter 7 asked you to create a conference registration application. In the current version of the application, write a registration record to a text file just as the main form is closing. The following sample shows the suggested format for your data:

    ```
    Conference Registration----------------------
    Name: John Smith
    Phone: 305-111-1111
    Company: ABC Consolidated
    Email: jsmith@cons.com
    Address: 2014 North Way, FL 33176
    Attending keynote address
    Workshop: The Future of the Web $295
    Total fees: $1,220.00
    ```

    Notice that the Workshop entry includes the workshop price because it was copied directly from the ListBox on the options form. Optionally, you can remove the price using methods from the String class.

16. **Solar Panel Installation**

    Programming Challenge 4 in Chapter 7 asked you to create an application that calculates the cost of installing solar panels. In that version, there was a base charge of $2,000 that pays for two panels, plus a $300 charge per panel for any panels after that. In the current version of the program, however, the panel prices vary depending on the geographical region in which the customer lives. Create a file containing region names and prices. Here is a suggested format for the file, which should contain at least five regions:

    > number of regions
    > name of region 1
    > base charge for region 1
    > charge per addition panel for region 1
    > express installation percentage for region 1
    > minimum deposit percentage for region 1
    > name of region 2
    > base charge for region 2
    > charge per addition panel for region 2
    > express installation percentage for region 2
    > minimum deposit percentage for region 2
    > *(and so on, for the other regions).*

    For region names in the United States, good choices might be Northeast, Southeast, Northwest, Southwest, and Midwest. We suggest you create a structure to hold the information for one region, and create an array of these structure objects. At runtime, fill a ComboBox control with the names of the regions. Use error checking to ensure that the user selects the region name before finishing the Customer Information step. If the customer's region is changed after prices have been calculated, close the Installation Options and Charges panels, so the user will have to validate the Installation Options values again.

10 Working with Databases

CHAPTER

TOPICS

10.1 Database Management Systems

10.2 Database Concepts

10.3 DataGridView Control

10.4 Data-Bound Controls

10.5 Structured Query Language (SQL)

10.6 Focus on Problem Solving: *Karate School Management* Application

10.7 Introduction to LINQ

10.8 Creating Your Own Database

Video Tutorial: Adding a Database to the *Kayak Rental* Application

Most businesses store their company data in databases. In this chapter you will learn basic database concepts and how to write Visual Basic applications that interact with databases. You will learn how to use a DataGridView control to display the data in a database. You will also learn how to sort and update database data. We will finish with an application that displays database data in list boxes, text boxes, labels, and combo boxes.

10.1 Database Management Systems

CONCEPT: Visual Basic applications use database management systems to make large amounts of data available to programs.

In Chapter 9 you learned how to perform input and output operations using simple text files. If an application needs to store only a small amount of data, those types of files work well. When a large amount of data must be stored and manipulated, however, they are not practical. Many businesses keep hundreds of thousands, or even millions of data items in files. When a text file contains this much data, simple operations such as searching, inserting, and deleting become slow, inefficient, and cumbersome.

When developing applications that work with a large amount of data, most developers prefer to use a database management system. A **database management system (DBMS)** is software that is specifically designed to store, retrieve, and manipulate large amounts of data in an organized and efficient manner. Once the data is stored using the database management system, applications may be written in Visual Basic or other languages to communicate with the DBMS. Rather than retrieving or manipulating the data directly, a Visual Basic application can send instructions to the DBMS. The DBMS carries out those instructions and sends the results back to the Visual Basic application. Figure 10-1 illustrates this.

Figure 10-1 A Visual Basic application interacts with a DBMS, which manipulates data

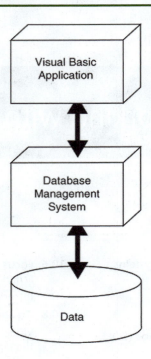

Although Figure 10-1 is greatly simplified, it illustrates the layered nature of an application that works with a database management system. The topmost layer of software, which in this case is written in Visual Basic, interacts with the user. It also sends instructions to the next layer of software, the DBMS. The DBMS works directly with the data and sends the results of operations back to the application.

For example, suppose a company keeps all of its product records in a database. The company has a Visual Basic application that allows the user to search for information on any product by entering its product ID number. The Visual Basic application instructs the DBMS to retrieve the record for the product with the specified product ID number. The DBMS retrieves the product record and sends the data back to the Visual Basic application. The Visual Basic application displays the data to the user.

The advantage of this layered approach to software development is that the Visual Basic programmer does not need know about the physical structure of the data. He or she only needs to know how to interact with the DBMS. The DBMS handles the actual reading, writing, and searching of data.

Visual Basic is capable of interacting with many DBMSs. Some of the more popular DBMSs are Microsoft SQL Server, Oracle, DB2, and MySQL. In this chapter we will use Microsoft SQL Server Express, which is installed with Visual Studio.

10.2 Database Concepts

CONCEPT: A database is a collection of one or more tables, each containing data related to a particular topic.

A **database** is a collection of one or more tables, each containing data related to a particular topic. A **table** is a logical grouping of related information. A database might, for example, have a table containing information about employees. Another table might list information about weekly sales. Another table might contain a list of the items in a store's inventory. Let's look at a database table named *Departments*, shown in Table 10-1, which contains information about departments within a company. Each row of the table corresponds to a single department. The sample table contains the ID number, name, and number of employees in each department.

Table 10-1 *Departments* table

Dept_Id	Dept_Name	Num_Employees
1	Human Resources	10
2	Accounting	5
3	Computer Support	30
4	Research & Development	15

Each database record appears as a row in the table. In the *Departments* table, shown in Table 10-1, the first row contains 1, Human Resources, 10. When discussing a table, we refer to the columns by name. The columns in Table 10-1 are named Dept_Id, Dept_Name, and Num_Employees. Table columns are also called **fields**. Each table has a **design**, which specifies each column's name, data type, and field size and/or range of valid values. Table 10-2 contains the design of our sample *Departments* table.

Table 10-2 *Departments* table design

Field	Type	Range/Size
Dept_Id	Integer	−32,768 to +32,767
Dept_Name	String	30 characters
Num_Employees	Integer	−32,768 to +32,767

The *Dept_Id* column is called a **primary key** because it uniquely identifies each department. No two departments can ever have the same department ID. Primary keys can be either numbers or strings, but numeric values are processed by the database software more efficiently. In this table, the primary key is one column. Sometimes a primary key will consist of two or more combined columns, creating what is called a **composite key**.

SQL Server Column Types

When you use Visual Basic to read a database, your program copies values from a database table into program variables. Therefore, it is important to select variable types that match the type of data in the table. Table 10-3 compares SQL Server column types to Visual Basic data types. The varchar and nvarchar types permit variable-length strings. Their *n* parameter specifies the longest string that can be stored in the column.

Table 10-3 Comparing SQL Server column types to Visual Basic types

SQL type(s)	Usage	Visual Basic Type
bit	True/false values	Boolean
datetime, smalldatetime	Dates and times	Date, DateTime
decimal, money	Financial values in which precision is important	Decimal
float	Real-number values	Double
image	Pictures, Word documents, Excel files, PDF files	Array of Byte
int	Integer values	Integer
nvarchar(n)	Variable-length strings containing 16-bit Unicode characters	String
smallint	Integers between −32,768 and +32,767	Short
text	Strings longer than 8,000 characters	String
varchar(n)	Variable-length strings containing ANSI (8-bit) characters	String

Choosing Column Names

A **database schema** is the design of tables, columns, and relationships between tables in a database. Let's look at some of the elements that belong to a schema, beginning with tables. Suppose you want to create a database to keep track of club members. First, you should choose meaningful names for each column.

Let's assume you want to store each member's first and last names, phone number, E-mail address, date joined, number of meetings attended, and a column indicating whether the person is an officer. Table 10-4 contains a possible design. Choosing the lengths of varchar columns involves some guesswork because you don't want to cut off any of the values stored in these columns. Disk space is relatively inexpensive, so it's usually better to make the columns a little larger than they need to be.

In most cases, you should never embed spaces in column names. If you do that, all references to the column name in database queries must be surrounded by brackets, as in [Last Name]. As an alternative use an underscore character between words, as in Last_Name.

Table 10-4 *Members* table sample design

Column Name	Type	Remarks
Member_ID	int	Primary key
First_Name	varchar(40)	
Last_Name	varchar(40)	
Phone	varchar(30)	
Email	varchar(50)	
Date_Joined	smalldatetime	Date only, no time values
Meetings_Attended	smallint	
Officer	bit	True/False values

Table 10-5 *Employees* table with department names

Emp_Id	First_Name	Last_Name	Department
001234	Ignacio	Fleta	Accounting
002000	Christian	Martin	Computer Support
002122	Orville	Gibson	Human Resources
003000	Jose	Ramirez	Research & Development
003400	Ben	Smith	Accounting
003780	Allison	Chong	Computer Support

Avoiding Redundancy by Using Linked Tables

Most well-designed databases keep redundant data to a minimum. It might be tempting when designing a table of employees, for example, to include the complete name of the department in which an employee works. A few sample rows are shown in Table 10-5. There are problems with this approach. We can imagine that the same department name appears many times within the *Employees* table, leading to wasted storage space. Also, someone typing in employee data might easily misspell a department name. Finally, if the company decides to rename a department, it would be necessary to find and correct every occurrence of the department name in the *Employees* table (and possibly other tables).

Rather than inserting a department name in each employee record, a good designer would store a department ID number in each row of the *Employees* table, as shown in Table 10-6. A data entry clerk would require less time to input a numeric department ID, and there would be less chance of a typing error. One would then create a separate table named *Departments*, containing all department names and IDs, as shown in Table 10-7. When looking up the name of an employee's department, we can use the department ID in the *Employees* table to find the same ID in the *Departments* table. The department name will be in the same table row. Relational databases make it easy to create links (called relationships) between tables such as *Employees* and *Departments*.

Table 10-6 *Employees* table with department ID numbers

Emp_Id	First_Name	Last_Name	Dept_Id
001234	Ignacio	Fleta	2
002000	Christian	Martin	3
002122	Orville	Gibson	1
003000	Jose	Ramirez	4
003400	Ben	Smith	2
003780	Allison	Chong	3

Table 10-7 *Departments* table

Dept_Id	Dept_Name	Dept_Size
1	Human Resources	10
2	Accounting	5
3	Computer Support	30
4	Research & Development	15

One-to-Many Relationship

Databases are usually designed around a **relational model,** meaning that relations exist between tables. A **relation** is a link or relationship that relies on a common field value to join rows from two different tables. In the relationship diagram shown in Figure 10-2, *Dept_Id* is the common field that links the *Departments* and *Employees* tables. The primary key field is always shown in bold.

In the *Departments* table, *Dept_Id* is the primary key. In the *Employees* table, *Dept_Id* is called a **foreign key.** A foreign key is a column in one table that references a primary key in another table. There can be multiple occurrences of a foreign key in a table. Along the line connecting the two tables, the ⚷ and ∞ symbols indicate a **one-to-many relationship.** A particular *Dept_Id* (such as 4) occurs only once in the *Departments* table, but it can appear many times (or not at all) in the *Employees* table. At first, we will work with only one table at a time. Later, we will show how to pull information from two related tables.

Figure 10-2 One-to-many relationship between *Departments* and *Employees*

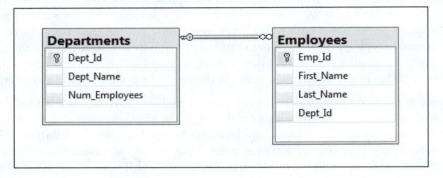

 **Checkpoint**

10.1   How is a table different from a database?

10.2   In a table of employees, what column would make a good primary key?

10.3   Which Visual Basic data type is equivalent to the *bit* column type in Microsoft SQL Server?

10.4   Why would we not want to spell out the name of each person's department in a table of employees?

10.5   How is a foreign key different from a primary key?

10.3 DataGridView Control

CONCEPT: The DataGridView control allows you to display a database table in a grid. The grid can be used at runtime to sort and edit the contents of a table.

VideoNote

The DataGridView Control

Visual Basic provides easy-to-use tools for displaying database tables in Windows forms and Web forms. In this chapter, we will show how to display data on a Windows form, and in Chapter 11, we will demonstrate Web forms.

Visual Basic uses a technique called **data binding** to link database tables to controls on a program's forms. Special controls, called **components,** provide the linking mechanism.

When you decide to bind a control to a database, a software tool named a **wizard** guides you through the process. Wizards are quite common in Microsoft Windows and many other applications such as Microsoft Word, so you have probably used one before.

We will use the following data-related components:

- **Data source.** A **data source** is usually a database, but can include text files, Excel spreadsheets, XML data, or Web services. Our data sources will be Microsoft SQL Server database files.
- **Binding source.** A **binding source** connects data bound controls to a dataset.
- **Table adapter.** A **table adapter** pulls data from one or more database tables and passes it to your program. It can select some or all table rows, add new rows, delete rows, and modify existing rows. It uses an industry standard language named **Structured Query Language (SQL)**, which is recognized by nearly all databases.
- **Dataset.** A **dataset** is an in-memory copy of the data pulled from database tables. The table adapter does the pulling, and it copies the data to the dataset. Your program can modify rows in the dataset, add new rows, and delete rows. None of your changes are permanent, unless you tell the table adapter to write the changes back to the database. Datasets can get data from more than one data source and from more than one table adapter.

Figure 10-3 shows the relationship between the data source, binding source, table adapter, dataset, and application. Data from a data source travels all the way to the dataset and application. The dataset's contents can be modified and viewed by the application. Updates to the dataset can be written back to the data source. In Tutorial 10-1, you show a database table in a **DataGridView control**.

Figure 10-3 Data flow from the data source to an application

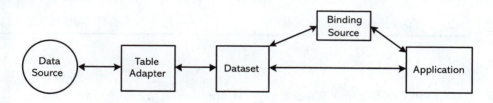

Tutorial 10-1:
Showing a database table in a DataGridView control

This tutorial leads you through the steps to display the contents of a database table in a DataGridView control. You will see all rows and columns of the data. You will see how easy it is for users of your program to sort on any column, delete rows, and insert new rows.

The *SalesStaff* table, located in the SQL Server database named *Company*, represents information collected about sales employees. Its design is shown in Table 10-8, and some sample rows are shown in Table 10-9.

Preparation Step: Make sure the database file named *Company.mdf* is located in the student sample programs folder named *Chap10*. This file must be located on your computer's hard drive, and not on a network drive. Visual Studio considers a network drive to be an unsafe location and will display a warning message if you connect to a database on a network.

Table 10-8 *SalesStaff* table design

Column Name	Type
ID	int(primary key)
Last_Name	varchar(40)
First_Name	varchar(40)
Full_Time	bit
Hire_Date	smalldatetime
Salary	decimal

Table 10-9 Sample rows in the *SalesStaff* table

ID	Last_Name	First_Name	Full_Time	Hire_Date	Salary
104	Adams	Adrian	True	01/01/2010	$35,007.00
114	Franklin	Fay	True	08/22/2005	$56,001.00
115	Franklin	Adiel	False	03/20/2010	$41,000.00
120	Baker	Barbara	True	04/22/2003	$32,000.00
135	Ferriere	Henri	True	01/01/2010	$57,000.00
292	Hasegawa	Danny	False	05/20/2007	$45,000.00
302	Easterbrook	Erin	False	07/09/2004	$22,000.00
305	Kawananakoa	Sam	True	10/20/2009	$42,000.00
396	Zabaleta	Maria	True	11/01/2009	$29,000.00
404	Del Terzo	Daniel	True	07/09/2007	$37,500.00
407	Greenwood	Charles	False	04/20/2008	$23,432.00

Step 1: Create a new Windows Forms Application project named *SalesStaff 1*.

Step 2: Set the Text property of Form1 to *Company Sales Staff Table*. Set the form's *Font.Size* property to 10 or 11.

Step 3: Save your project by selecting *Save All* from the File menu.

Step 4: Drag a DataGridView control from the *Data* section of the *Toolbox* window onto the form. In the *Properties* window, set the DataGridView control's Dock property to *Fill*.

TIP: If you select the DataGridView control and click on the Dock property in the *Properties* window, a small dialog window appears. Click on the center button, which causes the grid to fill the entire form.

Step 5: In the DataGridView control, click the small arrow pointing to the right in the upper right corner of the DataGridView. You should see a small pop-up window named *DataGridView Tasks*, as shown in Figure 10-4.

Step 6: Click the drop-down arrow next to *Choose Data Source*. In the dialog box that appears (see Figure 10-5), click *Add Project Data Source*.

Figure 10-4 *DataGridView Tasks window*

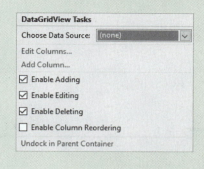

Figure 10-5 Choosing a data source, Step 1

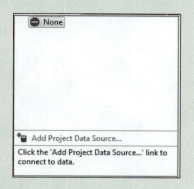

Step 7: When the *Data Source Configuration Wizard* displays, as shown in Figure 10-6, select the *Database* icon and click the *Next* button.

Figure 10-6 *Data Source Configuration Wizard*

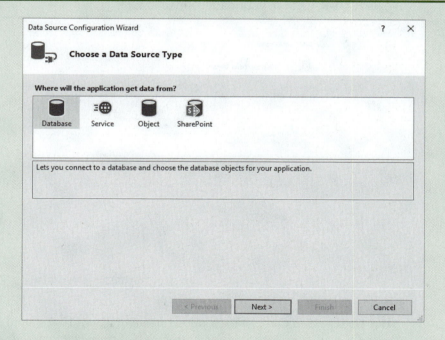

Step 8: Next, the wizard asks you to choose a database model, shown in Figure 10-7. Make sure the *Dataset* model is selected. Click the *Next* button to continue.

Step 9: Next, the wizard asks you to choose your data connection, as shown in Figure 10-8. If you had created data connections before, you could select one from the drop-down list. Because this is your first data connection, click the *New Connection* button.

Figure 10-7 Choose a database model

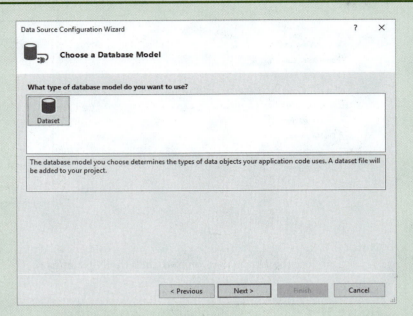

Figure 10-8 Choose your data connection

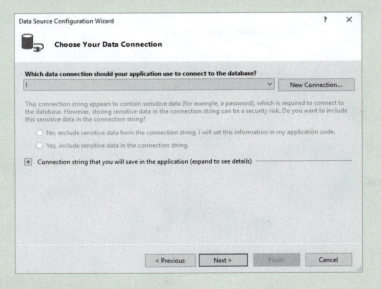

Step 10: The *Add Connection* window shown in Figure 10-9 should appear. As shown in the figure, make sure *Microsoft SQL Server Database File (SqlClient)* is shown as the *Data source*. (If it is not, click the *Change . . .* button. In the window that appears next, select *Microsoft SQL Server Database File* and click *OK*.)

TIP: When you create a connection for the first time, Visual Studio may display a popup window named *Choose Data Source*. In subsequent sessions, the same popup window will be entitled *Change Data Source*, as shown in Figure 10-10. Always select *Microsoft SQL Server Database File* from the list box, check the box next to *Always use this selection*, and click the *Continue* button to close the window.

Next, click the *Browse . . .* button, as indicated in Figure 10-9. Navigate to the student sample programs folder named *Chap10*, and select the *Company.mdf* database file. Figure 10-11 shows an example of the *Add Connection* window with the database file selected. (The path of the file shown on your system might look different.)

Figure 10-9 The Visual Studio *Add Connection* window

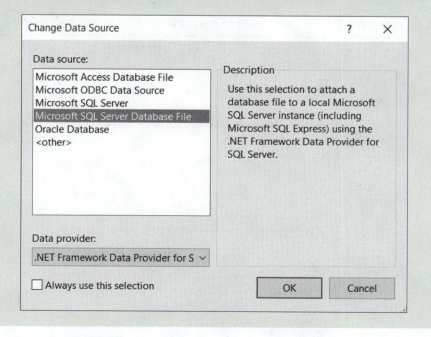

① Make sure this data source is selected. If it is not, click the *Change...* button and select *Microsoft SQL Server Database File (SqlClient)*.

② Click here to browse for the *Company.mdf* database file.

Figure 10-10 The *Change Data Source* window.

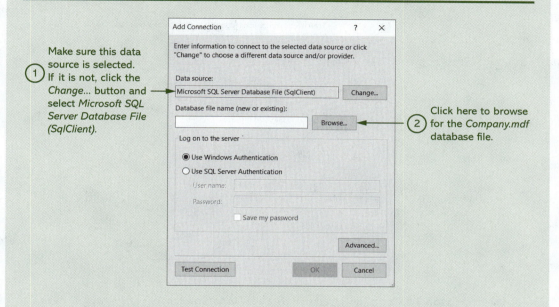

At this point you can optionally click the *Test Connection* button and wait for the message box that says *Test connection succeeded*. This message indicates that you successfully connected to the *Company.mdf* database file.

Click the *OK* button to close the *Add Connection* window.

Figure 10-11 The correct data source and database file selected in Visual Studio

Step 11: You will return to the *Data Source Configuration Wizard* window (in Figure 10-12), now showing the name of the connection as *Company.mdf*. Click the *Next* button to continue.

Figure 10-12 *Data Source Configuration Wizard* window with *Company.mdf*

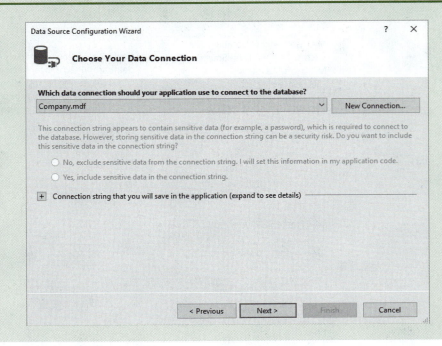

Step 12: Next you will see a dialog box with the following message:

> *The connection you selected uses a local data file that is not in the current project. Would you like to copy the file to your project and modify the connection?*
>
> *If you copy the data file to your project, it will be copied to the project's output directory each time you run the application. Press F1 for information on controlling this behavior.*

This dialog box is asking you if you want to copy the database file to the project directory. If you click *Yes*, you will be more easily able to copy your program and its database to another computer. When you hand in programming assignments, for example, it is a good idea to have the database stored with the project.

Click the *Yes* button to continue. After a moment, you might notice that a database icon with the name *Company.mdf* appears in your project's *Solution Explorer* window. This icon shows that the database file is now contained within your project.

Step 13: Next, the wizard asks if you want to save a named connection string to the application configuration file, as shown in Figure 10-13. This is a good idea because it means that the application will remember the location of the database, and you could use it on other forms later on. You could possibly change the name of the connection string, but let's leave it as is.

Click the *Next* button to continue.

Figure 10-13 Saving the connection string

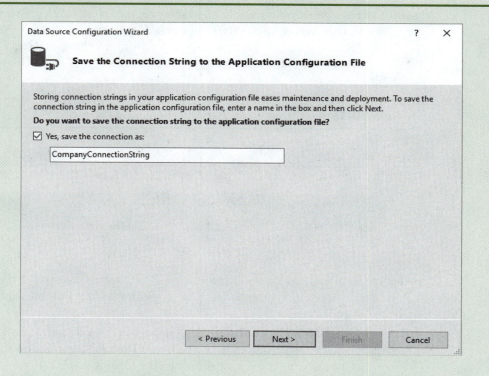

Step 14: Next, you are asked to select which database objects you want to include in your dataset. Expand the entry under *Tables*, and place a check mark next to *SalesStaff*, as shown in Figure 10-14.

Figure 10-14 Choosing the *SalesStaff* table

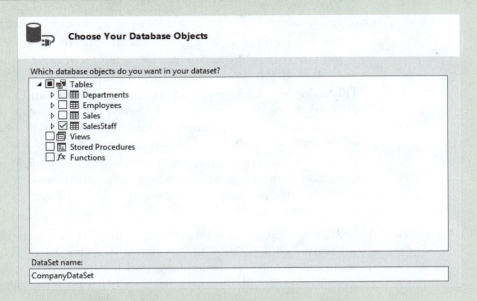

Click the *Finish* button to complete the wizard. If the *DataGridView Tasks* window appears next to the DataGridView, just click the mouse inside the grid to hide the tasks window.

Step 15: Now you should see column headings in the DataGridView control (Figure 10-15) that match the *SalesStaff* columns: *ID*, *Last_Name*, *First_Name*, *Full_Time*, *Hire_Date*, and *Salary*. Widen the form so the DataGridView control can expand, as shown in Figure 10-15.

Figure 10-15 Column headings in the DataGridView control

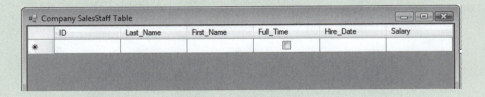

Step 16: Save and run the application. You should see all the rows of the *SalesStaff* table, as shown in Figure 10-16. Now you can experiment a bit while the application is running:

- Resize the form, and notice that the gray background area of the grid expands and contracts along with the form. The grid columns, on the other hand, do not expand automatically when the form is resized. If you want to change a column width while the application is running, hover the mouse over the divider between two column headings, press and hold the mouse button, and drag the mouse sideways. When you release the mouse button, the column will have a new width.

- Select individual rows in the grid by clicking on the buttons along the left side.
- Select multiple rows by holding down the Ctrl key or Shift key while clicking the selection buttons.
- Modify any of the cells by clicking the mouse inside the cell and typing new data.

When you are ready, close the window to exit the program.

Figure 10-16 Running the application, displaying the *SalesStaff* table

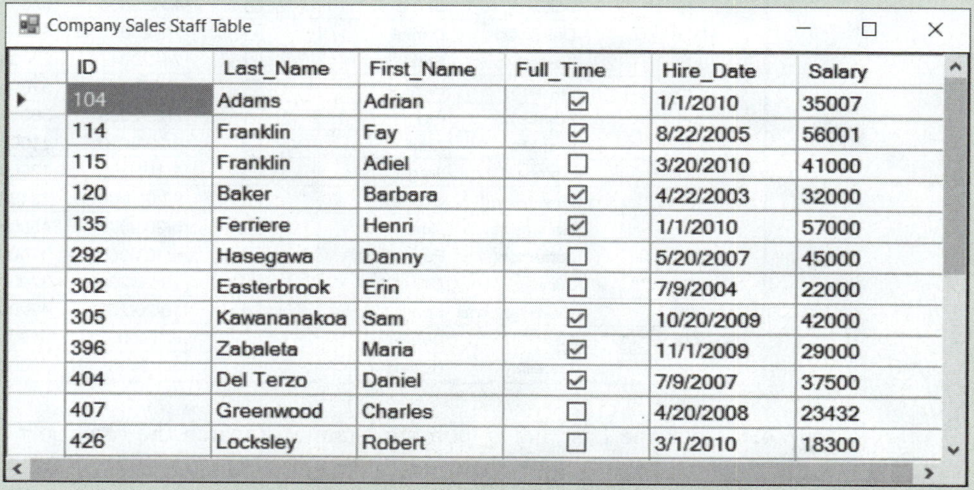

ID	Last_Name	First_Name	Full_Time	Hire_Date	Salary
104	Adams	Adrian	☑	1/1/2010	35007
114	Franklin	Fay	☑	8/22/2005	56001
115	Franklin	Adiel	☐	3/20/2010	41000
120	Baker	Barbara	☑	4/22/2003	32000
135	Ferriere	Henri	☑	1/1/2010	57000
292	Hasegawa	Danny	☐	5/20/2007	45000
302	Easterbrook	Erin	☐	7/9/2004	22000
305	Kawananakoa	Sam	☑	10/20/2009	42000
396	Zabaleta	Maria	☑	11/1/2009	29000
404	Del Terzo	Daniel	☑	7/9/2007	37500
407	Greenwood	Charles	☐	4/20/2008	23432
426	Locksley	Robert	☐	3/1/2010	18300

Window title: Company Sales Staff Table

In this tutorial, you have seen some of the power and convenience of the DataGridView control. This control, in fact, is the result of years of evolution, through the different versions of Visual Basic. At one time, people had to write a great deal of code in order to display data in a grid. But now, it is possible without any coding at all. However, we have only touched the surface of what the DataGridView can do. In Tutorial 10-2, you will use the DataGridView control to sort columns, add rows, and delete rows from the *SalesStaff* table.

Tutorial 10-2:
Sorting and updating the *SalesStaff* table

In this tutorial, you will learn more about the capabilities of the DataGridView control's ability to add, delete, and modify data.

Step 1: Open the *SalesStaff 1* project you created in Tutorial 10-1.

Step 2: Run the application.

The Full_Time column holds *True* and *False* values—such columns are designed as type bit in the SQL Server database. The DataGridView control always displays bit values in a CheckBox control.

Step 3: Currently, the rows are listed in ascending order by ID number. Click the Last_Name column heading and watch the grid sort the rows in ascending order by last name (see Figure 10-17).

Figure 10-17 Sorting on the Last_Name column

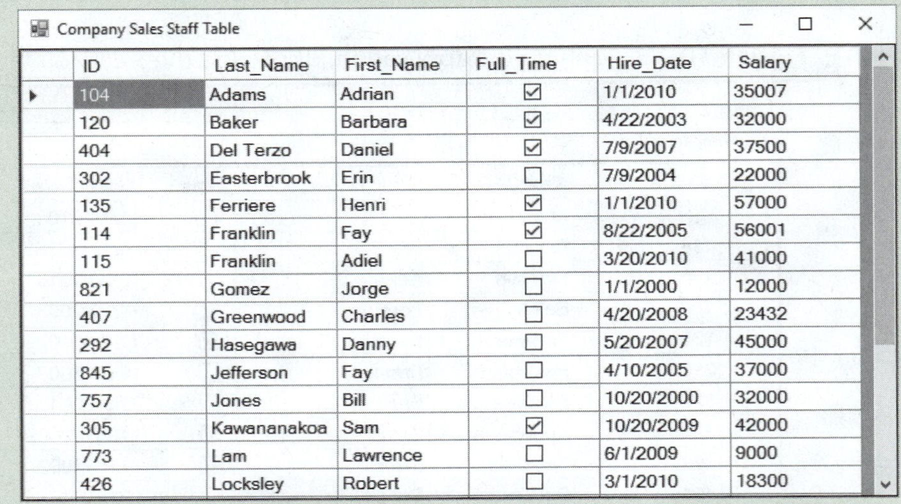

ID	Last_Name	First_Name	Full_Time	Hire_Date	Salary
104	Adams	Adrian	☑	1/1/2010	35007
120	Baker	Barbara	☑	4/22/2003	32000
404	Del Terzo	Daniel	☑	7/9/2007	37500
302	Easterbrook	Erin	☐	7/9/2004	22000
135	Ferriere	Henri	☑	1/1/2010	57000
114	Franklin	Fay	☑	8/22/2005	56001
115	Franklin	Adiel	☐	3/20/2010	41000
821	Gomez	Jorge	☐	1/1/2000	12000
407	Greenwood	Charles	☐	4/20/2008	23432
292	Hasegawa	Danny	☐	5/20/2007	45000
845	Jefferson	Fay	☐	4/10/2005	37000
757	Jones	Bill	☐	10/20/2000	32000
305	Kawananakoa	Sam	☑	10/20/2009	42000
773	Lam	Lawrence	☐	6/1/2009	9000
426	Locksley	Robert	☐	3/1/2010	18300

Step 4: Click the Last_Name column again and watch the rows sort in reverse on the same column.

Step 5: Place the mouse over the border between two column headings. When the mouse cursor changes to a horizontal arrow, press the mouse button and drag the border to the right or left. Doing this gives the user the opportunity to change the width of a column.

Step 6: Next, you will delete a row from the grid. Click the button to the left of one of the grid rows. The entire row will be selected (highlighted), as shown in Figure 10-18. Press Delete and watch the row disappear. The row has been removed from the in-memory dataset, but not the database. Remember which row you deleted, because you will rerun the program soon and verify that the deleted row has been restored.

Figure 10-18 Selecting a DataGridView row

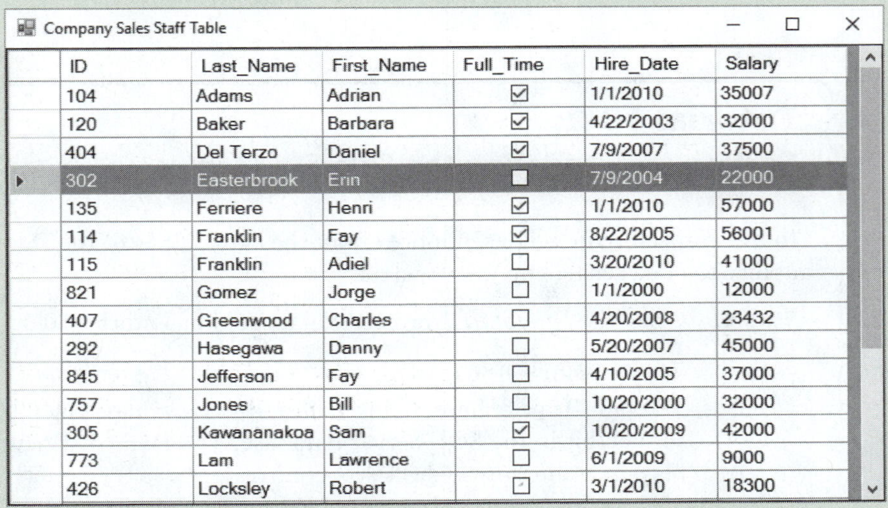

ID	Last_Name	First_Name	Full_Time	Hire_Date	Salary
104	Adams	Adrian	☑	1/1/2010	35007
120	Baker	Barbara	☑	4/22/2003	32000
404	Del Terzo	Daniel	☑	7/9/2007	37500
302	Easterbrook	Erin	☐	7/9/2004	22000
135	Ferriere	Henri	☑	1/1/2010	57000
114	Franklin	Fay	☑	8/22/2005	56001
115	Franklin	Adiel	☐	3/20/2010	41000
821	Gomez	Jorge	☐	1/1/2000	12000
407	Greenwood	Charles	☐	4/20/2008	23432
292	Hasegawa	Danny	☐	5/20/2007	45000
845	Jefferson	Fay	☐	4/10/2005	37000
757	Jones	Bill	☐	10/20/2000	32000
305	Kawananakoa	Sam	☑	10/20/2009	42000
773	Lam	Lawrence	☐	6/1/2009	9000
426	Locksley	Robert	☐	3/1/2010	18300

Step 7: Next, you will insert a row into the grid. First, sort the grid by the ID column. Next, scroll to the bottom row of the grid and enter the following information in the empty cells: 847, Jackson, Adele, (check Full_time), 6/1/2015, 65000. Figure 10-19 shows the new row added to the table. Press ⏎Enter to save your changes. Sort the grid on the Last_Name column and look for the row you inserted.

Figure 10-19 Adding a new row to the grid

ID ▲	Last_Name	First_Name	Full_Time	Hire_Date	Salary
396	Zabaleta	Maria	☑	11/1/2009	29000
404	Del Terzo	Daniel	☑	7/9/2007	37500
407	Greenwood	Charles	☐	4/20/2008	23432
426	Locksley	Robert	☐	3/1/2010	18300
565	Smith	Bill	☑	2/5/2009	50009
694	Rubenstein	Narida	☑	6/1/1999	22000
721	Molina	Marcos	☐	10/20/2008	15000
757	Jones	Bill	☐	10/20/2000	32000
773	Lam	Lawrence	☐	6/1/2009	9000
813	Wang	Li Chuan	☑	3/1/2010	29000
821	Gomez	Jorge	☐	1/1/2000	12000
845	Jefferson	Fay	☐	4/10/2005	37000
846	Zelinski	Danny	☑	5/1/2002	50000
847	Jackson	Adele	☑	6/1/2015	65000
			☐		

Step 8: Stop the program. Rerun the program, and notice that the changes you made to the dataset were not saved in the database. Later in the chapter we will show how to save changes directly into the database. The grid rows look exactly as they did when you first displayed the dataset.

Stop the program.

Step 9: In the *Designer* window, look at the three components placed in the form's component tray by Visual Studio when you added the connection to the *SalesStaff* table:

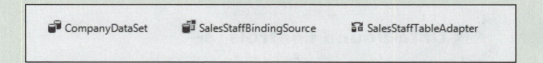

- `CompanyDataSet` is the dataset object that holds the table data in memory and passes the data to the DataGridView control.
- `SalesStaffBindingSource` is the BindingSource object that connects your program to the database.
- `SalesStaffTableAdapter` is the TableAdapter object that pulls data from the database into your program. It contains a command called an SQL Query that specifies which data is to be selected from the table. By default, all rows and columns are selected.

Step 10: Open the form's *Code* window and note the statement in Form_Load that tells the table adapter to fill the dataset (the comments were inserted by Visual Studio):

```
Private Sub Form1_Load(...) Handles MyBase.Load
    'TODO: This line of code loads data into the
    'CompanyDataSet.SalesStaff' table. You can move,
    'or remove it, as needed.
    Me.SalesStaffTableAdapter.Fill(Me.CompanyDataSet.SalesStaff)
End Sub
```

The TableAdapter's Fill method opens the database connection, reads the data from the database into the dataset, and closes the connection. The Me. qualifier used when naming the SalesStaffTableAdapter just indicates that it belongs to the current form. The argument passed to the Fill method is the *SalesStaff* table inside the CompanyDataSet. It may seem unnecessary to specify a table name when the dataset contains only one table. But datasets can contain multiple tables, so we must identify which table is to be filled.

This tutorial shows how easy it is to display database data in a Windows form. The DataGridView control is the ideal tool for giving users a quick view of data. In our example, the column names and ordering were taken directly from the database table. As you learn more about the DataGridView, you will be able to rename the columns and change their order.

Checkpoint

10.6 The technique called _____ links database tables to controls on Visual Basic forms.

10.7 Which component pulls data from one or more database tables and passes it into a dataset?

10.8 When changes are made to a dataset, what happens to the database that filled the dataset?

10.9 Which control displays datasets in a spreadsheet-like format?

10.10 What type of object connects a program to a database?

10.4 Data-Bound Controls

CONCEPT: Some controls can be bound to a dataset. A data-bound control can be used to display and edit the contents of a particular row and column.

VideoNote

Data-Bound
Controls

In this section, we will show you how to add new data sources to a project. Using a dataset, you can bind its fields to individual controls such as text boxes, labels, and list boxes. **Data-bound controls** are convenient because they update their contents automatically when you move from one row to the next in a dataset. They can also be used to update the contents of fields. You will learn how to bind a DataGridView control to an existing dataset. You will also learn how to use a ListBox control to navigate between different rows of a dataset.

Adding a New Data Source

To add a data source to an application that currently has no data sources, open the *Data Sources* window and click the *Add New Data Source* link, as shown in Figure 10-20. The *Data Source Configuration Wizard* window appears (see Figure 10-21), just as it did in Tutorial 10-1. Then you follow the steps to create a connection to a database, as was done in Tutorial 10-1. The data source entry added to the *Data Sources* window is shown in Figure 10-22. If the application already has a data source, you can right-click inside the Data Sources window and select Add New Data Source from the popup menu.

 TIP: If you cannot see the *Data Sources* window, do the following: From the *View* menu, select *Other Windows*, and then select *Data Sources*. The *Data Sources* window usually appears in the same area of the screen as the *ToolBox*, or the *Solution Explorer*.

Figure 10-20 About to add a new data source

Figure 10-21 *Data Source Configuration Wizard*

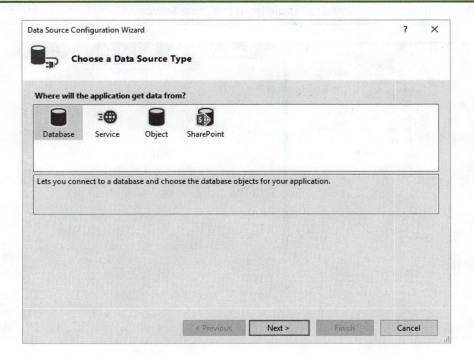

Figure 10-22 *SalesStaff* table in the *Data Sources* window

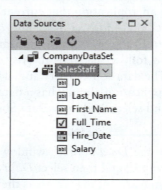

Deleting a Data Source

Suppose you were to create a data source and then later decide to rename it. Unfortunately, data sources are impossible to rename. But you can easily delete a data source and create a new one. To delete an existing data source, select its dataset name in the *Solution Explorer* window with the mouse, and then press Delete on the keyboard. A data source named *CompanyDataSet*, for example, is defined by a file named *CompanyDataSet.xsd*.

Binding a Dataset to a DataGridView Control

In Tutorial 10-1, you used the *DataGridView Tasks* window to guide you through creating a binding source, table adapter, and dataset. What if you already have a dataset, located in the *Data Sources* window? Then you can bind it to a DataGridView control just by dragging the *SalesStaff* table from the *Data Sources* window to the open area of a form, as shown in Figure 10-23. (The *Data Sources* window may be in a different location on your screen.) When you use this technique for data binding, Visual Studio adds a navigation toolbar to the form, as shown in Figure 10-24.

Figure 10-23 Dragging the *SalesStaff* table from the *Data Sources* window onto a form

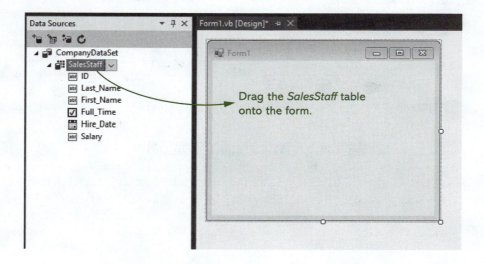

Figure 10-24 After dragging the *SalesStaff* table from the *DataSources* window onto a form

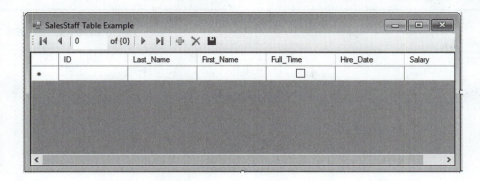

At the same time that Visual Studio builds a DataGridView on the form, it adds a number of important objects to the form's component tray, shown in Figure 10-25:

- *SalesStaffBindingNavigator*—Creates the ToolStrip at the top of the form, with buttons to carry out actions such as moving forward and backward, and adding and deleting rows.
- *CompanyDataSet*—An in-memory copy of the *SalesStaff* table
- *SalesStaffBindingSource*—Connects the DataGridView to the DataSet.
- *SalesStaffTableAdapter*—Pulls data from the database and places it in the DataSet.
- *TableAdapterManager*—A tool for saving data in related tables

 TIP: If you want to remove the ToolStrip from a form, all you have to do is select the SalesStaffBindingNavigator icon and press the [Delete] key on the keyboard.

Figure 10-25 Objects added to the form's component tray

Binding Individual Fields to Controls

If you have an existing dataset in the *Data Sources* window, you can easily create an individual data-bound control for each field by dragging a table from the dataset onto a form that is visible in Design mode. First, click the arrow just to the right of the table name and select *Details* in the drop-down list associated with the table, as shown in Figure 10-26. (The default control type is DataGridView, which we've already used.) Then, when you drag the table name onto a form, a separate control is created for each field. As shown in Figure 10-27, a navigation toolbar is also added to the form. (You may have to wait a few seconds for the controls to appear.)

Figure 10-26 Selecting a table's binding control, in the *Data Sources* window

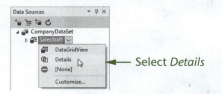

Select *Details*

Figure 10-27 After dragging a dataset table onto the form

Although the dataset column names have underscores between words, as in *First_Name*, Visual Studio removes the underscore between words when generating the labels next to the controls. You may want to modify the appearance or properties of the controls. For example, if you want the *Hire_Date* column to display in *mm/dd/yyyy* format, set the DateTimePicker control's Format property to *Short*.

By default, numeric database columns are bound to TextBox controls, bit (Boolean) fields are bound to CheckBox controls, and datetime fields are bound to **DateTimePicker controls**. The DateTimePicker control displays a date in different formats and lets the user select a date from a calendar-like popup dialog.

If you would prefer not to let the user modify a protected field such as *ID*, you can change the binding control type for individual fields in the *Data Sources* window. For example, if we click the *ID* field in the *SalesStaff* table in the *Data Sources* window, a list of control types appears (see Figure 10-28). If you choose a Label, the user can view the field, but cannot modify its contents.

In Figure 10-29, we show a sample of the same form with a Label control for the *ID* field, and some customizing of the appearance of the other controls. For example, we have cleared the Text property of the CheckBox control and shortened the Hire Date

Figure 10-28 Selecting the control binding type for the *ID* field in the *Data Sources* window

Figure 10-29 Displaying one row of the *SalesStaff* table in bound controls

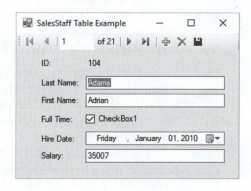

and Salary fields. The DateTimePicker control's Format property has four choices: *Long*, *Short*, *Time*, and *Custom*. Changing the format to *Short* causes the dates to be displayed in *mm/dd/yyyy* format, or the equivalent for other world locales.

If you want to include only one or two bound controls from a dataset, you can drag individual columns from the *Data Sources* window onto a form. To run and modify this sample program, see the *Binding Example* program located in the student sample programs folder named *Chap10\Binding Example*. Tutorial 10-3 shows you how to bind a DataGridView to the *SalesStaff* table.

Tutorial 10-3:
Binding a DataGridView to the *SalesStaff* table

In this tutorial, you will begin by adding a new data source to your application. Then you will bind the data source to a DataGridView control and tell Visual Studio to create a tool strip with buttons that let the user navigate, insert, delete, and save database rows.

Step 1: Create a new Windows Forms Application project named *SalesStaff Databound*.

Step 2: From the *View* menu, select *Other Windows*, and then select *Data Sources*. This will cause the *Data Sources* window to appear. (The *Data Sources* window usually appears on the left or right side of the Visual Studio window.)

Step 3: In the *Data Sources* window, click the *Add New Data Source* link.

Step 4: Repeat what you did in Tutorial 10-1, in Steps 7 through 13, to select the *Company.mdf* database from student sample programs folder for Chapter 10.

Step 5: In the *Choose Your Database Objects* step of the *Data Source Configuration Wizard* window (Figure 10-30), select the *SalesStaff* table and name the dataset *CompanyDataSet*. Click the *Finish* button.

Figure 10-30 *Data Source Configuration Wizard*

Choose Your Database Objects

Which database objects do you want in your dataset?

- ▲ ☑ Tables
  - ▷ ☐ Departments
  - ▷ ☐ Employees
  - ▷ ☐ Sales
  - ▷ ☑ SalesStaff
- ☐ Views
- ☐ Stored Procedures
- ☐ *fx* Functions

DataSet name:

CompanyDataSet

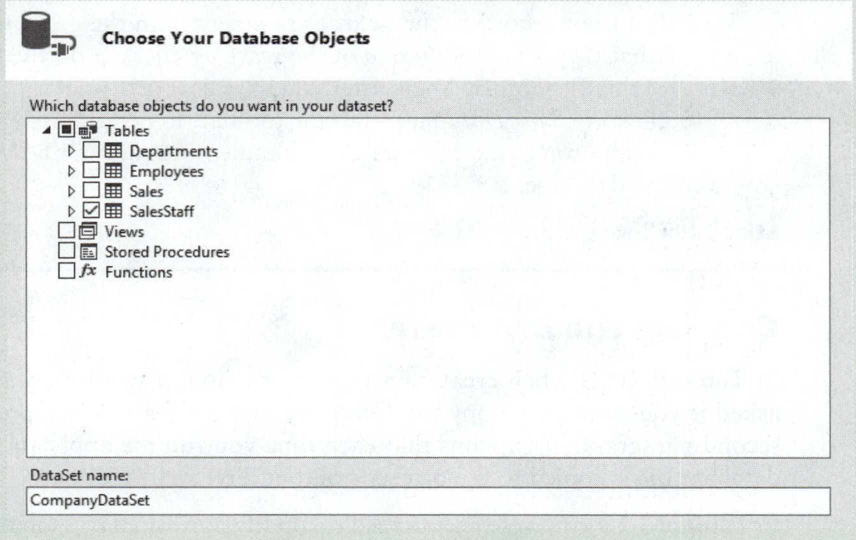

Step 6: Increase the width of the program's form to about 700 pixels and set its Text property to *SalesStaff Table*.

Step 7: Drag the *SalesStaff* table name from the *Data Sources* window onto your form. Notice how Visual Studio adds both a DataGridView control and a ToolStrip control to the form. The ToolStrip contains buttons that let the user perform operations on the DataGridView control's data.

Step 8: Set the DataGridView control's Dock property to *Fill*, so it anchors to all sides of the form.

Step 9: Save the project and run the application. You should see output similar to that shown in Figure 10-31.

Figure 10-31 Output from the *SalesStaff Databound* application

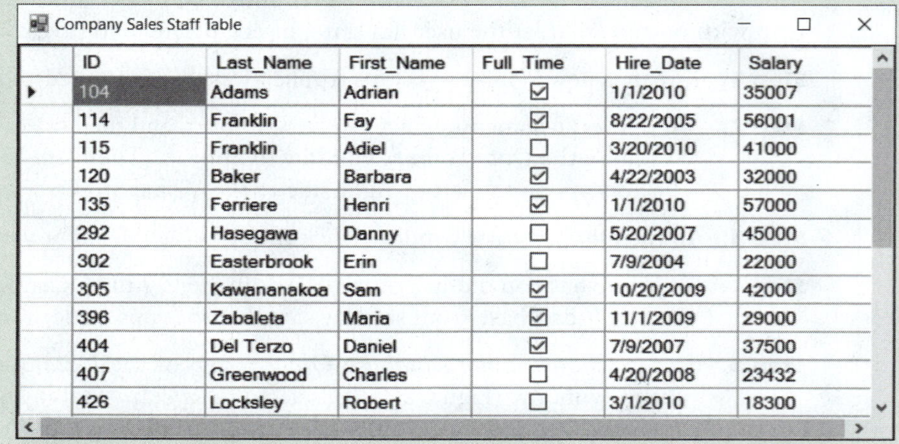

ID	Last_Name	First_Name	Full_Time	Hire_Date	Salary
104	Adams	Adrian	☑	1/1/2010	35007
114	Franklin	Fay	☑	8/22/2005	56001
115	Franklin	Adiel	☐	3/20/2010	41000
120	Baker	Barbara	☑	4/22/2003	32000
135	Ferriere	Henri	☑	1/1/2010	57000
292	Hasegawa	Danny	☐	5/20/2007	45000
302	Easterbrook	Erin	☐	7/9/2004	22000
305	Kawananakoa	Sam	☑	10/20/2009	42000
396	Zabaleta	Maria	☑	11/1/2009	29000
404	Del Terzo	Daniel	☑	7/9/2007	37500
407	Greenwood	Charles	☐	4/20/2008	23432
426	Locksley	Robert	☐	3/1/2010	18300

Step 10: Initially, the ID field of the first record is highlighted. Click the arrow buttons on the Navigation toolbar and notice that the highlighted selection bar moves from one record to the next. Experiment with the other toolbar buttons to see what they do. Modify one of the rows by clicking on the button just to the left of the ID number. Then, after you have changed the data in one of the row cells, click the *Save Data* button in the toolbar. In design mode, you can double-click this button to examine its Click handler and find out how changes are saved to the database.

Step 11: Close the program.

Copying the Database

In Tutorial 10-1, when creating a new connection, a window, shown in Figure 10-32, asked if you wanted to copy the *Company.mdf* database to the project directory. In the second paragraph, it explains that each time you run the application, a new copy of the database file is copied to the project's output directory.

In Tutorial 10-3 you were encouraged to modify individual rows in the DataGridView and save the changes in the database. But, if you ran the application again, it may have seemed that the changes you made earlier were not saved. If fact, the changes were saved, but when you ran the application, Visual Studio made a fresh copy of the database and put it in the project's output directory. By doing this, it erased the changes you made to the data.

Figure 10-32 Copying a database to the project director

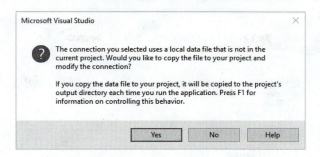

If you want changes to your database to be permanent, you can click the *No* button when the window in Figure 10-32 appears. This will cause Visual Studio to connect to the existing database rather than making a copy. There is only one disadvantage to this decision: If you give your project to another person (such as your instructor), the database will not be inside the project folder. Also, the database connection string in your project will have to be modified before the other person can execute your project. When creating a project to turn in for a grade, be sure to follow your instructor's instructions when answering either *Yes* or *No* in response to this window.

In Tutorial 10-4, you will display individual fields from the *SalesStaff* table.

Tutorial 10-4:

Binding individual controls to the *SalesStaff* table

VideoNote

Binding individual controls to the *SalesStaff* table

In this tutorial, you will select the *Details* option in the *Data Source* window so you can bind individual controls to fields in the *SalesStaff* table.

Step 1: Create a new Windows Forms Application project named *SalesStaff Details*.

Step 2: Set the form's Text property to *SalesStaff Details*.

Step 3: From the *View* menu, select *Other Windows*, and then select *Data Sources*. This will cause the *Data Sources* window to appear.

Step 4: In the *Data Sources* window, click the *Add New Data Source* link.

Step 5: Select the *Company.mdf* database from the student sample programs folder for Chapter 10. This is what you did in Steps 7 through 13 of Tutorial 10-1. When you are asked if the database should be copied to your project folder, answer *Yes*.

Step 6: In the *Choose Your Database Objects* step of the *Data Source Configuration Wizard* (Figure 10-33), select the *SalesStaff* table and name the dataset *CompanyDataSet*. Click the *Finish* button.

Step 7: In the *Data Sources* window, expand the list of fields under the *SalesStaff* table name by clicking the arrow to the left of the *SalesStaff* table name.

Step 8: Drag the *Last_Name* field from the *Data Sources* window onto your form. When you do this, you should see a TextBox control appear on the form with a label to its left side. Notice that Visual Studio automatically removes the underscore character between the two words in the field name. You will also see a new ToolStrip control on the form. An example is shown in Figure 10-34.

Figure 10-33 *Data Source Configuration Wizard*

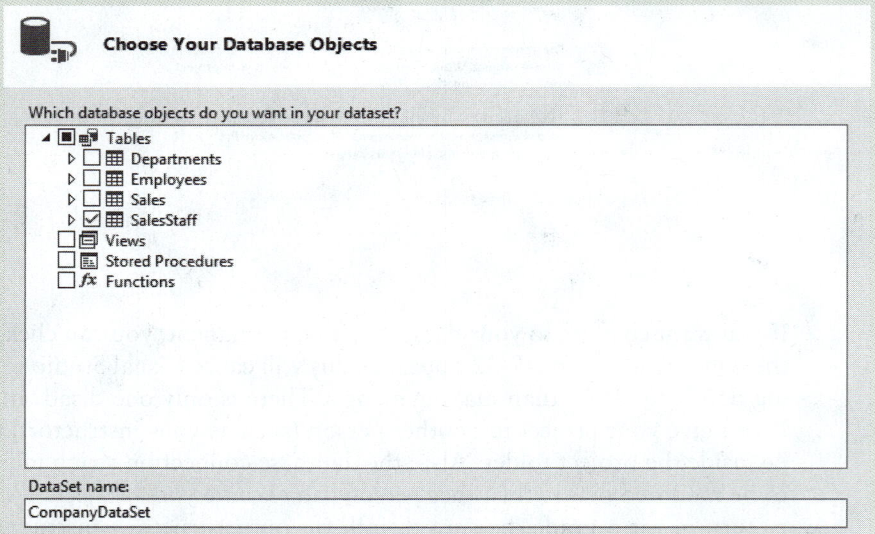

Choose Your Database Objects

Which database objects do you want in your dataset?

- ▲ ■ Tables
    - ▷ □ Departments
    - ▷ □ Employees
    - ▷ □ Sales
    - ▷ ☑ SalesStaff
- □ Views
- □ Stored Procedures
- □ *fx* Functions

DataSet name:

CompanyDataSet

Figure 10-34 After dragging the *Last_Name* field onto the form

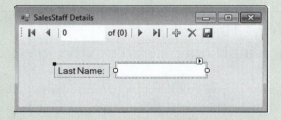

Step 9: Save the project and run the application. Click the navigation buttons in the tool strip and notice how the name changes. Also, the table's row number changes in the tool strip.

Step 10: Stop the application.

Step 11: Drag the remaining columns from the *SalesStaff* table onto the form. You might want to rearrange their order, expand some fields, remove the text from the Full Time check box, and change the *Hire_Date* control's Format property to *Short*. An example is shown in Figure 10-35.

Step 12: Save the project and run the application again. Notice how all the fields update at the same time when you click the navigation buttons on the tool strip.

Step 13: Experiment with adding, deleting, and editing individual rows from the table. Changes you make to individual fields will be saved only if you click the *Save Data* button on the tool strip.

Step 14: Close the application.

In this tutorial, you have seen how easy it is to work with data-bound tables in Visual Basic. You can display an entire table at once, or you can display each row of a table individually.

Figure 10-35 After dragging all *SalesStaff* fields onto the form

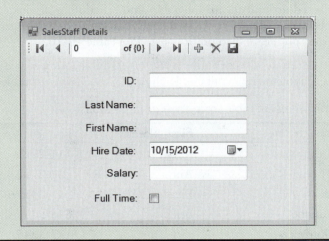

More about the ToolStrip in Data-Bound Forms

Filling the DataSet

You have seen how Visual Studio adds a ToolStrip control with buttons whenever you drag a table from the *Data Source* window onto a form. In fact, a certain amount of code is generated inside the form, which may be of interest to you.

The Form1_Load event handler contains comments, followed by a call to the Fill method of the SalesStaffTableAdapter object:

```
Private Sub Form1_Load(...) Handles MyBase.Load

    ' TODO: This line of code loads data into the
    ' CompanyDataSet.SalesStaff table. You can move,
    ' or remove it, as needed.

    Me.SalesStaffTableAdapter.Fill(Me.CompanyDataSet.SalesStaff)

End Sub
```

Earlier, we said that the job of a TableAdapter is to pull data from the database and copy it into the DataSet. In fact, this is exactly what the Fill method does, as it copies the data into the SalesStaff table of the CompanyDataSet object.

Saving Changes to the Data

The data binding examples we saw earlier also contained a procedure that saves changes made by the user when the *Save* button is clicked in the ToolStrip control:

```
Private Sub SalesStaffBindingNavigatorSaveItem_Click(...) Handles...
  Me.Validate()
  Me.SalesStaffBindingSource.EndEdit()
  Me.TableAdapterManager.UpdateAll(Me.CompanyDataSet)
End Sub
```

First, the Validate method is called, which checks to see if the database data is ready to be written to the database. Second, the EndEdit method is called, which applies any pending changes to the dataset. Finally, the UpdateAll method tells the TableAdapter to write the data changes back to the database.

Introducing the *Karate* Database

The database we will use for the next set of examples is called *Karate* (*Karate.mdf*), designed around the membership and scheduling of classes for a martial arts school. A table called *Members* contains information about members, such as their first and last names, phone, and so on. It is listed in Table 10-10.

The database also contains a *Payments* table, shown in Table 10-11, that holds recent dues payments by members. Each row in the *Payments* table contains a *Member_Id* value,

Table 10-10 The *Members* table from the *Karate* database

ID	Last_Name	First_Name	Phone	Date_Joined
1	Kahumanu	Keoki	111-2222	2/20/2002
2	Chong	Anne	232-2323	2/20/2010
3	Hasegawa	Elaine	313-3455	2/20/2004
4	Kahane	Brian	646-9387	5/20/2008
5	Gonzalez	Aldo	123-2345	6/6/2009
6	Kousevitzky	Jascha	414-2345	2/20/2010
7	Taliafea	Moses	545-2323	5/20/2005
8	Concepcion	Rafael	602-3312	5/20/2007
9	Taylor	Winifred	333-2222	2/20/2010

Table 10-11 The *Payments* table from the *Karate* database

ID	Member_Id	Payment_Date	Amount
1	1	10/20/2016	$48.00
2	2	02/20/2016	$80.00
3	6	03/20/2016	$75.00
4	4	12/16/2016	$50.00
5	5	04/11/2016	$65.00
6	3	02/16/2016	$75.00
7	9	03/20/2016	$77.00
8	8	02/27/2016	$44.00
9	6	04/20/2016	$77.00
10	5	01/16/2016	$66.00
11	8	05/11/2016	$77.00
13	6	02/20/2016	$77.00
14	7	07/16/2016	$77.00
15	1	03/11/2016	$44.00
16	3	03/28/2016	$43.00
17	4	03/27/2016	$44.00
19	9	02/20/2016	$44.00
22	2	03/20/2016	$55.00

which identifies the member (from the *Members* table) who made a dues payment. Their relationship is shown by the diagram in Figure 10-36. The line connects the *ID* field in the *Members* table to the *Member_Id* field in the *Payments* table. In Tutorials 10-5 and 10-6, you will work with these two tables.

Figure 10-36 Relationship between the *Members* and *Payments* tables

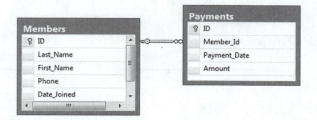

Binding to ListBox and ComboBox Controls

ListBox and ComboBox controls are ideal tools for displaying lists of items and permitting users to select individual items. When working with databases, you need to set the following properties:

- DataSource: The **DataSource property** identifies the table within the dataset that supplies the data.
- DisplayMember: The **DisplayMember property** identifies the column within the table that displays in the list box or combo box.

When you use the mouse to drag a table column from the *Data Sources* window onto a list box or combo box, Visual Studio automatically creates the necessary data components: a dataset, binding source, and table adapter.

Tutorial 10-5 shows you how to display the *Members* table in a list box.

Tutorial 10-5:
Displaying the *Karate Members* table in a ListBox Control

In this tutorial, you will use a ListBox control to display the last names of members from the *Members* table in the *Karate* database. When the user clicks a member name, the program will display the date when the member joined.

Step 1: Create a new Windows Forms Application project named *Member List*. Save the project immediately.

Step 2: Click *Add New Data Source* in the *Data Sources* window. (If you cannot see the *Data Sources* window, do the following: From the *View* menu, select *Other Windows*, and then select *Data Sources*.)

Step 3: Follow the steps in the *Data Source Configuration Wizard* to create a connection to the *Members* table in the *Karate.mdf* database, located in the student sample programs folder named *Chap10*. Name the dataset *MembersDataSet*.

Step 4: Set the form's Text property to *Member List*.

Step 5: Add a ListBox control to the form and name it 1stMembers. Set the ListBox control's Size.Width property to 125, and its Size.Height property to 134.

Step 6: Add a Label just above the list box and set its Text property to *Member Names*. Widen the form so it appears similar to the one shown in Figure 10-37.

Step 7: Select the list box, and then click the down-arrow next to its DataSource property in the *Properties* window. Expand the *Other Data Sources* group, expand *Project Data Sources*, expand *MembersDataSet*, and select *Members* (shown in Figure 10-38). Notice that Visual Studio immediately adds three components to the form's component tray: a dataset, a binding source, and a table adapter.

Figure 10-37 *Member List* program with list box

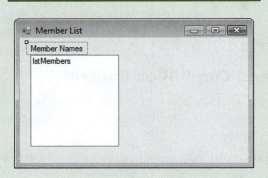

Figure 10-38 Setting the list box's DataSource property

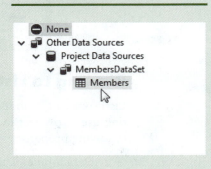

Step 8: Set the list box's DisplayMember property to *Last_Name*.

Step 9: Save and run the application. The list box should contain the last names of members, as shown in Figure 10-39. Close the window and return to Design mode.

Figure 10-39 List box filled, at runtime

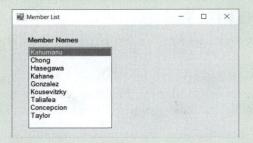

Step 10: Next, you will add a data-bound TextBox control to the form that displays the member's phone number. To do this, expand the *Members* table in the *Data Sources* window, and then use the mouse to drag the *Phone* field from the *Data Sources* window onto the form.

Step 11: Save and run the program. As you click each member's name, notice how the current phone number is displayed. For a sample, see Figure 10-40.

Let's analyze what's happening here. When the user selects a name in the list box, the form's data binding mechanism moves to the dataset row containing the person's name. The *Phone* TextBox control shares the same binding source as the ListBox, so it displays the phone number of the person selected in the list box.

Figure 10-40 Phone number of selected member displays in a TextBox control

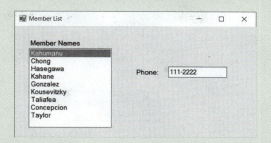

Step 12: Add the remaining fields by dragging the field names from the *Data Sources* window onto the form, as shown in Figure 10-41. Choose the Label control type for the *ID* field. In the figure, a DateTimePicker control was used for the *Date_Joined* field. The DateTimePicker control's Format property was set to *Short*. Reposition the controls and resize the form as necessary. The Label control displaying the *ID* field looks best with its BorderStyle property set to *Fixed3D* and its AutoSize property set to *False*.

Figure 10-41 Displaying the *Members* table in detail controls

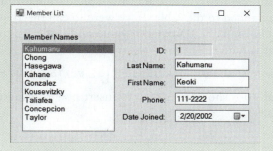

Step 13: Save and rerun the program. Now you have a way to navigate through dataset rows by selecting from a list box!

Step 14: End the program.

Adding Rows to a Database Table

The easiest way for an application to add a row to a database table is to call a procedure named Insert, which belongs to a TableAdapter. To find one, you have to open a dataset's **schema defintion**. When you add a data source to a project, a special file called a **DataSet Designer file** is created. This is a file with a designer window that displays the names and data types of fields in the table. It has a filename extension of *xsd*. In Tutorial 10-5, for example, the *Members* table was used as a data source and the *Solution Explorer* window contained a file named *MembersDataSet.xsd*. To edit a designer file, double-click its name in the *Solution Explorer* window. An editor window will open, as shown in Figure 10-42. A Data-Table named *Members* was created automatically when this data source was added to the project. Associated with every DataTable is a TableAdapter, which in this case is named *MembersTableAdapter*.

Figure 10-42 The MembersDataSet DataSet Designer file, containing the *Members* DataTable and the *MembersTableAdapter*

Suppose you would like the code in your application to add a new row to the *Members* table. You can call the TableAdapter's Insert method, passing it the column values for the row being added. Here is an example:

```
MembersTableAdapter.Insert(10, "Hasegawa", "Adrian",
                           "305-999-8888",#5/15/2010#)
```

Identity Columns

A database table can have what is known as an **identity column.** When new rows are added to the table, the identity column is assigned a new unique integer value. That is the case for the *Payments* table in the *Karate* database. The primary key column, named ID, is also an identity column. Its values are automatically generated in sequence when new rows are added to the table. If we were to call the Insert method for the *Payments* table, we would omit the ID column value and just pass the Member_Id, Payment_Date, and Amount values:

```
PaymentsTableAdapter.Insert(5, #5/15/2010#, 50D)
```

Tutorial 10-6 shows you how to insert new rows into the *Payments* table of the *Karate* database.

Tutorial 10-6:
Inserting *Karate* member payments

In this tutorial, you will write a program that inserts new rows into the *Payments* table of the *Karate* database.

Step 1: Create a new Windows Forms Application project named *Insert Karate Payments*.

Step 2: In the *Data Sources* window, add a new data source named PaymentsDataSet, which uses the *Payments* table from the *Karate* database. Answer *Yes* when Visual Studio asks if you want the database copied to the project directory.

Step 3: Add three text boxes to the form with appropriate labels. One is named txtMemberId, another is named txtDate, and the third is named txtAmount. Set the form's Text property to *Insert Karate Payments*. Use Figure 10-43 as a guide.

Figure 10-43 The startup form in the *Insert Karate Payments* application

txtDate

txtMemberId

btnInsert

txtAmount

Step 4: Add a Button control to the form, and set its name to `btnInsert`. Set the button's Text property to *Insert Payment*.

Step 5: Add a DataGridView control and set the following properties: Name = *dgvPayments*; BorderStyle = *None*; BackgroundColor = *Control*; ReadOnly = *True*; RowHeadersVisible = *False*; Anchor = *Top, Bottom, Left, Right*. The ReadOnly property prevents the user from making any changes to the grid's data at runtime.

Step 6: Click the grid's smart tag (the arrow in the grid's upper right corner) to display the *DataGridView Tasks* window. Set its data source to the *Payments* table of the `PaymentsDataSet`.

Step 7: Select the grid's Columns property, which opens the *Edit Columns* window, and remove the *ID* column. Figure 10-44 shows the *Edit Columns* window after the ID column was removed.

Figure 10-44 Editing the Columns property of the *dgvPayments* grid

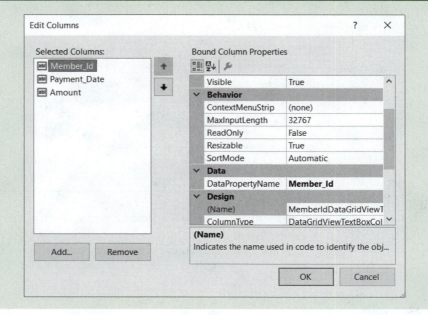

Step 8: Still in the *Edit Columns* window, select the *Member_Id* column, and open the DefaultCellStyle property in the right-hand list box. The *CellStyle Builder* window will appear, as shown in Figure 10-45.

Step 9: In the *CellStyle Builder* window, set the following properties: Alignment = *MiddleCenter*; ForeColor = *Blue*. Click the *OK* button to close the window.

Step 10: In the *Edit Columns* window, select the *Amount* column and open its DefaultCellStyle property.

Step 11: Open its Format property and select *Currency*. Click the *OK* button to close the dialog box.

Step 12: Click the *OK* button to close the *CellStyle Builder* window.

Step 13: Experiment with the three columns, changing colors and formats as you wish. When you finish, click the *OK* button to close the *Edit Columns* window.

Step 14: Save and run the program. You should see a list of payments in the grid. Halt the program.

Figure 10-45 Editing the *Member_Id* column in the *CellStyle Builder* window

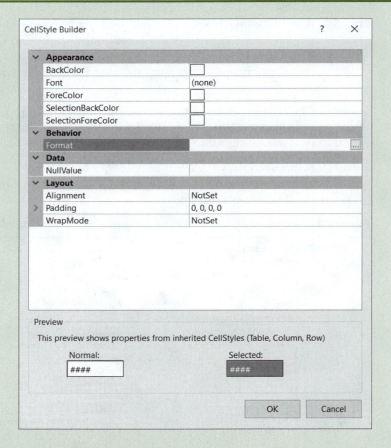

Step 15: Next, you will add code to the *Insert Payment* button that lets the program save new payments. In Design mode, double-click the *Insert Payment* button. Add the following code, shown in bold, to the button's Click event handler:

```
Private Sub btnInsert_Click(...) Handles btnInsert.Click
    Try
        Me.PaymentsTableAdapter.Insert(CShort(txtMemberID.Text),
            CDate(txtDate.Text), CDec(txtAmount.Text))
        Me.PaymentsTableAdapter.Fill(PaymentsDataSet.Payments)
    Catch ex As Exception
        MessageBox.Show(ex.Message, "Data Input Error")
    End Try
End Sub
```

The code you added calls the TableAdapter's Insert method, passing to the method the values of the three columns we want to add: *Member_Id*, *Date*, and *Amount*. Each must be converted to a type that matches the appropriate dataset column type. Then, the *Fill* method is called so you can see the new payment in the grid.

 TIP: The Me object referred to in Step 15 refers to the current Form object. Its use is optional.

Step 16: Add the following lines, marked in bold, to the Form1_Load event handler. As the comment says, we want the text box to display today's date.

```
Private Sub Form1_Load(...) Handles MyBase.Load
    'TODO: This line of code loads data into the...
    Me.PaymentsTableAdapter.Fill(Me.PaymentsDataSet.Payments)

    ' Set the text box to today's date.
    txtDate.Text = Today().ToString("d")
End Sub
```

Step 17: Save and run the application. Add a new payment, using a *Member_Id* value between 1 and 9. Verify that your payment appears in the grid after clicking the *Insert Payment* button. This payment was saved in the database.

Step 18: Add a payment that uses an invalid date format or a nonnumeric value for the amount. When you click the *Insert Payment* button, observe the error message (generated by the Try-Catch statement). An application should always recover gracefully when users enter invalid data.

Step 19: End the application.

Using Loops with DataTables

Techniques you've learned about loops and collections in previous chapters apply easily to database tables. You can iterate over the Rows collection of a table using the For Each statement. Usually, it's best to create a strongly typed row that matches the type of rows in the table.

The following code loops over the Rows collection of the *Payments* table of the PaymentsDataSet dataset, adding the *Amount* column to a total:

```
Dim row As PaymentsDataSet.PaymentsRow
Dim decTotal As Decimal = 0

For Each row In Me.PaymentsDataSet.Payments.Rows
    decTotal += row.Amount
Next
```

The dataset was built from the *Payments* table in the *Karate* database when we added a new data source to the project.

Tutorial 10-7 shows how to add a total to the *Insert Karate Payments* application.

Tutorial 10-7:
Adding a total to the *Insert Karate Payments* application

In this tutorial, you will add statements that calculate the total amount of payments made by students in the karate school.

Step 1: Open the *Insert Karate Payments* project you created in Tutorial 10-6.

Step 2: Add a new button to the form, just below the *Insert Payment* button. (You may have to move the *Insert Payment* button up a little to make room. See Figure 10-46 for an example.) Set its properties as follows: Name = btnTotal; Text = *Show Total*

Step 3: Double-click the *Show Total* button and insert the following code, shown in bold, in its Click event handler. This code uses a loop to get the payment amount value from each row in the dataset and add the value to a total:

```
Private Sub btnTotal_Click(...) Handles btnTotal.Click
    Dim decTotal As Decimal = 0
    Dim row As PaymentsDataSet.PaymentsRow

    For Each row In Me.PaymentsDataSet.Payments.Rows
        decTotal += row.Amount
    Next

    MessageBox.Show("Total payments are equal to " &
                    decTotal.ToString("c"), "Total")
End Sub
```

Step 4: Save and run the program. Click the *Show Total* button and observe the results. An example is shown in Figure 10-46.

Step 5: Insert a new payment. Then click the *Show Total* button, and note that the value of the total payments has increased.

Step 6: End the program.

Figure 10-46 Calculating the total payments

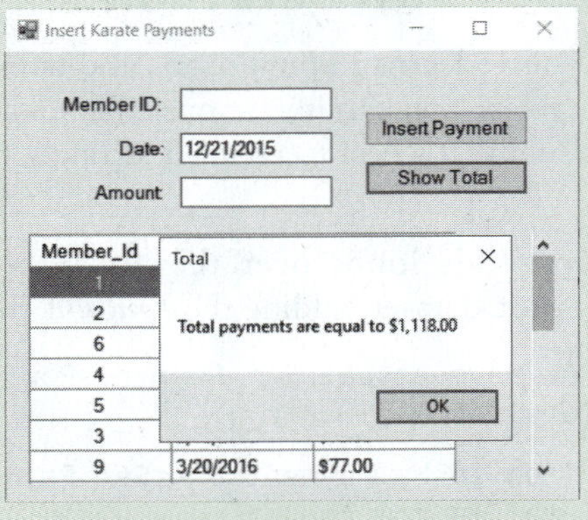

Checkpoint

10.11 Which Visual Studio window displays the list of datasets belonging to a project?

10.12 The _____ _____ *Configuration Wizard* is a tool you can use to create a connection to a database and select a database table.

10.13 If a certain data source exists, how do you bind it to a DataGridView control?

10.14 How do you bind a single data source column to a text box?

10.15 By default, which control binds to a DateTime field in a data source?

10.16 What is the Visual Studio menu command for adding a new data source to the current project?

10.5 Structured Query Language (SQL)

SQL, which stands for *Structured Query Language*, is a standard language for working with database management systems. SQL has been standardized by the American National Standards Institute (ANSI) and adopted by almost every database software vendor as the language of choice for interacting with their Database Management System (DBMS).

SQL consists of a limited set of keywords. You use the keywords to construct statements known as **database queries**. These statements are submitted to the DBMS, and in response, the DBMS carries out operations on its data.

 NOTE: Although SQL is a language, you don't use it to write applications. It is intended only as a standard means of interacting with a DBMS. You still need a general programming language such as Visual Basic to write database-related applications.

SELECT **Statement**

The **SELECT statement** retrieves data from a database. You can use it to select rows, columns, and tables. The most basic format for a single table is as follows:

```
SELECT ColumnList
FROM Table
```

The members of `ColumnList` must be table column names separated by commas. The following statement selects the *ID* and *Salary* columns from the *SalesStaff* table:

```
SELECT ID, Salary
FROM SalesStaff
```

In a Visual Basic program, the dataset produced by this query would have just two columns: *ID* and *Salary*. There is no required formatting or capitalization of SQL statements or field names. The following queries are equivalent:

```
SELECT ID, Salary FROM SalesStaff
select ID, Salary from SalesStaff
Select id, salary from salesstaff
```

As a matter of style and readability, you should try to use consistent capitalization.

If field names contain embedded spaces, they must be surrounded by square brackets, as in the following example:

```
SELECT [Last Name], [First Name]
FROM Employees
```

The * character in the column list selects all columns from a table, as shown in the following example:

```
SELECT *
FROM SalesStaff
```

Aliases for Column Names

Column names can be renamed, using the AS keyword. The new column name is called an *alias*, as in the following example that renames the Hire_Date column to Date_Hired:

```
SELECT
    Last_Name, Hire_Date AS Date_Hired
FROM
    SalesStaff
```

Renaming columns is useful for two reasons: First, you might want to hide the real column names from users for security purposes. Second, column headings in reports can be made more user friendly if you substitute your own names for the column names used inside the database.

Creating Alias Columns from Other Columns

A query can create a new column (called an *alias*) from other existing columns. For example, we might want to combine *Last_Name* and *First_Name* from a table named *Members*. We can insert a comma and space between the columns as follows:

```
SELECT Last_Name + ', ' + First_Name AS Full_Name
FROM Members
```

Now the *Full_Name* column can conveniently be inserted into a list box or combo box. In general, when strings occur in queries, they must always be surrounded by apostrophes. The + operator concatenates multiple strings into a single string.

Calculated Columns

You can create new columns, whose contents are calculated from existing column values. Suppose a table named *Payroll* contains columns named employeeId, hoursWorked, and hourlyRate. The following statement creates a new column named payAmount using hoursWorked and hourlyRate:

```
SELECT employeeId,
    hoursWorked * hourlyRate AS payAmount
FROM PayRoll
```

Setting the Row Order with ORDER BY

The SQL SELECT statement has an **ORDER BY clause** that lets you control the display order of the table rows. In other words, you can sort the data on one or more columns. The following is the general form for sorting on a single column:

```
ORDER BY ColumnName [ASC | DESC]
```

ASC indicates ascending order (the default), and DESC indicates descending order. Both are optional, and you can use only one at a time. The following clause sorts the output in ascending order by last name:

```
ORDER BY Last_Name ASC
```

We can do this more simply, as follows:

```
ORDER BY Last_Name
```

The following sorts the output in descending order by salary:

```
ORDER BY Salary DESC
```

You can sort on multiple columns. The following statement sorts in ascending order first by last name; then within each last name, it sorts in ascending order by first name:

```
ORDER BY Last_Name, First_Name
```

The following SELECT statement returns the first name, last name, and date joined, sorting by last name and first name in the *Members* table of the *Karate* database:

```
SELECT
   First_Name, Last_Name, Date_Joined
FROM
   Members
ORDER BY Last_Name, First_Name
```

Selecting Rows with the WHERE Clause

The SQL SELECT statement has an optional **WHERE clause** that you can use to *filter*, or select which rows you want to retrieve from a database table. The simplest form of the WHERE clause is as follows:

```
WHERE ColumnName = Value
```

In this format, *ColumnName* must be one of the table columns, and *Value* must be in a format that is consistent with the column type. The following SELECT statement, for example, specifies that *Last_Name* must be equal to *Gomez*:

```
SELECT First_Name, Last_Name, Salary
FROM SalesStaff
WHERE Last_Name = 'Gomez'
```

Because *Last_Name* is a *nvarchar* column, it must be compared to a string literal enclosed in apostrophes. If the person's name contains an apostrophe (such as O'Leary), the apostrophe must be repeated. The following is an example:

```
SELECT First_Name, Last_Name, Salary
FROM SalesStaff
WHERE Last_Name = 'O''Leary'
```

Relational Operators

Table 10-12 lists the operators that can be used in WHERE clauses. The following expression matches last names starting with letters B–Z:

```
WHERE Last_Name >= 'B'
```

The following expression matches non-zero salary values:

```
WHERE Salary <> 0
```

Table 10-12 SQL relational operators

Operator	Meaning
=	equal to
<>	not equal to
<	less than
<=	less than or equal to
>	greater than
>=	greater than or equal to

Numeric and Date Values

Numeric literals are not surrounded by quotation marks. The following expression matches all rows in which *Salary* is greater than $30,000. The use of parentheses is optional.

```
WHERE (Salary > 30000)
```

Date literals must be delimited by apostrophes:

```
WHERE (Hire_Date > '12/31/2016')
```

The following expression matches rows containing hire dates falling between (and including) January 1, 2016, and December 31, 2016:

```
WHERE (Hire_Date BETWEEN '1/1/2016' AND '12/31/2016')
```

The following is a complete SELECT statement using the WHERE clause that selects rows according to *Hire_Date* and sorts by last name:

```
SELECT First_Name, Last_Name, Hire_Date
FROM SalesStaff
WHERE (Hire_Date BETWEEN '1/1/2016' AND '12/31/2016')
ORDER BY Last_Name
```

LIKE Operator

The **LIKE operator** can be used to create partial matches with varchar column values. When combined with LIKE, the underscore character matches a single unknown character. For example, the following expression matches all three-character Account_ID values beginning with X and ending with 4:

```
WHERE Account_ID LIKE 'X_4'
```

The % character matches multiple unknown characters. We call % a **wildcard** symbol. For example, the following matches all last names starting with the letter A:

```
WHERE Last_Name LIKE 'A%'
```

Wildcard symbols can be combined. For example, the following matches all *First_Name* values in the table that have 'dr' in the second and third positions:

```
WHERE First_Name LIKE '_dr%'
```

Compound Expressions (AND, OR, and NOT)

SQL uses the AND, OR, and NOT operators to create compound expressions. In most cases, you should use parentheses to clarify the order of operations. The following expression matches rows in which the person was hired after 1/1/2016 and their salary is greater than $40,000.

```
WHERE (Hire_Date > '1/1/2016') AND (Salary > 40000)
```

The following expression matches rows in which the person was hired either before 2011 or after 2016:

```
WHERE (Hire_Date < '1/1/2011') OR (Hire_Date > '12/31/2016')
```

The following expression matches two types of employees: (1) employees hired after 1/1/2010 whose salaries are greater than $40,000; (2) part-time employees:

```
WHERE (Hire_Date > '1/1/2010') AND (Salary > 40000)
OR (Full_Time = 'False')
```

The following expression matches rows in which the hire date does not fall between 1/1/2010 and 12/31/2016:

```
WHERE (Hire_Date NOT BETWEEN '1/1/2010' AND '12/31/2016')
```

The following expression matches rows in which the last name does not begin with the letter A:

```
WHERE (Last_Name NOT LIKE 'A%')
```

Modifying the Query in a Data Source

To modify (edit) a query used by a data source, open its dataset designer file from the *Solution Explorer* window. Suppose an application contains a dataset named *CompanyDataSet*. Then the corresponding designer file would be named *CompanyDataSet.xsd*. You can open a designer file in *Solution Explorer* by double-clicking its filename. An example is shown in Figure 10-47. The top line shows the database name. The next several lines list the columns in the dataset, identifying the ID column as the primary key. The *SalesStaffTableAdapter* appears next, followed by a list of its database queries. By default, there is one query named *Fill, GetData()* that fills the dataset when the form loads.

Figure 10-47 SalesStaff TableAdapter, in the *Dataset Designer* window

If you right-click the name *SalesStaffTableAdapter* and select *Configure* from the pop-up menu, you can modify the currently selected query using the *TableAdapter Configuration Wizard*, as shown in Figure 10-48. If the query text is simple enough, you can modify it directly in this window. If the query is more complicated, you may want to use the *Query Builder*, which can be launched by clicking the *Query Builder* button. An example is shown in Figure 10-49.

To close the *Query Builder*, click the *OK* button. Then click the *Finish* button to close the *TableAdapter Configuration Wizard*. Finally, you should save the dataset in the *DataSet Designer* window before closing it. Let's take a closer look at the *Query Builder* tool.

Query Builder

Query Builder is a tool provided by Visual Studio for creating and modifying SQL queries. It consists of four sections, called *panes*, as shown in Figure 10-49.

- The **diagram pane** displays all the tables used in the query, with a check mark next to each field that will be used in the dataset.

- The **grid pane** (also known as the **criteria pane**) displays the query in a spreadsheet-like format, which is particularly well suited to choosing a sort order and entering selection criteria.
- The **SQL pane** displays the actual SQL query that corresponds to the tables and fields selected in the diagram and grid panes. Advanced SQL users usually write queries directly into this pane.
- The **results pane** displays the data rows returned by executing the current SQL query. To fill the results pane, click the *Execute Query* button.

Figure 10-48 Using the *TableAdapter Configuration Wizard*

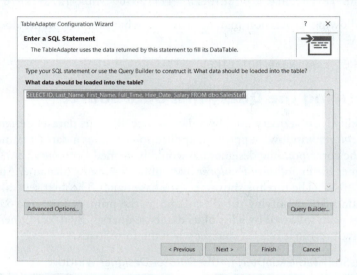

Figure 10-49 *Query Builder* window

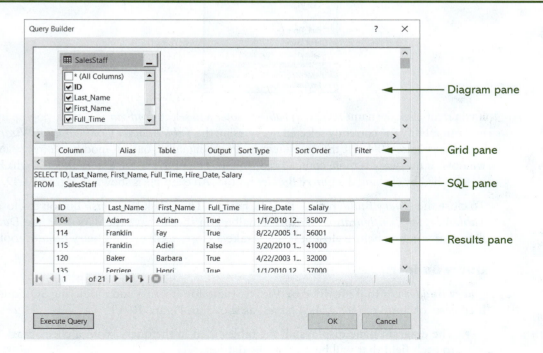

To remove and restore panes, do the following:

- To remove a pane, right-click it and select *Remove Pane* from the pop-up menu.
- To restore a pane that was removed, right-click in the window, select *Show Panes* from the pop-up menu, and select a pane from the list that appears.

To add a new table to the *Query Builder* window, right-click inside the diagram pane and select *Add Table* from the pop-up menu. To close *Query Builder*, click the *OK* button.

Adding a Query to a TableAdapter

If you want to filter (limit the display of) rows in a DataGridView control, the easiest way to do it is to add a new query to the TableAdapter attached to the grid. Suppose *Sales-StaffTableAdapter* is attached to a DataGridView displaying the *SalesStaff* table from the Company database. In the component tray at the bottom of the Form in the Design view, right-click the table adapter icon and select *Add Query* (shown in Figure 10-50). The *Search Criteria Builder* window appears, as shown in Figure 10-51. Let's modify the query so it looks as follows:

```
SELECT ID, Last_Name, First_Name, Full_Time, Hire_Date, Salary
FROM SalesStaff
WHERE Salary < 45000
```

Figure 10-52 shows what the window looks like after adding a WHERE clause to the SELECT statement. Notice that you can give a name to the query, which we called *Salary_query*. When you click the *OK* button, a ToolStrip control is added to the form, with a query button, as shown in Figure 10-53. When we run the program and click the *Salary_query* button on the tool strip, the results are as shown in Figure 10-54. Only rows with salaries less than $45,000 are displayed.

Figure 10-50 Adding a query to a TableAdapter

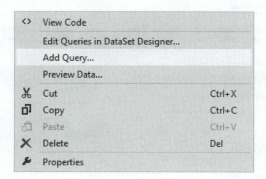

Figure 10-51 *Search Criteria Builder* window

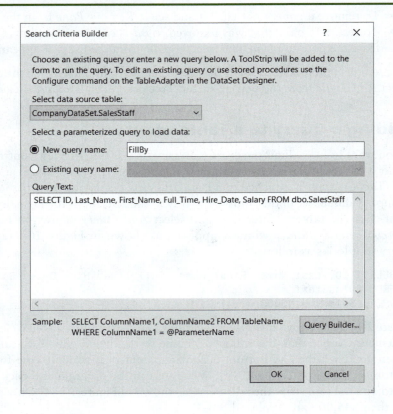

Figure 10-52 Entering a query in the *Search Criteria Builder*

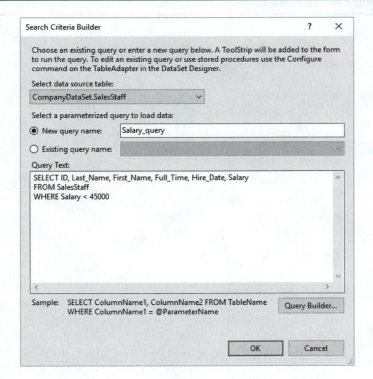

Figure 10-53 Tool strip added to the form, with a query button

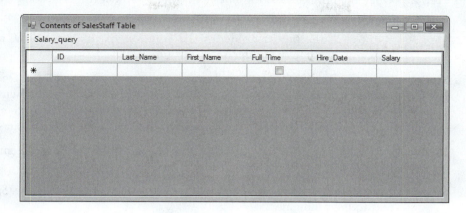

Figure 10-54 Rows filtered by a query named *Salary_query*

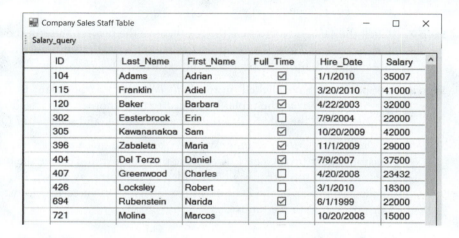

Tutorial 10-8 shows how to filter rows in the *SalesStaff* table.

Tutorial 10-8:
Filtering rows in the *SalesStaff* table

In this tutorial, you will create a query that changes the way *SalesStaff* rows display in a DataGridView control.

Step 1: Make sure Visual Studio is closed. Then, copy the *SalesStaff 1* project folder you created in Tutorial 10-1 to a new folder named *SalesStaff Queries*.

> **TIP:** To copy a folder in Windows Explorer, right-click its name with the mouse and select *Copy* from the pop-up menu; right-click again and select *Paste* from the pop-up menu. The new folder will be named *<name> - Copy*, where *<name>* is the original folder name. Right-click the copied folder and select *Rename* from the pop-up menu. Type the new folder name and press ⏎ Enter. (The same procedure works when copying files.)

Step 2: Open the project from the *SalesStaff Queries* folder (the solution file will still be named *SalesStaff 1.sln*).

Step 3: Right-click the project folder in the *Solution Explorer* window, and choose *Rename*. Rename the folder *SalesStaff Queries*.

Step 4: Select the DataGridView control in the *Designer* window and set its Dock property to None. Then, drag the top edge of the DataGridView control downward about three-quarters of an inch. This will leave room for two ToolStrip controls. Set the DataGridView control's Anchor property so that it anchors on all four sides.

Step 5: Right-click the SalesStaffTableAdapter control in the component tray, and select *Add Query* from the pop-up menu.

Step 6: In the *Search Criteria Builder* window, name the query *Full_Time*. Set its query text to the following:

```
SELECT ID, Last_Name, First_Name, Full_Time, Hire_Date, Salary
FROM dbo.SalesStaff
WHERE Full_Time = 'True'
```

Step 7: Click the *OK* button to save the query. Save the project and run the application. Click the *Full_Time* ToolStrip button and observe that only full time employees are displayed. Stop the program and return to *Design* mode.

Step 8: Suppose you have clicked on the *Full_Time* button, but want to return to displaying all rows in the table. You need to add another query to do that. To do so, right-click the SalesStaffTableAdapter control, and select *Add Query*.

Step 9: In the *Search Criteria Builder* window, name the query *All_Rows*, and keep the existing query text. Click *OK* to close the window and create the query. Notice that a second tool strip has been added to the form, as shown in Figure 10-55. If the upper part of the DataGridView has been covered up, adjust its top border position with the mouse.

Figure 10-55 *SalesStaff* table in a DataGridView, with two query buttons

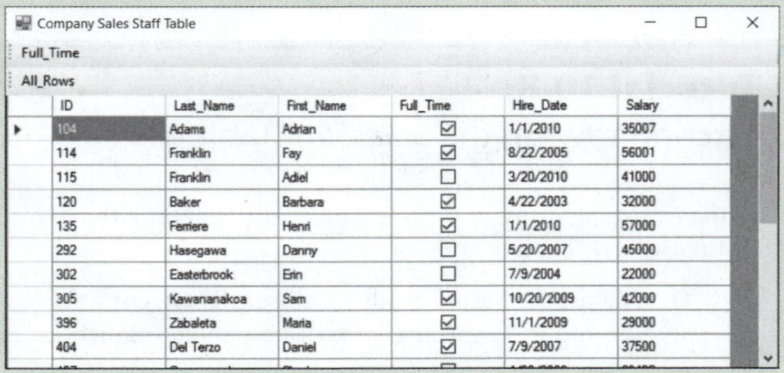

Step 10: Run the program, and click both query buttons. The display should alternate between displaying all rows and only rows for full-time employees.

Step 11: End the program and close the project.

This tutorial has shown you an easy way to create queries that select rows from a database table. Ease of use, however, can mean a lack of flexibility. Eventually, it would be a good idea to let the user modify query values at run time. Later in this chapter we will show you how to use query parameters to pass different values to SQL queries.

Checkpoint

10.17 What does the acronym SQL represent, in relation to databases?

10.18 Why do SQL queries work with any database?

10.19 Write an SQL SELECT statement that retrieves the *First_Name* and *Last_Name* columns from a table named *Employees*.

10.20 How do you add a query to a TableAdapter in the component tray of a form?

10.21 Write a WHERE clause that limits the returned data to rows in which the field named Salary is less than or equal to $85,000.

10.22 Write a SELECT statement that retrieves the *pay_rate*, *employee_id*, and *hours_worked* columns from a table named *Payroll*, and sorts the rows in descending order by *hours_worked*.

10.23 Write a SELECT statement that creates an alias named *Rate_of_Pay* for the existing column named *pay_rate* in the *Payroll* table.

10.24 Write a SELECT statement for the *Payroll* table that creates a new output column named *gross_pay* by multiplying the *pay_rate* column by the *hours_worked* column.

10.25 Write a SELECT statement for the *Payroll* table that returns only rows in which the pay rate is greater than 20,000 and less than or equal to 55,000.

10.26 Write a SELECT statement for the *Payroll* table that returns only rows in which the *employee_id* column begins with the characters *FT*. The remaining characters in the *employee_id* are unimportant.

10.6 Focus on Problem Solving: *Karate School Management* Application

Suppose you are a member of the Kyoshi Karate School and Sensei (the teacher) has asked you to create a management application with the following capabilities:

1. Displays a list of all members, and lets the user sort on any column, edit individual rows, and delete rows.
2. Adds new people to the *Members* table.
3. Displays members having similar last names.
4. Displays payments by all members, permitting the user to sort on any column.

Techniques for completing most of the tasks have already been demonstrated earlier in this chapter. Other tasks will require some new skills, which we will explain along the way. Before beginning to code an application, you would normally consult with the customer to clarify some user interface details. Your next step is to determine which types of controls would provide the most effective user interface. To illustrate, we will do that for the current application:

- For Requirement 1, we will use a DataGridView control. We will set options that permit modifying and removing rows. The user will be able to sort by clicking on column headings.
- For Requirement 2, we will create a data input form with TextBox controls and a DateTimePicker control.

- For Requirement 3, the user will type a partial last name into a text box. The application will display a grid containing all members whose last names begin with the name entered by the user.
- For Requirement 4, we will create an SQL query that combines the *Members* and *Payments* tables and displays the results in a DataGridView control.

When possible, we will avoid duplication of effort by using existing datasets and DataGridView controls.

General Design Guidelines

Each form will have a *File* menu with a *Close window* option. A startup form will display a menu and a program logo. Each major requirement will be carried out on a separate form to allow for future expansion. When the Karate teacher sees how easy the program is to use, he will surely want to add more capabilities.

Before we start to create the application, let's look at the finished version. Doing so will give you a better idea of how the detailed steps fit into the overall picture. In real life, programmers usually create a **prototype** or demonstration copy of their program. The prototype lets you try out different versions of the user interface, requiring some reworking, problem-solving, and discussions with the customer. To save time, we will skip the prototyping stage and move directly to the program implementation.

The startup form, called MainForm, displays a program logo and a menu with three major choices, as shown in Figure 10-56.

Figure 10-56 *Karate School Manager* startup form

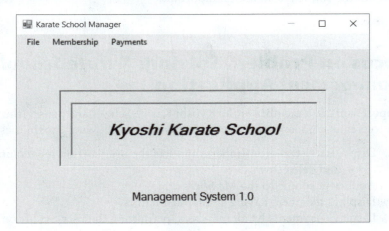

The startup form should be simple, to avoid overwhelming the user with details. The menu makes it clear that our system handles two major types of functions: membership and payments. The menu selections are as follows:

```
File
   Exit
Membership
   List All
   Find Member
   Add New Member
Payments
   All Members
```

Membership Forms

The Karate teacher wants to view a list of all members, so we have provided the *All Members* form, as shown in Figure 10-57. The grid allows users to sort on any column, select and delete rows, and modify individual cells within each row. If the user wants to save changes they've made back into the database, they select *Save changes* from the *File* menu.

The *Find Member by Last Name* form, shown in Figure 10-58, lets the user enter all or part of a member's last name. When the user clicks the *Go* button or presses Enter, a list of matching member rows displays in the grid. The Karate teacher has asked that name searches be case insensitive.

Figure 10-57 *All Members* form

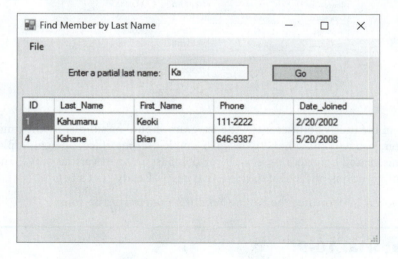

Figure 10-58 *Find Member by Last Name* form

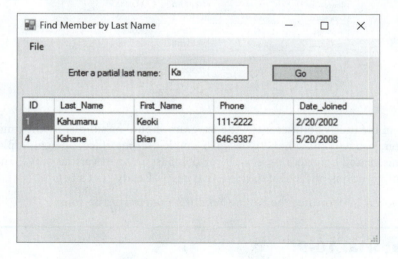

The *Add New Member* form, as shown in Figure 10-59, lets the user add a new person to the *Members* table. After entering the fields and choosing a data from the DateTimePicker control, the user selects *Save and close* from the *File* menu. Or, if the user wants to close the form without saving the data, he or she selects *Close without saving* from the *File* menu.

Figure 10-59 *Add New Member* form

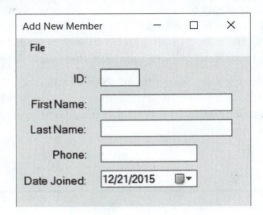

Payment Form

We now turn our attention to the *Payments* subsystem of our application. When the user selects *All members* from the *Payments* menu on the startup form, the *Payments by All Members* form appears, as shown in Figure 10-60. The rows are initially ordered by last name, but the user can sort on any column by clicking on the column header (once for an ascending sort, and a second time for a descending sort).

Figure 10-60 *Payments by All Members* form

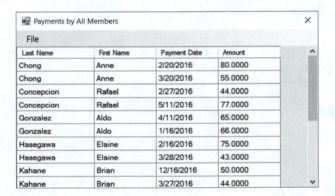

From the user's point of view, the program should be simple. By the time you finish creating it, you will know how to design a simple user interface, open multiple windows, create datasets and connections, search for database rows in various ways, and perform simple configurations of the DataGridView control. Ready? Let's begin.

Tutorial 10-9 creates the *Karate School Manager* startup form.

Tutorial 10-9:
Creating the *Karate School Manager* startup form

In this tutorial, you will create the startup form that first displays when the *Karate School Manager* runs. Although we suggest some font sizes to use in the next several tutorials, you can decide on the optimal font sizes based on your personal preferences.

Step 1: Create a new Windows Forms application named *Karate School Manager*.

Step 2: Change the name of *Form1.vb* to *MainForm.vb* in the *Solution Explorer* window.

Step 3: Open the form and set its Size.Width property to *530*, and its Size.Height property to *320*. Change its Text property to *Karate School Manager*. Change its StartPosition property to *CenterScreen*. Set its MaximizeBox property to *False*. Set the FormBorderStyle to *FixedSingle*.

Step 4: Insert a Panel control on the form and set its Size.Width and Size.Height properties to *390* and *115*, respectively. Insert another Panel control inside the first one, and set its Size property to *360, 80*. Set the BorderStyle property of both panels to *Fixed3D*. Use Figure 10-56 as a guide to the placement of the panels.

Step 5: Insert a Label control inside the smaller panel and set its Text property to *Kyoshi Karate School*. Set the font to Bold Italic 18 points, so it looks like the text shown in Figure 10-56.

Step 6: Add another Label control near the bottom of the form and set its Text property to *Management System 1.0*. Center the text, and use an 12-point font.

Step 7: Add a MenuStrip control to the form containing the top-level menu names *File*, *Membership*, and *Payments*. In the *File* submenu, insert *Exit*. In the *Membership* submenu, insert three items: *List all*, *Find Member*, and *Add New Member*. In the *Payments* menu, insert one item: *All Members*. Insert the & character in each menu item according to your preference.

Step 8: Rename the *File/Exit* menu item to `mnuFileExit`. Double-click the item and insert the following statement in its event handler:

```
Me.Close()
```

Step 9: Save the project. When you run the application, verify that the form closes when you click the *File/Exit* menu item.

> **NOTE:** Some early releases of Visual Studio 2015 have a bug that will cause the following error when you compile the project in Step 9: *'Form1' is not a member of 'Karate School Manager'*. If you see this error message, download the document titled **Startup Form Issue in VS2015** from this book's companion Web site for a simple solution. The companion Web site is at www.pearsonhighered.com/gaddisvb.

Tutorial 10-10 focuses on adding the Membership subsystem to the application.

Tutorial 10-10:
Adding the *Membership / List All* function to the *Karate School Manager*

In this tutorial, you will enable the part of the *Karate School Manager* application that lists all members.

Step 1: Open the *Karate School Manager* project, if it is not already open. Open the MainForm form in the *Designer* window.

Step 2: Add a new form to the project named *AllMembersForm.vb*. Resize the form so it looks similar to the one shown in Figure 10-57. Set its Text property to *All Members*.

Step 3: Open the MainForm form in the *Designer* window. Double-click the *Membership / List All* menu item and insert the following code in its event handler:

```
' Create an instance of AllMembersForm
Dim frmAllMembers As New AllMembersForm

' Display the form.
frmAllMembers.ShowDialog()
```

Step 4: In the *Data Sources* window, add a new data source that connects to the Members table in the *Karate* database. As shown in Figure 10-61, name the dataset *AllMembersDataSet*. Respond with *Yes* when asked to copy the database file into the project.

Figure 10-61 Creating the `AllMembersDataSet` dataset in the *Data Source Configuration Wizard*

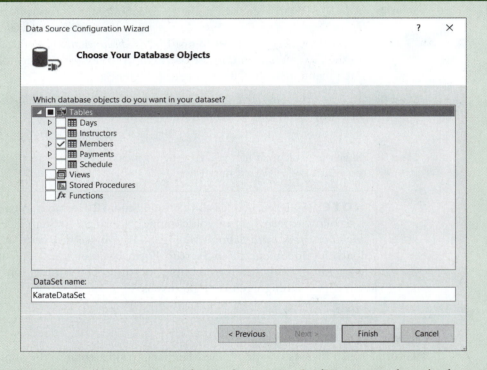

Step 5: In the AllMembersForm form, place a DataGridView control on the form and name it *dgvMembers*. Set its Dock property to *Fill*. Set its BackgroundColor property to *Control*. Set its BorderStyle property to *None*.

Step 6: Click the smart tag arrow icon in the upper right corner of *dgvMembers*, showing the *DataGridView Tasks* window, as shown in Figure 10-62. In the *Choose Data Source* drop-down list, select the *Members* table from the `AllMembersDataSet` dataset. Adjust the check boxes in the *Tasks* window so that only *Enable Editing* is checked.

Step 7: If the grid's columns do not appear as shown earlier in Figure 10-57, click the grid's Columns property. Use the arrows next to the column names list to adjust the column order, as shown in Figure 10-63.

Figure 10-62 Tasks for the *dgvMembers* DataGridView control

Figure 10-63 Adjusting the column order in the DataGridView control

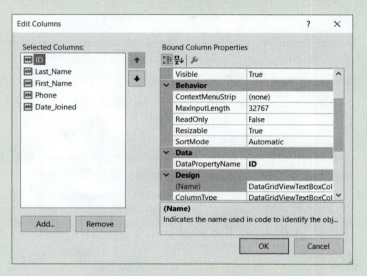

Step 8: Add a *File* menu to the AllMembersForm form, with two submenu items: *Save* and *Close*. In the *Close* menu item's Click handler, insert the `Me.Close()` statement. Insert the following statement in the Click handler for the *Save* menu item:

```
Me.MembersTableAdapter.Update(Me.AllMembersDataSet.Members)
```

Step 9: Save the project and run the application. From the MainForm menu, select *Membership / List All*. You should see a list of members similar to that shown earlier in Figure 10-57. Experiment by modifying one of the grid rows, and selecting *Save* from the *File* menu. Then, close the *All Members* form and reopen it to verify that your changes were saved.

Step 10: End the program and return to *Design* mode.

In Tutorial 10-11, you will add the *Membership / Add New Member* function to the *Karate School Manager* application.

Using a Binding Source to Add Table Rows

When you bind a data source to controls on a form, Visual Studio automatically adds a BindingSource component to the form. The name of the binding source is derived from the dataset name. If a dataset is named `MembersDataSet`, for instance, its binding source will be named `MembersBindingSource`.

A binding source's `AddNew` method adds a blank new row to a dataset. For example:

```
MembersBindingSource.AddNew()
```

The `AddNew` method clears the controls on the form that are bound to the dataset so the user can begin to enter data. The addition does not become permanent until the `EndEdit` method is called as follows:

```
MembersBindingSource.EndEdit()
```

Or, to cancel the operation and not add the new row, call the `CancelEdit` method as follows:

```
MembersBindingSource.CancelEdit()
```

In any case, you have complete control over whether the row is added to the dataset.

Tutorial 10-11:
Adding the *Membership / Add New Member* function to the *Karate School Manager*

In this tutorial, you will add a form to the *Karate School Manager* program that lets users add new students to the *Members* table.

Step 1: Open the *Karate School Manager* program if it is not already open.

Step 2: Add a new form to the project named AddMemberForm. Set its Text property to *Add New Member*. Set its FormBorderStyle property to *FixedDialog*, and optionally set its Font.Size property to 10.

Step 3: In the MainForm form's Design view, double-click the *Membership / Add New Member* menu item and insert the following code in its Click event handler:

```
' Create an instance of AddMemberForm
Dim frmAddMember As New AddMemberForm

' Display the form.
frmAddMember.ShowDialog()
```

Step 4: Open the AddMemberForm form in Design view. Then, in the *Data Sources* window, locate the *Members* table under the AllMembersDataSet entry. Click the down-arrow that appears next to *Members*, and select *Details*. Then drag the table onto the form. This will create a set of data-bound controls. Align the controls as necessary, and move the *First_Name* field above the *Last_Name* field. Set the Format property of the DateTimePicker control to *Short*. Adjust the form's tab stops as necessary. Figure 10-64 shows how the form should appear once you have completed the tutorial. Use the figure as a guide.

Figure 10-64 Adding a new member to the *Members* table

Add New Member	—	□	×

File

ID: [ ]

First Name: [ ]

Last Name: [ ]

Phone: [ ]

Date Joined: 12/21/2015

Step 5: Delete the `MembersBindingNavigator` component from the form's component tray. This will cause the ToolStrip (just under the menu) to disappear. You will not need it.

Step 6: Add a MenuStrip control to the AddMemberForm form. Then, add a *File* menu to the MenuStrip control and insert two submenu items: *Save and close*, and *Close without saving*. Double-click the *Save and close* item and insert the following statements in its event handler:

```
Try
   Me.MembersBindingSource.EndEdit()
   Me.MembersTableAdapter.Update(AllMembersDataSet.Members)
   Me.Close()
Catch ex As Exception
   MessageBox.Show(Me, "Error: " & ex.Message, "Save",
      MessageBoxButtons.OK, MessageBoxIcon.Warning)
End Try
```

These statements call `EndEdit`, which saves the new row in the dataset. Then the `Update` method call writes the dataset's modifications back to the database.

Step 7: Replace the current contents of the AddMemberForm_Load event handler with the following code:

```
Me.MembersBindingSource.AddNew()
Date_JoinedDateTimePicker.Value = Today()
```

The first line puts the dataset into *add new row* mode. The second line initializes the DateTimePicker control to today's date.

Step 8: Double-click the *Close without saving* menu item and insert the following statements in its handler:

```
Me.MembersBindingSource.CancelEdit()
Me.Close()
```

Step 9: Save the project and run the application. Click the *Membership / Add New Member* menu selection, and add a new member. Choose a member ID that did not appear when you listed all members in Tutorial 10-10. Or, if you're not sure, display a list of all members first. After you have added the new member, close the dialog (Save and close). Then select *List All* from the *Membership* menu and look for the member you added. Next, try adding a new member who has the same ID number as an existing member. You should see an error message dialog containing *Error: Violation of PRIMARY KEY contstraint. . .* etc.

Step 10: End the program.

Using Query Parameters

When you write SQL queries that search for selected records in database tables, you usually don't know ahead of time what values the user might want to find. While it is possible to modify an SQL query using program code at runtime, it's not easy because program variables must be concatenated with SQL statements. Instead, the designers of SQL included the ability to pass values to queries at runtime, using what are known as query parameters. A **query parameter** is a special variable (preceded by the @ symbol) that is embedded within an SQL query.

We can show why query parameters are useful. Suppose the user had entered a name in the `txtLastName` control, and you wanted to write a query that would locate all rows in the *Members* table having the same last name. You could write the following statements, but the resulting code is both messy and prone to typing errors:

```
Dim query As String
query = "SELECT ID, Last_Name, First_Name, Phone, Date_Joined " _
   & "FROM Members WHERE Last_Name = '" & txtLastName.Text & "'"
```

Instead, we will insert a query parameter named @Last_Name directly into the SELECT statement:

```
SELECT ID, Last_Name, First_Name, Phone, Date_Joined
FROM Members
WHERE Last_Name = @Last_Name
```

When you call the TableAdapter's Fill method, the second argument is assigned to the query's @Last_Name parameter as follows:

```
Me.MembersTableAdapter.Fill(Me.FindMemberDataSet.Members,
                         txtLastName.Text)
```

If a query contains more than one parameter, the additional required query parameter values are passed as arguments when calling the Fill method. We will use a parameterized query (a query containing a parameter) in Tutorial 10-12.

Tutorial 10-12:
Adding the *Membership / Find Member* function to the *Karate School Manager*

In this tutorial, you will add a form that lets users search for members by last name. You will use a partial string match, so if the user does not know the exact spelling of the member name, they can view a list of similar names.

Step 1: Open the *Karate School Manager* project.

Step 2: Add a new form to the project named *FindMemberForm.vb*. Set its Text property to *Find Member by Last Name*. Set the form's size to 470 by 300, and optionally set the form's Font.Size property to 10.

Step 3: In the MainForm form, double-click the *Membership / Find Member* menu item and insert the following code in its event handler:

```
' Create an instance of FindMemberForm
Dim frmFindMember As New FindMemberForm

' Display the form.
frmFindMember.ShowDialog()
```

Step 4: Add a MenuStrip control to the FindMemberForm form and create a *File* menu with one selection: *Close*. In this menu item's Click handler, insert the Me.Close() statement.

Step 5: Add a label, a text box named txtLastName, and a button named btnGo to the FindMemberForm form. Use Figure 10-58, shown earlier, as a guide.

Step 6: Right-click inside the *Data Sources* window and select *Add New Data Source* from the popup menu. Add a new data source that uses the existing *Karate* database connection. Select the *Members* table, and name the dataset *FindMemberDataSet*. Figure 10-65 shows the *Data Source Configuration Wizard* window, in which you name the dataset and select the *Members* table.

Figure 10-65 Adding the `FindMemberDataSet` dataset to the application

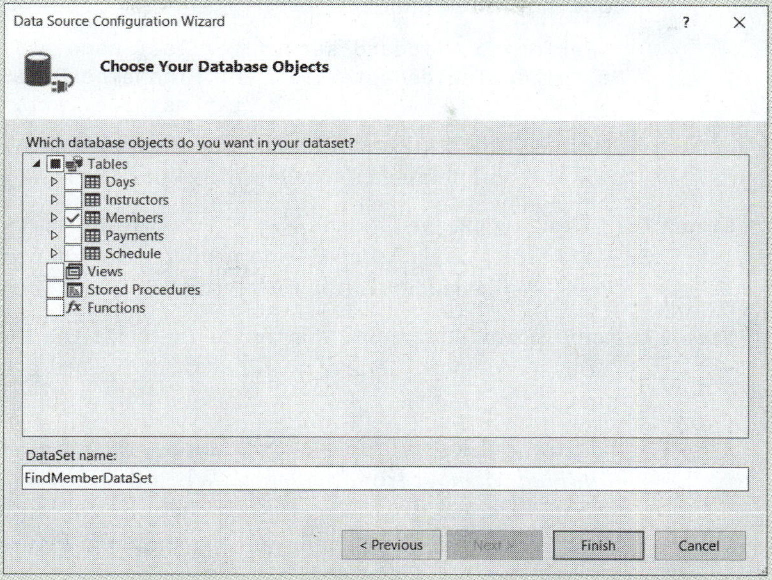

```
Data Source Configuration Wizard                              ?    ×

      🗄    Choose Your Database Objects


Which database objects do you want in your dataset?
  ▲ ■ 🗄 Tables
      ▷ □ ▦ Days
      ▷ □ ▦ Instructors
      ▷ ✓ ▦ Members
      ▷ □ ▦ Payments
      ▷ □ ▦ Schedule
        □ 📄 Views
        □ 📄 Stored Procedures
        □ ƒx Functions



DataSet name:
FindMemberDataSet

                         < Previous   Next >      Finish      Cancel
```

Step 7: Next, you will modify `FindMemberDataSet` by adding a query parameter that lets the program find members by their last names. In the *Solution Explorer* window, double-click to open the designer window for *FindMemberDataSet.xsd*. Right-click the entry labeled *Fill, GetData()*, and select *Configure* from the pop-up menu. Change the query text to the following, and click the *Finish* button:

```
SELECT ID, Last_Name, First_Name, Phone, Date_Joined
FROM dbo.Members
WHERE (Last_Name LIKE @Last_Name + '%')
```

Step 8: Back in the FindMemberForm form, place a DataGridView control on the form and name it *dgvMembers*. Set its properties as follows: BackgroundColor = *Control*; BorderStyle = *None*; Anchor = *Top, Bottom, Left, Right*; RowHeadersVisible = *False*. Use Figure 10-58, shown earlier, as a guide.

Step 9: Click the smart tag in the grid's upper right corner, displaying the *DataGridView Tasks* window. Bind the grid to the *Members* table belonging to the Find-MemberDataSet, as shown in Figure 10-66. Disable adding, editing, and deleting of rows by removing the appropriate check marks.

Figure 10-66 Selecting DataGridView *databinding* options

Step 10: Next, you will add a call to the `Fill` method in the event handler for the button that activates the search. Double-click the *Go* button and insert the following code in its event handler:

```
' Perform a wildcard search for last name.
Me.MembersTableAdapter.Fill(Me.FindMemberDataSet.Members,
                     txtLastName.Text)
```

Normally, the `Fill` method has only one parameter, the dataset. But here you pass a second parameter, which is the value to be assigned to the query parameter.

Step 11: In Design view for the *FindMemberForm* form, select the form with the mouse and set the Form's AcceptButton property to *btnGo*. This will allow the user to press [Enter] when activating the search.

Step 12: Remove any statements that might be inside the form's `Load` event handler. (You don't want the grid to fill with data until a member's name has been entered.)

Step 13: Save the project and run the application. From the startup form, click *Membership/Find Member* from the menu. When the *Find Member* form appears, enter a partial last name, such as *Ka* and click the *Go* button or press the [Enter] key. Your output should be similar to that shown in Figure 10-58.

Step 14: Experiment with other partial last names, checking your results against the grid that displays all members.

In Tutorial 10-13, you will add the *Payments / All Members* function to the *Karate School Manager*.

Tutorial 10-13:
Adding the *Payments / All Members* function to the *Karate School Manager*

In this tutorial, you will create a dataset by joining two tables: *Members* and *Payments*. The dataset will be displayed in a grid.

Step 1: Open the *Karate School Manager* project if it is not already open.

Step 2: Add a new form named *AllPaymentsForm.vb* to the project. Set its Text property to *Payments by All Members*.

Step 3: In the `MainForm` form, double-click the *Payments / All Members* menu item and insert the following code in its event handler:

```
' Create an instance of AllPaymentsForm
Dim frmPaymentsAll As New AllPaymentsForm

' Display the form.
frmPaymentsAll.ShowDialog()
```

Step 4: Back in the AllPaymentsForm form, add a MenuStrip control and create a *File* menu with one submenu item: *Close*. In its Click event handler, insert the `Me.Close()` statement.

Step 5: Right-click inside the *Data Sources* window and select *Add New Data Source* from the popup menu. Add a new data source that uses the existing *Karate* database connection. Select the *Payments* table, and name the dataset *AllPaymentsDataSet*. After the data source has been created, double-click the *AllPaymentsDataSet.xsd* file in the *Solution Explorer* window. Now, in the *DataSet Designer* window, right-click the *Fill, GetData()* entry, and choose *Configure* from the pop-up menu.

Step 6: In the *TableAdapter Configuration Wizard* window that says *Enter a SQL Statement*, click the *Query Builder* button.

Step 7: Add the *Members* table to the upper pane of the *Query Builder* by right-clicking inside the upper pane, and selecting *Add Table*. The *Add Table* window will appear. Select the *Members* table and then click *Add*. Click *Close* to close the *Add Table* window. After adding the *Members* table, a line should appear between the two tables, as shown in Figure 10-67. This line, with a diamond in the middle, indicates that the Member_Id column in the *Payments* table is related to the ID column in the *Members* table.

Figure 10-67 *Query Builder* window, after adding the *Members* table

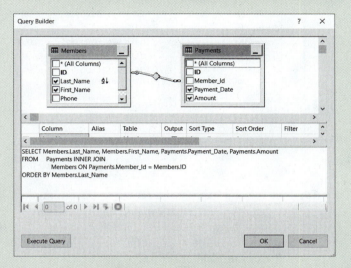

Step 8: Remove all checks from the boxes next to the column names in the upper pane. Then recheck the following fields, in order: *Last_Name*, *First_Name*, *Payment_Date*, and *Amount*.

Step 9: In the *Sort Type* column in the grid pane, select *Ascending* in the *Last_Name* row.

Step 10: Click the *Execute Query* button; a list of names and payments should appear in the bottom pane, as shown in Figure 10-68.

Step 11: Click the *OK* button to close *Query Builder*, and click the *Finish* button to save changes to the dataset. Save your project and close the *designer* window for *AllPaymentsDataSet*.

Step 12: Place a DataGridView control on the AllPaymentsForm form and name it *dgvPayments*. Set its properties as follows: BackgroundColor = *Control*; BorderStyle = *None*; Dock = Fill; RowHeadersVisible = *False*.

Step 13: Open the *DataGridView tasks* window. For the Data Source, choose the *Payments* table of `AllPaymentsDataSet`. Unselect the *Enable Adding*, *Enable Editing*, and *Enable Deleting* check boxes.

Step 14: Save the project and run the application. Display the *Payments by All Members* window. Although the payment information appears, the columns are not in the order we would like. Fortunately, it's easy to modify the column ordering in the DataGridView control.

Figure 10-68 Executing a query containing *Payments* and *Members* tables

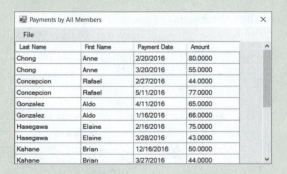

Step 15: Exit the application and return to Design mode. Click the Columns property of the *dgvPayments* grid, causing the *Edit Columns* dialog to open. Set the column order to: *Last Name*, *First Name*, *Payment Date*, and *Amount*. Use the arrows next to the Selected Columns list to change the column order. Optionally, you can use the HeaderText property of each column to modify its displayed column heading. A sample of the form at runtime is shown in Figure 10-69.

Figure 10-69 *Payments by All Members* form

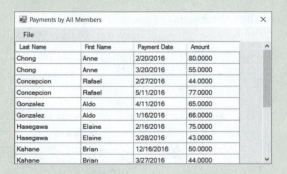

Step 16: Save the project and rerun it.

You've completed this tutorial. You have successfully joined two database tables, using a relation based on the Member_Id table column. You have seen how a dataset can easily join two database tables.

Complete Source Code

Here is a listing of all the source code in the *Karate School Manager* application. Some extraneous comment lines and portions of some procedure headers have been removed:

MainForm.vb:

```vb
Public Class MainForm
    Private Sub mnuFileExit_Click(...) Handles mnuFileExit.Click
        Me.Close()
    End Sub

    Private Sub ListAllToolStripMenuItem_Click(...) Handles ...
        ' Create an instance of AllMembersForm
        Dim frmAllMembers As New AllMembersForm

        ' Display the form.
        frmAllMembers.ShowDialog()
    End Sub

    Private Sub AddNewMemberToolStripMenuItem_Click(...) Handles ...
        ' Create an instance of AddMemberForm
        Dim frmAddMember As New AddMemberForm

        ' Display the form.
        frmAddMember.ShowDialog()
    End Sub

    Private Sub FindMemberToolStripMenuItem_Click(...) Handles ...
        ' Create an instance of FindMemberForm
        Dim frmFindMember As New FindMemberForm

        ' Display the form.
        frmFindMember.ShowDialog()
    End Sub

    Private Sub AllMembersToolStripMenuItem_Click(...) Handles ...
        ' Create an instance of AllPaymentsForm
        Dim frmPaymentsAll As New AllPaymentsForm

        ' Display the form.
        frmPaymentsAll.ShowDialog()
    End Sub
End Class
```

AllMembersForm.vb:

```vb
Public Class AllMembersForm

    Private Sub AllMembersForm_Load(...) Handles MyBase.Load
        'TODO: This line of code loads data into the
        'AllMembersDataSet.Members' table. You can move, or remove it,
        'as needed.
        Me.MembersTableAdapter.Fill(Me.AllMembersDataSet.Members)

    End Sub

    Private Sub SaveToolStripMenuItem_Click(...) Handles ...
        Me.MembersTableAdapter.Update(Me.AllMembersDataSet.Members)
    End Sub

    Private Sub CloseToolStripMenuItem_Click(...) Handles ...
        Me.Close()
    End Sub
End Class
```

FindMemberForm.vb:

```vb
Public Class FindMemberForm

    Private Sub CloseToolStripMenuItem_Click(...) Handles ...
        Me.Close()
    End Sub

    Private Sub btnGo_Click(...) Handles btnGo.Click
        ' Perform a wildcard search for last name.
        Me.MembersTableAdapter.Fill(Me.FindMemberDataSet.Members,
                            txtLastName.Text)

    End Sub
End Class
```

AddMemberForm.vb:

```vb
Public Class AddMemberForm

    Private Sub MembersBindingNavigatorSaveItem_Click(...)
        Me.Validate()
        Me.MembersBindingSource.EndEdit()
        Me.TableAdapterManager.UpdateAll(Me.AllMembersDataSet)
    End Sub

    Private Sub AddMemberForm_Load(...) Handles MyBase.Load
        Me.MembersBindingSource.AddNew()
        Date_JoinedDateTimePicker.Value = Today()
    End Sub

    Private Sub SaveAndCloseToolStripMenuItem_Click(...) Handles ...
        Try
            Me.MembersBindingSource.EndEdit()
            Me.MembersTableAdapter.Update(AllMembersDataSet.Members)
            Me.Close()
        Catch ex As Exception
            MessageBox.Show(Me, "Error: " & ex.Message, "Save",
                        MessageBoxButtons.OK, MessageBoxIcon.Warning)
        End Try
    End Sub

    Private Sub CloseWithoutSavingToolStripMenuItem_Click(...) Handles...
        Me.MembersBindingSource.CancelEdit()
        Me.Close()
    End Sub
End Class
```

AllPaymentsForm.vb:

```vb
Public Class AllPaymentsForm

    Private Sub CloseToolStripMenuItem_Click(...) Handles ...
        Me.Close()
    End Sub

    Private Sub AllPaymentsForm_Load(...) Handles MyBase.Load
        'TODO: This line of code loads data into the
        'AllPaymentsDataSet.Payments' table. You can move,
        'or remove it, as needed.
        Me.PaymentsTableAdapter.Fill(Me.AllPaymentsDataSet.Payments)
    End Sub
End Class
```

Using the ListBox's ValueMember Property

One of the most useful features of a data-bound ListBox control is its ValueMember property. This property identifies a column from the DataTable that is bound to the control. For example, using the *Karate* database, we could select member names from a List-Box and then use the ValueMember property to tell the ListBox to return the member's ID number. Let's see how this is done.

First, we create a data source that links to the *Members* table of the *Karate* database. We name this dataset *MembersDataSet*, shown in Figure 10-70.

Figure 10-70 *MembersDataSet* added to the *DataSources* window

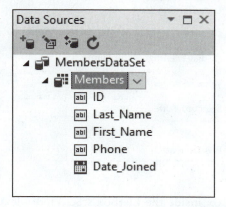

Next, we open the dataset in the *DataSet Designer* window, right-click *MembersTableAdapter*, and select *Configure*, as shown in Figure 10-71.

Figure 10-71 Configuring the query in the *MembersTableAdapter*

In the *TableAdapter Configuration Wizard*, we change the query by combining the Last_Name and First_Name columns into a single column named *Full_Name*. The only other column we need is ID:

```
SELECT ID, Last_Name + ', ' + First_Name AS Full_Name
FROM dbo.Members
ORDER BY Last_Name
```

TIP: The + operator in a SQL query lets you combine the values of two or more columns. When combining columns, you can insert other characters such as commas and spaces.

Next, we add a ListBox to the startup form and bind it to the data source, as shown in Figure 10-72. We set the DataSource property to the *Members* table of our new dataset. The DisplayMember property is set to *Full_Name*, so we can see both the first and last names of each person. We also set the ValueMember property to ID, so when the user selects a member name at runtime, we can get the selected member's ID number.

Figure 10-72 Binding the ListBox to the *Members* table

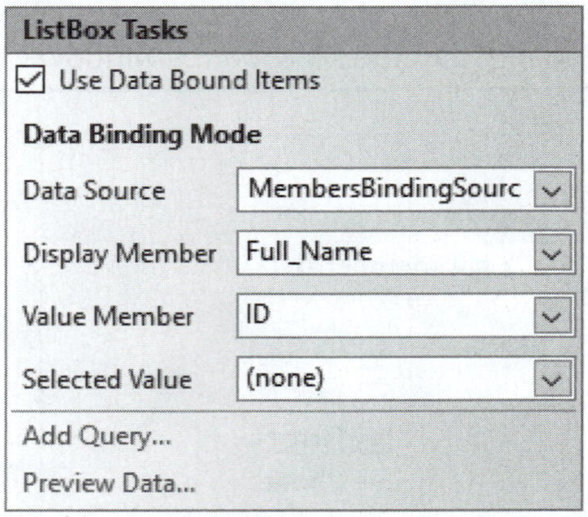

Next, a message box inside the ListBox's SelectedIndexChanged event handler displays the ID of the member selected by the user. The ID is obtained from the SelectedValue property of the ListBox, which is named lstMembers:

```
Private Sub lstMembers_SelectedIndexChanged(...) Handles...

    MessageBox.Show("The member's ID is " &
                    lstMembers.SelectedValue.ToString())
End Sub
```

So now when we run and program and select any member, a message box appears, displaying the member's ID.

A project named *ListBox SelectedValue* that does all of these tasks can be found in the student sample programs folder for this chapter.

Passing the SelectedValue to a Query with Parameters

There are interesting ways to use the SelectedValue property of a ListBox. For example, when a member is selected from a ListBox and we know its ID number, we could pass the ID to the input of a parameterized query. Suppose, for example, that we want to create a query that returns payments by a certain member of the *Payments* table in the *Karate* database. A SQL query to do this is:

```
SELECT Payment_Date, Amount
FROM Payments
WHERE Member_Id = @Member_Id
```

If this query were added to a TableAdapter connected to the *Payments* table, the TableAdapter's *Fill* method would have two parameters: the DataTable to be filled, and the Member_Id parameter that would be passed to the query.

Checkpoint

10.27 In the *Karate* database, which table contains the names and dates when students joined the school?

10.28 In the AllPaymentsForm form, which two tables are required when filling the grid?

10.29 Which property of a DataGridView control lets you alter the order in which columns appear?

10.30 What special operator is used in the WHERE clause of a query when you want to perform a wildcard comparison?

10.7 Introduction to LINQ

CONCEPT: LINQ (Language Integrated Query) is a query language that is built into Visual Basic and can be used to query data from many sources other than databases.

In this chapter you've learned about SQL, which allows you to query the data in a database. Visual Studio also provides another querying language named **LINQ** (which stands for **Language Integrated Query**). Whereas SQL allows you to query the data in a database, LINQ allows you to query many types of data from virtually any source. In this section we will look at how you can use LINQ to query the data in an array. Suppose we have declared the following array of Integers:

```
Dim intNumbers() As Integer = {4, 104, 2, 102, 1, 101, 3, 103}
```

If we want to query this array to get all of the values that are greater than 100, we can write the following statement:

```
Dim queryResults = From item In intNumbers
                   Where item > 100
                   Select item
```

Let's take a closer look at the statement. First, notice that the statement begins with Dim queryResults. We are declaring an object named queryResults, which will hold the results of the LINQ query. Notice that we have not specified a data type. Visual Basic will automatically determine the data type for the object. On the right side of the = operator is the LINQ query. The = operator will assign the results of the LINQ query to the queryResults object. The LINQ query reads:

```
From item In intNumbers
Where item > 100
Select item
```

The results of this query will be all the items in the intNumbers array that are greater than 100. After the statement executes, we can use a For Each loop to examine the values stored in the queryResults object. For example, the following code segment shows how we can add the values to a list box named lstResults.

```
' Create an array of integers.
Dim intNumbers() As Integer = {4, 104, 2, 102, 1, 101, 3, 103}

' Use LINQ to query the array for all numbers
' that are greater than 100.
```

```
        Dim queryResults = From item In intNumbers
                           Where item > 100
                           Select item

    ' Add the query results to the list box.
    For Each intNum As Integer In queryResults
      lstResults.Items.Add(intNum)
    Next
```

After this code executes, the values 104, 102, 101, and 103 will be added to the list box, in that order. If you want the results of the LINQ query to be sorted in ascending order, you can use the Order By operator as shown here:

```
        Dim queryResults = From item In intNumbers
                           Where item > 100
                           Select item
                           Order By item
```

Adding the Descending keyword to the Order By operator causes the results of the query to be sorted in descending order. Here is an example:

```
        Dim queryResults = From item In intNumbers
                           Where item > 100
                           Select item
                           Order By item Descending
```

As you can see from these examples, LINQ uses operators such as Where, Select, and Order By, which are similar to SQL operators. Unlike the SQL operators, however, the LINQ operators are built into the Visual Basic language. When you write a LINQ query, you write it directly into your Visual Basic program. As a result, the VB compiler checks the syntax of your query and you know immediately if you've made a mistake. An application named *LINQ Example* can be found in the *Chap10* student sample programs folder.

> **NOTE:** In this section we've looked only at how LINQ can be used to query the data in an array. LINQ can be used to query any data that is stored in memory as an object. This includes not only arrays and databases, but many other types of data collections.

10.8 Creating Your Own Database

CONCEPT: Visual Studio provides an easy to use tool for creating a database.

Up to this point, you have used existing databases to learn about SQL Server. But there are many advantages to being able to create your own database. You may want to create a database to keep track of your movie collection, or to build a schedule for team activities for one of your classes. Or, perhaps, you may want to keep track of customers for a new business you have started.

For our first example, we will show how to create a simple database to keep track of information about commercial films. It's a good idea to make a quick and easy design of the table structures for the database, using many of the principles discussed at the beginning of the chapter. You can use any ordinary text editor for this purpose. Let's start with a table named *Films*, which holds IDs, titles, directors, and the year of release:

Table name: Films

Field name	Column type
FilmId	primary key, type int, auto-generated starting at 1000
Title	type varchar(80)
Directors	type varchar(80)
Year	type int

Of course, many more fields could be added to this table, for things like the genre, the writers, the synopsis, and so on. But we suggest that you limit your first database tables to a small number of fields. Notice how we're allowing quite a bit of space for long film titles and names for multiple directors. Here's a sample row that could be inserted in the *Films* table:

1000, The Matrix, Andy and Lana Wachowski, 1999

In Tutorial 10-14 you will create the *Movie* database and the *Films* table.

Tutorial 10-14:
Creating the *Movie* database and the *Films* table

In this tutorial, you will create the *Movie* database and design the *Films* table.

Step 1: Create a new Windows Forms application named *Create Movie Database*.

Step 2: In the *Solution Explorer* window, right-click on the project name and select *Add*, then select *New Item . . . .* You should see the *Add New Item – Create Movie Database* dialog window, shown in Figure 10-73.

Figure 10-73 The *Add New Item* dialog window

Step 3: In the *Common Items* group in the left panel of the dialog window, select *Data*. Then select *Service-based Database* from the list of template types in the middle panel, and enter *Movie.mdf* into the *Name* input box on the bottom of the window. Figure 10-74 shows the *Add New Item* dialog with the correct settings. Then click the *Add* button to continue.

Figure 10-74 Creating the Movie.mdf database

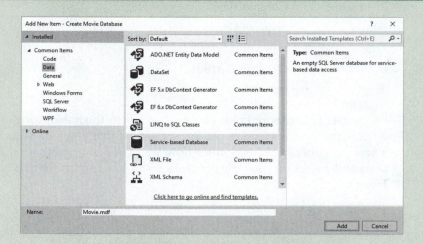

Step 4: Notice that the *Movie.mdf* database filename appears in the *Solution Explorer* window. Double-click this filename. The *Server Explorer* window should appear, containing *Movie.mdf* and a list of subfolders, shown in Figure 10-75. (The Azure entry at the top of this window refers to cloud-based services, which we will not be using.)

Figure 10-75 The *Movie* database, in the *Server Explorer* window

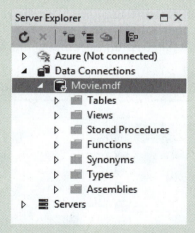

Step 5: In the *Server Explorer* window, right-click the *Tables* folder icon and select *Add New Table* from the pop-up menu. The database table designer panel should appear in your editing area.

Step 6: Insert the following columns for the *Films* table. A sample is shown in Figure 10-76.

Field Name	Column Type	Allow Nulls
FilmId	int	(unchecked)
Title	varchar(80)	(unchecked)
Directors	varchar(80)	(unchecked)
Year	int	(unchecked)

Figure 10-76 Defining the *Films* table columns

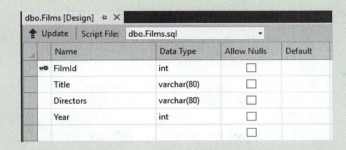

Step 7: Verify that a small key icon appears just to the left of the FilmId field. If not, right-click in the column just to the left of the FilmId name, and select *Set Primary Key*. After doing this, a small key icon should appear next to the field.

Step 8: Click the square just to the left of the key symbol next to the FilmId field to select the field. Then expand the lower panel of the window until you can see the T-SQL code that defines the table. Modify the first line until it looks like this:

```
CREATE TABLE [dbo].[Films]
```

This line tells Visual Studio to create a table named *Films*.

Step 9: Modify the line beginning with [FilmId] until it looks like this:

```
[FilmId] INT IDENTITY(1000,1) NOT NULL PRIMARY KEY,
```

The keyword IDENTITY means that a new FilmId value will be generated automatically each time you insert a row in this table. The (1000,1) notation means that the first FilmId value will be 1000, and each new value, as more rows are added to the table, will increase by 1.

Step 10: Click the *Update* button (⬆ Update Update) in the upper left corner of the table editor window (top pane). The *Preview Database Updates* dialog will appear, as in Figure 10-77. Click the *Update Database* button to confirm that you want to add the *Films* table to the database. After you do this, a confirmation message should appear in the bottom pane, shown in Figure 10-78. Close the table designer window.

Next, you will add some rows to the *Films* table.

Figure 10-77 Database update confirmed

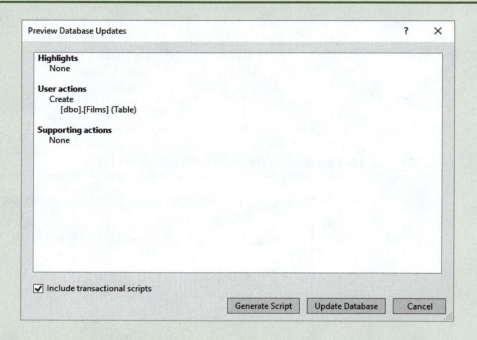

Figure 10-78 Confirmation message after adding the Films table

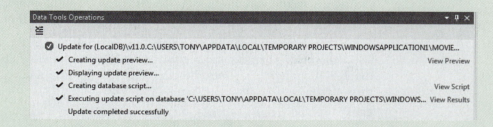

Step 11: In the *Server Explorer* window, double-click to expand the *Tables* folder, then right-click the *Films* table in the Server Explorer window and select *Show Table Data* from the pop-up menu.

Step 12: Add the following table data, beginning with the second row. Do not enter any values into the FilmId column, because the database will create its values automatically:

(Title)	(Directors)	(Year)
The Matrix	Andy and Lana Wachowski	1999
Argo	Ben Affleck	2012
Batman Forever	Joel Schumacher	1995
Rush	Ron Howard	2013
Karate Kid	John G. Avildsen	1984
Hero	Yimou Zhang	2002

Step 13: After entering the last line, click the mouse in any of the rows above it. That should save all of your data entries. Close the table editor. You are finished!

Summary

10.1 Database Management Systems

- A database is a collection of one or more tables, each containing data related to a particular topic. A table is a logical grouping of related information. Each row of a table is also called a *record*. Table columns are also called *fields*.
- Each table has a design, which specifies each column's name, data type, and range or size. A database schema is the design of tables, columns, and relationships between tables for the database.
- A primary key column uniquely identifies each row of a table. A primary key will sometimes consist of two or more combined columns.
- When you use Visual Basic to read a database table, you must select variable types that match the type of data in the table.
- Most well-designed databases keep redundant data to a minimum. They use key fields to link data stored in multiple tables. This reduces data entry errors and reduces the likelihood of inconsistenet data.
- A relationship is a link that relies on a common field value in the primary and foreign keys to join rows from two different tables. The most common type of relationship is a one-to-many relation.

10.2 Database Concepts

- A data source is usually a database, but can include text files and other sources of data outside a program.
- A binding source keeps track of the database name, location, username, password, and other connection information.
- A table adapter pulls data from one or more database tables and passes it to your program.
- A dataset is an in-memory copy of data pulled from database tables.
- A TableAdapter object's Fill method opens a database connection, reads data from a database into the dataset, and closes the connection.

10.3 DataGridView Control

- The DataGridView control allows you to display a database table in a grid. The grid can be used at runtime to sort and edit the contents of the table.
- Visual Basic uses a technique called *data binding* to link database tables to controls.
- A data source usually connects to a database, but can also connect to text files, Excel spreadsheets, XML data, and Web services.
- A binding source connects data-bound controls to a dataset.
- A table adapter pulls data from one or more database tables and passes it to your program.
- A dataset is an in-memory copy of the data pulled from database tables.
- The DataGridView's smart tag opens the DataGridView Tasks window. In this window, you can choose a data source, edit the grid columns, and enable operations on data such as adding, editing, and deleting.

10.4 Data-Bound Controls

- Using a data source, you can bind its fields to individual controls such as text boxes, labels, and list boxes.
- Data-bound controls update their contents automatically when you move from one row to the next in a dataset.
- You can bind an existing data source to a DataGridView control by dragging a table from the *Data Sources* window to an open area of a form. Similarly, you can individually create data-bound controls such as text boxes and labels by dragging individual fields in the *Data Sources* window onto the open area of a form.

- ListBox and ComboBox controls have two important properties that are required when using data binding: the DataSource property identifies the table within the dataset that supplies the data; the DisplayMember property identifies the column to be displayed.

10.5 Structured Query Language (SQL)

- SQL is a universal language for creating, updating, and retrieving data from databases.
- The SQL SELECT statement has an optional ORDER BY clause that lets you control the display order of the table rows.
- Applications often need to filter certain rows when retrieving data from data sources. Filtering, or choosing rows to display in a dataset, is done by creating a query. In SQL, the WHERE statement limits the rows retrieved from a database table.
- The *TableAdapter Configuration Wizard* and *Search Criteria Builder* can be used to modify queries.

10.6 Focus on Problem Solving: *Karate School Management* Application

- This section shows how to create the *Karate School Management* application, which displays a list of all members; permits the user to sort on any column, edit individual rows, and delete rows; adds new students to the *Members* table; displays members having similar last names; and displays payments by all members.

10.7 Introduction to LINQ

- LINQ, which stands for *Language Integrated Query*, is a query language that can be used to select, display, and filter data from virtually any source. The LINQ operators are built into .NET, and as a result, LINQ queries appear as statements in Visual Basic programs.

10.8 Creating Your Own Database

- Always design your database structure before starting to create the database in Visual Studio.
- In Visual Studio, choose the *Service-Based Database* template when creating a database file.
- Always click the *Update* button after entering your table design information.

Key Terms

binding source
components
composite key
criteria pane
data binding
data source
database
database management system (DBMS)
database query
database schema
data-bound controls
DataGridView control
dataset
Dataset designer file
DataSource property
DateTimePicker control

diagram pane design
DisplayMember property
field
foreign key
grid pane
identity column
Language Integrated Query (LINQ)
LIKE operator (SQL)
one-to-many relationship
ORDER BY clause (SQL)
primary key
prototype
query parameter
relation
relational model
results pane

schema definition   table
SELECT statement (SQL)   table adapter
SQL pane   WHERE clause (SQL)
Structured Query Language (SQL)   wildcard (SQL)

VideoNote

Adding a
Database to the
Kayak Rental
Application

Video Tutorial: Adding a Database to the *Kayak Rental* Application

In this sequence of video tutorials, we continue the *Kayak Rental* application by adding a database. We will show how to create a table containing the kayak inventory, a table of kayak tours, and a table that holds the rental history. We will permit the store manager to display and filter the rental history list by choosing either a customer name or a date range. Also, we will modify the code behind the store clerk interface, so rentals may be saved in the database.

- Part 1: Creating the database and adding the *Inventory* table
- Part 2: Adding the *Tours* and *Rentals* (rental history) tables
- Part 3: Saving rentals in the database
- Part 4: Displaying all rental history items
- Part 5: Filtering history items by customer names and rental dates

Review Questions and Exercises

Fill-in-the-Blank

1. A database _____ system is software that is specifically designed to store, retrieve, and manipulate large amounts of data.

2. A database is a collection of one or more _____, each containing data related to a particular topic.

3. A(n) _____ key is a column in one table that references a primary key in another related table.

4. A(n) _____ source connects data-bound controls to a dataset.

5. A table _____ pulls data from one or more database tables and passes it to your program

Multiple Choice

1. Which of the following is an in-memory copy of data pulled from one or more database tables?
    a. Table adapter
    b. Table relation
    c. Dataset
    d. Data record

2. Which of the following is not an SQL Server field type?
    a. bit
    b. datetime
    c. largedatetime
    d. float

3. A Visual Basic Double data type corresponds best to which of the following SQL Server column types?
    a. float
    b. currency
    c. integer
    d. real

4. Which of the following is not a property of a ListBox control?

   a. ValueMember
   b. DataSource
   c. DisplayMember
   d. DataMember

5. Which of the following keywords and relational operators is used by SQL when performing wildcard matches?

   a. `EQUAL`
   b. `LIKE`
   c. `MATCH`
   d. `=`

6. Which of the following structures describes the design of tables, columns, and relationships between tables in a database?

   a. database schema
   b. table template
   c. relationship diagram
   d. relational model

7. Which of the following creates a connection on an external data source such as a database?

   a. Connection manager
   b. Server explorer configuration wizard
   c. Data source connection wizard
   d. Data binding wizard

8. Which ToolBox control displays data directly from a dataset in a spreadsheet-like format, without any programming required?

   a. ControlGrid
   b. DataControlGrid
   c. DataGridControl
   d. DataGridView

9. Which control lets the user select a date using the mouse?

   a. DateSelector
   b. SelectDateControl
   c. DateTimePicker
   d. DateTimeSelector

10. Which of the following indicates a connection between two tables using matching columns?

    a. relationship
    b. column connection
    c. linked fields
    d. common fields

True or False

Indicate whether the following statements are true or false.

1. T F: A TableAdapter's `Fill` method receives a dataset argument.

2. T F: A one-to-many relationship involves associating a column in one table with a column of another table.

3. T F: A primary key can involve only a single column of a database table.

4. T F: A data source field such as *Last_Name* can be bound to a TextBox or Label control.

5. T F: The default type of control bound to DateTime fields is the TextBox.

6. T F: The *Karate School Manager* application joins the *Members* table to the *Payments* table when displaying payments by all members.

7. T F: The *Karate School Manager* application requires you to write special event handling code that makes sorting in a DataGridView possible.

8. T F: When the user makes changes to a dataset, the changes are not permanent unless other measures are taken to write the dataset back to a database.

9. T F: In an SQL Server, query parameter names always begin with the @ sign.

10. T F: Query parameters are passed to datasets as arguments when calling a TableAdapter's `Fill` method.

Short Answer

1. Which property of a ListBox control must be set before a program can use the SelectedValue property at runtime?

2. What type of relationship existed between the *Employees* and *Department* tables in Section 10.1?

3. If the *Employees* table contains a foreign key named *dept_id*, is it likely that the values in this field will be unique?

4. What type of component keeps track of the database name, location, username, password, and other connection information?

5. What happens when you drag a table name from the *Data Sources* window onto an open area of a form?

6. Write a statement that uses a TableAdapter named MembersTableAdapter to add a new row to its dataset. The fields to be inserted are MemberID, last name, first name, phone number, and date joined.

7. Which property of a DataGridView control causes the buttons at the beginning of each row to appear?

What Do You Think?

1. When displaying the contents of the *Payments* table in a DataGridView control, the *ID* column displays by default. What would you do to limit the columns to just *Payment_Date* and *Amount*?

2. Suppose you wanted to add a new row to the *Payments* table in the *Karate School Management* application. How would you determine which *Member_Id* value to insert in the row?

Algorithm Workbench

1. Suppose a database table named *Address* contains fields named *City* and *State*. Write an SQL SELECT statement that combines these fields into a new field named *CityState*.

2. Suppose a database table named *Students* contains the fields *FirstName*, *LastName*, and *IDNumber*. Write an SQL SELECT statement that retrieves the *IDNumber* field for all records that have a *LastName* equal to "Ford".

3. Write an SQL query that retrieves the *ID*, *Title*, *Artist*, and *Price* from a database table named *Albums*. The query should sort the rows in ascending order by *Artist*.

4. Write an SQL query that uses a query parameter to retrieve a row from the *Albums* table that has a particular *ID* value. Retrieve the *ID*, *Title*, *Artist*, and *Price*.

5. Write an SQL query that retrieves columns from the *Payments* table when the *Payment_Date* is earlier than January 1, 2000.

6. Write a statement that fills a table named *Members* in a dataset named *AllMembersDataSet*. The table adapter is named *MembersTableAdapter*.

7. Write an SQL query that retrieves the *ID*, *Last_Name*, and *First_Name* from the *Members* table. You only want rows having a *Date_Joined* value greater than or equal to the value of a query parameter.

Programming Challenges

VideoNote

The *Kayak Browser* Problem

1. Kayak Browser

Create an application named *Kayak Browser* that lets the user select different types of kayaks from a list box. When each ListBox entry is selected by the user, the application must display a description of the kayak type in a Label control. Figure 10-79 shows an example of how the application's form should appear. Use the *Kayaks* database supplied in the student sample programs folder named *Chap10*.

Figure 10-79 *Kayak Browser* application

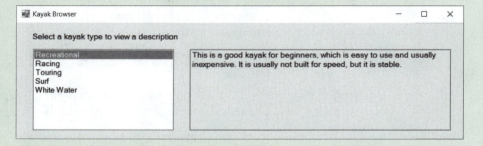

2. Kayak Rental Prices

Create an application named *Kayak Rental Prices* that displays a DataGridView containing kayak types, along with their hourly, daily, and weekly rental rates. Figure 10-80 shows an example of how the application's form should appear. Format all prices with two digits to the right of the decimal point. Use the *Kayaks* database supplied in the student sample programs folder named *Chap10*. Disable adding, editing, and deleting in the grid, and remove the row headers. Remove the underscore characters from the column headings. Suggestion: When you create the new data source, select the *KayakTypes* table. Then, in the *DataSet Designer* window, modify the *Fill, GetData* entry of the TableAdapter, open the *Query Builder* window, and add the *RentalPrices* table. Sort the entries by kayak name. This was the approach used in Tutorial 10-13.

Figure 10-80 *Kayak Rental Prices* application

Name	Hourly Rate	Daily Rate	Weekly Rate
Racing	30.00	80.00	450.00
Recreational	20.00	50.00	250.00
Surf	22.50	55.00	275.00
Touring	25.00	70.00	400.00
White Water	18.00	45.00	230.00

3. **Planning Vacations, Part 1**

   We all like to go on vacations, and sometimes it's fun to anticipate where we might travel in the future. For this exercise, you will open and modify an existing database table named **Locations**, in a database file named **vacations.mdf.** Each row contains a unique integer ID, the name of a vacation city (or landmark), the country containing the city or landmark, the date when you plan to visit, and the number of days you plan to stay. Next, create an application that displays this information in a DataGridView control. Open the database table in the *Server Explorer* window and add at least 10 different vacation spots to your list. Next, you will create an application that displays the database table in a DataGridView control, demonstrated in Figure 10-81.

Figure 10-81 Displaying the Locations table in a DataGridView control

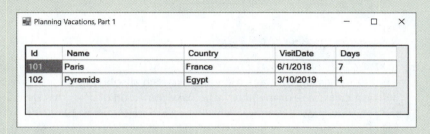

4. **Planning Vacations, Part 2**

   Using the database you created in *Planning Vacations, Part 1*, create an application that lets the user select the name of a vacation city or landmark from a ComboBox control. As the user selects each location name, the remaining labels on the form must display the corresponding country, date, and number of days in Label controls. Also, it is suggested that you group the labels inside a Panel control. A sample is shown in Figure 10-82.

Figure 10-82 Selecting Locations from a ComboBox control

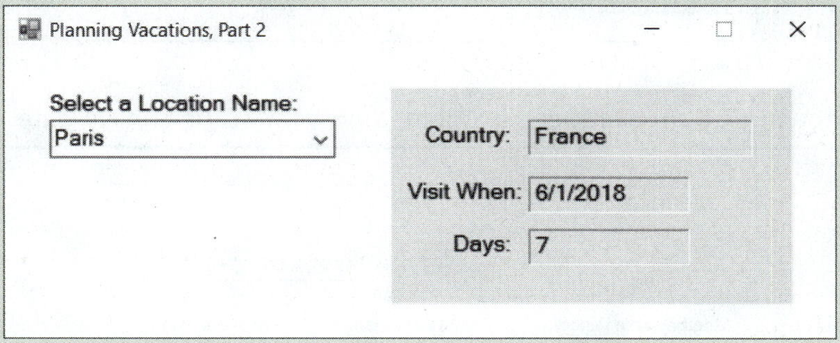

5. **Karate Member Dates**

   Create a program that uses the *Members* table of the *Karate* database. Let the user select a date from a DateTimePicker control. The program must display the first and last names, the phone numbers, and dates joined of all members who joined before the selected date (see Figure 10-83). Use a parameterized query to retrieve the matching table rows and display them in a DataGridView control.

Figure 10-83 Finding members who joined before a selected date

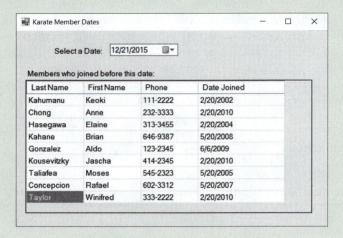

6. **Advanced Karate Member Dates**

   (*Extra challenge project*) Enhance the program you created in Programming Challenge 5 by giving the user a choice between displaying members who have joined before a given date or members who have joined on or after that date. In Figure 10-84, the program shows members who joined before October 20, 2008. In Figure 10-85, a list of members who joined on or after October 20, 2008 is displayed.

Figure 10-84 Showing members who joined before the chosen date

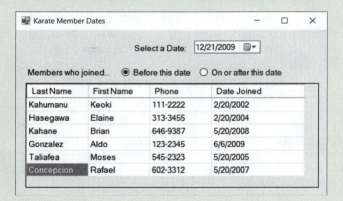

Figure 10-85 Showing *Karate* members who joined on or after the chosen date

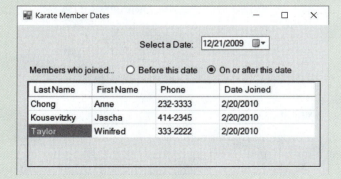

You should create two datasets, one for each type of search. After binding the grid to the first dataset, a component named `MembersBindingSource` is created. If you

then bind the grid to the second dataset, a second component named Members-
BindingSource1 is created. At runtime, when the user switches between the radio
buttons, their event handlers can assign one of the two binding sources to the Data-
Source property of the DataGridView control. That would be a good time to call the
Fill method of the appropriate DataAdapter.

7. **Modify Existing Karate School Payments**

Using the *Karate School* application from Tutorial 10-13 as a starting point, add a
new form, shown in Figure 10-86 that lets the user make modifications to the *Payments* table. The *Details* view works well for modifying the payments, but you also
must add a DataGridView to the form that displays member names and ID numbers. This grid helps the user to associate member IDs with member names.

Figure 10-86 Modifying existing Karate School payments

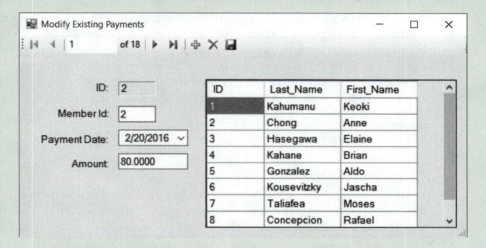

8. **Karate Payments by a Single Member**

Using the *Karate School* application from Tutorial 10-13 as a starting point, add a
new form, shown in Figure 10-87, that lets the user view all payments made by a
single member. The ListBox control displays a list of member names. When the user
selects a name in the ListBox, the DataGridView control on the same form displays
the payment date and amount of all payments made by the selected member.

VideoNote

**The *Karate
Payments by a
Single Member*
Problem**

Figure 10-87 Viewing Karate School payments by one member

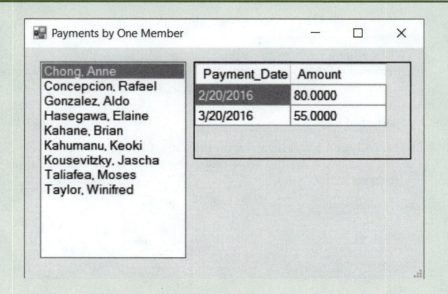

You will need two data sources for this form:

1. The first one selects ID and (Last_Name + ',' + First_Name) from the *Members* table, ordered by Last_Name.
2. The second data source selects Member_Id, Payment_Date, and Amount from the *Payments* table listed in ascending order by Payment_Date. You will need to add a query to the TableAdapter of this dataset. The query returns payment rows that match a particular member ID value.

When the user selects a name from the ListBox, your event handler will obtain the SelectedValue property from the ListBox and assign its value to the query parameter for the query that fills the grid. In that way, the grid shows only payments by the selected member. In Design mode, when you bind the ListBox to the data source, be sure to assign ID to the ListBox's ValueMember property.

9. **Creating the *Actors* Table in the *Movies* Database**

   Tutorial 10-14 showed how to create the *Movies* database and insert a table named *Films*. You may have noticed that the *Films* table did not contain the names of actors. It certainly would not be practical to add a list of actor names to the *Films* table, since the number of actors varies between films, and we might accidentally misspell an actor's name when typing it so many times! Instead, you will create a new table named *Actors* that holds the names and IDs of actors. Here are the table columns:

Column name	Column type
ActorId	primary key, type int, auto-generated starting at 100
LastName	varchar(40)
FirstName	varchar(40)

   Using an online movie database, you can look up names of actors that appeared in the films currently contained in our *Films* table. Here's a sample row, for example, that could be inserted into the *Actors* table, because he was an actor in *The Matrix*:

   100, Reeves, Keanu

   Add at least 10 rows to this table.

10. **Creating the *FilmsActors* table in the *Movies* database**

   Complete Programming Challenge 9 before beginning this challenge. In this challenge, you will add a new table named *FilmsActors* to the *Movies* database. This table links films to actors, since one film may contain many actors, and one actor may participate in many films. Here are the columns:

Field name	Column type
FilmId	type int (1000+)
ActorId	type int (100+)

   When adding rows to this table, be sure you use FilmId values that match those already in the *Films* table, and ActorId numbers that match rows from the *Actors* table. Here is a sample row, for example, indicating that Keanu Reeves (ActorId = 100) was an actor in *The Matrix* (FilmId = 1000):

   1000, 100

   You will need to create a row in this table for every actor in the *Actors* table that acted in a film from the *Films* table. This information is available in online movie databases.

11 Developing Web Applications

In this chapter, you will learn how to create ASP.NET applications that run under Web browsers such as Internet Explorer, Microsoft Edge, Chrome, Safari, and Firefox. Most of the time, we think of running browser-based applications on the Internet, but they can be just as effective on networks limited to a single organization. You can use any version of Visual Studio (Community, Professional, or Enterprise) to create Web applications.

11.1 Programming for the Web

CONCEPT: A Web application runs on a Web server and presents its content to the user across a network, in a Web browser.

HyperText Markup Language

When the Web first became popular, HTML was the only available tool for creating pages with text, graphics buttons, and input forms. **HTML**, which stands for **HyperText Markup Language**, is a standardized language that describes the appearance of pages. It uses special sequences of characters called tags to embed commands inside the text appearing on a Web page. For example, the following line instructs the browser to display "This text is in bold." in bold type.

```
<b>This text is in bold.</b>This text is normal.
```

The <b> tag begins the bold font, and the </b> tag ends it. There are a large number of markup tags, explained by many excellent books. Special Web design editors such as

Microsoft Expression Web and Adobe Dreamweaver make editing HTML easy without having to memorize HTML tags.

But what about Web programming? Rather than display static content such as pictures and text, many applications require Web pages to be fully functional programs. Companies like Microsoft and Sun Microsystems decided that Web applications should be written using advanced programming languages. Web-based technologies and tools such as Java Server Pages and Microsoft ASP.NET were created. Scripting languages such as JavaScript and PHP have made Web programming much easier.

ASP.NET

ASP.NET is the Microsoft platform for Web development. It is called a **platform** because it provides development tools, code libraries, and visual controls for browser-based applications. ASP.NET provides a way to separate ordinary HTML from object-oriented program code. It also provides many powerful controls, which are similar to Windows Forms controls. ASP.NET lets you transfer a lot of your Visual Basic knowledge to Web applications. Visual Studio checks your Web application's code for errors before running it. Visual Basic code can be stored in a separate file from a page's text and HTML, making it easier for you to code and maintain program logic.

Web applications written for ASP.NET consist of the following parts:

- Content: Web forms, HTML code, Web forms controls, images, and other multimedia
- Program logic, in compiled Visual Basic (or C#) code
- Configuration information

How Web Applications Work

Web applications are designed around a **client-server model**, which means that an entity called a **server** produces data consumed by another entity called a *client*. Put another way, clients make requests satisfied by responses from servers.

When you use a Web browser such as Internet Explorer to access a Web site, your browser is the client. A program called a *Web server* runs on the computer hosting the Web site. Web browsers, such as Internet Explorer, Safari, or Netscape, display data encoded in HTML. Web browsers connect to Web sites, causing HTML data to be sent to the client's computer. The browsers interpret, or render the HTML, displaying the fonts, colors, and images from the pages in the browser windows.

Uniform Resource Locator (URL)

A URL (**Uniform Resource Locator**) is the universal way of addressing objects and pages on a network. It always starts with a **protocol**, such as http://, https://, or ftp://. It is followed by a **domain name**, such as microsoft.com, ibm.com, or aw.com. A specially defined domain name for your local computer is called localhost. Then, the URL may end with a specific folder path and/or filename. The following is a complete URL with folder path and filename:

```
http://pearsonhighered.com
```

Displaying a Web Page

What happens when a Web page is displayed by a Web browser? In preparation, a computer must be running a **Web server**. The server waits for connection requests, which occur in two steps:

1. A user running a Web browser connects to the server by opening a network connection and passing a URL to the connection. An example is http://microsoft.com.
2. Using the URL it receives from the user's Web browser, the Web server translates the URL into a physical location within the server computer's file system. The server reads the requested file, now called a **Web page**. The server sends the Web page over the network connection to the user's computer. The user's Web browser renders (interprets) the HTML. Output consists of text, graphics, and sound.

After sending the Web page to the user, the server immediately breaks the connection. It becomes free to handle Web page requests from other users.

After a Web page is displayed, the user may click a **button control** or press Enter, causing the page contents to be sent back to the Web server. This action, callled a **postback**, occurs when the server processes the page contents and resends the modified page to the browser. The processing might involve updating controls and executing functions in the application's compiled code.

Web Forms

Web applications written in ASP.NET use special Web pages called Web forms. A **Web form**, which can be identified by its *.aspx* filename extension, contains text, **HTML tags**, **HTML controls** (such as buttons and text boxes), and special interactive controls called **Web server controls**. The latter, known also as **ASP.NET Server controls**, are interactive controls such as buttons, list boxes, and text boxes that execute on the server. Although they look like HTML controls, they are more powerful because they have a larger set of properties and they use event handler procedures to carry out actions based on user input. In effect, they behave a lot like Windows Forms controls.

The source code for a Web form is usually stored in a related file called a **code-behind file**, with the filename extension *aspx.vb*. This part of the application is called the **program logic**.

Configuration information can be stored in two files. One file, *Web.config*, contains information about the runtime environment. Another file, *Styles.css*, is a **Cascading Style Sheet (CSS)** file containing HTML styles for customizing the appearance of Web forms.

Web Servers

Web applications must be run using a Web server. You have three choices as follows:

- The local web server is installed automatically with Visual Studio. It is easy to use and requires no special security setup.
- **Internet Information Services (IIS)** is a professional production tool, which is available as an option with various versions of Microsoft Windows. It must be configured carefully to ensure security against hackers.
- A remote Web server is typically available through an Internet Service Provider (ISP) or a corporate Web server. You can copy your application to a remote Web server before running it. You must always have a username and password to publish on a remote server.

HTML Designer

HTML Designer is the tool in Visual Studio that simplifies the design of Web pages and Web forms. The designer generates HTML source code and embeds special codes that identify ASP.NET Web controls. It is possible to create Web forms using a plain text editor, but doing so requires considerable practice. We will use the designer in this book. The designer offers the following views of a Web page:

- *Design* view: You can visually edit Web pages, using the mouse to drag controls and table borders. This view most closely resembles Visual Studio's editor for Windows Forms projects.
- *Source* view: You use this view to directly edit the HTML source code that makes up a Web form.
- *Split* view: This view displays the page's *Design* view and *Source* view in separate panels.

Web Browser Support

Web pages would be easier to create if all end users ran the same Web browser. Unfortunately, browsers have different capabilities and characteristics. To make it easier to adapt to different browsers, the Web server automatically detects the browser type and makes the information available to ASP.NET programs. The programs automatically generate HTML that is appropriate for the user's browser.

TIP: Before publishing your Web applications for end users, test them with browsers other than Internet Explorer (the default). Chrome, Safari, and Firefox are good choices. Chrome can be downloaded from www.google.com/chrome, Safari can be downloaded from www.apple.com/safari, and Firefox can be downloaded from www.mozilla.com.

Types of Controls

When you are designing Web forms, the *Toolbox* window contains Web-related controls placed in the following groups:

- **Standard:** This group contains the most commonly used controls on Web forms. Some are close relatives of Windows forms controls, including Label, Button, List-Box, CheckBox, CheckBoxList, and RadioButton. Others are unique to Web programming, such as the LinkButton and HyperLink controls.
- **Data:** Controls for connecting to data sources; displaying database and XML data in grids and lists.
- **Validation:** Controls for validating user input into controls such as text boxes.
- **Navigation:** Advanced controls for navigating between Web pages.
- **Reporting:** Contains the Microsoft ReportViewer control for displaying Web-based reports.
- **Login:** Controls related to authenticating users when they log into a Web site with usernames and passwords.
- **WebParts:** Controls that let a Web site's users modify the content, appearance, and behavior of Web pages directly from a browser.
- **AJAX Extensions:** Controls that provide rich interface experiences in the user's Web browser.
- **Dynamic Data:** Controls that let you automatically generate Web pages from database tables.
- **HTML:** Controls found on HTML Web pages, such as buttons, check boxes, radio buttons, lists, and text boxes. They are compatible with standard HTML, have a limited number of properties, and have no associated classes. Most importantly, they do not generate user events such as Click or SelectedIndexChanged.

 **Checkpoint**

11.1   Describe a Web application in your own words.

11.2   Describe the client-server relationship in a Web application.

11.3   What is a postback?

11.4   Why is ASP.NET called a platform?

11.5   What is meant by *content* in an ASP.NET application?

 ## 11.2 Creating ASP.NET Applications

CONCEPT: You can use Visual Studio to create Web applications in Visual Basic.

Types of Web Sites

In Visual Studio, you select *Open Web Site* from the *File* menu when you want to open an existing Web application. The following types of Web sites are available in the *Open Web Site* dialog box in Figure 11-1: File System, Local IIS, FTP Site, and Remote Site. (You may see a fifth type, Source Control, which we do not discuss in this book.) ASP.NET applications are also known as Web sites or **Web applications**.

A **File System Web site** runs directly under the **local web server** supplied with Visual Studio. The application files can be stored in any disk directory you select, or on a network computer. The server is simple to use and does not leave your computer open to security attacks. This type of Web site is best suited to college laboratory environments and non-administrative users (students). We will use File System Web sites in this chapter.

Figure 11-1 The *Open Web Site* dialog

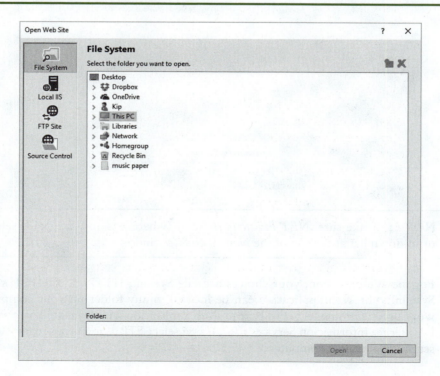

A Local IIS Web site runs under a Windows operating system utility named **Internet Information Services** (IIS). It is a professional-quality Web server with powerful security and configuration features, but requires some expertise to set up and maintain. IIS requires you to have administrative rights on the computer running the server in order to test and debug Web applications.

An **FTP Site** is a web site located on a different machine, usually on the Internet. If you were to sign up for an Internet hosting account, for example, they would assign you some disk storage, a Web address, and a username and password. You would use this information to copy your web site from your local computer to the remote hosting account. FTP stands for *File Transfer Protocol*, a way of copying files from one computer to another that is universally understood by all computer systems.

A **Remote Site** is also a web site located across a network, with a special requirement: It must be configured with Microsoft FrontPage Extensions. Many Internet service providers include this option. When FrontPage Extensions are enabled, you can very easily update your remote site directly from Visual Studio.

Creating a Web Application

VideoNote

Creating a Simple Web Application

In Visual Studio, you create a new Web application (Web site) by choosing *New Web Site* from the *File* menu. The *New Web Site* dialog box provides a list of possible Web sites, as shown in Figure 11-2. In this chapter, we will always select the *ASP.NET Empty Web Site* item when creating new Web sites.

Figure 11-2 *New Web Site* dialog box

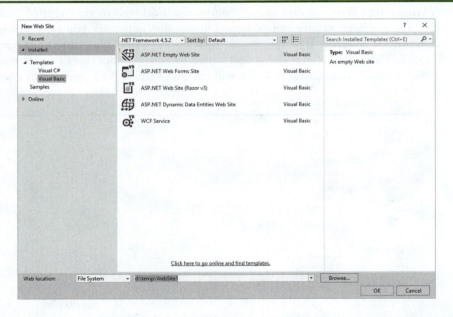

NOTE: Make sure *.NET Framework* 4.5.x (where *x* is any integer) is selected in the drop-down list at the top of the *New Web Site* window.

For the Web location, your choices are File System, HTTP, and FTP. If you select File System, your Web application can be located in any folder on your computer or a network drive. If you select HTTP, your Web application will be located on a Web site set up by Internet Information Services (IIS). If you select FTP, you must already have a Web site set up on a remote computer.

If you create a File System Web site, the edit box just to the right of the location lets you choose the path and folder name for your project. Suppose, for example, you wish to create an application named *Click* in the *C:\WebSites* folder. Then you should name your folder *C:\WebSites\Click*.

If, on the other hand, you were to create an **HTTP Web site**, you would choose a location determined by the Internet Information Services (IIS) Web Server. IIS is beyond the scope of this book.

Application Files

When an empty Web site is created, it contains only one file, named *Web.config*. The *Web.config* file contains necessary configuration data for the Web site. Figure 11-3 shows the *Solution Explorer* after we have created a sample Web site named *Click*. In the figure you can see entry for the *Web.config* file.

Figure 11-3 An empty Web site project

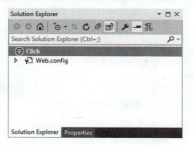

Once we have created an empty Web site, we will add a Web Form file named *Default.aspx* to the project. This is the Web page that will be displayed when running the Web application. When we add the *Default.aspx* Web form to the project, another file named *Default.aspx.vb* is automatically created. This is called a code-behind file because it will hold all of the Visual Basic code that we will write for event handlers and program logic. Figure 11-4 shows a project in the *Solution Explorer* window with a *Default.aspx* file, a *Default.aspx.vb* file, and a *Web.config* file.

Figure 11-4 *Solution Explorer* after adding *Default.aspx*

Displaying the Formatting Toolbar

The Visual Studio Formatting toolbar, shown in Figure 11-5, is useful when creating text on a Web page. If you do not see the Formatting toolbar, click *View* on the menu, then select *Toolbars*, and then select *Formatting*.

Figure 11-5 Formatting toolbar

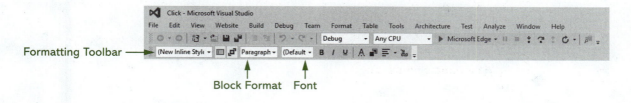

Opening an Existing Web Application Project

To open an existing Web application project, click *File* on the menu, and then click *Open Web Site*. This will display the *Open Web Site* window shown previously in Figure 11-1. Simply browse to and select the folder that contains the project, and click *Open*. The Web application project that is stored in that folder will be opened.

Selecting a Web Browser to Run the Application

When you run a Web application in Visual Studio, a default Web browser is selected for you. It's a good idea, however, to test programs with more than one browser. To see a list of available browsers, right-click your project name in the *Solution Explorer* window and select *Browse With . . .* from the *pop-up* menu. The *Browse With* dialog box shown in Figure 11-6 will appear.

Figure 11-6 Selecting a Web browser to run the application

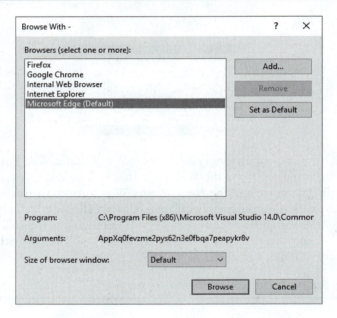

Running a Web Application Project

To run a Web application project you have two choices:

- **Start without debugging:** Press [Ctrl]+[F5] to run the Web application without being able to use the Visual Studio debugger.
- **Start with debugging:** Press [F5] to run the Web application with the ability to use the debugging tools. (Alternatively you can click *Debug* on the Visual Studio menu, and then select *Start Debugging*.) If debugging is not enabled for the project, you will see the window shown in Figure 11-7. To continue running the Web application with debugging enabled, select *Modify the Web.config file to enable debugging*, then click *OK*. (If you decide at this point that you do not want to use the debugging tools, you can select *Run without debugging* and click *OK*.)

Figure 11-7 *Debugging Not Enabled* window

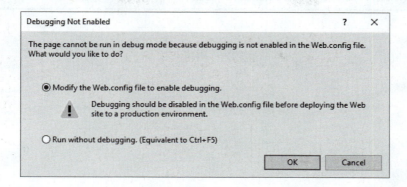

Static Text

Static text is text you type directly onto a form. Web forms behave like documents, similar to Microsoft Word. In Windows forms, labels are needed for all text displayed on forms; but Web forms do not need labels for that type of text. In Figure 11-8, for example, three lines of text were typed directly onto a Web form in *Design* view.

Figure 11-8 Static text typed directly on a form, in *Design* view

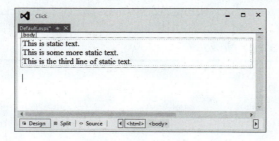

In Tutorial 11-1, you create the *Click* application.

Tutorial 11-1:
Creating the *Click* application

Now you're ready to create your first Web application. Microsoft went to great lengths to make Web development as similar as possible to Windows Forms programming. Your first application will have a short and simple name: *Click*.

As a preparation step, decide which directory you will use to save your Web projects. In our examples we will use a directory named *C:\WebSites*, but you can choose any name.

Step 1: Start Visual Studio.

Step 2: Select *New Web Site* from the *File* menu. Figure 11-9 shows the *New Web Site* window. Make sure *ASP.NET Empty Web Site* is selected. (You should also make sure some version of the *.NET Framework 4.5* is selected in the drop-down list at the top of the window.)

At the bottom of the window, enter the path of the folder where you want to save your new Web site, followed by **Click**. (In the example shown in Figure 11-9, we have entered *D:\WebSites\Click* as the location for the Web site. Choose an appropriate location that exists on your system.) Click *OK* to close the dialog box.

Figure 11-9 *New Web Site* dialog box

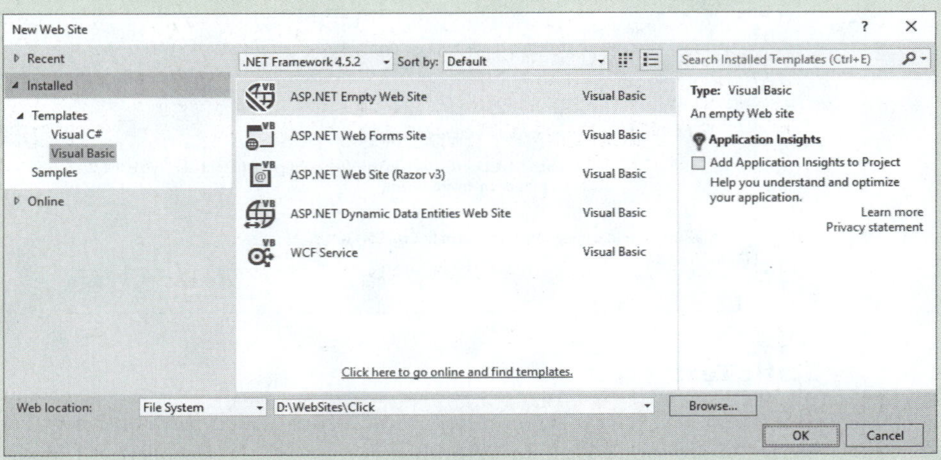

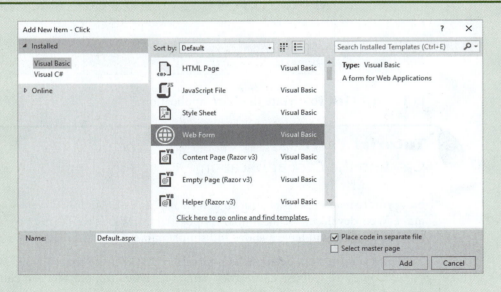

Step 3: Now you will add the *Default.aspx* Web Form file to the project. Click *Website* on the menu, and then select *Add New Item . . .* You will see the *Add New Item* window shown in Figure 11-10. As shown in the figure, make sure *Web Form* is the selected type, and the file is named *Default.aspx*. Also make sure *Place code in separate file* is checked, and *Select master page* is not checked. Click the *Add* button.

Figure 11-10 *Add New Item* window

Step 4: Figure 11-11 shows Visual Studio with the *Default.aspx* Web form open in *Source* view. At the bottom of the editor window you should see three tabs named *Design*, *Split*, and *Source*. The *Design* tab displays the Web form just as it would when running in a Web browser. If you select the *Split* tab, the view splits, showing the form's XHTML code in one window and the form in *Design* view in another. If you select the *Source* tab, you see only the form's XHTML code.

Figure 11-11 After adding the *Default.aspx* Web form

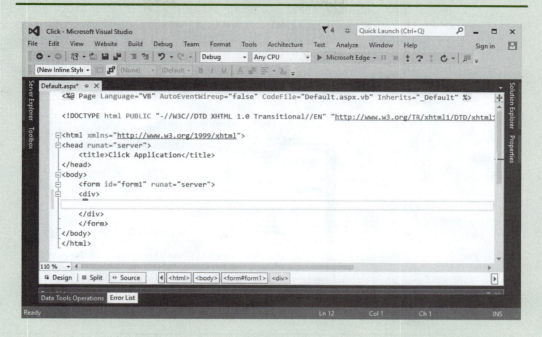

Step 5: Next, you will create a title that displays in the title bar of the Web browser when the application runs. Switch to *Design* view, click inside the Web page, select *DOCUMENT* from the drop-down list that appears in the *Properties* window, and then set the Title property to *Click Application*. Figure 11-12 shows the appearance of the *Properties* window.

Figure 11-12 Properties window for the Document object

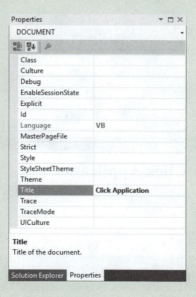

Step 6: Click inside the light blue box that appears on the form in *Design* view. Then, select *Toolbars* from the *View* menu, and then select *Formatting* (if it is not already selected). The formatting toolbar should appear just below the standard toolbar. Look for the *Block Format* drop-down list on the left side of the

formatting toolbar (see Figure 11-13). Select *Heading 1 <H1>*. This will cause a small tag labeled *h1* to appear in the upper-left corner of the light blue box on the form, as shown in Figure 11-14. The *Block Format* list contains a list of standard HTML formats that affect the font size, color, and other attributes.

Figure 11-13 Block format drop-down list, on formatting toolbar

Figure 11-14 *h1* tag displayed

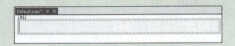

Step 7: Click the mouse inside the box labeled *h1* on the Web form and type *My Click Application*. Press Enter to move to the next line. Figure 11-15 shows a sample of your work so far.

Figure 11-15 After typing the program heading in *Heading 1* style

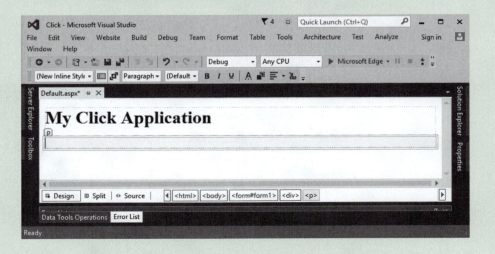

Step 8: Double-click the Button control icon in the *Toolbox* to create a Button control on your form. In the *Properties* window, set its Text property to *Click Here*. Set its ID property to btnClick.

Step 9: Click the mouse just to the right of the button and press [Enter] to move to the next line. Insert a Label control on the next line. Set its ID property to `lblMessage` and erase its Text property. A sample of the form in *Design* view is shown in Figure 11-16.

Figure 11-16 Design window, after adding Button and Label controls

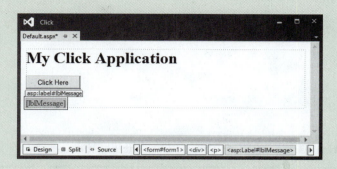

Step 10: Next, you will add code to the button's Click event handler that assigns a string to the label. Double-click the Button control and add the following statement (shown in bold) to its event handler:

```
Protected Sub btnClick_Click(...) Handles btnClick.Click
    lblMessage.Text = "Thank you for clicking the button!"
End Sub
```

You have opened the file named *Default.aspx.vb*, called the code-behind file for this Web form. The Visual Basic code in this file is contained in a class named `_Default` (the same name as the form). It works almost exactly the same as code written for Windows Forms applications.

Step 11: Save the project, and run the application by pressing [Ctrl]+[F5]. When the Web browser opens your application, click the *Click Here* button. A message should appear below the button, as shown in Figure 11-17. Our example uses the Microsoft Edge Web browser, but your computer may display a different browser, based on its default settings.

Step 12: Close the browser to end the application.

Let's take a final look at the contents of the Web page, which is in many ways like a text document. In the *Design* view, you can type text directly onto a Web page. Text typed directly on a page is called *static text* because it does not require the use of Label controls. The button on your Web page that says *Click Here* is an ASP.NET server control. The blank Label control named *lblMessage* is also an ASP.NET server control. You may want to try adding more random text, buttons, and labels to the Web page. Experiment with using HTML styles, available in the drop-down list on the left side of the formatting toolbar.

Figure 11-17 After clicking the button in the *Click* application

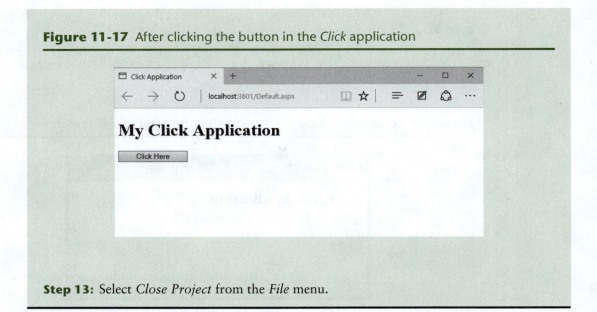

Step 13: Select *Close Project* from the *File* menu.

 Checkpoint

11.6 Name three types of Web sites you can create with Visual Studio.

11.7 When you edit a Web page, which tab must you click to switch from the page's *Source* view to *Design* view?

11.8 How do you select from a list of Web browsers when running your Web application?

11.9 What is static text, and is it similar to or different from Label controls in Windows forms?

11.10 In the *Click* application, how did you specify the block format named *Heading 1* for the first line of text in the Web form?

11.11 What happens the first time you run a Web application in Debug mode?

11.3 Web Server Controls

CONCEPT: Web Server controls are similar to controls used in Windows applications. You use Web Server controls to make ASP.NET Web applications interactive.

Web server controls make ASP.NET applications dynamic and interactive. The controls are powerful because each is defined by a class with a rich set of properties, methods, and events. The controls look and feel like Windows Forms controls, making them easy for Visual Basic programmers to learn. We often refer to Web server controls simply as *Web controls*.

The following Web controls are the ones you are likely to use often. Except where noted by an asterisk (*), all have counterparts among the controls used on Windows forms.

- Button
- ImageButton
- LinkButton
- TextBox
- Label
- RadioButton
- RadioButtonList*
- CheckBox

- CheckBoxList*
- ListBox
- DropDownList (similar to ComboBox control)
- Image (similar to PictureBox control)
- Calendar*
- HyperLink*

Web controls have similar properties to their Windows Forms counterparts. Examples of such properties are Text, Enabled, Visible, Font, BorderStyle, ReadOnly, and TabIndex. The following, however, are a few important differences between Web controls and Windows controls:

- The ID property of Web controls is the counterpart to the Name property of Windows controls.
- Web controls have an important new property named AutoPostBack.
- Web controls lose their runtime properties when the user moves away from the current page. Special programming techniques, called *saving state*, are available to overcome this challenge.

How Web Controls Are Processed

Web server controls are unique to ASP.NET. When a user connects to an ASP.NET Web page, a special process takes place, as shown in Figure 11-18. In Step 2, the Web server reads and interprets the Web controls on the page and executes Visual Basic statements in the application's code-behind file. In Step 3, the server creates a modified Web page consisting of standard HTML tags and controls. In Step 4, the modified Web page is sent back to the user and displayed in the Web browser.

Figure 11-18 Connecting to ASP Web pages

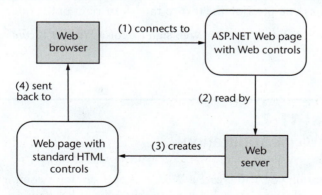

Label Control

The Web **Label control** is almost identical to the Label control on Windows forms. When displaying text, you need to use a Label only if its contents will change at runtime, or if you plan to change its Visible property. Always assign a name to a Label's ID property so you can access it in code. You can create interesting effects by varying the BorderStyle and BorderWidth properties, as shown in Figure 11-19.

Figure 11-19 *BorderStyle* and *BorderWidth* samples for the Label control

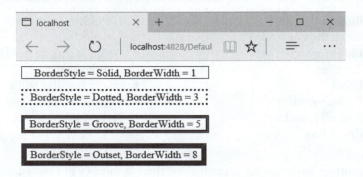

TextBox Control

The **TextBox Web control** is similar in many ways to the TextBox control for Windows forms. The Text property holds text input by the user. The MaxLength property lets you limit the number of characters the user is permitted to type. The TextMode property has the following choices:

- SingleLine: permits the user to enter only a single line of input
- MultiLine: permits the user to enter multiple lines of input
- Password: characters typed by the user appear as asterisks

Internet Explorer and other browsers behave differently when using the TextBox control. To be as compatible as possible with all Web browsers, you should use the Columns property to control the width of the text box. If you want the user to enter multiple lines of input, set the Rows property accordingly.

CheckBox Control

The **CheckBox control** is almost identical to the CheckBox in Windows forms applications. Use the Text property to set the visible text, and evaluate the Checked property at runtime to determine whether the control has been checked by the user. The TextAlign property lets you position the text to the left or right of the box.

In Tutorial 11-2, you create a Web sign-up for a *Student Picnic* application.

Tutorial 11-2:
Student Picnic application

VideoNote

The *Student Picnic* application

In this tutorial, you will create a Web sign-up form for a computer department picnic. It will have a title, text boxes for a user to enter his or her name, a check box, and a button that displays a confirmation message. Figure 11-20 shows the program's output after the *Confirm* button was clicked.

Figure 11-20 The *Student Picnic* application

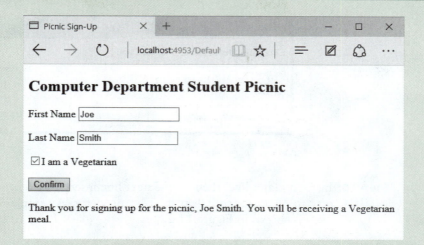

Step 1: Select *New Web Site* from the Visual Studio *File* menu. In the *New Web Site* window select *ASP.NET Empty Web Site* as the type, and set the project folder name to *Picnic*, using the same directory path you used in Tutorial 11-1. (If you are using Visual Studio, make sure *.NET Framework 4.5* is selected in the drop-down list at the top of the *New Web Site* window.)

Step 2: Add a new Web form named *Default.aspx* to the project.

Step 3: With *Default.aspx* open in *Design* view, select *DOCUMENT* in the *Properties* window and set its Title property to *Picnic Sign-Up*. This text will appear in the browser's title bar when the application runs.

Step 4: Type the heading *Computer Department Student Picnic* directly onto the form (inside the box that appears near the top of the form), and press [Enter]. Then select the first line of text with the mouse and set its block format style to *Heading 2 <H2>*. (The *Block Format* tool is located on the left side of the formatting toolbar.)

Step 5: Type *First Name* and *Last Name* on separate lines, leaving a blank line between them.

Step 6: Insert a single space and a TextBox control at the end of the same line as First Name. Set its ID property to `txtFirst`.

Step 7: Insert a single space and a TextBox control at the end of the same line as Last Name. Set its ID property to `txtLast`. A sample of the form in *Design* view is shown in Figure 11-21.

Step 8: After a blank line, insert a CheckBox control and set its ID property to `chkVegetarian`. Set its Text property to *I am a Vegetarian*.

Step 9: Insert a blank line, then on the next line insert a Button control. Set its ID property to `btnConfirm`, and set its Text property to *Confirm*.

Figure 11-21 *Picnic* application *Design* view, after inserting the TextBox controls

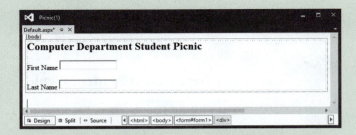

Step 10: Insert a blank line, then on the next line insert a Label control. Set its ID property to lblMessage. Clear its Text property. A sample of the form in *Design* view is shown in Figure 11-22.

Figure 11-22 *Picnic* application, after inserting all controls

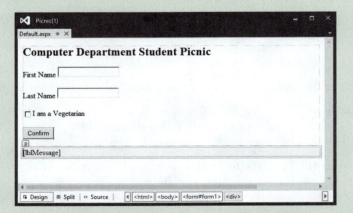

Step 11: Next, you will insert code in the *Confirm* button's Click event handler. Double-click the button and add the following statements, shown in bold:

```
Protected Sub btnConfirm_Click(...) Handles btnConfirm.Click
    lblMessage.Text = "Thank you for signing up for the " &
        "picnic, " & txtFirst.Text & " " & txtLast.Text & "."
    If chkVegetarian.Checked = True Then
        lblMessage.Text &= " You will be receiving a " &
            "Vegetarian meal."
    End If
End Sub
```

Step 12: Save the application and press Ctrl+F5 to run it. Enter a person's name, click the check box, and click the *Submit* button. The output should show the name and an additional comment about the meal because the check box was selected. The application's sample output was shown earlier in Figure 11-20.

Event Handling in Web Forms

Events are fired in a different sequence in Web forms than they are in Windows forms. In a Web form, the Page_Load event occurs when the page is first loaded into the user's browser, and again every time the page is posted back to the server. The Web form shown in Figure 11-23 inserts a message in the list box every time the Page_Load event fires. From the program display, we can see that Page_Load fired when the page was first displayed.

Figure 11-23 Loading a Web form

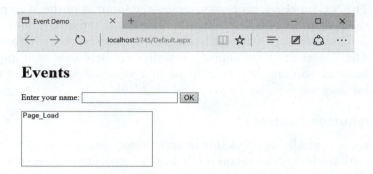

When the user types in a name and clicks the *OK* button, as shown in Figure 11-24, the Page_Load event fires again because a postback event occurs. Next, the TextChanged and Button Click event events are fired. This unusual event sequence can be unsettling if you expect the TextChanged event to fire immediately, as it does in Windows Forms applications. In particular, you must be careful not to execute any code in the Page_Load event handler that changes the states of controls whose event handlers have not yet had a chance to execute.

Figure 11-24 After entering a name and clicking the *OK* button

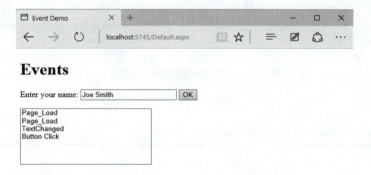

The AutoPostBack Property

When a control's **AutoPostBack property** equals *True*, clicking on the control causes the form to be posted back to the server. You might, for example, want to trigger a database row lookup when the user makes a selection in a list box. The server redisplays the form quickly or slowly, depending on how busy it is at the moment.

AutoPostBack defaults to *False* for the following controls: CheckBox, CheckBoxList, DropDownList, ListBox, ListControl, RadioButton, RadioButtonList, and TextBox. Not all controls have an AutoPostBack property. In particular, the Button, LinkButton, and ImageButton controls automatically post the current page back to the server.

HyperLink, ImageButton, LinkButton, and RadioButtonList

HyperLink Control

The **HyperLink control** provides a simple, easy way to add a link to your page that lets users navigate from the current page to another page. The link appears as underlined text. The HyperLink control does not generate any events, but it has three important properties as follows:

- The Text property contains the text shown to the user at runtime.
- The NavigateURL property contains the location of the Web page you would like the program to display when the user clicks the link. The property editor has a *Browse* button you can use to locate Web pages within your project.
- The Target property controls whether the new page will appear in the current browser window (the default) or in a separate window. To open in a separate browser window, set Target equal to *_blank*.

ImageButton Control

Web pages typically use clickable images as navigation tools. You can create the same effect with the **ImageButton control**. It does not look like or bounce like a typical button—instead, it simply shows an image. When the user hovers the mouse over the image, the mouse cursor changes shape. When the user clicks the image, a Click event is generated.

Assign an image's relative URL (path from the current page to the image file location) to the button's ImageUrl property. Ordinarily, you copy the image file into your project folder. The button generates a Click event when the image is clicked by the user. An example of a relative URL is *Images/photo.gif*, where the file named *photo.gif* is located in the *Images* subdirectory.

LinkButton Control

The **LinkButton control** looks and behaves much like a HyperLink control, with one major difference: it generates a Click event. You can write an event handler that executes when the user clicks the button. Figure 11-25 shows samples of HyperLink, ImageButton, and LinkButton controls. The latter two controls fire Click events, so the labels on the right side of the figure have been filled by the Click event handlers. See the *Button Demo* application in the student sample programs folder for this chapter.

Figure 11-25 Examples of button-type controls

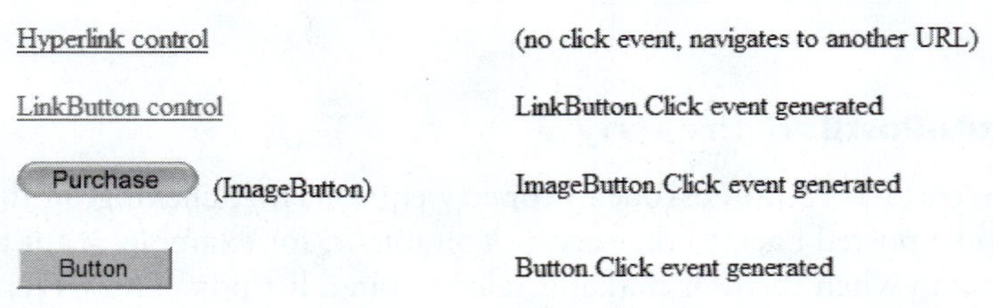

RadioButtonList Control

The **RadioButtonList control** displays a group of radio buttons, as shown in Figure 11-26. You can create individual **RadioButton controls**, but the RadioButtonList is easier to use. Similar to a ListBox, it has SelectedIndex, SelectedItem, and SelectedValue properties. You can arrange the buttons horizontally or vertically, using the RepeatDirection property. You can use the BorderStyle, BorderWidth, and BorderColor properties to create a frame around the buttons. It has an Items property containing ListItem objects. You can add items using the *ListItem Collection Editor* window, as shown in Figure 11-27.

The following event handler displays the selected item in a RadioButtonList control named radDrinks. Because we have set its AutoPostBack property to true, this event handler fires each time the user makes a selection:

```
Protected Sub radDrinks_SelectedIndexChanged(...) Handles
radDrinks.SelectedIndexChanged

    lblSelected.Text = radDrinks.SelectedItem.ToString()
End Sub
```

Figure 11-26 *RadioButtonList* example

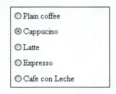

Figure 11-27 *ListItem Collection Editor* window

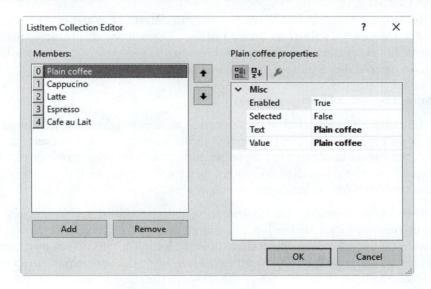

ListBox Control

In many ways, the Web **ListBox control** is similar to the Windows forms ListBox control. It has an Items collection and a SelectedIndexChanged event. You can retrieve the following properties at runtime:

- **SelectedIndex:** returns the index of the selected item
- **SelectedItem:** returns the currently selected item, a ListItem object
- **SelectedValue:** returns the contents of the selected item's Value property

In Figure 11-28, the selected item from a list of sales staff members is displayed in a label below the *OK* button.

Figure 11-28 Displaying the selected item of a ListBox control

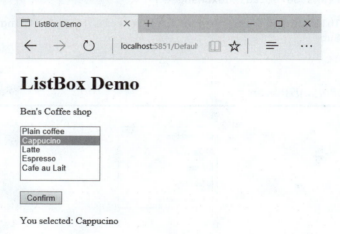

SelectionMode

You can use the SelectionMode property to determine whether users can select only a single item or multiple items from a ListBox. The two possible choices are *Single* and *Multiple*. In *Multiple* mode, the user can hold down the Ctrl key to select multiple individual items or hold down the Shift key to select a range of items.

SelectedIndexChanged Event

You can use a SelectedIndexChanged event handler to respond to selections by the user in any list-type control. There is one important consideration, however: the AutoPostBack property must be set to *True* if you want the user's selection to be detected immediately. Otherwise, the SelectedIndexChanged event will not fire until the form is posted back to the server by some other control (such as a button).

When you set AutoPostBack to *True* for a list-type control, users experience a short delay each time they click on the list. Depending on the Web server's response time, the delay could cause performance problems. Most Web applications do not post back to the server every time users select from list-type controls. Instead, the sites use button controls to post all selections on the page back to the server at the same time.

CheckBoxList Control

The **CheckBoxList control** looks like a group of check boxes, but works just like a List-Box. It has SelectedIndex, SelectedItem, and SelectedValue properties. It has an Items collection, and each item has a Selected property (*True* or *False*). Figure 11-29 shows a CheckBoxList control with a 1-pixel-wide solid border.

Figure 11-29 CheckBoxList control

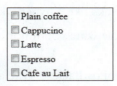

Usually, you will want to iterate over the Items collection to find out which boxes have been checked. The following code sample collects the captions from all selected Check-Boxes and places the captions in a Label.

```
Dim item As ListItem
lblResult.Text = "You selected "
For Each item In chkDrinks.Items
    If item.Selected Then
        lblResult.Text &= item.ToString() + ", "
    End If
Next
```

DropDownList Control

The **DropDownList control** lets the user select a single item from a list. There are two noticeable differences between the DropDownList and its Windows Forms counterpart, the ComboBox. First, in a DropDownList, the initial value of SelectedIndex is always 0, causing the first item to display when the form is loaded. Second, users cannot enter an arbitrary string into the DropDownList, as they can in a ComboBox.

Figure 11-30 shows a simple example of a `DropDownList` when first displayed on a Web form.

The following code shows how to find out which item was selected in a DropDownList named `ddlTours`. The DropDownList does not generate a postback event, so we must write code in a separate Click handler for a Button control to get the selected item.

```
Protected Sub btnCheck_Click(...) Handles btnCheck.Click

    lblResult.Text = "You selected: " &
      ddlTours.SelectedItem.ToString()
End Sub
```

Figure 11-30 Using the DropDownList control

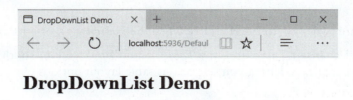

Checkpoint

11.12 Which Web control is the counterpart to the ComboBox in Windows forms?

11.13 Which Web control displays an image and fires a Click event?

11.14 Which Web control looks like a hyperlink and fires a Click event?

11.15 How can you determine which button in a RadioButtonList control was selected by the user?

11.16 How does setting AutoPostBack to *True* affect a ListBox control?

11.17 Which list-type control automatically initializes its SelectedIndex property to zero?

11.4 Designing Web Forms

CONCEPT: HTML tables can be used to design a Web application's user interface. HTML tables provide a convenient way to align the elements of a Web form.

Using Tables to Align Text and Controls

An **HTML table** is an essential tool for designing the layout of Web forms. You can use it to align text, graphics, and controls in rows and columns. In Figure 11-31, for example, a table contains five rows and three columns. Static text has been placed in column 1, and text boxes have been placed in column 3. The table cells in column 1 are right justified, and the cells in column 3 are left justified. Column 2 is intentionally left blank so it can be used as a spacer between the first and third columns.

Figure 11-31 Aligning text and text boxes with a table

First Name		
Last Name		
Street		
City		
State		Zip

There are two ways to insert a table when the *Design* view of a form is active:

- Select *Insert Table* from the *Table* menu. When you do so, the *Insert Table* dialog box appears, letting you set various table layout options (see Figure 11-32).

Figure 11-32 *Insert Table* dialog box

- Select the Table control from the HTML section of the *Toolbox* window. A basic 3 × 3 table is placed on the form, which you can resize by dragging the handles along its right and bottom sides. A sample is shown in Figure 11-33.

Figure 11-33 Empty HTML Table control, in *Design* view

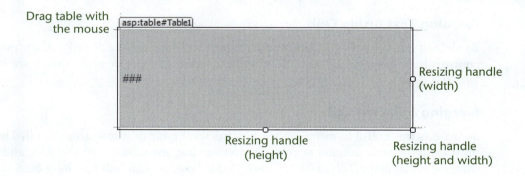

Although the table borders show in *Design* view, they are invisible at runtime because (by default) the border width equals zero. If you set the Border property to an integer value greater than zero, the table borders appear at runtime. An example is shown in Figure 11-34.

Figure 11-34 Table displayed at runtime with Border = *1* and text in each cell

A	B	C
D	E	F
G	H	I

Adjusting Row Heights and Column Widths

To adjust the width of a column, hover the mouse over the double bar along the column's right border. When the mouse cursor changes to a double vertical bar with arrows pointing left and right, hold down the mouse button and drag the border to its new location. As you do so, the column width (in pixels) displays inside the column. Often, the displayed number gives you a more accurate idea of the column width than the table's visual display.

To adjust the height of a row, hover the mouse over the row's lower border. When the mouse cursor changes to a double horizontal line with arrows pointing up and down, drag the mouse and the border up or down. As you do so, the column height (in pixels) displays inside the column. Often, the displayed number gives you a more accurate idea of the column height than the table's visual display.

Inserting Rows and Columns

The *Table* menu gives you tools to insert new rows and columns, relative to the currently selected cell:

- To insert a row above the current row, select *Insert* from the *Table* menu, and select *Row Above*. Or, press the Ctrl+Alt+↑ keyboard shortcut.
- To insert a row below the current row, select *Insert* from the *Table* menu, and select *Row Below*. Or, press the Ctrl+Alt+↓ keyboard shortcut.
- To insert a column to the left of the current column, select *Insert* from the *Table* menu, and select *Column to the Left*. Or, press the Ctrl+Alt+← keyboard shortcut.
- To insert a column to the right of the current column, select *Insert* from the *Table* menu, and select *Column to the Right*. Or, press the Ctrl+Alt+→ keyboard shortcut.

In each case, the inserted row or column will have the same attributes as the row or column that was selected when you issued the command. Use similar commands in the *Table* menu to delete rows and columns.

Aligning Text Inside Cells

By default, static text typed into table cells is left justified. Each cell's Align property controls the placement of text and graphics in the cell. The possible values are center, left, and right.

Merging Adjacent Cells

Sometimes it is useful to merge or combine adjacent table cells into a single cell. The cells must be in the same column or row. To do this, drag the mouse over the cells, and select *Merge Cells* from the *Table* menu. Figure 11-35 shows several cells that have been selected by the mouse, prior to being merged.

Figure 11-35 Selecting multiple cells

Final Notes

If the height of a row seems to change when you switch from *Design* view to Run mode, drag the bottom of the row with the mouse. This causes a specific row height to be encoded in the Style property of each cell in the row.

Start with more columns and rows than you think you need. It's much easier to delete an existing column than to insert a new one without messing up the existing table alignment.

In *Design* view, avoid pressing Enter as the last action while editing a cell. Doing so inserts a paragraph tag which is difficult to remove. A paragraph tag can be removed by editing the HTML directly, and removing the `<P>` and `</P>` tags from the cells. In HTML, a table cell is defined by the `<TD>` and `</TD>` tags.

If you're an expert, go ahead and edit the HTML in your forms. However, be careful, because it's easy to introduce errors. If Visual Studio is unable to understand your HTML, it will refuse to load some or all of the controls on your Web form.

In Tutorial 11-3, you write a program that allows users to sign up for a *Kayak Tour*.

Tutorial 11-3:
Signing up for a *Kayak Tour*

In this tutorial, you will write a program that lets the user sign up for kayak tours in Key Largo, Florida. You will use DropDownList, CheckBoxList, ListBox, and Button controls. You will use an HTML table to align the text and controls. You will write short event handlers for the buttons. A sample of the program when running is shown in Figure 11-36 (only the internal area of the browser window is shown).

Figure 11-36 Signing up for a *Kayak Tour*

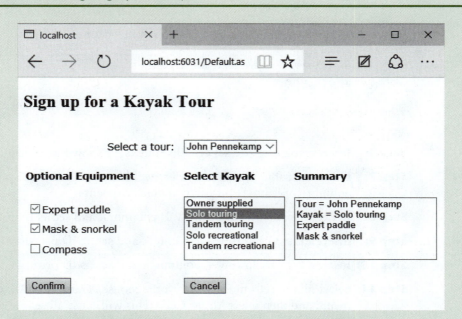

Step 1: Create a new empty Web site named *Kayak Tour*. Add a Web form named *Default.aspx* to the project. Click the *Design* tab at the bottom of the Default. aspx editor window to make sure you are in *Design* view of the form.

Step 2:   Select *Document* in the *Properties* window and set its Title property to *Kayak Tour*.

Step 3:   Type *Sign up for a Kayak Tour* in the first line of the Web page and set its block format to *Heading 2*. Press Enter at the end of the line.

Step 4:   Select *Insert Table* from the *Table* menu and set the size to 6 rows and 5 columns. Click the *OK* button to insert the table.

Step 5:   Select the entire table (choose *Select/Table* from the *Table* menu) and modify its Style property. In the *Modify Style* dialog box, shown in Figure 11-37, experiment with various fonts and colors. For our sample, we select Verdana from the font-family dropdown list, and set the font-size attribute to .85 em. Click *OK* to close the *Modify Style* dialog box.

Figure 11-37 Modifying the Style properties for the HTML table

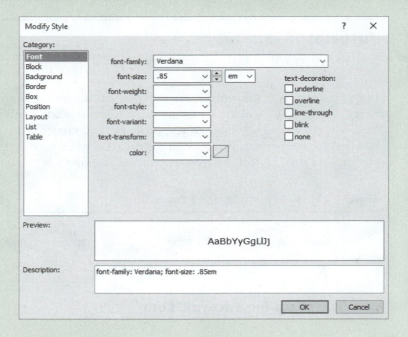

Step 6:   Insert static text and set cell alignments, as shown in Figure 11-38.

Step 7:   Using the same figure as a reference, insert a CheckBoxList control in row 4, column 1. Set its ID property to `chkEquipment`.

Step 8:   Insert a DropDownList in row 1, column 3, and set its ID property to `ddlTour`.

Step 9:   Insert a ListBox in row 4, column 3, and set its ID property to `lstKayak`.

Step 10: Insert a ListBox in row 4, column 5, and set its ID property to `lstSummary`.

Step 11: Select all the cells in Row 5 with the mouse. Then select *Modify* from the *Table* menu, and then select *Merge Cells*. This will cause all cells in row 5 to be merged into a single cell.

Figure 11-38 The Web form, in *Design* view

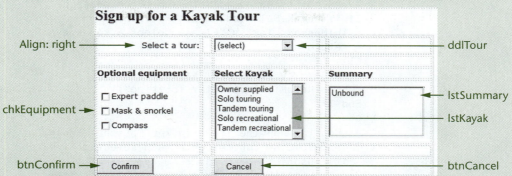

Step 12: Insert a Label control in Row 5 and name it `lblMessage`. Clear its Text property, and set its ForeColor property to red. (This label will be used to display error messages.)

Step 13: Insert a Button control in row 6, column 1, and set its ID property to `btnConfirm`. Set the button's Text property to *Confirm*.

Step 14: Insert a Button control in row 6, column 3, and set its ID property to `btnCancel`. Set the button's Text property to *Cancel*.

Step 15: This is a good time to adjust the column widths so they look approximately like those shown in Figure 11-38. Don't try to be too precise, because the column widths will change when you run the program.

Step 16: Insert the following items in `ddlTour`: *(select)*, *Key Largo*, *John Pennekamp*, *Flamingo Park*. We made the first entry *(select)* so we can tell when the user has not yet selected a tour.

Step 17: Insert items in `chkEquipment` and `lstKayak` according to the values displayed in Figure 11-38.

Step 18: Double-click the *Confirm* button and insert the following code in its Click event handler. The lines you must add are marked in bold. Read the comment lines carefully to understand the code following the comments:

```
Protected Sub btnConfirm_Click(...) Handles btnConfirm.Click

    ' This procedure creates a list containing the tour name,
    ' kayak type, and optional equipment. It adds the list to
    ' the lstSummary ListBox.

    ' Clear the lstSummary ListBox and message label.
    lstSummary.Items.Clear()
    lblMessage.Text = String.Empty

    ' If the user selects a tour from the
    ' DropDownList control, add the tour name to the
    ' summary ListBox. But if an item was not selected,
    ' display an error message.
    If ddlTour.SelectedIndex = 0 Then
        lblMessage.Text = "Please select a tour"
        Return
    Else
        lstSummary.Items.Add("Tour = " & ddlTour.Text)
    End If
```

```
       ' If the user selects a kayak type from the ListBox,
       ' add the kayak type to the summary. But if a kayak
       ' was not selected, display an error message.
       If lstKayak.SelectedIndex = -1 Then
         lblMessage.Text = "Please select a kayak type"
         Return
       Else
         lstSummary.Items.Add("Kayak = " &
           lstKayak.SelectedItem.ToString())
       End If

       ' Loop through the items in the Optional Equipment
       ' CheckBoxList control. For each selected item, add
       ' its description to the summary ListBox.
       For Each item As ListItem In chkEquipment.Items
         If item.Selected Then
           lstSummary.Items.Add(item.Text)
         End If
       Next
     End Sub
```

Step 19: In the *Design* window, double-click the *Cancel* button and insert the following code, shown in bold, in its Click event handler:

```
     Protected Sub btnCancel_Click(...) Handles btnCancel.Click
       ddlTour.SelectedIndex = 0
       lstKayak.SelectedIndex = -1
       lblMessage.Text = String.Empty

       ' Clear the CheckBoxList
       Dim item As ListItem
       For Each item In chkEquipment.Items
           item.Selected = False
       Next
       lstSummary.Items.Clear()
     End Sub
```

Step 20: Save and run the application by pressing Ctrl + F5 . Make several selections and compare your form's appearance to Figure 11-36, shown earlier. You can return to *Design* view, adjust the table column widths by dragging the borders, and rerun the program. After selecting a tour, click the *Cancel* button and verify that all selections are cleared.

Step 21: When you're done, close the project.

✓ Checkpoint

11.18   How do you merge several cells into a single table cell?

11.19   How do you select a column in a table?

11.20   How do you change a column width?

11.21   How do you set the default font for all cells in a table?

11.22   Which property of a CheckBoxList control contains the individual list items?

11.5 Applications with Multiple Web Pages

CONCEPT: A Web application may use multiple Web pages to display data and interact with the user.

Before long, you will want to create Web applications that have multiple pages. You might collect information on one page and display a summary on another page. Or, you might display supplementary information on a second page, which the user can select at will. First we will talk about how you add a new page to a project, and then we will show how your program can navigate from one page to another.

Adding New Web Forms to a Project

Each Web page in your application is designed using a Web form in Visual Studio. To add a Web form to your project, right-click the project name in *Solution Explorer*, select *Add*, then select *Web Form*.

The dialog window, shown in Figure 11-39, prompts you for the name of the web form. It is not necessary to type a filename extension.

Figure 11-39 Adding a Web form to a project

Specify Name for Item

Item name: MyForm

OK   Cancel

Moving between Pages

There are three common things you can do that will let a program move from a Web page we will call the *source page* to another Web page we will call the *target page*:

- Place the URL of the target page in the NavigateURL property of a HyperLink control. We discussed the HyperLink control in Section 11.3.
- Write code in the Click event handler of a Button, ImageButton, or LinkButton control. In a moment, we will show how to call the `Response.Redirect` method.
- Convert a block of static text to a hyperlink. Select a block of text with the mouse, click the *Convert to Hyperlink* button on the formatting toolbar (as shown in Figure 11-40), and enter the URL of the target page. Optionally, you can click the *Browse* button to locate a file within your project, as shown in Figure 11-41.

Figure 11-40 Converting a block of text to a hyperlink

Convert to Hyperlink

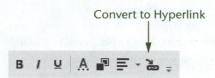

Figure 11-41 Selecting the target page for the hyperlink

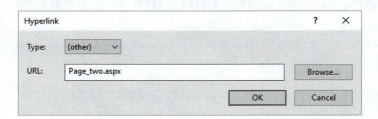

The major difference between these methods is that only one—the call to `Response.Redirect`—is initiated by program code. The other two require the user to click a hyperlink.

Calling `Response.Redirect`

In your program code, you can tell the browser to navigate to another page in your application, or any other page on the Web by calling the **Response.Redirect method**. A **Response object** automatically exists in every Web page. It is an instance of the `HttpResponse` class. Suppose, for example, a program must transfer to a page named *Page_two.aspx*. We would put the following statement in the Click event handler of a Button, ImageButton, or LinkButton control:

```
Response.Redirect("Page_two.aspx")
```

If the target page is on another Web server, we must supply a fully formed URL as follows:

```
Response.Redirect("http://microsoft.com")
```

The following, for example, launches a Google search for the word *horses*:

```
http://www.google.com/search?q=horses
```

In Tutorial 11-4, you add a description form to the *Kayak Tour* application.

Tutorial 11-4:
Adding a description form to the *Kayak Tour* application

In this tutorial, you will extend the *Kayak Tour* program you created in Tutorial 11-3. You will add a Web form that describes the different kayak tours and use a HyperLink control to navigate to the form.

Step 1: Open the *Kayak_Tour* project folder you created in Tutorial 11-3.

Step 2: Add a new Web form named *Tours.aspx*. Set the form's Title property to *Kayak Tour Descriptions*. Type the text shown in Figure 11-42, shortening it if necessary. We used a Verdana font.

Step 3: In the *Default.aspx* form, add a HyperLink control to the cell in row 1, column 5. Set its Text property to *Tour descriptions*. Set its NavigateURL property to *Tours.aspx*. Set its Target property to *_blank*, which will cause the new form to be displayed in a separate browser window.

Figure 11-42 The *Kayak Tour* description Web form

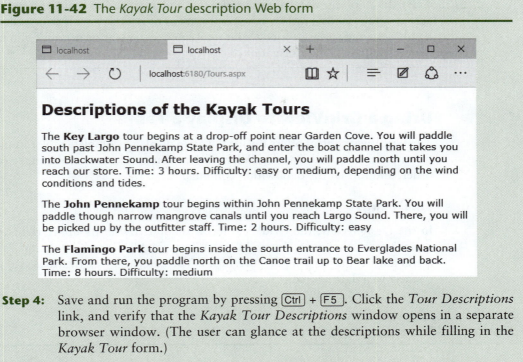

localhost:6180/Tours.aspx

Descriptions of the Kayak Tours

The **Key Largo** tour begins at a drop-off point near Garden Cove. You will paddle south past John Pennekamp State Park, and enter the boat channel that takes you into Blackwater Sound. After leaving the channel, you will paddle north until you reach our store. Time: 3 hours. Difficulty: easy or medium, depending on the wind conditions and tides.

The **John Pennekamp** tour begins within John Pennekamp State Park. You will paddle though narrow mangrove canals until you reach Largo Sound. There, you will be picked up by the outfitter staff. Time: 2 hours. Difficulty: easy

The **Flamingo Park** tour begins inside the sourth entrance to Everglades National Park. From there, you paddle north on the Canoe trail up to Bear lake and back. Time: 8 hours. Difficulty: medium

Step 4: Save and run the program by pressing Ctrl + F5 . Click the *Tour Descriptions* link, and verify that the *Kayak Tour Descriptions* window opens in a separate browser window. (The user can glance at the descriptions while filling in the *Kayak Tour* form.)

Step 5: Close both browser windows to end the application.

 Checkpoint

11.23 Which menu command adds a new Web form to a project?

11.24 How can a HyperLink control be used to navigate between Web pages?

11.25 How do you convert a block of static text to a hyperlink?

11.26 Which method in the Response object navigates to a different Web page?

11.6 Using Databases

CONCEPT: ASP.NET provides several Web controls for displaying and updating a database from a Web application.

You can display and update the contents of database tables very easily in ASP.NET applications. First, we will show how to use the GridView control to display database tables. Then we will show how to use the DetailsView control to display a single row at a time, and how to add a new row to a database table.

Web applications use a specialized type of ASP.NET control for accessing databases, generally called a *DataSource control*. Actually, there are two specific controls, depending on which type of database you're using. One control is named *AccessDataSource*, for MS Access databases. The other is named *SqlDataSource*, for SQL Server databases. We will use the latter. One important characteristic of the DataSource controls is that they directly update the database, with no separate Update method call required.

TIP: In all of our database examples, we will assume that you are connecting to SQL Server database files, rather than a full version of SQL Server. If your college lab uses a database server, please contact your classroom instructor or network administrator for database connection information.

Using a GridView to Display a Table

The **GridView control** offers the ideal way to display a complete table. Similar to the Windows control named DataGridView, it lets you sort on any column, select the column order, and format the data within columns.

Smart Tags

In the *Design* view, the GridView has a small arrow in its upper right corner called a *smart tag*, as shown in Figure 11-43. When you click on this tag, the *GridView Tasks* menu pops up, as shown in Figure 11-44. You can use it to set various grid properties and connect to a data source.

Figure 11-43 GridView control with smart tag (*Design* view)

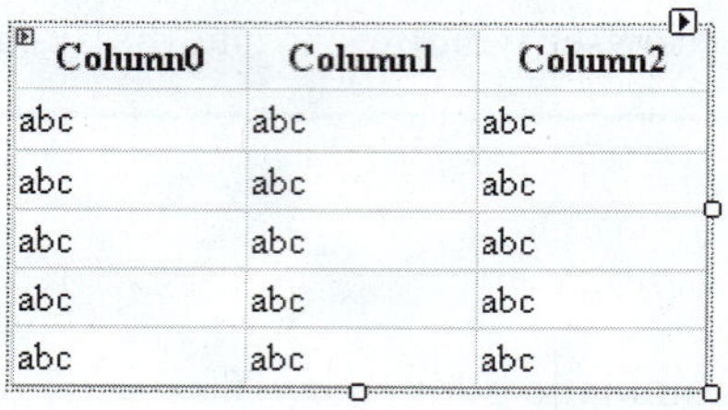

Figure 11-44 The smart tag activates the *GridView Tasks* menu

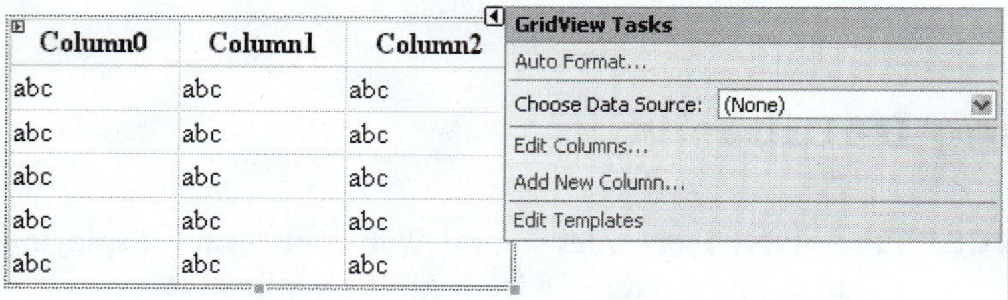

Setting Up a Connection

The general steps required to connect your Web form to a database follow. Don't try to do them yet, because we need to provide a few more details during the upcoming tutorial.

1. Inside the *Solution Explorer* window, add an *App_Data* folder to your project, and then in Windows Explorer, copy the database file to the *App_Data* folder.
2. Add a GridView control to the form, click its smart tag, and select *<New data source . . .>* from the *Choose Data Source* DropDown list.
3. Select the data source type, as shown in Figure 11-45.

Figure 11-45 Choosing a data source type

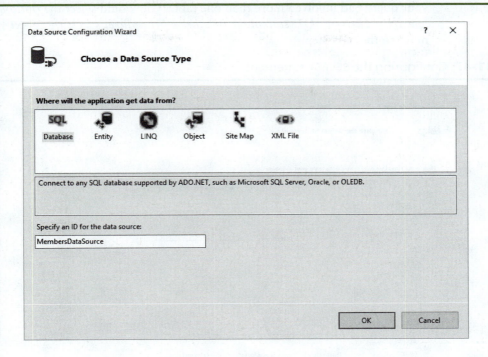

4. Select the database name within the *App_Data* folder, as shown in Figure 11-46. Your exact file path will be different from the one shown in the figure.

Figure 11-46 Identifying the *Database* file

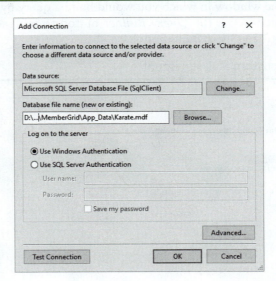

5. Configure the SELECT statement for the database query, as shown in Figure 11-47. If your query had involved more than one table, you would select the option that says *Specify a custom SQL statement or stored procedure*. Click the *Next* button to move to the next step.

Figure 11-47 Configuring the SELECT statement

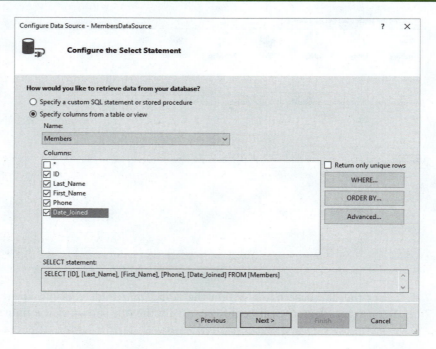

6. If you had specified a custom SQL statement in the previous step, Figure 11-48 shows the window in which you would build a query by joining tables. Usually, you will want to click the *Query Builder* button to take advantage of the convenient Visual Studio Query Builder tool.

Figure 11-48 Building a custom SQL statement

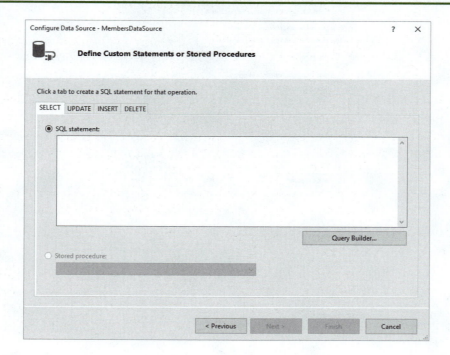

When you're finished with the *Data Source Configuration Wizard*, an **SqlDataSource Control** is placed on your Web form.

In Tutorial 11-5, you display the *Karate Members* table in a GridView.

Tutorial 11-5:
Displaying the *Karate Members* table in a GridView

In this tutorial, you will create a connection to the *Karate* database, and display the *Members* table in a GridView control. You will perform some basic configurations of the grid's appearance.

Step 1: Create a new emtpy Web site named *MemberGrid*. Add a new Web form named *Default.aspx* to the project.

Step 2: Right-click the project name in the *Solution Explorer* window. From the popup menu, select *Add*, then select *ASP.NET folder*, and then select *App_Data*.

Step 3: Open a *Windows Explorer* window and copy the *Karate.mdf* file from the student sample programs folder named *Chap11* to your project's *App_Data* folder.

Step 4: In the *Solution Explorer* window, right-click the project name and select *Refresh Folder*. Then expand the entry under *App_Data* and look for the *Karate.mdf* filename, as shown in Figure 11-49.

Figure 11-49 Locating the *Karate.mdf* file under *App_Data* in the *Solution Explorer* window

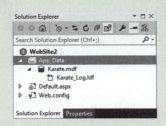

Step 5: In the *Design* view window of the Default.aspx form, select *Document* in the *Properties* window and set its Title property to *Karate Members*.

Step 6: On the first line of the Web page (in *Design* view) type *Members Table, Karate Database*. Set the block style to *Heading 2*, and press [Enter] at the end of the line.

Step 7: Place a GridView control on the form. You can find it in the *Data* section of the *Toolbox* window. Drag its right handle until its Width property equals about 640 pixels. Its Height property should be blank.

Step 8: Click the grid's smart tag, opening the *GridView Tasks* dialog box. Select *<New data source . . .>* from the *Choose Data Source* DropDown list.

Step 9: In the *Data Source Configuration Wizard*, select *Database*, change the ID value to *KarateDataSource*, and click the *OK* button.

Step 10: The next step in the wizard is named *Choose Your Data Connection*. Click the *New Connection* button. When the *Add Connection* window appears, as shown in Figure 11-50, make sure the *Data Source* field is set to *Microsoft SQL Server Database File (SqlClient)*. If some other value appears in the field, change it.

Figure 11-50 Select the *Karate.mdf* database file

Step 11: For the Database file name entry, click the *Browse* button, select your project's *App_Data* folder, select *Karate.mdf*, and click the *Open* button. Then, click the *OK* button to close the *Add Connection* dialog. When you return to the window that reads *Choose Your Data Connection*, click the *Next* button. When a window appears that reads *Save the Application Connection String to the Application Configuration File*, click the *Next* button.

Step 12: You will be asked to configure the SELECT statement that pulls rows and columns from the database. From the *Name* DropDown list, select the *Members* table, as shown in Figure 11-51.

Figure 11-51 Configuring the SELECT statement

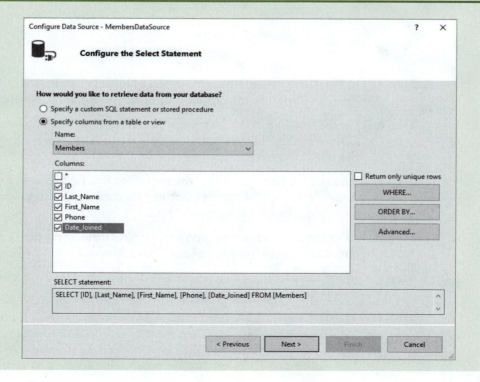

Step 13: Place check marks next to the following columns, in order: *ID*, *Last_Name*, *First_Name*, *Phone*, and *Date_Joined*.

Step 14: Click the *ORDER BY . . .* button. In the dialog box shown in Figure 11-52, sort by the *Last_Name* column. Click *OK* to close the dialog box.

Step 15: Returning to the *Configure the Select Statement* dialog box, click the *Next* button, which takes you to the *Test Query* dialog box. Click the *Test Query* button. If the displayed columns match those shown in Figure 11-53, click the *Finish* button to close the window.

Figure 11-52 Adding the `ORDER BY` clause

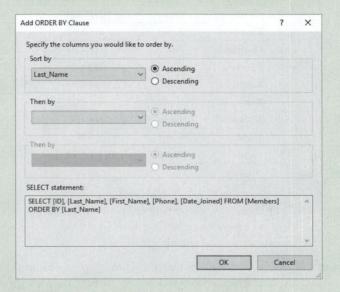

Figure 11-53 Testing the `SELECT` query

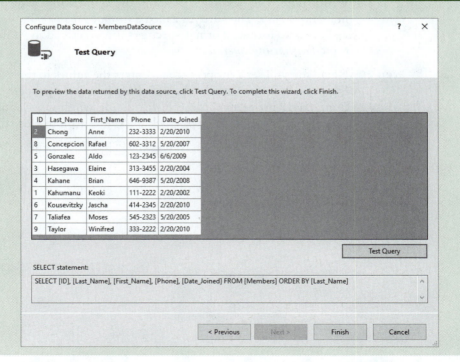

Step 16: Click the *GridView*'s smart tag again and check the *Enable Sorting* check box.

Step 17: Save and run the Web application by pressing Ctrl + F5 . The contents of your browser window should appear as shown in Figure 11-54, although some of the data in the rows may be different.

Figure 11-54 Running the Web application

Members Table, Karate Database

ID	Last Name	First Name	Phone	Date Joined
2	Chong	Anne	232-3333	2/20/2010 12:00:00 AM
8	Concepcion	Rafael	602-3312	5/20/2007 12:00:00 AM
5	Gonzalez	Aldo	123-2345	6/6/2009 12:00:00 AM
3	Hasegawa	Elaine	313-3455	2/20/2004 12:00:00 AM
4	Kahane	Brian	646-9387	5/20/2008 12:00:00 AM
1	Kahumanu	Keoki	111-2222	2/20/2002 12:00:00 AM
6	Kousevitzky	Jascha	414-2345	2/20/2010 12:00:00 AM
7	Taliafea	Moses	545-2323	5/20/2005 12:00:00 AM
9	Taylor	Winifred	333-2222	2/20/2010 12:00:00 AM

Step 18: Experiment with sorting columns by clicking each of the column headers. If you click the same column twice in a row, it reverses the sort order. Close the browser to end the application.

Step 19: Next, you will format the *Date_Joined* column. Select the grid with the mouse. In the *Properties* window, click the Columns property, which causes the *Fields* dialog box to display. In the lower left box, select *Date_Joined*. In the properties list for this column, enter {0:d} into the DataFormatString property, as shown in Figure 11-55. The {0:d} is called a *format specifier*. In this case, it says to use a *short date* format. Format specifiers are described in MSDN Help under the topic *Formatting overview*.

Step 20: Next, you will set a property that centers the values in the *Date_Joined* column. Expand the entries under the column's ItemStyle property (last in the list of *BoundField* properties in the *Fields* dialog window). Change the Horizontal-Align subproperty to *Center*. Click the *OK* button to close the dialog box.

Step 21: Save and run the application by pressing Ctrl + F5 . Your output should be similar to that shown in Figure 11-56.

Step 22: Close the browser window to end the program.

Figure 11-55 Formatting the *Date_Joined* column

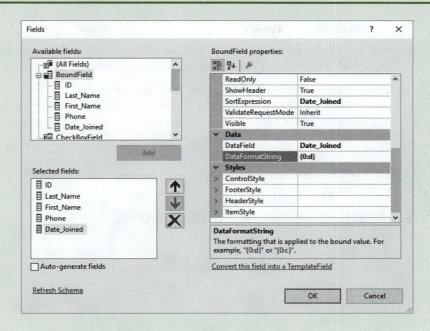

Figure 11-56 After formatting the *Date_Joined* column

Members Table, Karate Database

ID	Last Name	First Name	Phone	Date Joined
2	Chong	Anne	232-3333	2/20/2010
8	Concepcion	Rafael	602-3312	5/20/2007
5	Gonzalez	Aldo	123-2345	6/6/2009
3	Hasegawa	Elaine	313-3455	2/20/2004
4	Kahane	Brian	646-9387	5/20/2008
1	Kahumanu	Keoki	111-2222	2/20/2002
6	Kousevitzky	Jascha	414-2345	2/20/2010
7	Taliafea	Moses	545-2323	5/20/2005
9	Taylor	Winifred	333-2222	2/20/2010

In addition to the formats you modified just now, there are many detailed formatting changes you can make to a GridView control.

Using a DetailsView Control to Modify Table Rows

The **DetailsView control** makes it easy to view, edit, delete, or add rows to a database table. To use it, you must create a data source, as you did in Tutorial 11-5. When you connect the DetailsView to the data source, most of the work is done for you. Microsoft engineers have been working hard to automate as many menial tasks as they can, and database table editing is high on the list of tasks most programmers would prefer *not* to do repeatedly.

The DetailsView control is found in the Data section of the *Toolbox* window. When you place it on a Web form, use its smart tag (upper right-hand corner) to add a database connection and set various options. You did the same for the GridView control in Tutorial 11-5.

In Tutorial 11-6, you will update the *Karate Members* table using a DetailsView control.

Tutorial 11-6:
Updating the *Karate Members* table

In this tutorial, you will write an application that lets the user view, edit, insert, and delete individual rows in the *Members* table in the *Karate* database. You will create an SqlDataSource control and hook it up to a DetailsView control. You will not have to write any program code.

Figure 11-57 shows the finished program right after it starts, with rows sorted by last name. The underlined words *Edit*, *Delete*, and *New* are called *link buttons* (LinkButton controls). They look like HTML links, but function like ordinary button controls.

Figure 11-57 Adding a member at runtime

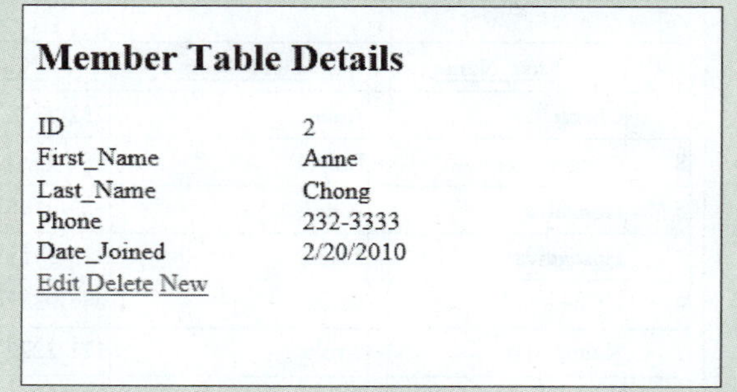

Member Table Details

ID	2
First_Name	Anne
Last_Name	Chong
Phone	232-3333
Date_Joined	2/20/2010

Edit Delete New

In Figure 11-58, the user has clicked the *New* button and begun to enter data for a new member. The user will soon click the *Insert (link)* button, which will save the new row in the database.

Figure 11-59 shows the same form after the user has clicked the *Insert* button. The new member (Eric Baker) appears in the detail fields.

If the user tries to add a row having an ID number equal to an existing ID in the table, an error page displays, as shown in Figure 11-60. The user can click the browser's *Back* button, enter a different ID, and try again.

Figure 11-58 About to insert a new member

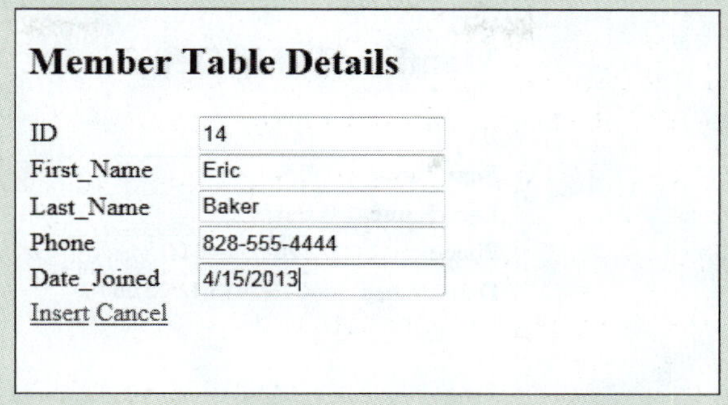

Member Table Details

ID	14
First_Name	Eric
Last_Name	Baker
Phone	828-555-4444
Date_Joined	4/15/2013

Insert Cancel

Figure 11-59 After clicking the *Insert* button

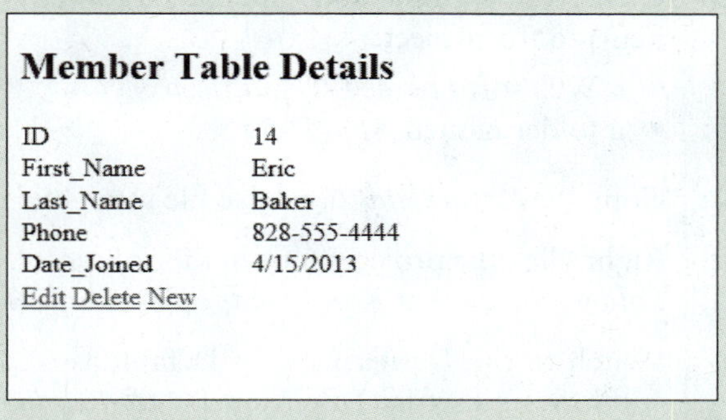

Member Table Details

ID	14
First_Name	Eric
Last_Name	Baker
Phone	828-555-4444
Date_Joined	4/15/2013

Edit Delete New

Figure 11-60 Error displayed when the user tries to add a row with a duplicate ID

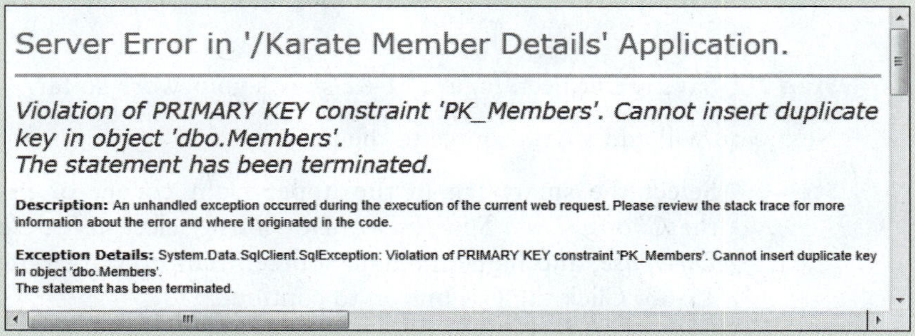

Server Error in '/Karate Member Details' Application.

Violation of PRIMARY KEY constraint 'PK_Members'. Cannot insert duplicate key in object 'dbo.Members'.
The statement has been terminated.

Description: An unhandled exception occurred during the execution of the current web request. Please review the stack trace for more information about the error and where it originated in the code.

Exception Details: System.Data.SqlClient.SqlException: Violation of PRIMARY KEY constraint 'PK_Members'. Cannot insert duplicate key in object 'dbo.Members'.
The statement has been terminated.

When the user clicks the *Edit* button, he or she can modify any of the member fields, as shown in Figure 11-61. When the user clicks the *Update* button, changes to the record are saved in the database.

Figure 11-61 After clicking the *Edit* button

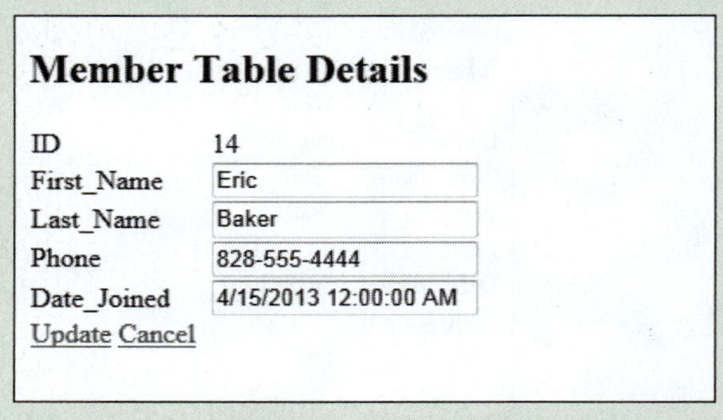

Now let's build the program.

Step 1: Create a new empty Web site named *Karate Member Details*. Add the following items to the project:
- a Web form named *Default.aspx*
- a folder named *App_Data*

Step 2: Copy the *Karate.mdf* database file into your project's *App_Data* folder.

Step 3: Right-click the project name in the *Solution Explorer* window and select *Refresh Folder*. Verify that *Karate.mdf* appears under the *App_Data* entry.

Step 4: Switch to the *Design* view of Default.aspx, select *Document* in the *Properties* window, and set its Title property to *Members Table Details*.

Step 5: On the first line of the page, insert *Members Table Details*, and give it a *Heading 2* block style. Then, press [Enter] to go to the next line.

Step 6: Add a DetailsView control to the page, and set its ID property to dvwAddMember. Widen it to about 300 pixels. Make sure its Height property is blank.

Step 7: Save the project. Figure 11-62 shows your work so far.

Next, you will add a data source to the project.

Step 8: Select the smart tag in the upper right corner of *dvwAddMember*. From the *Choose Data Source* DropDown list, select *<New data source . . .>*. Select *Database*, and name the data source MembersDataSource, as shown in Figure 11-63. Click the *OK* button to continue.

Step 9: As in the previous tutorial, create a connection to the *Karate.mdf* file in the project's *App_Data* folder.

Figure 11-62 Designing the *Karate Member Details* form

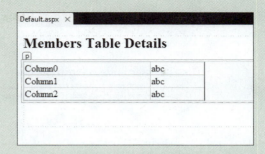

Figure 11-63 Creating the data source

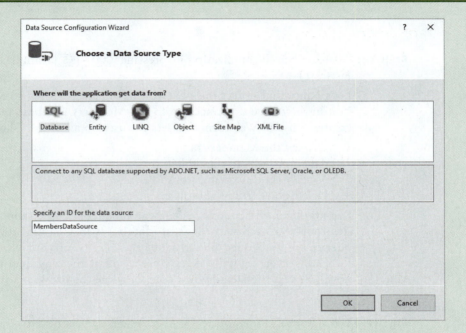

Step 10: When the window entitled *Save the Connection String to the Application Configuration File* appears, click the *Next* button.

Step 11: In the next window, select all columns in the *Members* table, and order the rows by *Last_Name* in ascending order. When you return to the window entitled *Configure the Select Statement*, click the *Advanced* button.

Step 12: In the *Advanced SQL Generation Options* dialog box, select the *Generate INSERT, UPDATE, and DELETE statements* option, as shown in Figure 11-64. Click the *OK* button, and then click the *Next* button.

Step 13: Click the *Finish* button to close the *Configure Data Source* window. Back in the *Smart Tag* menu for dvwAddMember, select the check boxes to enable *Inserting*, *Editing*, and *Deleting*.

Figure 11-64 Selecting *Advanced SQL Generation Options*

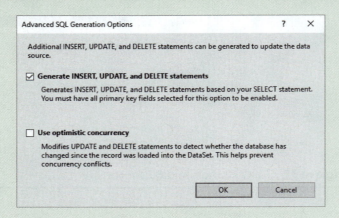

Step 14: Save and run the application by pressing ⌃Ctrl + F5 . Sample output is shown in Figure 11-65.

Let's pause and reflect on what you have accomplished so far in this tutorial. You have created a connection to the Members database table, and you have created a useful Web form that lets the user do all of the following:

1. Display the Members table
2. Add new rows to the table
3. Modify (Edit) existing rows
4. Delete rows from the table

Behind this useful control, as you can imagine, are the same types of SQL queries that you used with desktop databases in Chapter 10. In fact, the SQL queries are embedded directly into the HTML of your web page. When this tutorial is over, we will take a closer look at the way queries are stored. But, now, let's test the DetailsView control while the browser window is still open.

Figure 11-65 Running the *Karate Member Details* application for the first time

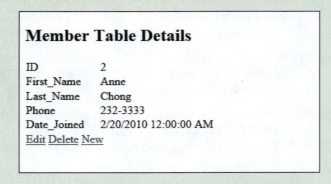

Step 15: Click the *Edit* button, change the values of one of the fields, and click the *Update* button. You should notice that the field value has been changed.

Step 16: Close the browser window and return to *Design* view. Let's improve the appearance of the DetailView just a bit. Select it, and set its BorderWidth property to

Figure 11-66 *Fields* dialog box for the DetailsView control

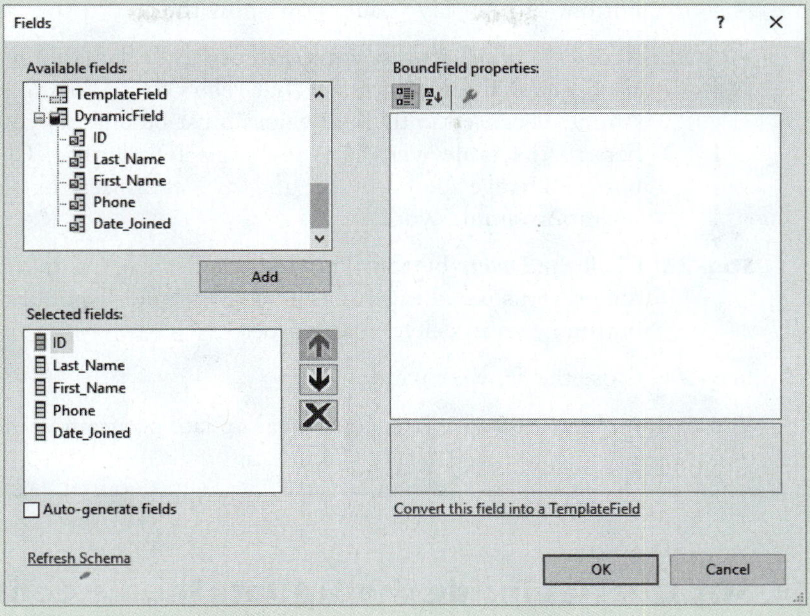

0px (zero pixels wide). Next, select its Fields property, causing the *Fields* dialog box to display (see Figure 11-66).

Step 17: In the *Fields* dialog box, select the *Date_Joined* field in the lower left list box. Then in the right-hand list box, set its DataFormatString property to *{0:d}*. You may recall this is the same short date format specifier we used in the GridView control in Tutorial 11-5.

Step 18: Next, you will change the field order slightly. Select the *First_Name* field in the lower left list box, and use the arrow button on the right side of the box to move the *First_Name* field above the *Last_Name* field.

Step 19: Click *OK* to close the *Fields* dialog box. Next, find the GridLines property and set it equal to *None*.

Step 20: Save and run the application by pressing `Ctrl` + `F5`. It should now appear as shown in Figure 11-67.

Figure 11-67 After modifying the field display in the DetailsView control

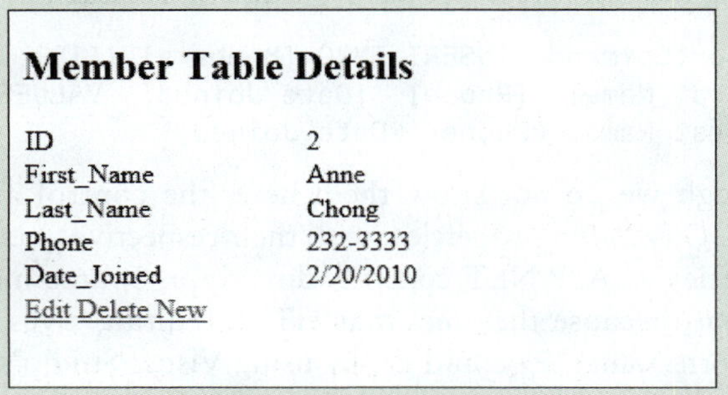

Step 21: Click the *New* button, and notice that all the text boxes become empty. Enter the following data: 14, Eric, Baker, 654–3210, 3/1/2013. Then click the *Insert* button. The display should now show the record you inserted.

Step 22: Again, try to insert a new record, using the same ID number (14). You should see a detailed error message that refers to a Violation of a primary key constraint. Because the ID field values must be unique, you cannot add two members to the table who have the same ID number. Click the browser's Back button, change the ID to 15, and click the *Insert* button. This time, the insert operation should work.

Step 23: Click the *Delete* button. The last member you inserted should disappear. Then, the previous member you inserted (Eric Baker) should display. Click the *Delete* button again to delete this member.

Step 24: Close the browser window.

You're done. You created a fully functional update program without writing a single line of code.

SQL Queries inside the SqlDataSource Control

In Tutorial 11-6, you created a simple web application that used the SqlDataSource control to populate a DetailsView control. The user was able to display, modify, insert, and delete rows from the Karate Members table. You might be interested to see how a SqlDataSource is represented in your web form's HTML code. You can click the *Source* tab for the Default.aspx page in the *Karate Member Details* application and then look for the SqlDataSource control named *MembersDataSource*. This is the beginning of the code that defines it:

```
<asp:SqlDataSource ID="MembersDataSource" runat="server"
```

The *asp:SqlDataSource* tag identifies the type of control and assigns it an ID (*MembersDataSource*). The *runat* property indicates that this control executes on the Web server. Next, you will see the name of the connection string that ties this control to the database:

```
ConnectionString="<%$ ConnectionStrings:karateConnectionString %>"
```

Next, you will find the *DeleteCommand* property, which contains an SQL query that deletes rows from the Members table. It uses a query parameter (named *@ID*) to identify exactly which member is to be deleted:

```
DeleteCommand="DELETE FROM [Members] WHERE [ID] = @ID"
```

Next is the *InsertCommand* property, which contains the query used to insert new rows into the Members table. It has a parameter for each column in the table:

```
InsertCommand="INSERT INTO [Members] ([ID], [Last_Name],
[First_Name], [Phone], [Date_Joined]) VALUES (@ID, @Last_Name,
@First_Name, @Phone, @Date_Joined)"
```

Although we do not show them here, the control also contains *SelectCommand* and *UpdateCommand* properties, with their respective queries. With practice, you can edit the properties of ASP.NET controls directly in Source mode. Expert web programmers do just that, because they feel that HTML editing gives them more precise control over a Web form than they could get by using Visual Studio's *Design* view.

✅ Checkpoint

11.27 Which Web control displays database table rows and columns in a grid-like format?

11.28 In a Web form, what type of object provides a connection to an SQL Server database?

11.29 Which property in a DetailsView control permits you to modify the formatting of a column containing a date?

11.30 Which property in a DetailsView control permits you to modify the order of the columns?

11.31 Which Web control lets you display individual fields in each row from a database, using text boxes?

Summary

11.1 Programming for the Web

- Web applications are designed around a client-server model: a server produces data consumed by another entity called a client. Web applications must be run using a Web server.
- When the Web first became popular, HTML was the only available encoding method for creating Web pages with text, graphics buttons, and input forms.
- ASP.NET is called a *platform* because it provides development tools, code libraries, and visual controls for browser-based applications.
- Web applications written for ASP.NET consist of content, in the form of Web forms, HTML code, Web forms controls, images, and other multimedia; program logic, in compiled Visual Basic (or C#) code; and configuration information.
- Visual Studio simplifies the way Web applications are developed, by providing a fully functional HTML editor, design viewer, and internal Web server.
- A URL (Uniform Resource Locator) provides a universal way of addressing objects and pages on a network.
- Web applications written in ASP.NET use special Web pages called *Web forms*. A Web form, which can be identified by the *aspx* file name extension, contains text, HTML tags, HTML controls (such as buttons and text boxes), and Web server controls.

11.2 Creating ASP.NET Applications

- Using Visual Studio, you can create a Web site in the local File System, Local or remote Web server, or remote FTP site.
- A File System Web site runs directly under the local web server supplied with Visual Studio. An HTTP Web site runs under a Windows operating system utility named Internet Information Services (IIS). An FTP Web site references an existing ASP.NET Web site located on a remote computer (network or Web).
- ASP.NET applications are also known as Web sites or Web applications.
- You can start a program in *Debug* mode by selecting *Start Debugging* from the *Debug* menu.

11.3 Web Server Controls

- Web server controls make ASP.NET applications dynamic and interactive. The controls are far more powerful than standard HTML controls because each is defined by a class with a rich set of properties, methods, and events.
- The ID property of Web controls is the counterpart to the Name property of Windows controls. Web controls lose their runtime properties when the user moves away from the current page.
- The Label control for Web forms is almost identical to the Label control on Windows forms. Use a Label only if its contents will change at runtime, or if you plan to change its Visible property.
- The TextBox control for Web forms is similar in many ways to the TextBox control for Windows forms. The Text property holds text input by the user.
- The CheckBox control for Web forms is almost identical to the CheckBox in Windows forms. Use the Text property to set the visible text and evaluate the Checked property at runtime.
- Events are fired in a different sequence in Web forms than they are in Windows forms. In a Web form, the Page_Load event occurs when the page is first loaded into the user's browser, and again every time the page is posted back to the server.
- When a control's AutoPostBack property equals *True*, clicking on the control causes the form to be posted back to the server.

11.4 Designing Web Forms

- An HTML table is an essential tool for designing the layout of Web forms. Use it to align text, graphics, and controls in rows and columns.
- To insert a table when viewing a form in *Design* view, select *Insert Table* from the *Table* menu or double-click the HTML Table control from the *Toolbox* window.
- To adjust the width of a column, hover the mouse over the double bar along the column's right-hand border. To adjust the height of a row, hover the mouse over the row's lower border. After finding the border in this way, hold down the left mouse button and drag the border to change the column or row size.

11.5 Applications with Multiple Web Pages

- Most Web applications have multiple pages. You might collect information on one page and display a summary on another page. Or, you might display supplementary information on a second page.
- There are two ways to add a new Web page to a project: select *Add New Item* from the *Website* menu, or right-click the project name in the *Solution Explorer* window and select *Add New Item*.
- To permit your application to navigate from one Web page to another, you can use a HyperLink control, code a call to `Response.Redirect`, or convert a block of static text to a hyperlink.

11.6 Using Databases

- Web applications use a different model for accessing databases than Windows Forms applications. Rather than using a dataset, Web applications often use a Data-Source Web server control.
- The GridView control, similar to the Windows control named DataGridView, lets you sort on any column, select the column order, and format the data within columns.
- The DetailsView, like the GridView, connects to a DataSource Web server control.
- Tutorial 11-6 shows how to view, edit, insert, and delete individual rows in the *Members* table of the *Karate* database.

Key Terms

ASP.NET
ASP.NET Server controls
AutoPostBack property
button control
Cascading Style Sheet (CSS)
CheckBox control
CheckBoxList control
client-server model
code-behind file
DataSource control
DetailsView control
domain name
DropDownList control
File System Web site
FTP Site
GridView control
HTML control

HTML Designer
HTML table
HTML tag
HTTP Web site
HyperLink control
HyperText Markup Language (HTML)
ImageButton control
Internet Information Services (IIS)
Label control
LinkButton control
ListBox control
Local IIS Web site
local web server
platform
postback
program logic

protocol
RadioButton controls
RadioButtonList control
Remote site
Response object
Response.Redirect method
server
static text

TextBox Web control
Uniform Resource Locator (URL)
Web application
Web form
Web page
Web server
Web server control

VideoNote

Building a Movie Tracking Application

Video Tutorial: Movie Tracking Application

In this sequence of video tutorials, we build a simple Movie Tracking application. We will let the user input his or her favorite film title and provide supplemental information such as the name of the director(s), some of the actors, the year produced, and related information. The user will also be able to modify and delete existing entries. The application will use the *Movies* database from Chapter 10.

- Part 1: Designing the Web interface

- Part 2: Learning about the *Movies* database

- Part 3: Filling a grid with film titles and dates

- Part 4: Adding, editing, and removing films

Review Questions and Exercises

Fill-in-the-Blank

1. Conventional Web pages contain tags based on the _____ Markup Language.

2. Microsoft's platform for Web development is named _____.

3. URL stands for Uniform _____ Locator.

4. Web server controls are also known as _____ server controls.

5. A powerful Web server used by Web developers is named Internet _____ Services (IIS).

6. The _____ control displays a sequence of check boxes.

7. The _____ control displays a hyperlink and has a property named NavigateURL.

8. When creating a new Web site, the choices of location type are _____, HTTP, and FTP.

9. Debugging configuration information is stored in a file named _____.

10. The _____ property of a Label control can be used to make its border solid, dotted, or dashed.

11. The _____ property of a TextBox control determines whether the box will permit multiple lines of input.

12. When a postback occurs on a Web page, the first event handler to execute is _____.

13. The _____ property of an ImageButton control holds the name of the image file.

Multiple Choice

1. Which of the following is the name of the grid-like control that displays database tables?
   a. DataGrid
   b. DataGridView
   c. GridView
   d. TableGrid

2. Which of the following is the standard file name extension for Web forms?
   a. *.aspx*
   b. *.asp*
   c. *.htm*
   d. *.html*

3. Which of the following is not a control category in the *Toolbox* window?
   a. Navigation
   b. Login
   c. WebParts
   d. FileServer

4. Which of the following Web site types requires running Internet Information Services on the local computer?
   a. File system
   b. Local IIS
   c. FTP
   d. Remote Web

5. Which of the following is not a Web server control described in this chapter?
   a. NavigateButton
   b. RadioButtonList
   c. CheckBoxList
   d. LinkButton

6. Which of the following cannot be assigned to the TextMode property of a TextBox control?
   a. MultiLine
   b. Hidden
   c. Password
   d. SingleLine

7. Which of the following properties is (are) found in both the RadioButtonList and ListBox controls?
   a. SelectedIndex
   b. ImageIndex
   c. RepeatDirection
   d. Items
   e. Two of the above are correct

True or False

Indicate whether the following statements are true or false.

1. T F: ASP.NET applications will only work if the user's Web browser is Internet Explorer Version 8.0 or above.

2. T F: The DropDownList control permits the user to type text directly into the first line.

768   Chapter 11   Developing Web Applications

3. T F: The AutoPostBack property does not affect the ListBox control.
4. T F: The ListBox control fires a SelectedIndexChanged event.
5. T F: To create Web sites on your local computer, you must be running Internet Information Services (IIS), a professional tool for handling Web sites.
6. T F: The default value of SelectedIndex for a DropDownList control is zero.
7. T F: The HyperLink control does not generate a Click event.
8. T F: The ImageButton control generates a Click event and does not look like a button.
9. T F: The `Response.NavigateTo` method lets your code transfer control to a different Web page.
10. T F: To fill a GridView control, you must create a data adapter and a dataset.
11. T F: The DetailsView control does not permit deleting a row from a database table.
12. T F: When adding text to a Web form, you can type static text directly onto the form.

Short Answer

1. What are the three basic parts of an ASP.NET application?
2. Which control has a NavigateURL property?
3. How are Web server controls different from HTML controls?
4. What special requirement do remote Web servers have, as opposed to local Web servers?
5. What are the two ways to view a Web form inside Visual Studio?
6. What command lets you select which Web browser will run your Web application?
7. How do you open an existing Web application?
8. What happens the first time you try to run a Web application in Debug mode?
9. How is the DropDownList control different from the ComboBox control?
10. How are the HyperLink and LinkButton controls different?
11. Which Web control property corresponds to the Name property in Windows controls?
12. When the user selects an item from a ListBox and then posts the page back to the server (called a postback), which method executes first: `Page_Load` or `SelectedIndexChanged`?
13. Which property in a ListBox governs whether or not the user's selection is posted back to the server immediately?
14. Which property of a HyperLink control affects whether the target page will display in a new browser window?

What Do You Think?

1. What advantages does a File System Web site have over an HTTP Web site?
2. Why is the HTML Table control useful when designing Web forms?
3. Why should you to test your application with different Web browsers?

4. Why should debugging be disabled when distributing your Web site to the general public?

5. What disadvantage is there to setting AutoPostBack to *True* for a DropDownList control?

Algorithm Workbench

1. Write a code statement that transfers control to a Web page named *PageTwo.aspx*.

2. Write a statement that checks if the first button in a RadioButtonList control named `radButtons` has been selected by the user.

3. Write a statement that removes all items from a ListBox named `lstSummary`.

4. Write a loop that selects all check boxes in a CheckBoxList control named `chkOptions`.

Programming Challenges

VideoNote

The *Stadium Seating* Problem

1. **Stadium Seating**

   Create an ASP.NET version of the solution program for Programming Challenge 2 in Chapter 3, named *Stadium Seating*.

2. **Room Charge Calculator**

   Implement the *Room Charge Calculator* application from Section 3.10 as a Web application. In place of Group boxes, use Panel Web controls.

3. **Sailboat Race Ranking**

   Create an ASP.NET version of the solution program for Programming Challenge 6 in Chapter 4, named *Sailboat Race Ranking*.

4. **Museum Tours**

   Create an ASP.NET version of the solution program for Programming Challenge 12 in Chapter 4, named *Museum Tours*. Create a hyperlink on the startup form that displays a second browser window containing the cost of the tour, the language, and the list of museum sections they plan to visit.

5. **Karate Payments Grid**

   Write an ASP.NET application that displays the first name, last name, payment date, and payment amounts paid by members in the *Karate.mdf* database. Permit the user to display payments, but not to perform any modifications to the data. Sort the rows by last name. Display the Payment Date column in mm/dd/yyyy format, and display the Amount column in Currency format, encoded as {0:c}. For each column except the payment date, left justify the heading by setting the HeaderStyle. HorizonalAlign property to *Left*. Put a blue border around the grid, 1 pixel wide. Use the grid's HeaderStyle property to give the headings white text on a dark blue background. A sample is shown in Figure 11-68.

Figure 11-68 Grid showing *Karate* members names, dates, and payments

Payments by Karate Students

First_Name	Last_Name	Payment_Date	Amount
Anne	Chong	2/20/2016	$80.00
Anne	Chong	3/20/2016	$55.00
Rafael	Concepcion	2/27/2016	$44.00
Rafael	Concepcion	5/11/2016	$77.00
Aldo	Gonzalez	4/11/2016	$65.00
Aldo	Gonzalez	1/16/2016	$66.00
Elaine	Hasegawa	2/16/2016	$75.00
Elaine	Hasegawa	3/28/2016	$43.00
Brian	Kahane	12/16/2016	$50.00
Brian	Kahane	3/27/2016	$44.00
Keoki	Kahumanu	10/20/2016	$48.00
Keoki	Kahumanu	3/11/2016	$44.00
Jascha	Kousevitzky	3/20/2016	$75.00
Jascha	Kousevitzky	4/20/2016	$77.00
Jascha	Kousevitzky	2/20/2016	$77.00
Moses	Taliafea	7/16/2016	$77.00
Winifred	Taylor	3/20/2016	$77.00
Winifred	Taylor	2/20/2016	$44.00

6. **Karate Schedule Details**

   The *Schedule* table in the *Karate.mdf* database contains the following columns: *ID*, *Day*, *Time*, and *Instructor_Id*. The *Day* value is an integer between 0 and 6, where 0 indicates Monday and 6 indicates Sunday. Display the table in a DetailsView control, and permit the user to add, remove, and update records. Also, display the same table in a GridView control just below the DetailsView. Center all grid columns, and format the time as {0:t}.

   A sample is shown in Figure 11-69.

Figure 11-69 DetailsView and GridView displays of the *Karate Schedule* table

Karate Schedule Details

ID	1000
Day	1
Time	9:30 AM
Instructor_Id	1
Edit Delete New	

ID	Day	Time	Instructor_Id
1000	1	9:30 AM	1
1001	1	10:30 AM	1
1002	1	1:00 PM	2
1003	1	5:00 PM	2
1004	2	4:00 PM	2
1005	2	5:00 PM	2
1006	3	4:00 PM	4
1007	3	5:00 PM	4
1008	4	4:00 PM	2
1009	4	5:00 PM	2

12 Classes, Collections, and Inheritance

This chapter introduces abstract data types and shows you how to create them with classes. The process of analyzing a problem and determining its classes is discussed, and techniques for creating objects, properties, and methods are introduced. Collections, which are structures for holding groups of objects, are also covered. The Object Browser, which allows you to see information about the classes, properties, methods, and events available to your project, is discussed. The chapter concludes by introducing inheritance, a way for new classes to be created from existing ones.

12.1 Classes and Objects

CONCEPT: Classes are program structures that define abstract data types and are used to create objects.

One of the most exciting developments in computer software over the last 30 years has been object-oriented programming. **Object-oriented programming** (OOP) is a way of designing and coding applications such that interchangeable software components can be used to build larger programs. Object-oriented programming languages, such as ALGOL, SmallTalk, and C++, first appeared in the early 1980s. The legacy from these languages has been the gradual development of object-like visual tools for building programs. In Visual Basic, for example, forms, buttons, check boxes, list boxes, and other controls are ideal examples of objects. Object-oriented designs help us produce programs that are well suited to ongoing development and expansion.

Abstract Data Types

An **abstract data type** (**ADT**) is a data type created by a programmer. ADTs are very important in computer science and especially significant in object-oriented programming. An **abstraction** is a general model of something—a definition that includes only the general characteristics of an object. For example, the term *dog* is an abstraction. It defines a general type of animal. The term captures the essence of what all dogs are without specifying the detailed characteristics of any particular breed of dog or any individual animal. According to *Webster's New Collegiate Dictionary*,* a dog is "a highly variable domestic mammal (*Canis familiaris*) closely related to the gray wolf."

In real life, however, there is no such thing as a mere dog. There are specific dogs, each sharing common characteristics such as paws, fur, whiskers, and a carnivorous diet. For example, Travis owns a rottweiler named Bailey, and Shirley owns a poodle named Snuggles. In this analogy, the abstraction (dog) is like a data type and the specific dogs (Bailey and Snuggles) are instances of the type.

Classes

A **class** is a program structure that defines an abstract data type. You create a class and then create instances of the class. All class instances share common characteristics. For example, Visual Basic controls and forms are classes. In the Visual Studio Toolbox, each icon represents a class. When you select the *Button* tool from the Toolbox and place it on a form, as shown in Figure 12-1, you create an instance of the Button class. An instance is also called an **object**.

Figure 12-1 Instances of the Button class

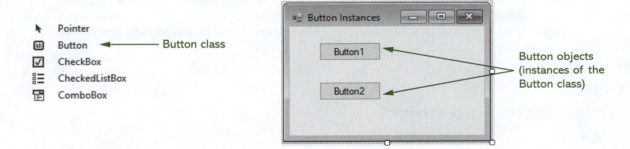

Properties, Methods, and Event Handlers

The way a program communicates with each object is determined by the properties and methods defined in the object's class. The Button class, for example, has properties such as Location, Text, and Name. Each Button object contains its own unique set of property values. In the example shown in Figure 12-1, the two buttons have different values in their Location and Text properties.

Methods are shared by all instances of a class. For example, the Button class has a method named Focus, which is the same for all Button objects.

Event handlers are also methods, but they are specific to individual objects. For example, a form with several buttons will almost always have different code written in each button's Click event procedure.

*By permission. From *Merriam-Webster's Collegiate® Dictionary, 11th Edition* © 2016 by Merriam-Webster, Inc. (www.Merriam-Webster.com).

Object-Oriented Design

Object-oriented design is focused on designing classes in such a way that the resulting objects will effectively cooperate and communicate. The primary goal of object-oriented design is to address the needs of the application or problem being solved. A secondary goal is to design classes that can outlive the current application and possibly be useful in future programs.

The first step, after creating the program specifications, is to analyze the application requirements. **Object-oriented analysis**, as it is called, often starts with a detailed specification of the problem to be solved. A term often applied to this process is **finding the classes**. A famous sculptor once said that inside every block of marble is a work of art waiting to be discovered. So, too, in every problem and every application there are classes waiting to be found. It is the designer's job to discover them.

Finding the Classes

Classes are the fundamental building blocks of object-oriented applications. When designing object-oriented programs, first we select classes that reflect physical entities in the application domain. For example, the user of a record-keeping program for a college might describe some of the application's requirements as follows:

> We need to keep a *list of students* that lets us track the courses they have completed. Each student has a *transcript* that contains all information about his or her completed courses. At the end of each semester, we will calculate the grade point average of each *student*. At times, users will search for a particular *course* taken by a student.

Notice the italicized nouns and noun phrases in this description: list of students, transcript, student, and course. These would ordinarily become classes in the program's design.

Looking for Control Structures

Classes can also be discovered in the description of processing done by an application or in the description of control structures. For example, if the application involved scheduling college classes for students, another description from the program specifications might be:

> We also want to schedule classes for students, using the college's master schedule to determine the times and room numbers for each student's class. When the optimal arrangement of classes for each student has been determined, each student's class schedule will be printed and distributed.

In this description, we anticipate a need for a controlling agent that could be implemented as a class. We might call it Scheduler, a class that matches each student's schedule with the college's master schedule.

Describing the Classes

The next step, after finding the classes in an application, is to describe the classes in terms of attributes and operations. **Attributes** are characteristics of each object that will be implemented as Visual Basic properties. Attributes describe the properties that all objects of the same class have in common. Classes also have **operations**, which are actions objects may perform or messages to which they can respond. Operations are implemented as Visual Basic methods. Table 12-1 describes some of the important attributes and operations of the record-keeping application that we described earlier.

Table 12-1 Sample attributes and operations

Class	Attributes (properties)	Operations (methods)
Student	LastName, FirstName, IdNumber	Display, Input
StudentList	AllStudents, Count	Add, Remove, FindStudent
Course	Semester, Name, Grade, Credits	Display, Input
Transcript	CourseList, Count	Display, Search, CalculateGPA

The complete set of attributes and operations is often incomplete during the early stages of design because it is difficult to anticipate all the application requirements. As a design develops, the need often arises for additional properties and methods that improve communication between objects. Rather than a weakness, however, this ability to accommodate ongoing modifications is one of the strengths of the object-oriented design process.

Interface and Implementation

The **class interface** is the portion of the class that is visible to the application programmer. The program written to use a class is sometimes called the **client program**, in reference to the client-server relationship between a class and the programs that use it. The class interface provides a way for clients to communicate (send messages) to class objects. In Visual Basic, the public properties, methods, and events of a class constitute its interface.

A **class implementation** is the portion of a class that is hidden from client programs; it is created from private member variables, private properties, and private methods. The hiding of data and procedures inside a class is achieved through a process called **encapsulation**. In this, it might be helpful to visualize the class as a *capsule* around its data and procedures.

 Checkpoint

12.1   Give some examples of classes in Visual Basic.

12.2   A TextBox icon appears in the Toolbox and a Textbox control has been placed on a form. Which represents the TextBox class and which is an instance of the TextBox class?

12.3   When analyzing a problem, how do we select useful classes?

12.4   What is an attribute of a class? How are attributes implemented?

12.5   What is an operation of a class? How are operations implemented?

12.6   What is a class interface?

12.7   What is the class implementation?

 ## 12.2   Creating a Class

CONCEPT: To define (create) a class in Visual Basic, you write a class declaration. The class declaration includes member variables, properties, methods, and events that belong to the class.

You define a class in Visual Basic by writing a **class declaration**. We will use the following general format when creating a class:

```
Public Class ClassName
    MemberDeclarations
End Class
```

ClassName is the name of the class. *MemberDeclarations* indicates the variables, constants, and methods (procedures) that will belong to the class. Follow these steps to add a new class to your project:

1. Right-click the project name in the *Solution Explorer* window, and then select *Add Class* from the popup menu. The *Add New Item* dialog box, shown in Figure 12-2, should appear. Make sure that *Class* is selected as the type. Notice that in the figure, the name *Class1.vb* appears in the *Name* text box. In this example, *Class1.vb* is the default name for the file that the class declaration will be stored in, and *Class1* is the default name for the class.

 NOTE: The default name may be different, depending on the number of classes already in the project.

2. Change the default name displayed in the *Name* text box to the name you wish to give the new class file. For example, if you wish to name the new class `Student`, enter *Student.vb* in the *Name* text box.
3. Click the *Add* button.

A new, empty class will be added to your project. The empty class will be displayed in the *Code* window and an entry for the new class file will appear in the *Solution Explorer* window. The *Solution Explorer* window in Figure 12-3 shows a form named `Form1`, and a class named `Student`.

Figure 12-2 *Add New Item dialog box*

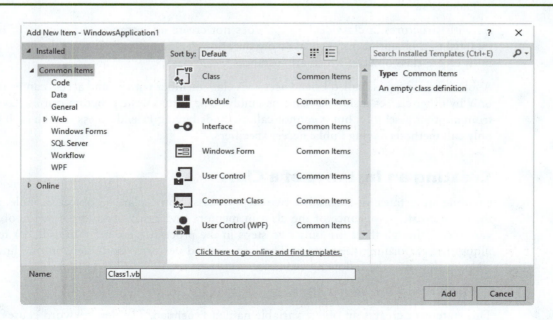

Figure 12-3 *Solution Explorer* window showing one form and one class

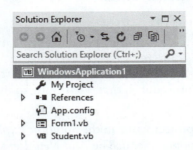

Member Variables

A **member variable** is a variable that is declared inside a class declaration. The variable is a member of the class. A member variable declaration has the following general format:

```
AccessSpecifer VariableName As DataType
```

AccessSpecifier determines the accessibility of the variable. Variables declared with the Public access specifier may be accessed by statements outside the class, and even outside the same assembly. An assembly is a container that holds a collection of classes. When you create a Visual Basic project, an assembly is created automatically by Visual Studio to hold the project's classes. Variables declared with the Private access specifier may be accessed only by statements inside the class declaration. *VariableName* is the name of the variable and *DataType* is the variable's data type. For example, the following code declares a class named Student. The class has three member variables: strLastName, strFirstName, and strId.

```
Public Class Student
    Private strLastName As String       ' Holds last name
    Private strFirstName As String      ' Holds first name
    Private strId As String             ' Holds ID number
End Class
```

As with structures, a class declaration does not create an instance of the class. It only establishes a blueprint for the class's organization. To actually work with the class, you must create **class objects**, which are instances of the class.

Another access type is called **Friend access**. A class member with Friend access can be used only by other classes inside the same assembly. One Visual Basic program can use classes from another assembly, but it cannot call methods having Friend access specifiers. It can only call methods having Public access specifiers.

Creating an Instance of a Class

Creating an instance of a class is a two-step process: You declare an object variable, and then you create an instance of the class in memory and assign its address to the object variable. Although there are only two steps in the process, there are two different techniques for performing these steps. The first method performs both steps in one line of code, as shown in the following example:

```
Dim freshman As New Student
```

This statement creates an object variable named freshman. The New keyword causes the class instance to be created in memory. The object's address is assigned to freshman.

The second method requires two lines of code, as shown in the following example:

```
Dim freshman As Student
freshman = New Student
```

The `Dim` statement in the first line creates an object variable named `freshman`. By default, the object variable is initialized to the value `Nothing`. The second line uses the `New` keyword to create an instance of the `Student` class and assigns its memory address to the `freshman` variable.

When you create instances of a class, each instance has its own copy of the class's member variables.

Accessing Members

Once you have created a class object, you can work with its `Public` members in code. You access the `Public` members of a class object with the dot (`.`) operator. Suppose the `Student` class was declared as follows:

```
Public Class Student
    Public strLastName As String
    Public strFirstName As String
    Public strId As String
End Class
```

In a Windows form, we might create a button `Click` handler procedure that declares `freshman` as a `Student` object. The following statements store values in the object's public member variables:

```
Private Sub btnOk_Click(...) Handles btnOk.Click
    ' Create an instance of the Student class.
    Dim freshman As New Student

    ' Assign values to the object's members.
    freshman.strFirstName = "Joy"
    freshman.strLastName = "Robinson"
    freshman.strId = "23G794"
End Sub
```

One might think that `strFirstName`, `strLastName`, and `strId` are properties of the `Student` class. But implementing properties as public member variables directly is not a good idea. Doing so allows users of the class to modify the variables directly and prevents the author of the class from including range checking or validating of values assigned to variables. Instead, a much better approach is to implement properties as property procedures.

Property Procedures

A **property procedure** is a function that defines a class property. The general format of a property procedure is as follows:

```
Public Property PropertyName() As DataType
    Get
        Statements
    End Get
    Set(ParameterDeclaration)
        Statements
    End Set
End Property
```

PropertyName is the name of the property procedure, and hence the name of the property that the procedure implements. *DataType* is the type of data (such as Integer, String, or

Decimal) that can be assigned to the property. Notice that the procedure has two sections: a `Get` section and a `Set` section. The **Get section** holds the code that is executed when the property value is retrieved, and the **Set section** holds the code that is executed when a value is stored in the property.

TIP: Properties are almost always declared with the `Public` access specifier so they can be accessed from outside their enclosing class module.

TIP: After you type the word `Get` inside a property procedure, Visual Basic will build a code template for the rest of the procedure.

For example, let's add a property to the `Student` class that holds the student's test score average. The modified code for the class follows:

```
Public Class Student
    Private strLastName As String      ' Holds last name
    Private strFirstName As String     ' Holds first name
    Private strId As String            ' Holds ID number
    Private dblTestAverage As Double   ' Holds test average

    Public Property TestAverage() As Double
      Get
        Return dblTestAverage
      End Get
      Set(ByVal value As Double)
        dblTestAverage = value
      End Set
    End Property
End Class
```

Notice that a private member variable named `dblTestAverage` was added to the class to hold the actual value stored in the TestAverage property. We have declared the variable private to prevent code outside the class from storing values directly in it. To store a test average in an object, the property procedure must be used. This allows us to perform validation on the value before it is stored in an object.

Let's look at the `Get` and `Set` sections of the property procedure. The `Get` section does only one thing: It returns the value stored in the `dblTestAverage` member variable. The code for the `Get` section follows:

```
Get
    Return dblTestAverage
End Get
```

Here is the code for the `Set` section:

```
Set(ByVal value As Double)
    dblTestAverage = value
End Set
```

The `Set` section has a declaration for a parameter named `value`. When a number is stored in the TestAverage property, the `Set` section is executed and the number being stored in the property is passed into the `value` parameter. The procedure then assigns the `value` parameter to the `dblTestAverage` member variable.

The following code shows an example of the TestAverage property in use:

```
Dim freshman As New Student
freshman.TestAverage = 82.3
```

The last statement stores the value 82.3 in the TestAverage property. Because a value is being stored in the property, this statement causes the Set section of the TestAverage property procedure to execute. The number 82.3 is passed into the value parameter. The value parameter is then assigned to the object's dblTestAverage member variable.

Any statement that retrieves the value in the TestAverage property causes the property procedure's Get section to execute. For example, the following code assigns the value in the TestAverage property to the variable dblAverage:

```
dblAverage = freshman.TestAverage
```

This statement causes the property's Get section to execute, which returns the value stored in the dblTestAverage member variable. The following code displays the value in the TestAverage property in a message box:

```
MessageBox.Show(freshman.TestAverage.ToString())
```

Creating Property Procedures for the Student Class

Now, let's modify the Student class by implementing the following property procedures: FirstName, LastName, IdNumber, and TestAverage. The code follows:

```
Public Class Student
    Private strLastName As String          ' Holds last name
    Private strFirstName As String         ' Holds first name
    Private strId As String                ' Holds ID number
    Private dblTestAverage As Double       ' Holds test average

    ' LastName property procedure

    Public Property LastName() As String
      Get
        Return strLastName
      End Get
      Set(ByVal value As String)
        strLastName = value
      End Set
    End Property

    ' FirstName property procedure

    Public Property FirstName() As String
      Get
        Return strFirstName
      End Get
      Set(ByVal value As String)
        strFirstName = value
      End Set
    End Property

    ' IdNumber property procedure

    Public Property IdNumber() As String
      Get
        Return strId
      End Get
      Set(ByVal value As String)
        strId = value
      End Set
    End Property
```

```
' TestAverage property procedure

Public Property TestAverage() As Double
  Get
    Return dblTestAverage
  End Get
  Set(ByVal value As Double)
    dblTestAverage = value
  End Set
End Property
End Class
```

Read-Only Properties

Sometimes it is useful to make a property read-only. Client programs can query a **read-only property** to get its value, but cannot modify it. The general format of a read-only property procedure is as follows:

```
Public ReadOnly Property PropertyName() As  DataType
  Get
    Statements
  End Get
End Property
```

The first line of a read-only property procedure contains the ReadOnly keyword. Notice that the procedure has no Set section. It is only capable of returning a value. For example, the following code demonstrates a read-only property named Grade that we might add to our Student class:

```
' Grade read-only property procedure

Public ReadOnly Property Grade() As String
  Get
    ' Variable to hold the grade.
    Dim strGrade As String

    ' Determine the grade.
    If dblTestAverage >= 90.0 Then
      strGrade = "A"
    ElseIf dblTestAverage >= 80.0 Then
      strGrade = "B"
    ElseIf dblTestAverage >= 70.0 Then
      strGrade = "C"
    ElseIf dblTestAverage >= 60.0 Then
      strGrade = "D"
    Else
      strGrade = "F"
    End If

    ' Return the grade.
    Return strGrade
  End Get
End Property
```

This property returns one of the following string values, depending on the contents of the dblTestAverage member variable: "A", "B", "C", "D", or "F".

A compiler error occurs if a client program attempts to store a value in a read-only property. For example, the following statement would result in an error:

```
freshman.Grade = "A"            ' Error
```

Auto-Implemented Properties

An **auto-implemented property** is a class property that is defined by only a single line of code. This is a great convenience, because it means that you do not have to create a private member field to hold the property data. There are two general formats for auto-implemented properties:

```
Public Property PropertyName As DataType
Public Property PropertyName As DataType = InitialValue
```

InitialValue is an optional value that you can assign to the property when it is created. When you declare an auto-implemented property, Visual Studio automatically creates a hidden private field called a *backing field* that contains the property value. The backing field's name is the property name preceded by an underscore character. For example, if you declare an auto-implemented property named ID, its backing field will be named _ID. The following are examples of auto-implemented properties that could be used in the Student class:

```
Public Property FirstName As String
Public Property LastName As String
Public Property IdNumber As String
Public Property TestAverage As Double
```

After learning about auto-implemented properties, why would you ever want to create the longer property definitions? It turns out that the longer property definitions let you include range checking and other validations on data assigned to the property.

Removing Objects and Garbage Collection

It is a good practice to remove objects that are no longer needed, allowing the application to free memory for other purposes. To remove an object, set all the object variables that reference it to Nothing. For example, the following statement sets the object variable freshman to Nothing:

```
freshman = Nothing
```

After this statement executes, the freshman variable will no longer reference an object. If the object that it previously referenced is no longer referenced by any other variables, it will be removed from memory by the .NET garbage collector. The **garbage collector** is a utility program that removes objects from memory when they are no longer needed.

NOTE: The garbage collector might not remove an object from memory immediately when the last reference to it has been removed. The system uses an algorithm to determine when it should periodically remove unused objects. As the amount of available memory decreases, the garbage collector removes unreferenced objects more often.

Going Out of Scope

Like all variables, an object variable declared inside a procedure is local to that procedure. If an object is referenced only by a procedure's local object variable, it becomes eligible to be removed from memory by the garbage collector after the procedure ends. This is called **going out of scope**. For example, look at the following procedure:

```
Sub CreateStudent()
   Dim sophomore As Student ' Object variable
```

```
          ' Create an instance of the Student class.
          sophomore = New Student()

          ' Assign values to its properties.
          sophomore.FirstName = "Travis"
          sophomore.LastName = "Barnes"
          sophomore.IdNumber = "17H495"
          sophomore.TestAverage = 94.7
      End Sub
```

This procedure declares an object variable named sophomore. An instance of the Student class is created and referenced by the sophomore variable. When this procedure ends, the object referenced by sophomore is no longer accessible.

An object is not removed from memory if there are still references to it. For example, assume an application has a global module-level variable named g_studentVar. Look at the following code:

```
      Sub CreateStudent()
          Dim sophomore As Student ' Object variable

          ' Create an instance of the Student class.
          sophomore = New Student()

          ' Assign values to its properties.
          sophomore.FirstName = "Travis"
          sophomore.LastName = "Barnes"
          sophomore.IdNumber = "17H495"
          sophomore.TestAverage = 94.7

          ' Assign the object to a global variable.
          g_studentVar = sophomore
      End Sub
```

The last statement in the procedure assigns g_studentVar the object referenced by sophomore. This means that both g_studentVar and sophomore reference the same object. When this procedure ends, the object referenced by sophomore will not be removed from memory because it is still referenced by the module-level variable g_studentVar.

Comparing Object Variables with the Is and IsNot Operators

Multiple object variables can reference the same object in memory. For example, the following code declares two object variables: collegeStudent and transferStudent. Both object variables are made to reference the same instance of the Student class.

```
      Dim collegeStudent As Student
      Dim transferStudent As Student
      collegeStudent = New Student
      transferStudent = collegeStudent
```

After this code executes, both collegeStudent and transferStudent reference the same object. You cannot use the = operator in an If statement to determine whether two object variables reference the same object. Instead, use the **Is operator**. For example, the following statement properly determines if collegeStudent and transferStudent reference the same object:

```
      If collegeStudent Is transferStudent Then
          ' Perform some action
      End If
```

You can use the **IsNot operator** to determine whether two variables do not reference the same object. The following is an example:

```
If collegeStudent IsNot transferStudent Then
  ' Perform some action
End If
```

If you wish to compare an object variable to the special value `Nothing`, use either the `Is` or `IsNot` operator, as shown in the following code:

```
If collegeStudent Is Nothing Then
  ' Perform some action
End If
If transferStudent IsNot Nothing Then
  ' Perform some action
End If
```

Creating an Array of Objects

You can create an array of object variables, and then create an object for each element of the array to reference. The following code declares `mathStudents` as an array of 10 `Student` objects. Then it uses a loop to assign a `Student` to each element of the array.

```
Dim mathStudents(9) As Student
Dim intCount As Integer
For intCount = 0 To 9
  mathStudents(intCount) = New Student
Next
```

You can use another loop to release the memory used by the array, as shown in the following statements:

```
Dim intCount As Integer

For intCount = 0 To 9
  mathStudents(intCount) = Nothing
Next
```

Writing Procedures and Functions That Work with Objects

Procedures and functions can accept object variables as arguments. For example, the following procedure accepts an object variable that references an instance of the `Student` class as its argument and displays the student's grade.

```
Sub DisplayStudentGrade(ByVal s As Student)
  ' Displays a student's grade.
  MessageBox.Show("The grade for " & s.FirstName &
                  " " & s.LastName & " is " &
                  s.TestGrade.ToString())
End Sub
```

The parameter named `s` references a `Student` object. To call the procedure, pass an object variable that references a `Student` object, as shown in the following code:

```
DisplayStudentGrade(freshman)
```

When this statement executes, the `DisplayStudentGrade` procedure is called, and the `freshman` object variable is passed as an argument. Inside the procedure, the parameter variable `s` references the same object that `freshman` references.

Passing Objects by Value and by Reference

Object variable parameters may be passed by *value* or by *reference*. As you may recall from Chapter 6, a parameter is passed by value when either it contains the ByVal qualifier, or it has no qualifier at all. On the other hand, if the ByRef qualifier is used, the parameter is passed by reference. Please review Section 6.2 for a complete explanation. Be aware, however, that passing by value does not prevent a procedure from accessing and modifying the object referenced by the variable that was passed to the procedure. For example, look at the following ClearStudent procedure:

```
Sub ClearStudent(ByVal s As Student)
  s.FirstName = String.Empty
  s.LastName = String.Empty
  s.IdNumber = String.Empty
  s.TestAverage = 0.0
End Sub
```

Let's assume that a variable referencing a Student object is passed to ClearStudent. The procedure clears the FirstName, LastName, IdNumber, and TestAverage properties of the object referenced by the parameter variable s. For example, look at the following code, which initializes various properties of a Student object and then passes the object to the ClearStudent procedure:

```
freshman.FirstName = "Joy"
freshman.LastName = "Robinson"
freshman.IdNumber = "23G794"
freshman.TestAverage = 82.3

' Clear the properties of the object.
ClearStudent(freshman)
```

After the ClearStudent procedure executes, the properties of the object referenced by the freshman variable are cleared.

If, inside the body of a procedure, we assign a different object to a parameter variable that is passed by value, the assignment does not affect the object that was passed as an argument into the parameter variable. For example, the following procedure accepts an object as its argument, and then assigns the parameter variable s to another object.

```
Sub ResetStudent(ByVal s As Student)
  ' Create an instance of the Student class.
  Dim newStudent As Student

  ' Assign values to the object's properties.
  newStudent.FirstName = "Bill"
  newStudent.LastName = "Owens"
  newStudent.IdNumber = "56K789"
  newStudent.TestAverage = 84.6

  ' Assign the new object to the s parameter.
  s = newStudent
End Sub
```

Suppose we call the procedure, as shown in the following code:

```
freshman.FirstName = "Joy"
freshman.LastName = "Robinson"
freshman.IdNumber = "23G794"
freshman.TestAverage = 82.3
ResetStudent(freshman)
```

After the `ResetStudent` procedure executes, the object referenced by the `freshman` variable still contains the data for Joy Robinson. If the parameter variable `s` was declared `ByRef`, on the other hand, the variable named `freshman` would contain Bill Owens' information after the procedure call.

Returning an Object from a Function

Functions can return objects. For example, the following function creates and initializes a `Student` object. The object is then returned to the caller.

```
' Get student data and return it as an object.

Function GetStudent() As Student
    ' Create an instance of the Student class.
    Dim s As New Student

    ' Get values for the object's properties.
    s.FirstName = InputBox("Enter the student's first name.")
    s.LastName = InputBox("Enter the student's last name.")
    s.IdNumber = InputBox("Enter the student's ID number.")
    s.TestAverage = CDbl(InputBox("Enter the student's test average."))

    ' Return the object's address.
    Return s
End Function
```

The following code assigns the function's return value to the `freshman` object variable:

```
Dim freshman As Student = GetStudent()
```

Methods

A **method** is a procedure or function that is a member of a class. In fact, all of the procedures and functions you have created so far, with the exception of those in modules, are commonly known as methods. The terms *sub procedure* and *function* are still used in Visual Basic for historical reasons. The method performs some operation on the data stored in the class. For example, suppose we wish to add a `Clear` method to the `Student` class, as shown in the following code. To simplify the code listing, the property procedures have been omitted.

```
Public Class Student
    ' Member variables
    Private strLastName As String        ' Holds last name
    Private strFirstName As String       ' Holds first name
    Private strId As String              ' Holds ID number
    Private dblTestAverage As Double     ' Holds test average

    (...Property procedures omitted...)

    ' Clear method
    Public Sub Clear()
        strFirstName = String.Empty
        strLastName = String.Empty
        strId = String.Empty
        dblTestAverage = 0.0
    End Sub
End Class
```

The `Clear` method clears the private member variables that hold the student's first name, last name, ID number, and test average. The following statement calls the method using the object referenced by `freshman`:

```
freshman.Clear()
```

Constructors

A **constructor** is a method that is automatically called when an instance of a class is created. It is helpful to think of constructors as initialization routines. They are useful for initializing member variables or performing other startup operations. To create a constructor, create a method named `New` inside the class. Each time an instance of the class is created, the `New` procedure is executed.

For example, let's add a constructor to the `Student` class that initializes the private member variables. The code follows:

```
Public Class Student
  ' Member variables
  Private strLastName As String        ' Holds last name
  Private strFirstName As String       ' Holds first name
  Private strId As String              ' Holds ID number
  Private dblTestAverage As Double     ' Holds test average

  ' Constructor
  Public Sub New()
    strFirstName = "(unknown)"
    strLastName = "(unknown)"
    strId = "(unknown)"
    dblTestAverage = 0.0
  End Sub

  (The rest of this class is omitted.)

End Class
```

The following statement creates a `Student` object:

```
Dim freshman As New Student
```

When this statement executes, an instance of the `Student` class is created and its constructor is executed. The result is that `freshman.LastName`, `freshman.FirstName`, and `freshman.IdNumber` will hold the string `"(unknown)"` and `freshman.TestAverage` will hold `0.0`.

The `CType` Method

The `CType` method provides a convenient type conversion for variables declared as a more general type, such as Object, which need to be assigned to a more specific variable type. Here's a short example:

```
1: Public obj As Object
2: Public stu As Student

   ' Somewhere else in the program, far away, this line executes:
   obj = new Student()

3: stu = obj           ' Option Strict does not allow this
```

The last line in our example seems like it should compile, since we know from the context that **obj** holds a reference to a student. But compilers like Visual Studio cannot reasonably be asked to search every possible execution path of a program, just in case **obj** was assigned a student! Therefore, we have to use the `CType` method to convince the VB compiler that it's okay to approve the code. And of course, if it turns out at runtime that we were wrong, and **obj** wasn't really referencing a Student after all, VB will throw an exception. CType is known in other programming languages as *casting*, or a *cast* from one type to another. Here's our correction to line 3 from the foregoing example:

```
3: stu = CType(obj, Student)      ' Option Strict allows this
```

The first argument is the variable that needs casting, and the second argument is the type we want to use. It turns out that this will be useful when using `Collection` objects (Section 12.3), since they automatically assume all their elements are type Object (the most general type). `CType` doesn't actually modify any data inside an object—it just convinces the VB compiler that the code should be allowed to compile. If you move ahead in your Visual Basic, C#, or Java programming, you will use the cast operator frequently.

Displaying Messages in the *Output* Window

Before beginning our class-building tutorial, let's discuss a valuable debugging tool: the ***Output* window**. The *Output* window, shown in Figure 12-4, normally appears at the bottom of the Visual Basic environment while an application is running. If you do not see the *Output* window, you can display it by clicking the *View* menu, then *Other Windows*, then *Output*. Alternatively you can press Ctrl+Alt+O. This window displays various messages while an application is being compiled.

Figure 12-4 *Output* window

You can display your own messages in the *Output* window with the `Debug.WriteLine` method. The method has the following general format:

```
Debug.WriteLine(expression)
```

Expression is an expression whose value is to be displayed in the *Output* window. To enable debug messages, insert the following line in your startup form's `Load` event handler:

```
Debug.Listeners.Add(New ConsoleTraceListener())
```

We will use this method in Tutorial 12-1 to display status messages from a class constructor. The constructor will be modified as follows:

```
' Constructor
Public Sub New()
   Debug.WriteLine("Student object was created.")
   strFirstName = String.Empty
   strLastName = String.Empty
   strId = String.Empty
   dblTestAverage = 0.0
End Sub
```

The `Debug.WriteLine` method displays a message in the *Output* window each time a Student object is created.

In Tutorial 12-1, you create the `Student` class we have been using as an example, and use it in an application that saves student data to a file.

Tutorial 12-1:
Creating the *Student Data* application

Step 1:   Create a new Windows Forms Application project named *Student Data*.

Step 2:   Set up the application's form as shown in Figure 12-5.

Step 3:   Perform the following steps to add a new class to the project:
- Right-click the project name in the *Solution Explorer* window, and then click *Add Class*.
- In the *Add New Item* dialog box, make sure *Class* is selected in the *Templates* pane. In the *Name* text box, type *Student.vb*.
- Click the *Add* button.

Figure 12-5 *Student Data* form

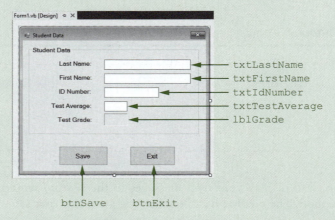

A new class file is created and opened in the *Code* window. The contents of the class appear as follows:

```
Public Class Student

End Class
```

Step 4:   Complete the class by entering the following code shown in bold, in lines 2 through 79. (Don't type the line numbers. They are shown only for reference.)

```
 1 Public Class Student
 2    ' Member variables
 3    Private strLastName As String        ' Holds last name
 4    Private strFirstName As String       ' Holds first name
 5    Private strId As String              ' Holds ID number
 6    Private dblTestAverage As Double     ' Holds test average
 7
 8    ' Constructor
 9    Public Sub New()
10       Debug.WriteLine("Student object being created.")
11       strFirstName = "(unknown)"
12       strLastName = "(unknown)"
13       strId = "(unknown)"
14       dblTestAverage = 0.0
15    End Sub
16
17    ' LastName property procedure
18    Public Property LastName() As String
19       Get
20          Return strLastName
21       End Get
```

```
22        Set(ByVal value As String)
23          strLastName = value
24        End Set
25      End Property
26
27      ' FirstName property procedure
28      Public Property FirstName() As String
29        Get
30          Return strFirstName
31        End Get
32        Set(ByVal value As String)
33          strFirstName = value
34        End Set
35      End Property
36
37      ' IdNumber property procedure
38      Public Property IdNumber() As String
39        Get
40          Return strId
41        End Get
42        Set(ByVal value As String)
43          strId = value
44        End Set
45      End Property
46
47      ' TestAverage property procedure
48      Public Property TestAverage() As Double
49        Get
50          Return dblTestAverage
51        End Get
52        Set(ByVal value As Double)
53          dblTestAverage = value
54        End Set
55      End Property
56
57      ' Grade read-only property procedure
58      Public ReadOnly Property Grade() As String
59        Get
60          ' Variable to hold the grade.
61          Dim strGrade As String
62
63          ' Determine the grade.
64          If dblTestAverage >= 90.0 Then
65            strGrade = "A"
66          ElseIf dblTestAverage >= 80.0 Then
67            strGrade = "B"
68          ElseIf dblTestAverage >= 70.0 Then
69            strGrade = "C"
70          ElseIf dblTestAverage >= 60.0 Then
71            strGrade = "D"
72          Else
73            strGrade = "F"
74          End If
75
76          ' Return the grade.
77          Return strGrade
78        End Get
79      End Property
80 End Class
```

Step 5: Now write the procedures and event handlers for Form1, shown here in bold. Notice the Imports statement in line 1. (Don't type the line numbers. They are shown only for reference.)

```
1  Imports System.IO
2
3  Public Class Form1
4
5    ' The GetData procedure gets data from the text boxes
6    ' and stores it in the object referenced by objStudent.
7    Private Sub GetData(ByVal objStudent As Student)
8      Try
9        ' Assign values from the form to the object properties.
10       objStudent.LastName = txtLastName.Text
11       objStudent.FirstName = txtFirstName.Text
12       objStudent.IdNumber = txtIdNumber.Text
13       objStudent.TestAverage = CDbl(txtTestAverage.Text)
14     Catch ex As Exception
15       ' Display an error message.
16       MessageBox.Show(ex.Message)
17     End Try
18   End Sub
19
20   Private Sub SaveRecord(ByVal objStudent As Student)
21     Dim writer As StreamWriter
22
23     Try
24       ' Open the file in Append mode.
25       writer = File.AppendText("Students.txt")
26
27       ' Save the Student object's properties.
28       writer.WriteLine(objStudent.IdNumber)
29       writer.WriteLine(objStudent.FirstName)
30       writer.WriteLine(objStudent.LastName)
31       writer.WriteLine(objStudent.TestAverage.ToString())
32       writer.WriteLine(objStudent.Grade)
33
34       ' Close the StreamWriter.
35       writer.Close()
36     Catch ex As Exception
37       ' Display an error message.
38       MessageBox.Show(ex.Message)
39     End Try
40   End Sub
41
42   ' The ClearForm procedure clears the form.
43   Private Sub ClearForm()
44     ' Clear the text boxes.
45     txtFirstName.Clear()
46     txtLastName.Clear()
47     txtIdNumber.Clear()
48     txtTestAverage.Clear()
49     lblGrade.Text = String.Empty
50
51     ' Reset the focus.
52     txtLastName.Focus()
53   End Sub
54
55   Private Sub btnSave_Click(...) Handles btnSave.Click
56     ' Create an instance of the Student class.
57     Dim objStudent As New Student
```

```
58
59      ' Get data from the form.
60      GetData(objStudent)
61
62      ' Display the student's grade.
63      lblGrade.Text = objStudent.Grade
64
65      ' Save this student's record.
66      SaveRecord(objStudent)
67
68      ' Confirm that the record was saved.
69      MessageBox.Show("Student record saved.")
70
71      ' Clear the form.
72      ClearForm()
73   End Sub
74
75   Private Sub btnExit_Click(...) Handles btnExit.Click
76      ' Close the form.
77      Me.Close()
78   End Sub
79
80   Private Sub Form1_Load(...) Handles MyBase.Load
81      ' Enable output to the Output window.
82      Debug.Listeners.Add(New ConsoleTraceListener())
83   End Sub
84 End Class
```

Step 6: Save the project and run the application. On the application's form, enter the following data:

Last name: Green
First name: Sara
ID number: 27R8974
Test average: 92.3

Click the *Save* button to save the student data to a file. A message box appears indicating that the record was saved. Notice that the message *Student object being created* is displayed in the *Output* window. This message was displayed by the Student class constructor. Click the *OK* button on the message box.

Step 7: Click the *Exit* button to close the application window.

Checkpoint

12.8 How do you add a class module to a project?

12.9 What two steps must you perform when creating an instance of a class?

12.10 How do you remove an object from memory?

12.11 If an object is created inside a procedure, it is automatically removed from memory when the procedure ends, if no variables declared at the class or module level reference it. What is the name of the process that removes the object?

12.12 What are member variables?

12.13 What is a property procedure?

12.14 What does the Get section of a property procedure do?

12.15 What does the Set section of a property procedure do?

12.16 What is a constructor?

12.3 Collections

> **CONCEPT:** A collection holds a group of items. It automatically expands and shrinks in size to accommodate the items added to it. It allows items to be stored with associated key values, which may then be used in searches.

VideoNote

Creating and using a Collection

A **collection** is similar to an array. It is a single unit that contains several items. You can access the individual items in a collection with an index, which is similar to an array subscript. The difference between an array's subscript and a collection's index is that the latter begins at 1. You might recall that an array's subscripts begin at 0.

Another difference between arrays and collections is that collections automatically expand as items are added and shrink as items are removed. Also, the items stored in a collection do not have to be of the same type.

Visual Basic provides a class named Collection. When you create a collection in an application you are creating an instance of the Collection class. So, creating a collection is identical to creating any other class object. The following statements declare an object variable named customers, and then assign a new Collection instance to it:

```
Dim customers As Collection
customers = New Collection
```

You can also create a Collection instance and assign it to an object variable in one statement as follows:

```
Dim customers As New Collection
```

Adding Items to a Collection

You add items to a collection with the **Add method**. We will use the following general format:

```
CollectionName.Add(Item [, Key])
```

CollectionName is the name of an object variable that references a collection. The *Item* argument is the object, variable, or value that is to be added to the collection. *Key* is an optional string expression that is associated with the item and can be used to search for it. (*Key* must be unique for each member of a collection.)

Let's define a simple class named Customer with two variables and corresponding properties. The properties are abbreviated to save space.

```
Public Class Customer
   Private strName As String
   Private strPhone As String

   Public Property Name As String
      ...
   End Property

   Public Property Phone As String
      ...
   End Property
End Class
```

Suppose we are writing code for a form in our application. At the top of the form, at the class level, we can declare a `Collection` object:

```
Private customers As New Collection
```

Then, in a button's `Click` event handler procedure, we will declare a `Customer` object and assign TextBox values to its properties:

```
Dim myCustomer As New Customer
myCustomer.Name = txtName.Text
myCustomer.Phone = txtPhone.Text
```

Next, we will insert the `Customer` in the customers collection:

```
customers.Add(myCustomer)
```

We have not provided a key value, so we probably do not plan to search for customers later on. The collection is simply acting as a convenient container to hold customers.

Suppose, however, that we plan to search for customers at a later time while the application is running. In that case, we can use a different form of the `Add` statement, which allows us to pass a key value as the second argument:

```
customers.Add(myCustomer, myCustomer.Name)
```

This statement adds the `myCustomer` object to the collection, using the `myCustomer.Name` property as a key. Later, we will be able to search the collection for this object by specifying the customer's name.

Handling Exceptions

An `ArgumentException` is thrown if you attempt to add a member with the same Key as an existing member. The following code example shows how to handle the exception:

```
Try
   customers.Add(myCustomer, myCustomer.Name)
Catch ex as ArgumentException
   MessageBox.Show(ex.Message)
End Try
```

Accessing Items by Their Indexes

You can access an item in a collection by passing an integer to the **Item method** as follows:

```
CollectionName.Item(index)
```

CollectionName is the name of the variable that references the collection, and *index* is the integer index of the item that you want to retrieve. The following statements locate the `Customer` object at index 1 in the collection named `customers`, assign the object to a `Customer` variable, and then display the customer's name in a message box:

```
Dim cust As Customer = CType(customers.Item(1), Customer)
MessageBox.Show("Customer found: " & cust.Name & ": " &
                cust.Phone)
```

Calling the `CType` method is necessary because the `Item` method of a collection returns an Object. We must cast (convert) the Object into a Customer.

Because `Item` is the default method for collections, you can use an abbreviated format such as the following to locate a collection item:

```
Dim cust As Customer = CType(customers(3), Customer)
```

Handling an `IndexOutOfRangeException`

An exception of the `IndexOutOfRangeException` type occurs if you use an index that does not match the index of any item in a collection. The following code example shows how to handle the exception:

```
Try
  Dim cust As Customer

  ' Get the collection index from user input
  Dim index As Integer = CInt(txtIndex.Text)

  ' Locate the customer in the collection
  cust = CType(customers.Item(index), Customer)

  ' Display the customer information
  MessageBox.Show("Customer found: " & cust.Name & ": " &
                  cust.Phone)

Catch ex As IndexOutOfRangeException
  MessageBox.Show(ex.Message)
End Try
```

The Count Property

Each collection has a Count property that holds the number of items stored in the collection. Suppose an application has a list box named `lstNames` and a collection named `names`. The following code uses the Count property as the upper limits of the `For Next` loop.

```
Dim intX As Integer
For intX = 1 To names.Count
  lstNames.Items.Add(names(intX).ToString())
Next
```

Searching for an Item by Key Value Using the `Item` Method

You have already seen how the `Item` method can be used to retrieve an item with a specific index. It can also be used to retrieve an item with a specific key value. When used this way, the general format of the method is as follows:

*CollectionName*Item.(*Expression*)

CollectionName is the name of a collection. *Expression* can be either a numeric or a string expression. If *Expression* is a string, the `Item` method returns the member with the key value that matches the string. If no member exists with an index or key value matching *Expression*, an exception of the type `IndexOutOfRangeException` occurs. (If *Expression* is a numeric expression, it is used as an index value and the `Item` method returns the member at the specified index location.)

For example, the following code searches the `studentCollection` collection for an item with the key value 49812:

```
Dim s as Student
s = CType(studentCollection.Item("49812"), Student)
```

After this code executes, if the item is found, the s variable will reference the object returned by the `Item` method.

The following code uses the Item method to retrieve members by index. It retrieves each member from the collection and displays the value of the LastName property in a message box.

```
Dim intIndex As Integer
Dim aStudent As Student
For intIndex = 1 To studentCollection.Count
   aStudent = CType(studentCollection.Item(intIndex), Student)
   MessageBox.Show(aStudent.LastName)
Next
```

Using References versus Copies

When an item in a collection is of a fundamental Visual Basic data type, such as Integer or Single, you retrieve a copy of the member only. For example, suppose the following code is used to add integers to a collection named numbers:

```
Dim intInput As Integer
intInput = InputBox("Enter an integer value.")
numbers.Add(intInput)
```

Suppose the following code is used to retrieve the integer stored at index 1 and to change its value. Because intNum is only a copy of a value in the collection, the item stored at index 1 is unchanged.

```
Dim intNum As Integer
intNum = CType(numbers(1), Integer)
intNum = 0
```

When an item in a collection is a class object, however, you retrieve a reference to it, not a copy. For example, the following code retrieves the member of the studentCollection collection with the key value 49812, and changes the value of its LastName property to *Griffin*.

```
Dim s as Student
s = CType(studentCollection.Item("49812"), Student)
s.LastName = "Griffin"
```

Because a reference to the member is returned, the LastName property of the object in the collection is modified.

Using the For Each...Next Loop with a Collection

You may also use a For Each...Next loop to access the individual members of a collection, eliminating the need to compare a counter variable against the collection's Count property. For example, the following code prints the LastName property of each member of the studentCollection collection.

```
Dim s As Student
For Each s In studentCollection
   MessageBox.Show(s.LastName)
Next
```

Removing Members

Use the **Remove method** to remove a member from a collection. The general format is:

```
CollectionName.Remove(Expression)
```

CollectionName is the name of a collection. *Expression* can be either a numeric or string expression. If it is a numeric expression, it is used as an index value and the member at the specified index location is removed. If *Expression* is a string, the member with the ¹ value that matches the string is removed. If an index is provided, and it does not ma⸱

index of any item in the collection, an exception of the `IndexOutOfRangeException` type occurs. If a key value is provided, and it does not match the key value of any item in the collection, an exception of the `ArgumentException` type occurs.

For example, the following statement removes the member with the key value "49812" from the `studentCollection` collection:

```
studentCollection.Remove("49812")
```

The following statement removes the member at index location 7 from the `studentCollection` collection:

```
studentCollection.Remove(7)
```

To avoid throwing an exception, always check the range of the index you pass to the `Remove` method. The following is an example:

```
Dim intIndex As Integer
' (assign value to intIndex...)

If intIndex > 0 and intIndex <= studentCollection.Count Then
    studentCollection.Remove(intIndex)
End If
```

Similarly, make sure a key value exists before using it to remove an item, as shown here:

```
Dim strKeyToRemove As String
' (assign value to strKeyToRemove...)

If studentCollection.Contains(strKeyToRemove) Then
    studentCollection.Remove(strKeyToRemove))
End If
```

Writing Sub Procedures and Functions That Use Collections

Sub procedures and functions can accept collections as arguments, and functions can return collections. Remember that a collection is an instance of a class, so follow the same guidelines for passing any class object as an argument, or returning a class object from a function.

Relating the Items in Parallel Collections

Sometimes it is useful to store related data in two or more parallel collections. For example, assume a company assigns a unique employee number to each employee. An application that calculates gross pay has the following collections:

```
Dim hoursWorked As New Collection    ' To hold hours worked
Dim payRates As New Collection       ' To hold hourly pay rates
```

The `hoursWorked` collection stores the number of hours each employee has worked, and the `payRates` collection stores each employee's hourly pay rate.

When an item is stored in the `hoursWorked` or `payRates` collections, the employee's number is the key. For instance, let's say James Bourne's ID number is 55678. He has worked 40 hours and his pay rate is $12.50. The following statements add his data to the appropriate collection:

```
hoursWorked.Add(40, "55678")
payRates.Add(12.5, "55678")
```

To calculate his gross pay, we retrieve his data from each collection, using his ID number as the key:

```
sngGrossPay = hoursWorked.Item("55678") * payRate.Item("55678")
```

Employee Collection Program Example

The following code expands this idea. In addition to using the hoursWorked and payRates collections, this code uses a collection to hold the employee names and a collection to hold the employee ID numbers.

```
Dim empNumbers As New Collection        ' Holds employee numbers
Dim employees As New Collection         ' Holds employee names
Dim hoursWorked As New Collection       ' Holds hours worked
Dim payRates As New Collection          ' Holds hourly pay rates

Dim strEmpNumber As String              ' Employee ID number
Dim strEmpName As String                ' Employee name
Dim decGrossPay, decHours, decRate As Decimal
Dim i As Integer                        ' Loop counter

' Add each employee's number to the empNumbers collection.
empNumbers.Add("55678")
empNumbers.Add("78944")
empNumbers.Add("84417")

' Add the employee names to the employees
' collection, with the employee ID number
' as the key.
employees.Add("James Bourne", "55678")
employees.Add("Jill Davis", "78944")
employees.Add("Kevin Franklin", "84417")

' Add each employee's hours worked to the
' hoursWorked collection, with the employee
' ID number as the key.
hoursWorked.Add(40, "55678")
hoursWorked.Add(35, "78944")
hoursWorked.Add(20, "84417")

' Add each employee's hourly pay rate to the
' payRates collection, with the employee
' ID number as the key.
payRates.Add(12.5, "55678")
payRates.Add(18.75, "78944")
payRates.Add(9.6, "84417")

' Compute and display each employee's
' gross pay.

For intIndex = 1 To employees.Count

    ' Get an employee ID number to use as a key.
    strEmpNumber = empNumbers(intIndex).ToString()

    ' Get this employee's name.
    strEmpName = employees.Item(strEmpNumber).ToString()

    ' Get the hours worked for this employee.
    decHours = CDec(hoursWorked.Item(strEmpNumber))

    ' Get the pay rate for this employee.
    decRate = CDec(payRates.Item(strEmpNumber))

    ' Calculate this employee's gross pay.
    decGrossPay = decHours * decRate

    ' Display the results for this employee.
    lblResult.Text &= "Gross pay for " & strEmpName &
        " is " & decGrossPay.ToString("c") & vbCrLf
Next
```

Checkpoint

12.17 How do collections differ from arrays?

12.18 How do you add members to a collection?

12.19 How is a key value useful when you are adding an item to a collection?

12.20 How do you search for a specific member of a collection?

12.21 How do you remove a member from a collection?

12.4   Focus on Problem Solving: Creating the *Student Collection* Application

Campus Systems, Inc. is developing software for a university and has hired you as a programmer. Your first assignment is to develop an application that allows the user to select a student's ID number from a list box to view information about the student. The user should also be able to add new student records and delete student records. The application will use the Student class and a collection of Student class objects. A test application with two forms has already been created for you.

In Tutorial 12-2, you examine the existing forms of the *Student Collection* application.

 Tutorial 12-2:
Completing the *Student Collection* application

VideoNote

Completing the *Student Collection* application

Step 1:   Open the *Student Collection* project from the student sample programs folder named *Chap12\Student Collection*.

The project already has two forms, as shown in Figures 12-6 and 12-7. The MainForm form has a list box, lstIdNumbers, which will display a list of student ID numbers. When a student's ID number is selected from the list box, the data for that student will be displayed in the following Label controls: lblLastName, lblFirstName, lblIdNumber, lblTestAverage, and lblGrade. The *Add Student* button causes the AddForm form to be displayed. The *Remove* button removes the student whose ID number is currently selected.

Figure 12-6 MainForm form

Figure 12-7 AddForm form

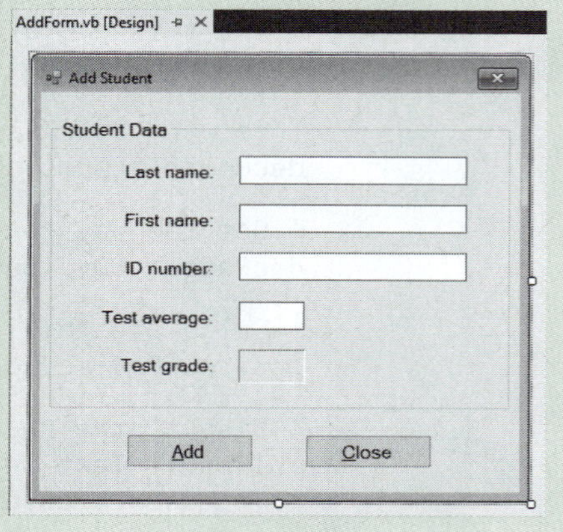

Step 2: Add the Student class you created in Tutorial 12-1 to the project. (Click *Project* on the menu bar, and then click *Add Existing Item*. Browse to the folder containing the *Student.vb* file. Select the *Student.vb* file and click the *Add* button.)

Step 3: Add a module to the project. Name the module *StudentCollectionModule.vb*. Complete the module by entering the following code, shown in bold. (Don't type the line numbers. They are shown only for reference.)

```
1 Module StudentCollectionModule
2   ' Create a collection to hold Student objects.
3   Public studentCollection As New Collection
4
5   ' The AddRecord procedure adds the object referenced
6   ' by s to the collection. It uses the student ID number
7   ' as the key.
8
9   Public Sub AddRecord(ByVal s As Student)
10    Try
11       studentCollection.Add(s, s.IdNumber)
12    Catch ex As Exception
13       MessageBox.Show(ex.Message)
14    End Try
15  End Sub
16 End Module
```

The statement in line 3 creates a collection, referenced by the object variable studentCollection. Because it is declared as Public, it will be available to all the forms in the project. The AddRecord procedure in lines 9 through 15, also declared as Public, accepts a Student object as an argument, and adds that object to the studentCollection collection.

Step 4: Now write the procedures and event handlers for the MainForm form, shown here. (Don't type the line numbers. They are shown only for reference.) Before you begin entering the code, make sure you understand how to create the code template for the lstIdNumbers_SelectedIndexChanged event handler in lines 84 through 101. This event handler will execute anytime the user selects an item in the lstIdNumbers list box. To create the code template, simply open MainForm in the *Designer* window and double-click the lstIdNumbers list box. (The comments that appear in lines 81 through 83 are there only as a reminder of how to create the code template. You do not need to type those comments into your code.)

```
1 Public Class MainForm
2   ' The ClearForm procedure clears the form.
3   Private Sub ClearForm()
4      lblFirstName.Text = String.Empty
5      lblLastName.Text = String.Empty
6      lblIdNumber.Text = String.Empty
7      lblTestAverage.Text = String.Empty
8      lblGrade.Text = String.Empty
9   End Sub
10
11  ' The UpdateListBox procedure updates the
12  ' contents of the list box.
13  Private Sub UpdateListBox()
14     ' Clear the list box.
15     lstIdNumbers.Items.Clear()
16
```

```
17        ' Load the ID numbers in the collection
18        ' into the list box.
19        Dim s As Student
20        For Each s In studentCollection
21          lstIdNumbers.Items.Add(s.IdNumber)
22        Next
23
24        ' Select the first item in the list.
25        If lstIdNumbers.Items.Count > 0 Then
26          lstIdNumbers.SelectedIndex = 0
27        Else
28          ClearForm()
29        End If
30    End Sub
31
32    ' The DisplayData procedure displays the data contained
33    ' in the Student object parameter.
34    Private Sub DisplayData(ByVal s As Student)
35        lblLastName.Text = s.LastName
36        lblFirstName.Text = s.FirstName
37        lblIdNumber.Text = s.IdNumber
38        lblTestAverage.Text = s.TestAverage.ToString()
39        lblGrade.Text = s.Grade
40    End Sub
41
42    Private Sub btnAdd_Click(...) Handles btnAdd.Click
43        ' Create an instance of the AddForm form.
44        Dim frmAdd As New AddForm
45
46        ' Display the form.
47        frmAdd.ShowDialog()
48
49        ' Update the contents of the list box.
50        UpdateListBox()
51    End Sub
52
53    Private Sub btnRemove_Click(...) Handles btnRemove.Click
54        Dim intIndex As Integer
55
56        ' Make sure an item is selected.
57        If lstIdNumbers.SelectedIndex <> -1 Then
58          ' Confirm that the user wants to remove the item.
59          If MessageBox.Show("Are you sure?", "Confirm Deletion",
60                        MessageBoxButtons.YesNo) =
61                        Windows.Forms.DialogResult.Yes Then
62
63            ' Retrieve the student's data from the collection.
64            intIndex = lstIdNumbers.SelectedIndex
65
66            Try
67              ' Remove the selected item from the collection.
68              studentCollection.Remove(
69                lstIdNumbers.SelectedItem.ToString())
70
71              ' Update the list box.
72              UpdateListBox()
73            Catch ex As Exception
```

```
74              ' Error message
75                MessageBox.Show(ex.Message)
76          End Try
77       End If
78     End If
79   End Sub
80
81   ' Note: To create the code template for the
82   ' following event handler, double-click the lstIdNumbers
83   ' list box in the Designer window.
84   Private Sub lstIdNumbers_SelectedIndexChanged(...) Handles...
85     Dim objStudent As Student
86
87     ' See if an item is selected.
88     If lstIdNumbers.SelectedIndex <> -1 Then
89       ' Retrieve the student's data from the collection.
90       Try
91         objStudent = CType(studentCollection.Item(
92           lstIdNumbers.SelectedItem), Student)
93
94         ' Display the student data.
95         DisplayData(objStudent)
96       Catch ex As Exception
97         ' Error message
98         MessageBox.Show(ex.Message)
99       End Try
100    End If
101  End Sub
102
103  Private Sub btnExit_Click(...) Handles btnExit.Click
104    ' Close the form.
105    Me.Close()
106  End Sub
107 End Class
```

Step 5: Now write the procedures and event handlers for the AddForm form, shown here. (Line numbers are shown only for reference.)

```
1 Public Class AddForm
2   ' The GetData procedure gets data from the form
3   ' and stores it in the Student object parameter.
4   Private Sub GetData(ByVal s As Student)
5     s.LastName = txtLastName.Text
6     s.FirstName = txtFirstName.Text
7     s.IdNumber = txtIdNumber.Text
8     s.TestAverage = CDbl(txtTestAverage.Text)
9   End Sub
10
11  ' The ClearForm procedure clears the form.
12  Private Sub ClearForm()
13    ' Clear the text boxes.
14    txtFirstName.Text = String.Empty
15    txtLastName.Text = String.Empty
16    txtIdNumber.Text = String.Empty
17    txtTestAverage.Text = String.Empty
18    lblGrade.Text = String.Empty
19
20    ' Reset the focus.
21    txtLastName.Focus()
22  End Sub
```

```
23
24     Private Sub btnAdd_Click(...) Handles btnAdd.Click
25        ' Create an instance of the Student class.
26        Dim objStudent As New Student
27
28        ' Get data from the form.
29        GetData(objStudent)
30
31        ' Display the student's grade.
32        lblGrade.Text = objStudent.Grade
33
34        ' Save the student's record.
35        AddRecord(objStudent)
36
37        ' Confirm that the record was saved.
38        MessageBox.Show("Record added.")
39
40        ' Clear the form.
41        ClearForm()
42     End Sub
43
44     Private Sub btnClose_Click(...) Handles btnClose.Click
45        ' Close the form.
46        Me.Close()
47     End Sub
48 End Class
```

Step 6: Save the project and run the application. Click the *Add Student* button and add the following students:

Student 1
Last name: Green
First name: Sara
ID number: 27R8974
Test average: 92.3

Student 2
Last name: Robinson
First name: Joy
ID number: 89G4561
Test average: 97.3

Student 3
Last name: Williams
First name: Jon
ID number: 71A4478
Test average: 78.6

Step 7: Close the AddForm form. The main form should now appear as shown in Figure 12-8.

Step 8: Select a student's ID number in the list box. That student's data is displayed in the Label controls.

Step 9: Remove each student by selecting an ID number and then clicking the *Remove* button. Click *Yes* when asked *Are you sure?*

Step 10: Exit the application. Leave the *Student Collection* project loaded for Tutorial 12-3.

Figure 12-8 `MainForm` with students added

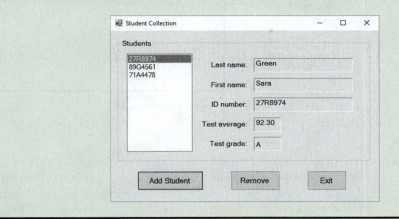

12.5 The Object Browser

> **CONCEPT:** The Object Browser is a dialog box that allows you to browse all classes and components available to your project.

The **Object Browser** is a dialog box that displays information about objects. You can use the Object Browser to examine classes you have created, as well as the namespaces, classes, and other components that Visual Basic makes available to your project. Tutorial 12-3 guides you through the process of using the Object Browser to examine the classes you created in the *Student Collection* project.

Tutorial 12-3:
Using the Object Browser

Step 1: Make sure that you have the *Student Collection* project you created in Tutorial 12-2 opened in Visual Studio.

Step 2: Open the Object Browser by performing one of the following actions:
- Click *View* on the menu bar, and then click *Object Browser*.
- Press the [F2] key.

The *Object Browser* window appears as shown in Figure 12-9 where we have typed *Student_Collection* into the Search input line and pressed the *Enter* key. The left pane is the *objects* pane, and the right pane is the *members* pane. When you select an item in the *objects* pane on the left, information about that item appears in the *members* pane on the right.

Figure 12-9 *Object Browser* window

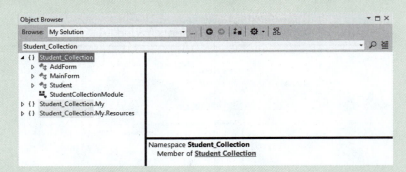

Step 3: Notice in Figure 12-9 that a *{} Student_Collection* entry appears in the objects pane. The braces *{}* indicate that Student_Collection is a namespace. Visual Studio has created a namespace for this project and named it Student_Collection. The contents of the project are stored in this namespace. Click the small arrow at the left of this entry to expand it. Now entries appear for AddForm, MainForm, Student, and StudentCollectionModule.

Step 4: Click the entry for Student. All members of the Student class should be listed in the *members* pane, as shown in Figure 12-10. If you click an entry in the *members* pane, a brief summary of the member is displayed below the pane. If you double-click an entry, the *Code* window appears with the cursor positioned at the selected item's declaration statement.

Figure 12-10 Members of the Student class displayed in the *members* pane

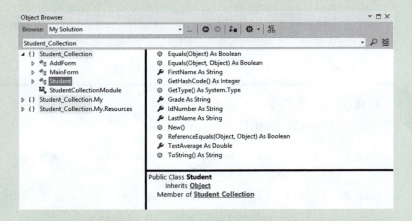

Step 5: Click some other entries under *{} Student_Collection* in the *object* window, such as MainForm and StudentCollectionModule, to view their members in the *members* window.

Step 6: Because forms and controls are classes, the Object Browser can be used to examine them as well. You can use this tool to quickly find out what methods and properties a control has. For example, type *TextBox* in the Search box and press Enter. The results of the search will appear in the left-hand pane. Double-click the entry for *System.Windows.Forms.TextBox*. The TextBox class should appear selected in the *objects* pane and the members of the TextBox class should appear in the *members* pane.

Step 7: Close the Object Browser and close the project.

12.6 Introduction to Inheritance

CONCEPT: Inheritance allows a new class to be based on an existing class. The new class inherits the accessible member variables, methods, and properties of the class on which it is based.

An important aspect of object-oriented programming is inheritance. **Inheritance** allows you to create new classes that inherit, or derive, characteristics of existing classes. For example, you might start with the Student class we discussed earlier, which has only general information for all types of students. But special types of students might require the creation of classes such as GraduateStudent, ExchangeStudent, StudentEmployee, and so on. These new classes would share all the characteristics of the Student class, and they would each add the new characteristics that make them specialized.

In an inheritance relationship, there is a base class and a derived class. The **base class** is a general-purpose class that other classes may be based on. The **derived class** is based on the base class and inherits characteristics from it. You can think of the base class as the parent and the derived class as the child.

Let's look at an example. The following Vehicle class has two private variables and two property procedures: Passengers and MilesPerGallon. The Passengers property uses the intPassengers member variable and the MilesPerGallon property uses the sngMPG member variable.

```
Public Class Vehicle
    ' Private member variables
    Private intPassengers As Integer        ' Number of passengers
    Private dblMPG As Double                ' Miles per gallon

    ' Passengers property
    Public Property Passengers() As Integer
      Get
        Return intPassengers
      End Get
      Set(ByVal value As Integer)
        intPassengers = value
      End Set
    End Property
```

```
    ' MilesPerGallon property
    Public Property MilesPerGallon() As Double
      Get
         Return dblMPG
      End Get
      Set(ByVal value As Double)
        dblMPG = value
      End Set
    End Property
  End Class
```

(The *Vehicle Inheritance* program in the Chapter 12 student sample programs folder contains the code examples shown here.) The Vehicle class holds only general data about a vehicle. By using it as a base class, however, we can create other classes that hold more specialized data about specific types of vehicles. For example, look at the following code for a Truck class:

```
Public Class Truck
  Inherits Vehicle

    ' Private member variables
    Private dblCargoWeight As Double      ' Maximum cargo weight
    Private blnFourWheelDrive As Boolean   ' Four wheel drive

    ' MaxCargoWeight property
    Public Property MaxCargoWeight() As Double
      Get
         Return dblCargoWeight
      End Get
      Set(ByVal value As Single)
        dblCargoWeight = value
      End Set
  End Property

    ' FourWheelDrive property
    Public Property FourWheelDrive() As Boolean
      Get
         Return blnFourWheelDrive
      End Get
      Set(ByVal value As Boolean)
        blnFourWheelDrive = value
      End Set
    End Property
  End Class
```

Notice the second line of this class declaration:

```
  Inherits Vehicle
```

This statement indicates that this class is derived from the Vehicle class. Because it is derived from the Vehicle class, the Truck class inherits all the Vehicle class member variables, methods, and properties that are not declared Private. In addition to the inherited base class members, the Truck class adds two properties of its own: MaxCargoWeight, which hold the maximum cargo weight, and FourWheelDrive, which indicates whether the truck uses four-wheel drive.

In the Form1 form, the following statements create an instance of the Truck class:

```
Dim pickUp as Truck
pickUp = New Truck
```

And the following statements store values in all of the object's properties:

```
pickUp.Passengers = 2
pickUp.MilesPerGallon = 18.0
pickUp.MaxCargoWeight = 2000.0
pickUp.FourWheelDrive = True
```

Notice that values are stored not only in the MaxCargoWeight and FourWheelDrive properties, but also in the Passengers and MilesPerGallon properties. The Truck class inherits the Passengers and MilesPerGallon properties from the Vehicle class.

Overriding Properties and Methods

Sometimes a property procedure or method in a base class is not appropriate for a derived class. If this is the case, you can **override** the base class property procedure or method by adding one with the same name to the derived class. When an object of the derived class accesses the property or calls the method, the overridden version in the derived class is executed rather than the version in the base class. For example, the Vehicle class has the following property procedure:

```
Public Property Passengers() As Integer
   Get
      Return intPassengers
   End Get
   Set(ByVal value As Integer)
      intPassengers = value
   End Set
End Property
```

The Set section of this property procedure stores any value passed to it in the intPassengers variable. Suppose that in the Truck class we want to restrict the number of passengers to either 1 or 2. We can override the Passengers property procedure by writing another version of it in the Truck class.

First, we must add the Overridable keyword to the property procedure in the Vehicle class, as follows:

```
Public Overridable Property Passengers() As Integer
   Get
      Return intPassengers
   End Get
   Set(ByVal value As Integer)
      intPassengers = value
   End Set
End Property
```

The **Overridable keyword** indicates that the procedure may be overridden in a derived class. If we do not add this keyword to the declaration, a compiler error will occur when we attempt to override the procedure. The general format of a property procedure with the Overridable keyword is as follows:

```
Public Overridable Property PropertyName() As DataType
   Get
      Statements
   End Get
   Set(ParameterDeclaration)
      Statements
   End Set
End Property
```

NOTE: A private property cannot be overridable.

Next, we add a property by the same name to the Truck class, as follows:

```
' Passengers property
Public Overrides Property Passengers() As Integer
  Get
    Return MyBase.Passengers
  End Get
  Set(ByVal value As Integer)
    If value >= 1 And value <= 2 Then
      MyBase.Passengers = value
    Else
      MessageBox.Show("Passengers must be 1 or 2.", "Error")
    End If
  End Set
End Property
```

This property declaration uses the **Overrides keyword**, indicating that it overrides a property in the base class. The general format of a property that overrides a base class property is as follows:

```
Public Overrides Property PropertyName() As DataType
  Get
    Statements
  End Get
  Set(ParameterDeclaration)
    Statements
  End Set
End Property
```

Let's see how the code in the property works. The Get section has the following statement:

```
Return MyBase.Passengers
```

The **MyBase keyword** refers to the base class. The expression MyBase.Passengers refers to the base class's Passengers property. This statement returns the same value returned from the base class's Passengers property.

The Set section uses an If statement to validate that value is 1 or 2. If value is 1 or 2, the following statement is executed:

```
MyBase.Passengers = value
```

This statement stores value in the base class's Passenger property. If value is not 1 or 2, an error message is displayed. So, the following code will cause the error message to appear:

```
Dim pickUp As New Truck
pickUp.Passengers = 5
```

The complete code for the modified Vehicle and Truck classes follows:

```
Public Class Vehicle
  ' Private member variables
  Private intPassengers As Integer      ' Number of passengers
  Private dblMPG As Double              ' Miles per gallon

  ' Passengers property
  Public Overridable Property Passengers() As Integer
    Get
      Return intPassengers
    End Get
    Set(ByVal value As Integer)
      intPassengers = value
    End Set
  End Property
```

```
      ' MilesPerGallon property
    Public Property MilesPerGallon() As Double
      Get
         Return dblMPG
      End Get
      Set(ByVal value As Double)
         dblMPG = value
      End Set
    End Property
End Class

Public Class Truck
    Inherits Vehicle

    ' Private member variables
    Private dblCargoWeight As Double       ' Maximum cargo weight
    Private blnFourWheelDrive As Boolean     ' Four wheel drive

    ' MaxCargoWeight property
    Public Property MaxCargoWeight() As Double
      Get
         Return dblCargoWeight
      End Get
      Set(ByVal value As Double)
         dblCargoWeight = value
      End Set
    End Property

    ' FourWheelDrive property
    Public Property FourWheelDrive() As Boolean
      Get
         Return blnFourWheelDrive
      End Get
      Set(ByVal value As Boolean)
         blnFourWheelDrive = value
      End Set
    End Property

    ' Passengers property
    Public Overrides Property Passengers() As Integer
      Get
         Return MyBase.Passengers
      End Get
      Set(ByVal value As Integer)
        If value >= 1 And value <= 2 Then
           MyBase.Passengers = value
        Else
           MessageBox.Show("Passengers must be 1 or 2.", "Error")
        End If
      End Set
    End Property
End Class
```

Overriding Methods

Class methods may be overridden in the same manner as property procedures. The general format of an overridable base class Sub procedure is as follows:

```
Public Overridable Sub ProcedureName()
    Statements
End Sub
```

The general format of an overridable base class function is as follows:

```
Public Overridable Function FunctionName() As DataType
    Statements
End Function
```

NOTE: A private procedure or function cannot be overridable.

The general format of a Sub procedure that overrides a base class Sub procedure is as follows:

```
AccessSpecifier Overrides Sub ProcedureName()
    Statements
End Sub
```

The general format of a function that overrides a base class function is as follows:

```
AccessSpecifier Overrides Function FunctionName() As DataType
    Statements
End Sub
```

Because a derived class cannot access the private members of its base class, the overridable methods in the base class cannot be declared Private. A derived class method that overrides a base class method must keep the same access level (such as Public).

Overriding the ToString Method

By now you are familiar with the ToString method that all Visual Basic data types provide. This method returns a string representation of the data stored in a variable or object.

Every class you create in Visual Basic is automatically derived from a built-in class named Object. The **Object class** has a method named ToString which returns a fully qualified class name (System.String), which includes the namespace named *System*. You can override this method so it returns a string representation of the data stored in an object. For example, we can add the following ToString method to the Vehicle class:

```
Public Overrides Function ToString() As String
    ' Return a string representation
    ' of a vehicle.
    Dim str As String
    str = "Passengers: " & intPassengers.ToString() &
        " MPG: " & dblMPG.ToString()
    Return str
End Function
```

Our ToString method must be declared Public because ToString has already been given public visibility in the Object class. The ToString implementation shown here returns a string showing a vehicle's number of passengers and the miles-per-gallon. When a method is declared with the Overrides keyword, it is also implicitly declared as Overridable. So, we can override this ToString method in the Truck class, as follows:

```
Public Overrides Function ToString() As String
    Dim str As String
    str = MyBase.ToString() & " Max. Cargo: " &
        dblCargoWeight.ToString() & " 4WD: " &
        blnFourWheelDrive.ToString()
    Return str
End Function
```

This method calls MyBase.ToString, which is the Vehicle class's ToString method. To that method's return value, it appends string versions of the sngCargoWeight and blnFourWheelDrive variables. The resulting string is then returned. The following statements, located in a separate class, create a Truck object, assign values to its properties, and call the ToString method:

```
Dim bigTruck As New Truck
bigTruck.Passengers = 2
bigTruck.MilesPerGallon = 14.0
bigTruck.MaxCargoWeight = 8000.0
bigTruck.FourWheelDrive = True
MessageBox.Show(bigTruck.ToString())
```

This code will display the following string in a message box:

```
Passengers: 2 MPG: 14.0 Max. Cargo: 8000.0 4WD: True
```

Base Class and Derived Class Constructors

Earlier in this chapter, you learned that a constructor is a special class method named New, and the constructor is automatically called when an instance of the class is created. It is possible for both a base class and a derived class to have constructors. For example, look at the following abbreviated versions of the Vehicle and Truck classes containing constructors:

```
Public Class Vehicle

  Public Sub New()
    MessageBox.Show("This is the base class constructor.")
  End Sub
  ' (other properties and methods...)
End Class

Public Class Truck
    Inherits Vehicle

  Public Sub New()
    MessageBox.Show("This is the derived class constructor.")
  End Sub
  ' (other properties and methods...)
End Class
```

When an instance of the derived class is created, the base class constructor is automatically called first and then the derived class constructor is called. So, creating an instance of the Truck class will cause the message *This is the base class constructor* to be displayed, followed by the message *This is the derived class constructor*.

 NOTE: The Overridable and Overrrides keywords are not used with constructors.

Protected Members

In addition to Private and Public, we will also study the Protected access specifier. The **Protected access specifier** may be used in the declaration of a base class member, such as the following:

```
Protected decCost As Decimal
```

This statement declares a protected variable named decCost. Protected base class members are like private members, except they may be accessed by methods and property procedures in derived classes. To all other classes, however, protected class members are just like private class members.

In Tutorial 12-4, you complete an application that uses inheritance.

Tutorial 12-4:
Completing an application that uses inheritance

In this tutorial, you will complete an application that keeps records about the number of course hours completed by computer science students. You will create a class named `GeneralStudent`, which will have properties to hold the following data: first name, last name, ID number, math hours completed, communications hours completed, humanities hours completed, elective hours completed, and total hours completed. This class will have a method named `UpdateHours` that will calculate the total hours completed when any of the other hours are changed. In addition, the class will override the `ToString` method.

You will also create a class named `CsStudent`, derived from the `GeneralStudent` class. The `CsStudent` class will have a property to hold the number of computer science hours completed. This class will override the `GeneralStudent` class's `UpdateHours` method to add the number of computer science hours.

Step 1: Open the *Computer Science Student* project from the *Chap12* student sample programs folder. The forms have already been built for you. Figure 12-11 shows the `MainForm` form and Figure 12-12 shows the `DisplayForm` form.

Figure 12-11 `MainForm` form

Figure 12-12 `DisplayForm` form

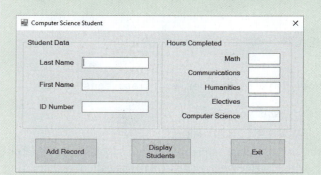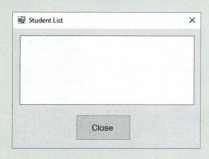

Step 2: Add a new class named `GeneralStudent` to the project. (Name the class file *GeneralStudent.vb*.) Complete the class by entering the following code, shown in bold. (Don't type the line numbers. They are shown only for reference.)

```
1 Public Class GeneralStudent
2    ' Member variables for last name, first name,
3    ' and ID number
4    Private strLastName As String
5    Private strFirstName As String
6    Private strIdNum As String
7
8    ' Member variables for hours completed
9    Private dblMathHours As Double
10   Private dblCommHours As Double
```

```
11    Private dblHumHours As Double
12    Private dblElectHours As Double
13    Protected dblTotalHours As Double
14
15    ' Constructor to initialize member variables
16    Public Sub New()
17      strLastName = "(Unknown)"
18      strFirstName = "(Unknown)"
19      strIdNum = "(Unknown)"
20      dblMathHours = 0.0
21      dblCommHours = 0.0
22      dblHumHours = 0.0
23      dblElectHours = 0.0
24      dblTotalHours = 0.0
25    End Sub
26
27    ' The UpdateHours procedure updates the hours completed.
28    Public Overridable Sub UpdateHours()
29      dblTotalHours = dblMathHours + dblCommHours +
30        dblHumHours + dblElectHours
31    End Sub
32
33    ' Last Name property
34    Public Property LastName() As String
35      Get
36        Return strLastName
37      End Get
38      Set(ByVal value As String)
39        strLastName = value
40      End Set
41    End Property
42
43    ' First name property
44    Public Property FirstName() As String
45      Get
46        Return strFirstName
47      End Get
48      Set(ByVal value As String)
49        strFirstName = value
50      End Set
51    End Property
52
53    ' IdNumber property
54    Public Property IdNumber() As String
55      Get
56        Return strIdNum
57      End Get
58      Set(ByVal value As String)
59        strIdNum = value
60      End Set
61    End Property
62
63    ' MathHours property
64    Public Property MathHours() As Double
65      Get
66        Return dblMathHours
67      End Get
68      Set(ByVal value As Double)
69        dblMathHours = value
```

```
70        UpdateHours()
71      End Set
72    End Property
73
74    ' CommunicationsHours property
75    Public Property CommunicationsHours() As Double
76      Get
77        Return dblCommHours
78      End Get
79      Set(ByVal value As Double)
80        dblCommHours = value
81        UpdateHours()
82      End Set
83    End Property
84
85    ' HumanitiesHours property
86    Public Property HumanitiesHours() As Double
87      Get
88        Return dblHumHours
89      End Get
90      Set(ByVal value As Double)
91        dblHumHours = value
92        UpdateHours()
93      End Set
94    End Property
95
96    ' ElectiveHours property
97    Public Property ElectiveHours() As Double
98      Get
99        Return dblElectHours
100     End Get
101     Set(ByVal value As Double)
102       dblElectHours = value
103       UpdateHours()
104     End Set
105   End Property
106
107   ' HoursCompleted property (read-only)
108   Public ReadOnly Property HoursCompleted() As Double
109     Get
110       Return dblTotalHours
111     End Get
112   End Property
113
114   ' Overridden ToString method
115   Public Overrides Function ToString() As String
116     Dim str As String
117     str = "Name: " & strLastName & ", " &
118       strFirstName & " Completed Hours: " &
119       dblTotalHours.ToString()
120     Return str
121   End Function
122 End Class
```

Step 3: Add another class named `CsStudent` to the project. (Name the class file *CsStudent.vb*.) This class will be derived from the `GeneralStudent` class.

Complete the class by entering the following code, shown in bold, without the line numbers.

```
1 Public Class CsStudent
2   Inherits GeneralStudent
3
4   ' Member variable for CS hours completed
5   Private dblCompSciHours As Double
6
7   ' Constructor
8   Public Sub New()
9     dblCompSciHours = 0.0
10  End Sub
11
12  ' Overridden UpdateHours method
13  Public Overrides Sub UpdateHours()
14    MyBase.UpdateHours()
15    dblTotalHours += dblCompSciHours
16  End Sub
17
18  ' CompSciHours property
19  Public Property CompSciHours() As Double
20    Get
21      Return dblCompSciHours
22    End Get
23    Set(ByVal value As Double)
24      dblCompSciHours = value
25      UpdateHours()
26    End Set
27  End Property
28 End Class
```

Step 4: Add a module named *CompSciStudentModule.vb* to the project. Complete the module by entering the following code, shown in bold, without the line numbers.

```
1 Module CompSciStudentModule
2   ' Collection for computer science students
3   Public csStudentCollection As New Collection
4
5   ' The AddStudent procedure adds a CsStudent object
6   ' to the collection and uses the IdNumber property
7   ' as the key.
8
9   Public Sub AddStudent(ByVal objCsStudent As CsStudent)
10    Try
11      csStudentCollection.Add(objCsStudent,
12                              objCsStudent.IdNumber)
13    Catch ex As Exception
14      MessageBox.Show(ex.Message)
15    End Try
16  End Sub
17 End Module
```

Line 3 creates a public collection named csStudentCollection. We will use this collection to hold CsStudent objects. The AddStudent public procedure in lines 9 through 16 accepts a CsStudent object as an argument and adds it to the csStudentCollection collection.

Step 5: Now you will write the procedures and event handlers for the `MainForm` form. Complete the form as follows by entering the code shown in bold, without the line numbers.

```
1 Public Class MainForm
2   ' The GetData procedure assigns values from the form
3   ' to a CsStudent object's properties.
4   Private Sub GetData(ByVal objCsStudent As CsStudent)
5     Try
6       ' Get name and ID number
7       objCsStudent.LastName = txtLastName.Text
8       objCsStudent.FirstName = txtFirstName.Text
9       objCsStudent.IdNumber = txtIdNumber.Text
10
11      ' Get hours
12      objCsStudent.MathHours = CDbl(txtMath.Text)
13      objCsStudent.CommunicationsHours = CDbl(txtComm.Text)
14      objCsStudent.HumanitiesHours = CDbl(txtHum.Text)
15      objCsStudent.ElectiveHours = CDbl(txtElect.Text)
16      objCsStudent.CompSciHours = CDbl(txtCompSci.Text)
17    Catch ex As Exception
18      ' Error message
19      MessageBox.Show("Enter valid numeric values for all hours.")
20    End Try
21  End Sub
22
23  ' The ClearForm procedure clears the form.
24  Private Sub ClearForm()
25    ' Clear the text boxes.
26    txtLastName.Clear()
27    txtFirstName.Clear()
28    txtIdNumber.Clear()
29    txtMath.Clear()
30    txtComm.Clear()
31    txtHum.Clear()
32    txtElect.Clear()
33    txtCompSci.Clear()
34
35    ' Set the focus.
36    txtLastName.Focus()
37  End Sub
38
39  Private Sub btnAdd_Click(...) Handles btnAdd.Click
40    ' Create an instance of the CsStudent class.
41    Dim objCsStudent As New CsStudent
42
43    ' Get data from the form.
44    GetData(objCsStudent)
45
46    ' Add the CsStudent object to the collection.
47    AddStudent(objCsStudent)
48
49    ' Clear the form.
50    ClearForm()
51
52    ' Display a confirmation message.
53    MessageBox.Show("Student record added successfully")
54  End Sub
55
56  Private Sub btnDisplay_Click(...) Handles btnDisplay.Click
```

```
57        ' Create an instance of the DisplayForm form.
58        Dim frmDisplay As New DisplayForm
59
60        ' Display the form.
61        frmDisplay.ShowDialog()
62    End Sub
63
64    Private Sub btnExit_Click(...) Handles btnExit.Click
65        ' Close the form.
66        Me.Close()
67    End Sub
68 End Class
```

Step 6:   Now you will write the event handlers for the `DisplayForm` form. Complete the form as follows by entering the code shown in bold. (Don't type the line numbers. They are shown only for reference.)

```
 1 Public Class DisplayForm
 2
 3    Private Sub DisplayForm_Load(...) Handles MyBase.Load
 4        ' Declare an object variable that can reference
 5        ' a CsStudent object.
 6        Dim objCsStudent As CsStudent
 7
 8        ' Get each object in the collection and add its
 9        ' data to the list box.
10        For Each objCsStudent In csStudentCollection
11            lstStudents.Items.Add(objCsStudent.ToString())
12        Next
13    End Sub
14
15    Private Sub btnClose_Click(...) Handles btnClose.Click
16        ' Close the form.
17        Me.Close()
18    End Sub
19 End Class
```

Step 7:   Save the project and run the application. On the main form, add data for a fictitious student, and then click the *Add Record* button. Repeat this for at least two more students. Click the *Display Students* button to see a list of the students you have added. Figure 12-13 shows an example.

Figure 12-13 *Student List* displayed

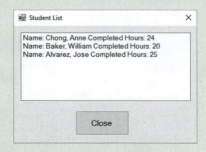

Step 8:   Click the *Close* button to close the application window.

✔ Checkpoint

12.22 The beginning of a class declaration follows. What is the name of the base class, and what is the name of the derived class?

```
Public Class Fly
    Inherits Insect
```

12.23 What does a derived class inherit from its base class?

12.24 What is *overriding*, when speaking of class declarations?

12.25 What keyword must you include in the declaration of a property procedure or method in order for it to be overridden in a derived class?

12.26 What keyword must you include in the declaration of a property or method in order for it to override one that exists in the base class?

12.27 When both a base class and its derived class have a constructor, which constructor executes first?

12.28 What is a protected base class member?

Summary

12.1 Classes and Objects

- Object-oriented programming is a way of designing and coding applications that allows interchangeable software components to be used to build larger programs.
- The primary goal of object-oriented design is to address the needs of the application or problem being solved. A secondary goal is to design classes that can outlive the current application and possibly be used in future programs.
- The class interface is the portion that is visible to the application programmer who uses the class. The program written by such a person is also called the client program, in reference to the client-server relationship between a class and the programs that use it.
- The class implementation is the portion of a class that is hidden from client programs; it is created from private member variables, private properties, and private methods.

12.2 Creating a Class

- The steps that must occur when an instance of a class is created are (1) declare an object variable and (2) create an instance of the class in memory and assign its address to the object variable. Each instance of a class has its own unique copy of the class's member variables.
- Members of an object are accessed with the dot (.) operator.
- Properties are usually implemented as property procedures. A property procedure is a function that behaves like a property. Property procedures have two sections: Get and Set. The Get section is executed when the value of the property is retrieved. The Set section is executed when a value is stored in the property. The value of a read-only property cannot be modified by a client program. A read-only property is implemented as a property procedure declared with the ReadOnly keyword, and the property does not have a Set section. An auto-implemented property is a simple, short way of declaring properties without having to create a corresponding private class variable.
- To remove an object, set all the object variables that reference it to Nothing; it will be removed from memory by the .NET garbage collector.
- An object variable declared inside a procedure is local to that procedure. If an object is referenced only by a procedure's local object variable, the object is automatically removed from memory by the garbage collector after the procedure ends.
- The Is and IsNot operators compare two object variables to determine if they reference the same object.
- You can create arrays of objects, and you can write Sub procedures and functions that work with arrays of objects.
- A method is a procedure or function that is a member of a class. The method performs some operation on the data stored in the class. You write methods inside the class declaration.
- A constructor is a method that is automatically called when an instance of the class is created. Constructors are useful for initializing member variables or performing other startup operations. To create a constructor, create a method named New in the class.
- Use the *Add Existing Item* dialog box to add an existing class to a project.

12.3 Collections

- A collection is a structure that holds a group of items. It automatically expands and shrinks to accommodate the items added to it, and allows items to be stored with an associated key value, which may be used when searching for collection members.

- The Count property indicates the number of items stored in a collection. The Add method stores an item in a collection. The Item method finds and returns an object in a collection. The Remove method is used to remove an item from a collection.

12.4 Focus on Problem Solving: Creating the *Student Collection* Application

- Tutorial 12-2 develops an application that builds a collection of students and allows the user to select a student's ID number from a list box to view information about the student.

12.5 The Object Browser

- The Object Browser displays information about the classes, properties, methods, and events available to a project.

12.6 Introduction to Inheritance

- Inheritance allows you to create new classes that inherit, or derive, characteristics of existing classes. In an inheritance relationship, there is a base class and a derived class. The base class can be thought of as the parent and the derived class as the child.
- Sometimes a property procedure or method in a base class does not work adequately for a derived class. When this happens, you can override the base class property procedure or method by writing one with the same name in the derived class.
- You must use the Overridable keyword in the declaration of a method or property procedure in a base class that is to be overridden. You must use the Overrides keyword in the declaration of a method or property procedure in a derived class that overrides another one in the base class.
- Every class you create in Visual Basic is automatically derived from a built-in class named Object. The Object class has a method named ToString that returns a fully qualified class name. You can override this method so it returns a string representation of the data stored in a class.
- It is possible for both a base class and a derived class to have constructors. When an instance of the derived class is created, the base class constructor is called before the derived class constructor.
- Protected base class members are like private members, except they may be accessed by methods and property procedures in derived classes. To all other classes, however, protected class members are just like private class members.

Key Terms

abstract data type (ADT)	constructor
abstraction	derived class
Add method	encapsulation
attributes	finding the classes
auto-implemented property	Friend access
base class	garbage collector
class	going out of scope
class declaration	inheritance
class implementation	Is operator
class interface	IsNot operator
class objects	Item method
client program	member variable
collection	method

MyBase keyword
object
Object Browser
Object class
object-oriented analysis
object-oriented programming
  (OOP)
operations
Output window

Overridable keyword
override
Overrides keyword
property procedure
Protected access specifier
read-only property
Remove method
Set section

VideoNote

***Kayak Rental*
Application
with Classes**

Video Tutorial: *Kayak Rental* Application with Classes

In this sequence of video tutorials, we continue the *Kayak Rental* Application from Chapter 9. We create different classes to hold kayak information, kayak tours, and rental history information. We also use a collection to hold all rental information when reading and writing the sequential data file.

- Part 1: Creating the Kayak and KayakTour classes

- Part 2: Building collections of kayaks and tours

- Part 3: Creating the RentalHistory class

- Part 4: Creating a collection of RentalHistory items

Review Questions and Exercises

Fill-in-the-Blank

1. A(n) _____ is a data type created by a programmer.

2. A(n) _____ is a program structure that defines an abstract data type.

3. An object is a(n) _____ of a class.

4. The _____ is the portion of a class that is visible to the client program that uses the class.

5. The _____ is the portion of a class that is hidden from client programs.

6. A(n) _____ procedure is a function that behaves like a class property.

7. The _____ section of a Property procedure is executed when a client program retrieves the value of a property.

8. The _____ section of a Property procedure executes when a client program stores a value in a property.

9. A(n) _____ property cannot be set by a client program.

10. A(n) _____ is a procedure or function that is a member of the class.

11. A(n) _____ is a class method that is automatically called when an instance of the class is created.

12. A(n) _____ is a class method that is automatically called just before an instance of the class is removed from memory.

13. You can display messages for debugging purposes in the _____ window.

14. A(n) _____ is a structure that holds a group of items.

15. The _____ window displays information about the classes, properties, methods, and events available to a project.

16. _____ is an object-oriented programming feature that allows you to create new classes that derive characteristics of existing classes.

17. A(n) _____ class is a general-purpose class on which other classes may be based.

18. A(n) _____ class is based on another class, and inherits characteristics from it.

19. You can _____ a base class property procedure or method by writing one with the same name in a derived class.

20. _____ base class members are like private members, except that they may be accessed by methods and property procedures in derived classes.

Multiple Choice

1. Which of the following program structures defines an abstract data type?
   a. Variable
   b. Exception
   c. Class
   d. Class object

2. If the variable `status` is declared inside a class, but not inside a method, which of the following describes `status`?
   a. Global variable
   b. Constructor
   c. Local variable
   d. Member variable

3. An object is automatically released when all references to it are set to which of the following?
   a. `Nothing`
   b. `Empty`
   c. `Clear`
   d. `Done`

4. This section of a property procedure returns the value of the property.
   a. `Value`
   b. `Property`
   c. `Get`
   d. `Set`

5. This section of a property procedure stores a value of the property.
   a. `Value`
   b. `Property`
   c. `Get`
   d. `Set`

6. In a class named `Student`, which of the following would be the name of its constructor?
   a. `New`
   b. `Constructor`
   c. `Student`
   d. `Main`

7. Class members declared with this access specifier are like private members, except that they may be accessed by methods and property procedures in derived classes.

   a. `Special`
   b. `Secret`
   c. `Public`
   d. `Protected`

8. Which section is missing from a read-only property procedure?

   a. `Get`
   b. `Set`
   c. `Store`
   d. `Save`

9. This process runs periodically to free the memory used by all unreferenced objects.

   a. Garbage collector
   b. Memory collector
   c. Housekeeper
   d. RAM dumper

10. Which of the following operators can be used to determine whether two object variables reference the same object?

    a. `=`
    b. `<>`
    c. `Is`
    d. `Equal`

11. Which method is used to store an item in a collection?

    a. `Store`
    b. `Insert`
    c. `Add`
    d. `Collect`

12. Which method is used to search for an item in a collection?

    a. `Find`
    b. `Item`
    c. `Search`
    d. `Member`

13. Which method removes an item from a collection?

    a. `Remove`
    b. `Item`
    c. `Delete`
    d. `Erase`

14. Which property indicates the number of items stored in a collection?

    a. Items
    b. Number
    c. Count
    d. Members

15. Which of the following displays information about the classes, properties, methods, and events available to a project?

    a. Object Browser
    b. Object Navigator
    c. Class Browser
    d. Class Resource List

16. In an inheritance relationship, which class is usually a generalized class from which other, more specialized, classes are derived?
    a. Derived
    b. Base
    c. Protected
    d. Public

17. Which type of class member is not visible to derived classes?
    a. Private
    b. Public
    c. Protected
    d. ReadOnly

18. Which keyword indicates that the procedure may be overridden in a derived class?
    a. Private
    b. Overrides
    c. Public
    d. Overridable

19. Which keyword indicates that a procedure in a derived class overrides a procedure in the base class?
    a. Private
    b. Overrides
    c. Public
    d. Overridable

20. When used in a derived class, which keyword refers to the base class?
    a. BaseClass
    b. Base
    c. MyBase
    d. Parent

21. Every class in Visual Basic is derived from a built-in class having which of the following names?
    a. Object
    b. SuperClass
    c. Parent
    d. System

True or False

Indicate whether the following statements are true or false.

1. T F: Public properties are part of the class interface.

2. T F: Private member variables are part of the class interface.

3. T F: A class's New procedure must be called from a client program.

4. T F: A class method may be either a procedure or a function.

5. T F: A runtime error will occur when you attempt to add a member with the same key to a collection as an existing member.

6. T F: You can use both the Before and After arguments of a collection's Add method at the same time.

7. T F: When retrieving an item from a collection, if the item is of the Integer data type, you can retrieve only a copy of the member.

8. T F: The Object Browser does not display information about the standard Visual Basic controls.

9. T F: If you attempt to retrieve an item from a collection and specify a nonexistent index, a runtime error is generated.

10. T F: A private property or method cannot be overridden.

11. T F: The ToString method cannot be overridden.

12. T F: Protected base class members cannot be accessed by derived classes.

Short Answer

1. How is a class interface created in Visual Basic?

2. What does the term *encapsulation* mean, in terms of object-oriented programming?

3. In the statement Dim newStudent As Student, which is the class and which is the object variable?

4. In a read-only property procedure, which section is missing, and which keyword is required?

5. How is an object different from a class?

6. Do the icons in the Visual Studio *Toolbox* represent classes or objects?

7. How are properties different from methods?

8. When you retrieve an integer from a collection and modify the integer, what happens to the corresponding integer stored in the collection? How is this different from retrieving and modifying an object?

9. What is encapsulation?

10. What happens to an object created inside a procedure when the procedure finishes?

11. Suppose class A has the following members:
    Private member variable x
    Public member variable y
    Public property Data
    Protected method UpdateData
    Suppose also that class B is derived from class A. Which of class A's members are inherited by class B?

12. When a property procedure or method in a base class is not appropriate for a derived class, what can you do?

13. Suppose class B is derived from class A. Class A's UpdateData method has been overridden in class B. How can the UpdateData method in class B call the UpdateData method in class A?

What Do You Think?

1. Suppose that when developing an application, you create a class named BankAccount and you declare an object variable of the BankAccount type named checking. Which is the abstract data type, BankAccount or checking?

2. Look at the following problem description and identify the potential classes.
    We need to keep a list of customers and record our business transactions with them. Each time a customer purchases a product, an order is filled out. Each order shows a list of items kept in our central warehouse.

3. Does each button on the same form have its own copy of the Visible property?

4. In a student record-keeping program, what attributes might be assigned to a college transcript class?

5. Why are member variables usually declared `Private` in classes?

6. At the end of the following example, how many `Student` objects exist?
```
Dim st1 As New Student
Dim st2 As Student
st2 = st1
```

7. At the end of the following example, how many `Student` objects exist?
```
Dim st1 As New Student
Dim st2 As Student
st2 = st1
st1 = Nothing
```

8. Suppose that an application at an animal hospital uses two classes: `Mammal` and `Dog`. Which do you think is the base class and which is the derived class? Why?

9. Why does it make sense that you cannot use the `Overridable` keyword in a private base class member declaration?

Find the Error

For each of the following questions, assume `Customer` is a class. Find the errors.

1. `Dim Customer as New customerData`

2.
```
Dim customerData as Customer
customerData.LastName = "Smith"
```

3.
```
customerData = Nothing
customerData.LastName = "Smith"
```

4.
```
Public Property LastName() As String
  Set
    Return lname
  End Get
  Get(ByVal value As String)
    lname = value
  End Set
End Property
```

5.
```
Dim customerCollection as Collection
customerCollection.Add customerData
```

6. The following code appears in a base class:
```
Private Overridable Function GetData() As Integer
  ' (statements...)
End Sub
```

7. The following code appears in a derived class:
```
' This function overrides the base class function.
Public Function GetData() As Integer
  ' (statements...)
End Sub
```

Algorithm Workbench

1. Suppose an application declares an array of objects with the following statement:

   `Dim employees(9) As Employee`

   Write a loop that creates ten instances of the class and assigns them to the elements of the array.

2. Code a `Dim` statement that declares an object variable of the class type `Transcript`. The statement should not create an instance of the class.

3. Code a statement that creates a `Transcript` object and assigns it to the variable from Question 2.

4. Code a statement that removes the reference used by the object variable used in Questions 2 and 3.

5. Code a single statement that declares an object variable and creates a new instance of the `Transcript` class.

6. Write the property procedures for a property named CustomerNumber that assigns a string value to a member variable named `strCustomerNumber`.

7. Look at the following code for the Book class:

```
Public Class Book
    ' Private member variables
    Private strTitle As String
    Private strAuthor As String
    Private strPublisher As String
    Private strIsbn As String

    ' Constructor
    Public Sub New()
        strTitle = String.Empty
        strAuthor = String.Empty
        strPublisher = String.Empty
        strIsbn = String.Empty
    End Sub

    ' Title Property
    Public Property Title() As String
        Get
            Return strTitle
        End Get
        Set(ByVal value As String)
            strTitle = value
        End Set
    End Property

    ' Author property
    Public Property Author() As String
        Get
            Return strAuthor
        End Get
        Set(ByVal value As String)
            strAuthor = value
        End Set
    End Property
```

```
       ' Publisher property
      Public Property Publisher() As String
        Get
          Return strPublisher
        End Get
        Set(ByVal value As String)
          strPublisher = value
        End Set
      End Property

       ' Isbn property
      Public Property Isbn() As String
        Get
          Return strIsbn
        End Get
        Set(ByVal value As String)
          strIsbn = value
        End Set
      End Property
    End Class
```

Design a class named `TextBook` that is derived from the `Book` class. The `TextBook` class should have the following properties:

- Course (string). This property holds the name of the course that the textbook is used for.
- OrderQuantity (integer). This property holds the number of books to order for the course.

The OrderQuantity property cannot be negative, so provide error checking in the property procedure.

Programming Challenges

1. **E-Mail Address Book**

   Write a program that lets the user display and modify an address book containing names, e-mail addresses, and phone numbers. The program should contain a class named `Address`. The `Address` class should contain the following information about one person: name, e-mail address, phone, and comments. The application should also have a collection named `addressList`, which stores a collection of `Address` objects.

   The main window, shown in Figure 12-14, displays the names from the address book in a list box. The user should be able to input new names and addresses, using a form similar to the one shown in Figure 12-15.

Figure 12-14 *E-mail Address Book* form   **Figure 12-15** *Add New Name* form

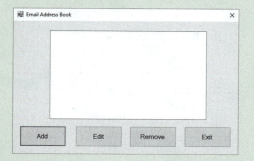

2. **Carpet Price Calculator**

The Westfield Carpet Company has asked you to write an application that calculates the price of carpeting. To calculate the price of a carpeting, you multiply the area of the floor (width × length) by the price per square foot of carpet. For example, the area of a floor that is 12 feet long and 10 feet wide is 120 feet. To cover that floor with carpet that costs $8 per square foot would cost $960.

You should create a class named `Rectangle` with the following properties:

Width: A single
Length: A single
Area: A single

The Area property should be read-only. Provide a method named `CalcArea` that calculates width × length and stores the result in the Area property.

Next, create a class named `Carpet` with the following properties:

Color: A string
Style: A string
Price: A decimal

The application should have a form similar to the one shown in Figure 12-16. (The carpet price is the price per square foot.) When the *Calculate* button is clicked, the application should copy the data in the text boxes into the appropriate object properties, and then display the area and price.

Figure 12-16 *Carpet Price Calculator* form

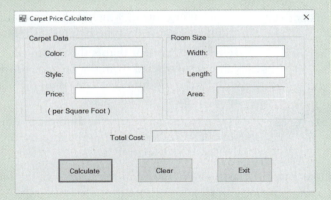

Design Your Own Forms

3. **Saving the Student Collection**

Modify the *Student Collection* application from this chapter so it saves the collection in a text file before the program exits. When the program starts up, load the collection from the file.

VideoNote
The *Motor Class* Problem

4. **Motor Class**

Create an application that tracks electric motors in a manufacturing plant. The application should have a `Motor` class with the following properties:

- MotorId: Five-digit string, such as "02340"
- Description: String
- RPM: Double, values in the range 10 to 10000
- Voltage: Double, values in the range 1 to 500
- Status: String, three characters

The Status values are:

- ON: Motor is online and running.
- OFF: Motor is online but not running.
- MNT: Motor is undergoing maintenance and cleaning.
- NA: Motor is not available.

The application should be able to store at least 10 Motor class objects in an array. Create an input form in the application that allows users to input new motor records to be added to the array. Create another form that displays all the motors in the array in a list box.

5. **MotorCollection Class**

Modify the application you created in Programming Challenge 4 so it uses a collection instead of an array to hold the Motor class objects. When the application ends, it should save the contents of the collection to a sequential text file. When the application starts up, it should load the data from the file into the collection. Be sure to write the appropriate error handlers.

6. **Account Class**

You are a programmer for the Home Software Company. You have been assigned to develop a class that models the basic workings of a bank account. The class should have the following properties:

- Balance: Holds the current account balance.
- IntRate: Holds the interest rate for the period.
- Interest: Holds the interest earned for the current period.
- Transactions: Holds the number of transactions for the current period.

The class should also have the following methods:

MakeDeposit   Takes an argument, which is the amount of the deposit. This argument is added to the Balance property.

Withdraw   Takes an argument that is the amount of the withdrawal. This value is subtracted from the Balance property, unless the withdrawal amount is greater than the balance. If this happens, an error message is displayed.

CalcInterest   This method calculates the amount of interest for the current period, stores this value in the Interest property, and adds it to the Balance property.

Demonstrate the class in an application that performs the following tasks:

- Allows deposits to be made to the account.
- Allows withdrawals to be taken from the account.
- Calculates interest for the period.
- Reports the current account balance at any time.
- Reports the current number of transactions at any time.

7. **Inventory Class**

Create an application that stores inventory records for a retail store. The application should have an Inventory class with the following properties:

InvNumber: A string used to hold an inventory number. Each item in the inventory should have a unique inventory number.

Description: A string that holds a brief description of the item.

Cost: A decimal value that holds the amount that the retail store paid for the item.

Retail: A decimal value that holds the retail price for the item.

OnHand: An integer value that holds the number of items on hand. This value cannot be less than 0.

The application should store `Inventory` class objects in a collection. Create an input form in the application that allows users to input new inventory items to be added to the collection. The user should also be able to look up items by their inventory number.

8. **Inventory Class Modification**

Modify the application you created in Programming Challenge 7 so it saves the contents of the collection to a file. When the application starts up, it should load the data from the file into the collection. Be sure to use exception handling.

9. **Cash Register**

Create an application that serves as a simple cash register for a retail store. Use the `Inventory` class you created in Programming Challenge 7 to store data about the items in the store's inventory. When the application starts up, it should load the entire store's inventory from a file into a collection of `Inventory` objects.

When a purchase is made, the cashier should select an item from a list box. (If an item's OnHand property is set to zero, the item should not be available in the list box.) The item's description, retail price, and number of units on hand should be displayed on the form when selected. The cashier should enter the quantity being purchased, and the application should display the sales tax and the total of the sale. (The quantity being purchased cannot exceed the number of units on hand.) The quantity being purchased should be subtracted from the item's OnHand property. When the application ends, the contents of the collection should be saved to the file.

10. **Person Class**

Begin a new project named *Customer Information*, and design a class named `Person` with the following properties:

- LastName (string)
- FirstName (string)
- Address (string)
- City (string)
- State (string)
- Zip (string)
- Phone (string)

Implement the properties as public property procedures.

Create a form that allows you to assign values to each property of a `Person` object.

11. **Derived `Customer` Class**

Open the *Person Class* project you created in Programming Challenge 10. Design a new class named `Customer`, which is derived from the `Person` class. The `Customer` class should have the following properties:

- CustomerNumber (integer)
- MailingList (Boolean)
- Comments (String)

The CustomerNumber property will be used to hold a unique number for each customer. The Mailing List property will be set to *True* if the customer wishes to be on a mailing list, or *False* if the customer does not wish to be on a mailing list. The Comments property holds miscellaneous comments about the customer.

Modify the form so that it allows you to store data in each property of a `Customer` object. To enter the customer comments, use a TextBox control with its Multiline and WordWrap properties set to *True*.

12. **Derived PreferredCustomer Class**

A retail store has a preferred customer plan where customers may earn discounts on all their purchases. The amount of a customer's discount is determined by the amount of the customer's cumulative purchases in the store.

- When a preferred customer spends $500, he or she gets a 5% discount on all future purchases.
- When a preferred customer spends $1000, he or she gets a 6% discount on all future purchases.
- When a preferred customer spends $1500, he or she gets a 7% discount on all future purchases.
- When a preferred customer spends $2000 or more, he or she gets a 10% discount on all future purchases.

Open the *Derived Customer Class* project that you modified in Programming Challenge 11. Design a new class named PreferredCustomer, which is derived from the Customer class. The PreferredCustomer class should have the following properties:

- PurchasesAmount (decimal)
- DiscountLevel (single)

Modify the application's form so it allows you to store data in each property of a PreferredCustomer object. Add the object to a collection, using the customer number as a key. Allow the user to look up a preferred customer by the customer number, edit the customer data, and remove a customer from the collection.

A Advanced User Interface Controls and Techniques

The chapters in this textbook have introduced you to the fundamental Visual Basic controls. There are many more controls available in Visual Basic and this appendix introduces you to several of them. It also discusses some advanced programming techniques, and user interface design guidelines. The examples shown in this appendix can be found in the Student Sample Programs folder named *Appendix A*.

Scroll Bars

Scroll bars provide a visual way to adjust a value within a range of values. These types of controls display a slider that may be dragged along a track. Visual Basic provides a horizontal scroll bar control named **HScrollBar**, and a vertical scroll bar control named **VScrollBar**. Figure A-1 shows examples of each of these controls. You can find these controls in the *Toolbox*, in the *All Windows Forms* group.

Here is a summary of the important properties of each of these controls:

- The Value property is an integer value that is adjusted as the user moves the control's slider. (The default value is 0.)
- The Minimum property is the lower limit of the scrollable range. (The default value is 0.)
- The Maximum property is the upper limit of the scrollable range. (The default value is 100.)
- The LargeChange property is the integer amount by which the Value property changes when the user clicks the scroll bar area that lies to either side of the slider. This is also the amount by which the Value property changes when the user presses the Page Up or Page Down keys on the keyboard while the control has the focus. (The default value is 10.)
- The SmallChange property is the integer amount by which the Value property changes when the user clicks one of the arrows that appear at either end of a scroll bar control. (The default value is 1.)

Figure A-1 Horizontal and vertical scroll bars

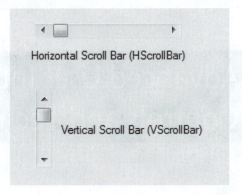

When a horizontal scroll bar's slider is moved toward its left side, the Value property is decreased. When the slider is moved toward the scroll bar's right side, the Value property is increased. When a vertical scroll bar's slider is moved toward its top, the Value property is decreased. When the slider is moved toward the scroll bar's bottom, the Value property is increased.

When the user moves the slider on a scroll bar control, a Scroll event occurs. If you write a Scroll event handler for the control, the event handler will execute any time the slider is moved. To generate a code template for the Scroll event handler, simply double-click the scroll bar control in the *Designer* window.

Figure A-2 shows the form in an example application that demonstrates the HScrollBar control. The HScrollBar control is named `hsbScrollBar` and the label that displays the value is named `lblValue`. The form's code follows. This project can be found in the Student Sample Programs folder for this Appendix. You will also find a similar project that demonstrates the VScrollBar control.

Figure A-2 *HScrollBar Demo* application form

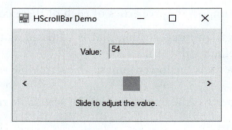

```
Public Class Form1

    Private Sub Form1_Load(...) Handles MyBase.Load
        ' Set the property values for the scroll bar control.
        ' These properties can also be set at Design
        ' time in the Properties window.
        hsbScrollBar.Value = 0
        hsbScrollBar.Minimum = 0
        hsbScrollBar.Maximum = 100
        hsbScrollBar.LargeChange = 10
        hsbScrollBar.SmallChange = 1
```

```
        ' Display the scroll bar's initial value
        ' in the label control.
        lblValue.Text = hsbScrollBar.Value.ToString()
    End Sub

    Private Sub hsbScrollBar_Scroll(...) Handles hsbScrollBar.Scroll
        ' Display the scroll bar value.
        lblValue.Text = hsbScrollBar.Value.ToString()
    End Sub
End Class
```

Using a TabControl to Organize a Form

A **TabControl** allows you to create a user interface that is made of multiple pages, with each page containing its own set of controls. The TabControl appears as a container on a form, with one or more tabs positioned along its top edge. Each tab represents a different page, known as a **TabPage**. When the user clicks a tab, the control displays that page. You can find the TabControl in the *Toolbox*, in the *Containers* group.

When you insert a new TabControl, it will contain two TabPage controls named Tab-Page1 and TabPage2. This is shown in Figure A-3. Keep in mind that a TabControl is a container that contains TabPage controls. When you are working with a TabControl in the *Designer* window, you can select the TabControl (the container) or you can select the individual TabPage controls that it contains. When you work with a TabControl for the first time, you should practice selecting each of the controls in the group so you know at all times which one you are working with.

Figure A-3 TabControl with two TabPages

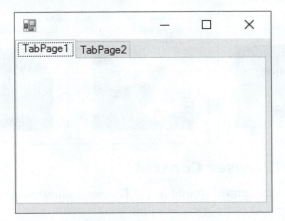

Each of the TabPage controls has its own set of properties that can be changed in the *Properties* window. For example, to change the text that is displayed on a TabPage's tab, you change that TabPage control's Text property.

As previously mentioned, a TabControl contains two TabPage controls when first inserted in a form. To add more TabPages, select the TabControl, and then select its TabPages property. (Click the ellipses button ⌊…⌋ that appears next to the TabPages property window.) This opens the *TabPage Collection Editor*, shown in Figure A-4. This window allows you to add new TabPages, remove existing TabPages, and edit each TabPage's properties.

Figure A-4 *TabPage Collection Editor* window

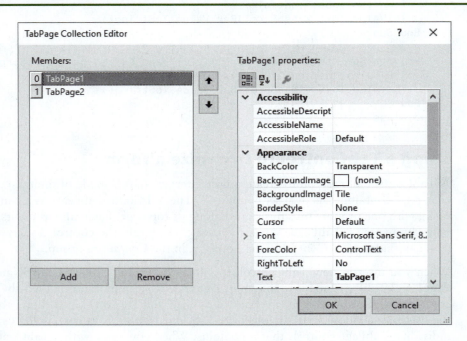

Figure A-5 shows the *TabControl Demo* application that can be found in the Student Sample Programs folder for this Appendix. The application's form has a TabControl with three TabPages. Each TabPage contains a PictureBox control displaying an image. (There is no code in the application.)

Figure A-5 *TabControl Demo* application

The WebBrowser Control

The **WebBrowser** control (found in the *Common Controls* group in the *Toolbox*) allows you to display a Web page on an application's form. The control has a property named Url that can be set to a Web page's URL (Uniform Resource Locator). At runtime, that Web page will be displayed in the control.

At design time, you can use the *Properties* window to set the Url property. You simply type a valid URL such as `http://www.gaddisbooks.com` into the property's value box. If you want to set the Url property in code, you must create a Uri object (Uniform Resource Identifier) and assign that object to the property. Here is an example:

```
WebBrowser1.Url = New Uri("http://www.gaddisbooks.com")
```

Alternatively, you can call the control's Navigate method to display a Web page, as shown here:

```
WebBrowser1.Navigate(New Uri("http://www.gaddisbooks.com"))
```

In either of these approaches, an exception will be thrown if an invalid Web address is used.

When a Web page has finished loading, a DocumentCompleted event occurs. If you want to perform some action after a page has loaded, you can write a handler for this event. (Just double-click the WebBrowser control in the *Designer* window to create a code template for the DocumentCompleted event handler.)

Figure A-6 shows the *WebBrowser Demo* application from the Student Sample Programs folder for this Appendix. The application's form has a WebBrowser control named WebBrowser1, a TextBox control named txtURL, and a Button control named btnGo. When the user clicks the btnGo button, the application sets the WebBrowser1 control's Url property to the address that has been typed into the txtURL text box. The application's code follows.

```
Public Class Form1

    Private Sub btnGo_Click(...) Handles btnGo.Click
        Try
            WebBrowser1.Url = New Uri(txtURL.Text)
        Catch ex As Exception
            ' Error message for an invalid Web address.
            MessageBox.Show(ex.Message)
        End Try
    End Sub
End Class
```

Figure A-6 *WebBrowser Demo* application

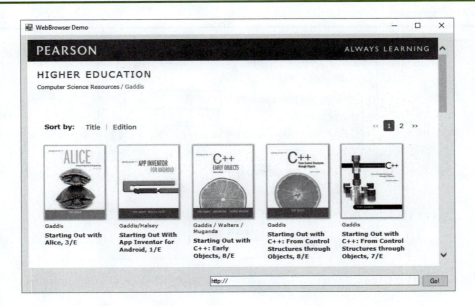

The ErrorProvider Component

The **ErrorProvider** component (found in the *Components* group in the *Toolbox*) allows you to indicate that the user has entered an invalid value by displaying a blinking error icon (🛑) next to a specific control on the application's form. When the user hovers the mouse pointer over the icon, an error message is displayed as a ToolTip.

When you insert an ErrorProvider component, it appears in the component tray at the bottom of the *Designer* window, with a default name such as ErrorProvider1. In code, when the user enters an invalid value with a specific control, you call the ErrorProvider component's SetError method. Here is the general format for calling the method:

```
ErrorProviderName.SetError(ControlName, ErrorMessage)
```

In the general format, *ErrorProviderName* is the name of the ErrorProvider component, *ControlName* is the name of the control that you want to display the error icon next to, and *ErrorMessage* is the error message to associate with the error. Here is an example:

```
ErrorProvider1.SetError(txtPayRate, "Invalid pay rate")
```

This statement uses the ErrorProvider1 component to display an error icon next to the txtPayRate control. When the user hovers the mouse pointer over the error icon, the message *Invalid pay rate* will be displayed as a ToolTip.

The error icon will remain displayed next to the specified control until you call the SetError method again, passing the same control name as the first argument, and String. Empty as the second argument. Here is an example:

```
ErrorProvider1.SetError(txtPayRate, String.Empty)
```

Figure A-7 shows the *ErrorProvider Demo* application in the Student Sample Programs folder for this Appendix. The user enters a number of hours in the txtHours TextBox, a numeric pay rate in the txtPayRate TextBox, and then clicks the btnCalc button to calculate gross pay. If a nonnumeric value is entered for either the hours or the pay rate, an ErrorProvider component displays an error icon next to the control containing the invalid value. In Figure A-7 the user has entered an invalid value for the pay rate. The application's code follows.

Figure A-7 *ErrorProvider Demo* application

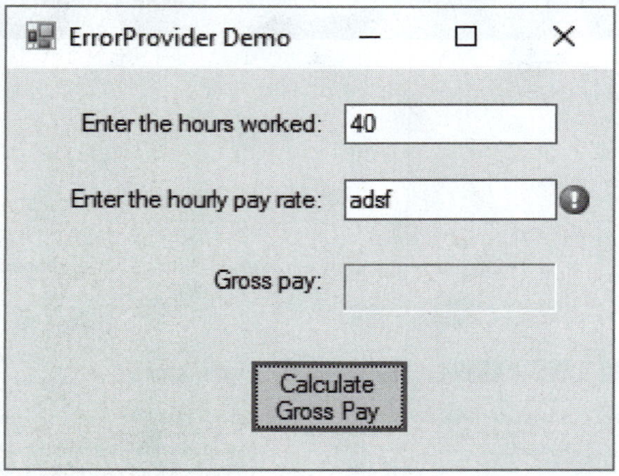

```
Public Class Form1

    Private Sub btnCalc_Click(...) Handles btnCalc.Click
        ' Variables for hours, pay rate, and gross pay
        Dim dblHours, dblPayRate, dblGrossPay As Double

        ' Clear any existing errors.
        ErrorProvider1.SetError(txtHours, String.Empty)
        ErrorProvider1.SetError(txtPayRate, String.Empty)

        ' Get values and calculate gross pay.
        Try
            ' Get the hours worked.
            dblHours = CDbl(txtHours.Text)
```

```
        Try
            ' Get the pay rate.
            dblPayRate = CDbl(txtPayRate.Text)

            ' Calculate the gross pay.
            dblGrossPay = dblHours * dblPayRate

            ' display the gross pay.
            lblGrossPay.Text = dblGrossPay.ToString("c")
        Catch ex As Exception
            ' Invalid pay rate
            ErrorProvider1.SetError(txtPayRate, "Pay rate must be numeric.")
        End Try
    Catch ex As Exception
        ' Invalid hours
        ErrorProvider1.SetError(txtHours, "Hours must be numeric.")
    End Try
    End Sub
End Class
```

Writing Code to Select Text in a TextBox

TextBox controls have a method named SelectAll that you can use to make the process of correcting invalid input more convenient for the user. When the user enters an invalid value, you can display an error message and then use these properties to automatically select the invalid input for the user. Then, the user can immediately retype the input without having to use the mouse to select the TextBox.

The SelectAll method in the TextBox class automatically selects all text in the box. For example, look at the following code and assume that txtName is a text box that the user has typed input into:

```
txtName.Focus()
txtName.SelectAll()
```

After these statements execute, all of the contents of the txtName TextBox will be selected. When the user types a key, that keystroke will immediately erase all of the selected text.

Figure A-8 shows the *Selected Text Demo* application in the Student Sample Programs folder for this Appendix. This is a modified version of the *ErrorProvider Demo* application previously shown. In this version, after the ErrorProvider displays an error icon, the content of the TextBox containing the invalid input is automatically selected. In the figure, the user has entered an invalid value for the hours. The application's code follows.

Figure A-8 *Selected Text Demo* application

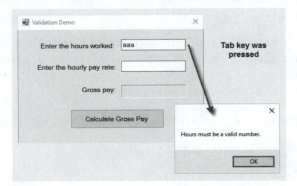

```
Public Class Form1

    Private Sub btnCalc_Click(...) Handles btnCalc.Click
        ' Variables for hours, pay rate, and gross pay
        Dim dblHours, dblPayRate, dblGrossPay As Double

        ' Clear any existing errors.
        ErrorProvider1.SetError(txtHours, String.Empty)
        ErrorProvider1.SetError(txtPayRate, String.Empty)

        ' Get values and calculate gross pay.
        Try
            ' Get the hours worked.
            dblHours = CDbl(txtHours.Text)

            Try
                ' Get the pay rate.
                dblPayRate = CDbl(txtPayRate.Text)

                ' Calculate the gross pay.
                dblGrossPay = dblHours * dblPayRate

                ' display the gross pay.
                lblGrossPay.Text = dblGrossPay.ToString("c")
            Catch ex As Exception
                ' Invalid pay rate
                ErrorProvider1.SetError(txtPayRate, "Pay rate must be numeric.")

                ' Select the invalid input.
                txtPayRate.Focus()
                txtPayRate.SelectAll()
            End Try
        Catch ex As Exception
            ' Invalid hours
            ErrorProvider1.SetError(txtHours, "Hours must be numeric.")
            ' Select the invalid input.
            txtHours.Focus()
            txtHours.SelectAll()
        End Try
    End Sub
End Class
```

Using Control-Level Validation

You've seen many examples in this book of code using Try-Catch statements to respond to the exceptions that occur when the user has entered invalid data in a TextBox. Visual Basic provides another approach to input validation that can be useful when a form contains many fields that must be validated, or when more complex validation must be applied to user input.

Most controls have a Boolean property named **CausesValidation** that is set to *True* by default. When the focus is shifting from one control to another, if the control that is receiving the focus has its CausesValidation property set to *True*, then a Validating event will occur for the control that is losing the focus.

Suppose an application has two text box controls: `txtFirst` and `txtSecond`. The user has just entered a value into `txtFirst` and pressed the `Tab` key, which should shift the focus from `txtFirst` to `txtSecond`. But `txtSecond`'s CausesValidation property is set to *True*, so `txtFirst`'s Validating event is triggered before the focus shifts. The `txtFirst` control has a Validating event handler, which is executed as a result of the Validating event being triggered.

The Validating event handler contains code that checks the value in `txtFirst`. If the value is invalid, the event handler does the following:

- It displays an error message instructing the user to reenter the data.
- It cancels the event, which prevents the focus from shifting. This lets the user correct the invalid value.

If the value is valid, however, the event handler allows the focus to shift.

The Validating event handler has a parameter named e. This parameter is a special type of object known as a `CancelEventArgs` object. It has a Boolean property named Cancel that, if set to *True*, will prevent the focus from shifting after the handler finishes executing. If the e.Cancel property is set to *False*, however, the focus will continue to shift after the handler finishes executing.

Figure A-9 shows the *Validation Demo* application in the Student Sample Programs folder for this Appendix. The user enters a number of hours in the `txtHours` TextBox, a numeric pay rate in the `txtPayRate` TextBox, and then clicks the `btnCalc` button to calculate gross pay. The CausesValidation property of all the controls on the form is set to *True*. The `txtHours` control has a Validating event handler that executes when focus shifts away from `txtHours`. It makes sure the hours entered is a valid number and within the range of 0 through 40. The `txtPayRate` control also has a Validating event handler, that executes when focus shifts away from `txtPayRate`. It makes sure the pay rate is a valid number and is 0 or greater. The application's code follows.

Figure A-9 *Validation Demo* application

 NOTE: The form has a FormClosing event handler that sets e.`Cancel` to *False*. This is a necessary workaround in case the user tries to close the form without entering a value into the `txtHours` TextBox. Without this statement in the FormClosing event handler, the user will not be able to close the form without entering a valid value in `txtHours`.

```
Public Class Form1

    Private Sub btnCalc_Click(...) Handles btnCalc.Click
        ' Variables for hours, pay rate, and gross pay
        Dim dblHours, dblPayRate, dblGrossPay As Double

        ' Get the hours worked.
        dblHours = CDbl(txtHours.Text)

        ' Get the pay rate.
        dblPayRate = CDbl(txtPayRate.Text)

        ' Calculate the gross pay.
        dblGrossPay = dblHours * dblPayRate

        ' display the gross pay.
        lblGrossPay.Text = dblGrossPay.ToString("c")
    End Sub

    Private Sub txtHours_Validating(...) Handles txtHours.Validating
      Try
          ' Get the hours, as a Double.
          Dim dblHours As Double = CDbl(txtHours.Text)

          ' Make sure it's in the range 0 - 40.
          If dblHours >= 0.0 And dblHours <= 40.0 Then
            ' The input is okay, so do NOT cancel the event.
            e.Cancel = False
          Else
            ' The input is out of range, so display an
            ' error message.
            MessageBox.Show("Hours must be in the range 0 through 40.")
            ' Now cancel the event.
            e.Cancel = True
          End If
      Catch ex As Exception
          ' The input is not a valid number, so display
          ' an error message.
          MessageBox.Show("Hours must be a valid number.")

          ' Cancel the event.
          e.Cancel = True
      End Try
    End Sub

    Private Sub txtPayRate_Validating(...) Handles txtPayRate.Validating
      Try
          ' Get the pay rate, as a Double.
          Dim dblPayRate As Double = CDbl(txtPayRate.Text)

          ' Make sure it's 0 or greater.
          If dblPayRate >= 0.0 Then
            ' The input is okay, so do NOT cancel the event.
            e.Cancel = False
```

```
        Else
            ' The input is out of range, so display an
            ' error message.
            MessageBox.Show("Pay rate must be 0 or greater.")

            ' Now cancel the event.
            e.Cancel = True
            End If
        Catch ex As Exception
            ' The input is not a valid number, so display
            ' an error message.
            MessageBox.Show("Pay rate must be a valid number.")

            ' Cancel the event.
            e.Cancel = True
        End Try
    End Sub

    Private Sub Form1_FormClosing(...) Handles Me.FormClosing
        e.Cancel = False
    End Sub
End Class
```

The DateTimePicker and MonthCalendar Controls

The DateTimePicker and MonthCalendar controls (found in the Toolbox's *Common Controls* group) provide a much simpler and more reliable way for users to enter dates on a form than typing them into a TextBox. Both of these controls display a small scrollable calendar, showing an entire month, that the user may pick a date from. The selected date is stored, as a Date value, in the control's Value property. Initially, the Value property is set to the current date, and the current date will appear selected in the control's calendar.

When the user selects a date from either of these controls, a ValueChanged event is triggered. If you write a ValueChanged event handler for the control, the event handler will execute any time a date is selected. To generate a code template for the ValueChanged event handler, simply double-click the DateTimePicker or MonthCalendar control in the *Designer* window.

The difference between the two controls is that a DateTimePicker is a drop-down control (showing the calendar only when the user clicks an arrow) and the MonthCalendar always displays the calendar.

Figure A-10 shows the *Date Demo* application in the Student Sample Programs folder for this Appendix. The user selects a date from the DateTimePicker control's drop-down calendar, and then the selected date is displayed in the lblDate label control. The application's code follows.

```
    Public Class Form1

      Private Sub DateTimePicker1_ValueChanged(...) Handles
          DateTimePicker1.ValueChanged
        lblDate.Text = DateTimePicker1.Value.ToShortDateString
      End Sub
    End Class
```

Figure A-10 The *Date Demo* application

User Interface Design Guidelines

When developing an application, you should carefully plan the design of its user interface. A correctly designed user interface should be simple, self explanatory, and without distracting features. This remainder of this appendix covers several important areas of user interface design.

Adhere to Windows Standards

The users of your application are probably experienced with other Windows applications. They will expect your application to provide the features and exhibit the behavior that is common to all Windows applications. The guidelines provided here cover many of the Windows standards. Additionally, you should carefully study applications such as Microsoft Word and Microsoft Excel to observe their forms, menus, controls, and behavior.

Provide a Menu System

Avoid using too many buttons on a form. If an application provides many commands or operations for the user to choose from, place them in a menu system. Of course, an application that uses a menu system will have some menus and menu commands that are unique to that application. However, there are many menu commands that are common to most, if not all, applications. Windows applications that use a menu system normally have the following standard menus:

- **File menu commands.** *New*, *Open*, *Close*, *Save*, *Save As*, *Print*, and *Exit*
- **Edit menu commands.** *Copy*, *Cut*, *Paste*, and *Select All*. If an application provides searching capabilities, such as *Find* or *Replace* commands, they are typically found on the *Edit* menu.
- **Help menu commands.** *About*

Color

Use of color should be tailored to your audience. Business applications should use at most one or two colors, preferably subdued. Multimedia applications (such as Windows Media player) tend to be more colorful and use more graphics. In any event, it's a good idea to show your program to potential users and get their feedback. The color combinations that you consider attractive may not be appealing to others. The following are some general color usage guidelines for business applications:

- **Use dark text on a light background.** Combining certain colors for text and background makes the text difficult to read. Use dark colors for the text and light colors for the background. The contrast between dark and light colors makes the text easier to read.
- **Use predefined Windows colors.** Microsoft Windows uses a predefined set of colors for forms, controls, text, and so on. These colors may be customized by the user. To ensure that your application conforms to a customized color scheme, you should use the predefined system colors. To find the system colors in the *Properties* window, select a color-related property such as *BackColor*. Then click the property's down-arrow button to display a pop-up list of colors. Select the *System* tab to display the system colors.
- **Avoid intense primary colors.** Primary colors are not recommended in business applications because they can distract the user and make the application appear cluttered and unprofessional. Additionally, users with color-defective vision can have difficulty trying to distinguish between certain colors.

Text

The use of nonstandard or multiple fonts can be distracting and makes your forms difficult to read. The following are some suggestions regarding font usage:

- **Use default fonts.** In most cases, stick with the default font for labels and text boxes. Avoid using italic and underlined styles, as they are less readable than plain fonts.
- **Use standard type sizes.** For ordinary text, Microsoft recommends 8, 9, or 11 point type. For window title bars, Microsoft recommends 10 point type.
- **Limit your exceptions to these rules.** If you insist on changing the font and/or font size, do so sparingly; do not use more than two fonts and two font sizes on a form.

Define a Logical Tab Order

Recall from Chapter 3 that a control's TabIndex property specifies the control's position in the tab order. The user expects the focus to shift logically when the ⟨Tab⟩ key is pressed. Typically, the control in the upper left corner of the form will be first in the tab order. The control that appears below it or next to it will be next. The tab order will continue in this fashion. If the focus shifts randomly around the form, a user may become confused and frustrated.

Assign Tool Tips

Recall from Chapter 5 that a tool tip is a small box that is displayed when you hold the mouse cursor over a control for a few seconds. The box gives a short description of what the button does. You can define tool tips for a form by creating a ToolTip control.

Provide Keyboard Access

Many users are proficient with the keyboard and can perform operations with it faster than with the mouse. For their convenience, you should develop your applications so they support both mouse and keyboard input. The following are some suggestions:

- **Use keyboard access keys.** Assign keyboard access keys to buttons, option buttons, check boxes, and menu items.
- **Assign a default button.** If a form uses buttons, you should always make the one that is most frequently clicked the default button. Do this by selecting that button as the form's AcceptButton. Recall from Chapter 3 that when a button is selected in a form's AcceptButton property, the button's Click event procedure is triggered when the user presses the Enter key while the form is active.
- **Assign a cancel button.** If a form has a cancel button, you should select it in the form's CancelButton property. Recall from Chapter 3 that when a button is selected in a form's CancelButton property, the button's Click event procedure is triggered when the user presses the Esc key while the form is active.

Group Controls

If a form has several controls, try to simplify the form's layout by grouping related controls inside group boxes. This visually divides the form's surface area into separate sections, making it more intuitive for the user.

Form Location

To center a form when it first appears, set its StartPosition property to *CenterScreen*.

B Windows Presentation Foundation (WPF)

Imagine a single application that has the usual set of menus and controls, along with rich text displayed in columns, a 3D bar chart, and live video. Imagine being able to combine all these elements on the same page. This is the type of capability provided to advanced developers using Microsoft's new **Windows Presentation Foundation (WPF)**. In the past, developers with a wide variety of specialties and skills would be required to create such an application. They would have to integrate different toolkits and spend a lot of time testing and debugging. To make matters worse, they might have to completely redo these applications for the Web.

Microsoft created the Windows Presentation Foundation (WPF) technology for a number of reasons: (1) They wanted developers to be able to create applications that could run both on the desktop and the Web. (2) They wanted to make it easy to incorporate advanced 2D and 3D graphics and multimedia into applications without having to manually link together separate tools.

WPF was first introduced in Visual Studio 2008. Microsoft has reworked the traditional Windows Forms technology (which we have covered throughout this book) to allow it to incorporate WPF forms within the same applications. In the future, WPF will be Microsoft's new solution for applications that run on both the desktop and the Web.

Visual Studio contains an interactive design surface that provides drag and drop support for WPF layout and controls, a new property editor, and Intellisense support for XAML editing. **Microsoft Expression Blend** is the tool used by designers to create advanced interactive visual elements in applications. Animation, multimedia, and advanced styles are often developed in this way.

XAML

XAML (*eXtensible Application Markup Language*) is used to describe the visual elements in an application. In some ways, it resembles the XHTML markup used in ASP.NET Web applications (see Chapter 11). It can be generated by both Expression Blend and Visual Studio. It can be referenced by coding statements at runtime.

In the past, artistic designers and programmers had great difficulty working together unless they were extensively trained to do so. The designer might create a graphic design for a Web page, and then pass it along to the programmer, who would then add the functions needed by the application. But the designer might not know whether their design vision could be implemented by the programmer. Making matters worse, once the programmer started to add code, it was nearly impossible to make any changes or improvements to the visual design.

By creating XAML and WPF, Microsoft allows designers and programmers to work together, each taking advantage of their special skills. The same project can be passed back and forth between the designer and the programmer as it gradually takes shape. Using XAML, the designer can create rich visual interfaces that lend themselves very neatly to coding by a programmer.

Layout and Controls

A WPF application controls its layout through the use of containers called *panels*. Each panel can contain child elements such as controls like buttons and checkboxes, or other panels. There are three types of panels:

- DockPanel—allows child elements to be positioned along the edges of the panel
- Grid—allows child elements to be positioned in predetermined rows and columns, much like one would with a table
- Canvas—allows child elements to be positioned anywhere in the panel.

All of the standard controls are available, such as TextBox, CheckBox, and ComboBox. More advanced controls are also available, including DocumentViewer, MediaElement, and ViewPort3D.

Types of Applications

Standalone WPF

A Standalone WPF application runs like any other Windows application. You do not need to use a Web browser to run it. This type of program runs with the same privileges as the current user, so it can access the computer's hard drive, use network sockets, and so on. It can be installed from a local disk, a network server, or by a method named **ClickOnce**. Using ClickOnce, the user can use a Web browser to connect to a page containing a button that lets them download and install the WPF application on their computer.

There is a clear advantage to creating ClickOnce applications. You can publish the application to a Web server for others to use. Later, when you have made improvements to the program, you can republish the application. This makes it easy for users to get the latest version of your work.

XAML Browser Applications (XBAPs)

A XAML Browser Application (XBAP) runs inside Internet Explorer. It can act as a client for Web applications. It can use most of the capabilities of WPF in a browser application.

An XBAP is silently loaded via ClickOnce, and looks just like a Web page. It is given only a limited amount of trust, so it does not have all the privileges normally given to desktop applications. For example, it cannot create other windows, display dialog boxes, access the full file system of the computer, or execute user interface code created with Windows Forms.

Tutorial 1:
Creating the Kayak Tour Reservations application

In this tutorial, you will begin to create a WPF application named **Kayak Tour Reservations** that lets the user sign up for a kayak tour. By the time you finish this set of tutorials, the user will be able to select the type of kayak they want to use, the tour location, and the tour date.

Step 1: On the File menu, select *New Project*. Select *WPF Application* from the list of application templates. Name the project *KayakTourWPF* and click the OK button.

Step 2: Select *Save All* from the File menu. When the *Save Project* dialog appears, choose a folder location for your project and click the *Save* button.

Step 3: The *MainWindow.xaml* Design window should appear, as shown in Figure B-1. You should also see another tab, labeled *MainWindow.xaml.vb*. When you click this tab, you see the code file for the MainWindow, where you will write event handlers.

Figure B-1 Design window, immediately after creating a new WPF project

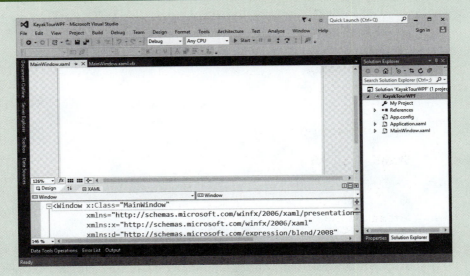

Step 4: Using the mouse, click the Zoom percent dropdown list on the left side of the divider line between the design view and the code view. The percent value you select will affect the size of the designer window. You can also use the scroll wheel on the mouse to do this. This adjustment does not change the actual size of the window object. Look for its Height and Width properties in the Properties window to verify that their values do not change.

Step 5: Using the mouse to drag the corner of the window, expand the window's size to about 380 units high and 600 units wide. Now you can see that Height and Width properties have changed.

Step 6: Set the window's Title property to *Register for a Kayak Tour*.

> The design surface automatically contains a single Grid control. The advantage to using a grid is that you can use the mouse to drag controls from the Toolbox onto the grid and position them anywhere you want. In some applications, you will insert additional rows and columns into the grid, to help you align the different controls.

Step 7: Open the Toolbox window and expand the *Common WPF Controls* group of controls.

Step 8: Drag a Label control from the Toolbox into the middle of the grid, near the top. Set the following properties for the Label: FontSize = 30; Content = *Our Featured Kayak Tours*. Drag the borders of the label with the mouse so that all the text in the label is visible. A sample is shown in Figure B-2.

Figure B-2 A Label containing the application title

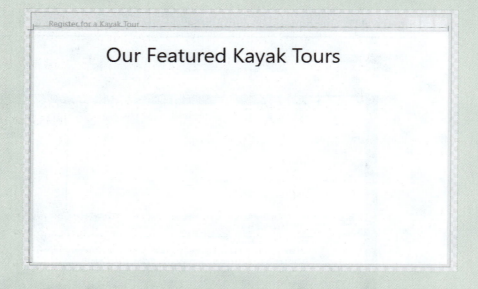

Step 9: Drag a Label control onto the grid near the left side, and set its Content property to *Select a Type of Kayak*.

Step 10: Drag a ListBox control on to the grid, just below the label on the left side. Set its Name property to *lstKayaks*. Select its Items property, which opens the Collection Editor window shown in Figure B-3. On the left side, select ListBoxItem from the dropdown list, and click the Add button three times. For each, you need to enter a value into its Content property. The values are:

Solo recreational
Tandem recreational
Solo sea kayak

Click the OK button to close the dialog. Figure B-4 shows the design of the form after adding the ListBox.

Figure B-3 Adding items to the lstKayak ListBox

Collection Editor: Items   ✕

Items	Properties
[0] ListBoxItem	▷ Brush
[1] ListBoxItem	▷ Appearance
[2] ListBoxItem	◢ Common

Content   Solo recreational   ▪

Cursor   ▾   ☐

DataContext   New   ☐

IsEnabled   ☑   ☐

IsSelected   ☐   ☐

ToolTip   ☐

⌄

▷ Layout

▷ Text

▷ Transform

▷ Miscellaneous

✕   ↑   ↓   Button   ▾   Add

OK   Cancel

Step 11: Add another label to the right side of the form and set its Content property to *Select a Kayak Tour*.

Step 12: Add a ComboBox control to the right side of the form and name it cboTour. Select its Items property, and add three items. Set the Content properties of the three items to the following:

Na Pali Coast tour
Hanalei Bay tour
Wailua River tour

Step 13: We would also like to let the user select the date of their tour. Just below the ComboBox control, add a DatePicker control. In the following figure, you can see the ComboBox control, with the DatePicker just below it:

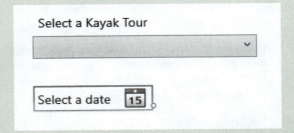

Step 14: Save the project and run the application by selecting *Start Debugging* from the Debug menu. Verify that you can select kayak types from the list box, and you can select tour names from the ComboBox. Click the ShowCalendar control, which causes the month calendar to appear, as shown in Figure B-4. When you select a date, the calendar closes and the date appears in the text box.

Step 15: Close the application window and return to Design mode.

Figure B-4 Select the DatePicker control, causing a month calendar to drop down

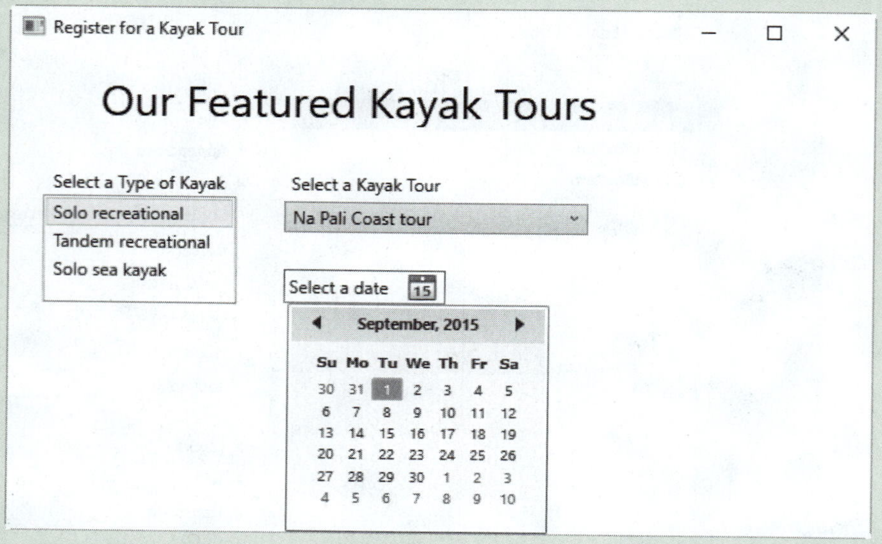

Register for a Kayak Tour   — □ ✕

Our Featured Kayak Tours

Select a Type of Kayak   Select a Kayak Tour

| Solo recreational |
| Tandem recreational |
| Solo sea kayak |

Na Pali Coast tour ⌄

Select a date `15`

◀	September, 2015				▶
Su	Mo	Tu	We	Th	Fr	Sa
30	31	1	2	3	4	5
6	7	8	9	10	11	12
13	14	15	16	17	18	19
20	21	22	23	24	25	26
27	28	29	30	1	2	3
4	5	6	7	8	9	10

Tutorial 2:
Adding Images to the Kayak Tour Reservations application

Most customers who go on kayak tours for the first time are not familiar with the various types of kayaks that they might be able to use. A well-designed reservation system should, therefore, display a picture of each kayak type to help the user make a selection. In this tutorial you will add three kayak images to the Kayak Tour Reservations application. The pictures will be displayed by a WPF Image control. When the user selects each type of kayak in the ListBox, the appropriate image will display at the bottom of the window.

Adding an image to a WPF application is a little different from the way it's done in Windows Forms. You must first add the image file to the project, using the Solution Explorer window. Then, when you want to display the image in an Image control, you select the image name from a list of images belonging to the project.

Step 1:   Copy three image files from the student sample programs folder for Appendix B into your application's directory (the directory containing the file named *MainWindow.xaml*). The image filenames are: *rec_kayak.jpg, sea_kayak.jpg,* and *tandem_rec_kayak.jpg.*

Step 2:   Right-click the project name in Solution Explorer, select *Add*, and select *Existing Item.* In the *Add Existing Item* dialog window, select *Image Files* in the *file type* dropdown list in the lower corner of the window, as shown here:

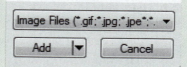

Select the three image files from your project directory, then click the *Add* button. The three filenames should appear in the list of files in your Solution Explorer window.

Step 3: Add three Image controls to the form, positioned near the bottom center area of the form. Set each Image control's Width property to 168 and Height property to 100.

Step 4: Select the first image control, set its Name property to *imgRecKayak*. Click its Source property, and select the *rec_kayak.jpg* image from the list of images shown in the dialog window.

Step 5: Select the second image control, set its Name property to *imgRecTandem*. Click its Source property, and select the *tandem_rec_kayak.jpg* image from the list of images shown in the dialog window.

Step 6: Select the third image control, set its Name property to *imgSeaKayak*. Click its Source property, and select the *sea_kayak.jpg* image from the list of images shown in the dialog window.

> If you were to run the application now, all of images would appear. But what we want to happen is for the images to pop out and become visible when the appropriate type of kayak is selected in the ListBox control.

Step 7: Select click the lstKayaks ListBox control with the mouse. At the top of the Properties window, click the events tab (lightning bolt icon) to display all the ListBox event types. Double click the box to the right of the **SelectionChanged** event in the Properties window. You should now see the code window editor for *MainWindow.xaml.vb*, containing the lstKayaks_SelectionChanged event handler procedure. Add the following code, listed in bold:

```
Private Sub lstKayaks_SelectionChanged(...)Handles lstKayaks.SelectionChanged

    imgRecKayak.Visibility = Visibility.Hidden
    imgRecTandem.Visibility = Visibility.Hidden
    imgSeaKayak.Visibility = Visibility.Hidden

    If lstKayaks.SelectedIndex = 0 Then
      imgRecKayak.Visibility = Visibility.Visible
    ElseIf lstKayaks.SelectedIndex = 1 Then
      imgRecTandem.Visibility = Visibility.Visible
    ElseIf lstKayaks.SelectedIndex = 2 Then
      imgSeaKayak.Visibility = Visibility.Visible
    End If

End Sub
```

Therefore, depending on the SelectedIndex of the kayak selected in the ListBox, we set one of the Image controls to *Visible*. The other two images remain set to *Hidden*.

Step 8: Create the following *Loaded* event handler for the main window. These statements hide all three kayak images when the form is first loaded into memory:

```
Private Sub Load() Handles Me.Loaded

  imgRecKayak.Visibility = Windows.Visibility.Hidden
  imgRecTandem.Visibility = Windows.Visibility.Hidden
  imgSeaKayak.Visibility = Windows.Visibility.Hidden
End Sub
```

Step 9: Save the project and run the application by selecting *Start Debugging* from the Debug menu. Experiment with selecting each of the kayak types from the ListBox. Notice that each time you do so, a different kayak photo appears. See Figure B-5 for a sample.

Figure B-5 Viewing the kayak photos while running the application

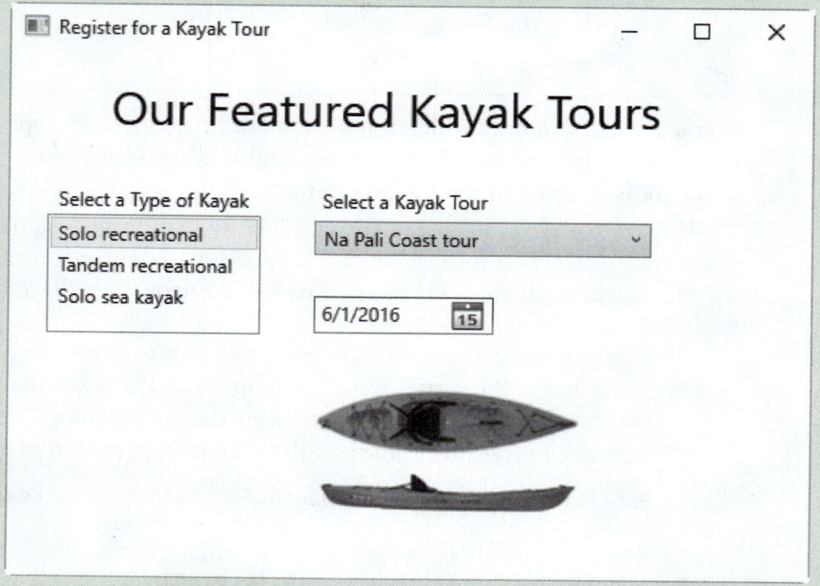

C Converting Mathematical Expressions to Programming Statements

In mathematical expressions, it is not always necessary to use an operator for multiplication. For example, the expression $2xy$ is understood to mean "2 times x times y." Visual Basic, however, requires an operator for any mathematical operation. Table C-1 shows some mathematical expressions that perform multiplication and the equivalent Visual Basic expression.

Table C-1 Math expressions in Visual Basic

Mathematical Expression	Operation	Visual Basic Equivalent
$6b$	6 times b	6 * b
(3)(12)	3 times 12	3 * 12
$4xy$	4 times x times y	4 * x * y

When converting mathematical expressions to Visual Basic programming statements, you may have to insert parentheses that do not appear in the mathematical expression. For example, look at the following expression:

$$x = \frac{a + b}{c}$$

To convert this to a Visual Basic statement, $a + b$ will have to be enclosed in parentheses:

```
x = (a + b) / c
```

Table C-2 shows more mathematical expressions and their Visual Basic equivalents.

Table C-2 More math expressions in Visual Basic

Mathematical Expression	Visual Basic Expression
$y = 3\dfrac{x}{2}$	y = x / 2 * 3
$z = 3bc + 4$	z = 3 * b * c + 4
$a = \dfrac{3x + 2}{4a - 1}$	a = (3 * x + 2) / (4 * a - 1)

Chapter 1

1.1 Central Processing Unit (CPU), main memory, secondary storage, input devices, and output devices

1.2 Main memory holds the sequences of instructions in the programs that are running and the data with which those programs are working. RAM is usually a volatile type of memory that is used only for temporary storage.

1.3 Program instructions and data are stored in main memory while the program is operating. Main memory is volatile and loses its content when power is removed from the computer. Secondary storage holds data for long periods of time—even when there is no power to the computer.

1.4 Operating systems and application software

1.5 A set of well-defined steps for performing a task or solving a problem

1.6 To ease the task of programming; programs may be written in a programming language and then converted to machine language

1.7 An object is an item in a program that contains data and has the ability to perform operations. A control is a specific type of object that usually appears in a program's graphical user interface.

1.8 An application responds to events that occur or actions that take place, such as the clicking of a mouse.

1.9 A property is a piece of data that determines some characteristics of a control.

1.10 The default name is not descriptive; it does not indicate the purpose of the control.

1.11 A Text Box

1.12 TextBox1

1.13 No; the + symbol is an illegal character for control names.

1.14 The program's purpose, information to be input, the processing to take place, and the desired output

1.15 Planning helps the programmer create a good design and avoid errors that may not otherwise be anticipated.

1.16 To imagine what the computer screen looks like when the program is running; it's the first step in creating an application's forms or windows.

1.17 A diagram that graphically depicts a program's flow

1.18 A cross between human language and a programming language

1.19 A mistake that does not prevent an application from executing, but causes it to produce incorrect results; a mistake in a mathematical formula is a common type of runtime error

1.20 To find and correct runtime errors.

1.21 Testing is a part of each design step. Flowcharts should be tested, code should be desk-checked, and the application should be run with test data to verify that it produces the correct output.

1.22 The *Solution Explorer* window shows a file-oriented view of a project. It allows quick navigation among the project files.

1.23 The *Properties* window shows and allows you to change most of the currently selected object's properties and their values.

1.24 The standard toolbar contains buttons that execute frequently used commands.

1.25 The toolbar contains buttons that execute frequently used menu commands. The *ToolBox* provides buttons for placing controls.

1.26 A ToolTip is a small box that is displayed when you hold the mouse cursor over a button on the toolbar or in the *ToolBox* for a few seconds. The box gives a short description of what the button does.

Chapter 2

2.1 An empty form (a Form object) that will be your program's main window.

2.2 The object's sizing handles appear on all sides.

2.3 Use them to drag the object's boundaries, making it larger and smaller.

2.4 A Name property

2.5 To view and modify properties of the control or form that is currently selected in the designer window.

2.6 It lists the property names in alphabetical order.

2.7 It lists the property names in order according to category.

2.8 The visible part of the control that commonly contains text.

2.9 The height and width of the object, in pixels.

2.10 The entire set of controls that can be added to a form.

2.11 Either double-click the control's name, or drag it onto the form with the mouse.

2.12 A hint to the user as to what the button does.

2.13 Event handlers that execute code.

2.14 Double-click the object to create the handler. This opens the *Code* window.

2.15 A window showing a separate file containing only Visual Basic code related to a form.

2.16 Data containing a sequence of characters.

2.17 The assignment operator is the = symbol. It assigns the value of the expression on its right side to the variable on its left side.

2.18 Look for the tabs near the top of the Visual Studio work area.

2.19 Design, Debug, and Run

2.20 A collection of files and resources relating to a single application.

2.21 A collection of projects

2.22 The name of the label

2.23 None

2.24 Select Borderstyle, and choose from three styles.

2.25 Autosize property

2.26 TextAlign property

2.27 The area behind the label's text changes color.

2.28 The label's Text changes color.

2.29 Custom, Web, System

2.30 A literal is a piece of data is written into a program's code. For example, a string enclosed in quotes, or a number.

2.31 Quotation marks

2.32 String

2.33 Assign an empty string ("") or the special value `String.Empty` to its Text property

2.34 Displaying images

2.35 Common Controls group

2.36 Assign an image (from an image file) to the control's Image property

2.37 Normal

2.38 The image expands to match the size of the PictureBox.

2.39 Add a Click event handler to the PictureBox control holding the image.

2.40 Makes the control visible at runtime.

2.41 No

2.42 `picPrize.Visible = False`

2.43 Sequentially, from first to last

2.44 To close the current form.

2.45 The current form

2.46 To document and explain the code.

2.47 Apostrophe (')

2.48 No

2.49   Blank lines help to separate important structural blocks, making the code more readable. Indentation helps to improve readability also.

2.50   Syntax, runtime, and Logic

2.51   The code shows a jagged red line.

2.52   Help appears, explaining the error and recommending fixes.

2.53   The program will not be compiled. Instead, error messages will be displayed.

2.54   Runtime

2.55   Divide by zero, file not found, invalid type conversion.

2.56   An error in the logical steps performed by the program.

2.57   The only way to find logic errors and runtime errors in your code is to test the application. To test an application, you run it many times, providing sample input and verifying that the output is correct. If the output is not correct, you know there is a logic error somewhere in your code. To find the logic error, you must debug the application.

2.58   A popup box with text and a button inside.

2.59   `MessageBox.Show("Welcome to our hotel!")`

2.60   Missing a period between "Box" and "Show".

2.61   A container that is usually docked along the bottom of a form. It holds several types of controls inside, including a ToolStripStatusLabel.

2.62   The controls cannot be moved on the form at Design time.

2.63   Right-click the form and choose Lock Controls from the popup menu.

2.64   Right-click the form and choose Lock Controls from the popup menu.

Chapter 3

3.1   Text

3.2   `lblMessage.Text = txtInput.Text`

3.3   Hello Jonathon, how are you?

3.4   Appending one string to another.

3.5   A variable is a storage location in the computer's memory; used for holding data while the program is running.

3.6   `Dim intUnitsSold As Integer`

3.7   `decInterestRate` is written with the convention used in this book.

3.8   a. `count`   Legal
      b. `rate*Pay`   Illegal; cannot use the * character
      c. `deposit.amount`   Illegal; cannot use a period
      d. `down_payment`   Legal

3.9   a. 0   d. 0
      b. 0.0   e. 12:00:00 AM, January 1 of year 1
      c. False

3.10 `#2/20/2017 5:35:00 PM#`

3.11 Charles Simonyi. He introduced the use of prefixes in variable names, called *Hungarian Notation*, a popular naming convention often used in Visual Basic and many other programming languages.

3.12 a. 21   e. 3.0
      b. 2   f. 36
      c. 17
      d. 18

3.13 a. 1
      b. 2

3.14 Integer division throws away any fractional part of the quotient. The result of integer division is always an integer.

3.15 `dblResult` will be set to `4.7`

3.16 `dblResult` will be set to `7.0`

3.17 `dblResult` will be set to `3.0`

3.18 a. 21
      b. 2
      c. 17
      d. 18

3.19 `dblResult` will be set to `28`

3.20 `dblResult` will be set to `186478.39`

3.21 A named constant is like a variable whose content is read-only, and cannot be changed by a programming statement while the program is running.

3.22 a. 27   c. 12
      b. 13   d. 18

3.23 `CDbl`

3.24 a. 48   (rounds to nearest even integer)
      b. 35   (rounds up)
      c. 2300
      d. cannot be converted

3.25 `dblSalary.ToString("c")`

3.26 a. `"c"`
      b. `"e"`
      c. `"n"`
      d. `"p"`
      e. `"f"`

3.27 `ToString("c")`

3.28
Number Value	Format String	ToString Value
12.3	n4	12.3000
12.348	n1	12.3
1234567.1	n3	1,234,567.100
123456.0	f1	123456.0
123456.0	e3	1.235E+005
.234	p2	23.40%
–1234567.8	c3	($1,234,567.800)

3.29   `datStart.ToString("T")`

3.30   `datBirth.ToString("D")`

3.31   Local variables are not visible to statements outside the procedure in which they are declared. Class-level variables are visible to all of the procedures in a class.

3.32   Class-level variables are declared at the class-level (inside the class, but not in any procedure).

3.33   An exception is an unexpected error that occurs while a program is running, causing the program to abruptly halt.

3.34   A block of code that is executed automatically when an exception is thrown.

3.35   Code related to the normal functioning of the application.

3.36   This happens when an exception is thrown.

3.37   You display the exception object's Message property in a message box or a label.

3.38
```
Try
    Dim intSum As Integer = CInt(txtValue1.Text) + CInt(txtValue2.Text)
    lblSum.Text = intSum.ToString()
Catch
    MessageBox.Show("Please enter integer values")
End Try
```

3.39   The control is accepting keyboard and/or mouse input from the user.

3.40   The button's Click event handler executes.

3.41   Select *Tab Order* from the *View* menu.

3.42   The control is skipped when the user presses the Tab key.

3.43   `txtNumber.Focus()`

3.44   Insert the & character in its Text.

3.45   Insert two consecutive && characters into its Text

3.46   AcceptButton refers to the control that will receive a Click event when the user presses the Enter key. CancelButton refers to the control that will receive a Click event when the user presses the Esc key. You identify the two buttons in form properties, named AcceptButton and CancelButton.

3.47   They are deleted also.

3.48   They form a subgroup of the GroupBox's own TabIndex value.

3.49   A Panel cannot display a title, and does not have a Text property.

3.50   The form's Load event

3.51   Double-click any area of the form in the *Designer* window, where there is no other control.

3.52   `Now`

3.53   `TimeOfDay`

3.54   `Today`

3.55   A syntax error will prevent an application from compiling and executing. Examples are misspelled keywords and incorrect use of operators or punctuation. Syntax errors are often reported as soon as you type them. A logic error is a programming mistake that does not prevent an application from starting, but causes the application to produce incorrect results. Examples are incorrect math statements and assigning the wrong value to a variable.

3.56   A breakpoint is a line of code that causes a running application to pause execution and enter break mode. While the application is paused, you may perform debugging operations, such as examining variable contents and the values stored in control properties.

3.57   Single-stepping is a useful debugging technique for locating logic errors. In single-stepping, you execute an application's code one line at a time. After each line executes, you can examine variable and property contents. This process allows you to identify the line or lines of code causing the error.

Chapter 4

4.1   a. T   e. T
      b. T   f. F
      c. F   g. T
      d. T

4.2   If the Boolean variable blnIsInvalid equals True.

4.3   Yes, they both perform the same operation. Only the indentation is different.

4.4   The following statement is preferred because the conditionally executed statement is indented. The indention makes the statement easier to read.

```
If decSales > 10000 Then
   decCommissionRate = 0.15
End If
```

4.5   a. 99
      b. 0
      c. 99

4.6   Three times

4.7   One time by the If...Then...ElseIf statement and four times by the set of If...Then statements

4.8 | Logical Expression | Result |
      |---|---|
      | True And False | False |
      | True And True | True |
      | False And True | False |
      | False And False | False |
      | True Or False | True |
      | True Or True | True |
      | False Or True | True |
      | False Or False | False |
      | True Xor False | True |
      | True Xor True | False |
      | Not True | False |
      | Not False | True |

4.9 a. *False*
    b. *False*
    c. *True*

4.10 f, g, a, b, i, h, e, c, d

4.11
```
Select Case intQuantity
    Case 0 To 9
       decDiscount = 0.1
    Case 10 To 19
       decDiscount = 0.2
    Case 20 To 29
       decDiscount = 0.3
    Case Is >= 30
       decDiscount = 0.4
    Case Else
       MessageBox.Show("Invalid Data")
End Select
```

4.12 `radBlue.Checked`

4.13 Only one

4.14 `chkCream.Checked`

4.15 Any or all of them

4.16 By pressing the spacebar

Chapter 5

5.1 `strInput = InputBox("Enter a number", "Please Respond", "500")`

5.2
```
Dim str As String = InputBox("Enter a value")
Dim intVal as Integer
    If Str.Length() > 0 Then
    intVal = CInt(str)
End If
```

5.3 0

5.4 `Items.Count`

5.5 11

5.6 SelectedItem

5.7 SelectedIndex

5.8 `strSelectedName = lstNames.Items(1).ToString()`

5.9 The loop is an infinite loop because it does not change the value of `intCount`.

5.10 Ten times

5.11 One time

5.12 `intX` is the counter and `intY` is the accumulator.

5.13 `Dim intCount As Integer = 5`

```
Do While intCount >= 1
  lstOutput.Items.Add(intCount)
  intCount -= 1
Loop
```

5.14
```
Dim intTotal As Integer = 0
Dim intNumber As Integer

Do While intTotal <= 300
  intNumber = CInt(InputBox("Enter a number"))
  intTotal += intNumber
Loop
```

5.15 Posttest

5.16 The loop will execute five times. The message box will display 10.

5.17
```
Dim intCount As Integer

For intCount = 0 To 100 Step 5
  lstOutput.Items.Add(intCount)
Next
```

5.18
```
Dim intCount As Integer
Dim intTotal As Integer
Dim intNum As Integer

intTotal = 0
For intCount = 0 To 7
  intNum = CInt(InputBox("Enter a number"))
  intTotal += intNum
Next
MessageBox.Show("The total is " & intTotal.ToString())
```

5.19 The For loop

5.20 The Do While loop

5.21 The Do Until loop

5.22 1, 1, 2, 2, 1, 2, 3, 1, 2

5.23 600 times

5.24 0

5.25 Items.Count

5.26 SelectedIndex

5.27 A drop-down combo box allows the user to type text into its text area. A drop-down list combo box does not allow the user to type text. The user can only select an item from the list.

5.28 By retrieving the value in the Text property

5.29 A drop-down list combo box

5.30 It returns a random integer value somewhere between 0 and 2,147,483,647.

5.31 It returns a random floating-point number between 0.0 and 1.0 (not including 1.0).

5.32
```
Dim rand as New Random

intRandomNumber = rand.Next(101)
```

5.33
```
Dim rand as New Random

intRandomNumber = rand.Next(301) + 100
```

5.34 When a Random object is created in memory, it retrieves the system time from the computer's internal clock, and uses that as the seed value.

5.35 If a Random object uses the same seed each time it is created, it will always generate the same series of random numbers.

Chapter 6

6.1 If you enter 10, the following will be displayed:

I saw Elba
Able was I

If you enter 5, the following will be displayed:

Able was I
I saw Elba

6.2 Most of the time, using procedures decreases the amount of duplicate code in a program.

6.3
```
Sub TimesTen(ByVal intValue As Integer)
    Dim intResult As Integer
    intResult = intValue * 10
    MessageBox.Show(intResult.ToString())
End Sub
```

6.4 `TimesTen(25)`

6.5
```
Sub PrintTotal(ByVal intNum1 As Integer, ByVal intNum2 As Integer,
               ByVal intNum3 As Integer)
    Dim intTotal As Integer
    intTotal = intNum1 + intNum2 + intNum3
    MessageBox.Show(intTotal.ToString())
End Sub
```

6.6 `PrintTotal(intUnits, intWeight, intCount)`

6.7 `ByVal`

6.8 a. Distance
b. Two
c. sngRate and sngTime; they are both Singles
d. Single

6.9
```
Function Days(ByVal intYears As Integer, ByVal intMonths As Integer,
              ByVal intWeeks As Integer) As Integer
```

6.10 `intNumDays = Days(intY, intM, intW)`

6.11 `Function LightYears(ByVal lngMiles As Long) As Single`

6.12 `sngDistance = LightYears(m)`

6.13
```
Function TimesTwo(intNumber As Integer) As Integer
    Return intNumber * 2
End Function
```

6.14 Step Out; Ctrl + Shift + F8

6.15 Step Into; F8

6.16 Step Over; Shift + F8

Chapter 7

7.1 Make it the startup form in the project's properties.

7.2 `frm`

7.3 To add a new form to a project either: Click the *Add New Item* button on the toolbar, and then select *Windows form,* or select *Add Windows Form* from the

PROJECT menu. In both cases, the *Add New Item* dialog appears. You can enter a form name and click the *Add* button.

7.4 To exclude a form from a project in Visual Studio: Right-click the form's entry in the *Solution Explorer* window. On the pop-up menu, click *Exclude From Project*.

7.5 A form file contains a form's code. It has the *.vb* extension.

7.6 When a modal form is displayed, no other form in the application can receive the focus until the modal form is closed. Also, when a statement displays a modal form, no other statements in that procedure will execute until the modal form is closed. A modeless form, however, allows the user to switch focus to another form while it is displayed. When a statement uses a method call to display a modeless form, the statements that follow the method call will continue to execute after the modeless form is displayed.

7.7 `frmResults.ShowDialog()`

7.8 `frmResults.Show()`

7.9 In the form's Activated event handler.

7.10 `frmInfo.lblCustomer.Text = "Jim Jones"`

7.11 The `Me` keyword indicates the currently active form. This can be useful when a form needs to call one of its own methods.

7.12 `Public dblAverage As Double`

7.13 It contains procedures, functions, and the declarations of variables and/or constants.

7.14 *.vb*

7.15 (1) Click the *Add New Item* button on the toolbar, or click *PROJECT* on the menu bar, and then click *Add Module*. The *Add New Item* dialog box should appear. (2) Select *Module* as the type of item. (3) Change the default name that is displayed in the *Name* text box to the name you wish to give the new module.

7.16 When you create a large application with multiple forms, quite often you will find that the code in several different forms needs to call the same general-purpose functions and/or procedures. These functions and/or procedures can be placed in a module to eliminate the duplication of code that would result if they were written into each form file.

7.17 1. Click *PROJECT* on the menu bar, and then click *Add Existing Item*.
      2. The *Add Existing Item* dialog box appears. Use the dialog box to locate the module file you want to add to the project. When you locate the file, select it and click the *Open* button. The module is now added to the project.

7.18 a. The name of a drop-down menu, which appears on the form's menu bar
      b. A command that appears on a drop-down menu, and may be selected by the user
      c. A menu item that appears dimmed and cannot be selected by the user
      d. A menu item that appears with a check mark to its left
      e. A key or combination of keys that causes a menu command to execute
      f. Another menu that appears when a command on a drop-down menu is selected
      g. A horizontal bar used to separate groups of commands on a menu

7.19   Shortcut keys are different from access keys in that a command's shortcut key may be used at any time the form is active, while a command's access key may only be used while the drop-down menu containing the command is visible.

7.20   `mnu`

7.21   `mnuFileSave`, `mnuFileSaveAs`, `mnuFilePrint`, and `mnuFileExit`

7.22   By placing an ampersand (&) before a character in the Text property.

7.23   The item initially appears as a checked menu item, meaning it appears with a check mark displayed next to it.

7.24   By setting its Enabled property to *False*.

7.25   By testing the value of the menu item's Checked property.

7.26   A Click event occurs for the ToolStripMenuItem.

7.27   By right-clicking a control

7.28   By setting the control's ContextMenuStrip property to the name of the ContextMenuStrip control.

Chapter 8

8.1   a. `Dim intEmpNums(99) As Integer`
b. `Dim decPayRate(23) As Decimal`
c. `Dim intMiles() As Integer = { 10, 20, 30, 40, 50 }`
d. `Dim strNames(12) As String`
e. `Dim strDivisions() As String = {"North", "South",`
`                                "East", "West"}`

8.2   The upper boundary (4) cannot appear inside the parentheses when an initialization list is provided.

8.3   a. 101
b. 3
c. 1

8.4   The runtime system throws an exception if a subscript is outside the range of subscripts for an array.

8.5
```
For intCount = 0 To intMAX_SUBSCRIPT
   MessageBox.Show(intPoints(intCount).ToString())
Next
```

8.6
```
Dim intNumber As Integer
For Each intNumber In intPoints
   MessageBox.Show(intNumber.ToString())
Next
```

8.7   a. 10.00
b. 25.00
c. 32.50
d. 50.00

8.8
```
intTotal = 0              ' Initialize accumulator.
For intCount = 0 To 99
  intTotal += intValues(intCount)
Next
```

8.9
```
intTotal = 0            ' Initialize accumulator.
For intCount= 0 To (points.Length - 1)
   intTotal += intPoints(intCount)
Next
dblAverage = intTotal / points.Length
```

8.10
```
Array.Sort(strSerialNumbers)
```

8.11
```
0 18 0
1 4 4
2 27 54
3 52 156
4 100 400
```

8.12
```
ReDim Preserve decSales(49)
```

8.13 (Code example)
```
blnFound = False
intCount = 0
Do While Not blnFound And intCount < intValidNumbers.Length
   If intValidNumbers (intCount) = 247 Then
      blnFound = True
      intPosition = intCount
   End If
   intCount+= 1
Loop
'Was 100 found in the array?
If blnFound Then
   MessageBox.Show("The value was found at position " &
                   intPosition.ToString())
Else
   MessageBox.Show("The value was not found.")
End If
```

8.14
```
Dim intGrades(29, 9) As Integer
```

8.15 24 elements (6 rows by 4 columns)

8.16
```
decSales(0, 0) = 56893.12
```

8.17
```
MessageBox.Show(decSales(5, 3).ToString())
```

8.18
```
Dim intSettings(2, 4) As Integer
```

8.19 Four rows and five columns

8.20
```
Dim strMovies(49, 9, 24) As String
```

8.21
```
If radLifeTimeMember.Checked = True Then
   chkFreePizza.Enabled = True
   chkFreeCola.Enabled = True
End If
```

8.22 500

8.23 It allows you to anchor the control to one or more edges of a form. When a control is anchored to a form's edge, the distance between the control's edge and the form's edge will remain constant, even when the user resizes the form.

8.24 It allows you to dock a control. When a control is docked, it is positioned directly against one of the edges of a form. Additionally, the length or width of a docked control is changed to match the length or width of the form's edge.

Chapter 9

9.1 (1) open the file, (2) write data to the file or read data from the file, and (3) close the file

9.2 `StreamWriter`, `StreamReader`

9.3 `outputFile = System.IO.File.CreateText("Test.txt")`

9.4 `outputFile.WriteLine(intX)`

9.5 `inputFile = System.IO.File.OpenText("Test.txt")`

9.6 `intX = inputFile.ReadLine`

9.7 With the `System.IO.File.Exists` method

9.8 With the `Peek` method; when `Peek` returns –1, the end of the file has been reached

9.9 Most Windows users are accustomed to using a dialog box to browse their disk for a file to open, or for a location to save a file.

9.10 Filter: These list boxes display a filter that specifies the type of files that are visible in the dialog box. You store a string in the Filter property that specifies the filter(s) available in the list boxes.

InitialDirectory: You store the path of the directory whose contents are to be initially displayed in the dialog box.

Title: The string stored in this property is displayed in the dialog box's title bar.

Filename: The filename selected or entered by the user is stored in this property.

9.11 `Text files (*.txt)|*.txt|Word files (*.doc)|*.doc|`
`All files(*.*)`

9.12 The ColorDialog control's Color property.

9.13 The FontDialog control's Font property.

9.14 By setting the FontDialog control's ShowColor property to *True* before calling the ShowDialog method.

9.15 In the FontDialog control's Color property.

9.16 By calling the control's Print method.

9.17 `e.Graphics.DrawString("Joe Smith", New Font("MS sans Serif",`
`    18, FontStyle.Bold), Brushes.Black, 100, 20)`

9.18 Header, body, and footer.

9.19 The characters in a proportionally spaced font do not occupy the same amount of horizontal space. All the characters in a monospaced font use the same amount of space.

9.20 `e.Graphics.DrawString(String.Format("{0,12} {1,8} ", a, b),`
`    New Font("Courier", 12, FontStyle.Regular),`
`    Brushes.Black, 10, 50)`

9.21 `e.Graphics.DrawString(String.Format("{0,–12} {1,8} ", a, b),`
`    New Font("Courier", 12, FontStyle.Regular),`
`    Brushes.Black, 10, 50)`

9.22
```
Structure Movie
    strName As String
    strDirector As String
    strProducer As String
    intYear As Integer
End Structure
```

9.23 `Dim film As Movie`

9.24 The following statements assume the variable is named `film`:

```
film.strName = "Wheels of Fury"
film.strDirector = "Arlen McGoo"
film.strProducer = "Vincent Van Dough"
film.intYear = 2016
```

9.25 The following statements assume the variable is named `film`:

```
With film

    .strName = "Wheels of Fury"
    .strDirector = "Arlen McGoo"
    .strProducer = "Vincent Van Dough"
    .intYear = 2010
End With
```

Chapter 10

10.1 A database is a container for one or more tables. A table is a set of rows and columns holding logically related data.

10.2 Employee_ID

10.3 Boolean

10.4 There would be too great a chance for misspellings by the data entry person. Also, the department name could change in the future, making maintenance a problem.

10.5 Individual values of a foreign key column can occur multiple times in a table, whereas a primary key can contain values that occur only once. Also, a foreign key links its table with some other table's primary key.

10.6 Data binding

10.7 TableAdapter

10.8 The database is not affected by changes to a dataset unless a special `Update` method is called.

10.9 DataGridView control

10.10 DataConnection object

10.11 Data Sources window

10.12 DataSource

10.13 Click the DataGridView's smart tag (arrow in the upper right corner), and select the data source. Alternatively, you can select the DataGridView's DataSource property in the Properties window and select the data source from a list.

10.14 Select the column in the *Data Sources* window and drag it onto the form.

10.15 DateTimePicker control

10.16 Select *Add New Data Source* from the *Data* menu.

10.17 Structured Query Language

10.18 SQL queries are written using an industry-standard language

10.19 `SELECT First_Name, Last_Name FROM Employees`

10.20 Right-click the table adapter icon in the form's component tray and select *Add Query*.

10.21 `WHERE Salary <= 85000`

10.22 `SELECT pay_rate, employee_id, hours_worked FROM Payroll`
`ORDER by hours_worked DESC`

10.23 `SELECT pay_rate AS Rate_of_Pay FROM Payroll`

10.24 `SELECT pay_rate, hours_worked, pay_rate * hours_worked`
`AS gross_pay FROM Payroll`

10.25 `SELECT * FROM Payroll WHERE pay_rate > 20000`
`AND pay_rate <= 55000`

10.26 `SELECT * FROM Payroll WHERE employee_id LIKE "FT%"`

10.27 *Members* table

10.28 *Payments* and *Members* tables

10.29 Columns property

10.30 `LIKE`

Chapter 11

11.1 A Web application is a program running on a Web server that interacts with Web browsers. The connection might be across the Internet, or it might be within a company intranet.

11.2 The Web server generates Web pages, which are consumed by clients (end users) running Web browsers. The clients make requests and the server satisfies the requests.

11.3 A postback occurs when the end user clicks a button or activates a control that sends the contents of the Web page back to the Web server.

11.4 ASP.NET is called a platform because it provides development tools, code libraries, and visual controls for browser-based applications.

11.5 Content is comprised of Web forms, HTML code, Web controls, images, and other multimedia.

11.6 File system, HTTP, and FTP

11.7 Click the *Design* tab.

11.8 Right-click the *Solution Explorer* window and select *Browse with* . . . .

11.9 Static text is text typed directly onto a form in *Design* mode. It can be used in place of Labels (the type used in Windows forms) when you do not need to access it at runtime in program code.

11.10 By selecting the text with the mouse, and then selecting *Heading 1* from the *Block format* pull-down list on the left side of the formatting toolbar

11.11 A dialog window explains that a confirmation option must be set in the *Web. config* file. It creates the file and adds it to the *Solution Explorer* window.

11.12 DropDownList

11.13 ImageButton

11.14 LinkButton

11.15 The SelectedIndex property contains an integer that indicates the selected button.

11.16 As soon as the user makes a ListBox selection, the page is posted back to the server.

11.17 DropDownList

11.18 Drag the mouse over the cells and select *Merge Cells* from the *Layout* menu.

11.19 Click the column select button just above the column along the table border.

11.20 Drag the right-hand border of the column with the mouse.

11.21 From the *Layout* menu, choose *Select*, and then choose *Table*. Open the Style property of the table, and modify the font in the *Style Builder* dialog.

11.22 Items collection

11.23 Select *Add New Item* from the Web site menu.

11.24 Assign the new Web page location to the NavigateURL property.

11.25 Select the block with the mouse and click the *HyperLink* button on the formatting toolbar.

11.26 The `Redirect` method

11.27 GridView control

11.28 SqlDataSource object

11.29 DataFormatString property

11.30 Fields property

11.31 DetailsView control

Chapter 12

12.1 Examples: Form, CheckBox, RadioButton, TextBox, ListBox, and every other control in the Visual Studio Toolbox window.

12.2 The TextBox tool represents the class and a specific TextBox control on the form is an instance of the class.

12.3 Select classes by finding the physical entities in the application domain.

12.4 Attributes describe the properties that all objects of the same class have in common. They are implemented as properties.

12.5 Operations are actions the class objects may perform or messages to which they can respond. They are implemented as methods.

12.6 A class interface is the portion that is visible to the application programmer who uses the class.

12.7 A class implementation is the portion of a class that is hidden from client programs.

12.8 (1) Click the *Add New Item* button () on the toolbar, or click *Project* on the menu bar, and then click *Add Class*. The *Add New Item* dialog box should appear. Make sure that *Class* is selected in the *Templates* pane. (2) Change the default class name in the Name text box to the name you wish to give the new class file. (3) Click the *Add* button.

12.9 Declare an object variable, and then create an instance of the class in memory and assign its address to the variable.

12.10 An object is removed by setting all variables that reference it to Nothing.

12.11 Garbage collection.

12.12 Variables declared in a class module, but outside of any class methods

12.13 A procedure that behaves like a Class property

12.14 It allows a client program to retrieve the value of a property.

12.15 It allows a client program to set the value of a property.

12.16 A constructor is a class method that is executed automatically when an instance of a class is created. A Finalize method is called just before the Garbage Collector removes an object from memory.

12.17 Unlike arrays, which have fixed sizes, collection objects automatically expand as items are added to them, and shrink as items are removed from them. Another difference is this: all elements in an array must be of the same type, but members of collections do not have to be of the same type.

12.18 Use the Add method to add members to a collection.

12.19 By adding a key value, you will be more easily able to search for items.

12.20 With the Item method

12.21 With the Remove method

12.22 Insect is the base class and Fly is the derived class.

12.23 All of the base class's members (variables, properties, and methods)

12.24 Overriding is replacing a base Class property procedure or method with one of the same name in the derived class.

12.25 Overridable

12.26 Overrides

12.27 The base class constructor executes first, followed by the derived class constructor.

12.28 Protected base class members are like private members, except they may be accessed by methods and property procedures in derived classes. To all other code, however, protected class members are just like private class members.

E Glossary

About box—a dialog box that usually displays brief information about the application

abstract data type (ADT)—a data type created by a programmer

abstraction—a model that includes only the general characteristics of an object

accept button—a button on a form that is clicked when the user presses the [Enter] key

access key—a key that is pressed in combination with the [Alt] key; access keys allow the user to access buttons and menu items using the keyboard; also known as a mnemonic

accumulator—the variable used to keep a running total

Activated event—a form event that occurs each time the user switches focus to a form from another form or another application

Activated event handler—created in response to an Activated event

Add method—used to add items to a collection

algorithm—a set of well-defined steps for performing a task or solving a problem

Alphabetical button—a button on the *Properties* window that causes properties to be displayed alphabetically

Anchor property—a control property that allows you to anchor the control to one or more edges of a form

And operator—a logical operator that combines two expressions into one; both expressions must be true for the overall expression to be true

AndAlso operator—uses short-circuit evaluation in compound expressions

append—to write new data immediately following existing data in a file

application software—programs that make the computer useful to the user by solving specific problems or performing general operations

argument—a value passed to a procedure or function

array—a group of variables with a single name

array bounds checking—a runtime feature of Visual Basic that does not allow a statement to use a subscript outside the range of subscripts for an array

ascending order—when items are arranged in order, from lowest to highest value

aspect ratio—the image's width to height ratio

ASP.NET—Microsoft's platform for Web applications; an improvement over Active Server Pages

ASP.NET Server Controls—interactive controls such as buttons, list boxes, and text boxes that execute on the server

assignment operator—the equal sign (=); it copies the value on its right into the item on its left in an assignment statement

assignment statement—a programming statement that uses the assignment operator to copy a value from one object to another

attributes—the data contained in an object; the characteristics of an object that will be implemented as properties

Auto Hide—when this feature is turned on, the window is displayed only as a tab along one of the edges of the Visual Studio window; click the pushpin icon to turn it on or off

Autos window—a debugging window that displays the value and data type of the variables that appear in the current statement, the three statements before, and the three statements after the current statement

Auto-implemented property—a class property that is defined by only a single line of code

AutoPostBack property—used on Web forms to force the page to be sent to the server when the user clicks on the control

AutoSize property—a Label control property that, when set to *True*, causes the label's size to display all the text in the Text property

BackColor property—establishes the background color for text

base class—the class that a derived class is based on

binary number—a number that is a sequence of 1s and 0s

binary operator—an operator that works with two operands

binding source—keeps track of a database name, location, username, password, and other connection information

Boolean expression—the expression tested in an If...Then statement; can be either *True* or *False*

Boolean property—a value that can be either *True* or *False*

BorderStyle property—a Label control property that determines the type of border, if any, that will appear around the control

bounding box—a transparent rectangular area that defines a control's size on a form

break mode—the mode in which an application has been suspended for debugging purposes

breakpoint—a line of code that causes a running application to pause execution and enter break mode; while the application is paused, you may examine variable contents and the values stored in certain control properties

buffer—a small holding section of memory that data is first written to; when the buffer is filled, all the information stored there is written to the file

button—a rectangular button-shaped control that performs an action when clicked with the mouse

Button control—when clicked by a user on a Web page, causes the page contents to be sent back to the Web server

ByRef—keyword used to declare a parameter variable, causing its argument to be passed by reference

by reference—when passing an argument to a procedure, the procedure has access to the original argument and can make changes to it

ByVal keyword—indicates that arguments passed into the variable are passed by value

by value—when passing an argument to a procedure, only a portion of the argument is passed to the procedure

Call keyword—a keyword that may be optionally used to call a procedure

cancel button—a button on a form that is clicked when the user presses the [Esc] key

Cascading Style Sheet (CSS)—file containing HTML styles that affect the appearance of text and graphics on Web pages

catch block—one or more statements following the Catch clause in a Try-Catch statement; execute only if an exception is thrown from the try block

Catch clause—part of a Try-Catch statement; appears after the last statement in a try block; marks the beginning of a catch block; program execution jumps here if an exception is thrown in the try block

Categorized button—a button on the *Properties* window that causes related properties to be displayed in groups

central processing unit (CPU)—the part of the computer that fetches instructions, carries out operations commanded by the instructions, and produces some outcome

CheckBox—a box that is checked or unchecked when clicked with the mouse

CheckBox control—allows the user to make yes/no or on/off selections; may appear alone or in groups

CheckBoxList control—looks like a group of check boxes, but works like a list box

CheckedChanged event—occurs when the state of a radio button or check box changes

CheckOnClick property—setting this property to *True* gives a menu item the ability to become checked or unchecked when it is clicked by the user

Checked property—a property of radio buttons and check boxes; it is set to *True* when the control is selected and *False* when the control is deselected. Also a MenuItem object property that may be set to *True* or *False*; when set to *True*, the object becomes a checked menu item

Chr function—an intrinsic function that accepts a character code as an argument and returns the character that corresponds to the code

class—a program structure that defines an abstract data type

class declaration—defines a class and member variables, properties, events, and methods

class implementation—the portion of a class that is hidden from client programs

class interface—the portion of a class that is visible to the application programmer who uses the class

class objects—instances of a class

client—entity that consumes data and makes requests of a server

client program—a program written to use a class; this term is in reference to the client-server relationship between a class and the programs that use it

client-server model—describes interaction between users of a program (the clients) and the server (as in a Web server)

Close method—closes a form and releases its visual par from memory

Closed event handler—a form event procedure that executes after a form has closed

Closing event handler—a form event procedure that executes as a form is in the process of closing, but before it has closed

code—the statements that are written in a program; commonly called source code, or simply code

code-behind file—stores the source code for a Web form

code outlining—a Visual Studio tool that lets you expand and collapse sections of code

code template—code that is automatically inserted into an event handler, consisting of the first and last lines of the procedure; you must add the code that appears between these two lines

Code window—a text-editing window in which you write code

collection—an object that is similar to an array; it is a single unit that contains several items and dynamically expands or shrinks in size as items are added or removed

Color dialog box—allows the user to select a color

ColorDialog control—displays a *Color* dialog box

columns—the vertical lists of data in a database table

combined assignment operators—combine an arithmetic operator with an assignment operator

combo box—similar to list boxes; display lists of items to the user

ComboBox—a control that is the combination of a ListBox and a TextBox

comments—notes of explanation that document lines or sections in a method; also known as remarks

Common Gateway Interface (CGI)—typically written in languages such as C or Perl; process information collected by HTML controls

compile errors—syntax errors, such as misspelled keywords and incorrect use of operators or punctuation; statements containing compile errors are underlined with a jagged blue line

compiler—special software that converts the program into machine language

components—special controls in Visual Basic that provide the linking mechanism in a database

Component tray—a resizable region at the bottom of the *Designer* window that holds invisible controls.

composite key—a primary key consisting of two or more combined columns in a database table

compound operators—*see* combined assignment operators

conditionally executed statements—statements that are executed only when certain conditions exist; usually determined by the value of a Boolean expression

connection object—provides the low-level functionality to interact with a data source

connector symbol—a flowcharting symbol used to connect two flowcharts when a flowchart does not fit on a single sheet of paper or must be divided into sections

constructor—a method that is automatically called when an instance of the class is created

Contents button—on the *Dynamic Help* window; displays a table of contents in which related help topics are organized into groups

context menu—a pop-up menu that is displayed when the user right-clicks a form or control

context-sensitive help—a help screen that is displayed when the F1 key is pressed (for the item that is currently selected)

control—a specific type of object that usually appears in a program's graphical user interface

ControlBox property—affects whether or not control buttons appear at the upper-right corner of a form's title bar

ControlChars.CrLf—a value that can be concatenated with a string to produce multiple line displays

Count property—a collection property that holds the number of items in the collection

counter—a variable that is regularly incremented or decremented each time a loop iterates

database—a collection of tables that hold related data

database management system (DBMS)—software that is specifically designed to store, retrieve, and manipulate large amounts of data in an organized and efficient manner

database schema—the design of tables, columns, and relationships between tables for the database

data binding—a Visual Basic technique that links database tables to controls on a program's forms

data-bound controls—update their contents automatically when you move from one row to the next in a dataset

DataGridView control—bound to DateTime fields

dataset—an in-memory cache of records that is separate from the data source but still allows you to work with the data

Dataset designer file—a file that holds information about datasets that are connected to the application

data source—usually a database, but can include text files, Excel spreadsheets, XML data, or Web services

DataSource control—visible only at design time; for example, AccessDataSource or SqlDataSource

DataSource property—identifies the table within the dataset that supplies the data

data type—the type of information that the variable can hold

DateTimePicker control—bound to DateTime fields

debugger—a tool that lets you step through a program, or part of a program, executing its code one line at a time. As you execute each line of code, you can observe the data that the program stores in memory, as well as the values of control properties.

debugging—the process of analyzing your code to determine where the error is taking place.

decision structure—a program structure that allows a program to have more than one path of execution

delimiter—an item that separates other items

derived class—a class that is based on another class

design—in a database table, specifies each column's name, data type, and range or size

Design mode—the mode in which you design and build an application

design time—see Design mode

Designer window—contains the application's forms; where one designs the application's user interface by creating forms and placing controls on them

DetailsView control—makes it easy to view, edit, delete, or add rows to a database table

diagram pane—part of the Query Builder tool in Visual Studio. It displays all the tables used in a query, with a check mark next to each field that will be used in the dataset.

dialog box—a small window that displays a message to the user; *see* message box

disk drive—stores information by magnetically encoding it onto a circular disk

DisplayMember property—identifies the column within the table that displays in the list box or combo box

DLLs—dynamic-link library files

docked—describes windows that are attached to each other or to one of the edges of the Visual Studio window

Dock property—a control property that allows you to dock a control against a form's edge

domain name—in a URL, the specific designation, such as microsoft.com

Do Until loop—a looping structure that causes one or more statements to repeat until its test expression is true

Do While loop—a looping structure that causes one or more statements to repeat as long as an expression is true

DropDownList control—permits the user to select a single item from a list

elements—variables stored within an array

empty string—represented by two quotation marks, with no space between them

Enabled property—a control property that, when set to *False*, disables the control; therefore the control cannot receive the focus, cannot respond to events generated by the user, and appears dimmed or grayed out on the form

encapsulation—the hiding of data and procedures inside a class

EndOfStream property—indicates whether or not the end of an input stream (usually a file) has been reached

event-driven—a type of program that responds to events or actions that occur while the program is running

event handler—a type of method that responds to events, such as mouse clicks and key presses at the keyboard

event procedure—*see* event handler

exception—an event or condition that happens unexpectedly and causes the application to halt

exception handler—in most modern programming languages, a simple mechanism for handling exceptions

exception object—contains various data about an exception; created when an exception is thrown; can optionally be assigned a name in the `Catch` clause of a `Try-Catch` statement to access properties

execution point—while single-stepping through an application's code, the next line of code that will execute

Exit Do statement—stops the execution of a `Do While` or `Do Until` loop

Exit For statement—stops the execution of a `For...Next` loop

field—*see* columns

file—a collection of data stored on a computer's disk

File.AppendText method—a method that opens a text file for data to be written to it; if the file method already exists, data is appended to its current contents

File.CreateText method—a method that opens a text file for data to be written to it; if the file does not exist, it is created

File.Exists method—a method that returns `True` if the specified file exists, or `False` if it does not

File.OpenText method—a method that opens a text file for reading

Filename property—a property of the OpenFileDialog and SaveFileDialog controls that holds the name of the file selected or entered by the user with the *Open* and *Save As* dialog boxes

File System Web site—runs directly under the ASP.NET development server supplied with Visual Studio and Visual Web Developer

Filter property—a property of the OpenFileDialog and SaveFileDialog controls used to set filters that control what file types are displayed in the *Open* and *Save As* dialog boxes

finding the classes—the object-oriented analysis process of discovering the classes within a problem

flag—a Boolean variable that signals when some condition exists in the program

floating—when windows, such as *Project Explorer, Properties,* or *Form Layout,* are not docked (attached)

flowchart—a diagram that graphically depicts the flow of a method

focus—the control that has the focus is the one that receives the user's keyboard input or mouse clicks

Focus method—gives the focus to a control

***Font* dialog box**—allows the user to select a font, style, and size

Font property—indicates the size and style of a text font

FontDialog control—displays a *Font* dialog box

For Each loop—a special loop designed specifically to access values from arrays and array-like structures

foreign key—a column in one table that references a primary key in another table

For...Next loop—a loop specifically designed to initialize, test, and increment a counter variable

ForeColor property—establishes the foreground color for text

Form—a window, onto which other controls may be placed

formatting—the way a value is printed or displayed

FormBorderStyle property—a property that configures a form's border; allows or prevents resizing, minimizing, or maximizing a window

FormClosed event handler—used to execute code immediately after a form has closed

FormClosing event handler—used to execute code in response to a form's closing

Friend access—an access type; a class member with Friend access can be used only by other classes inside the same assembly

FTP site—references an existing ASP.NET Web site located on a remote computer (network or Web)

function—a specialized routine that performs a specific operation, and then returns or produces information

function procedure—a collection of statements that performs an operation and returns a value

garbage collector—a process that destroys objects when they are no longer needed

Get section—located in a property procedure; permits a client program to retrieve the value of a property

global variable—a module-level or class-level variable that is declared with the `Public` access specifier

going out of scope—what happens when an object is created inside a procedure, and is automatically removed from memory when the procedure ends

graphical user interface (GUI)—the graphical interface used by modern operating systems

GridView control—displays database tables; allows you to sort on any column, select the column order, and format data within columns

GroupBox—a rectangular border that functions as a container for other controls

GroupBox control—a control that appears as a rectangular border with an optional title that appears in the upper left corner; you group other controls by drawing them inside a GroupBox control

hardware—a computer's physical components

Hello World program—a simple program that displays the words "Hello World" on the screen.

Hide method—removes a form or control, but does not remove it from memory

HScrollBar—a horizontal slider bar that, when moved with the mouse, increases or decreases a value

HTML control—controls found on most Web pages (not ASP.NET)

HTML designer—the tool in Visual Studio that simplifies the design of Web pages and Web forms

HTML Table control—an essential tool for designing the layout of Web forms; used to align text, graphics, and controls in rows and columns

HTML tag—used to design the layout of a Web form

HTTP Web site—runs under a Windows operating system utility named Internet Information Services (IIS)

Hungarian notation—system in which a three-letter prefix is used in variable names to identify their data type

HyperLink control—Web forms control that displays underlined text; when the user clicks on the text, the program navigates to a new Web page

Hypertext Markup Language (HTML)—the notation used when creating ordinary Web pages; determines fonts, images, and positioning of elements

identity column—a column in a database table that is assigned a unique integer value when new rows are added to the table

If...Then—a statement that can cause other statements to execute under certain conditions

If...Then...Else—a statement that will execute one group of statements if a condition is true, or another group of statements if a condition is false

If...Then...ElseIf—a statement that is like a chain of If...Then...ElseIf statements; they perform their tests, one after the other, until one of them is found to be true

Image property—specifies the image file that is to be displayed by the control

ImageButton control—Web forms control that displays an image on a clickable button

implicit type conversion—when you assign a value of one data type to a variable of another data type, Visual Basic attempts to convert the value being assigned to the data type of the variable

Immediate window—a debugging window used by advanced programmers; allows you to type debugging commands using the keyboard

index—see subscript

Index button—a button on the Dynamic Help window that displays a searchable alphabetized index of all help topics

IndexOf method—searches for a character or a string within a string

infinite loop—a loop that never stops repeating

inheritance—an object-oriented programming feature that allows you to create classes that are based on other classes

InitialDirectory property—a property of the OpenFileDialog and SaveFileDialog controls used to set the path of the directory initially displayed in Open and Save As dialog boxes

initialization—specifying an initial value for a variable

input—data the computer collects from the outside world

input box—a Windows dialog box that displays a message to the user; it provides a text box for the user to enter input

input device—a device that collects information and sends it to the computer

input file—file from which a program reads data

input validation—the process of inspecting input values and determining whether they are valid

integer division—a division operation performed with the \ operator in which the result is always an integer; if the result has a fractional part, it is discarded

integrated development environment (IDE)—an application that provides the necessary tools for creating, testing, and debugging software

IntelliSense—a feature of Visual Basic that provides help and some automatic code completion while you are developing an application

Internet Information Services (IIS)—Microsoft professional-level Web server

Interval property—a property of the timer control; the value stored in the Interval property is the number of milliseconds that elapse between timer events

intranet—network within a company, usually protected by a firewall

IPmt function—returns the required interest payment for a specific period on a loan

Is operator—used to compare two object variables to determine whether they reference the same object

IsNot operator—used to determine whether two variables do not reference the same object

IsNumeric function—an intrinsic function that accepts a string as its argument, and returns True if the string contains a number; the function returns False if the string's contents cannot be recognized as a number

Item method—a collection method that searches for a specific member of the collection and returns a reference to it

Items property—items that are displayed in a list box or combo box are stored as strings in the Items property

`Items.Add` method—a list box and combo box method that adds an item to the end of the control's Item property

`Items.Clear` method—a list box and combo box method that erases all the items in the control's Items property

`Items.Count` property—holds the number of items in a list box or combo box

`Items.Insert` method—a list box and combo box method that adds an item at a specific index of the control's Item property

`Items.Remove` method—a list box and combo box method that removes an item from the control's Item property

`Items.RemoveAt` method—a list box and combo box method that removes an item at a specific index of the control's Item property

iteration—one execution of a loop's conditionally-executed statements

JavaScript—scripting language used on Web pages, usually for client-side programming; runs under the control of the browser, not the Web server

keywords—programming language words that have a special meaning; keywords may only be used for their intended purpose

Label—text that cannot be changed or entered by the user; created with a Label control

Label control—used to create labels to display text on a Web form

Language Integrated Query (LINQ)—a query language that can be used to query many types of data from virtually any source

leading space—a space that appears at the beginning of a string

`Length` property—a string method that returns the number of characters in the string

lifetime—the time during which the variable exists in memory

`LIKE` operator (SQL)—used to create partial matches with Text column values

LinkButton control—used on Web forms; looks like a hyperlink, but generates a Click event

LINQ—*see* Language Integrated Query

List data type—a collection of items having the same type; like an array, but expandable at runtime

ListBox—a control that appears as a box containing a list of items

ListBox control—displays a list of items and allows the user to select one or more items from the list

literal—a piece of data is written into a program's code

`Load` event procedure—a procedure that is executed each time a form loads into memory

local variables—variables declared inside a procedure

local IIS Web site—a Web site that runs locally, under a Windows utility named Internet Information Services (IIS).

local Web server—a Web server that is supplied with Visual Studio, and runs on the local system.

Locals window—a debugging window that displays the current value and the data type of all the variables in the currently running procedure

logic error—a programming mistake that does not prevent an application from running but causes the application to produce incorrect results; *see* runtime error

logical operators—operators, such as And or Or, which connect two or more relational expressions into one, or Not, which reverse the logic of an expression

loop—one or more programming statements that repeat

machine language instructions—instructions that are stored in memory as a series of 1s and 0s and can only be processed by the CPU

main memory—also known as random-access memory, or RAM; where the computer stores information while programs are running

mathematical expression—an expression that uses multiple operators

MaximizeBox property—when set to *True*, causes a *Maximize* button to appear on the right side of a form's title bar

`Me` keyword—may be substituted for the name of the currently active form or object

member variable—declared inside a class declaration; the variable is a member of the class

menu designer—allows you to create a custom menu system for any form in an application

menu system—a collection of commands organized in one or more drop-down menus

MenuItem objects—menu names, menu commands, or separator bars on a menu system

MenuStrip control—consists of ToolStripMenuItem objects; used to construct a menu system on a form

message box—a dialog box that displays a message to the user

method call—statement that causes a method to execute

methods—procedures or functions that are members of a class; perform some operation on the data stored in the class

Microsoft Developer Network (MSDN) Library—provides complete documentation for Visual Basic, as well as other programming languages included in Visual Studio

millisecond—1/1000 of a second

MinimizeBox property—when set to *True*, causes a *Minimize* button to appear on the right side of a form's title bar

mnemonic—a key that you press in combination with the [Alt] key to access a control such as a button quickly; also called an *access key*

mnu—standard prefix for menu controls

modal form—when a modal form displayed, no other form in the application can receive the focus until the modal form is closed; no other statements in the procedure that displayed the modal form will execute until the modal form is closed

modeless form—Allows the user to switch focus to another form while it is displayed; statements that follow the modeless `Show` method call will continue to execute after the modeless form is displayed. Visual Basic will not wait until the modeless form is closed to execute these statements.

modularize—to break an application's code into small, manageable procedures

module—a Visual Basic file that contains only code; used for general-purpose procedures, functions, and declarations that are available to all forms in a project

module-level variable—a variable declared inside a module, but not inside a procedure or function

module scope—the scope of a module-level variable declared with the `Dim` keyword or the `Private` access specifier

Multiline property—a TextBox control property that, when set to *True*, allows the text box's text to span multiple lines

`MyBase` keyword—refers to a derived class's base class

Name property—a property that holds the control's name; controls are accessed and manipulated in code by their names

named constant—like a variable whose content is *read-only* and cannot be changed by a programming statement while the program is running

narrowing conversion—if you assign a real number to an integer variable, Visual Basic attempts to perform this conversion, which sometimes results in lost data

nested `If` statement—an `If` statement in the conditionally executed code of another `If` statement

nested loop—a loop inside another loop

newline character—an invisible character that separates text by breaking it into another line when displayed on the screen

`Next` method—a `Random` class method that is used to get a random integer number

`NextDouble` method—a `Random` class method that is used to get a random floating-point number between 0.0 and 1.0 (not including 1.0)

`Not` operator—a logical operator that reverses the *truth* of an expression; it makes a true expression false and a false expression true

object—a programming element that contains data and actions

object box—a drop-down list of the objects in the project that appears in the *Properties* window

Object Browser—a dialog box that allows you to browse the many classes and components available to your project

`Object` class—all classes are derived from the built-in `Object` class

object variable—a variable that holds the memory address of an object and allows you to work with the object

object-oriented analysis—during object-oriented design, the process of analyzing application requirements

object-oriented programming (OOP)—a programming technique centered on creating objects; a way of designing and coding applications that has led to using interchangeable software components

one-dimensional array—an array with one subscript

one-to-many relationship—when connecting two database tables indicates multiple occurrences of a foreign key

Open dialog box—gives users the capability of browsing their disks for a file to open, instead of typing a long path and filename

OpenFileDialog control—displays an *Open* dialog box

operand—a piece of data, such as a number, on which operators perform operations

operating system (OS)—a set of programs that manages the computer's hardware devices and controls their processes

operations—actions performed by class objects

operators—perform operations on one or more operands

Option Strict—in Visual Basic, a configuration option that determines whether certain implicit conversions are legal

`Or` operator—combines two expressions into one; one or both expressions must be true for the overall expression to be true (it is only necessary for one to be true, and it does not matter which one)

`ORDER BY` clause (SQL)—lets you control the display order of the table rows

`OrElse` operator—uses short-circuit evaluation in compound expressions

output—data a computer sends to the outside world

output device—a device that formats and presents output information

output file—a file into which a program writes data

Output window—displays various messages while an application is being compiled; you may write your own messages with the `Debug.WriteLine` method

`Overridable` keyword—in a procedure declaration, indicates that the procedure may be overridden in a derived class

override—to override a property or method in a base class means to create one of the same name in a derived class; when an object of the derived class accesses the property or procedure, it accesses the one in the derived class instead of the one in the base class

`Overrides` keyword—in a procedure declaration, indicates that the procedure overrides a procedure in the base class

panel control—a rectangular container for other controls, similar to a GroupBox

parallel arrays—two or more arrays that hold related data; the related elements in each array are accessed with a common subscript

parameter—a special variable that receives an argument being passed into a method, procedure, or function

parse—to analyze a string of characters for some purpose

Pascal casing—a style of mixing uppercase and lowercase characters in procedure, method, and class names; the first character in the name and the first character of each subsequent word in the name are capitalized and all other characters are lowercase

PHP—popular server-side scripting language used for many Web applications; major competitor of ASP.NET

PictureBox—displays a graphic image

PictureBox control—a control that can be used to display a graphic image

platform—Operating system + computer hardware; creates a complete environment under which programs can run. May also mean a virtual machine such as JVM (Java Virtual Machine) or CLR (Common Language Runtime).

Pmt function—returns the periodic payment amount for a loan

postback—when a Web page is sent back to the Web server for more processing

posttest loop—evaluates its test-expression after each iteration

PPmt function—returns the principal payment for a specific period on a loan

precedence—a ranking system that determines which operator works first in an expression where two operators share an operand

pretest loop—evaluates its test-expression before each iteration

primary key—a field, or the combination of multiple fields, that uniquely identifies each row in a database table

Print method—a method of the PrintDocument control that triggers a PrintPage event

PrintDialog control—displays a dialog box that allows you to select a printer, the number of copies to print, and establish other settings.

PrintDocument control—gives an application the ability to print output on a printer

PrintPage event handler—a PrintDocument control event procedure in which you write code that sends printed output to the printer

Private keyword—used to explicitly declare class-level variables private, making the source code more self-documenting

procedure—a set of programming language statements that are executed by the computer

procedure call—a statement that calls, or executes, a procedure

procedure declaration—specifies the name, parameter list, and statements that make up a procedure

program—a sequence of instructions stored in the computer's memory; the instructions enable the computer to solve a problem or perform a task

program code—generally, statements inside methods

program logic—program source code, written in languages such as Visual Basic and C#; in ASP.NET, the program logic is stored in the *code-behind* file

programmer-defined name—word or name defined by the programmer

programming languages—languages that use words instead of numbers to program the computer

project—a group of files that make up a Visual Basic application

project file—a file ending with the .vbproj extension that contains data describing the Visual Basic project

project folder—a folder that contains various files related to the project.

Prompt—a string displayed, typically on a Form or in an Input Box, requesting the user to enter a value

properties—in Visual Basic, pieces of data that determine the attributes of an object.

Properties window—shows and allows you to change most of the currently selected object's properties, and those properties' values

property—a piece of data that determines some characteristic of the control.

Property Get section—located in a property procedure; permits a client program to retrieve the value of a property

property procedure—a function that is a member of a class, and behaves like a property

Property Set section—located in a property procedure; permits a client program to set the value of a property

Protected access specifier—Protected base class members are like private members, except they may be accessed by methods and property procedures in derived classes. To all other code, however, protected class members are just like private class members.

protocol—in a URL, the designation http://, https://, or ftp://

prototype—a demonstration copy of a program

pseudocode—statements that are a cross between human language and a programming language

pseudo-random—numbers that only seem to be random

Public keyword—used in the declaration of a module level variable or procedure, which makes it available to statements outside the module

query—an SQL statement that retrieves and/or manipulates data in a database

query parameter—when a query contains more than one parameter, these required values are passed as arguments when calling the Fill method

RadioButton—a round button that is either selected or deselected when clicked with the mouse

RadioButton control—usually appears in groups and allows the user to select one of several possible options

RadioButtonList control—Web control that displays a grouped list of radio buttons

RadioChecked property—a MenuItem object property that may be set to *True* or *False*; when set to *True* for a checked menu item, the item appears with a radio button instead of a check mark

random-access memory (RAM)—*see* main memory

Random object—a special type of object that has methods and properties that make generating random numbers fairly easy

Read method—a StreamReader method that reads the next character from a file

read position—the position of the next item to be read from a file

ReadLine method—a StreamReader method that reads a line of data from a file

read-only property—a property whose value may be read, but may not be set by a client program

ReadToEnd method—a StreamReader method that reads and returns the entire contents of a file, beginning at the current read position

record—a complete set of data about a single item, consisting of one or more fields

relation—a link or relationship that relies on a common field value to join rows from two different tables

relational model—in databases; relations exist between tables

relational operator—determines if a specific relationship, such as less than or greater than, exists between two values

remarks—also known as comments; notes of explanation that document lines or sections in a method

remote site—a Web site located across a network

Remove method—a collection method that removes a member

repetition structure—*see* loop

report body—the part of a report that contains the report's data, and is often formatted in columns

report footer—an optional part of a report that contains the sum of one or more columns of data

report header—the part of a report that is printed first and usually contains the name of the report, the date and time the report was printed, and other general information about the data in the report

reserved words—*see* keywords

Response object—automatically exists in every Web page; its Redirect method is used to navigate to other Web pages

Response.Redirect method—transfers control from the current Web form to another Web page or URL on the Internet

returning a value—the term used when a function returns a value as output

Rnd function—generates a single precision random number in the range of 0.0 to 1.0

row—*see* record

Run mode—the runtime mode in which you run and test an application

running total—a sum of numbers that accumulates with each iteration of a loop

runtime—*see* run mode

runtime error—a mistake, such as an incorrect mathematical formula, that does not prevent the application from executing; *see* runtime errors

runtime errors—mistakes that do not prevent an application from executing, but cause it to produce incorrect results

Save As dialog box—gives users the capability of browsing their disks for a location to save a file to, as well as specifying a file's name

SaveFileDialog control—displays a standard Windows *Save As* dialog box

SaveFileDialog property—displays a *Save As* dialog box

scope—the part of the program where the variable is visible, and may be accessed by programming statements

Search button—a button on the *Dynamic Help* window that allows you to search for help topics using keywords

secondary storage—a device, such as a disk drive, that can hold information for long periods of time

SD (Secure Digital) memory cards—small devices that appear to the system as disk drives.

seed value—used in the calculation that returns the next random number in the series; a value from the system timer is used by default; a value can be specified when creating a Random object

Select Case statement—a statement in which one of several possible actions is taken, depending on the value of an expression

SELECT statement (SQL)—used to find records within a database table

SelectedIndex property—holds the index of the selected item in a list box or combo box

SelectedItem property—holds the currently selected item of a list box or combo box

separator bar—a horizontal bar used to separate groups of commands on a menu

sequence structure—a code structure where the statements are executed in sequence, without branching off in another direction

sequential-access file—a file whose contents must be read from beginning to end

sequential search—an algorithm that uses a loop to search for a value in an array; it examines the elements in the array, one after the other, starting with the first one

server—entity that produces data consumed by a client

Set section—located in a property procedure; permits a client program to set the value of a property

short-circuit evaluation—allows you to skirt the CheckValue function; it is the default in languages such as C#, C++, and Java

shortcut key—a key or combination of keys that causes a menu command to execute

ShortcutKeys property—a ToolStripMenuItem object property used to select a shortcut key

ShowDialog method—displays a modal form and causes it to receive the focus

Show method—displays a modeless form and causes it to receive the focus

ShowShortcut property—a ToolStripMenuItem object property; values may be *True* or *False*; when *True*, the menu item's shortcut key (selected with the ShortcutKeys property) is displayed; when *False*, the shortcut key is not displayed

single dimension array—an array with one subscript, which is useful for storing and working with a single set of data

single-step—a debugging technique where you execute an application's programming statements one at a time; after each statement executes you can examine variable and property contents, which allows you to identify code causing a logic error

SizeMode property—a PictureBox property that determines how the control will position and scale its graphic image

sizing handles—small boxes that appear around a control when it is selected during design mode; used to enlarge or shrink the control

software—programs that run on a computer

Solid-state drive—a drive that stores data in solid-state memory

Solution—a container for holding Visual Basic projects

Solution Explorer window—allows quick navigation among the files in the application

solution file—a file that ends with the .sln extension and contains data describing a solution

solution folder—a folder that contains various files related to a solution.

Sorted property—causes the items in the Items property of a list box to be displayed alphabetically

source code—the statements that are written in a program

SQL—*see* Structured Query Language

SQL pane—displays the actual SQL query that corresponds to the tables and fields selected in the diagram and grid panes; advanced SQL users usually write queries directly into this pane

standard toolbar—situated below the menu bar; contains buttons that execute frequently used commands

startup form—the form that is displayed when the project executes

statement—an instruction that you write in a program; can consist of keywords, operators, punctuation, and other allowable programming elements, arranged in the proper sequence to perform an operation

static text—ordinary text typed directly onto a Web form in Design mode

StatusStrip control—displays a toolstrip with buttons and text, usually at the bottom of a form

Step Into command—a debugging command that allows you to execute a single programming statement (*see* single-step); if the statement contains a call to a procedure or function, the next execution point that will be displayed is the first line of code in that procedure or function

Step Out command—a debugging command executed while the application is in Break mode; it causes the remainder of the current procedure or function to complete execution without single stepping; after the procedure or function has completed, the line following the procedure or function call is highlighted, and single-stepping may resume

Step Over command—a debugging command executed while the application is in Break mode; it causes the currently highlighted line to execute; if the line contains a procedure or function call, however, the procedure or function is executed and there is no opportunity to single-step through its statements; the entire procedure or function is executed, and the next line in the current procedure is highlighted

step value—the value added to the counter variable at the end of each iteration of a For...Next loop

StreamReader class—a class that provides methods for reading data to sequential files

StreamReader object—an instance of the StreamReader class; used to read data to sequential files

StreamWriter class—a class that provides methods for writing data to sequential files

StreamWriter object—an instance of the StreamWriter class, used to write data to sequential files

string—a sequence of characters

string concatenation—when one string is appended to another

string literal—a group of characters inside quotation marks

structure—a data type created by the programmer that contains one or more variables, which are known as members

Structure statement—used to create a structure

Structured Query Language (SQL)—the standard database language for data storage, retrieval, and (SQL) manipulation

Sub—a keyword that precedes the name of a procedure

Sub procedure—a collection of statements that performs a specific task and does not return a value; *see* procedure

subscript—a number that identifies a specific element within an array; also known as an index

Substring method—returns a substring, or a string within a string

syntax—rules that must be followed when constructing a method; dictate how keywords, operators, and programmer-defined names may be used

syntax error—an error such as a misspelled keyword, or the incorrect use of operators or punctuation; statements containing syntax errors are underlined with a jagged blue line

tab order—the order in which controls receive the focus

tab order selection mode—establishes a tab order when you click controls in the desired sequence

TabIndex property—contains a numeric value, which indicates the control's position in the tab order

table—holds data in a database; organized in rows and columns

table adapter—pulls data from one or more database tables and passes it to the program

TabStop property—when set to *True*, causes a control to be skipped in the tab order

TextAlign property—a property that aligns text within a control

test—To test an application, you run it many times, providing sample input and verifying that the output is correct.

text box—a rectangular area on a form in which the user can enter text, or the program can display text

text file—contains plain text and may be opened in a text editor

Text property—in Visual Basic, stores the value that becomes the text in a control

TextBox control—allows you to capture input that the user has typed on the keyboard

TextBox Web control—similar in many ways to the TextBox control for Windows forms; the Text property holds text input by the user

Timer control—allows an application to automatically execute code at regular time intervals

Title property—a property of the OpenFileDialog and SaveFileDialog controls used to set the string displayed in the *Open* and *Save As* dialog box title bars

ToLower method—a string method that returns a lowercase version of a string

Toolbar, layout—contains buttons for formatting the layout of controls on a form

Toolbar, standard—contains buttons that execute frequently used commands

Toolbox window—contains buttons, or tools, for Visual Basic controls

ToolStripMenuItem objects—items added to a menu in the menu designer; each item has properties such as Name and Text

ToolStripStatusLabel control—The part of a StatusStrip control that displays messages.

ToolTip—a small box that pops up when you hover the mouse over a button on the toolbar in the *Toolbox*; it contains a short description of the button's purpose

ToolTip control—a control that allows you to create ToolTips for the other controls on a form

ToString method—a method that returns the string representation of a variable

ToUpper method—a string method that returns an uppercase version of a string

trailing space—a space that appears at the end of a string

Trim method—returns a copy of the string without leading or trailing spaces

TrimEnd method—returns a copy of the string without trailing spaces

TrimStart method—returns a copy of the string without leading spaces

truncation—occurs when the fractional part of a number is dropped

try block—one or more statements that follow the Try clause in a Try-Catch statement and can potentially throw an exception

Try-Catch statement—a construct used for handling exceptions

TryParse method—a method that lets you determine whether a string (such as a TextBox's Text property) contains a value that can be successfully converted to a specific data type.

twip—1/1440th of an inch; twips are used as a measurement for positioning input boxes on the screen

two-dimensional array—an array of arrays; can be used to hold multiple sets of values

type conversion error—a runtime error that is generated when a nonnumeric value that cannot be automatically converted to a numeric value is assigned to a numeric variable or property

type mismatch error—*see* type conversion error

unary operator—an operator that requires only a single operand

Unicode—A set of numeric codes that represent all the letters of the alphabet (both lowercase and uppercase), the printable digits 0 through 9, punctuation symbols, and special characters. The Unicode system is extensive enough to encompass all the world's alphabets.

Uniform Resource Locator (URL)—universal way of addressing objects and pages on a network

USB (Universal Serial Bus) drives—small devices that appear to the system as disk drives.

user—the person who uses a program

user interface—the part of the program that users interact with

variable—a storage location in the computer's memory, used for holding information while the program is running

variable array—a group of variables with a single name

variable declaration—a statement that causes Visual Basic to create a variable in memory

variable scope—the area of a program in which a variable is visible

Visible property—a Boolean property that causes a control to be visible on the form when set to *True*, or hidden when set to *False*

Visual Studio—an integrated development environment (IDE) that provides all the necessary tools for creating, testing, and debugging software.

VScrollBar—a vertical slider bar that, when moved with the mouse, increases or decreases a value

VScrollBar control—used to create a vertical scroll bar

Watch window—a debugging window that allows you to add the names of variables that you want to watch; displays only the variables that you have added

Web application—an application that runs on a Web server and presents its content to the user across a network, in a Web browser

Web form—a Web page that contains text, HTML tags, HTML controls, and Web server controls

Web page—information requested by a Web browser; sent by a Web server; displayed to the user in the form of text, graphics, and sound

Web server—the program running on a host Web site that processes requests from end users running Web browsers

Web server controls—same as Web forms controls—type of interactive controls used on Web forms that must be decoded and processed by a Web server; generate runtime events such as Click, SelectedIndexChanged, and TextChanged

WHERE clause (SQL)—used to filter, or select zero or more rows retrieved from a database table

widening conversion—a conversion in which no data is lost

wildcard—a symbol that matches unknown characters

window—a rectangular area that contains other visual elements such as text, buttons that can be clicked with the mouse, boxes that accept keyboard input, and so forth

With...End With statement—allows you to create a With block; statements inside a With block may perform several operations on the same object without specifying the name of the object each time

wizard—software tool that guides you through the process of linking a control to a database

WordWrap property—a TextBox control property that causes the contents of a multiline text box to word wrap

Write method—a StreamWriter method that writes data to a file

WriteLine method—a StreamWriter method used to write a line of data to a file

Xor operator—Combines two expressions into one. One expression (not both) must be true for the overall expression to be true. If both expressions are true, or both expressions are false, the overall expression is false.

Index

Credits

Photo:

Cover: Stargatechris/123RF.

Chapter 1:

Pg. 2, Fig. 1-1a (Digital webcam in a white background with reflection): Iko/Shutterstock.

Pg. 2, Fig. 1-1b (Modern flight joystick isolated on white background): Nikita Rogul/Shutterstock.

Pg. 2, Fig. 1-1c (Scanner close up shot, business concept): Feng Yu/Shutterstock.

Pg. 2, Fig. 1-1d (Black Wireless Computer Keyboard and Mouse Isolated on White): Chiyacat/Shutterstock.

Pg. 2, Fig. 1-1e (Compact photo camera): Shutterstock.

Pg. 2, Fig. 1-1f (Computer drawing tablet with pen): Tkemot/Shutterstock.

Pg. 2, Fig. 1-1g (Illustration of Hard disk drive HDD isolated on white background with soft shadow): Vitaly Korovin/Shutterstock.

Pg. 2, Fig. 1-1h (Small computer speakers isolated on a white background): StockPhotosArt/Shutterstock.

Pg. 2, Fig. 1-1i (Color Printer): Jocic/Shutterstock.

Pg. 2, Fig. 1-1j (Four monitors): Art gallery/Shutterstock.

Pg. 2, Fig. 1-1k (Stick of computer random access memory, RAM): Peter Guess/Shutterstock.

Pg. 2, Fig. 1-1l (Chip processor radiator): Aquila/Shutterstock.

Chapter 2:

Pg. 85, Fig. 2-74; Pg. 86, Fig. 2-75; Pg. 96, Fig. 2-83; Pg. 97, Fig. 2-84: Library of Congress.
All other Images in Chapter 2, Tony Gaddis.

Chapter 7:

All other Images in Chapter 7, Tony Gaddis.

Text:

Chapter 1:

Pg. 21, Fig. 1-11; Pg. 21, Fig. 1-12; Pg. 22, Fig. 1-14; Pg. 23, Fig. 1-15; Pg. 25, Fig. 1-17; Pg. 26, Fig. 1-20; Pg. 27, Fig. 1-22; Pg. 29, Fig. 1-24; Pg. 31, Fig. 1-26; Pg. 31, Fig. 1-27; Pg. 32, Fig. 1-28; Pg. 32, Fig. 1-29; Pg. 39, Fig. 1-30: Screenshot from Microsoft® Visual Studio®.
All other Figures and Tables in Chapter 1, Tony Gaddis, Kip Irvine.

Chapter 2:

Pg. 42, Fig. 2-01; Pg. 54, Fig. 2-19; Pg. 64, Fig. 2-41; Pg. 62, Fig. 2-37; Pg. 65, Fig. 2-43; Pg. 68, Fig. 2-48; Pg. 69, Fig. 2-49; Pg. 70, Fig. 2-52; Pg. 100, Fig. 2-86; Pg. 111, Fig. 2-96: Screenshot from Microsoft® Visual Studio®.
All other Figures and Tables in Chapter 2, Tony Gaddis, Kip Irvine.

Chapter 3:

Pg. 126, Fig. 3-1; Pg. 126, Fig. 3-2; Pg. 127, Fig. 3-3; Pg. 129, Fig. 3-4; Pg. 130, Fig. 3-5; Pg. 138, Fig. 3-7; Pg. 139, Fig. 3-8; Pg. 149, Fig. 3-11; Pg. 155, Fig. 3-14; Pg. 156, Fig. 3-15; Pg. 158, Fig. 3-16; Pg. 164, Fig. 3-17; Pg. 166, Fig. 3-18; Pg. 169, Fig. 3-19; Pg. 170, Fig. 3-20; Pg. 174, Fig. 3-21; Pg. 174, Fig. 3-22; Pg. 175, Fig. 3-23; Pg. 177, Fig. 3-25; Pg. 178, Fig. 3-26; Pg. 179, Fig. 3-27; Pg. 180, Fig. 3-28; Pg. 183, Fig. 3-29; Pg. 185, Fig. 3-30; Pg. 187, Fig. 3-31; Pg. 189, Fig. 3-35; Pg. 190, Fig. 3-36; Pg. 190, Fig. 3-37; Pg. 191, Fig. 3-38; Pg. 192, Fig. 3-39; Pg. 193, Fig. 3-40; Pg. 194, Fig. 3-41; Pg. 195, Fig. 3-42; Pg. 201, Fig. 3-48; Pg. 204, Fig. 3-50; Pg. 209, Fig. 3-51; Pg. 210, Fig. 3-52; Pg. 210, Fig. 3-53; Pg. 211, Fig. 3-54; Pg. 212, Fig. 3-56; Pg. 224, Fig. 3-58; Pg. 225, Fig. 3-59; Pg. 226, Fig. 3-60; Pg. 227, Fig. 3-61; Pg. 228, Fig. 3-62: Screenshot from Microsoft® Visual Studio®.
All other Figures and Tables in Chapter 3, Tony Gaddis, Kip Irvine.

Chapter 4:

Pg. 238, Fig. 4-4; Pg. 238, Fig. 4-5; Pg. 243, Fig. 4-7; Pg. 245, Fig. 4-8; Pg. 248, Fig. 4-10; Pg. 249, Fig. 4-11; Pg. 251, Fig. 4-12; Pg. 263, Fig. 4-15; Pg. 268, Fig. 4-16; Pg. 268, Fig. 4-17; Pg. 268, Fig. 4-18; Pg. 274, Fig. 4-21;

Pg. 275, Fig. 4-22; Pg. 278, Fig. 4-23; Pg. 281, Fig. 4-25; Pg. 283, Fig. 4-27; Pg. 290, Fig. 4-32; Pg. 301, Fig. 4-33; Pg. 302, Fig. 4-34; Pg. 302, Fig. 4-35; Pg. 303, Fig. 4-36; Pg. 304, Fig. 4-37; Pg. 304, Fig. 4-38; Pg. 305, Fig. 4-39; Pg. 305, Fig. 4-40: Screenshot from Microsoft® Visual Studio®.
All other Figures and Tables in Chapter 4, Tony Gaddis, Kip Irvine.

Chapter 5:

Pg. 312, Fig. 5-5; Pg. 317, Fig. 5-8; Pg. 317, Fig. 5-10; Pg. 322, Fig. 5-12; Pg. 329, Fig. 5-15; Pg. 329, Fig. 5-16; Pg. 330, Fig. 5-17; Pg. 332, Fig. 5-18; Pg. 336, Fig. 5-21; Pg. 336, Fig. 5-22; Pg. 337, Fig. 5-24; Pg. 344, Fig. 5-28; Pg. 344, Fig. 5-29; Pg. 347, Fig. 5-35; Pg. 350, Fig. 5-36; Pg. 351, Fig. 5-37; Pg. 353, Fig. 5-38; Pg. 354, Fig. 5-39; Pg. 357, Fig. 5-40; Pg. 357, Fig. 5-41; Pg. 358, Fig. 5-42; Pg. 359, Fig. 5-43; Pg. 370, Fig. 5-44; Pg. 371, Fig. 5-47; Pg. 371, Fig. 5-48; Pg. 372, Fig. 5-49; Pg. 373, Fig. 5-50; Pg. 373, Fig. 5-51; Pg. 374, Fig. 5-52; Pg. 375, Fig. 5-53; Pg. 375, Fig. 5-54: Screenshot from Microsoft® Visual Studio®.
All other Figures and Tables in Chapter 5, Tony Gaddis, Kip Irvine.

Chapter 6:

Pg. 380, Fig. 6-1; Pg. 382, Fig. 6-4; Pg. 384, Fig. 6-5; Pg. 386, Fig. 6-6; Pg. 387, Fig. 6-7; Pg. 389, Fig. 6-9; Pg. 392, Fig. 6-11; Pg. 393, Fig. 6-12; Pg. 394, Fig. 6-13; Pg. 397, Fig. 6-15; Pg. 401, Fig. 6-16; Pg. 408, Fig. 6-20; Pg. 413, Fig. 6-21; Pg. 421, Fig. 6-22; Pg. 421, Fig. 6-23; Pg. 422, Fig. 6-24; Pg. 423, Fig. 6-25; Pg. 423, Fig. 6-26; Pg. 424, Fig. 6-27: Screenshot from Microsoft® Visual Studio®.
All other Figures and Tables in Chapter 6, Tony Gaddis, Kip Irvine.

Chapter 7:

Pg. 431, Fig. 7-4; Pg. 432, Fig. 7-6; Pg. 434, Fig. 7-8; Pg. 437, Fig. 7-11; Pg. 438, Fig. 7-12; Pg. 438, Fig. 7-13; Pg. 441, Fig. 7-18; Pg. 441, Fig. 7-19; Pg. 442, Fig. 7-20; Pg. 443, Fig. 7-21; Pg. 443, Fig. 7-22; Pg. 444, Fig. 7-24; Pg. 447, Fig. 7-26; Pg. 447, Fig. 7-27; Pg. 449, Fig. 7-28; Pg. 452, Fig. 7-29; Pg. 454, Fig. 7-31; Pg. 454, Fig. 7-32; Pg. 455, Fig. 7-33; Pg. 457, Fig. 7-35; Pg. 458, Fig. 7-36; Pg. 458, Fig. 7-37; Pg. 459, Fig. 7-38; Pg. 459, Fig. 7-39; Pg. 460, Fig. 7-40; Pg. 461, Fig. 7-41; Pg. 462, Fig. 7-42; Pg. 462, Fig. 7-43; Pg. 463, Fig. 7-45; Pg. 464, Fig. 7-46; Pg. 463, Fig. 7-47; Pg. 467, Fig. 7-50; Pg. 469, Fig. 7-52; Pg. 469, Fig. 7-53; Pg. 470, Fig. 7-54; Pg. 470, Fig. 7-55; Pg. 470, Fig. 7-56; Pg. 470, Fig. 7-57; Pg. 473, Fig. 7-59; Pg. 474, Fig. 7-61; Pg. 475, Fig. 7-62; Pg. 487, Fig. 7-63; Pg. 488, Fig. 7-64; Pg. 488, Fig. 7-65; Pg. 489, Fig. 7-67; Pg. 489, Fig. 7-68; Pg. 490, Fig. 7-69; Pg. 490, Fig. 7-70; Pg. 491, Fig. 7-71; Pg. 492, Fig. 07-72; Pg. 492, Fig. 7-73; Pg. 493, Fig. 7-74; Pg. 493, Fig. 7-75; Pg. 494, Fig. 7-76; Pg. 494, Fig. 7-77; Pg. 496, Fig. 7-79: Screenshot from Microsoft® Visual Studio®.
All other Figures and Tables in Chapter 7, Tony Gaddis, Kip Irvine.

Chapter 8:

Pg. 505, Fig. 8-07; Pg. 506, Fig. 8-9; Pg. 507, Fig. 8-10; Pg. 509, Fig. 8-12; Pg. 510, Fig. 8-13; Pg. 512, Fig. 8-14; Pg. 513, Fig. 8-15; Pg. 518, Fig. 8-17; Pg. 519, Fig. 8-19; Pg. 527, Fig. 8-21; Pg. 527, Fig. 8-22; Pg. 535, Fig. 8-26; Pg. 538, Fig. 8-27; Pg. 541, Fig. 8-30; Pg. 541, Fig. 8-31; Pg. 543, Fig. 8-33; Pg. 545, Fig. 8-34; Pg. 546, Fig. 8-37; Pg. 546, Fig. 8-38; Pg. 547, Fig. 8-39; Pg. 551, Fig. 8-43; Pg. 554, Fig. 8-44; Pg. 556, Fig. 8-45; Pg. 566, Fig. 8-46; Pg. 567, Fig. 8-47; Pg. 567, Fig. 8-48; Pg. 568, Fig. 8-49; Pg. 569, Fig. 8-50; Pg. 570, Fig. 8-51; Pg. 570, Fig. 8-52; Pg. 572, Fig. 8-53: Screenshot from Microsoft® Visual Studio®.
All other Figures and Tables in Chapter 8, Tony Gaddis, Kip Irvine.

Chapter 9:

Pg. 577, Fig. 9-3; Pg. 580, Fig. 9-5; Pg. 582, Fig. 9-6; Pg. 593, Fig. 9-15; Pg. 594, Fig. 9-16; Pg. 596, Fig. 9-17; Pg. 604, Fig. 9-23; Pg. 607, Fig. 9-24: Windows 10, Microsoft Corporation.
Pg. 578, Fig. 9-4; Pg. 583, Fig. 9-9; Pg. 585, Fig. 9-10; Pg. 586, Fig. 9-11; Pg. 587, Fig. 9-12; Pg. 588, Fig. 9-13; Pg. 588, Fig. 9-14; Pg. 598, Fig. 9-19; Pg. 598, Fig. 9-20; Pg. 600, Fig. 9-21; Pg. 609, Fig. 9-25; Pg. 625, Fig. 9-30; Pg. 625, Fig. 9-31; Pg. 626, Fig. 9-32; Pg. 626, Fig. 9-33: Screenshot from Microsoft ®Visual Studio®.
All other Figures and Tables in Chapter 9, Tony Gaddis, Kip Irvine.

Chapter 10:

Pg. 655, Fig. 10-32: Screenshot from Microsoft®Visual Studio®.
All other Figures and Tables in Chapter 10, Tony Gaddis, Kip Irvine.

Chapter 11:

Pg. 717, Fig. 11-05; Pg. 721, Fig. 11-11; Pg. 722, Fig. 11-13; Pg. 722, Fig. 11-15: Screenshot from Microsoft® Visual Studio®.
All other Figures and Tables in Chapter 11, Tony Gaddis, Kip Irvine.

Appendix A:

Pg. 831, Fig. A-3; Pg. 832, Fig. A-5; Pg. 834, Fig. A-7; Pg. 835, Fig. A-8; Pg. 837, Fig. A-9; Pg. 840, Fig. A-10: Screenshots from Microsoft® Visual Studio®. Used by permission of Microsoft Corporation.

Appendix B:

Pg. 845, Fig. B-1: Screenshot from Microsoft® Visual Studio®. Used by permission of Microsoft Corporation.